C

HOW TO PROGRAM

FOURTH EDITION

Deitel® Books, Cyber Classrooms, Complete Tra published by

How To Program Series
Advanced Java™ 2 Platform How to Program
C How to Program, 4/E
C++ How to Program, 4/E
C#® How to Program
e-Business and e-Commerce How to Program
Internet and World Wide Web How to Program, 2/E
Java™ How to Program, 5/E
Perl How to Program
Python How to Program
Visual Basic® 6 How to Program
Visual Basic® .NET How to Program, 2/E
Visual C++® .NET How to Program
Wireless Internet & Mobile Business How to Program
XML How to Program

.NET How to Program Series
C# How to Program
Visual Basic® .NET How to Program, 2/E
Visual C++® .NET How to Program

Visual Studio® Series
C# How to Program
Getting Started with Microsoft® Visual C++® 6 with an Introduction to MFC
Simply C#: An Application-Driven Tutorial Approach
Simply Visual Basic® .NET: An Application-Driven Tutorial Approach (Visual Studio .NET 2002 Edition)
Simply Visual Basic® .NET: An Application-Driven Tutorial Approach (Visual Studio .NET 2003 Edition)
Visual Basic® 6 How to Program
Visual Basic® .NET How to Program, 2/E
Visual C++® .NET How to Program

CS1 Programming Series
Java™ Software Design

Simply Series
Simply C#: An Application-Driven Tutorial Approach
Simply Java™ Programming: An Application-Driven Tutorial Approach
Simply Visual Basic® .NET: An Application Driven Tutorial Approach (Visual Studio .NET 2002 Edition)
Simply Visual Basic® .NET: An Application Driven Tutorial Approach (Visual Studio .NET 2003 Edition)

Deitel® Developer Series
Java™ Web Services for Experienced Programmers
Web Services A Technical Introduction

Computer Science Series
Operating Systems, 3/E

For Managers Series
e-Business and e-Commerce for Managers

ining Courses and Web-Based Training Courses
Prentice Hall

To follow the Deitel publishing program, please register at:

> www.deitel.com/newsletter/subscribe.html

for the free *Deitel® Buzz Online* e-mail newsletter.

To communicate with the authors, send e-mail to:

> deitel@deitel.com

For information on Deitel instructor-led, corporate training seminars offered worldwide visit:

> www.deitel.com

For continuing updates on Prentice Hall and Deitel publications visit:

> www.deitel.com,
> www.prenhall.com/deitel or
> www.InformIT.com/deitel

Library of Congress Cataloging-in-Publication Data

On file

Vice President and Editorial Director: *Marcia Horton*
Senior Acquisitions Editor: *Kate Hargett*
Assistant Editor: *Sarah Parker*
Editorial Assistant: *Michael Giacobbe*
Vice President and Director of Production and Manufacturing, ESM: *David W. Riccardi*
Executive Managing Editor: *Vince O'Brien*
Managing Editor: *Tom Manshreck*
Production Editor: *Chirag Thakkar*
Production Editor, Media: *Bob Engelhardt*
Director of Creative Services: *Paul Belfanti*
Creative Director: *Carole Anson*
Art Director: *Geoff Cassar*
Chapter Opener and Cover Designer: *Dr. Harvey Deitel and David Merrell*
Manufacturing Manager: *Trudy Pisciotti*
Manufacturing Buyer: *Lisa McDowell*
Marketing Manager: *Pamela Shaffer*

 © 2004 by Prentice-Hall, Inc.
Upper Saddle River, New Jersey 07458

Printed in the United States of America

10 9 8 7 6 5 4 3 2

ISBN 0-13-142644-3

Pearson Education Ltd., *London*
Pearson Education Australia Pty. Ltd., *Sydney*
Pearson Education Singapore, Pte. Ltd.
Pearson Education North Asia Ltd., *Hong Kong*
Pearson Education Canada, Inc., *Toronto*
Pearson Educacion de Mexico, S.A. de C.V.
Pearson Education–Japan, *Tokyo*
Pearson Education Malaysia, Pte. Ltd.
Pearson Education, Inc., *Upper Saddle River, New Jersey*

C

HOW TO PROGRAM
FOURTH EDITION

H. M. Deitel
Deitel & Associates, Inc.

P. J. Deitel
Deitel & Associates, Inc.

PEARSON EDUCATION, INC., Upper Saddle River, New Jersey 07458

Trademarks

To Marcia Horton,

Editorial Director of Engineering and
Computer Science at Prentice Hall:

It has been a privilege and a joy
building the Deitel publishing program with you
over the last 18 years. Thank you
for being our mentor and our friend.

Harvey and Paul Deitel

Contents

10   C Structures, Unions, Bit Manipulations and Enumerations   **393**

11   C File Processing   **429**

12   C Data Structures   **466**

Preface

Welcome to ANSI/ISO Standard C, and to C++ and Java™, too! At Deitel & Associates, we write college-level programming-language textbooks and professional books and work hard to keep our published books up-to-date with a steady flow of new editions. Writing *C How to Program, Fourth Edition*, (*4/e* for short), was a joy. This book and its support materials have everything instructors and students need for an informative, interesting, challenging and entertaining educational experience. We have tuned the writing, the pedagogy, our coding style and the book's ancillary package. Also, we have included a Tour of the Book in this Preface. This will help instructors, students and professionals get a sense of the rich coverage this book provides of C, C++ and Java programming.

In this Preface, we overview the conventions we use in *C How to Program, 4/e*, such as syntax coloring the code examples, "code washing" and highlighting important code segments to help focus students' attention on key concepts introduced in each chapter. We also overview the new features of *C How to Program, 4/e*.

Prentice Hall has bundled Microsoft's Visual C++® 6 Introductory Edition software with the text. To further support novice programmers, we offer several of our new *Dive-Into™ Series* publications that are available free for download at www.deitel.com. These materials explain how to compile, execute and debug C, C++ and Java programs using various popular development environments.

We discuss *C How to Program, 4/e*'s comprehensive suite of educational materials that help instructors maximize their students' learning experience. These include an Instructor's Resource CD with solutions to the book's chapter exercises and a Test-Item File with hundreds of multiple-choice examination questions and answers. Additional instructor resources are available at the book's Companion Web Site (www.prenhall.com/deitel), which includes a Syllabus Manager and customizable PowerPoint® Lecture Notes. PowerPoint slides and additional support materials are available for students at the Companion Web Site, as well.

We also discuss the new *Student Solutions Manual* to accompany this textbook. This additional resource provides solutions to about half of the exercises in the textbook.

C How to Program, 4/e, was reviewed by a team of distinguished academics and industry professionals, including the head and former head of the C standards committee; we list their names and affiliations so you can get a sense of how carefully this book was scrutinized. The Preface concludes with information about the authors and about Deitel & Associates, Inc. As you read this book, if you have any questions, please send an e-mail to deitel@deitel.com; we will respond promptly. Please visit our Web site, www.deitel.com, regularly and be sure to sign up for the *Deitel® Buzz Online* e-mail newsletter at www.deitel.com/newsletter/subscribe.html. We use the Web site and the newsletter to keep our readers current on all Deitel publications and services.

Features of C How to Program, Fourth Edition

Syntax Highlighting

We syntax highlight all the C, C++ and Java code, as do many integrated-development environments and code editors. This greatly improves code readability—an especially important goal, given that this book contains over 13,280 lines of code. Our syntax-highlighting conventions are as follows:

```
comments appear like this
keywords appear like this
errors appear like this
constants and literal values appear like this
all other code appears in black
```

Code Highlighting and User-Input Highlighting

We have added extensive code highlighting to make it easier for readers to spot the featured segments of each program. This feature also helps students review the material rapidly when preparing for exams or labs. We have also highlighted in our screen dialogs all user inputs to distinguish them from program outputs.

"Code Washing"

"Code washing" is our term for applying comments, using meaningful identifiers, applying indentation and using vertical spacing to separate meaningful program units. This process results in programs that are much more readable and self-documenting. We have added extensive and descriptive comments to all of the code, including a comment before and after every major control statement, to help the student clearly understand the flow of the program. We have done extensive code washing of all the source code programs in the text, the ancillaries and the *Student Solutions Manual*.

To promote good programming practices, we updated all the source code programs in the C portion of this book with new coding standards. Variable definitions are now placed on separate lines to increase readability and every control statement has an opening and closing brace even when this is redundant. This will help the reader when he or she is beginning to develop large and complex programs. Every function prototype now matches the first line of the function definition, including the parameter names (which help document the program and reduce errors—especially for novice programmers).

Use of Terminology/Presentation

We have updated our use of terminology throughout the text to comply with the various language standards and specification.

Teaching Approach

Many educators believe that the complexity of C, and a number of other difficulties, make C unworthy for a first programming course—precisely the target course for this book. So why did we write this text?

Dr. Harvey M. Deitel (HMD) taught introductory programming courses in college environments for two decades with an emphasis on developing clearly written, well-structured programs. Much of what is taught in these courses is the basic principles of structured programming, with an emphasis on the effective use of control statements and functionalization. We have presented this material exactly the way HMD has done in his college courses. Students are motivated by the fact that they are learning a language that will be immediately useful to them as they enter industry.

Our goal was clear: Produce a C programming textbook for introductory university-level courses in computer programming for students with little or no programming experience, yet offer the deep and rigorous treatment of theory and practice demanded by traditional C courses. To meet these goals, we produced a book larger than other C texts—this because our text also patiently teaches structured programming principles. Hundreds of thousands of students worldwide have learned C from the earlier editions of this book.

C How to Program, 4/e, contains a rich collection of examples, exercises and projects drawn from many fields and designed to provide students with a chance to solve interesting, real-world problems. The code examples in the text have been tested on multiple compilers.

The book concentrates on the principles of good software engineering and stresses program clarity. We are educators who teach edge-of-the-practice topics in industry classrooms worldwide. This text emphasizes good pedagogy.

Live-Code Approach

C How to Program, 4/e, is loaded with numerous live-code examples— each new concept is presented in the context of a complete, working program that is immediately followed by one or more sample executions showing the program's input/output dialog. This style exemplifies the way we teach and write about programming. We call this method of teaching and writing the live-code approach. *We use programming languages to teach programming languages.* Reading the examples in the text is much like typing and running them on a computer.

World Wide Web Access

All of the source-code examples for *C How to Program, 4/e,* (and our other publications) are available on the Internet as downloads from the following Web sites:

```
www.deitel.com
www.prenhall.com/deitel
```

Registration is quick and easy and the downloads are free. We suggest downloading all the examples, then running each program as you read the corresponding text. Making changes to the examples and immediately seeing the effects of those changes is a great way to enhance your learning experience.

Objectives

Each chapter begins with a statement of objectives. This tells the student what to expect and gives the student an opportunity, after reading the chapter, to determine if he or she has met these objectives. It is a confidence builder and a source of positive reinforcement.

Quotations

The learning objectives are followed by a series of quotations. Some are humorous, some are philosophical and some offer interesting insights. Our students enjoy relating the quotations to the chapter material. You may appreciate some of the quotations more *after* reading the chapters.

Outline

The chapter outline helps the student approach the material in top-down fashion. This, too, helps students anticipate what is to come and set a comfortable and effective learning pace.

Sections

Each chapter is organized into small sections that address key C, C++ or Java topics.

13, 280 Lines of Syntax-Highlighted Code in 268 Example Programs (with Outputs)

We present C, C++ and Java features in the context of complete, working programs using our our live-code approach. Each program is immediately followed by a window containing the outputs produced when the program is run. This enables the student to confirm that the programs run as expected. Relating outputs to the program statements that produce those outputs is an excellent way to learn and to reinforce concepts. Our programs exercise many features of C, C++ and Java. Reading the book carefully is much like entering and running these programs on a computer. The code is "syntax highlighted" with keywords appearing in bold blue, comments appearing in italic blue, constants and literal values appearing in a lighter shade of bold blue and the rest of each program appearing in black. This makes it much easier to read the code—students will especially appreciate the syntax highlighting when they read the more substantial programs we present.

469 Illustrations/Figures

An abundance of colorized charts and line drawings is included. The discussions of control statements in Chapters 3 and 4 feature carefully drawn flowcharts. [*Note:* We do not teach the use of flowcharting as a program development tool, but we do use a brief flowchart-oriented presentation to specify the precise operation of C's control statements.] Chapter 12, Data Structures, uses colorized line drawings to illustrate creating and maintaining linked lists, queues, stacks and binary trees. The remainder of the book is abundantly illustrated.

768 Programming Tips

We have included seven programming tip elements to help students focus on important aspects of program development, testing and debugging, performance and portability. We highlight hundreds of these tips in the form of *Common Programming Errors, Error-Prevention Tips, Good Programming Practices, Look-and-Feel Observations, Performance Tips, Portability Tips* and *Software Engineering Observations*. These tips and practices represent the best we have been able to glean from six decades (combined) of programming and teaching experience. One of our students—a mathematics major—told us that she feels this approach is like the highlighting of axioms, theorems and corollaries in mathematics books; it provides a basis on which to build good software.

259 Common Programming Errors

Students learning a language—especially in their first programming course—tend to make certain kinds of errors frequently. Focusing on these Common Programming Errors *helps students avoid making the same errors. It also helps reduce long lines outside instructors' offices during office hours!*

132 Good Programming Practices

Good Programming Practices *are tips for writing clear programs. These techniques help students produce programs that are more readable, self-documenting and easier to maintain.*

49 Error-Prevention Tips

When we first designed this "tip type," we thought we would use it strictly to tell people how to test and debug programs and in previous editions have labelled this tip as "Testing and Debugging Tips." In fact, many of the tips describe aspects of C, C++ and Java that reduce the likelihood of "bugs" and thus simplify the testing and debugging processes. In addition, we also changed many of the Good Programming Practices *throughout the book to this tip type.*

32 Look-and-Feel Observations

In the Java portion of this book, we provide Look-and-Feel Observations *to highlight graphical user interface conventions. These observations help students design their own graphical user interfaces to conform with industry norms.*

68 Performance Tips

In our experience, teaching students to write clear and understandable programs is by far the most important goal for a first programming course. But students want to write the programs that run the fastest, use the least memory, require the smallest number of keystrokes, or dazzle in other nifty ways. Students really care about performance. They want to know what they can do to "turbo charge" their programs. So we highlight opportunities for improving program performance—making programs run faster or minimizing the amount of memory that they occupy.

38 Portability Tips

Software development is a complex and expensive activity. Organizations that develop software must often produce versions customized to a variety of computers and operating systems. So there is a strong emphasis today on portability, i.e., on producing software that will run on a variety of computer systems with few, if any, changes. Many people tout C, C++ and Java as appropriate languages for developing portable software. Some people assume that if they implement an application in one of the languages, the application will automatically be portable. This is simply not the case. Achieving portability requires careful and cautious design. There are many pitfalls. We include numerous Portability Tips *to help students write portable code. Java was designed from the start to maximize portability, but Java programs can also require modifications to "port" them.*

189 Software Engineering Observations

The Software Engineering Observations *highlight techniques, architectural issues and design issues, etc. that affect the architecture and construction of software systems, especially large-scale systems. Much of what the student learns here will be useful in upper-level courses and in industry as the student begins to work with large, complex real-world systems. C, C++ and Java are especially effective software engineering languages.*

Summary

Each chapter ends with additional pedagogical devices. We present an extensive, bullet-list-style *Summary* in every chapter. This helps the student review and reinforce key concepts. There is an average of 37 summary bullets per chapter.

Terminology

We include a *Terminology* section with an alphabetized list of the important terms defined in the chapter—again, further reinforcement. There is an average of 73 terms per chapter.

Summary of Tips, Practices and Errors

We collect and list from the chapter the *Good Programming Practices, Common Programming Errors, Look-and-Feel Observations, Performance Tips, Portability Tips, Software Engineering Observations* and *Error-Prevention Tips.*

728 Self-Review Exercises and Answers (Count Includes Separate Parts)

Extensive *Self-Review Exercises* and *Answers to Self-Review Exercises* are included for self study. This gives the student a chance to build confidence with the material and prepare to attempt the regular exercises.

993 Exercises (Count Includes Separate Parts; 1722 Total Exercises)

Each chapter concludes with a substantial set of exercises including simple recall of important terminology and concepts; writing individual program statements; writing small portions of functions and C++/Java classes; writing complete functions, C++/Java classes and programs;and writing major term projects. The large number of exercises enables instructors to tailor their courses to the unique needs of their audiences and to vary course assignments each semester. Instructors can use these exercises to form homework assignments, short quizzes and major examinations.

4800+ Index Entries (Total of 7500+ Entries Counting Multiple References)

We have included an extensive *Index* at the back of the book. This helps the student find any term or concept by keyword. The *Index* is useful to people reading the book for the first time and is especially useful to practicing programmers who use the book as a reference. Most of the terms in the *Terminology* sections appear in the *Index* (along with many more index entries from each chapter). Thus, the student can use the *Index* in conjunction with the *Terminology* sections to be sure he or she has covered the key material of each chapter.

Software Included with C How to Program, 4/e

In writing this book, we have used a variety of C compilers. For the most part, the programs in the text will work on all ANSI/ISO C and C++ compilers, including the Visual C++ 6.0 Introductory Edition compiler included with this book.

The C material (Chapters 2–14) follows the ANSI C standard published in 1990. See the reference manuals for your particular system for more details about the language, or obtain a copy of ANSI/ISO 9899: 1990, "American National Standard for Information Systems—Programming Language C," from the American National Standards Institute, 11 West 42nd Street, New York, New York 10036.

In 1999, ISO approved a new version of C, C99, which is not as yet widely used. Appendix B contains a comprehensive list of C99 Web resources. For more information on C99—and to purchase a copy of the C99 standards document (ISO/IEC 9899:1999)—visit the Web site of the American National Standards Institute (ANSI) at www.ansi.org.

The C++ material is based on the C++ programming language as developed by the Accredited Standards Committee INCITS, Information Technology and its Technical Committee J11, Programming Language C++, respectively. The C and C++ languages were approved by the International Standards Organization (ISO).

The serious programmer should read these documents carefully and reference them regularly. These documents are not tutorials. Rather they define their respective languages with the extraordinary level of precision that compiler implementors and "heavy-duty" developers demand.

The Java chapters are based on Sun Microsystem's Java programming language. Sun provides an implementation of the Java 2 Platform called the Java 2 Software Development Kit (J2SDK) that includes the minimum set of tools you need to write software in Java. You can download the most recent version the J2SDK from

```
java.sun.com/j2se/downloads.html
```

Information on installing and configuring the J2SDK is located at

```
developer.java.sun.com/developer/onlineTraining/new2java/
gettingstartedjava.html
```

We have carefully audited our presentation against these documents and documentation. Our book is intended to be used at the introductory and intermediate levels. We have not attempted to cover every feature discussed in these comprehensive documents.

DIVE-INTO™ Series Tutorials for Popular C, C++ and Java Environments
We have launched our new *DIVE-INTO™ SERIES* of tutorials to help our readers get started with many popular program-development environments. These are available free for download at www.deitel.com/books/downloads.html.

Currently, we have the following *DIVE-INTO™ SERIES* publications:

- *DIVE-INTO Microsoft® Visual C++® 6*
- *DIVE-INTO Microsoft® Visual C++® .NET*
- *DIVE-INTO Borland™ C++Builder™ Compiler* (command-line version)
- *DIVE-INTO Borland™ C++Builder™ Personal* (IDE version)
- *DIVE-INTO GNU C++ on Linux*
- *DIVE-INTO GNU C++ via Cygwin on Windows* (Cygwin is a UNIX emulator for Windows that includes the GNU C++ compiler.)
- *DIVE-INTO Forte for Java Community Edition 3.0*
- *DIVE-INTO SunOne Studio Community Edition 4.0*

Each of these tutorials shows how to compile, execute and debug C, C++ and Java applications in that particular compiler product. Many of these documents also provide step-by-step instructions with screen shots to help readers install the software. Each document overviews the compiler and its online documentation.

Ancillary Package for C How to Program, 4/e

C How to Program, 4/e, has extensive ancillary materials for instructors. The *Instructor's Resource CD (IRCD)* contains solutions to most of the end-of-chapter exercises. This CD is available only to instructors through their Prentice Hall representatives. [*NOTE:* **Please do not write to us requesting the instructor's CD. Distribution of this CD is limited strictly to college professors teaching from the book. Instructors may obtain the solutions manual only from their Prentice Hall representatives.**] The ancillaries for this book also include a *Test Item File* of multiple-choice questions. In addition, we provide PowerPoint® slides containing all the code and figures in the text and bulleted items that summarize the key points in the text. Instructors can customize the slides. The Power-Point® slides are downloadable from `www.deitel.com` and are available as part of Prentice Hall's Companion Web Site (`www.prenhall.com/deitel`) for *C How to Program, 4/e*, which offers resources for both instructors and students. For instructors, the Companion Web Site offers a Syllabus Manager, which helps instructors plan courses interactively and create online syllabi.

Students also benefit from the functionality of the *Companion Web Site*. Book-specific resources for students include:

- Customizable PowerPoint® slides
- Source code for all example programs
- Reference materials from the book appendices (such as operator-precedence chart, character set and Web resources)

Chapter-specific resources available for students include:

- Chapter objectives
- Highlights (e.g., chapter summary)
- Outline
- Tips (e.g., *Common Programming Errors*, *Good Programming Practices*, *Portability Tips*, *Performance Tips*, *Look-and-Feel Observations*, *Software Engineering Observations* and *Error-Prevention Tips*)
- Online Study Guide—contains additional short-answer self-review exercises (e.g., true/false and matching questions) with answers and provides immediate feedback to the student

Students can track their results and course performance on quizzes using the *Student Profile* feature, which records and manages all feedback and results from tests taken on the *Companion Web Site*. To access DEITEL® *Companion Web Site*, visit `www.prenhall.com/deitel`.

Student Solutions Manual

The *C Student Solutions Manual* (ISBN 0-13-145245-2) to accompany *C How to Program, 4/e* provides solutions to approximately half of the exercises in the text. Many of the solved exercises are similar to the unsolved exercises, which will help students when completing homework assignments.

Deitel® e-Learning Initiatives

e-Books and Support for Wireless Devices

Wireless devices will have an enormous role in the future of the Internet. Given recent bandwidth enhancements and the emergence of 2.5 and 3G technologies, it is projected that, within a few years, more people will access the Internet through wireless devices than through desktop computers. Deitel & Associates is committed to wireless accessibility and has published *Wireless Internet & Mobile Business How to Program*. We are investigating new electronic formats, such as wireless e-books so that students and professors can access content virtually anytime, anywhere. For periodic updates on these initiatives subscribe to the *Deitel® Buzz Online* e-mail newsletter, www.deitel.com/newsletter/subscribe.html or visit www.deitel.com.

Deitel® Buzz Online E-mail Newsletter

Our free e-mail newsletter, the *Deitel® Buzz Online*, includes commentary on industry trends and developments, links to free articles and resources from our published books and upcoming publications, product-release schedules, errata, challenges, anecdotes, information on our corporate instructor-led training courses and more. To subscribe, visit

> www.deitel.com/newsletter/subscribe.html

The New Deitel® Developer Series

Deitel & Associates, Inc., is making a major commitment to covering leading-edge technologies for industry software professionals through the launch of our *Deitel® Developer Series*. The first books in the series are *Web Services A Technical Introduction* and *Java Web Services for Experienced Programmers*. We are working on *ASP .NET with Visual Basic .NET for Experienced Programmers*, *ASP .NET with C# for Experienced Programmers* and many more. Please visit www.deitel.com or subscribe to our e-mail newsletter at www.deitel.com/newsletter/subscribe.html for continuous updates on all published and forthcoming *Deitel Developer Series* titles.

The *Deitel Developer Series* is divided into three subseries. The *A Technical Introduction* subseries provides IT managers and developers with detailed overviews of emerging technologies. The *A Programmer's Introduction* subseries is designed to teach the fundamentals of new languages and software technologies to programmers and novices from the ground up; these books discuss programming fundamentals, followed by brief introductions to more sophisticated topics. The *For Experienced Programmers* subseries is designed for seasoned developers seeking a deeper treatment of new programming languages and technologies, without the encumbrance of introductory material; the books in this subseries move quickly to in-depth coverage of the features of the programming languages and software technologies being covered.

A Tour of the Book

The book is divided into four major parts. The first part, Chapters 1 through 14, presents a thorough treatment of the C programming language including a formal introduction to structured programming. The second part (Chapters 15 through 23)—unique among C textbooks—presents a substantial treatment of C++ and object-oriented programming sufficient for an upper-level undergraduate college course. The third part—Chapters 24 through

30 (and also unique among C books)—presents a thorough introduction to Java, including graphics programming, graphical user interface (GUI) programming using Java Swing, multimedia programming and event-driven programming. The fourth part, Appendices A through F, presents a variety of reference materials that support the main text.

Part 1: Procedural Programming in C

Chapter 1—Introduction to Computers, the Internet and the World Wide Web— discusses what computers are, how they work and how they are programmed. It introduces the notion of structured programming and explains why this set of techniques has fostered a revolution in the way programs are written. The chapter gives a brief history of the development of programming languages from machine languages, to assembly languages, to high-level languages. The origins of the C, C++ and Java programming languages are discussed. The chapter includes an introduction to a typical C programming environment. We discuss the explosion in interest in the Internet that has occurred with the advent of the World Wide Web and the Java programming language.

Chapter 2—Introduction to C Programming—gives a concise introduction to writing C programs. A detailed treatment of decision making and arithmetic operations in C is presented. After studying this chapter, the student will understand how to write simple, but complete, C programs.

Chapter 3—Structured Program Development—is probably the most important chapter in the text, especially for the serious student of computer science. It introduces the notion of algorithms (procedures) for solving problems. It explains the importance of structured programming in producing programs that are understandable, debuggable, maintainable and likely to work properly on the first try. It introduces the fundamental control statements of structured programming, namely the sequence, selection (`if` and `if...else`) and repetition (`while`) statements. It explains the technique of top-down, stepwise refinement that is critical to the production of properly structured programs. It presents the popular program design aid, structured pseudocode. The methods and approaches used in Chapter 3 are applicable to structured programming in any programming language, not just C. This chapter helps the student develop good programming habits in preparation for dealing with the more substantial programming tasks in the remainder of the text.

Chapter 4—C Program Control—refines the notions of structured programming and introduces additional control statements. It examines repetition in detail and compares the alternatives of counter-controlled loops and sentinel-controlled loops. The `for` statement is introduced as a convenient means for implementing counter-controlled loops. The `switch` selection statement and the `do...while` repetition statement are presented. The chapter concludes with a discussion of logical operators.

Chapter 5—C Functions—discusses the design and construction of program modules. C's function-related capabilities include standard library functions, programmer-defined functions, recursion and call-by-value capabilities. The techniques presented in Chapter 5 are essential to the production and appreciation of properly structured programs, especially the kinds of larger programs and software that system programmers and application programmers are likely to develop in real-world applications. The "divide and conquer" strategy is presented as an effective means for solving complex problems by dividing them into simpler interacting components. Students enjoy the treatment of random numbers and simulation, and they appreciate the discussion of the dice game of craps which makes elegant use of control statements. We introduce enumerations in this chapter and provide a more detailed discussion in Chapter 10. Chapter 5 offers a solid introduction to recursion and includes a table summarizing the dozens of recursion examples and exercises distributed throughout the remainder of the book. Some books leave recursion for a chapter late in the book; we feel this topic is best covered gradually throughout the text. The extensive exercises include several classical recursion problems such as the Towers of Hanoi.

Chapter 6—C Arrays—discusses the structuring of data into arrays, or groups, of related data items of the same type. The chapter presents numerous examples of both single-subscripted arrays and double-subscripted arrays. It is widely recognized that structuring data properly is just as important as using control statements effectively in developing properly structured programs. The examples investigate various common array manipulations, printing histograms, sorting data, passing arrays to functions and an introduction to the field of survey data analysis (with simple statistics). A feature of this chapter is the careful discussion of elementary sorting and searching techniques and the presentation of binary searching as a dramatic improvement over linear searching. The end-of-chapter exercises include a variety of interesting and challenging problems, such as improved sorting techniques, the design of an airline reservations system, an introduction to the concept of turtle graphics (made famous in the LOGO language) and the Knight's Tour and Eight Queens problems that introduce the notions of heuristic programming so widely employed in the field of artificial intelligence.

Chapter 7—C Pointers—presents one of the most powerful and difficult to master features of the C language: pointers. The chapter provides detailed explanations of pointer operators, call by reference, pointer expressions, pointer arithmetic, the relationship between pointers and arrays, arrays of pointers and pointers to functions. The chapter exercises include a delightful simulation of the classic race between the tortoise and the hare, card shuffling and dealing algorithms and recursive maze traversals. A special section entitled "Building Your Own Computer" is also included. This section explains machine language programming and proceeds with a project involving the design and implementation of a computer simulator that allows the reader to write and run machine language programs. This unique feature of the text will be especially useful to the reader who wants to understand how computers really work. Our students enjoy this project and often implement substantial enhancements, many of which are suggested in the exercises. In Chapter 12, another special section guides the reader through building a compiler; the machine language produced by the compiler is then executed on the machine language simulator produced in Chapter 7.

Chapter 8—C Characters and Strings—deals with the fundamentals of processing nonnumeric data. The chapter includes a thorough walkthrough of the character and string processing functions available in C's libraries. The techniques discussed here are widely used in building word processors, page layout and typesetting software and text-processing applications. The chapter includes a variety of exercises that explore text-processing applications. The student will enjoy the exercises on writing limericks, writing random poetry, converting English to pig Latin, generating seven-letter words that are equivalent to a given telephone number, text justification, check protection, writing a check amount in words, generating Morse Code, metric conversions and dunning letters. The last exercise challenges the student to use a computerized dictionary to create a crossword puzzle generator.

Chapter 9—C Formatted Input/Output—presents all the powerful formatting capabilities of `printf` and `scanf`. We discuss `printf`'s output formatting capabilities such as rounding floating point values to a given number of decimal places, aligning columns of numbers, right-justification and left-justification, insertion of literal information, forcing a plus sign, printing leading zeros, using exponential notation, using octal and hexadecimal numbers and controlling field widths and precisions. We discuss all of `printf`'s escape sequences for cursor movement, printing special characters and causing an audible alert. We examine all of `scanf`'s input formatting capabilities, including inputting specific types of data and skipping specific characters in an input stream. We discuss all of `scanf`'s conversion specifiers for reading decimal, octal, hexadecimal, floating point, character and string values. We discuss scanning inputs to match (or not match) the characters in a scan set. The chapter exercises test virtually all of C's formatted input/output capabilities.

Chapter 10—C Structures, Unions, Bit Manipulations and Enumerations—presents a variety of important features. Structures are like records in other programming languages—they group data items of various types. Structures are used in Chapter 11 to form files consisting of records of information. Structures are used in conjunction with pointers and dynamic memory allocation in Chapter 12 to form dynamic data structures such as linked lists, queues, stacks and trees. Unions enable an area of memory to be used for different types of data at different times; such sharing can reduce a program's memory requirements or secondary-storage requirements. Enumerations provide a convenient means of defining useful symbolic constants; this helps make programs more self-documenting. C's powerful bit manipulation capabilities enable programmers to write programs that exercise lower-level hardware capabilities. This helps programs process bit strings, set individual bits on or off and store information more compactly. Such capabilities, often found only in low-level assembly languages, are valued by programmers writing system software such as operating systems and networking software. A feature of the chapter is its revised, high-performance card shuffling and dealing simulation. This is an excellent opportunity for the instructor to emphasize the quality of algorithms.

Chapter 11—C File Processing—discusses the techniques used to process text files with sequential access and random access. The chapter begins with an introduction to the data hierarchy from bits, to bytes, to fields, to records, to files. Next, C's simple view of files and streams is presented. Sequential-access files are discussed using programs that show how to open and close files, how to store data sequentially in a file and how to read data sequentially from a file. Random-access files are discussed using programs that show how to create a file sequentially for random access, how to read and write data to a file with random access and how to read data sequentially from a randomly accessed file. The fourth random-access program combines many of the techniques of accessing files both sequentially and randomly into a complete transaction-processing program.

Chapter 12—C Data Structures—discusses the techniques used to create and manipulate dynamic data structures. The chapter begins with discussions of self-referential structures and dynamic memory allocation and proceeds with a discussion of how to create and maintain various dynamic data structures including linked lists, queues (or waiting lines), stacks and trees. For each type of data structure, we present complete, working programs and show sample outputs. The chapter helps the student master pointers. It includes abundant examples using indirection and double indirection—a particularly difficult concept. One problem when working with pointers is that students have trouble visualizing the data structures and how their nodes are linked together. So we have included illustrations that show the links, and the sequence in which they are created. The binary tree example is a nice capstone for the study of pointers and dynamic data structures. This example creates a binary tree; enforces duplicate elimination; and introduces recursive preorder, inorder and postorder tree traversals. Students have a genuine sense of accomplishment when they study and implement this example. They particularly appreciate seeing that the inorder traversal prints the node values in sorted order. The chapter includes a substantial collection of exercises. A highlight of the exercises is the special section "Building Your Own Compiler." The exercises walk the student through the development of an infix-to-postfix-conversion program and a postfix-expression-evaluation program. We then modify the postfix evaluation algorithm to generate machine-language code. The compiler places this code in a file (using the techniques of Chapter 11). Students can run the machine language produced by their compilers on the software simulators they built in the exercises of Chapter 7!

Chapter 13—The C Preprocessor—provides detailed discussions of the preprocessor directives. The chapter includes detailed information on the `#include` directive (that causes a copy of a specified file to be included in place of the directive in the source code file before the file is compiled) and the `#define` directive that creates symbolic constants and macros. The chapter explains conditional compilation for enabling the programmer to control the execution of preprocessor directives and the compilation of program code. The `#` operator that converts its operand to a string and the `##` operator that concatenates two tokens are discussed. Predefined symbolic constants __LINE__, __FILE__, __DATE__ and __TIME__ are presented. Finally, macro `assert` of the `assert.h` header is discussed. Macro `assert` is valuable in program testing, debugging, verification and validation.

Chapter 14—Other C Topics—presents additional topics including several advanced topics not ordinarily covered in introductory courses. We show how to redirect program input to come from a file, redirect program output to be placed in a file, redirect the output of one program to be the input of another (called "piping"), append the output of a program to an existing file, develop functions that use variable-length argument lists, pass command-line arguments to function `main` and use them in a program, compile programs whose components are spread across multiple files, register functions with `atexit` to be executed at program termination, terminate program execution with function `exit`, use the `const` and `volatile` type qualifiers, specify the type of a numeric constant using the integer and floating-point suffixes, use the signal-handling library to trap unexpected events, create and use dynamic arrays with `calloc` and `realloc`, and use `unions` as a space-saving technique.

Part 2: Object-Based, Object-Oriented and Generic Programming in C++

Chapter 15—C++ as a "Better C"—introduces the non-object-oriented features of C++. These features improve the process of writing procedural programs. The chapter discusses single-line comments, stream input/output, declarations, creating new data types, function prototypes and type checking, `inline` functions (as a replacement for macros), reference parameters, the `const` qualifier, dynamic memory allocation, default arguments, the unary scope resolution operator, function overloading, linkage specifications and function templates.

Chapter 16—C++ Classes and Data Abstraction—begins our discussion of object-based programming. The chapter represents a wonderful opportunity for teaching data abstraction the "right way"—through a language (C++) expressly devoted to implementing abstract data types (ADTs). In recent years, data abstraction has become a major topic in introductory computing courses. Chapters 16 through 18 include a solid treatment of data abstraction. Chapter 16 discusses implementing ADTs as C++-style classes and why this approach is superior to using structs, accessing class members, separating interface from implementation, using access functions and utility functions, initializing objects with constructors, destroying objects with destructors, assignment by default memberwise copy and software reusability. One of the chapter exercises challenges the reader to develop a class for complex numbers.

Chapter 17—C++ Classes Part II—continues the study of classes and data abstraction. The chapter discusses declaring and using constant objects, constant member functions, composition—the process of building classes that have objects of other classes as members, friend functions and friend classes that have special access rights to the private and protected members of classes, the this pointer that enables an object to know its own address, dynamic memory allocation, static class members for containing and manipulating class-wide data, examples of popular abstract data types (arrays, strings and queues), container classes and iterators. The chapter exercises ask the student to develop a savings account class and a class for holding sets of integers. We discuss dynamic memory allocation with new and delete. When new fails, it returns a 0 pointer in pre-standard C++. We use this pre-standard style in Chapters 17 through 22. We defer to Chapter 23 the discussion of the new style of new failure in which new now "throws an exception." We motivate the discussion of static class members with a video-game-based example. We emphasize throughout the book and in our professional seminars how important it is to hide implementation details from clients of a class.

Chapter 18—C++ Operator Overloading—is one of the most popular topics in our C++ courses. Students really enjoy this material. They find it a perfect match with the discussion of abstract data types in Chapters 16 and 17. Operator overloading enables the programmer to tell the compiler how to use existing operators with objects of new class types. C++ already knows how to use these operators with objects of built-in types such as integers, floating point numbers and characters. But suppose we create a new string class— what would the plus sign mean when used between string objects? Many programmers use plus with strings to mean concatenation. The chapter discusses the fundamentals of operator overloading, restrictions in operator overloading, overloading with class member functions vs. with nonmember functions, overloading unary and binary operators and converting between types. A feature of the chapter is the substantial case study of an array class, a huge-integer class and a complex numbers class (the last two appear with full source code in the exercises). This material is different from what you do in most programming languages and courses. Operator overloading is a complex topic, but an enriching one. Using operator overloading wisely helps you add that extra "polish" to your classes. With the techniques of Chapters 16, 17 and 18, it is possible to craft a Date class that, if we had been using it for the last two decades, could easily have eliminated a major portion of the so-called "Year 2000 (or Y2K) Problem." One of the exercises encourages the reader to add operator overloading to class Complex to enable convenient manipulation of objects of this class with operator symbols—as in mathematics—rather than with function calls as the student did in the Chapter 17 exercises.

Chapter 19—C++ Inheritance—deals with one of the most fundamental capabilities of object-oriented programming languages. Inheritance is a form of software reusability in which new classes are developed quickly and easily by absorbing the capabilities of existing classes and adding appropriate new capabilities. The chapter discusses the notions of base classes and derived classes, `protected` members, `public` inheritance, `protected` inheritance, `private` inheritance, direct base classes, indirect base classes, constructors and destructors in base classes and derived classes and software engineering with inheritance. The chapter compares inheritance (*is a* relationships) with composition (*has a* relationships) and introduces *uses a* and *knows a* relationships. A feature of the chapter is its several substantial case studies. In particular, a lengthy case study implements a point, circle, cylinder class hierarchy. The exercises ask the student to compare the creation of new classes by inheritance vs. composition; to extend the various inheritance hierarchies discussed in the chapter; to write an inheritance hierarchy for quadrilaterals, trapezoids, parallelograms, rectangles and squares; and to create a more general shape hierarchy with two-dimensional shapes and three-dimensional shapes.

Chapter 20—C++ Virtual Functions and Polymorphism—deals with another of the fundamental capabilities of object-oriented programming, namely polymorphic behavior. When many classes are related through inheritance to a common base class, each derived-class object may be treated as a base-class object. This enables programs to be written in a general manner independent of the specific types of the derived-class objects. New kinds of objects can be handled by the same program, thus making systems more extensible. Polymorphism enables programs to eliminate complex `switch` logic in favor of simpler "straight-line" logic. A screen manager of a video game, for example, can simply send a draw message to every object in a linked list of objects to be drawn. Each object knows how to draw itself. A new object can be added to the program without modifying that program as long as that new object also knows how to draw itself. This style of programming is typically used to implement today's popular graphical user interfaces (GUIs). The chapter discusses the mechanics of achieving polymorphic behavior through the use of `virtual` functions. It distinguishes between abstract classes (from which objects cannot be instantiated) and concrete classes (from which objects can be instantiated). Abstract classes are useful for providing an inheritable interface to classes throughout the hierarchy. A feature of the chapter is its polymorphism case study of the point, circle, cylinder shape hierarchy discussed in Chapter 19. The chapter exercises ask the student to discuss a number of conceptual issues and approaches, add abstract classes to the shape hierarchy and develop a basic graphics package—and pursue all these projects with `virtual` functions and polymorphic programming. Our professional audiences insisted that we explain precisely how polymorphism is implemented in C++, and what execution time and memory "costs" one must pay when programming with this powerful capability. We responded by developing an illustration in the section entitled "Polymorphism, `virtual` Functions and Dynamic Binding "Under the Hood" that shows the *vtables* (`virtual` function tables) that the C++ compiler automatically builds to support the polymorphic programming style. We drew these tables in our classes in which we discussed the point, circle, cylinder shape hierarchy. Our audiences indicated that this indeed gave them the information to decide whether polymorphism was an appropriate programming style for each new project they would tackle. We have included this presentation in Section 20.9 and the *vtable* illustration in Fig. 20.2. Please study this presentation carefully. It will give you a much deeper understanding of what is really occurring in the computer when you program with inheritance and polymorphism.

Chapter 21—C++ Stream Input/Output—contains a comprehensive treatment of C++ object-oriented input/output. The chapter discusses the various I/O capabilities of C++ including output with the stream insertion operator, input with the stream extraction operator, type-safe I/O (a nice improvement over C), formatted I/O, unformatted I/O (for performance), stream manipulators for controlling the stream base (decimal, octal, or hexadecimal), floating-point numbers, controlling field widths, user-defined manipulators, stream format states, stream error states, I/O of objects of user-defined types and tying output streams to input streams (to ensure that prompts actually appear before the user is expected to enter responses). The extensive exercise set asks the student to write various programs that test most of the I/O capabilities discussed in the text.

Chapter 22—C++ Templates—discusses one of the more recent additions to C++. Function templates were introduced in Chapter 15. Class templates enable the programmer to capture the essence of an abstract data type (such as a stack, an array, or a queue) and then create—with minimal additional code—versions of that ADT for particular types (such as a queue of `int`, a queue of `float`, a queue of strings, etc.). For this reason, template classes are often called parameterized types. The chapter discusses using type parameters and nontype parameters and considers the interaction between templates and other C++ concepts, such as inheritance, `friends` and `static` members. The exercises challenge the student to write a variety of function templates and class templates, and to employ these in complete programs.

Chapter 23—C++ Exception Handling—discusses one of the more recent enhancements to the C++ language. Exception handling enables the programmer to write programs that are more robust, more fault tolerant and more appropriate for business-critical and mission-critical environments. The chapter discusses when exception handling is appropriate; introduces the basics of exception handling with `try` blocks, `throw` statements and `catch` blocks; indicates how and when to rethrow an exception; explains how to write an exception specification and process unexpected exceptions; and discusses the important ties between exceptions and constructors, destructors and inheritance. We discuss rethrowing an exception and we illustrate both ways `new` can fail when memory is exhausted. Prior to the C++ draft standard `new` failed by returning 0, much as `malloc` fails in C by returning a `NULL` pointer value. We show the new style of `new` failing by throwing a `bad_alloc` (bad allocation) exception. We illustrate how to use `set_new_handler` to specify a custom function to be called to deal with memory exhaustion situations. We discuss the `auto_ptr` class template to guarantee that dynamically allocated memory will be properly `deleted` to avoid memory leaks.

Part 3: Object-Oriented, GUI Event-Driven, Graphics and Multimedia Programming in Java

Chapter 24—Introduction to Java Applications and Applets—introduces a typical Java programming environment and provides a lightweight introduction to programming applications and applets in the Java programming language. Some of the input and output is performed using a new graphical user interface (GUI) element called `JOptionPane` that provides predefined windows (called dialogs) for input and output. `JOptionPane` handles ouputting data to windows and inputting data from windows. The chapter introduces applets using several of the sample demonstration applets supplied with the Java 2 Software Development Kit (J2SDK). We use `appletviewer` (a utility supplied with the J2SDK) to execute several sample applets. We then write Java applets that perform tasks similar to the applications written earlier in the chapter, and we explain the similarities and differences between applets and applications. After studying this chapter, the student will understand how to write simple, but complete, Java applications and applets. The next several chapters use both applets and applications to demonstrate additional key programming concepts.

Chapter 25—Beyond C & C++: Operators, Methods & Arrays—focuses on both the similarities and differences among Java, C and C++. The chapter discusses the primitive types in Java and how they differ from C/C++, as well as some differences in terminology. For example, what we call a function in C/C++ is called a method in Java. The chapter also contains a discussion of logical operators—&& (logical AND), & (boolean logical AND), | | (logical OR), | (boolean logical inclusive OR), ∧ (boolean logical exclusive OR) and ! (NOT) applications. The topic of method overloading (as compared to function overloading in C++) is motivated and explained. In this chapter, we also introduce events and event handling—elements required for programming graphical user interfaces. Events are notifications of state change such as button clicks, mouse clicks, pressing a keyboard key, etc. Java allows programmers to respond to various events by coding methods called event handlers. We also introduce arrays in Java, which are processed as full-fledged objects. This is further evidence of Java's commitment to nearly 100% object-orientation. We discuss the structuring of data into arrays, or groups, of related data items of the same type. The chapter presents numerous examples of both single-subscripted arrays and double-subscripted arrays.

Chapter 26—Java Object-Based Programming—begins our deeper discussion of classes. The chapter focuses on the essence and terminology of classes and objects. What is an object? What is a class of objects? What does the inside of an object look like? How are objects created? How are they destroyed? How do objects communicate with one another? Why are classes such a natural mechanism for packaging software as reusable componentry? The chapter discusses implementing abstract data types as Java-style classes, accessing class members, enforcing information hiding with `private` instance variables, separating interface from implementation, using access methods and utility methods, initializing objects with constructors and using overloaded constructors. The chapter discusses declaring and using constant references, composition—the process of building classes that have as members references to objects, the `this` reference that enables an object to "know itself," dynamic memory allocation, `static` class members for containing and manipulating class-wide data and examples of popular abstract data types such as stacks and queues. The chapter also introduces the `package` statement and discusses how to create reusable packages. The chapter exercises challenge the student to develop classes for complex numbers, rational numbers, times, dates, rectangles, huge integers, a class for playing Tic-Tac-Toe, a savings account class and a class for holding sets of integers.

Chapter 27—Java Object-Oriented Programming—discusses the relationships among classes of objects, and programming with related classes. How can we exploit commonality between classes of objects to minimize the amount of work it takes to build large software systems? What is polymorphism? What does it mean to "program in the general" rather than "programming in the specific?" How does programming in the general make it easy to modify systems and add new features with minimal effort? How can we program for a whole category of objects rather than programming individually for each type of object? The chapter deals with one of the most fundamental capabilities of object-oriented programming languages, inheritance, which is a form of software reusability in which new classes are developed quickly and easily by absorbing the capabilities of existing classes and adding appropriate new capabilities. The chapter discusses the notions of superclasses and subclasses, `protected` members, direct superclasses, indirect superclasses, use of constructors in superclasses and subclasses, and software engineering with inheritance. We introduce inner classes that help hide implementation details. Inner classes are most frequently used to create GUI event handlers. Named inner classes can be declared inside other classes and are useful in defining common event handlers for several GUI components. Anonymous inner classes are declared inside methods and are used to create one object—typically an event handler for a specific GUI component. The chapter compares inheritance (*is a* relationships) with composition (*has a* relationships). A feature of the chapter is its case study implementation of a point, circle, cylinder class hierarchy. The exercises ask the student to compare the creation of new classes by inheritance vs. composition; to extend the inheritance hierarchies discussed in the chapter; to write an inheritance hierarchy for quadrilaterals, trapezoids, parallelograms, rectangles and squares; and to create a more general shape hierarchy with two-dimensional shapes and three-dimensional shapes. The chapter explains polymorphic behavior. When many classes are related through inheritance to a common superclass, each subclass object may be treated as a superclass object. This enables programs to be written in a general manner independent of the specific types of the subclass objects. New kinds of objects can be handled by the same program, thus making systems more extensible. Polymorphism enables programs to eliminate complex `switch` logic in favor of simpler "straight-line" logic. A video game screen manager, for example, can send a "draw" message to every object in a linked list of objects to be drawn. Each object knows how to draw itself. A new type of object can be added to the program without modifying that program as long as that new object also knows how to draw itself. This style of programming is typically used to implement today's popular graphical user interfaces. The chapter distinguishes between `abstract` classes (from which objects cannot be instantiated) and concrete classes (from which objects can be instantiated). The chapter also introduces interfaces—sets of methods that must be defined by any class that `implements` the interface.

Chapter 28—Java Graphics and Java2D—begins a run of three chapters that present the multimedia "sizzle" of Java. Traditional C and C++ programming are pretty much confined to character-mode input/output. Some versions of C++ are supported by platform-dependent class libraries that can do graphics, but using these libraries makes your applications nonportable. Java's graphics capabilities are platform independent and hence, portable—and we mean portable in a worldwide sense. You can develop graphics-intensive Java applets and distribute them over the World Wide Web to colleagues everywhere and they will run nicely on the local Java platforms. We discuss graphics contexts and graphics objects; drawing strings, characters and bytes; color and font control; screen manipulation and paint modes; and drawing lines, rectangles, rounded rectangles, 3-dimensional rectangles, ovals, arcs and polygons. We introduce the Java2D API, new in Java 2, which provides powerful graphical manipulation tools. The chapter has many figures that painstakingly illustrate each of these graphics capabilities with live-code examples, appealing screen outputs, detailed features tables and detailed line art.

Chapter 29—Java Graphical User Interface Components—introduces the creation of applets and applications with user-friendly graphical user interfaces (GUIs). This chapter focuses on Java's new Swing GUI components. These platform-independent GUI components are written entirely in Java. This provides Swing GUI components with great flexibility—they can be customized to look like the computer platform on which the program executes, or they can use the standard Java look-and-feel that provides an identical user interface across all computer platforms. We discuss the `javax.swing` package, which provides especially powerful GUI components. The chapter illustrates GUI design principles, the `javax.swing` hierarchy, labels, push buttons, text fields, text areas, combo boxes, check boxes, panels, scrolling panels, custom panels, handling mouse events, windows, menus and using three of Java's simpler GUI layout managers: `FlowLayout`, `BorderLayout` and `GridLayout`. The chapter concentrates on Java's delegation event model for GUI processing. The exercises challenge the student to create specific GUIs, exercise various GUI features, develop drawing programs that let the user draw with the mouse and control fonts.

Chapter 30—Java Multimedia: Images, Animation, Audio and Video—deals with Java's capabilities for making computer applications "come alive." It is remarkable that students in first programming courses will be writing applications with all these capabilities. The possibilities are intriguing. Students now access (over the Internet and through CD-ROM technology) vast libraries of graphics images, audios and videos, and can weave their own together with those in the libraries to form creative applications. Already most new computers come "multimedia equipped." Dazzling term papers and classroom presentations are being prepared by students with access to vast public domain libraries of images, drawings, voices, pictures, videos, animations and the like. A "paper" when most of us were in the earlier grades was a collection of characters, possibly handwritten, possibly typewritten. A "paper" can be a multimedia "extravaganza." It can hold your interest, pique your curiosity, make you feel what the subjects of the paper felt when they were making history. Multimedia can make your science labs much more exciting. Textbooks can come alive. Instead of looking at a static picture of some phenomenon, you can watch that phenomenon occur in a colorful, animated, presentation with sounds, videos and various other effects. People can learn more, learn it in more depth and experience more viewpoints. A feature of the chapter is the image maps discussion that enable a program to sense the presence of the mouse pointer over a region of an image, without clicking the mouse. We present a live-code image map application with the icons Prentice Hall artists created for our *Java Multimedia Cyber Classroom* programming tips. As the user moves the mouse pointer across the six icon images, the type of tip is displayed, either "Good Programming Practice" for the thumbs-up icon, "Portability Tip" for the bug with the suitcase icon, and so on.

Part 4: Appendices

Several Appendices provide valuable reference material. We present Internet and Web resources for C, C++ and Java in Appendix A; a list of C99 Internet and Web resources in Appendix B; complete operator precedence and associativity charts for C, C++ and Java in Appendix C; the set of ASCII character codes in Appendix D. Appendix E is a complete tutorial on number systems including many self-review exercises with answers. Appendix F provides an overview of the C Standard Libraries and Web resources for these libraries.

Acknowledgments

One of the great pleasures of writing a textbook is acknowledging the efforts of many people whose names may not appear on the cover, but whose hard work, cooperation, friendship and understanding were crucial to the production of the book. Many people at Deitel & Associates, Inc. devoted long hours to this project.

- Abbey Deitel, President
- Barbara Deitel, Chief Financial Officer
- Christi Kelsey, Director of Business Development
- Jeff Listfield, Senior Developer
- Su Zhang, Senior Developer

We would also like to thank the participants in the Deitel & Associates, Inc., College Internship Program: Mike Oliver, Brian O'Connor and Adam Burke who worked on the book's ancillary package.[1] We would especially like to thank Tim Christensen. Tim, a senior at Boston College majoring in Business Management with a concentration in Computer Science, tested all the source code for the entire book, added comments to all of the C code (Chapters 2–14) and updated the programs to our standard coding conventions. He created Appendix F (C Standard Libraries Internet and Web Resources) and revised Appendix B (C99 Internet and Web Resources). Tim also worked on the ancillary package for the textbook.

We are fortunate to have worked on this project with the talented and dedicated team of publishing professionals at Prentice Hall. We especially appreciate the extraordinary efforts of our Computer Science Editor, Kate Hargett and her boss and our mentor in publishing—Marcia Horton, Editorial Director of Prentice-Hall's Engineering and Computer Science Division. Vince O'Brien and Tom Manshreck did a marvelous job managing the production of the book. Sarah Parker managed the publication of the book's extensive ancillary package.

We wish to acknowledge the efforts of our *Fourth Edition* reviewers and to give a special note of thanks to Carole Snyder of Prentice Hall who managed this extraordinary review effort. [Please note that the first two editions of *C How to Program* included only C and C++; Java was added in the *Third Edition*.]

- Rex Jaeschke (Independent Consultant; former chair of the ANSI C Committee)
- John Benito (Convener of the ISO working group that is responsible for the C programming language)
- Deena Engel (New York University)
- Geb Thomas (University of Iowa)
- Jim Brzowski (University of Massachusetts – Lowell)

We wish to acknowledge again the efforts of our previous edition reviewers (some first edition, some second edition, some third edition and some all three); the affiliations were current at the time of the review):

---

1. This highly competitive program (we received 1000+ applications for 11 internship positions in 2003) offers a limited number of salaried positions to Boston-area college students majoring in Computer Science, Information Technology, Marketing, Management and English. Students work at our corporate headquarters in Maynard, Massachusetts full-time in the summers and (for those attending college in the Boston area) part-time during the academic year. We also offer full-time internship positions for students interested in taking a semester off from school to gain industry experience. Regular full-time positions are available from time to time to college graduates. For more information, please contact our president—abbey.deitel@deitel.com—and visit our Web site, www.deitel.com.

- Rex Jaeshke (Independent Consultant; former chair of the ANSI C Committee)
- Randy Meyers (NetCom; ANSI C Committee Chair; former ANSI C++ Committee Member)
- Simon North (Synopsis, XML Author)
- Fred Tydeman (Consultant)
- Kevin Wayne (Princeton University)
- Eugene Katzin (Montgomery College)
- Sam Harbison (Texas Instruments, PH Author)
- Chuck Allison (Tydeman Consulting)
- Catherine Dwyer (Pace University)
- Glen Lancaster (DePaul University)
- David Falconer (California State University at Fullerton)
- David Finkel (Worcester Polytechnic)
- H. E. Dunsmore (Purdue University)
- Jim Schmolze (Tufts University)
- Gene Spafford (Purdue University)
- Clovis Tondo (IBM Corporation and visiting professor at Nova University)
- Jeffrey Esakov (University of Pennsylvania)
- Tom Slezak (University of California, Lawrence Livermore National Laboratory)
- Gary A. Wilson (Gary A Wilson & Associates and University of California Berkeley Extension)
- Mike Kogan (IBM Corporation; chief architect of 32-bit OS/2 2.0)
- Don Kostuch (IBM Corporation retired; worldwide instructor in C, C++ and object-oriented programming)
- Ed Lieblein (Nova University)
- John Carroll (San Diego State University)
- Alan Filipski (Arizona State University)
- Greg Hidley (University of California, San Diego)
- Daniel Hirschberg (University of California, Irvine)
- Jack Tan (University of Houston)
- Richard Alpert (Boston University)
- Eric Bloom (Bentley College)

These reviewers scrutinized every aspect of the text and made countless suggestions for improving the accuracy and completeness of the presentation.

Contacting Deitel & Associates

We would sincerely appreciate your comments, criticisms, corrections and suggestions for improving the text. Please address all correspondence to:

    deitel@deitel.com

We will respond promptly.

Errata

We will post all errata for the *Fourth Edition* at www.deitel.com.

Customer Support

Please direct all software and installation questions to Pearson Education Technical Support:

- By phone: 1-800-677-6337
- By email: media.support@pearsoned.com
- On the Web: 247.prenhall.com

Please direct all C, C++ and Java language questions to deitel@deitel.com. We will respond promptly.

Welcome to the exciting worlds of procedural programming in C; object-based, object-oriented and generic programming in C++; and graphics, graphical user interface, multimedia and event-driven programming in Java. We sincerely hope you enjoy learning with this book.

Dr. Harvey M. Deitel
Paul J. Deitel

About the Authors

Dr. Harvey M. Deitel, Chairman and Chief Strategy Officer of Deitel & Associates, Inc., has 42 years experience in the computing field, including extensive industry and academic experience. Dr. Deitel earned B.S. and M.S. degrees from the Massachusetts Institute of Technology and a Ph.D. from Boston University. He worked on the pioneering virtual-memory operating-systems projects at IBM and MIT that developed techniques now widely implemented in systems such as UNIX, Linux and Windows XP. He has 20 years of college teaching experience, including earning tenure and serving as the Chairman of the Computer Science Department at Boston College before founding Deitel & Associates, Inc., with his son, Paul J. Deitel. He and Paul are the co-authors of several dozen books and multimedia packages and they are writing many more. With translations published in Japanese, German, Russian, Spanish, Traditional Chinese, Simplified Chinese, Korean, French, Polish, Italian, Portuguese, Greek, Urdu and Turkish, the Deitels' texts have earned international recognition. Dr. Deitel has delivered professional seminars to major corporations, government organizations and the military.

Paul J. Deitel, CEO and Chief Technical Officer of Deitel & Associates, Inc., is a graduate of the Massachusetts Institute of Technology's Sloan School of Management, where he studied Information Technology. Through Deitel & Associates, Inc., he has delivered C, C++, Java, Internet and World Wide Web courses to industry clients, including IBM, Sun Microsystems, Dell, Lucent Technologies, Fidelity, NASA at the Kennedy Space Center, the National Severe Storm Laboratory, Compaq, White Sands Missile Range, Rogue Wave Software, Boeing, Stratus, Cambridge Technology Partners, Open Environment Corporation, One Wave, Hyperion Software, Adra Systems, Entergy, Cable-Data Systems and many other organizations. He has lectured on C++ and Java for the Boston Chapter of the Association for Computing Machinery and has taught satellite-based Java courses through a cooperative venture of Deitel & Associates, Prentice Hall and the

Technology Education Network. He and his father, Dr. Harvey M. Deitel, are the world's best-selling Computer Science textbook authors.

About Deitel & Associates, Inc.

Deitel & Associates, Inc., is an internationally recognized corporate training and content-creation organization specializing in Internet/World Wide Web software technology, e-business/e-commerce software technology, object technology and computer programming languages education. The company provides instructor-led courses on Internet and World Wide Web programming, wireless Internet programming, object technology, and major programming languages and platforms, such as C, C++, Visual C++® .NET, Visual Basic® .NET, C#, Java, Advanced Java, XML, Perl, Python and more. The founders of Deitel & Associates, Inc., are Dr. Harvey M. Deitel and Paul J. Deitel. The company's clients include many of the world's largest computer companies, government agencies, branches of the military and business organizations. Through its 27-year publishing partnership with Prentice Hall, Deitel & Associates, Inc., publishes leading-edge programming textbooks, professional books, interactive CD-based multimedia *Cyber Classrooms*, *Complete Training Courses*, Web-based training courses and course management systems e-content for popular CMSs such as WebCT™, Blackboard™ and CourseCompass^SM. Deitel & Associates, Inc., and the authors can be reached via e-mail at:

    deitel@deitel.com

To learn more about Deitel & Associates, Inc., its publications and its worldwide corporate on-site training curriculum, see the last few pages of this book or visit:

    www.deitel.com

Individuals wishing to purchase Deitel® books, *Cyber Classrooms*, *Complete Training Courses* and Web-based training courses can do so through bookstores, online booksellers and:

    www.deitel.com
    www.prenhall.com/deitel
    www.InformIT.com/deitel
    www.InformIT.com/cyberclassrooms

Bulk orders by corporations and academic institutions should be placed directly with Prentice Hall. See the last few pages of this book for worldwide ordering instructions.

1

Introduction to Computers, the Internet and the World Wide Web

Objectives

- To understand basic computer concepts.
- To become familiar with different types of programming languages.
- To become familiar with the history of the C programming language.
- To become aware of the C Standard Library.
- To understand the elements of a typical C program development environment.
- To appreciate why it is appropriate to learn C in a first programming course.
- To appreciate why C provides a foundation for further study of programming languages in general and of C++, Java and C# in particular.
- To become familiar with the history of the Internet and the World Wide Web.

Things are always at their best in their beginning.
Blaise Pascal

High thoughts must have high language.
Aristophanes

Our life is frittered away by detail … Simplify, simplify.
Henry Thoreau

Outline

1.1 Introduction

Welcome to C, C++ and Java! We have worked hard to create what we sincerely hope will be an informative and entertaining learning experience for you. This book is unique among C textbooks in that:

- It is appropriate for technically oriented people with little or no programming experience.

- It is appropriate for experienced programmers who want a deep and rigorous treatment of the language.

How can one book appeal to both groups? The answer is that the common core of the book emphasizes achieving program *clarity* through the proven techniques of *structured programming*. Non-programmers learn programming the right way from the beginning. We have attempted to write in a clear and straightforward manner. The book is abundantly illustrated. Perhaps most importantly, the book presents hundreds of complete working programs and shows the outputs produced when those programs are run on a computer. We call this the "live-code approach." All of these example programs are provided on the CD that accompanies this book. You may also download all these examples from our Web site `www.deitel.com`.

The first four chapters introduce the fundamentals of computing, computer programming and the C computer programming language. Novices who have taken our courses tell us that the material in these chapters presents a solid foundation for the deeper treatment of C in Chapters 5 through 14. Experienced programmers typically read the first four chapters quickly and then discover that the treatment of C in Chapters 5 through 14 is both rigorous and challenging. They particularly appreciate the detailed treatments of pointers, strings, files and data structures in the later chapters.

Many experienced programmers appreciate the treatment of structured programming. Often they have been programming in a structured language such as Pascal, but because they were never formally introduced to structured programming, they are not writing the best possible code. As they learn C with this book, they are able to improve their programming style. So whether you are a novice or an experienced programmer, there is much here to inform, entertain and challenge you.

Most people are familiar with the exciting tasks computers perform. Using this textbook, you will learn how to command computers to perform those tasks. It is *software* (i.e., the instructions you write to command computers to perform *actions* and make *decisions*) that controls computers (often referred to as *hardware*). This text provides an introduction to programming in C, which was standardized in 1989 in the United States through the *American National Standards Institute (ANSI)* and worldwide through the efforts of the *International Standards Organization (ISO)*.

Computer use is increasing in almost every field of endeavor. In an era of steadily rising costs, computing costs have been decreasing dramatically due to rapid developments in both hardware and software technologies. Computers that might have filled large rooms and cost millions of dollars two decades ago can now be inscribed on the surfaces of silicon chips smaller than a fingernail, costing perhaps a few dollars each. Ironically, silicon is one of the most abundant materials on earth—it is an ingredient in common sand. Silicon-chip technology has made computing so economical that hundreds of millions of general-purpose computers are in use worldwide helping people in business, industry and government, and in their personal lives. That number could easily double in the next few years.

C++ and Java—object-oriented programming languages based on C—receive so much interest today that we have included a detailed introduction to C++ and object-oriented programming in Chapters 15–23 and a detailed introduction to object-oriented programming in Java in Chapters 24–30. In the programming languages marketplace, many key vendors market a combined C/C++ product rather than offering separate products. This gives users the ability to continue programming in C if they wish, then gradually migrate to C++ when it is appropriate. All the software you need to develop and run the C, C++ and Java programs in this book is available on the CD that accompanies this book or free for download on the Internet. [See the Preface.]

You are about to start on a challenging and rewarding path. As you proceed, if you would like to communicate with us, please send us email at

deitel@deitel.com

or browse our World Wide Web site at

www.deitel.com

We will respond promptly. We hope you enjoy learning C, C++ and Java with *C How to Program: Fourth Edition.*

1.2 What Is a Computer?

A *computer* is a device capable of performing computations and making logical decisions at speeds millions (even billions) of times faster than human beings can. For example, many of today's personal computers can perform a billion additions per second. A person operating a desk calculator might require a lifetime to complete the same number of calculations a powerful personal computer can perform in one second. (Points to ponder: How would you know whether the person added the numbers correctly? How would you know whether the computer added the numbers correctly?) Today's fastest *supercomputers* can perform hundreds of billions of additions per second! And trillion-instruction-per-second computers are already functioning in research laboratories!

Computers process *data* under the control of sets of instructions called *computer programs.* These computer programs guide the computer through orderly sets of actions specified by people called *computer programmers.*

A computer is comprised of various devices (such as the keyboard, screen, "mouse," disks, memory, DVD, CD-ROM and processing units) that are referred to as *hardware.* The computer programs that run on a computer are referred to as *software.* Hardware costs have been declining dramatically in recent years, to the point that personal computers have become commodities. Unfortunately, for decades software-development costs rose steadily as programmers developed ever more powerful and complex applications, without significantly improved technology for software development. In this book, you will learn proven software-development methods that are helping organizations control, and even reduce, software-development costs—structured programming, top-down stepwise refinement, functionalization, object-based programming and object-oriented programming.

1.3 Computer Organization

Regardless of differences in physical appearance, virtually every computer may be envisioned as being divided into six *logical units* or sections:

1. *Input unit.* This is the "receiving" section of the computer. It obtains information (data and computer programs) from *input devices* and places this information at the disposal of the other units so that the information can be processed. Most information is entered into computers through keyboards and mouse devices. Information also can be entered by speaking to your computer, by scanning images and by having your computer receive information from a network, such as the Internet.

2. *Output unit.* This is the "shipping" section of the computer. It takes information that has been processed by the computer and places it on various *output devices* to make the information available for use outside the computer. Most information output from computers today is displayed on screens, printed on paper or used to control other devices. Computers also can output their information to networks, such as the Internet.

3. *Memory unit.* This is the rapid access, relatively low-capacity "warehouse" section of the computer. It retains information that has been entered through the input

unit, so the information may be made immediately available for processing when it is needed. The memory unit also retains processed information until that information can be placed on output devices by the output unit. The memory unit is often called either *memory* or *primary memory.*

4. *Arithmetic and logic unit (ALU).* This is the "manufacturing" section of the computer. It is responsible for performing calculations such as addition, subtraction, multiplication and division. It contains the decision mechanisms that allow the computer, for example, to compare two items from the memory unit to determine whether they are equal.

5. *Central processing unit (CPU).* This is the "administrative" section of the computer. It is the computer's coordinator and is responsible for supervising the operation of the other sections. The CPU tells the input unit when information should be read into the memory unit, tells the ALU when information from the memory unit should be used in calculations and tells the output unit when to send information from the memory unit to certain output devices. Many of today's computers have multiple processing units and, hence, can perform many operations simultaneously—such computers are called *multiprocessors.*

6. *Secondary storage unit.* This is the long-term, high-capacity "warehousing" section of the computer. Programs or data not actively being used by the other units normally are placed on secondary storage devices (such as disks) until they are again needed, possibly hours, days, months or even years later. Information in secondary storage takes much longer to access than information in primary memory, but the cost per unit of secondary storage is much less than the cost per unit of primary memory.

1.4 Evolution of Operating Systems

Early computers were capable of performing only one *job* or *task* at a time. This form of computer operation is often called single-user *batch processing.* The computer runs a single program at a time while processing data in groups or *batches.* In these early systems, users generally submitted their jobs to a computer center on decks of punched cards. Users often had to wait hours or even days before printouts were returned to their desks.

Software systems called *operating systems* were developed to help make it more convenient to use computers. Early operating systems managed the smooth transition between jobs. This minimized the time it took for computer operators to switch between jobs and hence increased the amount of work, or *throughput*, computers could process.

As computers became more powerful, it became evident that single-user batch processing rarely utilized the computer's resources efficiently because most of the time was spent waiting for slow input/output devices to complete their tasks. Instead, it was thought that many jobs or tasks could be made to *share* the resources of the computer to achieve better utilization. This is called *multiprogramming.* Multiprogramming involves the "simultaneous" operation of many jobs on the computer—the computer shares its resources among the jobs competing for its attention. With early multiprogramming operating systems, users still submitted jobs on decks of punched cards and waited hours or days for results.

In the 1960s, several groups in industry and the universities pioneered *timesharing* operating systems. Timesharing is a special case of multiprogramming, in which users access the computer through *terminals*, typically devices with keyboards and screens. In a typical timesharing computer system, there may be dozens or even hundreds of users sharing the computer at once. The computer actually does not run all the users simultaneously. Rather, it runs a small portion of one user's job then moves on to service the next user. The computer does this so quickly that it may provide service to each user several times per second. Thus, the users' programs *appear* to be running simultaneously. An advantage of timesharing is that the user receives almost immediate responses to requests rather than having to wait long periods for results as with previous modes of computing.

1.5 Personal, Distributed and Client/Server Computing

In 1977, Apple Computer popularized the phenomenon of *personal computing*. Initially, it was a hobbyist's dream. Computers became economical enough for people to buy them for their own personal or business use. In 1981, IBM, the world's largest computer vendor, introduced the IBM Personal Computer. This quickly legitimized personal computing in business, industry and government organizations.

These computers were "standalone" units—people did their work on their own computers then transported disks back and forth to share information (often called "sneakernet"). Although early personal computers were not powerful enough to timeshare several users, these machines could be linked together in computer networks, sometimes over telephone lines and sometimes in *local area networks (LANs)* within an organization. This led to the phenomenon of *distributed computing,* in which an organization's computing, instead of being performed strictly at some central computer installation, is distributed over networks to the sites at which the work of the organization is performed. Personal computers were powerful enough to handle the computing requirements of individual users, and to handle the basic communications tasks of passing information between one another electronically.

Today's personal computers are as powerful as the million dollar machines of just 10–15 years ago. The most powerful desktop machines—called *workstations*—provide individual users with enormous capabilities. Information is shared easily across computer networks where computers called *file servers* offer a common store data that may be used by *client* computers distributed throughout the network, hence the term *client/server computing*. C, C++ and Java are among the programming languages of choice for writing software for operating systems, computer networking and distributed client/server applications. Today's popular operating systems such as UNIX, Linux, Mac OS X (pronounced "OS ten") and Windows provide the kinds of capabilities discussed in this section.

1.6 Machine Languages, Assembly Languages and High-Level Languages

Programmers write instructions in various programming languages, some directly understandable by computers and others that require intermediate *translation* steps. Hundreds of computer languages are in use today. These may be divided into three general types:

1. Machine languages
2. Assembly languages
3. High-level languages

Any computer can directly understand only its own *machine language*. Machine language is the "natural language" of a particular computer. It is defined by the hardware design of that computer. Machine languages generally consist of strings of numbers (ultimately reduced to 1s and 0s) that instruct computers to perform their most elementary operations one at a time. Machine languages are *machine dependent* (i.e., a particular machine language can be used on only one type of computer). Such languages are cumbersome for humans, as can be seen by the following section of a machine-language program that adds overtime pay to base pay and stores the result in gross pay:

```
+1300042774
+1400593419
+1200274027
```

Machine-language programming was simply too slow and tedious for most programmers. Instead of using the strings of numbers that computers could directly understand, programmers began using English-like abbreviations to represent elementary operations. These abbreviations formed the basis of *assembly languages. Translator programs* called *assemblers* were developed to convert assembly-language programs to machine language at computer speeds. The following section of an assembly-language program also adds overtime pay to base pay and stores the result in gross pay, but more clearly than its machine-language equivalent:

```
LOAD    BASEPAY
ADD     OVERPAY
STORE   GROSSPAY
```

Although such code is clearer to humans, it is incomprehensible to computers until translated to machine language.

Computer usage increased rapidly with the advent of assembly languages, but programming in these languages still required many instructions to accomplish even the simplest tasks. To speed the programming process, *high-level languages* were developed in which single statements could be written to accomplish substantial tasks. The translator programs that convert high-level language programs into machine language are called *compilers*. High-level languages allow programmers to write instructions that look almost like everyday English and contain commonly used mathematical notations. A payroll program written in a high-level language might contain a statement such as

```
grossPay = basePay + overTimePay
```

Obviously, high-level languages are much more desirable from the programmer's standpoint than either machine languages or assembly languages. C, C++ and Java are among the most powerful and most widely used high-level programming languages.

The process of compiling a high-level language program into machine language can take a considerable amount of computer time. *Interpreter* programs were developed to execute high-level language programs directly without the need for compiling those programs into machine language. Although compiled programs execute much faster than interpreted programs, interpreters are popular in program-development environments in which programs are recompiled frequently as new features are added and errors are corrected. Once a program is developed, a compiled version can be produced to run most efficiently.

1.7 FORTRAN, COBOL, Pascal and Ada

Hundreds of high-level languages have been developed, but only a few have achieved broad acceptance. *FORTRAN* (FORmula TRANslator) was developed by IBM Corporation in the 1950s to be used for scientific and engineering applications that require complex mathematical computations. FORTRAN is still widely used, especially in engineering applications.

COBOL (COmmon Business Oriented Language) was developed in 1959 by computer manufacturers, the government and industrial computer users. COBOL is used for commercial applications that require precise and efficient manipulation of large amounts of data. A significant percentage of business software is still programmed in COBOL.

During the 1960s, many large software development efforts encountered severe difficulties. Software schedules were typically late, costs greatly exceeded budgets and the finished products were unreliable. People began to realize that software development was a far more complex activity than they had imagined. Research activity in the 1960s resulted in the evolution of *structured programming*—a disciplined approach to writing programs that are clearer than unstructured programs, easier to test and debug and easier to modify.

One of the more tangible results of this research was the development of the *Pascal* programming language by Professor Niklaus Wirth in 1971. Pascal, named after the seventeenth-century mathematician and philosopher Blaise Pascal, was designed for teaching structured programming and rapidly became the preferred programming language in most colleges. Unfortunately, the language lacks many features needed to make it useful in commercial, industrial and government applications, so it has not been widely accepted in these environments.

The *Ada* programming language was developed under the sponsorship of the U.S. Department of Defense (DOD) during the 1970s and early 1980s. Hundreds of separate languages were being used to produce the DOD's massive command-and-control software systems. The DOD wanted a single language that would fill most of its needs. The language was named after Lady Ada Lovelace, daughter of the poet Lord Byron. Lady Lovelace is credited with writing the world's first computer program in the early 1800s (for the Analytical Engine mechanical computing device designed by Charles Babbage). One important capability of Ada is called *multitasking*, which allows programmers to specify that many activities are to occur in parallel. Some widely used high-level languages we have discussed—including C and C++—allow the programmer to write programs that perform only one activity at a time. Java, through a technique called *multithreading*, enables programmers to write programs with parallel activities.

1.8 History of C

C evolved from two previous languages, BCPL and B. BCPL was developed in 1967 by Martin Richards as a language for writing operating systems software and compilers. Ken Thompson modeled many features in his B language after their counterparts in BCPL and used B in 1970 to create early versions of the UNIX operating system at Bell Laboratories on a DEC PDP-7 computer. Both BCPL and B were "typeless" languages—every data item occupied one "word" in memory and the burden of typing variables fell on the shoulders of the programmer.

The C language was evolved from B by Dennis Ritchie at Bell Laboratories and was originally implemented on a DEC PDP-11 computer in 1972. C uses many of the important concepts of BCPL and B while adding data typing and other powerful features. C initially became widely known as the development language of the UNIX operating system. Today, virtually all new major operating systems are written in C and/or C++. C is available for most computers. C is also hardware independent. With careful design, it is possible to write C programs that are *portable* to most computers.

By the late 1970s, C had evolved into what is now referred to as "traditional C." The publication in 1978 of Kernighan and Ritchie's book, *The C Programming Language*, brought wide attention to the language. This publication became one of the most successful computer science books of all time.

The rapid expansion of C over various types of computers (sometimes called *hardware platforms*) led to many variations that were similar but often incompatible. This was a serious problem for program developers who needed to develop code that would run on several platforms. It became clear that a standard version of C was needed. In 1983, the X3J11 technical committee was created under the American National Standards Committee on Computers and Information Processing (X3) to "provide an unambiguous and machine-independent definition of the language." In 1989, the standard was approved; this standard was updated in 1999. The standards document is referred to as *INCITS/ISO/IEC 9899-1999*. Copies of this document may be ordered from the American National Standards Institute (www.ansi.org) at webstore.ansi.org/ansidocstore.

Portability Tip 1.1

Because C is a hardware-independent, widely available language, applications written in C can run with little or no modifications on a wide range of different computer systems.

[*Note*: We will include many of these *Portability Tips* to highlight techniques that will help you write programs that can run, with little or no modification, on a variety of computers. We will also highlight *Good Programming Practices* (practices that can help you write programs that are clear, understandable, maintainable and easy to test and debug—that is, eliminate errors), *Common Programming Errors* (problems to watch out for, so you do not make these same errors in your programs), *Performance Tips* (techniques that will help you write programs that run faster and use less memory), *Error-Prevention Tips* (techniques that will help you remove bugs from your programs, and more important, techniques that will help you write bug-free programs in the first place) and *Software Engineering Observations* (concepts that affect and improve the overall architecture and quality of a software system, and particularly, of large software systems). Many of these techniques and practices are only guidelines; you will, no doubt, develop your own preferred programming style.]

1.9 C Standard Library

As you will learn in Chapter 5, C programs consist of modules or pieces called *functions*. You can program all the functions you need to form a C program, but most C programmers take advantage of a rich collection of existing functions called the *C Standard Library*. Thus, there are really two pieces to learning how to program in C. The first is learning the C language itself, and the second is learning how to use the functions in the C Standard Library. Throughout the book, we discuss many of these functions. P.J. Plauger's *The Standard C Library* is required reading for programmers who need a deep understanding of the library functions, how to implement them and how to use them to write portable code.

This textbook encourages a *building block approach* to creating programs. Avoid reinventing the wheel. Use existing pieces—this is called *software reusability*, and it is a key to the developing field of object-oriented programming, as we will see in Chapters 15 through 30. When programming in C you will typically use the following building blocks:

- C Standard Library functions
- Functions you create yourself
- Functions other people have created and made available to you

The advantage of creating your own functions is that you will know exactly how they work. You will be able to examine the C code. The disadvantage is the time-consuming effort that goes into designing and developing new functions.

If you use existing functions, you can avoid reinventing the wheel. In the case of the ANSI standard functions, you know that they are carefully written, and you know that because you are using functions that are available on virtually all ANSI C implementations, your programs will have a greater chance of being portable.

Performance Tip 1.1

Using ANSI standard library functions instead of writing your own comparable versions can improve program performance because these functions are carefully written to perform efficiently.

Portability Tip 1.2

Using ANSI standard library functions instead of writing your own comparable versions can improve program portability because these functions are used in virtually all ANSI C implementations.

1.10 C++

C++ is a superset of C developed by Bjarne Stroustrup at Bell Laboratories. C++ provides a number of features that "spruce up" the C language. More importantly, it provides capabilities for *object-oriented programming*. C++ has become a dominant language in both industry and universities.

Objects are essentially reusable software *components* that model items in the real world. There is a revolution brewing in the software industry. Building software quickly, correctly and economically remains an elusive goal, and at a time when demands for new and more powerful software are soaring.

Software developers are discovering that using a modular, object-oriented design and implementation approach can make software development groups much more productive than is possible with conventional programming techniques.

Many people feel that the best educational strategy today is to master C, then study C++. Therefore, in Chapters 15–23 of *C How to Program: Fourth Edition*, we present a condensed treatment of C++ selected from our book *C++ How to Program*. We hope that you find this valuable and that it will encourage you to pursue further study of C++ after completing this book.

1.11 Java

Many people believe that the next major area in which microprocessors will have a profound impact is intelligent consumer electronic devices. Recognizing this, Sun Microsystems funded an internal corporate research project code-named Green in 1991. The project resulted in the development of a language based on C and C++ which its creator, James Gosling, called Oak after an oak tree outside his window at Sun. It was later discovered that there already was a computer language called Oak. When a group of Sun people visited a local coffee place, the name *Java* was suggested and it stuck.

However, the Green project ran into some difficulties. The marketplace for intelligent consumer electronic devices was not developing as quickly as Sun had anticipated. Worse yet, a major contract for which Sun had competed was awarded to another company, putting the project in danger of being canceled. By sheer good fortune, the World Wide Web exploded in popularity in 1993, and Sun saw the immediate potential of using Java to create Web pages with so-called *dynamic content*.

Sun formally announced Java at a trade show in May 1995. Ordinarily, an event such as this would not have generated much attention. However, Java generated immediate interest in the business community because of the phenomenal interest in the World Wide Web. Java is now used to create Web pages with dynamic and interactive content, develop large-scale enterprise applications, enhance the functionality of Web servers (the computers that provide the content we see in our Web browsers), provide applications for consumer devices (such as cell phones, pagers and personal digital assistants) and do many more things.

In 1995, we were following the development of Java by Sun Microsystems. In November of that year, we attended an Internet conference in Boston. A representative from Sun Microsystems gave a rousing presentation on Java. As the talk proceeded, it became clear to us that Java would certainly play a significant part in the development of interactive, multimedia Web pages. But we immediately saw a much greater potential for the language. We saw Java as a superb language for teaching first-year programming language students the essentials of graphics, images, animation, audio, video, database, networking, multithreading and collaborative computing.

Chapters 24–30 of this book present a detailed introduction to Java graphics programming, graphical user interface (GUI) programming, multimedia programming and event-driven programming. This material was carefully condensed from our textbook *Java How to Program*. We hope you find this material valuable and that it will encourage you to pursue further study in Java.

In addition to its prominence in developing Internet- and intranet-based applications, Java has become the language of choice for implementing software for devices that communicate over a network (such as cellular phones, pagers and personal digital assistants). Do not be surprised when your new stereo and other devices in your home are networked together using Java technology!

1.12 BASIC, Visual Basic, Visual C++, C# and .NET

The BASIC (Beginner's All-Purpose Symbolic Instruction Code) programming language was developed in the mid-1960s by Professors John Kemeny and Thomas Kurtz of Dartmouth College as a language for writing simple programs. BASIC's primary purpose was to familiarize novices with programming techniques. Visual Basic was introduced by Microsoft in 1991 to simplify the process of developing Microsoft Windows applications.

Visual Basic .NET, Visual C++ .NET and C# are designed for Microsoft's new *.NET programming platform*. All three languages make use of .NET's powerful library of reusable software components called the Framework Class Library (FCL).

Comparably to Java, the .NET platform enables Web-based applications to be distributed to many devices (even cell phones) and to desktop computers. The C# programming language was designed specifically for the .NET platform as a language that would enable programmers to migrate easily to .NET. C++, Java and C# all have their roots in the C programming language.

1.13 Key Software Trend: Object Technology

One of the authors, HMD, remembers the great frustration that was felt in the 1960s by software-development organizations, especially those developing large-scale projects. During his undergraduate years, HMD had the privilege of working summers at a leading computer vendor on the teams developing time-sharing, virtual memory operating systems. This was a great experience for a college student. But, in the summer of 1967, reality set in when the company "decommitted" from producing as a commercial product the particular system on which hundreds of people had been working for many years. It was difficult to get this software right. Software is "complex stuff."

Improvements to software technology did start to appear with the benefits of so-called *structured programming* (and the related disciplines of *structured systems analysis and design)* being realized in the 1970s. But it was not until the technology of object-oriented programming became widely used in the 1990s, that software developers finally felt they had the necessary tools for making major strides in the software-development process.

Actually, object technology dates back to the mid 1960s. The C++ programming language, developed at AT&T by Bjarne Stroustrup in the early 1980s, is based on two languages—C and Simula 67, a simulation programming language developed in Europe and released in 1967. C++ absorbed the features of C and added Simula's capabilities for creating and manipulating objects. Neither C nor C++ was originally intended for wide use beyond the AT&T research laboratories. But grass roots support rapidly developed for each.

What are objects and why are they special? Actually, object technology is a packaging scheme that enables programmers to create meaningful software units. These are large and highly focussed on particular applications areas. There are date objects, time objects, paycheck objects, invoice objects, audio objects, video objects, file objects, record objects and so on. In fact, almost any noun can be reasonably represented as an object.

We live in a world of objects. Just look around you. There are cars, planes, people, animals, buildings, traffic lights, elevators, and the like. Before object-oriented languages appeared, programming languages (such as FORTRAN, Pascal, Basic and C) were focussed on actions (verbs) rather than on things or objects (nouns). Programmers living in a world of objects program primarily using nouns. This paradigm shift made it awkward to write programs. Now, with the availability of popular object-oriented languages such as Java and C++, programmers continue to live in an object-oriented world and can program in an object-oriented manner. This is a more natural process than procedural programming and has resulted in significant productivity enhancements.

A key problem with procedural programming is that the program units do not easily mirror real-world entities effectively, so these units are not particularly reusable. It is not unusual for programmers to "start fresh" on each new project and have to write similar software "from scratch." This wastes time and money as people repeatedly "reinvent the wheel." With object technology, the software entities created (called *classes*), if properly designed, tend to be much more reusable on future projects. Using libraries of reusable componentry, such as *MFC (Microsoft Foundation Classes)* and those produced by many other software development organizations, can greatly reduce the amount of effort required to implement certain kinds of systems (compared to the effort that would be required to reinvent these capabilities on new projects).

Some organizations report that software reuse is not, in fact, the key benefit they get from object-oriented programming. Rather, they indicate that object-oriented programming tends to produce software that is more understandable, better organized and easier to maintain, modify and debug. This can be significant because it has been estimated that as much as 80% of software costs are not associated with the original efforts to develop the software, but with the continued evolution and maintenance of that software throughout its lifetime.

Whatever the perceived benefits of object-orientation are, it is clear that object-oriented programming will be the key programming methodology for the next several decades.

1.14 Basics of a Typical C Program Development Environment

C systems generally consist of several parts: a program development environment, the language and the C Standard Library. The following discussion explains the typical C development environment shown in Figure 1.1.

C programs typically go through six phases to be executed (Fig. 1.1). These are: *edit, preprocess, compile, link, load* and *execute*. Although *C How to Program: Fourth Edition* is a generic C textbook (written independently of the details of any particular operating system), we concentrate in this section on a typical UNIX-based C system. [*Note:* The programs in this book will run with little or no modification on most current C systems, including Microsoft Windows-based systems.] If you are not using a UNIX system, refer to the manuals for your system or ask your instructor how to accomplish these tasks in your environment.

The first phase consists of editing a file. This is accomplished with an *editor program.* Two editors widely used on UNIX systems are vi and emacs. Software packages for the C/C++ integrated program development environments such as Borland C++ Builder and Microsoft Visual Studio have editors that are integrated into the programming environment. We assume that the reader knows how to edit a program. The programmer types a C program with the editor, makes corrections if necessary, then stores the program on a secondary storage device such as a disk. C program file names should end with the .c extension.

Next, the programmer gives the command to *compile* the program. The compiler translates the C program into machine language code (also referred to as *object code*). In a C system, a *preprocessor* program executes automatically before the compiler's translation phase begins. The C preprocessor obeys special commands called *preprocessor directives*, which indicate that certain manipulations are to be performed on the program before compilation. These manipulations usually consist of including other files in the file to be compiled and performing various text replacements. The most common preprocessor directives are discussed in the early chapters; a detailed discussion of preprocessor features appears in Chapter 13. The preprocessor is automatically invoked by the compiler before the program is converted to machine language.

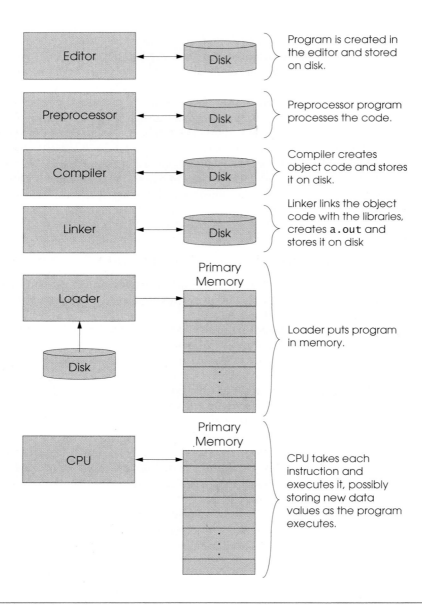

Fig. 1.1   Typical C environment.

The next phase is called *linking*. C programs typically contain references to functions defined elsewhere, such as in the standard libraries or in the private libraries of groups of programmers working on a particular project. The object code produced by the C compiler typically contains "holes" due to these missing parts. A *linker* links the object code with the code for the missing functions to produce an *executable image* (with no missing pieces). On a typical UNIX system, the command to compile and link a program is called *cc*. To compile and link a program named welcome.c type

```
cc welcome.c
```

at the UNIX prompt and press the *Enter* key (or *Return* key). [*Note:* UNIX commands are case sensitive; make sure that you type lowercase *c's* and that the letters in the filename are in the appropriate case.] If the program compiles and links correctly, a file called `a.out` is produced. This is the executable image of our `welcome.c` program.

The next phase is called *loading.* Before a program can be executed, the program must first be placed in memory. This is done by the *loader,* which takes the executable image from disk and transfers it to memory. Additional components from shared libraries that support the program are also loaded.

Finally, the computer, under the control of its CPU, *executes* the program one instruction at a time. To load and execute the program on a UNIX system, type `a.out` at the UNIX prompt and press *Enter.*

Programs do not always work on the first try. Each of the preceding phases can fail because of various errors that we will discuss. For example, an executing program might attempt to divide by zero (an illegal operation on computers just as in arithmetic). This would cause the computer to print an error message. The programmer would then return to the edit phase, make the necessary corrections and proceed through the remaining phases again to determine that the corrections work properly.

Common Programming Error 1.1

Errors like division-by-zero occur as a program runs, so these errors are called run-time errors or execution-time errors. Divide-by-zero is generally a fatal error, i.e., an error that causes the program to terminate immediately without successfully performing its job. Non-fatal errors allow programs to run to completion, often producing incorrect results. [*Note:* On some systems, divide-by-zero is not a fatal error. Please see your system documentation.]

Most programs in C input and/or output data. Certain C functions take their input from `stdin` (the *standard input stream*) which is normally the keyboard, but `stdin` can be connected to another stream. Data is often output to `stdout` (the *standard output stream*) which is normally the computer screen, but `stdout` can be connected to another stream. When we say that a program prints a result, we normally mean that the result is displayed on a screen. Data may be output to devices such as disks and printers. There is also a *standard error stream* referred to as `stderr`. The `stderr` stream (normally connected to the screen) is used for displaying error messages. It is common to route regular output data, i.e., `stdout`, to a device other than the screen while keeping `stderr` assigned to the screen so that the user can be immediately informed of errors.

1.15 Hardware Trends

The programming community thrives on a continuing stream of dramatic improvements in hardware, software and communications technologies. Every year, people generally expect to pay at least a little more for new products and services. The opposite has been the case in the computer and communications fields, especially with regard to the hardware costs of supporting these technologies. For many decades, and with no change in the foreseeable future, hardware costs have fallen rapidly, if not precipitously, every year. This is a phenomenon of technology. Every year or two, computer performance tends to double while computer prices continue drop. The sharp decrease in computer systems' cost/performance ratio is driven by the increasing speed and capacity of the memory in which computers execute programs, the exponential rise in amount of secondary storage (such as disk storage) they have to hold programs and data over the longer term, and the continuing increases in processor speeds—the speeds at which computers execute their programs (i.e., do their work).

The same growth has occurred in the communications field, with costs plummeting, especially in recent years as the enormous demand for communications bandwidth has attracted tremendous competition. We know of no other fields in which technology moves so quickly and costs fall so rapidly. When computer use exploded in the sixties and seventies, there was talk of huge improvements in human productivity that computing and communications would bring about. However, these improvements did not materialize. Organizations were spending vast sums on computers and certainly employing them effectively, but without realizing the productivity gains that had been expected. It was the invention of microprocessor chip technology and its wide deployment in the late 1970s and 1980s that laid the groundwork for the productivity improvements of the 1990s and today.

1.16 History of the Internet

In the late 1960s, one of the authors (HMD) was a graduate student at MIT. His research at MIT's Project Mac (now the Laboratory for Computer Science—the home of the World Wide Web Consortium) was funded by ARPA—the Advanced Research Projects Agency of the Department of Defense. ARPA sponsored a conference at which several dozen ARPA-funded graduate students were brought together at the University of Illinois at Urbana-Champaign to meet and share ideas. During this conference, ARPA rolled out the blueprints for networking the main computer systems of about a dozen ARPA-funded universities and research institutions. They were to be connected with communications lines operating at a then-stunning 56KB (i.e., 56,000 bits per second), at a time when most people (of the few who could) were connecting over telephone lines to computers at a rate of 110 bits per second. HMD vividly recalls the excitement at that conference. Researchers at Harvard in Massachusetts talked about communication with the Univac 1108 "supercomputer" across the country at the University of Utah to handle calculations related to their computer graphics research. Many other intriguing possibilities were raised. Academic research was about to take a giant leap forward. Shortly after this conference, ARPA proceeded to implement what quickly became called the *ARPAnet*, the grandparent of today's *Internet*.

Things worked out differently than originally planned. Although the ARPAnet did enable researchers to share each others' computers, its chief benefit proved to be its capability of quick and easy communication via what came to be known as *electronic mail (e-mail)*. This is true even today on the Internet, with e-mail facilitating communications of all kinds among hundreds of millions of people worldwide.

One of ARPA's primary goals for the network was to allow multiple users to send and receive information at the same time over the same communications paths (such as phone lines). The network operated with a technique called *packet switching* in which digital data was sent in small packages called *packets*. The packets contained data, address information, error-control information and sequencing information. The address information was used to route the packets of data to their destination. The sequencing information was used to help reassemble the packets (which—because of complex routing mechanisms—could actually arrive out of order) into their original order for presentation to the recipient. Packets of many people were intermixed on the same lines. This packet-switching technique greatly reduced transmission costs as compared to those of dedicated communications lines.

The network was designed to operate without centralized control. This meant that if a portion of the network should fail, the remaining working portions would still be able to route packets from senders to receivers over alternate paths.

The protocol for communicating over the ARPAnet became known as *TCP—the Transmission Control Protocol*. TCP ensured that messages were properly routed from sender to receiver and that those messages arrived intact.

In parallel with the early evolution of the Internet, organizations worldwide were implementing their own networks for both intra-organization (i.e., within the organization) and inter-organization (i.e., between organizations) communication. A huge variety of networking hardware and software appeared. One challenge was to get these to intercommunicate. ARPA accomplished this with the development of *IP—the Internetworking Protocol*), truly creating a "network of networks," the current architecture of the Internet. The combined set of protocols is now commonly called *TCP/IP*.

Initially, use of the Internet was limited to colleges and research institutions; then the military became a big user. Eventually, the government decided to allow access to the Internet for commercial purposes. Initially, there was resentment among the research and military communities—it was felt that response times would become poor as "the net" became saturated with so many users.

In fact, the exact opposite has occurred. Businesses rapidly realized that, by making effective use of the Internet, they could tune their operations and offer new and better services to their clients, so they started spending vasts amounts of money to develop and enhance the Internet. This generated fierce competition among the communications carriers and the hardware and software suppliers to meet the demand. The result is that *bandwidth* (i.e., the information carrying capacity of communications lines) on the Internet has increased tremendously and costs have plummeted. Countries worldwide now realize that the Internet is crucial to their economic prosperity and competitiveness.

1.17 History of the World Wide Web

The *World Wide Web* allows computer users to locate and view over the Internet multimedia-based documents (i.e., documents with text, graphics, animations, audios and/or videos) on almost any subject. Even though the Internet was developed more than three decades ago, the introduction of the *World Wide Web* was a relatively recent event. In 1990, *Tim Berners-Lee* of CERN (the European Laboratory for Particle Physics) developed the World Wide Web and several communication protocols that form its backbone.

The Internet and the World Wide Web will surely be listed among the most important and profound creations of humankind. In the past, most computer applications ran on "standalone" computers, i.e., computers that were not connected to one another. Today's applications can be written to communicate among the world's hundreds of millions of computers. The Internet mixes computing and communications technologies. It makes our work easier. It makes information instantly and conveniently accessible worldwide. It makes it possible for individuals and small businesses to get worldwide exposure. It is changing the way business is done. People can search for the best prices on virtually any product or service. Special-interest communities can stay in touch with one another. Researchers can be made instantly aware of the latest breakthroughs worldwide.

1.18 General Notes About C and this Book

Experienced C programmers sometimes take pride in being able to create weird, contorted, convoluted usages of the language. This is a poor programming practice. It makes programs more difficult to read, more likely to behave strangely, more difficult to test and debug and more difficult to adapt to changing requirements. This book is geared for novice programmers, so we stress program *clarity*. The following is our first "good programming practice."

Good Programming Practice 1.1

Write your C programs in a simple and straightforward manner. This is sometimes referred to as KIS ("keep it simple"). Do not "stretch" the language by trying bizarre usages.

You may have heard that C is a portable language and that programs written in C can run on many different computers. *Portability is an elusive goal.* The ANSI C standard document contains a lengthy list of portability issues, and complete books have been written that discuss portability.

Portability Tip 1.3

Although it is possible to write portable programs, there are many problems between different C compilers and different computers that make portability difficult to achieve. Simply writing programs in C does not guarantee portability. The progammer will often need to deal directly with complex computer variations.

We have done a careful walkthrough of the C standard document and audited our presentation against it for completeness and accuracy. However, C is a rich language, and there are some subtleties in the language and some advanced subjects we have not covered. If you need additional technical details on C, we suggest that you read the C standard document itself or the book by Kernighan and Ritchie.

We have limited our discussions to ANSI/ISO C. Many features of this version of C are not compatible with older C implementations, so you may find that some of the programs in this text do not work on older C compilers.

Software Engineering Observation 1.1

Read the manuals for the version of C you are using. Reference these manuals frequently to be sure you are aware of the rich collection of C features and that you are using these features correctly.

Software Engineering Observation 1.2

Your computer and compiler are good teachers. If you are not sure how a feature of C works, write a sample program with that feature, compile and run the program and see what happens.

SUMMARY

- Software (i.e., the instructions you write to command the computer to perform actions and make decisions) controls computers (often referred to as hardware).
- ANSI C is the version of the C programming language standardized in 1989 in both the United States through the American National Standards Institute (ANSI) and around the world through the International Standards Organization (ISO).
- Computers that might have filled large rooms and cost millions of dollars years ago can now be inscribed on the surfaces of silicon chips smaller than a fingernail and that cost perhaps a few dollars each.

- Hundreds of millions of general-purpose computers are in use worldwide helping people in business, industry, government and in their personal lives. That number could easily double in a few years.
- A computer is a device capable of performing computations and making logical decisions at speeds millions and even billions of times faster than human beings can.
- Computers process data under the control of computer programs.
- The various devices (such as the keyboard, screen, disks, memory and processing units) that comprise a computer system are referred to as hardware.
- The computer programs that run on a computer are referred to as software.
- The input unit is the "receiving" section of the computer. Most information is entered into computers today through typewriter-like keyboards.
- The output unit is the "shipping" section of the computer. Most information is output from computers today by displaying it on screens or by printing it on paper.
- The memory unit is the "warehouse" section of the computer and is often called either memory or primary memory.
- The arithmetic and logic unit (ALU) performs calculations and makes decisions.
- The central processing unit (CPU) is the computer's administrator and is responsible for supervising the operation of the other sections.
- Programs or data not actively being used by the other units are normally placed on secondary storage devices (such as disks) until they are again needed.
- Operating systems are software systems that make it more convenient to use computers and to get the best performance from computers.
- Multiprogramming operating systems enable the "simultaneous" operation of many jobs on the computer—the computer shares its resources among the jobs.
- Timesharing is a special case of multiprogramming in which users access the computer through terminals. The users appear to be running simultaneously.
- With distributed computing, an organization's computing is distributed via networking to the sites at which the work of the organization is performed.
- Servers store programs and data that may be shared by client computers distributed throughout the network, hence the term client/server computing.
- Any computer can directly understand only its own machine language. Machine languages generally consist of strings of numbers (ultimately reduced to 1s and 0s) that instruct computers to perform their most elementary operations one at a time. Machine languages are machine dependent.
- English-like abbreviations form the basis of assembly languages. Assemblers translate assembly language programs into machine language.
- Compilers translate high-level language programs into machine language. High-level languages contain English words and conventional mathematical notations.
- Interpreter programs directly execute high-level language programs without the need for compiling those programs into machine language.
- Although compiled programs execute faster than interpreted programs, interpreters are popular in program development environments, in which programs are recompiled frequently as new features are added and errors are corrected. Once a program is developed, a compiled version can then be produced to run more efficiently.
- FORTRAN (FORmula TRANslator) is used for mathematical applications. COBOL (COmmon Business Oriented Language) is used primarily for commercial applications that require precise and efficient manipulation of large amounts of data.

- Structured programming is a disciplined approach to writing programs that are clearer than unstructured programs, easier to test and debug and easier to modify.
- Pascal was designed for teaching structured programming.
- Ada was developed under the sponsorship of the United States Department of Defense (DoD) using Pascal as a base. Lady Lovelace is credited with writing the world's first computer program in the early 1800s (for the Analytical Engine mechanical computing device designed by Charles Babbage).
- Multitasking allows programmers to specify parallel activities.
- C is known as the development language of the UNIX operating system.
- It is possible to write programs in C that are portable to most computers.
- There are two pieces to learning how to program in C. The first is learning the C language itself, and the second is learning how to use the functions in the C Standard Library.
- C++ is a superset of C developed by Bjarne Stroustrup at Bell Laboratories. C++ provides capabilities for object-oriented programming.
- Objects are essentially reusable software components that model items in the real world.
- Using a modular, object-oriented design and implementation approach can make software development groups much more productive than is possible with conventional programming techniques.
- Java is used to create Web pages with dynamic and interactive content, develop large-scale enterprise applications, enhance the functionality of Web servers (the computers that provide the content we see in our Web browsers), provide applications for consumer devices (such as cell phones, pagers and personal digital assistants).
- The BASIC (Beginner's All-Purpose Symbolic Instruction Code) programming language was developed in the mid-1960s by Professors John Kemeny and Thomas Kurtz of Dartmouth College as a language for writing simple programs. BASIC's primary purpose was to familiarize novices with programming techniques.
- Visual Basic .NET, Visual C++ .NET and C# are designed for Microsoft's new .NET programming platform. All three languages make use of .NET's powerful library of reusable software components called the Framework Class Library (FCL).
- The C# programming language was designed by microsoft specifically for its .NET platform as a language that would enable programmers to migrate easily to .NET.
- Comparably to Java, the .NET platform enables Web-based applications to be distributed to many devices (even cell phones) and to desktop computers.
- C++, Java and C# all have their roots in the C programming language.
- Object technology is a packaging scheme that helps us create meaningful software units. These are large and highly focussed on particular applications areas.
- A key problem with procedural programming is that the program units do not easily mirror real-world entities effectively, so these units are not particularly reusable. It is not unusual for programmers to "start fresh" on each new project and have to write similar software "from scratch."
- With object technology, the software entities created (called classes), if properly designed, tend to be much more reusable on future projects. Using libraries of reusable componentry can greatly reduce the amount of effort required to implement certain kinds of systems (compared to the effort that would be required to reinvent these capabilities on new projects).
- Object-oriented programming tends to produce software that is more understandable, better organized and easier to maintain, modify and debug. This can be significant because it has been estimated that as much as 80% of software costs are associated with the continued evolution and maintenance of that software throughout its lifetime.

- All C systems consist of three parts: the environment, the language and the standard libraries. Library functions are not part of the C language itself; these functions perform operations such as input/output and mathematical calculations.
- C programs typically go through six phases to be executed: edit, preprocess, compile, link, load and execute.
- The programmer types a program with an editor and makes corrections if necessary. C file names typically end with the .c extension.
- A compiler translates a C program into machine language code (or object code).
- The C preprocessor obeys preprocessor directives which typically indicate that other files are to be included in the file to be compiled and special symbols are to be replaced with program text.
- A linker links the object code with the code for missing functions to produce an executable image (with no missing pieces). On a typical UNIX-based system, the command to compile and link a C++ program is cc. If the program compiles and links correctly, a file called a.out is produced. This is the executable image of the program.
- A loader takes an executable image from disk and transfers it to memory.
- Errors like division-by-zero occur as a program runs, so they are called run-time errors or execution-time errors.
- Divide-by-zero is generally a fatal error, i.e., an error that causes the program to terminate immediately without having successfully performed its job. Non-fatal errors allow programs to run to completion, often producing incorrect results.
- A computer, under the control of its CPU, executes a program one instruction at a time.
- Certain C functions (such as scanf) take their input from stdin (the standard input stream) which is normally assigned to the keyboard. Data is output to stdout (the standard output stream) which is normally the computer screen.
- There is also a standard error stream referred to as stderr. The stderr stream (normally the screen) is used for displaying error messages.
- There are many variations between different C implementations and different computers that make portability an elusive goal.

TERMINOLOGY

Ada
ALU
ANSI/ISO Standard C
arithmetic and logic unit (ALU)
assembler
assembly language
BASIC
batch processing
building block approach
C
.c extension
C preprocessor
C Standard Library
C#
C++
central processing unit (CPU)
clarity

class library
client
client/server computing
COBOL
compiler
computer
computer networking
computer program
computer programmer
CPU
data
debug
distributed computing
editor
environment
executable image
execute a program

fatal error
file server
FORTRAN
Framework Class Library (FCL)
function
functionalization
hardware
hardware platform
high-level language
input device
input stream
input unit
input/output (I/O)
Internet
interpreter
Java
KIS ("keep it simple")
Lady Ada Lovelace
library function
linker
Linux
loader
logical units
Mac OS X
machine dependent
machine independent
machine language
memory
memory unit
multiprocessor
multiprogramming
multitasking
multithreading
natural language of a computer
nonfatal error
.NET
object
object code
object-oriented programming (OOP)

operating system
output device
output stream
output unit
Pascal
performance
personal computer
portability
preprocessor
primary memory
program
programming language
reusable software components
run a program
runtime error
screen
secondary storage unit
software
software reusability
standard error stream (`stderr`)
standard input stream (`stdin`)
standard libraries
standard output stream (`stdout`)
stored program
structured programming
supercomputer
task
TCP/IP
terminal
timesharing
top-down, stepwise refinement
translator program
UNIX
Visual Basic .NET
Visual C++
Visual C++ .NET
Windows
World Wide Web
workstation

COMMON PROGRAMMING ERROR

1.1   Errors like division-by-zero errors occur as a program runs, so these errors are called run-time errors or execution-time errors. Divide-by-zero is generally a fatal error, i.e., an error that causes the program to terminate immediately without successfully performing its job. Non-fatal errors allow programs to run to completion, often producing incorrect results. [*Note:* On some systems, divide-by-zero is not a fatal error. Please see your system documentation.]

GOOD PROGRAMMING PRACTICE

1.1   Write your C programs in a simple and straightforward manner. This is sometimes referred to as KIS ("keep it simple"). Do not "stretch" the language by trying "weirdisms."

PERFORMANCE TIP

1.1   Using ANSI standard library functions instead of writing your own comparable versions can improve program performance because these functions are carefully written to perform efficiently.

PORTABILITY TIPS

1.1   Because C is a hardware-independent, widely available language, applications written in C can run with little or no modifications on a wide range of different computer systems.

1.2   Using ANSI standard library functions instead of writing your own comparable versions can improve program portability because these functions are implemented on virtually all ANSI C implementations.

1.3   Although it is possible to write portable programs, there are many problems between different C implementations and different computers that make portability difficult to achieve. Simply writing programs in C does not guarantee portability. The program will often need to deal directly with complex computer variations.

SOFTWARE ENGINEERING OBSERVATIONS

1.1   Read the manuals for the version of C you are using. Reference these manuals frequently to be sure you are aware of the rich collection of C features and that you are using these features correctly.

1.2   Your computer and compiler are good teachers. If you are not sure how a feature of C works, write a sample program with that feature, compile and run the program and see what happens.

SELF-REVIEW EXERCISES

1.1   Fill in the blanks in each of the following:

    a) The company that brought the phenomenon of personal computing to the world was _____.

    b) The computer that made personal computing legitimate in business and industry was the _____.

    c) Computers process data under the control of sets of instructions called computer _____.

    d) The six key logical units of the computer are the _____, _____, _____, _____, _____ and the _____.

    e) _____ is a special case of multiprogramming in which users access the computer through devices called terminals.

    f) The three classes of languages discussed in the chapter are _____, _____ and _____.

    g) The programs that translate high-level language programs into machine language are called _____.

    h) C is widely known as the development language of the _____ operating system.

    i) This book presents the version of C called _____ C that was recently standardized through the American National Standards Institute.

    j) The _____ language was developed by Wirth for teaching structured programming.

    k) The Department of Defense developed the Ada language with a capability called _____ which allows programmers to specify that many activities can proceed in parallel.

1.2   Fill in the blanks in each of the following sentences about the C environment.
a) C programs are normally typed into a computer using an _____ program.
b) In a C system, a _____ program automatically executes before the translation phase begins.
c) The two most common kinds of preprocessor directives are _____ and _____.
d) The _____ program combines the output of the compiler with various library functions to produce an executable image.
e) The _____ program transfers the executable image from disk to memory.
f) To load and execute the most recently compiled program on a UNIX system, type _____.

ANSWERS TO SELF-REVIEW EXERCISES

1.1   a) Apple. b) IBM Personal Computer. c) programs. d) input unit, output unit, memory unit, arithmetic and logic unit (ALU), central processing unit (CPU), secondary storage unit. e) timesharing. f) machine languages, assembly languages, high-level languages. g) compilers. h) UNIX. i) ANSI. j) Pascal. k) multitasking.

1.2   a) editor. b) preprocessor. c) including other files in the file to be compiled, replacing special symbols with program text. d) linker. e) loader. f) a.out.

EXERCISES

1.3   Categorize each of the following items as either hardware or software:
a) CPU
b) C compiler
c) ALU
d) C preprocessor
e) input unit
f) a word processor program

1.4   Why might you want to write a program in a machine-independent language instead of a machine-dependent language? Why might a machine-dependent language be more appropriate for writing certain types of programs?

1.5   Translator programs such as assemblers and compilers convert programs from one language (referred to as the *source* language) to another language (referred to as the *object* language). Determine which of the following statements are true and which are false:
a) A compiler translates high-level language programs into object language.
b) An assembler translates source language programs into machine language programs.
c) A compiler converts source language programs into object language programs.
d) High-level languages are generally machine dependent.
e) A machine language program requires translation before the program can be run on a computer.

1.6   Fill in the blanks in each of the following statements:
a) Devices from which users access timesharing computer systems are usually called _____.
b) A computer program that converts assembly language programs to machine language programs is called _____.
c) The logical unit of the computer that receives information from outside the computer for use by the computer is called _____.
d) The process of instructing the computer to solve specific problems is called _____.

    e) What type of computer language uses English-like abbreviations for machine language instructions? _____.

    f) Which logical unit of the computer sends information that has already been processed by the computer to various devices, so that the information may be used outside the computer? _____.

    g) The general name for a program that converts programs written in a certain computer language into machine language is _____.

    h) Which logical unit of the computer retains information? _____.

    i) Which logical unit of the computer performs calculations? _____.

    j) Which logical unit of the computer makes logical decisions? _____.

    k) The commonly used abbreviation for the computer's control unit is _____.

    l) The level of computer language most convenient to the programmer for writing programs quickly and easily is _____.

    m) The only language that a computer can directly understand is called that computer's _____.

    n) Which logical unit of the computer coordinates the activities of all the other logical units? _____.

1.7   State whether each of the following is *true* or *false*. If *false*, explain your answer.

    a) Machine languages are generally machine dependent.

    b) Timesharing truly runs several users simultaneously on a computer.

    c) Like other high-level languages, C is generally considered to be machine independent.

1.8   Discuss the meaning of each of the following names:

    a) `stdin`

    b) `stdout`

    c) `stderr`

1.9   Why is so much attention today focused on object-oriented programming in general and C++ in particular?

1.10   Which programming language is best described by each of the following?

    a) Developed by IBM for scientific and engineering applications.

    b) Developed specifically for business applications.

    c) Developed for teaching structured programming.

    d) Named after the world's first computer programmer.

    e) Developed to familiarize novices with programming techniques.

    f) Specifically developed to help programmers migrate to .NET.

    g) Known as the development language of UNIX.

    h) Formed primarily by adding object-oriented programming to C.

    i) Succeeded initially because of its ability to create Web pages with dynamic content.

Introduction to C Programming

Objectives

- To be able to write simple computer programs in C.
- To be able to use simple input and output statements.
- To become familiar with fundamental data types.
- To understand computer memory concepts.
- To be able to use arithmetic operators.
- To understand the precedence of arithmetic operators.
- To be able to write simple decision-making statements.

What's in a name? That which we call a rose
By any other name would smell as sweet.
William Shakespeare
Romeo and Juliet

I only took the regular course … the different branches of
arithmetic—Ambition, Distraction, Uglification, and
Derision.
Lewis Carroll

Precedents deliberately established by wise men are entitled
to great weight.
Henry Clay

2.1 Introduction

The C language facilitates a structured and disciplined approach to computer program design. In this chapter we introduce C programming and present several examples that illustrate many important features of C. Each example is carefully analyzed one statement at a time. In Chapter 3 and Chapter 4 we present an introduction to *structured programming* in C. We then use the structured approach throughout the remainder of the text.

2.2 A Simple C Program: Printing a Line of Text

C uses some notations that may appear strange to people who have not programmed computers. We begin by considering a simple C program. Our first example prints a line of text. The program and the program's screen output are shown in Fig. 2.1.

```
1    /* Fig. 2.1: fig02_01.c
2       A first program in C */                   Comment - ignored by compiler
3    #include <stdio.h>
4
5    /* function main begins program execution */
6    int main()
7    {
8       printf( "Welcome to C!\n" );
9
10      return 0; /* indicate that program ended successfully */
11
12   } /* end function main */
```

```
Welcome to C!
```

Fig. 2.1   Text printing program.

Even though this program is simple, it illustrates several important features of the C language. We now consider each line of the program in detail. Lines 1 and 2

```
/* Fig. 2.1: fig02_01.c
   A first program in C */
```

begin with **/*** and end with ***/** indicating that these two lines are a *comment*. Programmers insert comments to *document* programs and improve program readability. Comments do not cause the computer to perform any action when the program is run. Comments are ignored by the C compiler and do not cause any machine language object code to be generated. The preceding comment simply describes the figure number, file name and purpose of the program. Comments also help other people read and understand your program, but too many comments can make a program difficult to read.

Common Programming Error 2.1

Forgetting to terminate a comment with */.

Common Programming Error 2.2

Starting a comment with the characters */ or ending a comment with the characters /*.

Line 3

```
#include <stdio.h>
```

is a directive to the *C preprocessor.* Lines beginning with **#** are processed by the preprocessor before the program is compiled. This specific line tells the preprocessor to include the contents of the *standard input/output header* (`stdio.h`) in the program. This header contains information used by the compiler when compiling calls to standard input/output library functions such as `printf`. We will explain the contents of headers in more detail in Chapter 5.

Line 6

```
int main()
```

is a part of every C program. The parentheses after `main` indicate that `main` is a program building block called a *function.* C programs contain one or more functions, one of which must be `main`. Every program in C begins executing at the function `main`.

Good Programming Practice 2.1

Every function should be preceded by a comment describing the purpose of the function.

The *left brace,* {, must begin the *body* of every function (line 7). A corresponding *right brace* must end each function (line 12). This pair of *braces* and the portion of the program between the braces is called a *block.* The block is an important program unit in C.

Line 8

```
printf( "Welcome to C!\n" );
```

instructs the computer to perform an *action,* namely to print on the screen the *string* of characters marked by the quotation marks. A string is sometimes called a *character string,* a *message* or a *literal.* The entire line, including `printf`, its *argument* within the parentheses and the *semicolon* (**;**), is called a *statement.* Every statement must end with a semicolon (also known as the *statement terminator*). When the preceding `printf` statement is executed, it prints the message `Welcome to C!` on the screen. The characters normally print exactly as they appear between the double quotes in the `printf` statement. Notice that the characters \n were not printed on the screen. The backslash (\) is called an *escape charac-*

ter. It indicates that printf is supposed to do something out of the ordinary. When encountering a backslash in a string, the compiler looks ahead at the next character and combines it with the backslash to form an *escape sequence.* The escape sequence \n means *newline.* When a newline appears in the string output by a printf, the newline causes the cursor to position to the beginning of the next line on the screen. Some common escape sequences are listed in Fig. 2.2.

Escape Sequence	Description
\n	Newline. Position the cursor at the beginning of the next line.
\t	Horizontal tab. Move the cursor to the next tab stop.
\a	Alert. Sound the system bell.
\\	Backslash. Insert a backslash character in a string.
\"	Double quote. Insert a double quote character in a string.

Fig. 2.2   Some common escape sequences .

The last two escape sequences in Fig. 2.2 may seem strange. Because the backslash has special meaning in a string, i.e., the compiler recognizes it as an escape character, we use a double backslash (\\) to place a single backslash in a string. Printing a double quote also presents a problem because double quotes mark the boundary of a string—such quotes are not in fact printed. By using the escape sequence \" in a string to be output by printf, we indicate that printf should display a double quote.

Line 10

```
return 0; /* indicate that program ended successfully */
```

is included at the end of every main function. The keyword return is one of several means we will use to *exit a function.* When the return statement is used at the end of main as shown here, the value 0 indicates that the program has terminated successfully. In Chapter 5, we discuss functions in detail and the reasons for including this statement will become clear. For now, simply include this statement in each program, or the compiler might produce a warning on some systems. The *right brace,* }, (line 12) indicates that the end of main has been reached.

Good Programming Practice 2.2

Add a comment to the line containing the right brace, }, that closes every function, including main.

We said that printf causes the computer to perform an *action.* As any program executes, it performs a variety of actions and makes *decisions.* At the end of this chapter, we discuss decision making. In Chapter 3, we discuss this *action/decision model* of programming in depth.

Common Programming Error 2.3

Typing the name of the output function printf *as* print *in a program.*

It is important to note that standard library functions like `printf` and `scanf` are not part of the C programming language. For example, the compiler cannot find a spelling error in `printf` or `scanf`. When the compiler compiles a `printf` statement, it merely provides space in the object program for a "call" to the library function. But the compiler does not know where the library functions are—the linker does. When the linker runs, it locates the library functions and inserts the proper calls to these library functions in the object program. Now the object program is "complete" and ready to be executed. In fact, the linked program is often called an *executable*. If the function name is misspelled, it is the linker that will spot the error, because it will not be able to match the name in the C program with the name of any known function in the libraries.

Good Programming Practice 2.3

The last character printed by a function that does any printing should be a newline (\n). This ensures that the function will leave the screen cursor positioned at the beginning of a new line. Conventions of this nature encourage software reusability—a key goal in software development environments.

Good Programming Practice 2.4

Indent the entire body of each function one level of indentation (we recommend three spaces) within the braces that define the body of the function. This emphasizes the functional structure of programs and helps make programs easier to read.

Good Programming Practice 2.5

Set a convention for the size of indent you prefer and then uniformly apply that convention. The tab key may be used to create indents, but tab stops may vary. We recommend using either 1/4-inch tab stops or hand counting three spaces per level of indent.

The `printf` function can print `Welcome to C!` several different ways. For example, the program of Fig. 2.3 produces the same output as the program of Fig. 2.1. This works because each `printf` resumes printing where the previous `printf` stopped printing. The first `printf` (line 8) prints `Welcome` followed by a space and the second `printf` (line 9) begins printing on the same line immediately following the space.

```
1   /* Fig. 2.3: fig02_03.c
2      Printing on one line with two printf statements */
3   #include <stdio.h>
4
5   /* function main begins program execution */
6   int main()
7   {
8      printf( "Welcome " );
9      printf( "to C!\n" );
10
11     return 0; /* indicate that program ended successfully */
12
13  } /* end function main */
```

```
Welcome to C!
```

Fig. 2.3 Printing on one line with separate `printf` statements.

One `printf` can print several lines by using additional newline characters as in Fig. 2.4. Each time the \n (newline) escape sequence is encountered, output continues at the beginning of the next line.

```
1   /* Fig. 2.4: fig02_04.c
2      Printing multiple lines with a single printf */
3   #include <stdio.h>
4
5   /* function main begins program execution */
6   int main()
7   {
8      printf( "Welcome\nto\nC!\n" );
9
10     return 0; /* indicate that program ended successfully */
11
12  } /* end function main */
```

```
Welcome
to
C!
```

Fig. 2.4   Printing on multiple lines with a single `printf`.

2.3 Another Simple C Program: Adding Two Integers

Our next program uses the standard library function `scanf` to obtain two integers typed by a user at the keyboard, computes the sum of these values and prints the result using `printf`. The program and sample output are shown in Fig. 2.5. [Note that in the input/output dialog of Fig. 2.5, we highlight the numbers input by the user.]

```
1   /* Fig. 2.5: fig02_05.c
2      Addition program */
3   #include <stdio.h>
4
5   /* function main begins program execution */
6   int main()
7   {
8      int integer1; /* first number to be input by user  */
9      int integer2; /* second number to be input by user */
10     int sum;      /* variable in which sum will be stored */
11
12     printf( "Enter first integer\n" ); /* prompt */
13     scanf( "%d", &integer1 );          /* read an integer */   input statement
14
15     printf( "Enter second integer\n" ); /* prompt */
16     scanf( "%d", &integer2 );          /* read an integer */
17
18     sum = integer1 + integer2; /* assign total to sum */
19
20     printf( "Sum is %d\n", sum ); /* print sum */
```
      ← sets up variable

Fig. 2.5   Addition program. (Part 1 of 2.)

```
21
22      return 0;    /* indicate that program ended successfully */
23
24  } /* end function main */
```

```
Enter first integer
45
Enter second integer
72
Sum is 117
```

Fig. 2.5   Addition program. (Part 2 of 2.)

The comment in lines 1–2 states the purpose of the program. As we stated earlier, every program begins execution with `main`. The left brace { (line 7) marks the beginning of the body of `main` and the corresponding right brace (line 24) marks the end of `main`.

Lines 8–10

```
int integer1; /* first number to be input by user  */
int integer2; /* second number to be input by user */
int sum;      /* variable in which sum will be stored */
```

are *definitions*. The names `integer1`, `integer2` and `sum` are the names of *variables*. A variable is a location in memory where a value can be stored for use by a program. This definition specifies that the variables `integer1`, `integer2` and `sum` are of type *int* which means that these variables will hold *integer* values, i.e., whole numbers such as 7, –11, 0, 31914 and the like. All variables must be defined with a name and a data type immediately after the left brace that begins the body of `main` before they can be used in a program. There are other data types besides `int` in C. Note that the preceding definitions could have been combined into a single definition statement as follows:

```
int integer1, integer2, sum;
```

A variable name in C is any valid *identifier*. An identifier is a series of characters consisting of letters, digits and underscores (_) that does not begin with a digit. An identifier can be any length, but, only the first 31 characters are required to be recognized by C compilers according to the ANSI C standard. C is *case sensitive*—uppercase and lowercase letters are different in C, so `a1` and `A1` are different identifiers.

Common Programming Error 2.4

Using a capital letter where a lowercase letter should be used (for example, typing Main instead of main).

Portability Tip 2.1

Use identifiers of 31 or fewer characters. This helps ensure portability and can avoid some subtle programming errors.

Good Programming Practice 2.6

Choosing meaningful variable names helps make a program self documenting, i.e., fewer comments are needed.

Good Programming Practice 2.7

The first letter of an identifier used as a simple variable name should be a lowercase letter. Later in the text we will assign special significance to identifiers that begin with a capital letter and to identifiers that use all capital letters.

Good Programming Practice 2.8

Multiple-word variable names can help make a program be more readable. Avoid running the separate words together as in `totalcommissions`. *Rather separate the words with underscores as in* `total_commissions`, *or, if you do wish to run the words together, begin each word after the first with a capital letter as in* `totalCommissions`. *The latter style is preferred.*

Definitions must be placed after the left brace of a function and before *any* executable statements. For example, in the program of Fig. 2.5, inserting the definitions after the first `printf` would cause a syntax error. A *syntax error* is caused when the compiler can not recognize a statement. The compiler normally issues an error message to help the programmer locate and fix the incorrect statement. Syntax errors are violations of the language. Syntax errors are also called *compile errors,* or *compile-time errors.*

Common Programming Error 2.5

Placing variable definitions among executable statements causes syntax errors.

Good Programming Practice 2.9

Separate the definitions and executable statements in a function with one blank line to emphasize where the definitions end and the executable statements begin.

Line 12

```
printf( "Enter first integer\n" ); /* prompt */
```

prints the literal `Enter first integer` on the screen and positions the cursor to the beginning of the next line. This message is called a *prompt* because it tells the user to take a specific action.

The next statement

```
scanf( "%d", &integer1 ); /* read an integer */
```

uses *scanf* to obtain a value from the user. The `scanf` function takes input from the standard input which is usually the keyboard. This `scanf` has two arguments, `"%d"` and `&integer1`. The first argument, the *format control string,* indicates the type of data that should be input by the user. The `%d` *conversion specifier* indicates that the data should be an integer (the letter d stands for "decimal integer"). The `%` in this context is treated by `scanf` (and `printf` as we will see) as a special character that begins a conversion specifier. The second argument of `scanf` begins with an ampersand (&)—called the *address operator* in C—followed by the variable name. The ampersand, when combined with the variable name, tells `scanf` the location in memory at which the variable `integer1` is located. The computer then stores the value for `integer1` at that location. The use of ampersand (&) is often confusing to novice programmers or to people who have programmed in other languages that do not require this notation. For now, just remember to precede each variable in every `scanf` statement with an ampersand. Some exceptions to this rule are dis-

cussed in Chapter 6 and Chapter 7. The use of the ampersand will become clear after we
study pointers in Chapter 7.

Good Programming Practice 2.10

Place a space after each comma (,) to make programs more readable.

When the computer executes the preceding scanf, it waits for the user to enter a value
for variable integer1. The user responds by typing an integer then pressing the *Return*
key (sometimes called the *Enter* key) to send the number to the computer. The computer
then assigns this number, or *value,* to the variable integer1. Any subsequent references
to integer1 in the program will use this same value. Functions printf and scanf facilitate interaction between the user and the computer. Because this interaction resembles a
dialogue, it is often called *conversational computing* or *interactive computing.*

Line 15

```
printf( "Enter second integer\n" ); /* prompt */
```

displays the message Enter second integer on the screen, then positions the cursor to
the beginning of the next line. This printf also prompts the user to take action.

The statement

```
scanf( "%d", &integer2 ); /* read an integer */
```

obtains a value for variable integer2 from the user. Line 18's *assignment statement*

```
sum = integer1 + integer2; /* assign total to sum */
```

calculates the sum of variables integer1 and integer2 and assigns the result to variable
sum using the *assignment operator* =. The statement is read as, "sum *gets* the value of
integer1 + integer2." Most calculations are performed in assignment statements. The
= operator and the + operator are called *binary operators* because they each have two *operands.* In the case of the + operator, the two operands are integer1 and integer2. In
the case of the = operator, the two operands are sum and the value of the expression
integer1 + integer2.

Good Programming Practice 2.11

*Place spaces on either side of a binary operator. This makes the operator stand out and
makes the program more readable.*

Common Programming Error 2.6

*The calculation in an assignment statement must be on the right side of the = operator. It is
a syntax error to place a calculation on the left side of an assignment operator.*

Line 20

```
printf( "Sum is %d\n", sum ); /* print sum */
```

calls function printf to print the literal Sum is followed by the numerical value of variable sum on the screen. This printf has two arguments, "Sum is %d\n" and sum. The
first argument is the format control string. It contains some literal characters to be displayed, and it contains the conversion specifier %d indicating that an integer will be printed.
The second argument specifies the value to be printed. Notice that the conversion specifier
for an integer is the same in both printf and scanf. This is the case for most C data types.

Calculations can also be performed inside `printf` statements. We could have combined the previous two statements into the statement

```
printf( "Sum is %d\n", integer1 + integer2 );
```

Line 22

```
return 0; /* indicate that program ended successfully */
```

passes the value 0 back to the operating system environment in which the program is being executed. This indicates to the operating system that the program executed successfully. For information on how to report a program failure, see the manuals for your particular operating system environment.

The right brace, }, at line 24 indicates that the end of function `main` has been reached.

Common Programming Error 2.7
Forgetting one or both of the double quotes surrounding the format control string in a `printf` *or* `scanf`.

Common Programming Error 2.8
Forgetting the % in a conversion specification in the format control string of a `printf` *or* `scanf`.

Common Programming Error 2.9
Placing an escape sequence such as \n *outside the format control string of a* `printf` *or* `scanf`.

Common Programming Error 2.10
Forgetting to include the expressions whose values are to be printed in a `printf` *containing conversion specifiers.*

Common Programming Error 2.11
Not providing in a `printf` *format control string a conversion specifier when one is needed to print the value of an expression.*

Common Programming Error 2.12
Placing inside the format control string the comma that is supposed to separate the format control string from the expressions to be printed.

Common Programming Error 2.13
Forgetting to precede a variable in a `scanf` *statement with an ampersand when that variable should, in fact, be preceded by an ampersand.*

On many systems, the preceding execution-time error causes a "segmentation fault" or "access violation." Such an error occurs when a user's program attempts to access a part of the computer's memory to which the user's program does not have access privileges. The precise cause of this error will be explained in Chapter 7.

Common Programming Error 2.14
Preceding a variable included in a `printf` *statement with an ampersand when, in fact, that variable should not be preceded by an ampersand.*

2.4 Memory Concepts

Variable names such as `integer1`, `integer2` and `sum` actually correspond to *locations* in the computer's memory. Every variable has a *name,* a *type and* a *value.*

In the addition program of Fig. 2.5, when the statement (line 13)

```
scanf( "%d", &integer1 ); /* read an integer */
```

is executed, the value typed by the user is placed into a memory location to which the name `integer1` has been assigned. Suppose the user enters the number 45 as the value for `integer1`. The computer will place 45 into location `integer1` as shown in Fig. 2.6.

integer1   45

Fig. 2.6   Memory location showing the name and value of a variable.

Whenever a value is placed in a memory location, the value replaces the previous value in that location. Because this previous information is destroyed, the process of reading information into a memory location is called *destructive read-in.*

Returning to our addition program again, when the statement (line 16)

```
scanf( "%d", &integer2 ); /* read an integer */
```

is executed, suppose the user enters the value 72. This value is placed into location `integer2` and memory appears as in Fig. 2.7. Note that these locations are not necessarily adjacent in memory.

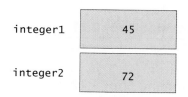

integer1   45

integer2   72

Fig. 2.7   Memory locations after both variables are input.

Once the program has obtained values for `integer1` and `integer2`, it adds these values and places the sum into variable `sum`. The statement (line 18)

```
sum = integer1 + integer2; /* assign total to sum */
```

that performs the addition also involves destructive read-in. This occurs when the calculated sum of `integer1` and `integer2` is placed into location `sum` (destroying the value that may already be in `sum`). After `sum` is calculated, memory appears as in Fig. 2.8. Note that the values of `integer1` and `integer2` appear exactly as they did before they were used in the calculation of `sum`. These values were used, but not destroyed, as the computer performed the calculation. Thus, when a value is read out of a memory location, the process is referred to as *nondestructive read-out.*

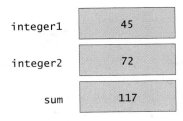

integer1   45

integer2   72

sum   117

Fig. 2.8   Memory locations after a calculation.

2.5 Arithmetic in C

Most C programs perform arithmetic calculations. The C *arithmetic operators* are summarized in Fig. 2.9. Note the use of various special symbols not used in algebra. The *asterisk* (*) indicates multiplication and the *percent sign* (%) denotes the *remainder* operator which is introduced below. In algebra, if we want to multiply *a* times *b,* we can simply place these single-letter variable names side by side as in *ab*. In C, however, if we were to do this, ab would be interpreted as a single, two-letter name (or identifier). Therefore, C (and other programming languages, in general) require that multiplication be explicitly denoted by using the * operator as in a * b.

C Operation	Arithmetic operator	Algebraic expression	C expression
Addition	+	$f + 7$	f + 7
Subtraction	−	$p - c$	p - c
Multiplication	*	bm	b * m
Division	/	x / y or $\dfrac{x}{y}$ or $x \div y$	x / y
Remainder	%	$r \bmod s$	r % s

Fig. 2.9   Arithmetic operators.

The arithmetic operators are all binary operators. For example, the expression 3 + 7 contains the binary operator + and the operands 3 and 7.

Integer division yields an integer result. For example, the expression 7 / 4 evaluates to 1 and the expression 17 / 5 evaluates to 3. C provides the remainder operator, %, which yields the remainder after integer division. The remainder operator is an integer operator that can be used only with integer operands. The expression x % y yields the remainder after x is divided by y. Thus, 7 % 4 yields 3 and 17 % 5 yields 2. We will discuss many interesting applications of the remainder operator.

Common Programming Error 2.15

An attempt to divide by zero is normally undefined on computer systems and generally results in a fatal error, i.e., an error that causes the program to terminate immediately without having successfully performed its job. Non-fatal errors allow programs to run to completion, often producing incorrect results.

Arithmetic expressions in C must be written in *straight-line form* to facilitate entering programs into the computer. Thus, expressions such as "a divided by b" must be written as a/b so that all operators and operands appear in a straight line. The algebraic notation

$$\frac{a}{b}$$

is generally not acceptable to compilers, although some special-purpose software packages do exist that support more natural notation for complex mathematical expressions.

Parentheses are used to group terms in C expressions in much the same manner as in algebraic expressions. For example, to multiply a times the quantity b + c we write:

```
a * ( b + c )
```

C evaluates arithmetic expressions in a precise sequence determined by the following *rules of operator precedence,* which are generally the same as those followed in algebra:

1. Multiplication, division and remainder operations are applied first. If an expression contains several multiplication, division and remainder operations, evaluation proceeds from left to right. Multiplication, division and remainder are said to be on the same level of precedence.

2. Addition and subtraction operations are evaluated next. If an expression contains several addition and subtraction operations, evaluation proceeds from left to right. Addition and subtraction also have the same level of precedence, which is lower than the precedence of the multiplication, division and remainder operators.

The rules of operator precedence are guidelines that enable C to evaluate expressions in the correct order. When we say evaluation proceeds from left to right, we are referring to the *associativity* of the operators. We will see that some operators associate from right to left. Figure 2.10 summarizes these rules of operator precedence.

Operator(s)	Operation(s)	Order of evaluation (precedence)
* / %	Multiplication Division Remainder	Evaluated first. If there are several, they are evaluated left to right.
+ –	Addition Subtraction	Evaluated next. If there are several, they are evaluated left to right.

Fig. 2.10   Precedence of arithmetic operators.

Now let us consider several expressions in light of the rules of operator precedence. Each example lists an algebraic expression and its C equivalent.

The following example calculates the arithmetic mean (average) of five terms:

Algebra: $m = \dfrac{a + b + c + d + e}{5}$

C: `m = ( a + b + c + d + e ) / 5;`

The parentheses are required to group the additions because division has higher precedence than addition. The entire quantity (a + b + c + d + e) should be divided by 5. If the parentheses are erroneously omitted, we obtain a + b + c + d + e / 5 which evaluates incorrectly as

$$a + b + c + d + \frac{e}{5}$$

The following example is the equation of a straight line:

Algebra: $y = mx + b$

C: y = m * x + b;

No parentheses are required. The multiplication is evaluated first because multiplication has a higher precedence than addition.

The following example contains remainder (%), multiplication, division, addition, subtraction and assignment operations:

Algebra: $z = pr\%q + w/x - y$

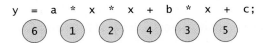

C: z = p * r % q + w / x - y;

The circled numbers under the statement indicate the order in which C evaluates the operators. The multiplication, remainder and division are evaluated first in left-to-right order (i.e., they associate from left to right) since they have higher precedence than addition and subtraction. The addition and subtraction are evaluated next. These are also evaluated left to right.

Not all expressions with several pairs of parentheses contain nested parentheses. The expression

a * (b + c) + c * (d + e)

does not contain nested parentheses. Instead, the parentheses are said to be "on the same level."

To develop a better understanding of the rules of operator precedence, let us see how C evaluates a second-degree polynomial.

y = a * x * x + b * x + c;

The circled numbers under the statement indicate the order in which C performs the operations. There is no arithmetic operator for exponentiation in C, so we have represented x^2 as x * x. The C Standard Library includes the pow ("power") function to perform exponentiation. Because of some subtle issues related to the data types required by pow, we defer a detailed explanation of pow until Chapter 4.

Suppose a = 2, b = 3, c = 7 and x = 5. Figure 2.11 illustrates how the preceding second-degree polynomial is evaluated.

Step 1.   y = 2 * 5 * 5 + 3 * 5 + 7;   (Leftmost multiplication)
          2 * 5 is 10

Step 2.   y = 10 * 5 + 3 * 5 + 7;   (Leftmost multiplication)
          10 * 5 is 50

Step 3.   y = 50 + 3 * 5 + 7;   (Multiplication before addition)
                   3 * 5 is 15

Step 4.   y = 50 + 15 + 7;   (Leftmost addition)
          50 + 15 is 65

Step 5.   y = 65 + 7;   (Last addition)
          65 + 7 is 72

Step 6.   y = 72;   (Last operation—place 72 in y)

Fig. 2.11   Order in which a second-degree polynomial is evaluated.

2.6 Decision Making: Equality and Relational Operators

Executable C statements either perform *actions* (such as calculations or input or output of data), or make *decisions* (we will soon see several examples of these). We might make a decision in a program, for example, to determine if a person's grade on an exam is greater than or equal to 60 and if it is to print the message "Congratulations! You passed." This section introduces a simple version of C's *if statement* that allows a program to make a decision based on the truth or falsity of a statement of fact called a *condition*. If the condition is met (i.e., the condition is *true*) the statement in the body of the if statement is executed. If the condition is not met (i.e., the condition is *false*) the body statement is not executed. Whether the body statement is executed or not, after the if statement completes, execution proceeds with the next statement after the if statement.

Conditions in if statements are formed by using the *equality operators* and *relational operators* summarized in Fig. 2.12. The relational operators all have the same level of precedence and they associate left to right. The equality operators have a lower level of precedence than the relational operators and they also associate left to right. [*Note:* In C, a condition may actually be any expression that generates a zero (false) or nonzero (true) value. We will see many applications of this throughout the book.]

Standard algebraic equality operator or relational operator	C equality or relational operator	Example of C condition	Meaning of C condition
Equality operators			
=	==	x == y	x is equal to y
≠	!=	x != y	x is not equal to y
Relational operators			
>	>	x > y	x is greater than y
<	<	x < y	x is less than y
≥0	>=	x >= y	x is greater than or equal to y
≤	<=	x <= y	x is less than or equal to y

Fig. 2.12   Equality and relational operators.

Common Programming Error 2.16

A syntax error will occur if the two symbols in any of the operators ==, !=, >= and <= are separated by spaces.

Common Programming Error 2.17

A syntax error will occur if the two symbols in any of the operators !=, >= and <= are reversed as in =!, => and =<, respectively.

Common Programming Error 2.18

Confusing the equality operator == with the assignment operator =.

To avoid this confusion, the equality operator should be read "double equals" and the assignment operator should be read "gets." As we will soon see, confusing these operators may not necessarily cause an easy-to-recognize syntax error, but may cause extremely subtle logic errors.

Common Programming Error 2.19

Placing a semicolon immediately to the right of the right parenthesis after the condition in an if statement.

Figure 2.13 uses six if statements to compare two numbers input by the user. If the condition in any of these if statements is satisfied, the printf statement associated with that if is executed. The program and three sample execution outputs are shown in the figure.

```
1   /* Fig. 2.13: fig02_13.c
2      Using if statements, relational
3      operators, and equality operators */
4   #include <stdio.h>
5
```

Fig. 2.13   Using equality and relational operators. (Part 1 of 3.)

```
6   /* function main begins program execution */
7   int main()
8   {
9      int num1, /* first number to be read from user  */
10     int num2; /* second number to be read from user */
11
12     printf( "Enter two integers, and I will tell you\n" );
13     printf( "the relationships they satisfy: " );
14
15     scanf( "%d%d", &num1, &num2 ); /* read two integers */
16
17     if ( num1 == num2 ) {
18        printf( "%d is equal to %d\n", num1, num2 );
19     } /* end if */
20
21     if ( num1 != num2 ) {
22        printf( "%d is not equal to %d\n", num1, num2 );
23     } /* end if */
24
25     if ( num1 < num2 ) {
26        printf( "%d is less than %d\n", num1, num2 );
27     } /* end if */
28
29     if ( num1 > num2 ) {
30        printf( "%d is greater than %d\n", num1, num2 );
31     } /* end if */
32
33     if ( num1 <= num2 ) {
34        printf( "%d is less than or equal to %d\n", num1, num2 );
35     } /* end if */
36
37     if ( num1 >= num2 ) {
38        printf( "%d is greater than or equal to %d\n", num1, num2 );
39     } /* end if */
40
41     return 0;   /* indicate that program ended successfully */
42
43  } /* end function main */
```

```
Enter two integers, and I will tell you
the relationships they satisfy: 3 7
3 is not equal to 7
3 is less than 7
3 is less than or equal to 7
```

```
Enter two integers, and I will tell you
the relationships they satisfy: 22 12
22 is not equal to 12
22 is greater than 12
22 is greater than or equal to 12
```

Fig. 2.13   Using equality and relational operators. (Part 2 of 3.)

```
Enter two integers, and I will tell you
the relationships they satisfy: 7 7
7 is equal to 7
7 is less than or equal to 7
7 is greater than or equal to 7
```

Fig. 2.13   Using equality and relational operators. (Part 3 of 3.)

Note that the program in Fig. 2.13 uses `scanf` (line 15) to input two numbers. Each conversion specifier has a corresponding argument in which a value will be stored. The first `%d` converts a value to be stored in variable `num1`, and the second `%d` converts a value to be stored in variable `num2`. Indenting the body of each `if` statement and placing blank lines above and below each `if` statement enhances program readability. Also, notice that each `if` statement in Fig. 2.13 has a single statement in its body. In Chapter 3, we show how to specify `if` statements with multiple-statement bodies.

Good Programming Practice 2.12

Indent the statement(s) in the body of an `if` statement.

Good Programming Practice 2.13

Place a blank line before and after every `if` statement in a program for readability.

Good Programming Practice 2.14

Although it is allowed, there should be no more than one statement per line in a program.

Common Programming Error 2.20

Placing commas (when none are needed) between conversion specifiers in the format control string of a `scanf` statement.

The comment (lines 1–3) in Fig. 2.13 is split over three lines. In C programs, *white space* characters such as tabs, newlines and spaces are normally ignored. So, statements and comments may be split over several lines. It is not correct, however, to split identifiers.

Good Programming Practice 2.15

A lengthy statement may be spread over several lines. If a statement must be split across lines, choose breaking points that make sense (such as after a comma in a comma-separated list). If a statement is split across two or more lines, indent all subsequent lines.

Figure 2.14 lists the precedence of the operators introduced in this chapter. Operators are shown top to bottom in decreasing order of precedence. Note that the equals sign is also an operator. All these operators, with the exception of the assignment operator =, associate from left to right. The assignment operator (=) associates from right to left.

Good Programming Practice 2.16

Refer to the operator precedence chart when writing expressions containing many operators. Confirm that the operators in the expression are applied in the proper order. If you are uncertain about the order of evaluation in a complex expression, use parentheses to group expressions. Be sure to observe that some of C's operators such as the assignment operator (=) associate from right to left rather than from left to right.

Operators	Associativity
* / %	left to right
+ -	left to right
< <= > >=	left to right
== !=	left to right
=	right to left

Fig. 2.14 Precedence and associativity of the operators discussed so far.

Some of the words we have used in the C programs in this chapter—in particular `int`, `return` and `if`—are *keyword*s or *reserved words* of the language. The C keywords are shown in Fig. 2.15. These words have special meaning to the C compiler, so the programmer must be careful not to use these words as identifiers such as variable names. In this book, we will discuss all of these keywords.

Keywords			
auto	double	int	struct
break	else	long	switch
case	enum	register	typedef
char	extern	return	union
const	float	short	unsigned
continue	for	signed	void
default	goto - *do not use*	sizeof	volatile
do	if	static	while

Fig. 2.15 C's keywords.

In this chapter, we have introduced many important features of the C programming language, including printing data on the screen, inputting data from the user, performing calculations and making decisions. In the next chapter, we build upon these techniques as we introduce *structured programming.* You will become more familiar with indentation techniques. We will study how to specify the order in which statements are executed—this is called *flow of control.*

SUMMARY

- Comments begin with /* and end with */. Programmers insert comments to document programs and improve their readability. Comments do not cause the computer to perform any action when the program is run.
- The preprocessor directive #include <stdio.h> tells the compiler to include the standard input/output header in the program. This file contains information used by the compiler to verify the accuracy of calls to input and output functions such as scanf and printf.

- C programs consist of functions one of which must be `main`. Every C program begins executing at the function `main`.

- Function `printf` can be used to print a string contained in quotation marks and to print the values of expressions. When printing an integer value, the first argument of the `printf` function—the format control string—contains the conversion specifier %d and any other characters that will be printed; the second argument is the expression whose value will be printed. If more than one integer will be printed, then the format control string contains a %d for each integer, and the comma-separated arguments following the format control string contain the expressions whose values are to be printed.

- Function `scanf` obtains values the user normally enters at the keyboard. Its first argument is the format control string that tells the computer what type of data should be input by the user. The conversion specifier %d indicates that the data should be an integer. Each of the remaining arguments corresponds to one of the conversion specifiers in the format control string. Each variable name is normally preceded by an ampersand (&), called the address operator. The ampersand, when combined with the variable name, tells the computer the location in memory where the value will be stored. The computer then stores the value at that location.

- All variables must be defined before they can be used in the program.

- A variable name is any valid identifier. An identifier is a series of characters consisting of letters, digits and underscores (_). Identifiers cannot start with a digit. Identifiers can be any length; however, only the first 31 characters are significant.

- C is case sensitive.

- Most calculations are performed in assignment statements.

- Every variable stored in the computer's memory has a name, a value and a type.

- Whenever a new value is placed in a memory location, it replaces the previous value in that location. Since this previous information is destroyed, the process of reading information into a memory location is called destructive read-in.

- The process of reading a value from memory is referred to as nondestructive read-out.

- Arithmetic expressions must be written in straight-line form to facilitate entering programs into the computer.

- The compiler evaluates arithmetic expressions in a precise sequence determined by the rules of operator precedence and associativity.

- The `if` statement allows the programmer to make a decision when a certain condition is met.

- If the condition is true, the statement in the body of the `if` is executed. If the condition is false, the body statement is skipped.

- Conditions in `if` statements are commonly formed by using equality operators and relational operators. The result of using these operators is always simply the observation of "true" or "false." Note that conditions may be any expression that generates a zero (false) or nonzero (true) value.

TERMINOLOGY

action
action/decision model
address operator
ampersand (&)
argument
arithmetic operators
assignment operator (=)

assignment statement
associativity of operators
asterisk (*)
backslash (\) escape character
binary operators
block
body of a function

braces {}
case sensitive
character string
C keywords
comment
compile error
compile-time error
condition
control string
conversational computing
conversion specifier
C preprocessor
C Standard Library
%d conversion specifier
decision
decision making
definition
division by zero
Enter key
equal sign (=) assignment operator
equality operators
    == "is equal to"
    != "is not equal to"
escape character
escape sequence
false
fatal error
flow of control
format control string
function
identifier
`if` control statement
indentation
`int`
integer
integer division
interactive computing
keywords
left-to-right associativity
literal
location
`main`
memory
memory location

message
multiplication operator (*)
name
nested parentheses
newline character (\n)
nondestructive read-out
nonfatal error
nonzero (true) value
operand
operator
parentheses ()
percent sign (%) to begin a conversion specifier
precedence
`printf` function
prompt
relational operators
    > "is greater than"
    < "is less than"
    >= "is greater than or equal to"
    <= "is less than or equal to"
remainder operator (%)
reserved words
Return key
right-to-left associativity
rules of operator precedence
`scanf` function
semicolon (;) statement terminator
standard input/output header
statement
statement terminator (;)
`stdio.h`
straight-line form
string
structured programming
syntax error
true
underscore (_)
value
variable
variable name
variable type
variable value
white-space character
zero (false) value

COMMON PROGRAMMING ERRORS

2.1   Forgetting to terminate a comment with */.

2.2   Starting a comment with the characters */ or ending a comment with the characters /*.

2.3   Typing the name of the output function printf as print in a program.

2.4   Using a capital letter where a lowercase letter should be used (for example, typing Main instead of main).

2.5   Placing variable definitions among executable statements causes syntax errors.

2.6   The calculation in an assignment statement must be on the right side of the = operator. It is a syntax error to place a calculation on the left side of an assignment operator.

2.7   Forgetting one or both of the double quotes surrounding the format control string in a printf or scanf.

2.8   Forgetting the % in a conversion specification in the format control string of a printf or scanf.

2.9   Placing an escape sequence such as \n outside the format control string of a printf or scanf.

2.10   Forgetting to include the expressions whose values are to be printed in a printf that contains conversion specifiers.

2.11   Not providing in a printf format control string a conversion specifier when one is needed to print an expression.

2.12   Placing inside the format control string the comma that is supposed to separate the format control string from the expressions to be printed.

2.13   Forgetting to precede a variable in a scanf statement with an ampersand when that variable should, in fact, be preceded by an ampersand.

2.14   Preceding a variable included in a printf statement with an ampersand when, in fact, that variable should not be preceded by an ampersand.

2.15   An attempt to divide by zero is normally undefined on computer systems and generally results in a fatal error, i.e., an error that causes the program to terminate immediately without having successfully performed its job. Nonfatal errors allow programs to run to completion, often producing incorrect results.

2.16   A syntax error will occur if the two symbols in any of the operators ==, !=, >= and <= are separated by spaces.

2.17   A syntax error will occur if the two symbols in any of the operators !=, >= and <= are reversed as in =!, => and =<, respectively.

2.18   Confusing the equality operator == with the assignment operator =.

2.19   Placing a semicolon immediately to the right of the right parenthesis after the condition in an if statement.

2.20   Placing commas (when none are needed) between conversion specifiers in the format control string of a scanf statement.

GOOD PROGRAMMING PRACTICES

2.1   Every function should be preceded by a comment describing the purpose of the function.

2.2   Add a comment to the line containing the right brace, }, that closes every function, including main.

2.3   The last character printed by a function that does any printing should be a newline (\n). This ensures that the function will leave the screen cursor positioned at the beginning of a new line. Conventions of this nature encourage software reusability—a key goal in software development environments.

2.4   Indent the entire body of each function one level of indentation (we recommend three spaces) within the braces that define the body of the function. This emphasizes the functional structure of programs and helps make programs easier to read.

2.5   Set a convention for the size of indent you prefer and then uniformly apply that convention. The tab key may be used to create indents, but tab stops may vary. We recommend using either 1/4-inch tab stops or hand counting three spaces per level of indent.

2.6   Choosing meaningful variable names helps make a program self documenting, i.e., fewer comments are needed.

2.7   The first letter of an identifier used as a simple variable name should be a lowercase letter. Later in the text we will assign special significance to identifiers that begin with a capital letter and to identifiers that use all capital letters.

2.8   Multiple-word variable names can help make a program be more readable. Avoid running the separate words together as in `totalcommissions`. Rather separate the words with underscores as in `total_commissions`, or, if you do wish to run the words together, begin each word after the first with a capital letter as in `totalCommissions`. The latter style is preferred.

2.9   Separate the definitions and executable statements in a function with one blank line to emphasize where the definitions end and the executable statements begin.

2.10   Place a space after each comma (`,`) to make programs more readable.

2.11   Place spaces on either side of a binary operator. This makes the operator stand out and makes the program more readable.

2.12   Indent the statement(s) in the body of an `if` statement.

2.13   Place a blank line before and after every `if` statement in a program for readability.

2.14   Although it is allowed, there should be no more than one statement per line in a program.

2.15   A lengthy statement may be spread over several lines. If a statement must be split across lines, choose breaking points that make sense such as after a comma in a comma-separated list. If a statement is split across two or more lines, indent all subsequent lines.

2.16   Refer to the operator precedence chart when writing expressions containing many operators. Confirm that the operators in the expression are applied in the proper order. If you are uncertain about the order of evaluation in a complex expression, use parentheses to group expressions. Be sure to observe that some of C's operators such as the assignment operator (`=`) associate from right to left rather than from left to right.

PORTABILITY TIP

2.1   Use identifiers of 31 or fewer characters. This helps ensure portability and can avoid some subtle programming errors.

SELF-REVIEW EXERCISES

2.1   Fill in the blanks in each of the following.
  a) Every C program begins execution at the function _____.
  b) The _____ begins the body of every function and the _____ ends the body of every function.
  c) Every statement ends with a(n) _____.
  d) The _____ standard library function displays information on the screen.
  e) The escape sequence \n represents the _____ character which causes the cursor to position to the beginning of the next line on the screen.
  f) The _____ standard library function is used to obtain data from the keyboard.
  g) The conversion specifier _____ is used in a `scanf` format control string to indicate that an integer will be input and in a `printf` format control string to indicate that an integer will be output.
  h) Whenever a new value is placed in a memory location, that value overrides the previous value in that location. This process is known as _____ read-in.

    i) When a value is read out of a memory location the value in that location is preserved; this is called _____ read-out.

    j) The _____ statement is used to make decisions.

2.2 State whether each of the following is *true* or *false*. If *false*, explain why.

    a) When the `printf` function is called, it always begins printing at the beginning of a new line.

    b) Comments cause the computer to print the text enclosed between `/*` and `*/` on the screen when the program is executed.

    c) The escape sequence \n when used in a `printf` format control string causes the cursor to position to the beginning of the next line on the screen.

    d) All variables must be defined before they are used.

    e) All variables must be given a type when they are defined.

    f) C considers the variables `number` and `NuMbEr` to be identical.

    g) Definitions can appear anywhere in the body of a function.

    h) All arguments following the format control string in a `printf` function must be preceded by an ampersand (&).

    i) The remainder operator (%) can be used only with integer operands.

    j) The arithmetic operators *, /, %, + and – all have the same level of precedence.

    k) The following variable names are identical on all ANSI C systems.

```
thisisasuperduperlongname1234567
thisisasuperduperlongname1234568
```

    l) A program that prints three lines of output must contain three `printf` statements.

2.3 Write a single C statement to accomplish each of the following:

    a) Define the variables `c`, `thisVariable`, `q76354` and `number` to be of type `int`.

    b) Prompt the user to enter an integer. End your prompting message with a colon (`:`) followed by a space and leave the cursor positioned after the space.

    c) Read an integer from the keyboard and store the value entered in integer variable a.

    d) If `number` is not equal to 7, print `"The variable number is not equal to 7."`

    e) Print the message `"This is a C program."` on one line.

    f) Print the message `"This is a C program."` on two lines so that the first line ends with C.

    g) Print the message `"This is a C program."` with each word on a separate line.

    h) Print the message `"This is a C program."` with each word separated by tabs.

2.4 Write a statement (or comment) to accomplish each of the following:

    a) State that a program will calculate the product of three integers.

    b) Define the variables `x`, `y`, `z` and `result` to be of type `int`.

    c) Prompt the user to enter three integers.

    d) Read three integers from the keyboard and store them in the variables `x`, `y` and `z`.

    e) Compute the product of the three integers contained in variables `x`, `y` and `z`, and assign the result to the variable `result`.

    f) Print `"The product is"` followed by the value of the integer variable `result`.

2.5 Using the statements you wrote in Exercise 2.4, write a complete program that calculates the product of three integers.

2.6 Identify and correct the errors in each of the following statements:

    a) `printf( "The value is %d\n", &number );`

    b) `scanf( "%d%d", &number1, number2 );`

    c) `if ( c < 7 );`
       `printf( "C is less than 7\n" );`

    d) `if ( c => 7 )`
       `printf( "C is equal to or less than 7\n" );`

ANSWERS TO SELF-REVIEW EXERCISES

2.1   a) main. b) left brace. ({), right brace (}). c) semicolon. d) printf. e) newline. f) scanf. g) %d. h) destructive. i) nondestructive. j) if.

2.2   a) False. Function printf always begins printing where the cursor is positioned, and this may be anywhere on a line of the screen.
    b) False. Comments do not cause any action to be performed when the program is executed. They are used to document programs and improve their readability.
    c) True.
    d) True.
    e) True.
    f) False. C is case sensitive, so these variables are unique.
    g) False. The definitions must appear after the left brace of the body of a function and before any executable statements.
    h) False. Arguments in a printf function ordinarily should not be preceded by an ampersand. Arguments following the format control string in a scanf function ordinarily should be preceded by an ampersand. We will discuss exceptions to these rules in Chapter 6 and Chapter 7.
    i) True.
    j) False. The operators *, / and % are on the same level of precedence, and the operators + and − are on a lower level of precedence.
    k) False. Some systems may distinguish between identifiers longer than 31 characters.
    l) False. A printf statement with multiple \n escape sequences can print several lines.

2.3   a) int c, thisVariable, q76354, number;
    b) printf("Enter an integer: ");
    c) scanf("%d", &a);
    d) if (number != 7)
           printf("The variable number is not equal to 7.\n");
    e) printf("This is a C program.\n");
    f) printf("This is a C\nprogram.\n");
    g) printf("This\nis\na\nC\nprogram.\n");
    h) printf("This\tis\ta\tC\tprogram.\n");

2.4   a) /* Calculate the product of three integers */
    b) int x, y, z, result;
    c) printf("Enter three integers: ");
    d) scanf("%d%d%d", &x, &y, &z);
    e) result = x * y * z;
    f) printf("The product is %d\n", result);

2.5   See below.

```
1   /* Calculate the product of three integers */
2   #include <stdio.h>
3
4   int main()
5   {
6       int x, y, z, result; /* declare variables */
7
```

```
 8      printf( "Enter three integers: " );   /* prompt */
 9      scanf( "%d%d%d", &x, &y, &z );          /* read three integers */
10      result = x * y * z; /* multiply values */
11      printf( "The product is %d\n", result ); /* display result */
12
13      return 0;
14   }
```

(Part 2 of 2.)

2.6 a) Error: &number. Correction: Eliminate the &. Later in the text we discuss exceptions to this.

   b) Error: `number2` does not have an ampersand. Correction: `number2` should be `&number2`. Later in the text we discuss exceptions to this.

   c) Error: Semicolon after the right parenthesis of the condition in the `if` statement. Correction: Remove the semicolon after the right parenthesis. [*Note:* The result of this error is that the `printf` statement will be executed whether or not the condition in the `if` statement is true. The semicolon after the right parenthesis is considered an empty statement—a statement that does nothing.]

   d) Error: The relational operator => should be changed to >= (greater than or equal to).

EXERCISES

2.7 Identify and correct the errors in each of the following statements (*Note:* there may be more than one error per statement):

   a) `scanf( "d", value );`
   b) `printf( "The product of %d and %d is %d"\n, x, y );`
   c) `firstNumber + secondNumber = sumOfNumbers`
   d) `if ( number => largest )`
       `    largest == number;`
   e) `*/ Program to determine the largest of three integers /*`
   f) `Scanf( "%d", anInteger );`
   g) `printf( "Remainder of %d divided by %d is\n", x, y, x % y );`
   h) `if ( x = y );`
       `    printf( %d is equal to %d\n", x, y );`
   i) `print( "The sum is %d\n," x + y );`
   j) `Printf( "The value you entered is: %d\n, &value );`

2.8 Fill in the blanks in each of the following:

   a) _____ are used to document a program and improve its readability.
   b) The function used to display information on the screen is _____.
   c) A C statement that makes a decision is _____.
   d) Calculations are normally performed by _____ statements.
   e) The _____ function inputs values from the keyboard.

2.9 Write a single C statement or line that accomplishes each of the following:

   a) Print the message "Enter two numbers."
   b) Assign the product of variables b and c to variable a.
   c) State that a program performs a sample payroll calculation (i.e., use text that helps to document a program).
   d) Input three integer values from the keyboard and place these values in integer variables a, b and c.

2.10 State which of the following are *true* and which are *false*. If *false*, explain your answer.

   a) C operators are evaluated from left to right.

b) The following are all valid variable names: _under_bar_, m928134, t5, j7, her_sales, his_account_total, a, b, c, z, z2.
c) The statement printf("a = 5;"); is a typical example of an assignment statement.
d) A valid arithmetic expression containing no parentheses is evaluated from left to right.
e) The following are all invalid variable names: 3g, 87, 67h2, h22, 2h.

2.11   Fill in the blanks in each of the following:
a) What arithmetic operations are on the same level of precedence as multiplication? _____.
b) When parentheses are nested, which set of parentheses is evaluated first in an arithmetic expression? _____.
c) A location in the computer's memory that may contain different values at various times throughout the execution of a program is called a _____.

2.12   What, if anything, prints when each of the following statements is performed? If nothing prints, then answer "nothing." Assume x = 2 and y = 3.
a) printf("%d", x);
b) printf("%d", x + x);
c) printf("x=");
d) printf("x=%d", x);
e) printf("%d = %d", x + y, y + x);
f) z = x + y;
g) scanf("%d%d", &x, &y);
h) /* printf("x + y = %d", x + y); */
i) printf("\n");

2.13   Which, if any, of the following C statements contain variables involved in destructive read-in?
a) scanf("%d%d%d%d%d", &b, &c, &d, &e, &f);
b) p = i + j + k + 7;
c) printf("Destructive read-in");
d) printf("a = 5");

2.14   Given the equation $y = ax^3 + 7$, which of the following, if any, are correct C statements for this equation?
a) y = a * x * x * x + 7;
b) y = a * x * x * (x + 7);
c) y = (a * x) * x * (x + 7);
d) y = (a * x) * x * x + 7;
e) y = a * (x * x * x) + 7;
f) y = a * x * (x * x + 7);

2.15   State the order of evaluation of the operators in each of the following C statements and show the value of x after each statement is performed.
a) x = 7 + 3 * 6 / 2 - 1;
b) x = 2 % 2 + 2 * 2 - 2 / 2;
c) x = (3 * 9 * (3 + (9 * 3 / (3))));

2.16   Write a program that asks the user to enter two numbers, obtains the two numbers from the user and prints the sum, product, difference, quotient and remainder of the two numbers.

2.17   Write a program that prints the numbers 1 to 4 on the same line. Write the program using the following methods.
a) Using one printf statement with no conversion specifiers.

     b) Using one `printf` statement with four conversion specifiers.

     c) Using four `printf` statements.

2.18   Write a program that asks the user to enter two integers, obtains the numbers from the user, then prints the larger number followed by the words "`is larger.`" If the numbers are equal, print the message "`These numbers are equal.`" Use only the single-selection form of the `if` statement you learned in this chapter.

2.19   Write a program that inputs three different integers from the keyboard, then prints the sum, the average, the product, the smallest and the largest of these numbers. Use only the single-selection form of the `if` statement you learned in this chapter. The screen dialogue should appear as follows:

```
Input three different integers: 13 27 14
Sum is 54
Average is 18
Product is 4914
Smallest is 13
Largest is 27
```

2.20   Write a program that reads in the radius of a circle and prints the circle's diameter, circumference and area. Use the constant value 3.14159 for π. Perform each of these calculations inside the `printf` statement(s) and use the conversion specifier %f. [*Note*: In this chapter, we have discussed only integer constants and variables. In Chapter 3 we will discuss floating-point numbers, i.e., values that can have decimal points.]

2.21   Write a program that prints a box, an oval, an arrow and a diamond as follows:

```
*********          ***          *            *
*       *        *     *       ***          * *
*       *       *       *     *****         *   *
*       *       *       *      *           *     *
*       *       *       *      *          *       *
*       *       *       *      *          *       *
*       *       *       *      *           *     *
*       *        *     *       *            * *
*********          ***          *            *
```

2.22   What does the following code print?

```
printf( "*\n**\n***\n****\n*****\n" );
```

2.23   Write a program that reads in five integers and then determines and prints the largest and the smallest integers in the group. Use only the programming techniques you have learned in this chapter.

2.24   Write a program that reads an integer and determines and prints whether it is odd or even. [*Hint*: Use the remainder operator. An even number is a multiple of two. Any multiple of two leaves a remainder of zero when divided by 2.]

2.25   Print your initials in block letters down the page. Construct each block letter out of the letter it represents as shown below.

```
PPPPPPPP
     P   P
     P   P
     P   P
      P P

  JJ
  J
 J
  J
   JJJJJJJ

DDDDDDDD
D        D
D        D
 D      D
   DDDDD
```

2.26   Write a program that reads in two integers and determines and prints if the first is a multiple of the second. [*Hint*: Use the remainder operator.]

2.27   Display the following checkerboard pattern with eight `printf` statements and then display the same pattern with as few `printf` statements as possible.

```
* * * * * * * *
 * * * * * * * *
* * * * * * * *
 * * * * * * * *
* * * * * * * *
 * * * * * * * *
* * * * * * * *
 * * * * * * * *
```

2.28   Distinguish between the terms fatal error and non-fatal error. Why might you prefer to experience a fatal error rather than a non-fatal error?

2.29   Here's a peek ahead. In this chapter you learned about integers and the type `int`. C can also represent uppercase letters, lowercase letters and a considerable variety of special symbols. C uses small integers internally to represent each different character. The set of characters a computer uses and the corresponding integer representations for those characters is called that computer's character set. You can print the integer equivalent of uppercase A for example, by executing the statement

```
printf( "%d", 'A' );
```

Write a C program that prints the integer equivalents of some uppercase letters, lowercase letters, digits and special symbols. As a minimum, determine the integer equivalents of the following: A B C a b c 0 1 2 $ * + / and the blank character.

2.30   Write a program that inputs one five-digit number, separates the number into its individual digits and prints the digits separated from one another by three spaces each. [*Hint*: Use combinations of integer division and the remainder operation.] For example, if the user types in 42139, the program should print

```
4   2   1   3   9
```

2.31   Using only the techniques you learned in this chapter, write a program that calculates the squares and cubes of the numbers from 0 to 10 and uses tabs to print the following table of values:

```
number  square  cube
0       0       0
1       1       1
2       4       8
3       9       27
4       16      64
5       25      125
6       36      216
7       49      343
8       64      512
9       81      729
10      100     1000
```

Structured Program Development in C

Objectives

- To understand basic problem-solving techniques.
- To be able to develop algorithms through the process of top-down, stepwise refinement.
- To be able to use the if selection statement and if...else selection statement to select actions.
- To be able to use the while repetition statement to execute statements in a program repeatedly.
- To understand counter-controlled repetition and sentinel-controlled repetition.
- To understand structured programming.
- To be able to use the increment, decrement and assignment operators.

The secret to success is constancy to purpose.
Benjamin Disraeli

Let's all move one place on.
Lewis Carroll

The wheel is come full circle.
William Shakespeare
King Lear

How many apples fell on Newton's head before he took the hint!
Robert Frost
Comment

Outline

3.1 Introduction

Before writing a program to solve a particular problem, it is essential to have a thorough understanding of the problem and a carefully planned approach to solving the problem. The next two chapters discuss techniques that facilitate the development of structured computer programs. In Section 4.12, we present a summary of structured programming that ties together the techniques developed here and in Chapter 4.

3.2 Algorithms

The solution to any computing problem involves executing a series of actions in a specific order. A *procedure* for solving a problem in terms of

1. the *actions* to be executed, and

2. the *order* in which these actions are to be executed

is called an *algorithm*. The following example demonstrates that correctly specifying the order in which the actions are to be executed is important.

Consider the "rise-and-shine algorithm" followed by one junior executive for getting out of bed and going to work:

Get out of bed.
Take off pajamas.
Take a shower.

Get dressed.
Eat breakfast.
Carpool to work.

This routine gets the executive to work well prepared to make critical decisions. Suppose, however, that the same steps are performed in a slightly different order:

Get out of bed.
Take off pajamas.
Get dressed.
Take a shower.
Eat breakfast.
Carpool to work.

In this case, our junior executive shows up for work soaking wet. Specifying the order in which statements are to be executed in a computer program is called *program control*. In this and the next chapter, we investigate the program control capabilities of C.

3.3 Pseudocode

Pseudocode is an artificial and informal language that helps programmers develop algorithms. The pseudocode we present here is particularly useful for developing algorithms that will be converted to structured C programs. Pseudocode is similar to everyday English; it is convenient and user-friendly although it is not an actual computer programming language.

Pseudocode programs are not executed on computers. Rather, they merely help the programmer "think out" a program before attempting to write it in a programming language such as C. In this chapter, we give several examples of how pseudocode may be used effectively in developing structured C programs.

Pseudocode consists purely of characters, so programmers may conveniently type pseudocode programs into a computer using an editor program. The computer can display or print a fresh copy of a pseudocode program on demand. A carefully prepared pseudocode program may be converted easily to a corresponding C program. This is done in many cases simply by replacing pseudocode statements with their C equivalents.

Pseudocode consists only of action statements—those that are executed when the program has been converted from pseudocode to C and is run in C. Definitions are not executable statements. They are messages to the compiler. For example, the definition

```
int i;
```

simply tells the compiler the type of variable i and instructs the compiler to reserve space in memory for the variable. But this definition does not cause any action—such as input, output, or a calculation—to occur when the program is executed. Some programmers choose to list each variable and briefly mention the purpose of each at the beginning of a pseudocode program. Again, pseudocode is an informal program development aid.

3.4 Control Structures

Normally, statements in a program are executed one after the other in the order in which they are written. This is called *sequential execution*. Various C statements we will soon discuss enable the programmer to specify that the next statement to be executed may be other than the next one in sequence. This is called *transfer of control*.

During the 1960s, it became clear that the indiscriminate use of transfers of control was the root of a great deal of difficulty experienced by software development groups. The finger of blame was pointed at the *goto statement* that allows the programmer to specify a transfer of control to one of a wide range of possible destinations in a program. The notion of so-called structured programming became almost synonymous with *"goto elimination."*

The research of Bohm and Jacopini[1] had demonstrated that programs could be written without any goto statements. The challenge of the era was for programmers to shift their styles to "goto-less programming." It was not until well into the 1970s that the programming profession started taking structured programming seriously. The results were impressive, as software development groups reported reduced development times, more frequent on-time delivery of systems and more frequent within-budget completion of software projects. The key to these successes was simply that programs produced with structured techniques were clearer, easier to debug and modify and more likely to be bug-free in the first place.

Bohm and Jacopini's work demonstrated that all programs could be written in terms of only three *control structures*, namely the *sequence structure*, the *selection structure* and the *repetition structure*. The sequence structure is essentially built into C. Unless directed otherwise, the computer automatically executes C statements one after the other in the order in which they are written. The *flowchart* segment of Fig. 3.1 illustrates C's sequence structure.

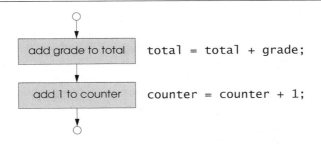

Fig. 3.1   Flowcharting C's sequence structure.

A flowchart is a graphical representation of an algorithm or of a portion of an algorithm. Flowcharts are drawn using certain special-purpose symbols such as rectangles, diamonds, ovals, and small circles; these symbols are connected by arrows called *flowlines*.

Like pseudocode, flowcharts are useful for developing and representing algorithms, although pseudocode is preferred by most programmers. Flowcharts clearly show how control structures operate; that is all we use them for in this text.

Consider the flowchart for the sequence structure in Fig. 3.1. We use the *rectangle symbol*, also called the *action symbol*, to indicate any type of action including a calculation or an input/output operation. The flowlines in the figure indicate the order in which the actions are performed—first, grade is to be added to total and then 1 is to be added to counter. C allows us to have as many actions as we want in a sequence structure. As we will soon see, anywhere a single action may be placed, we may place several actions in sequence.

When drawing a flowchart that represents a complete algorithm, an *oval symbol* containing the word "Begin" is the first symbol used in the flowchart; an oval symbol con-

1. Bohm, C., and G. Jacopini, "Flow Diagrams, Turing Machines, and Languages with Only Two Formation Rules," *Communications of the ACM*, Vol. 9, No. 5, May 1966, pp. 336-371.

taining the word "End" is the last symbol used. When drawing only a portion of an algorithm as in Fig. 3.1, the oval symbols are omitted in favor of using *small circle symbols* also called *connector symbols*.

Perhaps the most important flowcharting symbol is the *diamond symbol*, also called the *decision symbol,* which indicates that a decision is to be made. We will discuss the diamond symbol in the next section.

C provides three types of selection structures in the form of statements. The `if` selection statement (Section 3.5) either performs (selects) an action if a condition is true or skips the action if the condition is false. The `if...else` selection statement (Section 3.6) performs an action if a condition is true and performs a different action if the condition is false. The `switch` selection statement (discussed in Chapter 4) performs one of many different actions depending on the value of an expression. The `if` statement is called a *single-selection statement* because it selects or ignores a single action. The `if...else` statement is called a *double-selection statement* because it selects between two different actions. The `switch` statement is called a *multiple-selection statement* because it selects among many different actions.

C provides three types of repetition structures in the form of statements, namely `while` (Section 3.7), and `do...while` and `for` (both discussed in Chapter 4).

That is all there is. C has only seven control statements: Sequence, three types of selection and three types of repetition. Each C program is formed by combining as many of each type of control statement as is appropriate for the algorithm the program implements. As with the sequence structure of Fig. 3.1, we will see that the flowchart representation of each control statement has two small circle symbols, one at the entry point to the control statement and one at the exit point. These *single-entry/single-exit control statements* make it easy to build programs. The control statement flowchart segments can be attached to one another by connecting the exit point of one control statement to the entry point of the next. This is much like the way in which a child stacks building blocks, so we call this *control-statement stacking*. We will learn that there is only one other way control statements may be connected—a method called *control-statement nesting*. Thus, any C program we will ever need to build can be constructed from only seven different types of control statements combined in only two ways. This is the essence of simplicity.

3.5 The `if` Selection Statement

Selection structures are used to choose among alternative courses of action. For example, suppose the passing grade on an exam is 60. The pseudocode statement

> *If student's grade is greater than or equal to 60*
>   *Print "Passed"*

determines if the condition "student's grade is greater than or equal to 60" is true or false. If the condition is true, then "Passed" is printed, and the next pseudocode statement in order is "performed" (remember that pseudocode is not a real programming language). If the condition is false, the printing is ignored, and the next pseudocode statement in order is performed. Note that the second line of this selection structure is indented. Such indentation is optional, but it is highly recommended as it helps emphasize the inherent structure of structured programs. We will apply indentation conventions carefully throughout this text. The C compiler ignores *whitespace characters* like blanks, tabs and newlines used for indentation and vertical spacing.

Good Programming Practice 3.1

Consistently applying responsible indentation conventions greatly improves program readability. We suggest a fixed-size tab of about 1/4 inch or three blanks per indent. In this book, we use three blanks per indent.

The preceding pseudocode *If* statement may be written in C as

```
if ( grade >= 60 )
   printf( "Passed\n" );
```

Notice that the C code corresponds closely to the pseudocode. This is one of the properties of pseudocode that makes it such a useful program development tool.

Good Programming Practice 3.2

Pseudocode is often used to "think out" a program during the program design process. Then the pseudocode program is converted to C.

The flowchart of Fig. 3.2 illustrates the single selection `if` statement. This flowchart contains what is perhaps the most important flowcharting symbol—the *diamond symbol*, also called the *decision symbol*, which indicates that a decision is to be made. The decision symbol contains an expression, such as a condition, that can be either true or false. The decision symbol has two flowlines emerging from it. One indicates the direction to be taken when the expression in the symbol is true; the other indicates the direction to be taken when the expression is false. We learned in Chapter 2 that decisions can be based on conditions containing relational or equality operators. Actually, a decision can be based on any expression—if the expression evaluates to zero, it is treated as false, and if the expression evaluates to nonzero, it is treated as true.

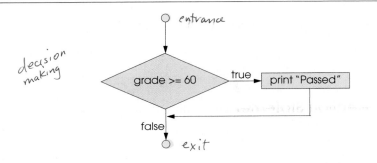

Fig. 3.2   Flowcharting the single-selection `if` statement.

Note that the `if` statement, too, is a single-entry/single-exit structure. We will soon learn that the flowcharts for the remaining control structures can also contain (besides small circle symbols and flowlines) only rectangle symbols to indicate the actions to be performed, and diamond symbols to indicate decisions to be made. This is the action/decision model of programming we have been emphasizing.

We can envision seven bins, each containing only control statement flowcharts of one of the seven types. These flowchart segments are empty—nothing is written in the rectangles and nothing is written in the diamonds. The programmer's task, then, is assembling a program from as many of each type of control statement as the algorithm demands, combining those control statements in only two possible ways (stacking or nesting), and then filling in the actions and decisions in a manner appropriate for the algorithm. We will discuss the variety of ways in which actions and decisions may be written.

3.6 The if...else Selection Statement

The if selection statement performs an indicated action only when the condition is true; otherwise the action is skipped. The if...else selection statement allows the programmer to specify that different actions are to be performed when the condition is true than when the condition is false. For example, the pseudocode statement

> *If student's grade is greater than or equal to 60*
>   *Print "Passed"*
> *else*
>   *Print "Failed"*

prints *Passed* if the student's grade is greater than or equal to 60 and prints *Failed* if the student's grade is less than 60. In either case, after printing occurs, the next pseudocode statement in sequence is "performed." Note that the body of the *else* is also indented. Whatever indentation convention you choose should be carefully applied throughout your programs. It is difficult to read a program that does not obey uniform spacing conventions.

Good Programming Practice 3.3

Indent both body statements of an if...else statement.

Good Programming Practice 3.4

If there are several levels of indentation, each level should be indented the same additional amount of space.

The preceding pseudocode *If...else* statement may be written in C as

```
if ( grade >= 60 )
    printf( "Passed\n" );
else
    printf( "Failed\n" );
```

The flowchart of Fig. 3.3 nicely illustrates the flow of control in the if...else statement. Once again, note that (besides small circles and arrows) the only symbols in the flowchart are rectangles (for actions) and a diamond (for a decision). We continue to emphasize this action/decision model of computing. Imagine again a deep bin containing as many empty double-selection statements (represented as flowchart segments) as might be needed to build any C program. The programmer's job, again, is to assemble these selection statements (by stacking and nesting) with any other control statements required by the algorithm, and to fill in the empty rectangles and empty diamonds with actions and decisions appropriate to the algorithm being implemented.

C provides the *conditional operator (?:)* which is closely related to the if...else statement. The conditional operator is C's only *ternary operator*—it takes three operands. The operands together with the conditional operator form a *conditional expression*. The first operand is a condition. The second operand is the value for the entire conditional expression if the condition is true and the third operand is the value for the entire conditional expression if the condition is false. For example, the printf statement

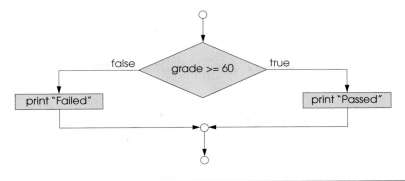

Fig. 3.3   Flowcharting the double-selection if...else statement.

```
printf( "%s\n", grade >= 60 ? "Passed" : "Failed" );
```

contains a conditional expression that evaluates to the string literal `"Passed"` if the condition `grade >= 60` is true and evaluates to the string literal `"Failed"` if the condition is false. The format control string of the `printf` contains the conversion specification `%s` for printing a character string. So the preceding `printf` statement performs in essentially the same way as the preceding if...else statement.

The values in a conditional expression can also be actions to be executed. For example, the conditional expression

```
grade >= 60 ? printf( "Passed\n" ) : printf( "Failed\n" );
```

is read, "If `grade` is greater than or equal to 60 then `printf("Passed\n")`, otherwise `printf( "Failed\n" )`." This, too, is comparable to the preceding if...else statement. We will see that conditional operators can be used in some situations where if...else statements cannot.

Nested if...else *statements* test for multiple cases by placing if...else statements inside if...else statements. For example, the following pseudocode statement will print A for exam grades greater than or equal to 90, B for grades greater than or equal to 80, C for grades greater than or equal to 70, D for grades greater than or equal to 60, and F for all other grades.

> *If student's grade is greater than or equal to 90*
> > *Print "A"*
> *else*
> > *If student's grade is greater than or equal to 80*
> > > *Print "B"*
> > *else*
> > > *If student's grade is greater than or equal to 70*
> > > > *Print "C"*
> > > *else*
> > > > *If student's grade is greater than or equal to 60*
> > > > > *Print "D"*
> > > > *else*
> > > > > *Print "F"*

This pseudocode may be written in C as

```
if ( grade >= 90 )
   printf( "A\n" );
else
   if ( grade >= 80 )
      printf("B\n");
   else
      if ( grade >= 70 )
         printf("C\n");
      else
         if ( grade >= 60 )
            printf( "D\n" );
         else
            printf( "F\n" );
```

If the variable grade is greater than or equal to 90, the first four conditions will be true, but only the printf statement after the first test will be executed. After that printf is executed, the else part of the "outer" if...else statement is skipped. Many C programmers prefer to write the preceding if statement as

```
if ( grade >= 90 )
   printf( "A\n" );
else if ( grade >= 80 )
   printf( "B\n" );
else if ( grade >= 70 )
   printf( "C\n" );
else if ( grade >= 60 )
   printf( "D\n" );
else
   printf( "F\n" );
```

As far as the C compiler is concerned, both forms are equivalent. The latter form is popular because it avoids the deep indentation of the code to the right. Such indentation often leaves little room on a line, forcing lines to be split and decreasing program readability.

The if selection statement expects only one statement in its body. To include several statements in the body of an if, enclose the set of statements in braces ({ and }). A set of statements contained within a pair of braces is called a *compound statement* or a *block*.

Software Engineering Observation 3.1

A compound statement can be placed anywhere in a program that a single statement can be placed.

The following example includes a compound statement in the else part of an if...else statement.

```
if ( grade >= 60 )
   printf( "Passed.\n" );
else {
   printf( "Failed.\n" );
   printf( "You must take this course again.\n" );
}
```

In this case, if grade is less than 60, the program executes both printf statements in the body of the else and prints

```
Failed.
You must take this course again.
```

Notice the braces surrounding the two statements in the `else` clause. These braces are important. Without the braces, the statement

```
printf( "You must take this course again.\n" );
```

would be outside the body of the `else` part of the `if`, and would execute regardless of whether the grade is less than 60.

Common Programming Error 3.1

Forgetting one or both of the braces that delimit a compound statement.

A syntax error is caught by the compiler. A logic error has its effect at execution time. A fatal logic error causes a program to fail and terminate prematurely. A nonfatal logic error allows a program to continue executing but to produce incorrect results.

Common Programming Error 3.2

Placing a semicolon after the condition in an if *statement leads to a logic error in single-selection* if *statements and a syntax error in double-selection* if *statements.*

Error-Prevention Tip 3.1

Typing the beginning and ending braces of compound statements before typing the individual statements within the braces, helps avoid omitting one or both of the braces, preventing syntax errors and logic errors (where both braces are indeed required).

Software Engineering Observation 3.2

Just as a compound statement can be placed anywhere a single statement can be placed, it is also possible to have no statement at all, i.e., the empty statement. The empty statement is represented by placing a semicolon (; *) where a statement would normally be.*

3.7 The while Repetition Statement

A *repetition statement* allows the programmer to specify that an action is to be repeated while some condition remains true. The pseudocode statement

> *While there are more items on my shopping list*
> *Purchase next item and cross it off my list*

describes the repetition that occurs during a shopping trip. The condition, "there are more items on my shopping list" may be true or false. If it is true, then the action, "Purchase next item and cross it off my list" is performed. This action will be performed repeatedly while the condition remains true. The statement(s) contained in the *while* repetition statement constitute the body of the *while*. The *while* statement body may be a single statement or a compound statement.

Eventually, the condition will become false (when the last item on the shopping list has been purchased and crossed off the list). At this point, the repetition terminates, and the first pseudocode statement after the repetition structure is executed.

Common Programming Error 3.3

Not providing in the body of a while statement with an action that eventually causes the condition in the while to become false. Normally, such a repetition structure will never terminate—an error called an "infinite loop."

Common Programming Error 3.4

Spelling the keyword while with an uppercase W as in While (remember that C is a case-sensitive language). All of C's reserved keywords such as while, if and else contain only lowercase letters.

As an example of an actual while, consider a program segment designed to find the first power of 2 larger than 1000. Suppose the integer variable product has been initialized to 2. When the following while repetition statement finishes executing, product will contain the desired answer:

```
product = 2;

while ( product <= 1000 )
    product = 2 * product;
```

The flowchart of Fig. 3.4 nicely illustrates the flow of control in the while repetition statement. Once again, note that (besides small circles and arrows) the flowchart contains only a rectangle symbol and a diamond symbol. The flowchart clearly shows the repetition. The flowline emerging from the rectangle wraps back to the decision which is tested each time through the loop until the decision eventually becomes false. At this point, the while statement is exited and control passes to the next statement in the program.

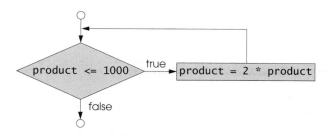

Fig. 3.4   Flowcharting the while repetition statement.

When the while statement is entered, the value of product is 2. The variable product is repeatedly multiplied by 2, taking on the values 4, 8, 16, 32, 64, 128, 256, 512, and 1024 successively. When product becomes 1024, the condition in the while statement, product <= 1000, becomes false. This terminates the repetition, and the final value of product is 1024. Program execution continues with the next statement after the while.

3.8 Formulating Algorithms: Case Study 1 (Counter-Controlled Repetition)

To illustrate how algorithms are developed, we solve several variations of a class averaging problem. Consider the following problem statement:

> *A class of ten students took a quiz. The grades (integers in the range 0 to 100) for this quiz are available to you. Determine the class average on the quiz.*

The class average is equal to the sum of the grades divided by the number of students. The algorithm for solving this problem on a computer must input each of the grades, perform the averaging calculation, and print the result.

Let us use pseudocode, list the actions to be executed, and specify the order in which these actions should be executed. We use *counter-controlled repetition* to input the grades one at a time. This technique uses a variable called a *counter* to specify the number of times a set of statements should execute. In this example, repetition terminates when the counter exceeds 10. In this section we simply present the pseudocode algorithm (Fig. 3.5) and the corresponding C program (Fig. 3.6). In the next section, we show how pseudocode algorithms are developed. Counter-controlled repetition is often called *definite repetition* because the number of repetitions is known before the loop begins executing.

Set total to zero
Set grade counter to one

While grade counter is less than or equal to ten
    Input the next grade
    Add the grade into the total
    Add one to the grade counter

Set the class average to the total divided by ten
Print the class average

Fig. 3.5   Pseudocode algorithm that uses counter-controlled repetition to solve the class average problem.

```
1   /* Fig. 3.6: fig03_06.c
2      Class average program with counter-controlled repetition */
3   #include <stdio.h>
4
5   /* function main begins program execution */
6   int main()
7   {
8      int counter; /* number of grade to be entered next */
9      int grade;   /* grade value */
10     int total;   /* sum of grades input by user */
11     int average; /* average of grades */
12
```

Fig. 3.6   C program and sample execution for the class average problem with counter-controlled repetition. (Part 1 of 2.)

```
13      /* initialization phase */
14      total = 0;     /* initialize total */
15      counter = 1; /* initialize loop counter */
16
17      /* processing phase */
18      while ( counter <= 10 ) {      /* loop 10 times */
19         printf( "Enter grade: " );  /* prompt for input */
20         scanf( "%d", &grade );      /* read grade from user */
21         total = total + grade;      /* add grade to total */
22         counter = counter + 1;      /* increment counter */
23      } /* end while */
24
25      /* termination phase */
26      average = total / 10; /* integer division */
27
28      printf( "Class average is %d\n", average ); /* display result */
29
30      return 0; /* indicate program ended successfully */
31
32   } /* end function main */
```

```
Enter grade: 98
Enter grade: 76
Enter grade: 71
Enter grade: 87
Enter grade: 83
Enter grade: 90
Enter grade: 57
Enter grade: 79
Enter grade: 82
Enter grade: 94
Class average is 81
```

Fig. 3.6   C program and sample execution for the class average problem with counter-controlled repetition. (Part 2 of 2.)

Note the references in the algorithm to a total and a counter. A *total* is a variable used to accumulate the sum of a series of values. A counter is a variable used to count—in this case, to count the number of grades entered. Variables used to store totals should normally be initialized to zero before being used in a program; otherwise the sum would include the previous value stored in the total's memory location. Counter variables are normally initialized to zero or one, depending on their use (we will present examples showing each of these uses). An uninitialized variable contains a *"garbage" value*—the value last stored in the memory location reserved for that variable.

Common Programming Error 3.5

If a counter or total is not initialized, the results of your program will probably be incorrect. This is an example of a logic error.

Error-Prevention Tip 3.2

Initialize counters and totals.

Note that the averaging calculation in the program produced an integer result of 81. Actually, the sum of the grades in this example is 817 which when divided by 10 should yield 81.7, i.e., a number with a decimal point. We will see how to deal with such numbers (called floating-point numbers) in the next section.

3.9 Formulating Algorithms with Top-Down, Stepwise Refinement: Case Study 2 (Sentinel-Controlled Repetition)

Let us generalize the class average problem. Consider the following problem:

> *Develop a class averaging program that will process an arbitrary number of grades each time the program is run.*

In the first class average example, the number of grades (10) was known in advance. In this example, no indication is given of how many grades are to be entered. The program must process an arbitrary number of grades. How can the program determine when to stop the input of grades? How will it know when to calculate and print the class average?

One way to solve this problem is to use a special value called a *sentinel value* (also called a *signal value,* a *dummy value,* or a *flag value*) to indicate "end of data entry." The user types grades in until all legitimate grades have been entered. The user then types the sentinel value to indicate that the last grade has been entered. Sentinel-controlled repetition is often called *indefinite repetition* because the number of repetitions is not known before the loop begins executing.

Clearly, the sentinel value must be chosen so that it cannot be confused with an acceptable input value. Since grades on a quiz are normally nonnegative integers, –1 is an acceptable sentinel value for this problem. Thus, a run of the class average program might process a stream of inputs such as 95, 96, 75, 74, 89 and –1. The program would then compute and print the class average for the grades 95, 96, 75, 74, and 89 (–1 is the sentinel value, so it should not enter into the averaging calculation).

 Common Programming Error 3.6

Choosing a sentinel value that is also a legitimate data value.

We approach the class average program with a technique called *top-down, stepwise refinement,* a technique that is essential to the development of well structured programs. We begin with a pseudocode representation of the *top:*

> *Determine the class average for the quiz*

The top is a single statement that conveys the program's overall function. As such, the top is, in effect, a complete representation of a program. Unfortunately, the top rarely conveys a sufficient amount of detail for writing the C program. So we now begin the refinement process. We divide the top into a series of smaller tasks and list these in the order in which they need to be performed. This results in the following *first refinement.*

> *Initialize variables*
> *Input, sum, and count the quiz grades*
> *Calculate and print the class average*

Here, only the sequence structure has been used—the steps listed are to be executed in order, one after the other.

Software Engineering Observation 3.3

Each refinement, as well as the top itself, is a complete specification of the algorithm; only the level of detail varies.

To proceed to the next level of refinement, i.e., the *second refinement*, we commit to specific variables. We need a running total of the numbers, a count of how many numbers have been processed, a variable to receive the value of each grade as it is input and a variable to hold the calculated average. The pseudocode statement

> *Initialize variables*

may be refined as follows:

> *Initialize total to zero*
> *Initialize counter to zero*

Notice that only total and counter need to be initialized; the variables average and grade (for the calculated average and the user input, respectively) need not be initialized because their values will be written over by the process of destructive read-in discussed in Chapter 2. The pseudocode statement

> *Input, sum, and count the quiz grades*

requires a repetition structure (i.e., a loop) that successively inputs each grade. Since we do not know in advance how many grades are to be processed, we will use sentinel-controlled repetition. The user will type legitimate grades in one at a time. After the last legitimate grade is typed, the user will type the sentinel value. The program will test for this value after each grade is input and will terminate the loop when the sentinel is entered. The refinement of the preceding pseudocode statement is then

> *Input the first grade*
> *While the user has not as yet entered the sentinel*
>   *Add this grade into the running total*
>   *Add one to the grade counter*
>   *Input the next grade (possibly the sentinel)*

Notice that in pseudocode, we do not use braces around the set of statements that form the body of the *while* statement. We simply indent all these statements under the *while* to show that they all belong to the *while*. Again, pseudocode is only an informal program development aid.

The pseudocode statement

> *Calculate and print the class average*

may be refined as follows:

> *If the counter is not equal to zero*
>   *Set the average to the total divided by the counter*
>   *Print the average*
> *else*
>   *Print "No grades were entered"*

Notice that we are being careful here to test for the possibility of division by zero—a *fatal error* that if undetected would cause the program to fail (often called *"bombing"* or *"crashing"*). The complete second refinement is shown in Fig. 3.7.

Initialize total to zero
Initialize counter to zero

Input the first grade
While the user has not as yet entered the sentinel
      Add this grade into the running total
      Add one to the grade counter
      Input the next grade (possibly the sentinel)

If the counter is not equal to zero
      Set the average to the total divided by the counter
      Print the average
else
      Print "No grades were entered"

Fig. 3.7   Pseudocode algorithm that uses sentinel-controlled repetition to solve the class average problem.

Common Programming Error 3.7
An attempt to divide by zero causes a fatal error.

Good Programming Practice 3.5
When performing division by an expression whose value could be zero, explicitly test for this case and handle it appropriately in your program (such as printing an error message) rather than allowing the fatal error to occur.

In Fig. 3.5 and Fig. 3.7, we include some completely blank lines in the pseudocode for readability. Actually, the blank lines separate these programs into their various phases.

Software Engineering Observation 3.4
Many programs can be divided logically into three phases: An initialization phase that initializes the program variables; a processing phase that inputs data values and adjusts program variables accordingly; and a termination phase that calculates and prints the final results.

The pseudocode algorithm in Fig. 3.7 solves the more general class averaging problem. This algorithm was developed after only two levels of refinement. Sometimes more levels are necessary.

Software Engineering Observation 3.5
The programmer terminates the top-down, stepwise refinement process when the pseudocode algorithm is specified in sufficient detail for the programmer to be able to convert the pseudocode to C. Implementing the C program is then normally straightforward.

The C program and a sample execution are shown in Fig. 3.8. Although only integer grades are entered, the averaging calculation is likely to produce a decimal number with a decimal point. The type int can not represent such a number. The program introduces the data type *float* to handle numbers with decimal points (called *floating-point numbers*) and introduces a special operator called a *cast operator* to handle the averaging calculation. These features are explained in detail after the program is presented.

```c
1   /* Fig. 3.8: fig03_08.c
2      Class average program with sentinel-controlled repetition */
3   #include <stdio.h>
4
5   /* function main begins program execution */
6   int main()
7   {
8      int counter; /* number of grades entered */
9      int grade;   /* grade value */
10     int total;   /* sum of grades */
11
12     float average; /* number with decimal point for average */
13
14     /* initialization phase */
15     total = 0;     /* initialize total */
16     counter = 0; /* initialize loop counter */
17
18     /* processing phase */
19     /* get first grade from user */
20     printf( "Enter grade, -1 to end: " ); /* prompt for input */
21     scanf( "%d", &grade );               /* read grade from user */
22
23     /* loop while sentinel value not yet read from user */
24     while ( grade != -1 ) {
25        total = total + grade; /* add grade to total */
26        counter = counter + 1; /* increment counter */
27
28        /* get next grade from user */
29        printf( "Enter grade, -1 to end: " /* prompt for input */
30        scanf("%d", &grade);            /* read next grade */
31     } /* end while */
32
33     /* termination phase */
34     /* if user entered at least one grade */
35     if ( counter != 0 ) {
36
37        /* calculate average of all grades entered */
38        average = ( float ) total / counter; /* avoid truncation */
39
40        /* display average with two digits of precision */
41        printf( "Class average is %.2f\n", average );
42     } /* end if */
43     else { /* if no grades were entered, output message */
44        printf( "No grades were entered\n" );
45     } /* end else */
46
47     return 0; /* indicate program ended successfully */
48
49  } /* end function main */
```

Fig. 3.8   C program and sample execution for the class average problem with sentinel-controlled repetition. (Part 1 of 2.)

```
Enter grade, -1 to end: 75
Enter grade, -1 to end: 94
Enter grade, -1 to end: 97
Enter grade, -1 to end: 88
Enter grade, -1 to end: 70
Enter grade, -1 to end: 64
Enter grade, -1 to end: 83
Enter grade, -1 to end: 89
Enter grade, -1 to end: -1
Class average is 82.50
```

```
Enter grade, -1 to end: -1
No grades were entered
```

Fig. 3.8   C program and sample execution for the class average problem with sentinel-controlled repetition. (Part 2 of 2.)

Notice the compound statement in the `while` loop (line 24) in Fig. 3.8. Once again, the braces are necessary for all four statements to be executed within the loop. Without the braces, the last three statements in the body of the loop would fall outside the loop, causing the computer to interpret this code incorrectly as follows.

```
while( grade != -1 )
    total = total + grade;            /* add grade to total */
counter = counter + 1;                /* increment counter */
printf( "Enter grade, -1 to end: " ); /* prompt for input */
scanf( "%d", &grade );                /* read next grade */
```

This would cause an infinite loop if the user does not input −1 for the first grade.

Good Programming Practice 3.6

In a sentinel-controlled loop, the prompts requesting data entry should explicitly remind the user what the sentinel value is.

Averages do not always evaluate to integer values. Often, an average is a value such as 7.2 or -93.5 that contains a fractional part. These values are referred to as floating-point numbers and are represented by the data type `float`. The variable `average` is defined to be of type `float` (line 12) to capture the fractional result of our calculation. However, the result of the calculation `total / counter` is an integer because `total` and `counter` are both integer variables. Dividing two integers results in *integer division* in which any fractional part of the calculation is lost (i.e., *truncated*). Since the calculation is performed first, the fractional part is lost before the result is assigned to `average`. To produce a floating-point calculation with integer values, we must create temporary values that are floating-point numbers for the calculation. C provides the *unary cast operator* to accomplish this task. Line 38

```
average = ( float ) total / counter;
```

includes the cast operator (`float`) which creates a temporary floating point copy of its operand, `total`. The value stored in `total` is still an integer. Using a cast operator in this manner is called *explicit conversion.* The calculation now consists of a floating-point value (the temporary `float` version of `total`) divided by the integer value stored in `counter`. The C compiler knows how to evaluate expressions only in which the data types of the operands are identical. To ensure that the operands are of the same type, the compiler performs an operation called *promotion* (also called *implicit conversion*) on selected operands. For example, in an expression containing the data types `int` and `float`, copies of `int` operands are made and *promoted* to `float`. In our example, after a copy of `counter` is made and promoted to `float`, the calculation is performed and the result of the floating-point division is assigned to `average`. C provides a set of rules for promotion of operands of different types. Chapter 5 presents a discussion of all the standard data types and their order of promotion.

Cast operators are available for most data types. The cast operator is formed by placing parentheses around a data type name. The cast operator is a *unary operator*, i.e., an operator that takes only one operand. In Chapter 2, we studied the binary arithmetic operators. C also supports unary versions of the plus (+) and minus (-) operators, so the programmer can write expressions like -7 or +5. Cast operators associate from right to left and have the same precedence as other unary operators such as unary + and unary -. This precedence is one level higher than that of the *multiplicative operators* *, / and %.

Figure 3.8 uses the `printf` conversion specifier `%.2f` (line 41) to print the value of `average`. The f specifies that a floating-point value will be printed. The `.2` is the *precision* with which the value will be displayed. It states that the value will be displayed with 2 digits to the right of the decimal point. If the `%f` conversion specifier is used (without specifying the precision), the *default precision* of 6 is used—exactly as if the conversion specifier `%.6f` had been used. When floating-point values are printed with precision, the printed value is *rounded* to the indicated number of decimal positions. The value in memory is unaltered. When the following statements are executed, the values 3.45 and 3.4 are printed.

```
printf( "%.2f\n", 3.446 );   /* prints 3.45 */
printf( "%.1f\n", 3.446 );   /* prints 3.4  */
```

Common Programming Error 3.8

Using precision in a conversion specification in the format control string of a scanf statement is wrong. Precisions are used only in printf conversion specifications.

Common Programming Error 3.9

Using floating-point numbers in a manner that assumes they are represented precisely can lead to incorrect results. Floating-point numbers are represented only approximately by most computers.

Error-Prevention Tip 3.3

Do not compare floating-point values for equality.

Despite the fact that floating-point numbers are not always "100% precise," they have numerous applications. For example, when we speak of a "normal" body temperature of 98.6 we do not need to be precise to a large number of digits. When we view the temperature on a thermometer and read it as 98.6, it may actually be 98.5999473210643. The point here is that calling this number simply 98.6 is fine for most applications. We will say more about this issue later.

Another way floating-point numbers develop is through division. When we divide 10 by 3, the result is 3.3333333... with the sequence of 3s repeating infinitely. The computer allocates only a fixed amount of space to hold such a value, so clearly the stored floating-point value can only be an approximation.

3.10 Formulating Algorithms with Top-Down, Stepwise Refinement: Case Study 3 (Nested Control Structures)

Let us work another complete problem. We will once again formulate the algorithm using pseudocode and top-down, stepwise refinement, and write a corresponding C program. We have seen that control statements may be stacked on top of one another (in sequence) just as a child stacks building blocks. In this case study we will see the only other structured way control statements may be connected in C, namely through *nesting* of one control statement within another.

Consider the following problem statement:

A college offers a course that prepares students for the state licensing exam for real estate brokers. Last year, several of the students who completed this course took the licensing examination. Naturally, the college wants to know how well its students did on the exam. You have been asked to write a program to summarize the results. You have been given a list of these 10 students. Next to each name a 1 is written if the student passed the exam and a 2 if the student failed.

Your program should analyze the results of the exam as follows:

1. *Input each test result (i.e., a 1 or a 2). Display the message "Enter result" on the screen each time the program requests another test result.*

2. *Count the number of test results of each type.*

3. *Display a summary of the test results indicating the number of students who passed and the number of students who failed.*

4. *If more than 8 students passed the exam, print the message "Raise tuition."*

After reading the problem statement carefully, we make the following observations:

1. The program must process 10 test results. A counter-controlled loop will be used.

2. Each test result is a number—either a 1 or a 2. Each time the program reads a test result, the program must determine if the number is a 1 or a 2. We test for a 1 in our algorithm. If the number is not a 1, we assume that it is a 2. (An exercise at the end of the chapter considers the consequences of this assumption.)

3. Two counters are used—one to count the number of students who passed the exam and one to count the number of students who failed the exam.

4. After the program has processed all the results, it must decide if more than 8 students passed the exam.

Let us proceed with top-down, stepwise refinement. We begin with a pseudocode representation of the top:

> *Analyze exam results and decide if tuition should be raised*

Once again, it is important to emphasize that the top is a complete representation of the program, but several refinements are likely to be needed before the pseudocode can be naturally evolved into a C program. Our first refinement is

Initialize variables
Input the ten quiz grades and count passes and failures
Print a summary of the exam results and decide if tuition should be raised

Here, too, even though we have a complete representation of the entire program, further refinement is necessary. We now commit to specific variables. Counters are needed to record the passes and failures, a counter will be used to control the looping process, and a variable is needed to store the user input. The pseudocode statement

Initialize variables

may be refined as follows:

Initialize passes to zero
Initialize failures to zero
Initialize student to one

Notice only the counters and totals are initialized. The pseudocode statement

Input the ten quiz grades and count passes and failures

requires a loop that successively inputs the result of each exam. Here it is known in advance that there are precisely ten exam results, so counter-controlled looping is appropriate. Inside the loop (i.e., *nested* within the loop) a double-selection statement will determine whether each exam result is a pass or a failure, and will increment the appropriate counters accordingly. The refinement of the preceding pseudocode statement is then

While student counter is less than or equal to ten
*   Input the next exam result*

*   If the student passed*
*   Add one to passes*
*   else*
*   Add one to failures*

*   Add one to student counter*

Notice the use of blank lines to set off the *If...else* to improve program readability. The pseudocode statement

Print a summary of the exam results and decide if tuition should be raised

may be refined as follows:

Print the number of passes
Print the number of failures
If more than eight students passed
*   Print "Raise tuition"*

The complete second refinement appears in Fig. 3.9. Notice that blank lines are also used to set off the *while* statement for program readability.

This pseudocode is now sufficiently refined for conversion to C. The C program and two sample executions are shown in Fig. 3.10. Note that we have taken advantage of a feature of C that allows initialization to be incorporated into definitions. Such initialization occurs at compile time.

Initialize passes to zero
Initialize failures to zero
Initialize student to one

While student counter is less than or equal to ten
        Input the next exam result

            If the student passed
                Add one to passes
            else
                    Add one to failures

            Add one to student counter

Print the number of passes
Print the number of failures
If more than eight students passed
            Print "Raise tuition"

Fig. 3.9   Pseudocode for examination results problem.

```
1   /* Fig. 3.10: fig03_10.c
2      Analysis of examination results */
3   #include <stdio.h>
4
5   /* function main begins program execution */
6   int main()
7   {
8      /* initialize variables in definitions */
9      int passes = 0;    /* number of passes */
10     int failures = 0; /* number of failures */
11     int student = 1;   /* student counter */
12     int result;        /* one exam result */
13
14     /* process 10 students using counter-controlled loop */
15     while ( student <= 10 ) {
16
17        /* prompt user for input and obtain value from user */
18        printf( "Enter result ( 1=pass,2=fail ): " );
19        scanf( "%d", &result );
20
21        /* if result 1, increment passes */
22        if ( result == 1 ) {
23           passes = passes + 1;
24        } /* end if */
25        else {/* otherwise, increment failures */
26           failures = failures + 1;
27        } /* end else */
```

Fig. 3.10   C program and sample executions for examination results problem. (Part 1 of 2.).

```
28
29          student = student + 1; /* increment student counter */
30      } /* end while */
31
32      /* termination phase; display number of passes and failures */
33      printf( "Passed %d\n", passes );
34      printf( "Failed %d\n", failures );
35
36      /* if more than eight students passed, print "raise tuition" */
37      if ( passes > 8 ) {
38          printf( "Raise tuition\n" );
39      } /* end if */
40
41      return 0; /* indicate program ended successfully */
42
43   } /* end function main */
```

```
Enter Result (1=pass,2=fail): 1
Enter Result (1=pass,2=fail): 2
Enter Result (1=pass,2=fail): 2
Enter Result (1=pass,2=fail): 1
Enter Result (1=pass,2=fail): 1
Enter Result (1=pass,2=fail): 1
Enter Result (1=pass,2=fail): 2
Enter Result (1=pass,2=fail): 1
Enter Result (1=pass,2=fail): 1
Enter Result (1=pass,2=fail): 2
Passed 6
Failed 4
```

```
Enter Result (1=pass,2=fail): 1
Enter Result (1=pass,2=fail): 1
Enter Result (1=pass,2=fail): 1
Enter Result (1=pass,2=fail): 2
Enter Result (1=pass,2=fail): 1
Enter Result (1=pass,2=fail): 1
Enter Result (1=pass,2=fail): 1
Enter Result (1=pass,2=fail): 1
Enter Result (1=pass,2=fail): 1
Enter Result (1=pass,2=fail): 1
Passed 9
Failed 1
Raise tuition
```

Fig. 3.10   C program and sample executions for examination results problem. (Part 2 of 2.).

Performance Tip 3.1

Initializing variables when they are defined can help reduce a program's execution time.

Performance Tip 3.2

Many of the performance tips we mention in this text result in nominal improvements, so the reader may be tempted to ignore them. Note that the cumulative effect of all these performance enhancements that can make a program perform significantly faster. Also, significant improvement is realized when a supposedly nominal improvement is placed in a loop that may repeat a large number of times.

Software Engineering Observation 3.6

Experience has shown that the most difficult part of solving a problem on a computer is developing the algorithm for the solution. Once a correct algorithm has been specified, the process of producing a working C program is normally straightforward.

Software Engineering Observation 3.7

Many programmers write programs without ever using program development tools such as pseudocode. They feel that their ultimate goal is to solve the problem on a computer and that writing pseudocode merely delays the production of final outputs.

3.11 Assignment Operators

C provides several assignment operators for abbreviating assignment expressions. For example the statement

```
c = c + 3;
```

can be abbreviated with the *addition assignment operator* += as

```
c += 3;
```

The += operator adds the value of the expression on the right of the operator to the value of the variable on the left of the operator and stores the result in the variable on the left of the operator. Any statement of the form

variable = variable operator expression;

where *operator* is one of the binary operators +, -, *, / or % (or others we will discuss in Chapter 10), can be written in the form

variable operator= expression;

Thus the assignment c += 3 adds 3 to c. Figure 3.11 shows the arithmetic assignment operators, sample expressions using these operators and explanations.

Assignment operator	Sample expression	Explanation	Assigns
Assume: int c = 3, d = 5, e = 4, f = 6, g = 12;			
+=	c += 7	c = c + 7	10 to c
-=	d -= 4	d = d - 4	1 to d

Fig. 3.11 Arithmetic assignment operators. (Part 1 of 2.)

Assignment operator	Sample expression	Explanation	Assigns
*=	e *= 5	e = e * 5	20 to e
/=	f /= 3	f = f / 3	2 to f
%=	g %= 9	g = g % 9	3 to g

Fig. 3.11   Arithmetic assignment operators. (Part 2 of 2.)

3.12 Increment and Decrement Operators

C also provides the unary *increment operator*, **++**, and the unary *decrement operator*, **--**, which are summarized in Fig. 3.12. If a variable c is incremented by 1, the increment operator ++ can be used rather than the expressions c = c + 1 or c += 1. If increment or decrement operators are placed before a variable, they are referred to as the *preincrement* or *predecrement operators,* respectively. If increment or decrement operators are placed after a variable, they are referred to as the *postincrement* or *postdecrement operators,* respectively. Preincrementing (predecrementing) a variable causes the variable to be incremented (decremented) by 1, then the new value of the variable is used in the expression in which it appears. Postincrementing (postdecrementing) the variable causes the current value of the variable to be used in the expression in which it appears, then the variable value is incremented (decremented) by 1.

Operator	Sample expression	Explanation
++	++a	Increment a by 1 then use the new value of a in the expression in which a resides.
++	a++	Use the current value of a in the expression in which a resides, then increment a by 1.
--	--b	Decrement b by 1 then use the new value of b in the expression in which b resides.
--	b--	Use the current value of b in the expression in which b resides, then decrement b by 1.

Fig. 3.12   Increment and decrement operators

Figure 3.13 demonstrates the difference between the preincrementing and the postincrementing versions of the ++ operator. Postincrementing the variable c causes it to be incremented after it is used in the printf statement. Preincrementing the variable c causes it to be incremented before it is used in the printf statement.

```
1    /* Fig. 3.13: fig03_13.c
2       Preincrementing and postincrementing */
3    #include <stdio.h>
```

Fig. 3.13   Preincrementing vs. postincrementing. (Part 1 of 2.)

```
4
5   /* function main begins program execution */
6   int main()
7   {
8      int c;                  /* define variable */
9
10     /* demonstrate postincrement */
11     c = 5;                  /* assign 5 to c */
12     printf( "%d\n", c );    /* print 5 */
13     printf( "%d\n", c++ );  /* print 5 then postincrement */
14     printf( "%d\n\n", c );  /* print 6 */
15
16     /* demonstrate preincrement */
17     c = 5;                  /* assign 5 to c */
18     printf( "%d\n", c );    /* print 5 */
19     printf( "%d\n", ++c );  /* preincrement then print 6 */
20     printf( "%d\n", c );    /* print 6 */
21
22     return 0; /* indicate program ended successfully */
23
24  } /* end function main */
```

```
5
5
6

5
6
6
```

Fig. 3.13   Preincrementing vs. postincrementing. (Part 2 of 2.)

The program displays the value of c before and after the ++ operator is used. The decrement operator (--) works similarly.

 Good Programming Practice 3.7

Unary operators should be placed directly next to their operands with no intervening spaces.

The three assignment statements in Fig. 3.10

```
passes = passes + 1;
failures = failures + 1;
student = student + 1;
```

can be written more concisely with assignment operators as

```
passes += 1;
failures += 1;
student += 1;
```

with preincrement operators as

```
++passes;
++failures;
++student;
```

or with postincrement operators as

```
passes++;
failures++;
student++;
```

It is important to note here that when incrementing or decrementing a variable in a statement by itself, the preincrement and postincrement forms have the same effect. It is only when a variable appears in the context of a larger expression that preincrementing and postincrementing have different effects (and similarly for predecrementing and post-decrementing). Only a simple variable name may be used as the operand of an increment or decrement operator.

Common Programming Error 3.10

Attempting to use the increment or decrement operator on an expression other than a simple variable name is a syntax error, e.g., writing ++(x + 1).

Error-Prevention Tip 3.4

C generally does not specify the order in which an operator's operands will be evaluated (although we will see exceptions to this for a few operators in Chapter 4). Therefore the programmer should avoid using statements with increment or decrement operators in which a particular variable being incremented or decremented appears more than once.

Figure 3.14 lists the precedence and associativity of the operators introduced to this point. The operators are shown top to bottom in decreasing order of precedence. The second column describes the associativity of the operators at each level of precedence. Notice that the conditional operator (?:), the unary operators increment (++), decrement (--), plus (+), minus (-) and casts, and the assignment operators =, +=, -=, *=, /= and %= associate from right to left. The third column names the various groups of operators. All other operators in Fig. 3.14 associate from left to right.

Operators	Associativity	Type
++ -- + - (*type*)	right to left	unary
* / %	left to right	multiplicative
+ -	left to right	additive
< <= > >=	left to right	relational
== !=	left to right	equality
?:	right to left	conditional
= += -= *= /= %=	right to left	assignment

Fig. 3.14   Precedence of the operators encountered so far in the text.

SUMMARY

- The solution to any computing problem involves performing a series of actions in a specific order. A procedure for solving a problem in terms of the actions to be executed and the order in which these actions should be executed is called an algorithm.

- Specifying the order in which statements are to be executed in a computer program is called program control.
- Pseudocode is an artificial and informal language that helps programmers develop algorithms. It is similar to everyday English. Pseudocode programs are not actually executed on computers. Rather, pseudocode merely helps the programmer to "think out" a program before attempting to write it in a programming language such as C.
- Pseudocode consists purely of characters, so programmers may type pseudocode programs into the computer, edit them, and save them.
- Pseudocode consists only of executable statements. Definitions are messages to the compiler telling it the attributes of variables and telling it to reserve space for variables.
- A selection statement is used to choose among alternative courses of action.
- The if selection statement executes an indicated action only when the condition is true.
- The if...else selection statement specifies separate actions to be executed when the condition is true and when the condition is false.
- A nested if...else selection statement can test for many different cases. If more than one condition is true, only the statements after the first true condition will be executed.
- Whenever more than one statement is to be executed where normally only a single statement is expected, these statements must be enclosed in braces forming a compound statement. A compound statement can be placed anywhere a single statement can be placed.
- An empty statement indicating that no action is to be taken is indicated by placing a semicolon (;) where a statement would normally be.
- A repetition statement specifies that an action is to be repeated while some condition remains true.
- The statement (or compound statement or block) contained in the while repetition statement constitutes the body of the loop.
- Normally, some action specified within the body of a while statement must eventually cause the condition to become false. Otherwise, the loop will never terminate—an error called an infinite loop.
- Counter-controlled looping uses a variable as a counter to determine when a loop should terminate.
- A total is a variable that accumulates the sum of a series of numbers. Totals should normally be initialized to zero before a program is run.
- A flowchart is a graphical representation of an algorithm. Flowcharts are drawn using certain special symbols such as ovals, rectangles, diamonds, and small circles connected by arrows called flowlines. Symbols indicate the actions to be performed. Flowlines indicate the order in which actions are to be performed.
- The oval symbol, also called the termination symbol, indicates the beginning and end of every algorithm.
- The rectangle symbol, also called the action symbol, indicates any type of calculation or input/output operation. Rectangle symbols correspond to the actions that are normally performed by assignment statements or to the input/output operations that are normally performed by standard library functions like printf and scanf.
- The diamond symbol, also called the decision symbol, indicates that a decision is to be made. The decision symbol contains an expression that can be either true or false. Two flowlines emerge from it. One flowline indicates the direction to be taken when the condition is true; the other indicates the direction to be taken when the condition is false.
- A value that contains a fractional part is referred to as a floating-point number and is represented by the data type float.

- When dividing two integers, any fractional part of the calculation is lost (i.e., truncated).
- C provides the unary cast operator (float) to create a temporary floating-point copy of its operand. Using a cast operator in this manner is called explicit conversion. Cast operators are available for most data types.
- The C compiler knows how to evaluate expressions only in which the data types of the operands are identical. To ensure that the operands are of the same type, the compiler performs an operation called promotion (also called implicit conversion) on selected operands. In particular, int operands are promoted to float. C provides a set of rules for promotion of operands of different types.
- Floating-point values are output with a specific number of digits following the decimal point by using a precision with the %f conversion specifier in a printf statement. The value 3.456 output with the conversion specifier %.2f is displayed as 3.46. If the %f conversion specifier is used (without specifying the precision), the default precision of 6 is used.
- C provides various assignment operators that help abbreviate certain common types of arithmetic assignment expressions. These operators are: +=, -=, *=, /=, and %=. In general, any statement of the form

    variable = variable operator expression;

where operator is one of the operators +, -, *, /, or %, can be written in the form

    variable operator= expression;

- C provides the increment operator, ++, and the decrement operator, --, to increment or decrement a variable by 1. These operators can be prefixed or postfixed to a variable. If the operator is prefixed to the variable, the variable is incremented or decremented by 1 first, then used in its expression. If the operator is postfixed to the variable, the variable is used in its expression, then incremented or decremented by 1.

TERMINOLOGY

action
action symbol
algorithm
arithmetic assignment operators:
    +=, -=, *=, /=, and %=
arrow symbol
block
body of a loop
"bombing"
cast operator
compound statement
conditional expression
conditional operator (?:)
connector symbol
control structure
counter
counter-controlled repetition
"crashing"
decision
decision symbol
decrement operator (--)

default precision
definite repetition
diamond symbol
division by zero
double-selection statement
dummy value
empty statement (;)
"end of data entry"
end symbol
explicit conversion
fatal error
first refinement
flag value
float
floating-point number
flowchart
flowchart symbol
flowline
"garbage" value
goto elimination
goto statement

COMMON PROGRAMMING ERRORS

3.1 Forgetting one or both of the braces that delimit a compound statement.

3.2 Placing a semicolon after the condition in an if statement leads to a logic error in single selection if statements and a syntax error in double selection if statements.

3.3 Not providing in the body of a while statement with an action that eventually causes the condition in the while to become false. Normally, such a repetition structure will never terminate—an error called an "infinite loop."

3.4 Spelling the keyword while with an uppercase W as in While (remember that C is a case-sensitive language). All of C's reserved keywords such as while, if and else contain only lowercase letters.

3.5 If a counter or total is not initialized, the results of your program will probably be incorrect. This is an example of a logic error.

3.6 Choosing a sentinel value that is also a legitimate data value.

3.7 An attempt to divide by zero causes a fatal error.

3.8 Using precision in a conversion specification in the format control string of a scanf statement is wrong. Precisions are used only in printf conversion specifications.

3.9 Using floating-point numbers in a manner that assumes they are represented precisely can lead to incorrect results. Floating-point numbers are represented only approximately by most computers.

3.10 Attempting to use the increment or decrement operator on an expression other than a simple variable name is a syntax error, e.g., writing ++(x + 1).

ERROR-PREVENTION TIPS

3.1 Typing the beginning and ending braces of compound statements before typing the individual statements within the braces, helps avoid omitting one or both of the braces, preventing syntax errors and logic errors (where both braces are indeed required).

3.2 Initialize counters and totals.

3.3 Do not compare floating-point values for equality.

3.4 C generally does not specify the order in which an operator's operands will be evaluated (although we will see exceptions to this for a few operators in Chapter 4). Therefore the programmer should avoid using statements with increment or decrement operators in which a particular variable being incremented or decremented appears more than once.

GOOD PROGRAMMING PRACTICES

3.1 Consistently applying responsible indentation conventions greatly improves program readability. We suggest a fixed-size tab of about 1/4 inch or three blanks per indent. In this book, we use three blanks per indent.

3.2 Pseudocode is often used to "think out" a program during the program design process. Then the pseudocode program is converted to C.

3.3 Indent both body statements of an if...else statement.

3.4 If there are several levels of indentation, each level should be indented the same additional amount of space.

3.5 When performing division by an expression whose value could be zero, explicitly test for this case and handle it appropriately in your program (such as printing an error message) rather than allowing the fatal error to occur.

3.6 In a sentinel-controlled loop, the prompts requesting data entry should explicitly remind the user what the sentinel value is.

3.7 Unary operators should be placed directly next to their operands with no intervening spaces.

PERFORMANCE TIPS

3.1 Initializing variables when they are defined can help reduce a program's execution time.

3.2 Many of the performance tips we mention in this text result in nominal improvements, so the reader may be tempted to ignore them. Note that the cumulative effect of all these performance enhancements can make a program perform significantly faster. Also, significant improvement is realized when a supposedly nominal improvement is placed in a loop that may repeat a large number of times.

SOFTWARE ENGINEERING OBSERVATIONS

3.1 A compound statement can be placed anywhere in a program that a single statement can be placed.

3.2 Just as a compound statement can be placed anywhere a single statement can be placed, it is also possible to have no statement at all, i.e., the empty statement. The empty statement is represented by placing a semicolon (;) where a statement would normally be.

3.3 Each refinement, as well as the top itself, is a complete specification of the algorithm; only the level of detail varies.

3.4 Many programs can be divided logically into three phases: An initialization phase that initializes the program variables; a processing phase that inputs data values and adjusts program variables accordingly; and a termination phase that calculates and prints the final results.

3.5 The programmer terminates the top-down, stepwise refinement process when the pseudocode algorithm is specified in sufficient detail for the programmer to be able to convert the pseudocode to C. Implementing the C program is then normally straightforward.

3.6 Experience has shown that the most difficult part of solving a problem on a computer is developing the algorithm for the solution. Once a correct algorithm has been specified, the process of producing a working C program is normally straightforward.

3.7 Many programmers write programs without ever using program development tools such as pseudocode. They feel that their ultimate goal is to solve the problem on a computer and that writing pseudocode merely delays the production of final outputs.

SELF-REVIEW EXERCISES

3.1 Fill in the blanks in each of the following questions.
a) A procedure for solving a problem in terms of the actions to be executed and the order in which the actions should be executed is called a(n) _____.
b) Specifying the execution order of statements by the computer is called _____.
c) All programs can be written in terms of three types of control statements: _____, _____ and _____.
d) The _____ selection statement is used to execute one action when a condition is true and another action when that condition is false.
e) Several statements grouped together in braces ({ and }) are called a(n) _____.
f) The _____ repetition statement specifies that a statement or group of statements is to be executed repeatedly while some condition remains true.
g) Repetition of a set of instructions a specific number of times is called_____ repetition.
h) When it is not known in advance how many times a set of statements will be repeated, a(n) _____ value can be used to terminate the repetition.

3.2 Write four different C statements that each add 1 to integer variable x.

3.3 Write a single C statement to accomplish each of the following:
a) Assign the sum of x and y to z and increment the value of x by 1 after the calculation.
b) Multiply the variable product by 2 using the *= operator.
c) Multiply the variable product by 2 using the = and * operators.
d) Test if the value of the variable count is greater than 10. If it is, print "Count is greater than 10."
e) Decrement the variable x by 1, then subtract it from the variable total.
f) Add the variable x to the variable total, then decrement x by 1.
g) Calculate the remainder after q is divided by divisor and assign the result to q. Write this statement two different ways.
h) Print the value 123.4567 with 2 digits of precision. What value is printed?
i) Print the floating point value 3.14159 with three digits to the right of the decimal point. What value is printed?

3.4 Write a C statement to accomplish each of the following tasks.
a) Define variables sum and x to be of type int.
b) Initialize variable x to 1.
c) Initialize variable sum to 0.
d) Add variable x to variable sum and assign the result to variable sum.
e) Print "The sum is: " followed by the value of variable sum.

3.5   Combine the statements that you wrote in Exercise 3.4 into a program that calculates the sum of the integers from 1 to 10. Use the `while` statement to loop through the calculation and increment statements. The loop should terminate when the value of x becomes 11.

3.6   Determine the values of variables `product` and x after the following calculation is performed. Assume that `product` and x each have the value 5 when the statement begins executing.

```
product *= x++;
```

3.7   Write single C statements that
a) Input integer variable x with `scanf`.
b) Input integer variable y with `scanf`.
c) Initialize integer variable i to 1.
d) Initialize integer variable `power` to 1.
e) Multiply variable `power` by x and assign the result to `power`.
f) Increment variable i by 1.
g) Test i to see if it is less than or equal to y in the condition of a `while` statement.
h) Output integer variable `power` with `printf`.

3.8   Write a C program that uses the statements in Exercise 3.7 to calculate x raised to the y power. The program should have a `while` repetition control statement.

3.9   Identify and correct the errors in each of the following:
a) ```
    while (c <= 5) {
         product *= c;
         ++c;
    ```
b)  ```
    scanf( "%.4f", &value );
    ```
c) ```
    if (gender == 1)
            printf("Woman\n");
       else;
            printf("Man\n");
    ```

**3.10**    What is wrong with the following `while` repetition statement (assume z has value 100), which is supposed to calculate the sum of the integers from 100 down to 1:
a)  ```
    while ( z >= 0 )
         sum += z;
    ```

ANSWERS TO SELF-REVIEW EXERCISES

3.1   a) Algorithm. b) Program control. c) Sequence, selection, repetition. d) `if…else`. e) Compound statement. f) `while`. g) Counter-controlled. h) Sentinel.

3.2
```
x = x + 1;
x += 1;
++x;
x++;
```

3.3
a) ```
   z = x++ + y;
   ```
b) ```
   product *= 2;
   ```
c) ```
   product = product * 2;
   ```
d) ```
   if ( count > 10 )
        printf( "Count is greater than 10.\n" );
   ```
e) ```
   total -= --x;
   ```
f) ```
   total += x--;
   ```
g) ```
   q %= divisor;
   q = q % divisor;
   ```
   ```

h) printf("%.2f", 123.4567);
123.46 is displayed.
i) printf("%.3f\n", 3.14159);
3.142 is displayed.

3.4   a) int sum, x;
       b) x = 1;
       c) sum = 0;
       d) sum += x; or sum = sum + x;
       e) printf("The sum is: %d\n", sum);

3.5   See below.

```
1    /* Calculate the sum of the integers from 1 to 10 */
2    #include <stdio.h>
3
4    int main()
5    {
6       int sum, x; /* define variables sum and x */
7
8       x = 1;   /* initialize x */
9       sum = 0; /* initialize sum */
10
11      while ( x <= 10 ) { /* loop while x is less than or equal to 10 */
12         sum += x; /* add x to sum */
13         ++x; /* increment x */
14      } /* end while */
15
16      printf( "The sum is: %d\n", sum ); /* display sum */
17
18      return 0;
19   } /* end main function */
```

3.6   product = 25, x = 6;

3.7   a) scanf("%d", &x);
       b) scanf("%d", &y);
       c) i = 1;
       d) power = 1;
       e) power *= x;
       f) y++;
       g) if (y <= x)
       h) printf("%d", power);

3.8   See below.

```
1    /* raise x to the y power */
2    #include <stdio.h>
3
4    int main()
5    {
6       int x, y, i, power; /* define variables */
```

(Part 1 of 2.)

```
7
8      i = 1;      /* initialize i */
9      power = 1; /* initialize power */
10     scanf( "%d", &x ); /* read value for x from user */
11     scanf( "%d", &y ); /* read value for y from user */
12
13     while ( i <= y ) { /* loop while i is less than or equal to y */
14        power *= x; /* multiply power by x */
15        ++i; /* increment i */
16     } /* end while */
17
18     printf( "%d", power ); /* display power */
19
20     return 0;
21  } /* end main function */
```

(Part 2 of 2.)

3.9 a) Error: Missing the closing right brace of the `while` body.
Correction: Add closing right brace after the statement `++c;`.
b) Error: Precision used in a `scanf` conversion specification.
Correction: Remove `.4` from the conversion specification.
c) Error: Semicolon after the `else` part of the `if...else` statement results in a logic error.
The second `printf` will always be executed.
Correction: Remove the semicolon after `else`.

3.10 The value of the variable `z` is never changed in the `while` statement. Therefore, an infinite loop is created. To prevent the infinite loop, `z` must be decremented so that it eventually becomes 0.

EXERCISES

3.11 Identify and correct the errors in each of the following [*Note*: There may be more than one error in each piece of code]:
a)
```
if ( age >= 65 );
    printf( "Age is greater than or equal to 65\n" );
else
    printf( "Age is less than 65\n" );
```
b)
```
int x = 1, total;

while ( x <= 10 ) {
    total += x;
    ++x;
}
```
c)
```
While ( x <= 100 )
    total += x;
    ++x;
```
d)
```
while ( y > 0 ) {
    printf( "%d\n", y );
    ++y;
}
```

3.12 Fill in the blanks in each of the following:
a) The solution to any problem involves performing a series of actions in a specific _____.

b) A synonym for procedure is _____.
c) A variable that accumulates the sum of several numbers is a(n) _____.
d) The process of setting certain variables to specific values at the beginning of a program is called _____.
e) A special value used to indicate "end of data entry" is called a(n) _____, a(n) _____, a(n) _____ or a(n) _____ value.
f) A(n) _____ is a graphical representation of an algorithm.
g) In a flowchart, the order in which the steps should be performed is indicated by _____ symbols.
h) The termination symbol indicates the _____ and _____ of every algorithm.
i) Rectangle symbols correspond to calculations that are normally performed by _____ statements and input/output operations that are normally performed by calls to the _____ and _____ standard library functions.
j) The item written inside a decision symbol is called a(n) _____.

3.13   What does the following program print?

```
1   #include <stdio.h>
2
3   int main()
4   {
5       int x = 1, total = 0, y;
6
7       while ( x <= 10 ) {
8          y = x * x;
9          printf( "%d\n", y );
10         total += y;
11         ++x;
12      }
13
14      printf("Total is %d\n", total);
15
16      return 0;
17   }
```

3.14   Write a single pseudocode statement that indicates each of the following:
a) Display the message "Enter two numbers".
b) Assign the sum of variables x, y, and z to variable p.
c) The following condition is to be tested in an if...else selection statement: The current value of variable m is greater than twice the current value of variable v.
d) Obtain values for variables s, r, and t from the keyboard.

3.15   Formulate a pseudocode algorithm for each of the following:
a) Obtain two numbers from the keyboard, compute the sum of the numbers and display the result.
b) Obtain two numbers from the keyboard, and determine and display which (if either) is the larger of the two numbers.
c) Obtain a series of positive numbers from the keyboard, and determine and display the sum of the numbers. Assume that the user types the sentinel value –1 to indicate "end of data entry."

3.16   State which of the following are *true* and which are *false*. If a statement is *false*, explain why.
a) Experience has shown that the most difficult part of solving a problem on a computer is producing a working C program.

b) A sentinel value must be a value that cannot be confused with a legitimate data value.

c) Flowlines indicate the actions to be performed.

d) Conditions written inside decision symbols always contain arithmetic operators (i.e., +, -, *, /, and %).

e) In top-down, stepwise refinement, each refinement is a complete representation of the algorithm.

For Exercises 3.17 to 3.21, perform each of these steps:

1. Read the problem statement.

2. Formulate the algorithm using pseudocode and top-down, stepwise refinement.

3. Write a C program.

4. Test, debug and execute the C program.

3.17   Drivers are concerned with the mileage obtained by their automobiles. One driver has kept track of several tankfuls of gasoline by recording miles driven and gallons used for each tankful. Develop a program that will input the miles driven and gallons used for each tankful. The program should calculate and display the miles per gallon obtained for each tankful. After processing all input information, the program should calculate and print the combined miles per gallon obtained for all tankfuls. Here is a sample input/output dialog:

```
Enter the gallons used (-1 to end): 12.8
Enter the miles driven: 287
The miles / gallon for this tank was 22.421875

Enter the gallons used (-1 to end): 10.3
Enter the miles driven: 200
The miles / gallon for this tank was 19.417475

Enter the gallons used (-1 to end): 5
Enter the miles driven: 120
The miles / gallon for this tank was 24.000000

Enter the gallons used (-1 to end): -1

The overall average miles/gallon was 21.601423
```

3.18   Develop a C program that will determine if a department store customer has exceeded the credit limit on a charge account. For each customer, the following facts are available:

1. Account number

2. Balance at the beginning of the month

3. Total of all items charged by this customer this month

4. Total of all credits applied to this customer's account this month

5. Allowed credit limit

The program should input each of these facts, calculate the new balance (= *beginning balance + charges – credits*), and determine if the new balance exceeds the customer's credit limit. For those customers whose credit limit is exceeded, the program should display the customer's account number, credit limit, new balance and the message "Credit limit exceeded." Here is a sample input/output dialog:

```
Enter account number (-1 to end): 100
Enter beginning balance: 5394.78
Enter total charges: 1000.00
Enter total credits: 500.00
Enter credit limit: 5500.00
Account:      100
Credit limit: 5500.00
Balance:      5894.78
Credit Limit Exceeded.

Enter account number (-1 to end): 200
Enter beginning balance: 1000.00
Enter total charges: 123.45
Enter total credits: 321.00
Enter credit limit: 1500.00

Enter account number (-1 to end): 300
Enter beginning balance: 500.00
Enter total charges: 274.73
Enter total credits: 100.00
Enter credit limit: 800.00

Enter account number (-1 to end): -1
```

3.19   One large chemical company pays its salespeople on a commission basis. The salespeople receive $200 per week plus 9% of their gross sales for that week. For example, a salesperson who sells $5000 worth of chemicals in a week receives $200 plus 9% of $5000, or a total of $650. Develop a program that will input each salesperson's gross sales for last week and will calculate and display that salesperson's earnings. Process one salesperson's figures at a time. Here is a sample input/output dialog:

```
Enter sales in dollars (-1 to end): 5000.00
Salary is: $650.00

Enter sales in dollars (-1 to end): 1234.56
Salary is: $311.11

Enter sales in dollars (-1 to end): 1088.89
Salary is: $298.00

Enter sales in dollars (-1 to end): -1
```

3.20   The simple interest on a loan is calculated by the formula

```
interest = principal * rate * days / 365;
```

The preceding formula assumes that rate is the annual interest rate, and therefore includes the division by 365 (days). Develop a program that will input principal, rate and days for several loans, and will calculate and display the simple interest for each loan, using the preceding formula. Here is a sample input/output dialog:

```
Enter loan principal (-1 to end): 1000.00
Enter interest rate: .1
Enter term of the loan in days: 365
The interest charge is $100.00


Enter loan principal (-1 to end): 1000.00
Enter interest rate: .08375
Enter term of the loan in days: 224
The interest charge is $51.40


Enter loan principal (-1 to end): 10000.00
Enter interest rate: .09
Enter term of the loan in days: 1460
The interest charge is $3600.00


Enter loan principal (-1 to end): -1
```

3.21   Develop a program that will determine the gross pay for each of several employees. The company pays "straight-time" for the first 40 hours worked by each employee and pays "time-and-a-half" for all hours worked in excess of 40 hours. You are given a list of the employees of the company, the number of hours each employee worked last week and the hourly rate of each employee. Your program should input this information for each employee, and should determine and display the employee's gross pay. Here is a sample input/output dialog:

```
Enter # of hours worked (-1 to end): 39
Enter hourly rate of the worker ($00.00): 10.00
Salary is $390.00


Enter # of hours worked (-1 to end): 40
Enter hourly rate of the worker ($00.00): 10.00
Salary is $400.00


Enter # of hours worked (-1 to end): 41
Enter hourly rate of the worker ($00.00): 10.00
Salary is $415.00


Enter # of hours worked (-1 to end): -1
```

3.22   Write a program that demonstrates the difference between predecrementing and post-decrementing using the decrement operator --.

3.23   Write a program that utilizes looping to print the numbers from 1 to 10 side-by-side on the same line with 3 spaces between each number.

3.24   The process of finding the largest number (i.e., the maximum of a group of numbers) is used frequently in computer applications. For example, a program that determines the winner of a sales contest would input the number of units sold by each salesperson. The salesperson who sells the most units wins the contest. Write a pseudocode program and then a program that inputs a series of 10 numbers, and determines and prints the largest of the numbers. [*Hint*: Your program should use three variables as follows]:

counter:	A counter to count to 10 (i.e., to keep track of how many numbers have been input and to determine when all 10 numbers have been processed)
number:	The current number input to the program
largest:	The largest number found so far

3.25 Write a program that utilizes looping to print the following table of values:

N	10*N	100*N	1000*N
1	10	100	1000
2	20	200	2000
3	30	300	3000
4	40	400	4000
5	50	500	5000
6	60	600	6000
7	70	700	7000
8	80	800	8000
9	90	900	9000
10	100	1000	10000

The tab escape sequence, \t, may be used in the printf statement to separate the columns with tabs.

3.26 Write a program that utilizes looping to produce the following table of values:

A	A+2	A+4	A+6
3	5	7	9
6	8	10	12
9	11	13	15
12	14	16	18
15	17	19	21

3.27 Using an approach similar to Exercise 3.24, find the *two* largest values of the 10 numbers. [*Note*: You may input each number only once.]

3.28 Modify the program in Figure 3.10 to validate its inputs. On any input, if the value entered is other than 1 or 2, keep looping until the user enters a correct value.

3.29 What does the following program print?

```
1   #include <stdio.h>
2
3   /* function main begins program execution */
4   int main()
5   {
```

(Part 1 of 2.)

```
 6        int count = 1; /* initialize count */
 7
 8        while ( count <= 10 ) { /* loop 10 times */
 9
10           /* output line of text */
11           printf( "%s\n", count % 2 ? "****" : "++++++++" );
12           count++; /* increment count */
13        } /* end while */
14
15        return 0; /* indicate program ended successfully */
16
17     } /* end function main */
```

(Part 2 of 2.)

3.30   What does the following program print?

```
 1    #include <stdio.h>
 2
 3    /* function main begins program execution */
 4    int main()
 5    {
 6       int row = 10; /* initialize row */
 7       int column;    /* define column */
 8
 9       while ( row >= 1 ) { /* loop until row < 1 */
10          column = 1;        /* set column to 1 as iteration begins */
11
12          while ( column <= 10 ) {              /* loop 10 times */
13             printf( "%s", row % 2 ? "<": ">" ); /* output */
14             column++;                          /* increment column */
15          } /* end inner while */
16
17          row--;             /* decrement row */
18          printf( "\n" ); /* begin new output line */
19       } /* end outer while */
20
21       return 0; /* indicate program ended successfully */
22
23    } /* end function main */
```

3.31   *(Dangling Else Problem)* Determine the output for each of the following when x is 9 and y is 11 and when x is 11 and y is 9. Note that the compiler ignores the indentation in a C program. Also, the compiler always associates an else with the previous if unless told to do otherwise by the placement of braces {}. Because, on first glance, the programmer may not be sure which if an else matches, this is referred to as the "dangling else" problem. We have eliminated the indentation from the following code to make the problem more challenging. [*Hint:* Apply indentation conventions you have learned.]

```
a)  if ( x < 10 )
    if ( y > 10 )
    printf( "*****\n" );
    else
    printf( "#####\n" );
    printf( "$$$$$\n" );
```

b)
```
if ( x < 10 ) {
if ( y > 10 )
printf( "*****\n" );
}
else {
printf( "#####\n" );
printf( "$$$$$\n" );
}
```

3.32 *(Another Dangling Else Problem)* Modify the following code to produce the output shown. Use proper indentation techniques. You might not make any changes other than inserting braces. The compiler ignores the indentation in a program. We have eliminated the indentation from the following code to make the problem more challenging. [*Note*: It is possible that no modification is necessary.]

```
if ( y == 8 )
if ( x == 5 )
printf( "@@@@@\n" );
else
printf( "#####\n" );
printf( "$$$$$\n" );
printf( "&&&&&\n" );
```

a) Assuming x = 5 and y = 8, the following output is produced.

```
@@@@@
$$$$$
&&&&&
```

b) Assuming x = 5 and y = 8, the following output is produced.

```
@@@@@
```

c) Assuming x = 5 and y = 8, the following output is produced.

```
@@@@@
&&&&&
```

d) Assuming x = 5 and y = 7, the following output is produced. [*Note*: The last three `printf` statements are all part of a compound statement.]

```
#####
$$$$$
&&&&&
```

3.33 Write a program that reads in the side of a square and then prints that square out of asterisks. Your program should work for squares of all side sizes between 1 and 20. For example, if your program reads a size of 4, it should print

```
****
****
****
****
```

3.34   Modify the program you wrote in Exercise 3.33 so that it prints a hollow square. For example, if your program reads a size of 5, it should print

```
*****
*   *
*   *
*   *
*****
```

3.35   A palindrome is a number or a text phrase that reads the same backwards as forwards. For example, each of the following five-digit integers are palindromes: 12321, 55555, 45554 and 11611. Write a program that reads in a five-digit integer and determines whether or not it is a palindrome. [*Hint*: Use the division and remainder operators to separate the number into its individual digits.]

3.36   Input an integer containing only 0s and 1s (i.e., a "binary" integer) and print its decimal equivalent. [*Hint*: Use the remainder and division operators to pick off the "binary" number's digits one at a time from right to left. Just as in the decimal number system in which the rightmost digit has a positional value of 1, and the next digit left has a positional value of 10, then 100, then 1000, etc., in the binary number system the rightmost digit has a positional value of 1, the next digit left has a positional value of 2, then 4, then 8, etc. Thus the decimal number 234 can be interpreted as 4 * 1 + 3 * 10 + 2 * 100. The decimal equivalent of binary 1101 is 1 * 1 + 0 * 2 + 1 * 4 + 1 * 8 or 1 + 0 + 4 + 8 or 13.]

3.37   How can you determine how fast your own computer really operates? Write a program with a `while` loop that counts from 1 to 300,000,000 by 1s. Every time the count reaches a multiple of 100,000,000 print that number on the screen. Use your watch to time how long each million repetitions of the loop takes.

3.38   Write a program that prints 100 asterisks, one at a time. After every tenth asterisk, your program should print a newline character. [*Hint*: Count from 1 to 100. Use the remainder operator to recognize each time the counter reaches a multiple of 10.]

3.39   Write a program that reads an integer and determines and prints how many digits in the integer are 7s.

3.40   Write a program that displays the following checkerboard pattern:

```
* * * * * * * *
 * * * * * * * *
* * * * * * * *
 * * * * * * * *
* * * * * * * *
 * * * * * * * *
* * * * * * * *
 * * * * * * * *
```

Your program must use only three output statements, one of each of the following forms:

```
printf( "* " );
printf( "  " );
printf( "\n" );
```

3.41　Write a program that keeps printing the multiples of the integer 2, namely 2, 4, 8, 16, 32, 64, etc. Your loop should not terminate (i.e., you should create an infinite loop). What happens when you run this program?

3.42　Write a program that reads the radius of a circle (as a `float` value) and computes and prints the diameter, the circumference and the area. Use the value 3.14159 for π.

3.43　What is wrong with the following statement? Rewrite the statement to accomplish what the programmer was probably trying to do.

```
printf( "%d", ++( x + y ) );
```

3.44　Write a program that reads three nonzero `float` values and determines and prints if they could represent the sides of a triangle.

3.45　Write a program that reads three nonzero integers and determines and prints if they could be the sides of a right triangle.

3.46　A company wants to transmit data over the telephone, but they are concerned that their phones may be tapped. All of their data is transmitted as four-digit integers. They have asked you to write a program that will encrypt their data so that it may be transmitted more securely. Your program should read a four-digit integer and encrypt it as follows: Replace each digit by the remainder after *(the sum of that digit plus 7)* is divided by *10*. Then, swap the first digit with the third, and swap the second digit with the fourth. Then print the encrypted integer. Write a separate program that inputs an encrypted four-digit integer and decrypts it to form the original number.

3.47　The factorial of a nonnegative integer *n* is written *n*! (pronounced "*n* factorial") and is defined as follows:

$$n! = n \cdot (n - 1) \cdot (n - 2) \cdot \ldots \cdot 1 \quad \text{(for values of } n \text{ greater than or equal to 1)}$$

and

$$n! = 1 \quad \text{(for } n = 0\text{)}.$$

For example, *5!* = 5 · 4 · 3 · 2 · 1, which is 120.

　　a)　Write a program that reads a nonnegative integer and computes and prints its factorial.

　　b)　Write a program that estimates the value of the mathematical constant *e* by using the formula:

$$e = 1 + \frac{1}{1!} + \frac{1}{2!} + \frac{1}{3!} + \ldots$$

　　c)　Write a program that computes the value of e^x by using the formula

$$e^x = 1 + \frac{x}{1!} + \frac{x^2}{2!} + \frac{x^3}{3!} + \ldots$$

C Program Control

Objectives

- To be able to use the `for` and `do...while` repetition statements.
- To understand multiple selection using the `switch` selection statement.
- To be able to use the `break` and `continue` program control statements
- To be able to use the logical operators.

Who can control his fate?
William Shakespeare
Othello

The used key is always bright.
Benjamin Franklin

Man is a tool-making animal.
Benjamin Franklin

*Intelligence ... is the faculty of making artificial objects,
especially tools to make tools.*
Henry Bergson

Outline

4.1 Introduction

The reader should now be comfortable with the process of writing simple but complete C programs. In this chapter, repetition is considered in greater detail, and additional repetition control statements, namely the for statement and the do...while statement, are presented. The switch multiple-selection statement is introduced. We discuss the break statement for exiting immediately and rapidly from certain control statements, and the continue statement for skipping the remainder of the body of a repetition statement and proceeding with the next iteration of the loop. The chapter discusses logical operators used for combining conditions, and concludes with a summary of the principles of structured programming as presented in Chapter 3 and Chapter 4.

4.2 Repetition Essentials

Most programs involve repetition, or *looping*. A *loop* is a group of instructions the computer executes repeatedly while some *loop-continuation condition* remains true. We have discussed two means of repetition:

1. Counter-controlled repetition
2. Sentinel-controlled repetition

Counter-controlled repetition is sometimes called *definite repetition* because we know in advance exactly how many times the loop will be executed. Sentinel-controlled repetition is sometimes called *indefinite repetition* because it is not known in advance how many times the loop will be executed.

In counter-controlled repetition, a *control variable* is used to count the number of repetitions. The control variable is incremented (usually by 1) each time the group of instructions is performed. When the value of the control variable indicates that the correct number of repetitions has been performed, the loop terminates and the computer continues executing with the statement after the repetition statement.

Sentinel values are used to control repetition when:

1. The precise number of repetitions is not known in advance, and

2. The loop includes statements that obtain data each time the loop is performed.

The sentinel value indicates "end of data." The sentinel is entered after all regular data items have been supplied to the program. Sentinels must be distinct from regular data items.

4.3 Counter-Controlled Repetition

Counter-controlled repetition requires:

1. The *name* of a control variable (or loop counter).

2. The *initial value* of the control variable.

3. The *increment* (or *decrement*) by which the control variable is modified each time through the loop.

4. The condition that tests for the *final value* of the control variable (i.e., whether looping should continue).

Consider the simple program shown in Fig. 4.1, which prints the numbers from 1 to 10. The definition

```
int counter = 1; /* initialization */
```

names the control variable (`counter`), defines it to be an integer, reserves memory space for it, and sets it to an *initial value* of 1. This definition is not an executable statement.

```
1   /* Fig. 4.1: fig04_01.c
2      Counter-controlled repetition */
3   #include <stdio.h>
4
5   /* function main begins program execution */
6   int main()
7   {
8      int counter = 1; /* initialization */
9
10     while ( counter <= 10 ) { /* repetition condition */
11        printf ( "%d\n", counter ); /* display counter */
12        ++counter; /* increment */
13     } /* end while */
14
15     return 0; /* indicate program ended successfully */
16
17  } /* end function main */
```

Fig. 4.1   Counter-controlled repetition. (Part 1 of 2.)

```
1
2
3
4
5
6
7
8
9
10
```

Fig. 4.1   Counter-controlled repetition. (Part 2 of 2.)

The definition and initialization of `counter` could also have been accomplished with the statements

```
int counter;
counter = 1;
```

The definition is not executable, but the assignment is. We use both methods of initializing variables.

The statement

```
++counter; /* increment */
```

increments the loop counter by 1 each time the loop is performed. The loop-continuation condition in the `while` statement tests if the value of the control variable is less than or equal to 10 (the last value for which the condition is true). Note that the body of this `while` is performed even when the control variable is 10. The loop terminates when the control variable exceeds 10 (i.e., `counter` becomes 11).

C programmers would normally make the program in Fig. 4.1 more concise by initializing `counter` to 0 and by replacing the `while` statement with

```
while ( ++counter <= 10 )
    printf( "%d\n", counter );
```

This code saves a statement because the incrementing is done directly in the `while` condition before the condition is tested. Also, this code eliminates the need for the braces around the body of the `while` because the `while` now contains only one statement. Coding in such a condensed fashion takes some practice.

Common Programming Error 4.1

Because floating-point values may be approximate, controlling counting loops with floating-point variables may result in imprecise counter values and inaccurate tests for termination.

Error-Prevention Tip 4.1

Control counting loops with integer values.

Good Programming Practice 4.1

Indent the statements in the body of each control statement.

Good Programming Practice 4.2

Put a blank line before and after each control statement to make it stand out in a program.

Good Programming Practice 4.3

Too many levels of nesting can make a program difficult to understand. As a general rule, try to avoid using more than three levels of nesting.

Good Programming Practice 4.4

The combination of vertical spacing before and after control statements and indentation of the bodies of control statements within the control statement headers gives programs a two-dimensional appearance that greatly improves program readability.

4.4 for Repetition Statement

The for repetition statement handles all the details of counter-controlled repetition. To illustrate the power of for, let us rewrite the program of Fig. 4.1. The result is shown in Fig. 4.2.

```
1   /* Fig. 4.2: fig04_02.c
2      Counter-controlled repetition with the for statement */
3   #include <stdio.h>
4
5   /* function main begins program execution */
6   int main()
7   {
8      int counter; /* define counter */
9
10     /* initialization, repetition condition, and increment
11        are all included in the for statement header. */
12     for ( counter = 1; counter <= 10; counter++ ) {
13        printf( "%d\n", counter );
14     } /* end for */
15
16     return 0; /* indicate program ended successfully */
17
18  } /* end function main */
```

Fig. 4.2   Counter-controlled repetition with the for statement.

The program operates as follows. When the for statement begins executing, the control variable counter is initialized to 1. Then, the loop-continuation condition counter <= 10 is checked. Because the initial value of counter is 1, the condition is satisfied, so the printf statement (line 13) prints the value of counter, namely 1. The control variable counter is then incremented by the expression counter++, and the loop begins again with the loop-continuation test. Since the control variable is now equal to 2, the final value is not exceeded, so the program performs the printf statement again. This process continues until the control variable counter is incremented to its final value of 11—this causes the loop-continuation test to fail, and repetition terminates. The program continues by performing the first statement after the for statement (in this case, the return statement at the end of the program).

Figure 4.3 takes a closer look at the for statement of Fig. 4.2. Notice that the for statement "does it all"—it specifies each of the items needed for counter-controlled repetition with a control variable. If there is more than one statement in the body of the for, braces are required to define the body of the loop.

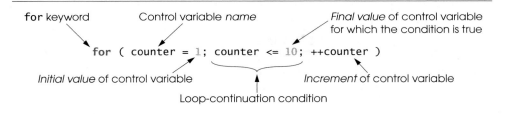

Fig. 4.3 for header components.

Notice that Fig. 4.2 uses the loop-continuation condition counter <= 10. If the programmer incorrectly wrote counter < 10, then the loop would be executed only 9 times. This is a common logic error called an *off-by-one error*.

 Common Programming Error 4.2

Using an incorrect relational operator or using an incorrect final value of a loop counter in the condition of a while or for statement can cause off-by-one errors.

 Error-Prevention Tip 4.2

Using the final value in the condition of a while or for statement and using the <= relational operator will help avoid off-by-one errors. For a loop used to print the values 1 to 10, for example, the loop-continuation condition should be counter <= 10 rather than counter < 11 or counter < 10.

The general format of the for statement is

> for (*expression1*; *expression2*; *expression3*)
>   *statement*

where *expression1* initializes the loop-control variable, *expression2* is the loop-continuation condition, and *expression3* increments the control variable. In most cases, the for statement can be represented with an equivalent while statement as follows:

> *expression1*;
> while (*expression2*) {
>   *statement*
>   *expression3*;
> }

There is an exception to this rule, which we will discuss in Section 4.9.

Often, *expression1* and *expression3* are comma-separated lists of expressions. The commas as used here are actually *comma operators* that guarantee that lists of expressions evaluate from left to right. The value and type of a comma-separated list of expressions is the value and type of the rightmost expression in the list. The comma operator is most often used in for statement. Its primary use is to enable the programmer to use multiple initialization and/or multiple increment expressions. For example, there may be two control variables in a single for statement that must be initialized and incremented.

Software Engineering Observation 4.1

Place only expressions involving the control variables in the initialization and increment sections of a for statement. Manipulations of other variables should appear either before the loop (if they execute only once, like initialization statements) or in the loop body (if they execute once per repetition, like incrementing or decrementing statements).

The three expressions in the for statement are optional. If *expression2* is omitted, C assumes that the condition is true, thus creating an infinite loop. One might omit *expression1* if the control variable is initialized elsewhere in the program. *expression3* might be omitted if the increment is calculated by statements in the body of the for statement or if no increment is needed. The increment expression in the for statement acts like a standalone C statement at the end of the body of the for. Therefore, the expressions

```
counter = counter + 1
counter += 1
++counter
counter++
```

are all equivalent in the incrementing portion of the for statement. Many C programmers prefer the form counter++ because the incrementing occurs after the loop body is executed, and the postincrementing form seems more natural. Because the variable being preincremented or postincremented here does not appear in an expression, both forms of incrementing have the same effect. The two semicolons in the for statement are required.

Common Programming Error 4.3

Using commas instead of semicolons in a for header is a syntax error.

Common Programming Error 4.4

Placing a semicolon immediately to the right of a for header makes the body of that for statement an empty statement. This is normally a logic error.

4.5 for Statement: Notes and Observations

1. The initialization, loop-continuation condition and increment can contain arithmetic expressions. For example, if x = 2 and y = 10, the statement

   ```
   for ( j = x; j <= 4 * x * y; j += y / x )
   ```

   is equivalent to the statement

   ```
   for ( j = 2; j <= 80; j += 5 )
   ```

2. The "increment" may be negative (in which case it is really a decrement and the loop actually counts downwards).

3. If the loop-continuation condition is initially false, the body portion of the loop is not performed. Instead, execution proceeds with the statement following the for statement.

4. The control variable is frequently printed or used in calculations in the body of a loop, but it does not need to be. It is common to use the control variable for controlling repetition while never mentioning it in the body of the loop.

5. The `for` statement is flowcharted much like the `while` statement. For example, the flowchart of the `for` statement

```
for ( counter = 1; counter <= 10; counter++ )
    printf( "%d", counter );
```

is shown in Fig. 4.4. This flowchart makes it clear that the initialization occurs only once and that incrementing occurs after the body statement is performed. Note that (besides small circles and arrows) the flowchart contains only rectangle symbols and a diamond symbol. Imagine, again, that the programmer has access to a deep bin of empty `for` statements (represented as flowchart segments)—as many as the programmer might need to stack and nest with other control statements to form a structured implementation of an algorithm's flow of control. And again, the rectangles and diamonds are then filled with actions and decisions appropriate to the algorithm.

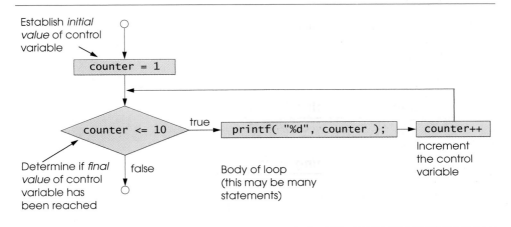

Fig. 4.4   Flowcharting a typical `for` repetition statement.

Error-Prevention Tip 4.3

Although the value of the control variable can be changed in the body of a for loop, this can lead to subtle errors. It is best not to change it.

4.6 Examples Using the for Statement

The following examples show methods of varying the control variable in a `for` statement.

1. Vary the control variable from 1 to 100 in increments of 1.

```
for ( i = 1; i <= 100; i++ )
```

2. Vary the control variable from 100 to 1 in increments of -1 (decrements of 1).

```
for ( i = 100; i >= 1; i-- )
```

3. Vary the control variable from 7 to 77 in steps of 7.

```
for ( i = 7; i <= 77; i += 7 )
```

4. Vary the control variable from 20 to 2 in steps of -2.

```
for ( i = 20; i >= 2; i -= 2 )
```

5. Vary the control variable over the following sequence of values: 2, 5, 8, 11, 14, 17, 20.

```
for ( j = 2; j <= 20; j += 3 )
```

6. Vary the control variable over the following sequence of values: 99, 88, 77, 66, 55, 44, 33, 22, 11, 0.

```
for ( j = 99; j >= 0; j -= 11 )
```

The next two examples provide simple applications of the for statement. Figure 4.2 uses the for statement to sum all the even integers from 2 to 100.

```
1   /* Fig. 4.5: fig04_05.c
2      Summation with for */
3   #include <stdio.h>
4
5   /* function main begins program execution */
6   int main()
7   {
8      int sum = 0; /* initialize sum */
9      int number;  /* number to be added to sum */
10
11     for ( number = 2; number <= 100; number += 2 ) {
12        sum += number; /* add number to sum */
13     } /* end for */
14
15     printf( "Sum is %d\n", sum ); /* output sum */
16
17     return 0; /* indicate program ended successfully */
18
19  } /* end function main */
```

```
Sum is 2550
```

Fig. 4.5   Using for to sum numbers.

Note that the body of the for statement in Fig. 4.5 could actually be merged into the rightmost portion of the for header by using the comma operator as follows:

```
for ( number = 2; number <= 100; sum += number, number += 2 )
   ; /* empty statement */
```

The initialization sum = 0 could also be merged into the initialization section of the for.

Good Programming Practice 4.5

Although statements preceding a for and statements in the body of a for can often be merged into the for header, avoid doing so because it makes the program more difficult to read.

Good Programming Practice 4.6

Limit the size of control statement headers to a single line if possible.

The next example computes compound interest using the for statement. Consider the following problem statement:

A person invests $1000.00 in a savings account yielding 5 percent interest. Assuming that all interest is left on deposit in the account, calculate and print the amount of money in the account at the end of each year for 10 years. Use the following formula for determining these amounts:

$$a = p(1 + r)^n$$

where

p   *is the original amount invested (i.e., the principal)*
r   *is the annual interest rate*
n   *is the number of years*
a   *is the amount on deposit at the end of the nth year.*

This problem involves a loop that performs the indicated calculation for each of the 10 years the money remains on deposit. The solution is shown in Fig. 4.6. [*Note:* On many UNIX C compilers, you must include the -*lm* option (e.g., cc -lm fig04_06.c) when compiling Fig. 4.6. This links the math library to the program.]

```
1   /* Fig. 4.6: fig04_06.c
2      Calculating compound interest */
3   #include <stdio.h>
4   #include <math.h>
5
6   /* function main begins program execution */
7   int main()
8   {
9      double amount;              /* amount on deposit */
10     double principal = 1000.0;  /* starting principal */
11     double rate = .05;          /* annual interest rate */
12     int year;                   /* year counter */
13
14     /* output table column head */
15     printf( "%4s%21s\n", "Year", "Amount on deposit" );
16
17     /* calculate amount on deposit for each of ten years */
18     for ( year = 1; year <= 10; year++ ) {
19
20        /* calculate new amount for specified year */
21        amount = principal * pow( 1.0 + rate, year );
22
```

Fig. 4.6   Calculating compound interest with for. (Part 1 of 2.)

```
23              /* output one table row */
24              printf( "%4d%21.2f\n", year, amount );
25          } /* end for */
26
27          return 0; /* indicate program ended successfully */
28
29      } /* end function main */
```

```
Year     Amount on deposit
   1            1050.00
   2            1102.50
   3            1157.63
   4            1215.51
   5            1276.28
   6            1340.10
   7            1407.10
   8            1477.46
   9            1551.33
  10            1628.89
```

Fig. 4.6   Calculating compound interest with `for`. (Part 2 of 2.)

The `for` statement executes the body of the loop 10 times, varying a control variable from 1 to 10 in increments of 1. Although C does not include an exponentiation operator, we can use the standard library function `pow` for this purpose. The function `pow(x, y)` calculates the value of x raised to the yth power. It takes two arguments of type *double* and returns a `double` value. Type `double` is a floating-point type much like `float`, but typically a variable of type `double` can store a value of much greater magnitude with greater precision than `float`. Note that the header `math.h` (line 4) should be included whenever a math function such as `pow` is used. Actually, this program would malfunction without the inclusion of `math.h`. Function `pow` requires two `double` arguments. Note that `year` is an integer. The `math.h` file includes information that tells the compiler to convert the value of `year` to a temporary `double` representation before calling the function. This information is contained in something called `pow`'s *function prototype*. Function prototypes are explained in Chapter 5. We also provide a summary of the `pow` function and other math library functions in Chapter 5.

Notice that we defined the variables `amount`, `principal` and `rate` to be of type `double`. We did this for simplicity because we are dealing with fractional parts of dollars.

Error-Prevention Tip 4.4

Do not use variables of type `float` or `double` to perform monetary calculations. The impreciseness of floating-point numbers can cause errors that will result in incorrect monetary values. [In the exercises, we explore the use of integers to perform monetary calculations.]

Here is a simple explanation of what can go wrong when using `float` or `double` to represent dollar amounts.

Two `float` dollar amounts stored in the machine could be 14.234 (which with `%.2f` prints as 14.23) and 18.673 (which with `%.2f` prints as 18.67). When these amounts are added, they produce the sum 32.907, which with `%.2f` prints as 32.91. Thus your printout could appear as

```
    14.23
+ 18.67
  -------
   32.91
```

but clearly the sum of the individual numbers as printed should be 32.90! You have been warned!

The conversion specifier %21.2f is used to print the value of the variable amount in the program. The 21 in the conversion specifier denotes the *field width* in which the value will be printed. A field width of 21 specifies that the value printed will appear in 21 print positions. The 2 specifies the precision (i.e., the number of decimal positions). If the number of characters displayed is less than the field width, then the value will automatically be *right justified* in the field. This is particularly useful for aligning floating-point values with the same precision (so that their decimal points align vertically). To *left justify* a value in a field, place a - (minus sign) between the % and the field width. Note that the minus sign may also be used to left justify integers (such as in %-6d) and character strings (such as in %-8s). We will discuss the powerful formatting capabilities of printf and scanf in detail in Chapter 9.

4.7 switch Multiple-Selection Statement

In Chapter 3, we discussed the if single-selection statement and the if...else double-selection statement. Occasionally, an algorithm will contain a series of decisions in which a variable or expression is tested separately for each of the constant integral values it may assume, and different actions are taken. This is called multiple selection. C provides the switch multiple-selection statement to handle such decision making.

The switch statement consists of a series of case labels, and an optional default case. Figure 4.7 uses switch to count the number of each different letter grade students earned on an exam.

```
1   /* Fig. 4.7: fig04_07.c
2      Counting letter grades */
3   #include <stdio.h>
4
5   /* function main begins program execution */
6   int main()
7   {
8      int grade;        /* one grade */
9      int aCount = 0;   /* number of As */
10     int bCount = 0;   /* number of Bs */
11     int cCount = 0;   /* number of Cs */
12     int dCount = 0;   /* number of Ds */
13     int fCount = 0;   /* number of Fs */
14
15     printf( "Enter the letter grades.\n" );
16     printf( "Enter the EOF character to end input.\n" );
17
18     /* loop until user types end-of-file key sequence */
19     while ( ( grade = getchar() ) != EOF ) {
20
```

Fig. 4.7   switch example. (Part 1 of 3.)

```
21          /* determine which grade was input */
22          switch ( grade ) { /* switch nested in while */
23
24              case 'A': /* grade was uppercase A */
25              case 'a': /* or lowercase a */
26                  ++aCount; /* increment aCount */
27                  break; /* necessary to exit switch */
28
29              case 'B': /* grade was uppercase B */
30              case 'b': /* or lowercase b */
31                  ++bCount; /* increment bCount */
32                  break; /* exit switch */
33
34              case 'C': /* grade was uppercase C */
35              case 'c': /* or lowercase c */
36                  ++cCount; /* increment cCount */
37                  break; /* exit switch */
38
39              case 'D': /* grade was uppercase D */
40              case 'd': /* or lowercase d */
41                  ++dCount; /* increment dCount */
42                  break; /* exit switch */
43
44              case 'F': /* grade was uppercase F */
45              case 'f': /* or lowercase f */
46                  ++fCount; /* increment fCount */
47                  break; /* exit switch */
48
49              case '\n': /* ignore newlines, */
50              case '\t': /* tabs, */
51              case ' ':  /* and spaces in input */
52                  break; /* exit switch */
53
54              default: /* catch all other characters */
55                  printf( "Incorrect letter grade entered." );
56                  printf( " Enter a new grade.\n" );
57                  break; /* optional; will exit switch anyway */
58          } /* end switch */
59
60      } /* end while */
61
62      /* output summary of results */
63      printf( "\nTotals for each letter grade are:\n" );
64      printf( "A: %d\n", aCount ); /* display number of A grades */
65      printf( "B: %d\n", bCount ); /* display number of B grades */
66      printf( "C: %d\n", cCount ); /* display number of C grades */
67      printf( "D: %d\n", dCount ); /* display number of D grades */
68      printf( "F: %d\n", fCount ); /* display number of F grades */
69
70      return 0; /* indicate program ended successfully */
71
72  } /* end function main */
```

Fig. 4.7   switch example. (Part 2 of 3.)

```
Enter the letter grades.
Enter the EOF character to end input.
a
b
c
C
A
d
f
C
E
Incorrect letter grade entered. Enter a new grade.
D
A
b
^Z

Totals for each letter grade are:
A: 3
B: 2
C: 3
D: 2
F: 1
```

Fig. 4.7   switch example. (Part 3 of 3.)

In the program, the user enters letter grades for a class. In the while header (line 19),

```
while ( ( grade = getchar() ) != EOF )
```

the parenthesized assignment (grade = getchar()) is executed first. The getchar function (from the standard input/output library) reads one character from the keyboard and stores that character in integer variable grade. Characters are normally stored in variables of type *char*. However, an important feature of C is that characters can be stored in any integer data type because they are usually represented as one-byte integers in the computer. Thus, we can treat a character as either an integer or a character depending on its use. For example, the statement

```
printf( "The character (%c) has the value %d.\n", 'a', 'a' );
```

uses the conversion specifiers %c and %d to print the character a and its integer value, respectively. The result is

```
The character (a) has the value 97.
```

The integer 97 is the character's numerical representation in the computer. Many computers today use the *ASCII (American Standard Code for Information Interchange) character set* in which 97 represents the lower case letter 'a'. A list of the ASCII characters and their decimal values is presented in Appendix D. Characters can be read with scanf by using the conversion specifier %c.

Assignment statements as a whole actually have a value. This is the value that is assigned to the variable on the left side of the =. The value of the assignment expression grade = getchar() is the character that is returned by getchar and assigned to the variable grade.

The fact that assignment statements have values can be useful for initializing several variables to the same value. For example,

    a = b = c = 0;

first evaluates the assignment c = 0 (because the = operator associates from right to left). The variable b is then assigned the value of the assignment c = 0 (which is 0). Then, the variable a is assigned the value of the assignment b = (c = 0) (which is also 0). In the program, the value of the assignment grade = getchar() is compared with the value of EOF (a symbol whose acronym stands for "end of file"). We use EOF (which normally has the value -1) as the sentinel value. The user types a system-dependent keystroke combination to mean "end of file"—i.e., "I have no more data to enter." EOF is a symbolic integer constant defined in the <stdio.h> header (we will see how symbolic constants are defined in Chapter 6). If the value assigned to grade is equal to EOF, the program terminates. We have chosen to represent characters in this program as ints because EOF has an integer value (again, normally -1).

Portability Tip 4.1

The keystroke combinations for entering EOF (end of file) are system dependent.

Portability Tip 4.2

Testing for the symbolic constant EOF rather than –1 makes programs more portable. The C standard states that EOF is a negative integral value (but not necessarily –1). Thus, EOF could have different values on different systems.

On UNIX systems and many others, the EOF indicator is entered by typing the sequence

    <return> <ctrl-d>

This notation means to press the return key and then simultaneously press both the ctrl key and the d key. On other systems, such as Microsoft Corporation's Windows, the EOF indicator can be entered by typing

    <ctrl-z>

The user enters grades at the keyboard. When the *Return* (or *Enter*) key is pressed, the characters are read by function getchar one character at a time. If the character entered is not equal to EOF, the switch statement (line 22) is entered. Keyword switch is followed by the variable name grade in parentheses. This is called the *controlling expression*. The value of this expression is compared with each of the *case labels*. Assume the user has entered the letter C as a grade. C is automatically compared to each case in the switch. If a match occurs (case 'C':), the statements for that case are executed. In the case of the letter C, cCount is incremented by 1 (line 36), and the switch statement is exited immediately with the break statement.

The break statement causes program control to continue with the first statement after the switch statement. The break statement is used because the cases in a switch statement would otherwise run together. If `break` is not used anywhere in a `switch` statement, then each time a match occurs in the statement, the statements for all the remaining `case`s will be executed. (This feature is rarely useful, although it is perfect for programming the iterative song *The Twelve Days of Christmas*!) If no match occurs, the `default` case is executed, and an error message is printed.

Each `case` can have one or more actions. The `switch` statement is different from all other control statements in that braces are not required around multiple actions in a `case` of a `switch`. The general `switch` multiple-selection statement (using a `break` in each `case`) is flowcharted in Fig. 4.8.

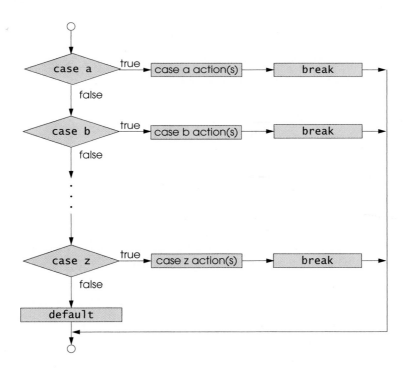

Fig. 4.8   `switch` multiple-selection statement with `break`s.

The flowchart makes it clear that each `break` statement at the end of a `case` causes control to immediately exit the `switch` statement. Again, note that (besides small circles and arrows) the flowchart contains only rectangle symbols and diamond symbols. Imagine, again, that the programmer has access to a deep bin of empty `switch` statements (represented as flowchart segments)—as many as the programmer might need to stack and nest with other control statements to form a structured implementation of an algorithm's flow of control. And again, the rectangles and diamonds are then filled with actions and decisions appropriate to the algorithm.

Common Programming Error 4.5

Forgetting a `break` *statement when one is needed in a* `switch` *statement is a logic error.*

Good Programming Practice 4.7

Provide a `default` *case in* `switch` *statements. Cases not explicitly tested in a* `switch` *are ignored. The* `default` *case helps prevent this by focusing the programmer on the need to process exceptional conditions. There are situations in which no* `default` *processing is needed.*

Good Programming Practice 4.8

Although the `case` *clauses and the* `default` *case clause in a* `switch` *statement can occur in any order, it is considered good programming practice to place the* `default` *clause last.*

Good Programming Practice 4.9

In a `switch` *statement when the* `default` *clause is listed last, the* `break` *statement is not required. But some programmers include this* `break` *for clarity and symmetry with other* `cases`.

In the `switch` statement of Fig. 4.7, the lines

```
case '\n': /* ignore newlines, */
case '\t': /* tabs, */
case ' ':  /* and spaces in input */
    break;  /* exit switch */
```

cause the program to skip newline and blank characters. Reading characters one at a time can cause some problems. To have the program read the characters, they must be sent to the computer by pressing the *Return* key. This causes the newline character to be placed in the input after the character we wish to process. Often, this newline character must be specially processed to make the program work correctly. By including the preceding cases in our `switch` statement, we prevent the error message in the `default` case from being printed each time a newline or space is encountered in the input.

Common Programming Error 4.6

Not processing newline characters in the input when reading characters one at a time can cause logic errors.

Error-Prevention Tip 4.5

Remember to provide processing capabilities for newline characters in the input when processing characters one at a time.

Note that several case labels listed together (such as `case "D": case "d":` in Fig. 4.7) simply means that the same set of actions is to occur for either of these cases.

When using the `switch` statement, remember that it can only be used for testing a *constant integral expression*—i.e., any combination of character constants and integer constants that evaluates to a constant integer value. A character constant is represented as the specific character in single quotes, such as "A". Characters must be enclosed within single quotes to be recognized as character constants. Integer constants are simply integer values. In our example, we have used character constants. Remember that characters are actually small integer values.

Portable languages like C must have flexible data type sizes. Different applications may need integers of different sizes. C provides several data types to represent integers. The range of integer values for each type depends on the particular computer's hardware. In addition to the types `int` and `char`, C provides types `short` (an abbreviation of `short int`) and `long` (an abbreviation of `long int`). C specifies that the minimum range of values for `short` integers is ±32767. For the vast majority of integer calculations, `long` integers are sufficient. The standard specifies that the minimum range of values for `long` integers is ±2147483647. The standard states that the range of values for an `int` is at least the same as the range for `short` integers and no larger than the range for `long` integers. The data type `char` can be used to represent integers in the range ±127 or any of the characters in the computer's character set.

4.8 do...while Repetition Statement

The do...while repetition statement is similar to the `while` statement. In the `while` statement, the loop-continuation condition is tested at the beginning of the loop before the body of the loop is performed. The do...while statement tests the loop-continuation condition *after* the loop body is performed. Therefore, the loop body will be executed at least once. When a do...while terminates, execution continues with the statement after the `while` clause. Note that it is not necessary to use braces in the do...while statement if there is only one statement in the body. However, the braces are usually included to avoid confusion between the `while` and do...while statements. For example,

```
while( condition )
```

is normally regarded as the header to a `while` statement. A do...while with no braces around the single statement body appears as

```
do
    statement
while( condition );
```

which can be confusing. The last line—`while( condition );`—may be misinterpreted by the reader as a `while` statement containing an empty statement. Thus, the do...while with one statement is often written as follows to avoid confusion:

```
do {
    statement
} while (condition);
```

Good Programming Practice 4.10

Some programmers always include braces in a do...while *statement even if the braces are not necessary. This helps eliminate ambiguity between the* do...while *statement containing one statement and the* while *statement.*

Common Programming Error 4.7

Infinite loops are caused when the loop-continuation condition in a while, *for or* do...while *statement never becomes false. To prevent this, make sure there is not a semicolon immediately after the header of a* while *or* for *statement. In a counter-controlled loop, make sure the control variable is incremented (or decremented) in the body of the loop. In a sentinel-controlled loop, make sure the sentinel value is eventually input.*

Figure 4.9 uses a do...while statement to print the numbers from 1 to 10. Note that the control variable counter is preincremented in the loop-continuation test. Note also the use of the braces to enclose the single-statement body of the do...while.

```
1   /* Fig. 4.9: fig04_09.c
2      Using the do/while repetition statement */
3   #include <stdio.h>
4
5   /* function main begins program execution */
6   int main()
7   {
8      int counter = 1; /* initialize counter */
9
10     do {
11        printf( "%d  ", counter ); /* display counter */
12     } while ( ++counter <= 10 );   /* end do...while */
13
14     return 0; /* indicate program ended successfully */
15
16  } /* end function main */
```

```
1   2   3   4   5   6   7   8   9   10
```

Fig. 4.9   do...while statement example.

The do...while statement is flowcharted in Fig. 4.10. This flowchart makes it clear that the loop-continuation condition is not executed until after the action is performed at least once. Again, note that (besides small circles and arrows) the flowchart contains only a rectangle symbol and a diamond symbol. Imagine, again, that the programmer has access to a deep bin of empty do...while statements (represented as flowchart segments)—as many as the programmer might need to stack and nest with other control statements to form a structured implementation of an algorithm's flow of control. And again, the rectangles and diamonds are then filled with actions and decisions appropriate to the algorithm.

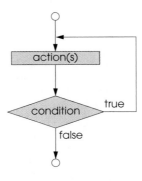

Fig. 4.10   Flowcharting the do...while repetition statement.

4.9 break and continue Statements

The break and continue statements are used to alter the flow of control. The break statement, when executed in a while, for, do...while or switch statement, causes immediate exit from that statement. Program execution continues with the next statement. Common uses of the break statement are to escape early from a loop or to skip the remainder of a switch statement (as in Fig. 4.7). Figure 4.11 demonstrates the break statement in a for repetition statement. When the if statement detects that x has become 5, break is executed. This terminates the for statement and the program continues with the printf after the for. The loop fully executes only four times.

```
1   /* Fig. 4.11: fig04_11.c
2      Using the break statement in a for statement */
3   #include <stdio.h>
4
5   /* function main begins program execution */
6   int main()
7   {
8      int x; /* counter */
9
10     /* loop 10 times */
11     for ( x = 1; x <= 10; x++ ) {
12
13        /* if x is 5, terminate loop */
14        if ( x == 5 ) {
15           break; /* break loop only if x is 5 */
16        } /* end if */
17
18        printf( "%d ", x ); /* display value of x */
19     } /* end for */
20
21     printf( "\nBroke out of loop at x == %d\n", x );
22
23     return 0; /* indicate program ended successfully */
24
25  } /* end function main */
```

```
1 2 3 4
Broke out of loop at x == 5
```

Fig. 4.11 Using the break statement in a for statement.

The continue statement, when executed in a while, for or do...while statement, skips the remaining statements in the body of that control statement and performs the next iteration of the loop. In while and do...while statements, the loop-continuation test is evaluated immediately after the continue statement is executed. In the for statement, the increment expression is executed, then the loop-continuation test is evaluated. Earlier, we stated that the while statement could be used in most cases to represent the for statement. The one exception occurs when the increment expression in the while statement follows the continue statement. In this case, the increment is not executed before the repetition-continuation condition is tested, and the while does not execute in the same manner as the for. Figure 4.12 uses the continue statement in a for statement to skip the printf statement and begin the next iteration of the loop.

```
1   /* Fig. 4.12: fig04_12.c
2      Using the continue statement in a for statement */
3   #include <stdio.h>
4
5   /* function main begins program execution */
6   int main()
7   {
8      int x; /* counter */
9
10     /* loop 10 times */
11     for ( x = 1; x <= 10; x++ ) {
12
13        /* if x is 5, continue with next iteration of loop */
14        if ( x == 5 ) {
15           continue; /* skip remaining code in loop body */
16        } /* end if */
17
18        printf( "%d ", x ); /* display value of x */
19     } /* end for */
20
21     printf( "\nUsed continue to skip printing the value 5\n" );
22
23     return 0; /* indicate program ended successfully */
24
25  } /* end function main */
```

```
1 2 3 4 6 7 8 9 10
Used continue to skip printing the value 5
```

Fig. 4.12   Using the continue statement in a for statement.

Software Engineering Observation 4.2

Some programmers feel that break *and* continue *violate the norms of structured programming. Because the effects of these statements can be achieved by structured programming techniques we will soon learn, these programmers do not use* break *and* continue.

Performance Tip 4.1

The break *and* continue *statements, when used properly, perform faster than the corresponding structured techniques that we will soon learn.*

Software Engineering Observation 4.3

There is a tension between achieving quality software engineering and achieving the best performing software. Often one of these goals is achieved at the expense of the other.

4.10 Logical Operators

So far we have studied only *simple conditions*, such as counter <= 10, total > 1000, and number != sentinelValue. We have expressed these conditions in terms of the relational operators, >, <, >= and <=, and the equality operators, == and !=. Each decision tested precisely one condition. If we wanted to test multiple conditions in the process of making a decision, we had to perform these tests in separate statements or in nested if or if...else statements.

C provides *logical operators* that may be used to form more complex conditions by combining simple conditions. The logical operators are && *(logical AND)*, || *(logical OR)* and ! *(logical NOT* also called *logical negation)*. We will consider examples of each of these.

Suppose we wish to ensure that two conditions are *both* true before we choose a certain path of execution. In this case, we can use the logical && operator as follows:

```
if ( gender == 1 && age >= 65 )
    ++seniorFemales;
```

This if statement contains two simple conditions. The condition gender == 1 might be evaluated, for example, to determine if a person is a female. The condition age >= 65 is evaluated to determine if a person is a senior citizen. The two simple conditions are evaluated first because the precedences of == and >= are both higher than the precedence of &&. The if statement then considers the combined condition

```
gender == 1 && age >= 65
```

This condition is true if and only if both of the simple conditions are true. Finally, if this combined condition is indeed true, then the count of seniorFemales is incremented by 1. If either or both of the simple conditions are false, then the program skips the incrementing and proceeds to the statement following the if.

Figure 4.13 summarizes the && operator. The table shows all four possible combinations of zero (false) and nonzero (true) values for expression1 and expression2. Such tables are often called *truth tables*. C evaluates all expressions that include relational operators, equality operators, and/or logical operators to 0 or 1. Although C sets a true value to 1, it accepts *any* nonzero value as true.

expression1	expression2	expression1 && expression2
0	0	0
0	nonzero	0
nonzero	0	0
nonzero	nonzero	1

Fig. 4.13   Truth table for the && (logical AND) operator.

Now let us consider the || (logical OR) operator. Suppose we wish to ensure at some point in a program that either *or* both of two conditions are true before we choose a certain path of execution. In this case, we use the || operator as in the following program segment:

```
if ( semesterAverage >= 90 || finalExam >= 90 )
    printf( "Student grade is A\n" );
```

This statement also contains two simple conditions. The condition `semesterAverage >= 90` is evaluated to determine if the student deserves an "A" in the course because of a solid performance throughout the semester. The condition `finalExam >= 90` is evaluated to determine if the student deserves an "A" in the course because of an outstanding performance on the final exam. The `if` statement then considers the combined condition

```
semesterAverage >= 90 || finalExam >= 90
```

and awards the student an "A" if either or both of the simple conditions are true. Note that the message "`Student grade is A`" is not printed only when both of the simple conditions are false (zero). Figure 4.14 is a truth table for the logical OR operator (`||`).

expression1	expression2	expression1 || expression2
0	0	0
0	nonzero	1
nonzero	0	1
nonzero	nonzero	1

Fig. 4.14   Truth table for the logical OR (`||`) operator.

The `&&` operator has a higher precedence than `||`. Both operators associate from left to right. An expression containing `&&` or `||` operators is evaluated only until truth or falsehood is known. Thus, evaluation of the condition

```
gender == 1 && age >= 65
```

will stop if `gender` is not equal to 1 (i.e., the entire expression is false), and continue if `gender` is equal to 1 (i.e., the entire expression could still be true if `age >= 65`).

Performance Tip 4.2

*In expressions using operator **&&**, make the condition that is most likely to be false the leftmost condition. In expressions using operator `||`, make the condition that is most likely to be true the leftmost condition. This can reduce a program's execution time.*

C provides `!` (logical negation) to enable a programmer to "reverse" the meaning of a condition. Unlike the `&&` and `||` operators, which combine two conditions (and are therefore binary operators), the logical negation operator has only a single condition as an operand (and is therefore a unary operator). The logical negation operator is placed before a condition when we are interested in choosing a path of execution if the original condition (without the logical negation operator) is false, such as in the following program segment:

```
if ( !( grade == sentinelValue ) )
    printf( "The next grade is %f\n", grade );
```

The parentheses around the condition `grade == sentinelValue` are needed because the logical negation operator has a higher precedence than the equality operator. Figure 4.15 is a truth table for the logical negation operator.

expression	! expression
0	1
nonzero	0

Fig. 4.15 Truth table for operator ! (logical negation).

In most cases, the programmer can avoid using logical negation by expressing the condition differently with an appropriate relational operator. For example, the preceding statement may also be written as follows:

```
if ( grade != sentinelValue )
    printf( "The next grade is %f\n", grade );
```

Figure 4.16 shows the precedence and associativity of the various operators introduced to this point. The operators are shown from top to bottom in decreasing order of precedence.

Operators						Associativity	Type
++	--	+	-	!	(type)	right to left	unary
*	/	%				left to right	multiplicative
+	-					left to right	additive
<	<=	>	>=			left to right	relational
==	!=					left to right	equality
&&						left to right	logical AND
||						left to right	logical OR
?:						right to left	conditional
=	+=	-=	*=	/=	%=	right to left	assignment
,						left to right	comma

Fig. 4.16 Operator precedence and associativity.

4.11 Confusing Equality (==) and Assignment (=) Operators

There is one type of error that C programmers, no matter how experienced, tend to make so frequently that we felt it was worth a separate section. That error is accidentally swapping the operators == (equality) and = (assignment). What makes these swaps so damaging is the fact that they do not ordinarily cause syntax errors. Rather, statements with these errors ordinarily compile correctly, allowing programs to run to completion while likely generating incorrect results through runtime logic errors.

There are two aspects of C that cause these problems. One is that any expression in C that produces a value can be used in the decision portion of any control statement. If the value is 0, it is treated as false, and if the value is nonzero, it is treated as true. The second is that assignments in C produce a value, namely the value that is assigned to the variable on the left side of the assignment operator. For example, suppose we intend to write

```
if ( payCode == 4 )
    printf( "You get a bonus!" );
```

but we accidentally write

```
if ( payCode = 4 )
    printf( "You get a bonus!" );
```

The first **if** statement properly awards a bonus to the person whose paycode is equal to 4. The second **if** statement—the one with the error—evaluates the assignment expression in the **if** condition. This expression is a simple assignment whose value is the constant 4. Because any nonzero value is interpreted as "true," the condition in this **if** statement is always true, and the person always receives a bonus regardless of what the actual paycode is!

 Common Programming Error 4.8

Using operator == for assignment or using operator = for equality is a logic error.

Programmers normally write conditions such as **x == 7** with the variable name on the left and the constant on the right. By reversing these so that the constant is on the left and the variable name is on the right, as in **7 == x**, the programmer who accidentally replaces the **==** operator with **=** will be protected by the compiler. The compiler will treat this as a syntax error because only a variable name can be placed on the left-hand side of an assignment statement. At least this will prevent the potential devastation of a runtime logic error.

Variable names are said to be *lvalues* (for "left values") because they can be used on the left side of an assignment operator. Constants are said to be *rvalues* (for "right values") because they can be used on only the right side of an assignment operator. Note that lvalues can also be used as rvalues, but not vice versa.

Good Programming Practice 4.11

When an equality expression has a variable and a constant, as in x == 1, some programmers prefer to write the expression with the constant on the left and the variable name on the right as protection against the logic error that occurs when the programmer accidentally replaces the == operator with =.

The other side of the coin can be equally unpleasant. Suppose the programmer wants to assign a value to a variable with a simple statement like

```
x = 1;
```

but instead writes

```
x == 1;
```

Here, too, this is not a syntax error. Rather the compiler simply evaluates the conditional expression. If **x** is equal to 1, the condition is true and the expression returns the value 1. If **x** is not equal to 1, the condition is false and the expression returns the value 0. Regardless of what value is returned, there is no assignment operator, so the value is simply lost, and the value of **x** remains unaltered, probably causing an execution-time logic error. Unfortunately, we do not have a handy trick available to help you with this problem!

 Error-Prevention Tip 4.6

After you write a program, text search it for every = and check that it is being used properly.

4.12 Structured Programming Summary

Just as architects design buildings by employing the collective wisdom of their profession, so should programmers design programs. Our field is younger than architecture is, and our collective wisdom is considerably sparser. We have learned a great deal in a mere five decades. Perhaps most importantly, we have learned that structured programming produces programs that are easier (than unstructured programs) to understand and hence are easier to test, debug, modify, and even prove correct in a mathematical sense.

Chapter 3 and Chapter 4 have concentrated on C's control statements. Each statement has been presented, flowcharted and discussed separately with examples. Now, we summarize the results of Chapter 3 and Chapter 4 and introduce a simple set of rules for the formation and properties of structured programs.

Figure 4.17 summarizes the control statements discussed in Chapter 3 and Chapter 4. Small circles are used in the figure to indicate the single entry point and the single exit point of each statement. Connecting individual flowchart symbols arbitrarily can lead to unstructured programs. Therefore, the programming profession has chosen to combine flowchart symbols to form a limited set of control statements, and to build only structured programs by properly combining control statements in only two simple ways. For simplicity, only single-entry/single-exit control statements are used—there is only one way to enter and only one way to exit each control statement. Connecting control statements in sequence to form structured programs is simple—the exit point of one control statement is connected directly to the entry point of the next control statement, i.e., the control statements are simply placed one after another in a program—we have called this "control statement stacking." The rules for forming structured programs also allow for control statements to be nested.

Figure 4.18 shows the rules for forming structured programs. The rules assume that the rectangle flowchart symbol may be used to indicate any action including input/output.

Applying the rules of Fig. 4.18 always results in a structured flowchart with a neat, building-block appearance. Repeatedly applying rule 2 to the simplest flowchart (Fig. 4.19) results in a structured flowchart containing many rectangles in sequence (Fig. 4.20). Notice that rule 2 generates a stack of control statements; so we call rule 2 the *stacking rule*.

Rule 3 is called the *nesting rule*. Repeatedly applying rule 3 to the simplest flowchart results in a flowchart with neatly nested control statements. For example, in Fig. 4.21, the rectangle in the simplest flowchart is first replaced with a double-selection (if…else) statement. Then rule 3 is applied again to both of the rectangles in the double-selection statement, replacing each of these rectangles with double-selection statements. The dashed boxes around each of the double-selection statements represent the rectangle that was replaced in the original flowchart.

Rule 4 generates larger, more involved, and more deeply nested structures. The flowcharts that emerge from applying the rules in Fig. 4.18 constitute the set of all possible structured flowcharts and hence the set of all possible structured programs.

It is because of the elimination of the goto statement that these building blocks never overlap one another. The beauty of the structured approach is that we use only a small number of simple single-entry/single-exit pieces, and we assemble them in only two simple ways. Figure 4.22 shows the kinds of stacked building blocks that emerge from applying rule 2 and the kinds of nested building blocks that emerge from applying rule 3. The figure also shows the kind of overlapped building blocks that cannot appear in structured flowcharts (because of the elimination of the goto statement).

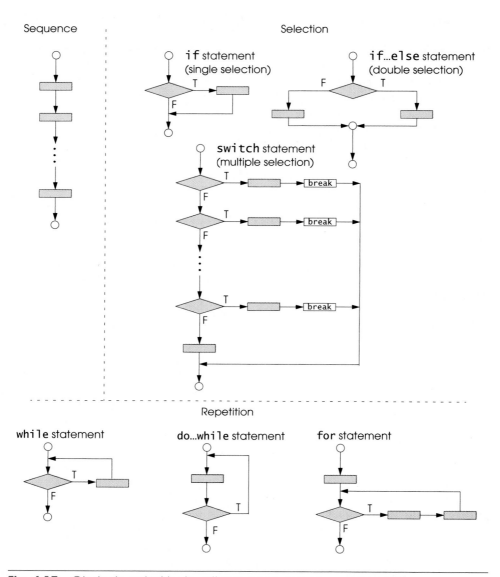

Fig. 4.17 C's single-entry/single-exit sequence, selection and repetition statements.

Rules for Forming Structured Programs

1) Begin with the "simplest flowchart" (Fig. 4.19).

2) Any rectangle (action) can be replaced by two rectangles (actions) in sequence.

Fig. 4.18 Rules for forming structured programs. (Part 1 of 2.)

Rules for Forming Structured Programs

3) Any rectangle (action) can be replaced by any control statement (sequence, `if`, `if...else`, `switch`, `while`, `do...while` or `for`).

4) Rules 2 and 3 may be applied as often as you like and in any order.

Fig. 4.18   Rules for forming structured programs. (Part 2 of 2.)

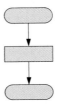

Fig. 4.19   Simplest flowchart.

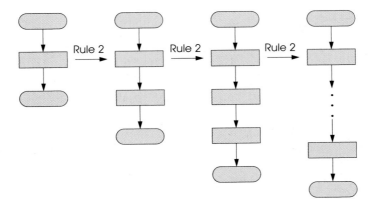

Fig. 4.20   Repeatedly applying rule 2 of Fig. 4.18 to the simplest flowchart.

If the rules in Fig. 4.18 are followed, an unstructured flowchart (such as that in Fig. 4.23) cannot be created. If you are uncertain if a particular flowchart is structured, apply the rules of Fig. 4.18 in reverse to try to reduce the flowchart to the simplest flowchart. If the flowchart is reducible to the simplest flowchart, the original flowchart is structured; otherwise, it is not.

Structured programming promotes simplicity. Bohm and Jacopini showed that only three forms of control are needed:

- Sequence
- Selection
- Repetition

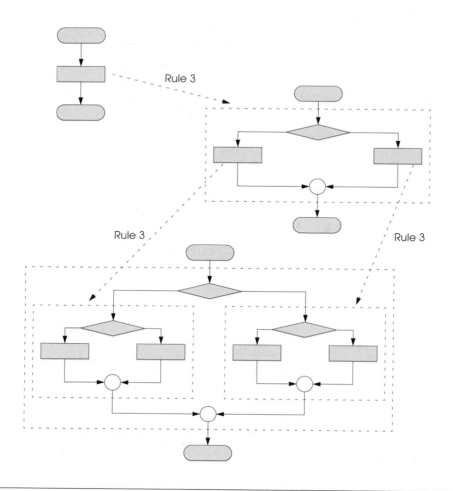

Fig. 4.21   Applying rule 3 of Fig. 4.18 to the simplest flowchart.

Sequence is straighforward. Selection is implemented in one of three ways:

- `if` statement (single selection)
- `if...else` statement (double selection)
- `switch` statement (multiple selection)

In fact, it is straightforward to prove that the simple `if` statement is sufficient to provide any form of selection—everything that can be done with the `if...else` statement and the `switch` statement can be implemented with one or more `if` statements.

Repetition is implemented in one of three ways:

- `while` statement
- `do...while` statement
- `for` statement

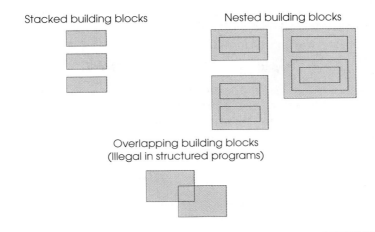

Fig. 4.22   Stacked, nested and overlapped building blocks.

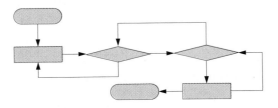

Fig. 4.23   An unstructured flowchart.

It is straightforward to prove that the while statement is sufficient to provide any form of repetition. Everything that can be done with the do...while statement and the for statement can be done with the while statement.

Combining these results illustrates that any form of control ever needed in a C program can be expressed in terms of only three forms of control:

- sequence
- if statement (selection)
- while statement (repetition)

And these control statements can be combined in only two ways—stacking and nesting. Indeed, structured programming promotes simplicity.

In Chapter 3 and Chapter 4, we discussed how to compose programs from control statements containing actions and decisions. In Chapter 5, we introduce another program structuring unit called the *function*. We will learn to compose large programs by combining functions, which, in turn, are composed of control statements. We will also discuss how using functions promotes software reusability.

SUMMARY

- A loop is a set of instructions the computer executes repeatedly until some terminating condition is satisfied. Two forms of repetition are counter-controlled repetition and sentinel-controlled repetition.

- A loop counter is used to count the number of times a group of instructions should be repeated. It is incremented (usually by 1) each time the group of instructions is performed.

- Sentinel values are generally used to control repetition when the precise number of repetitions is not known in advance and the loop includes statements that obtain data each time the loop is performed.

- A sentinel value is entered after all regular data items have been supplied to the program. Sentinels must be chosen carefully so that there is no possibility of confusing them with valid data items.

- The for repetition statement handles all the details of counter-controlled repetition. The general form of the for statement is

      for (*expression1*; *expression2*; *expression3*)
          statement

  where *expression1* initializes the loop's control variable, *expression2* is the loop-continuation condition, and *expression3* increments (or decrements) the control variable.

- The do...while repetition statement is similar to the while repetition statement, but the do...while statement tests the loop-continuation condition at the end of the loop, so the body of the loop will be executed at least once. The form of the do...while statement is

      do
          statement
      while (*condition*);

- The break statement, when executed in one of the repetition statements (for, while and do...while), causes immediate exit from the statement. Execution continues with the first statement after the loop. The break can also be used to exit a switch.

- The continue statement, when executed in one of the repetition statements (for, while and do...while), skips any remaining statements in the body of the control statement, and proceeds with the next iteration of the loop.

- The switch statement handles a series of decisions in which a particular variable or expression is tested for each of the values it may assume, and different actions are taken. Each case in a switch statement may cause many statements to be performed. In most programs, it is necessary to include a break statement after the statements for each case, otherwise the program will execute the statements in each case until a break statement is encountered or the end of the switch statement is reached. Several cases can execute the same statements by listing the case labels together before the statements. The switch statement can only test constant integral expressions.

- Function getchar returns one character from the keyboard (the standard input) as an integer.

- On UNIX systems and many others, the EOF character is entered by typing the sequence

      <return> <ctrl-d>

  On Microsoft Windows systems, the EOF character is entered by typing

      <ctrl-z>

- Logical operators may be used to form complex conditions by combining conditions. The logical operators are &&, ||, and !, meaning logical AND, logical OR, and logical NOT (negation), respectively.

- A true value is any nonzero value.

- A false value is 0 (zero).

TERMINOLOGY

ASCII character set
body of a loop
break control statement
case label
char
continue control statement
control variable
counter-controlled repetition
<ctrl-z>
decrement control variable
default case in switch
definite repetition
double
do...while repetition statement
end of file
EOF
field width
final value of control variable
for repetition statement
getchar function
increment control variable
indefinite repetition
infinite loop
initial value of control variable
left justify
logical AND (&&)

logical negation (!)
logical operators
logical OR (| |)
long
loop-continuation condition
loop-control variable
loop counter
lvalue ("left value")
minus sign for left justification
multiple selection
nested control statements
nesting rule
off-by-one error
pow function
repetition statements
<return> <ctrl-d>
right justify
rvalue ("right value")
short
simple condition
single-entry/single-exit control statements
stacking rule
switch selection statement
truth table
unary operator
while repetition statement

COMMON PROGRAMMING ERRORS

4.1   Because floating-point values may be approximate, controlling counting loops with floating point variables may result in imprecise counter values and inaccurate tests for termination.

4.2   Using an incorrect relational operator or using an incorrect final value of a loop counter in the condition of a while or for statement can cause off-by-one errors.

4.3   Using commas instead of semicolons in a for header is a syntax error.

4.4   Placing a semicolon immediately to the right of a for header makes the body of that for statement an empty statement. This is normally a logic error.

4.5   Forgetting a break statement when one is needed in a switch statement is a logic error.

4.6   Not processing newline characters in the input when reading characters one at a time can cause logic errors.

4.7   Infinite loops are caused when the loop-continuation condition in a while, for or do...while statement never becomes false. To prevent this, make sure there is not a semicolon immediately after the header of a while or for statement. In a counter-controlled loop, make sure the control variable is incremented (or decremented) in the body of the loop. In a sentinel-controlled loop, make sure the sentinel value is eventually input.

4.8   Using operator == for assignment or using operator = for equality is a logic error.

ERROR-PREVENTION TIPS

4.1   Control counting loops with integer values.

4.2 Using the final value in the condition of a `while` or `for` statement and using the `<=` relational operator will help avoid off-by-one errors. For a loop used to print the values 1 to 10, for example, the loop-continuation condition should be `counter <= 10` rather than `counter < 11` or `counter < 10`.

4.3 Although the value of the control variable can be changed in the body of a `for` loop, this can lead to subtle errors; so it is best not to change it.

4.4 Do not use variables of type `float` or `double` to perform monetary calculations. The impreciseness of floating-point numbers can cause errors that will result in incorrect monetary values. [In the exercises, we explore the use of integers to perform monetary calculations.]

4.5 Remember to provide processing capabilities for newline characters in the input when processing characters one at a time.

4.6 After you write a program, text search it for every = and check that it is being used properly.

GOOD PROGRAMMING PRACTICES

4.1 Indent the statements in the body of each control statement.

4.2 Put a blank line before and after each control statement to make it stand out in a program.

4.3 Too many levels of nesting can make a program difficult to understand. As a general rule, try to avoid using more than three levels of indentation.

4.4 The combination of vertical spacing before and after control statements and indentation of the bodies of control statements within the control statement headers gives programs a two-dimensional appearance that greatly improves program readability.

4.5 Although statements preceding a `for` and statements in the body of a `for` can often be merged into the `for` header, avoid doing so because it makes the program more difficult to read.

4.6 Limit the size of control statement headers to a single line if possible.

4.7 Provide a `default` case in `switch` statements. Cases not explicitly tested are ignored. The `default` case helps prevent this by focusing the programmer on the need to process exceptional conditions. There are situations in which no default processing is needed.

4.8 Although the `case` clauses and the `default` case clause in a `switch` statement can occur in any order, it is considered good programming practice to place the `default` clause last.

4.9 In a `switch` statement when the `default` clause is listed last, the `break` statement is not required. But some programmers include this `break` for clarity and symmetry with other `cases`.

4.10 Some programmers always include braces in a `do…while` statement even if the braces are not necessary. This helps eliminate ambiguity between the `do…while` statement containing one statement and the `while` statement.

4.11 When an equality expression has a variable and a constant as in `x == 1`, some programmers prefer to write the expression with the constant on the left and the variable name on the right as protection against the logic error that occurs when the programmer accidentally replaces the `==` operator with `=`.

PERFORMANCE TIPS

4.1 The `break` and `continue` statements, when used properly, perform faster than the corresponding structured techniques that we will soon learn.

4.2 In expressions using operator `&&`, make the condition that is most likely to be false the leftmost condition. In expressions using operator `||`, make the condition that is most likely to be true the leftmost condition. This can reduce a program's execution time.

PORTABILITY TIPS

4.1   The keystroke combinations for entering EOF (end of file) are system dependent.

4.2   Testing for the symbolic constant EOF rather than –1 makes programs more portable. The C standard states that EOF is a negative integral value (but not necessarily –1). Thus, EOF could have different values on different systems.

SOFTWARE ENGINEERING OBSERVATIONS

4.1   Place only expressions involving the control variables in the initialization and increment sections of a for statement. Manipulations of other variables should appear either before the loop (if they execute only once, like initialization statements) or in the loop body (if they execute once per repetition, like incrementing or decrementing statements).

4.2   Some programmers feel that break and continue violate the norms of structured programming. Because the effects of these statements can be achieved by structured programming techniques we will soon learn, these programmers do not use break and continue.

4.3   There is a tension between achieving quality software engineering and achieving the best software peformance. Often one of these goals is achieved at the expense of the other.

SELF-REVIEW EXERCISES

4.1   Fill in the blanks in each of the following statements.
    a) Counter-controlled repetition is also known as _____ repetition because it is known in advance how many times the loop will be executed.
    b) Sentinel-controlled repetition is also known as _____ repetition because it is not known in advance how many times the loop will be executed.
    c) In counter-controlled repetition, a(n) _____ is used to count the number of times a group of instructions should be repeated.
    d) The _____ statement, when executed in a repetition statement, causes the next iteration of the loop to be performed immediately.
    e) The _____ statement, when executed in a repetition statement or a switch, causes immediate exit from the statement.
    f) The _____ is used to test a particular variable or expression for each of the constant integral values it may assume.

4.2   State whether the following are *true* or *false*. If the answer is *false*, explain why.
    a) The default case is required in the switch selection statement.
    b) The break statement is required in the default case of a switch selection statement.
    c) The expression (x > y && a < b) is true if either x > y is true or a < b is true.
    d) An expression containing the || operator is true if either or both of its operands is true.

4.3   Write a statement or a set of statements to accomplish each of the following tasks:
    a) Sum the odd integers between 1 and 99 using a for statement. Assume the integer variables sum and count have been defined.
    b) Print the value 333.546372 in a field width of 15 characters with precisions of 1, 2, 3, 4 and 5. Left justify the output. What are the five values that print?
    c) Calculate the value of 2.5 raised to the power of 3 using the pow function. Print the result with a precision of 2 in a field width of 10 positions. What is the value that prints?
    d) Print the integers from 1 to 20 using a while loop and the counter variable x. Assume that the variable x has been defined, but not initialized. Print only five integers per line. [*Hint:* Use the calculation x % 5. When the value of this is 0, print a newline character, otherwise print a tab character.]
    e) Repeat Exercise 4.3 (d) using a for statement.

4.4   Find the error in each of the following code segments and explain how to correct it.

a)
```
x = 1;
while ( x <= 10 );
    x++;
}
```

b)
```
for ( y = .1; y != 1.0; y += .1 )
    printf( "%f\n", y );
```

c)
```
switch ( n ) {
    case 1:
        printf( "The number is 1\n" );
    case 2:
        printf( "The number is 2\n" );
        break;
    default:
        printf( "The number is not 1 or 2\n" );
        break;
}
```

d) The following code should print the values 1 to 10.

```
n = 1;
while ( n < 10 )
    printf( "%d ", n++ );
```

ANSWERS TO SELF-REVIEW EXERCISES

4.1   a) definite. b) indefinite. c) control variable or counter. d) `continue`. e) `break`. f) `switch` selection statement.

4.2   a) False. The `default` case is optional. If no default action is needed, then there is no need for a `default` case.

b) False. The `break` statement is used to exit the `switch` statement. The `break` statement is not required when the `default` case is the last case.

c) False. Both of the relational expressions must be true in order for the entire expression to be true when using the `&&` operator.

d) True.

4.3   a)
```
sum = 0;
for ( count = 1; count <= 99; count += 2 )
    sum += count;
```

b)
```
printf( "%-15.1f\n", 333.546372 );   /* prints 333.5       */
printf( "%-15.2f\n", 333.546372 );   /* prints 333.55      */
printf( "%-15.3f\n", 333.546372 );   /* prints 333.546     */
printf( "%-15.4f\n", 333.546372 );   /* prints 333.5464    */
printf( "%-15.5f\n", 333.546372 );   /* prints 333.54637 */
```

c)
```
printf( "%10.2f\n", pow( 2.5, 3 ) );   /* prints 15.63       */
```

d)
```
x = 1;
while ( x <= 20 ) {
    printf( "%d", x );
    if ( x % 5 == 0 )
        printf( "\n" );
    else
        printf( "\t" );
    x++;
}
```

or

```
x = 1;
while ( x <= 20 )
    if ( x % 5 == 0 )
        printf( "%d\n", x++ );
    else
        printf( "%d\t", x++ );
```

or

```
x = 0;
while ( ++x <= 20 )
    if ( x % 5 == 0 )
        printf( "%d\n", x );
    else
        printf( "%d\t", x );
```
e) ```
for (x = 1; x <= 20; x++) {
    printf("%d", x);
    if (x % 5 == 0)
        printf("\n");
    else
        printf("\t");
}
```

or

```
for ( x = 1; x <= 20; x++ )
    if ( x % 5 == 0 )
        printf( "%d\n", x );
    else
        printf( "%d\t", x );
```

4.4   a) Error: The semicolon after the while header causes an infinite loop.
          Correction: Replace the semicolon with a { or remove both the ; and the }.
       b) Error: Using a floating-point number to control a for repetition statement.
          Correction: Use an integer, and perform the proper calculation in order to get the values
          you desire.

```
for ( y = 1; y != 10; y++ )
    printf( "%f\n", ( float ) y / 10 );
```

       c) Error: Missing break statement in the statements for the first case.
          Correction: Add a break statement at the end of the statements for the first case. Note
          that this is not necessarily an error if the programmer wants the statement of case 2: to
          execute every time the case 1: statement executes.
       d) Error: Improper relational operator used in the while repetition-continuation condition.
          Correction: Use <= rather than <.

EXERCISES

4.5   Find the error in each of the following (Note: there may be more than one error):
       a) ```
For (x = 100, x >= 1, x++)
    printf("%d\n", x);
```

b) The following code should print whether a given integer is odd or even:

```
switch ( value % 2 ) {
   case 0:
      printf( "Even integer\n" );
   case 1:
      printf( "Odd integer\n" );
}
```

c) The following code should input an integer and a character and print them. Assume the user types as input 100 A.

```
scanf( "%d", &intVal );
charVal = getchar();
printf( "Integer: %d\nCharacter: %c\n", intVal, charVal );
```

d)
```
for ( x = .000001; x <= .0001; x += .000001 )
   printf( "%.7f\n", x );
```

e) The following code should output the odd integers from 999 to 1:

```
for ( x = 999; x >= 1; x += 2 )
   printf( "%d\n", x );
```

f) The following code should output the even integers from 2 to 100:

```
counter = 2;

Do {
   if ( counter % 2 == 0 )
      printf( "%d\n", counter );

   counter += 2;
} While ( counter < 100 );
```

g) The following code should sum the integers from 100 to 150 (assume total is initialized to 0):

```
for ( x = 100; x <= 150; x++ );
   total += x;
```

4.6 State which values of the control variable x are printed by each of the following for statements:

a)
```
for ( x = 2; x <= 13; x += 2 )
   printf( "%d\n", x );
```

b)
```
for ( x = 5; x <= 22; x += 7 )
   printf( "%d\n", x );
```

c)
```
for ( x = 3; x <= 15; x += 3 )
   printf( "%d\n", x );
```

d)
```
for ( x = 1; x <= 5; x += 7 )
   printf( "%d\n", x );
```

e)
```
for ( x = 12; x >= 2; x -= 3 )
   printf( "%d\n", x );
```

4.7 Write for statements that print the following sequences of values:

a) 1, 2, 3, 4, 5, 6, 7

b) 3, 8, 13, 18, 23

    c) 20, 14, 8, 2, -4, -10

    d) 19, 27, 35, 43, 51

4.8 What does the following program do?

```
1    #include <stdio.h>
2
3    /* function main begins program execution */
4    int main()
5    {
6       int x;
7       int y;
8       int i;
9       int j;
10
11      /* prompt user for input */
12      printf( "Enter two integers in the range 1-20: " );
13      scanf( "%d%d", &x, &y ); /* read values for x and y */
14
15      for ( i = 1; i <= y; i++ ) { /* count from 1 to y */
16
17         for ( j = 1; j <= x; j++ ) { /* count from 1 to x */
18            printf( "@" ); /* output @ */
19         } /* end inner for */
20
21         printf( "\n" ); /* begin new line */
22      } /* end outer for */
23
24      return 0; /* indicate program ended successfully */
25
26   } /* end function main */
```

4.9 Write a program that sums a sequence of integers. Assume that the first integer read with scanf specifies the number of values remaining to be entered. Your program should read only one value each time scanf is executed. A typical input sequence might be

    5 100 200 300 400 500

where the 5 indicates that the subsequent five values are to be summed.

4.10 Write a program that calculates and prints the average of several integers. Assume the last value read with scanf is the sentinel 9999. A typical input sequence might be

    10 8 11 7 9 9999

indicating that the average of all the values preceding 9999 is to be calculated.

4.11 Write a program that finds the smallest of several integers. Assume that the first value read specifies the number of values remaining.

4.12 Write a program that calculates and prints the sum of the even integers from 2 to 30.

4.13 Write a program that calculates and prints the product of the odd integers from 1 to 15.

4.14 The *factorial* function is used frequently in probability problems. The factorial of a positive integer *n* (written *n!* and pronounced "n factorial") is equal to the product of the positive integers from 1 to *n*. Write a program that evaluates the factorials of the integers from 1 to 5. Print the results in tabular format. What difficulty might prevent you from calculating the factorial of 20?

4.15   Modify the compound interest program of Section 4.6 to repeat its steps for interest rates of 5 percent, 6 percent, 7 percent, 8 percent, 9 percent, and 10 percent. Use a `for` loop to vary the interest rate.

4.16   Write a program that prints the following patterns separately one below the other. Use `for` loops to generate the patterns. All asterisks (*) should be printed by a single `printf` statement of the form `printf( "*" );` (this causes the asterisks to print side by side). Hint: The last two patterns require that each line begin with an appropriate number of blanks.

```
(A)                 (B)                 (C)                 (D)
*                   **********          **********                   *
**                  *********           *********                   **
***                 ********            ********                   ***
****                *******             *******                   ****
*****               ******              ******                   *****
******              *****               *****                   ******
*******             ****                ****                   *******
********            ***                 ***                   ********
*********           **                  **                   *********
**********          *                   *                   **********
```

4.17   Collecting money becomes increasingly difficult during periods of recession, so companies may tighten their credit limits to prevent their accounts receivable (money owed to them) from becoming too large. In response to a prolonged recession, one company has cut its customer's credit limits in half. Thus, if a particular customer had a credit limit of $2000, this customer's credit limit is now $1000. If a customer had a credit limit of $5000, this customer's credit limit is now $2500. Write a program that analyzes the credit status of three customers of this company. For each customer you are given:

   a) The customer's account number
   b) The customer's credit limit before the recession
   c) The customer's current balance (i.e., the amount the customer owes the company).

   Your program should calculate and print the new credit limit for each customer and should determine (and print) which customers have current balances that exceed their new credit limits.

4.18   One interesting application of computers is drawing graphs and bar charts (sometimes called "histograms"). Write a program that reads five numbers (each between 1 and 30). For each number read, your program should print a line containing that number of adjacent asterisks. For example, if your program reads the number seven, it should print *******.

4.19   A mail order house sells five different products whose retail prices are shown in the following table:

Product number	Retail price
1	$ 2.98
2	$ 4.50
3	$ 9.98
4	$ 4.49
5	$ 6.87

Write a program that reads a series of pairs of numbers as follows:
    a) Product number
    b) Quantity sold for one day

Your program should use a `switch` statement to help determine the retail price for each product. Your program should calculate and display the total retail value of all products sold last week.

4.20   Complete the following truth tables by filling in each blank with 0 or 1.

Condition1	Condition2	Condition1 && Condition2
0	0	0
0	nonzero	0
nonzero	0	_____
nonzero	nonzero	_____

Condition1	Condition2	Condition1 || Condition2
0	0	0
0	nonzero	1
nonzero	0	_____
nonzero	nonzero	_____

Condition1	! Condition1
0	1
nonzero	_____

4.21   Rewrite the program of Fig. 4.2 so that the initialization of the variable `counter` is done in the definition instead of the `for` statement.

4.22   Modify the program of Fig. 4.7 so that it calculates the average grade for the class.

4.23   Modify the program of Fig. 4.6 so that it uses only integers to calculate the compound interest. [*Hint*: Treat all monetary amounts as integral numbers of pennies. Then "break" the result into its dollar portion and cents portion by using the division and remainder operations, respectively. Insert a period.]

4.24   Assume i = 1, j = 2, k = 3 and m = 2. What does each of the following statements print?
    a) `printf( "%d", i == 1 );`
    b) `printf( "%d", j == 3 );`
    c) `printf( "%d", i >= 1 && j < 4 );`
    d) `printf( "%d", m < = 99 && k < m );`
    e) `printf( "%d", j >= i || k == m );`
    f) `printf( "%d", k + m < j || 3 - j >= k );`
    g) `printf( "%d", !m );`
    h) `printf( "%d", !( j - m ) );`

```
    i) printf( "%d", !( k > m ) );
    j) printf( "%d", !( j > k ) );
```

4.25   Print a table of decimal, binary, octal, and hexadecimal equivalents. If you are not familiar with these number systems, read Appendix E first if you would like to attempt this exercise.

4.26   Calculate the value of π from the infinite series

$$\pi = 4 - \frac{4}{3} + \frac{4}{5} - \frac{4}{7} + \frac{4}{9} - \frac{4}{11} + \cdots$$

Print a table that shows the value of π approximated by one term of this series, by two terms, by three terms, etc. How many terms of this series do you have to use before you first get 3.14? 3.141? 3.1415? 3.14159?

4.27   *(Pythagorean Triples)* A right triangle can have sides that are all integers. The set of three integer values for the sides of a right triangle is called a Pythagorean triple. These three sides must satisfy the relationship that the sum of the squares of two of the sides is equal to the square of the hypotenuse. Find all Pythagorean triples for side1, side2, and the hypotenuse all no larger than 500. Use a triple-nested for loop that simply tries all possibilities. This is an example of "brute force" computing. It is not aesthetically pleasing to many people. But there are many reasons why these techniques are important. First, with computing power increasing at such a phenomenal pace, solutions that would have taken years or even centuries of computer time to produce with the technology of just a few years ago can now be produced in hours, minutes or even seconds. Recent microprocessor chips can process a billion instructions per second! Second, as you will learn in more advanced computer science courses, there are large numbers of interesting problems for which there is no known algorithmic approach other than sheer brute force. We investigate many kinds of problem-solving methodologies in this book. We will consider many brute force approaches to various interesting problems.

4.28   A company pays its employees as managers (who receive a fixed weekly salary), hourly workers (who receive a fixed hourly wage for up to the first 40 hours they work and "time-and-a-half"—i.e., 1.5 times their hourly wage—for overtime hours worked), commission workers (who receive a $250 plus 5.7% of their gross weekly sales), or pieceworkers (who receive a fixed amount of money per item for each of the items they produce—each pieceworker in this company works on only one type of item). Write a program to compute the weekly pay for each employee. You do not know the number of employees in advance. Each type of employee has its own pay code: Managers have paycode 1, hourly workers have code 2, commission workers have code 3 and pieceworkers have code 4. Use a switch to compute each employee's pay based on that employee's paycode. Within the switch, prompt the user (i.e., the payroll clerk) to enter the appropriate facts your program needs to calculate each employee's pay based on that employee's paycode.

4.29   *(De Morgan's Laws)* In this chapter, we discussed the logical operators &&, ||, and !. De Morgan's Laws can sometimes make it more convenient for us to express a logical expression. These laws state that the expression !(*condition1* && *condition2*) is logically equivalent to the expression (!*condition1* || !*condition2*). Also, the expression !(*condition1* || *condition2*) is logically equivalent to the expression (!*condition1* && !*condition2*). Use De Morgan's Laws to write equivalent expressions for each of the following, and then write a program to show that both the original expression and the new expression in each case are equivalent.

```
    a) !( x < 5 ) && !( y >= 7 )
    b) !( a == b ) || !( g != 5 )
    c) !( ( x <= 8 ) && ( y > 4 ) )
    d) !( ( i > 4 ) || ( j <= 6 ) )
```

4.30   Rewrite the program of Fig. 4.7 by replacing the `switch` statement with a nested `if...else` statement; be careful to deal with the `default` case properly. Then rewrite this new version by replacing the nested `if...else` statement with a series of `if` statements; here, too, be careful to deal with the `default` case properly (this is more difficult than in the nested `if...else` version). This exercise demonstrates that `switch` is a convenience and that any `switch` statement can be written with only single-selection statements.

4.31   Write a program that prints the following diamond shape. You may use `printf` statements that print either a single asterisk (*) or a single blank. Maximize your use of repetition (with nested `for` statements) and minimize the number of `printf` statements.

```
        *
       ***
      *****
     *******
    *********
     *******
      *****
       ***
        *
```

4.32   Modify the program you wrote in Exercise 4.31 to read an odd number in the range 1 to 19 to specify the number of rows in the diamond. Your program should then display a diamond of the appropriate size.

4.33   Write a program that prints a table of all the Roman numeral equivalents of the decimal numbers in the range 1 to 100.

4.34   Write a program that prints a table of the binary, octal and hexadecimal equivalents of the decimal numbers in the range 1 through 256. If you are not familiar with these number systems, read Appendix E before you attempt this exercise.

4.35   Describe the process you would use to replace a `do...while` loop with an equivalent `while` loop. What problem occurs when you try to replace a `while` loop with an equivalent `do...while` loop? Suppose you have been told that you must remove a `while` loop and replace it with a `do...while`. What additional control statement would you need to use and how would you use it to ensure that the resulting program behaves exactly as the original?

4.36   Write a program that inputs the year in the range 1994 through 1999 and uses `for`-loop repetition to produce a condensed, neatly printed calendar. Watch out for leap years.

4.37   A criticism of the `break` statement and the `continue` statement is that each is unstructured. Actually, `break` statements and `continue` statements can always be replaced by structured statements, although doing so can be awkward. Describe in general how you would remove any `break` statement from a loop in a program and replace that statement with some structured equivalent. [*Hint*: The `break` statement leaves a loop from within the body of the loop. The other way to leave is by failing the loop-continuation test. Consider using in the loop-continuation test a second test that indicates "early exit because of a 'break' condition."] Use the technique you developed here to remove the break statement from the program of Fig. 4.11.

4.38   What does the following program segment do?

```
1    for ( i = 1; i <= 5; i++ ) {
2       for ( j = 1; j <= 3; j++ ) {
3          for ( k = 1; k <= 4; k++ )
4             printf( "*" );
5          printf( "\n" );
6       }
7       printf( "\n" );
8    }
```

4.39   Describe in general how you would remove any `continue` statement from a loop in a program and replace that statement with some structured equivalent. Use the technique you developed here to remove the `continue` statement from the program of Fig. 4.12.

C Functions

Objectives

- To understand how to construct programs modularly from small pieces called functions.
- To introduce the common math functions available in the C standard library.
- To be able to create new functions.
- To understand the mechanisms used to pass information between functions.
- To introduce simulation techniques using random number generation.
- To understand how to write and use functions that call themselves.

Form ever follows function.
Louis Henri Sullivan

E pluribus unum.
(One composed of many.)
Virgil

O! call back yesterday, bid time return.
William Shakespeare
Richard II

Call me Ishmael.
Herman Melville
Moby Dick

When you call me that, smile.
Owen Wister

Outline

Summary • Terminology • Common Programming Errors • Error-Prevention Tips • Good Programming Practices • Performance Tips • Portability Tips • Software Engineering Observations • Self-Review Exercises • Answers to Self-Review Exercises • Exercises

5.1 Introduction

Most computer programs that solve real-world problems are much larger than the programs presented in the first few chapters. Experience has shown that the best way to develop and maintain a large program is to construct it from smaller pieces or *modules* each of which is more manageable than the original program. This technique is called *divide and conquer.* This chapter describes the features of the C language that facilitate the design, implementation, operation, and maintenance of large programs.

5.2 Program Modules in C

Modules in C are called *functions.* C programs are typically written by combining new functions the programmer writes with "pre-packaged" functions available in the *C standard library.* We discuss both kinds of functions in this chapter. The C standard library provides a rich collection of functions for performing common mathematical calculations, string manipulations, character manipulations, input/output, and many other useful operations. This makes the programmer's job easier because these functions provide many of the capabilities programmers need.

Good Programming Practice 5.1

Familiarize yourself with the rich collection of functions in the C standard library.

Software Engineering Observation 5.1

Avoid "reinventing the wheel." When possible, use C standard library functions instead of writing new functions. This can reduce program development time.

Portability Tip 5.1

Using the functions in the C standard library helps make programs more portable.

Although the standard library functions are technically not a part of the C language, they are invariably provided with C systems. The functions printf, scanf and pow that we have used in previous chapters are standard library functions.

The programmer can write functions to define specific tasks that may be used at many points in a program. These are sometimes referred to as *programmer-defined functions*. The actual statements defining the function are written only once, and the statements are hidden from other functions.

Functions are *invoked* by a *function call*, which specifies the function name and provides information (as *arguments*) that the called function needs in order to perform its designated task. A common analogy for this is the hierarchical form of management. A boss (the *calling function* or *caller*) asks a worker (the *called function*) to perform a task and report back when the task is done (Fig. 5.1). For example, a function that wants to display information on the screen calls the worker function printf to perform that task, then printf displays the information and reports back—or *returns*—to the calling function when its task is completed. The boss function does not know how the worker function performs its designated tasks. The worker may call other worker functions, and the boss will be unaware of this. We will soon see how this "hiding" of implementation details promotes good software engineering. Figure 5.1 shows the main function communicating with several worker functions in a hierarchical manner. Note that worker1 acts as a boss function to worker4 and worker5. Relationships among functions may be other than the hierarchical structure shown in this figure.

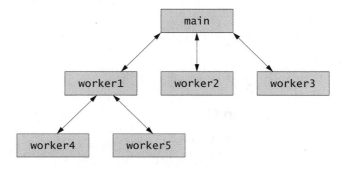

Fig. 5.1   Hierarchical boss function/worker function relationship.

5.3 Math Library Functions

Math library functions allow the programmer to perform certain common mathematical calculations. We use various math library functions here to introduce the concept of functions. Later in the book, we will discuss many of the other functions in the C standard library.

Functions are normally used in a program by writing the name of the function followed by a left parenthesis followed by the *argument* (or a comma separated list of arguments) of the function followed by a right parenthesis. For example, a programmer desiring to calculate and print the square root of 900.0 might write

```
printf( "%.2f", sqrt( 900.0 ) );
```

When this statement is executed, the math library function sqrt is called to calculate the square root of the number contained in the parentheses (900.0). The number 900.0 is the argument of the sqrt function. The preceding statement would print 30.00. The sqrt function takes an argument of type double and returns a result of type double. All functions in the math library return the data type double. Note that double values, like float values, can be output using the %f conversion specification.

Error-Prevention Tip 5.1

Include the math header by using the preprocessor directive #include <math.h> when using functions in the math library.

Function arguments may be constants, variables, or expressions. If c1 = 13.0, d = 3.0 and f = 4.0, then the statement

```
printf( "%.2f", sqrt( c1 + d * f ) );
```

calculates and prints the square root of 13.0 + 3.0 * 4.0 = 25.0, namely 5.00.

Some C math library functions are summarized in Fig. 5.2. In the figure, the variables x and y are of type double.

Function	Description	Example
sqrt(x)	square root of x	sqrt(900.0) is 30.0 sqrt(9.0) is 3.0
exp(x)	exponential function e^x	exp(1.0) is 2.718282 exp(2.0) is 7.389056
log(x)	natural logarithm of x (base e)	log(2.718282) is 1.0 log(7.389056) is 2.0
log10(x)	logarithm of x (base 10)	log10(1.0) is 0.0 log10(10.0) is 1.0 log10(100.0) is 2.0
fabs(x)	absolute value of x	fabs(5.0) is 5.0 fabs(0.0) is 0.0 fabs(-5.0) is 5.0
ceil(x)	rounds x to the smallest integer not less than x	ceil(9.2) is 10.0 ceil(-9.8) is -9.0
floor(x)	rounds x to the largest integer not greater than x	floor(9.2) is 9.0 floor(-9.8) is -10.0
pow(x, y)	x raised to power y (x^y)	pow(2, 7) is 128.0 pow(9, .5) is 3.0

Fig. 5.2   Commonly used math library functions. (Part 1 of 2.)

Function	Description	Example
fmod(x, y)	remainder of *x*/*y* as a floating point number	fmod(13.657, 2.333) is 1.992
sin(x)	trigonometric sine of *x* (*x* in radians)	sin(0.0) is 0.0
cos(x)	trigonometric cosine of *x* (*x* in radians)	cos(0.0) is 1.0
tan(x)	trigonometric tangent of *x* (*x* in radians)	tan(0.0) is 0.0

Fig. 5.2   Commonly used math library functions. (Part 2 of 2.)

5.4 Functions

Functions allow the programmer to modularize a program. All variables defined in function definitions are *local variables*—they are known only in the function in which they are defined. Most functions have a list of *parameters*. The parameters provide the means for communicating information between functions. A function's parameters are also local variables of that function.

Software Engineering Observation 5.2

In programs containing many functions, main *is often implemented as a group of calls to functions that perform the bulk of the program's work.*

There are several motivations for "functionalizing" a program. The divide-and-conquer approach makes program development more manageable. Another motivation is *software reusability*—using existing functions as building blocks to create new programs. Software reusability is a major factor in the object-oriented programming movement that you will learn more about when you study languages derived from C such as C++, Java and C# (pronounced "C sharp"). With good function naming and definition, programs can be created from standardized functions that accomplish specific tasks, rather than being built by using customized code. This technique is known as *abstraction*. We use abstraction each time we write programs including standard library functions like printf, scanf and pow. A third motivation is to avoid repeating code in a program. Packaging code as a function allows the code to be executed from several locations in a program simply by calling the function.

Software Engineering Observation 5.3

Each function should be limited to performing a single, well-defined task, and the function name should effectively express that task. This facilitates abstraction and promotes software reusability.

Software Engineering Observation 5.4

If you cannot choose a concise name that expresses what the function does, it is possible that your function is attempting to perform too many diverse tasks. It is usually best to break such a function into several smaller functions.

5.5 Function Definitions

Each program we have presented has consisted of a function called `main` that called standard library functions to accomplish its tasks. We now consider how programmers write their own customized functions.

Consider a program that uses a function `square` to calculate and print the squares of the integers from 1 to 10 (Fig. 5.3).

```c
1   /* Fig. 5.3: fig05_03.c
2      Creating and using a programmer-defined function */
3   #include <stdio.h>
4
5   int square( int y ); /* function prototype */
6
7   /* function main begins program execution */
8   int main()
9   {
10     int x; /* counter */
11
12     /* loop 10 times and calculate and output square of x each time */
13     for ( x = 1; x <= 10; x++ ) {
14        printf( "%d  ", square( x ) ); /* function call */
15     } /* end for */
16
17     printf( "\n" );
18
19     return 0; /* indicates successful termination */
20
21   } /* end main */
22
23   /* square function definition returns square of parameter */
24   int square( int y ) /* y is a copy of argument to function */
25   {
26     return y * y; /* returns square of y as an int */
27
28   } /* end function square */
```

```
1  4  9  16  25  36  49  64  81  100
```

Fig. 5.3   Using a programmer-defined function.

Good Programming Practice 5.2

Place a blank line between function definitions to separate the functions and enhance program readability.

Function `square` is *invoked* or *called* in `main` within the `printf` statement (line 14)

```c
printf( "%d  ", square( x ) ); /* function call */
```

Function `square` receives a copy of the value of `x` in the *parameter* `y` (line 24). Then `square` calculates `y * y` (line 26). The result is passed back to function `printf` in `main` where `square` was invoked, and `printf` displays the result. This process is repeated ten times using the `for` repetition statement.

The definition of function `square` shows that `square` expects an integer parameter y. The keyword `int` preceding the function name (line 24) indicates that `square` returns an integer result. The `return` statement in `square` passes the result of the calculation back to the calling function.

Line 5

```
int square( int y ); /* function prototype */
```

is a *function prototype*. The `int` in parentheses informs the compiler that `square` expects to receive an integer value from the caller. The `int` to the left of the function name `square` informs the compiler that `square` returns an integer result to the caller. The compiler refers to the function prototype to check that calls to `square` (line 14) contain the correct return type, the correct number of arguments, the correct argument types, and that the arguments are in the correct order. Function prototypes are discussed in detail in Section 5.6.

The format of a function definition is

> *return-value-type function-name(parameter-list)*
> {
>   *definitions*
>   *statements*
> }

The *function-name* is any valid identifier. The *return-value-type* is the data type of the result returned to the caller. The *return-value-type* `void` indicates that a function does not return a value. An unspecified *return-value-type* is assumed by the compiler to be `int`. However, omitting the return type is discouraged. Together, the *return-value-type*, *function-name* and *parameter-list* are sometimes referred to as the *function header*.

Common Programming Error 5.1

Omitting the return-value-type in a function definition is a syntax error if the function prototype specifies a return type other than `int`.

Common Programming Error 5.2

Forgetting to return a value from a function that is supposed to return a value can lead to unexpected errors. The C standard states that the result of this omission is undefined.

Common Programming Error 5.3

Returning a value from a function with a `void` return type is a syntax error.

Good Programming Practice 5.3

Even though an omitted return type defaults to `int`, always state the return type explicitly.

The *parameter-list* is a comma-separated list that specifies the parameters received by the function when it is called. If a function does not receive any values, *parameter-list* is `void`. A type must be listed explicitly for each parameter unless the parameter is of type `int`. If a type is not listed, `int` is assumed.

Common Programming Error 5.4

Specifying function parameters of the same type as `double x, y` *instead of* `double x, double y` *might cause errors in your programs. The parameter declaration* `double x, y` *would actually make* `y` *a parameter of type* `int` *because* `int` *is the default.*

Common Programming Error 5.5

Placing a semicolon after the right parenthesis enclosing the parameter list of a function definition is a syntax error.

Common Programming Error 5.6

Defining a function parameter again as a local variable within the function is a syntax error.

Good Programming Practice 5.4

Include the type of each parameter in the parameter list, even if that parameter is of the default type `int`.

Good Programming Practice 5.5

Although it is not incorrect to do so, do not use the same names for the arguments passed to a function and the corresponding parameters in the function definition. This helps avoid ambiguity.

The *definitions* and *statements* within braces form the *function body*. The function body is also referred to as a *block*. Variables can be declared in any block, and blocks can be nested. *A function cannot be defined inside another function under any circumstances.*

Common Programming Error 5.7

Defining a function inside another function is a syntax error.

Good Programming Practice 5.6

Choosing meaningful function names and meaningful parameter names makes programs more readable and helps avoid excessive use of comments.

Software Engineering Observation 5.5

A function should be no longer than one page. Better yet, a function should be no longer than half a page. Small functions promote software reusability.

Software Engineering Observation 5.6

Programs should be written as collections of small functions. This makes programs easier to write, debug, maintain and modify.

Software Engineering Observation 5.7

A function requiring a large number of parameters may be performing too many tasks. Consider dividing the function into smaller functions that perform the separate tasks. The function header should fit on one line if possible.

Software Engineering Observation 5.8

The function prototype, function header and function calls should all agree in the number, type, and order of arguments and parameters, and in the type of return value.

There are three ways to return control from a called function to the point at which a function was invoked. If the function does not return a result, control is returned simply when the function-ending right brace is reached, or by executing the statement

```
return;
```

If the function does return a result, the statement

```
return expression;
```

returns the value of *expression* to the caller.

Our second example uses a programmer-defined function `maximum` to determine and return the largest of three integers (Fig. 5.4). The three integers are input with `scanf` (line 15). Next, the integers are passed to `maximum` (line 19) which determines the largest integer. This value is returned to main by the `return` statement in `maximum` (line 39). The value returned is then printed in the `printf` statement (line 19).

```c
1   /* Fig. 5.4: fig05_04.c
2      Finding the maximum of three integers */
3   #include <stdio.h>
4
5   int maximum( int x, int y, int z ); /* function prototype */
6
7   /* function main begins program execution */
8   int main()
9   {
10     int number1; /* first integer */
11     int number2; /* second integer */
12     int number3; /* third integer */
13
14     printf( "Enter three integers: " );
15     scanf( "%d%d%d", &number1, &number2, &number3 );
16
17     /* number1, number2 and number3 are arguments
18        to the maximum function call */
19     printf( "Maximum is: %d\n", maximum( number1, number2, number3 ) );
20
21     return 0; /* indicates successful termination */
22
23   } /* end main */
24
25   /* Function maximum definition */
26   /* x, y and z are parameters */
27   int maximum( int x, int y, int z )
28   {
29      int max = x;      /* assume x is largest */
30
31      if ( y > max ) { /* if y is larger than max, assign y to max */
32         max = y;
33      } /* end if */
34
```

Fig. 5.4   Programmer-defined `maximum` function. (Part 1 of 2.)

```
35      if ( z > max ) { /* if z is larger than max, assign z to max */
36         max = z;
37      } /* end if */
38
39      return max;        /* max is largest value */
40
41  } /* end function maximum */
```

```
Enter three integers: 22 85 17
Maximum is: 85
```

```
Enter three integers: 85 22 17
Maximum is: 85
```

```
Enter three integers: 22 17 85
Maximum is: 85
```

Fig. 5.4   Programmer-defined `maximum` function. (Part 2 of 2.)

5.6 Function Prototypes

One of the most important features of C is the *function prototype.* This feature was borrowed by the C standard committee from the developers of C++. A function prototype tells the compiler the type of data returned by the function, the number of parameters the function expects to receive, the types of the parameters, and the order in which these parameters are expected. The compiler uses function prototypes to validate function calls. Previous versions of C did not perform this kind of checking, so it was possible to call functions improperly without the compiler detecting the errors. Such calls could result in fatal execution-time errors or nonfatal errors that caused subtle, difficult to detect logic errors. Function prototypes correct this deficiency.

Good Programming Practice 5.7

Include function prototypes for all functions to take advantage of C's type checking capabilities. Use `#include` preprocessor directives to obtain function prototypes for the standard library functions from the headers for the appropriate libraries, or to obtain headers containing function prototypes for functions developed by you and/or your group members.

The function prototype for `maximum` in Fig. 5.4 (line 5) is

```
int maximum( int x, int y, int z ); /* function prototype */
```

This function prototype states that `maximum` takes three arguments of type `int`, and returns a result of type `int`. Notice that the function prototype is the same as the first line of the function definition of `maximum`.

Good Programming Practice 5.8

Parameter names are sometimes included in function prototypes (our preference) for documentation purposes. The compiler ignores these names.

Common Programming Error 5.8

Forgetting the semicolon at the end of a function prototype is a syntax error.

A function call that does not match the function prototype is a syntax error. An error is also generated if the function prototype and the function definition disagree. For example, in Fig. 5.4, if the function prototype had been written

```
void maximum( int x, int y, int z );
```

the compiler would generate an error because the void return type in the function prototype would differ from the int return type in the function header.

Another important feature of function prototypes is the *coercion of arguments,* i.e., the forcing of arguments to the appropriate type. For example, the math library function sqrt can be called with an integer argument even though the function prototype in math.h specifies a double argument, and the function will still work correctly. The statement

```
printf( "%.3f\n", sqrt( 4 ) );
```

correctly evaluates sqrt(4), and prints the value 2.000. The function prototype causes the compiler to convert the integer value 4 to the double value 4.0 before the value is passed to sqrt. In general, argument values that do not correspond precisely to the parameter types in the function prototype are converted to the proper type before the function is called. These conversions can lead to incorrect results if C's *promotion rules* are not followed. The promotion rules specify how types can be converted to other types without losing data. In our sqrt example above, an int is automatically converted to a double without changing its value. However, a double converted to an int truncates the fractional part of the double value. Converting large integer types to small integer types (e.g., long to short) may also result in changed values.

The promotion rules automatically apply to expressions containing values of two or more data types (also referred to as *mixed-type* expressions). The type of each value in a mixed-type expression is automatically promoted to the "highest" type in the expression (actually a temporary version of each value is created and used for the expression—the original values remain unchanged). Figure 5.5 lists the data types in order from highest type to lowest type with each type's printf and scanf conversion specifications.

Data type	printf conversion specification	scanf conversion specification
long double	%Lf	%Lf
double	%f	%lf
float	%f	%f
unsigned long int	%lu	%lu
long int	%ld	%ld
unsigned int	%u	%u
int	%d	%d
short	%hd	%hd
char	%c	%c

Fig. 5.5   Promotion hierarchy for data types.

Converting values to lower types normally results in an incorrect value. Therefore, a value can only be converted to a lower type by explicitly assigning the value to a variable of lower type, or by using a cast operator. Function argument values are converted to the parameter types in a function prototype as if they are being assigned directly to variables of those types. If our `square` function that uses an integer parameter (Fig. 5.3) is called with a floating point argument, the argument is converted to `int` (a lower type), and `square` usually returns an incorrect value. For example, `square( 4.5 )` returns `16` not `20.25`.

Common Programming Error 5.9

Converting from a higher data type in the promotion hierarchy to a lower type can change the data value.

If the function prototype for a function has not been included in a program, the compiler forms its own function prototype using the first occurrence of the function—either the function definition or a call to the function. By default, the compiler assumes the function returns an `int`, and nothing is assumed about the arguments. Therefore, if the arguments passed to the function are incorrect, the errors are not detected by the compiler.

Common Programming Error 5.10

Forgetting a function prototype causes a syntax error if the return type of the function is not `int` and the function definition appears after the function call in the program. Otherwise, forgetting a function prototype may cause a run-time error or an unexpected result.

Software Engineering Observation 5.9

A function prototype placed outside any function definition applies to all calls to the function appearing after the function prototype in the file. A function prototype placed in a function applies only to calls made in that function.

5.7 Headers

Each standard library has a corresponding *header* containing the function prototypes for all the functions in that library and definitions of various data types and constants needed by those functions. Figure 5.6 lists alphabetically some of the standard library headers that may be included in programs. The term "macros" that is used several times in Fig. 5.6 is discussed in detail in Chapter 13, C Preprocessor.

Standard library header	Explanation
`<assert.h>`	Contains macros and information for adding diagnostics that aid program debugging.
`<ctype.h>`	Contains function prototypes for functions that test characters for certain properties, and function prototypes for functions that can be used to convert lowercase letters to uppercase letters and vice versa.
`<errno.h>`	Defines macros that are useful for reporting error conditions.
`<float.h>`	Contains the floating point size limits of the system.
`<limits.h>`	Contains the integral size limits of the system.

Fig. 5.6   Some of the standard library headers. (Part 1 of 2.)

Standard library header	Explanation
`<locale.h>`	Contains function prototypes and other information that enables a program to be modified for the current locale on which it is running. The notion of locale enables the computer system to handle different conventions for expressing data like dates, times, dollar amounts and large numbers throughout the world.
`<math.h>`	Contains function prototypes for math library functions.
`<setjmp.h>`	Contains function prototypes for functions that allow bypassing of the usual function call and return sequence.
`<signal.h>`	Contains function prototypes and macros to handle various conditions that may arise during program execution.
`<stdarg.h>`	Defines macros for dealing with a list of arguments to a function whose number and types are unknown.
`<stddef.h>`	Contains common definitions of types used by C for performing certain calculations.
`<stdio.h>`	Contains function prototypes for the standard input/output library functions, and information used by them.
`<stdlib.h>`	Contains function prototypes for conversions of numbers to text and text to numbers, memory allocation, random numbers, and other utility functions.
`<string.h>`	Contains function prototypes for string processing functions.
`<time.h>`	Contains function prototypes and types for manipulating the time and date.

Fig. 5.6 Some of the standard library headers. (Part 2 of 2.)

The programmer can create custom headers. Programmer-defined headers should also end in `.h`. A programmer-defined header can be included by using the `#include` preprocessor directive. For example, if the prototype for our square function was located in the header `square.h`, we would include that header in our program by using the following directive at the top of the program:

```
#include "square.h"
```

Section 13.2 presents additional information on including headers.

5.8 Calling Functions: Call by Value and Call by Reference

Two ways to invoke functions in many programming languages are *call by value* and *call by reference*. When arguments are passed by value, a *copy* of the argument's value is made and passed to the called function. Changes to the copy do not affect an original variable's value in the caller. When an argument is passed by reference, the caller actually allows the called function to modify the original variable's value.

Call by value should be used whenever the called function does not need to modify the value of the caller's original variable. This prevents the accidental *side effects* that so greatly hinder the development of correct and reliable software systems. Call by reference should only be used with trusted called functions that need to modify the original variable.

In C, all calls are by value. As we will see in Chapter 7, it is possible to *simulate* call by reference by using address operators and indirection operators. In Chapter 6, we will see that arrays are automatically passed simulated call by reference. We will have to wait until Chapter 7 for a full understanding of this complex issue. For now, we concentrate on call by value.

5.9 Random Number Generation

We now take a brief and, hopefully, entertaining diversion into a popular programming application, namely simulation and game playing. In this and the next section, we will develop a nicely structured game-playing program that includes multiple functions. The program uses most of the control structures we have studied.

There is something in the air of a gambling casino that invigorates every type of person from the high-rollers at the plush mahogany-and-felt craps tables to the quarter-poppers at the one-armed bandits. It is the *element of chance,* the possibility that luck will convert a mere pocketful of money into a mountain of wealth. The element of chance can be introduced into computer applications by using the `rand` function in the C standard library.

Consider the following statement:

```
i = rand();
```

The `rand` function generates an integer between 0 and RAND_MAX (a symbolic constant defined in the `<stdlib.h>` header). The ANSI standard states that the value of RAND_MAX must be at least 32767 which is the maximum value for a two-byte (i.e., 16-bit) integer. The programs in this section were tested on a C system with a maximum value of 32767 for RAND_MAX. If `rand` truly produces integers at random, every number between 0 and RAND_MAX has an equal *chance* (or *probability*) of being chosen each time `rand` is called.

The range of values produced directly by `rand` is often different than what is needed in a specific application. For example, a program that simulates coin tossing might require only 0 for "heads" and 1 for "tails." A dice-rolling program that simulates a six-sided die would require random integers in range 1 to 6.

To demonstrate `rand`, let us develop a program to simulate 20 rolls of a six-sided die and print the value of each roll. The function prototype for function `rand` can be found in `<stdlib.h>`. We use the remainder operator (%) in conjunction with `rand` as follows

```
rand() % 6
```

to produce integers in the range 0 to 5. This is called *scaling*. The number 6 is called the *scaling factor*. We then *shift* the range of numbers produced by adding 1 to our previous result. The output of Fig. 5.7 confirms that the results are in the range 1 to 6.

```
1   /* Fig. 5.7: fig05_07.c
2      Shifted, scaled integers produced by 1 + rand() % 6 */
3   #include <stdio.h>
4   #include <stdlib.h>
5
6   /* function main begins program execution */
7   int main()
8   {
```

Fig. 5.7   Shifted, scaled random integers produced by `1 + rand() % 6`. (Part 1 of 2.)

```
 9      int i; /* counter */
10
11      /* loop 20 times */
12      for ( i = 1; i <= 20; i++ ) {
13
14         /* pick random number from 1 to 6 and output it */
15         printf( "%10d", 1 + ( rand() % 6 ) );
16
17         /* if counter is divisible by 5, begin new line of output */
18         if ( i % 5 == 0 ) {
19            printf( "\n" );
20         } /* end if */
21
22      } /* end for */
23
24      return 0; /* indicates successful termination */
25
26   } /* end main */
```

6	6	5	5	6
5	1	1	5	3
6	6	2	4	2
6	2	3	4	1

Fig. 5.7   Shifted, scaled random integers produced by 1 + rand() % 6. (Part 2 of 2.)

To show that these numbers occur approximately with equal likelihood, let us simulate 6000 rolls of a die with the program of Fig. 5.8. Each integer from 1 to 6 should appear approximately 1000 times.

```
 1   /* Fig. 5.8: fig05_08.c
 2      Roll a six-sided die 6000 times */
 3   #include <stdio.h>
 4   #include <stdlib.h>
 5
 6   /* function main begins program execution */
 7   int main()
 8   {
 9      int frequency1 = 0; /* rolled 1 counter */
10      int frequency2 = 0; /* rolled 2 counter */
11      int frequency3 = 0; /* rolled 3 counter */
12      int frequency4 = 0; /* rolled 4 counter */
13      int frequency5 = 0; /* rolled 5 counter */
14      int frequency6 = 0; /* rolled 6 counter */
15
16      int roll; /* roll counter, value 1 to 6000 */
17      int face; /* represents one roll of the die, value 1 to 6 */
18
19      /* loop 6000 times and summarize results */
20      for ( roll = 1; roll <= 6000; roll++ ) {
```

Fig. 5.8   Rolling a six-sided die 6000 times. (Part 1 of 2.)

```
21          face = 1 + rand() % 6; /* random number from 1 to 6 */
22
23          /* determine face value and increment appropriate counter */
24          switch ( face ) {
25
26             case 1: /* rolled 1 */
27                ++frequency1;
28                break;
29
30             case 2: /* rolled 2 */
31                ++frequency2;
32                break;
33
34             case 3: /* rolled 3 */
35                ++frequency3;
36                break;
37
38             case 4: /* rolled 4 */
39                ++frequency4;
40                break;
41
42             case 5: /* rolled 5 */
43                ++frequency5;
44                break;
45
46             case 6: /* rolled 6 */
47                ++frequency6;
48                break; /* optional */
49          } /* end switch */
50
51       } /* end for */
52
53       /* display results in tabular format */
54       printf( "%s%13s\n", "Face", "Frequency" );
55       printf( "   1%13d\n", frequency1 );
56       printf( "   2%13d\n", frequency2 );
57       printf( "   3%13d\n", frequency3 );
58       printf( "   4%13d\n", frequency4 );
59       printf( "   5%13d\n", frequency5 );
60       printf( "   6%13d\n", frequency6 );
61
62       return 0; /* indicates successful termination */
63
64    } /* end main */
```

```
Face      Frequency
   1          1003
   2          1017
   3           983
   4           994
   5          1004
   6           999
```

Fig. 5.8   Rolling a six-sided die 6000 times. (Part 2 of 2.)

As the program output shows, by scaling and shifting we have utilized the rand function to realistically simulate the rolling of a six-sided die. Note that *no* default case is provided in the switch statement. Also note the use of the %s conversion specifier to print the character strings "Face" and "Frequency" as column headers (line 54). After we study arrays in Chapter 6, we will show how to replace this entire switch statement elegantly with a single-line statement. Executing the program of Fig. 5.7 again produces

```
6        6        5        5        6
5        1        1        5        3
6        6        2        4        2
6        2        3        4        1
```

Notice that exactly the same sequence of values was printed. How can these be random numbers? Ironically, this repeatability is an important characteristic of function rand. When debugging a program, this repeatability is essential for proving that corrections to a program work properly.

Function rand actually generates *pseudo-random numbers.* Calling rand repeatedly produces a sequence of numbers that appears to be random. However, the sequence repeats itself each time the program is executed. Once a program has been thoroughly debugged, it can be conditioned to produce a different sequence of random numbers for each execution. This is called *randomizing,* and is accomplished with the standard library function srand. Function srand takes an unsigned integer argument and *seeds* function rand to produce a different sequence of random numbers for each execution of the program.

The use of srand is demonstrated in Fig. 5.9. In the program, we use the data type unsigned which is short for unsigned int. An int is stored in at least two bytes of memory, and can have positive and negative values. A variable of type unsigned is also stored in at least two bytes of memory. A two-byte unsigned int can have only positive values in the range 0 to 65535. A four-byte unsigned int can have only positive values in the range 0 to 4294967295. Function srand takes an unsigned value as an argument. The conversion specifier %u is used to read an unsigned value with scanf. The function prototype for srand is found in <stdlib.h>.

```
1   /* Fig. 5.9: fig05_09.c
2      Randomizing die-rolling program */
3   #include <stdlib.h>
4   #include <stdio.h>
5
6   /* function main begins program execution */
7   int main()
8   {
9      int i;          /* counter */
10     unsigned seed;  /* number used to seed random number generator */
11
12     printf( "Enter seed: " );
13     scanf( "%u", &seed ); /* note %u for unsigned */
14
15     srand( seed ) /* seed random number generator */
```

Fig. 5.9   Randomizing the die-rolling program. (Part 1 of 2.)

```
16
17        /* loop 10 times */
18        for ( i = 1; i <= 10; i++ ) {
19
20            /* pick a random number from 1 to 6 and output it */
21            printf( "%10d", 1 + ( rand() % 6 ) );
22
23            /* if counter is divisible by 5, begin a new line of output */
24            if ( i % 5 == 0 ) {
25                printf( "\n" );
26            } /* end if */
27
28        } /* end for */
29
30        return 0; /* indicates successful termination */
31
32    } /* end main */
```

```
Enter seed: 67
         6         1         4         6         2
         1         6         1         6         4
```

```
Enter seed: 867
         2         4         6         1         6
         1         1         3         6         2
```

```
Enter seed: 67
         6         1         4         6         2
         1         6         1         6         4
```

Fig. 5.9   Randomizing the die-rolling program. (Part 2 of 2.)

Let us run the program several times and observe the results. Notice that a *different* sequence of random numbers is obtained each time the program is run, provided that a different seed is supplied.

If we wish to randomize without the need for entering a seed each time, we may use a statement like

```
srand( time( NULL ) );
```

This causes the computer to read its clock to obtain the value for the seed automatically. Function time returns the current time of day in seconds. This value is converted to an unsigned integer and used as the seed to the random number generator. Function time takes NULL as an argument (time is capable of providing the programmer with a string representing the time of day; NULL disables this capability for a specific call to time). The function prototype for time is in <time.h>.

The values produced directly by rand are always in the range:

```
0 ≤ rand() ≤ RAND_MAX
```

Previously we demonstrated how to write a single statement to simulate the rolling of a six-sided die:

```
face = 1 + rand() % 6;
```

This statement always assigns an integer value (at random) to the variable face in the range $1 \le face \le 6$. Note that the width of this range (i.e., the number of consecutive integers in the range) is 6 and the starting number in the range is 1. Referring to the preceding statement, we see that the width of the range is determined by the number used to scale rand with the remainder operator (i.e., 6), and the starting number of the range is equal to the number (i.e., 1) that is added to rand % 6. We can generalize this result as follows

```
n = a + rand() % b;
```

where a is the *shifting value* (which is equal to the first number in the desired range of consecutive integers), and b is the scaling factor (which is equal to the width of the desired range of consecutive integers). In the exercises, we will see that it is possible to choose integers at random from sets of values other than ranges of consecutive integers.

Common Programming Error 5.11

Using srand in place of rand to generate random numbers.

5.10 Example: A Game of Chance

One of the most popular games of chance is a dice game known as "craps," which is played in casinos and back alleys throughout the world. The rules of the game are straightforward:

> *A player rolls two dice. Each die has six faces. These faces contain 1, 2, 3, 4, 5, and 6 spots. After the dice have come to rest, the sum of the spots on the two upward faces is calculated. If the sum is 7 or 11 on the first throw, the player wins. If the sum is 2, 3, or 12 on the first throw (called "craps"), the player loses (i.e., the "house" wins). If the sum is 4, 5, 6, 8, 9, or 10 on the first throw, then that sum becomes the player's "point." To win, you must continue rolling the dice until you "make your point." The player loses by rolling a 7 before making the point.*

Figure 5.10 simulates the game of craps and Fig. 5.11 shows several sample executions.

```
1   /* Fig. 5.10: fig05_10.c
2      Craps */
3   #include <stdio.h>
4   #include <stdlib.h>
5   #include <time.h> /* contains prototype for function time */
6
7   /* enumeration constants represent game status */
8   enum Status { CONTINUE, WON, LOST };
9
10  int rollDice( void ); /* function prototype */
11
12  /* function main begins program execution */
13  int main()
14  {
15      int sum;          /* sum of rolled dice */
```

Fig. 5.10   Program to simulate the game of craps. (Part 1 of 3.)

```
16      int myPoint;    /* point earned */
17
18      enum Status gameStatus /* can contain CONTINUE, WON, or LOST */
19
20      /* randomize random number generator using current time */
21      srand( time( NULL ) );
22
23      sum = rollDice(); /* first roll of the dice */
24
25      /* determine game status based on sum of dice */
26      switch( sum ) {
27
28         /* win on first roll */
29         case 7:
30         case 11:
31            gameStatus = WON;
32            break;
33
34         /* lose on first roll */
35         case 2:
36         case 3:
37         case 12:
38            gameStatus = LOST;
39            break;
40
41         /* remember point */
42         default:
43            gameStatus = CONTINUE;
44            myPoint = sum;
45            printf( "Point is %d\n", myPoint );
46            break; /* optional */
47      } /* end switch */
48
49      /* while game not complete */
50      while ( gameStatus == CONTINUE ) {
51         sum = rollDice(); /* roll dice again */
52
53         /* determine game status */
54         if ( sum == myPoint ) { /* win by making point */
55            gameStatus = WON; /* game over, player won */
56         } /* end if */
57         else {
58
59            if ( sum == 7 ) { /* lose by rolling 7 */
60               gameStatus = LOST; /* game over, player lost */
61            } /* end if */
62
63         } /* end else */
64
65      } /* end while */
66
67      /* display won or lost message */
68      if ( gameStatus == WON ) { /* did player win? */
```

Fig. 5.10   Program to simulate the game of craps. (Part 2 of 3.)

```
69          printf( "Player wins\n" );
70       } /* end if */
71       else { /* player lost */
72          printf( "Player loses\n" );
73       } /* end else */
74
75       return 0; /* indicates successful termination */
76
77    } /* end main */
78
79    /* roll dice, calculate sum and display results */
80    int rollDice( void )
81    {
82       int die1;    /* first die */
83       int die2;    /* second die */
84       int workSum; /* sum of dice */
85
86       die1 = 1 + ( rand() % 6 ); /* pick random die1 value */
87       die2 = 1 + ( rand() % 6 ); /* pick random die2 value */
88       workSum = die1 + die2;     /* sum die1 and die2 */
89
90       /* display results of this roll */
91       printf( "Player rolled %d + %d = %d\n", die1, die2, workSum );
92
93       return workSum; /* return sum of dice */
94
95    } /* end function rollRice */
```

Fig. 5.10   Program to simulate the game of craps. (Part 3 of 3.)

```
Player rolled 5 + 6 = 11
Player wins
```

```
Player rolled 4 + 1 = 5
Point is 5
Player rolled 6 + 2 = 8
Player rolled 2 + 1 = 3
Player rolled 3 + 2 = 5
Player wins
```

```
Player rolled 1 + 1 = 2
Player loses
```

```
Player rolled 6 + 4 = 10
Point is 10
Player rolled 3 + 4 = 7
Player loses
```

Fig. 5.11   Sample runs for the game of craps.

In the rules of the game, notice that the player must roll two dice on the first roll, and must do so later on all subsequent rolls. We define a function `rollDice` to roll the dice and compute and print their sum. Function `rollDice` is defined once, but it is called from two places in the program (lines 23 and 51). Interestingly, `rollDice` takes no arguments, so we have indicated `void` in the parameter list (line 80). Function `rollDice` does return the sum of the two dice, so a return type of `int` is indicated in the function header.

The game is reasonably involved. The player may win or lose on the first roll, or may win or lose on any subsequent roll. Variable `gameStatus`, defined to be of a new type `enum Status`, stores the current status. Line 8 creates a programmer-defined type called an *enumeration*. An enumeration, introduced by the keyword *enum*, is a set of integer constants represented by identifiers. *Enumeration constants* are sometimes called symbolic constants—constants represented as symbols. Values in an `enum` start with 0 and are incremented by 1. In line 8, the constant CONTINUE has the value 0, WON has the value 1 and LOST has the value 2. It is also possible to assign an integer value to each identifier in an `enum` (see Chapter 13). The identifiers in an enumeration must be unique, but the values may be duplicated.

Common Programming Error 5.12

Assigning a value to an enumeration constant after it has been defined is a syntax error.

Good Programming Practice 5.9

Use only uppercase letters in the names of enumeration constants to make these constants stand out in a program and to indicate that enumeration constants are not variables.

When the game is won, either on the first roll or on a subsequent roll, `gameStatus` is set to WON. When the game is lost, either on the first roll or on a subsequent roll, `gameStatus` is set to LOST. Otherwise `gameStatus` is set to CONTINUE and the game continues.

After the first roll, if the game is over, the `while` statement (line 50) is skipped because `gameStatus` is not CONTINUE. The program proceeds to the `if...else` statement at line 68 which prints "Player wins" if `gameStatus` is WON and "Player loses" otherwise.

After the first roll, if the game is not over, then `sum` is saved in `myPoint`. Execution proceeds with the `while` statement (line 50) because `gameStatus` is CONTINUE. Each time through the `while`, `rollDice` is called to produce a new `sum`. If `sum` matches `myPoint`, `gameStatus` is set to WON to indicate that the player won, the `while`-test fails, the `if...else` statement (line 68) prints "Player wins" and execution terminates. If `sum` is equal to 7 (line 59), `gameStatus` is set to LOST to indicate that the player lost, the `while`-test fails, the `if...else` statement (line 68) prints "Player loses" and execution terminates.

Note the interesting control architecture of the program. We have used two functions—`main` and `rollDice`—and the `switch`, `while`, nested `if...else` and nested `if` statements. In the exercises, we will investigate various interesting characteristics of the game of craps.

5.11 Storage Classes

In Chapters 2 through 4, we used identifiers for variable names. The attributes of variables include name, type, size and value. In this chapter, we also use identifiers as names for user-defined functions. Actually, each identifier in a program has other attributes including *storage class*, *storage duration*, *scope* and *linkage*.

C provides four storage classes indicated by the *storage class specifiers: auto, register, extern* and *static*. An identifier's *storage class* determines its *storage duration*, *scope* and *linkage*. An identifier's *storage duration* is the period during which that identifier exists in memory. Some identifiers exist briefly, some are repeatedly created and destroyed, and others exist for the entire execution of a program. An identifier's *scope* is where the identifier can be referenced in a program. Some identifiers can be referenced throughout a program, others from only portions of a program. An identifier's *linkage* determines for a multiple-source-file program (a topic we will investigate in Chapter 14) whether the identifier is known only in the current source file or in any source file with proper declarations. This section discusses the four storage classes and storage duration. Section 5.12 discusses the scope of identifiers. Chapter 14, Other C Topics, discusses identifier linkage and programming with multiple source files.

The four storage class specifiers can be split into two storage durations: *automatic storage duration* and *static storage duration*. Keywords `auto` and `register` are used to declare variables of automatic storage duration. Variables with automatic storage duration are created when the block in which they are defined is entered; they exist while the block is active, and they are destroyed when the block is exited.

Only variables can have automatic storage duration. A function's local variables (those declared in the parameter list or in the function body) normally have automatic storage duration. Keyword `auto` explicitly declares variables of automatic storage duration. For example, the following declaration indicates that `double` variables x and y are automatic local variables and they exist only in the body of the function in which the declaration appears:

```
auto double x, y;
```

Local variables have automatic storage duration by default, so keyword `auto` is rarely used. For the remainder of the text, we will refer to variables with automatic storage duration simply as *automatic variables*.

Performance Tip 5.1

Automatic storage is a means of conserving memory because automatic variables exist only when they are needed. They are created when the function in which they are defined is entered and they are destroyed when the function is exited.

Software Engineering Observation 5.10

Automatic storage is an example of the principle of least privilege—*allowing access to data only when it is absolutely needed. Why have variables stored in memory and accessible when in fact they are not needed?*

Data in the machine language version of a program is normally loaded into registers for calculations and other processing.

Performance Tip 5.2

The storage class specifier `register` *can be placed before an automatic variable declaration to suggest that the compiler maintain the variable in one of the computer's high-speed hardware registers. If intensely used variables such as counters or totals can be maintained in hardware registers, the overhead of repeatedly loading the variables from memory into the registers and storing the results back into memory can be eliminated.*

The compiler may ignore `register` declarations. For example, there may not be a sufficient number of registers available for the compiler to use. The following declaration suggests that the integer variable `counter` be placed in one of the computer's registers and initialized to 1:

```
register int counter = 1;
```

Keyword `register` can be used only with variables of automatic storage duration.

Performance Tip 5.3

Often, `register` declarations are unnecessary. Today's optimizing compilers are capable of recognizing frequently used variables and can decide to place them in registers without the need for a `register` declaration from the programmer.

Keywords `extern` and `static` are used to declare identifiers for variables and functions of static storage duration. Identifiers of static storage duration exist from the point at which the program begins execution. For variables, storage is allocated and initialized once, when the program begins execution. For functions, the name of the function exists when the program begins execution. However, even though the variables and the function names exist from the start of program execution, this does not mean that these identifiers can be accessed throughout the program. Storage duration and scope (where a name can be used) are separate issues as we will see in Section 5.12.

There are two types of identifiers with static storage duration: external identifiers (such as global variables and function names) and local variables declared with the storage class specifier `static`. Global variables and function names are of storage class `extern` by default. Global variables are created by placing variable declarations outside any function definition, and they retain their values throughout the execution of the program. Global variables and functions can be referenced by any function that follows their declarations or definitions in the file. This is one reason for using function prototypes—when we include `stdio.h` in a program that calls `printf`, the function prototype is placed at the start of our file to make the name `printf` known to the rest of the file.

Software Engineering Observation 5.11

Defining a variable as global rather than local allows unintended side effects to occur when a function that does not need access to the variable accidentally or maliciously modifies it. In general, use of global variables should be avoided except in certain situations with unique performance requirements (as discussed in Chapter 14).

Software Engineering Observation 5.12

Variables used only in a particular function should be defined as local variables in that function rather than as external variables.

Local variables declared with the keyword `static` are still known only in the function in which they are defined, but unlike automatic variables, `static` local variables retain their value when the function is exited. The next time the function is called, the `static` local variable contains the value it had when the function last exited. The following statement declares local variable `count` to be `static` and to be initialized to 1.

```
static int count = 1;
```

All numeric variables of static storage duration are initialized to zero if they are not explicitly initialized by the programmer.

Common Programming Error 5.13

Using multiple storage class specifiers for an identifier. Only one storage class specifier can be applied to an identifier.

Keywords `extern` and `static` have special meaning when explicitly applied to external identifiers. In Chapter 14, Other C Topics, we discuss the explicit use of `extern` and `static` with external identifiers and multiple-source-file programs.

5.12 Scope Rules

The *scope* of an identifier is the portion of the program in which the identifier can be referenced. For example, when we define a local variable in a block, it can be referenced only in that block or in blocks nested within that block. The four scopes for an identifier are *function scope, file scope, block scope,* and *function-prototype scope.*

Labels (an identifier followed by a colon such as `start:`) are the only identifiers with *function scope.* Labels can be used anywhere in the function in which they appear, but can not be referenced outside the function body. Labels are used in `switch` statements (as `case` labels) and in `goto` statements (see Chapter 14, Other C Topics). Labels are implementation details that functions hide from one another. This hiding—more formally called *information hiding*—is a means of implementing the *principle of least privilege*, one of the most fundamental principles of good software engineering.

An identifier declared outside any function has *file scope.* Such an identifier is "known" (i.e., accessible) in all functions from the point at which the identifier is declared until the end of the file. Global variables, function definitions, and function prototypes placed outside a function all have file scope.

Identifiers defined inside a block have *block scope.* Block scope ends at the terminating right brace (}) of the block. Local variables defined at the beginning of a function have block scope as do function parameters, which are considered local variables by the function. Any block may contain variable definitions. When blocks are nested, and an identifier in an outer block has the same name as an identifier in an inner block, the identifier in the outer block is "hidden" until the inner block terminates. This means that while executing in the inner block, the inner block sees the value of its own local identifier and not the value of the identically named identifier in the enclosing block. Local variables declared `static` still have block scope even though they exist from the time the program begins execution. Thus, storage duration does not affect the scope of an identifier.

The only identifiers with *function-prototype scope* are those used in the parameter list of a function prototype. As mentioned previously, function prototypes do not require names in the parameter list—only types are required. If a name is used in the parameter list of a function prototype, the compiler ignores the name. Identifiers used in a function prototype can be reused elsewhere in the program without ambiguity.

Common Programming Error 5.14

Accidentally using the same name for an identifier in an inner block as is used for an identifier in an outer block, when in fact, the programmer wants the identifier in the outer block to be active for the duration of the inner block.

Error-Prevention Tip 5.2

Avoid variable names that hide names in outer scopes. This can be accomplished simply by avoiding the use of duplicate identifiers in a program.

Figure 5.12 demonstrates scoping issues with global variables, automatic local variables, and `static` local variables. A global variable `x` is defined and initialized to 1 (line 9). This global variable is hidden in any block (or function) in which a variable named `x` is defined. In main, a local variable x is defined and initialized to 5 (line 14). This variable is then printed to show that the global x is hidden in main. Next, a new block is defined in main with another local variable x initialized to 7 (line 19). This variable is printed to show that it hides x in the outer block of main. The variable x with value 7 is automatically destroyed when the block is exited, and the local variable x in the outer block of main is printed again to show that it is no longer hidden. The program defines three functions that each take no arguments and return nothing. Function useLocal defines an automatic variable x and initializes it to 25 (line 42). When useLocal is called, the variable is printed, incremented, and printed again before exiting the function. Each time this function is called, automatic variable x is reinitialized to 25. Function useStaticLocal defines a static variable x and initializes it to 50 (line 55). Local variables declared as static retain their values even when they are out of scope. When useStaticLocal is called, x is printed, incremented, and printed again before exiting the function. In the next call to this function, static local variable x will contain the value 51. Function useGlobal does not define any variables. Therefore, when it refers to variable x, the global x (line 9) is used. When useGlobal is called, the global variable is printed, multiplied by 10, and printed again before exiting the function. The next time function useGlobal is called, the global variable still has its modified value, 10. Finally, the program prints the local variable x in main again (line 33) to show that none of the function calls modified the value of x because the functions all referred to variables in other scopes.

```
1   /* Fig. 5.12: fig05_12.c
2      A scoping example */
3   #include <stdio.h>
4
5   void useLocal( void );        /* function prototype */
6   void useStaticLocal( void );  /* function prototype */
7   void useGlobal( void );       /* function prototype */
8
9   int x = 1; /* global variable */    Seen by entire program
10
11  /* function main begins program execution */
12  int main()
13  {
14     int x = 5; /* local variable to main */    local variable
15
16     printf("local x in outer scope of main is %d\n", x );
17
18     { /* start new scope */
19        int x = 7; /* local variable to new scope */
20
21        printf( "local x in inner scope of main is %d\n", x );
22     } /* end new scope */
23
24     printf( "local x in outer scope of main is %d\n", x );
25
26     useLocal();        /* useLocal has automatic local x */
27     useStaticLocal();  /* useStaticLocal has static local x */
28     useGlobal();       /* useGlobal uses global x */
29     useLocal();        /* useLocal reinitializes automatic local x */
```

Fig. 5.12   Scoping example. (Part 1 of 3.)

```
30      useStaticLocal(); /* static local x retains its prior value */
31      useGlobal();      /* global x also retains its value */
32
33      printf( "\nlocal x in main is %d\n", x );
34
35      return 0; /* indicates successful termination */
36
37   } /* end main */
38
39   /* useLocal reinitializes local variable x during each call */
40   void useLocal( void )
41   {
42      int x = 25;  /* initialized each time useLocal is called */
43
44      printf( "\nlocal x in useLocal is %d after entering useLocal\n", x );
45      x++;
46      printf( "local x in useLocal is %d before exiting useLocal\n", x );
47   } /* end function useLocal */
48
49   /* useStaticLocal initializes static local variable x only the first time
50      the function is called; value of x is saved between calls to this
51      function */
52   void useStaticLocal( void )
53   {
54      /* initialized only first time useStaticLocal is called */
55      static int x = 50;
56
57      printf( "\nlocal static x is %d on entering useStaticLocal\n", x );
58      x++;
59      printf( "local static x is %d on exiting useStaticLocal\n", x );
60   } /* end function useStaticLocal */
61
62   /* function useGlobal modifies global variable x during each call */
63   void useGlobal( void )
64   {
65      printf( "\nglobal x is %d on entering useGlobal\n", x );
66      x *= 10;
67      printf( "global x is %d on exiting useGlobal\n", x );
68   } /* end function useGlobal */
```

```
local x in outer scope of main is 5
local x in inner scope of main is 7
local x in outer scope of main is 5

local x in a is 25 after entering useLocal
local x in a is 26 before exiting useLocal

local static x is 50 on entering useStaticLocal
local static x is 51 on exiting useStaticLocal

global x is 1 on entering useGlobal
global x is 10 on exiting useGlobal                    (continued next page)
```

Fig. 5.12   Scoping example. (Part 2 of 3.)

```
local x in a is 25 after entering useLocal
local x in a is 26 before exiting useLocal

local static x is 51 on entering useStaticLocal
local static x is 52 on exiting useStaticLocal

global x is 10 on entering useGlobal
global x is 100 on exiting useGlobal

local x in main is 5
```

Fig. 5.12   Scoping example. (Part 3 of 3.)

5.13 Recursion

The programs we have discussed are generally structured as functions that call one another in a disciplined, hierarchical manner. For some types of problems, it is useful to have functions call themselves. A *recursive function* is a function that calls itself either directly or indirectly through another function. Recursion is a complex topic discussed at length in upper-level computer science courses. In this section and the next, simple examples of recursion are presented. This book contains an extensive treatment of recursion which is spread throughout Chapters 5 through 12. Figure 5.17, in Section 5.15, summarizes the 31 recursion examples and exercises in the book.

We consider recursion conceptually first, and then examine several programs containing recursive functions. Recursive problem solving approaches have a number of elements in common. A recursive function is called to solve a problem. The function actually knows how to solve only the simplest case(s), or so-called *base case(s)*. If the function is called with a base case, the function simply returns a result. If the function is called with a more complex problem, the function divides the problem into two conceptual pieces: A piece that the function knows how to do and a piece that the function does not know how to do. To make recursion feasible, the latter piece must resemble the original problem, but be a slightly simpler or slightly smaller version of the original problem. Because this new problem looks like the original problem, the function launches (calls) a fresh copy of itself to go to work on the smaller problem—this is referred to as a *recursive call* and is also called the *recursion step*. The recursion step also includes the keyword `return` because its result will be combined with the portion of the problem the function knew how to solve to form a result that will be passed back to the original caller, possibly `main`.

The recursion step executes while the original call to the function is still open, i.e., it has not yet finished executing. The recursion step can result in many more such recursive calls as the function keeps dividing each problem it is called with into two conceptual pieces. In order for the recursion to terminate, each time the function calls itself with a slightly simpler version of the original problem, this sequence of smaller problems must eventually converge on the base case. At that point, the function recognizes the base case, returns a result to the previous copy of the function, and a sequence of returns ensues all the way up the line until the original call of the function eventually returns the final result to `main`. All of this sounds quite exotic compared to the kind of problem solving we have been using with conventional function calls to this point. Indeed, it takes a great deal of practice writing recursive programs before the process will appear natural. As an example of these concepts at work, let us write a recursive program to perform a popular mathematical calculation.

The factorial of a nonnegative integer *n*, written *n!* (and pronounced "*n* factorial"), is the product

$$n \cdot (n - 1) \cdot (n - 2) \cdot \ldots \cdot 1$$

with 1! equal to 1, and 0! defined to be 1. For example, 5! is the product $5 * 4 * 3 * 2 * 1$, which is equal to 120.

The factorial of an integer, `number`, greater than or equal to 0, can be calculated *iteratively* (nonrecursively) using a `for` statement as follows:

```
factorial = 1;

for ( counter = number; counter >= 1; counter-- )
    factorial *= counter;
```

A recursive definition of the factorial function is arrived at by observing the following relationship:

$$n! = n \cdot (n - 1)!$$

For example, 5! is clearly equal to 5 * 4! as is shown by the following:

$$5! = 5 \cdot 4 \cdot 3 \cdot 2 \cdot 1$$
$$5! = 5 \cdot (4 \cdot 3 \cdot 2 \cdot 1)$$
$$5! = 5 \cdot (4!)$$

The evaluation of 5! would proceed as shown in Fig. 5.13. Figure 5.13a shows how the succession of recursive calls proceeds until 1! is evaluated to be 1, which terminates the recursion. Figure 5.13b shows the values returned from each recursive call to its caller until the final value is calculated and returned.

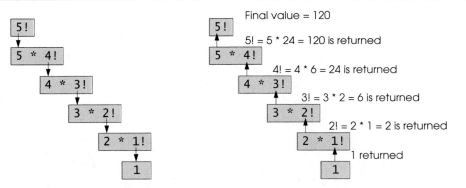

(a) Sequence of recursive calls.   (b) Values returned from each recursive call.

Fig. 5.13   Recursive evaluation of 5!.

Figure 5.14 uses recursion to calculate and print the factorials of the integers 0 to 10 (the choice of the data type `long` will be explained momentarily). The recursive function `factorial` first tests to see if a terminating condition is true, i.e., is `number` less than or equal to 1. If `number` is indeed less than or equal to 1, `factorial` returns 1, no further recursion is necessary, and the program terminates. If `number` is greater than 1, the statement

```
    return number * factorial( number - 1 );
```

expresses the problem as the product of number and a recursive call to factorial evaluating the factorial of number - 1. Note that factorial(number - 1) is a slightly simpler problem than the original calculation factorial(number).

```
1   /* Fig. 5.14: fig05_14.c
2      Recursive factorial function */
3   #include <stdio.h>
4
5   long factorial( long number ); /* function prototype */
6
7   /* function main begins program execution */
8   int main()
9   {
10      int i; /* counter */
11
12      /* loop 11 times; during each iteration, calculate
13         factorial( i ) and display result */
14      for ( i = 0; i <= 10; i++ ) {
15         printf( "%2d! = %ld\n", i, factorial( i ) );
16      } /* end for */
17
18      return 0; /* indicates successful termination */
19
20   } /* end main */
21
22   /* recursive definition of function factorial */
23   long factorial( long number )
24   {
25      /* base case */
26      if ( number <= 1 ) {
27         return 1;
28      } /* end if */
29      else { /* recursive step */
30         return ( number * factorial( number - 1 ) );
31      } /* end else */
32
33   } /* end function factorial */
```

```
 0! = 1
 1! = 1
 2! = 2
 3! = 6
 4! = 24
 5! = 120
 6! = 720
 7! = 5040
 8! = 40320
 9! = 362880
10! = 3628800
```

Fig. 5.14   Calculating factorials with a recursive function.

Function `factorial` (line 23) has been declared to receive a parameter of type `long` and return a result of type `long`. This is shorthand notation for `long int`. The C standard specifies that a variable of type `long int` is stored in at least 4 bytes, and thus may hold a value as large as +2147483647. As can be seen in Fig. 5.14, factorial values become large quickly. We have chosen the data type `long` so the program can calculate factorials greater than 7! on computers with small (such as 2-byte) integers. The conversion specifier `%ld` is used to print `long` values. Unfortunately, the `factorial` function produces large values so quickly that even `long int` does not help us print many factorial values before the size of a `long int` variable is exceeded.

As we explore in the exercises, `double` may ultimately be needed by the user desiring to calculate factorials of larger numbers. This points to a weakness in C (and most other programming languages), namely that the language is not easily extended to handle the unique requirements of various applications. As we will see later, C++ is an extensible language that allows us to create arbitrarily large integers if we wish.

Common Programming Error 5.15

Forgetting to return a value from a recursive function when one is needed.

Common Programming Error 5.16

Either omitting the base case, or writing the recursion step incorrectly so that it does not converge on the base case, will cause infinite recursion, eventually exhausting memory. This is analogous to the problem of an infinite loop in an iterative (nonrecursive) solution. Infinite recursion can also be caused by providing an unexpected input.

5.14 Example Using Recursion: Fibonacci Series

The Fibonacci series

$$0, 1, 1, 2, 3, 5, 8, 13, 21, \ldots$$

begins with 0 and 1 and has the property that each subsequent Fibonacci number is the sum of the previous two Fibonacci numbers.

The series occurs in nature and, in particular, describes a form of spiral. The ratio of successive Fibonacci numbers converges on a constant value of 1.618.... This number, too, repeatedly occurs in nature and has been called the *golden ratio* or the *golden mean*. Humans tend to find the golden mean aesthetically pleasing. Architects often design windows, rooms, and buildings whose length and width are in the ratio of the golden mean. Postcards are often designed with a golden mean length/width ratio.

The Fibonacci series may be defined recursively as follows:

fibonacci(0) = 0
fibonacci(1) = 1
fibonacci(n) = fibonacci(n – 1) + fibonacci(n – 2)

Figure 5.15 calculates the nth Fibonacci number recursively using function `fibonacci`. Notice that Fibonacci numbers tend to become large quickly. Therefore, we have chosen the data type `long` for the parameter type and the return type in function `fibonacci`. In Fig. 5.15, each pair of output lines shows a separate run of the program.

```
1    /* Fig. 5.15: fig05_15.c
2       Recursive fibonacci function */
3    #include <stdio.h>
4
5    long fibonacci( long n ); /* function prototype */
6
7    /* function main begins program execution */
8    int main()
9    {
10      long result; /* fibonacci value */
11      long number; /* number input by user */
12
13      /* obtain integer from user */
14      printf( "Enter an integer: " );
15      scanf( "%ld", &number );
16
17      /* calculate fibonacci value for number input by user */
18      result = fibonacci( number );
19
20      /* display result */
21      printf( "Fibonacci( %ld ) = %ld\n", number, result );
22
23      return 0; /* indicates successful termination */
24
25   } /* end main */
26
27   /* Recursive definition of function fibonacci */
28   long fibonacci( long n )
29   {
30      /* base case */
31      if ( n == 0 || n == 1 ) {
32         return n;
33      } /* end if */
34      else { /* recursive step */
35         return fibonacci( n - 1 ) + fibonacci( n - 2 );
36      } /* end else */
37
38   } /* end function fibonacci */
```

```
Enter an integer: 0
Fibonacci( 0 ) = 0
```

```
Enter an integer: 1
Fibonacci( 1 ) = 1
```

```
Enter an integer: 2
Fibonacci( 2 ) = 1
```

Fig. 5.15   Recursively generating Fibonacci numbers. (Part 1 of 2.)

```
Enter an integer: 3
Fibonacci( 3 ) = 2
```

```
Enter an integer: 4
Fibonacci( 4 ) = 3
```

```
Enter an integer: 5
Fibonacci( 5 ) = 5
```

```
Enter an integer: 6
Fibonacci( 6 ) = 8
```

```
Enter an integer: 10
Fibonacci( 10 ) = 55
```

```
Enter an integer: 20
Fibonacci( 20 ) = 6765
```

```
Enter an integer: 30
Fibonacci( 30 ) = 832040
```

```
Enter an integer: 35
Fibonacci( 35 ) = 9227465
```

Fig. 5.15   Recursively generating Fibonacci numbers. (Part 2 of 2.)

The call to fibonacci from main is not a recursive call (line 18), but all subsequent calls to fibonacci are recursive (line 35). Each time fibonacci is invoked, it immediately tests for the base case—n is equal to 0 or 1. If this is true, n is returned. Interestingly, if n is greater than 1, the recursion step generates *two* recursive calls, each of which is for a slightly simpler problem than the original call to fibonacci. Figure 5.16 shows how function fibonacci would evaluate fibonacci(3).

This figure raises some interesting issues about the order in which C compilers will evaluate the operands of operators. This is a different issue from the order in which operators are applied to their operands, namely the order dictated by the rules of operator precedence. From Fig. 5.16 it appears that while evaluating fibonacci(3), two recursive calls will be made, namely fibonacci(2) and fibonacci(1). But in what order will these calls be made? Most programmers simply assume the operands will be evaluated left to right. Strangely, the ANSI standard does not specify the order in which the operands of most operators (including +) are to be evaluated. Therefore, the programmer may make no assumption about the order in which these calls will execute. The calls could in fact execute `fibonacci( 2 )` first and then `fibonacci( 1 )`, or the calls could execute in the reverse order, `fibonacci( 1 )` then `fibonacci( 2 )`. In this program and in most other programs, it turns out the final result would be the same. But in some programs the evaluation of an operand may have side effects that could affect the final result of the expression. Of C's many operators, the ANSI standard specifies the order of evaluation of the operands of only four operators—namely &&, ||, the comma (,) operator and ?:. The first three of these are binary operators whose two operands are guaranteed to be evaluated left to right. [*Note:* The commas used to separate the arguments in a function call are not comma operators.] The last operator is C's only ternary operator. Its leftmost operand is always evaluated first; if the leftmost operand evaluates to nonzero, the middle operand is evaluated next and the last operand is ignored; if the leftmost operand evaluates to zero, the third operand is evaluated next and the middle operand is ignored.

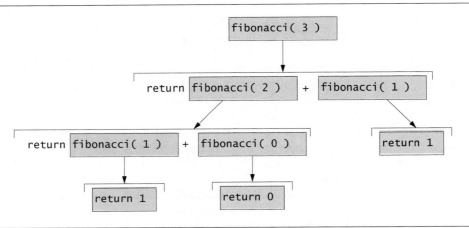

Fig. 5.16   Set of recursive calls for `fibonacci( 3 )`.

Common Programming Error 5.17

Writing programs that depend on the order of evaluation of the operands of operators other than &&*,* ||*,* ?:*, and the comma (,) operator can lead to errors because compilers may not necessarily evaluate the operands in the order the programmer expects.*

Portability Tip 5.2

Programs that depend on the order of evaluation of the operands of operators other than &&*,* ||*,* ?:*, and the comma (,) operator can function differently on systems with different compilers.*

A word of caution is in order about recursive programs like the one we use here to generate Fibonacci numbers. Each level of recursion in the `fibonacci` function has a doubling effect on the number of calls, i.e., the number of recursive calls that will be executed to calculate the nth Fibonacci number is on the order of 2^n. This rapidly gets out of hand. Calculating only the 20th Fibonacci number would require on the order of 2^{20} or about a million calls, calculating the 30th Fibonacci number would require on the order of 2^{30} or about a billion calls, and so on. Computer scientists refer to this as *exponential complexity*. Problems of this nature humble even the world's most powerful computers! Complexity issues in general, and exponential complexity in particular, are discussed in detail in the upper-level computer science curriculum course generally called "Algorithms."

Performance Tip 5.4

Avoid Fibonacci-style recursive programs which result in an exponential "explosion" of calls.

5.15 Recursion vs. Iteration

In the previous sections, we studied two functions that can easily be implemented either recursively or iteratively. In this section we compare the two approaches and discuss why the programmer might choose one approach over the other in a particular situation.

Both iteration and recursion are based on a control structure: Iteration uses a repetition structure; recursion uses a selection structure. Both iteration and recursion involve repetition: Iteration explicitly uses a repetition structure; recursion achieves repetition through repeated function calls. Iteration and recursion each involve a termination test: Iteration terminates when the loop-continuation condition fails; recursion terminates when a base case is recognized. Iteration with counter-controlled repetition and recursion each gradually approach termination: Iteration keeps modifying a counter until the counter assumes a value that makes the loop-continuation condition fail; recursion keeps producing simpler versions of the original problem until the base case is reached. Both iteration and recursion can occur infinitely: An infinite loop occurs with iteration if the loop-continuation test never becomes false; infinite recursion occurs if the recursion step does not reduce the problem each time in a manner that converges on the base case.

Recursion has many negatives. It repeatedly invokes the mechanism, and consequently the overhead, of function calls. This can be expensive in both processor time and memory space. Each recursive call causes another copy of the function (actually only the function's variables) to be created; this can consume considerable memory. Iteration normally occurs within a function so the overhead of repeated function calls and extra memory assignment is omitted. So why choose recursion?

Software Engineering Observation 5.13

Any problem that can be solved recursively can also be solved iteratively (nonrecursively). A recursive approach is normally chosen in preference to an iterative approach when the recursive approach more naturally mirrors the problem and results in a program that is easier to understand and debug. Another reason to choose a recursive solution is that an iterative solution may not be apparent.

Performance Tip 5.5

Avoid using recursion in performance situations. Recursive calls take time and consume additional memory.

Common Programming Error 5.18

Accidentally having a nonrecursive function call itself either directly, or indirectly through another function.

Most programming textbooks introduce recursion much later than we have done here. We feel that recursion is a sufficiently rich and complex topic that it is better to introduce it earlier and spread the examples over the remainder of the text. Figure 5.17 summarizes by chapter the 31 recursion examples and exercises in the text.

Let us close this chapter with some observations that we make repeatedly throughout the book. Good software engineering is important. High performance is important. Unfortunately, these goals are often at odds with one another. Good software engineering is key to making more manageable the task of developing the larger and more complex software systems we need. High performance is key to realizing the systems of the future that will place ever greater computing demands on hardware. Where do functions fit in here?

Chapter	Recursion Examples and Exercises
Chapter 5	Factorial function Fibonacci function Greatest common divisor Sum of two integers Multiply two integers Raising an integer to an integer power Towers of Hanoi Recursive `main` Printing keyboard inputs in reverse Visualizing recursion
Chapter 6	Sum the elements of an array Print an array Print an array backwards Print a string backwards Check if a string is a palindrome Minimum value in an array Selection sort Quicksort Linear search Binary search
Chapter 7	Eight Queens Maze traversal
Chapter 8	Printing a string input at the keyboard backwards
Chapter 12	Linked list insert Linked list delete Search a linked list Print a linked list backwards Binary tree insert Preorder traversal of a binary tree Inorder traversal of a binary tree Postorder traversal of a binary tree

Fig. 5.17 Recursion examples and exercises in the text.

Performance Tip 5.6

Functionalizing programs in a neat, hierarchical manner promotes good software engineering. But it has a price. A heavily functionalized program—as compared to a monolithic (i.e., one-piece) program without functions—makes potentially large numbers of function calls and these consume execution time on a computer's processor(s). So although monolithic programs may perform better, they are more difficult to program, test, debug, maintain, and evolve.

So functionalize your programs judiciously, always keeping in mind the delicate balance between performance and good software engineering.

SUMMARY

- The best way to develop and maintain a large program is to divide it into several smaller program modules each of which is more manageable than the original program. Modules are written as functions in C.

- A function is invoked by a function call. The function call mentions the function by name and provides information (as arguments) that the called function needs to perform its task.

- The purpose of information hiding is for functions to have access only to the information they need to complete their tasks. This is a means of implementing the principle of least privilege, one of the most important principles of good software engineering.

- Functions are normally invoked in a program by writing the name of the function followed by a left parenthesis followed by the argument (or a comma separated list of arguments) of the function followed by a right parenthesis.

- Data type `double` is a floating point type like `float`. A variable of type `double` can store a value of much greater magnitude and precision than `float` can store.

- Each argument of a function may be a constant, a variable, or an expression.

- A local variable is known only in a function definition. Other functions are not allowed to know the names of a function's local variables, nor is any function allowed to know the implementation details of any other function.

- The general format for a function definition is

      return-value-type function-name(*parameter-list*)
      {
          definitions
          statements
      }

  The *return-value-type* states the type of the value returned to the calling function. If a function does not return a value, the *return-value-type* is declared as `void`. The *function-name* is any valid identifier. The *parameter-list* is a comma-separated list containing the definitions of the variables that will be passed to the function. If a function does not receive any values, *parameter-list* is declared as `void`. The *function-body* is the set of definitions and statements that constitute the function.

- The arguments passed to a function should match in number, type and order with the parameters in the function definition.

- When a program encounters a function call, control is transferred from the point of invocation to the called function, the statements of the called function are executed and control returns to the caller.

- A called function can return control to the caller in one of three ways. If the function does not return a value, control is returned when the function-ending right brace is reached, or by executing the statement

      return;

  If the function does return a value, the statement

      return *expression*;

  returns the value of *expression*.

- A function prototype declares the return type of the function and declares the number, the types, and order of the parameters the function expects to receive.

- Function prototypes enable the compiler to verify that functions are called correctly.

- The compiler ignores variable names mentioned in the function prototype.

- Each standard library has a corresponding header containing the function prototypes for all the functions in that library, as well as definitions of various symbolic constants needed by those functions.

- Programmers can create and include their own headers.

- When an argument is passed by value, a copy of the variable's value is made and the copy is passed to the called function. Changes to the copy in the called function do not affect the original variable's value.

- All calls in C are call by value.

- Function `rand` generates an integer between 0 and RAND_MAX which is defined by the C standard to be at least 32767.

- The function prototypes for `rand` and `srand` are contained in `<stdlib.h>`.

- Values produced by `rand` can be scaled and shifted to produce values in a specific range.

- To randomize a program, use the C standard library function `srand`.

- The `srand` function call is ordinarily inserted in a program only after it has been thoroughly debugged. While debugging, it is better to omit `srand`. This ensures repeatability, which is essential to proving that corrections to a random number generation program work properly.

- To randomize without the need for entering a seed each time, we use `srand( time( NULL ) )`. Function `time` returns the number of seconds since the start of the day. The `time` function prototype is located in the header `<time.h>`.

- The general equation for scaling and shifting a random number is

      n = a + rand() % b;

  where `a` is the shifting value (i.e., the first number in the desired range of consecutive integers), and `b` is the scaling factor (i.e,. the width of the desired range of consecutive integers).

- An enumeration, introduced by the keyword `enum`, is a set of integer constants represented by identifiers. Values in an `enum` start with 0 and are incremented by 1. It is also possible to assign an integer value to each identifier in an `enum`. The identifiers in an enumeration must be unique, but the values may be duplicated.

- Each identifier in a program has the attributes storage class, storage duration, scope and linkage.

- C provides four storage classes indicated by the storage class specifiers: `auto`, `register`, `extern` and `static`.

- An identifier's storage duration is when that identifier exists in memory.

- An identifier's scope is where the identifier can be referenced in a program.

- An identifier's linkage determines for a multiple-source-file program if an identifier is known only in the current source file or in any source file with proper declarations.

- Variables with automatic storage duration are created when the block in which they are defined is entered, exist while the block is active and are destroyed when the block is exited. A function's local variables normally have automatic storage duration.

- The storage class specifier `register` can be placed before an automatic variable declaration to suggest that the compiler maintain the variable in one of the computer's high-speed hardware registers. The compiler may ignore `register` declarations. Keyword `register` can be used only with variables of automatic storage duration.

- Keywords `extern` and `static` are used to declare identifiers for variables and functions of static storage duration.

- Variables with static storage duration are allocated and initialized once when the program begins execution.

- There are two types of identifiers with static storage duration: external identifiers (such as global variables and function names) and local variables declared with the storage class specifier `static`.

- Global variables are created by placing variable definitions outside any function definition. Global variables retain their values throughout the execution of the program.

- Local variables declared `static` retain their value between calls to the function in which they are defined.

- All numeric variables of static storage duration are initialized to zero if they are not explicitly initialized by the programmer.

- The four scopes for an identifier are function scope, file scope, block scope and function-prototype scope.

- Labels are the only identifiers with function scope. Labels can be used anywhere in the function in which they appear, but can not be referenced outside the function body.

- An identifier declared outside any function has file scope. Such an identifier is "known" in all functions from the point at which the identifier is declared until the end of the file.

- Identifiers defined inside a block have block scope. Block scope ends at the terminating right brace (}) of the block.

- Local variables defined at the beginning of a function have block scope as do function parameters, which are considered local variables by the function.

- Any block may contain variable definitions. When blocks are nested, and an identifier in an outer block has the same name as an identifier in an inner block, the identifier in the outer block is "hidden" until the inner block terminates.

- The only identifiers with function-prototype scope are those used in the parameter list of a function prototype. Identifiers used in a function prototype can be reused elsewhere in the program without ambiguity.

- A recursive function is a function that calls itself either directly or indirectly.

- If a recursive function is called with a base case, the function simply returns a result. If the function is called with a more complex problem, the function divides the problem into two conceptual pieces: A piece that the function knows how to do and a slightly smaller version of the original problem. Because this new problem looks like the original problem, the function launches a recursive call to work on the smaller problem.

- For recursion to terminate, each time the recursive function calls itself with a slightly simpler version of the original problem, the sequence of smaller and smaller problems must converge on the base case. When the function recognizes the base case, the result is returned to the previous function call, and a sequence of returns ensues all the way up the line until the original call of the function eventually returns the final result.

- The ANSI standard does not specify the order in which the operands of most operators (including +) are to be evaluated. Of C's many operators, the standard specifies the order of evaluation of the operands of the operators &&, | |, the comma (,) operator and ? : . The first three of these are binary operators whose two operands are evaluated left to right. The last operator is C's only ternary operator. Its leftmost operand is evaluated first; if the leftmost operand evaluates to nonzero, the middle operand is evaluated next and the last operand is ignored; if the leftmost operand evaluates to zero, the third operand is evaluated next and the middle operand is ignored.

- Both iteration and recursion are based on a control structure: Iteration uses a repetition structure; recursion uses a selection structure.

- Both iteration and recursion involve repetition: Iteration explicitly uses a repetition structure; recursion achieves repetition through repeated function calls.

- Iteration and recursion each involve a termination test: Iteration terminates when the loop-continuation condition fails; recursion terminates when a base case is recognized.

- Iteration and recursion can occur infinitely: An infinite loop occurs with iteration if the loop-continuation test never becomes false; infinite recursion occurs if the recursion step does not reduce the problem in a manner that converges on the base case.

- Recursion repeatedly invokes the mechanism, and consequently the overhead, of function calls. This can be expensive in both processor time and memory space.

TERMINOLOGY

abstraction
argument in a function call
automatic storage
automatic storage duration
automatic variable
`auto` storage class specifier
base case in recursion
block
block scope
C standard library
call a function
call by reference
call by value
called function
caller
calling function
coercion of arguments
copy of a value
divide and conquer
`enum` (enumeration)
`extern` storage class specifier
factorial function
file scope
function
function call
function definition
function prototype
function prototype scope
function scope

global variable
header
information hiding
invoke a function
iteration
linkage
local variable
math library functions
mixed-type expression
optimizing compiler
parameter list
principle of least privilege
programmer-defined function
promotion hierarchy
pseudo-random numbers
`rand`
RAND_MAX
randomize
random number generation
recursion
recursive call
recursive function
`register` storage class specifier
`return`
return-value-type
scaling
%s conversion specifier
scope
shifting

side effects	`static` variable
simulation	storage classes
software engineering	storage class specifier
software reusability	storage duration
`srand`	`time`
standard library headers	`unsigned`
`static` storage class specifier	`void`

COMMON PROGRAMMING ERRORS

5.1   Omitting the return-value-type in a function definition is a syntax error if the function proto-type specifies a return type other than `int`.

5.2   Forgetting to return a value from a function that is supposed to return a value can lead to un-expected errors. The C standard states that the result of this omission is undefined.

5.3   Returning a value from a function with a `void` return type is a syntax error.

5.4   Specifying function parameters of the same type as `double x, y` instead of `double x, double y` might cause errors in your programs. The parameter declaration `double x, y` would actually make `y` a parameter of type `int` because `int` is the default.

5.5   Placing a semicolon after the right parenthesis enclosing the parameter list of a function def-inition is a syntax error.

5.6   Defining a function parameter again as a local variable within the function is a syntax error.

5.7   Defining a function inside another function is a syntax error.

5.8   Forgetting the semicolon at the end of a function prototype is a syntax error.

5.9   Converting from a higher data type in the promotion hierarchy to a lower type can change the data value.

5.10   Forgetting a function prototype causes a syntax error if the return type of the function is not `int` and the function definition appears after the function call in the program. Otherwise, for-getting a function prototype may cause a run-time error or an unexpected result.

5.11   Using `srand` in place of `rand` to generate random numbers.

5.12   Assigning a value to an enumeration constant after it has been defined is a syntax error.

5.13   Using multiple storage class specifiers for an identifier. Only one storage class specifier can be applied to an identifier.

5.14   Accidentally using the same name for an identifier in an inner block as is used for an iden-tifier in an outer block, when in fact, the programmer wants the identifier in the outer block to be active for the duration of the inner block.

5.15   Forgetting to return a value from a recursive function when one is needed.

5.16   Either omitting the base case or writing the recursion step incorrectly so that it does not con-verge on the base case will cause infinite recursion, eventually exhausting memory. This is analogous to the problem of an infinite loop in an iterative (nonrecursive) solution. Infinite recursion can also be caused by providing an unexpected input.

5.17   Writing programs that depend on the order of evaluation of the operands of operators other than `&&`, `||`, `?:` and the comma (`,`) operator can lead to errors because compilers may not necessarily evaluate the operands in the order the programmer expects.

5.18   Accidentally having a nonrecursive function call itself either directly or indirectly through another function.

ERROR-PREVENTION TIPS

5.1   Include the math header by using the preprocessor directive `#include <math.h>` when us-ing functions in the math library.

5.2   Avoid variable names that hide names in outer scopes. This can be accomplished simply by avoiding the use of duplicate identifiers in a program.

GOOD PROGRAMMING PRACTICES

5.1   Familiarize yourself with the rich collection of functions in the C standard library.

5.2   Place a blank line between function definitions to separate the functions and enhance program readability.

5.3   Even though an omitted return type defaults to `int`, always state the return type explicitly.

5.4   Include the type of each parameter in the parameter list, even if that parameter is of the default type `int`.

5.5   Although it is not incorrect to do so, do not use the same names for the arguments passed to a function and the corresponding parameters in the function definition. This helps avoid ambiguity.

5.6   Choosing meaningful function names and meaningful parameter names makes programs more readable and helps avoid excessive use of comments.

5.7   Include function prototypes for all functions to take advantage of C's type checking capabilities. Use `#include` preprocessor directives to obtain function prototypes for the standard library functions from the headers for the appropriate libraries, or to obtain headers containing function prototypes for functions developed by you and/or your group members.

5.8   Parameter names are sometimes included in function prototypes for documentation purposes. The compiler ignores these names.

5.9   Use only uppercase letters in the names of enumeration constants to make these constants stand out in a program and to indicate that enumeration constants are not variables.

PERFORMANCE TIPS

5.1   Automatic storage is a means of conserving memory because automatic variables exist only when they are needed. They are created when the function in which they are defined is entered and they are destroyed when the function is exited.

5.2   The storage class specifier `register` can be placed before an automatic variable declaration to suggest that the compiler maintain the variable in one of the computer's high-speed hardware registers. If intensely used variables such as counters or totals can be maintained in hardware registers, the overhead of repeatedly loading the variables from memory into the registers and storing the results back into memory can be eliminated.

5.3   Often, `register` declarations are unnecessary. Today's optimizing compilers are capable of recognizing frequently used variables and can decide to place them in registers without the need for a `register` declaration from the programmer.

5.4   Avoid Fibonacci-style recursive programs which result in an exponential "explosion" of calls.

5.5   Avoid using recursion in performance situations. Recursive calls take time and consume additional memory.

5.6   Functionalizing programs in a neat, hierarchical manner promotes good software engineering. But it has a price. A heavily functionalized program—as compared to a monolithic (i.e., one-piece) program without functions—makes potentially large numbers of function calls and these consume execution time on a computer's processor(s). So although monolithic programs may perform better, they are more difficult to program, test, debug, maintain, and evolve.

PORTABILITY TIPS

5.1   Using the functions in the C standard library helps make programs more portable.

5.2   Programs that depend on the order of evaluation of the operands of operators other than &&, ||, ?: and the comma (,) operator can function differently on systems with different compilers.

SOFTWARE ENGINEERING OBSERVATIONS

5.1   Avoid "reinventing the wheel". When possible, use C standard library functions instead of writing new functions. This reduces program development time.

5.2   In programs containing many functions, main should be implemented as a group of calls to functions that perform the bulk of the program's work.

5.3   Each function should be limited to performing a single, well-defined task, and the function name should effectively express that task. This facilitates abstraction and promotes software reusability.

5.4   If you cannot choose a concise name that expresses what the function does, it is possible that your function is attempting to perform too many diverse tasks. It is usually best to break such a function into several smaller functions.

5.5   A function should be no longer than one page. Better yet, a function should be no longer than half a page. Small functions promote software reusability.

5.6   Programs should be written as collections of small functions. This makes programs easier to write, debug, maintain and modify.

5.7   A function requiring a large number of parameters may be performing too many tasks. Consider dividing the function into smaller functions that perform the separate tasks. The function header should fit on one line if possible.

5.8   The function prototype, function header and function calls should all agree in the number, type, and order of arguments and parameters, and in the type of return value.

5.9   A function prototype placed outside any function definition applies to all calls to the function appearing after the function prototype in the file. A function prototype placed in a function applies only to calls made in that function.

5.10   Automatic storage is an example of the principle of least privilege—allowing access to data only when it is absolutely needed. Why have variables stored in memory and accessible when in fact they are not needed?

5.11   Defining a variable as global rather than local allows unintended side effects to occur when a function that does not need access to the variable accidentally or maliciously modifies it. In general, use of global variables should be avoided except in certain situations with unique performance requirements (as discussed in Chapter 14).

5.12   Variables used only in a particular function should be defined as local variables in that function rather than as global variables.

5.13   Any problem that can be solved recursively can also be solved iteratively (nonrecursively). A recursive approach is normally chosen in preference to an iterative approach when the recursive approach more naturally mirrors the problem and results in a program that is easier to understand and debug. Another reason to choose a recursive solution is that an iterative solution may not be apparent.

SELF-REVIEW EXERCISES

5.1   Answer each of the following:
        a) A program module in C is called a(n) _____.
        b) A function is invoked with a(n) _____.
        c) A variable that is known only within the function in which it is defined is called a(n) _____.

d) The _____ statement in a called function is used to pass the value of an expression back to the calling function.

e) Keyword _____ is used in a function header to indicate that a function does not return a value or to indicate that a function contains no parameters.

f) The _____ of an identifier is the portion of the program in which the identifier can be used.

g) The three ways to return control from a called function to a caller are _____, _____ and _____.

h) A(n) _____ allows the compiler to check the number, types, and order of the arguments passed to a function.

i) The _____ function is used to produce random numbers.

j) The _____ function is used to set the random number seed to randomize a program.

k) The storage class specifiers are _____, _____, _____ and _____.

l) Variables declared in a block or in the parameter list of a function are assumed to be of storage class _____ unless specified otherwise.

m) The storage class specifier _____ is a recommendation to the compiler to store a variable in one of the computer's registers.

n) A variable defined outside any block or function is a(n) _____ variable.

o) For a local variable in a function to retain its value between calls to the function, it must be declared with the _____ storage class specifier.

p) The four possible scopes of an identifier are _____, _____, _____ and _____.

q) A function that calls itself either directly or indirectly is a(n) _____ function.

r) A recursive function typically has two components: One that provides a means for the recursion to terminate by testing for a(n) _____ case, and one that expresses the problem as a recursive call for a slightly simpler problem than the original call.

5.2   For the following program, state the scope (either function scope, file scope, block scope or function prototype scope) of each of the following elements.

a) The variable x in main.

b) The variable y in cube.

c) The function cube.

d) The function main.

e) The function prototype for cube.

f) The identifier y in the function prototype for cube.

```c
#include <stdio.h>
int cube( int y );

int main()
{
    int x;

    for ( x = 1; x <= 10; x++ )
        printf( "%d\n", cube( x ) );
    return 0;
}

int cube( int y )
{
    return y * y * y;
}
```

5.3   Write a program that tests if the examples of the math library function calls shown in Fig. 5.2 actually produce the indicated results.

5.4   Give the function header for each of the following functions.
  a) Function `hypotenuse` that takes two double-precision floating point arguments, `side1` and `side2`, and returns a double-precision floating point result.
  b) Function `smallest` that takes three integers, x, y, z, and returns an integer.
  c) Function `instructions` that does not receive any arguments and does not return a value. [*Note:* Such functions are commonly used to display instructions to a user.]
  d) Function `intToFloat` that takes an integer argument, `number`, and returns a floating point result.

5.5   Give the function prototype for each of the following:
  a) The function described in Exercise 5.4a.
  b) The function described in Exercise 5.4b.
  c) The function described in Exercise 5.4c.
  d) The function described in Exercise 5.4d.

5.6   Write a declaration for each of the following:
  a) Integer `count` that should be maintained in a register. Initialize `count` to 0.
  b) Floating point variable `lastVal` that is to retain its value between calls to the function in which it is defined.
  c) External integer `number` whose scope should be restricted to the remainder of the file in which it is defined.

5.7   Find the error in each of the following program segments and explain how the error can be corrected (see also Exercise 5.50):

  a)
```
int g( void )
{
    printf( "Inside function g\n" );
    int h( void )
    {
        printf( "Inside function h\n" );
    }
}
```

  b)
```
int sum( int x, int y )
{
    int result;
    result = x + y;
}
```

  c)
```
int sum( int n )
{
    if ( n == 0 )
        return 0;
    else
        n + sum( n - 1 );
}
```

  d)
```
void f( float a );
{
    float a;
    printf( "%f", a );
}
```

  e)
```
void product( void )
{
    int a, b, c, result;
```

```
        printf( "Enter three integers: " )
        scanf( "%d%d%d", &a, &b, &c );
        result = a * b * c;
        printf( "Result is %d", result );
        return result;
    }
```

ANSWERS TO SELF-REVIEW EXERCISES

5.1   a) Function.   b) Function call.   c) Local variable.   d) `return`.   e) `void`.   f) Scope.
g) `return;` or `return expression;` or encountering the closing right brace of a function.
h) Function prototype.   i) `rand`.   j) `srand`.   k) `auto, register, extern, static`.   l) `auto`.
m) `register`. n) External, global. o) `static`. p) Function scope, file scope, block scope, function
prototype scope. q) Recursive. r) Base.

5.2   a)   Block scope. b) Block Scope. c) File scope. d) File scope. e) File scope. f) Function prototype scope.

5.3

```
1   /* ex05_03.c */
2   /* Testing the math library functions */
3   #include <stdio.h>
4   #include <math.h>
5
6   /* function main begins program execution */
7   int main()
8   {
9      /* calculates and outputs the square root */
10     printf( "sqrt(%.1f) = %.1f\n", 900.0, sqrt( 900.0 ) );
11     printf( "sqrt(%.1f) = %.1f\n", 9.0, sqrt( 9.0 ) );
12
13     /* calculates and outputs the exponential function e to the x */
14     printf( "exp(%.1f) = %f\n", 1.0, exp( 1.0 ) );
15     printf( "exp(%.1f) = %f\n", 2.0, exp( 2.0 ) );
16
17     /* calculates and outputs the logorithm (base e) */
18     printf( "log(%f) = %.1f\n", 2.718282, log( 2.718282 ) );
19     printf( "log(%f) = %.1f\n", 7.389056, log( 7.389056 ) );
20
21     /* calculates and outputs the logorithm (base 10) */
22     printf( "log10(%.1f) = %.1f\n", 1.0, log10( 1.0 ) );
23     printf( "log10(%.1f) = %.1f\n", 10.0, log10( 10.0 ) );
24     printf( "log10(%.1f) = %.1f\n", 100.0, log10( 100.0 ) );
25
26     /* calculates and outputs the absolute value */
27     printf( "fabs(%.1f) = %.1f\n", 13.5, fabs( 13.5 ) );
28     printf( "fabs(%.1f) = %.1f\n", 0.0, fabs( 0.0 ) );
29     printf( "fabs(%.1f) = %.1f\n", -13.5, fabs( -13.5 ) );
30
31     /* calculates and outputs ceil( x ) */
32     printf( "ceil(%.1f) = %.1f\n", 9.2, ceil( 9.2 ) );
33     printf( "ceil(%.1f) = %.1f\n", -9.8, ceil( -9.8 ) );
34
```

(continued next page)

```
35        /* calculates and outputs floor( x ) */
36        printf( "floor(%.1f) = %.1f\n", 9.2, floor( 9.2 ) );
37        printf( "floor(%.1f) = %.1f\n", -9.8, floor( -9.8 ) );
38
39        /* calculates and outputs pow( x, y ) */
40        printf( "pow(%.1f, %.1f) = %.1f\n", 2.0, 7.0, pow( 2.0, 7.0 ) );
41        printf( "pow(%.1f, %.1f) = %.1f\n", 9.0, 0.5, pow( 9.0, 0.5 ) );
42
43        /* calculates and outputs fmod( x, y ) */
44        printf( "fmod(%.3f/%.3f) = %.3f\n", 13.675, 2.333,
45              fmod( 13.675, 2.333 ) );
46
47        /* calculates and outputs sin( x ) */
48        printf( "sin(%.1f) = %.1f\n", 0.0, sin( 0.0 ) );
49
50        /* calculates and outputs cos( x ) */
51        printf( "cos(%.1f) = %.1f\n", 0.0, cos( 0.0 ) );
52
53        /* calculates and outputs tan( x ) */
54        printf( "tan(%.1f) = %.1f\n", 0.0, tan( 0.0 ) );
55
56        return 0; /* indicates successful termination */
57
58   } /* end main */
```

```
sqrt(900.0) = 30.0
sqrt(9.0) = 3.0
exp(1.0) = 2.718282
exp(2.0) = 7.389056
log(2.718282) = 1.0
log(7.389056) = 2.0
log10(1.0) = 0.0
log10(10.0) = 1.0
log10(100.0) = 2.0
fabs(13.5) = 13.5
fabs(0.0) = 0.0
fabs(-13.5) = 13.5
ceil(9.2) = 10.0
ceil(-9.8) = -9.0
floor(9.2) = 9.0
floor(-9.8) = -10.0
pow(2.0, 7.0) = 128.0
pow(9.0, 0.5) = 3.0
fmod(13.675/2.333) = 2.010
sin(0.0) = 0.0
cos(0.0) = 1.0
tan(0.0) = 0.0
```

5.4   a) `double hypotenuse( double side1, double side2 )`
       b) `int smallest( int x, int y, int z )`
       c) `void instructions( void )`
       d) `float intToFloat( int number )`

5.5   a   `double hypotenuse( double side1, double side2 );`

    b) `int smallest( int x, int y, int z );`
    c) `void instructions( void );`
    d) `float intToFloat( int number );`

5.6   a) `register int count = 0;`
    b) `static float lastVal;`
    c) `static int number;`
       [*Note:* This would appear outside any function definition.]

5.7   a) Error: Function h is defined in function g.
       Correction: Move the definition of h out of the definition of g.
    b) Error: The body of the function is supposed to return an integer, but does not.
       Correction: Delete variable `result` and place the following statement in the function:

          `return x + y;`

    c) Error: The result of n + sum(n − 1) is not returned; sum returns an improper result.
       Correction: Rewrite the statement in the `else` clause as

          `return n + sum( n - 1 );`

    d) Error: Semicolon after the right parenthesis that encloses the parameter list, and re-defining the parameter a in the function definition.
       Correction: Delete the semicolon after the right parenthesis of the parameter list, and delete the declaration `float a;` in the function body.
    e) Error: The function returns a value when it is not supposed to.
       Correction: Eliminate the `return` statement.

EXERCISES

5.8   Show the value of x after each of the following statements is performed:
    a) `x = fabs( 7.5 );`
    b) `x = floor( 7.5 );`
    c) `x = fabs( 0.0 );`
    d) `x = ceil( 0.0 );`
    e) `x = fabs( -6.4 );`
    f) `x = ceil( -6.4 );`
    g) `x = ceil( -fabs( -8 + floor( -5.5 ) ) );`

5.9   A parking garage charges a $2.00 minimum fee to park for up to three hours. The garage charges an additional $0.50 per hour for each hour *or part thereof* in excess of three hours. The maximum charge for any given 24-hour period is $10.00. Assume that no car parks for longer than 24 hours at a time. Write a program that will calculate and print the parking charges for each of 3 customers who parked their cars in this garage yesterday. You should enter the hours parked for each customer. Your program should print the results in a neat tabular format, and should calculate and print the total of yesterday's receipts. The program should use the function `calculateCharges` to determine the charge for each customer. Your outputs should appear in the following format:

Car	Hours	Charge
1	1.5	2.00
2	4.0	2.50
3	24.0	10.00
TOTAL	29.5	14.50

5.10   An application of function `floor` is rounding a value to the nearest integer. The statement

        y = floor(x + .5);

will round the number x to the nearest integer, and assign the result to y. Write a program that reads several numbers and uses the preceding statement to round each of these numbers to the nearest integer. For each number processed, print both the original number and the rounded number.

5.11   Function `floor` may be used to round a number to a specific decimal place. The statement

        y = floor(x * 10 + .5) / 10;

rounds x to the tenths position (the first position to the right of the decimal point). The statement

        y = floor(x * 100 + .5) / 100;

rounds x to the hundredths position (i.e., the second position to the right of the decimal point). Write a program that defines four functions to round a number x in various ways
   a) `roundToInteger( number )`
   b) `roundToTenths( number )`
   c) `roundToHundreths( number )`
   d) `roundToThousandths( number )`
For each value read, your program should print the original value, the number rounded to the nearest integer, the number rounded to the nearest tenth, the number rounded to the nearest hundredth, and the number rounded to the nearest thousandth.

5.12   Answer each of the following questions.
   a) What does it mean to choose numbers "at random?"
   b) Why is the `rand` function useful for simulating games of chance?
   c) Why would you randomize a program by using `srand`? Under what circumstances is it desirable not to randomize?
   d) Why is it often necessary to scale and/or shift the values produced by `rand`?
   e) Why is computerized simulation of real-world situations a useful technique?

5.13   Write statements that assign random integers to the variable n in the following ranges:
   a) $1 \leq n \leq 2$
   b) $1 \leq n \leq 100$
   c) $0 \leq n \leq 9$
   d) $1000 \leq n \leq 1112$
   e) $-1 \leq n \leq 1$
   f) $-3 \leq n \leq 11$

5.14   For each of the following sets of integers, write a single statement that will print a number at random from the set.
   a) 2, 4, 6, 8, 10.
   b) 3, 5, 7, 9, 11.
   c) 6, 10, 14, 18, 22.

5.15   Define a function called `hypotenuse` that calculates the length of the hypotenuse of a right triangle when the other two sides are given. Use this function in a program to determine the length of the hypotenuse for each of the following triangles. The function should take two arguments of type `double` and return the hypotenuse as a `double`. Test your program with the side values specified in Fig. 5.18.

Triangle	Side 1	Side 2
1	3.0	4.0
2	5.0	12.0
3	8.0	15.0

Fig. 5.18 *Sample triangle side values for Exercise 5.15.*

5.16   Write a function `integerPower( base, exponent )` that returns the value of

$$base^{exponent}$$

For example, `integerPower( 3, 4 )` = 3 * 3 * 3 * 3. Assume that `exponent` is a positive, nonzero integer, and `base` is an integer. Function `integerPower` should use `for` to control the calculation. Do not use any math library functions.

5.17   Write a function `multiple` that determines for a pair of integers whether the second integer is a multiple of the first. The function should take two integer arguments and return 1 (true) if the second is a multiple of the first, and 0 (false) otherwise. Use this function in a program that inputs a series of pairs of integers.

5.18   Write a program that inputs a series of integers and passes them one at a time to function `even` which uses the remainder operator to determine if an integer is even. The function should take an integer argument and return 1 if the integer is even and 0 otherwise.

5.19   Write a function that displays at the left margin of the screen a solid square of asterisks whose side is specified in integer parameter `side`. For example, if `side` is 4, the function displays:

```
****
****
****
****
```

5.20   Modify the function created in Exercise 5.19 to form the square out of whatever character is contained in character parameter `fillCharacter`. Thus if `side` is 5 and `fillCharacter` is "#" then this function should print:

```
#####
#####
#####
#####
#####
```

5.21   Use techniques similar to those developed in Exercises 5.19 and 5.20 to produce a program that graphs a wide range of shapes.

5.22   Write program segments that accomplish each of the following:
   a) Calculate the integer part of the quotient when integer a is divided by integer b.
   b) Calculate the integer remainder when integer a is divided by integer b.

c) Use the program pieces developed in a) and b) to write a function that inputs an integer between 1 and 32767 and prints it as a series of digits, each pair of which is separated by two spaces. For example, the integer 4562 should be printed as:

```
4   5   6   2
```

5.23 Write a function that takes the time as three integer arguments (for hours, minutes, and seconds), and returns the number of seconds since the last time the clock "struck 12." Use this function to calculate the amount of time in seconds between two times, both of which are within one 12-hour cycle of the clock.

5.24 Implement the following integer functions:
  a) Function `celsius` returns the Celsius equivalent of a Fahrenheit temperature.
  b) Function `fahrenheit` returns the Fahrenheit equivalent of a Celsius temperature.
  c) Use these functions to write a program that prints charts showing the Fahrenheit equivalents of all Celsius temperatures from 0 to 100 degrees, and the Celsius equivalents of all Fahrenheit temperatures from 32 to 212 degrees. Print the outputs in a neat tabular format that minimizes the number of lines of output while remaining readable.

5.25 Write a function that returns the smallest of three floating point numbers.

5.26 An integer number is said to be a *perfect number* if its factors, including 1 (but not the number itself), sum to the number. For example, 6 is a perfect number because 6 = 1 + 2 + 3. Write a function `perfect` that determines if parameter `number` is a perfect number. Use this function in a program that determines and prints all the perfect numbers between 1 and 1000. Print the factors of each perfect number to confirm that the number is indeed perfect. Challenge the power of your computer by testing numbers much larger than 1000.

5.27 An integer is said to be *prime* if it is divisible only by 1 and itself. For example, 2, 3, 5 and 7 are prime, but 4, 6, 8 and 9 are not.
  a) Write a function that determines if a number is prime.
  b) Use this function in a program that determines and prints all the prime numbers between 1 and 10,000. How many of these 10,000 numbers do you really have to test before being sure that you have found all the primes?
  c) Initially you might think that $n/2$ is the upper limit for which you must test to see if a number is prime, but you need only go as high as the square root of n. Why? Rewrite the program, and run it both ways. Estimate the performance improvement.

5.28 Write a function that takes an integer value and returns the number with its digits reversed. For example, given the number 7631, the function should return 1367.

5.29 The *greatest common divisor (GCD)* of two integers is the largest integer that evenly divides each of the two numbers. Write function `gcd` that returns the greatest common divisor of two integers.

5.30 Write a function `qualityPoints` that inputs a student's average and returns 4 if a student's average is 90-100, 3 if the average is 80-89, 2 if the average is 70-79, 1 if the average is 60-69, and 0 if the average is lower than 60.

5.31 Write a program that simulates coin tossing. For each toss of the coin the program should print Heads or Tails. Let the program toss the coin 100 times, and count the number of times each side of the coin appears. Print the results. The program should call a separate function `flip` that takes no arguments and returns 0 for tails and 1 for heads. [*Note:* If the program realistically simulates the coin tossing, then each side of the coin should appear approximately half the time for a total of approximately 50 heads and 50 tails.]

5.32   Computers are playing an increasing role in education. Write a program that will help an elementary school student learn multiplication. Use `rand` to produce two positive one-digit integers. It should then type a question such as:

```
How much is 6 times 7?
```

The student then types the answer. Your program checks the student's answer. If it is correct, print `"Very good!"` and then ask another multiplication question. If the answer is wrong, print `"No. Please try again."` and then let the student try the same question again repeatedly until the student finally gets it right.

5.33   The use of computers in education is referred to as *computer-assisted instruction* (CAI). One problem that develops in CAI environments is student fatigue. This can be eliminated by varying the computer's dialogue to hold the student's attention. Modify the program of Exercise 5.32 so the various comments are printed for each correct answer and each incorrect answer as follows:

Responses to a correct answer

```
Very good!
Excellent!
Nice work!
Keep up the good work!
```

Responses to an incorrect answer

```
No. Please try again.
Wrong. Try once more.
Don't give up!
No. Keep trying.
```

Use the random number generator to choose a number from 1 to 4 to select an appropriate response to each answer. Use a `switch` statement with `printf` statements to issue the responses.

5.34   More sophisticated computer-aided instructions systems monitor the student's performance over a period of time. The decision to begin a new topic is often based on the student's success with previous topics. Modify the program of Exercise 5.33 to count the number of correct and incorrect responses typed by the student. After the student types 10 answers, your program should calculate the percentage of correct responses. If the percentage is lower than 75 percent, your program should print `"Please ask your instructor for extra help"` and then terminate.

5.35   Write a C program that plays the game of "guess the number" as follows: Your program chooses the number to be guessed by selecting an integer at random in the range 1 to 1000. The program then types:

```
I have a number between 1 and 1000.
Can you guess my number?
Please type your first guess.
```

The player then types a first guess. The program responds with one of the following:

```
1. Excellent! You guessed the number!
   Would you like to play again (y or n)?
2. Too low. Try again.
3. Too high. Try again.
```

If the player's guess is incorrect, your program should loop until the player finally gets the number right. Your program should keep telling the player Too high or Too low to help the player "zero in" on the correct answer. [*Note:* The searching technique employed in this problem is called binary search. We will say more about this in the next problem.]

5.36   Modify the program of Exercise 5.35 to count the number of guesses the player makes. If the number is 10 or fewer, print Either you know the secret or you got lucky! If the player guesses the number in 10 tries, then print Ahah! You know the secret! If the player makes more than 10 guesses, then print You should be able to do better! Why should it take no more than 10 guesses? Well with each "good guess" the player should be able to eliminate half of the numbers. Now show why any number 1 to 1000 can be guessed in 10 or fewer tries.

5.37   Write a recursive function power(base, exponent) that when invoked returns

$$base^{exponent}$$

For example, power(3, 4) = 3 * 3 * 3 * 3. Assume that exponent is an integer greater than or equal to 1. *Hint:* The recursion step would use the relationship

$$base^{exponent} = base * base^{exponent - 1}$$

and the terminating condition occurs when exponent is equal to 1 because

$$base^1 = base$$

5.38   The Fibonacci series

0, 1, 1, 2, 3, 5, 8, 13, 21, ...

begins with the terms 0 and 1 and has the property that each succeeding term is the sum of the two preceding terms. a) Write a *nonrecursive* function fibonacci(n) that calculates the nth Fibonacci number. b) Determine the largest Fibonacci number that can be printed on your system. Modify the program of part a) to use double instead of int to calculate and return Fibonacci numbers. Let the program loop until it fails because of an excessively high value.

5.39   (*Towers of Hanoi*) Every budding computer scientist must grapple with certain classic problems, and the Towers of Hanoi (see Fig. 5.19) is one of the most famous of these. Legend has it that in a temple in the Far East, priests are attempting to move a stack of disks from one peg to another. The initial stack had 64 disks threaded onto one peg and arranged from bottom to top by decreasing size. The priests are attempting to move the stack from this peg to a second peg under the constraints that exactly one disk is moved at a time, and at no time may a larger disk be placed above a smaller disk. A third peg is available for temporarily holding the disks. Supposedly the world will end when the priests complete their task, so there is little incentive for us to facilitate their efforts.

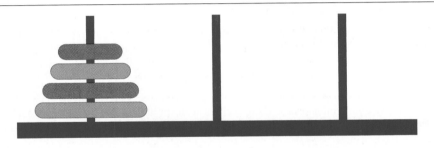

Fig. 5.19   Towers of Hanoi for the case with four disks.

Let us assume that the priests are attempting to move the disks from peg 1 to peg 3. We wish to develop an algorithm that will print the precise sequence of disk-to-disk peg transfers.

If we were to approach this problem with conventional methods, we would rapidly find ourselves hopelessly knotted up in managing the disks. Instead, if we attack the problem with recursion in mind, it immediately becomes tractable. Moving n disks can be viewed in terms of moving only $n - 1$ disks (and hence the recursion) as follows:

a)   Move $n - 1$ disks from peg 1 to peg 2, using peg 3 as a temporary holding area.

b)   Move the last disk (the largest) from peg 1 to peg 3.

c)   Move the $n - 1$ disks from peg 2 to peg 3, using peg 1 as a temporary holding area.

The process ends when the last task involves moving $n = 1$ disk, i.e., the base case. This is accomplished by trivially moving the disk without the need for a temporary holding area.

Write a program to solve the Towers of Hanoi problem. Use a recursive function with four parameters:

a)   The number of disks to be moved

b)   The peg on which these disks are initially threaded

c)   The peg to which this stack of disks is to be moved

d)   The peg to be used as a temporary holding area

Your program should print the precise instructions it will take to move the disks from the starting peg to the destination peg. For example, to move a stack of three disks from peg 1 to peg 3, your program should print the following series of moves:

$1 \rightarrow 3$ (This means move one disk from peg 1 to peg 3.)
$1 \rightarrow 2$
$3 \rightarrow 2$
$1 \rightarrow 3$
$2 \rightarrow 1$
$2 \rightarrow 3$
$1 \rightarrow 3$

5.40   Any program that can be implemented recursively can be implemented iteratively, although sometimes with considerably more difficulty and considerably less clarity. Try writing an iterative version of the Towers of Hanoi. If you succeed, compare your iterative version with the recursive version you developed in Exercise 5.39. Investigate issues of performance, clarity, and your ability to demonstrate the correctness of the programs.

5.41   (*Visualizing Recursion*) It is interesting to watch recursion "in action." Modify the factorial function of Fig. 5.14 to print its local variable and recursive call parameter. For each recursive call, display the outputs on a separate line and add a level of indentation. Do your utmost to make the outputs clear, interesting, and meaningful. Your goal here is to design and implement an output format that helps a person understand recursion better. You may want to add such display capabilities to the many other recursion examples and exercises throughout the text.

5.42   The greatest common divisor of integers x and y is the largest integer that evenly divides both x and y. Write a recursive function gcd that returns the greatest common divisor of x and y. The gcd of x and y is defined recursively as follows: If y is equal to 0, then gcd(x, y) is x; otherwise gcd(x, y) is gcd(y, x % y) where % is the remainder operator.

5.43   Can main be called recursively? Write a program containing a function main. Include static local variable count initialized to 1. Postincrement and print the value of count each time main is called. Run your program. What happens?

5.44   Exercises 5.32 through 5.34 developed a computer-assisted instruction program to teach an elementary school student multiplication. This exercise suggests enhancements to that program.

a) Modify the program to allow the user to enter a grade-level capability. A grade level of 1 means to use only single-digit numbers in the problems, a grade level of two means to use numbers as large as two-digits, etc.
b) Modify the program to allow the user to pick the type of arithmetic problems he or she wishes to study. An option of 1 means addition problems only, 2 means subtraction problems only, 3 means multiplication problems only, 4 means division problems only, and 5 means to randomly intermix problems of all these types.

5.45 Write function distance that calculates the distance between two points *(x1, y1)* and *(x2, y2)*. All numbers and return values should be of type double.

5.46 What does the following program do?

```
1    #include <stdio.h>
2
3    /* function main begins program execution */
4    int main()
5    {
6       int c; /* variable to hold character input by user */
7
8       if ( ( c = getchar() ) != EOF ) {
9          main();
10          printf( "%c", c );
11       } /* end if */
12
13       return 0; /* indicates successful termination */
14
15    } /* end main */
```

5.47 What does the following program do?

```
1    #include <stdio.h>
2
3    int mystery( int a, int b ); /* function prototype */
4
5    /* function main begins program execution */
6    int main()
7    {
8       int x; /* first integer */
9       int y; /* second integer */
10
11       printf( "Enter two integers: " );
12       scanf( "%d%d", &x, &y );
13
14       printf( "The result is %d\n", mystery( x, y ) );
15
16       return 0; /* indicates successful termination */
17
18    } /* end main */
19
20    /* Parameter b must be a positive integer
21       to prevent infinite recursion */
22    int mystery( int a, int b )
23    {
```

(continued on next page)

```
24      /* base case */
25      if ( b == 1 ) {
26         return a;
27      } /* end if */
28      else { /* recursive step */
29         return a + mystery( a, b - 1 );
30      } /* end else */
31
32   } /* end function mystery */
```

5.48   After you determine what the program of Exercise 5.47 does, modify the program to function properly after removing the restriction of the second argument being nonnegative.

5.49   Write a program that tests as many of the math library functions in Fig. 5.2 as you can. Exercise each of these functions by having your program print out tables of return values for a diversity of argument values.

5.50   Find the error in each of the following program segments and explain how to correct it:

a) ```
double cube(float);   /* function prototype */
...
cube(float number)   /* function definition */
{
    return number * number * number;
}
```

b) `register auto int x = 7;`

c) `int randomNumber = srand();`

d) ```
double y = 123.45678;
int x;
x = y;
printf( "%f\n", (double) x );
```

e) ```
double square(double number)
{
    double number;

    return number * number;
}
```

f) ```
int sum( int n )
{
    if ( n == 0 )
        return 0;
    else
        return n + sum( n );
}
```

5.51   Modify the craps program of Fig. 5.10 to allow wagering. Package as a function the portion of the program that runs one game of craps. Initialize variable bankBalance to 1000 dollars. Prompt the player to enter a wager. Use a while loop to check that wager is less than or equal to bankBalance and if not prompt the user to reenter wager until a valid wager is entered. After a correct wager is entered, run one game of craps. If the player wins, increase bankBalance by wager and print the new bankBalance. If the player loses, decrease bankBalance by wager, print the new bankBalance, check if bankBalance has become zero, and if so print the message "Sorry. You busted!" As the game progresses, print various messages to create some "chatter" such as "Oh, you're going for broke, huh?", or "Aw cmon, take a chance!", or "You're up big. Now's the time to cash in your chips!".

6

C Arrays

Objectives

- To introduce the array data structure.
- To understand the use of arrays to store, sort and search lists and tables of values.
- To understand how to define an array, initialize an array and refer to individual elements of an array.
- To be able to pass arrays to functions.
- To understand basic sorting techniques.
- To be able to define and manipulate multiple subscripted arrays.

With sobs and tears he sorted out
Those of the largest size …
Lewis Carroll

Attempt the end, and never stand to doubt;
Nothing's so hard, but search will find it out.
Robert Herrick

Now go, write it before them in a table,
and note it in a book.
Isaiah 30:8

'Tis in my memory lock'd,
And you yourself shall keep the key of it.
William Shakespeare

6.1 Introduction

This chapter serves as an introduction to the important topic of data structures. *Arrays* are
data structures consisting of related data items of the same type. In Chapter 10, we discuss
C's notion of `struct` (structure)—a data structure consisting of related data items of possibly different types. Arrays and structures are "static" entities in that they remain the same
size throughout program execution (they may, of course, be of automatic storage class and
hence created and destroyed each time the blocks in which they are defined are entered and
exited). In Chapter 12, we introduce dynamic data structures such as lists, queues, stacks
and trees that may grow and shrink as programs execute.

6.2 Arrays

An array is a group of memory locations related by the fact that they all have the same name
and the same type. To refer to a particular location or element in the array, we specify the
name of the array and the *position number* of the particular element in the array.

Figure 6.1 shows an integer array called c. This array contains 12 *elements.* Any one
of these elements may be referred to by giving the name of the array followed by the position number of the particular element in square brackets (`[]`). The first element in every
array is the *zeroth element.* Thus, the first element of array c is referred to as c[0], the
second element of array c is referred to as c[1], the seventh element of array c is referred
to as c[6], and, in general, the *i*th element of array c is referred to as c[i - 1]. Array
names, like other variable names, can contain only letters, digits and underscores. Array
names cannot begin with a digit.

The position number contained within square brackets is more formally called a *subscript.* A subscript must be an integer or an integer expression. If a program uses an
expression as a subscript, then the expression is evaluated to determine the subscript. For
example, if a = 5 and b = 6, then the statement

```
c[ a + b ] += 2;
```

Name of array (Note that all elements
of this array have the same name, c)

c[0]	-45
c[1]	6
c[2]	0
c[3]	72
c[4]	1543
c[5]	-89
c[6]	0
c[7]	62
c[8]	-3
c[9]	1
c[10]	6453
c[11]	78

Position number of the element within array c

Fig. 6.1 12-element array.

adds 2 to array element c[11]. Note that a subscripted array name is an lvalue—it can be used on the left side of an assignment.

Let us examine array c in Fig. 6.1 more closely. The *name* of the array is c. Its 12 elements are referred to as c[0], c[1], c[2], ..., c[11]. The *value* stored in c[0] is -45, the value of c[1] is 6, the value of c[2] is 0, the value of c[7] is 62 and the value of c[11] is 78. To print the sum of the values contained in the first three elements of array c, we would write

```
printf( "%d", c[ 0 ] + c[ 1 ] + c[ 2 ] );
```

To divide the value of the seventh element of array c by 2 and assign the result to the variable x, we would write

```
x = c[ 6 ] / 2;
```

Common Programming Error 6.1

It is important to note the difference between the "seventh element of the array" and "array element seven." Because array subscripts begin at 0, the "seventh element of the array" has a subscript of 6, while "array element seven" has a subscript of 7 and is actually the eighth element of the array. This is a source of "off-by-one" errors.

The brackets used to enclose the subscript of an array are actually considered to be an operator in C. They have the same level of precedence as the function call operator (i.e., the parentheses that are placed following a function name to call that function). Figure 6.2 shows the precedence and associativity of the operators introduced to this point in the text. They are shown top to bottom in decreasing order of precedence.

Operators						Associativity	Type
[]	()					left to right	highest
++	--	!	(type)			right to left	unary
*	/	%				left to right	multiplicative
+	-					left to right	additive
<	<=	>	>=			left to right	relational
==	!=					left to right	equality
&&						left to right	logical and
||						left to right	logical or
?:						right to left	conditional
=	+=	-=	*=	/=	%=	right to left	assignment
,						left to right	comma

Fig. 6.2   Operator precedence.

6.3 Defining Arrays

Arrays occupy space in memory. The programmer specifies the type of each element and the number of elements required by each array so that the computer may reserve the appropriate amount of memory. To tell the computer to reserve 12 elements for integer array c, the definition

```
int c[ 12 ];
```

is used. The following definition

```
int b[ 100 ], x[ 27 ];
```

reserves 100 elements for integer array b and 27 elements for integer array x.

Arrays may be defined to contain other data types. For example, an array of type char can be used to store a character string. Character strings and their similarity to arrays are discussed in Chapter 8. The relationship between pointers and arrays is discussed in Chapter 7.

6.4 Array Examples

This section presents several examples that demonstrate how to define arrays, how to initialize arrays and how to perform many common array manipulations.

Defining an Array and Using a Loop to Initialize the Array's Elements

Figure 6.3 uses `for` statements to initialize the elements of a 10-element integer array n to zeros and print the array in tabular format. The first `printf` statement (line 16) displays the column heads for the two columns printed in the subsequent `for` statement.

```
1   /* Fig. 6.3: fig06_03.c
2      initializing an array */
3   #include <stdio.h>
4
5   /* function main begins program execution */
6   int main()
7   {
8      int n[ 10 ]; /* n is an array of 10 integers */
9      int i; /* counter */
10
11     /* initialize elements of array n to 0 */
12     for ( i = 0; i < 10; i++ ) {
13        n[ i ] = 0; /* set element at location i to 0 */
14     } /* end for */
15
16     printf( "%s%13s\n", "Element", "Value" );
17
18     /* output contents of array n in tabular format */
19     for ( i = 0; i < 10; i++ ) {
20        printf( "%7d%13d\n", i, n[ i ] );
21     } /* end for */
22
23     return 0; /* indicates successful termination */
24
25  } /* end main */
```

```
Element        Value
      0            0
      1            0
      2            0
      3            0
      4            0
      5            0
      6            0
      7            0
      8            0
      9            0
```

Fig. 6.3   Initializing the elements of an array to zeros.

Initializing an Array in a Definition with an Initializer List

The elements of an array can also be initialized when the array is defined by following the definition with an equal sign and braces, {}, containing a comma-separated list of *initializers*. Figure 6.4 initializes an integer array with ten values (line 9) and prints the array in tabular format.

```
1   /* Fig. 6.4: fig06_04.c
2      Initializing an array with an initializer list */
3   #include <stdio.h>
4
5   /* function main begins program execution */
6   int main()
7   {
8      /* use initializer list to initialize array n */
9      int n[ 10 ] = { 32, 27, 64, 18, 95, 14, 90, 70, 60, 37 };
10     int i; /* counter */
11
12     printf( "%s%13s\n", "Element", "Value" );
13
14     /* output contents of array in tabular format */
15     for ( i = 0; i < 10; i++ ) {
16        printf( "%7d%13d\n", i, n[ i ] );
17     } /* end for */
18
19     return 0; /* indicates successful termination */
20
21  } /* end main */
```

```
Element        Value
      0           32
      1           27
      2           64
      3           18
      4           95
      5           14
      6           90
      7           70
      8           60
      9           37
```

Fig. 6.4   Initializing the elements of an array with an initializer list.

If there are fewer initializers than elements in the array, the remaining elements are initialized to zero. For example, the elements of the array n in Fig. 6.3 could have been initialized to zero as follows:

```
int n[ 10 ] = { 0 };
```

This explicitly initializes the first element to zero and initializes the remaining nine elements to zero because there are fewer initializers than there are elements in the array. It is important to remember that arrays are not automatically initialized to zero. The programmer must at least initialize the first element to zero for the remaining elements to be automatically zeroed. This method of initializing the array elements to 0 is performed at compile time for static arrays and at run time for automatic arrays.

Common Programming Error 6.2

Forgetting to initialize the elements of an array whose elements should be initialized.

The array definition

```
int n[ 5 ] = { 32, 27, 64, 18, 95, 14 };
```

causes a syntax error because there are six initializers and only five array elements.

Common Programming Error 6.3

Providing more initializers in an array initializer list than there are elements in the array is a syntax error.

If the array size is omitted from a definition with an initializer list, the number of elements in the array will be the number of elements in the initializer list. For example,

```
int n[] = { 1, 2, 3, 4, 5 };
```

would create a five-element array.

Specifying an Array's Size with a Symbolic Constant and Initializing Array Elements with Calculations
Figure 6.5 initializes the elements of a 10-element array s to the values 2, 4, 6, …, 20 and prints the array in tabular format. The values are generated by multiplying the loop counter by 2 and adding 2.

```c
1   /* Fig. 6.5: fig06_05.c
2      Initialize the elements of array s to the even integers from 2 to 20 */
3   #include <stdio.h>
4   #define SIZE 10
5
6   /* function main begins program execution */
7   int main()
8   {
9      /* symbolic constant SIZE can be used to specify array size */
10     int s[ SIZE ]; /* array s has 10 elements */
11     int j; /* counter */
12
13     for ( j = 0; j < SIZE; j++ ) { /* set the values */
14        s[ j ] = 2 + 2 * j;
15     } /* end for */
16
17     printf( "%s%13s\n", "Element", "Value" );
18
19     /* output contents of array s in tabular format */
20     for ( j = 0; j < SIZE; j++ ) {
21        printf( "%7d%13d\n", j, s[ j ] );
22     } /* end for */
23
24     return 0; /* indicates successful termination */
25
26  } /* end main */
```

Fig. 6.5　Generating the values to be placed into elements of an array. (Part 1 of 2.)

Element	Value
0	2
1	4
2	6
3	8
4	10
5	12
6	14
7	16
8	18
9	20

Fig. 6.5   Generating the values to be placed into elements of an array. (Part 2 of 2.)

The `#define` preprocessor directive is introduced in this program. Line 4

```
#define SIZE 10
```

defines a *symbolic constant* `SIZE` whose value is `10`. A symbolic constant is an identifier that is replaced with *replacement text* by the C preprocessor before the program is compiled. When the program is preprocessed, all occurrences of the symbolic constant `SIZE` are replaced with the replacement text `10`. Using symbolic constants to specify array sizes makes programs more *scalable*. In Fig. 6.5, the first `for` loop (line 13) could fill a 1000-element array by simply changing the value of `SIZE` in the `#define` directive from `10` to `1000`. If the symbolic constant `SIZE` had not been used, we would have to change the program in three separate places to scale the program to handle 1000 array elements. As programs get larger, this technique becomes more useful for writing clear programs.

Common Programming Error 6.4

Ending a #define or #include preprocessor directive with a semicolon. Remember that preprocessor directives are not C statements.

If the `#define` preprocessor directive in line 4 is terminated with a semicolon, all occurrences of the symbolic constant `SIZE` in the program are replaced with the text `10;` by the preprocessor. This may lead to syntax errors at compile time, or logic errors at execution time. Remember that the preprocessor is not C—it is only a text manipulator.

Common Programming Error 6.5

Assigning a value to a symbolic constant in an executable statement is a syntax error. A symbolic constant is not a variable. No space is reserved for it by the compiler as with variables that hold values at execution time.

Software Engineering Observation 6.1

Defining the size of each array as a symbolic constant makes programs more scalable.

Good Programming Practice 6.1

Use only uppercase letters for symbolic constant names. This makes these constants stand out in a program and reminds the programmer that symbolic constants are not variables.

Good Programming Practice 6.2

In multiword symbolic constant names, use underscores to separate the words for readability.

Summing the Elements of an Array

Figure 6.6 sums the values contained in the 12-element integer array a. The for statement's body (line 16) does the totaling.

```
1   /* Fig. 6.6: fig06_06.c
2      Compute the sum of the elements of the array */
3   #include <stdio.h>
4   #define SIZE 12
5
6   /* function main begins program execution */
7   int main()
8   {
9      /* use initializer list to initialize array */
10     int a[ SIZE ] = { 1, 3, 5, 4, 7, 2, 99, 16, 45, 67, 89, 45 };
11     int i; /* counter */
12     int total = 0; /* sum of array */
13
14     /* sum contents of array a */
15     for ( i = 0; i < SIZE; i++ ) {
16        total += a[ i ];
17     } /* end for */
18
19     printf( "Total of array element values is %d\n", total );
20
21     return 0; /* indicates successful termination */
22
23  } /* end main */
```

```
Total of array element values is 383
```

Fig. 6.6   Computing the sum of the elements of an array.

Using Arrays to Summarize Survey Results

Our next example uses arrays to summarize the results of data collected in a survey. Consider the problem statement.

> *Forty students were asked to rate the quality of the food in the student cafeteria on a scale of 1 to 10 (1 means awful and 10 means excellent). Place the 40 responses in an integer array and summarize the results of the poll.*

This is a typical array application (see Fig. 6.7). We wish to summarize the number of responses of each type (i.e., 1 through 10). The array responses (line 17) is a 40-element array of the students' responses. We use an 11-element array frequency (line 14) to count the number of occurrences of each response. We ignore frequency[0] because it is logical to have the response 1 increment frequency[1] rather than frequency[0]. This allows us to use each response directly as the subscript in the frequency array.

```
1   /* Fig. 6.7: fig06_07.c
2      Student poll program */
3   #include <stdio.h>
4   #define RESPONSE_SIZE 40 /* define array sizes */
5   #define FREQUENCY_SIZE 11
6
7   /* function main begins program execution */
8   int main()
9   {
10     int answer; /* counter to loop through 40 responses */
11     int rating; /* counter to loop through frequencies 1-10 */
12
13     /* initialize frequency counters to 0 */
14     int frequency[ FREQUENCY_SIZE ] = { 0 };
15
16     /* place the survey responses in the responses array */
17     int responses[ RESPONSE_SIZE ] = { 1, 2, 6, 4, 8, 5, 9, 7, 8, 10,
18        1, 6, 3, 8, 6, 10, 3, 8, 2, 7, 6, 5, 7, 6, 8, 6, 7, 5, 6, 6,
19        5, 6, 7, 5, 6, 4, 8, 6, 8, 10 };
20
21     /* for each answer, select value of an element of array responses
22        and use that value as subscript in array frequency to
23        determine element to increment */
24     for ( answer = 0; answer < RESPONSE_SIZE; answer++ ) {
25        ++frequency[ responses [ answer ] ];
26     } /* end for */
27
28     /* display results */
29     printf( "%s%17s\n", "Rating", "Frequency" );
30
31     /* output the frequencies in a tabular format */
32     for ( rating = 1; rating < FREQUENCY_SIZE; rating++ ) {
33        printf( "%6d%17d\n", rating, frequency[ rating ] );
34     } /* end for */
35
36     return 0; /* indicates successful termination */
37
38   } /* end main */
```

Rating	Frequency
1	2
2	2
3	2
4	2
5	5
6	11
7	5
8	7
9	1
10	3

Fig. 6.7   Student poll analysis program.

Good Programming Practice 6.3

Strive for program clarity. Sometimes it may be worthwhile to trade off the most efficient use of memory or processor time in favor of writing clearer programs.

Performance Tip 6.1

Sometimes performance considerations far outweigh clarity considerations.

The `for` loop (line 24) takes the responses one at a time from the array `responses` and increments one of the 10 counters (`frequency[ 1 ]` to `frequency[ 10 ]`) in the frequency array. The key statement in the loop is line 25

```
++frequency[ responses[ answer ] ];
```

which increments the appropriate `frequency` counter depending on the value of `responses[ answer ]`. When the counter variable `answer` is 0, `responses[ answer ]` is `responses[ 0 ]` which is 1, so `++frequency[ responses[ answer ] ];` is actually interpreted as

```
++frequency[ 1 ];
```

which increments array element one. When `answer` is 1, `responses[ answer ]` is `responses[ 1 ]` which is 2, so `++frequency[ responses[ answer ] ];` is actually interpreted as

```
++frequency[ 2 ];
```

which increments array element two. When `answer` is 2, `responses[ answer ]` is `responses[ 2 ]` which is 6, so `++frequency[ responses[ answer ] ];` is actually interpreted as

```
++frequency[ 6 ];
```

which increments array element six, and so on. Note that regardless of the number of responses processed in the survey, only an 11-element array is required (ignoring element zero) to summarize the results. If the data contained invalid values such as 13, the program would attempt to add 1 to `frequency[ 13 ]`. This would be outside the bounds of the array. *C has no array bounds checking to prevent the computer from referring to an element that does not exist.* Thus, an executing program can "walk off" the end of an array without warning. The programmer should ensure that all array references remain within the bounds of the array.

Common Programming Error 6.6

Referring to an element outside the array bounds.

Error-Prevention Tip 6.1

When looping through an array, the array subscript never goes below 0 and is always less than the total number of elements in the array (size – 1). Make sure the loop terminating condition prevents accessing elements outside this range.

Error-Prevention Tip 6.2

Programs should validate the correctness of all input values to prevent erroneous information from effecting a program's calculations.

Graphing Array Element Values with Histograms

Our next example (Fig. 6.8) reads numbers from an array and graphs the information in the form of a bar chart or histogram—each number is printed, then a bar consisting of that many asterisks is printed beside the number. The nested `for` statement (line 20) draws the bars. Note the use of `printf( "\n" )` to end a histogram bar (line 24).

```c
1   /* Fig. 6.8: fig06_08.c
2      Histogram printing program */
3   #include <stdio.h>
4   #define SIZE 10
5
6   /* function main begins program execution */
7   int main()
8   {
9      /* use initializer list to initialize array n */
10     int n[ SIZE ] = { 19, 3, 15, 7, 11, 9, 13, 5, 17, 1 };
11     int i; /* outer for counter for array elements */
12     int j; /* inner for counter counts *s in each histogram bar */
13
14     printf( "%s%13s%17s\n", "Element", "Value", "Histogram" );
15
16     /* for each element of array n, output a bar of the histogram */
17     for ( i = 0; i < SIZE; i++ ) {
18        printf( "%7d%13d           ", i, n[ i ]) ;
19
20        for ( j = 1; j <= n[ i ]; j++ ) { /* print one bar */
21           printf( "%c", '*' );
22        } /* end inner for */
23
24        printf( "\n" ); /* end a histogram bar */
25     } /* end outer for */
26
27     return 0; /* indicates successful termination */
28
29  } /* end main */
```

```
Element        Value    Histogram
      0           19    *******************
      1            3    ***
      2           15    ***************
      3            7    *******
      4           11    ***********
      5            9    *********
      6           13    *************
      7            5    *****
      8           17    *****************
      9            1    *
```

Fig. 6.8   Histogram printing.

Rolling a Die 6000 Times and Summarizing the Results in an Array

In Chapter 5, we stated that we would show a more elegant method of writing the dice-rolling program of Fig. 5.8. The problem was to roll a single six-sided die 6000 times to test whether the random number generator actually produces random numbers. An array version of this program is shown in Fig. 6.9.

```c
1   /* Fig. 6.9: fig06_09.c
2      Roll a six-sided die 6000 times */
3   #include <stdio.h>
4   #include <stdlib.h>
5   #include <time.h>
6   #define SIZE 7
7
8   /* function main begins program execution */
9   int main()
10  {
11     int face; /* random die value 1 - 6 */
12     int roll; /* roll counter 1-6000 */
13     int frequency[ SIZE ] = { 0 }; /* clear counts */
14
15     srand( time( NULL ) ); /* seed random-number generator */
16
17     /* roll die 6000 times */
18     for ( roll = 1; roll <= 6000; roll++ ) {
19        face = 1 + rand() % 6;
20        ++frequency[ face ]; /* replaces 26-line switch of Fig. 5.8 */
21     } /* end for */
22
23     printf( "%s%17s\n", "Face", "Frequency" );
24
25     /* output frequency elements 1-6 in tabular format */
26     for ( face = 1; face < SIZE; face++ ) {
27        printf( "%4d%17d\n", face, frequency[ face ] );
28     } /* end for */
29
30     return 0; /* indicates successful termination */
31
32  } /* end main */
```

Face	Frequency
1	1029
2	951
3	987
4	1033
5	1010
6	990

Fig. 6.9   Dice-rolling program using arrays instead of switch.

Using Character Arrays to Store and Manipulate Strings

We have discussed only integer arrays. However, arrays are capable of holding data of any type. We now discuss storing strings in character arrays. So far, the only string processing capability we have is outputting a string with `printf`. A string such as "hello" is really a `static` array of individual characters in C.

Character arrays have several unique features. A character array can be initialized using a string literal. For example,

```
char string1[] = "first";
```

initializes the elements of array `string1` to the individual characters in the string literal "first". In this case, the size of array `string1` is determined by the compiler based on the length of the string. It is important to note that the string "first" contains five characters *plus* a special string termination character called the *null character*. Thus, array `string1` actually contains six elements. The character constant representing the null character is '\0'. All strings in C end with this character. A character array representing a string should always be defined large enough to hold the number of characters in the string and the terminating null character.

Character arrays also can be initialized with individual character constants in an initializer list. The preceding definition is equivalent to

```
char string1[] = { 'f', 'i', 'r', 's', 't', '\0' };
```

Because a string is really an array of characters, we can access individual characters in a string directly using array subscript notation. For example, `string1[ 0 ]` is the character 'f' and `string1[ 3 ]` is the character 's'.

We also can input a string directly into a character array from the keyboard using `scanf` and the conversion specifier %s. For example,

```
char string2[ 20 ];
```

creates a character array capable of storing a string of at most 19 characters and a terminating null character. The statement

```
scanf( "%s", string2 );
```

reads a string from the keyboard into `string2`. Note that the name of the array is passed to `scanf` without the preceding & used with non-string variables. The & is normally used to provide `scanf` with a variable's location in memory so a value can be stored there. In Section 6.5, when we discuss passing arrays to functions, we will see that an array name is the address of the start of the array; therefore, the & is not necessary.

It is the programmer's responsibility to ensure that the array into which the string is read is capable of holding any string that the user types at the keyboard. Function `scanf` reads characters from the keyboard until the first whitespace character is encountered—it does not check how large the array is. Thus, `scanf` can write beyond the end of the array.

Common Programming Error 6.7

Not providing `scanf` with a character array large enough to store a string typed at the keyboard can result in destruction of data in a program and other run-time errors.

A character array representing a string can be output with `printf` and the %s conversion specifier. The array `string2` is printed with the statement

```
printf( "%s\n", string2 );
```

Note that `printf`, like `scanf`, does not check how large the character array is. The characters of the string are printed until a terminating null character is encountered.

Figure 6.10 demonstrates initializing a character array with a string literal, reading a string into a character array, printing a character array as a string and accessing individual characters of a string.

```
1   /* Fig. 6.10: fig06_10.c
2      Treating character arrays as strings */
3   #include <stdio.h>
4
5   /* function main begins program execution */
6   int main()
7   {
8      char string1[ 20 ]; /* reserves 20 characters */
9      char string2[] = "string literal"; /* reserves 15 characters */
10     int i; /* counter */
11
12     /* read string from user into array string1 */
13     printf("Enter a string: ");
14     scanf( "%s", string1 ); /* input ended by whitespace character */
15
16     /* output strings */
17     printf( "string1 is: %s\nstring2 is: %s\n"
18             "string1 with spaces between characters is:\n",
19             string1, string2 );
20
21     /* output characters until null character is reached */
22     for ( i = 0; string1[ i ] != '\0'; i++ ) {
23        printf( "%c ", string1[ i ] );
24     } /* end for */
25
26     printf( "\n" );
27
28     return 0; /* indicates successful termination */
29
30  } /* end main */
```

```
Enter a string: Hello there
string1 is: Hello
string2 is: string literal
string1 with spaces between characters is:
H e l l o
```

Fig. 6.10   Treating character arrays as strings.

Figure 6.10 uses a `for` statement (line 22) to loop through the `string1` array and print the individual characters separated by spaces using the `%c` conversion specifier. The condition in the `for` statement, `string1[ i ] != '\0'`, is true while the terminating null character has not been encountered in the string.

Static Local Arrays and Automatic Local Arrays

Chapter 5 discussed the storage class specifier `static`. A `static` local variable exists for the duration of the program, but is only visible in the function body. We can apply `static` to a local array definition so the array is not created and initialized each time the function is called and the array is not destroyed each time the function is exited in the program. This reduces program execution time particularly for programs with frequently called functions that contain large arrays.

Performance Tip 6.2

In functions that contain automatic arrays where the function is in and out of scope frequently, make the array `static` so it is not created each time the function is called.

Arrays that are `static` are automatically initialized once at compile time. If a `static` array is not explicitly initialized by the programmer, that array's elements are initialized to zero by the compiler.

Figure 6.11 demonstrates function `staticArrayInit` (line 24) with a local `static` array (line 27) and function `automaticArrayInit` (line 47) with a local automatic array (line 50). Function `staticArrayInit` is called twice (lines 12 and 16). The local `static` array in the function is initialized to zero by the compiler (line 27). The function prints the array, adds 5 to each element and prints the array again. The second time the function is called, the `static` array contains the values stored during the first function call. Function `automaticArrayInit` is also called twice (lines 13 and 17). The elements of the automatic local array in the function are initialized with the values 1, 2 and 3 (line 50). The function prints the array, adds 5 to each element and prints the array again. The second time the function is called, the array elements are initialized to 1, 2 and 3 again because the array has automatic storage duration.

Common Programming Error 6.8

Assuming that elements of a local `static` array are initialized to zero every time the function in which the array is defined is called.

```
1   /* Fig. 6.11: fig06_11.c
2      Static arrays are initialized to zero */
3   #include <stdio.h>
4
5   void staticArrayInit( void );    /* function prototype */
6   void automaticArrayInit( void ); /* function prototype */
7
8   /* function main begins program execution */
9   int main()
10  {
11     printf( "First call to each function:\n" );
12     staticArrayInit();
13     automaticArrayInit();
14
15     printf( "\n\nSecond call to each function:\n" );
16     staticArrayInit();
17     automaticArrayInit();
18
19     return 0; /* indicates successful termination */
20
21  } /* end main */
22
```

Fig. 6.11   Static arrays are automatically initialized to zero if not explicitly initialized by the programmer. (Part 1 of 3.)

```
23    /* function to demonstrate a static local array */
24    void staticArrayInit( void )
25    {
26       /* initializes elements to 0 first time function is called */
27       static int array1[ 3 ];
28       int i; /* counter */
29
30       printf( "\nValues on entering staticArrayInit:\n" );
31
32       /* output contents of array1 */
33       for ( i = 0; i <= 2; i++ ) {
34          printf( "array1[ %d ] = %d  ", i, array1[ i ] );
35       } /* end for */
36
37       printf( "\nValues on exiting staticArrayInit:\n" );
38
39       /* modify and output contents of array1 */
40       for ( i = 0; i <= 2; i++ ) {
41          printf( "array1[ %d ] = %d  ", i, array1[ i ] += 5 );
42       } /* end for */
43
44    } /* end function staticArrayInit */
45
46    /* function to demonstrate an automatic local array */
47    void automaticArrayInit( void )
48    {
49       /* initializes elements each time function is called */
50       int array2[ 3 ] = { 1, 2, 3 };
51       int i; /* counter */
52
53       printf( "\n\nValues on entering automaticArrayInit:\n" );
54
55       /* output contents of array2 */
56       for ( i = 0; i <= 2; i++ ) {
57          printf("array2[ %d ] = %d  ", i, array2[ i ] );
58       } /* end for */
59
60       printf( "\nValues on exiting automaticArrayInit:\n" );
61
62       /* modify and output contents of array2 */
63       for ( i = 0; i <= 2; i++ ) {
64          printf( "array2[ %d ] = %d  ", i, array2[ i ] += 5 );
65       } /* end for */
66
67    } /* end function automaticArrayInit */
```

```
First call to each function:

Values on entering staticArrayInit:
array1[ 0 ] = 0  array1[ 1 ] = 0  array1[ 2 ] = 0
Values on exiting staticArrayInit:
array1[ 0 ] = 5  array1[ 1 ] = 5  array1[ 2 ] = 5
```

Fig. 6.11   Static arrays are automatically initialized to zero if not explicitly initialized by the programmer. (Part 2 of 3.)

```
Values on entering automaticArrayInit:
array2[ 0 ] = 1  array2[ 1 ] = 2  array2[ 2 ] = 3
Values on exiting automaticArrayInit:
array2[ 0 ] = 6  array2[ 1 ] = 7  array2[ 2 ] = 8

Second call to each function:

Values on entering staticArrayInit:
array1[ 0 ] = 5  array1[ 1 ] = 5  array1[ 2 ] = 5
Values on exiting staticArrayInit:
array1[ 0 ] = 10  array1[ 1 ] = 10  array1[ 2 ] = 10

Values on entering automaticArrayInit:
array2[ 0 ] = 1  array2[ 1 ] = 2  array2[ 2 ] = 3
Values on exiting automaticArrayInit:
array2[ 0 ] = 6  array2[ 1 ] = 7  array2[ 2 ] = 8
```

Fig. 6.11 Static arrays are automatically initialized to zero if not explicitly initialized by the programmer. (Part 3 of 3.)

6.5 Passing Arrays to Functions

To pass an array argument to a function, specify the name of the array without any brackets. For example, if array hourlyTemperatures has been defined as

```
int hourlyTemperatures[ 24 ];
```

the function call

```
modifyArray( hourlyTemperatures, 24 )
```

passes array hourlyTemperatures and its size to function modifyArray. Unlike char arrays that contain strings, other array types do not have a special terminator. For this reason, the size of an array is passed to the function, so the function can process the proper number of elements.

C automatically passes arrays to functions by reference—the called functions can modify the element values in the callers' original arrays. The name of the array is actually the address of the first element of the array. Because the starting address of the array is passed, the called function knows precisely where the array is stored. Therefore, when the called function modifies array elements in its function body, it is modifying the actual elements of the array in their original memory locations.

Figure 6.12 demonstrates that an array name is really the address of the first element of an array by printing array, &array[0] and &array using the %p conversion specifier—a special conversion specifier for printing addresses. The %p conversion specifier normally outputs addresses as hexadecimal numbers. Hexadecimal (base 16) numbers consist of the digits 0 through 9 and the letters A through F (these letters are the hexadecimal equivalents of the numbers 10–15). They are often used as shorthand notation for large integer values. Appendix E, Number Systems, provides an in-depth discussion of the relationships between binary (base 2), octal (base 8), decimal (base 10; standard integers) and hexadecimal integers. The output shows that both array and &array[0] have the same value, namely 0012FF78. The output of this program is system dependent, but the addresses are always identical for a particular execution of this program on a particular computer.

```
1    /* Fig. 6.12: fig06_12.c
2       The name of an array is the same as &array[ 0 ] */
3    #include <stdio.h>
4
5    /* function main begins program execution */
6    int main()
7    {
8       char array[ 5 ]; /* define an array of size 5 */
9
10      printf( "    array = %p\n&array[0] = %p\n"
11          "    &array = %p\n",
12          array, &array[ 0 ], &array );
13
14      return 0; /* indicates successful termination */
15
16   } /* end main */
```

```
      array = 0012FF78
&array[0] = 0012FF78
   &array = 0012FF78
```

Fig. 6.12   Array name is the same as the address of the array's first element.

Performance Tip 6.3

Passing arrays by reference makes sense for performance reasons. If arrays were passed by value, a copy of each element would be passed. For large, frequently passed arrays, this would be time consuming and would consume considerable storage for the copies of the arrays.

Software Engineering Observation 6.2

It is possible to pass an array by value (by using a simple trick we explain in Chapter 10).

Although entire arrays are passed by reference, individual array elements are passed by value exactly as simple variables are. Such simple single pieces of data (such as individual `int`s, `float`s and `char`s) are called *scalars*. To pass an element of an array to a function, use the subscripted name of the array element as an argument in the function call. In Chapter 7, we show how to pass scalars (i.e., individual variables and array elements) to functions by reference.

For a function to receive an array through a function call, the function's parameter list must specify that an array will be received. For example, the function header for function `modifyArray` (that we called earlier in this section) might be written as

```
void modifyArray( int b[], int size )
```

indicating that `modifyArray` expects to receive an array of integers in parameter b and the number of array elements in parameter `size`. The size of the array is not required between the array brackets. If it is included, the compiler checks that it is greater than zero then ignores it. Specifying a negative size is a compile error. Because arrays are automatically passed by reference, when the called function uses the array name b, it will be referring to the array in the caller (array `hourlyTemperatures` in the preceding call). In Chapter 7, we introduce other notations for indicating that an array is being received by a function. As we will see, these notations are based on the intimate relationship between arrays and pointers in C.

Figure 6.13 demonstrates the difference between passing an entire array and passing an array element. The program first prints the five elements of integer array a (lines 20–22). Next, a and its size are passed to function modifyArray (line 27) where each of a's elements is multiplied by 2 (lines 56–57). Then a is reprinted in main (lines 32–34). As the output shows, the elements of a are indeed modified by modifyArray. Now the program prints the value of a[3] (line 38) and passes it to function modifyElement (line 40). Function modifyElement multiplies its argument by 2 (line 67) and prints the new value. Note that when a[3] is reprinted in main (line 43), it has not been modified because individual array elements are passed by value.

```
1   /* Fig. 6.13: fig06_13.c
2      Passing arrays and individual array elements to functions */
3   #include <stdio.h>
4   #define SIZE 5
5
6   /* function prototypes */
7   void modifyArray( int b[], int size );
8   void modifyElement( int e );
9
10  /* function main begins program execution */
11  int main()
12  {
13     int a[ SIZE ] = { 0, 1, 2, 3, 4 }; /* initialize a */
14     int i; /* counter */
15
16     printf( "Effects of passing entire array by reference:\n\nThe "
17             "values of the original array are:\n" );
18
19     /* output original array */
20     for ( i = 0; i < SIZE; i++ ) {
21        printf( "%3d", a[ i ] );
22     } /* end for */
23
24     printf( "\n" );
25
26     /* pass array a to modifyArray by reference */
27     modifyArray( a, SIZE );
28
29     printf( "The values of the modified array are:\n" );
30
31     /* output modified array */
32     for ( i = 0; i < SIZE; i++ ) {
33        printf( "%3d", a[ i ] );
34     } /* end for */
35
36     /* output value of a[ 3 ] */
37     printf( "\n\n\nEffects of passing array element "
38             "by value:\n\nThe value of a[3] is %d\n", a[ 3 ] );
39
```

Fig. 6.13 Passing arrays and individual array elements to functions. (Part 1 of 2.)

```
40        modifyElement( a[ 3 ] );  /* pass array element a[ 3 ] by value */
41
42        /* output value of a[ 3 ] */
43        printf( "The value of a[ 3 ] is %d\n", a[ 3 ] );
44
45        return 0;  /* indicates successful termination */
46
47  }  /* end main */
48
49  /* in function modifyArray, "b" points to the original array "a"
50        in memory */
51  void modifyArray( int b[], int size )
52  {
53        int j;  /* counter */
54
55        /* multiply each array element by 2 */
56        for ( j = 0; j < size; j++ ) {
57              b[ j ] *= 2;
58        }  /* end for */
59
60  }  /* end function modifyArray */
61
62  /* in function modifyElement, "e" is a local copy of array element
63        a[ 3 ] passed from main */
64  void modifyElement( int e )
65  {
66        /* multiply parameter by 2 */
67        printf( "Value in modifyElement is %d\n", e *= 2 );
68  }  /* end function modifyElement */
```

```
Effects of passing entire array by reference:

The values of the original array are:
   0   1   2   3   4
The values of the modified array are:
   0   2   4   6   8


Effects of passing array element by value:

The value of a[3] is 6
Value in modifyElement is 12
The value of a[ 3 ] is 6
```

Fig. 6.13 Passing arrays and individual array elements to functions. (Part 2 of 2.)

There may be situations in your programs in which a function should not be allowed to modify array elements. Because arrays are always passed by reference, modification of values in an array is difficult to control. C provides the type qualifier *const* to prevent modification of array values in a function. When an array parameter is preceded by the const qualifier, the elements of the array become constant in the function body and any attempt to modify an element of the array in the function body results in a compile time error. This enables the programmer to correct a program so it does not attempt to modify array elements.

Figure 6.14 demonstrates the const qualifier. Function tryToModifyArray (line 22) is defined with parameter const int b[] which specifies that array b is constant and cannot be modified. The output shows the error messages produced by the compiler—the errors may be different on your system. Each of the three attempts by the function to modify array elements results in the compiler error "l-value specifies a const object." The const qualifier is discussed again in Chapter 7.

Software Engineering Observation 6.3

The const type qualifier can be applied to an array parameter in a function definition to prevent the original array from being modified in the function body. This is another example of the principle of least privilege. Functions should not be given the capability to modify an array unless it is absolutely necessary.

```c
1   /* Fig. 6.14: fig06_14.c
2      Demonstrating the const type qualifier with arrays */
3   #include <stdio.h>
4
5   void tryToModifyArray( const int b[]  /* function prototype */
6
7   /* function main begins program execution */
8   int main()
9   {
10      int a[] = { 10, 20, 30 }; /* initialize a */
11
12      tryToModifyArray( a );
13
14      printf("%d %d %d\n", a[ 0 ], a[ 1 ], a[ 2 ] );
15
16      return 0; /* indicates successful termination */
17
18   } /* end main */
19
20   /* in function tryToModifyArray, array b is const, so it cannot be
21      used to modify the original array a in main. */
22   void tryToModifyArray( const int b[] )
23   {
24      b[ 0 ] /= 2;    /* error */
25      b[ 1 ] /= 2;    /* error */
26      b[ 2 ] /= 2;    /* error */
27   } /* end function tryToModifyArray */
```

```
Compiling...
FIG06_14.C
fig06_14.c(24) : error C2166: l-value specifies const object
fig06_14.c(25) : error C2166: l-value specifies const object
fig06_14.c(26) : error C2166: l-value specifies const object
```

Fig. 6.14   const type qualifier.

6.6 Sorting Arrays

Sorting data (i.e., placing the data into a particular order such as ascending or descending) is one of the most important computing applications. A bank sorts all checks by account number so that it can prepare individual bank statements at the end of each month. Telephone companies sort their lists of accounts by last name and, within that, by first name to make it easy to find phone numbers. Virtually every organization must sort some data and in many cases massive amounts of data. Sorting data is an intriguing problem which has attracted some of the most intense research efforts in the field of computer science. In this chapter we discuss what is perhaps the simplest known sorting scheme. In the exercises and in Chapter 12, we investigate more complex schemes that yield far superior performance.

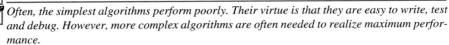

Performance Tip 6.4

Often, the simplest algorithms perform poorly. Their virtue is that they are easy to write, test and debug. However, more complex algorithms are often needed to realize maximum performance.

Figure 6.15 sorts the values in the elements of the 10-element array a (line 10) into ascending order. The technique we use is called the *bubble sort* or the *sinking sort* because the smaller values gradually "bubble" their way upward to the top of the array like air bubbles rising in water, while the larger values sink to the bottom of the array. The technique is to make several passes through the array. On each pass, successive pairs of elements are compared. If a pair is in increasing order (or if the values are identical), we leave the values as they are. If a pair is in decreasing order, their values are swapped in the array.

```c
1    /* Fig. 6.15: fig06_15.c
2       This program sorts an array's values into ascending order */
3    #include <stdio.h>
4    #define SIZE 10
5
6    /* function main begins program execution */
7    int main()
8    {
9       /* initialize a */
10      int a[ SIZE ] = { 2, 6, 4, 8, 10, 12, 89, 68, 45, 37 };
11      int pass; /* passes counter */
12      int i;    /* comparisons counter */
13      int hold; /* temporary location used to swap array elements */
14
15      printf( "Data items in original order\n" );
16
17      /* output original array */
18      for ( i = 0; i < SIZE; i++ ) {
19         printf( "%4d", a[ i ] );
20      } /* end for */
21
22      /* bubble sort */
23      /* loop to control number of passes */
24      for ( pass = 1; pass < SIZE; pass++ ) {
25
26         /* loop to control number of comparisons per pass */
27         for ( i = 0; i < SIZE - 1; i++ ) {
28
29            /* compare adjacent elements and swap them if first
30               element is greater than second element */
```

Fig. 6.15 Sorting an array with bubble sort. (Part 1 of 2.)

```
31              if ( a[ i ] > a[ i + 1 ] ) {
32                  hold = a[ i ];
33                  a[ i ] = a[ i + 1 ];
34                  a[ i + 1 ] = hold;
35              } /* end if */
36
37          } /* end inner for */
38
39      } /* end outer for */
40
41      printf( "\nData items in ascending order\n" );
42
43      /* output sorted array */
44      for ( i = 0; i < SIZE; i++ ) {
45          printf( "%4d", a[ i ] );
46      } /* end for */
47
48      printf( "\n" );
49
50      return 0; /* indicates successful termination */
51
```

```
Data items in original order
   2    6    4    8   10   12   89   68   45   37
Data items in ascending order
   2    4    6    8   10   12   37   45   68   89
```

Fig. 6.15   Sorting an array with bubble sort. (Part 2 of 2.)

First the program compares a[0] to a[1], then a[1] to a[2], then a[2] to a[3], and so on until it completes the pass by comparing a[8] to a[9]. Note that although there are 10 elements, only nine comparisons are performed. Because of the way the successive comparisons are made, a large value may move down the array many positions on a single pass, but a small value may move up only one position. On the first pass, the largest value is guaranteed to sink to the bottom element of the array, a[9]. On the second pass, the second largest value is guaranteed to sink to a[8]. On the ninth pass, the ninth largest value sinks to a[1]. This leaves the smallest value in a[0], so only nine passes of the array are needed to sort the array even though there are ten elements.

The sorting is performed by the nested for loop (lines 24–39). If a swap is necessary, it is performed by the three assignments

```
hold = a[ i ];
a[ i ] = a[ i + 1 ];
a[ i + 1 ] = hold;
```

where the extra variable hold temporarily stores one of the two values being swapped. The swap cannot be performed with only the two assignments

```
a[ i ] = a[ i + 1 ];
a[ i + 1 ] = a[ i ];
```

If, for example, a[i] is 7 and a[i + 1] is 5, after the first assignment both values will be 5 and the value 7 will be lost. Hence the need for the extra variable hold.

The chief virtue of the bubble sort is that it is easy to program. However, the bubble sort runs slowly. This becomes apparent when sorting large arrays. In the exercises, we will develop more efficient versions of the bubble sort. Far more efficient sorts than the bubble sort have been developed. We will investigate a few of these in the exercises. More advanced courses investigate sorting and searching in greater depth.

6.7 Case Study: Computing Mean, Median and Mode Using Arrays

We now consider a larger example. Computers are commonly used for *survey data analysis* to compile and analyze the results of surveys and opinion polls. Figure 6.16 uses array response initialized with 99 responses to a survey. Each response is a number from 1 to 9. The program computes the mean, median and mode of the 99 values.

```
1   /* Fig. 6.16: fig06_16.c
2       This program introduces the topic of survey data analysis.
3       It computes the mean, median and mode of the data */
4   #include <stdio.h>
5   #define SIZE 99
6
7   /* function prototypes */
8   void mean( const int answer[] );
9   void median( int answer[] );
10  void mode( int freq[], const int answer[] ) ;
11  void bubbleSort( int a[] );
12  void printArray( const int a[] );
13
14  /* function main begins program execution */
15  int main()
16  {
17     int frequency[ 10 ] = { 0 }; /* initialize array frequency */
18
19     /* initialize array response */
20     int response[ SIZE ] =
21        { 6, 7, 8, 9, 8, 7, 8, 9, 8, 9,
22          7, 8, 9, 5, 9, 8, 7, 8, 7, 8,
23          6, 7, 8, 9, 3, 9, 8, 7, 8, 7,
24          7, 8, 9, 8, 9, 8, 9, 7, 8, 9,
25          6, 7, 8, 7, 8, 7, 9, 8, 9, 2,
26          7, 8, 9, 8, 9, 8, 9, 7, 5, 3,
27          5, 6, 7, 2, 5, 3, 9, 4, 6, 4,
28          7, 8, 9, 6, 8, 7, 8, 9, 7, 8,
29          7, 4, 4, 2, 5, 3, 8, 7, 5, 6,
30          4, 5, 6, 1, 6, 5, 7, 8, 7 };
31
32     /* process responses */
33     mean( response );
34     median( response );
35     mode( frequency, response );
36
```

Fig. 6.16 Survey data analysis program. (Part 1 of 4.)

```
37        return 0; /* indicates successful termination */
38
39   } /* end main */
40
41   /* calculate average of all response values */
42   void mean( const int answer[] )
43   {
44        int j; /* counter for totaling array elements */
45        int total = 0; /* variable to hold sum of array elements */
46
47        printf( "%s\n%s\n%s\n", "********", "  Mean", "********" );
48
49        /* total response values */
50        for ( j = 0; j < SIZE; j++ ) {
51           total += answer[ j ];
52        } /* end for */
53
54        printf( "The mean is the average value of the data\n"
55                "items. The mean is equal to the total of\n"
56                "all the data items divided by the number\n"
57                "of data items ( %d ). The mean value for\n"
58                "this run is: %d / %d = %.4f\n\n",
59                SIZE, total, SIZE, ( double ) total / SIZE );
60   } /* end function mean */
61
62   /* sort array and determine median element's value */
63   void median( int answer[] )
64   {
65        printf( "\n%s\n%s\n%s\n%s",
66                "********", "  Median", "********",
67                "The unsorted array of responses is" );
68
69        printArray( answer ); /* output unsorted array */
70
71        bubbleSort( answer ); /* sort array */
72
73        printf( "\n\nThe sorted array is" );
74        printArray( answer ); /* output sorted array */
75
76        /* display median element */
77        printf( "\n\nThe median is element %d of\n"
78                "the sorted %d element array.\n"
79                "For this run the median is %d\n\n",
80                SIZE / 2, SIZE, answer[ SIZE / 2 ] );
81   } /* end function median */
82
83   /* determine most frequent response */
84   void mode( int freq[], const int answer[] )
85   {
86        int rating; /* counter for accessing elements 1-9 of array freq */
87        int j; /* counter for summarizing elements 0-98 of array answer */
88        int h; /* counter for diplaying histograms of elements in array freq */
89        int largest = 0; /* represents largest frequency */
```

Fig. 6.16 Survey data analysis program. (Part 2 of 4.)

```
90       int modeValue = 0; /* respesents most frequent response */
91
92       printf( "\n%s\n%s\n%s\n",
93               "*********", "   Mode", "*********" );
94
95       /* initialize frequencies to 0 */
96       for ( rating = 1; rating <= 9; rating++ ) {
97          freq[ rating ] = 0;
98       } /* end for */
99
100      /* summarize frequencies */
101      for ( j = 0; j < SIZE; j++ ) {
102         ++freq[ answer[ j ] ];
103      } /* end for */
104
105      /* output headers for result columns */
106      printf( "%s%11s%19s\n\n%54s\n%54s\n\n",
107              "Response", "Frequency", "Histogram",
108              "1    1    2    2", "5    0    5    0    5" );
109
110      /* output results */
111      for ( rating = 1; rating <= 9; rating++ ) {
112         printf( "%8d%11d           ", rating, freq[ rating ] );
113
114         /* keep track of mode value and largest frequency value */
115         if ( freq[ rating ] > largest ) {
116            largest = freq[ rating ];
117            modeValue = rating;
118         } /* end if */
119
120         /* output histogram bar representing frequency value */
121         for ( h = 1; h <= freq[ rating ]; h++ ) {
122            printf( "*" );
123         } /* end inner for */
124
125         printf( "\n" ); /* being new line of output */
126      } /* end outer for */
127
128      /* display the mode value */
129      printf( "The mode is the most frequent value.\n"
130              "For this run the mode is %d which occurred"
131              " %d times.\n", modeValue, largest );
132   } /* end function mode */
133
134   /* function that sorts an array with bubble sort algorithm */
135   void bubbleSort( int a[] )
136   {
137      int pass; /* pass counter */
138      int j;    /* comparison counter */
139      int hold; /* temporary location used to swap elements */
140
141      /* loop to control number of passes */
142      for ( pass = 1; pass < SIZE; pass++ ) {
```

Fig. 6.16 Survey data analysis program. (Part 3 of 4.)

```
143
144        /* loop to control number of comparisons per pass */
145        for ( j = 0; j < SIZE - 1; j++ ) {
146
147           /* swap elements if out of order */
148           if ( a[ j ] > a[ j + 1 ] ) {
149              hold = a[ j ];
150              a[ j ] = a[ j + 1 ];
151              a[ j + 1 ] = hold;
152           } /* end if */
153
154        } /* end inner for */
155
156     } /* end outer for */
157
158  } /* end function bubbleSort */
159
160  /* output array contents (20 values per row) */
161  void printArray( const int a[] )
162  {
163     int j; /* counter */
164
165     /* output array contents */
166     for ( j = 0; j < SIZE; j++ ) {
167
168        if ( j % 20 == 0 ) { /* begin new line every 20 values */
169           printf( "\n" );
170        } /* end if */
171
172        printf( "%2d", a[ j ] );
173     } /* end for */
174
175  } /* end function printArray */
```

Fig. 6.16   Survey data analysis program. (Part 4 of 4.)

The mean is the arithmetic average of the 99 values. Function mean (line 42) computes the mean by totaling the 99 elements and dividing the result by 99.

The median is the "middle value." Function median (line 63) determines the median by calling function bubbleSort (defined in line 135) to sort the array of responses into ascending order then picking the middle element, answer[SIZE / 2], of the sorted array. Note that when there is an even number of elements, the median should be calculated as the mean of the two middle elements. Function median does not currently provide this capability. Function printArray (line 161) is called to output the response array.

The mode is the value that occurs most frequently among the 99 responses. Function mode (line 84) determines the mode by counting the number of responses of each type, then selecting the value with the greatest count. This version of function mode does not handle a tie (see Exercise 6.14). Function mode also produces a histogram to aid in determining the mode graphically. Figure 6.17 contains a sample run of this program. This example includes most of the common manipulations usually required in array problems, including passing arrays to functions.

```
********
  Mean
********
The mean is the average value of the data
items. The mean is equal to the total of
all the data items divided by the number
of data items ( 99 ). The mean value for
this run is: 681 / 99 = 6.8788


********
  Median
********
The unsorted array of responses is
6 7 8 9 8 7 8 9 8 9 7 8 9 5 9 8 7 8 7 8
6 7 8 9 3 9 8 7 8 7 7 8 9 8 9 8 9 7 8 9
6 7 8 7 8 7 9 8 9 2 7 8 9 8 9 8 9 7 5 3
5 6 7 2 5 3 9 4 6 4 7 8 9 6 8 7 8 9 7 8
7 4 4 2 5 3 8 7 5 6 4 5 6 1 6 5 7 8 7

The sorted array is
1 2 2 2 3 3 3 3 4 4 4 4 5 5 5 5 5 5 5 5
5 6 6 6 6 6 6 6 6 7 7 7 7 7 7 7 7 7 7 7
7 7 7 7 7 7 7 7 7 7 7 7 7 8 8 8 8 8 8 8
8 8 8 8 8 8 8 8 8 8 8 8 8 8 8 8 8 8 8 8
9 9 9 9 9 9 9 9 9 9 9 9 9 9 9 9 9 9 9

The median is element 49 of
the sorted 99 element array.
For this run the median is 7


********
  Mode
********
Response   Frequency        Histogram

                                 1    1    2    2
                            5    0    5    0    5


      1           1         *
      2           3         ***
      3           4         ****
      4           5         *****
      5           8         ********
      6           9         *********
      7          23         ***********************
      8          27         ***************************
      9          19         *******************
The mode is the most frequent value.
For this run the mode is 8 which occurred 27 times.
```

Fig. 6.17   Sample run for the survey data analysis program.

6.8 Searching Arrays

Often, a programmer will be working with large amounts of data stored in arrays. It may be necessary to determine whether an array contains a value that matches a certain *key value*. The process of finding a particular element of an array is called *searching*. In this section we discuss two searching techniques—the simple *linear search* technique and the more efficient (but more complex) *binary search* technique. Exercise 6.34 and Exercise 6.35 at the end of this chapter ask you to implement recursive versions of the linear search and the binary search.

Searching an Array with Linear Search
The linear search (Fig. 6.18) compares each element of the array with the *search key*. Since the array is not in any particular order, it is just as likely that the value will be found in the first element as the last. On average, therefore, the program will have to compare the search key with half the elements of the array.

```
1   /* Fig. 6.18: fig06_18.c
2      Linear search of an array */
3   #include <stdio.h>
4   #define SIZE 100
5
6   /* function prototype */
7   int linearSearch( const int array[], int key, int size );
8
9   /* function main begins program execution */
10  int main()
11  {
12     int a[ SIZE ]; /* create array a */
13     int x; /* counter for initializing elements 0-99 of array a */
14     int searchKey; /* value to locate in array a */
15     int element; /* variable to hold location of searchKey or -1 */
16
17     /* create data */
18     for ( x = 0; x < SIZE; x++ ) {
19        a[ x ] = 2 * x;
20     } /* end for */
21
22     printf( "Enter integer search key:\n" );
23     scanf( "%d", &searchKey );
24
25     /* attempt to locate searchKey in array a */
26     element = linearSearch( a, searchKey, SIZE );
27
28     /* display results */
29     if ( element != -1 ) {
30        printf( "Found value in element %d\n", element );
31     } /* end if */
32     else {
33        printf( "Value not found\n" );
34     } /* end else */
```

Fig. 6.18 Linear search of an array. (Part 1 of 2.)

```
35
36        return 0; /* indicates successful termination */
37
38   } /* end main */
39
40   /* compare key to every element of array until the location is found
41      or until the end of array is reached; return subscript of element
42      if key or -1 if key is not found */
43   int linearSearch( const int array[], int key, int size )
44   {
45      int n; /* counter */
46
47      /* loop through array */
48      for ( n = 0; n < size; ++n ) {
49
50         if ( array[ n ] == key ) {
51            return n; /* return location of key */
52         } /* end if */
53
54      } /* end for */
55
56      return -1; /* key not found */
57
58   } /* end function linearSearch */
```

```
Enter integer search key:
36
Found value in element 18
```

```
Enter integer search key:
37
Value not found
```

Fig. 6.18 Linear search of an array. (Part 2 of 2.)

Searching an Array with Binary Search

The linear searching method works well for small or unsorted arrays. However, for large arrays linear searching is inefficient. If the array is sorted, the high-speed binary search technique can be used.

The binary search algorithm eliminates from consideration one half of the elements in a sorted array after each comparison. The algorithm locates the middle element of the array and compares it to the search key. If they are equal, the search key is found and the array subscript of that element is returned. If they are not equal, the problem is reduced to searching one half of the array. If the search key is less than the middle element of the array, the first half of the array is searched, otherwise the second half of the array is searched. If the search key is not found in the specified subarray (piece of the original array), the algorithm is repeated on one quarter of the original array. The search continues until the search key is equal to the middle element of a subarray, or until the subarray consists of one element that is not equal to the search key (i.e., the search key is not found).

In a worst case scenario, searching an array of 1023 elements will take only 10 comparisons using a binary search. Repeatedly dividing 1024 by 2 yields the values 512, 256, 128, 64, 32, 16, 8, 4, 2 and 1. The number 1024 (2^{10}) is divided by 2 only 10 times to get the value 1. Dividing by 2 is equivalent to one comparison in the binary search algorithm. An array of 1048576 (2^{20}) elements takes a maximum of 20 comparisons to find the search key. An array of one billion elements takes a maximum of 30 comparisons to find the search key. This is a tremendous increase in performance over the linear search that required comparing the search key to an average of half the elements in the array. For a one billion element array, this is a difference between an average of 500 million comparisons and a maximum of 30 comparisons! The maximum comparisons for any array can be determined by finding the first power of 2 greater than the number of elements in the array.

Figure 6.19 presents the iterative version of function binarySearch (lines 45–77). The function receives four arguments—an integer array b to be searched, an integer searchKey, the low array subscript and the high array subscript (these define the portion of the array to be searched). If the search key does not match the middle element of a subarray, the low subscript or high subscript is modified so a smaller subarray can be searched. If the search key is less than the middle element, the high subscript is set to middle - 1 and the search is continued on the elements from low to middle - 1. If the search key is greater than the middle element, the low subscript is set to middle + 1 and the search is continued on the elements from middle + 1 to high. The program uses an array of 15 elements. The first power of 2 greater than the number of elements in this array is 16 (2^4), so a maximum of 4 comparisons are required to find the search key. The program uses function printHeader (lines 80–99) to output the array subscripts and function printRow (lines 103–124) to output each subarray during the binary search process. The middle element in each subarray is marked with an asterisk (*) to indicate the element to which the search key is compared.

```
1   /* Fig. 6.19: fig06_19.c
2      Binary search of an array */
3   #include <stdio.h>
4   #define SIZE 15
5
6   /* function prototypes */
7   int binarySearch( const int b[], int searchKey, int low, int high );
8   void printHeader( void );
9   void printRow( const int b[], int low, int mid, int high );
10
11  /* function main begins program execution */
12  int main()
13  {
14     int a[ SIZE ]; /* create array a */
15     int i; /* counter for initializing elements 0-14 of array a */
16     int key; /* value to locate in array a */
17     int result; /* variable to hold location of key or -1 */
18
```

Fig. 6.19 Binary search of a sorted array. (Part 1 of 4.)

```
19      /* create data */
20      for ( i = 0; i < SIZE; i++ ) {
21         a[ i ] = 2 * i;
22      } /* end for */
23
24      printf( "Enter a number between 0 and 28: " );
25      scanf( "%d", &key );
26
27      printHeader();
28
29      /* search for key in array a */
30      result = binarySearch( a, key, 0, SIZE - 1 );
31
32      /* display results */
33      if ( result != -1 ) {
34         printf( "\n%d found in array element %d\n", key, result );
35      } /* end if */
36      else {
37         printf( "\n%d not found\n", key );
38      } /* end else */
39
40      return 0; /* indicates successful termination */
41
42   } /* end main */
43
44   /* function to perform binary search of an array */
45   int binarySearch( const int b[], int searchKey, int low, int high )
46   {
47      int middle; /* variable to hold middle element of array */
48
49      /* loop until low subscript is greater than high subscript */
50      while ( low <= high ) {
51
52         /* determine middle element of subarray being searched */
53         middle = ( low + high ) / 2;
54
55         /* display subarray used in this loop iteration */
56         printRow( b, low, middle, high );
57
58         /* if searchKey matched middle element, return middle */
59         if ( searchKey == b[ middle ] ) {
60            return middle;
61         } /* end if */
62
63         /* if searchKey less than middle element, set new high */
64         else if ( searchKey < b[ middle ] ) {
65            high = middle - 1; /* search low end of array */
66         } /* end else if */
67
68         /* if searchKey greater than middle element, set new low */
69         else {
70            low = middle + 1; /* search high end of array */
71         } /* end else */
```

Fig. 6.19   Binary search of a sorted array. (Part 2 of 4.)

```
72
73     } /* end while */
74
75     return -1;   /* searchKey not found */
76
77  } /* end function binarySearch */
78
79  /* Print a header for the output */
80  void printHeader( void )
81  {
82     int i; /* counter */
83
84     printf( "\nSubscripts:\n" );
85
86     /* output column head */
87     for ( i = 0; i < SIZE; i++ ) {
88        printf( "%3d ", i );
89     } /* end for */
90
91     printf( "\n" ); /* start new line of output */
92
93     /* output line of - characters */
94     for ( i = 1; i <= 4 * SIZE; i++ ) {
95        printf( "-" );
96     } /* end for */
97
98     printf( "\n" ); /* start new line of output */
99  } /* end function printHeader */
100
101 /* Print one row of output showing the current
102    part of the array being processed. */
103 void printRow( const int b[], int low, int mid, int high )
104 {
105    int i; /* counter for iterating through array b */
106
107    /* loop through entire array */
108    for ( i = 0; i < SIZE; i++ ) {
109
110       /* display spaces if outside current subarray range */
111       if ( i < low || i > high ) {
112          printf( "    " );
113       } /* end if */
114       else if ( i == mid ) { /* display middle element */
115          printf( "%3d*", b[ i ] ); /* mark middle value */
116       } /* end else if */
117       else { /* display other elements in subarray */
118          printf( "%3d ", b[ i ] );
119       } /* end else */
120
121    } /* end for */
122
123    printf( "\n" ); /* start new line of output */
124 } /* end function printRow */
```

Fig. 6.19   Binary search of a sorted array. (Part 3 of 4.)

```
Enter a number between 0 and 28: 25

Subscripts:
  0   1   2   3   4   5   6   7   8   9  10  11  12  13  14
-------------------------------------------------------------
  0   2   4   6   8  10  12  14* 16  18  20  22  24  26  28
                              16  18  20  22* 24  26  28
                                          24  26* 28
                                          24*

25 not found
```

```
Enter a number between 0 and 28: 8

Subscripts:
  0   1   2   3   4   5   6   7   8   9  10  11  12  13  14
-------------------------------------------------------------
  0   2   4   6   8  10  12  14* 16  18  20  22  24  26  28
  0   2   4   6*  8  10  12
                   8  10* 12
                   8*

8 found in array element 4
```

```
Enter a number between 0 and 28: 6

Subscripts:
  0   1   2   3   4   5   6   7   8   9  10  11  12  13  14
-------------------------------------------------------------
  0   2   4   6   8  10  12  14* 16  18  20  22  24  26  28
  0   2   4   6*  8  10  12

6 found in array element 3
```

Fig. 6.19   Binary search of a sorted array. (Part 4 of 4.)

6.9 Multiple-Subscripted Arrays

Arrays in C can have multiple subscripts. A common use of multiple-subscripted arrays is to represent *tables* of values consisting of information arranged in *rows* and *columns*. To identify a particular table element, we must specify two subscripts: The first (by convention) identifies the element's row and the second (by convention) identifies the element's column. Tables or arrays that require two subscripts to identify a particular element are called *double-subscripted arrays*. Note that multiple-subscripted arrays can have more than two subscripts.

Figure 6.20 illustrates a double-subscripted array, a. The array contains three rows and four columns, so it is said to be a 3-by-4 array. In general, an array with *m* rows and *n* columns is called an *m-by-n array*.

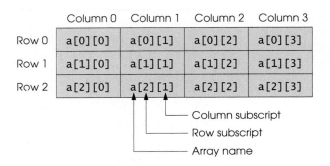

Fig. 6.20 Double-subscripted array with three rows and four columns.

Every element in array a is identified in Fig. 6.20 by an element name of the form a[i][j]; a is the name of the array, and i and j are the subscripts that uniquely identify each element in a. Notice that the names of the elements in the first row all have a first subscript of 0; the names of the elements in the fourth column all have a second subscript of 3.

Common Programming Error 6.9

Referencing a double-subscripted array element a[x, y] instead of a[x][y].

A multiple-subscripted array can be initialized when it is defined much like a single subscripted array. For example, a double-subscripted array int b[2][2] could be defined and initialized with

```
int b[ 2 ][ 2 ] = { { 1, 2 }, { 3, 4 } };
```

The values are grouped by row in braces. The values in the first set of braces initialize row 0 and the values in the second set of braces initialize row 1. So, the values 1 and 2 initialize elements b[0][0] and b[0][1], respectively, and the values 3 and 4 initialize elements b[1][0] and b[1][1], respectively. If there are not enough initializers for a given row, the remaining elements of that row are initialized to 0. Thus,

```
int b[ 2 ][ 2 ] = { { 1 }, { 3, 4 } };
```

would initialize b[0][0] to 1, b[0][1] to 0, b[1][0] to 3 and b[1][1] to 4. Figure 6.21 demonstrates defining and initializing double-subscripted arrays.

```
1   /* Fig. 6.21: fig06_21.c
2      Initializing multidimensional arrays */
3   #include <stdio.h>
4
5   void printArray( const int a[][ 3 ] ); /* function prototype */
6
7   /* function main begins program execution */
8   int main()
9   {
```

Fig. 6.21 Initializing multidimensional arrays. (Part 1 of 2.)

```
10      /* initialize array1, array2, array3 */
11      int array1[ 2 ][ 3 ] = { { 1, 2, 3 }, { 4, 5, 6 } };
12      int array2[ 2 ][ 3 ] = { 1, 2, 3, 4, 5 };
13      int array3[ 2 ][ 3 ] = { { 1, 2 }, { 4 } };
14
15      printf( "Values in array1 by row are:\n" );
16      printArray( array1 );
17
18      printf( "Values in array2 by row are:\n" );
19      printArray( array2 );
20
21      printf( "Values in array3 by row are:\n" );
22      printArray( array3 );
23
24      return 0; /* indicates successful termination */
25
26   } /* end main */
27
28   /* function to output array with two rows and three columns */
29   void printArray( const int a[][ 3 ] )
30   {
31      int i; /* row counter */
32      int j; /* column counter */
33
34      /* loop through rows */
35      for ( i = 0; i <= 1; i++ ) {
36
37         /* output column values */
38         for ( j = 0; j <= 2; j++ ) {
39            printf( "%d ", a[ i ][ j ] );
40         } /* end inner for */
41
42         printf( "\n" ); /* start new line of output */
43      } /* end outer for */
44
45   } /* end function printArray */
```

```
Values in array1 by row are:
1 2 3
4 5 6
Values in array2 by row are:
1 2 3
4 5 0
Values in array3 by row are:
1 2 0
4 0 0
```

Fig. 6.21   Initializing multidimensional arrays. (Part 2 of 2.)

The program defines three arrays of two rows and three columns (six elements each). The definition of `array1` (line 11) provides six initializers in two sublists. The first sublist initializes the first row (i.e., row 0) of the array to the values 1, 2 and 3; and the second sublist initializes the second row (i.e., row 1) of the array to the values 4, 5 and 6.

If the braces around each sublist are removed from the array1 initializer list, the compiler initializes the elements of the first row followed by the elements of the second row. The definition of array2 (line 12) provides five initializers. The initializers are assigned to the first row then the second row. Any elements that do not have an explicit initializer are initialized to zero automatically, so array2[1][2] is initialized to 0.

The definition of array3 (line 13) provides three initializers in two sublists. The sublist for the first row explicitly initializes the first two elements of the first row to 1 and 2. The third element is initialized to zero. The sublist for the second row explicitly initializes the first element to 4. The last two elements are initialized to zero.

The program calls function printArray (lines 29–45) to output each array's elements. Notice that the function definition specifies the array parameter as const int a[][3]. When we receive a single-subscripted array as an argument to a function, the array brackets are empty in the function's parameter list. The first subscript of a multiple-subscripted array is not required either, but all subsequent subscripts are required. The compiler uses these subscripts to determine the locations in memory of elements in multiple-subscripted arrays. All array elements are stored consecutively in memory regardless of the number of subscripts. In a double-subscripted array, the first row is stored in memory followed by the second row.

Providing the subscript values in a parameter declaration enables the compiler to tell the function how to locate an element in the array. In a double-subscripted array, each row is basically a single-subscripted array. To locate an element in a particular row, the compiler must know exactly how many elements are in each row so it can skip the proper number of memory locations when accessing the array. Thus, when accessing a[1][2] in our example, the compiler knows to skip the three elements of the first row in memory to get to the second row (row 1). Then, the compiler accesses the third element of that row (element 2).

Many common array manipulations use for repetition statements. For example, the following statement sets all the elements in the third row of array a in Fig. 6.20 to zero:

```
for ( column = 0; column <= 3; column++ )
    a[ 2 ][ column ] = 0;
```

We specified the *third* row, therefore we know that the first subscript is always 2 (again, 0 is the first row and 1 is the second row). The for statement varies only the second subscript (i.e., the column subscript). The preceding for statement is equivalent to the assignment statements:

```
a[ 2 ][ 0 ] = 0;
a[ 2 ][ 1 ] = 0;
a[ 2 ][ 2 ] = 0;
a[ 2 ][ 3 ] = 0;
```

The following nested for statement determines the total of all the elements in array a.

```
total = 0;

for ( row = 0; row <= 2; row++ )
    for ( column = 0; column <= 3; column++ )
        total += a[ row ][ column ];
```

The for statement totals the elements of the array one row at a time. The outer for statement begins by setting row (i.e., the row subscript) to 0 so the elements of the first row may be totaled by the inner for statement. The outer for statement then increments row to 1, so the elements of the second row can be totaled. Then, the outer for statement increments row to 2, so the elements of the third row can be totaled. The result is printed when the nested for statement terminates.

Figure 6.22 performs several other common array manipulations on 3-by-4 array studentGrades using for statements. Each row of the array represents a student and each column represents a grade on one of the four exams the students took during the semester. The array manipulations are performed by four functions. Function minimum (lines 44–66) determines the lowest grade of any student for the semester. Function maximum (lines 69–91) determines the highest grade of any student for the semester. Function average (lines 94–106) determines a particular student's semester average. Function printArray (lines 109–130) outputs the double-subscripted array in a neat, tabular format.

```c
1   /* Fig. 6.22: fig06_22.c
2      Double-subscripted array example */
3   #include <stdio.h>
4   #define STUDENTS 3
5   #define EXAMS 4
6
7   /* function prototypes */
8   int minimum( const int grades[][ EXAMS ], int pupils, int tests );
9   int maximum( const int grades[][ EXAMS ], int pupils, int tests );
10  double average( const int setOfGrades[], int tests );
11  void printArray( const int grades[][ EXAMS ], int pupils, int tests );
12
13  /* function main begins program execution */
14  int main()
15  {
16     int student; /* student counter */
17
18     /* initialize student grades for three students (rows) */
19     const int studentGrades[ STUDENTS ][ EXAMS ] =
20        { { 77, 68, 86, 73 },
21          { 96, 87, 89, 78 },
22          { 70, 90, 86, 81 } };
23
24     /* output array studentGrades */
25     printf( "The array is:\n" );
26     printArray( studentGrades, STUDENTS, EXAMS );
27
28     /* determine smallest and largest grade values */
29     printf( "\n\nLowest grade: %d\nHighest grade: %d\n",
30        minimum( studentGrades, STUDENTS, EXAMS ),
31        maximum( studentGrades, STUDENTS, EXAMS ) );
32
33     /* calculate average grade for each student */
34     for ( student = 0; student < STUDENTS; student++ ) {
35        printf( "The average grade for student %d is %.2f\n",
36           student, average( studentGrades[ student ], EXAMS ) );
37     } /* end for */
38
```

Fig. 6.22 Double-subscripted arrays example. (Part 1 of 3.)

```
39      return 0; /* indicates successful termination */
40
41   } /* end main */
42
43   /* Find the minimum grade */
44   int minimum( const int grades[][ EXAMS ], int pupils, int tests )
45   {
46      int i; /* student counter */
47      int j; /* exam counter */
48      int lowGrade = 100; /* initialize to highest possible grade */
49
50      /* loop through rows of grades */
51      for ( i = 0; i < pupils; i++ ) {
52
53         /* loop through columns of grades */
54         for ( j = 0; j < tests; j++ ) {
55
56            if ( grades[ i ][ j ] < lowGrade ) {
57               lowGrade = grades[ i ][ j ];
58            } /* end if */
59
60         } /* end inner for */
61
62      } /* end outer for */
63
64      return lowGrade; /* return minimum grade */
65
66   } /* end function minimum */
67
68   /* Find the maximum grade */
69   int maximum( const int grades[][ EXAMS ], int pupils, int tests )
70   {
71      int i; /* student counter */
72      int j; /* exam counter */
73      int highGrade = 0; /* initialize to lowest possible grade */
74
75      /* loop through rows of grades */
76      for ( i = 0; i < pupils; i++ ) {
77
78         /* loop through columns of grades */
79         for ( j = 0; j < tests; j++ ) {
80
81            if ( grades[ i ][ j ] > highGrade ) {
82               highGrade = grades[ i ][ j ];
83            } /* end if */
84
85         } /* end inner for */
86
87      } /* end outer for */
88
89      return highGrade; /* return maximum grade */
90
91   } /* end function maximum */
```

Fig. 6.22   Double-subscripted arrays example. (Part 2 of 3.)

```
92
93      /* Determine the average grade for a particular student */
94      double average( const int setOfGrades[], int tests )
95      {
96          int i; /* exam counter */
97          int total = 0; /* sum of test grades */
98
99          /* total all grades for one student */
100         for ( i = 0; i < tests; i++ ) {
101             total += setOfGrades[ i ];
102         } /* end for */
103
104         return ( double ) total / tests; /* average */
105
106     } /* end function average */
107
108     /* Print the array */
109     void printArray( const int grades[][ EXAMS ], int pupils, int tests )
110     {
111         int i; /* student counter */
112         int j; /* exam counter */
113
114         /* output column heads */
115         printf( "                    [0]   [1]   [2]   [3]" );
116
117         /* output grades in tabular format */
118         for ( i = 0; i < pupils; i++ ) {
119
120             /* output label for row */
121             printf( "\nstudentGrades[%d] ", i );
122
123             /* output grades for one student */
124             for ( j = 0; j < tests; j++ ) {
125                 printf( "%-5d", grades[ i ][ j ] );
126             } /* end inner for */
127
128         } /* end outer for */
129
130     } /* end function printArray */
```

```
The array is:
                 [0]   [1]   [2]   [3]
studentGrades[0] 77    68    86    73
studentGrades[1] 96    87    89    78
studentGrades[2] 70    90    86    81

Lowest grade: 68
Highest grade: 96
The average grade for student 0 is 76.00
The average grade for student 1 is 87.50
The average grade for student 2 is 81.75
```

Fig. 6.22   Double-subscripted arrays example. (Part 3 of 3.)

Functions `minimum`, `maximum` and `printArray` each receive three arguments—the `studentGrades` array (called `grades` in each function), the number of students (rows of the array) and the number of exams (columns of the array). Each function loops through array `grades` using nested `for` statements. The following nested `for` statement is from the function `minimum` definition:

```
/* loop through rows of grades */
for ( i = 0; i < pupils; i++ ) {

   /* loop through columns of grades */
   for ( j = 0; j < tests; j++ ) {

      if ( grades[ i ][ j ] < lowGrade ) {
         lowGrade = grades[ i ][ j ];

      } /* end if */

   } /* end inner for */

} /* end outer for */
```

The outer `for` statement begins by setting i (i.e., the row subscript) to 0 so the elements of the first row (i.e., the grades of the first student) can be compared to variable `lowGrade` in the body of the inner `for` statement. The inner `for` statement loops through the four grades of a particular row and compares each grade to `lowGrade`. If a grade is less than `lowGrade`, `lowGrade` is set to that grade. The outer `for` statement then increments the row subscript to 1. The elements of the second row are compared to variable `lowGrade`. The outer `for` statement then increments the row subscript to 2. The elements of the third row are compared to variable `lowGrade`. When execution of the nested structure is complete, `lowGrade` contains the smallest grade in the double-subscripted array. Function `maximum` works similarly to function `minimum`.

Function `average` (line 63) takes two arguments—a single-subscripted array of test results for a particular student called `setOfGrades` and the number of test results in the array. When `average` is called, the first argument `studentGrades[ student ]` is passed. This causes the address of one row of the double-subscripted array to be passed to `average`. The argument `studentGrades[ 1 ]` is the starting address of the second row of the array. Remember that a double-subscripted array is basically an array of single-subscripted arrays and that the name of a single-subscripted array is the address of the array in memory. Function `average` calculates the sum of the array elements, divides the total by the number of test results and returns the floating-point result.

SUMMARY

- C stores lists of values in arrays. An array is a group of related memory locations. These locations are related by the fact that they all have the same name and the same type. To refer to a particular location or element within the array, we specify the name of the array and the subscript.

- A subscript may be an integer or an integer expression. If a program uses an expression as a subscript, then the expression is evaluated to determine the particular element of the array.

- It is important to note the difference when referring to the seventh element of the array as opposed to array element seven. The seventh element has a subscript of 6, while array element seven has a subscript of 7 (actually the eighth element of the array). This is a source of "off-by-one" errors.

- Arrays occupy space in memory. To reserve 100 elements for integer array b and 27 elements for integer array x, the programmer writes

  ```
  int b[ 100 ], x[ 27 ];
  ```
- An array of type char can be used to store a character string.
- The elements of an array can be initialized in a definition, in assignment statements and by inputting the values directly into the elements of the array.
- If there are fewer initializers than elements in the array, C initializes the remaining elements to zero.
- C does not prevent referencing elements beyond the bounds of an array.
- A character array can be initialized using a string literal.
- All strings in C end with the null character. The character constant representing the null character is '\0'.
- Character arrays can be initialized with character constants in an initializer list.
- Individual characters in a string stored in an array can be accessed directly using array subscript notation.
- A string can be input directly into a character array from the keyboard using scanf and the conversion specifier %s.
- A character array representing a string can be output with printf and the %s conversion specifier.
- Apply static to a local array definition so the array is not created each time the function is called and the array is not destroyed each time the function exits.
- Arrays that are static are automatically initialized once at compile time. If the programmer does not explicitly initialize a static array, it is initialized to zero by the compiler.
- To pass an array to a function, the name of the array is passed. To pass a single element of an array to a function, simply pass the name of the array followed by the subscript (contained in square brackets) of the particular element.
- C passes arrays to functions by reference—the called functions can modify the element values in the callers' original arrays. The name of the array is actually the address of the first element of the array. Because the starting address of the array is passed, the called function knows precisely where the array is stored.
- To receive an array argument, the function's parameter list must specify that an array will be received. The size of the array is not required (for single-subscripted arrays) in the array brackets.
- When used with printf, the %p conversion specifier normally outputs addresses as hexadecimal numbers, but this is platform dependent.
- C provides the special type qualifier const to prevent modification of array values in a function. When an array parameter is preceded by the const qualifier, the elements of the array become constant in the function body and any attempt to modify an element of the array in the function body results in a compile time error.
- An array can be sorted using the bubble sort technique. Several passes of the array are made. On each pass, successive pairs of elements are compared. If a pair is in order (or if the values are identical), it is left as is. If a pair is out of order, the values are swapped. For small arrays, the bubble sort is acceptable, but for larger arrays it is inefficient compared to other more sophisticated sorting algorithms.
- The linear search compares each element of the array with the search key. Since the array is not in any particular order, it is just as likely that the value will be found in the first element as the last. On average, therefore, the program will have to compare the search key with half the elements of the array. The linear searching method works well for small arrays or for unsorted arrays.

- The binary search algorithm eliminates one half of the elements in a sorted array after each comparison. The algorithm locates the middle element of the array and compares it to the search key. If they are equal, the search key is found and the array subscript of that element is returned. If they are not equal, the problem is reduced to searching one half of the array.

- In a worst case scenario, searching an array of 1023 elements will take only 10 comparisons using a binary search. An array of 1048576 (2^{20}) elements takes a maximum of 20 comparisons to find the search key. An array of one billion elements takes a maximum of 30 comparisons to find the key.

- Arrays may be used to represent tables of values consisting of information arranged in rows and columns. To identify a particular element of a table, two subscripts are specified: The first (by convention) identifies the row in which the element is contained and the second (by convention) identifies the column in which the element is contained. Tables or arrays that require two subscripts to identify a particular element are called double-subscripted arrays.

- A multiple-subscripted array can be initialized when it is defined by using an initializer list.

- When a function receives a single-subscripted array as an argument, the array brackets are empty in the function's parameter list. The first subscript of a multiple-subscripted array is not required either, but all subsequent subscripts are required. The compiler uses these subscripts to determine the locations in memory of elements in multiple-subscripted arrays.

- To pass one row of a double-subscripted array to a function that receives a single-subscripted array, simply pass the name of the array followed by the subscript (in square brackets) of that row.

TERMINOLOGY

a[i]

a[i][j]

array

array initializer list

bar chart

binary search

bounds checking

bubble sort

character array

column subscript

const qualifier

define an array

#define preprocessor directive

double precision

double-subscripted array

element of an array

expression as a subscript

initialize an array

initializer list

linear search

m-by-*n* array

mean

median

mode

multiple-subscripted array

name of an array

null character '\0'

off-by-one error

pass-by-reference

passing arrays to functions

%p conversion specifier

position number

replacement text

row subscript

scalability

scalar

search key

searching an array

single-subscripted array

sinking sort

sorting

sorting pass

sorting the elements of an array

square brackets

string

subscript

survey data analysis

symbolic constant

table of values

tabular format

temporary area for exchange of values

terminating null character

totaling the elements of an array

value of an element

walk off an array

zeroth element

COMMON PROGRAMMING ERRORS

6.1   It is important to note the difference between the "seventh element of the array" and "array element seven." Because array subscripts begin at 0, the "seventh element of the array" has a subscript of 6, while "array element seven" has a subscript of 7 and is actually the eighth element of the array. This is a source of "off-by-one" errors.

6.2   Forgetting to initialize the elements of an array whose elements should be initialized.

6.3   Providing more initializers in an array initializer list than there are elements in the array is a syntax error.

6.4   Ending a `#define` or `#include` preprocessor directive with a semicolon. Remember that preprocessor directives are not C statements.

6.5   Assigning a value to a symbolic constant in an executable statement is a syntax error. A symbolic constant is not a variable. No space is reserved for it by the compiler as with variables that hold values at execution time.

6.6   Referring to an element outside the array bounds.

6.7   Not providing `scanf` with a character array large enough to store a string typed at the keyboard can result in destruction of data in a program and other run-time errors.

6.8   Assuming that elements of a local `static` array are initialized to zero every time the function in which the array is defined is called.

6.9   Referencing a double-subscripted array element as `a[ x, y ]` instead of `a[ x ][ y ]`.

ERROR-PREVENTION TIPS

6.1   When looping through an array, the array subscript should never go below 0 and should always be less than the total number of elements in the array (size − 1). Make sure the loop terminating condition prevents accessing elements outside this range.

6.2   Programs should validate the correctness of all input values to prevent erroneous information from affecting a program's calculations.

GOOD PROGRAMMING PRACTICES

6.1   Use only uppercase letters for symbolic constant names. This makes these constants stand out in a program and reminds the programmer that symbolic constants are not variables.

6.2   In multiword symbolic constant names, use underscores to separate the words for readability.

6.3   Strive for program clarity. Sometimes it may be worthwhile to trade off the most efficient use of memory or processor time in favor of writing clearer programs.

PERFORMANCE TIPS

6.1   Sometimes performance considerations far outweigh clarity considerations.

6.2   In functions that contain automatic arrays where the function is in and out of scope frequently, make the array `static` so it is not created each time the function is called.

6.3   Passing arrays by reference makes sense for performance reasons. If arrays were passed by value, a copy of each element would be passed. For large, frequently passed arrays, this would be time consuming and would consume considerable storage for the copies of the arrays.

6.4   Often, the simplest algorithms perform poorly. Their virtue is that they are easy to write, test and debug. However, more complex algorithms are often needed to realize maximum performance.

SOFTWARE ENGINEERING OBSERVATIONS

6.1   Defining the size of each array as a symbolic constant makes programs more scalable.

6.2   It is possible to pass an array by value (by using a simple trick we explain in Chapter 10).

6.3   The `const` type qualifier can be applied to an array parameter in a function definition to prevent the original array from being modified in the function body. This is another example of the principle of least privilege. Functions should not be given the capability to modify an array unless it is absolutely necessary.

SELF-REVIEW EXERCISES

6.1   Answer each of the following:
   a) Lists and tables of values are stored in _____.
   b) The elements of an array are related by the fact that they have the same _____ and
      _____.
   c) The number used to refer to a particular element of an array is called its _____.
   d) A(n) _____ should be used to specify the size of an array because it makes the program more scalable.
   e) The process of placing the elements of an array in order is called _____ the array.
   f) Determining if an array contains a certain key value is called _____ the array.
   g) An array that uses two subscripts is referred to as a(n) _____ array.

6.2   State whether the following are *true* or *false*. If the answer is *false*, explain why.
   a) An array can store many different types of values.
   b) An array subscript can be of data type `double`.
   c) If there are fewer initializers in an initializer list than the number of elements in the array, C automatically initializes the remaining elements to the last value in the list of initializers.
   d) It is an error if an initializer list contains more initializers than there are elements in the array.
   e) An individual array element that is passed to a function and modified in the called function will contain the modified value in the calling function.

6.3   Answer the following questions regarding an array called `fractions`.
   a) Define a symbolic constant `SIZE` to be replaced with the replacement text 10.
   b) Define an array with `SIZE` elements of type `double` and initialize the elements to 0.
   c) Name the fourth element from the beginning of the array.
   d) Refer to array element 4.
   e) Assign the value `1.667` to array element nine.
   f) Assign the value `3.333` to the seventh element of the array.
   g) Print array elements 6 and 9 with two digits of precision to the right of the decimal point, and show the output that is actually displayed on the screen.
   h) Print all the elements of the array using a `for` repetition statement. Assume the integer variable `x` has been defined as a control variable for the loop. Show the output.

6.4   Write statements to accomplish the following:
   a) Define `table` to be an integer array and to have 3 rows and 3 columns. Assume the symbolic constant `SIZE` has been defined to be 3.
   b) How many elements does the array `table` contain? Print the total number of elements.
   c) Use a `for` repetition statement to initialize each element of `table` to the sum of its subscripts. Assume the integer variables `x` and `y` are defined as control variables.
   d) Print the values of each element of array `table`. Assume the array was initialized with the definition:

```
int table[ SIZE ][ SIZE ] =
   { { 1, 8 }, { 2, 4, 6 }, { 5 } };
```

6.5   Find the error in each of the following program segments and correct the error.
   a) `#define SIZE 100;`
   b) `SIZE = 10;`
   c) *Assume* `int b[ 10 ] = { 0 }, i;`
       ```
       for ( i = 0; i <= 10; i++ )
           b[ i ] = 1;
       ```
   d) `#include <stdio.h>;`
   e) *Assume* `int a[ 2 ][ 2 ] = { { 1, 2 }, { 3, 4 } };`
       ```
       a[ 1, 1 ] = 5;
       ```
   f) `#define VALUE = 120`

ANSWERS TO SELF-REVIEW EXERCISES

6.1   a) Arrays. b) Name, type. c) Subscript. d) Symbolic constant. e) Sorting. f) Searching.
g) Double-subscripted.

6.2   a) False. An array can store only values of the same type.
   b) False. An array subscript must be an integer or an integer expression.
   c) False. C automatically initializes the remaining elements to zero.
   d) True.
   e) False. Individual elements of an array are passed by value. If the entire array is passed to
       a function, then any modifications will be reflected in the original.

6.3   a) `#define SIZE 10`
   b) `double fractions[ SIZE ] = { 0 };`
   c) `fractions[ 3 ]`
   d) `fractions[ 4 ]`
   e) `fractions[ 9 ] = 1.667;`
   f) `fractions[ 6 ] = 3.333;`
   g) `printf( "%.2f %.2f\n", fractions[ 6 ], fractions[ 9 ] );`
       Output: 3.33 1.67.
   h) ```
       for (x = 0; x < SIZE; x++)
           printf("fractions[%d] = %f\n", x, fractions[x]);
       ```
       *Output:*
       ```
       fractions[0] = 0.000000
       fractions[1] = 0.000000
       fractions[2] = 0.000000
       fractions[3] = 0.000000
       fractions[4] = 0.000000
       fractions[5] = 0.000000
       fractions[6] = 3.333000
       fractions[7] = 0.000000
       fractions[8] = 0.000000
       fractions[9] = 1.667000
       ```

**6.4**    a)  `int table[ SIZE ][ SIZE ];`
   b)  Nine elements. `printf( "%d\n", SIZE * SIZE );`
   c)  ```
       for ( x = 0; x < SIZE; x++ )
           for ( y = 0; y < SIZE; y++ )
               table[ x ][ y ] = x + y;
       ```
   d) ```
       for (x = 0; x < SIZE; x++)
           for (y = 0; y < SIZE; y++)
               printf("table[%d][%d] = %d\n", x, y, table[x][y]);
       ```
       ```

Output:

```
table[0][0] = 1
table[0][1] = 8
table[0][2] = 0
table[1][0] = 2
table[1][1] = 4
table[1][2] = 6
table[2][0] = 5
table[2][1] = 0
table[2][2] = 0
```

6.5   a) Error: Semicolon at end of #define preprocessor directive.
          Correction: Eliminate semicolon.
      b) Error: Assigning a value to a symbolic constant using an assignment statement.
          Correction: Assign a value to the symbolic constant in a #define preprocessor directive
          without using the assignment operator as in #define SIZE 10.
      c) Error: Referencing an array element outside the bounds of the array (b[10]).
          Correction: Change the final value of the control variable to 9.
      d) Error: Semicolon at end of #include preprocessor directive.
          Correction: Eliminate semicolon.
      e) Error: Array subscripting done incorrectly.
          Correction: Change the statement to a[1][1] = 5;
      g) Error: Assigning a value to a symbolic constant using an assignment statement.
          Correction: Assign a value to the symbolic constant in a #define preprocessor
          directive without using the assignment operator as in #define VALUE 120.

EXERCISES

6.6   Fill in the blanks in each of the following:
      a) C stores lists of values in _____.
      b) The elements of an array are related by the fact that they _____.
      c) When referring to an array element, the position number contained within parentheses is
          called a(n) _____.
      d) The names of the five elements of array p are _____, _____, _____,
          _____ and _____.
      e) The contents of a particular element of an array is called the _____ of that element.
      f) Naming an array, stating its type and specifying the number of elements in the array is
          called _____ the array.
      g) The process of placing the elements of an array into either ascending or descending order
          is called _____.
      h) In a double-subscripted array, the first subscript (by convention) identifies the
          _____ of an element and the second subscript (by convention) identifies the
          _____ of an element.
      i) An *m*-by-*n* array contains _____ rows, _____ columns and _____ ele-
          ments.
      j) The name of the element in row 3 and column 5 of array d is _____.

6.7   State which of the following are *true* and which are *false*. If *false*, explain why.
      a) To refer to a particular location or element within an array, we specify the name of the
          array and the value of the particular element.
      b) An array definition reserves space for the array.

c) To indicate that 100 locations should be reserved for integer array p, the programmer writes the definition

p[100];

d) A C program that initializes the elements of a 15-element array to zero must contain one for statement.

e) A C program that totals the elements of a double-subscripted array must contain nested for statements.

f) The mean, median and mode of the following set of values are 5, 6 and 7, respectively: 1, 2, 5, 6, 7, 7, 7.

6.8   Write statements to accomplish each of the following:
a) Display the value of the seventh element of character array f.
b) Input a value into element 4 of single-subscripted floating-point array b.
c) Initialize each of the 5 elements of single-subscripted integer array g to 8.
d) Total the elements of floating-point array c of 100 elements.
e) Copy array a into the first portion of array b. Assume double a[11], b[34];
f) Determine and print the smallest and largest values contained in 99-element floating-point array w.

6.9   Consider a 2-by-5 integer array t.
a) Write a definition for t.
b) How many rows does t have?
c) How many columns does t have?
d) How many elements does t have?
e) Write the names of all the elements in the second row of t.
f) Write the names of all the elements in the third column of t.
g) Write a single statement that sets the element of t in row 1 and column 2 to zero.
h) Write a series of statements that initialize each element of t to zero. Do not use a repetition structure.
i) Write a nested for statement that initializes each element of t to zero.
j) Write a statement that inputs the values for the elements of t from the terminal.
k) Write a series of statements that determine and print the smallest value in array t.
l) Write a statement that displays the elements of the first row of t.
m) Write a statement that totals the elements of the fourth column of t.
n) Write a series of statements that print the array t in tabular format. List the column subscripts as headings across the top and list the row subscripts at the left of each row.

6.10   Use a single-subscripted array to solve the following problem. A company pays its salespeople on a commission basis. The salespeople receive $200 per week plus 9 percent of their gross sales for that week. For example, a salesperson who grosses $3000 in sales in a week receives $200 plus 9 percent of $3000, or a total of $470. Write a C program (using an array of counters) that determines how many of the salespeople earned salaries in each of the following ranges (assume that each salesperson's salary is truncated to an integer amount):
a) $200–299
b) $300–399
c) $400–499
d) $500–599
e) $600–699
f) $700–799
g) $800–899
h) $900–999
i) $1000 and over

6.11   The bubble sort presented in Fig. 6.15 is inefficient for large arrays. Make the following simple modifications to improve the performance of the bubble sort.

  a) After the first pass, the largest number is guaranteed to be in the highest-numbered element of the array; after the second pass, the two highest numbers are "in place," and so on. Instead of making nine comparisons on every pass, modify the bubble sort to make eight comparisons on the second pass, seven on the third pass and so on.

  b) The data in the array may already be in the proper order or near-proper order, so why make nine passes if fewer will suffice? Modify the sort to check at the end of each pass if any swaps have been made. If none has been made, then the data must already be in the proper order, so the program should terminate. If swaps have been made, then at least one more pass is needed.

6.12   Write single statements that perform each of the following single-subscripted array operations:

  a) Initialize the 10 elements of integer array `counts` to zeros.
  b) Add 1 to each of the 15 elements of integer array `bonus`.
  c) Read the 12 values of floating-point array `monthlyTemperatures` from the keyboard.
  d) Print the 5 values of integer array `bestScores` in column format.

6.13   Find the error(s) in each of the following statements:

  a) Assume: `char str[ 5 ];`
```
     scanf( "%s", str );      /* User types hello */
```
  b) Assume: `int a[ 3 ];`
```
     printf( "$d  %d  %d\n", a[ 1 ], a[ 2 ], a[ 3 ] );
```
  c) `double f[ 3 ] = { 1.1, 10.01, 100.001, 1000.0001 };`
  d) Assume: `double d[ 2 ][ 10 ];`
```
     d[ 1, 9 ] = 2.345;
```

6.14   Modify the program of Fig. 6.16 so function `mode` is capable of handling a tie for the mode value. Also modify function `median` so the two middle elements are averaged in an array with an even number of elements.

6.15   Use a single-subscripted array to solve the following problem. Read in 20 numbers, each of which is between 10 and 100, inclusive. As each number is read, print it only if it is not a duplicate of a number already read. Provide for the "worst case" in which all 20 numbers are different. Use the smallest possible array to solve this problem.

6.16   Label the elements of 3-by-5 double-subscripted array `sales` to indicate the order in which they are set to zero by the following program segment:

```
for ( row = 0; row <= 2; row++ )
   for ( column = 0; column <= 4; column++ )
      sales[ row ][ column ] = 0;
```

6.17   What does the following program do?

```
1   /* ex06_17.c */
2   /* What does this program do? */
3   #include <stdio.h>
4   #define SIZE 10
5
6   int whatIsThis( const int b[], int p ); /* function prototype */
7
```

(Part 1 of 2.)

```
8    /* function main begins program execution */
9    int main()
10   {
11      int x; /* holds return value of function whatIsThis */
12
13      /* initialize array a */
14      int a[ SIZE ] = { 1, 2, 3, 4, 5, 6, 7, 8, 9, 10 };
15
16      x = whatIsThis( a, SIZE );
17
18      printf( "Result is %d\n", x );
19
20      return 0; /* indicates successful termination */
21
22   } /* end main */
23
24   /* what does this function do? */
25   int whatIsThis( const int b[], int p )
26   {
27      /* base case */
28      if ( p == 1 ) {
29         return b[ 0 ];
30      } /* end if */
31      else { /* recursion step */
32
33         return b[ p - 1 ] + whatIsThis( b, p - 1 );
34      } /* end else */
35
36   } /* end function whatIsThis */
```

(Part 2 of 2.)

6.18   What does the following program do?

```
1    /* ex06_18.c */
2    /* What does this program do? */
3    #include <stdio.h>
4    #define SIZE 10
5
6    /* function prototype */
7    void someFunction( const int b[], int startIndex, int size );
8
9    /* function main begins program execution */
10   int main()
11   {
12      int a[ SIZE ] = { 8, 3, 1, 2, 6, 0, 9, 7, 4, 5 }; /* initialize a */
13
14      printf( "Answer is:\n" );
15      someFunction( a, 0, SIZE );
16      printf( "\n" );
17
```

(Part 1 of 2.)

```
18        return 0; /* indicates successful termination */
19
20   } /* end main */
21
22   /* What does this function do? */
23   void someFunction( const int b[], int startIndex, int size )
24   {
25      if ( startIndex < size ) {
26         someFunction( b, startIndex + 1, size );
27         printf( "%d  ", b[ startIndex ] );
28      } /* end if */
29
30   } /* end function someFunction */
```

(Part 2 of 2.)

6.19   Write a program that simulates the rolling of two dice. The program should use rand to roll the first die, and should use rand again to roll the second die. The sum of the two values should then be calculated. [*Note:* Since each die can show an integer value from 1 to 6, then the sum of the two values will vary from 2 to 12 with 7 being the most frequent sum and 2 and 12 being the least frequent sums.] Figure 6.23 shows the 36 possible combinations of the two dice. Your program should roll the two dice 36,000 times. Use a single-subscripted array to tally the numbers of times each possible sum appears. Print the results in a tabular format. Also, determine if the totals are reasonable; i.e., there are six ways to roll a 7, so approximately one sixth of all the rolls should be 7.

	1	2	3	4	5	6
1	2	3	4	5	6	7
2	3	4	5	6	7	8
3	4	5	6	7	8	9
4	5	6	7	8	9	10
5	6	7	8	9	10	11
6	7	8	9	10	11	12

Fig. 6.23   Dice rolling outcomes.

6.20   Write a program that runs 1000 games of craps (without human intervention) and answers each of the following questions:
   a)   How many games are won on the first roll, second roll, ..., twentieth roll and after the twentieth roll?
   b)   How many games are lost on the first roll, second roll, ..., twentieth roll and after the twentieth roll?
   c)   What are the chances of winning at craps? [*Note:* You should discover that craps is one of the fairest casino games. What do you suppose this means?]
   d)   What is the average length of a game of craps?
   e)   Do the chances of winning improve with the length of the game?

6.21   (*Airline Reservations System*) A small airline has just purchased a computer for its new automated reservations system. The president has asked you to program the new system. You are to write a program to assign seats on each flight of the airline's only plane (capacity: 10 seats).

Your program should display the following menu of alternatives:

```
Please type 1 for "first class"
Please type 2 for "economy"
```

If the person types 1, then your program should assign a seat in the first class section (seats 1-5). If the person types 2, then your program should assign a seat in the economy section (seats 6-10). Your program should then print a boarding pass indicating the person's seat number and whether it is in the first class or economy section of the plane.

Use a single-subscripted array to represent the seating chart of the plane. Initialize all the elements of the array to 0 to indicate that all seats are empty. As each seat is assigned, set the corresponding elements of the array to 1 to indicate that the seat is no longer available.

Your program should, of course, never assign a seat that has already been assigned. When the first class section is full, your program should ask the person if it is acceptable to be placed in the economy section (and vice versa). If yes, then make the appropriate seat assignment. If no, then print the message `"Next flight leaves in 3 hours."`

6.22   Use a double-subscripted array to solve the following problem. A company has four salespeople (1 to 4) who sell five different products (1 to 5). Once a day, each salesperson passes in a slip for each different type of product sold. Each slip contains:

  a) The salesperson number
  b) The product number
  c) The total dollar value of that product sold that day

Thus, each salesperson passes in between 0 and 5 sales slips per day. Assume that the information from all of the slips for last month is available. Write a program that will read all this information for last month's sales and summarize the total sales by salesperson by product. All totals should be stored in the double-subscripted array `sales`. After processing all the information for last month, print the results in tabular format with each of the columns representing a particular salesperson and each of the rows representing a particular product. Cross total each row to get the total sales of each product for last month; cross total each column to get the total sales by salesperson for last month. Your tabular printout should include these cross totals to the right of the totaled rows and to the bottom of the totaled columns.

6.23   (*Turtle Graphics*) The Logo language, which is particularly popular among personal computer users, made the concept of *turtle graphics* famous. Imagine a mechanical turtle that walks around the room under the control of a C program. The turtle holds a pen in one of two positions, up or down. While the pen is down, the turtle traces out shapes as it moves; while the pen is up, the turtle moves about freely without writing anything. In this problem you will simulate the operation of the turtle and create a computerized sketchpad as well.

Use a 50-by-50 array `floor` which is initialized to zeros. Read commands from an array that contains them. Keep track of the current position of the turtle at all times and whether the pen is currently up or down. Assume that the turtle always starts at position 0,0 of the floor with its pen up. The set of turtle commands your program must process are shown in Fig. 6.24. Suppose that the turtle is somewhere near the center of the floor. The following "program" would draw and print a 12-by-12-square:

```
2
5,12
3
5,12
```

```
3
5,12
3
5,12
1
6
9
```

As the turtle moves with the pen down, set the appropriate elements of array floor to 1s. When the 6 command (print) is given, wherever there is a 1 in the array, display an asterisk, or some other character you choose. Wherever there is a zero, display a blank. Write a program to implement the turtle graphics capabilities discussed here. Write several turtle graphics programs to draw interesting shapes. Add other commands to increase the power of your turtle graphics language.

Command	Meaning
1	Pen up
2	Pen down
3	Turn right
4	Turn left
5, 10	Move forward 10 spaces (or a number other than 10)
6	Print the 20-by-20 array
9	End of data (sentinel)

Fig. 6.24 Turtle commands.

6.24   (*Knight's Tour*) One of the more interesting puzzlers for chess buffs is the Knight's Tour problem, originally proposed by the mathematician Euler. The question is this: Can the chess piece called the knight move around an empty chessboard and touch each of the 64 squares once and only once? We study this intriguing problem in depth here.

The knight makes L-shaped moves (over two in one direction and then over one in a perpendicular direction). Thus, from a square in the middle of an empty chessboard, the knight can make eight different moves (numbered 0 through 7) as shown in Fig. 6.25.

a) Draw an 8-by-8 chessboard on a sheet of paper and attempt a Knight's Tour by hand. Put a 1 in the first square you move to, a 2 in the second square, a 3 in the third, etc. Before starting the tour, estimate how far you think you will get, remembering that a full tour consists of 64 moves. How far did you get? Were you close to the estimate?

b) Now let us develop a program that will move the knight around a chessboard. The board itself is represented by an 8-by-8 double-subscripted array board. Each of the squares is initialized to zero. We describe each of the eight possible moves in terms of both their horizontal and vertical components. For example, a move of type 0 as shown in Fig. 6.25 consists of moving two squares horizontally to the right and one square vertically upward. Move 2 consists of moving one square horizontally to the left and two squares vertically upward. Horizontal moves to the left and vertical moves upward are indicated with negative numbers. The eight moves may be described by two single-subscripted arrays, horizontal and vertical, as follows:

	0	1	2	3	4	5	6	7
0								
1				2		1		
2			3				0	
3					K			
4			4				7	
5				5		6		
6								
7								

Fig. 6.25 The eight possible moves of the knight.

```
horizontal[ 0 ] = 2
horizontal[ 1 ] = 1
horizontal[ 2 ] = -1
horizontal[ 3 ] = -2
horizontal[ 4 ] = -2
horizontal[ 5 ] = -1
horizontal[ 6 ] = 1
horizontal[ 7 ] = 2

vertical[ 0 ] = -1
vertical[ 1 ] = -2
vertical[ 2 ] = -2
vertical[ 3 ] = -1
vertical[ 4 ] = 1
vertical[ 5 ] = 2
vertical[ 6 ] = 2
vertical[ 7 ] = 1
```

Let the variables `currentRow` and `currentColumn` indicate the row and column of the knight's current position on the board. To make a move of type `moveNumber`, where `moveNumber` is between 0 and 7, your program uses the statements

```
currentRow += vertical[ moveNumber ];
currentColumn += horizontal[ moveNumber ];
```

Keep a counter that varies from `1` to `64`. Record the latest count in each square the knight moves to. Remember to test each potential move to see if the knight has already visited that square. And, of course, test every potential move to make sure that the knight does not land off the chessboard. Now write a program to move the knight around the chessboard. Run the program. How many moves did the knight make?

c) After attempting to write and run a Knight's Tour program, you have probably developed some valuable insights. We will use these to develop a *heuristic* (or strategy) for moving the knight. Heuristics do not guarantee success, but a carefully developed heuristic greatly improves the chance of success. You may have observed that the outer squares are in some sense more troublesome than the squares nearer the center of the board. In fact, the most troublesome, or inaccessible, squares are the four corners.

   Intuition may suggest that you should attempt to move the knight to the most troublesome squares first and leave open those that are easiest to get to so that when the board gets congested near the end of the tour there will be a greater chance of success.

   We may develop an "accessibility heuristic" by classifying each of the squares according to how accessible they are and always moving the knight to the square (within the knight's L-shaped moves, of course) that is most inaccessible. We label a double-subscripted array `accessibility` with numbers indicating from how many squares each particular square is accessible. On a blank chessboard, the center squares are therefore rated as 8s, the corner squares are rated as 2s, and the other squares have accessibility numbers of 3, 4, or 6 as follows:

```
2  3  4  4  4  4  3  2
3  4  6  6  6  6  4  3
4  6  8  8  8  8  6  4
4  6  8  8  8  8  6  4
4  6  8  8  8  8  6  4
4  6  8  8  8  8  6  4
3  4  6  6  6  6  4  3
2  3  4  4  4  4  3  2
```

Now write a version of the Knight's Tour program using the accessibility heuristic. At any time, the knight should move to the square with the lowest accessibility number. In case of a tie, the knight may move to any of the tied squares. Therefore, the tour may begin in any of the four corners. [*Note:* As the knight moves around the chessboard, your program should reduce the accessibility numbers as more and more squares become occupied. In this way, at any given time during the tour, each available square's accessibility number will remain equal to precisely the number of squares from which that square may be reached.] Run this version of your program. Did you get a full tour? Now modify the program to run 64 tours, one from each square of the chessboard. How many full tours did you get?

d) Write a version of the Knight's Tour program which, when encountering a tie between two or more squares, decides what square to choose by looking ahead to those squares reachable from the "tied" squares. Your program should move to the square for which the next move would arrive at a square with the lowest accessibility number.

6.25 (*Knight's Tour: Brute Force Approaches*) In Exercise 6.24 we developed a solution to the Knight's Tour problem. The approach used, called the "accessibility heuristic," generates many solutions and executes efficiently.

As computers continue increasing in power, we will be able to solve many problems with sheer computer power and relatively unsophisticated algorithms. Let us call this approach "brute force" problem solving.

a) Use random number generation to enable the knight to walk around the chess board (in its legitimate L-shaped moves, of course) at random. Your program should run one tour and print the final chessboard. How far did the knight get?

b) Most likely, the preceding program produced a relatively short tour. Now modify your program to attempt 1000 tours. Use a single-subscripted array to keep track of the number of tours of each length. When your program finishes attempting the 1000 tours, it should print this information in neat tabular format. What was the best result?

c) Most likely, the preceding program gave you some "respectable" tours but no full tours. Now "pull all the stops out" and simply let your program run until it produces a full tour. [*Caution:* This version of the program could run for hours on a powerful computer.] Once again, keep a table of the number of tours of each length and print this table when the first full tour is found. How many tours did your program attempt before producing a full tour? How much time did it take?

d) Compare the brute force version of the Knight's Tour with the accessibility heuristic version. Which required a more careful study of the problem? Which algorithm was more difficult to develop? Which required more computer power? Could we be certain (in advance) of obtaining a full tour with the accessibility heuristic approach? Could we be certain (in advance) of obtaining a full tour with the brute force approach? Argue the pros and cons of brute force problem solving in general.

6.26 (*Eight Queens*) Another puzzler for chess buffs is the Eight Queens problem. Simply stated: Is it possible to place eight queens on an empty chessboard so that no queen is "attacking" any other—that is, so that no two queens are in the same row, the same column, or along the same diagonal? Use the kind of thinking developed in Exercise 6.24 to formulate a heuristic for solving the Eight Queens problem. Run your program. [*Hint:* It is possible to assign a numeric value to each square of the chessboard indicating how many squares of an empty chessboard are "eliminated" once a queen is placed in that square. For example, each of the four corners would be assigned the value 22, as in Fig. 6.26.]

```
*  *  *  *  *  *  *  *
*  *
*     *
*        *
*           *
*              *
*                 *
*                    *
```

Fig. 6.26 *The 22 squares eliminated by placing a queen in the upper-left corner.*

Once these "elimination numbers" are placed in all 64 squares, an appropriate heuristic might be: Place the next queen in the square with the smallest elimination number. Why is this strategy intuitively appealing?

6.27 (*Eight Queens: Brute Force Approaches*) In this problem you will develop several brute force approaches to solving the Eight Queens problem introduced in Exercise 6.26.

a) Solve the Eight Queens problem, using the random brute force technique developed in Exercise 6.25.

b) Use an exhaustive technique (i.e., try all possible combinations of eight queens on the chessboard).

c) Why do you suppose the exhaustive brute force approach may not be appropriate for solving the Knight's Tour problem?

d) Compare and contrast the random brute force and exhaustive brute force approaches in general.

6.28 (*Duplicate elimination*) In Chapter 12, we explore the high-speed binary search tree data structure. One feature of a binary search tree is that duplicate values are discarded when insertions are made into the tree. This is referred to as duplicate elimination. Write a program that produces 20 random numbers between 1 and 20. The program should store all nonduplicate values in an array. Use the smallest possible array to accomplish this task.

6.29   (*Knight's Tour: Closed Tour Test*) In the Knight's Tour, a full tour is when the knight makes 64 moves touching each square of the chess board once and only once. A closed tour occurs when the 64th move is one move away from the location in which the knight started the tour. Modify the Knight's Tour program you wrote in Exercise 6.24 to test for a closed tour if a full tour has occurred.

6.30   (*The Sieve of Eratosthenes*) A prime integer is any integer that can be divided evenly only by itself and 1. The Sieve of Eratosthenes is a method of finding prime numbers. It works as follows:
  1) Create an array with all elements initialized to 1 (true). Array elements with prime subscripts will remain 1. All other array elements will eventually be set to zero.
  2) Starting with array subscript 2 (subscript 1 must be prime), every time an array element is found whose value is 1, loop through the remainder of the array and set to zero every element whose subscript is a multiple of the subscript for the element with value 1. For array subscript 2, all elements beyond 2 in the array that are multiples of 2 will be set to zero (subscripts 4, 6, 8, 10, etc.). For array subscript 3, all elements beyond 3 in the array that are multiples of 3 will be set to zero (subscripts 6, 9, 12, 15, etc.).

When this process is complete, the array elements that are still set to one indicate that the subscript is a prime number. These subscripts can then be printed. Write a program that uses an array of 1000 elements to determine and print the prime numbers between 1 and 999. Ignore element 0 of the array.

6.31   (*Bucket Sort*) A bucket sort begins with an single-subscripted array of positive integers to be sorted, and a double-subscripted array of integers with rows subscripted from 0 to 9 and columns subscripted from 0 to *n* - 1 where *n* is the number of values in the array to be sorted. Each row of the double-subscripted array is referred to as a bucket. Write a function bucketSort that takes an integer array and the array size as arguments.
  The algorithm is as follows:
  1) Loop through the single-subscripted array and place each of its values in a row of the bucket array based on its ones digit. For example, 97 is placed in row 7, 3 is placed in row 3 and 100 is placed in row 0.
  2) Loop through the bucket array and copy the values back to the original array. The new order of the above values in the single-subscripted array is 100, 3 and 97.
  3) Repeat this process for each subsequent digit position (tens, hundreds, thousands, etc.) and stop when the leftmost digit of the largest number has be processed.

On the second pass of the array, 100 is placed in row 0, 3 is placed in row 0 (it had only one digit) and 97 is placed in row 9. The order of the values in the single-subscripted array is 100, 3 and 97. On the third pass, 100 is placed in row 1, 3 is placed in row zero and 97 is placed in row zero (after 3). The bucket sort is guaranteed to have all the values properly sorted after processing the leftmost digit of the largest number. The bucket sort knows it is done when all the values are copied into row zero of the double-subscripted array.

  Note that the double-subscripted array of buckets is ten times the size of the integer array being sorted. This sorting technique provides better performance than a bubble sort, but requires much larger storage capacity. Bubble sort requires only one additional memory location for the type of data being sorted. Bucket sort is an example of a space-time trade-off. It uses more memory, but performs better. This version of the bucket sort requires copying all the data back to the original array on each pass. Another possibility is to create a second double-subscripted bucket array and repeatedly move the data between the two bucket arrays until all the data is copied into row zero of one of the arrays. Row zero then contains the sorted array.

RECURSION EXERCISES

6.32   (*Selection Sort*) A selection sort searches an array looking for the smallest element in the array. When the smallest element is found, it is swapped with the first element of the array. The process is then repeated for the subarray beginning with the second element of the array. Each pass of the array results in one element being placed in its proper location. This sort requires similar processing capabilities to the bubble sort—for an array of n elements, $n - 1$ passes must be made, and for each subarray, $n - 1$ comparisons must be made to find the smallest value. When the subarray being processed contains one element, the array is sorted. Write a recursive function `selectionSort` to perform this algorithm.

6.33   (*Palindromes*) A palindrome is a string that is spelled the same way forwards and backwards. Some examples of palindromes are: "radar," "able was i ere i saw elba," and, if you ignore blanks, "a man a plan a canal panama." Write a recursive function `testPalindrome` that returns 1 if the string stored in the array is a palindrome and 0 otherwise. The function should ignore spaces and punctuation in the string.

6.34   (*Linear Search*) Modify the program of Fig. 6.18 to use a recursive `linearSearch` function to perform the linear search of the array. The function should receive an integer array and the size of the array as arguments. If the search key is found, return the array subscript; otherwise, return –1.

6.35   (*Binary Search*) Modify the program of Fig. 6.19 to use a recursive `binarySearch` function to perform the binary search of the array. The function should receive an integer array and the starting subscript and ending subscript as arguments. If the search key is found, return the array subscript; otherwise, return –1.

6.36   (*Eight Queens*) Modify the Eight Queens program you created in Exercise 6.26 to solve the problem recursively.

6.37   (*Print an array*) Write a recursive function `printArray` that takes an array and the size of the array as arguments, and returns nothing. The function should stop processing and return when it receives an array of size zero.

6.38   (*Print a string backwards*) Write a recursive function `stringReverse` that takes a character array as an argument, prints it back to front and returns nothing. The function should stop processing and return when the terminating null character of the string is encountered.

6.39   (*Find the minimum value in an array*) Write a recursive function `recursiveMinimum` that takes an integer array and the array size as arguments and returns the smallest element of the array. The function should stop processing and return when it receives an array of one element.

7

C Pointers

Objectives

- To understand pointers and pointer operators.
- To be able to use pointers to pass arguments to functions by reference.
- To understand the close relationships among pointers, arrays and strings.
- To understand the use of pointers to functions.
- To be able to define and use arrays of strings.

Addresses are given to us to conceal our whereabouts.
Saki (H. H. Munro)

By indirections find directions out.
William Shakespeare
Hamlet

Many things, having full reference
To one consent, may work contrariously.
William Shakespeare
King Henry V

You will find it a very good practice always to verify your references, sir!
Dr. Routh

You can't trust code that you did not totally create yourself.
(Especially code from companies that employ people like me.)
Ken Thompson
1983 Turing Award Lecture
Association for Computing Machinery, Inc.

Outline

7.1 Introduction

In this chapter, we discuss one of the most powerful features of the C programming language, the *pointer*. Pointers are among C's most difficult capabilities to master. Pointers enable programs to simulate call-by-reference, and to create and manipulate dynamic data structures, i.e., data structures that can grow and shrink at execution time, such as *linked lists*, queues, stacks and trees. This chapter explains basic pointer concepts. Chapter 10 examines the use of pointers with structures. Chapter 12 introduces *dynamic memory management* techniques and presents examples of creating and using dynamic data structures.

7.2 Pointer Variable Definitions and Initialization

Pointers are variables whose values are memory addresses. Normally, a variable directly contains a specific value. A pointer, on the other hand, contains an address of a variable that contains a specific value. In this sense, a variable name *directly* references a value, and a pointer *indirectly* references a value (Fig. 7.1). Referencing a value through a pointer is called *indirection*.

Pointers, like all variables, must be defined before they can be used. The definition

```
int *countPtr, count;
```

specifies that variable `countPtr` is of type `int *` (i.e., a pointer to an integer) and is read, "`countPtr` is a pointer to `int`" or "`countPtr` points to an object of type `int`." Also, the variable `count` is defined to be an `int`, not a pointer to an `int`. The * only applies to `countPtr` in the definition. When * is used in this manner in a definition, it indicates that the variable being defined is a pointer. Pointers can be defined to point to objects of any data type.

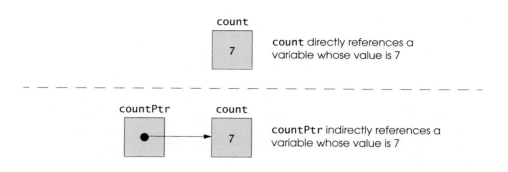

Fig. 7.1   Directly and indirectly referencing a variable.

Common Programming Error 7.1

The asterisk (*) notation used to declare pointer variables does not distribute to all variable names in a declaration. Each pointer must be declared with the * prefixed to the name, e.g., if you wish to declare xPtr and yPtr as int pointers, use int *xPtr, *yPtr;.

Good Programming Practice 7.1

Include the letters ptr *in pointer variable names to make it clear that these variables are pointers and thus need to be handled appropriately.*

Pointers should be initialized either when they are defined or in an assignment statement. A pointer may be initialized to 0, NULL or an address. A pointer with the value NULL, points to nothing. NULL is a symbolic constant defined in the <stddef.h> header (which is included by several other headers, such as <stdio.h>). Initializing a pointer to 0 is equivalent to initializing a pointer to NULL, but NULL is preferred. When 0 is assigned, it is first converted to a pointer of the appropriate type. The value 0 is the only integer value that can be assigned directly to a pointer variable. Assigning a variable's address to a pointer is discussed in Section 7.3.

Error-Prevention Tip 7.1

Initialize pointers to prevent unexpected results.

7.3 Pointer Operators

The &, or *address operator*, is a unary operator that returns the address of its operand. For example, assuming the definitions

```
int y = 5;
int *yPtr;
```

the statement

```
yPtr = &y;
```

assigns the address of the variable y to pointer variable yPtr. Variable yPtr is then said to "point to" y. Figure 7.2 shows a schematic representation of memory after the preceding assignment is executed.

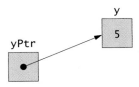

Fig. 7.2   Graphical representation of a pointer pointing to an integer variable in memory.

Figure 7.3 shows the representation of the pointer in memory, assuming that integer variable y is stored at location 600000, and pointer variable yPtr is stored at location 500000. The operand of the address operator must be a variable; the address operator can not be applied to constants, to expressions or to variables declared with the storage class register.

	yptr			y
500000	600000		600000	5

Fig. 7.3   Representation of y and yPtr in memory.

The * operator, commonly referred to as the *indirection operator* or *dereferencing operator,* returns the value of the object to which its operand (i.e., a pointer) points. For example, the statement

```
printf( "%d", *yPtr );
```

prints the value of variable y, namely 5. Using * in this manner is called *dereferencing a pointer.*

Common Programming Error 7.2

Dereferencing a pointer that has not been properly initialized or that has not been assigned to point to a specific location in memory is an error. This could cause a fatal execution-time error, or it could accidentally modify important data and allow the program to run to completion with incorrect results.

Figure 7.4 demonstrates the pointer operators & and *. The printf conversion specifier %p outputs the memory location as a hexadecimal integer on most platforms. (See Appendix E, Number Systems, for more information on hexadecimal integers.) Notice that the address of a and the value of aPtr are identical in the output, thus confirming that the address of a is indeed assigned to the pointer variable aPtr (line 11). The & and * operators are complements of one another—when they are both applied consecutively to aPtr in either order (line 21), the same result is printed. Figure 7.5 lists the precedence and associativity of the operators introduced to this point.

```
1   /* Fig. 7.4: fig07_04.c
2      Using the & and * operators */
3   #include <stdio.h>
4
5   int main()
6   {
7      int a;          /* a is an integer */
8      int *aPtr;      /* aPtr is a pointer to an integer */
9
10     a = 7;
11     aPtr = &a;      /* aPtr set to address of a */
12
13     printf( "The address of a is %p"
14             "\nThe value of aPtr is %p", &a, aPtr );
15
16     printf( "\n\nThe value of a is %d"
17             "\nThe value of *aPtr is %d", a, *aPtr );
18
19     printf( "\n\nShowing that * and & are complements of "
20             "each other\n&*aPtr = %p"
21             "\n*&aPtr = %p\n", &*aPtr, *&aPtr );
22
23     return 0; /* indicates successful termination */
24
25  } /* end main */
```

```
The address of a is 0012FF7C
The value of aPtr is 0012FF7C

The value of a is 7
The value of *aPtr is 7

Showing that * and & are complements of each other.
&*aPtr = 0012FF7C
*&aPtr = 0012FF7C
```

Fig. 7.4   & and * pointer operators.

Operators									Associativity	Type
() []									left to right	highest
+ - ++ -- ! * & (type)									right to left	unary
* / %									left to right	multiplicative
+ -									left to right	additive
< <= > >=									left to right	relational
== !=									left to right	equality
&&									left to right	logical and

Fig. 7.5   Operator precedence. (Part 1 of 2.)

Operators	Associativity	Type
||	left to right	logical or
?:	right to left	conditional
= += -= *= /= %=	right to left	assignment
,	left to right	comma

Fig. 7.5   Operator precedence. (Part 2 of 2.)

7.4 Calling Functions by Reference

There are two ways to pass arguments to a function—*call-by-value* and *call-by-reference*. All arguments in C are passed by value. As we saw in Chapter 5, `return` may be used to return one value from a called function to a caller (or to return control from a called function without passing back a value). Many functions require the capability to modify one or more variables in the caller or to pass a pointer to a large data object to avoid the overhead of passing the object by value (which incurs the overhead of making a copy of the object). For these purposes, C provides the capabilities for *simulating call-by-reference*.

In C, programmers use pointers and the indirection operator to simulate call-by-reference. When calling a function with arguments that should be modified, the addresses of the arguments are passed. This is normally accomplished by applying the address operator (&) to the variable (in the caller) whose value will be modified. As we saw in Chapter 6, arrays are not passed using operator & because C automatically passes the starting location in memory of the array (the name of an array is equivalent to `&arrayName[ 0 ]`). When the address of a variable is passed to a function, the indirection operator (*) may be used in the function to modify the value at that location in the caller's memory.

The programs in Fig. 7.6 and Fig. 7.7 present two versions of a function that cubes an integer—`cubeByValue` and `cubeByReference`. Figure 7.6 passes the variable `number` to function `cubeByValue` using call-by-value (line 14). The `cubeByValue` function cubes its argument and passes the new value back to `main` using a `return` statement. The new value is assigned to `number` in `main` (line 14).

```
1   /* Fig. 7.6: fig07_06.c
2      Cube a variable using call-by-value */
3   #include <stdio.h>
4
5   int cubeByValue( int n ); /* prototype */
6
7   int main()
8   {
9       int number = 5; /* initialize number */
10
11      printf( "The original value of number is %d", number );
12
```

Fig. 7.6   Cube a variable using call-by-value. (Part 1 of 2.)

```
13       /* pass number by value to cubeByValue */
14       number = cubeByValue( number );
15
16       printf( "\nThe new value of number is %d\n", number );
17
18       return 0; /* indicates successful termination */
19
20    } /* end main */
21
22    /* calculate and return cube of integer argument */
23    int cubeByValue( int n )
24    {
25       return n * n * n;    /* cube local variable n and return result */
26
27    } /* end function cubeByValue */
```

```
The original value of number is 5
The new value of number is 125
```

Fig. 7.6   Cube a variable using call-by-value. (Part 2 of 2.)

Figure 7.7 passes the variable `number` using call-by-reference (line 15)—the address of `number` is passed—to function `cubeByReference`. Function `cubeByReference` takes as a parameter a pointer to an `int` called `nPtr` (line 24). The function dereferences the pointer and cubes the value to which `nPtr` points (line 26), then assigns the result to `*nPtr` (which is really `number` in `main`), thus changing the value of `number` in `main`. Figure 7.8 and Fig. 7.9 analyze graphically the programs in Fig. 7.6 and Fig. 7.7, respectively.

 Common Programming Error 7.3

> *Not dereferencing a pointer when it is necessary to do so in order to obtain the value to which the pointer points is a syntax error.*

```
1     /* Fig. 7.7: fig07_07.c
2        Cube a variable using call-by-reference with a pointer argument */
3
4     #include <stdio.h>
5
6     void cubeByReference( int *nPtr ); /* prototype */
7
8     int main()
9     {
10       int number = 5; /* initialize number */
11
12       printf( "The original value of number is %d", number );
13
14       /* pass address of number to cubeByReference */
15       cubeByReference( &number );
16
17       printf( "\nThe new value of number is %d\n", number );
18
```

Fig. 7.7   Cube a variable using call-by-reference.   (Part 1 of 2.)

```
19        return 0; /* indicates successful termination */
20
21    } /* end main */
22
23    /* calculate cube of *nPtr; modifies variable number in main */
24    void cubeByReference( int *nPtr )
25    {
26        *nPtr = *nPtr * *nPtr * *nPtr;   /* cube *nPtr */
27    } /* end function cubeByReference */
```

```
The original value of number is 5
The new value of number is 125
```

Fig. 7.7   Cube a variable using call-by-reference.   (Part 2 of 2.)

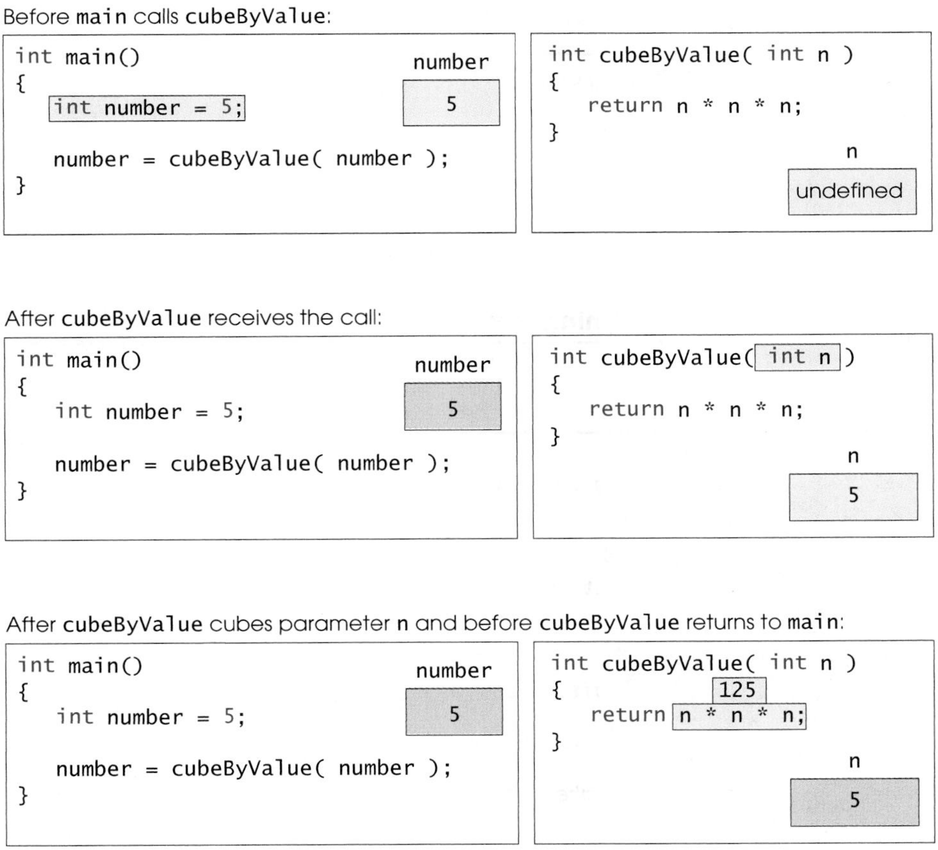

Before main calls cubeByValue:

```
int main()                      number
{
    int number = 5;                5

    number = cubeByValue( number );
}
```

```
int cubeByValue( int n )
{
    return n * n * n;
}
                                      n
                               undefined
```

After cubeByValue receives the call:

```
int main()                      number
{
    int number = 5;                5

    number = cubeByValue( number );
}
```

```
int cubeByValue( int n )
{
    return n * n * n;
}
                                      n
                                      5
```

After cubeByValue cubes parameter n and before cubeByValue returns to main:

```
int main()                      number
{
    int number = 5;                5

    number = cubeByValue( number );
}
```

```
int cubeByValue( int n )
{               125
    return n * n * n;
}
                                      n
                                      5
```

Fig. 7.8   Analysis of a typical call-by-value. (Part 1 of 2.)

After `cubeByValue` returns to `main` and before assigning the result to `number`:

```
int main()                          number
{                                      ┌──────────┐
    int number = 5;                    │    5     │
                 ┌─────┐               └──────────┘
                 │ 125 │
    number = ┌───────────────────────┐
             │cubeByValue( number );  │
             └───────────────────────┘
}
```

```
int cubeByValue( int n )
{
    return n * n * n;
}
                                    n
                          ┌──────────────┐
                          │  undefined   │
                          └──────────────┘
```

After `main` completes the assignment to `number`:

```
int main()                          number
{                                      ┌──────────┐
    int number = 5;                    │   125    │
         ┌─────┐           ┌─────┐     └──────────┘
         │ 125 │           │ 125 │
    ┌──────────────────────────────┐
    │ number = cubeByValue( number ); │
    └──────────────────────────────┘
}
```

```
int cubeByValue( int n )
{
    return n * n * n;
}
                                    n
                          ┌──────────────┐
                          │  undefined   │
                          └──────────────┘
```

Fig. 7.8   Analysis of a typical call-by-value. (Part 2 of 2.)

Before `main` calls `cubeByReference`:

```
int main()                     number
{                                ┌──────────┐
    ┌───────────────┐            │    5     │
    │int number = 5;│            └──────────┘
    └───────────────┘
    cubeByReference( &number );
}
```

```
void cubeByReference( int *nPtr )
{
    *nPtr = *nPtr * *nPtr * *nPtr;
}
                                    nPtr
                          ┌──────────────┐
                          │  undefined   │
                          └──────────────┘
```

After `cubeByReference` receives the call and before `*nPtr` is cubed:

```
int main()                     number
{                                ┌──────────┐
    int number = 5;              │    5     │
                                 └──────────┘
    cubeByReference( &number );
}
```

```
void cubeByReference( ┌───────────┐ )
                      │ int *nPtr │
                      └───────────┘
{
    *nPtr = *nPtr * *nPtr * *nPtr;
}
                                    nPtr
call establishes this pointer  ┌──────────────┐
                               │      ●       │
                               └──────────────┘
```

After `*nPtr` is cubed and before program control returns to `main`:

```
int main()                     number
{                                ┌──────────┐
    int number = 5;              │   125    │
                                 └──────────┘
    cubeByReference( &number );
}
```

```
void cubeByReference( int *nPtr )
                              ┌─────┐
                              │ 125 │
{                             └─────┘
┌────────────────────────────────────┐
│ *nPtr = *nPtr * *nPtr * *nPtr;      │
└────────────────────────────────────┘
called function modifies            nPtr
caller's variable          ┌──────────────┐
                           │      ●       │
                           └──────────────┘
```

Fig. 7.9   Analysis of a typical call-by-reference with a pointer argument.

A function receiving an address as an argument must define a pointer parameter to receive the address. For example, in Fig. 7.7 the header for function `cubeByReference` (line 24) is:

```
void cubeByReference( int *nPtr )
```

The header specifies that `cubeByReference` receives the address of an integer variable as an argument, stores the address locally in `nPtr` and does not return a value.

The function prototype for `cubeByReference` contains `int  *` in parentheses. As with other variable types, it is not necessary to include names of pointers in function prototypes. Names included for documentation purposes are ignored by the C compiler.

In the function header and in the prototype for a function that expects a single-subscripted array as an argument, the pointer notation in the parameter list of function `cubeByReference` may be used. The compiler does not differentiate between a function that receives a pointer and a function that receives a single-subscripted array. This, of course, means that the function must "know" when it is receiving an array or simply a single variable for which it is to perform call by reference. When the compiler encounters a function parameter for a single-subscripted array of the form `int b[]`, the compiler converts the parameter to the pointer notation `int *b`. The two forms are interchangeable.

Error-Prevention Tip 7.2

Use call-by-value to pass arguments to a function unless the caller explicitly requires the called function to modify the value of the argument variable in the caller's environment. This prevents accidental modification of the caller's arguments and is another example of the principle of least privilege.

7.5 Using the `const` Qualifier with Pointers

The `const` *qualifier* enables the programmer to inform the compiler that the value of a particular variable should not be modified. The `const` qualifier did not exist in early versions of C; it was added to the language by the ANSI C committee.

Software Engineering Observation 7.1

The `const` qualifier can be used to enforce the principle of least privilege. Using the principle of least privilege to properly design software reduces debugging time and improper side effects, making a program easier to modify and maintain.

Portability Tip 7.1

Although `const` is well defined in ANSI C, some compilers do not enforce it.

Over the years, a large base of legacy code was written in early versions of C that did not use `const` because it was not available. For this reason, there are significant opportunities for improvement in the software engineering of old C code.

Six possibilities exist for using (or not using) `const` with function parameters—two with call-by-value parameter passing and four with call-by-reference parameter passing. How do you choose one of the six possibilities? Let the *principle of least privilege* be your guide. Always award a function enough access to the data in its parameters to accomplish its specified task, but no more.

In Chapter 5, we explained that all calls in C are call-by-value—a copy of the argument in the function call is made and passed to the function. If the copy is modified in the function, the original value in the caller does not change. In many cases, a value passed to a function is modified so the function can accomplish its task. However, in some instances, the value should not be altered in the called function even though it manipulates a only copy of the original value.

Consider a function that takes a single-subscripted array and its size as arguments and prints the array. Such a function should loop through the array and output each array element individually. The size of the array is used in the function body to determine the high subscript of the array, so the loop can terminate when the printing is completed. Neither the size of the array nor its contents should change in the function body.

Error-Prevention Tip 7.3

If a variable does not (or should not) change in the body of a function to which it is passed, the variable should be declared const *to ensure that it is not accidentally modified.*

If an attempt is made to modify a value that is declared const, the compiler catches it and issues either a warning or an error depending on the particular compiler.

Software Engineering Observation 7.2

Only one value can be altered in a calling function when call-by-value is used. That value must be assigned from the return value of the function. To modify multiple values in a calling function, call-by-reference must be used.

Error-Prevention Tip 7.4

Before using a function, check its function prototype to determine if the function is able to modify the values passed to it.

Common Programming Error 7.4

Being unaware that a function is expecting pointers as arguments for call by reference and passing arguments call by value. Some compilers take the values assuming they are pointers and dereference the values as pointers. At run-time, memory access violations or segmentation faults are often generated. Other compilers catch the mismatch in types between arguments and parameters and generate error messages.

There are four ways to pass a pointer to a function: *a non-constant pointer to non-constant data*, *a constant pointer to non-constant data*, *a non-constant pointer to constant data*, and *a constant pointer to constant data*. Each of the four combinations provides different access privileges. These are discussed in the next several examples.

Converting a String to Uppercase Using Non-Constant Pointer to Non-Constant Data

The highest level of data access is granted by a non-constant pointer to non-constant data. In this case, the data can be modified through the dereferenced pointer, and the pointer can be modified to point to other data items. A declaration for a non-constant pointer to non-constant data does not include const. Such a pointer might be used to receive a string as an argument to a function that uses *pointer arithmetic* to process (and possibly modify) each character in the string. Function convertToUppercase of Fig. 7.10 declares its parameter, a non-constant pointer to non-constant data called sPtr (char *sPtr), in line 23. The function processes the array string (pointed to by sPtr) one character at a time using pointer arithmetic. C standard library function islower (called in line 27) tests the character contents of the address pointed to by sPtr. If a character is in the range a to z, islower returns true and C standard library function toupper (line 28) is called to convert the character to its corresponding uppercase letter; otherwise, islower returns false and the next character in the string is processed.

```
1    /* Fig. 7.10: fig07_10.c
2       Converting lowercase letters to uppercase letters
3       using a non-constant pointer to non-constant data */
4
5    #include <stdio.h>
6    #include <ctype.h>
7
8    void convertToUppercase( char *sPtr ); /* prototype */
9
10   int main()
11   {
12      char string[] = "characters and $32.98"; /* initialize char array */
13
14      printf( "The string before conversion is: %s", string );
15      convertToUppercase( string );
16      printf( "\nThe string after conversion is: %s\n", string );
17
18      return 0; /* indicates successful termination */
19
20   } /* end main */
21
22   /* convert string to uppercase letters */
23   void convertToUppercase( char *sPtr )
24   {
25      while ( *sPtr != '\0' ) { /* current character is not '\0' */
26
27         if ( islower( *sPtr ) ) {      /* if character is lowercase, */
28            *sPtr = toupper( *sPtr ); /* convert to uppercase */
29         } /* end if */
30
31         ++sPtr;   /* move sPtr to the next character */
32      } /* end while */
33
34   } /* end function convertToUppercase */
```

```
The string before conversion is: characters and $32.98
The string after conversion is: CHARACTERS AND $32.98
```

Fig. 7.10 Converting a string to uppercase using a non-constant pointer to non-constant data.

Printing a String One Character at a Time Using a Non-Constant Pointer to Constant Data
A non-constant pointer to constant data can be modified to point to any data item of the appropriate type, but the data to which it points cannot be modified. Such a pointer might be used to receive an array argument to a function that will process each element of the array without modifying the data. For example, the printCharacters function of Fig. 7.11 declares parameter sPtr to be of type const char * (line 24). The declaration is read from right to left as "sPtr is a pointer to a character constant." The body of the function uses a for statement to output each character in the string until the null character is encountered.

After each character is printed, pointer `sPtr` is incremented to point to the next character in the string.

```c
1   /* Fig. 7.11: fig07_11.c
2      Printing a string one character at a time using
3      a non-constant pointer to constant data */
4
5   #include <stdio.h>
6
7   void printCharacters( const char *sPtr );
8
9   int main()
10  {
11     /* initialize char array */
12     char string[] = "print characters of a string";
13
14     printf( "The string is:\n" );
15     printCharacters( string );
16     printf( "\n" );
17
18     return 0; /* indicates successful termination */
19
20  } /* end main */
21
22  /* sPtr cannot modify the character to which it points,
23     i.e., sPtr is a "read-only" pointer */
24  void printCharacters( const char *sPtr )
25  {
26     /* loop through entire string */
27     for ( ; *sPtr != '\0'; sPtr++ ) { /* no initialization */
28        printf( "%c", *sPtr );
29     } /* end for */
30
31  } /* end function printCharacters */
```

```
The string is:
print characters of a string
```

Fig. 7.11   Printing a string one character at a time using a non-constant pointer to constant data.

Figure 7.12 demonstrates the error messages when attempting to compile a function that receives a non-constant pointer (xPtr) to constant data. This function attempts to modify the data pointed to by xPtr in line 22—which results in a compilation error. [*Note:* The actual error message you see will be compiler specific.]

```c
1   /* Fig. 7.12: fig07_12.c
2      Attempting to modify data through a
3      non-constant pointer to constant data. */
4   #include <stdio.h>
```

Fig. 7.12   Attempting to modify data through a non-constant pointer to constant data. (Part 1 of 2.)

```
 5
 6   void f( const int *xPtr ); /* prototype */
 7
 8   int main()
 9   {
10      int y;        /* define y */
11
12      f( &y );       /* f attempts illegal modification */
13
14      return 0;      /* indicates successful termination */
15
16   } /* end main */
17
18   /* xPtr cannot be used to modify the
19      value of the variable to which it points */
20   void f( const int *xPtr )
21   {
22      *xPtr = 100;  /* error: cannot modify a const object */
23   } /* end function f */
```

```
Compiling...
FIG07_12.c
d:\books\2003\chtp4\examples\ch07\fig07_12.c(22) : error C2166: l-value
   specifies const object
Error executing cl.exe.

FIG07_12.exe - 1 error(s), 0 warning(s)
```

Fig. 7.12   Attempting to modify data through a non-constant pointer to constant data. (Part 2 of 2.)

As we know, arrays are aggregate data types that store related data items of the same type under one name. In Chapter 10, we will discuss another form of aggregate data type called a *structure* (sometimes called a *record* in other languages). A structure is capable of storing related data items of different data types under one name (e.g., storing information about each employee of a company). When a function is called with an array as an argument, the array is automatically passed to the function by reference. However, structures are always passed by value—a copy of the entire structure is passed. This requires the execution-time overhead of making a copy of each data item in the structure and storing it on the computer's function call stack. When structure data must be passed to a function, we can use pointers to constant data to get the performance of call-by-reference and the protection of call-by-value. When a pointer to a structure is passed, only a copy of the address at which the structure is stored must be made. On a machine with 4-byte addresses, a copy of 4 bytes of memory is made rather than a copy of possibly hundreds or thousands of bytes of the structure.

Performance Tip 7.1

Pass large objects such as structures using pointers to constant data to obtain the performance benefits of call-by-reference and the security of call-by-value.

Using pointers to constant data in this manner is an example of a *time/space trade-off*. If memory is low and execution efficiency is a major concern, pointers should be used. If memory is in abundance and efficiency is not a major concern, data should be passed by value to enforce the principle of least privilege. Remember that some systems do not enforce `const` well, so call-by-value is still the best way to prevent data from being modified.

Attempting to Modify a Constant Pointer to Non-Constant Data

A constant pointer to non-constant data always points to the same memory location, and the data at that location can be modified through the pointer. This is the default for an array name. An array name is a constant pointer to the beginning of the array. All data in the array can be accessed and changed by using the array name and array subscripting. A constant pointer to non-constant data can be used to receive an array as an argument to a function that accesses array elements using only array subscript notation. Pointers that are declared `const` must be initialized when they are defined (if the pointer is a function parameter, it is initialized with a pointer that is passed to the function). Figure 7.13 attempts to modify a constant pointer. Pointer `ptr` is defined in line 12 to be of type `int * const`. The definition is read from right to left as "`ptr` is a constant pointer to an integer." The pointer is initialized (line 12) with the address of integer variable `x`. The program attempts to assign the address of `y` to `ptr` (line 15), but an error message is generated.

```
1   /* Fig. 7.13: fig07_13.c
2      Attempting to modify a constant pointer to non-constant data */
3   #include <stdio.h>
4
5   int main()
6   {
7      int x; /* define x */
8      int y; /* define y */
9
10     /* ptr is a constant pointer to an integer that can be modified
11        through ptr, but ptr always points to the same memory location */
12     int * const ptr = &x;
13
14     *ptr = 7; /* allowed: *ptr is not const */
15     ptr = &y; /* error: ptr is const; cannot assign new address */
16
17     return 0; /* indicates successful termination */
18
19   } /* end main */
```

```
Compiling...
FIG07_13.c
D:\books\2003\chtp4\Examples\ch07\FIG07_13.c(15) : error C2166: l-value
   specifies const object
Error executing cl.exe.

FIG07_13.exe - 1 error(s), 0 warning(s)
```

Fig. 7.13   Attempting to modify a constant pointer to non-constant data.

Attempting to Modify a Constant Pointer to Constant Data

The least access privilege is granted by a constant pointer to constant data. Such a pointer always points to the same memory location, and the data at that memory location cannot be modified. This is how an array should be passed to a function that only looks at the array using array subscript notation and does not modify the array. Figure 7.14 defines pointer variable ptr (line 13) to be of type const int *const, which is read from right to left as "ptr is a constant pointer to an integer constant." The figure shows the error messages generated when an attempt is made to modify the data to which ptr points (line 17) and when an attempt is made to modify the address stored in the pointer variable (line 18).

```
1   /* Fig. 7.14: fig07_14.c
2      Attempting to modify a constant pointer to constant data. */
3   #include <stdio.h>
4
5   int main()
6   {
7      int x = 5; /* initialize x */
8      int y;     /* define y */
9
10     /* ptr is a constant pointer to a constant integer. ptr always
11        points to the same location; the integer at that location
12        cannot be modified */
13     const int *const ptr = &x;
14
15     printf( "%d\n", *ptr );
16
17     *ptr = 7; /* error: *ptr is const; cannot assign new value */
18     ptr = &y; /* error: ptr is const; cannot assign new address */
19
20     return 0; /* indicates successful termination */
21
22  } /* end main */
```

```
Compiling...
FIG07_14.c
D:\books\2003\chtp4\Examples\ch07\FIG07_14.c(17) : error C2166: l-value
   specifies const object
D:\books\2003\chtp4\Examples\ch07\FIG07_14.c(18) : error C2166: l-value
   specifies const object
Error executing cl.exe.

FIG07_12.exe - 2 error(s), 0 warning(s)
```

Fig. 7.14   Attempting to modify a constant pointer to constant data.

7.6 Bubble Sort Using Call-by-Reference

Let us modify the bubble sort program of Fig. 6.15 to use two functions—bubbleSort and swap. Function bubbleSort sorts the array. It calls function swap (line 53) to exchange the array elements array[j] and array[j + 1] (see Fig. 7.15). Remember that C enforces information hiding between functions, so swap does not have access to individual array elements in bubbleSort. Because bubbleSort *wants* swap to have access to the array elements to be swapped, bubbleSort passes each of these elements call-by-reference to swap—the address of each array element is passed explicitly. Although entire arrays are automatically passed by reference, individual array elements are scalars, and are ordinarily passed by value. Therefore, bubbleSort uses the address operator (&) on each of the array elements in the swap call (line 53) as follows

```
swap( &array[ j ], &array[ j + 1 ] );
```

to effect call-by-reference. Function swap receives &array[j] in pointer variable element1Ptr (line 64). Even though swap—because of information hiding—is not allowed to know the name array[j], swap may use *element1Ptr as a synonym for array[j]. Therefore, when swap references *element1Ptr, it is actually referencing array[j] in bubbleSort. Similarly, when swap references *element2Ptr, it is actually referencing array[j + 1] in bubbleSort. Even though swap is not allowed to say

```
hold = array[ j ];
array[ j ] = array[ j + 1 ];
array[ j + 1 ] = hold;
```

precisely the same effect is achieved by lines 66 through 68

```
int hold = *element1Ptr;
*element1Ptr = *element2Ptr;
*element2Ptr = hold;
```

in the swap function of Fig. 7.15.

```
1   /* Fig. 7.15: fig07_15.c
2      This program puts values into an array, sorts the values into
3      ascending order, and prints the resulting array. */
4   #include <stdio.h>
5   #define SIZE 10
6
7   void bubbleSort( int * const array, const int size ); /* prototype */
8
9   int main()
10  {
11     /* initialize array a */
12     int a[ SIZE ] = { 2, 6, 4, 8, 10, 12, 89, 68, 45, 37 };
13
14     int i; /* counter */
15
16     printf( "Data items in original order\n" );
17
18     /* loop through array a */
19     for ( i = 0; i < SIZE; i++ ) {
20        printf( "%4d", a[ i ] );
21     } /* end for */
22
23     bubbleSort( a, SIZE ); /* sort the array */
24
25     printf( "\nData items in ascending order\n" );
26
```

Fig. 7.15 Bubble sort with call-by-reference. (Part 1 of 2.)

```
27        /* loop through array a */
28        for ( i = 0; i < SIZE; i++ ) {
29           printf( "%4d", a[ i ] );
30        } /* end for */
31
32        printf( "\n" );
33
34        return 0; /* indicates successful termination */
35
36     } /* end main */
37
38     /* sort an array of integers using bubble sort algorithm */
39     void bubbleSort( int * const array, const int size )
40     {
41        void swap( int *element1Ptr, int *element2Ptr ); /* prototype */
42        int pass; /* pass counter */
43        int j;    /* comparison counter */
44
45        /* loop to control passes */
46        for ( pass = 0; pass < size - 1; pass++ ) {
47
48           /* loop to control comparisons during each pass */
49           for ( j = 0; j < size - 1; j++ ) {
50
51              /* swap adjacent elements if they are out of order */
52              if ( array[ j ] > array[ j + 1 ] ) {
53                 swap( &array[ j ], &array[ j + 1 ] );
54              } /* end if */
55
56           } /* end inner for */
57
58        } /* end outer for */
59
60     } /* end function bubbleSort */
61
62     /* swap values at memory locations to which element1Ptr and
63        element2Ptr point */
64     void swap( int *element1Ptr, int *element2Ptr )
65     {
66        int hold = *element1Ptr;
67        *element1Ptr = *element2Ptr;
68        *element2Ptr = hold;
69     } /* end function swap */
```

```
Data items in original order
   2   6   4   8  10  12  89  68  45  37
Data items in ascending order
   2   4   6   8  10  12  37  45  68  89
```

Fig. 7.15   Bubble sort with call-by-reference. (Part 2 of 2.)

Several features of function bubbleSort should be noted. The function header (line 39) declares array as int *array rather than int array[] to indicate that bubbleSort receives a single-subscripted array as an argument (again, these notations are interchangeable). Parameter `size` is declared `const` to enforce the principle of least privilege. Although parameter `size` receives a copy of a value in `main`, and modifying the copy cannot change the value in `main`, `bubbleSort` does not need to alter `size` to accomplish its task. The size of the array remains fixed during the execution of function `bubbleSort`. Therefore, `size` is declared `const` to ensure that it is not modified. If the size of the array is modified during the sorting process, the sorting algorithm might not run correctly.

The prototype for function `swap` (line 41) is included in the body of function `bubble-Sort` because `bubbleSort` is the only function that calls `swap`. Placing the prototype in `bubbleSort` restricts proper calls of `swap` to those made from `bubbleSort`. Other functions that attempt to call `swap` do not have access to a proper function prototype, so the compiler generates one automatically. This normally results in a prototype that does not match the function header (and generates a compiler error) because the compiler assumes `int` for the return type and the parameter types.

Software Engineering Observation 7.3

Placing function prototypes in the definitions of other functions enforces the principle of least privilege by restricting proper function calls to the functions in which the prototypes appear.

Note that function `bubbleSort` receives the size of the array as a parameter (line 39). The function must know the size of the array to sort the array. When an array is passed to a function, the memory address of the first element of the array is received by the function. The address, of course, does not convey the number of elements in the array. Therefore, the programmer must pass to the function the array size.

In the program, the size of the array is explicitly passed to function `bubbleSort`. There are two main benefits to this approach—software reusability and proper software engineering. By defining the function to receive the array size as an argument, we enable the function to be used by any program that sorts single-subscripted integer arrays of any size.

Software Engineering Observation 7.4

When passing an array to a function, also pass the size of the array. This helps make the function reusable in many programs.

We could have stored the size of the array in a global variable that is accessible to the entire program. This would be more efficient because a copy of the size is not made to pass to the function. However, other programs that require an integer array-sorting capability may not have the same global variable, so the function cannot be used in those programs.

Software Engineering Observation 7.5

Global variables often violate the principle of least privilege and can lead to poor software engineering.

Performance Tip 7.2

Passing the size of an array to a function takes time and requires additional stack space because a copy of the size is made to pass to the function. Global variables require no additional time or space because they can be accessed directly by any function.

The size of the array could have been programmed directly into the function. This restricts the use of the function to an array of a specific size and significantly reduces its reusability. Only programs processing single-subscripted integer arrays of the specific size coded into the function can use the function.

7.7 sizeof Operator

C provides the special unary operator *sizeof* to determine the size in bytes of an array (or any other data type) during program compilation. When applied to the name of an array as in Fig. 7.16 (line 14), the sizeof operator returns the total number of bytes in the array as an integer. Note that variables of type float are normally stored in 4 bytes of memory, and array is defined to have 20 elements. Therefore, there are a total of 80 bytes in array.

Performance Tip 7.3

sizeof is a compile-time operator, so it does not incur any execution-time overhead.

```
1    /* Fig. 7.16: fig07_16.c
2       Sizeof operator when used on an array name
3       returns the number of bytes in the array. */
4    #include <stdio.h>
5
6    size_t getSize( float *ptr ); /* prototype */
7
8    int main()
9    {
10       float array[ 20 ]; /* create array */
11
12       printf( "The number of bytes in the array is %d"
13               "\nThe number of bytes returned by getSize is %d\n",
14               sizeof( array ), getSize( array ) );
15
16       return 0; /* indicates successful termination */
17
18   } /* end main */
19
20   /* return size of ptr */
21   size_t getSize( float *ptr )
22   {
23       return sizeof( ptr );
24
25   } /* end function getSize */
```

```
The number of bytes in the array is 80
The number of bytes returned by getSize is 4
```

Fig. 7.16 Operator sizeof when applied to an array name returns the number of bytes in the array.

The number of elements in an array also can be determined with sizeof. For example, consider the following array definition:

```
double real[ 22 ];
```

Variables of type double normally are stored in 8 bytes of memory. Thus, array real contains a total of 176 bytes. To determine the number of elements in the array, the following expression can be used:

```
sizeof( real ) / sizeof( double )
```

The expression determines the number of bytes in array `real` and divides that value by the number of bytes used in memory to store a `double` value.

Note that function `getSize` returns type `size_t`. Type *size_t* is a type defined by the C standard as the integral type (`unsigned` or `unsigned long`) of the value returned by operator `sizeof`. Type `size_t` is defined in header `<stddef.h>` (which is included by several headers, such as `<stdio.h>`). Figure 7.17 calculates the number of bytes used to store each of the standard data types. The results could be different between computers.

```
1   /* Fig. 7.17: fig07_17.c
2      Demonstrating the sizeof operator */
3   #include <stdio.h>
4
5   int main()
6   {
7      char c;
8      short s;
9      int i;
10     long l;
11     float f;
12     double d;
13     long double ld;
14     int array[ 20 ];   /* create array of 20 int elements */
15     int *ptr = array; /* create pointer to array */
16
17     printf( "        sizeof c = %d\tsizeof(char)   = %d"
18             "\n        sizeof s = %d\tsizeof(short) = %d"
19             "\n        sizeof i = %d\tsizeof(int) = %d"
20             "\n        sizeof l = %d\tsizeof(long) = %d"
21             "\n        sizeof f = %d\tsizeof(float) = %d"
22             "\n        sizeof d = %d\tsizeof(double) = %d"
23             "\n       sizeof ld = %d\tsizeof(long double) = %d"
24             "\n sizeof array = %d"
25             "\n     sizeof ptr = %d\n",
26          sizeof c, sizeof( char ), sizeof s, sizeof( short ), sizeof i,
27          sizeof( int ), sizeof l, sizeof( long ), sizeof f,
28          sizeof( float ), sizeof d, sizeof( double ), sizeof ld,
29          sizeof( long double ), sizeof array, sizeof ptr );
30
31     return 0; /* indicates successful termination */
32
33  } /* end main */
```

```
    sizeof c = 1       sizeof(char)   = 1
    sizeof s = 2       sizeof(short) = 2
    sizeof i = 4       sizeof(int) = 4
    sizeof l = 4       sizeof(long) = 4
    sizeof f = 4       sizeof(float) = 4
    sizeof d = 8       sizeof(double) = 8
   sizeof ld = 8       sizeof(long double) = 8
sizeof array = 80
  sizeof ptr = 4
```

Fig. 7.17   Using operator `sizeof` to determine standard data type sizes.

Portability Tip 7.2

The number of bytes used to store a particular data type may vary between systems. When writing programs that depend on data type sizes and that will run on several computer systems, use `sizeof` *to determine the number of bytes used to store the data types.*

Operator `sizeof` can be applied to any variable name, type or value (including the value of an expression). When applied to a variable name (that is not an array name) or a constant, the number of bytes used to store the specific type of variable or constant is returned. Note that the parentheses used with `sizeof` are required if a type name is supplied as its operand. Omitting the parentheses in this case results in a syntax error. The parentheses are not required if a variable name is supplied as its operand.

7.8 Pointer Expressions and Pointer Arithmetic

Pointers are valid operands in arithmetic expressions, assignment expressions and comparison expressions. However, not all the operators normally used in these expressions are valid in conjunction with pointer variables. This section describes the operators that can have pointers as operands, and how these operators are used.

A limited set of arithmetic operations may be performed on pointers. A pointer may be *incremented* (++) or *decremented* (--), *an integer may be added to a pointer* (+ or +=), *an integer may be subtracted from a pointer* (- or -=) and *one pointer may be subtracted from another.*

Assume that array `int v[ 5 ]` has been defined and its first element is at location 3000 in memory. Assume pointer `vPtr` has been initialized to point to `v[ 0 ]`—i.e., the value of `vPtr` is 3000. Figure 7.18 illustrates this situation for a machine with 4-byte integers. Note that `vPtr` can be initialized to point to array `v` with either of the statements

```
vPtr = v;
vPtr = &v[ 0 ];
```

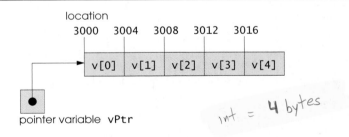

Fig. 7.18 Array v and a pointer variable vPtr that points to v.

Portability Tip 7.3

Most computers today have 2-byte or 4-byte integers. Some of the newer machines use 8-byte integers. Because the results of pointer arithmetic depend on the size of the objects a pointer points to, pointer arithmetic is machine dependent.

In conventional arithmetic, 3000 + 2 yields the value 3002. This is normally not the case with *pointer arithmetic*. When an integer is added to or subtracted from a pointer, the pointer is not simply incremented or decremented by that integer, but by that integer times the size of the object to which the pointer refers. The number of bytes depends on the object's data type. For example, the statement

```
vPtr += 2;
```

would produce 3008 (3000 + 2 * 4) assuming an integer is stored in 4 bytes of memory. In the array v, vPtr would now point to v[2] (Fig. 7.19). If an integer is stored in 2 bytes of memory, then the preceding calculation would result in memory location 3004 (3000 + 2 * 2). If the array were of a different data type, the preceding statement would increment the pointer by twice the number of bytes that it takes to store an object of that data type. When performing pointer arithmetic on a character array, the results will be consistent with regular arithmetic because each character is 1 byte long.

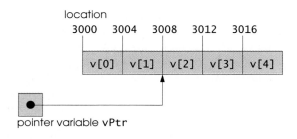

Fig. 7.19 The pointer vPtr after pointer arithmetic.

If vPtr had been incremented to 3016, which points to v[4], the statement

```
vPtr -= 4;
```

would set vPtr back to 3000—the beginning of the array. If a pointer is being incremented or decremented by one, the increment (++) and decrement (--) operators can be used. Either of the statements

```
++vPtr;
vPtr++;
```

increment the pointer to point to the next location in the array. Either of the statements

```
--vPtr;
vPtr--;
```

decrement the pointer to point to the previous element of the array.

Pointer variables may be subtracted from one another. For example, if vPtr contains the location 3000, and v2Ptr contains the address 3008, the statement

```
x = v2Ptr - vPtr;
```

would assign to x the number of array elements from vPtr to v2Ptr, in this case 2 (not 8). Pointer arithmetic is meaningless unless performed on an array. We can not assume that two variables of the same type are stored contiguously in memory unless they are adjacent elements of an array.

Common Programming Error 7.5

Using pointer arithmetic on a pointer that does not refer to an element in an array.

Common Programming Error 7.6

Subtracting or comparing two pointers that do not refer to elements in the same array.

Common Programming Error 7.7

Running off either end of an array when using pointer arithmetic.

A pointer can be assigned to another pointer if both pointers are of the same type. The exception to this rule is the *pointer to void* (i.e., *void* *), which is a generic pointer that can represent any pointer type. All pointer types can be assigned a pointer to void, and a pointer to void can be assigned a pointer of any type. In both cases, a cast operation is not required.

A pointer to void cannot be dereferenced. For example, the compiler knows that a pointer to int refers to four bytes of memory on a machine with 4-byte integers, but a pointer to void simply contains a memory location for an unknown data type—the precise number of bytes to which the pointer refers is not known by the compiler. The compiler must know the data type to determine the number of bytes to be dereferenced for a particular pointer.

Common Programming Error 7.8

Assigning a pointer of one type to a pointer of another type if neither is of type void * is a syntax error.

Common Programming Error 7.9

Dereferencing a void * pointer is a syntax error.

Pointers can be compared using equality and relational operators, but such comparisons are meaningless unless the pointers point to elements of the same array. Pointer comparisons compare the addresses stored in the pointers. A comparison of two pointers pointing to elements in the same array could show, for example, that one pointer points to a higher-numbered element of the array than the other pointer does. A common use of pointer comparison is determining whether a pointer is NULL.

7.9 Relationship between Pointers and Arrays

Arrays and pointers are intimately related in C and often may be used interchangeably. An array name can be thought of as a constant pointer. Pointers can be used to do any operation involving array subscripting.

Assume that integer array b[5] and integer pointer variable bPtr have been defined. Since the array name (without a subscript) is a pointer to the first element of the array, we can set bPtr equal to the address of the first element in array b with the statement

```
bPtr = b;
```

This statement is equivalent to taking the address of the first element of the array as follows

```
bPtr = &b[ 0 ];
```

Array element b[3] can alternatively be referenced with the pointer expression

```
*( bPtr + 3 )
```

The 3 in the above expression is the *offset* to the pointer. When the pointer points to the beginning of an array, the offset indicates which element of the array should be referenced, and the offset value is identical to the array subscript. The preceding notation is referred to as *pointer/offset notation*. The parentheses are necessary because the precedence of * is higher than the precedence of +. Without the parentheses, the above expression would add 3 to the value of the expression *bPtr (i.e., 3 would be added to b[0] assuming bPtr points to the beginning of the array). Just as the array element can be referenced with a pointer expression, the address

```
&b[ 3 ]
```

can be written with the pointer expression

```
bPtr + 3
```

The array itself can be treated as a pointer and used in pointer arithmetic. For example, the expression

```
*( b + 3 )
```

also refers to the array element b[3]. In general, all subscripted array expressions can be written with a pointer and an offset. In this case, pointer/offset notation was used with the name of the array as a pointer. Note that the preceding statement does not modify the array name in any way; b still points to the first element in the array.

Pointers can be subscripted exactly as arrays can. For example, if bPtr has the value b, the expression

```
bPtr[ 1 ]
```

refers to the array element b[1]. This is referred to as *pointer/subscript notation.*

Remember that an array name is essentially a constant pointer; it always points to the beginning of the array. Thus, the expression

```
b += 3
```

is invalid because it attempts to modify the value of the array name with pointer arithmetic.

 Common Programming Error 7.10

Attempting to modify an array name with pointer arithmetic is a syntax error.

Figure 7.20 uses the four methods we have discussed for referring to array elements— array subscripting, pointer/offset with the array name as a pointer, *pointer subscripting*, and pointer/offset with a pointer—to print the four elements of the integer array b.

```
1   /* Fig. 7.20: fig07_20.cpp
2      Using subscripting and pointer notations with arrays */
3
4   #include <stdio.h>
```

Fig. 7.20 Using four methods of referencing array elements. (Part 1 of 3.)

```
5
6   int main()
7   {
8      int b[] = { 10, 20, 30, 40 }; /* initialize array b */
9      int *bPtr = b;                 /* set bPtr to point to array b */
10     int i;                         /* counter */
11     int offset;                    /* counter */
12
13     /* output array b using array subscript notation */
14     printf( "Array b printed with:\nArray subscript notation\n" );
15
16     /* loop through array b */
17     for ( i = 0; i < 4; i++ ) {
18        printf( "b[ %d ] = %d\n", i, b[ i ] );
19     } /* end for */
20
21     /* output array b using array name and pointer/offset notation */
22     printf( "\nPointer/offset notation where\n"
23             "the pointer is the array name\n" );
24
25     /* loop through array b */
26     for ( offset = 0; offset < 4; offset++ ) {
27        printf( "*( b + %d ) = %d\n", offset, *( b + offset ) );
28     } /* end for */
29
30     /* output array b using bPtr and array subscript notation */
31     printf( "\nPointer subscript notation\n" );
32
33     /* loop through array b */
34     for ( i = 0; i < 4; i++ ) {
35        printf( "bPtr[ %d ] = %d\n", i, bPtr[ i ] );
36     } /* end for */
37
38     /* output array b using bPtr and pointer/offset notation */
39     printf( "\nPointer/offset notation\n" );
40
41     /* loop through array b */
42     for ( offset = 0; offset < 4; offset++ ) {
43        printf( "*( bPtr + %d ) = %d\n", offset, *( bPtr + offset ) );
44     } /* end for */
45
46     return 0; /* indicates successful termination */
47
48  } /* end main */
```

```
Array b printed with:
Array subscript notation
b[ 0 ] = 10
b[ 1 ] = 20
b[ 2 ] = 30
b[ 3 ] = 40
```

Fig. 7.20   Using four methods of referencing array elements. (Part 2 of 3.)

```
Pointer/offset notation where
the pointer is the array name
*( b + 0 ) = 10
*( b + 1 ) = 20
*( b + 2 ) = 30
*( b + 3 ) = 40

Pointer subscript notation
bPtr[ 0 ] = 10
bPtr[ 1 ] = 20
bPtr[ 2 ] = 30
bPtr[ 3 ] = 40

Pointer/offset notation
*( bPtr + 0 ) = 10
*( bPtr + 1 ) = 20
*( bPtr + 2 ) = 30
*( bPtr + 3 ) = 40
```

Fig. 7.20   Using four methods of referencing array elements. (Part 3 of 3.)

To further illustrate the interchangeability of arrays and pointers, let us look at the two string copying functions—copy1 and copy2—in the program of Fig. 7.21. Both functions copy a string (possibly a character array) into a character array. After a comparison of the function prototypes for copy1 and copy2, the functions appear identical. They accomplish the same task; however, they are implemented differently.

```
1   /* Fig. 7.21: fig07_21.c
2      Copying a string using array notation and pointer notation. */
3   #include <stdio.h>
4
5   void copy1( char *s1, const char *s2 ); /* prototype */
6   void copy2( char *s1, const char *s2 ); /* prototype */
7
8   int main()
9   {
10     char string1[ 10 ];          /* create array string1 */
11     char *string2 = "Hello";     /* create a pointer to a string */
12     char string3[ 10 ];          /* create array string3 */
13     char string4[] = "Good Bye"; /* create a pointer to a string */
14
15     copy1( string1, string2 );
16     printf( "string1 = %s\n", string1 );
17
18     copy2( string3, string4 );
19     printf( "string3 = %s\n", string3 );
20
21     return 0; /* indicates successful termination */
22
23   } /* end main */
```

Fig. 7.21   Copying a string using array notation and pointer notation. (Part 1 of 2.)

```
24
25    /* copy s2 to s1 using array notation */
26    void copy1( char *s1, const char *s2 )
27    {
28       int i; /* counter */
29
30       /* loop through strings */
31       for ( i = 0; ( s1[ i ] = s2[ i ] ) != '\0'; i++ ) {
32          ; /* do nothing in body */
33       } /* end for */
34
35    } /* end function copy1 */
36
37    /* copy s2 to s1 using pointer notation */
38    void copy2( char *s1, const char *s2 )
39    {
40       /* loop through strings */
41       for ( ; ( *s1 = *s2 ) != '\0'; s1++, s2++ ) {
42          ; /* do nothing in body */
43       } /* end for */
44
45    } /* end function copy2 */
```

```
string1 = Hello
string3 = Good Bye
```

Fig. 7.21   Copying a string using array notation and pointer notation. (Part 2 of 2.)

Function `copy1` uses array subscript notation to copy the string in `s2` to the character array `s1`. The function defines an integer counter variable `i` as the array subscript. The `for` statement header (line 31) performs the entire copy operation—its body is the empty statement. The header specifies that `i` is initialized to zero and incremented by one on each iteration of the loop. The condition in the `for` statement, `s1[ i ] = s2[ i ]`, performs the copy operation character-by-character from `s2` to `s1`. When the null character is encountered in `s2`, it is assigned to `s1` and the value of the assignment becomes the value assigned to the left operand (`s1`). The loop terminates because the integer value of the null character is zero (false).

Function `copy2` uses pointers and pointer arithmetic to copy the string in `s2` to the character array `s1`. Again, the `for` statement header (line 41) performs the entire copy operation. The header does not include any variable initialization. As in function `copy1`, the condition (`*s1 = *s2`) performs the copy operation. Pointer `s2` is dereferenced, and the resulting character is assigned to the dereferenced pointer `s1`. After the assignment in the condition, the pointers are incremented to point to the next element of array `s1` and the next character of string `s2`, respectively. When the null character is encountered in `s2`, it is assigned to the dereferenced pointer `s1` and the loop terminates.

Note that the first argument to both `copy1` and `copy2` must be an array large enough to hold the string in the second argument. Otherwise, an error may occur when an attempt is made to write into a memory location that is not part of the array. Also, note that the second parameter of each function is declared as `const char *` (a constant string). In both functions, the second argument is copied into the first argument—characters are read from it one at a time, but the characters are never modified. Therefore, the second parameter is declared to point to a constant value so the principle of least privilege is enforced—neither function requires the capability of modifying the second argument, so neither function is provided with that capability.

7.10 Arrays of Pointers

Arrays may contain pointers. A common use of an *array of pointers* is to form an *array of strings*, referred to simply as a *string array*. Each entry in the array is a string, but in C a string is essentially a pointer to its first character. So each entry in an array of strings is actually a pointer to the first character of a string. Consider the definition of string array `suit`, which might be useful in representing a deck of cards.

```
const char *suit[ 4 ] = { "Hearts", "Diamonds", "Clubs", "Spades" };
```

The `suit[ 4 ]` portion of the definition indicates an array of 4 elements. The `char *` portion of the declaration indicates that each element of array `suit` is of type "pointer to `char`." Qualifier `const` indicates that the strings pointed to by each element pointer will not be modified. The four values to be placed in the array are `"Hearts"`, `"Diamonds"`, `"Clubs"` and `"Spades"`. Each of these is stored in memory as a null-terminated character string that is one character longer than the number of characters between quotes. The four strings are 7, 9, 6 and 7 characters long, respectively. Although it appears as though these strings are being placed in the `suit` array, only pointers are actually stored in the array (Fig. 7.22). Each pointer points to the first character of its corresponding string. Thus, even though the `suit` array is fixed in size, it provides access to character strings of any length. This flexibility is one example of C's powerful data-structuring capabilities.

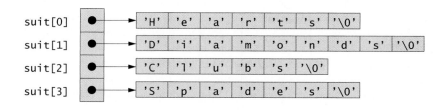

Fig. 7.22   Graphical representation of the `suit` array.

The suits could have been placed into a two-dimensional array in which each row would represent one suit, and each column would represent one of the letters of a suit name. Such a data structure would have to have a fixed number of columns per row, and that number would have to be as large as the largest string. Therefore, considerable memory could be wasted when a large number of strings being stored with most strings shorter than the longest string. We use string arrays to represent a deck of cards in the next section.

7.11 Case Study: Card Shuffling and Dealing Simulation

In this section, we use random number generation to develop a card shuffling and dealing simulation program. This program can then be used to implement programs that play specific card games. To reveal some subtle performance problems, we have intentionally used suboptimal shuffling and dealing algorithms. In the exercises and in Chapter 10, we develop more efficient algorithms.

Using the *top-down, stepwise refinement* approach, we develop a program that will shuffle a deck of 52 playing cards, and then deal each of the 52 cards. The top-down approach is particularly useful in attacking larger, more complex problems than we have seen in the early chapters.

We use 4-by-13 double-subscripted array deck to represent the deck of playing cards (Fig. 7.23). The rows correspond to the suits—row 0 corresponds to hearts, row 1 to diamonds, row 2 to clubs and row 3 to spades. The columns correspond to the face values of the cards—columns 0 through 9 correspond to faces ace through ten respectively, and columns 10 through 12 correspond to jack, queen and king. We shall load string array suit with character strings representing the four suits, and string array face with character strings representing the thirteen face values.

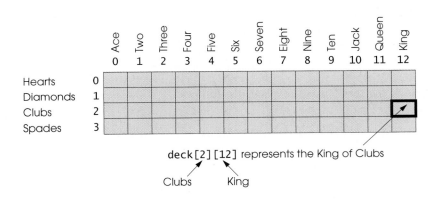

Fig. 7.23   Double-subscripted array representation of a deck of cards.

This simulated deck of cards may be shuffled as follows. First the array deck is cleared to zeros. Then, a row (0–3) and a column (0–12) are each chosen at random. The number 1 is inserted in array element deck[row][column] to indicate that this card is going to be the first one dealt from the shuffled deck. This process continues with the numbers 2, 3, …, 52 being randomly inserted in the deck array to indicate which cards are to be placed second, third, …, and fifty-second in the shuffled deck. As the deck array begins to fill with card numbers, it is possible that a card will be selected twice, i.e.—deck[row][column] will be nonzero when it is selected. This selection is simply ignored and other rows and columns are repeatedly chosen at random until an unselected card is found. Eventually, the numbers 1 through 52 will occupy the 52 slots of the deck array. At this point, the deck of cards is fully shuffled.

This shuffling algorithm could execute indefinitely if cards that have already been shuffled are repeatedly selected at random. This phenomenon is known as *indefinite postponement*. In the exercises, we discuss a better shuffling algorithm that eliminates the possibility of indefinite postponement.

Performance Tip 7.4

Sometimes an algorithm that emerges in a "natural" way can contain subtle performance problems, such as indefinite postponement. Seek algorithms that avoid indefinite postponement.

To deal the first card, we search the array for deck[row][column] equal to 1. This is accomplished with a nested for statement that varies row from 0 to 3 and column from 0 to 12. What card does that element of the array correspond to? The suit array has been preloaded with the four suits, so to get the suit, we print the character string suit[row]. Similarly, to get the face value of the card, we print the character string face[column]. We also print the character string " of ". Printing this information in the proper order enables us to print each card in the form "King of Clubs", "Ace of Diamonds" and so on.

Let us proceed with the top-down, stepwise refinement process. The top is simply

> *Shuffle and deal 52 cards*

Our first refinement yields:

> *Initialize the suit array*
> *Initialize the face array*
> *Initialize the deck array*
> *Shuffle the deck*
> *Deal 52 cards*

"Shuffle the deck" may be expanded as follows:

> *For each of the 52 cards*
> > *Place card number in randomly selected unoccupied slot of deck*

"Deal 52 cards" may be expanded as follows:

> *For each of the 52 cards*
> > *Find card number in deck array and print face and suit of card*

Incorporating these expansions yields our complete second refinement:

> *Initialize the suit array*
> *Initialize the face array*
> *Initialize the deck array*
>
> *For each of the 52 cards*
> > *Place card number in randomly selected unoccupied slot of deck*
>
> *For each of the 52 cards*
> > *Find card number in deck array and print face and suit of card*

"Place card number in randomly selected unoccupied slot of deck" may be expanded as follows:

> *Choose slot of deck randomly*
>
> *While chosen slot of deck has been previously chosen*
> > *Choose slot of deck randomly*
>
> *Place card number in chosen slot of deck*

"Find card number in deck array and print face and suit of card" may be expanded as follows:

For each slot of the deck array
    If slot contains card number
        Print the face and suit of the card

Incorporating these expansions yields our third refinement:

Initialize the suit array
Initialize the face array
Initialize the deck array

For each of the 52 cards
    Choose slot of deck randomly

    While slot of deck has been previously chosen
        Choose slot of deck randomly

    Place card number in chosen slot of deck

For each of the 52 cards
    For each slot of deck array
        If slot contains desired card number
            Print the face and suit of the card

This completes the refinement process. Note that this program is more efficient if the shuffle and deal portions of the algorithm are combined so each card is dealt as it is placed in the deck. We have chosen to program these operations separately because normally cards are dealt after they are shuffled (not while they are shuffled).

The card shuffling and dealing program is shown in Fig. 7.24, and a sample execution is shown in Fig. 7.25. Note the use of the conversion specifier %s to print strings of characters in the calls to printf. The corresponding argument in the printf call must be a pointer to char (or a char array). In the deal function, the format specification "%5s of %-8s" (line 76) prints a character string right-justified in a field of five characters followed by " of " and a character string left-justified in a field of eight characters. The minus sign in %-8s signifies that the string is left-justified in a field of width 8.

```
1    /* Fig. 7.24: fig07_24.c
2       Card shuffling dealing program */
3    #include <stdio.h>
4    #include <stdlib.h>
5    #include <time.h>
6
7    /* prototypes */
8    void shuffle( int wDeck[][ 13 ] );
9    void deal( const int wDeck[][ 13 ], const char *wFace[],
10              const char *wSuit[] );
11
12   int main()
13   {
```

Fig. 7.24 Card dealing program. (Part 1 of 3.)

```
14        /* initialize suit array */
15        const char *suit[ 4 ] = { "Hearts", "Diamonds", "Clubs", "Spades" };
16
17        /* initialize face array */
18        const char *face[ 13 ] =
19           { "Ace", "Deuce", "Three", "Four",
20             "Five", "Six", "Seven", "Eight",
21             "Nine", "Ten", "Jack", "Queen", "King" };
22
23        /* initialize deck array */
24        int deck[ 4 ][ 13 ] = { 0 };
25
26        srand( time( 0 ) ); /* seed random-number generator */
27
28        shuffle( deck );
29        deal( deck, face, suit );
30
31        return 0; /* indicates successful termination */
32
33     } /* end main */
34
35     /* shuffle cards in deck */
36     void shuffle( int wDeck[][ 13 ] )
37     {
38        int row;     /* row number */
39        int column;  /* column number */
40        int card;    /* counter */
41
42        /* for each of the 52 cards, choose slot of deck randomly */
43        for ( card = 1; card <= 52; card++ ) {
44
45           /* choose new random location until unoccupied slot found */
46           do {
47              row = rand() % 4;
48              column = rand() % 13;
49           } while( wDeck[ row ][ column ] != 0 ); /* end do...while */
50
51           /* place card number in chosen slot of deck */
52           wDeck[ row ][ column ] = card;
53        } /* end for */
54
55     } /* end function shuffle */
56
57     /* deal cards in deck */
58     void deal( const int wDeck[][ 13 ], const char *wFace[],
59               const char *wSuit[] )
60     {
61        int card;    /* card counter */
62        int row;     /* row counter */
63        int column;  /* column counter */
64
65        /* deal each of the 52 cards */
66        for ( card = 1; card <= 52; card++ ) {
```

Fig. 7.24 Card dealing program. (Part 2 of 3.)

```
67
68          /* loop through rows of wDeck */
69          for ( row = 0; row <= 3; row++ ) {
70
71              /* loop through columns of wDeck for current row */
72              for ( column = 0; column <= 12; column++ ) {
73
74                  /* if slot contains current card, display card */
75                  if ( wDeck[ row ][ column ] == card ) {
76                      printf( "%5s of %-8s%c", wFace[ column ], wSuit[ row ],
77                          card % 2 == 0 ? '\n' : '\t' );
78                  } /* end if */
79
80              } /* end for */
81
82          } /* end for */
83
84      } /* end for */
85
86  } /* end function deal */
```

Fig. 7.24   Card dealing program. (Part 3 of 3.)

```
Nine of Hearts        Five of Clubs
Queen of Spades       Three of Spades
Queen of Hearts       Ace of Clubs
 King of Hearts       Six of Spades
 Jack of Diamonds     Five of Spades
Seven of Hearts       King of Clubs
Three of Clubs        Eight of Hearts
Three of Diamonds     Four of Diamonds
Queen of Diamonds     Five of Diamonds
  Six of Diamonds     Five of Hearts
  Ace of Spades       Six of Hearts
 Nine of Diamonds     Queen of Clubs
Eight of Spades       Nine of Clubs
Deuce of Clubs        Six of Clubs
Deuce of Spades       Jack of Clubs
 Four of Clubs        Eight of Clubs
 Four of Spades       Seven of Spades
Seven of Diamonds     Seven of Clubs
 King of Spades        Ten of Diamonds
 Jack of Hearts       Ace of Hearts
 Jack of Spades       Ten of Clubs
Eight of Diamonds     Deuce of Diamonds
  Ace of Diamonds     Nine of Spades
 Four of Hearts       Deuce of Hearts
 King of Diamonds     Ten of Spades
Three of Hearts       Ten of Hearts
```

Fig. 7.25   Sample run of card dealing program.

There is a weakness in the dealing algorithm. Once a match is found, even if it is found on the first try, the two inner `for` statements continue searching the remaining elements of `deck` for a match. We correct this deficiency in the exercises and in a case study in Chapter 10.

7.12 Pointers to Functions   *Not on Exam*

A *pointer to a function* contains the address of the function in memory. In Chapter 6, we saw that an array name is really the address in memory of the first element of the array. Similarly, a function name is really the starting address in memory of the code that performs the function's task. Pointers to functions can be passed to functions, returned from functions, stored in arrays and assigned to other function pointers.

To illustrate the use of pointers to functions, Fig. 7.26 presents a modified version of the bubble sort program in Fig. 7.15. The new version consists of `main` and functions `bubble`, `swap`, `ascending` and `descending`. Function `bubbleSort` receives a pointer to a function—either function `ascending` or function `descending`—as an argument, in addition to an integer array and the size of the array. The program prompts the user to choose if the array should be sorted in ascending order or in descending order. If the user enters 1, a pointer to function `ascending` is passed to function `bubble`, causing the array to be sorted into increasing order. If the user enters 2, a pointer to function `descending` is passed to function `bubble`, causing the array to be sorted into decreasing order. The output of the program is shown in Fig. 7.27.

```
1   /* Fig. 7.26: fig07_26.c
2      Multipurpose sorting program using function pointers */
3   #include <stdio.h>
4   #define SIZE 10
5
6   /* prototypes */
7   void bubble( int work[], const int size, int (*compare)( int a, int b ) );
8   int ascending( int a, int b );
9   int descending( int a, int b );
10
11  int main()
12  {
13     int order;   /* 1 for ascending order or 2 for descending order */
14     int counter; /* counter */
15
16     /* initialize array a */
17     int a[ SIZE ] = { 2, 6, 4, 8, 10, 12, 89, 68, 45, 37 };
18
19     printf( "Enter 1 to sort in ascending order,\n"
20             "Enter 2 to sort in descending order: " );
21     scanf( "%d", &order );
22
23     printf( "\nData items in original order\n" );
24
```

Fig. 7.26   Multipurpose sorting program using function pointers. (Part 1 of 3.)

```
25       /* output original array */
26       for ( counter = 0; counter < SIZE; counter++ ) {
27          printf( "%5d", a[ counter ] );
28       } /* end for */
29
30       /* sort array in ascending order; pass function ascending as an
31          argument to specify ascending sorting order */
32       if ( order == 1 ) {
33          bubble( a, SIZE, ascending );
34          printf( "\nData items in ascending order\n" );
35       } /* end if */
36       else { /* pass function descending */
37          bubble( a, SIZE, descending );
38          printf( "\nData items in descending order\n" );
39       } /* end else */
40
41       /* output sorted array */
42       for ( counter = 0; counter < SIZE; counter++ ) {
43          printf( "%5d", a[ counter ] );
44       } /* end for */
45
46       printf( "\n" );
47
48       return 0; /* indicates successful termination */
49
50    } /* end main */
51
52    /* multipurpose bubble sort; parameter compare is a pointer to
53       the comparison function that determines sorting order */
54    void bubble( int work[], const int size, int (*compare)( int a, int b ) )
55    {
56       int pass;  /* pass counter */
57       int count; /* comparison counter */
58
59       void swap( int *element1Ptr, int *element2ptr ); /* prototype */
60
61       /* loop to control passes */
62       for ( pass = 1; pass < size; pass++ ) {
63
64          /* loop to control number of comparisons per pass */
65          for ( count = 0; count < size - 1; count++ ) {
66
67             /* if adjacent elements are out of order, swap them */
68             if ( (*compare)( work[ count ], work[ count + 1 ] ) ) {
69                swap( &work[ count ], &work[ count + 1 ] );
70             } /* end if */
71
72          } /* end for */
73
74       } /* end for */
75
76    } /* end function bubble */
77
```

Fig. 7.26 Multipurpose sorting program using function pointers. (Part 2 of 3.)

```
78    /* swap values at memory locations to which element1Ptr and
79       element2Ptr point */
80    void swap( int *element1Ptr, int *element2Ptr )
81    {
82       int hold; /* temporary holding variable */
83
84       hold = *element1Ptr;
85       *element1Ptr = *element2Ptr;
86       *element2Ptr = hold;
87    } /* end function swap */
88
89    /* determine whether elements are out of order for an ascending
90       order sort */
91    int ascending( int a, int b )
92    {
93       return b < a; /* swap if b is less than a */
94
95    } /* end function ascending */
96
97    /* determine whether elements are out of order for a descending
98       order sort */
99    int descending( int a, int b )
100   {
101      return b > a; /* swap if b is greater than a */
102
103   } /* end function descending */
```

Fig. 7.26   Multipurpose sorting program using function pointers. (Part 3 of 3.)

```
Enter 1 to sort in ascending order,
Enter 2 to sort in descending order: 1

Data items in original order
    2    6    4    8   10   12   89   68   45   37
Data items in ascending order
    2    4    6    8   10   12   37   45   68   89
```

```
Enter 1 to sort in ascending order,
Enter 2 to sort in descending order: 2

Data items in original order
    2    6    4    8   10   12   89   68   45   37
Data items in descending order
   89   68   45   37   12   10    8    6    4    2
```

Fig. 7.27   The outputs of the bubble sort program in Fig. 7.26.

The following parameter appears in the function header for bubble (line 54)

```
int (*compare)( int a, int b )
```

This tells `bubble` to expect a parameter (`compare`) that is a pointer to a function that receives two integer parameters and returns an integer result. Parentheses are needed around `*compare` to group `*` with `compare` to indicate that `compare` is a pointer. If we had not included the parentheses, the declaration would have been

```
int *compare( int a, int b )
```

which declares a function that receives two integers as parameters and returns a pointer to an integer.

The function prototype for `bubble` is shown in line 7. Note that the prototype could have been written as

```
int (*)( int, int );
```

without the function pointer name and parameter names.

The function passed to `bubble` is called in an `if` statement (line 68) as follows

```
if ( (*compare)( work[ count ], work[ count + 1 ] ) )
```

Just as a pointer to a variable is dereferenced to access the value of the variable, a pointer to a function is dereferenced to use the function.

The call to the function could have been made without dereferencing the pointer as in

```
if ( compare( work[ count ], work[ count + 1 ] ) )
```

which uses the pointer directly as the function name. We prefer the first method of calling a function through a pointer because it explicitly illustrates that `compare` is a pointer to a function that is dereferenced to call the function. The second method of calling a function through a pointer makes it appear as though `compare` is an actual function. This may be confusing to a user of the program who would like to see the definition of function `compare` and finds that it is never defined in the file.

Using Function Pointers to Create a Menu-Driven System

A common use of *function pointers* is in so-called menu-driven systems. A user is prompted to select an option from a menu (possibly from 1 to 5). Each option is serviced by a different function. Pointers to each function are stored in an array of pointers to functions. The user's choice is used as a subscript in the array, and the pointer in the array is used to call the function.

Figure 7.28 provides a generic example of the mechanics of defining and using an array of pointers to functions. Three functions are defined—`function1`, `function2` and `function3`—that each take an integer argument and return nothing. Pointers to these three functions are stored in array `f`, which is defined (line 14) as follows:

```
void ( *f[ 3 ] )( int ) = { function1, function2, function3 };
```

The definition is read beginning in the leftmost set of parentheses, "`f` is an array of 3 pointers to functions that take an `int` as an argument and that return `void`." The array is initialized with the names of the three functions. When the user enters a value between 0 and 2, the value is used as the subscript in the array of pointers to functions. The function call (line 26) is made as follows:

```
(*f[ choice ])( choice );
```

```
1   /* Fig. 7.28: fig07_28.c
2      Demonstrating an array of pointers to functions */
3   #include <stdio.h>
4
5   /* prototypes */
6   void function1( int a );
7   void function2( int b );
8   void function3( int c );
9
10  int main()
11  {
12     /* initialize array of 3 pointer to functions that each take an
13        int argument and return void */
14     void (*f[ 3 ])( int ) = { function1, function2, function3 };
15
16     int choice; /* variable to hold user's choice */
17
18     printf( "Enter a number between 0 and 2, 3 to end: " );
19     scanf( "%d", &choice );
20
21     /* process user's choice */
22     while ( choice >= 0 && choice < 3 ) {
23
24        /* invoke function at location choice in array f and pass
25           choice as an argument */
26        (*f[ choice ])( choice );
27
28        printf( "Enter a number between 0 and 2, 3 to end: ");
29        scanf( "%d", &choice );
30     } /* end while */
31
32     printf( "Program execution completed.\n" );
33
34     return 0; /* indicates successful termination */
35
36  } /* end main */
37
38  void function1( int a )
39  {
40     printf( "You entered %d so function1 was called\n\n", a );
41  } /* end function1 */
42
43  void function2( int b )
44  {
45     printf( "You entered %d so function2 was called\n\n", b );
46  } /* end function2 */
47
48  void function3( int c )
49  {
50     printf( "You entered %d so function3 was called\n\n", c );
51  } /* end function3 */
```

Fig. 7.28   Demonstrating an array of pointers to functions. (Part 1 of 2.)

```
Enter a number between 0 and 2, 3 to end: 0
You entered 0 so function1 was called

Enter a number between 0 and 2, 3 to end: 1
You entered 1 so function2 was called

Enter a number between 0 and 2, 3 to end: 2
You entered 2 so function3 was called

Enter a number between 0 and 2, 3 to end: 3
Program execution completed.
```

Fig. 7.28   Demonstrating an array of pointers to functions. (Part 2 of 2.)

In the function call, f[choice] selects the pointer at location choice in the array. The pointer is dereferenced to call the function and choice is passed as the argument to the function. Each function prints its argument's value and its function name to demonstrate that the function is called correctly. In the exercises, you will develop a menu-driven system.

SUMMARY

- Pointers are variables that contain as their values addresses of other variables.
- Pointers must be defined before they can be used.
- The definition

    int *ptr;

  defines ptr to be a pointer to an object of type int and is read, "ptr is a pointer to int." The * as used here indicates that the variable is a pointer.
- There are three values that can be used to initialize a pointer; 0, NULL, or an address. Initializing a pointer to 0 and initializing that same pointer to NULL are identical.
- The only integer that can be assigned to a pointer is 0.
- The & (address) operator returns the address of its operand.
- The operand of the address operator must be a variable; the address operator cannot be applied to constants, to expressions, or to variables declared with the storage class register.
- The * operator, referred to as the indirection or dereferencing operator, returns the value of the object that its operand points to in memory. This is called dereferencing the pointer.
- When calling a function with an argument that the caller wants the called function to modify, the address of the argument is passed. The called function then uses the indirection operator (*) to modify the value of the argument in the calling function.
- A function receiving an address as an argument must include a pointer as its corresponding formal parameter.
- It is not necessary to include the names of pointers in function prototypes; it is only necessary to include the pointer types. Pointer names may be included for documentation reasons, but the compiler ignores them.
- The const qualifier enables the programmer to inform the compiler that the value of a particular variable should not be modified.

- If an attempt is made to modify a value that is declared `const`, the compiler catches it and issues either a warning or an error, depending on the particular compiler.

- There are four ways to pass a pointer to a function: a non-constant pointer to non-constant data, a constant pointer to non-constant data, a non-constant pointer to constant data and a constant pointer to constant data.

- Arrays are automatically passed by reference because the value of the array name is the address of the array.

- To pass a single element of an array to a function by reference, the address of the specific array element must be passed.

- C provides the special unary operator `sizeof` to determine the size in bytes of an array (or any other data type) at compilation time.

- When applied to the name of an array, the operator `sizeof` returns an integer representing the total number of bytes in the array.

- Operator `sizeof` can be applied to any variable name, type or constant.

- Type `size_t` is a type defined by the standard (in `<stddef.h>`) as the integral type (`unsigned` or `unsigned long`) of the value returned by operator `sizeof`.

- The arithmetic operations that may be performed on pointers are incrementing (`++`) a pointer, decrementing (`--`) a pointer, adding (`+` or `+=`) a pointer and an integer, subtracting (`-` or `-=`) a pointer and an integer, and subtracting one pointer from another.

- When an integer is added to or subtracted from a pointer, the pointer is incremented or decremented by that integer times the size of the object pointed to.

- Pointer arithmetic operations should only be performed on contiguous portions of memory such as an array. All elements of an array are stored contiguously in memory.

- When performing pointer arithmetic on a character array, the results are like regular arithmetic because each character is stored in one byte of memory.

- Pointers can be assigned to one another if both pointers are of the same type. The exception to this is a pointer to `void`, which is a generic pointer type that can hold pointers of any type. Pointers to `void` can be assigned pointers of other types and can be assigned to pointers of other types without a cast.

- A pointer to `void` may not be dereferenced.

- Pointers can be compared using the equality and relational operators. Pointer comparisons are normally meaningful only if the pointers point to members of the same array.

- Pointers can be subscripted exactly as array names can.

- An array name without a subscript is a pointer to the first element of the array.

- In pointer/offset notation, the offset is the same as an array subscript.

- All subscripted array expressions can be written with a pointer and an offset, using either the name of the array as a pointer or a separate pointer that points to the array.

- An array name is a constant pointer that always points to the same location in memory. Array names cannot be modified as conventional pointers can.

- It is possible to have arrays of pointers.

- It is possible to have pointers to functions.

- A pointer to a function is the address where the code for the function resides.

- Pointers to functions can be passed to functions, returned from functions, stored in arrays and assigned to other pointers.

- A common use of function pointers is in so-called menu-driven systems.

TERMINOLOGY

adding a pointer and an integer

address operator (&)

array of pointers

array of strings

call by reference

call by value

character pointer

`const`

constant pointer

constant pointer to constant data

constant pointer to non-constant data

decrement a pointer

dereference a pointer

dereferencing operator (*)

directly reference a variable

dynamic memory allocation

function pointer

increment a pointer

indefinite postponement

indirection

indirection operator (*)

indirectly reference a variable

initializing pointers

linked list

non-constant pointer to constant data

non-constant pointer to non-constant data

NULL pointer

offset

pointer

pointer arithmetic

pointer assignment

pointer comparison

pointer expression

pointer indexing

pointer/offset notation

pointer subscripting

pointer to a function

pointer to `void` (`void *`)

pointer types

principle of least privilege

simulated call by reference

`sizeof` operator

`size_t` type

string array

subtracting an integer from a pointer

subtracting two pointers

top-down, stepwise refinement

`void *` (pointer to `void`)

COMMON PROGRAMMING ERRORS

7.1   The asterisk (*) notation used to declare pointer variables does not distribute to all variable names in a declaration. Each pointer must be declared with the * prefixed to the name, e.g., if you wish to declare xPtr and yPtr as int pointers, use `int *xPtr, *yPtr;`.

7.2   Dereferencing a pointer that has not been properly initialized or that has not been assigned to point to a specific location in memory is an error. This could cause a fatal execution-time error, or it could accidentally modify important data and allow the program to run to completion with incorrect results.

7.3   Not dereferencing a pointer when it is necessary to do so in order to obtain the value to which the pointer points is a syntax error.

7.4   Being unaware that a function is expecting pointers as arguments for call by reference and passing arguments call by value. Some compilers take the values assuming they are pointers and dereference the values as pointers. At run-time, memory access violations or segmentation faults are often generated. Other compilers catch the mismatch in types between arguments and parameters and generate error messages.

7.5   Using pointer arithmetic on a pointer that does not refer to an element in an array of values.

7.6   Subtracting or comparing two pointers that do not refer to elements in the same array.

7.7   Running off either end of an array when using pointer arithmetic.

7.8   Assigning a pointer of one type to a pointer of another type if neither is of type void * is a syntax error.

7.9   Dereferencing a void * pointer is a syntax error.

7.10   Attempting to modify an array name with pointer arithmetic is a syntax error.

GOOD PROGRAMMING PRACTICES

7.1   Initialize pointers to prevent unexpected results.

7.2   Use call-by-value to pass arguments to a function unless the caller explicitly requires the called function to modify the value of the argument variable in the caller's environment. This prevents accidental modification of the caller's arguments and is another example of the principle of least privilege.

7.3   If a variable does not (or should not) change in the body of a function to which it is passed, the variable should be declared `const` to ensure that it is not accidentally modified.

7.4   Before using a function, check its function prototype to determine if the function is able to modify the values passed to it.

GOOD PROGRAMMING PRACTICE

7.1   Include the letters `ptr` in pointer variable names to make it clear that these variables are pointers and thus need to be handled appropriately.

PERFORMANCE TIPS

7.1   Pass large objects such as structures using pointers to constant data to obtain the performance benefits of call by reference and the security of call-by-value.

7.2   Passing the size of an array to a function takes time and requires additional stack space because a copy of the size is made to pass to the function. Global variables require no additional time or space because they can be accessed directly by any function.

7.3   `sizeof` is a compile-time operator, so it does not incur any execution-time overhead.

7.4   Sometimes an algorithm that emerges in a "natural" way can contain subtle performance problems, such as indefinite postponement. Seek algorithms that avoid indefinite postponement.

PORTABILITY TIPS

7.1   Although `const` is well defined in ANSI C, some compilers do not enforce it.

7.2   The number of bytes used to store a particular data type may vary between systems. When writing programs that depend on data type sizes and that will run on several computer systems, use `sizeof` to determine the number of bytes used to store the data types.

7.3   Most computers today have 2-byte or 4-byte integers. Some of the newer machines use 8-byte integers. Because the results of pointer arithmetic depend on the size of the objects a pointer points to, pointer arithmetic is machine dependent.

SOFTWARE ENGINEERING OBSERVATIONS

7.1   The `const` qualifier can be used to enforce the principle of least privilege. Using the principle of least privilege to properly design software reduces debugging time and improper side effects, making a program easier to modify and maintain.

7.2   Only one value can be altered in a calling function when call-by-value is used. That value must be assigned from the return value of the function. To modify multiple values in a calling function, call-by-reference must be used.

7.3   Placing function prototypes in the definitions of other functions enforces the principle of least privilege by restricting proper function calls to the functions in which the prototypes appear.

7.4   When passing an array to a function, also pass the size of the array. This helps make the function reusable in many programs.

7.5   Global variables often violate the principle of least privilege and can lead to poor software engineering.

SELF-REVIEW EXERCISES

7.1   Answer each of the following:
a) A pointer variable contains as its value the _____ of another variable.
b) The three values that can be used to initialize a pointer are _____, _____ or a(n) _____.
c) The only integer that can be assigned to a pointer is _____.

7.2   State whether the following are *true* or *false*. If the answer is *false*, explain why.
a) The address operator (&) can be applied only to constants, to expressions and to variables declared with the storage class `register`.
b) A pointer that is declared to be `void` can be dereferenced.
c) Pointers of different types may not be assigned to one another without a cast operation.

7.3   Answer each of the following. Assume that single-precision floating-point numbers are stored in 4 bytes, and that the starting address of the array is at location 1002500 in memory. Each part of the exercise should use the results of previous parts where appropriate.
a) Define an array of type `float` called `numbers` with 10 elements, and initialize the elements to the values 0.0, 1.1, 2.2, ..., 9.9. Assume the symbolic constant SIZE has been defined as 10.
b) Define a pointer, `nPtr`, that points to an object of type `float`.
c) Print the elements of array `numbers` using array subscript notation. Use a `for` statement and assume the integer control variable `i` has been defined. Print each number with 1 position of precision to the right of the decimal point.
d) Give two separate statements that assign the starting address of array `numbers` to the pointer variable `nPtr`.
e) Print the elements of array `numbers` using pointer/offset notation with the pointer `nPtr`.
f) Print the elements of array `numbers` using pointer/offset notation with the array name as the pointer.
g) Print the elements of array `numbers` by subscripting pointer `nPtr`.
h) Refer to element 4 of array `numbers` using array subscript notation, pointer/offset notation with the array name as the pointer, pointer subscript notation with `nPtr` and pointer/offset notation with `nPtr`.
i) Assuming that `nPtr` points to the beginning of array `numbers`, what address is referenced by `nPtr + 8`? What value is stored at that location?
j) Assuming that `nPtr` points to `numbers[ 5 ]`, what address is referenced by `nPtr -= 4`. What is the value stored at that location?

7.4   For each of the following, write a statement that performs the indicated task. Assume that floating-point variables `number1` and `number2` are defined and that `number1` is initialized to 7.3.
a) Define the variable `fPtr` to be a pointer to an object of type `float`.
b) Assign the address of variable `number1` to pointer variable `fPtr`.
c) Print the value of the object pointed to by `fPtr`.
d) Assign the value of the object pointed to by `fPtr` to variable `number2`.
e) Print the value of `number2`.
f) Print the address of `number1`. Use the %p conversion specifier.
g) Print the address stored in `fPtr`. Use the %p conversion specifier. Is the value printed the same as the address of `number1`?

7.5   Do each of the following:
a) Write the function header for a function called `exchange` that takes two pointers to floating-point numbers x and y as parameters and does not return a value.
b) Write the function prototype for the function in part (a).

c) Write the function header for a function called `evaluate` that returns an integer and that takes as parameters integer x and a pointer to function `poly`. Function `poly` takes an integer parameter and returns an integer.

d) Write the function prototype for the function in part (c).

7.6 Find the error in each of the following program segments. Assume

```
int *zPtr; /* zPtr will reference array z */
int *aPtr = NULL;
void *sPtr = NULL;
int number, i;
int z[ 5 ] = { 1, 2, 3, 4, 5 };
sPtr = z;
```

a) `++zptr;`

b) `/* use pointer to get first value of array */`
   `number = zPtr;`

c) `/* assign array element 2 (the value 3) to number */`
   `number = *zPtr[ 2 ];`

d) `/* print entire array z */`
   `for ( i = 0; i <= 5; i++ )`
   `    printf( "%d ", zPtr[ i ] );`

e) `/* assign the value pointed to by sPtr to number */`
   `number = *sPtr;`

f) `++z;`

ANSWERS TO SELF-REVIEW EXERCISES

7.1 a) address. b) 0, NULL, an address. c) 0.

7.2 a) False. The address operator can be applied only to variables. The address operator cannot be applied to variables declared with storage class `register`.

b) False. A pointer to `void` cannot be dereferenced because there is no way to know exactly how many bytes of memory to dereference.

c) False. Pointers of type `void` can be assigned pointers of other types, and pointers of type `void` can be assigned to pointers of other types.

7.3 a) `float numbers[ SIZE ] =`
       `    { 0.0, 1.1, 2.2, 3.3, 4.4, 5.5, 6.6, 7.7, 8.8, 9.9 };`

b) `float *nPtr;`

c) `for ( i = 0; i < SIZE; i++ )`
   `    printf( "%.1f ", numbers[ i ] );`

d) `nPtr = numbers;`
   `nPtr = &numbers[ 0 ];`

e) `for ( i = 0; i < SIZE; i++ )`
   `    printf( "%.1f ", *( nPtr + i ) );`

f) `for ( i = 0; i < SIZE; i++ )`
   `    printf( "%.1f ", *( numbers + i ) );`

g) `for ( i = 0; i < SIZE; i++ )`
   `    printf( "%.1f ", nPtr[ i ] );`

h) `numbers[ 4 ]`
   `*( numbers + 4 )`
   `nPtr[ 4 ]`
   `*( nPtr + 4 )`

i) The address is 1002500 + 8 * 4 = 1002532. The value is 8.8.

j)   The address of `numbers[ 5 ]` is $1002500 + 5 * 4 = 1002520$.
     The address of `nPtr -= 4` is $1002520 - 4 * 4 = 1002504$.
     The value at that location is `1.1`.

7.4   a) `float *fPtr;`
          b) `fPtr = &number1;`
          c) `printf( "The value of *fPtr is %f\n", *fPtr );`
          d) `number2 = *fPtr;`
          e) `printf( "The value of number2 is %f\n", number2 );`
          f) `printf( "The address of number1 is %p\n", &number1 );`
          g) `printf( "The address stored in fptr is %p\n", fPtr );`
              Yes, the value is the same.

7.5   a) `void exchange( float *x, float *y )`
          b) `void exchange( float *x, float *y );`
          c) `int evaluate( int x, int (*poly)( int ) )`
          d) `int evaluate( int x, int (*poly)( int ) );`

7.6   a) Error: `zPtr` has not been initialized.
              Correction: Initialize `zPtr` with `zPtr = z;`
          b) Error: The pointer is not dereferenced.
              Correction: Change the statement to `number = *zPtr;`
          c) Error: `zPtr[ 2 ]` is not a pointer and should not be dereferenced.
              Correction: Change `*zPtr[ 2 ]` to `zPtr[ 2 ]`.
          d) Error: Referring to an array element outside the array bounds with pointer subscripting.
              Correction: Change the operator `<=` in the `for` condition to `<`.
          e) Error: Dereferencing a void pointer.
              Correction: In order to dereference the pointer, it must first be cast to an integer pointer.
              Change the statement to `number = *( ( int * ) sPtr );`
          f) Error: Trying to modify an array name with pointer arithmetic.
              Correction: Use a pointer variable instead of the array name to accomplish pointer arith-
              metic, or subscript the array name to refer to a specific element.

EXERCISES

7.7   Answer each of the following:
          a) The _____ operator returns the location in memory where its operand is stored.
          b) The _____ operator returns the value of the object to which its operand points.
          c) To simulate call-by-reference when passing a nonarray variable to a function, it is nec-
              essary to pass the _____ of the variable to the function.

7.8   State whether the following are *true* or *false*. If *false*, explain why.
          a) Two pointers that point to different arrays cannot be compared meaningfully.
          b) Because the name of an array is a pointer to the first element of the array, array names
              may be manipulated in precisely the same manner as pointers.

7.9   Answer each of the following. Assume that unsigned integers are stored in 2 bytes and that
the starting address of the array is at location `1002500` in memory.
          a) Define an array of type `unsigned int` called `values` with five elements, and initialize
              the elements to the even integers from 2 to 10. Assume the symbolic constant `SIZE` has
              been defined as `5`.
          b) Define a pointer `vPtr` that points to an object of type `unsigned int`.
          c) Print the elements of array `values` using array subscript notation. Use a `for` statement
              and assume integer control variable `i` has been defined.

d) Give two separate statements that assign the starting address of array `values` to pointer variable `vPtr`.

e) Print the elements of array `values` using pointer/offset notation.

f) Print the elements of array `values` using pointer/offset notation with the array name as the pointer.

g) Print the elements of array `values` by subscripting the pointer to the array.

h) Refer to element 5 of array `values` using array subscript notation, pointer/offset notation with the array name as the pointer, pointer subscript notation, and pointer/offset notation.

i) What address is referenced by `vPtr + 3`? What value is stored at that location?

j) Assuming `vPtr` points to `values[ 4 ]`, what address is referenced by `vPtr -= 4`. What value is stored at that location?

7.10 For each of the following, write a single statement that performs the indicated task. Assume that long integer variables `value1` and `value2` have been defined and that `value1` has been initialized to 200000.

a) Define the variable `lPtr` to be a pointer to an object of type `long`.

b) Assign the address of variable `value1` to pointer variable `lPtr`.

c) Print the value of the object pointed to by `lPtr`.

d) Assign the value of the object pointed to by `lPtr` to variable `value2`.

e) Print the value of `value2`.

f) Print the address of `value1`.

g) Print the address stored in `lPtr`. Is the value printed the same as the address of `value1`?

7.11 Do each of the following.

a) Write the function header for function `zero`, which takes a long integer array parameter `bigIntegers` and does not return a value.

b) Write the function prototype for the function in *Part a*.

c) Write the function header for function `add1AndSum`, which takes an integer array parameter `oneTooSmall` and returns an integer.

d) Write the function prototype for the function described in *Part c*.

Note: Exercise 7.12 through Exercise 7.15 are reasonably challenging. Once you have done these problems, you ought to be able to implement most popular card games easily.

7.12 Modify the program in Fig. 7.24 so that the card-dealing function deals a five-card poker hand. Then write the following additional functions:

a) Determine if the hand contains a pair.

b) Determine if the hand contains two pairs.

c) Determine if the hand contains three of a kind (e.g., three jacks).

d) Determine if the hand contains four of a kind (e.g., four aces).

e) Determine if the hand contains a flush (i.e., all five cards of the same suit).

f) Determine if the hand contains a straight (i.e., five cards of consecutive face values).

7.13 Use the functions developed in Exercise 7.12 to write a program that deals two five-card poker hands, evaluates each hand, and determines which is the better hand.

7.14 Modify the program developed in Exercise 7.13 so that it can simulate the dealer. The dealer's five-card hand is dealt "face down" so the player cannot see it. The program should then evaluate the dealer's hand, and based on the quality of the hand, the dealer should draw one, two or three more cards to replace the corresponding number of unneeded cards in the original hand. The program should then re-evaluate the dealer's hand. [*Caution:* This is a difficult problem!]

7.15 Modify the program developed in Exercise 7.14 so that it can handle the dealer's hand automatically, but the player is allowed to decide which cards of the player's hand to replace. The program should then evaluate both hands and determine who wins. Now use this new program to play 20 games against the computer. Who wins more games, you or the computer? Have one of your friends play 20 games against the computer. Who wins more games? Based on the results of these games, make appropriate modifications to refine your poker playing program (this, too, is a difficult problem). Play 20 more games. Does your modified program play a better game?

7.16   In the card shuffling and dealing program of Fig. 7.24, we intentionally used an inefficient shuffling algorithm that introduced the possibility of indefinite postponement. In this problem, you will create a high-performance shuffling algorithm that avoids indefinite postponement.

Modify the program of Fig. 7.24 as follows. Begin by initializing the deck array as shown in Fig. 7.29. Modify the shuffle function to loop row-by-row and column-by-column through the array touching every element once. Each element should be swapped with a randomly selected element of the array.

Unshuffled deck array												
	0	**1**	**2**	**3**	**4**	**5**	**6**	**7**	**8**	**9**	**10**	**11**	**12**
0	1	2	3	4	5	6	7	8	9	10	11	12	13
1	14	15	16	17	18	19	20	21	22	23	24	25	26
2	27	28	29	30	31	32	33	34	35	36	37	38	39
3	40	41	42	43	44	45	46	47	48	49	50	51	52

Fig. 7.29   Unshuffled deck array.

Print the resulting array to determine if the deck is satisfactorily shuffled (as in Fig. 7.30, for example). You may want your program to call the shuffle function several times to ensure a satisfactory shuffle.

Sample shuffled deck array												
	0	**1**	**2**	**3**	**4**	**5**	**6**	**7**	**8**	**9**	**10**	**11**	**12**
0	19	40	27	25	36	46	10	34	35	41	18	2	44
1	13	28	14	16	21	30	8	11	31	17	24	7	1
2	12	33	15	42	43	23	45	3	29	32	4	47	26
3	50	38	52	39	48	51	9	5	37	49	22	6	20

Fig. 7.30   Sample shuffled deck array.

Note that although the approach in this problem improves the shuffling algorithm, the dealing algorithm still requires searching the deck array for card 1, then card 2, then card 3, and so on. Worse yet, even after the dealing algorithm locates and deals the card, the algorithm continues searching through the remainder of the deck. Modify the program of Fig. 7.24 so that once a card is dealt, no further attempts are made to match that card number, and the program immediately proceeds with dealing the next card. In Chapter 10, we develop a dealing algorithm that requires only one operation per card.

7.17   (*Simulation: The Tortoise and the Hare*) In this problem, you will recreate one of the truly great moments in history, namely the classic race of the tortoise and the hare. You will use random number generation to develop a simulation of this memorable event.

Our contenders begin the race at "square 1" of 70 squares. Each square represents a possible position along the race course. The finish line is at square 70. The first contender to reach or pass square 70 is rewarded with a pail of fresh carrots and lettuce. The course weaves its way up the side of a slippery mountain, so occasionally the contenders lose ground.

There is a clock that ticks once per second. With each tick of the clock, your program should adjust the position of the animals according to the rules of Fig. 7.31.

Animal	Move type	Percentage of the time	Actual move
Tortoise	Fast plod	50%	3 squares to the right
	Slip	20%	6 squares to the left
	Slow plod	30%	1 square to the right
Hare	Sleep	20%	No move at all
	Big hop	20%	9 squares to the right
	Big slip	10%	12 squares to the left
	Small hop	30%	1 square to the right
	Small slip	20%	2 squares to the left

Fig. 7.31 Tortoise and hare rules for adjusting positions.

Use variables to keep track of the positions of the animals (i.e., position numbers are 1–70). Start each animal at position 1 (i.e., the "starting gate"). If an animal slips left before square 1, move the animal back to square 1.

Generate the percentages in the preceding table by producing a random integer, i, in the range $1 \leq i \leq 10$. For the tortoise, perform a "fast plod" when $1 \leq i \leq 5$, a "slip" when $6 \leq i \leq 7$, or a "slow plod" when $8 \leq i \leq 10$. Use a similar technique to move the hare.

Begin the race by printing

```
BANG !!!!!
AND THEY'RE OFF !!!!!
```

Then, for each tick of the clock (i.e., each repetition of a loop), print a 70 position line showing the letter T in the position of the tortoise and the letter H in the position of the hare. Occasionally, the contenders will land on the same square. In this case, the tortoise bites the hare and your program should print OUCH!!! beginning at that position. All print positions other than the T, the H, or the OUCH!!! (in case of a tie) should be blank.

After each line is printed, test if either animal has reached or passed square 70. If so, then print the winner and terminate the simulation. If the tortoise wins, print TORTOISE WINS!!! YAY!!! If the hare wins, print Hare wins. Yuch. If both animals win on the same tick of the clock, you may want to favor the turtle (the "underdog"), or you may want to print It's a tie. If neither animal wins, perform the loop again to simulate the next tick of the clock. When you are ready to run your program, assemble a group of fans to watch the race. You'll be amazed at how involved your audience gets!

SPECIAL SECTION: BUILDING YOUR OWN COMPUTER

In the next several problems, we take a temporary diversion away from the world of high-level language programming. We "peel open" a computer and look at its internal structure. We introduce machine language programming and write several machine language programs. To make this an especially valuable experience, we then build a computer (through the technique of software-based *simulation*) on which you can execute your machine language programs!

7.18   (*Machine Language Programming*) Let us create a computer we will call the Simpletron. As its name implies, it is a simple machine, but as we will soon see, a powerful one as well. The Simpletron runs programs written in the only language it directly understands—that is, Simpletron Machine Language, or SML for short.

The Simpletron contains an *accumulator*—a "special register" in which information is put before the Simpletron uses that information in calculations or examines it in various ways. All information in the Simpletron is handled in terms of *words*. A word is a signed four-digit decimal number such as +3364, -1293, +0007, -0001, etc. The Simpletron is equipped with a 100-word memory, and these words are referenced by their location numbers 00, 01, ..., 99.

Before running an SML program, we must *load* or place the program into memory. The first instruction (or statement) of every SML program is always placed in location 00.

Each instruction written in SML occupies one word of the Simpletron's memory (and hence instructions are signed four-digit decimal numbers). We assume that the sign of an SML instruction is always plus, but the sign of a data word may be either plus or minus. Each location in the Simpletron's memory may contain either an instruction, a data value used by a program or an unused (and hence undefined) area of memory. The first two digits of each SML instruction are the *operation code*, which specifies the operation to be performed. SML operation codes are summarized in Fig. 7.32.

Operation code	Meaning
Input/output operations:	
#define READ 10	Read a word from the terminal into a specific location in memory.
#define WRITE 11	Write a word from a specific location in memory to the terminal.
Load/store operations:	
#define LOAD 20	Load a word from a specific location in memory into the accumulator.
#define STORE 21	Store a word from the accumulator into a specific location in memory.
Arithmetic operations:	
#define ADD 30	Add a word from a specific location in memory to the word in the accumulator (leave result in accumulator).
#define SUBTRACT 31	Subtract a word from a specific location in memory from the word in the accumulator (leave result in accumulator).
#define DIVIDE 32	Divide a word from a specific location in memory into the word in the accumulator (leave result in accumulator).
#define MULTIPLY 33	Multiply a word from a specific location in memory by the word in the accumulator (leave result in accumulator).
Transfer of control operations:	
#define BRANCH 40	Branch to a specific location in memory.
#define BRANCHNEG 41	Branch to a specific location in memory if the accumulator is negative.
#define BRANCHZERO 42	Branch to a specific location in memory if the accumulator is zero.
#define HALT 43	Halt—i.e., the program has completed its task.

Fig. 7.32   Simpletron Machine Language (SML) operation codes.

The last two digits of an SML instruction are the *operand,* which is the address of the memory location containing the word to which the operation applies. Now let us consider several simple SML programs.

Example 1 Location	Number	Instruction
00	+1007	*(Read A)*
01	+1008	*(Read B)*
02	+2007	*(Load A)*
03	+3008	*(Add B)*
04	+2109	*(Store C)*
05	+1109	*(Write C)*
06	+4300	*(Halt)*
07	+0000	*(Variable A)*
08	+0000	*(Variable B)*
09	+0000	*(Result C)*

The preceding SML program reads two numbers from the keyboard, and computes and prints their sum. The instruction +1007 reads the first number from the keyboard and places it into location 07 (which has been initialized to zero). Then +1008 reads the next number into location 08. The *load* instruction, +2007, puts the first number into the accumulator, and the *add* instruction, +3008, adds the second number to the number in the accumulator. *All SML arithmetic instructions leave their results in the accumulator.* The *store* instruction, +2109, places the result back into memory location 09 from which the *write* instruction, +1109, takes the number and prints it (as a signed four-digit decimal number). The *halt* instruction, +4300, terminates execution.

Example 2 Location	Number	Instruction
00	+1009	*(Read A)*
01	+1010	*(Read B)*
02	+2009	*(Load A)*
03	+3110	*(Subtract B)*
04	+4107	*(Branch negative to 07)*
05	+1109	*(Write A)*
06	+4300	*(Halt)*
07	+1110	*(Write B)*
08	+4300	*(Halt)*
09	+0000	*(Variable A)*
10	+0000	*(Variable B)*

The preceding SML program reads two numbers from the keyboard, and determines and prints the larger value. Note the use of the instruction +4107 as a conditional transfer of control, much the same as C's `if` statement. Now write SML programs to accomplish each of the following tasks.

   a) Use a sentinel-controlled loop to read 10 positive integers and compute and print their sum.

b) Use a counter-controlled loop to read seven numbers, some positive and some negative, and compute and print their average.

c) Read a series of numbers and determine and print the largest number. The first number read indicates how many numbers should be processed.

7.19   (*A Computer Simulator*) It may at first seem outrageous, but in this problem you are going to build your own computer. No, you will not be soldering components together. Rather, you will use the powerful technique of *software-based simulation* to create a *software model* of the Simpletron. You will not be disappointed. Your Simpletron simulator will turn the computer you are using into a Simpletron, and you will actually be able to run, test and debug the SML programs you wrote in Exercise 7.18.

When you run your Simpletron simulator, it should begin by printing:

```
*** Welcome to Simpletron! ***
*** Please enter your program one instruction ***
*** (or data word) at a time. I will type the ***
*** location number and a question mark (?).   ***
*** You then type the word for that location.  ***
*** Type the sentinel -99999 to stop entering ***
*** your program. ***
```

Simulate the memory of the Simpletron with a single-subscripted array `memory` that has 100 elements. Now assume that the simulator is running, and let us examine the dialog as we enter the program of Example 2 of Exercise 7.18:

```
00 ? +1009
01 ? +1010
02 ? +2009
03 ? +3110
04 ? +4107
05 ? +1109
06 ? +4300
07 ? +1110
08 ? +4300
09 ? +0000
10 ? +0000
11 ? -99999
*** Program loading completed ***
*** Program execution begins  ***
```

The SML program has now been placed (or loaded) into the array `memory`. Now the Simpletron executes your SML program. Execution begins with the instruction in location 00 and, like C, continues sequentially, unless directed to some other part of the program by a transfer of control.

Use the variable `accumulator` to represent the accumulator register. Use the variable `instructionCounter` to keep track of the location in memory that contains the instruction being performed. Use the variable `operationCode` to indicate the operation currently being performed—i.e., the left two digits of the instruction word. Use the variable `operand` to indicate the memory location on which the current instruction operates. Thus, `operand` is the rightmost two digits of the instruction currently being performed. Do not execute instructions directly from memory. Rather, transfer the next instruction to be performed from memory to a variable called `instructionRegister`. Then "pick off" the left two digits and place them in the variable `operationCode,` and "pick off" the right two digits and place them in `operand`.

When Simpletron begins execution, the special registers are initialized as follows:

```
accumulator             +0000
instructionCounter        00
instructionRegister     +0000
```

```
operationCode                    00
operand                          00
```

Now let us "walk through" the execution of the first SML instruction, +1009 in memory location 00. This is called an *instruction execution cycle*.

The `instructionCounter` tells us the location of the next instruction to be performed. We *fetch* the contents of that location from `memory` by using the C statement

```
instructionRegister = memory[ instructionCounter ];
```

The operation code and the operand are extracted from the instruction register by the statements

```
operationCode = instructionRegister / 100;
operand = instructionRegister % 100;
```

Now the Simpletron must determine that the operation code is actually a *read* (versus a *write*, a *load*, etc.). A `switch` differentiates among the twelve operations of SML.

In the `switch` statement, the behavior of various SML instructions is simulated as follows (we leave the others to the reader):

read:	`scanf( "%d", &memory[ operand ] );`
load:	`accumulator = memory[ operand ];`
add:	`accumulator += memory[ operand ];`

Various branch instructions: We'll discuss these shortly.

halt: This instruction prints the message

```
          *** Simpletron execution terminated ***
```

then prints the name and contents of each register as well as the complete contents of memory. Such a printout is often called a *computer dump*. To help you program your dump function, a sample dump format is shown in Fig. 7.33. Note that a dump after executing a Simpletron program would show the actual values of instructions and data values at the moment execution terminated.

```
REGISTERS:
accumulator                      +0000
instructionCounter                  00
instructionRegister              +0000
operationCode                       00
operand                             00

MEMORY:
        0       1       2       3       4       5       6       7       8       9
 0  +0000   +0000   +0000   +0000   +0000   +0000   +0000   +0000   +0000   +0000
10  +0000   +0000   +0000   +0000   +0000   +0000   +0000   +0000   +0000   +0000
20  +0000   +0000   +0000   +0000   +0000   +0000   +0000   +0000   +0000   +0000
30  +0000   +0000   +0000   +0000   +0000   +0000   +0000   +0000   +0000   +0000
40  +0000   +0000   +0000   +0000   +0000   +0000   +0000   +0000   +0000   +0000
50  +0000   +0000   +0000   +0000   +0000   +0000   +0000   +0000   +0000   +0000
60  +0000   +0000   +0000   +0000   +0000   +0000   +0000   +0000   +0000   +0000
70  +0000   +0000   +0000   +0000   +0000   +0000   +0000   +0000   +0000   +0000
80  +0000   +0000   +0000   +0000   +0000   +0000   +0000   +0000   +0000   +0000
90  +0000   +0000   +0000   +0000   +0000   +0000   +0000   +0000   +0000   +0000
```

Fig. 7.33   *Sample dump of Simpletron's memory.*

Let us proceed with the execution of our program's first instruction, namely the +1009 in location 00. As we have indicated, the `switch` statement simulates this by performing the C statement

```
scanf( "%d", &memory[ operand ] );
```

A question mark (?) should be displayed on the screen before the `scanf` is executed to prompt the user for input. The Simpletron waits for the user to type a value and then press the *Return* key. The value is then read into location 09.

At this point, simulation of the first instruction is completed. All that remains is to prepare the Simpletron to execute the next instruction. Since the instruction just performed was not a transfer of control, we need merely increment the instruction counter register as follows:

```
++instructionCounter;
```

This completes the simulated execution of the first instruction. The entire process (i.e., the instruction execution cycle) begins anew with the fetch of the next instruction to be executed.

Now let us consider how the branching instructions—the transfers of control—are simulated. All we need to do is adjust the value in the instruction counter appropriately. Therefore, the unconditional branch instruction (40) is simulated within the `switch` as

```
instructionCounter = operand;
```

The conditional "branch if accumulator is zero" instruction is simulated as

```
if ( accumulator == 0 )
    instructionCounter = operand;
```

At this point, you should implement your Simpletron simulator and run the SML programs you wrote in Exercise 7.18. You may embellish SML with additional features and provide for these in your simulator.

Your simulator should check for various types of errors. During the program loading phase, for example, each number the user types into the Simpletron's `memory` must be in the range –9999 to +9999. Your simulator should use a `while` loop to test that each number entered is in this range, and, if not, keep prompting the user to reenter the number until the user enters a correct number.

During the execution phase, your simulator should check for various serious errors, such as attempts to divide by zero, attempts to execute invalid operation codes and accumulator overflows (i.e., arithmetic operations resulting in values larger than +9999 or smaller than –9999). Such serious errors are called *fatal errors*. When a fatal error is detected, your simulator should print an error message such as:

```
*** Attempt to divide by zero ***
*** Simpletron execution abnormally terminated ***
```

and should print a full computer dump in the format we have discussed previously. This will help the user locate the error in the program.

7.20 Modify the card shuffling and dealing program of Fig. 7.24 so the shuffling and dealing operations are performed by the same function (`shuffleAndDeal`). The function should contain one nested looping structure that is similar to function `shuffle` in Fig. 7.24.

7.21 What does this program do?

```
1   /* ex07_21.c */
2   /* What does this program do? */
3   #include <stdio.h>
4
```

```
 5   void mystery1( char *s1, const char *s2 ); /* prototype */
 6
 7   int main()
 8   {
 9      char string1[ 80 ]; /* create char array */
10      char string2[ 80 ]; /* create char array */
11
12      printf( "Enter two strings: " );
13      scanf( "%s%s" , string1, string2 );
14
15      mystery1( string1, string2 );
16
17      printf("%s", string1 );
18
19      return 0; /* indicates successful termination */
20
21   } /* end main */
22
23   /* What does this function do? */
24   void mystery1( char *s1, const char *s2 )
25   {
26      while ( *s1 != '\0' ) {
27         s1++;
28      } /* end while */
29
30      for ( ; *s1 = *s2; s1++, s2++ ) {
31         ;    /* empty statement */
32      } /* end for */
33
34   } /* end function mystery1 */
```

(Part 2 of 2.)

7.22   What does this program do?

```
 1   /* ex07_22.c */
 2   /* what does this program do? */
 3   #include <stdio.h>
 4
 5   int mystery2( const char *s ); /* prototype */
 6
 7   int main()
 8   {
 9      char string[ 80 ]; /* create char array */
10
11      printf( "Enter a string: ");
12      scanf( "%s", string );
13
14      printf( "%d\n", mystery2( string ) );
15
16      return 0; /* indicates successful termination */
```

(Part 1 of 2.)

```
17    } /* end main */
18
19    /* What does this function do? */
20    int mystery2( const char *s )
21    {
22       int x; /* counter */
23
24       /* loop through string */
25       for ( x = 0; *s != '\0'; s++ ) {
26          x++;
27       } /* end for */
28
29       return x;
30
31    } /* end function mystery2 */
```

(Part 2 of 2.)

7.23   Find the error in each of the following program segments. If the error can be corrected, explain how.

    a) `int *number;`
           `printf( "%d\n", *number );`

    b) `float *realPtr;`
           `long *integerPtr;`
           `integerPtr = realPtr;`

    c) `int * x, y;`
           `x = y;`

    d) `char s[] = "this is a character array";`
           `int count;`
           `for ( ; *s != '\0'; s++)`
              `printf( "%c ", *s );`

    e) `short *numPtr, result;`
           `void *genericPtr = numPtr;`
           `result = *genericPtr + 7;`

    f) `float x = 19.34;`
           `float xPtr = &x;`
           `printf( "%f\n", xPtr );`

    g) `char *s;`
           `printf( "%s\n", s );`

7.24   (*Quicksort*) In the examples and exercises of Chapter 6, we discussed the sorting techniques bubble sort, bucket sort and selection sort. We now present the recursive sorting technique called Quicksort. The basic algorithm for a single-subscripted array of values is as follows:

    a) *Partitioning Step:* Take the first element of the unsorted array and determine its final location in the sorted array (i.e., all values to the left of the element in the array are less than the element, and all values to the right of the element in the array are greater than the element). We now have one element in its proper location and two unsorted subarrays.

    b) *Recursive Step:* Perform *Step 1* on each unsorted subarray.

Each time *Step 1* is performed on a subarray, another element is placed in its final location of the sorted array, and two unsorted subarrays are created. When a subarray consists of one element, it must be sorted; therefore, that element is in its final location.

The basic algorithm seems simple enough, but how do we determine the final position of the first element of each subarray. As an example, consider the following set of values (the element in bold is the partitioning element—it will be placed in its final location in the sorted array):

37 2 6 4 89 8 10 12 68 45

a) Starting from the rightmost element of the array, compare each element with **37** until an element less than **37** is found. Then swap **37** and that element. The first element less than **37** is 12, so **37** and 12 are swapped. The new array is

12 2 6 4 89 8 10 **37** 68 45

Element 12 is in italic to indicate that it was just swapped with **37**.

b) Starting from the left of the array, but beginning with the element after 12, compare each element with **37** until an element greater than **37** is found. Then swap **37** and that element. The first element greater than **37** is 89, so **37** and 89 are swapped. The new array is

12 2 6 4 **37** 8 10 *89* 68 45

c) Starting from the right, but beginning with the element before 89, compare each element with **37** until an element less than **37** is found. Then swap **37** and that element. The first element less than **37** is 10, so **37** and 10 are swapped. The new array is

12 2 6 4 *10* 8 **37** 89 68 45

d) Starting from the left, but beginning with the element after 10, compare each element with **37** until an element greater than **37** is found. Then swap **37** and that element. There are no more elements greater than **37**, so when we compare **37** with itself, we know that **37** has been placed in its final location of the sorted array.

Once the partition has been applied to the array, there are two unsorted subarrays. The subarray with values less than 37 contains 12, 2, 6, 4, 10 and 8. The subarray with values greater than 37 contains 89, 68 and 45. The sort continues by partitioning both subarrays in the same manner as the original array.

Write recursive function `quicksort` to sort a single-subscripted integer array. The function should receive as arguments an integer array, a starting subscript and an ending subscript. Function `partition` should be called by `quicksort` to perform the partitioning step.

7.25   (*Maze Traversal*) The following grid is a double-subscripted array representation of a maze.

```
# # # # # # # # # # #
# . . . # . . . . . #
. . # . # . # # # # . #
# # # . # . . . . # . #
# . . . . # # # . # . .
# # # # . # . # . # . #
# . . # . # . # . # . #
# # . # . # . # . # . #
# . . . . . . . . # . #
# # # # # . # # # . # #
# . . . . . # . . . . #
# # # # # # # # # # #
```

The # symbols represent the walls of the maze, and the periods (.) represent squares in the possible paths through the maze.

There is a simple algorithm for walking through a maze that guarantees finding the exit (assuming there is an exit). If there is not an exit, you will arrive at the starting location again. Place your right hand on the wall to your right and begin walking forward. Never remove your hand from the wall. If the maze turns to the right, you follow the wall to the right. As long as you do not remove your hand from the wall, eventually you will arrive at the exit of the maze. There may be a shorter path than the one you have taken, but you are guaranteed to get out of the maze.

Write recursive function `mazeTraverse` to walk through the maze. The function should receive as arguments a 12-by-12 character array representing the maze and the starting location of the maze. As `mazeTraverse` attempts to locate the exit from the maze, it should place the character X in each square in the path. The function should display the maze after each move so the user can watch as the maze is solved.

7.26 (*Generating Mazes Randomly*) Write a function `mazeGenerator` that takes as an argument a double-subscripted 12-by-12 character array and randomly produces a maze. The function should also provide the starting and ending locations of the maze. Try your function `mazeTraverse` from Exercise 7.25 using several randomly generated mazes.

7.27 (*Mazes of Any Size*) Generalize functions `mazeTraverse` and `mazeGenerator` of Exercise 7.25 and Exercise 7.26 to process mazes of any width and height.

7.28 (*Arrays of Pointers to Functions*) Rewrite the program of Fig. 6.22 to use a menu driven interface. The program should offer the user four options as follows:

```
Enter a choice:
  0  Print the array of grades
  1  Find the minimum grade
  2  Find the maximum grade
  3  Print the average on all tests for each student
  4  End program
```

One restriction on using arrays of pointers to functions is that all the pointers must have the same type. The pointers must be to functions of the same return type that receive arguments of the same type. For this reason, the functions in Fig. 6.22 must be modified so that they each return the same type and take the same parameters. Modify functions `minimum` and `maximum` to print the minimum or maximum value and return nothing. For option 3, modify function `average` of Fig. 6.22 to output the average for each student (not a specific student). Function `average` should return nothing and take the same parameters as `printArray`, `minimum` and `maximum`. Store the pointers to the four functions in array `processGrades` and use the choice made by the user as the subscript into the array for calling each function.

7.29 (*Modifications to the Simpletron Simulator*) In Exercise 7.19, you wrote a software simulation of a computer that executes programs written in Simpletron Machine Language (SML). In this exercise, we propose several modifications and enhancements to the Simpletron Simulator. In Exercises 12.26 and 12.27, we propose building a compiler that converts programs written in a high-level programming language (a variation of BASIC) to Simpletron Machine Language. Some of the following modifications and enhancements may be required to execute the programs produced by the compiler.

    a) Extend the Simpletron Simulator's memory to contain 1000 memory locations to enable the Simpletron to handle larger programs.

    b) Allow the simulator to perform remainder calculations. This requires an additional Simpletron Machine Language instruction.

    c) Allow the simulator to perform exponentiation calculations. This requires an additional Simpletron Machine Language instruction.

    d) Modify the simulator to use hexadecimal values rather than integer values to represent Simpletron Machine Language instructions.

e) Modify the simulator to allow output of a newline. This requires an additional Simpletron Machine Language instruction.

f) Modify the simulator to process floating-point values in addition to integer values.

g) Modify the simulator to handle string input. [*Hint:* Each Simpletron word can be divided into two groups, each holding a two-digit integer. Each two-digit integer represents the ASCII decimal equivalent of a character. Add a machine language instruction that will input a string and store the string beginning at a specific Simpletron memory location. The first half of the word at that location will be a count of the number of characters in the string (i.e., the length of the string). Each succeeding half word contains one ASCII character expressed as two decimal digits. The machine language instruction converts each character into its ASCII equivalent and assigns it to a half word.]

h) Modify the simulator to handle output of strings stored in the format of part (g). [*Hint:* Add a machine language instruction that prints a string beginning at a specified Simpletron memory location. The first half of the word at that location is the length of the string in characters. Each succeeding half word contains one ASCII character expressed as two decimal digits. The machine language instruction checks the length and prints the string by translating each two-digit number into its equivalent character.]

7.30   What does this program do?

```
1   /* ex07_30.c */
2   /* What does this program do? */
3   #include <stdio.h>
4
5   int mystery3( const char *s1, const char *s2 ); /* prototype */
6
7   int main()
8   {
9      char string1[ 80 ]; /* create char array */
10     char string2[ 80 ]; /* create char array */
11
12     printf( "Enter two strings: " );
13     scanf( "%s%s", string1 , string2 );
14
15     printf( "The result is %d\n", mystery3( string1, string2 ) );
16
17     return 0; /* indicates successful termination */
18
19  } /* end main */
20
21  int mystery3( const char *s1, const char *s2 )
22  {
23     for ( ; *s1 != '\0' && *s2 != '\0'; s1++, s2++ ) {
24
25        if ( *s1 != *s2 ) {
26           return 0;
27        } /* end if */
28
29     } /* end for */
30
31     return 1;
32
33  } /* end function mystery3 */
```

C Characters and Strings

Objectives

- To be able to use the functions of the character handling library (`ctype`).
- To be able to use the string and character input/output functions of the standard input/output library (`stdio`).
- To be able to use the string conversion functions of the general utilities library (`stdlib`).
- To be able to use the string processing functions of the string handling library (`string`).
- To appreciate the power of function libraries as a means of achieving software reusability.

The chief defect of Henry King
Was chewing little bits of string.
Hilaire Belloc

Suit the action to the word, the word to the action.
William Shakespeare

Vigorous writing is concise. A sentence should contain no unnecessary words, a paragraph no unnecessary sentences.
William Strunk, Jr.

In a concatenation accordingly.
Oliver Goldsmith

Outline

8.1 Introduction

In this chapter, we introduce the C standard library functions that facilitate string and character processing. The functions enable programs to process characters, strings, lines of text and blocks of memory.

The chapter discusses the techniques used to develop editors, word processors, page layout software, computerized typesetting systems and other kinds of text-processing software. The text manipulations performed by formatted input/output functions like `printf` and `scanf` can be implemented using the functions discussed in this chapter.

8.2 Fundamentals of Strings and Characters

Characters are the fundamental building blocks of source programs. Every program is composed of a sequence of characters that—when grouped together meaningfully—is interpreted by the computer as a series of instructions used to accomplish a task. A program may contain *character constants*. A character constant is an `int` value represented as a character in single quotes. The value of a character constant is the integer value of the character in the machine's *character set*. For example, `'z'` represents the integer value of z, and `'\n'` represents the integer value of newline.

A *string* is a series of characters treated as a single unit. A string may include letters, digits and various *special characters* such as +, -, *, / and $. *String literals,* or *string constants,* in C are written in double quotation marks as follows:

"John Q. Doe"	(a name)
"99999 Main Street"	(a street address)
"Waltham, Massachusetts"	(a city and state)
"(201) 555-1212"	(a telephone number)

A string in C is an array of characters ending in the *null character (*`'\0'`*)*. A string is accessed via a pointer to the first character in the string. The value of a string is the address of its first character. Thus, in C, it is appropriate to say that *a string is a pointer*—in fact, a pointer to the string's first character. In this sense, strings are like arrays, because an array is also a pointer to its first element.

A character array or a variable of type `char *` can be initialized with a string in a definition. The definitions

```
char color[] = "blue";
const char *colorPtr = "blue";
```

each initialize a variable to the string `"blue"`. The first definition creates a 5-element array `color` containing the characters `'b'`, `'l'`, `'u'`, `'e'` and `'\0'`. The second definition creates, pointer variable, `colorPtr` that points to the string `"blue"` somewhere in memory.

Portability Tip 8.1

When a variable of type `char *` is initialized with a string literal, some compilers may place the string in a location in memory where the string cannot be modified. If you might need to modify a string literal, it should be stored in a character array to ensure modifiability on all systems.

The preceding array definition could also have been written

```
char color[] = { 'b', 'l', 'u', 'e', '\0' };
```

When defining a character array to contain a string, the array must be large enough to store the string and its terminating null character. The preceding definition automatically determines the size of the array based on the number of initializers in the initializer list.

Common Programming Error 8.1

Not allocating sufficient space in a character array to store the null character that terminates a string is an error.

Common Programming Error 8.2

Printing a "string" that does not contain a terminating null character is an error.

Error-Prevention Tip 8.1

When storing a string of characters in a character array, be sure that the array is large enough to hold the largest string that will be stored. C allows strings of any length to be stored. If a string is longer than the character array in which it is to be stored, characters beyond the end of the array will overwrite data in memory following the array.

A string can be stored in an array using `scanf`. For example, the following statement stores a string in character array `word[ 20 ]`:

```
scanf( "%s", word );
```

The string entered by the user is stored in `word`. Note that `word` is an array, which is, of course, a pointer, so the `&` is not needed with argument `word`. Function `scanf` will read characters until a space, tab, newline or end-of-file indicator is encountered. Note that the string should be no longer than 19 characters to leave room for the terminating null character. For a character array to be printed as a string, the array must contain a terminating null character.

Common Programming Error 8.3

Processing a single character as a string. A string is a pointer—probably a respectably large integer. However, a character is a small integer (ASCII values range 0–255). On many systems this causes an error, because low memory addresses are reserved for special purposes such as operating system interrupt handlers—so "access violations" occur.

Common Programming Error 8.4

Passing a character as an argument to a function when a string is expected is a syntax error.

Common Programming Error 8.5

Passing a string as an argument to a function when a character is expected is a syntax error.

8.3 Character Handling Library

The *character handling library* includes several functions that perform useful tests and manipulations of character data. Each function receives a character—represented as an `int`—or EOF as an argument. As we discussed in Chapter 4, characters are often manipulated as integers, because a character in C is usually a 1-byte integer. EOF normally has the value –1 and some hardware architectures do not allow negative values to be stored in `char` variables, so the character handling functions manipulate characters as integers. Figure 8.1 summarizes the functions of the character handling library.

Prototype	Function description
`int isdigit( int c );`	Returns a true value if c is a digit and 0 (false) otherwise.
`int isalpha( int c );`	Returns a true value if c is a letter and 0 otherwise.
`int isalnum( int c );`	Returns a true value if c is a digit or a letter and 0 otherwise.
`int isxdigit( int c );`	Returns a true value if c is a hexadecimal digit character and 0 otherwise. (See Appendix E, Number Systems, for a detailed explanation of binary numbers, octal numbers, decimal numbers and hexadecimal numbers.)
`int islower( int c );`	Returns a true value if c is a lowercase letter and 0 otherwise.
`int isupper( int c );`	Returns a true value if c is an uppercase letter and 0 otherwise.
`int tolower( int c );`	If c is an uppercase letter, `tolower` returns c as a lowercase letter. Otherwise, `tolower` returns the argument unchanged.
`int toupper( int c );`	If c is a lowercase letter, `toupper` returns c as an uppercase letter. Otherwise, `toupper` returns the argument unchanged.
`int isspace( int c );`	Returns a true value if c is a whitespace character—newline (`'\n'`), space (`' '`), form feed (`'\f'`), carriage return (`'\r'`), horizontal tab (`'\t'`) or vertical tab (`'\v'`)—and 0 otherwise.
`int iscntrl( int c );`	Returns a true value if c is a control character and 0 otherwise.

Fig. 8.1   Character handling library functions. (Part 1 of 2.)

Prototype	Function description
`int ispunct( int c );`	Returns a true value if c is a printing character other than a space, a digit, or a letter and 0 otherwise.
`int isprint( int c );`	Returns a true value if c is a printing character including a space (' ') and 0 otherwise.
`int isgraph( int c );`	Returns a true value if c is a printing character other than a space (' ') and 0 otherwise.

Fig. 8.1   Character handling library functions. (Part 2 of 2.)

Error-Prevention Tip 8.2

When using functions from the character handling library, include the `<ctype.h>` header.

Figure 8.2 demonstrates functions *isdigit, isalpha, isalnum* and *isxdigit.* Function isdigit determines whether its argument is a digit (0–9). Function isalpha determines whether its argument is an uppercase letter (A–Z) or a lowercase letter (a–z). Function isalnum determines whether its argument is an uppercase letter, a lowercase letter or a digit. Function isxdigit determines whether its argument is a *hexadecimal digit* (A–F, a–f, 0–9).

```
1   /* Fig. 8.2: fig08_02.c
2      Using functions isdigit, isalpha, isalnum, and isxdigit */
3   #include <stdio.h>
4   #include <ctype.h>
5
6   int main()
7   {
8      printf( "%s\n%s%s\n%s%s\n\n", "According to isdigit: ",
9         isdigit( '8' ) ? "8 is a " : "8 is not a ", "digit",
10        isdigit( '#' ) ? "# is a " : "# is not a ", "digit" );
11
12     printf( "%s\n%s%s\n%s%s\n%s%s\n%s%s\n\n",
13        "According to isalpha:",
14        isalpha( 'A' ) ? "A is a " : "A is not a ", "letter",
15        isalpha( 'b' ) ? "b is a " : "b is not a ", "letter",
16        isalpha( '&' ) ? "& is a " : "& is not a ", "letter",
17        isalpha( '4' ) ? "4 is a " : "4 is not a ", "letter" );
18
19     printf( "%s\n%s%s\n%s%s\n%s%s\n\n",
20        "According to isalnum:",
21        isalnum( 'A' ) ? "A is a " : "A is not a ",
22        "digit or a letter",
23        isalnum( '8' ) ? "8 is a " : "8 is not a ",
24        "digit or a letter",
25        isalnum( '#' ) ? "# is a " : "# is not a ",
26        "digit or a letter" );
```

Fig. 8.2   Using isdigit, isalpha, isalnum and isxdigit. (Part 1 of 2.)

```
27
28      printf( "%s\n%s%s\n%s%s\n%s%s\n%s%s\n%s%s\n",
29         "According to isxdigit:",
30         isxdigit( 'F' ) ? "F is a " : "F is not a ",
31         "hexadecimal digit",
32         isxdigit( 'J' ) ? "J is a " : "J is not a ",
33         "hexadecimal digit",
34         isxdigit( '7' ) ? "7 is a " : "7 is not a ",
35         "hexadecimal digit",
36         isxdigit( '$' ) ? "$ is a " : "$ is not a ",
37         "hexadecimal digit",
38         isxdigit( 'f' ) ? "f is a " : "f is not a ",
39         "hexadecimal digit" );
40
41      return 0; /* indicates successful termination */
42
43   } /* end main */
```

```
According to isdigit:
8 is a digit
# is not a digit

According to isalpha:
A is a letter
b is a letter
& is not a letter
4 is not a letter

According to isalnum:
A is a digit or a letter
8 is a digit or a letter
# is not a digit or a letter

According to isxdigit:
F is a hexadecimal digit
J is not a hexadecimal digit
7 is a hexadecimal digit
$ is not a hexadecimal digit
f is a hexadecimal digit
```

Fig. 8.2   Using isdigit, isalpha, isalnum and isxdigit. (Part 2 of 2.)

Figure 8.2 uses the conditional operator (?:) with each function to determine whether the string " is a " or the string " is not a " should be printed in the output for each character tested. For example, the expression

```
isdigit( '8' ) ? "8 is a " : "8 is not a "
```

indicates that if '8' is a digit (i.e., isdigit returns a true (nonzero) value), the string "8 is a " is printed, and if '8' is not a digit (i.e., isdigit returns 0), the string "8 is not a " is printed.

Figure 8.3 demonstrates functions *islower*, *isupper*, *tolower* and *toupper*. Function islower determines whether its argument is a lowercase letter (a–z). Function isupper determines whether its argument is an uppercase letter (A–Z). Function tolower converts an uppercase letter to a lowercase letter and returns the lowercase letter. If the argument is not an uppercase letter, tolower returns the argument unchanged. Function toupper converts a lowercase letter to an uppercase letter and returns the uppercase letter. If the argument is not a lowercase letter, toupper returns the argument unchanged.

```
1   /* Fig. 8.3: fig08_03.c
2      Using functions islower, isupper, tolower, toupper */
3   #include <stdio.h>
4   #include <ctype.h>
5
6   int main()
7   {
8      printf( "%s\n%s%s\n%s%s\n%s%s\n%s%s\n\n",
9              "According to islower:",
10             islower( 'p' ) ? "p is a " : "p is not a ",
11             "lowercase letter",
12             islower( 'P' ) ? "P is a " : "P is not a ",
13             "lowercase letter",
14             islower( '5' ) ? "5 is a " : "5 is not a ",
15             "lowercase letter",
16             islower( '!' ) ? "! is a " : "! is not a ",
17             "lowercase letter" );
18
19     printf( "%s\n%s%s\n%s%s\n%s%s\n%s%s\n\n",
20             "According to isupper:",
21             isupper( 'D' ) ? "D is an " : "D is not an ",
22             "uppercase letter",
23             isupper( 'd' ) ? "d is an " : "d is not an ",
24             "uppercase letter",
25             isupper( '8' ) ? "8 is an " : "8 is not an ",
26             "uppercase letter",
27             isupper( '$' ) ? "$ is an " : "$ is not an ",
28             "uppercase letter" );
29
30     printf( "%s%c\n%s%c\n%s%c\n%s%c\n",
31             "u converted to uppercase is ", toupper( 'u' ),
32             "7 converted to uppercase is ", toupper( '7' ),
33             "$ converted to uppercase is ", toupper( '$' ),
34             "L converted to lowercase is ", tolower( 'L' ) );
35
36     return 0; /* indicates successful termination */
37
38  } /* end main */
```

```
According to islower:
p is a lowercase letter
P is not a lowercase letter
5 is not a lowercase letter
! is not a lowercase letter
```

Fig. 8.3   Using functions islower, isupper, tolower and toupper. (Part 1 of 2.)

```
According to isupper:
D is an uppercase letter
d is not an uppercase letter
8 is not an uppercase letter
$ is not an uppercase letter

u converted to uppercase is U
7 converted to uppercase is 7
$ converted to uppercase is $
L converted to lowercase is l
```

Fig. 8.3   Using functions `islower`, `isupper`, `tolower` and `toupper`. (Part 2 of 2.)

Figure 8.4 demonstrates functions *isspace*, *iscntrl*, *ispunct*, *isprint* and *isgraph*. Function `isspace` determines whether its argument is one of the following whitespace characters: space (`' '`), form feed (`'\f'`), newline (`'\n'`), carriage return (`'\r'`), horizontal tab (`'\t'`) or vertical tab (`'\v'`). Function `iscntrl` determines whether its argument is one of the following *control characters*: horizontal tab (`'\t'`), vertical tab (`'\v'`), form feed (`'\f'`), alert (`'\a'`), backspace (`'\b'`), carriage return (`'\r'`) or newline (`'\n'`). Function `ispunct` determines whether its argument is a *printing character* other than a space, a digit or a letter, such as $, #, (,), [,], {, }, ;, : or %. Function `isprint` determines whether its argument is a character that can be displayed on the screen (including the space character). Function `isgraph` tests for the same characters as `isprint`; however, the space character is not included.

```
1   /* Fig. 8.4: fig08_04.c
2      Using functions isspace, iscntrl, ispunct, isprint, isgraph */
3   #include <stdio.h>
4   #include <ctype.h>
5
6   int main()
7   {
8      printf( "%s\n%s%s%s\n%s%s%s\n%s%s\n\n",
9          "According to isspace:",
10         "Newline", isspace( '\n' ) ? " is a " : " is not a ",
11         "whitespace character", "Horizontal tab",
12         isspace( '\t' ) ? " is a " : " is not a ",
13         "whitespace character",
14         isspace( '%' ) ? "% is a " : "% is not a ",
15         "whitespace character" );
16
17     printf( "%s\n%s%s%s\n%s%s\n\n", "According to iscntrl:",
18         "Newline", iscntrl( '\n' ) ? " is a " : " is not a ",
19         "control character", iscntrl( '$' ) ? "$ is a " :
20         "$ is not a ", "control character" );
21
22     printf( "%s\n%s%s\n%s%s\n%s%s\n\n",
23         "According to ispunct:",
24         ispunct( ';' ) ? "; is a " : "; is not a ",
25         "punctuation character",
```

Fig. 8.4   Using `isspace`, `iscntrl`, `ispunct`, `isprint` and `isgraph`. (Part 1 of 2.)

```
26          ispunct( 'Y' ) ? "Y is a " : "Y is not a ",
27          "punctuation character",
28          ispunct( '#' ) ? "# is a " : "# is not a ",
29          "punctuation character" );
30
31      printf( "%s\n%s%s\n%s%s%s\n\n", "According to isprint:",
32          isprint( '$' ) ? "$ is a " : "$ is not a ",
33          "printing character",
34          "Alert", isprint( '\a' ) ? " is a " : " is not a ",
35          "printing character" );
36
37      printf( "%s\n%s%s\n%s%s%s\n",  "According to isgraph:",
38          isgraph( 'Q' ) ? "Q is a " : "Q is not a ",
39          "printing character other than a space",
40          "Space", isgraph( ' ' ) ? " is a " : " is not a ",
41          "printing character other than a space" );
42
43      return 0; /* indicates successful termination */
44
45  } /* end main */
```

```
According to isspace:
Newline is a whitespace character
Horizontal tab is a whitespace character
% is not a whitespace character

According to iscntrl:
Newline is a control character
$ is not a control character

According to ispunct:
; is a punctuation character
Y is not a punctuation character
# is a punctuation character

According to isprint:
$ is a printing character
Alert is not a printing character

According to isgraph:
Q is a printing character other than a space
Space is not a printing character other than a space
```

Fig. 8.4   Using isspace, iscntrl, ispunct, isprint and isgraph. (Part 2 of 2.)

8.4 String Conversion Functions

This section presents the *string conversion functions* from the *general utilities library* (*<stdlib.h>*). These functions convert strings of digits to integer and floating-point values. Figure 8.5 summarizes the string conversion functions. Note the use of const to declare variable nPtr in the function headers (read from right to left as "nPtr is a pointer to a character constant"); const specifies that the argument value will not be modified.

Function prototype	Function description
`double atof( const char *nPtr );`	Converts the string `nPtr` to `double`.
`int atoi( const char *nPtr );`	Converts the string `nPtr` to `int`.
`long atol( const char *nPtr );`	Converts the string `nPtr` to `long int`.
`double strtod( const char *nPtr, char **endPtr );`	
	Converts the string `nPtr` to `double`.
`long strtol( const char *nPtr, char **endPtr, int base );`	
	Converts the string `nPtr` to `long`.
`unsigned long strtoul( const char *nPtr, char **endPtr, int base );`	
	Converts the string `nPtr` to `unsigned long`.

Fig. 8.5   String conversion functions of the general utilities library.

Error-Prevention Tip 8.3

When using functions from the general utilities library, include the `<stdlib.h>` header.

Function *atof* (Fig. 8.6) converts its argument—a string that represents a floating-point number—to a `double` value. The function returns the `double` value. If the converted value cannot be represented—for example, if the first character of the string is not a digit—the behavior of function `atof` is undefined.

```c
1   /* Fig. 8.6: fig08_06.c
2      Using atof */
3   #include <stdio.h>
4   #include <stdlib.h>
5
6   int main()
7   {
8      double d; /* variable to hold converted string */
9
10     d = atof( "99.0" );
11
12     printf( "%s%.3f\n%s%.3f\n",
13             "The string \"99.0\" converted to double is ", d,
14             "The converted value divided by 2 is ",
15             d / 2.0 );
16
17     return 0; /* indicates successful termination */
18
19  } /* end main */
```

```
The string "99.0" converted to double is 99.000
The converted value divided by 2 is 49.500
```

Fig. 8.6   Using `atof`.

Function *atoi* (Fig. 8.7) converts its argument—a string of digits that represents an integer—to an int value. The function returns the int value. If the converted value cannot be represented, the behavior of function atoi is undefined.

```
1   /* Fig. 8.7: fig08_07.c
2      Using atoi */
3   #include <stdio.h>
4   #include <stdlib.h>
5
6   int main()
7   {
8      int i; /* variable to hold converted string */
9
10     i = atoi( "2593" );
11
12     printf( "%s%d\n%s%d\n",
13             "The string \"2593\" converted to int is ", i,
14             "The converted value minus 593 is ", i - 593 );
15
16     return 0; /* indicates successful termination */
17
18  } /* end main */
```

```
The string "2593" converted to int is 2593
The converted value minus 593 is 2000
```

Fig. 8.7   Using atoi.

Function *atol* (Fig. 8.8) converts its argument—a string of digits representing a long integer—to a long value. The function returns the long value. If the converted value cannot be represented, the behavior of function atol is undefined. If int and long are both stored in 4 bytes, function atoi and function atol work identically.

```
1   /* Fig. 8.8: fig08_08.c
2      Using atol */
3   #include <stdio.h>
4   #include <stdlib.h>
5
6   int main()
7   {
8      long l; /* variable to hold converted string */
9
10     l = atol( "1000000" );
11
12     printf( "%s%ld\n%s%ld\n",
13             "The string \"1000000\" converted to long int is ", l,
14             "The converted value divided by 2 is ", l / 2 );
15
16     return 0; /* indicates successful termination */
17
18  } /* end main */
```

Fig. 8.8   Using atol. (Part 1 of 2.)

```
The string "1000000" converted to long int is 1000000
The converted value divided by 2 is 500000
```

Fig. 8.8   Using atol. (Part 2 of 2.)

Function *strtod* (Fig. 8.9) converts a sequence of characters representing a floating-point value to double. The function receives two arguments—a string (char *) and a pointer to a string (char **). The string contains the character sequence to be converted to double. The pointer is assigned the location of the first character after the converted portion of the string. Line 14

```
    d = strtod( string, &stringPtr );
```

indicates that d is assigned the double value converted from string, and stringPtr is assigned the location of the first character after the converted value (51.2) in string.

```
1    /* Fig. 8.9: fig08_09.c
2       Using strtod */
3    #include <stdio.h>
4    #include <stdlib.h>
5
6    int main()
7    {
8       /* initialize string pointer */
9       const char *string = "51.2% are admitted"; /* initialize string */
10
11      double d;          /* variable to hold converted sequence */
12      char *stringPtr; /* create char pointer */
13
14      d = strtod( string, &stringPtr );
15
16      printf( "The string \"%s\" is converted to the\n", string );
17      printf( "double value %.2f and the string \"%s\"\n", d, stringPtr );
18
19      return 0; /* indicates successful termination */
20
21   } /* end main */
```

```
The string "51.2% are admitted" is converted to the
double value 51.20 and the string "% are admitted"
```

Fig. 8.9   Using strtod.

Function *strtol* (Fig. 8.10) converts to long a sequence of characters representing an integer. The function receives three arguments—a string (char *), a pointer to a string and an integer. The string contains the character sequence to be converted. The pointer is assigned the location of the first character after the converted portion of the string. The integer specifies the *base* of the value being converted. The statement

```
    x = strtol( string, &remainderPtr, 0 );
```

in Fig. 8.10 indicates that x is assigned the long value converted from string. The second argument, remainderPtr, is assigned the remainder of string after the conversion. Using NULL for the second argument causes the remainder of the string to be ignored. The third argument, 0, indicates that the value to be converted can be in octal (base 8), decimal (base 10) or hexadecimal (base 16) format. The base can be specified as 0 or any value between 2 and 36. See Appendix E, Number Systems, for a detailed explanation of the octal, decimal and hexadecimal number systems. Numeric representations of integers from base 11 to base 36 use the characters A–Z to represent the values 10 to 35. For example, hexadecimal values can consist of the digits 0–9 and the characters A–F. A base-11 integer can consist of the digits 0–9 and the character A. A base-24 integer can consist of the digits 0–9 and the characters A–N. A base-36 integer can consist of the digits 0–9 and the characters A–Z.

```
1   /* Fig. 8.10: fig08_10.c
2      Using strtol */
3   #include <stdio.h>
4   #include <stdlib.h>
5
6   int main()
7   {
8      const char *string = "-1234567abc"; /* initialize string pointer */
9
10     char *remainderPtr; /* create char pointer */
11     long x;             /* variable to hold converted sequence */
12
13     x = strtol( string, &remainderPtr, 0 );
14
15     printf( "%s\"%s\"\n%s%ld\n%s\"%s\"\n%s%ld\n",
16             "The original string is ", string,
17             "The converted value is ", x,
18             "The remainder of the original string is ",
19             remainderPtr,
20             "The converted value plus 567 is ", x + 567 );
21
22     return 0; /* indicates successful termination */
23
24  } /* end main */
```

```
The original string is "-1234567abc"
The converted value is -1234567
The remainder of the original string is "abc"
The converted value plus 567 is -1234000
```

Fig. 8.10   Using strtol.

Function *strtoul* (Fig. 8.11) converts to unsigned long a sequence of characters representing an unsigned long integer. The function works identically to function strtol. The statement

        x = strtoul(string, &remainderPtr, 0);

in Fig. 8.11 indicates that x is assigned the unsigned long value converted from string. The second argument, &remainderPtr, is assigned the remainder of string after the conversion. The third argument, 0, indicates that the value to be converted can be in octal, decimal or hexadecimal format.

```
1   /* Fig. 8.11: fig08_11.c
2      Using strtoul */
3   #include <stdio.h>
4   #include <stdlib.h>
5
6   int main()
7   {
8      const char *string = "1234567abc"; /* initialize string pointer */
9      unsigned long x;    /* variable to hold converted sequence */
10     char *remainderPtr; /* create char pointer */
11
12     x = strtoul( string, &remainderPtr, 0 );
13
14     printf( "%s\"%s\"\n%s%lu\n%s\"%s\"\n%s%lu\n",
15             "The original string is ", string,
16             "The converted value is ", x,
17             "The remainder of the original string is ",
18             remainderPtr,
19             "The converted value minus 567 is ", x - 567 );
20
21     return 0; /* indicates successful termination */
22
23  } /* end main */
```

```
The original string is "1234567abc"
The converted value is 1234567
The remainder of the original string is "abc"
The converted value minus 567 is 1234000
```

Fig. 8.11   Using strtoul.

8.5 Standard Input/Output Library Functions

This section presents several functions from the standard input/output library (<stdio.h>) specifically for manipulating character and string data. Figure 8.12 summarizes the character and string input/output functions of the standard input/output library.

 **Error-Prevention Tip 8.4**

When using functions from the standard input/output library, include the <stdio.h> header.

Function prototype	Function description
int getchar(void);	Inputs the next character from the standard input and returns it as an integer.

Fig. 8.12   Standard input/output library character and string functions. (Part 1 of 2.)

Function prototype	Function description
`char *gets( char *s );`	Inputs characters from the standard input into the array `s` until a newline or end-of-file character is encountered. A terminating null character is appended to the array.
`int putchar( int c );`	Prints the character stored in `c`.
`int puts( const char *s );`	Prints the string `s` followed by a newline character.
`int sprintf( char *s, const char *format, ... );`	
	Equivalent to `printf`, except the output is stored in the array `s` instead of printed on the screen.
`int sscanf( char *s, const char *format, ... );`	
	Equivalent to `scanf`, except the input is read from the array `s` instead of read from the keyboard.

Fig. 8.12 Standard input/output library character and string functions. (Part 2 of 2.)

Figure 8.13 uses functions *gets* and *putchar* to read a line of text from the standard input (keyboard) and recursively output the characters of the line in reverse order. Function `gets` reads characters from the standard input into its argument—an array of type `char`—until a newline character or the end-of-file indicator is encountered. A null character (`'\0'`) is appended to the array when reading terminates. Function `putchar` prints its character argument. The program calls recursive function `reverse` to print the line of text backwards. If the first character of the array received by `reverse` is the null character `'\0'`, `reverse` returns. Otherwise, `reverse` is called again with the address of the subarray beginning at element `s[1]`, and character `s[0]` is output with `putchar` when the recursive call is completed. The order of the two statements in the `else` portion of the `if` statement causes `reverse` to walk to the terminating null character of the string before a character is printed. As the recursive calls are completed, the characters are output in reverse order.

```
1   /* Fig. 8.13: fig08_13.c
2      Using gets and putchar */
3   #include <stdio.h>
4
5   void reverse( const char * const sPtr ); /* prototype */
6
7   int main()
8   {
9      char sentence[ 80 ]; /* create char array */
10
11     printf( "Enter a line of text:\n" );
12
13     /* use gets to read line of text */
14     gets( sentence );
15
```

Fig. 8.13 Using `gets` and `putchar`. (Part 1 of 2.)

```
16        printf( "\nThe line printed backwards is:\n" );
17        reverse( sentence );
18
19        return 0; /* indicates successful termination */
20
21   } /* end main */
22
23   /* recursively outputs characters in string in reverse order */
24   void reverse( const char * const sPtr )
25   {
26        /* if end of the string */
27        if ( sPtr[ 0 ] == '\0' ) { /* base case */
28           return;
29        } /* end if */
30        else { /* if not end of the string */
31           reverse( &sPtr[ 1 ] ); /* recursion step */
32
33           putchar( sPtr[ 0 ] ); /* use putchar to display character */
34        } /* end else */
35
36   } /* end function reverse */
```

```
Enter a line of text:
Characters and Strings

The line printed backwards is:
sgnirtS dna sretcarahC
```

```
Enter a line of text:
able was I ere I saw elba

The line printed backwards is:
able was I ere I saw elba
```

Fig. 8.13   Using gets and putchar. (Part 2 of 2.)

Figure 8.14 uses functions *getchar* and *puts* to read characters from the standard input into character array sentence and print the array of characters as a string. Function getchar reads a character from the standard input and returns the character as an integer. Function puts takes a string (char *) as an argument and prints the string followed by a newline character.

```
1    /* Fig. 8.14: fig08_14.c
2       Using getchar and puts */
3    #include <stdio.h>
4
5    int main()
6    {
```

Fig. 8.14   Using getchar and puts. (Part 1 of 2.)

```
7       char c;                 /* variable to hold character input by user */
8       char sentence[ 80 ]; /* create char array */
9       int i = 0;              /* initialize counter i */
10
11      /* prompt user to enter line of text */
12      puts( "Enter a line of text:" );
13
14      /* use getchar to read each character */
15      while ( ( c = getchar() ) != '\n') {
16         sentence[ i++ ] = c;
17      } /* end while */
18
19      sentence[ i ] = '\0'; /* terminate string */
20
21      /* use puts to display sentence */
22      puts( "\nThe line entered was:" );
23      puts( sentence );
24
25      return 0; /* indicates successful termination */
26
27   } /* end main */
```

```
Enter a line of text:
This is a test.

The line entered was:
This is a test.
```

Fig. 8.14 Using `getchar` and `puts`. (Part 2 of 2.)

The program stops inputting characters when `getchar` reads the newline character entered by the user to end the line of text. A null character is appended to array `sentence` (line 19) so that the array may be treated as a string. Then, function `puts` prints the string contained in `sentence`.

Figure 8.15 uses function *sprintf* to print formatted data into array s—an array of characters. The function uses the same conversion specifiers as `printf` (see Chapter 9 for a detailed discussion of all print formatting features). The program inputs an `int` value and a `double` value to be formatted and printed to array s. Array s is the first argument of `sprintf`.

```
1    /* Fig. 8.15: fig08_15.c
2       Using sprintf */
3    #include <stdio.h>
4
5    int main()
6    {
7       char s[ 80 ]; /* create char array */
8       int x;        /* x value to be input */
9       double y;     /* y value to be input */
```

Fig. 8.15 Using `sprintf`. (Part 1 of 2.)

```
10
11        printf( "Enter an integer and a double:\n" );
12        scanf( "%d%lf", &x, &y );
13
14        sprintf( s, "integer:%6d\ndouble:%8.2f", x, y );
15
16        printf( "%s\n%s\n",
17                "The formatted output stored in array s is:", s );
18
19        return 0; /* indicates successful termination */
20
21    } /* end main */
```

```
Enter an integer and a double:
298 87.375
The formatted output stored in array s is:
integer:   298
double:   87.38
```

Fig. 8.15   Using `sprintf`. (Part 2 of 2.)

Figure 8.16 uses function *sscanf* to read formatted data from character array s. The function uses the same conversion specifiers as `scanf`. The program reads an int and a double from array s and stores the values in x and y, respectively. The values of x and y are printed. Array s is the first argument of `sscanf`.

```
1    /* Fig. 8.16: fig08_16.c
2       Using sscanf */
3    #include <stdio.h>
4
5    int main()
6    {
7        char s[] = "31298 87.375"; /* initialize array s */
8        int x;    /* x value to be input */
9        double y; /* y value to be input */
10
11        sscanf( s, "%d%lf", &x, &y );
12
13        printf( "%s\n%s%6d\n%s%8.3f\n",
14                "The values stored in character array s are:",
15                "integer:", x, "double:", y );
16
17        return 0; /* indicates successful termination */
18
19    } /* end main */
```

```
The values stored in character array s are:
integer: 31298
double:   87.375
```

Fig. 8.16   Using `sscanf`.

8.6 String Manipulation Functions of the String Handling Library

The string handling library (`<string.h>`) provides many useful functions for manipulating string data (*copying strings* and *concatenating strings*), *comparing strings*, *searching strings* for characters and other strings, *tokenizing strings* (separating strings into logical pieces) and *determining the length of strings*. This section presents the string manipulation functions of the string handling library. The functions are summarized in Fig. 8.17. Every function—except for `strncpy`—appends the null character to its result.

Function prototype	Function description
`char *strcpy( char *s1, const char *s2 )`	
	Copies string `s2` into array `s1`. The value of `s1` is returned.
`char *strncpy( char *s1, const char *s2, size_t n )`	
	Copies at most n characters of string `s2` into array `s1`. The value of `s1` is returned.
`char *strcat( char *s1, const char *s2 )`	
	Appends string `s2` to array `s1`. The first character of `s2` overwrites the terminating null character of `s1`. The value of `s1` is returned.
`char *strncat( char *s1, const char *s2, size_t n )`	
	Appends at most n characters of string `s2` to array `s1`. The first character of `s2` overwrites the terminating null character of `s1`. The value of `s1` is returned.

Fig. 8.17   String manipulation functions of the string handling library.

Functions *strncpy* and *strncat* specify a parameter of type `size_t`, which is a type defined by the C standard as the integral type of the value returned by operator `sizeof`.

Portability Tip 8.2

Type `size_t` is a system-dependent synonym for either type `unsigned long` or type unsigned int.

Error-Prevention Tip 8.5

When using functions from the string handling library, include the `<string.h>` header.

Function `strcpy` copies its second argument (a string) into its first argument (a character array that must be large enough to store the string and its terminating null character, which is also copied). Function `strncpy` is equivalent to `strcpy`, except that `strncpy` specifies the number of characters to be copied from the string into the array. Note that function `strncpy` does not necessarily copy the terminating null character of its second argument. A terminating null character is written only if the number of characters to be copied is at least one more than the length of the string. For example, if `"test"` is the second argument, a terminating null character is written only if the third argument to `strncpy` is at least 5 (four characters in `"test"` plus a terminating null character). If the third argument is larger than 5, null characters are appended to the array until the total number of characters specified by the third argument are written.

 Common Programming Error 8.6

Not appending a terminating null character to the first argument of a strncpy when the third argument is less than or equal to the length of the string in the second argument.

Figure 8.18 uses strcpy to copy the entire string in array x into array y and uses strncpy to copy the first 14 characters of array x into array z. A null character ('\0') is appended to array z, because the call to strncpy in the program does not write a terminating null character (the third argument is less than the string length of the second argument).

```c
1   /* Fig. 8.18: fig08_18.c
2      Using strcpy and strncpy */
3   #include <stdio.h>
4   #include <string.h>
5
6   int main()
7   {
8      char x[] = "Happy Birthday to You"; /* initialize char array x */
9      char y[ 25 ]; /* create char array y */
10     char z[ 15 ]; /* create char array z */
11
12     /* copy contents of x into y */
13     printf( "%s%s\n%s%s\n",
14        "The string in array x is: ", x,
15        "The string in array y is: ", strcpy( y, x ) );
16
17     /* copy first 14 characters of x into z. Does not copy null
18        character */
19     strncpy( z, x, 14 );
20
21     z[ 14 ] = '\0'; /* terminate string in z */
22     printf( "The string in array z is: %s\n", z );
23
24     return 0; /* indicates successful termination */
25
26  } /* end main */
```

```
The string in array x is: Happy Birthday to You
The string in array y is: Happy Birthday to You
The string in array z is: Happy Birthday
```

Fig. 8.18   Using strcpy and strncpy .

Function *strcat appends* its second argument (a string) to its first argument (a character array containing a string). The first character of the second argument replaces the null ('\0') that terminates the string in the first argument. The programmer must ensure that the array used to store the first string is large enough to store the first string, the second string and the terminating null character copied from the second string. Function strncat appends a specified number of characters from the second string to the first string. A terminating null character is automatically appended to the result. Figure 8.19 demonstrates function `strcat` and function `strncat`.

```
1   /* Fig. 8.19: fig08_19.c
2      Using strcat and strncat */
3   #include <stdio.h>
4   #include <string.h>
5
6   int main()
7   {
8      char s1[ 20 ] = "Happy "; /* initialize char array s1 */
9      char s2[] = "New Year "; /* initialize char array s2 */
10     char s3[ 40 ] = "";      /* initialize char array s3 to empty */
11
12     printf( "s1 = %s\ns2 = %s\n", s1, s2 );
13
14     /* concatenate s2 to s1 */
15     printf( "strcat( s1, s2 ) = %s\n", strcat( s1, s2 ) );
16
17     /* concatenate first 6 characters of s1 to s3. Place '\0'
18        after last character */
19     printf( "strncat( s3, s1, 6 ) = %s\n", strncat( s3, s1, 6 ) );
20
21     /* concatenate s1 to s3 */
22     printf( "strcat( s3, s1 ) = %s\n", strcat( s3, s1 ) );
23
24     return 0; /* indicates successful termination */
25
26  } /* end main */
```

```
s1 = Happy
s2 = New Year
strcat( s1, s2 ) = Happy New Year
strncat( s3, s1, 6 ) = Happy
strcat( s3, s1 ) = Happy Happy New Year
```

Fig. 8.19   Using `strcat` and `strncat`.

8.7 Comparison Functions of the String Handling Library

This section presents the *string comparison functions*, `strcmp` and `strncmp`, of the string handling library. Fig. 8.20 contains the function prototypes and a brief description of each function.

Figure 8.21 compares three strings using functions `strcmp` and `strncmp`. Function `strcmp` compares its first string argument with its second string argument character-by-character. The function returns 0 if the strings are equal, a negative value if the first string is less than the second string and a positive value if the first string is greater than the second string. Function `strncmp` is equivalent to `strcmp`, except that `strncmp` compares up to a specified number of characters. Function `strncmp` does not compare characters following a null character in a string. The program prints the integer value returned by each function call.

Function prototype	Function description

```
int strcmp( const char *s1, const char *s2 );
```
Compares the string s1 with the string s2. The function returns 0, less than 0 or greater than 0 if s1 is equal to, less than or greater than s2, respectively.

```
int strncmp( const char *s1, const char *s2, size_t n );
```
Compares up to n characters of the string s1 with the string s2. The function returns 0, less than 0 or greater than 0 if s1 is equal to, less than or greater than s2, respectively.

Fig. 8.20 String comparison functions of the string handling library.

```
1   /* Fig. 8.21: fig08_21.c
2      Using strcmp and strncmp */
3   #include <stdio.h>
4   #include <string.h>
5
6   int main()
7   {
8      const char *s1 = "Happy New Year"; /* initialize char pointer */
9      const char *s2 = "Happy New Year"; /* initialize char pointer */
10     const char *s3 = "Happy Holidays"; /* initialize char pointer */
11
12     printf("%s%s\n%s%s\n%s%s\n\n%s%2d\n%s%2d\n%s%2d\n\n",
13            "s1 = ", s1, "s2 = ", s2, "s3 = ", s3,
14            "strcmp(s1, s2) = ", strcmp( s1, s2 ),
15            "strcmp(s1, s3) = ", strcmp( s1, s3 ),
16            "strcmp(s3, s1) = ", strcmp( s3, s1 ) );
17
18     printf("%s%2d\n%s%2d\n%s%2d\n",
19            "strncmp(s1, s3, 6) = ", strncmp( s1, s3, 6 ),
20            "strncmp(s1, s3, 7) = ", strncmp( s1, s3, 7 ),
21            "strncmp(s3, s1, 7) = ", strncmp( s3, s1, 7 ) );
22
23     return 0; /* indicates successful termination */
24
25  } /* end main */
```

```
s1 = Happy New Year
s2 = Happy New Year
s3 = Happy Holidays

strcmp(s1, s2) =  0
strcmp(s1, s3) =  1
strcmp(s3, s1) = -1
```

Fig. 8.21 Using strcmp and strncmp. (Part 1 of 2.)

```
strncmp(s1, s3, 6) =   0
strncmp(s1, s3, 7) =   1
strncmp(s3, s1, 7) = -1
```

Fig. 8.21   Using `strcmp` and `strncmp`. (Part 2 of 2.)

Common Programming Error 8.7

Assuming that `strcmp` and `strncmp` return 1 when their arguments are equal is a logic error. Both functions return 0 (strangely, the equivalent of C's false value) for equality. Therefore, when testing two strings for equality, the result of function `strcmp` or `strncmp` should be compared with 0 to determine if the strings are equal.

To understand just what it means for one string to be "greater than" or "less than" another string, consider the process of alphabetizing a series of last names. The reader would, no doubt, place "Jones" before "Smith," because the first letter of "Jones" comes before the first letter of "Smith" in the alphabet. But the alphabet is more than just a list of 26 letters—it is an ordered list of characters. Each letter occurs in a specific position within the list. "Z" is more than merely a letter of the alphabet; "Z" is specifically the 26th letter of the alphabet.

How does the computer know that one particular letter comes before another? All characters are represented inside the computer as *numeric codes*; when the computer compares two strings, it actually compares the numeric codes of the characters in the strings.

Portability Tip 8.3

The internal numeric codes used to represent characters may be different on different computers.

In an effort to standardize character representations, most computer manufacturers have designed their machines to utilize one of two popular coding schemes—*ASCII* or *EBCDIC*. ASCII stands for "American Standard Code for Information Interchange," and EBCDIC stands for "Extended Binary Coded Decimal Interchange Code." There are other coding schemes, but these two are the most popular. The recent Unicode Standard outlines a specification to produce consistent encoding of the vast majority of the world's characters and symbols. To learn more about the Unicode Standard, visit `www.unicode.org`.

ASCII, EBCDIC and Unicode are called *character sets*. String and character manipulations actually involve the manipulation of the appropriate numeric codes and not the characters themselves. This explains the interchangeability of characters and small integers in C. Since it is meaningful to say that one numeric code is greater than, less than or equal to another numeric code, it becomes possible to relate various characters or strings to one another by referring to the character codes. Appendix D lists the ASCII character codes.

8.8 Search Functions of the String Handling Library

This section presents the functions of the string handling library used to search strings for characters and other strings. The functions are summarized in Fig. 8.22. Note that functions `strcspn` and `strspn` return `size_t`.

Function prototype	Function description

char *strchr(const char *s, int c);

Locates the first occurrence of character c in string s. If c is found, a pointer to c in s is returned. Otherwise, a NULL pointer is returned.

size_t strcspn(const char *s1, const char *s2);

Determines and returns the length of the initial segment of string s1 consisting of characters not contained in string s2.

size_t strspn(const char *s1, const char *s2);

Determines and returns the length of the initial segment of string s1 consisting only of characters contained in string s2.

char *strpbrk(const char *s1, const char *s2);

Locates the first occurrence in string s1 of any character in string s2. If a character from string s2 is found, a pointer to the character in string s1 is returned. Otherwise, a NULL pointer is returned.

char *strrchr(const char *s, int c);

Locates the last occurrence of c in string s. If c is found, a pointer to c in string s is returned. Otherwise, a NULL pointer is returned.

char *strstr(const char *s1, const char *s2);

Locates the first occurrence in string s1 of string s2. If the string is found, a pointer to the string in s1 is returned. Otherwise, a NULL pointer is returned.

char *strtok(char *s1, const char *s2);

A sequence of calls to strtok breaks string s1 into "tokens"—logical pieces such as words in a line of text—separated by characters contained in string s2. The first call contains s1 as the first argument, and subsequent calls to continue tokenizing the same string contain NULL as the first argument. A pointer to the current token is returned by each call. If there are no more tokens when the function is called, NULL is returned.

Fig. 8.22   String manipulation functions of the string handling library .

Function *strchr* searches for the first occurrence of a character in a string. If the character is found, strchr returns a pointer to the character in the string; otherwise, strchr returns NULL. Figure 8.23 uses strchr to search for the first occurrences of 'a' and 'z' in the string "This is a test".

```
1   /* Fig. 8.23: fig08_23.c
2      Using strchr */
3   #include <stdio.h>
4   #include <string.h>
5
6   int main()
7   {
```

Fig. 8.23   Using strchr. (Part 1 of 2.)

```
8       const char *string = "This is a test"; /* initialize char pointer */
9       char character1 = 'a'; /* initialize character1 */
10      char character2 = 'z'; /* initialize character2 */
11
12      /* if character1 was found in string */
13      if ( strchr( string, character1 ) != NULL ) {
14         printf( "\'%c\' was found in \"%s\".\n",
15            character1, string );
16      } /* end if */
17      else { /* if character1 was not found */
18         printf( "\'%c\' was not found in \"%s\".\n",
19            character1, string );
20      } /* end else */
21
22      /* if character2 was found in string */
23      if ( strchr( string, character2 ) != NULL ) {
24         printf( "\'%c\' was found in \"%s\".\n",
25            character2, string );
26      } /* end if */
27      else { /* if character2 was not found */
28         printf( "\'%c\' was not found in \"%s\".\n",
29            character2, string );
30      } /* end else */
31
32      return 0; /* indicates successful termination */
33
34   } /* end main */
```

```
'a' was found in "This is a test".
'z' was not found in "This is a test".
```

Fig. 8.23   Using `strchr`. (Part 2 of 2.)

Function *strcspn* (Fig. 8.24) determines the length of the initial part of the string in its first argument that does not contain any characters from the string in its second argument. The function returns the length of the segment.

```
1   /* Fig. 8.24: fig08_24.c
2      Using strcspn */
3   #include <stdio.h>
4   #include <string.h>
5
6   int main()
7   {
8      /* initialize two char pointers */
9      const char *string1 = "The value is 3.14159";
10     const char *string2 = "1234567890";
11
12     printf( "%s%s\n%s%s\n\n%s\n%s%u",
13        "string1 = ", string1, "string2 = ", string2,
```

Fig. 8.24   Using `strcspn`. (Part 1 of 2.)

```
14            "The length of the initial segment of string1",
15            "containing no characters from string2 = ",
16            strcspn( string1, string2 ) );
17
18     return 0; /* indicates successful termination */
19
20   } /* end main */
```

```
string1 = The value is 3.14159
string2 = 1234567890

The length of the initial segment of string1
containing no characters from string2 = 13
```

Fig. 8.24   Using strcspn. (Part 2 of 2.)

Function *strpbrk* searches its first string argument for the first occurrence of any character in its second string argument. If a character from the second argument is found, strpbrk returns a pointer to the character in the first argument; otherwise, strpbrk returns NULL. Figure 8.25 shows a program that locates the first occurrence in string1 of any character from string2.

```
1   /* Fig. 8.25: fig08_25.c
2      Using strpbrk */
3   #include <stdio.h>
4   #include <string.h>
5
6   int main()
7   {
8      const char *string1 = "This is a test"; /* initialize char pointer */
9      const char *string2 = "beware";         /* initialize char pointer */
10
11     printf( "%s\"%s\"\n'%c'%s\n\"%s\"\n",
12        "Of the characters in ", string2,
13        *strpbrk( string1, string2 ),
14        " appears earliest in ", string1 );
15
16     return 0; /* indicates successful termination */
17
18   } /* end main */
```

```
Of the characters in "beware"
'a' appears earliest in
"This is a test"
```

Fig. 8.25   Using strpbrk.

Function *strrchr* searches for the last occurrence of the specified character in a string. If the character is found, strrchr returns a pointer to the character in the string; otherwise, strrchr returns NULL. Figure 8.26 shows a program that searches for the last occurrence of the character 'z' in the string "A zoo has many animals including zebras."

```
1   /* Fig. 8.26: fig08_26.c
2      Using strrchr */
3   #include <stdio.h>
4   #include <string.h>
5
6   int main()
7   {
8      /* initialize char pointer */
9      const char *string1 = "A zoo has many animals including zebras";
10
11     int c = 'z'; /* character to search for */
12
13     printf( "%s\n%s'%c'%s\"%s\"\n",
14             "The remainder of string1 beginning with the",
15             "last occurrence of character ", c,
16             " is: ", strrchr( string1, c ) );
17
18     return 0; /* indicates successful termination */
19
20   } /* end main */
```

```
The remainder of string1 beginning with the
last occurrence of character 'z' is: "zebras"
```

Fig. 8.26   Using strrchr.

Function *strspn* (Fig. 8.27) determines the length of the initial part of the string in its first argument that contains only characters from the string in its second argument. The function returns the length of the segment.

```
1   /* Fig. 8.27: fig08_27.c
2      Using strspn */
3   #include <stdio.h>
4   #include <string.h>
5
6   int main()
7   {
8      /* initialize two char pointers */
9      const char *string1 = "The value is 3.14159";
10     const char *string2 = "aehi lsTuv";
11
12     printf( "%s%s\n%s%s\n\n%s\n%s%u\n",
13             "string1 = ", string1, "string2 = ", string2,
14             "The length of the initial segment of string1",
15             "containing only characters from string2 = ",
16             strspn( string1, string2 ) );
17
18     return 0; /* indicates successful termination */
19
20   } /* end main */
```

Fig. 8.27   Using strspn. (Part 1 of 2.)

```
string1 = The value is 3.14159
string2 = aehi lsTuv

The length of the initial segment of string1
containing only characters from string2 = 13
```

Fig. 8.27   Using strspn. (Part 2 of 2.)

Function *strstr* searches for the first occurrence of its second string argument in its first string argument. If the second string is found in the first string, a pointer to the location of the string in the first argument is returned. Figure 8.28 uses strstr to find the string "def" in the string "abcdefabcdef".

```
1    /* Fig. 8.28: fig08_28.c
2       Using strstr */
3    #include <stdio.h>
4    #include <string.h>
5
6    int main()
7    {
8       const char *string1 = "abcdefabcdef"; /* string to search */
9       const char *string2 = "def"; /* string to search for */
10
11      printf( "%s%s\n%s%s\n\n%s\n%s%s\n",
12         "string1 = ", string1, "string2 = ", string2,
13         "The remainder of string1 beginning with the",
14         "first occurrence of string2 is: ",
15         strstr( string1, string2 ) );
16
17      return 0; /* indicates successful termination */
18
19   } /* end main */
```

```
string1 = abcdefabcdef
string2 = def

The remainder of string1 beginning with the
first occurrence of string2 is: defabcdef
```

Fig. 8.28   Using strstr.

Function *strtok* (Fig. 8.29) is used to break a string into a series of *tokens*. A token is a sequence of characters separated by *delimiters* (usually spaces or punctuation marks). For example, in a line of text, each word can be considered a token, and the spaces separating the words can be considered delimiters.

```
1    /* Fig. 8.29: fig08_29.c
2       Using strtok */
3    #include <stdio.h>
```

Fig. 8.29   Using strtok. (Part 1 of 2.)

```
 4   #include <string.h>
 5
 6   int main()
 7   {
 8      /* initialize array string */
 9      char string[] = "This is a sentence with 7 tokens";
10      char *tokenPtr; /* create char pointer */
11
12      printf( "%s\n%s\n\n%s\n",
13         "The string to be tokenized is:", string,
14         "The tokens are:" );
15
16      tokenPtr = strtok( string, " " ); /* begin tokenizing sentence */
17
18      /* continue tokenizing sentence until tokenPtr becomes NULL */
19      while ( tokenPtr != NULL ) {
20         printf( "%s\n", tokenPtr );
21         tokenPtr = strtok( NULL, " " ); /* get next token */
22      } /* end while */
23
24      return 0; /* indicates successful termination */
25
26   } /* end main */
```

```
The string to be tokenized is:
This is a sentence with 7 tokens

The tokens are:
This
is
a
sentence
with
7
tokens
```

Fig. 8.29 Using strtok. (Part 2 of 2.)

Multiple calls to strtok are required to tokenize a string, break it into tokens (assuming that the string contains more than one token). The first call to strtok contains two arguments, a string to be tokenized, and a string containing characters that separate the tokens. In Fig. 8.29, the statement

```
tokenPtr = strtok( string, " " ); /* begin tokenizing sentence */
```

assigns tokenPtr a pointer to the first token in string. The second argument of strtok, " ", indicates that tokens in string are separated by spaces. Function strtok searches for the first character in string that is not a delimiting character (space). This begins the first token. The function then finds the next delimiting character in the string and replaces it with a null ('\0') character to terminate the current token. Function strtok saves a pointer to the next character following the token in string and returns a pointer to the current token.

Subsequent strtok calls continue tokenizing string. These calls contain NULL as their first argument. The NULL argument indicates that the call to strtok should continue tokenizing from the location in `string` saved by the last call to `strtok`. If no tokens remain when `strtok` is called, `strtok` returns NULL. Figure 8.29 uses `strtok` to tokenize the string `"This is a sentence with 7 tokens"`. Each token is printed separately. Note that `strtok` modifies the input string; therefore, a copy of the string should be made if the string will be used again in the program after the calls to `strtok`.

8.9 Memory Functions of the String Handling Library

The string handling library functions presented in this section manipulate, compare and search blocks of memory. The functions treat blocks of memory as character arrays and can manipulate any block of data. Figure 8.30 summarizes the memory functions of the string handling library. In the function discussions, "object" refers to a block of data.

Function prototype	Function description
`void *memcpy( void *s1, const void *s2, size_t n );`	
	Copies n characters from the object pointed to by s2 into the object pointed to by s1. A pointer to the resulting object is returned.
`void *memmove( void *s1, const void *s2, size_t n );`	
	Copies n characters from the object pointed to by s2 into the object pointed to by s1. The copy is performed as if the characters were first copied from the object pointed to by s2 into a temporary array and then from the temporary array into the object pointed to by s1. A pointer to the resulting object is returned.
`int memcmp( const void *s1, const void *s2, size_t n );`	
	Compares the first n characters of the objects pointed to by s1 and s2. The function returns 0, less than 0 or greater than 0 if s1 is equal to, less than or greater than s2.
`void *memchr( const void *s, int c, size_t n );`	
	Locates the first occurrence of c (converted to `unsigned char`) in the first n characters of the object pointed to by s. If c is found, a pointer to c in the object is returned. Otherwise, NULL is returned.
`void *memset( void *s, int c, size_t n );`	
	Copies c (converted to `unsigned char`) into the first n characters of the object pointed to by s. A pointer to the result is returned.

Fig. 8.30   Memory functions of the string handling library.

The pointer parameters to these functions are declared `void *`. In Chapter 7, we saw that a pointer to any data type can be assigned directly to a pointer of type `void *`, and a pointer of type `void *` can be assigned directly to a pointer to any data type. For this reason, these functions can receive pointers to any data type. Because a `void *` pointer cannot be dereferenced, each function receives a size argument that specifies the number of characters (bytes) the function will process. For simplicity, the examples in this section manipulate character arrays (blocks of characters).

Function *memcpy* copies a specified number of characters from the object pointed to by its second argument into the object pointed to by its first argument. The function can receive a pointer to any type of object. The result of this function is undefined if the two objects overlap in memory (i.e., if they are parts of the same object)—in such cases, use memmove. Figure 8.31 uses `memcpy` to copy the string in array `s2` to array `s1`.

```
1   /* Fig. 8.31: fig08_31.c
2      Using memcpy */
3   #include <stdio.h>
4   #include <string.h>
5
6   int main()
7   {
8      char s1[ 17 ];                 /* create char array s1 */
9      char s2[]  = "Copy this string"; /* initialize char array s2 */
10
11     memcpy( s1, s2, 17 );
12     printf( "%s\n%s\"%s\"\n",
13             "After s2 is copied into s1 with memcpy,",
14             "s1 contains ", s1 );
15
16     return 0; /* indicates successful termination */
17
18  } /* end main */
```

```
After s2 is copied into s1 with memcpy,
s1 contains "Copy this string"
```

Fig. 8.31   Using memcpy.

Function *memmove*, like memcpy, copies a specified number of bytes from the object pointed to by its second argument into the object pointed to by its first argument. Copying is performed as if the bytes are copied from the second argument into a temporary array of characters, then copied from the temporary array into the first argument. This allows characters from one part of a string to be copied into another part of the same string. Figure 8.32 uses memmove to copy the last 10 bytes of array x into the first 10 bytes of array x.

Common Programming Error 8.8

String manipulation functions other than memmove that copy characters have undefined results when copying takes place between parts of the same string.

```
1   /* Fig. 8.32: fig08_32.c
2      Using memmove */
3   #include <stdio.h>
4   #include <string.h>
5
6   int main()
7   {
```

Fig. 8.32   Using memmove. (Part 1 of 2.)

```
8       char x[] = "Home Sweet Home"; /* initialize char array x */
9
10      printf( "%s%s\n", "The string in array x before memmove is: ", x );
11      printf( "%s%s\n", "The string in array x after memmove is: ",
12              memmove( x, &x[ 5 ], 10 ) );
13
14      return 0; /* indicates successful termination */
15
16   } /* end main */
```

```
The string in array x before memmove is: Home Sweet Home
The string in array x after memmove is: Sweet Home Home
```

Fig. 8.32   Using memmove. (Part 2 of 2.)

Function memcmp (Fig. 8.33) compares the specified number of characters of its first argument with the corresponding characters of its second argument. The function returns a value greater than 0 if the first argument is greater than the second argument, returns 0 if the arguments are equal and returns a value less than 0 if the first argument is less than the second argument.

```
1    /* Fig. 8.33: fig08_33.c
2       Using memcmp */
3    #include <stdio.h>
4    #include <string.h>
5
6    int main()
7    {
8       char s1[] = "ABCDEFG"; /* initialize char array s1 */
9       char s2[] = "ABCDXYZ"; /* initialize char array s2 */
10
11      printf( "%s%s\n%s%s\n\n%s%2d\n%s%2d\n%s%2d\n",
12              "s1 = ", s1, "s2 = ", s2,
13              "memcmp( s1, s2, 4 ) = ", memcmp( s1, s2, 4 ),
14              "memcmp( s1, s2, 7 ) = ", memcmp( s1, s2, 7 ),
15              "memcmp( s2, s1, 7 ) = ", memcmp( s2, s1, 7 ) );
16
17      return 0; /* indicate successful termination */
18
19   } /* end main */
```

```
s1 = ABCDEFG
s2 = ABCDXYZ

memcmp( s1, s2, 4 ) =  0
memcmp( s1, s2, 7 ) = -1
memcmp( s2, s1, 7 ) =  1
```

Fig. 8.33   Using memcmp.

Function *memchr* searches for the first occurrence of a byte, represented as `unsigned char`, in the specified number of bytes of an object. If the byte is found, a pointer to the byte in the object is returned; otherwise, a NULL pointer is returned. Figure 8.34 searches for the character (byte) `'r'` in the string `"This is a string"`.

```
1   /* Fig. 8.34: fig08_34.c
2      Using memchr */
3   #include <stdio.h>
4   #include <string.h>
5
6   int main()
7   {
8      const char *s = "This is a string"; /* initialize char pointer */
9
10     printf( "%s\'%c\'%s\"%s\"\n",
11             "The remainder of s after character ", 'r',
12             " is found is ", memchr( s, 'r', 16 ) );
13
14     return 0; /* indicates successful termination */
15
16  } /* end main */
```

```
The remainder of s after character 'r' is found is "ring"
```

Fig. 8.34   Using `memchr`.

Function *memset* copies the value of the byte in its second argument into a specified number of bytes of the object pointed to by its first argument. Figure 8.35 uses `memset` to copy `'b'` into the first 7 bytes of `string1`.

```
1   /* Fig. 8.35: fig08_35.c
2      Using memset */
3   #include <stdio.h>
4   #include <string.h>
5
6   int main()
7   {
8      char string1[ 15 ] = "BBBBBBBBBBBBBB"; /* initialize string1 */
9
10     printf( "string1 = %s\n", string1 );
11     printf( "string1 after memset = %s\n", memset( string1, 'b', 7 ) );
12
13     return 0; /* indicates successful termination */
14
15  } /* end main */
```

```
string1 = BBBBBBBBBBBBBB
string1 after memset = bbbbbbbBBBBBBB
```

Fig. 8.35   Using `memset`.

8.10 Other Functions of the String Handling Library

The two remaining functions of the string handling library are strerror and strlen. Figure 8.36 summarizes the strerror and strlen functions.

Function prototype	Function description
char *strerror(int errornum);	
	Maps errornum into a full text string in a system-dependent manner. A pointer to the string is returned.
size_t strlen(const char *s);	
	Determines the length of string s. The number of characters preceding the terminating null character is returned.

Fig. 8.36   Other functions of the string handling library.

Function *strerror* takes an error number and creates an error message string. A pointer to the string is returned. Figure 8.37 demonstrates strerror.

Portability Tip 8.4

The message generated by strerror is system dependent.

```
1   /* Fig. 8.37: fig08_37.c
2      Using strerror */
3   #include <stdio.h>
4   #include <string.h>
5
6   int main()
7   {
8      printf( "%s\n", strerror( 2 ) );
9
10     return 0; /* indicates successful termination */
11
12  } /* end main */
```

```
No such file or directory
```

Fig. 8.37   Using strerror.

Function *strlen* takes a string as an argument and returns the number of characters in the string—the terminating null character is not included in the length. Figure 8.38 demonstrates function strlen.

```
1   /* Fig. 8.38: fig08_38.c
2      Using strlen */
3   #include <stdio.h>
```

Fig. 8.38   Using strlen. (Part 1 of 2.)

```
4    #include <string.h>
5
6    int main()
7    {
8        /* initialize 3 char pointers */
9        const char *string1 = "abcdefghijklmnopqrstuvwxyz";
10       const char *string2 = "four";
11       const char *string3 = "Boston";
12
13       printf("%s\"%s\"%s%lu\n%s\"%s\"%s%lu\n%s\"%s\"%s%lu\n",
14           "The length of ", string1, " is ",
15           ( unsigned long ) strlen( string1 ),
16           "The length of ", string2, " is ",
17           ( unsigned long ) strlen( string2 ),
18           "The length of ", string3, " is ",
19           ( unsigned long ) strlen( string3 ) );
20
21       return 0; /* indicates successful termination */
22
23   } /* end main */
```

```
The length of "abcdefghijklmnopqrstuvwxyz" is 26
The length of "four" is 4
The length of "Boston" is 6
```

Fig. 8.38   Using `strlen`. (Part 2 of 2.)

SUMMARY

- Function `islower` determines whether its argument is a lowercase letter (a–z).

- Function `isupper` determines whether its argument is an uppercase letter (A–Z).

- Function `isdigit` determines whether its argument is a digit (0–9).

- Function `isalpha` determines whether its argument is an uppercase letter (A–Z) or a lowercase letter (a–z).

- Function `isalnum` determines whether its argument is an uppercase letter (A–Z), a lowercase letter (a–z) or a digit (0–9).

- Function `isxdigit` determines whether its argument is a hexadecimal digit (A–F, a–f, 0–9).

- Function `toupper` converts a lowercase letter to an uppercase letter and returns the uppercase letter.

- Function `tolower` converts an uppercase letter to a lowercase letter and returns the lowercase letter.

- Function `isspace` determines whether its argument is one of the following whitespace characters: ' ' (space), '\f', '\n', '\r', '\t' or '\v'.

- Function `iscntrl` determines whether its argument is one of the following control characters: '\t', '\v', '\f', '\a', '\b', '\r' or '\n'.

- Function `ispunct` determines whether its argument is a printing character other than a space, a digit or a letter.

- Function `isprint` determines whether its argument is any printing character including the space character.

- Function `isgraph` determines whether its argument is a printing character other than the space character.

- Function `atof` converts its argument—a string beginning with a series of digits that represents a floating-point number—to a `double` value.

- Function `atoi` converts its argument—a string beginning with a series of digits that represents an integer—to an `int` value.

- Function `atol` converts its argument—a string beginning with a series of digits that represents a long integer—to a `long` value.

- Function `strtod` converts a sequence of characters representing a floating-point value to `double`. The function receives two arguments—a string (`char *`) and a pointer to `char *`. The string contains the character sequence to be converted and the pointer to `char *` is assigned the remainder of the string after the conversion.

- Function `strtol` converts a sequence of characters representing an integer to `long`. The function receives three arguments—a string (`char *`), a pointer to `char *` and an integer. The string contains the character sequence to be converted, the pointer to `char *` is assigned the remainder of the string after the conversion and the integer specifies the base of the value being converted.

- Function `strtoul` converts a sequence of characters representing an integer to `unsigned long`. The function receives three arguments—a string (`char *`), a pointer to `char *` and an integer. The string contains the character sequence to be converted, the pointer to `char *` is assigned the remainder of the string after the conversion and the integer specifies the base of the value being converted.

- Function `gets` reads characters from the standard input (keyboard) until a newline character or the end-of-file indicator is encountered. The argument to `gets` is an array of type `char`. A null character (`'\0'`) is appended to the array after reading terminates.

- Function `putchar` prints its character argument.

- Function `getchar` reads a single character from the standard input and returns the character as an integer. If the end-of-file indicator is encountered, `getchar` returns EOF.

- Function `puts` takes a string (`char *`) as an argument and prints the string followed by a newline character.

- Function `sprintf` uses the same conversion specifications as function `printf` to print formatted data into an array of type `char`.

- Function `sscanf` uses the same conversion specifications as function `scanf` to read formatted data from a string.

- Function `strcpy` copies its second argument (a string) into its first argument (a character). The programmer must ensure that the array is large enough to store the string and its terminating null character.

- Function `strncpy` is equivalent to `strcpy`, except that a call to `strncpy` specifies the number of characters to be copied from the string into the array. The terminating null character will only be copied if the number of characters to be copied is one more than the length of the string.

- Function `strcat` appends its second string argument—including the terminating null character—to its first string argument. The first character of the second string replaces the null (`'\0'`) character of the first string. The programmer must ensure that the array used to store the first string is large enough to store both the first string and the second string.

- Function `strncat` appends a specified number of characters from the second string to the first string. A terminating null character is appended to the result.

- Function `strcmp` compares its first string argument to its second string argument character-by-character. The function returns 0 if the strings are equal, returns a negative value if the first string is less than the second string and returns a positive value if the first string is greater than the second string.

- Function `strncmp` is equivalent to `strcmp`, except that `strncmp` compares a specified number of characters. If the number of characters in one of the strings is less than the number of characters specified, `strncmp` compares characters until the null character in the shorter string is encountered.

- Function `strchr` searches for the first occurrence of a character in a string. If the character is found, `strchr` returns a pointer to the character in the string; otherwise, `strchr` returns NULL.

- Function `strcspn` determines the length of the initial part of the string in its first argument that does not contain any characters from the string in its second argument. The function returns the length of the segment.

- Function `strpbrk` searches for the first occurrence in its first argument of any character in its second argument. If a character from the second argument is found, `strpbrk` returns a pointer to the character; otherwise, `strpbrk` returns NULL.

- Function `strrchr` searches for the last occurrence of a character in a string. If the character is found, `strrchr` returns a pointer to the character in the string; otherwise, `strrchr` returns NULL.

- Function `strspn` determines the length of the initial part of the string in its first argument that contains only characters from the string in its second argument. The function returns the length of the segment.

- Function `strstr` searches for the first occurrence of its second string argument in its first string argument. If the second string is found in the first string, a pointer to the location of the string in the first argument is returned.

- A sequence of calls to `strtok` breaks the string `s1` into tokens that are separated by characters contained in the string `s2`. The first call contains `s1` as the first argument, and subsequent calls to continue tokenizing the same string contain NULL as the first argument. A pointer to the current token is returned by each call. If there are no more tokens when the function is called, a NULL pointer is returned.

- Function `memcpy` copies a specified number of characters from the object to which its second argument points into the object to which its first argument points. The function can receive a pointer to any type of object. The pointers are received by `memcpy` as `void` pointers and converted to `char` pointers for use in the function. Function `memcpy` manipulates the bytes of the object as characters.

- Function `memmove` copies a specified number of bytes from the object pointed to by its second argument to the object pointed to by its first argument. Copying is accomplished as if the bytes were copied from the second argument to a temporary character array and then copied from the temporary array to the first argument.

- Function `memcmp` compares the specified number of characters of its first and second arguments.

- Function `memchr` searches for the first occurrence of a byte, represented as `unsigned char`, in the specified number of bytes of an object. If the byte is found, a pointer to the byte is returned; otherwise, a NULL pointer is returned.

- Function `memset` copies its second argument, treated as an `unsigned char`, to a specified number of bytes of the object pointed to by the first argument.

- Function `strerror` maps an integer error number into a full text string in a system-dependent manner. A pointer to the string is returned.

- Function `strlen` takes a string as an argument and returns the number of characters in the string—the terminating null character is not included in the length of the string.

TERMINOLOGY

appending strings to other strings
ASCII

atof
atoi

COMMON PROGRAMMING ERRORS

8.1 Not allocating sufficient space in a character array to store the null character that terminates a string is an error.

8.2 Printing a "string" that does not contain a terminating null character is an error.

8.3 Processing a single character as a string. A string is a pointer—probably a respectably large integer. However, a character is a small integer (ASCII values range 0–255). On many systems this causes an error, because low memory addresses are reserved for special purposes such as operating system interrupt handlers—so "access violations" occur.

8.4 Passing a character as an argument to a function when a string is expected is a syntax error.

8.5 Passing a string as an argument to a function when a character is expected is a syntax error.

8.6 Not appending a terminating null character to the first argument of a `strncpy` when the third argument is less than or equal to the length of the string in the second argument.

8.7   Assuming that `strcmp` and `strncmp` return 1 when their arguments are equal. Both functions return 0 (strangely, the equivalent of C's false value) for equality. Therefore, when testing two strings for equality, the result of function `strcmp` or `strncmp` should be compared with 0 to determine if the strings are equal.

8.8   String manipulation functions other than `memmove` that copy characters have undefined results when copying takes place between parts of the same string.

ERROR-PREVENTION TIPS

8.1   When storing a string of characters in a character array, be sure that the array is large enough to hold the largest string that will be stored. C allows strings of any length to be stored. If a string is longer than the character array in which it is to be stored, characters beyond the end of the array will overwrite data in memory following the array.

GOOD PROGRAMMING PRACTICES

8.1   When using functions from the character handling library, include the `<ctype.h>` header.

8.2   When using functions from the general utilities library, include the `<stdlib.h>` header.

8.3   When using functions from the standard input/output library, include the `<stdio.h>` header.

8.4   When using functions from the string handling library, include the `<string.h>` header.

PORTABILITY TIPS

8.1   When a variable of type `char *` is initialized with a string literal, some compilers may place the string in a location in memory where the string cannot be modified. If you might need to modify a string literal, it should be stored in a character array to ensure modifiability on all systems.

8.2   Type `size_t` is a system-dependent synonym for either `unsigned long` or `unsigned int`.

8.3   The internal numeric codes used to represent characters may be different on different computers.

8.4   The message generated by `strerror` is system dependent.

SELF-REVIEW EXERCISES

8.1   Write a single statement to accomplish each of the following. Assume that variables c (which stores a character), x, y and z are of type `int`, variables d, e and f are of type `double`, variable ptr is of type `char *` and arrays s1[100] and s2[100] are of type `char`.

   a) Convert the character stored in variable c to an uppercase letter. Assign the result to variable c.

   b) Determine if the value of variable c is a digit. Use the conditional operator as shown in Fig. 8.2–Fig. 8.4 to print " is a " or " is not a " when the result is displayed.

   c) Convert the string "1234567" to long and print the value.

   d) Determine if the value of variable c is a control character. Use the conditional operator to print " is a " or " is not a " when the result is displayed.

   e) Read a line of text into array s1 from the keyboard. Do not use `scanf`.

   f) Print the line of text stored in array s1. Do not use `printf`.

   g) Assign ptr the location of the last occurrence of c in s1.

   h) Print the value of variable c. Do not use `printf`.

   i) Convert the string "8.63582" to double and print the value.

   j) Determine if the value of c is a letter. Use the conditional operator to print " is a " or " is not a " when the result is displayed.

   k) Read a character from the keyboard and store the character in variable c.

l) Assign ptr the location of the first occurrence of s2 in s1.

m) Determine if the value of variable c is a printing character. Use the conditional operator to print " is a " or " is not a " when the result is displayed.

n) Read three double values into variables d, e and f from the string "1.27 10.3 9.432".

o) Copy the string stored in array s2 into array s1.

p) Assign ptr the location of the first occurrence in s1 of any character from s2.

q) Compare the string in s1 with the string in s2. Print the result.

r) Assign ptr the location of the first occurrence of c in s1.

s) Use sprintf to print the values of integer variables x, y and z into array s1. Each value should be printed with a field width of 7.

t) Append 10 characters from the string in s2 to the string in s1.

u) Determine the length of the string in s1. Print the result.

v) Convert the string "-21" to int and print the value.

w) Assign ptr to the location of the first token in s2. Tokens in the string s2 are separated by commas (,).

8.2 Show two different methods of initializing character array vowel with the string of vowels "AEIOU".

8.3 What, if anything, prints when each of the following C statements is performed? If the statement contains an error, describe the error and indicate how to correct it. Assume the following variable definitions:

```
char s1[ 50 ] = "jack", s2[ 50 ] = " jill", s3[ 50 ], *sptr;
```

```
a) printf( "%c%s", toupper( s1[ 0 ] ), &s1[ 1 ] );
b) printf( "%s", strcpy( s3, s2 ) );
c) printf( "%s",
       strcat( strcat( strcpy( s3, s1 ), " and " ), s2 ) );
d) printf( "%u", strlen( s1 ) + strlen( s2 ) );
e) printf( "%u", strlen( s3 ) );
```

8.4 Find the error in each of the following program segments and explain how to correct it:

```
a) char s[ 10 ];
   strncpy( s, "hello", 5 );
   printf( "%s\n", s );
b) printf( "%s", 'a' );
c) char s[ 12 ];
   strcpy( s, "Welcome Home" );
d) if ( strcmp( string1, string2 ) )
       printf( "The strings are equal\n" );
```

ANSWERS TO SELF-REVIEW EXERCISES

8.1
```
a) c = toupper( c );
b) printf( "'%c'%sdigit\n",
        c, isdigit( c ) ? " is a " : " is not a " );
c) printf( "%ld\n", atol( "1234567" ) );
d) printf( "'%c'%scontrol character\n",
        c, iscntrl( c ) ? " is a " : " is not a " );
e) gets( s1 );
f) puts( s1 );
g) ptr = strrchr( s1, c );
h) putchar( c );
```

i) `printf( "%f\n", atof( "8.63582" ) );`

j) `printf( "'%c'%sletter\n",`
`        c, isalpha( c ) ? " is a " : " is not a " );`

k) `c = getchar();`

l) `ptr = strstr( s1, s2 );`

m) `printf( "'%c'%sprinting character\n",`
`        c, isprint( c ) ? " is a " : " is not a " );`

n) `sscanf( "1.27 10.3 9.432", "%f%f%f", &d, &e, &f );`

o) `strcpy( s1, s2 );`

p) `ptr = strpbrk( s1, s2 );`

q) `printf( "strcmp( s1, s2 ) = %d\n", strcmp( s1, s2 ) );`

r) `ptr = strchr( s1, c );`

s) `sprintf( s1, "%7d%7d%7d", x, y, z );`

t) `strncat( s1, s2, 10 );`

u) `printf( "strlen(s1) = %u\n", strlen( s1 ) );`

v) `printf( "%d\n", atoi( "-21" ) ); *`

w) `ptr = strtok( s2, "," );`

8.2   `char vowel[] = "AEIOU";`
`char vowel[] = { 'A', 'E', 'I', 'O', 'U', '\0' };`

8.3   a) `Jack`
b) `jill`
c) `jack and jill`
d) `8`
e) `13`

8.4   a) Error: Function `strncpy` does not write a terminating null character to array `s` because its third argument is equal to the length of the string `"hello"`.
Correction: Make the third argument of `strncpy` 6, or assign `'\0'` to `s[ 5 ]`.

b) Error: Attempting to print a character constant as a string.
Correction: Use `%c` to output the character, or replace `'a'` with `"a"`.

a) Error: Character array `s` is not large enough to store the terminating null character.
Correction: Declare the array with more elements.

b) Error: Function `strcmp` returns 0 if the strings are equal; therefore, the condition in the `if` statement is false, and the `printf` will not be executed.
Correction: Compare the result of `strcmp` with 0 in the condition.

EXERCISES

8.5   Write a program that inputs a character from the keyboard and tests the character with each of the functions in the character handling library. The program should print the value returned by each function.

8.6   Write a program that inputs a line of text with function `gets` into `char` array `s[ 100 ]`. Output the line in uppercase letters and in lowercase letters.

8.7   Write a program that inputs four strings that represent integers, converts the strings to integers, sums the values and prints the total of the four values.

8.8   Write a program that inputs four strings that represent floating-point values, converts the strings to double values, sums the values and prints the total of the four values.

8.9   Write a program that uses function `strcmp` to compare two strings input by the user. The program should state whether the first string is less than, equal to or greater than the second string.

8.10   Write a program that uses function `strncmp` to compare two strings input by the user. The program should input the number of characters to be compared. The program should state whether the first string is less than, equal to or greater than the second string.

8.11   Write a program that uses random number generation to create sentences. The program should use four arrays of pointers to `char` called `article`, `noun`, `verb` and `preposition`. The program should create a sentence by selecting a word at random from each array in the following order: `article`, `noun`, `verb`, `preposition`, `article` and `noun`. As each word is picked, it should be concatenated to the previous words in an array large enough to hold the entire sentence. The words should be separated by spaces. When the final sentence is output, it should start with a capital letter and end with a period. The program should generate 20 such sentences.

The arrays should be filled as follows: The `article` array should contain the articles `"the"`, `"a"`, `"one"`, `"some"` and `"any"`; the `noun` array should contain the nouns `"boy"`, `"girl"`, `"dog"`, `"town"` and `"car"`; the `verb` array should contain the verbs `"drove"`, `"jumped"`, `"ran"`, `"walked"` and `"skipped"`; the `preposition` array should contain the prepositions `"to"`, `"from"`, `"over"`, `"under"` and `"on"`.

After the preceding program is written and working, modify the program to produce a short story consisting of several of these sentences. (How about the possibility of a random term paper writer?)

8.12   *(Limericks)* A limerick is a humorous five-line verse in which the first and second lines rhyme with the fifth, and the third line rhymes with the fourth. Using techniques similar to those developed in Exercise 8.11, write a program that produces random limericks. Polishing this program to produce good limericks is a challenging problem, but the result will be worth the effort!

8.13   Write a program that encodes English language phrases into pig Latin. Pig Latin is a form of coded language often used for amusement. Many variations exist in the methods used to form pig Latin phrases. For simplicity, use the following algorithm:

To form a pig Latin phrase from an English language phrase, tokenize the phrase into words with function `strtok`. To translate each English word into a pig Latin word, place the first letter of the English word at the end of the English word, and add the letters "ay." Thus the word "`jump`" becomes "umpjay," the word "`the`" becomes "hetay" and the word "`computer`" becomes "omputercay." Blanks between words remain as blanks. Assume the following: The English phrase consists of words separated by blanks, there are no punctuation marks, and all words have two or more letters. Function `printLatinWord` should display each word. [*Hint:* Each time a token is found in a call to `strtok`, pass the token pointer to function `printLatinWord`, and print the pig Latin word.]

8.14   Write a program that inputs a telephone number as a string in the form `(555) 555-5555`. The program should use function `strtok` to extract the area code as a token, the first three digits of the phone number as a token and the last four digits of the phone number as a token. The seven digits of the phone number should be concatenated into one string. The program should convert the area-code string to `int` and convert the phone number string to `long`. Both the area code and the phone number should be printed.

8.15   Write a program that inputs a line of text, tokenizes the line with function `strtok` and outputs the tokens in reverse order.

8.16   Write a program that inputs a line of text and a search string from the keyboard. Using function `strstr`, locate the first occurrence of the search string in the line of text, and assign the location to variable `searchPtr` of type char `*`. If the search string is found, print the remainder of the line of text beginning with the search string. Then, use `strstr` again to locate the next occurrence of the search string in the line of text. If a second occurrence is found, print the remainder of the line of text beginning with the second occurrence. [*Hint:* The second call to `strstr` should contain `searchPtr + 1` as its first argument.]

8.17   Write a program based on the program of Exercise 8.16 that inputs several lines of text and a search string, and uses function `strstr` to determine the total occurrences of the string in the lines of text. Print the result.

8.18   Write a program that inputs several lines of text and a search character, and uses function `strchr` to determine the total occurrences of the character in the lines of text.

8.19   Write a program based on the program of Exercise 8.18 that inputs several lines of text and uses function `strchr` to determine the total occurrences of each letter of the alphabet in the lines of text. Uppercase and lowercase letters should be counted together. Store the totals for each letter in an array and print the values in tabular format after the totals have been determined.

8.20   Write a program that inputs several lines of text and uses `strtok` to count the total number of words. Assume that the words are separated either by spaces or newline characters.

8.21   Use the string comparison functions discussed in Section 8.6 and the techniques for sorting arrays developed in Chapter 6 to write a program that alphabetizes a list of strings. Use the names of 10 or 15 towns in your area as data for your program.

8.22   The chart in Appendix D shows the numeric code representations for the characters in the ASCII character set. Study this chart and then state whether each of the following is *true* or *false*.

    a)   The letter "A" comes before the letter "B."
    b)   The digit "9" comes before the digit "0."
    c)   The commonly used symbols for addition, subtraction, multiplication and division all come before any of the digits.
    d)   The digits come before the letters.
    e)   If a sort program sorts strings into ascending sequence, then the program will place the symbol for a right parenthesis before the symbol for a left parenthesis.

8.23   Write a program that reads a series of strings and prints only those strings beginning with the letter "b."

8.24   Write a program that reads a series of strings and prints only those strings that end with the letters "ed."

8.25   Write a program that inputs an ASCII code and prints the corresponding character. Modify this program so that it generates all possible three-digit codes in the range 000 to 255 and attempts to print the corresponding characters. What happens when this program is run?

8.26   Using the ASCII character chart in Appendix D as a guide, write your own versions of the character handling functions in Fig. 8.1.

8.27   Write your own versions of the functions in Fig. 8.5 for converting strings to numbers.

8.28   Write two versions of each of the string copy and string concatenation functions in Fig. 8.17. The first version should use array subscripting, and the second version should use pointers and pointer arithmetic.

8.29   Write your own versions of the functions `getchar`, `gets`, `putchar` and `puts` described in Fig. 8.12.

8.30   Write two versions of each string comparison function in Fig. 8.20. The first version should use array subscripting, and the second version should use pointers and pointer arithmetic.

8.31   Write your own versions of the functions in Fig. 8.22 for searching strings.

8.32   Write your own versions of the functions in Fig. 8.30 for manipulating blocks of memory.

8.33   Write two versions of function `strlen` in Fig. 8.36. The first version should use array subscripting, and the second version should use pointers and pointer arithmetic.

SPECIAL SECTION: ADVANCED STRING MANIPULATION EXERCISES

The preceding exercises are keyed to the text and designed to test the reader's understanding of fundamental string manipulation concepts. This section includes a collection of intermediate and advanced problems. The reader should find these problems challenging yet enjoyable. The problems vary considerably in difficulty. Some require an hour or two of program writing and implementation. Others are useful for lab assignments that might require two or three weeks of study and implementation. Some are challenging term projects.

8.34   *(Text Analysis)* The availability of computers with string manipulation capabilities has resulted in some rather interesting approaches to analyzing the writings of great authors. Much attention has been focused on whether William Shakespeare ever lived. Some scholars believe that there is substantial evidence indicating that Christopher Marlowe actually penned the masterpieces attributed to Shakespeare. Researchers have used computers to find similarities in the writings of these two authors. This exercise examines three methods for analyzing texts with a computer.

   a) Write a program that reads several lines of text and prints a table indicating the number of occurrences of each letter of the alphabet in the text. For example, the phrase

```
To be, or not to be: that is the question:
```

   contains one "a," two "b's," no "c's," etc.

   b) Write a program that reads several lines of text and prints a table indicating the number of one-letter words, two-letter words, three-letter words, etc., appearing in the text. For example, the phrase

```
Whether 'tis nobler in the mind to suffer
```

   contains

Word length	Occurrences
1	0
2	2
3	1
4	2 (including 'tis)
5	0
6	2
7	1

   c) Write a program that reads several lines of text and prints a table indicating the number of occurrences of each different word in the text. The first version of your program should include the words in the table in the same order in which they appear in the text. A more interesting (and useful) printout should then be attempted in which the words are sorted alphabetically. For example, the lines

```
To be, or not to be: that is the question:
Whether 'tis nobler in the mind to suffer
```

   contain the words "to" three times, the word "be" two times, the word "or" once, etc.

8.35   *(Word Processing)* The detailed treatment of string manipulation in this text is greatly attributable to the exciting growth in word processing in recent years. One important function in word processing systems is *type-justification*—the alignment of words to both the left and right margins of a page. This generates a professional-looking document that gives the appearance of being set in type, rather than prepared on a typewriter. Type-justification can be accomplished on computer systems by inserting one or more blank characters between each of the words in a line so that the rightmost word aligns with the right margin.

Write a program that reads several lines of text and prints this text in type-justified format. Assume that the text is to be printed on 8 1/2-inch-wide paper and that one-inch margins are to be allowed on both the left and right sides of the printed page. Assume that the computer prints 10 characters to the horizontal inch. Therefore, your program should print 6 1/2 inches of text or 65 characters per line.

8.36 *(Printing Dates in Various Formats)* Dates are commonly printed in several different formats in business correspondence. Two of the more common formats are

> 07/21/2003 and `July 21, 2003`

Write a program that reads a date in the first format and prints that date in the second format.

8.37 *(Check Protection)* Computers are frequently used in check-writing systems, such as payroll and accounts payable applications. Many strange stories circulate regarding weekly paychecks being printed (by mistake) for amounts in excess of $1 million. Weird amounts are printed by computerized check-writing systems because of human error and/or machine failure. Systems designers, of course, make every effort to build controls into their systems to prevent erroneous checks from being issued.

Another serious problem is the intentional alteration of a check amount by someone who intends to cash a check fraudulently. To prevent a dollar amount from being altered, most computerized check-writing systems employ a technique called *check protection.*

Checks designed for imprinting by computer contain a fixed number of spaces in which the computer may print an amount. Suppose a paycheck contains nine blank spaces in which the computer is supposed to print the amount of a weekly paycheck. If the amount is large, then all nine of those spaces will be filled, for example:

```
11,230.60  (check amount)
---------
123456789  (position numbers)
```

On the other hand, if the amount is less than $1000, then several of the spaces would ordinarily be left blank. For example,

```
   99.87
---------
123456789
```

contains three blank spaces. If a check is printed with blank spaces, it is easier for someone to alter the amount of the check. To prevent a check from being altered, many check-writing systems insert *leading asterisks* to protect the amount as follows:

```
****99.87
---------
123456789
```

Write a program that inputs a dollar amount to be printed on a check and then prints the amount in check-protected format with leading asterisks if necessary. Assume that nine spaces are available for printing an amount.

8.38 *(Writing the Word Equivalent of a Check Amount)* Continuing the discussion of the previous example, we reiterate the importance of designing check-writing systems to prevent alteration of check amounts. One common security method requires that the check amount be both written in numbers and "spelled out" in words. Even if someone is able to alter the numerical amount of the check, it is extremely difficult to change the amount in words.

Many computerized check-writing systems do not print the amount of the check in words. Perhaps the main reason for this omission is the fact that most high-level languages used in commercial applications do not contain adequate string manipulation features. Another reason is that the logic for writing word equivalents of check amounts is somewhat involved.

Write a program that inputs a numeric check amount and writes the word equivalent of the amount. For example, the amount 112.43 should be written as

ONE HUNDRED TWELVE and 43/100

8.39   *(Morse Code)* Perhaps the most famous of all coding schemes is Morse code, developed by Samuel Morse in 1832 for use with the telegraph system. Morse code assigns a series of dots and dashes to each letter of the alphabet, each digit, and a few special characters (such as period, comma, colon and semicolon). In sound-oriented systems, the dot represents a short sound and the dash represents a long sound. Other representations of dots and dashes are used with light-oriented systems and signal-flag systems.

Separation between words is indicated by a space,—quite simply, the absence of a dot or dash. In a sound-oriented system, a space is indicated by a short period of time during which no sound is transmitted. The international version of Morse code appears in Fig. 8.39.

Character	Code	Character	Code
A	.–	T	–
B	–...	U	..–
C	–.–.	V	...–
D	–..	W	.––
E	.	X	–..–
F	..–.	Y	–.––
G	––.	Z	––..
H	....		
I	..	*Digits*	
J	.–––	1	.––––
K	–.–	2	..–––
L	.–..	3	...––
M	––	4	....–
N	–.	5	.....
O	–––	6	–....
P	.––.	7	––...
Q	––.–	8	–––..
R	.–.	9	––––.
S	...	0	–––––

Fig. 8.39   The letters of the alphabet as expressed in international Morse code.

Write a program that reads an English-language phrase and encodes the phrase into Morse code. Also write a program that reads a phrase in Morse code and converts the phrase into the English-language equivalent. Use one blank between each Morse-coded letter and three blanks between each Morse-coded word.

8.40   *(A Metric Conversion Program)* Write a program that will assist the user with metric conversions. Your program should allow the user to specify the names of the units as strings (i.e., centimeters, liters, grams, etc., for the metric system and inches, quarts, pounds, etc., for the English system) and should respond to simple questions such as

```
"How many inches are in 2 meters?"
"How many liters are in 10 quarts?"
```

Your program should recognize invalid conversions. For example, the question

```
"How many feet in 5 kilograms?"
```

is not meaningful, because `"feet"` are units of length while `"kilograms"` are units of mass.

8.41   *(Dunning Letters)* Many businesses spend a great deal of time and money collecting overdue debts. *Dunning* is the process of making repeated and insistent demands upon a debtor in an attempt to collect a debt.

Computers are often used to generate dunning letters automatically and in increasing degrees of severity as a debt ages. The theory is that as a debt becomes older, it becomes more difficult to collect, and therefore the dunning letters must become more threatening.

Write a program that contains the texts of five dunning letters of increasing severity. Your program should accept as input the following:
   a) Debtor's name
   b) Debtor's address
   c) Debtor's account
   d) Amount owed
   e) Age of the amount owed (i.e., one month overdue, two months overdue, etc.).

Use the age of the amount owed to select one of the five message texts, and then print the dunning letter inserting the other user-supplied information where appropriate.

A CHALLENGING STRING MANIPULATION PROJECT

8.42   *(A Crossword-Puzzle Generator)* Most people have worked a crossword puzzle at one time or another, but few have ever attempted to generate one. Generating a crossword puzzle is a difficult problem. It is suggested here as a string manipulation project requiring substantial sophistication and effort. There are many issues the programmer must resolve to get even the simplest crossword-puzzle generator program working. For example, how does one represent the grid of a crossword puzzle inside the computer? Should one use a series of strings, or should double-subscripted arrays be used? The programmer needs a source of words (i.e., a computerized dictionary) that can be directly referenced by the program. In what form should these words be stored to facilitate the complex manipulations required by the program? The really ambitious reader will want to generate the "clues" portion of the puzzle in which the brief hints for each "across" word and each "down" word are printed for the puzzle worker. Merely printing a version of the blank puzzle itself is not a simple problem.

C Formatted Input/Output

Objectives

- To understand input and output streams.
- To be able to use all print formatting capabilities.
- To be able to use all input formatting capabilities.
- To be able to print with field widths and precisions.
- To be able to use formatting flags in the `printf` format control string.
- To be able to output literals and escape sequences.

All the news that's fit to print.
Adolph S. Ochs

What mad pursuit? What struggle to escape?
John Keats

Remove not the landmark on the boundary of the fields.
Amenemope

Outline

9.1 Introduction

An important part of the solution to any problem is the presentation of the results. In this chapter, we discuss in depth the formatting features of *scanf* and *printf*. These functions input data from the *standard input stream* and output data to the *standard output stream,* respectively. Four other functions that use the standard input and standard output—gets, puts, getchar and putchar–were discussed in Chapter 8. Include the header <stdio.h> in programs that call these functions.

Many features of `printf` and `scanf` were discussed earlier in the text. This chapter summarizes those features and introduces others. Chapter 11 discusses several additional functions included in the standard input/output (stdio) library.

9.2 Streams

All input and output is performed with *streams*, which are sequences of bytes. In input operations, the bytes flow from a device (e.g., a keyboard, a disk drive, a network connection) to main memory. In output operations, bytes flow from main memory to a device (e.g., a display screen, a printer, a disk drive, a network connection, etc.).

When program execution begins, three streams are connected to the program automatically. Normally, the standard input stream is connected to the keyboard and the standard output stream is connected to the screen. Operating systems often allow these streams to be *redirected* to other devices. A third stream, the *standard error stream,* is connected to the screen. Error messages are output to the standard error stream. Streams are discussed in detail in Chapter 11, File Processing.

9.3 Formatting Output with `printf`

Precise output formatting is accomplished with `printf`. Every `printf` call contains a *format control string* that describes the output format. The format control string consists of *conversion specifiers, flags, field widths, precisions* and *literal characters.* Together with the percent sign (%), these form *conversion specifications.* Function `printf` can perform the following formatting capabilities, each of which is discussed in this chapter:

1. *Rounding* floating-point values to an indicated number of decimal places.

2. *Aligning* a column of numbers with decimal points appearing one above the other.

3. *Right-justification* and *left-justification* of outputs.

4. *Inserting literal characters* at precise locations in a line of output.

5. Representing *floating-point numbers* in exponential format.

6. Representing unsigned integers in octal and hexadecimal format. See Appendix E, Number Systems, for more information on octal and hexadecimal values.

7. Displaying all types of data with fixed-size field widths and precisions.

The `printf` function has the form

```
printf( format-control-string, other-arguments );
```

format-control-string describes the output format, and *other-arguments* (which are optional) correspond to each conversion specification in *format-control-string.* Each conversion specification begins with a percent sign and ends with a conversion specifier. There can be many conversion specifications in one format control string.

Common Programming Error 9.1

Forgetting to enclose a format-control-string in quotation marks is a syntax error.

Good Programming Practice 9.1

Edit outputs neatly for presentation to make program outputs more readable and reduce user errors.

9.4 Printing Integers

An integer is a whole number, such as 776, 0 or -52, that contains no decimal point. Integer values are displayed in one of several formats. Figure 9.1 describes the *integer conversion* specifiers.

Conversion Specifier	Description
d	Display a signed decimal integer.
i	Display a signed decimal integer. [*Note:* The i and d specifiers are different when used with `scanf`.]
o	Display an unsigned octal integer.
u	Display an unsigned decimal integer.
x or X	Display an unsigned hexadecimal integer. X causes the digits 0-9 and the letters A-F to be displayed and x causes the digits 0-9 and a-f to be displayed.

Fig. 9.1   Integer conversion specifiers. (Part 1 of 2.)

Conversion Specifier	Description
h or 1 (letter 1)	Place before any integer conversion specifier to indicate that a short or long integer is displayed respectively. Letters h and 1 are more precisely called *length modifiers*.

Fig. 9.1   Integer conversion specifiers. (Part 2 of 2.)

Figure 9.2 prints an integer using each of the integer conversion specifiers. Note that only the minus sign prints; plus signs are suppressed. Later in this chapter we will see how to force plus signs to print. Also note that the value −455, when read by %u, is converted to the unsigned value 4294966841.

```
1   /* Fig 9.2: fig09_02.c */
2   /* Using the integer conversion specifiers */
3   #include <stdio.h>
4
5   int main()
6   {
7      printf( "%d\n", 455 );
8      printf( "%i\n", 455 );   /* i same as d in printf */
9      printf( "%d\n", +455 );
10     printf( "%d\n", -455 );
11     printf( "%hd\n", 32000 );
12     printf( "%ld\n", 2000000000 );
13     printf( "%o\n", 455 );
14     printf( "%u\n", 455 );
15     printf( "%u\n", -455 );
16     printf( "%x\n", 455 );
17     printf( "%X\n", 455 );
18
19     return 0; /* indicates successful termination */
20
21  } /* end main */
```

```
455
455
455
-455
32000
2000000000
707
455
4294966841
1c7
1C7
```

Fig. 9.2   Using integer conversion specifiers.

 Common Programming Error 9.2

Printing a negative value with a conversion specifier that expects an unsigned value.

9.5 Printing Floating-Point Numbers

A floating-point value contains a decimal point as in 33.5, 0.0 or -657.983. Floating-point values are displayed in one of several formats. Figure 9.3 describes the floating-point conversion specifiers. The *conversion specifiers e and E* display floating-point values in *exponential notation.* Exponential notation is the computer equivalent of *scientific notation* used in mathematics. For example, the value 150.4582 is represented in scientific notation as

$$1.504582 \times 10^2$$

and is represented in exponential notation as

1.504582E+02

by the computer. This notation indicates that 1.504582 is multiplied by 10 raised to the second power (E+02). The E stands for "exponent."

Conversion specifier	Description
e or E	Display a floating-point value in exponential notation.
f	Display floating-point values in fixed-point notation.
g or G	Display a floating-point value in either the floating-point form f or the exponential form e (or E) based on the magnitude of the value.
L	Place before any floating-point conversion specifier to indicate that a long double floating-point value is displayed.

Fig. 9.3   Floating-point conversion specifiers.

Values printed with the conversion specifiers e, E and f are output with six digits of precision to the right of the decimal point by default (e.g., 1.04592); other precisions can be specified explicitly. *Conversion specifier f* always prints at least one digit to the left of the decimal point. Conversion specifiers e and E print lowercase e and uppercase E preceding the exponent respectively and always print exactly one digit to the left of the decimal point.

Conversion specifier g (or G) prints in either e (E) or f format with no trailing zeros (1.234000 is printed as 1.234). Values are printed with e (E) if, after converting the value to exponential notation, the value's exponent is less than -4, or the exponent is greater than or equal to the specified precision (six significant digits by default for g and G). Otherwise, conversion specifier f is used to print the value. Trailing zeros are not printed in the fractional part of a value output with g or G. At least one decimal digit is required for the decimal point to be output. The values 0.0000875, 8750000.0, 8.75, 87.50 and 875 are printed as 8.75e-05, 8.75e+06, 8.75, 87.5 and 875 with the conversion specifier g . The value 0.0000875 uses e notation because, when it is converted to exponential notation, its exponent (-5) is less than -4. The value 8750000.0 uses e notation because its exponent (6) is equal to the default precision.

The precision for conversion specifiers g and G indicates the maximum number of significant digits printed, including the digit to the left of the decimal point. The value 1234567.0 is printed as 1.23457e+06, using conversion specifier %g (remember that all floating-point conversion specifiers have a default precision of 6). Note that there are 6 significant digits in the result. The difference between g and G is identical to the difference between e and E when the value is printed in exponential notation—lowercase g causes a lowercase e to be output, and uppercase G causes an uppercase E to be output.

Error-Prevention Tip 9.1

When outputting data, be sure that the user is aware of situations in which data may be imprecise due to formatting (e.g., rounding errors from specifying precisions).

Figure 9.4 demonstrates each of the floating-point conversion specifiers. Note that the %E, %e and %g conversion specifiers cause the value to be rounded in the output and the conversion specifier %f does not.

```
1   /* Fig 9.4: fig09_04.c */
2   /* Printing floating-point numbers with
3      floating-point conversion specifiers */
4
5   #include <stdio.h>
6
7   int main()
8   {
9      printf( "%e\n", 1234567.89 );
10     printf( "%e\n", +1234567.89 );
11     printf( "%e\n", -1234567.89 );
12     printf( "%E\n", 1234567.89 );
13     printf( "%f\n", 1234567.89 );
14     printf( "%g\n", 1234567.89 );
15     printf( "%G\n", 1234567.89 );
16
17     return 0; /* indicates successful termination */
18
19  } /* end main */
```

```
1.234568e+006
1.234568e+006
-1.234568e+006
1.234568E+006
1234567.890000
1.23457e+006
1.23457E+006
```

Fig. 9.4   Using floating-point conversion specifiers.

9.6 Printing Strings and Characters

The c and s conversion specifiers are used to print individual characters and strings, respectively. *Conversion specifier c* requires a char argument. *Conversion specifier s* requires a pointer to char as an argument. Conversion specifier s causes characters to be printed until a terminating null ('\0') character is encountered. The program shown in Fig. 9.5 displays characters and strings with conversion specifiers c and s.

```
1    /* Fig 9.5: fig09_05c */
2    /* Printing strings and characters */
3    #include <stdio.h>
4
5    int main()
6    {
7       char character = 'A'; /* initialize char */
8       char string[] = "This is a string"; /* initialize char array */
9       const char *stringPtr = "This is also a string"; /* char pointer */
10
11      printf( "%c\n", character );
12      printf( "%s\n", "This is a string" );
13      printf( "%s\n", string );
14      printf( "%s\n", stringPtr );
15
16      return 0; /* indicates successful termination */
17
18   } /* end main */
```

```
A
This is a string
This is a string
This is also a string
```

Fig. 9.5   Using the character and string conversion specifiers.

Common Programming Error 9.3

Using %c to print a string is an error. The conversion specifier %c expects a char *argument. A string is a pointer to* char *(i.e., a* char **).*

Common Programming Error 9.4

Using %s to print a char *argument, on some systems, causes a fatal execution-time error called an access violation. The conversion specifier %s expects an argument of type pointer to* char.

Common Programming Error 9.5

Using single quotes around character strings is a syntax error. Character strings must be enclosed in double quotes.

Common Programming Error 9.6

Using double quotes around a character constant creates a string consisting of two characters, the second of which is the terminating null. A character constant is a single character enclosed in single quotes.

9.7 Other Conversion Specifiers

The three remaining conversion specifiers are p, n and % (Fig. 9.6).

Portability Tip 9.1

The conversion specifier p *displays an address in an implementation-defined manner (on many systems, hexadecimal notation is used rather than decimal notation).*

Conversion specifier	Description
p	Display a pointer value in an implementation-defined manner.
n	Store the number of characters already output in the current printf statement. A pointer to an integer is supplied as the corresponding argument. Nothing is displayed.
%	Display the percent character.

Fig. 9.6 Other conversion specifiers.

The *conversion specifier n* stores the number of characters already output in the current printf statement—the corresponding argument is a pointer to an integer variable in which the value is stored. Nothing is printed by a %n conversion specifier. The conversion specifier % causes a percent sign to be output.

Figure 9.7's %p prints the value of ptr and the address of x; these values are identical because ptr is assigned the address of x. Next, %n stores the number of characters output by the third printf statement (line 15) in integer variable y, and the value of y is printed. The last printf statement (line 21) uses %% to print the % character in a character string. Note that every printf call returns a value—either the number of characters output, or a negative value if an output error occurs.

```
1   /* Fig 9.7: fig09_07.c */
2   /* Using the p, n, and % conversion specifiers */
3   #include <stdio.h>
4
5   int main()
6   {
7      int *ptr;      /* define pointer to int */
8      int x = 12345; /* initialize int x */
9      int y;         /* define int y */
10
11     ptr = &x;      /* assign address of x to ptr */
12     printf( "The value of ptr is %p\n", ptr );
13     printf( "The address of x is %p\n\n", &x );
14
15     printf( "Total characters printed on this line:%n", &y );
16     printf( " %d\n\n", y );
17
18     y = printf( "This line has 28 characters\n" );
19     printf( "%d characters were printed\n\n", y );
20
21     printf( "Printing a %% in a format control string\n" );
22
23     return 0; /* indicates successful termination */
24
25  } /* end main */
```

Fig. 9.7 Using the p, n and % conversion specifiers. (Part 1 of 2.)

```
The value of ptr is 0012FF78
The address of x is 0012FF78

Total characters printed on this line: 38

This line has 28 characters
28 characters were printed

Printing a % in a format control string
```

Fig. 9.7   Using the p, n and % conversion specifiers. (Part 2 of 2.)

 Common Programming Error 9.7

Trying to print a literal percent character using % rather than %% in the format control string. When % appears in a format control string, it must be followed by a conversion specifier.

9.8 Printing with Field Widths and Precision

The exact size of a field in which data is printed is specified by a *field width*. If the field width is larger than the data being printed, the data will normally be right-justified within that field. An integer representing the field width is inserted between the percent sign (%) and the conversion specifier (e.g., %4d). Figure 9.8 prints two groups of five numbers each, right-justifying those numbers that contain fewer digits than the field width. Note that the field width is increased to print values wider than the field and that the minus sign for a negative value uses one character position in the field width. Field widths can be used with all conversion specifiers.

```
1   /* Fig 9.8: fig09_08.c */
2   /* Printing integers right-justified */
3   #include <stdio.h>
4
5   int main()
6   {
7      printf( "%4d\n", 1 );
8      printf( "%4d\n", 12 );
9      printf( "%4d\n", 123 );
10     printf( "%4d\n", 1234 );
11     printf( "%4d\n\n", 12345 );
12
13     printf( "%4d\n", -1 );
14     printf( "%4d\n", -12 );
15     printf( "%4d\n", -123 );
16     printf( "%4d\n", -1234 );
17     printf( "%4d\n", -12345 );
18
19     return 0; /* indicates successful termination */
20
21  } /* end main */
```

Fig. 9.8   Right-justifying integers in a field. (Part 1 of 2.)

```
    1
   12
  123
 1234
12345

   -1
  -12
 -123
-1234
-12345
```

Fig. 9.8   Right-justifying integers in a field. (Part 2 of 2.)

Common Programming Error 9.8

Not providing a sufficiently large field width to handle a value to be printed can offset other data being printed and can produce confusing outputs. Know your data!

Function `printf` also provides the ability to specify the precision with which data is printed. Precision has different meanings for different data types. When used with integer conversion specifiers, precision indicates the minimum number of digits to be printed. If the printed value contains fewer digits than the specified precision, zeros are prefixed to the printed value until the total number of digits is equivalent to the precision. The default precision for integers is 1. When used with floating-point conversion specifiers e, E and f, the precision is the number of digits to appear after the decimal point. When used with conversion specifiers g and G, the precision is the maximum number of significant digits to be printed. When used with conversion specifier s, the precision is the maximum number of characters to be written from the string. To use precision, place a decimal point (.), followed by an integer representing the precision between the percent sign and the conversion specifier. Figure 9.9 demonstrates the use of precision in format control strings. Note that when a floating-point value is printed with a precision smaller than the original number of decimal places in the value, the value is rounded.

```
1   /* Fig 9.9: fig09_09.c */
2   /* Using precision while printing integers,
3      floating-point numbers, and strings */
4   #include <stdio.h>
5
6   int main()
7   {
8      int i = 873;                 /* initialize int i */
9      double f = 123.94536;        /* initialize double f */
10     char s[] = "Happy Birthday"; /* initialize char array s */
11
12     printf( "Using precision for integers\n" );
13     printf( "\t%.4d\n\t%.9d\n\n", i, i );
14
15     printf( "Using precision for floating-point numbers\n" );
16     printf( "\t%.3f\n\t%.3e\n\t%.3g\n\n", f, f, f );
```

Fig. 9.9   Using precisions to display information of several types (Part 1 of 2.).

```
17
18        printf( "Using precision for strings\n" );
19        printf( "\t%.11s\n", s );
20
21        return 0; /* indicates successful termination */
22
23    } /* end main */
```

```
Using precision for integers
        0873
        000000873

Using precision for floating-point numbers
        123.945
        1.239e+002
        124

Using precision for strings
        Happy Birth
```

Fig. 9.9   Using precisions to display information of several types (Part 2 of 2.).

The field width and the precision can be combined by placing the field width, followed by a decimal point, followed by a precision between the percent sign and the conversion specifier, as in the statement

```
printf( "%9.3f", 123.456789 );
```

which displays 123.457 with three digits to the right of the decimal point right-justified in a nine-digit field.

It is possible to specify the field width and the precision using integer expressions in the argument list following the format control string. To use this feature, insert an asterisk (*) in place of the field width or precision (or both). The matching int argument in the argument list is evaluated and used in place of the asterisk. A field width's value may be either positive or negative (which causes the output to be left-justified in the field as described in the next section). The statement

```
printf( "%*.*f", 7, 2, 98.736 );
```

uses 7 for the field width, 2 for the precision and outputs the value 98.74 right justified.

9.9 Using Flags in the `printf` Format Control String

Function printf also provides flags to supplement its output formatting capabilities. Five flags are available for use in format control strings (Fig. 9.10).

Flag	Description
– (minus sign)	Left-justify the output within the specified field.

Fig. 9.10   Format control string flags. (Part 1 of 2.)

Flag	Description
+ (plus sign)	Display a plus sign preceding positive values and a minus sign preceding negative values.
space	Print a space before a positive value not printed with the + flag.
#	Prefix 0 to the output value when used with the octal conversion specifier o.
	Prefix 0x or 0X to the output value when used with the hexadecimal conversion specifiers x or X.
	Force a decimal point for a floating-point number printed with e, E, f, g or G that does not contain a fractional part. (Normally the decimal point is only printed if a digit follows it.) For g and G specifiers, trailing zeros are not eliminated.
0 (zero)	Pad a field with leading zeros.

Fig. 9.10   Format control string flags. (Part 2 of 2.)

To use a flag in a format control string, place the flag immediately to the right of the percent sign. Several flags may be combined in one conversion specifier.

Figure 9.11 demonstrates right-justification and left-justification of a string, an integer, a character and a floating-point number.

```
1   /* Fig 9.11: fig09_11.c */
2   /* Right justifying and left justifying values */
3   #include <stdio.h>
4
5   int main()
6   {
7      printf( "%10s%10d%10c%10f\n\n", "hello", 7, 'a', 1.23 );
8      printf( "%-10s%-10d%-10c%-10f\n", "hello", 7, 'a', 1.23 );
9
10     return 0; /* indicates successful termination */
11
12  } /* end main */
```

```
     hello         7         a  1.230000

hello     7         a         1.230000
```

Fig. 9.11   Left-justifying strings in a field.

Figure 9.12 prints a positive number and a negative number, each with and without the *+ flag*. Note that the minus sign is displayed in both cases, but the plus sign is only displayed when the + flag is used.

```
1   /* Fig 9.12: fig09_12.c */
2   /* Printing numbers with and without the + flag */
3   #include <stdio.h>
4
5   int main()
6   {
7      printf( "%d\n%d\n", 786, -786 );
8      printf( "%+d\n%+d\n", 786, -786 );
9
10     return 0; /* indicates successful termination */
11
12  } /* end main */
```

```
786
-786
+786
-786
```

Fig. 9.12   Printing positive and negative numbers with and without the + flag.

Figure 9.13 prefixes a space to the positive number with the *space flag*. This is useful for aligning positive and negative numbers with the same number of digits. Note that the value -547 is not preceded by a space in the output because of its minus sign.

```
1   /* Fig 9.13: fig09_13.c */
2   /* Printing a space before signed values
3      not preceded by + or - */
4   #include <stdio.h>
5
6   int main()
7   {
8      printf( "% d\n% d\n", 547, -547 );
9
10     return 0; /* indicates successful termination */
11
12  } /* end main */
```

```
 547
-547
```

Fig. 9.13   Using the space flag.

Figure 9.14 uses the *# flag* to prefix 0 to the octal value and 0x and 0X to the hexadecimal values, and to force the decimal point on a value printed with g.

```
1   /* Fig 9.14: fig09_14.c */
2   /* Using the # flag with conversion specifiers
3      o, x, X and any floating-point specifier */
4   #include <stdio.h>
```

Fig. 9.14   Using the # flag. (Part 1 of 2.)

```
5
6   int main()
7   {
8      int c = 1427;        /* initialize c */
9      double p = 1427.0;  /* initialize p */
10
11     printf( "%#o\n", c );
12     printf( "%#x\n", c );
13     printf( "%#X\n", c );
14     printf( "\n%g\n", p );
15     printf( "%#g\n", p );
16
17     return 0; /* indicates successful termination */
18
19  } /* end main */
```

```
02623
0x593
0X593

1427
1427.00
```

Fig. 9.14   Using the # flag. (Part 2 of 2.)

Figure 9.15 combines the + flag and the 0 (zero) flag to print 452 in a 9-space field with a + sign and leading zeros, then prints 452 again using only the 0 flag and a 9-space field.

```
1   /* Fig 9.15: fig09_15.c */
2   /* Printing with the 0( zero ) flag fills in leading zeros */
3   #include <stdio.h>
4
5   int main()
6   {
7      printf( "%+09d\n", 452 );
8      printf( "%09d\n", 452 );
9
10     return 0; /* indicates successful termination */
11
12  } /* end main */
```

```
+00000452
000000452
```

Fig. 9.15   Using the 0 (zero) flag.

9.10 Printing Literals and Escape Sequences

Most literal characters to be printed in a printf statement can simply be included in the format control string. However, there are several "problem" characters, such as the quotation mark (") that delimits the format control string itself. Various control characters, such as newline and tab, must be represented by *escape sequences*. An escape sequence is represented by a backslash (\), followed by a particular *escape character*. Figure 9.16 lists the escape sequences and the actions they cause.

Common Programming Error 9.9

Attempting to print as literal data in a printf *statement a single quote, double quote, question mark or backslash character without preceding that character with a backslash to form a proper escape sequence is an error.*

Escape sequence	Description
\' (single quote)	Output the single quote (') character.
\" (double quote)	Output the double quote (") character.
\? (question mark)	Output the question mark (?) character.
\\ (backslash)	Output the backslash (\) character.
\a (alert or bell)	Cause an audible (bell) or visual alert.
\b (backspace)	Move the cursor back one position on the current line.
\f (new page or form feed)	Move the cursor to the start of the next logical page.
\n (newline)	Move the cursor to the beginning of the next line.
\r (carriage return)	Move the cursor to the beginning of the current line.
\t (horizontal tab)	Move the cursor to the next horizontal tab position.
\v (vertical tab)	Move the cursor to the next vertical tab position.

Fig. 9.16   Escape sequences.

9.11 Formatting Input with scanf

Precise input formatting can be accomplished with scanf. Every scanf statement contains a format control string that describes the format of the data to be input. The format control string consists of conversion specifiers and literal characters. Function scanf has the following input formatting capabilities:

1. Inputting all types of data.

2. Inputting specific characters from an input stream.

3. Skipping specific characters in the input stream.

Function scanf is written in the following form:

scanf(*format-control-string*, *other-arguments*);

format-control-string describes the formats of the input, and *other-arguments* are pointers to variables in which the input will be stored.

Good Programming Practice 9.2

When inputting data, prompt the user for one data item or a few data items at a time. Avoid asking the user to enter many data items in response to a single prompt.

Figure 9.17 summarizes the conversion specifiers used to input all types of data. The remainder of this section provides programs that demonstrate reading data with the various `scanf` conversion specifiers.

Conversion specifier	Description
Integers	
d	Read an optionally signed decimal integer. The corresponding argument is a pointer to an integer.
i	Read an optionally signed decimal, octal or hexadecimal integer. The corresponding argument is a pointer to an integer.
o	Read an octal integer. The corresponding argument is a pointer to an unsigned integer.
u	Read an unsigned decimal integer. The corresponding argument is a pointer to an unsigned integer.
x or X	Read a hexadecimal integer. The corresponding argument is a pointer to an unsigned integer.
h or l	Place before any of the integer conversion specifiers to indicate that a `short` or `long` integer is to be input.
Floating-point numbers	
e, E, f, g or G	Read a floating-point value. The corresponding argument is a pointer to a floating-point variable.
l or L	Place before any of the floating-point conversion specifiers to indicate that a `double` or `long double` value is to be input. The corresponding argument is a pointer to a `double` or `long double` variable.
Characters and strings	
c	Read a character. The corresponding argument is a pointer to a `char`; no null (`'\0'`) is added.
s	Read a string. The corresponding argument is a pointer to an array of type `char` that is large enough to hold the string and a terminating null (`'\0'`) character—which is automatically added.
Scan set	
[scan characters]	Scan a string for a set of characters that are stored in an array.
Miscellaneous	
p	Read an address of the same form produced when an address is output with %p in a `printf` statement.
n	Store the number of characters input so far in this `scanf`. The corresponding argument is a pointer to integer
%	Skip a percent sign (%) in the input.

Fig. 9.17 Conversion specifiers for `scanf`.

Figure 9.18 reads integers with the various integer conversion specifiers and displays the integers as decimal numbers. Note that %i is capable of inputting decimal, octal and hexadecimal integers.

```
1   /* Fig 9.18: fig09_18.c */
2   /* Reading integers */
3   #include <stdio.h>
4
5   int main()
6   {
7      int a;
8      int b;
9      int c;
10     int d;
11     int e;
12     int f;
13     int g;
14
15     printf( "Enter seven integers: " );
16     scanf( "%d%i%i%i%o%u%x", &a, &b, &c, &d, &e, &f, &g );
17
18     printf( "The input displayed as decimal integers is:\n" );
19     printf( "%d %d %d %d %d %d %d\n", a, b, c, d, e, f, g );
20
21     return 0; /* indicates successful termination */
22
23  } /* end main */
```

```
Enter seven integers: -70 -70 070 0x70 70 70 70
The input displayed as decimal integers is:
-70 -70 56 112 56 70 112
```

Fig. 9.18   Reading input with integer conversion specifiers.

When inputting floating-point numbers, any of the floating-point conversion specifiers e, E, f, g or G can be used. Figure 9.19 reads three floating-point numbers, one with each of the three types of floating conversion specifiers, and displays all three numbers with conversion specifier f. Note that the program output confirms the fact that floating-point values are imprecise—this fact is highlighted by the third value printed.

```
1   /* Fig 9.19: fig09_19.c */
2   /* Reading floating-point numbers */
3   #include <stdio.h>
4
5   /* function main begins program execution */
6   int main()
7   {
8      double a;
9      double b;
10     double c;
```

Fig. 9.19   Reading input with floating-point conversion specifiers. (Part 1 of 2.)

```
11
12      printf( "Enter three floating-point numbers: \n" );
13      scanf( "%le%lf%lg", &a, &b, &c );
14
15      printf( "Here are the numbers entered in plain\n" );
16      printf( "floating-point notation:\n" );
17      printf( "%f\n%f\n%f\n", a, b, c );
18
19      return 0; /* indicates successful termination */
20
21   } /* end main */
```

```
Enter three floating-point numbers:
1.27987 1.27987e+03 3.38476e-06
Here are the numbers entered in plain
floating-point notation:
1.279870
1279.870000
0.000003
```

Fig. 9.19   Reading input with floating-point conversion specifiers. (Part 2 of 2.)

Characters and strings are input using the conversion specifiers c and s, respectively. Figure 9.20 prompts the user to enter a string. The program inputs the first character of the string with %c and stores it in the character variable x, then inputs the remainder of the string with %s and stores it in character array y.

```
1    /* Fig 9.20: fig09_20.c */
2    /* Reading characters and strings */
3    #include <stdio.h>
4
5    int main()
6    {
7       char x;
8       char y[ 9 ];
9
10      printf( "Enter a string: " );
11      scanf( "%c%s", &x, y );
12
13      printf( "The input was:\n" );
14      printf( "the character \"%c\" ", x );
15      printf( "and the string \"%s\"\n", y );
16
17      return 0; /* indicates successful termination */
18
19   } /* end main */
```

```
Enter a string: Sunday
The input was:
the character "S" and the string "unday"
```

Fig. 9.20   Inputting characters and strings.

A sequence of characters can be input using a *scan set*. A scan set is a set of characters enclosed in square brackets, [], and preceded by a percent sign in the format control string. A scan set scans the characters in the input stream, looking only for those characters that match characters contained in the scan set. Each time a character is matched, it is stored in the scan set's corresponding argument—a pointer to a character array. The scan set stops inputting characters when a character that is not contained in the scan set is encountered. If the first character in the input stream does not match a character in the scan set, only the null character is stored in the array. Figure 9.21 uses the scan set [aeiou] to scan the input stream for vowels. Notice that the first seven letters of the input are read. The eighth letter (h) is not in the scan set and therefore the scanning is terminated.

```c
1   /* Fig 9.21: fig09_21.c */
2   /* Using a scan set */
3   #include <stdio.h>
4
5   /* function main begins program execution */
6   int main()
7   {
8      char z[ 9 ]; /* define array z */
9
10     printf( "Enter string: " );
11     scanf( "%[aeiou]", z ); /* search for set of characters */
12
13     printf( "The input was \"%s\"\n", z );
14
15     return 0; /* indicates successful termination */
16
17  } /* end main */
```

```
Enter string: ooeeooahah
The input was "ooeeooa"
```

Fig. 9.21   Using a scan set.

The scan set can also be used to scan for characters not contained in the scan set by using an *inverted scan set*. To create an inverted scan set, place a *caret (^)* in the square brackets before the scan characters. This causes characters not appearing in the scan set to be stored. When a character contained in the inverted scan set is encountered, input terminates. Figure 9.22 uses the inverted scan set [^aeiou] to search for consonants—more properly to search for "nonvowels."

```c
1   /* Fig 9.22: fig09_22.c */
2   /* Using an inverted scan set */
3   #include <stdio.h>
4
5   int main()
6   {
7      char z[ 9 ];
```

Fig. 9.22   Using an inverted scan set. (Part 1 of 2.)

```
8
9       printf( "Enter a string: " );
10      scanf( "%[^aeiou]", z ); /* inverted scan set */
11
12      printf( "The input was \"%s\"\n", z );
13
14      return 0; /* indicates successful termination */
15
16   } /* end main */
```

```
Enter a string: String
The input was "Str"
```

Fig. 9.22 Using an inverted scan set. (Part 2 of 2.)

A field width can be used in a `scanf` conversion specifier to read a specific number of characters from the input stream. Figure 9.23 inputs a series of consecutive digits as a two-digit integer and an integer consisting of the remaining digits in the input stream.

```
1    /* Fig 9.23: fig09_23.c */
2    /* inputting data with a field width */
3    #include <stdio.h>
4
5    int main()
6    {
7       int x;
8       int y;
9
10      printf( "Enter a six digit integer: " );
11      scanf( "%2d%d", &x, &y );
12
13      printf( "The integers input were %d and %d\n", x, y );
14
15      return 0; /* indicates successful termination */
16
17   } /* end main */
```

```
Enter a six digit integer: 123456
The integers input were 12 and 3456
```

Fig. 9.23 Inputting data with a field width.

Often it is necessary to skip certain characters in the input stream. For example, a date could be entered as

11-10-1999

Each number in the date needs to be stored, but the dashes that separate the numbers can be discarded. To eliminate unnecessary characters, include them in the format control string of `scanf` (*whitespace* characters—such as space, newline and tab—skip all leading whitespace). For example, to skip the dashes in the input, use the statement

```
scanf( "%d-%d-%d", &month, &day, &year );
```

Although, this `scanf` does eliminate the dashes in the preceding input, it is possible that the date could be entered as

10/11/1999

In this case, the preceding `scanf` would not eliminate the unnecessary characters. For this reason, `scanf` provides the *assignment suppression character* *. The assignment suppression character enables `scanf` to read any type of data from the input and discard it without assigning it to a variable. Figure 9.24 uses the assignment suppression character in the %c conversion specifier to indicate that a character appearing in the input stream should be read and discarded. Only the month, day and year are stored. The values of the variables are printed to demonstrate that they are in fact input correctly. Note that the argument lists for each `scanf` call do not contain variables for the conversion specifiers that use the assignment suppression character. The corresponding characters are simply discarded.

```
1   /* Fig 9.24: fig09_24.c */
2   /* Reading and discarding characters from the input stream */
3   #include <stdio.h>
4
5   int main()
6   {
7      int month1;
8      int day1;
9      int year1;
10     int month2;
11     int day2;
12     int year2;
13
14     printf( "Enter a date in the form mm-dd-yyyy: " );
15     scanf( "%d%*c%d%*c%d", &month1, &day1, &year1 );
16
17     printf( "month = %d  day = %d  year = %d\n\n", month1, day1, year1 );
18
19     printf( "Enter a date in the form mm/dd/yyyy: " );
20     scanf( "%d%*c%d%*c%d", &month2, &day2, &year2 );
21
22     printf( "month = %d  day = %d  year = %d\n", month2, day2, year2 );
23
24     return 0; /* indicates successful termination */
25
26  } /* end main */
```

```
Enter a date in the form mm-dd-yyyy: 11-18-2003
month = 11   day = 18   year = 2003

Enter a date in the form mm/dd/yyyy: 11/18/2003
month = 11   day = 18   year = 2003
```

Fig. 9.24   Reading and discarding characters from the input stream.

SUMMARY

- All input and output is dealt with in streams—sequences of characters organized into lines. Each line consists of zero or more characters and ends with a newline character.

- Normally, the standard input steam is connected to the keyboard, and the standard output stream is connected to the computer screen.

- Operating systems often allow the standard input and standard output streams to be redirected to other devices.

- The printf format control string describes the formats in which the output values appear. The format control string consists of conversion specifiers, flags, field widths, precisions and literal characters.

- Integers are printed with the following conversion specifiers: d or i for optionally signed integers, o for unsigned integers in octal form, u for unsigned integers in decimal form and x or X for unsigned integers in hexadecimal form. The modifier h or l is prefixed to the preceding conversion specifiers to indicate a short or long integer, respectively.

- Floating-point values are printed with the following conversion specifiers: e or E for exponential notation, f for regular floating-point notation, and g or G for either e (or E) notation or f notation. When the g (or G) conversion specifier is indicated, the e (or E) conversion specifier is used if the value's exponent is less than –4 or greater than or equal to the precision with which the value is printed.

- The precision for the g and G conversion specifiers indicates the maximum number of significant digits printed.

- The conversion specifier c prints a character.

- The conversion specifier s prints a string of characters ending in the null character.

- The conversion specifier p displays an address in an implementation-defined manner (on many systems, hexadecimal notation is used).

- The conversion specifier n stores the number of characters already output in the current printf statement. The corresponding argument is a pointer to an integer.

- The conversion specifier %% causes a literal % to be output.

- If the field width is larger than the object being printed, the object is right-justified in the field by default.

- Field widths can be used with all conversion specifiers.

- Precision used with integer conversion specifiers indicates the minimum number of digits printed. If the value contains fewer digits than the precision specified, zeros are prefixed to the printed value until the number of digits is equivalent to the precision.

- Precision used with floating-point conversion specifiers e, E and f indicates the number of digits that appear after the decimal point. Precision used with floating-point conversion specifiers g and G indicates the number of significant digits to appear.

- Precision used with conversion specifier s indicates the number of characters to be printed.

- The field width and the precision can be combined by placing the field width, followed by a decimal point, followed by the precision between the percent sign and the conversion specifier.

- It is possible to specify the field width and the precision through integer expressions in the argument list following the format control string. To use this feature, insert an asterisk (*) in place of the field width or precision. The matching argument in the argument list is evaluated and used in place of the asterisk. The value of the argument can be negative for the field width, but must be positive for the precision.

- The – flag left-justifies its argument in a field.

- The + flag prints a plus sign for positive values and a minus sign for negative values. The space flag prints a space preceding a positive value not displayed with the + flag.
- The # flag prefixes 0 to octal values and 0x or 0X to hexadecimal values, and forces the decimal point to be printed for floating-point values printed with e, E, f, g or G (normally the decimal point is displayed only if the value contains a fractional part).
- The 0 flag prints leading zeros for a value that does not occupy its entire field width.
- Precise input formatting is accomplished with the scanf library function.
- Integers are input with scanf with the conversion specifiers d and i for optionally signed integers and o, u, x or X for unsigned integers. The modifiers h and l are placed before an integer conversion specifier to input a short or long integer, respectively.
- Floating-point values are input with scanf with the conversion specifiers e, E, f, g or G. The modifiers l and L are placed before any of the floating-point conversion specifiers to indicate that the input value is a double or long double value, respectively.
- Characters are input with scanf with the conversion specifier c.
- Strings are input with scanf with the conversion specifier s.
- A scan set in a scanf scans the characters in the input, looking only for those characters that match characters contained in the scan set. When a character is matched, it is stored in a character array. The scan set stops inputting characters when a character not contained in the scan set is encountered.
- To create an inverted scan set, place a caret (∧) in the square brackets before the scan characters. This causes characters input with scanf and not appearing in the scan set to be stored until a character contained in the inverted scan set is encountered.
- Address values are input with scanf with the conversion specifier p.
- Conversion specifier n stores the number of characters input previously in the current scanf. The corresponding argument is a pointer to int.
- The conversion specifier %% with scanf matches a single % character in the input.
- The assignment suppression character reads data from the input stream and discards the data.
- A field width is used in scanf to read a specific number of characters from the input stream.

TERMINOLOGY

# flag	\t escape sequence
% conversion specifier	\v escape sequence
* in field width	alignment
* in precision	assignment suppression character (*)
+ (plus sign) flag	blank insertion
– (minus sign) flag	c conversion specifier
0 (zero) flag	caret (∧)
<stdio.h>	conversion specification
\" escape sequence	conversion specifiers
\' escape sequence	d conversion specifier
\? escape sequence	e or E conversion specifier
\\ escape sequence	escape sequence
\a escape sequence	exponential floating-point format
\b escape sequence	f conversion specifier
\f escape sequence	field width
\n escape sequence	flag
\r escape sequence	floating-point

COMMON PROGRAMMING ERRORS

9.1 Forgetting to enclose a format control string in quotation marks is a syntax error.

9.2 Printing a negative value with a conversion specifier that expects an `unsigned` value.

9.3 Using `%c` to print a string is an error. The conversion specifier `%c` expects a `char` argument. A string is a pointer to `char` (i.e., a `char *`).

9.4 Using `%s` to print a `char` argument, on some systems, causes a fatal execution-time error called an access violation. The conversion specifier `%s` expects an argument of type pointer to `char`.

9.5 Using single quotes around character strings is a syntax error. Character strings must be enclosed in double quotes.

9.6 Using double quotes around a character constant creates a string consisting of two characters, the second of which is the terminating null. A character constant is a single character enclosed in single quotes.

9.7 Trying to print a literal percent character using `%` rather than `%%` in the format control string. When `%` appears in a format control string, it must be followed by a conversion specifier.

9.8 Not providing a sufficiently large field width to handle a value to be printed can offset other data being printed and can produce confusing outputs. Know your data!

9.9 Attempting to print as literal data in a `printf` statement a single quote, double quote, question mark or backslash character without preceding that character with a backslash to form a proper escape sequence is an error.

ERROR-PREVENTION TIP

9.1 When outputting data, be sure that the user is aware of situations in which data may be imprecise due to formatting (e.g., rounding errors from specifying precisions).

GOOD PROGRAMMING PRACTICES

9.1 Edit outputs neatly for presentation to make program outputs more readable and reduce user errors.

9.2 When inputting data, prompt the user for one data item or a few data items at a time. Avoid asking the user to enter many data items in response to a single prompt.

PORTABILITY TIP

9.1 The conversion specifier p displays an address in an implementation-defined manner (on many systems, hexadecimal notation is used rather than decimal notation).

SELF-REVIEW EXERCISES

9.1 Fill in the blanks in each of the following:
a) All input and output is dealt with in the form of _____.
b) The _____ stream is normally connected to the keyboard.
c) The _____ stream is normally connected to the computer screen.
d) Precise output formatting is accomplished with the _____ function.
e) The format control string may contain _____, _____, _____, and _____.
f) The conversion specifier _____ or _____ may be used to output a signed decimal integer.
g) The conversion specifiers _____, _____ and _____ are used to display unsigned integers in octal, decimal and hexadecimal form, respectively.
h) The modifiers _____ and _____ are placed before the integer conversion specifiers to indicate that short or long integer values are to be displayed.
i) The conversion specifier _____ is used to display a floating-point value in exponential notation.
j) The modifier _____ is placed before any floating-point conversion specifier to indicate that a long double value is to be displayed.
k) The conversion specifiers e, E and f are displayed with _____ digits of precision to the right of the decimal point if no precision is specified.
l) The conversion specifiers _____ and _____ are used to print strings and characters, respectively.
m) All strings end in the _____ character.
n) The field width and precision in a printf conversion specifier can be controlled with integer expressions by substituting a(n) _____ for the field width or for the precision and placing an integer expression in the corresponding argument of the argument list.
o) The _____ flag causes output to be left-justified in a field.
p) The _____ flag causes values to be displayed with either a plus sign or a minus sign.
q) Precise input formatting is accomplished with the _____ function.
r) A(n) _____ is used to scan a string for specific characters and store the characters in an array.
s) The conversion specifier _____ can be used to input optionally signed octal, decimal and hexadecimal integers.
t) The conversion specifier _____ can be used to input a double value.
u) The _____ is used to read data from the input stream and discard it without assigning it to a variable.
v) A(n) _____ can be used in a scanf conversion specifier to indicate that a specific number of characters or digits should be read from the input stream.

9.2 Find the error in each of the following and explain how the error can be corrected.
a) The following statement should print the character 'c'.
```
printf( "%s\n", 'c' );
```
b) The following statement should print 9.375%.

```
    printf( "%.3f%", 9.375 );
```
c) The following statement should print the first character of the string "Monday".
```
    printf( "%c\n", "Monday" );
```
d) `printf( ""A string in quotes"" );`
e) `printf( %d%d, 12, 20 );`
f) `printf( "%c", "x" );`
g) `printf( "%s\n", 'Richard' );`

9.3   Write a statement for each of the following:
  a) Print 1234 right-justified in a 10 digit field.
  b) Print 123.456789 in exponential notation with a sign (+ or -) and 3 digits of precision.
  c) Read a double value into variable number.
  d) Print 100 in octal form preceded by 0.
  e) Read a string into character array string.
  f) Read characters into array n until a nondigit character is encountered.
  g) Use integer variables x and y to specify the field width and precision used to display the double value 87.4573.
  h) Read a value of the form 3.5%. Store the percentage in float variable percent and eliminate the % from the input stream. Do not use the assignment suppression character.
  i) Print 3.333333 as a long double value with a sign (+ or -)in a field of 20 characters with a precision of 3.

ANSWERS TO SELF-REVIEW EXERCISES

9.1   a) Streams. b) Standard input. c) Standard output. d) printf. e) Conversion specifiers, flags, field widths, precisions, literal characters. f) d, i. g) o, u, x (or X). h) h, l. i) e (or E). j) L. k) 6. l) s, c. m) NULL ('\0'). n) asterisk (*). o) – (minus). p) + (plus). q) scanf. r) Scan set. s) i. t) le, lE, lf, lg or lG. u) Assignment suppression character (*). v) Field width.

9.2   a) Error: Conversion specifier s expects an argument of type pointer to char.
          Correction: To print the character 'c', use the conversion specifier %c or change 'c' to "c".
  b) Error: Trying to print the literal character % without using the conversion specifier %%.
          Correction: Use %% to print a literal % character.
  a) Error: Conversion specifier c expects an argument of type char.
          Correction: To print the first character of "Monday" use the conversion specifier %1s.
  b) Error: Trying to print the literal character " without using the \" escape sequence.
          Correction: Replace each quote in the inner set of quotes with \".
  c) Error: The format control string is not enclosed in double quotes.
          Correction: Enclose %d%d in double quotes.
  d) Error: The character x is enclosed in double quotes.
          Correction: Character constants to be printed with %c must be enclosed in single quotes.
  e) Error: The string to be printed is enclosed in single quotes.
          Correction: Use double quotes instead of single quotes to represent a string.

9.3   a) `printf( "%10d\n", 1234 );`
  b) `printf( "%+.3e\n", 123.456789 );`
  c) `scanf( "%lf", &number );`
  d) `printf( "%#o\n", 100 );`
  e) `scanf( "%s", string );`
  f) `scanf( "%[0123456789]", n );`
  g) `printf( "%*.*f\n", x, y, 87.4573 );`

h) `scanf( "%f%%", &percent );`
i) `printf( "%+20.3Lf\n", 3.333333 );`

EXERCISES

9.4 Write a `printf` or `scanf` statement for each of the following:
a) Print unsigned integer 40000 left justified in a 15-digit field with 8 digits.
b) Read a hexadecimal value into variable `hex`.
c) Print 200 with and without a sign.
d) Print 100 in hexadecimal form preceded by 0x.
e) Read characters into array `s` until the letter `p` is encountered.
f) Print 1.234 in a 9-digit field with preceding zeros.
g) Read a time of the form `hh:mm:ss`, storing the parts of the time in the integer variables `hour`, `minute` and `second`. Skip the colons (:) in the input stream. Use the assignment suppression character.
h) Read a string of the form `"characters"` from the standard input. Store the string in character array `s`. Eliminate the quotation marks from the input stream.
i) Read a time of the form `hh:mm:ss`, storing the parts of the time in the integer variables `hour`, `minute` and `second`. Skip the colons (:) in the input stream. Do not use the assignment-suppression character.

9.5 Show what is printed by each of the following statements. If a statement is incorrect, indicate why.
a) `printf( "%-10d\n", 10000 );`
b) `printf( "%c\n", "This is a string" );`
c) `printf( "%*.*1f\n", 8, 3, 1024.987654 );`
d) `printf( "%#o\n%#X\n%#e\n", 17, 17, 1008.83689 );`
e) `printf( "% 1d\n%+1d\n", 1000000, 1000000 );`
f) `printf( "%10.2E\n", 444.93738 );`
g) `printf( "%10.2g\n", 444.93738 );`
h) `printf( "%d\n", 10.987 );`

9.6 Find the error(s) in each of the following program segments. Explain how each error can be corrected.
a) `printf( "%s\n", 'Happy Birthday' );`
b) `printf( "%c\n", 'Hello' );`
c) `printf( "%c\n", "This is a string" );`
d) The following statement should print "Bon Voyage":
`printf( ""%s"", "Bon Voyage" );`
e) `char day[] = "Sunday";`
`printf( "%s\n", day[ 3 ] );`
f) `printf( 'Enter your name: ' );`
g) `printf( %f, 123.456 );`
h) The following statement should print the characters 'O' and 'K':
`printf( "%s%s\n", 'O', 'K' );`
i) `char s[ 10 ];`
`scanf( "%c", s[ 7 ] );`

9.7 Write a program that loads 10-element array `number` with random integers from 1 to 1000. For each value, print the value and a running total of the number of characters printed. Use the %n conversion specifier to determine the number of characters output for each value. Print the total number of characters output for all values up to and including the current value each time the current value is printed. The output should have the following format:

```
Value       Total characters
342         3
1000        7
963         10
6           11
etc.
```

9.8   Write a program to test the difference between the %d and %i conversion specifiers when used in scanf statements. Use the statements

```
scanf( "%i%d", &x, &y );
printf( "%d %d\n", x, y );
```

to input and print the values. Test the program with the following sets of input data:

```
    10       10
   -10      -10
   010      010
  0x10     0x10
```

9.9   Write a program that prints pointer values using all the integer conversion specifiers and the %p conversion specifier. Which ones print strange values? Which ones cause errors? In which format does the %p conversion specifier display the address on your system?

9.10   Write a program to test the results of printing the integer value 12345 and the floating-point value 1.2345 in various size fields. What happens when the values are printed in fields containing fewer digits than the values?

9.11   Write a program that prints the value 100.453627 rounded to the nearest digit, tenth, hundredth, thousandth and ten thousandth.

9.12   Write a program that inputs a string from the keyboard and determines the length of the string. Print the string using twice the length as the field width.

9.13   Write a program that converts integer Fahrenheit temperatures from 0 to 212 degrees to floating-point Celsius temperatures with 3 digits of precision. Use the formula

```
celsius = 5.0 / 9.0 * ( fahrenheit - 32 );
```

to perform the calculation. The output should be printed in two right-justified columns of 10 characters each, and the Celsius temperatures should be preceded by a sign for both positive and negative values.

9.14   Write a program to test all the escape sequences in Figure 9.16. For the escape sequences that move the cursor, print a character before and after printing the escape sequence so it is clear where the cursor has moved.

9.15   Write a program that determines whether ? can be printed as part of a printf format control string as a literal character rather than using the \? escape sequence.

9.16   Write a program that inputs the value 437 using each of the scanf integer conversion specifiers. Print each input value using all the integer conversion specifiers.

9.17   Write a program that uses each of the conversion specifiers e, f and g to input the value 1.2345. Print the values of each variable to prove that each conversion specifier can be used to input this same value.

9.18   In some programming languages, strings are entered surrounded by either single *or* double quotation marks. Write a program that reads the three strings suzy, "suzy" and 'suzy'. Are the single and double quotes ignored by C or read as part of the string?

9.19   Write a program that determines whether ? can be printed as the character constant '?' rather than the character constant escape sequence '\?' using conversion specifier %c in the format control string of a printf statement.

9.20   Write a program that uses the conversion specifier g to output the value 9876.12345. Print the value with precisions ranging from 1 to 9.

10

C Structures, Unions, Bit Manipulations and Enumerations

Objectives

- To be able to create and use structures, unions and enumerations.
- To be able to pass structures to functions by value and by reference.
- To be able to manipulate data with the bitwise operators.
- To be able to create bit fields for storing data compactly.

I could never make out what those damned dots meant.
Winston Churchill

But yet an union in partition.
William Shakespeare

You can include me out.
Samuel Goldwyn

The same old charitable lie
Repeated as the years scoot by
Perpetually makes a hit—
"You really haven't changed a bit!"
Margaret Fishback

Outline

10.1 Introduction

Structures—sometimes referred to as *aggregates*—are collections of related variables under one name. Structures may contain variables of many different data types—in contrast to arrays that contain only elements of the same data type. Structures are commonly used to define records to be stored in files (see Chapter 11, File Processing). Pointers and structures facilitate the formation of more complex data structures such as linked lists, queues, stacks and trees (see Chapter 12, Data Structures).

10.2 Structure Definitions

Structures are *derived data types*—they are constructed using objects of other types. Consider the following structure definition:

```
struct card {
   char *face;
   char *suit;
};
```

Keyword `struct` introduces the structure definition. The identifier `card` is the *structure tag*, which names the structure definition and is used with the keyword `struct` to declare variables of the *structure type*. In this example, the structure type is `struct card`. Variables declared within the braces of the structure definition are the structure's *members*. Members of the same structure type must have unique names, but two different structure types may contain members of the same name without conflict (we will soon see why). Each structure definition must end with a semicolon.

Common Programming Error 10.1

Forgetting the semicolon that terminates a structure definition is a syntax error.

The definition of struct card contains two members of type char *—face and suit. Structure members can be variables of the primitive data types (e.g., int, float, etc.), or aggregates, such as arrays and other structures. As we saw in Chapter 6, each element of an array must be of the same type. Structure members, however, can be of a variety of data types. For example,

```
struct employee {
    char firstName[ 20 ];
    char lastName[ 20 ];
    int age;
    char gender;
    double hourlySalary;
};
```

contains character array members for the first and last names, an int member for the employee's age, a char member that would contain 'M' or 'F' for the employee's gender and a double member for the employee's hourly salary.

A structure cannot contain an instance of itself. For example, a variable of type struct employee cannot be declared in the definition for struct employee. A pointer to struct employee, however, may be included. For example,

```
struct employee2 {
    char firstName[ 20 ];
    char lastName[ 20 ];
    int age;
    char gender;
    double hourlySalary;
    struct employee2 person;   /* ERROR */
    struct employee2 *ePtr;    /* pointer */
};
```

struct employee2 contains an instance of itself (person), which is an error. Because ePtr is a pointer (to type struct employee2), it is permitted in the definition. A structure containing a member that is a pointer to the same structure type is referred to as a *self-referential structure*. Self-referential structures are used in Chapter 12 to build linked data structures.

Structure definitions do not reserve any space in memory, rather each definition creates a new data type that is used to define variables. Structure variables are defined like variables of other types. The definition

```
struct card aCard, deck[ 52 ], *cardPtr;
```

declares aCard to be a variable of type struct card, declares deck to be an array with 52 elements of type struct card and declares cardPtr to be a pointer to struct card. Variables of a given structure type may also be declared by placing a comma-separated list of the variable names between the closing brace of the structure definition and the semicolon that ends the structure definition. For example, the preceding definition could have been incorporated into the struct card structure definition as follows:

```
struct card {
    char *face;
    char *suit;
} aCard, deck[ 52 ], *cardPtr;
```

The structure tag name is optional. If a structure definition does not contain a structure tag name, variables of the structure type may be declared only in the structure definition—not in a separate declaration.

Good Programming Practice 10.1

Always provide a structure tag name when creating a structure type. The structure tag name is convenient for declaring new variables of the structure type later in the program.

Good Programming Practice 10.2

Choosing a meaningful structure tag name helps make a program self-documenting.

The only valid operations that may be performed on structures are the following: assigning structure variables to structure variables of the same type, taking the address (&) of a structure variable, accessing the members of a structure variable (see Section 10.4) and using the `sizeof` operator to determine the size of a structure variable.

Common Programming Error 10.2

Assigning a structure of one type to a structure of a different type is a compilation error.

Structures may not be compared using operators == and != because structure members are not necessarily stored in consecutive bytes of memory. Sometimes there are "holes" in a structure because computers may store specific data types only on certain memory boundaries such as halfword, word or doubleword boundaries. A word is a standard memory unit used to store data in a computer—usually 2 bytes or 4 bytes. Consider the following structure definition in which `sample1` and `sample2` of type `struct example` are declared:

```
struct example {
    char c;
    int i;
} sample1, sample2;
```

A computer with 2-byte words may require that each member of `struct example` be aligned on a word boundary, i.e., at the beginning of a word (this is machine dependent). Figure 10.1 shows a sample storage alignment for a variable of type `struct example` that has been assigned the character `'a'` and the integer 97 (the bit representations of the values are shown). If the members are stored beginning at word boundaries, there is a 1-byte hole (byte 1 in the figure) in the storage for variables of type `struct example`. The value in the 1-byte hole is undefined. Even if the member values of `sample1` and `sample2` are in fact equal, the structures are not necessarily, equal because the undefined 1-byte holes are not likely to contain identical values.

Byte	0	1	2	3
	01100001		00000000	01100001

Fig. 10.1   Possible storage alignment for a variable of type `struct example` showing an undefined area in memory.

Common Programming Error 10.3

Comparing structures is a syntax error.

Portability Tip 10.1

Because the size of data items of a particular type is machine dependent and because storage alignment considerations are machine dependent, so too is the representation of a structure.

10.3 Initializing Structures

Structures can be initialized using initializer lists as with arrays. To initialize a structure, follow the variable name in the definition with an equals sign and a brace-enclosed, comma-separated list of initializers. For example, the declaration

```
struct card aCard = { "Three", "Hearts" };
```

creates variable `aCard` to be of type `struct card` (as defined in Section 10.2) and initializes member `face` to `"Three"` and member `suit` to `"Hearts"`. If there are fewer initializers in the list than members in the structure, the remaining members are automatically initialized to 0 (or NULL if the member is a pointer). Structure variables defined outside a function definition (i.e., externally) are initialized to 0 or NULL if they are not explicitly initialized in the external definition. Structure variables may also be initialized in assignment statements by assigning a structure variable of the same type, or by assigning values to the individual members of the structure.

10.4 Accessing Members of Structures

Two operators are used to access members of structures: The *structure member operator* (`.`)—also called the *dot operator*—and the *structure pointer operator* (`->`)—also called the *arrow operator*. The structure member operator accesses a structure member via the structure variable name. For example, to print member `suit` of structure variable `aCard` defined in Section 10.3, use the statement

```
printf( "%s", aCard.suit ); /* displays Hearts */
```

The structure pointer operator—consisting of a minus (-) sign and a greater than (>) sign with no intervening spaces—accesses a structure member via a *pointer to the structure*. Assume that the pointer `cardPtr` has been declared to point to `struct card` and that the address of structure `aCard` has been assigned to `cardPtr`. To print member `suit` of structure `aCard` with pointer `cardPtr`, use the statement

```
printf( "%s", cardPtr->suit ); /* displays Hearts */
```

The expression `cardPtr->suit` is equivalent to `(*cardPtr).suit`, which dereferences the pointer and accesses the member `suit` using the structure member operator. The parentheses are needed here because the structure member operator (`.`) has a higher precedence than the pointer dereferencing operator (`*`). The structure pointer operator and structure member operator, along with parentheses (for calling functions) and brackets (`[]`) used for array subscripting, have the highest operator precedence and associate from left to right.

Error-Prevention Tip 10.1
Avoid using the same names for members of structures of different types. This is allowed, but it may cause confusion.

Good Programming Practice 10.3
Do not put spaces around the -> and . operators. Omitting spaces helps emphasize that the expressions the operators are contained in are essentially single variable names.

Common Programming Error 10.4
Inserting space between the - and > components of the structure pointer operator (or inserting spaces between the components of any other multiple keystroke operator except ?:) is a syntax error.

Common Programming Error 10.5
Attempting to refer to a member of a structure by using only the member's name is a syntax error.

Common Programming Error 10.6
Not using parentheses when referring to a structure member that uses a pointer and the structure member operator (e.g., *cardPtr.suit) is a syntax error.

The program of Fig. 10.2 demonstrates the use of the structure member and structure pointer operators. Using the structure member operator, the members of structure aCard are assigned the values "Ace" and "Spades", respectively (lines 18 and 19). Pointer cardPtr is assigned the address of structure aCard (line 21). Function printf prints the members of structure variable aCard using the structure member operator with variable name aCard, the structure pointer operator with pointer cardPtr and the structure member operator with dereferenced pointer cardPtr (lines 23 through 25).

```
1   /* Fig. 10.2: fig10_02.c
2      Using the structure member and
3      structure pointer operators */
4   #include <stdio.h>
5
6   /* card structure definition */
7   struct card {
8      char *face; /* define pointer face */
9      char *suit; /* define pointer suit */
10  }; /* end structure card */
11
12  int main()
13  {
14     struct card aCard; /* define one struct card variable */
15     struct card *cardPtr; /* define a pointer to a struct card */
16
17     /* place strings into aCard */
18     aCard.face = "Ace";
19     aCard.suit = "Spades";
```

Fig. 10.2   Structure member operator and structure pointer operator. (Part 1 of 2.)

```
20
21      cardPtr = &aCard; /* assign address of aCard to cardPtr */
22
23      printf( "%s%s%s\n%s%s%s\n%s%s%s\n", aCard.face, " of ", aCard.suit,
24         cardPtr->face, " of ", cardPtr->suit,
25         ( *cardPtr ).face, " of ", ( *cardPtr ).suit );
26
27      return 0; /* indicates successful termination */
28
29   } /* end main */
```

```
Ace of Spades
Ace of Spades
Ace of Spades
```

Fig. 10.2   Structure member operator and structure pointer operator. (Part 2 of 2.)

10.5 Using Structures with Functions

Structures may be passed to functions by passing individual structure members, by passing an entire structure or by passing a pointer to a structure. When structures or individual structure members are passed to a function, they are passed by value. Therefore, the members of a caller's structure cannot be modified by the called function.

To pass a structure by reference, pass the address of the structure variable. Arrays of structures—like all other arrays—are automatically passed by reference.

In Chapter 6, we stated that an array could be passed by value by using a structure. To pass an array by value, create a structure with the array as a member. Structures are passed by value, so the array is passed by value.

Common Programming Error 10.7

Assuming that structures, like arrays, are automatically passed by reference and trying to modify the caller's structure values in the called function is a logic error.

Performance Tip 10.1

Passing structures by reference is more efficient than passing structures by value (which requires the entire structure to be copied).

10.6 typedef

The keyword `typedef` provides a mechanism for creating synonyms (or aliases) for previously defined data types. Names for structure types are often defined with `typedef` to create shorter type names. For example, the statement

```
typedef struct card Card;
```

defines the new type name `Card` as a synonym for type `struct card`. C programmers often use `typedef` to define a structure type so a structure tag is not required. For example, the following definition

```
typedef struct {
    char *face;
    char *suit;
} Card;
```

creates the structure type `Card` without the need for a separate `typedef` statement.

Good Programming Practice 10.4

Capitalize the first letter of `typedef` names to emphasize that these names are synonyms for other type names.

`Card` can now be used to declare variables of type `struct card`. The declaration

```
Card deck[ 52 ];
```

declares an array of 52 `Card` structures (i.e., variables of type `struct card`). Creating a new name with `typedef` does not create a new type; `typedef` simply creates a new type name, which may be used as an alias for an existing type name. A meaningful name helps make the program self-documenting. For example, when we read the previous declaration, we know "`deck` is an array of 52 `Card`s."

Often, `typedef` is used to create synonyms for the basic data types. For example, a program requiring 4-byte integers may use type `int` on one system and type `long` on another. Programs designed for portability often use `typedef` to create an alias for 4-byte integers such as `Integer`. The alias `Integer` can be changed once in the program to make the program work on both systems.

Portability Tip 10.2

Use `typedef` to help make a program more portable.

10.7 Example: High-Performance Card Shuffling and Dealing Simulation

The program in Fig. 10.3 is based on the card shuffling and dealing simulation discussed in Chapter 7. The program represents the deck of cards as an array of structures. The program uses high-performance shuffling and dealing algorithms. The output for the high-performance card shuffling and dealing program is shown in Fig. 10.4.

```
1   /* Fig. 10.3: fig10_03.c
2      The card shuffling and dealing program using structures */
3   #include <stdio.h>
4   #include <stdlib.h>
5   #include <time.h>
6
7   /* card structure definition */
8   struct card {
9      const char *face; /* define pointer face */
10     const char *suit; /* define pointer suit */
11  }; /* end structure card */
```

Fig. 10.3   High-performance card shuffling and dealing simulation. (Part 1 of 3.)

```
12
13   typedef struct card Card; /* new type name for struct card */
14
15   /* prototypes */
16   void fillDeck( Card * const wDeck, const char * wFace[],
17      const char * wSuit[] );
18   void shuffle( Card * const wDeck );
19   void deal( const Card * const wDeck );
20
21   int main()
22   {
23      Card deck[ 52 ]; /* define array of Cards */
24
25      /* initialize array of pointers */
26      const char *face[] = { "Ace", "Deuce", "Three", "Four", "Five",
27         "Six", "Seven", "Eight", "Nine", "Ten",
28         "Jack", "Queen", "King"};
29
30      /* initialize array of pointers */
31      const char *suit[] = { "Hearts", "Diamonds", "Clubs", "Spades"};
32
33      srand( time( NULL ) ); /* randomize */
34
35      fillDeck( deck, face, suit ); /* load the deck with Cards */
36      shuffle( deck ); /* put Cards in random order */
37      deal( deck ); /* deal all 52 Cards */
38
39      return 0; /* indicates successful termination */
40
41   } /* end main */
42
43   /* place strings into Card structures */
44   void fillDeck( Card * const wDeck, const char * wFace[],
45      const char * wSuit[] )
46   {
47      int i; /* counter */
48
49      /* loop through wDeck */
50      for ( i = 0; i <= 51; i++ ) {
51         wDeck[ i ].face = wFace[ i % 13 ];
52         wDeck[ i ].suit = wSuit[ i / 13 ];
53      } /* end for */
54
55   } /* end function fillDeck */
56
57   /* shuffle cards */
58   void shuffle( Card * const wDeck )
59   {
60      int i;     /* counter */
61      int j;     /* variable to hold random value between 0 - 51 */
62      Card temp; /* define temporary structure for swapping Cards */
63
```

Fig. 10.3   High-performance card shuffling and dealing simulation. (Part 2 of 3.)

```
64        /* loop through wDeck randomly swapping Cards */
65        for ( i = 0; i <= 51; i++ ) {
66            j = rand() % 52;
67            temp = wDeck[ i ];
68            wDeck[ i ] = wDeck[ j ];
69            wDeck[ j ] = temp;
70        } /* end for */
71
72    } /* end function shuffle */
73
74    /* deal cards */
75    void deal( const Card * const wDeck )
76    {
77        int i; /* counter */
78
79        /* loop through wDeck */
80        for ( i = 0; i <= 51; i++ ) {
81            printf( "%5s of %-8s%c", wDeck[ i ].face, wDeck[ i ].suit,
82                ( i + 1 ) % 2 ? '\t' : '\n' );
83        } /* end for */
84
85    } /* end function deal */
```

Fig. 10.3   High-performance card shuffling and dealing simulation. (Part 3 of 3.)

```
  Four of Clubs        Three of Hearts
Three of Diamonds      Three of Spades
  Four of Diamonds       Ace of Diamonds
  Nine of Hearts         Ten of Clubs
Three of Clubs         Four of Hearts
Eight of Clubs         Nine of Diamonds
Deuce of Clubs        Queen of Clubs
Seven of Clubs         Jack of Spades
  Ace of Clubs          Five of Diamonds
  Ace of Spades         Five of Clubs
Seven of Diamonds       Six of Spades
Eight of Spades       Queen of Hearts
 Five of Spades        Deuce of Diamonds
Queen of Spades         Six of Hearts
Queen of Diamonds      Seven of Hearts
 Jack of Diamonds      Nine of Spades
Eight of Hearts        Five of Hearts
 King of Spades         Six of Clubs
Eight of Diamonds       Ten of Spades
  Ace of Hearts        King of Hearts
 Four of Spades        Jack of Hearts
Deuce of Hearts        Jack of Clubs
Deuce of Spades         Ten of Diamonds
Seven of Spades       Nine of Clubs
 King of Clubs          Six of Diamonds
  Ten of Hearts        King of Diamonds
```

Fig. 10.4   Output for the high-performance card shuffling and dealing simulation.

In the program, function `fillDeck` (lines 44–55) initializes the `Card` array in order with Ace through King of each suit. The `Card` array is passed (in line 36) to function `shuffle` (lines 58–72), where the high-performance shuffling algorithm is implemented. Function `shuffle` takes an array of 52 `Card` structures as an argument. The function loops through the 52 cards (array subscripts 0 to 51) using a `for` statement in lines 65–70. For each card, a number between 0 and 51 is picked randomly. Next, the current `Card` structure and the randomly selected `Card` structure are swapped in the array (lines 67 through 69). A total of 52 swaps are made in a single pass of the entire array, and the array of `Card` structures is shuffled! This algorithm cannot suffer from indefinite postponement like the shuffling algorithm presented in Chapter 7. Since the `Card` structures were swapped in place in the array, the high-performance dealing algorithm implemented in function `deal` (lines 75–85) requires only one pass of the array to deal the shuffled cards.

Common Programming Error 10.8

Forgetting to include the array subscript when referring to individual structures in an array of structures is a syntax error.

10.8 Unions

A *union* is a derived data type—like a structure—with members that share the same storage space. For different situations in a program, some variables may not be relevant, but other variables are—so a union shares the space instead of wasting storage on variables that are not being used. The members of a union can be of any data type. The number of bytes used to store a union must be at least enough to hold the largest member. In most cases, unions contain two or more data types. Only one member, and thus one data type, can be referenced at a time. It is the programmer's responsibility to ensure that the data in a union is referenced with the proper data type.

Common Programming Error 10.9

Referencing data in a union with a variable of the wrong type is a logic error.

Portability Tip 10.3

If data is stored in a union as one type and referenced as another type, the results are implementation dependent.

A union is declared with keyword `union` in the same format as a structure. The `union` definition

```
union number {
    int x;
    double y;
};
```

indicates that `number` is a `union` type with members `int x` and `double y`. The union definition is normally placed in a header and included in all source files that use the union type.

Software Engineering Observation 10.1

As with a `struct` definition, a `union` definition simply creates a new type. Placing a `union` or `struct` definition outside any function does not create a global variable.

The operations that can be performed on a union are the following: assigning a union to another union of the same type, taking the address (&) of a union variable, and accessing union members using the structure member operator and the structure pointer operator. Unions may not be compared using operators == and != for the same reasons that structures cannot be compared.

In a declaration, a union may be initialized with a value of the same type as the first union member. For example, with the preceding union, the declaration

```
union number value = { 10 };
```

is a valid initialization of union variable value because the union is initialized with an int, but the following declaration would truncate the floating-point part of the initializer value and normally would produce a warning from the compiler:

```
union number value = { 1.43 };
```

Common Programming Error 10.10

Comparing unions is a syntax error.

Portability Tip 10.4

The amount of storage required to store a union is implementation dependent.

Portability Tip 10.5

Some unions may not port easily to other computer systems. Whether a union is portable or not often depends on the storage alignment requirements for the union member data types on a given system.

Performance Tip 10.2

Unions conserve storage.

The program in Fig. 10.5 uses the variable value (line 13) of type union number to display the value stored in the union as both an int and a double. The program output is implementation dependent. The program output shows that the internal representation of a double value can be quite different from the representation of int.

```
1   /* Fig. 10.5: fig10_05.c
2      An example of a union */
3   #include <stdio.h>
4
5   /* number union definition */
6   union number {
7      int x;
8      double y;
9   }; /* end union number */
10
11  int main()
12  {
```

Fig. 10.5   Displaying the value of a union in both member data types. (Part 1 of 2.)

```
13        union number value; /* define union variable */
14
15        value.x = 100; /* put an integer into the union */
16        printf( "%s\n%s\n%s%d\n%s%f\n\n",
17           "Put a value in the integer member",
18           "and print both members.",
19           "int:    ", value.x,
20           "double:\n", value.y );
21
22        value.y = 100.0; /* put a double into the same union */
23        printf( "%s\n%s\n%s%d\n%s%f\n",
24           "Put a value in the floating member",
25           "and print both members.",
26           "int:    ", value.x,
27           "double:\n", value.y );
28
29        return 0; /* indicates successful termination */
30
31     } /* end main */
```

```
Put a value in the integer member
and print both members.
int:    100
double:
-9255959211743313600000000000000000000000000000000000000000000.000000

Put a value in the floating member
and print both members.
int:    0
double:
100.000000
```

Fig. 10.5   Displaying the value of a union in both member data types. (Part 2 of 2.)

10.9 Bitwise Operators

Computers represent all data internally as sequences of bits. Each bit can assume the value 0 or the value 1. On most systems, a sequence of 8 bits form a byte—the standard storage unit for a variable of type char. Other data types are stored in larger numbers of bytes. The bitwise operators are used to manipulate the bits of integral operands (char, short, int and long; both signed and unsigned). Unsigned integers are normally used with the bitwise operators.

Portability Tip 10.6

Bitwise data manipulations are machine dependent.

Note that the bitwise operator discussions in this section show the binary representations of the integer operands. For a detailed explanation of the binary (also called base 2) number system see Appendix E, Number Systems. Also, the programs in Section 10.9 and 10.10 were tested using Microsoft Visual C++. Because of the machine-dependent nature of bitwise manipulations, these programs may not work on your system.

The bitwise operators are *bitwise AND (&), bitwise inclusive OR (|), bitwise exclusive OR (^), left shift (<<), right shift (>>) and complement (~).* The bitwise AND, bitwise inclusive OR and bitwise exclusive OR operators compare their two operands bit by bit. The bitwise AND operator sets each bit in the result to 1 if the corresponding bit in both operands is 1. The bitwise inclusive OR operator sets each bit in the result to 1 if the corresponding bit in either (or both) operand(s) is 1. The bitwise exclusive OR operator sets each bit in the result to 1 if the corresponding bit in exactly one operand is 1. The left-shift operator shifts the bits of its left operand to the left by the number of bits specified in its right operand. The right-shift operator shifts the bits in its left operand to the right by the number of bits specified in its right operand. The bitwise complement operator sets all 0 bits in its operand to 1 in the result and sets all 1 bits to 0 in the result. Detailed discussions of each bitwise operator appear in the following examples. The bitwise operators are summarized in Fig. 10.6.

Operator		Description
&	bitwise AND	The bits in the result are set to 1 if the corresponding bits in the two operands are both 1.
|	bitwise inclusive OR	The bits in the result are set to 1 if at least one of the corresponding bits in the two operands is 1.
^	bitwise exclusive OR	The bits in the result are set to 1 if exactly one of the corresponding bits in the two operands is 1.
<<	left shift	Shifts the bits of the first operand left by the number of bits specified by the second operand; fill from the right with 0 bits.
>>	right shift	Shifts the bits of the first operand right by the number of bits specified by the second operand; the method of filling from the left is machine dependent.
~	one's complement	All 0 bits are set to 1 and all 1 bits are set to 0.

Fig. 10.6 Bitwise operators.

Displaying an Unsigned Integer in Bits

When using the bitwise operators, it is useful to print values in their binary representation to illustrate the precise effects of these operators. The program of Fig. 10.7 prints an unsigned integer in its binary representation in groups of eight bits each.

```
1   /* Fig. 10.7: fig10_07.c
2      Printing an unsigned integer in bits */
3   #include <stdio.h>
4
5   void displayBits( unsigned value ); /* prototype */
6
7   int main()
8   {
9      unsigned x; /* variable to hold user input */
10
```

Fig. 10.7 Displaying an unsigned integer in bits. (Part 1 of 2.)

```
11        printf( "Enter an unsigned integer: " );
12        scanf( "%u", &x );
13
14        displayBits( x );
15
16        return 0; /* indicates successful termination */
17
18     } /* end main */
19
20     /* display bits of an unsigned integer value */
21     void displayBits( unsigned value )
22     {
23        unsigned c; /* counter */
24
25        /* define displayMask and left shift 31 bits */
26        unsigned displayMask = 1 << 31;
27
28        printf( "%10u = ", value );
29
30        /* loop through bits */
31        for ( c = 1; c <= 32; c++ ) {
32           putchar( value & displayMask ? '1' : '0' );
33           value <<= 1; /* shift value left by 1 */
34
35           if ( c % 8 == 0 ) { /* output space after 8 bits */
36              putchar( ' ' );
37           } /* end if */
38
39        } /* end for */
40
41        putchar( '\n' );
42     } /* end function displayBits */
```

```
Enter an unsigned integer: 65000
   65000 = 00000000 00000000 11111101 11101000
```

Fig. 10.7 Displaying an unsigned integer in bits. (Part 2 of 2.)

Function displayBits (lines 21–42) uses the bitwise AND operator to combine variable value with variable displayMask (line 32). Often, the bitwise AND operator is used with an operand called a *mask*—an integer value with specific bits set to 1. Masks are used to hide some bits in a value while selecting other bits. In function displayBits, mask variable displayMask is assigned the value

     1 << 31   (10000000 00000000 00000000 00000000)

The left shift operator shifts the value 1 from the low order (rightmost) bit to the high order (leftmost) bit in displayMask and fills in 0 bits from the right. Line 32

     putchar(value & displayMask ? '1' : '0');

determines whether a 1 or a 0 should be printed for the current leftmost bit of variable value. When value and displayMask are combined using &, all the bits except the high-order bit in variable value are "masked off" (hidden), because any bit "ANDed" with 0 yields 0. If the leftmost bit is 1, `value & displayMask` evaluates to a nonzero (true) value and 1 is printed—otherwise, 0 is printed. Variable `value` is then left shifted one bit by the expression `value <<= 1` (this is equivalent to `value = value << 1`). These steps are repeated for each bit in `unsigned` variable `value`. Fig. 10.8 summarizes the results of combining two bits with the bitwise AND operator.

Bit 1	Bit 2	Bit 1 & Bit 2
0	0	0
1	0	0
0	1	0
1	1	1

Fig. 10.8   Results of combining two bits with the bitwise AND operator &.

Common Programming Error 10.11

Using the logical AND operator (&&) for the bitwise AND operator (&) and vice versa is an error.

Using the Bitwise AND, Inclusive OR, Exclusive OR and Complement Operators

Figure 10.9 demonstrates the use of the bitwise AND operator, the bitwise inclusive OR operator, the bitwise exclusive OR operator and the bitwise complement operator. The program uses function `displayBits` (lines 53–74) to print the `unsigned` integer values. The output is shown in Fig. 10.10.

```
1   /* Fig. 10.9: fig10_09.c
2      Using the bitwise AND, bitwise inclusive OR, bitwise
3      exclusive OR and bitwise complement operators */
4   #include <stdio.h>
5
6   void displayBits( unsigned value ); /* prototype */
7
8   int main()
9   {
10      unsigned number1;
11      unsigned number2;
12      unsigned mask;
13      unsigned setBits;
14
15      /* demonstrate bitwise AND (&) */
16      number1 = 65535;
17      mask = 1;
18      printf( "The result of combining the following\n" );
19      displayBits( number1 );
20      displayBits( mask );
21      printf( "using the bitwise AND operator & is\n" );
22      displayBits( number1 & mask );
```

Fig. 10.9   Bitwise AND, bitwise inclusive OR, bitwise exclusive OR and bitwise complement operators. (Part 1 of 2.)

```
23
24       /* demonstrate bitwise inclusive OR (|) */
25       number1 = 15;
26       setBits = 241;
27       printf( "\nThe result of combining the following\n" );
28       displayBits( number1 );
29       displayBits( setBits );
30       printf( "using the bitwise inclusive OR operator | is\n" );
31       displayBits( number1 | setBits );
32
33       /* demonstrate bitwise exclusive OR (^) */
34       number1 = 139;
35       number2 = 199;
36       printf( "\nThe result of combining the following\n" );
37       displayBits( number1 );
38       displayBits( number2 );
39       printf( "using the bitwise exclusive OR operator ^ is\n" );
40       displayBits( number1 ^ number2 );
41
42       /* demonstrate bitwise complement (~)*/
43       number1 = 21845;
44       printf( "\nThe one's complement of\n" );
45       displayBits( number1 );
46       printf( "is\n" );
47       displayBits( ~number1 );
48
49       return 0; /* indicates successful termination */
50    } /* end main */
51
52    /* display bits of an unsigned integer value */
53    void displayBits( unsigned value )
54    {
55       unsigned c; /* counter */
56
57       /* declare displayMask and left shift 31 bits */
58       unsigned displayMask = 1 << 31;
59
60       printf( "%10u = ", value );
61
62       /* loop through bits */
63       for ( c = 1; c <= 32; c++ ) {
64          putchar( value & displayMask ? '1' : '0' );
65          value <<= 1; /* shift value left by 1 */
66
67          if ( c % 8 == 0 ) { /* output a space after 8 bits */
68             putchar( ' ' );
69          } /* end if */
70
71       } /* end for */
72
73       putchar( '\n' );
74    } /* end function displayBits */
```

Fig. 10.9 Bitwise AND, bitwise inclusive OR, bitwise exclusive OR and bitwise complement operators. (Part 2 of 2.)

```
The result of combining the following
    65535 = 00000000 00000000 11111111 11111111
        1 = 00000000 00000000 00000000 00000001
using the bitwise AND operator & is
        1 = 00000000 00000000 00000000 00000001

The result of combining the following
       15 = 00000000 00000000 00000000 00001111
      241 = 00000000 00000000 00000000 11110001
using the bitwise inclusive OR operator | is
      255 = 00000000 00000000 00000000 11111111

The result of combining the following
      139 = 00000000 00000000 00000000 10001011
      199 = 00000000 00000000 00000000 11000111
using the bitwise exclusive OR operator ^ is
       76 = 00000000 00000000 00000000 01001100

The one's complement of
    21845 = 00000000 00000000 01010101 01010101
is
4294945450 = 11111111 11111111 10101010 10101010
```

Fig. 10.10 Output for the program of Fig. 10.9.

In Fig. 10.9, integer variable number1 is assigned value 65535 (00000000 00000000 11111111 11111111) in line 16 and variable mask is assigned the value 1 (00000000 00000000 00000000 00000001) in line 17. When number1 and mask are combined using the bitwise AND operator (&) in the expression number1 & mask (line 22), the result is 00000000 00000000 00000000 00000001. All the bits except the low-order bit in variable number1 are "masked off" (hidden) by "ANDing" with variable mask.

The bitwise inclusive OR operator is used to set specific bits to 1 in an operand. In Fig. 10.9, variable number1 is assigned 15 (00000000 00000000 00000000 00001111) in line 25, and variable setBits is assigned 241 (00000000 00000000 00000000 11110001) in line 26. When number1 and setBits are combined using the bitwise OR operator in the expression number1 | setBits (line 31), the result is 255 (00000000 00000000 00000000 11111111). Figure 10.11 summarizes the results of combining two bits with the bitwise inclusive OR operator.

Bit 1	Bit 2	Bit 1 | Bit 2
0	0	0
1	0	1
0	1	1
1	1	1

Fig. 10.11 Results of combining two bits with the bitwise inclusive OR operator |.

Common Programming Error 10.12

Using the logical OR operator (| |) for the bitwise OR operator (|) and vice versa is an error.

The bitwise exclusive OR operator (^) sets each bit in the result to 1 if *exactly* one of the corresponding bits in its two operands is 1. In Fig. 10.9, variables `number1` and `number2` are assigned the values 139 (00000000 00000000 00000000 10001011) and 199 (00000000 00000000 00000000 11000111) in lines 34–35. When these variables are combined with the exclusive OR operator in the expression `number1 ^ number2` (line 40), the result is 00000000 00000000 00000000 01001100. Figure 10.12 summarizes the results of combining two bits with the bitwise exclusive OR operator.

Bit 1	Bit 2	Bit 1 ^ Bit 2
0	0	0
1	0	1
0	1	1
1	1	0

Fig. 10.12 Results of combining two bits with the bitwise exclusive OR operator ^.

The *bitwise* complement operator (~) sets all 1 bits in its operand to 0 in the result and sets all 0 bits to 1 in the result—otherwise referred to as "taking the *one's complement* of the value." In Fig. 10.9, variable `number1` is assigned the value 21845 (00000000 00000000 01010101 01010101) in line 43. When the expression `~number1` (line 47) is evaluated, the result is 00000000 00000000 10101010 10101010.

Using the Bitwise Left and Right Shift Operators
The program of Fig. 10.13 demonstrates the left-shift operator (<<) and the right-shift operator (>>). Function `displayBits` is used to print the `unsigned` integer values.

```
1   /* Fig. 10.13: fig10_13.c
2      Using the bitwise shift operators */
3   #include <stdio.h>
4
5   void displayBits( unsigned value ); /* prototype */
6
7   int main()
8   {
9      unsigned number1 = 960; /* initialize number1 */
10
11     /* demonstrate bitwise left shift */
12     printf( "\nThe result of left shifting\n" );
13     displayBits( number1 );
14     printf( "8 bit positions using the " );
15     printf( "left shift operator << is\n" );
16     displayBits( number1 << 8 );
```

Fig. 10.13 Bitwise shift operators. (Part 1 of 2.)

```
17
18      /* demonstrate bitwise right shift */
19      printf( "\nThe result of right shifting\n" );
20      displayBits( number1 );
21      printf( "8 bit positions using the " );
22      printf( "right shift operator >> is\n" );
23      displayBits( number1 >> 8 );
24
25      return 0; /* indicates successful termination */
26   } /* end main */
27
28   /* display bits of an unsigned integer value */
29   void displayBits( unsigned value )
30   {
31      unsigned c; /* counter */
32
33      /* declare displayMask and left shift 31 bits */
34      unsigned displayMask = 1 << 31;
35
36      printf( "%7u = ", value );
37
38      /* loop through bits */
39      for ( c = 1; c <= 32; c++ ) {
40         putchar( value & displayMask ? '1' : '0' );
41         value <<= 1; /* shift value left by 1 */
42
43         if ( c % 8 == 0 ) { /* output a space after 8 bits */
44            putchar( ' ' );
45         } /* end if */
46
47      } /* end for */
48
49      putchar( '\n' );
50   } /* end function displayBits */
```

```
The result of left shifting
     960 = 00000000 00000000 00000011 11000000
8 bit positions using the left shift operator << is
 245760 = 00000000 00000011 11000000 00000000

The result of right shifting
     960 = 00000000 00000000 00000011 11000000
8 bit positions using the right shift operator >> is
       3 = 00000000 00000000 00000000 00000011
```

Fig. 10.13 Bitwise shift operators. (Part 2 of 2.)

The left-shift operator (<<) shifts the bits of its left operand to the left by the number of bits specified in its right operand. Bits vacated to the right are replaced with 0s; 1s shifted off the left are lost. In Fig. 10.13, variable number1 is assigned the value 960 (00000000 00000000 00000011 11000000) in line 9. The result of left-shifting variable number1 8 bits in the expression number1 << 8 (line 16) is 49152 (00000000 00000000 11000000 00000000).

The right-shift operator (>>) shifts the bits of its left operand to the right by the number of bits specified in its right operand. Performing a right shift on an `unsigned` integer causes the vacated bits at the left to be replaced by 0s; 1s shifted off the right are lost. In Fig. 10.13, the result of right-shifting `number1` in the expression `number1 >> 8` (line 23) is 3 (00000000 00000000 00000000 00000011).

Common Programming Error 10.13

The result of shifting a value is undefined if the right operand is negative or if the right operand is larger than the number of bits in which the left operand is stored.

Portability Tip 10.7

Right shifting is machine dependent. Right shifting a signed integer fills the vacated bits with 0s on some machines and 1s on others.

Bitwise Assignment Operators

Each binary bitwise operator has a corresponding assignment operator. These *bitwise assignment operators* are shown in Fig. 10.14 and are used in a manner similar to the arithmetic assignment operators introduced in Chapter 3.

Bitwise assignment operators
&=   Bitwise AND assignment operator.
|=   Bitwise inclusive OR assignment operator.
^=   Bitwise exclusive OR assignment operator.
<<=   Left-shift assignment operator.
>>=   Right-shift assignment operator.

Fig. 10.14 The bitwise assignment operators.

Fig. 10.15 shows the precedence and associativity of the various operators introduced to this point in the text. They are shown top to bottom in decreasing order of precedence.

Operator	Associativity	Type
() [] . ->	left to right	highest
+ - ++ -- ! & * ~ sizeof (*type*)	right to left	unary
* / %	left to right	multiplicative
+ -	left to right	additive
<< >>	left to right	shifting
< <= > >=	left to right	relational
== !=	left to right	equality
&	left to right	bitwise AND

Fig. 10.15 Operator precedence and associativity. (Part 1 of 2.)

Operator											Associativity	Type
^											left to right	bitwise OR
|											left to right	bitwise OR
&&											left to right	logical AND
||											left to right	logical OR
?:											right to left	conditional
=	+=	-=	*=	/=	&=	|=	^=	<<=	>>=	%=	right to left	assignment
,											left to right	comma

Fig. 10.15 Operator precedence and associativity. (Part 2 of 2.)

10.10 Bit Fields

C enables programmers to specify the number of bits in which an `unsigned` or `int` member of a structure or union is stored. This is referred to as a *bit field*. Bit fields enable better memory utilization by storing data in the minimum number of bits required. Bit field members *must* be declared as `int` or `unsigned`

Performance Tip 10.3

Bit fields help conserve storage.

Consider the following structure definition:

```
struct bitCard {
    unsigned face : 4;
    unsigned suit : 2;
    unsigned color : 1;
};
```

The definition contains three `unsigned` bit fields—`face`, `suit` and `color`—used to represent a card from a deck of 52 cards. A bit field is declared by following an `unsigned` or `int` *member name* with a colon (`:`) and an integer constant representing the *width* of the field (i.e., the number of bits in which the member is stored). The constant representing the width must be an integer between 0 and the total number of bits used to store an `int` on your system. Our examples were tested on a computer with 4-byte (32 bit) integers.

The preceding structure definition indicates that member `face` is stored in 4 bits, member `suit` is stored in 2 bits and member `color` is stored in 1 bit. The number of bits is based on the desired range of values for each structure member. Member `face` stores values from 0 (Ace) through 12 (King)—4 bits can store values in the range 0–15. Member suit stores values from 0 through 3 (0 = Diamonds, 1 = Hearts, 2 = Clubs, 3 = Spades)—2 bits can store values in the range 0–3. Finally, member `color` stores either 0 (Red) or 1 (Black)—1 bit can store either 0 or 1.

Figure 10.16 (output shown in Fig. 10.17) creates array `deck` containing 52 `struct` `bitCard` structures in line 20. Function `fillDeck` (lines 30–41) inserts the 52 cards in the `deck` array and function `deal` (lines 45–58) prints the 52 cards. Notice that bit field members of structures are accessed exactly as any other structure member. Member `color` is included as a means of indicating the card color on a system that allows color displays.

```c
1   /* Fig. 10.16: fig10_16.c
2      Representing cards with bit fields in a struct */
3
4   #include <stdio.h>
5
6   /* bitCard structure definition with bit fields */
7   struct bitCard {
8      unsigned face : 4;   /* 4 bits; 0-15 */
9      unsigned suit : 2;   /* 2 bits; 0-3 */
10     unsigned color : 1;  /* 1 bit; 0-1 */
11  }; /* end struct bitCard */
12
13  typedef struct bitCard Card; /* new type name for struct bitCard */
14
15  void fillDeck( Card * const wDeck );    /* prototype */
16  void deal( const Card * const wDeck );  /* prototype */
17
18  int main()
19  {
20     Card deck[ 52 ]; /* create array of Cards */
21
22     fillDeck( deck );
23     deal( deck );
24
25     return 0; /* indicates successful termination */
26
27  } /* end main */
28
29  /* initialize Cards */
30  void fillDeck( Card * const wDeck )
31  {
32     int i; /* counter */
33
34     /* loop through wDeck */
35     for ( i = 0; i <= 51; i++ ) {
36        wDeck[ i ].face = i % 13;
37        wDeck[ i ].suit = i / 13;
38        wDeck[ i ].color = i / 26;
39     } /* end for */
40
41  } /* end function fillDeck */
42
43  /* output cards in two column format; cards 0-25 subscripted with
44     k1 (column 1); cards 26-51 subscripted k2 (column 2) */
45  void deal( const Card * const wDeck )
46  {
47     int k1; /* subscripts 0-25 */
48     int k2; /* subscripts 26-51 */
49
```

Fig. 10.16 Bit fields to store a deck of cards. (Part 1 of 2.)

```
50          /* loop through wDeck */
51          for ( k1 = 0, k2 = k1 + 26; k1 <= 25; k1++, k2++ ) {
52              printf( "Card:%3d  Suit:%2d  Color:%2d    ",
53                  wDeck[ k1 ].face, wDeck[ k1 ].suit, wDeck[ k1 ].color );
54              printf( "Card:%3d  Suit:%2d  Color:%2d\n",
55                  wDeck[ k2 ].face, wDeck[ k2 ].suit, wDeck[ k2 ].color );
56          } /* end for */
57
58      } /* end function deal */
```

Fig. 10.16 Bit fields to store a deck of cards. (Part 2 of 2.)

```
Card:  0  Suit: 0  Color: 0    Card:  0  Suit: 2  Color: 1
Card:  1  Suit: 0  Color: 0    Card:  1  Suit: 2  Color: 1
Card:  2  Suit: 0  Color: 0    Card:  2  Suit: 2  Color: 1
Card:  3  Suit: 0  Color: 0    Card:  3  Suit: 2  Color: 1
Card:  4  Suit: 0  Color: 0    Card:  4  Suit: 2  Color: 1
Card:  5  Suit: 0  Color: 0    Card:  5  Suit: 2  Color: 1
Card:  6  Suit: 0  Color: 0    Card:  6  Suit: 2  Color: 1
Card:  7  Suit: 0  Color: 0    Card:  7  Suit: 2  Color: 1
Card:  8  Suit: 0  Color: 0    Card:  8  Suit: 2  Color: 1
Card:  9  Suit: 0  Color: 0    Card:  9  Suit: 2  Color: 1
Card: 10  Suit: 0  Color: 0    Card: 10  Suit: 2  Color: 1
Card: 11  Suit: 0  Color: 0    Card: 11  Suit: 2  Color: 1
Card: 12  Suit: 0  Color: 0    Card: 12  Suit: 2  Color: 1
Card:  0  Suit: 1  Color: 0    Card:  0  Suit: 3  Color: 1
Card:  1  Suit: 1  Color: 0    Card:  1  Suit: 3  Color: 1
Card:  2  Suit: 1  Color: 0    Card:  2  Suit: 3  Color: 1
Card:  3  Suit: 1  Color: 0    Card:  3  Suit: 3  Color: 1
Card:  4  Suit: 1  Color: 0    Card:  4  Suit: 3  Color: 1
Card:  5  Suit: 1  Color: 0    Card:  5  Suit: 3  Color: 1
Card:  6  Suit: 1  Color: 0    Card:  6  Suit: 3  Color: 1
Card:  7  Suit: 1  Color: 0    Card:  7  Suit: 3  Color: 1
Card:  8  Suit: 1  Color: 0    Card:  8  Suit: 3  Color: 1
Card:  9  Suit: 1  Color: 0    Card:  9  Suit: 3  Color: 1
Card: 10  Suit: 1  Color: 0    Card: 10  Suit: 3  Color: 1
Card: 11  Suit: 1  Color: 0    Card: 11  Suit: 3  Color: 1
Card: 12  Suit: 1  Color: 0    Card: 12  Suit: 3  Color: 1
```

Fig. 10.17 Output of the program in Fig. 10.16.

It is possible to specify an *unnamed bit field* to be used as *padding* in the structure. For example, the structure definition

```
struct example {
    unsigned a : 13;
    unsigned   : 19;
    unsigned b : 4;
};
```

uses an unnamed 19-bit field as padding—nothing can be stored in those 19 bits. Member b (on our 4-byte word computer) is stored in another storage unit.

An *unnamed bit field with a zero width* is used to align the next bit field on a new storage unit boundary. For example, the structure definition

```
struct example {
    unsigned a : 13;
    unsigned   : 0;
    unsigned b : 4;
};
```

uses an unnamed 0-bit field to skip the remaining bits (as many as there are) of the storage unit in which a is stored and to align b on the next storage unit boundary.

Portability Tip 10.8

Bit field manipulations are machine dependent. For example, some computers allow bit fields to cross word boundaries, whereas others do not.

Common Programming Error 10.14

Attempting to access individual bits of a bit field as if they were elements of an array is a syntax error. Bit fields are not "arrays of bits."

Common Programming Error 10.15

Attempting to take the address of a bit field (the & operator may not be used with bit fields because they do not have addresses).

Performance Tip 10.4

Although bit fields save space, using them can cause the compiler to generate slower-executing machine language code. This occurs because it takes extra machine language operations to access only portions of an addressable storage unit. This is one of many examples of the kinds of space–time trade-offs that occur in computer science.

10.11 Enumeration Constants

C provides one final user-defined type called an *enumeration*. An enumeration, introduced by the keyword enum, is a set of integer *enumeration constants* represented by identifiers. \Values in an enum start with 0, unless specified otherwise, and are incremented by 1. For example, the enumeration

```
enum months {
    JAN, FEB, MAR, APR, MAY, JUN, JUL, AUG, SEP, OCT, NOV, DEC };
```

creates a new type, enum months, in which the identifiers are set to the integers 0 to 11, respectively. To number the months 1 to 12, use the following enumeration:

```
enum months {
    JAN = 1, FEB, MAR, APR, MAY, JUN, JUL, AUG, SEP, OCT, NOV, DEC };
```

Since the first value in the preceding enumeration is explicitly set to 1, the remaining values are incremented from 1 resulting in the values 1 through 12. The identifiers in an enumeration must be unique. The value of each enumeration constant of an enumeration can be set explicitly in the definition by assigning a value to the identifier. Multiple members of an enumeration can have the same constant value. In the program of Fig. 10.18, the enumeration variable month is used in a for statement to print the months of the year from the array monthName. Note that we have made monthName[0] the empty string "". Some programmers might prefer to set monthName[0] to a value such as ***ERROR*** to indicate that a logic error occurred.

```
1   /* Fig. 10.18: fig10_18.c
2      Using an enumeration type */
3   #include <stdio.h>
4
5   /* enumeration constants represent months of the year */
6   enum months {
7      JAN = 1, FEB, MAR, APR, MAY, JUN, JUL, AUG, SEP, OCT, NOV, DEC };
8
9   int main()
10  {
11     enum months month; /* can contain any of the 12 months */
12
13     /* initialize array of pointers */
14     const char *monthName[] = { "", "January", "February", "March",
15        "April", "May", "June", "July", "August", "September", "October",
16        "November", "December" };
17
18     /* loop through months */
19     for ( month = JAN; month <= DEC; month++ ) {
20        printf( "%2d%11s\n", month, monthName[ month ] );
21     } /* end for */
22
23     return 0; /* indicates successful termination */
24  } /* end main */
```

```
 1    January
 2   February
 3      March
 4      April
 5        May
 6       June
 7       July
 8     August
 9  September
10    October
11   November
12   December
```

Fig. 10.18 Using an enumeration.

 Common Programming Error 10.16

Assigning a value to an enumeration constant after it has been defined is a syntax error.

 Good Programming Practice 10.5

Use only uppercase letters in the names of enumeration constants. This makes these constants stand out in a program and reminds the programmer that enumeration constants are not variables.

SUMMARY

- Structures, sometimes referred to as aggregates, are collections of related variables under one name.
- Structures can contain variables of different data types.
- Keyword `struct` begins every structure definition. Within the braces of the structure definition are the structure member declarations.
- Members of the same structure must have unique names.
- A structure definition creates a new data type that can be used to define variables.
- There are two methods for defining structure variables. The first method is to define the variables as is done with variables of other data types using `struct tagName` as the type. The second method is to include the variables between the closing brace of the structure definition and the semicolon that ends the structure definition.
- The tag name of the structure is optional. If the structure is defined without a tag name, the variables of the derived data type must be defined in the structure definition, and no other variables of the new structure type can be defined.
- A structure can be initialized with an initializer list by following the variable name in the variable definition with an equals sign and a comma-separated list of initializers enclosed in braces. If there are fewer initializers in the list than members in the structure, the remaining members are automatically initialized to zero (or `NULL` if the member is a pointer).
- Entire structures may be assigned to structure variables of the same type.
- A structure variable may be initialized with a structure variable of the same type.
- The structure member operator is used when accessing a member of a structure via the structure variable name.
- The structure pointer operator (`->`)—created with a minus (-) sign and a greater than (>) sign—is used when accessing a member of a structure via a pointer to the structure.
- Structures and individual members of structures are passed to functions by value.
- To pass a structure by reference, pass the address of the structure variable.
- An array of structures is automatically passed by reference.
- To pass an array by value, create a structure with the array as a member.
- Creating a new name with `typedef` does not create a new type; it creates a name that is synonymous to a type defined previously.
- A union is a derived data type with members that share the same storage space. The members can be any type.
- The storage reserved for a union is large enough to store its largest member. In most cases, unions contain variables of two or more data types. Only one member and thus one data type, can be referenced at a time.
- A union is declared with keyword `union` in the same format as a structure.
- A union can be initialized with a value of the type of its first member.
- The bitwise AND operator (&) takes two integral operands. A bit in the result is set to 1 if the corresponding bits in each of the operands are 1.
- Masks are used to hide some bits while preserving others.
- The bitwise inclusive OR operator (|) takes two operands. A bit in the result is set to 1 if the corresponding bit in either operand is set to 1.
- Each of the binary bitwise operators has a corresponding assignment operator.

- The bitwise exclusive OR operator (^) takes two operands. A bit in the result is set to 1 if exactly one of the corresponding bits in the two operands is set to 1.
- The left-shift operator (<<) shifts the bits of its left operand left by the number of bits specified by its right operand. Bits vacated to the right are replaced with 0s.
- The right-shift operator (>>) shifts the bits of its left operand right by the number of bits specified in its right operand. Performing a right shift on an unsigned integer causes bits vacated at the left to be replaced by 0s. Vacated bits in signed integers can be replaced with 0s or 1s—this is machine dependent.
- The bitwise complement operator (~) takes one operand and reverses its bits—this produces the one's complement of the operand.
- Bit fields reduce storage use by storing data in the minimum number of bits required.
- Bit field members must be declared as int or unsigned.
- A bit field is declared by following an unsigned or int member name with a colon and the width of the bit field.
- The bit field width must be an integer constant between 0 and the total number of bits used to store an int variable on your system.
- If a bit field is specified without a name, the field is used as padding in the structure.
- An unnamed bit field with width 0 aligns the next bit field on a new machine word boundary.
- An enumeration, designated by the keyword enum, is a set of integers that are represented by identifiers. The values in an enum start with 0 unless specified otherwise and are incremented by 1.

TERMINOLOGY

^ bitwise exclusive OR operator
^= bitwise exclusive OR assignment operator
~ one's complement operator
& bitwise AND operator
&= bitwise AND assignment operator
| bitwise inclusive OR operator
|= bitwise inclusive OR assignment operator
<< left-shift operator
<<= left-shift assignment operator
>> right-shift operator
>>= right-shift assignment operator
accessing members of structures
aggregates
array of structures
bit field
bitwise operator
complementing
derived data type
enumeration
enumeration constant
structure initialization
initialization of structures
left shift
mask
masking off bits
member

member name
nested structures
one's complement
padding
pointer to a structure
programmer-defined data types
right shift
self-referential structure
shifting
space–time trade-offs
struct
structure
structure assignment
structure declaration
structure definition
structure member (dot) operator (.)
structure name
structure pointer (arrow) operator (->)
structure tag
structure type
tag name
typedef
union
unnamed bit field
width of a bit field
zero-width bit field

COMMON PROGRAMMING ERRORS

10.1 Forgetting the semicolon that terminates a structure definition is a syntax error.

10.2 Assigning a structure of one type to a structure of a different type is a compilation error.

10.3 Comparing structures is a syntax error.

10.4 Inserting space between the – and > components of the structure pointer operator (or inserting spaces between the components of other multiple keystroke operators except ? :) is a syntax error.

10.5 Attempting to refer to a member of a structure by using only the member's name is a syntax error.

10.6 Not using parentheses when referring to a structure member that uses a pointer and the structure member operator (e.g., *cardPtr.suit) is a syntax error.

10.7 Assuming that structures, like arrays, are automatically passed by reference and by trying to modify the caller's structure values in the called function is a logic error.

10.8 Forgetting to include the array subscript when referring to individual structures in an array of structures is a syntax error.

10.9 Referencing data in a union with a variable of the wrong type is a logic error.

10.10 Comparing unions is a syntax error.

10.11 Using the logical AND operator (&&) for the bitwise AND operator (&) and vice versa is an error.

10.12 Using the logical OR operator (| |) for the bitwise OR operator (|) and vice versa is an error.

10.13 The result of shifting a value is undefined if the right operand is negative or if the right operand is larger than the number of bits in which the left operand is stored.

10.14 Attempting to access individual bits of a bit field as if they were elements of an array is a syntax error. Bit fields are not "arrays of bits."

10.15 Attempting to take the address of a bit field (the & operator may not be used with bit fields because they do not have addresses).

10.16 Assigning a value to an enumeration constant after it has been defined is a syntax error.

ERROR-PREVENTION TIP

10.1 Avoid using the same names for members of structures of different types. This is allowed, but it may cause confusion.

GOOD PROGRAMMING PRACTICES

10.1 Always provide a structure tag name when creating a structure type. The structure tag name is convenient for declaring new variables of the structure type later in the program.

10.2 Choosing a meaningful structure tag name helps make a program self-documenting.

10.3 Do not put spaces around the -> and . operators. Omitting spaces helps emphasize that the expressions the operators are contained in are essentially single variable names.

10.4 Capitalize the first letter of typedef names to emphasize that these names are synonyms for other type names.

10.5 Use only uppercase letters in the names of enumeration constants. This makes these constants stand out in a program and reminds the programmer that enumeration constants are not variables.

PERFORMANCE TIPS

10.1 Passing structures by reference is more efficient than passing structures by value (which requires the entire structure to be copied).

10.2 Unions conserve storage.

10.3 Bit fields help conserve storage.

10.4 Although bit fields save space, using them can cause the compiler to generate slower-executing machine language code. This occurs because it takes extra machine language operations to access only portions of an addressable storage unit. This is one of many examples of the kinds of space–time trade-offs that occur in computer science.

PORTABILITY TIPS

10.1 Because the size of data items of a particular type is machine dependent and because storage alignment considerations are machine dependent, so too is the representation of a structure.

10.2 Use `typedef` to help make a program more portable.

10.3 If data is stored in a union as one type and referenced as another type, the results are implementation dependent.

10.4 The amount of storage required to store a union is implementation dependent.

10.5 Some unions may not port easily to other computer systems. Whether a union is portable or not often depends on the storage alignment requirements for the union member data types on a given system.

10.6 Bitwise data manipulations are machine dependent.

10.7 Right shifting is machine dependent. Right shifting a signed integer fills the vacated bits with 0s on some machines and 1s on others.

10.8 Bit field manipulations are machine dependent. For example, some computers allow bit fields to cross word boundaries, whereas others do not.

SOFTWARE ENGINEERING OBSERVATION

10.1 As with a `struct` declaration, a `union` declaration simply creates a new type. Placing a `union` or `struct` declaration outside any function does not create a global variable.

SELF-REVIEW EXERCISES

10.1 Fill in the blanks in each of the following:

a) A(n) _____ is a collection of related variables under one name.

b) A(n) _____ is a collection of variables under one name in which the variables share the same storage.

c) The bits in the result of an expression using the _____ operator are set to 1 if the corresponding bits in each operand are set to 1. Otherwise, the bits are set to zero.

d) The variables declared in a structure definition are called its _____ .

e) The bits in the result of an expression using the _____ operator are set to 1 if at least one of the corresponding bits in either operand is set to 1. Otherwise, the bits are set to zero.

f) Keyword _____ introduces a structure declaration.

g) Keyword _____ is used to create a synonym for a previously defined data type.

h) The bits in the result of an expression using the _____ operator are set to 1 if exactly one of the corresponding bits in either operand is set to 1. Otherwise, the bits are set to zero.

i) The bitwise AND operator `&` is often used to _____ bits, that is to select certain bits while zeroing others.

j) Keyword _____ is used to introduce a union definition.

k) The name of the structure is referred to as the structure _____.

l) A structure member is accessed with either the _____ or the _____ operator.

m) The _____ and _____ operators are used to shift the bits of a value to the left or to the right, respectively.

n) A(n) _____ is a set of integers represented by identifiers.

10.2 State whether each of the following is *true* or *false*. If *false*, explain why.

a) Structures may contain variables of only one data type.

b) Two unions can be compared (using ==) to determine if they are equal.

c) The tag name of a structure is optional.

d) Members of different structures must have unique names.

e) Keyword `typedef` is used to define new data types.

f) Structures are always passed to functions by reference.

g) Structures may not be compared by using operators == and !=.

10.3 Write code to accomplish each of the following:

a) Define a structure called `part` containing `int` variable `partNumber` and `char` array `partName` with values that may be as long as 25 characters (including the terminating null character).

b) Define `Part` to be a synonym for the type `struct part`.

c) Use `Part` to declare variable `a` to be of type `struct part`, array `b[ 10 ]` to be of type `struct part` and variable `ptr` to be of type pointer to `struct part`.

d) Read a part number and a part name from the keyboard into the individual members of variable `a`.

e) Assign the member values of variable `a` to element 3 of array `b`.

f) Assign the address of array `b` to the pointer variable `ptr`.

g) Print the member values of element 3 of array `b` using the variable `ptr` and the structure pointer operator to refer to the members.

10.4 Find the error in each of the following:

a) Assume that `struct card` has been defined containing two pointers to type `char`, namely `face` and `suit`. Also, the variable `c` has been defined to be of type `struct card` and the variable `cPtr` has been defined to be of type pointer to `struct card`. Variable `cPtr` has been assigned the address of `c`.

```
printf( "%s\n", *cPtr->face );
```

b) Assume that `struct card` has been defined containing two pointers to type `char`, namely `face` and `suit`. Also, the array `hearts[ 13 ]` has been defined to be of type `struct card`. The following statement should print the member `face` of element 10 of the array.

```
printf( "%s\n", hearts.face );
```

c)
```
union values {
    char w;
    float x;
    double y;
};

union values v = { 1.27 };
```

d)
```
struct person {
    char lastName[ 15 ];
    char firstName[ 15 ];
    int age;
}
```

e) Assume `struct person` has been defined as in part (d) but with the appropriate correction.

> `person d;`

f) Assume variable `p` has been declared as type `struct person` and variable `c` has been declared as type `struct card`.

> `p = c;`

ANSWERS TO SELF-REVIEW EXERCISES

10.1   a) structure. b) union. c) bitwise AND (`&`). d) members. e) bitwise inclusive OR (`|`). f) `struct`. g) `typedef`. h) bitwise exclusive OR (`^`). i) mask. j) `union`. k) tag name. l) structure member, structure pointer. m) left-shift operator (`<<`), right-shift operator (`>>`). n) enumeration.

10.2   a) False. A structure can contain variables of many data types.
   b) False. Unions can not be compared because there might be bytes of undefined data with different values in union variables that are otherwise identical.
   c) True.
   d) False. The members of separate structures can have the same names, but the members of the same structure must have unique names.
   e) False. Keyword `typedef` is used to define new names (synonyms) for previously defined data types.
   f) False. Structures are always passed to functions call by value.
   g) True, because of alignment problems.

10.3   a) `struct part {`
           `int partNumber;`
           `char partName[25];`
        `};`
   b) `typedef struct part Part;`
   c) `Part a, b[ 10 ], *ptr;`
   d) `scanf( "%d%s", &a.partNumber, &a.partName };`
   e) `b[ 3 ] = a;`
   f) `ptr = b;`
   g) `printf( "%d %s\n", ( ptr + 3 )->partNumber, ( ptr + 3 )->partName);`

10.4   a) The parentheses that should enclose `*cPtr` have been omitted causing the order of evaluation of the expression to be incorrect. The expression should be
            `( *cPtr )->face`
   b) The array subscript has been omitted. The expression should be
            `hearts[ 10 ].face.`
   c) A union can only be initialized with a value that has the same type as the union's first member.
   d) A semicolon is required to end a structure definition.
   e) Keyword `struct` was omitted from the variable declaration. The declaration should be
            `struct person d;`
   f) Variables of different structure types cannot be assigned to one another.

EXERCISES

10.5   Provide the definition for each of the following structures and unions:
   a) Structure `inventory` containing character array `partName[ 30 ]`, integer `partNumber`, floating point `price`, integer `stock` and integer `reorder`.

    b) Union data containing char c, short s, long b, float f and double d.

    c) A structure called address that contains character arrays
streetAddress[25], city[20], state[3] and zipCode[6].

    d) Structure student that contains arrays firstName[15] and
lastName[15] and variable homeAddress of type struct address from part (c).

    e) Structure test containing 16 bit fields with widths of 1 bit. The names of the bit fields
are the letters a to p.

10.6   Given the following structure and variable definitions,

```
struct customer {
    char lastName[ 15 ];
    char firstName[ 15 ];
    int customerNumber;

    struct {
        char phoneNumber[ 11 ];
        char address[ 50 ];
        char city[ 15 ];
        char state[ 3 ];
        char zipCode[ 6 ];
    } personal;

} customerRecord, *customerPtr;

customerPtr = &customerRecord;
```

write an expression that can be used to access the structure members in each of the following parts:

    a) Member lastName of structure customerRecord.

    b) Member lastName of the structure pointed to by customerPtr.

    c) Member firstName of structure customerRecord.

    d) Member firstName of the structure pointed to by customerPtr.

    e) Member customerNumber of structure customerRecord.

    f) Member customerNumber of the structure pointed to by customerPtr.

    g) Member phoneNumber of member personal of structure customerRecord.

    h) Member phoneNumber of member personal of the structure pointed to by customer-
Ptr.

    i) Member address of member personal of structure customerRecord.

    j) Member address of member personal of the structure pointed to by customerPtr.

    k) Member city of member personal of structure customerRecord.

    l) Member city of member personal of the structure pointed to by customerPtr.

    m) Member state of member personal of structure customerRecord.

    n) Member state of member personal of the structure pointed to by customerPtr.

    o) Member zipCode of member personal of customerRecord.

    p) Member zipCode of member personal of the structure pointed to by customerPtr.

10.7   Modify the program of Fig. 10.16 to shuffle the cards using a high performance shuffle (as shown in Fig. 10.3). Print the resulting deck in two column format as in Fig. 10.4. Precede each card with its color.

10.8   Create union integer with members char c, short s, int i and long b. Write a program that inputs value of type char, short, int and long and stores the values in union variables of type union integer. Each union variable should be printed as a char, a short, an int and a long. Do the values always print correctly?

10.9   Create union floatingPoint with members float f, double d and long double x. Write a program that inputs value of type float, double and long double and stores the values in union variables of type `union floatingPoint`. Each union variable should be printed as a `float`, a `double` and a `long double`. Do the values always print correctly?

10.10 Write a program that right shifts an integer variable 4 bits. The program should print the integer in bits before and after the shift operation. Does your system place 0s or 1s in the vacated bits?

10.11 If your computer uses 2-byte integers, modify the program of Fig. 10.7 so that it works with 2-byte integers.

10.12 Left shifting an `unsigned` integer by 1 bit is equivalent to multiplying the value 2. Write function `power2` that takes two integer arguments `number` and `pow` and calculates

$$number \ * \ 2^{pow}$$

Use the shift operator to calculate the result. Print the values as integers and as bits.

10.13 The left-shift operator can be used to pack two character values into an `unsigned` integer variable. Write a program that inputs two characters from the keyboard and passes them to function `packCharacters`. To pack two characters into an `unsigned` integer variable, assign the first character to the `unsigned` variable, shift the `unsigned` variable left by 8 bit positions and combine the `unsigned` variable with the second character using the bitwise inclusive OR operator. The program should output the characters in their bit format before and after they are packed into the `unsigned` integer to prove that the characters are in fact packed correctly in the `unsigned` variable.

10.14 Using the right-shift operator, the bitwise AND operator and a mask, write function `unpackCharacters` that takes the `unsigned` integer from Exercise 10.13 and unpacks it into two characters. To unpack two characters from an `unsigned` integer, combine the unsigned integer with the mask 65280 (00000000 00000000 11111111 00000000) and right shift the result 8 bits. Assign the resulting value to a `char` variable. Then combine the `unsigned` integer with the mask 255 (00000000 00000000 00000000 11111111). Assign the result to another `char` variable. The program should print the `unsigned` integer in bits before it is unpacked, then print the characters in bits to confirm that they were unpacked correctly.

10.15 If your system uses 4-byte integers, rewrite the program of Exercise 10.13 to pack 4 characters.

10.16 If your system uses 4-byte integers, rewrite the function `unpackCharacters` of Exercise 10.14 to unpack 4 characters. Create the masks you need to unpack the 4 characters by left shifting the value `255` in the mask variable by 8 bits 0, 1, 2 or 3 times (depending on the byte you are unpacking).

10.17 Write a program that reverses the order of the bits in an `unsigned` integer value. The program should input the value from the user and call function `reverseBits` to print the bits in reverse order. Print the value in bits both before and after the bits are reversed to confirm that the bits are reversed properly.

10.18 Modify function `displayBits` of Fig. 10.7 so it is portable between systems using 2-byte integers and systems using 4-byte integers. [*Hint:* Use the `sizeof` operator to determine the size of an integer on a particular machine.]

10.19 The following program uses function `multiple` to determine if the integer entered from the keyboard is a multiple of some integer X. Examine the function multiple, then determine the value of X.

```
1   /* ex10_19.c */
2   /* This program determines if a value is a multiple of X. */
3   #include <stdio.h>
4
```

```
5    int multiple( int num ); /* prototype */
6
7    int main()
8    {
9       int y; /* y will hold an integer entered by the user  */
10
11      printf( "Enter an integer between 1 and 32000: " );
12      scanf( "%d", &y );
13
14      /* if y is a multiple of X */
15      if ( multiple( y ) ) {
16         printf( "%d is a multiple of X\n", y );
17      } /* end if */
18      else {
19         printf( "%d is not a multiple of X\n", y );
20      } /* end else */
21
22      return 0; /* indicates successful termination */
23   } /* end main */
24
25   /* determine if num is a multiple of X */
26   int multiple( int num )
27   {
28      int i;        /* counter */
29      int mask = 1; /* initialize mask */
30      int mult = 1; /* initialize mult */
31
32      for ( i = 1; i <= 10; i++, mask <<= 1 ) {
33
34         if ( ( num & mask ) != 0 ) {
35            mult = 0;
36            break;
37         } /* end if */
38
39      } /* end for */
40
41      return mult;
42   } /* end function multiple */
```

(Part 2 of 2.)

10.20 What does the following program do?

```
1    /* ex10_20.c */
2    #include <stdio.h>
3
4    int mystery( unsigned bits ); /* prototype */
5
6    int main()
7    {
8       unsigned x; /* x will hold an integer entered by the user */
9
```

(Part 1 of 2.)

```
10      printf( "Enter an integer: " );
11      scanf( "%u", &x );
12
13      printf( "The result is %d\n", mystery( x ) );
14
15      return 0; /* indicates successful termination */
16   } /* end main */
17
18   /* What does this function do? */
19   int mystery( unsigned bits )
20   {
21      unsigned i;                  /* counter */
22      unsigned mask = 1 << 31; /* initialize mask */
23      unsigned total = 0;       /* initialize total */
24
25      for ( i = 1; i <= 32; i++, bits <<= 1 ) {
26
27         if ( ( bits & mask ) == mask ) {
28            total++;
29         } /* end if */
30
31      } /* end for */
32
33      return !( total % 2 ) ? 1 : 0;
34   } /* end function mystery */
```

(Part 2 of 2.)

11

C File Processing

Objectives

- To be able to create, read, write and update files.
- To become familiar with sequential access file processing.
- To become familiar with random-access file processing.

I read part of it all the way through.
Samuel Goldwyn

Hats off!
The flag is passing by.
Henry Holcomb Bennett

Consciousness … does not appear to itself chopped up in bits. … A "river" or a "stream" are the metaphors by which it is most naturally described.
William James

I can only assume that a "Do Not File" document is filed in a "Do Not File" file.
Senator Frank Church
Senate Intelligence Subcommittee Hearing, 1975

11.1 Introduction

Storage of data in variables and arrays is temporary—all such data are lost when a program terminates. *Files* are used for permanent retention of large amounts of data. Computers store files on secondary storage devices, especially disk storage devices. In this chapter, we explain how data files are created, updated and processed by C programs. We consider sequential-access files and random-access files.

11.2 Data Hierarchy

Ultimately, all data items processed by a computer are reduced to combinations of *zeros and ones*. This occurs because it is simple and economical to build electronic devices that can assume two stable states—one of the states represents 0 and the other represents 1. It is remarkable that the impressive functions performed by computers involve only the most fundamental manipulations of 0s and 1s.

The smallest data item in a computer can assume the value 0 or the value 1. Such a data item is called a *bit* (short for *"binary digit"*—a digit that can assume one of two values). Computer circuitry performs various simple bit manipulations such as determining the value of a bit, setting the value of a bit and reversing a bit (from 1 to 0 or from 0 to 1).

It is cumbersome for programmers to work with data in the low-level form of bits. Instead, programmers prefer to work with data in the form of *decimal digits* (i.e., 0, 1, 2, 3, 4, 5, 6, 7, 8, and 9), *letters* (i.e., A–Z, and a–z), and *special symbols* (i.e., $, @, %, &, *, (,), -, +, ", :, ?, /, and others). Digits, letters, and special symbols are referred to as *characters*. The set of all characters that may be used to write programs and represent data items on a particular computer is called that computer's *character set*. Since computers can process only 1s and 0s, every character in a computer's character set is represented as a pattern of 1s and 0s (called a *byte*). Today, bytes are most commonly composed of eight bits. Programmers create programs and data items as characters; computers then manipulate and process these characters as patterns of bits.

Just as characters are composed of bits, *fields* are composed of characters. A field is a group of characters that conveys meaning. For example, a field consisting solely of uppercase and lowercase letters can be used to represent a person's name.

Data items processed by computers form a *data hierarchy* in which data items become larger and more complex in structure as we progress from bits, to characters (bytes), to fields, and so on.

A *record* (i.e., a `struct` in C) is composed of several fields. In a payroll system, for example, a record for a particular employee might consist of the following fields:

1. Social Security number (alphanumeric field)

2. Name (alphabetic field)

3. Address (alphanumeric field)

4. Hourly salary rate (numeric field)

5. Number of exemptions claimed (numeric field)

6. Year-to-date earnings (numeric field)

7. Amount of Federal taxes withheld (numeric field)

Thus, a record is a group of related fields. In the preceding example, each of the fields belongs to the same employee. Of course, a particular company may have many employees and will have a payroll record for each employee. A *file* is a group of related records. A company's payroll file normally contains one record for each employee. Thus, a payroll file for a small company might contain only 22 records, whereas a payroll file for a large company might contain 100,000 records. It is not unusual for an organization to have hundreds or even thousands of files, with some containing billions or even trillions of characters of information. Figure 11.1 illustrates the data hierarchy.

To facilitate the retrieval of specific records from a file, at least one field in each record is chosen as a *record key*. A record key identifies a record as belonging to a particular person or entity. For example, in the payroll record described in this section, the Social Security number would normally be chosen as the record key.

There are many ways of organizing records in a file. The most popular type of organization is called a *sequential file*, in which records are typically stored in order by the record key field. In a payroll file, records are usually placed in order by Social Security Number. The first employee record in the file contains the lowest Social Security number, and subsequent records contain increasingly higher Social Security numbers.

Most businesses store date in many different files. For example, companies may have payroll files, accounts receivable files (listing money due from clients), accounts payable files (listing money due to suppliers), inventory files (listing facts about all the items handled by the business) and many other types of files. A group of related files is sometimes called a *database*. A collection of programs designed to create and manage databases is called a *database management system* (DBMS).

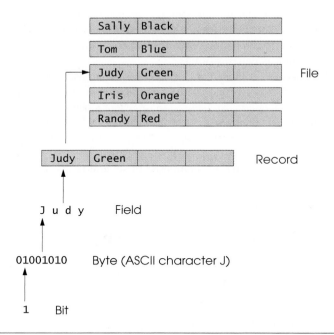

Fig. 11.1 Data hierarchy.

11.3 Files and Streams

C views each file simply as a sequential stream of bytes (Fig. 11.2). Each file ends either with an *end-of-file marker* or at a specific byte number recorded in a system-maintained, administrative data structure. When a file is *opened,* a *stream* is associated with the file. Three files and their associated streams are automatically opened when program execution begins—the *standard input,* the *standard output* and the *standard error.* Streams provide communication channels between files and programs. For example, the standard input stream enables a program to read data from the keyboard, and the standard output stream enables a program to print data on the screen. Opening a file returns a pointer to a FILE structure (defined in <stdio.h>) that contains information used to process the file. This structure includes a *file descriptor,* i.e., an index into an operating system array called the *open file table.* Each array element contains a *file control block (FCB)* that the operating system uses to administer a particular file. The standard input, standard output and standard error are manipulated using file pointers stdin, stdout and stderr.

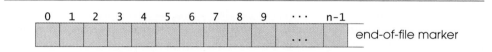

Fig. 11.2 C's view of a file of *n* bytes.

The standard library provides many functions for reading data from files and for writing data to files. Function fgetc, like getchar, reads one character from a file. Function fgetc receives as an argument a FILE pointer for the file from which a character will be read. The call fgetc(stdin) reads one character from stdin—the standard input. This call is equivalent to the call getchar(). Function fputc, like putchar, writes one character to a file. Function fputc receives as arguments a character to be written and a pointer for the file to which the character will be written. The function call fputc('a', stdout) writes the character 'a' to stdout—the standard output. This call is equivalent to putchar('a').

Several other functions used to read data from standard input and write data to standard output have similarly named file processing functions. The fgets and fputs functions, for example, can be used to read a line from a file and write a line to a file, respectively. Their counterparts for reading from standard input and writing to standard output, gets and puts, were discussed in Chapter 8. In the next several sections, we introduce the file processing equivalents of functions scanf and printf—fscanf and fprintf. Later in the chapter we discuss functions fread and fwrite.

11.4 Creating a Sequential-Access File

C imposes no structure on a file. Thus, notions such as a record of a file do not exist as part of the C language. Therefore, the programmer must provide a file structure to meet the requirements of a particular application. In the following example, we see how the programmer may impose a record structure on a file.

Figure 11.3 creates a simple sequential-access file that might be used in an accounts receivable system to help keep track of the amounts owed by a company's credit clients. For each client, the program obtains an account number, the client's name and the client's balance (i.e., the amount the client owes the company for goods and services received in the past). The data obtained for each client constitutes a "record" for that client. The account number is used as the record key in this application—the file will be created and maintained in account number order. This program assumes the user enters the records in account number order. In a comprehensive accounts receivable system, a sorting capability would be provided so the user could enter the records in any order. The records would then be sorted and written to the file.

```
1   /* Fig. 11.3: fig11_03.c
2      Create a sequential file */
3   #include <stdio.h>
4
5   int main()
6   {
7      int account;      /* account number */
8      char name[ 30 ]; /* account name */
9      double balance;  /* account balance */
10
11     FILE *cfPtr;      /* cfPtr = clients.dat file pointer */
12
13     /* fopen opens file. Exit program if unable to create file  */
14     if ( ( cfPtr = fopen( "clients.dat", "w" ) ) == NULL ) {
15        printf( "File could not be opened\n" );
16     } /* end if */
```

Fig. 11.3   Creating a sequential file. (Part 1 of 2.)

```
17     else {
18        printf( "Enter the account, name, and balance.\n" );
19        printf( "Enter EOF to end input.\n" );
20        printf( "? " );
21        scanf( "%d%s%lf", &account, name, &balance );
22
23        /* write account, name and balance into file with fprintf */
24        while ( !feof( stdin ) ) {
25           fprintf( cfPtr, "%d %s %.2f\n", account, name, balance );
26           printf( "? " );
27           scanf( "%d%s%lf", &account, name, &balance );
28        } /* end while */
29
30        fclose( cfPtr ); /* fclose closes file */
31     } /* end else */
32
33     return 0; /* indicates successful termination */
34
35  } /* end main */
```

```
Enter the account, name, and balance.
Enter EOF to end input.
? 100 Jones 24.98
? 200 Doe 345.67
? 300 White 0.00
? 400 Stone -42.16
? 500 Rich 224.62
? ^Z
```

Fig. 11.3   Creating a sequential file. (Part 2 of 2.)

Now let us examine this program. Line 11

```
FILE *cfPtr;
```

states that cfptr is a pointer to a FILE structure. A C program administers each file with a separate FILE structure. The programmer need not know the specifics of the FILE structure to use files. We will soon see precisely how the FILE structure leads indirectly to the operating system's file control block (FCB) for a file.

Each open file must have a separately declared pointer of type FILE that is used to refer to the file. Line 14

```
if ( ( cfPtr = fopen( "clients.dat", "w" ) ) == NULL )
```

names the file—"clients.dat"—to be used by the program and establishes a "line of communication" with the file. The file pointer cfPtr is assigned a pointer to the FILE structure for the file opened with fopen. Function fopen takes two arguments: a file name and a *file open mode*. The file open mode "w" indicates that the file is to be opened for *writing*. If a file does not exist and it is opened for writing, fopen creates the file. If an existing file is opened for writing, the contents of the file are discarded without warning. In the program, the if statement is used to determine whether the file pointer cfPtr is NULL (i.e., the file is not opened). If it is NULL, the program prints an error message and terminates. Otherwise, the program processes the input and writes it to the file.

Common Programming Error 11.1

Opening an existing file for writing ("w") when, in fact, the user wants to preserve the file discards the contents of the file without warning.

Common Programming Error 11.2

Forgetting to open a file before attempting to reference it in a program is a logic error.

The program prompts the user to enter the various fields for each record or to enter end-of-file when data entry is complete. Figure 11.4 lists the key combinations for entering end-of-file for various computer systems.

Operating system	Key combination
UNIX	*<return> <ctrl> d*
Windows	*<ctrl> z*
Macintosh	*<ctrl> d*

Fig. 11.4   End-of-file key combinations for various popular operating systems.

Line 24

```
while ( !feof( stdin ) )
```

uses function **feof** to determine whether the *end-of-file indicator* is set for the file to which **stdin** refers. The end-of-file indicator informs the program that there is no more data to be processed. In Fig. 11.3, the end-of-file indicator is set for the standard input when the user enters the end-of-file key combination. The argument to function **feof** is a pointer to the file being tested for the end-of-file indicator (**stdin** in this case). The function returns a nonzero (true) value when the end-of-file indicator has been set; otherwise, the function returns zero. The **while** statement that includes the **feof** call in this program continues executing while the end-of-file indicator is not set.

Line 25

```
fprintf( cfPtr, "%d %s %.2f\n", account, name, balance );
```

writes data to the file **clients.dat**. The data may be retrieved later by a program designed to read the file (see Section 11.5). Function **fprintf** is equivalent to **printf** except that **fprintf** also receives as an argument a file pointer for the file to which the data will be written.

Common Programming Error 11.3

Using the wrong file pointer to refer to a file is a logic error.

Error-Prevention Tip 11.1

Be sure that calls to file processing functions in a program contain the correct file pointers.

After the user enters end-of-file, the program closes the `clients.dat` file with `fclose` and terminates. Function `fclose` also receives the file pointer (rather than the file name) as an argument. If function `fclose` is not called explicitly, the operating system normally will close the file when program execution terminates. This is an example of operating system "housekeeping."

Good Programming Practice 11.1

Explicitly close each file as soon as it is known that the program will not reference the file again.

Performance Tip 11.1

Closing a file can free resources for which other users or programs may be waiting.

In the sample execution for the program of Fig. 11.3, the user enters information for five accounts, then enters end-of-file to signal that data entry is complete. The sample execution does not show how the data records actually appear in the file. To verify that the file has been created successfully, in the next section we present a program that reads the file and prints its contents.

Figure 11.5 illustrates the relationship between FILE pointers, FILE structures and FCBs in memory. When the file `"clients.dat"` is opened, an FCB for the file is copied into memory. The figure shows the connection between the file pointer returned by `fopen` and the FCB used by the operating system to administer the file.

Programs may process no files, one file or several files. Each file used in a program must have a unique name and will have a different file pointer returned by `fopen`. All subsequent file processing functions after the file is opened must refer to the file with the appropriate file pointer. Files may be opened in one of several modes (Fig. 11.6). To create a file, or to discard the contents of a file before writing data, open the file for writing (`"w"`). To read an existing file, open it for reading (`"r"`). To add records to the end of an existing file, open the file for appending (`"a"`). To open a file so that it may be written to and read from, open the file for updating in one of the three update modes—`"r+"`, `"w+"` or `"a+"`. Mode `"r+"` opens a file for reading and writing. Mode `"w+"` creates a file for reading and writing. If the file already exists, the file is opened and the current contents of the file are discarded. Mode `"a+"` opens a file for reading and writing—all writing is done at the end of the file. If the file does not exist, it is created. Note that each file open mode has a corresponding binary mode (containing the letter b) for manipulating binary files. The binary modes are used in Section 11.6–Section 11.10 when we introduce random-access files.

If an error occurs while opening a file in any mode, `fopen` returns NULL.

Common Programming Error 11.4

Opening a nonexistent file for reading is an error.

Common Programming Error 11.5

Opening a file for reading or writing without having been granted the appropriate access rights to the file (this is operating-system dependent) is an error.

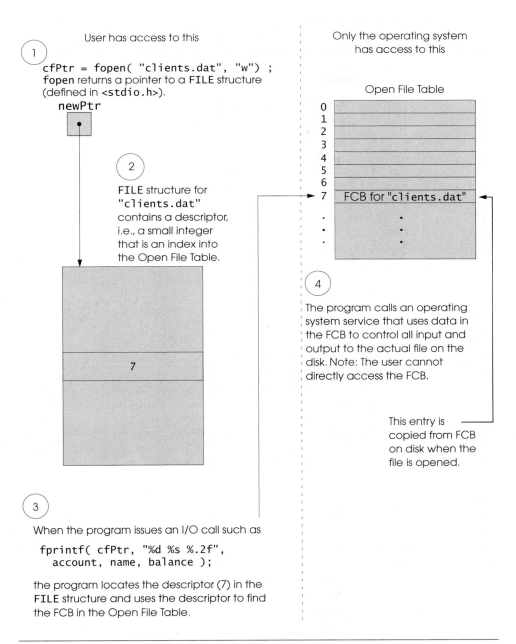

Fig. 11.5   Relationship between FILE pointers, FILE structures and FCBs.

Common Programming Error 11.6

Opening a file for writing when no disk space is available is an error.

Mode	Description
r	Open a file for reading.
w	Create a file for writing. If the file already exists, discard the current contents.
a	Append; open or create a file for writing at the end of the file.
r+	Open a file for update (reading and writing).
w+	Create a file for update. If the file already exists, discard the current contents.
a+	Append: open or create a file for update; writing is done at the end of the file.
rb	Open a file for reading in binary mode.
wb	Create a file for writing in binary mode. If the file already exists, discard the current contents.
ab	Append; open or create a file for writing at the end of the file in binary mode.
rb+	Open a file for update (reading and writing) in binary mode.
wb+	Create a file for update in binary mode. If the file already exists, discard the current contents.
ab+	Append: open or create a file for update in binary mode; writing is done at the end of the file.

Fig. 11.6 File opening modes.

Common Programming Error 11.7

Opening a file with the incorrect file mode is a logic error. For example, opening a file in write mode ("w") when it should be opened in update mode ("r+") causes the contents of the file to be discarded.

Error-Prevention Tip 11.2

Open a file only for reading (and not update) if the contents of the file should not be modified. This prevents unintentional modification of the file's contents. This is another example of the principle of least privilege.

11.5 Reading Data from a Sequential-Access File

Data is stored in files so that the data can be retrieved for processing when needed. The previous section demonstrated how to create a file for sequential access. This section shows how to read data sequentially from a file.

Figure 11.7 reads records from the file "clients.dat" created by the program of Fig. 11.3 and prints the contents of the records. Line 11

```
FILE *cfPtr;
```

indicates that cfPtr is a pointer to a FILE. Line 14

```
if ( ( cfPtr = fopen( "clients.dat", "r" ) ) == NULL )
```

attempts to open the file "clients.dat" for reading ("r") and determines whether the file is opened successfully (i.e., fopen does not return NULL). Line 19

```
fscanf( cfPtr, "%d%s%f", &account, name, &balance );
```

reads a "record" from the file. Function fscanf is equivalent to function scanf except fscanf receives as an argument a file pointer for the file from which the data are read. After this statement executes the first time, account will have the value 100, name will have the value "Jones" and balance will have the value 24.98. Each time the second fscanf statement (line 24) executes, the program reads another record from the file and account, name and balance take on new values. When the program reaches the end of the file, the file is closed (line 27) and the program terminates.

```
1   /* Fig. 11.7: fig11_07.c
2      Reading and printing a sequential file */
3   #include <stdio.h>
4
5   int main()
6   {
7      int account;      /* account number */
8      char name[ 30 ]; /* account name */
9      double balance;   /* account balance */
10
11     FILE *cfPtr;       /* cfPtr = clients.dat file pointer */
12
13     /* fopen opens file; exits program if file cannot be opened */
14     if ( ( cfPtr = fopen( "clients.dat", "r" ) ) == NULL ) {
15        printf( "File could not be opened\n" );
16     } /* end if */
17     else { /* read account, name and balance from file */
18        printf( "%-10s%-13s%s\n", "Account", "Name", "Balance" );
19        fscanf( cfPtr, "%d%s%lf", &account, name, &balance );
20
21        /* while not end of file */
22        while ( !feof( cfPtr ) ) {
23           printf( "%-10d%-13s%7.2f\n", account, name, balance );
24           fscanf( cfPtr, "%d%s%lf", &account, name, &balance );
25        } /* end while */
26
27        fclose( cfPtr ); /* fclose closes the file */
28     } /* end else */
29
30     return 0; /* indicates successful termination */
31
32   } /* end main */
```

```
Account    Name         Balance
100        Jones          24.98
200        Doe           345.67
300        White           0.00
400        Stone         -42.16
500        Rich          224.62
```

Fig. 11.7 Reading and printing a sequential file.

To retrieve data sequentially from a file, a program normally starts reading from the beginning of the file and reads all data consecutively until the desired data are found. It may be desirable to process the data sequentially in a file several times (from the beginning of the file) during the execution of a program. A statement such as

```
rewind( cfPtr );
```

causes a program's *file position pointer*—which indicates the number of the next byte in the file to be read or written—to be repositioned to the beginning of the file (i.e., byte 0) pointed to by `cfPtr`. The file position pointer is not really a pointer. Rather it is an integer value that specifies the byte location in the file at which the next read or write is to occur. This is sometimes referred to as the *file offset*. The file position pointer is a member of the `FILE` structure associated with each file.

The program of Fig. 11.8 allows a credit manager to obtain lists of customers with zero balances (i.e., customers who do not owe any money), customers with credit balances (i.e., customers to whom the company owes money) and customers with debit balances (i.e., customers who owe the company money for goods and services received). A credit balance is a negative amount; a debit balance is a positive amount.

```c
1   /* Fig. 11.8: fig11_08.c
2      Credit inquiry program */
3   #include <stdio.h>
4
5   /* function main begins program execution */
6   int main()
7   {
8      int request;     /* request number */
9      int account;     /* account number */
10     double balance;  /* account balance */
11     char name[ 30 ]; /* account name */
12     FILE *cfPtr;     /* clients.dat file pointer */
13
14     /* fopen opens the file; exits program if file cannot be opened */
15     if ( ( cfPtr = fopen( "clients.dat", "r" ) ) == NULL ) {
16        printf( "File could not be opened\n" );
17     } /* end if */
18     else {
19
20        /* display request options */
21        printf( "Enter request\n"
22           " 1 - List accounts with zero balances\n"
23           " 2 - List accounts with credit balances\n"
24           " 3 - List accounts with debit balances\n"
25           " 4 - End of run\n? " );
26        scanf( "%d", &request );
27
28        /* process user's request */
29        while ( request != 4 ) {
30
31           /* read account, name and balance from file */
32           fscanf( cfPtr, "%d%s%lf", &account, name, &balance );
33
34           switch ( request ) {
```

Fig. 11.8 Credit inquiry program. (Part 1 of 3.)

```
35
36              case 1:
37                  printf( "\nAccounts with zero balances:\n" );
38
39                  /* read file contents (until eof) */
40                  while ( !feof( cfPtr ) ) {
41
42                      if ( balance == 0 ) {
43                          printf( "%-10d%-13s%7.2f\n",
44                              account, name, balance );
45                      } /* end if */
46
47                      /* read account, name and balance from file */
48                      fscanf( cfPtr, "%d%s%lf",
49                          &account, name, &balance );
50                  } /* end while */
51
52                  break;
53
54              case 2:
55                  printf( "\nAccounts with credit balances:\n" );
56
57                  /* read file contents (until eof) */
58                  while ( !feof( cfPtr ) ) {
59
60                      if ( balance < 0 ) {
61                          printf( "%-10d%-13s%7.2f\n",
62                              account, name, balance );
63                      } /* end if */
64
65                      /* read account, name and balance from file */
66                      fscanf( cfPtr, "%d%s%lf",
67                          &account, name, &balance );
68                  } /* end while */
69
70                  break;
71
72              case 3:
73                  printf( "\nAccounts with debit balances:\n" );
74
75                  /* read file contents (until eof) */
76                  while ( !feof( cfPtr ) ) {
77
78                      if ( balance > 0 ) {
79                          printf( "%-10d%-13s%7.2f\n",
80                              account, name, balance );
81                      } /* end if */
82
83                      /* read account, name and balance from file */
84                      fscanf( cfPtr, "%d%s%lf",
85                          &account, name, &balance );
86                  } /* end while */
87
```

Fig. 11.8   Credit inquiry program. (Part 2 of 3.)

```
88                      break;
89
90              } /* end switch */
91
92              rewind( cfPtr ); /* return cfPtr to beginning of file */
93
94              printf( "\n? " );
95              scanf( "%d", &request );
96          } /* end while */
97
98          printf( "End of run.\n" );
99          fclose( cfPtr ); /* fclose closes the file */
100     } /* end else */
101
102     return 0; /* indicates successful termination */
103
104 } /* end main */
```

Fig. 11.8   Credit inquiry program. (Part 3 of 3.)

The program displays a menu and allows the credit manager to enter one of three options to obtain credit information. Option 1 produces a list of accounts with zero balances. Option 2 produces a list of accounts with credit balances. Option 3 produces a list of accounts with debit balances. Option 4 terminates program execution. A sample output is shown in Fig. 11.9.

```
Enter request
 1 - List accounts with zero balances
 2 - List accounts with credit balances
 3 - List accounts with debit balances
 4 - End of run
? 1

Accounts with zero balances:
300        White           0.00

? 2

Accounts with credit balances:
400        Stone         -42.16

? 3

Accounts with debit balances:
100        Jones          24.98
200        Doe           345.67
500        Rich          224.62

? 4
End of run.
```

Fig. 11.9   Sample output of the credit inquiry program of Fig. 11.8.

Note that data in this type of sequential file cannot be modified without the risk of destroying other data in the file. For example, if the name "White" needed to be changed to "Worthington," the old name cannot simply be overwritten. The record for White was written to the file as

```
300 White 0.00
```

If the record is rewritten beginning at the same location in the file using the new name, the record would be

```
300 Worthington 0.00
```

The new record is larger (has more characters) than the original record. The characters beyond the second "o" in "Worthington" would overwrite the beginning of the next sequential record in the file. The problem here is that in the *formatted input/output model* using fprintf and fscanf, fields—and hence records—can vary in size. For example, 7, 14, −117, 2074 and 27383 are all ints stored in the same number of bytes internally, but they are different-sized fields when displayed on the screen or written to a file as text.

Therefore, sequential access with fprintf and fscanf is not usually used to update records in place. Instead, the entire file is usually rewritten. To make the preceding name change, the records before 300 White 0.00 in such a sequential-access file would be copied to a new file, the new record would be written and the records after 300 White 0.00 would be copied to the new file. This requires processing every record in the file to update one record.

11.6 Random-Access Files

As we stated previously, records in a file created with the formatted output function fprintf are not necessarily the same length. However, individual records of a *random-access file* are normally fixed in length and may be accessed directly (and thus quickly) without searching through other records. This makes random-access files appropriate for airline reservation systems, banking systems, point-of-sale systems, and other kinds of *transaction processing systems* that require rapid access to specific data. There are other ways of implementing random-access files, but we will limit our discussion to this straightforward approach using fixed-length records.

Because every record in a random-access file normally has the same length, the exact location of a record relative to the beginning of the file can be calculated as a function of the record key. We will soon see how this facilitates immediate access to specific records, even in large files.

Figure 11.10 illustrates one way to implement a random-access file. Such a file is like a freight train with many cars—some empty and some with cargo. Each car in the train is the same length.

Data can be inserted in a random-access file without destroying other data in the file. Data stored previously can also be updated or deleted without rewriting the entire file. In the following sections we explain how to create a random-access file, enter data, read the data both sequentially and randomly, update the data, and delete data no longer needed.

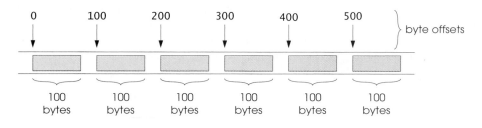

Fig. 11.10 C's view of a random-access file.

11.7 Creating a Random-Access File

Function `fwrite` transfers a specified number of bytes beginning at a specified location in memory to a file. The data are written beginning at the location in the file indicated by the file position pointer. Function `fread` transfers a specified number of bytes from the location in the file specified by the file position pointer to an area in memory beginning with a specified address. Now, when writing an integer, instead of using

```
fprintf( fPtr, "%d", number );
```

which could print a single digit or as many as 11 digits (10 digits plus a sign, each of which requires 1 byte of storage) for a 4-byte integer, we can use

```
fwrite( &number, sizeof( int ), 1, fPtr );
```

which always writes 4 bytes (or 2 bytes on a system with 2-byte integers) from a variable `number` to the file represented by `fPtr` (we will explain the `1` argument shortly). Later, `fread` can be used to read 4 of those bytes into an integer variable `number`. Although `fread` and `fwrite` read and write data, such as integers, in fixed-size rather than variable-size format, the data they handle are processed in computer "raw data" format (i.e., bytes of data) rather than in `printf`'s and `scanf`'s human-readable text format.

Functions `fwrite` and `fread` are capable of reading and writing arrays of data to and from disk. The third argument of both `fread` and `fwrite` is the number of elements in the array that should be read from disk or written to disk. The preceding `fwrite` function call writes a single integer to disk, so the third argument is `1` (as if one element of an array is being written).

File processing programs rarely write a single field to a file. Normally, they write one `struct` at a time, as we show in the following examples.

Consider the following problem statement:

> *Create a credit processing system capable of storing up to 100 fixed-length records. Each record should consist of an account number that will be used as the record key, a last name, a first name and a balance. The resulting program should be able to update an account, insert a new account record, delete an account and list all the account records in a formatted text file for printing. Use a random-access file.*

The next several sections introduce the techniques necessary to create the credit processing program. Figure 11.11 shows how to open a random-access file, define a record format using a `struct`, write data to the disk and close the file. This program initializes all 100 records of the file `"credit.dat"` with empty `struct`s using the function `fwrite`. Each empty `struct` contains 0 for the account number, "" (the empty string) for the last name, "" for the first name and 0.0 for the balance. The file is initialized in this manner to create space on the disk in which the file will be stored and to make it possible to determine if a record contains data.

```c
1   /* Fig. 11.11: fig11_11.c
2      Creating a random-access file sequentially */
3   #include <stdio.h>
4
5   /* clientData structure definition */
6   struct clientData {
7      int acctNum;           /* account number */
8      char lastName[ 15 ];   /* account last name */
9      char firstName[ 10 ];  /* account first name */
10     double balance;        /* account balance */
11  }; /* end structure clientData */
12
13  int main()
14  {
15     int i; /* counter used to count from 1-100 */
16
17     /* create clientData with default information */
18     struct clientData blankClient = { 0, "", "", 0.0 };
19
20     FILE *cfPtr; /* credit.dat file pointer */
21
22     /* fopen opens the file; exits if file cannot be opened */
23     if ( ( cfPtr = fopen( "credit.dat", "wb" ) ) == NULL ) {
24        printf( "File could not be opened.\n" );
25     } /* end if */
26     else {
27
28        /* output 100 blank records to file */
29        for ( i = 1; i <= 100; i++ ) {
30           fwrite( &blankClient, sizeof( struct clientData ), 1, cfPtr );
31        } /* end for */
32
33        fclose ( cfPtr ); /* fclose closes the file */
34     } /* end else */
35
36     return 0; /* indicates successful termination */
37
38  } /* end main */
```

Fig. 11.11 Creating a random access file sequentially.

Function `fwrite` writes a block (specific number of bytes) of data to a file. In our program, line 30

```c
fwrite( &blankClient, sizeof( struct clientData ), 1, cfPtr);
```

causes the structure blankClient of size sizeof(struct clientData) to be written to the file pointed to by cfPtr. The operator sizeof returns the size in bytes of its operand in parentheses (in this case struct clientData). The sizeof operator returns an unsigned integer and can be used to determine the size in bytes of any data type or expression. For example, sizeof(int) can be used to determine whether an integer is stored in 2 or 4 bytes on a particular computer.

Function fwrite can actually be used to write several elements of an array of objects. To write several array elements, the programmer supplies a pointer to an array as the first argument in the call to fwrite and specifies the number of elements to be written as the third argument in the call to fwrite. In the preceding statement, fwrite was used to write a single object that was not an array element. Writing a single object is equivalent to writing one element of an array, hence the 1 in the fwrite call.

11.8 Writing Data Randomly to a Random-Access File

Figure 11.12 writes data to the file "credit.dat". It uses the combination of fseek and fwrite to store data at specific locations in the file. Function fseek sets the file position pointer to a specific position in the file, then fwrite writes the data. A sample execution is shown in Fig. 11.13.

```
1   /* Fig. 11.12: fig11_12.c
2      Writing to a random access file */
3   #include <stdio.h>
4
5   /* clientData structure definition */
6   struct clientData {
7       int acctNum;           /* account number */
8       char lastName[ 15 ];   /* account last name */
9       char firstName[ 10 ];  /* account first name */
10      double balance;        /* account balance */
11  }; /* end structure clientData */
12
13  int main()
14  {
15      FILE *cfPtr; /* credit.dat file pointer */
16
17      /* create clientData with default information */
18      struct clientData client = { 0, "", "", 0.0 };
19
20      /* fopen opens the file; exits if file cannot be opened */
21      if ( ( cfPtr = fopen( "credit.dat", "rb+" ) ) == NULL ) {
22          printf( "File could not be opened.\n" );
23      } /* end if */
24      else {
25
```

Fig. 11.12 Writing data randomly to a random-access file. (Part 1 of 2.)

```
26          /* require user to specify account number */
27          printf( "Enter account number"
28             " ( 1 to 100, 0 to end input )\n? " );
29          scanf( "%d", &client.acctNum );
30
31          /* user enters information, which is copied into file */
32          while ( client.acctNum != 0 ) {
33
34             /* user enters last name, first name and balance */
35             printf( "Enter lastname, firstname, balance\n? " );
36
37             /* set record lastName, firstName and balance value */
38             fscanf( stdin, "%s%s%lf", client.lastName,
39                client.firstName, &client.balance );
40
41             /* seek position in file to user-specified record */
42             fseek( cfPtr, ( client.acctNum - 1 ) *
43                sizeof( struct clientData ), SEEK_SET );
44
45             /* write user-specified information in file */
46             fwrite( &client, sizeof( struct clientData ), 1, cfPtr );
47
48             /* enable user to input another account number */
49             printf( "Enter account number\n? " );
50             scanf( "%d", &client.acctNum );
51          } /* end while */
52
53          fclose( cfPtr ); /* fclose closes the file */
54       } /* end else */
55
56       return 0; /* indicates successful termination */
57
58    } /* end main */
```

Fig. 11.12 Writing data randomly to a random-access file. (Part 2 of 2.)

```
Enter account number ( 1 to 100, 0 to end input )
? 37
Enter lastname, firstname, balance
? Barker Doug 0.00
Enter account number
? 29
Enter lastname, firstname, balance
? Brown Nancy -24.54
Enter account number
? 96
Enter lastname, firstname, balance
? Stone Sam 34.98
Enter account number
? 88
Enter lastname, firstname, balance
? Smith Dave 258.34
```

Fig. 11.13 Sample execution of the program in Fig. 11.12. (Part 1 of 2.)

```
Enter account number
? 33
Enter lastname, firstname, balance
? Dunn Stacey 314.33
Enter account number
? 0
```

Fig. 11.13 Sample execution of the program in Fig. 11.12. (Part 2 of 2.)

Lines 42–43

```
fseek( cfPtr, ( client.acctNum - 1 ) *
    sizeof( struct clientData ), SEEK_SET );
```

position the file position pointer for the file referenced by `cfPtr` to the byte location calculated by (client.accountNum - 1) * sizeof(struct clientData). The value of this expression is called the *offset* or the *displacement*. Because the account number is between 1 and 100 but the byte positions in the file start with 0, 1 is subtracted from the account number when calculating the byte location of the record. Thus, for record 1, the file position pointer is set to byte 0 of the file. The symbolic constant SEEK_SET indicates that the file position pointer is positioned relative to the beginning of the file by the amount of the offset. As the above statement indicates, a seek for account number 1 in the file sets the file position pointer to the beginning of the file because the byte location calculated is 0. Figure 11.14 illustrates the file pointer referring to a FILE structure in memory. The file position pointer in this diagram indicates that the next byte to be read or written is 5 bytes from the beginning of the file.

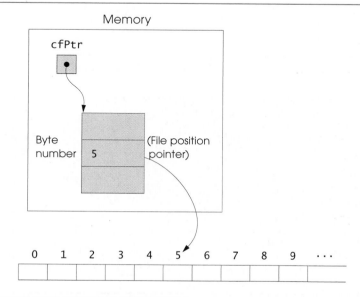

Fig. 11.14 File position pointer indicating an offset of 5 bytes from the beginning of the file.

The function prototype for `fseek` is

```
int fseek( FILE *stream, long int offset, int whence );
```

where `offset` is the number of bytes to seek from location `whence` in the file pointed to by `stream`. The argument `whence` can have one of three values—SEEK_SET, SEEK_CUR or SEEK_END (all defined in `<stdio.h>`)—indicating the location in the file from which the seek begins. SEEK_SET indicates that the seek starts at the beginning of the file; SEEK_CUR indicates that the seek starts at the current location in the file; and SEEK_END indicates that the seek starts at the end of the file.

11.9 Reading Data from a Random-Access File

Function `fread` reads a specified number of bytes from a file into memory. For example, the statement

```
fread( &client, sizeof( struct clientData ), 1, cfPtr );
```

reads the number of bytes determined by `sizeof( struct clientData )` from the file referenced by `cfPtr` and stores the data in the structure `client`. The bytes are read from the location in the file specified by the file position pointer. Function `fread` can be used to read several fixed-size array elements by providing a pointer to the array in which the elements will be stored and by indicating the number of elements to be read. The preceding statement specifies that one element should be read. To read more than one element, specify the number of elements in the third argument of the `fread` statement.

Figure 11.15 reads sequentially every record in the `"credit.dat"` file, determines whether each record contains data and displays the formatted data for records containing data. Function `feof` determines when the end of the file is reached, and the `fread` function transfers data from the disk to the `clientData` structure `client`.

```
1   /* Fig. 11.15: fig11_15.c
2      Reading a random access file sequentially */
3   #include <stdio.h>
4
5   /* clientData structure definition */
6   struct clientData {
7      int acctNum;          /* account number */
8      char lastName[ 15 ];  /* account last name */
9      char firstName[ 10 ]; /* account first name */
10     double balance;       /* account balance */
11  }; /* end structure clientData */
12
13  int main()
14  {
15     FILE *cfPtr; /* credit.dat file pointer */
16
```

Fig. 11.15 Reading a random-access file sequentially. (Part 1 of 2.)

```
17        /* create clientData with default information */
18        struct clientData client = { 0, "", "", 0.0 };
19
20        /* fopen opens the file; exits if file cannot be opened */
21        if ( ( cfPtr = fopen( "credit.dat", "rb" ) ) == NULL ) {
22           printf( "File could not be opened.\n" );
23        } /* end if */
24        else {
25           printf( "%-6s%-16s%-11s%10s\n", "Acct", "Last Name",
26              "First Name", "Balance" );
27
28           /* read all records from file (until eof) */
29           while ( !feof( cfPtr ) ) {
30              fread( &client, sizeof( struct clientData ), 1, cfPtr );
31
32              /* display record */
33              if ( client.acctNum != 0 ) {
34                 printf( "%-6d%-16s%-11s%10.2f\n",
35                    client.acctNum, client.lastName,
36                    client.firstName, client.balance );
37              } /* end if */
38
39           } /* end while */
40
41           fclose( cfPtr ); /* fclose closes the file */
42        } /* end else */
43
44        return 0; /* indicates successful termination */
45
46     } /* end main */
```

```
Acct   Last Name        First Name     Balance
29     Brown            Nancy           -24.54
33     Dunn             Stacey          314.33
37     Barker           Doug              0.00
88     Smith            Dave            258.34
96     Stone            Sam              34.98
```

Fig. 11.15 Reading a random-access file sequentially. (Part 2 of 2.)

11.10 Case Study: Transaction-Processing Program

We now present a substantial transaction-processing program using random-access files. The program maintains a bank's account information. The program updates existing accounts, adds new accounts, deletes accounts and stores a listing of all the current accounts in a text file for printing. We assume that the program of Fig. 11.11 has been executed to create the file credit.dat.

The program has five options. Option 1 calls function textFile to store a formatted list of all the accounts in a text file called accounts.txt that may be printed later. The function uses fread and the sequential file access techniques used in the program of Fig. 11.15. After choosing option 1 the file accounts.txt contains:

```
Acct   Last Name         First Name      Balance
29     Brown             Nancy            -24.54
33     Dunn              Stacey           314.33
37     Barker            Doug               0.00
88     Smith             Dave             258.34
96     Stone             Sam               34.98
```

Option 2 calls the function updateRecord to update an account. The function will only update a record that already exists, so the function first checks to see if the record specified by the user is empty. The record is read into structure client with fread, then member acctNum is compared to 0. If it is 0, the record contains no information, and a message is printed stating that the record is empty. Then, the menu choices are displayed. If the record contains information, function updateRecord inputs the transaction amount, calculates the new balance and rewrites the record to the file. A typical output for option 2 is

```
Enter account to update ( 1 - 100 ): 37
37     Barker            Doug               0.00

Enter charge ( + ) or payment ( - ): +87.99
37     Barker            Doug              87.99
```

Option 3 calls the function newRecord to add a new account to the file. If the user enters an account number for an existing account, newRecord displays an error message that the record already contains information, and the menu choices are printed again. This function uses the same process to add a new account as does the program in Fig. 11.12. A typical output for option 3 is

```
Enter new account number ( 1 - 100 ): 22
Enter lastname, firstname, balance
? Johnston Sarah 247.45
```

Option 4 calls function deleteRecord to delete a record from the file. Deletion is accomplished by asking the user for the account number and reinitializing the record. If the account contains no information, deleteRecord displays an error message that the account does not exist. Option 5 terminates program execution. The program is shown in Fig. 11.16. Note that the file "credit.dat" is opened for update (reading and writing) using "rb+" mode.

```
1    /* Fig. 11.16: fig11_16.c
2       This program reads a random access file sequentially, updates data
3       already written to the file, creates new data to be placed in the
4       file, and deletes data previously in the file. */
5    #include <stdio.h>
```

Fig. 11.16 Bank account program. (Part 1 of 6.)

```
6
7    /* clientData structure definition */
8    struct clientData {
9       int acctNum;           /* account number */
10      char lastName[ 15 ];   /* account last name */
11      char firstName[ 10 ];  /* account first name */
12      double balance;        /* account balance */
13   }; /* end structure clientData */
14
15   /* prototypes */
16   int enterChoice( void );
17   void textFile( FILE *readPtr );
18   void updateRecord( FILE *fPtr );
19   void newRecord( FILE *fPtr );
20   void deleteRecord( FILE *fPtr );
21
22   int main()
23   {
24      FILE *cfPtr; /* credit.dat file pointer */
25      int choice;  /* user's choice */
26
27      /* fopen opens the file; exits if file cannot be opened */
28      if ( ( cfPtr = fopen( "credit.dat", "rb+" ) ) == NULL ) {
29         printf( "File could not be opened.\n" );
30      } /* end if */
31      else {
32
33         /* enable user to specify action */
34         while ( ( choice = enterChoice() ) != 5 ) {
35
36            switch ( choice ) {
37
38               /* create text file from record file */
39               case 1:
40                  textFile( cfPtr );
41                  break;
42
43               /* update record */
44               case 2:
45                  updateRecord( cfPtr );
46                  break;
47
48               /* create record */
49               case 3:
50                  newRecord( cfPtr );
51                  break;
52
53               /* delete existing record */
54               case 4:
55                  deleteRecord( cfPtr );
56                  break;
57
```

Fig. 11.16 Bank account program. (Part 2 of 6.)

```
58                    /* display message if user does not select valid choice */
59                    default:
60                        printf( "Incorrect choice\n" );
61                        break;
62
63            } /* end switch */
64
65        } /* end while */
66
67        fclose( cfPtr ); /* fclose closes the file */
68    } /* end else */
69
70    return 0; /* indicates successful termination */
71
72 } /* end main */
73
74 /* create formatted text file for printing */
75 void textFile( FILE *readPtr )
76 {
77    FILE *writePtr; /* accounts.txt file pointer */
78
79    /* create clientData with default information */
80    struct clientData client = { 0, "", "", 0.0 };
81
82    /* fopen opens the file; exits if file cannot be opened */
83    if ( ( writePtr = fopen( "accounts.txt", "w" ) ) == NULL ) {
84        printf( "File could not be opened.\n" );
85    } /* end if */
86    else {
87        rewind( readPtr ); /* sets pointer to beginning of file */
88        fprintf( writePtr, "%-6s%-16s%-11s%10s\n",
89            "Acct", "Last Name", "First Name","Balance" );
90
91        /* copy all records from random-access file into text file */
92        while ( !feof( readPtr ) ) {
93            fread( &client, sizeof( struct clientData ), 1, readPtr );
94
95            /* write single record to text file */
96            if ( client.acctNum != 0 ) {
97                fprintf( writePtr, "%-6d%-16s%-11s%10.2f\n",
98                    client.acctNum, client.lastName,
99                    client.firstName, client.balance );
100           } /* end if */
101
102       } /* end while */
103
104       fclose( writePtr ); /* fclose closes the file */
105    } /* end else */
106
107 } /* end function textFile */
108
```

Fig. 11.16 Bank account program. (Part 3 of 6.)

```
109    /* update balance in record */
110    void updateRecord( FILE *fPtr )
111    {
112       int account;          /* account number */
113       double transaction; /* transaction amount */
114
115       /* create clientData with no information */
116       struct clientData client = { 0, "", "", 0.0 };
117
118       /* obtain number of account to update */
119       printf( "Enter account to update ( 1 - 100 ): " );
120       scanf( "%d", &account );
121
122       /* move file pointer to correct record in file */
123       fseek( fPtr, ( account - 1 ) * sizeof( struct clientData ),
124          SEEK_SET );
125
126       /* read record from file */
127       fread( &client, sizeof( struct clientData ), 1, fPtr );
128
129       /* display error if account does not exist */
130       if ( client.acctNum == 0 ) {
131          printf( "Acount #%d has no information.\n", account );
132       } /* end if */
133       else { /* update record */
134          printf( "%-6d%-16s%-11s%10.2f\n\n",
135             client.acctNum, client.lastName,
136             client.firstName, client.balance );
137
138          /* request transaction amount from user */
139          printf( "Enter charge ( + ) or payment ( - ): " );
140          scanf( "%lf", &transaction );
141          client.balance += transaction; /* update record balance */
142
143          printf( "%-6d%-16s%-11s%10.2f\n",
144             client.acctNum, client.lastName,
145             client.firstName, client.balance );
146
147          /* move file pointer to correct record in file */
148          fseek( fPtr, ( account - 1 ) * sizeof( struct clientData ),
149             SEEK_SET );
150
151          /* write updated record over old record in file */
152          fwrite( &client, sizeof( struct clientData ), 1, fPtr );
153       } /* end else */
154
155    } /* end function updateRecord */
156
157    /* delete an existing record */
158    void deleteRecord( FILE *fPtr )
159    {
160
161       struct clientData client; /* stores record read from file */
```

Fig. 11.16 Bank account program. (Part 4 of 6.)

```
162      struct clientData blankClient = { 0, "", "", 0 }; /* blank client */
163
164      int accountNum; /* account number */
165
166      /* obtain number of account to delete */
167      printf( "Enter account number to delete ( 1 - 100 ): " );
168      scanf( "%d", &accountNum );
169
170      /* move file pointer to correct record in file */
171      fseek( fPtr, ( accountNum - 1 ) * sizeof( struct clientData ),
172         SEEK_SET );
173
174      /* read record from file */
175      fread( &client, sizeof( struct clientData ), 1, fPtr );
176
177      /* display error if record does not exist */
178      if ( client.acctNum == 0 ) {
179         printf( "Account %d does not exist.\n", accountNum );
180      } /* end if */
181      else { /* delete record */
182
183         /* move file pointer to correct record in file */
184         fseek( fPtr, ( accountNum - 1 ) * sizeof( struct clientData ),
185            SEEK_SET );
186
187         /* replace existing record with blank record */
188         fwrite( &blankClient,
189            sizeof( struct clientData ), 1, fPtr );
190      } /* end else */
191
192   } /* end function deleteRecord */
193
194   /* create and insert record */
195   void newRecord( FILE *fPtr )
196   {
197      /* create clientData with default information */
198      struct clientData client = { 0, "", "", 0.0 };
199
200      int accountNum; /* account number */
201
202      /* obtain number of account to create */
203      printf( "Enter new account number ( 1 - 100 ): " );
204      scanf( "%d", &accountNum );
205
206      /* move file pointer to correct record in file */
207      fseek( fPtr, ( accountNum - 1 ) * sizeof( struct clientData ),
208         SEEK_SET );
209
210      /* read record from file */
211      fread( &client, sizeof( struct clientData ), 1, fPtr );
212
213      /* display error if account already exists */
214      if ( client.acctNum != 0 ) {
```

Fig. 11.16 Bank account program. (Part 5 of 6.)

```
215            printf( "Account #%d already contains information.\n",
216               client.acctNum );
217         } /* end if */
218         else { /* create record */
219
220            /* user enters last name, first name and balance */
221            printf( "Enter lastname, firstname, balance\n? " );
222            scanf( "%s%s%lf", &client.lastName, &client.firstName,
223               &client.balance );
224
225            client.acctNum = accountNum;
226
227            /* move file pointer to correct record in file */
228            fseek( fPtr, ( client.acctNum - 1 ) *
229               sizeof( struct clientData ), SEEK_SET );
230
231            /* insert record in file */
232            fwrite( &client,
233               sizeof( struct clientData ), 1, fPtr );
234         } /* end else */
235
236      } /* end function newRecord */
237
238      /* enable user to input menu choice */
239      int enterChoice( void )
240      {
241         int menuChoice; /* variable to store user's choice */
242
243         /* display available options */
244         printf( "\nEnter your choice\n"
245            "1 - store a formatted text file of acounts called\n"
246            "    \"accounts.txt\" for printing\n"
247            "2 - update an account\n"
248            "3 - add a new account\n"
249            "4 - delete an account\n"
250            "5 - end program\n? " );
251
252         scanf( "%d", &menuChoice ); /* receive choice from user */
253
254         return menuChoice;
255
256      } /* end function enterChoice */
```

Fig. 11.16 Bank account program. (Part 6 of 6.)

SUMMARY

- All data items processed by a computer are reduced to combinations of zeros and ones.

- The smallest data item in a computer can assume the value 0 or the value 1. Such a data item is called a bit (short for "binary digit"—a digit that can assume one of two values).

- Digits, letters and special symbols are referred to as characters. The character set is the set of all characters that may be used to write programs and represent data items on a particular computer. Every character in the computer's character set is represented as a pattern of eight 1s and 0s (called a byte).

- A field is a group of characters that conveys meaning.
- A record is a group of related fields.
- At least one field in each record is normally chosen as a record key. The record key identifies a record as belonging to a particular person or entity.
- The most popular type of organization for records in a file is called a sequential-access file, in which records are accessed consecutively until the desired data are located.
- A group of related files is sometimes called a database. A collection of programs designed to create and manage databases is called a database management system (DBMS).
- C views each file simply as a sequential stream of bytes.
- C opens three files and their associated streams—standard input, standard output and standard error—when program execution begins.
- The file pointers assigned to the standard input, standard output and standard error are stdin, stdout and stderr, respectively.
- Function fgetc reads a character from a specified file. Function fputc writes a character to a specified file.
- Function fgets reads a line from a specified file. Function fputs writes a line to a specified file.
- FILE is a structure type defined in the stdio.h header. The programmer need not know the specifics of this structure to use files. As a file is opened, a pointer to the file's FILE structure is returned.
- Function fopen takes two arguments—a file name and a file open mode—and opens the file. If the file exists, the contents of the file are discarded without warning. If the file does not exist and the file is being opened for writing, fopen creates the file.
- Function feof determines whether the end-of-file indicator for a file has been set.
- Function fprintf is equivalent to printf, except fprintf receives as an argument a pointer to the file to which the data will be written.
- Function fclose closes the file pointed to by its argument.
- To create a file, or to discard the contents of a file before writing data, open the file for writing ("w"). To read an existing file, open it for reading ("r"). To add records to the end of an existing file, open the file for appending ("a"). To open a file so that it may be written to and read from, open the file for updating in one of the three updating modes—"r+", "w+" or "a+". Mode "r+" simply opens the file for reading and writing. Mode "w+" creates the file if it does not exist and discards the current contents of the file if it does exist. Mode "a+" creates the file if it does not exist, and writing is done at the end of the file.
- Function fscanf is equivalent to scanf, except fscanf receives as an argument a pointer to the file (normally other than stdin) from which the data will be read.
- Function rewind causes the program to reposition the file position pointer for the specified file to the beginning of the file.
- Random-access file processing is used to access a record directly.
- To facilitate random access, data are stored in fixed-length records. Since every record is the same length, the computer can quickly calculate (as a function of the record key) the exact location of a record in relation to the beginning of the file.
- Data can be added easily to a random-access file without destroying other data in the file. Data stored previously in a file with fixed-length records can also be changed and deleted without rewriting the entire file.
- Function fwrite writes a block (specific number of bytes) of data to a file.

- The compile-time operator sizeof returns the size in bytes of its operand.
- Function fseek sets the file position pointer to a specific position in a file based on the starting location of the seek in the file. The seek can start from one of three locations—SEEK_SET starts from the beginning of the file, SEEK_CUR starts from the current position in the file and SEEK_END starts from the end of the file.
- Function fread reads a block (specific number of bytes) of data from a file.

TERMINOLOGY

a file open mode	fscanf
a+ file open mode	fseek
binary digit	fwrite
bit	getchar
byte	gets
character	letter
character set	NULL
close a file	offset
data hierarchy	open a file
database	open file table
database management system	printf
decimal digit	putchar
displacement	puts
end-of-file marker	r file open mode
fclose	random-access file
feof	record
fgetc	record key
fgets	rewind
field	r+ file open mode
file	scanf
file control block	SEEK_CUR
file descriptor	SEEK_END
file name	SEEK_SET
file offset	sequential-access file
file open mode	special symbol
file pointer	stderr (standard error)
file position pointer	stdin (standard input)
FILE structure	stdout (standard output)
fopen	stream
formatted input/output	transaction processing
fprintf	w file open mode
fputc	w+ file open mode
fputs	writing to a file
fread	zeros and ones

COMMON PROGRAMMING ERRORS

11.1 Opening an existing file for writing ("w") when, in fact, the user wants to preserve the file discards the contents of the file without warning.

11.2 Forgetting to open a file before attempting to reference it in a program is a logic error.

11.3 Using the wrong file pointer to refer to a file is a logic error.

11.4 Opening a nonexistent file for reading is an error.

11.5 Opening a file for reading or writing without having been granted the appropriate access rights to the file (this is operating-system dependent) is an error.

11.6 Opening a file for writing when no disk space is available is an error.

11.7 Opening a file with the incorrect file mode is a logic error. For example, opening a file in write mode ("w") when it should be opened in update mode ("r+") causes the contents of the file to be discarded.

ERROR-PREVENTION TIPS

11.1 Be sure that calls to file processing functions in a program contain the correct file pointers.

11.2 Open a file only for reading (and not update) if the contents of the file should not be modified. This prevents unintentional modification of the file's contents. This is another example of the principle of least privilege.

GOOD PROGRAMMING PRACTICE

11.1 Explicitly close each file as soon as it is known that the program will not reference the file again.

PERFORMANCE TIP

11.1 Closing a file can free resources for which other users or programs may be waiting.

SELF-REVIEW EXERCISES

11.1 Fill in the blanks in each of the following:
  a) Ultimately, all data items processed by a computer are reduced to combinations of _____ and _____.
  b) The smallest data item a computer can process is called a(n) _____.
  c) A(n) _____ is a group of related records.
  d) Digits, letters and special symbols are referred to as _____.
  e) A group of related files is called a _____.
  f) Function _____ closes a file.
  g) The _____ function reads data from a file in a manner similar to how scanf reads from stdin.
  h) Function _____ reads a character from a specified file.
  i) Function _____ reads a line from a specified file.
  j) Function _____ opens a file.
  k) Function _____ is normally used when reading data from a file in random-access applications.
  l) Function _____ repositions the file position pointer to a specific location in the file.

11.2 State which of the following are *true* and which are *false*. If *false*, explain why.
  a) Function fscanf cannot be used to read data from the standard input.
  b) The programmer must explicitly use fopen to open the standard input, standard output and standard error streams.
  c) A program must explicitly call function fclose to close a file.
  d) If the file position pointer points to a location in a sequential file other than the beginning of the file, the file must be closed and reopened to read from the beginning of the file.
  e) Function fprintf can write to the standard output.
  f) Data in sequential-access files are always updated without overwriting other data.

g) It is not necessary to search through all the records in a random-access file to find a specific record.

h) Records in random-access files are not of uniform length.

i) Function `fseek` may only seek relative to the beginning of a file.

11.3 Write a single statement to accomplish each of the following. Assume that each of these statements applies to the same program.

a) Write a statement that opens the file `"oldmast.dat"` for reading and assigns the returned file pointer to `ofPtr`.

b) Write a statement that opens the file `"trans.dat"` for reading and assigns the returned
file pointer to `tfPtr`.

c) Write a statement that opens the file `"newmast.dat"` for writing (and creation) and assigns the returned file pointer to `nfPtr`.

d) Write a statement that reads a record from the file `"oldmast.dat"`. The record consists
of integer `accountNum`, string `name` and floating-point `currentBalance`.

e) Write a statement that reads a record from the file `"trans.dat"`. The record consists of
the integer `accountNum` and floating-point `dollarAmount`.

f) Write a statement that writes a record to the file `"newmast.dat"`. The record consists of
the integer `accountNum`, string `name` and floating-point `currentBalance`.

11.4 Find the error in each of the following program segments. Explain how the error can be corrected.

a) The file referred to by `fPtr` (`"payables.dat"`) has not been opened.
```
printf( fPtr, "%d%s%d\n", account, company, amount );
```

b) `open( "receive.dat", "r+" );`

c) The following statement should read a record from the file `"payables.dat"`. File pointer `payPtr` refers to this file, and file pointer `recPtr` refers to the file `"receive.dat"`:
```
scanf( recPtr, "%d%s%d\n", &account, company, &amount );
```

d) The file `"tools.dat"` should be opened to add data to the file without discarding the
current data.
```
if ( ( tfPtr = fopen( "tools.dat", "w" ) ) != NULL )
```

e) The file `"courses.dat"` should be opened for appending without modifying the current
contents of the file.
```
if ( ( cfPtr = fopen( "courses.dat", "w+" ) ) != NULL )
```

ANSWERS TO SELF-REVIEW EXERCISES

11.1   a) 1s, 0s. b) Bit. c) File. d) Characters. e) Database. f) `fclose`. g) `fscanf`. h) `fgetc`.
i) `fgets`. j) `fopen`. k) `fread`. l) `fseek`.

11.2   a) False. Function `fscanf` can be used to read from the standard input by including the
pointer to the standard input stream, `stdin`, in the call to `fscanf`.

b) False. These three streams are opened automatically by C when program execution begins.

c) False. The files will be closed when program execution terminates, but all files should be
explicitly closed with `fclose`.

d) False. Function `rewind` can be used to reposition the file position pointer to the beginning of the file.

e) True.

f) False. In most cases, sequential file records are not of uniform length. Therefore, it is possible that updating a record will cause other data to be overwritten.

g) True.

h) False. Records in a random-access file are normally of uniform length.

i) False. It is possible to seek from the beginning of the file, from the end of the file and from the current location in the file.

11.3   a) `ofPtr = fopen( "oldmast.dat", "r" );`
       b) `tfPtr = fopen( "trans.dat", "r" );`
       c) `nfPtr = fopen( "newmast.dat", "w" );`
       d) `fscanf( ofPtr, "%d%s%f", &accountNum, name, &currentBalance );`
       e) `fscanf( tfPtr, "%d%f", &accountNum, &dollarAmount );`
       f) `fprintf( nfPtr, "%d %s %.2f", accountNum, name, currentBalance );`

11.4   a) Error: The file `"payables.dat"` has not been opened before the reference to its file pointer.
          Correction: Use `fopen` to open `"payables.dat"` for writing, appending or updating.
       b) Error: Function `open` is not an ANSI C function.
          Correction: Use function `fopen`.
       c) Error: Function `fscanf` uses the incorrect file pointer to refer to file `"payables.dat"`.
          Correction: Use file pointer `payPtr` to refer to `"payables.dat"`.
       d) Error: The contents of the file are discarded because the file is opened for writing (`"w"`).
          Correction: To add data to the file, either open the file for updating (`"r+"`) or open the file for appending (`"a"`).
       e) Error: File `"courses.dat"` is opened for updating in `"w+"` mode which discards the current contents of the file.
          Correction: Open the file `"a"` mode.

EXERCISES

11.5   Fill in the blanks in each of the following:
       a) Computers store large amounts of data on secondary storage devices as _____.
       b) A(n) _____ is composed of several fields.
       c) A field that may contain digits, letters and blanks is called a(n) _____ field.
       d) To facilitate the retrieval of specific records from a file, one field in each record is chosen as a(n) _____.
       e) The vast majority of information stored in computer systems is stored in _____ files.
       f) A group of related characters that conveys meaning is called a(n) _____.
       g) The file pointers for the three files that are opened automatically when program execution begins are named _____, _____ and _____.
       h) Function _____ writes a character to a specified file.
       i) Function _____ writes a line to a specified file.
       j) Function _____ is generally used to write data to a random-access file.
       k) Function _____ repositions the file position pointer to the beginning of the file.

11.6   State which of the following are *true* and which are *false*. If *false*, explain why.
       a) The impressive functions performed by computers essentially involve the manipulation of zeros and ones.
       b) People prefer to manipulate bits instead of characters and fields because bits are more compact.
       c) People specify programs and data items as characters; computers then manipulate and process these characters as groups of zeros and ones.
       d) A person's zip code is an example of a numeric field.
       e) A person's street address is generally considered to be an alphabetic field in computer applications.

   f) Data items processed by a computer form a data hierarchy in which data items become larger and more complex as we progress from fields to characters to bits etc.

   g) A record key identifies a record as belonging to a particular field.

   h) Most organizations store all their information in a single file to facilitate computer processing.

   i) Files are always referred to by name in C programs.

   j) When a program creates a file, the file is automatically retained by the computer for future reference.

11.7   Exercise 11.3 asked the reader to write a series of single statements. Actually, these statements form the core of an important type of file-processing program, namely, a file-matching program. In commercial data processing, it is common to have several files in each system. In an accounts receivable system, for example, there is generally a master file containing detailed information about each customer such as the customer's name, address, telephone number, outstanding balance, credit limit, discount terms, contract arrangements and possibly a condensed history of recent purchases and cash payments.

As transactions occur (i.e., sales are made and cash payments arrive in the mail), they are entered into a file. At the end of each business period (i.e., a month for some companies, a week for others and a day in some cases) the file of transactions (called "trans.dat" in Exercise 11.3) is applied to the master file (called "oldmast.dat" in Exercise 11.3), thus updating each account's record of purchases and payments. After each of these updatings run, the master file is rewritten as a new file ("newmast.dat"), which is then used at the end of the next business period to begin the updating process again.

File-matching programs must deal with certain problems that do not exist in single-file programs. For example, a match does not always occur. A customer on the master file might not have made any purchases or cash payments in the current business period, and therefore no record for this customer will appear on the transaction file. Similarly, a customer who did make some purchases or cash payments might have just moved to this community, and the company may not have had a chance to create a master record for this customer.

Use the statements written in Exercise 11.3 as a basis for writing a complete file-matching accounts receivable program. Use the account number on each file as the record key for matching purposes. Assume that each file is a sequential file with records stored in increasing account number order.

When a match occurs (i.e., records with the same account number appear on both the master file and the transaction file), add the dollar amount on the transaction file to the current balance on the master file and write the "newmast.dat" record. (Assume that purchases are indicated by positive amounts on the transaction file, and that payments are indicated by negative amounts.) When there is a master record for a particular account but no corresponding transaction record, merely write the master record to "newmast.dat". When there is a transaction record but no corresponding master record, print the message "Unmatched transaction record for account number ..." (fill in the account number from the transaction record).

11.8   After writing the program of Exercise 11.7, write a simple program to create some test data for checking out the program of Exercise 11.7. Use the following sample account data:

Master File: Account number	Name	Balance
100	Alan Jones	348.17
300	Mary Smith	27.19
500	Sam Sharp	0.00
700	Suzy Green	-14.22

Transaction File: Account number	Dollar amount
100	27.14
300	62.11
400	100.56
900	82.17

11.9 Run the program of Exercise 11.7 using the files of test data created in Exercise 11.8. Use the listing program of Section 11.7 to print the new master file. Check the results carefully.

11.10 It is possible (actually common) to have several transaction records with the same record key. This occurs because a particular customer might make several purchases and cash payments during a business period. Rewrite your accounts receivable file-matching program of Exercise 11.7 to provide for the possibility of handling several transaction records with the same record key. Modify the test data of Exercise 11.8 to include the following additional transaction records:

Account number	Dollar amount
300	83.89
700	80.78
700	1.53

11.11 Write statements that accomplish each of the following. Assume that the structure

```
struct person {
    char lastName[ 15 ];
    char firstName[ 15 ];
    char age[ 4 ];
};
```

has been defined and that the file is already open for writing.
     a) Initialize the file "nameage.dat" so that there are 100 records with lastName = "unassigned", firstname = "" and age = "0".
     b) Input 10 last names, first names and ages, and write them to the file.
     c) Update a record; if there is no information in the record, tell the user "No info".
     d) Delete a record that has information by reinitializing that particular record.

11.12 You are the owner of a hardware store and need to keep an inventory that can tell you what tools you have, how many you have and the cost of each one. Write a program that initializes the file "hardware.dat" to 100 empty records, lets you input the data concerning each tool, enables you to list all your tools, lets you delete a record for a tool that you no longer have and lets you update *any* information in the file. The tool identification number should be the record number. Use the following information to start your file:

Record #	Tool name	Quantity	Cost
3	Electric sander	7	57.98
17	Hammer	76	11.99
24	Jig saw	21	11.00
39	Lawn mower	3	79.50
56	Power saw	18	99.99
68	Screwdriver	106	6.99
77	Sledge hammer	11	21.50
83	Wrench	34	7.50

11.13 *Telephone Number Word Generator.* Standard telephone keypads contain the digits 0 through 9. The numbers 2 through 9 each have three letters associated with them, as is indicated by the following table:

Digit	Letter
2	A B C
3	D E F
4	G H I
5	J K L
6	M N O
7	P R S
8	T U V
9	W X Y

Many people find it difficult to memorize phone numbers, so they use the correspondence between digits and letters to develop seven-letter words that correspond to their phone numbers. For example, a person whose telephone number is 686-2377 might use the correspondence indicated in the above table to develop the seven-letter word "NUMBERS."

Businesses frequently attempt to get telephone numbers that are easy for their clients to remember. If a business can advertise a simple word for its customers to dial, then no doubt the business will receive a few more calls.

Each seven-letter word corresponds to exactly one seven-digit telephone number. The restaurant wishing to increase its take-home business could surely do so with the number 825-3688 (i.e., "TAKEOUT").

Each seven-digit phone number corresponds to many separate seven-letter words. Unfortunately, most of these represent unrecognizable juxtapositions of letters. It is possible, however, that the owner of a barber shop would be pleased to know that the shop's telephone number, 424-7288, corresponds to "HAIRCUT." The owner of a liquor store would, no doubt, be delighted to find that the store's telephone number, 233-7226, corresponds to "BEERCAN." A veterinarian with the phone number 738-2273 would be pleased to know that the number corresponds to the letters "PETCARE."

Write a C program that, given a seven-digit number, writes to a file every possible seven-letter word corresponding to that number. There are 2187 (3 to the seventh power) such words. Avoid phone numbers with the digits 0 and 1.

11.14 If you have a computerized dictionary available, modify the program you wrote in Exercise 11.13 to look up the words in the dictionary. Some seven-letter combinations created by this program consist of two or more words (the phone number 843-2677 produces "THEBOSS").

11.15 Modify the example of Fig. 8.14 to use functions `fgetc` and `fputs` rather than `getchar` and `puts`. The program should give the user the option to read from the standard input and write to the standard output or to read from a specified file and write to a specified file. If the user chooses the second option, have the user enter the file names for the input and output files.

11.16 Write a program that uses the `sizeof` operator to determine the sizes in bytes of the various data types on your computer system. Write the results to the file `"datasize.dat"` so you may print the results later. The format for the results in the file should be as follows:

```
Data type              Size
char                      1
unsigned char             1
short int                 2
unsigned short int        2
int                       4
unsigned int              4
long int                  4
unsigned long int         4
float                     4
double                    8
long double              16
```

[*Note:* The type sizes on your computer might be different from those listed above.]

11.17 In Exercise 7.19, you wrote a software simulation of a computer that used a special machine language called Simpletron Machine Language (SML). In the simulation, each time you wanted to run an SML program, you entered the program into the simulator from the keyboard. If you made a mistake while typing the SML program, the simulator was restarted and the SML code was reentered. It would be nice to be able to read the SML program from a file rather than type it each time. This would reduce time and mistakes in preparing to run SML programs.

    a) Modify the simulator you wrote in Exercise 7.19 to read SML programs from a file specified by the user at the keyboard.

    b) After the Simpletron executes, it outputs the contents of its registers and memory on the screen. It would be nice to capture the output in a file, so modify the simulator to write its output to a file in addition to displaying the output on the screen.

12

C Data Structures

Objectives

- To be able to allocate and free memory dynamically for data objects.
- To be able to form linked data structures using pointers, self-referential structures and recursion.
- To be able to create and manipulate linked lists, queues, stacks and binary trees.
- To understand various important applications of linked data structures.

Much that I bound, I could not free;

Much that I freed returned to me.

Lee Wilson Dodd

'Will you walk a little faster?' said a whiting to a snail,

'There's a porpoise close behind us, and he's treading on my tail.'

Lewis Carroll

There is always room at the top.

Daniel Webster

Push on — keep moving.

Thomas Morton

I think that I shall never see

A poem lovely as a tree.

Joyce Kilmer

Outline

12.1 Introduction

We have studied fixed-size *data structures* such as single-subscripted arrays, double-subscripted arrays and `struct`s. This chapter introduces *dynamic data structures* with sizes that grow and shrink at execution time. *Linked lists* are collections of data items "lined up in a row"—insertions and deletions are made anywhere in a linked list. *Stacks* are important in compilers and operating systems—insertions and deletions are made only at one end of a stack—its *top*. *Queues* represent waiting lines; insertions are made at the back (also referred to as the *tail*) of a queue and deletions are made from the front (also referred to as the *head*) of a queue. *Binary trees* facilitate high-speed searching and sorting of data, efficient elimination of duplicate data items, representing file system directories and compiling expressions into machine language. Each of these data structures has many other interesting applications.

We will discuss each of the major types of data structures and implement programs that create and manipulate these data structures. In the next part of the book—the introduction to C++ and object-oriented programming—we will study data abstraction. This technique will enable us to build these data structures in a dramatically different manner designed for producing software that is much easier to maintain and reuse.

This is a challenging chapter. The programs are substantial and they incorporate most of what you have learned in the earlier chapters. The programs are especially heavy on pointer manipulation, a subject many people consider to be among the most difficult topics in C. The chapter is loaded with highly practical programs that you will be able to use in more advanced courses; the chapter includes a rich collection of exercises that emphasize practical applications of the data structures.

We sincerely hope that you will attempt the major project described in the special section entitled "Building Your Own Compiler." You have been using a compiler to translate your C programs to machine language so that you could execute your programs on your computer. In this project, you will actually build your own compiler. It will read a file of statements written in a simple, yet powerful, high-level language similar to early versions of the popular language BASIC. Your compiler will translate these statements into a file of Simpletron Machine Language (SML) instructions. SML is the language you learned in the

Chapter 7 special section, "Building Your Own Computer." Your Simpletron Simulator program will then execute the SML program produced by your compiler! This project will give you a wonderful opportunity to exercise most of what you have learned in this course. The special section carefully walks you through the specifications of the high-level language, and describes the algorithms you will need to convert each type of high-level language statement into machine language instructions. If you enjoy being challenged, you might attempt the many enhancements to both the compiler and the Simpletron Simulator suggested in the Exercises.

12.2 Self-Referential Structures

A *self-referential structure* contains a pointer member that points to a structure of the same structure type. For example, the definition

```
struct node {
    int data;
    struct node *nextPtr;
};
```

defines a type, `struct node`. A structure of type `struct node` has two members—integer member `data` and pointer member `nextPtr`. Member `nextPtr` points to a structure of type `struct node`—a structure of the same type as the one being declared here, hence the term "self-referential structure." Member `nextPtr` is referred to as a *link*—i.e., `nextPtr` can be used to "tie" a structure of type `struct node` to another structure of the same type. Self-referential structures can be linked together to form useful data structures such as lists, queues, stacks and trees. Figure 12.1 illustrates two self-referential structure objects linked together to form a list. Note that a slash—representing a `NULL` pointer—is placed in the link member of the second self-referential structure to indicate that the link does not point to another structure. [*Note:* The slash is only for illustration purposes; it does not correspond to the backslash character in C.] A `NULL` pointer normally indicates the end of a data structure just as the null character indicates the end of a string.

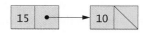

Fig. 12.1   Self-referential structures linked together.

 Common Programming Error 12.1

Not setting the link in the last node of a list to NULL can lead to runtime errors.

12.3 Dynamic Memory Allocation

Creating and maintaining dynamic data structures requires *dynamic memory allocation*—the ability for a program to obtain more memory space at execution time to hold new nodes, and to release space no longer needed. The limit for dynamic memory allocation can be as large as the amount of available physical memory in the computer or the amount of available virtual memory in a virtual memory system. Often, the limits are much smaller because available memory must be shared among many applications.

Functions `malloc` and `free`, and operator `sizeof`, are essential to dynamic memory allocation. Function `malloc` takes as an argument the number of bytes to be allocated and returns a pointer of type `void *` *(pointer to void)* to the allocated memory. A `void *` pointer may be assigned to a variable of any pointer type. Function `malloc` is normally used with the `sizeof` operator. For example, the statement

```
newPtr = malloc( sizeof( struct node ) );
```

evaluates `sizeof( struct node )` to determine the size in bytes of a structure of type `struct node`, allocates a new area in memory of that number of bytes and stores a pointer to the allocated memory in variable `newPtr`. The allocated memory is not initialized. If no memory is available, `malloc` returns NULL.

Function `free` deallocates memory—i.e., the memory is returned to the system so that the memory can be reallocated in the future. To free memory dynamically allocated by the preceding `malloc` call, use the statement

```
free( newPtr );
```

The following sections discuss lists, stacks, queues and trees, each of which is created and maintained with dynamic memory allocation and self-referential structures.

Portability Tip 12.1
A structure's size is not necessarily the sum of the sizes of its members. This is so because of various machine-dependent boundary alignment requirements (see Chapter 10).

Common Programming Error 12.2
Assuming that the size of a structure is simply the sum of the sizes of its members is a logic error.

Good Programming Practice 12.1
Use the `sizeof` operator to determine the size of a structure.

Error-Prevention Tip 12.1
When using `malloc`, test for a NULL pointer return value. Print an error message if the requested memory is not allocated.

Common Programming Error 12.3
Not returning dynamically allocated memory when it is no longer needed can cause the system to run out of memory prematurely. This is sometimes called a "memory leak."

Good Programming Practice 12.2
When memory that was dynamically allocated is no longer needed, use `free` to return the memory to the system immediately.

Common Programming Error 12.4
Freeing memory not allocated dynamically with `malloc` is an error.

Common Programming Error 12.5
Referring to memory that has been freed is an error.

12.4 Linked Lists

A *linked list* is a linear collection of self-referential structures, called *nodes,* connected by pointer *links*—hence, the term "linked" list. A linked list is accessed via a pointer to the first node of the list. Subsequent nodes are accessed via the link pointer member stored in each node. By convention, the link pointer in the last node of a list is set to NULL to mark the end of the list. Data is stored in a linked list dynamically—each node is created as necessary. A node can contain data of any type including other struct objects. Stacks and queues are also linear data structures, and, as we will see, are constrained versions of linked lists. Trees are nonlinear data structures.

Lists of data can be stored in arrays, but linked lists provide several advantages. A linked list is appropriate when the number of data elements to be represented in the data structure is unpredictable. Linked lists are dynamic, so the length of a list can increase or decrease as necessary. The size of an array, however cannot be altered once memory is allocated. Arrays can become full. Linked lists become full only when the system has insufficient memory to satisfy dynamic storage allocation requests.

Performance Tip 12.1

An array can be declared to contain more elements than the number of data items expected, but this can waste memory. Linked lists can provide better memory utilization in these situations.

Linked lists can be maintained in sorted order by inserting each new element at the proper point in the list.

Performance Tip 12.2

Insertion and deletion in a sorted array can be time consuming—all the elements following the inserted or deleted element must be shifted appropriately.

Performance Tip 12.3

The elements of an array are stored contiguously in memory. This allows immediate access to any array element because the address of any element can be calculated directly based on its position relative to the beginning of the array. Linked lists do not afford such immediate access to their elements.

Linked list nodes are normally not stored contiguously in memory. Logically, however, the nodes of a linked list appear to be contiguous. Figure 12.2 illustrates a linked list with several nodes.

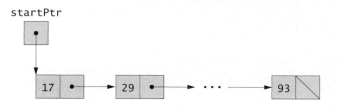

Fig. 12.2 Linked list graphical representation.

Performance Tip 12.4

Using dynamic memory allocation (instead of arrays) for data structures that grow and shrink at execution time can save memory. Keep in mind, however, that the pointers take up space, and that dynamic memory allocation incurs the overhead of function calls.

Figure 12.3 (output shown in Fig. 12.4) manipulates a list of characters. The program provides two options: 1) insert a character in the list in alphabetical order (function `insert`), and 2) delete a character from the list (function `delete`). This is a large and complex program. A detailed discussion of the program follows. Exercise 12.20 asks the reader to implement a recursive function that prints a list backwards. Exercise 12.21 asks the reader to implement a recursive function that searches a linked list for a particular data item.

```c
1   /* Fig. 12.3: fig12_03.c
2      Operating and maintaining a list */
3   #include <stdio.h>
4   #include <stdlib.h>
5
6   /* self-referential structure */
7   struct listNode {
8      char data; /* each listNode contains a character */
9      struct listNode *nextPtr; /* pointer to next node */
10  }; /* end structure listNode */
11
12  typedef struct listNode ListNode; /* synonym for struct listNode */
13  typedef ListNode *ListNodePtr; /* synonym for ListNode* */
14
15  /* prototypes */
16  void insert( ListNodePtr *sPtr, char value );
17  char delete( ListNodePtr *sPtr, char value );
18  int isEmpty( ListNodePtr sPtr );
19  void printList( ListNodePtr currentPtr );
20  void instructions( void );
21
22  int main()
23  {
24     ListNodePtr startPtr = NULL; /* initially there are no nodes */
25     int choice; /* user's choice */
26     char item;  /* char entered by user */
27
28     instructions(); /* display the menu */
29     printf( "? " );
30     scanf( "%d", &choice );
31
32     /* loop while user does not choose 3 */
33     while ( choice != 3 ) {
34
35        switch ( choice ) {
36
37           case 1:
38              printf( "Enter a character: " );
39              scanf( "\n%c", &item );
```

Fig. 12.3 Inserting and deleting nodes in a list. (Part 1 of 4.)

```
40              insert( &startPtr, item ); /* insert item in list */
41              printList( startPtr );
42              break;
43
44          case 2:
45
46              /* if list is not empty */
47              if ( !isEmpty( startPtr ) ) {
48                  printf( "Enter character to be deleted: " );
49                  scanf( "\n%c", &item );
50
51                  /* if character is found, remove it*/
52                  if ( delete( &startPtr, item ) ) { /* remove item */
53                      printf( "%c deleted.\n", item );
54                      printList( startPtr );
55                  } /* end if */
56                  else {
57                      printf( "%c not found.\n\n", item );
58                  } /* end else */
59
60              } /* end if */
61              else {
62                  printf( "List is empty.\n\n" );
63              } /* end else */
64
65              break;
66
67          default:
68              printf( "Invalid choice.\n\n" );
69              instructions();
70              break;
71
72          } /* end switch */
73
74          printf( "? " );
75          scanf( "%d", &choice );
76      } /* end while */
77
78      printf( "End of run.\n" );
79
80      return 0; /* indicates successful termination */
81
82  } /* end main */
83
84  /* display program instructions to user */
85  void instructions( void )
86  {
87      printf( "Enter your choice:\n"
88          "   1 to insert an element into the list.\n"
89          "   2 to delete an element from the list.\n"
90          "   3 to end.\n" );
91  } /* end function instructions */
92
```

Fig. 12.3   Inserting and deleting nodes in a list. (Part 2 of 4.)

```
93   /* Insert a new value into the list in sorted order */
94   void insert( ListNodePtr *sPtr, char value )
95   {
96      ListNodePtr newPtr;        /* pointer to new node */
97      ListNodePtr previousPtr;   /* pointer to previous node in list */
98      ListNodePtr currentPtr;    /* pointer to current node in list */
99
100     newPtr = malloc( sizeof( ListNode ) ); /* create node */
101
102     if ( newPtr != NULL ) { /* is space available */
103        newPtr->data = value; /* place value in node */
104        newPtr->nextPtr = NULL; /* node does not link to another node */
105
106        previousPtr = NULL;
107        currentPtr = *sPtr;
108
109        /* loop to find the correct location in the list */
110        while ( currentPtr != NULL && value > currentPtr->data ) {
111           previousPtr = currentPtr;           /* walk to ...   */
112           currentPtr = currentPtr->nextPtr;   /* ... next node */
113        } /* end while */
114
115        /* insert new node at beginning of list */
116        if ( previousPtr == NULL ) {
117           newPtr->nextPtr = *sPtr;
118           *sPtr = newPtr;
119        } /* end if */
120        else { /* insert new node between previousPtr and currentPtr */
121           previousPtr->nextPtr = newPtr;
122           newPtr->nextPtr = currentPtr;
123        } /* end else */
124
125     } /* end if */
126     else {
127        printf( "%c not inserted. No memory available.\n", value );
128     } /* end else */
129
130  } /* end function insert */
131
132  /* Delete a list element */
133  char delete( ListNodePtr *sPtr, char value )
134  {
135     ListNodePtr previousPtr; /* pointer to previous node in list */
136     ListNodePtr currentPtr;  /* pointer to current node in list */
137     ListNodePtr tempPtr;     /* temporary node pointer */
138
139     /* delete first node */
140     if ( value == ( *sPtr )->data ) {
141        tempPtr = *sPtr; /* hold onto node being removed */
142        *sPtr = ( *sPtr )->nextPtr; /* de-thread the node */
143        free( tempPtr ); /* free the de-threaded node */
144        return value;
145     } /* end if */
```

Fig. 12.3   Inserting and deleting nodes in a list. (Part 3 of 4.)

```
146     else {
147        previousPtr = *sPtr;
148        currentPtr = ( *sPtr )->nextPtr;
149
150        /* loop to find the correct location in the list */
151        while ( currentPtr != NULL && currentPtr->data != value ) {
152           previousPtr = currentPtr;         /* walk to ...   */
153           currentPtr = currentPtr->nextPtr; /* ... next node */
154        } /* end while */
155
156        /* delete node at currentPtr */
157        if ( currentPtr != NULL ) {
158           tempPtr = currentPtr;
159           previousPtr->nextPtr = currentPtr->nextPtr;
160           free( tempPtr );
161           return value;
162        } /* end if */
163
164     } /* end else */
165
166     return '\0';
167
168  } /* end function delete */
169
170  /* Return 1 if the list is empty, 0 otherwise */
171  int isEmpty( ListNodePtr sPtr )
172  {
173     return sPtr == NULL;
174
175  } /* end function isEmpty */
176
177  /* Print the list */
178  void printList( ListNodePtr currentPtr )
179  {
180
181     /* if list is empty */
182     if ( currentPtr == NULL ) {
183        printf( "List is empty.\n\n" );
184     } /* end if */
185     else {
186        printf( "The list is:\n" );
187
188        /* while not the end of the list */
189        while ( currentPtr != NULL ) {
190           printf( "%c --> ", currentPtr->data );
191           currentPtr = currentPtr->nextPtr;
192        } /* end while */
193
194        printf( "NULL\n\n" );
195     } /* end else */
196
197  } /* end function printList */
```

Fig. 12.3   Inserting and deleting nodes in a list. (Part 4 of 4.)

```
Enter your choice:
   1 to insert an element into the list.
   2 to delete an element from the list.
   3 to end.
? 1
Enter a character: B
The list is:
B --> NULL

? 1
Enter a character: A
The list is:
A --> B --> NULL

? 1
Enter a character: C
The list is:
A --> B --> C --> NULL

? 2
Enter character to be deleted: D
D not found.

? 2
Enter character to be deleted: B
B deleted.
The list is:
A --> C --> NULL

? 2
Enter character to be deleted: C
C deleted.
The list is:
A --> NULL

? 2
Enter character to be deleted: A
A deleted.
List is empty.

? 4
Invalid choice.

Enter your choice:
   1 to insert an element into the list.
   2 to delete an element from the list.
   3 to end.
? 3
End of run.

? 2
Enter character to be deleted: C
```

Fig. 12.4 Sample output for the program of Fig. 12.3. (Part 1 of 2.)

```
C deleted.
The list is:
A --> NULL

? 2
Enter character to be deleted: A
A deleted.
List is empty.

? 4
Invalid choice.

Enter your choice:
   1 to insert an element into the list.
   2 to delete an element from the list.
   3 to end.
? 3
End of run.
```

Fig. 12.4   Sample output for the program of Fig. 12.3. (Part 2 of 2.)

The primary functions of linked lists are `insert` (lines 94–130) and `delete` (lines 133–168). Function `isEmpty` (lines 171–175) is called a *predicate function*—it does not alter the list in any way; rather it determines if the list is empty (i.e., the pointer to the first node of the list is NULL). If the list is empty, 1 is returned; otherwise, 0 is returned. Function `printList` (lines 178–197) prints the list.

Characters are inserted in the list in alphabetical order. Function `insert` (lines 94–130) receives the *address* of the list and a character to be inserted. The address of the list is necessary when a value is to be inserted at the start of the list. Providing the address of the list enables the list (i.e., the pointer to the first node of the list) to be modified via a call by reference. Since the list itself is a pointer (to its first element), passing the address of the list creates a *pointer to a pointer* (i.e., *double indirection*). This is a complex notion and requires careful programming. The steps for inserting a character in the list are as follows (see Fig. 12.5):

1. Create a node by calling `malloc`, assigning to `newPtr` the address of the allocated memory (line 100), assigning the character to be inserted to `newPtr->data` (line 103), and assigning NULL to `newPtr->nextPtr` (line 104).

2. Initialize `previousPtr` to NULL (line 106) and `currentPtr` to `*sPtr` (line 107)—the pointer to the start of the list. Pointers `previousPtr` and `currentPtr` store the locations of the node preceding the insertion point and the node after the insertion point.

3. While `currentPtr` is not NULL and the value to be inserted is greater than `currentPtr->data` (line 110), assign `currentPtr` to `previousPtr` (line 111) and advance `currentPtr` to the next node in the list (line 112). This locates the insertion point for the value.

4. If `previousPtr` is NULL (line 116), insert the new node as the first node in the list (lines 117–118). Assign `*sPtr` to `newPtr->nextPtr` (the new node link points to the former first node) and assign `newPtr` to `*sPtr` (`*sPtr` points to the new node). Otherwise, if `previousPtr` is not NULL, the new node is inserted in place (lines 121–122). Assign `newPtr` to `previousPtr->nextPtr` (the previous node points

to the new node) and assign `currentPtr` to `newPtr->nextPtr` (the new node link points to the current node).

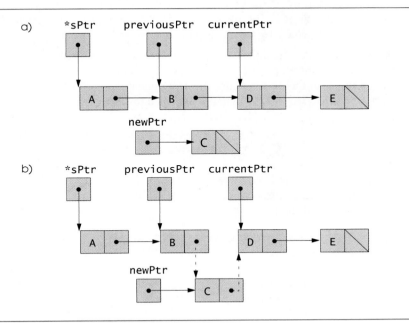

Fig. 12.5   Inserting a node in order in a list.

   Error-Prevention Tip 12.2

Assign NULL to the link member of a new node. Pointers should be initialized before they are used.

Figure 12.5 illustrates the insertion of a node containing the character `'C'` into an ordered list. Part a) of the figure shows the list and the new node before the insertion. Part b) of the figure shows the result of inserting the new node. The reassigned pointers are dotted arrows.

Function `delete` (lines 137–168) receives the address of the pointer to the start of the list and a character to be deleted. The steps for deleting a character from the list are as follows:

1. If the character to be deleted matches the character in the first node of the list (line 140), assign `*sPtr` to `tempPtr` (`tempPtr` will be used to `free` the unneeded memory), assign `(*sPtr)->nextPtr` to `*sPtr` (`*sPtr` now points to the second node in the list), `free` the memory pointed to by `tempPtr`, and return the character that was deleted.

2. Otherwise, initialize `previousPtr` with `*sPtr` and initialize `currentPtr` with `(*sPtr)->nextPtr` (lines 147–148).

3. While `currentPtr` is not `NULL` and the value to be deleted is not equal to `currentPtr->data` (Line 151), assign `currentPtr` to `previousPtr` (line 152), and assign `currentPtr->nextPtr` to `currentPtr` (line 153). This locates the character to be deleted if it is contained in the list.

4. If currentPtr is not NULL (line 157), assign currentPtr to tempPtr (line 158), assign currentPtr->nextPtr to previousPtr->nextPtr (line 159), free the node pointed to by tempPtr (line 160), and return the character that was deleted from the list (line 161). If currentPtr is NULL, return the null character ('\0') to signify that the character to be deleted was not found in the list (line 166).

Figure 12.6 illustrates the deletion of a node from a linked list. Part a) of the figure shows the linked list after the preceding insert operation. Part b) shows the reassignment of the link element of previousPtr and the assignment of currentPtr to tempPtr. Pointer tempPtr is used to free the memory allocated to store 'C'.

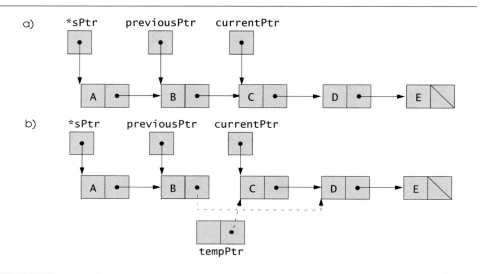

Fig. 12.6 Deleting a node from a list.

Function printList (lines 178–197) receives a pointer to the start of the list as an argument and refers to the pointer as currentPtr. The function first determines if the list is empty (lines 182–184) and, if so, prints "The list is empty." and terminates. Otherwise, it prints the data in the list (lines 185–195). While currentPtr is not NULL, currentPtr->data is printed by the function, and currentPtr->nextPtr is assigned to currentPtr. Note that if the link in the last node of the list is not NULL, the printing algorithm will try to print past the end of the list, and an error will occur. The printing algorithm is identical for linked lists, stacks and queues.

12.5 Stacks

A *stack* is a constrained version of a linked list. New nodes can be added to a stack and removed from a stack only at the top. For this reason, a stack is referred to as a *last-in, first-out (LIFO)* data structure. A stack is referenced via a pointer to the top element of the stack. The link member in the last node of the stack is set to NULL to indicate the bottom of the stack.

Figure 12.7 illustrates a stack with several nodes. Note that stacks and linked lists are represented identically. The difference between stacks and linked lists is that insertions and deletions may occur anywhere in a linked list, but only at the top of a stack.

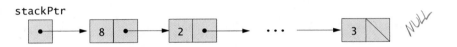

Fig. 12.7 Stack graphical representation.

 Common Programming Error 12.6

Not setting the link in the bottom node of a stack to NULL can lead to runtime errors.

The primary functions used to manipulate a stack are push and pop. Function push creates a new node and places it on top of the stack. Function pop removes a node from the top of the stack, frees the memory that was allocated to the popped node and returns the popped value.

Figure 12.8 (output shown in Fig. 12.9) implements a simple stack of integers. The program provides three options: 1) push a value onto the stack (function push), 2) pop a value off the stack (function pop) and 3) terminate the program.

```c
1   /* Fig. 12.8: fig12_08.c
2      dynamic stack program */
3   #include <stdio.h>
4   #include <stdlib.h>
5
6   /* self-referential structure */
7   struct stackNode {
8      int data;                  /* define data as an int */
9      struct stackNode *nextPtr; /* stackNode pointer */
10  }; /* end structure stackNode */
11
12  typedef struct stackNode StackNode; /* synonym for struct stackNode */
13  typedef StackNode *StackNodePtr; /* synonym for StackNode* */
14
15  /* prototypes */
16  void push( StackNodePtr *topPtr, int info );
17  int pop( StackNodePtr *topPtr );
18  int isEmpty( StackNodePtr topPtr );
19  void printStack( StackNodePtr currentPtr );
20  void instructions( void );
21
22  /* function main begins program execution */
23  int main()
24  {
25     StackNodePtr stackPtr = NULL; /* points to stack top */
26     int choice; /* user's menu choice */
27     int value;  /* int input by user */
28
29     instructions(); /* display the menu */
30     printf( "? " );
31     scanf( "%d", &choice );
32
```

Fig. 12.8 A simple stack program. (Part 1 of 4.)

```
33       /* while user does not enter 3 */
34       while ( choice != 3 ) {
35
36          switch ( choice ) {
37
38             /* push value onto stack */
39             case 1:
40                printf( "Enter an integer: " );
41                scanf( "%d", &value );
42                push( &stackPtr, value );
43                printStack( stackPtr );
44                break;
45
46             /* pop value off stack */
47             case 2:
48
49                /* if stack is not empty */
50                if ( !isEmpty( stackPtr ) ) {
51                   printf( "The popped value is %d.\n", pop( &stackPtr ) );
52                } /* end if */
53
54                printStack( stackPtr );
55                break;
56
57             default:
58                printf( "Invalid choice.\n\n" );
59                instructions();
60                break;
61
62          } /* end switch */
63
64          printf( "? " );
65          scanf( "%d", &choice );
66       } /* end while */
67
68       printf( "End of run.\n" );
69
70       return 0; /* indicates successful termination */
71
72    } /* end main */
73
74    /* display program instructions to user */
75    void instructions( void )
76    {
77       printf( "Enter choice:\n"
78          "1 to push a value on the stack\n"
79          "2 to pop a value off the stack\n"
80          "3 to end program\n" );
81    } /* end function instructions */
82
83    /* Insert a node at the stack top */
84    void push( StackNodePtr *topPtr, int info )
85    {
```

Fig. 12.8 A simple stack program. (Part 2 of 4.)

```
86         StackNodePtr newPtr; /* pointer to new node */
87
88         newPtr = malloc( sizeof( StackNode ) );
89
90         /* insert the node at stack top */
91         if ( newPtr != NULL ) {
92            newPtr->data = info;
93            newPtr->nextPtr = *topPtr;
94            *topPtr = newPtr;
95         } /* end if */
96         else { /* no space available */
97            printf( "%d not inserted. No memory available.\n", info );
98         } /* end else */
99
100  } /* end function push */
101
102  /* Remove a node from the stack top */
103  int pop( StackNodePtr *topPtr )
104  {
105         StackNodePtr tempPtr; /* temporary node pointer */
106         int popValue; /* node value */
107
108         tempPtr = *topPtr;
109         popValue = ( *topPtr )->data;
110         *topPtr = ( *topPtr )->nextPtr;
111         free( tempPtr );
112
113         return popValue;
114
115  } /* end function pop */
116
117  /* Print the stack */
118  void printStack( StackNodePtr currentPtr )
119  {
120
121         /* if stack is empty */
122         if ( currentPtr == NULL ) {
123            printf( "The stack is empty.\n\n" );
124         } /* end if */
125         else {
126            printf( "The stack is:\n" );
127
128            /* while not the end of the stack */
129            while ( currentPtr != NULL ) {
130               printf( "%d --> ", currentPtr->data );
131               currentPtr = currentPtr->nextPtr;
132            } /* end while */
133
134            printf( "NULL\n\n" );
135         } /* end else */
136
137  } /* end function printList */
138
```

Fig. 12.8   A simple stack program. (Part 3 of 4.)

```
139   /* Return 1 if the stack is empty, 0 otherwise */
140   int isEmpty( StackNodePtr topPtr )
141   {
142      return topPtr == NULL;
143
144   } /* end function isEmpty */
```

Fig. 12.8 A simple stack program. (Part 4 of 4.)

```
Enter choice:
1 to push a value on the stack
2 to pop a value off the stack
3 to end program
? 1
Enter an integer: 5
The stack is:
5 --> NULL

Enter an integer: 6
The stack is:
6 --> 5 --> NULL

? 1
Enter an integer: 4
The stack is:
4 --> 6 --> 5 --> NULL

? 2
The popped value is 4.
The stack is:
6 --> 5 --> NULL

? 2
The popped value is 6.
The stack is:
5 --> NULL

? 2
The popped value is 5.
The stack is empty.

? 2
The stack is empty.

? 4
Invalid choice.

Enter choice:
1 to push a value on the stack
2 to pop a value off the stack
3 to end program
? 3
End of run.
```

Fig. 12.9 Sample output from the program of Fig. 12.8.

Function `push` (lines 84–100) places a new node at the top of the stack. The function consists of three steps:

1. Create a new node by calling `malloc` and assign the location of the allocated memory to `newPtr` (line 88).

2. Assign to `newPtr->data` the value to be placed on the stack (line 92) and assign `*topPtr` (the stack top pointer) to `newPtr->nextPtr` (line 93)—the link member of `newPtr` now points to the previous top node.

3. Assign `newPtr` to `*topPtr` (line 94)—`*topPtr` now points to the new stack top.

Manipulations involving `*topPtr` change the value of `stackPtr` in `main`. Figure 12.10 illustrates function `push`. Part a) of the figure shows the stack and the new node before the `push` operation. The dotted arrows in part b) illustrate steps 2 and 3 of the `push` operation that enable the node containing `12` to become the new stack top.

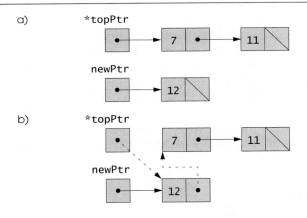

Fig. 12.10 push operation.

Function pop (lines 103–115) removes a node from the top of the stack. Note that `main` determines if the stack is empty before calling `pop`. The `pop` operation consists of five steps:

1. Assign `*topPtr` to `tempPtr` (line 108); `tempPtr` will be used to free the unneeded memory.

2. Assign `(*topPtr)->data` to `popValue` (line 109) to save the value in the top node.

3. Assign `(*topPtr)->nextPtr` to `*topPtr` (line 110) so `*topPtr` contains address of the new top node.

4. Free the memory pointed to by `tempPtr` (line 111).

5. Return `popValue` to the caller (line 113).

Figure 12.11 illustrates function pop. Part a) shows the stack after the previous `push` operation. Part b) shows `tempPtr` pointing to the first node of the stack and `topPtr` pointing to the second node of the stack. Function `free` is used to free the memory pointed to by `tempPtr`.

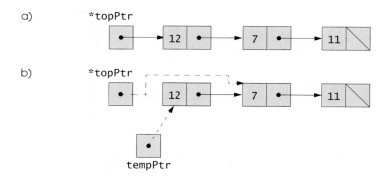

Fig. 12.11 pop operation.

Stacks have many interesting applications. For example, whenever a function call is made, the called function must know how to return to its caller, so the return address is pushed onto a stack. If a series of function calls occurs, the successive return values are pushed onto the stack in last-in, first-out order so that each function can return to its caller. Stacks support recursive function calls in the same manner as conventional nonrecursive calls.

Stacks contain the space created for automatic variables on each invocation of a function. When the function returns to its caller, the space for that function's automatic variables is popped off the stack, and these variables no longer are known to the program. Stacks are used by compilers in the process of evaluating expressions and generating machine language code. The Exercises explore several applications of stacks.

12.6 Queues

Another common data structure is the *queue.* A queue is similar to a checkout line in a grocery store—the first person in line is serviced first, and other customers enter the line only at the end and wait to be serviced. Queue nodes are removed only from the *head of the queue* and are inserted only at the *tail of the queue.* For this reason, a queue is referred to as a *first-in, first-out (FIFO)* data structure. The insert and remove operations are known as enqueue and dequeue.

Queues have many applications in computer systems. Many computers have only a single processor, so only one user at a time may be serviced. Entries for the other users are placed in a queue. Each entry gradually advances to the front of the queue as users receive service. The entry at the front of the queue is the next to receive service.

Queues are also used to support print spooling. A multiuser environment may have only a single printer. Many users may be generating outputs to be printed. If the printer is busy, other outputs may still be generated. These are spooled to disk where they wait in a queue until the printer becomes available.

Information packets also wait in queues in computer networks. Each time a packet arrives at a network node, it must be routed to the next node on the network along the path to the packet's final destination. The routing node routes one packet at a time, so additional packets are enqueued until the router can route them. Figure 12.12 illustrates a queue with several nodes. Note the pointers to the head of the queue and the tail of the queue.

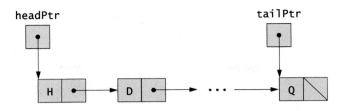

Fig. 12.12 Queue graphical representation.

 Common Programming Error 12.7

Not setting the link in the last node of a queue to NULL can lead to runtime errors.

Figure 12.13 (output in Fig. 12.14) performs queue manipulations. The program provides several options: insert a node in the queue (function **enqueue**), remove a node from the queue (function **dequeue**) and terminate the program.

```c
1   /* Fig. 12.13: fig12_13.c
2      Operating and maintaining a queue */
3
4   #include <stdio.h>
5   #include <stdlib.h>
6
7   /* self-referential structure */
8   struct queueNode {
9      char data;                   /* define data as a char */
10     struct queueNode *nextPtr;   /* queueNode pointer */
11  }; /* end structure queueNode */
12
13  typedef struct queueNode QueueNode;
14  typedef QueueNode *QueueNodePtr;
15
16  /* function prototypes */
17  void printQueue( QueueNodePtr currentPtr );
18  int isEmpty( QueueNodePtr headPtr );
19  char dequeue( QueueNodePtr *headPtr, QueueNodePtr *tailPtr );
20  void enqueue( QueueNodePtr *headPtr, QueueNodePtr *tailPtr,
21                char value );
22  void instructions( void );
23
24  /* function main begins program execution */
25  int main()
26  {
27     QueueNodePtr headPtr = NULL; /* initialize headPtr */
28     QueueNodePtr tailPtr = NULL; /* initialize tailPtr */
29     int choice;                  /* user's menu choice */
30     char item;                   /* char input by user */
31
32     instructions(); /* display the menu */
33     printf( "? " );
```

Fig. 12.13 Processing a queue. (Part 1 of 4.)

```
34        scanf( "%d", &choice );
35
36     /* while user does not enter 3 */
37     while ( choice != 3 ) {
38
39        switch( choice ) {
40
41           /* enqueue value */
42           case 1:
43              printf( "Enter a character: " );
44              scanf( "\n%c", &item );
45              enqueue( &headPtr, &tailPtr, item );
46              printQueue( headPtr );
47              break;
48
49           /* dequeue value */
50           case 2:
51
52              /* if queue is not empty */
53              if ( !isEmpty( headPtr ) ) {
54                 item = dequeue( &headPtr, &tailPtr );
55                 printf( "%c has been dequeued.\n", item );
56              } /* end if */
57
58              printQueue( headPtr );
59              break;
60
61           default:
62              printf( "Invalid choice.\n\n" );
63              instructions();
64              break;
65
66        } /* end switch */
67
68        printf( "? " );
69        scanf( "%d", &choice );
70     } /* end while */
71
72     printf( "End of run.\n" );
73
74     return 0; /* indicates successful termination */
75
76  } /* end main */
77
78  /* display program instructions to user */
79  void instructions( void )
80  {
81     printf ( "Enter your choice:\n"
82             "   1 to add an item to the queue\n"
83             "   2 to remove an item from the queue\n"
84             "   3 to end\n" );
85  } /* end function instructions */
86
```

Fig. 12.13 Processing a queue. (Part 2 of 4.)

```
87    /* insert a node a queue tail */
88    void enqueue( QueueNodePtr *headPtr, QueueNodePtr *tailPtr,
89                   char value )
90    {
91       QueueNodePtr newPtr; /* pointer to new node */
92
93       newPtr = malloc( sizeof( QueueNode ) );
94
95       if ( newPtr != NULL ) { /* is space available */
96          newPtr->data = value;
97          newPtr->nextPtr = NULL;
98
99          /* if empty, insert node at head */
100         if ( isEmpty( *headPtr ) ) {
101            *headPtr = newPtr;
102         } /* end if */
103         else {
104            ( *tailPtr )->nextPtr = newPtr;
105         } /* end else */
106
107         *tailPtr = newPtr;
108      } /* end if */
109      else {
110         printf( "%c not inserted. No memory available.\n", value );
111      } /* end else */
112
113   } /* end function enqueue */
114
115   /* remove node from queue head */
116   char dequeue( QueueNodePtr *headPtr, QueueNodePtr *tailPtr )
117   {
118      char value;               /* node value */
119      QueueNodePtr tempPtr; /* temporary node pointer */
120
121      value = ( *headPtr )->data;
122      tempPtr = *headPtr;
123      *headPtr = ( *headPtr )->nextPtr;
124
125      /* if queue is empty */
126      if ( *headPtr == NULL ) {
127         *tailPtr = NULL;
128      } /* end if */
129
130      free( tempPtr );
131
132      return value;
133
134   } /* end function dequeue */
135
136   /* Return 1 if the list is empty, 0 otherwise */
137   int isEmpty( QueueNodePtr headPtr )
138   {
139      return headPtr == NULL;
```

Fig. 12.13 Processing a queue. (Part 3 of 4.)

```
140
141  } /* end function isEmpty */
142
143  /* Print the queue */
144  void printQueue( QueueNodePtr currentPtr )
145  {
146
147     /* if queue is empty */
148     if ( currentPtr == NULL ) {
149        printf( "Queue is empty.\n\n" );
150     } /* end if */
151     else {
152        printf( "The queue is:\n" );
153
154        /* while not end of queue */
155        while ( currentPtr != NULL ) {
156           printf( "%c --> ", currentPtr->data );
157           currentPtr = currentPtr->nextPtr;
158        } /* end while */
159
160        printf( "NULL\n\n" );
161     } /* end else */
162
163  } /* end function printQueue */
```

Fig. 12.13 Processing a queue. (Part 4 of 4.)

```
Enter your choice:
   1 to add an item to the queue
   2 to remove an item from the queue
   3 to end
? 1
Enter a character: A
The queue is:
A --> NULL

? 1
Enter a character: B
The queue is:
A --> B --> NULL

? 1
Enter a character: C
The queue is:
A --> B --> C --> NULL

? 2
A has been dequeued.
The queue is:
B --> C --> NULL
```

Fig. 12.14 Sample output from the program in Fig. 12.13. (Part 1 of 2.)

```
? 2
B has been dequeued.
The queue is:
C --> NULL

? 2
C has been dequeued.
Queue is empty.

? 2
Queue is empty.

? 4
Invalid choice.

Enter your choice:
   1 to add an item to the queue
   2 to remove an item from the queue
   3 to end
? 3
End of run.
```

Fig. 12.14 Sample output from the program in Fig. 12.13. (Part 2 of 2.)

Function enqueue (lines 88–113) receives three arguments from main: the address of the pointer to the head of the queue, the address of the pointer to the tail of the queue and the value to be inserted in the queue. The function consists of three steps:

1. To create a new node: Call malloc, assign the allocated memory location to newPtr (line 93), assign the value to be inserted in the queue to newPtr->data (line 96) and assign NULL to newPtr->nextPtr (line 97).

2. If the queue is empty (line 100), assign newPtr to *headPtr (line 101); otherwise, assign pointer newPtr to (*tailPtr)->nextPtr (line 104).

3. Assign newPtr to *tailPtr (line 107).

Figure 12.15 illustrates an enqueue operation. Part a) shows the queue and the new node before the operation. The dotted arrows in part b) illustrate steps 2 and 3 of function enqueue that enable a new node to be added to the end of a queue that is not empty.

Function dequeue (lines 116–134) receives the address of the pointer to the head of the queue and the address of the pointer to the tail of the queue as arguments and removes the first node from the queue. The dequeue operation consists of six steps:

1. Assign (*headPtr)->data to value to save the data (line 121).

2. Assign *headPtr to tempPtr (line 122), which will be used to free the unneeded memory.

3. Assign (*headPtr)->nextPtr to *headPtr (line 123) so that *headPtr now points to the new first node in the queue.

4. If *headPtr is NULL (line 126), assign NULL to *tailPtr (line 127).

5. Free the memory pointed to by tempPtr (line 130).

6. Return value to the caller (line 132).

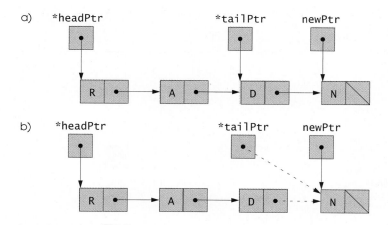

Fig. 12.15 enqueue operation.

Figure 12.16 illustrates function `dequeue`. Part a) shows the queue after the preceding `enqueue` operation. Part b) shows `tempPtr` pointing to the dequeued node, and `headPtr` pointing to the new first node of the queue. Function `free` is used to reclaim the memory pointed to by `tempPtr`.

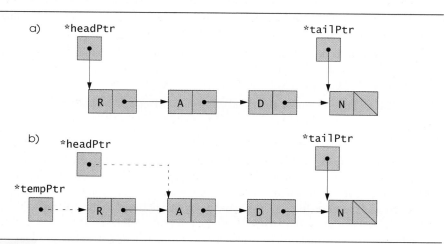

Fig. 12.16 dequeue operation.

12.7 Trees

Linked lists, stacks and queues are *linear data structures.* A *tree* is a nonlinear, two-dimensional data structure with special properties. Tree nodes contain two or more links. This section discusses *binary trees* (Fig. 12.17)—trees whose nodes all contain two links (none, one, or both of which may be NULL). The *root node* is the first node in a tree. Each link in the root node refers to a *child.* The *left child* is the first node in the *left subtree,* and the *right child* is the first node in the *right subtree.* The children of a node are called *siblings.* A node with no children is called a *leaf node*. Computer scientists normally draw trees from the root node down—exactly the opposite of trees in nature.

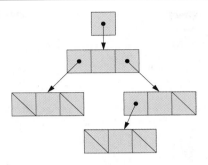

Fig. 12.17 Binary tree graphical representation.

In this section, a special binary tree called a *binary search tree* is created. A binary search tree (with no duplicate node values) has the characteristic that the values in any left subtree are less than the value in its parent node, and the values in any right subtree are greater than the value in its *parent node*. Figure 12.18 illustrates a binary search tree with 12 values. Note that the shape of the binary search tree that corresponds to a set of data can vary, depending on the order in which the values are inserted into the tree.

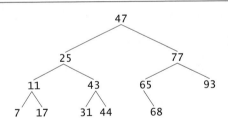

Fig. 12.18 Binary search tree.

Common Programming Error 12.8

Not setting to NULL the links in leaf nodes of a tree can lead to runtime errors.

Figure 12.19 (output shown in Fig. 12.20) creates a binary search tree and traverses it three ways—*inorder, preorder* and *postorder*. The program generates 10 random numbers and inserts each in the tree, except that duplicate values are discarded.

```
1   /* Fig. 12.19: fig12_19.c
2      Create a binary tree and traverse it
3      preorder, inorder, and postorder */
```

Fig. 12.19 Creating and traversing a binary tree. (Part 1 of 4.)

```c
 4   #include <stdio.h>
 5   #include <stdlib.h>
 6   #include <time.h>
 7
 8   /* self-referential structure */
 9   struct treeNode {
10      struct treeNode *leftPtr;  /* pointer to left subtree */
11      int data; /* node value */
12      struct treeNode *rightPtr; /* pointer to right subtree */
13   }; /* end structure treeNode */
14
15   typedef struct treeNode TreeNode; /* synonym for struct treeNode */
16   typedef TreeNode *TreeNodePtr; /* synonym for TreeNode* */
17
18   /* prototypes */
19   void insertNode( TreeNodePtr *treePtr, int value );
20   void inOrder( TreeNodePtr treePtr );
21   void preOrder( TreeNodePtr treePtr );
22   void postOrder( TreeNodePtr treePtr );
23
24   /* function main begins program execution */
25   int main()
26   {
27      int i; /* counter to loop from 1-10 */
28      int item; /* variable to hold random values */
29      TreeNodePtr rootPtr = NULL; /* tree initially empty */
30
31      srand( time( NULL ) );
32      printf( "The numbers being placed in the tree are:\n" );
33
34      /* insert random values between 1 and 15 in the tree */
35      for ( i = 1; i <= 10; i++ ) {
36         item = rand() % 15;
37         printf( "%3d", item );
38         insertNode( &rootPtr, item );
39      } /* end for */
40
41      /* traverse the tree preOrder */
42      printf( "\n\nThe preOrder traversal is:\n" );
43      preOrder( rootPtr );
44
45      /* traverse the tree inOrder */
46      printf( "\n\nThe inOrder traversal is:\n" );
47      inOrder( rootPtr );
48
49      /* traverse the tree postOrder */
50      printf( "\n\nThe postOrder traversal is:\n" );
51      postOrder( rootPtr );
52
53      return 0; /* indicates successful termination */
54
55   } /* end main */
56
```

Fig. 12.19 Creating and traversing a binary tree. (Part 2 of 4.)

```
57   /* insert node into tree */
58   void insertNode( TreeNodePtr *treePtr, int value )
59   {
60
61      /* if tree is empty */
62      if ( *treePtr == NULL ) {
63         *treePtr = malloc( sizeof( TreeNode ) );
64
65         /* if memory was allocated then assign data */
66         if ( *treePtr != NULL ) {
67            ( *treePtr )->data = value;
68            ( *treePtr )->leftPtr = NULL;
69            ( *treePtr )->rightPtr = NULL;
70         } /* end if */
71         else {
72            printf( "%d not inserted. No memory available.\n", value );
73         } /* end else */
74
75      } /* end if */
76      else { /* tree is not empty */
77
78         /* data to insert is less than data in current node */
79         if ( value < ( *treePtr )->data ) {
80            insertNode( &( ( *treePtr )->leftPtr ), value );
81         } /* end if */
82
83         /* data to insert is greater than data in current node */
84         else if ( value > ( *treePtr )->data ) {
85            insertNode( &( ( *treePtr )->rightPtr ), value );
86         } /* end else if */
87         else { /* duplicate data value ignored */
88            printf( "dup" );
89         } /* end else */
90
91      } /* end else */
92
93   } /* end function insertNode */
94
95   /* begin inorder traversal of tree */
96   void inOrder( TreeNodePtr treePtr )
97   {
98
99      /* if tree is not empty then traverse */
100     if ( treePtr != NULL ) {
101        inOrder( treePtr->leftPtr );
102        printf( "%3d", treePtr->data );
103        inOrder( treePtr->rightPtr );
104     } /* end if */
105
106  } /* end function inOrder */
107
```

Fig. 12.19 Creating and traversing a binary tree. (Part 3 of 4.)

```
108   /* begin preorder traversal of tree */
109   void preOrder( TreeNodePtr treePtr )
110   {
111
112      /* if tree is not empty then traverse */
113      if ( treePtr != NULL ) {
114         printf( "%3d", treePtr->data );
115         preOrder( treePtr->leftPtr );
116         preOrder( treePtr->rightPtr );
117      } /* end if */
118
119   } /* end function preOrder */
120
121   /* begin postorder traversal of tree */
122   void postOrder( TreeNodePtr treePtr )
123   {
124
125      /* if tree is not empty then traverse */
126      if ( treePtr != NULL ) {
127         postOrder( treePtr->leftPtr );
128         postOrder( treePtr->rightPtr );
129         printf( "%3d", treePtr->data );
130      } /* end if */
131
132   } /* end function postOrder */
```

Fig. 12.19 Creating and traversing a binary tree. (Part 4 of 4.)

```
The numbers being placed in the tree are:
  6   7   4  12   7dup  2   2dup  5   7dup  11

The preOrder traversal is:
  6   4   2   5   7  12  11

The inOrder traversal is:
  2   4   5   6   7  11  12

The postOrder traversal is:
  2   5   4  11  12   7   6
```

Fig. 12.20 Sample output from the program of Fig. 12.19.

The functions used in Fig. 12.19 to create a binary search tree and traverse the tree are recursive. Function insertNode (lines 58–93) receives the address of the tree and an integer to be stored in the tree as arguments. *A node can only be inserted as a leaf node in a binary search tree.* The steps for inserting a node in a binary search tree are as follows:

1. If *treePtr is NULL (line 62), create a new node (line 63). Call malloc, assign the allocated memory to *treePtr, assign to (*treePtr)->data the integer to be stored (line 67), assign to (*treePtr)->leftPtr and (*treePtr)->rightPtr the value NULL (lines 68–69, and return control to the caller (either main or a previous call to insertNode).

2. If the value of *treePtr is not NULL and the value to be inserted is less than (*treePtr)->data, function insertNode is called with the address of (*treePtr)->leftPtr (line 80). If the value to be inserted is greater than (*treePtr)->data, function insertNode is called with the address of (*treePtr)->rightPtr (line 85). Otherwise, the recursive steps continue until a NULL pointer is found, then step 1) is executed to insert the new node.

Functions inOrder (lines 96–106), preOrder (lines 109–119) and postOrder (lines 122–132) each receive a tree (i.e., the pointer to the root node of the tree) and traverse the tree. The steps for an inOrder traversal are:

1. Traverse the left subtree inOrder.

2. Process the value in the node.

3. Traverse the right subtree inOrder.

The value in a node is not processed until the values in its left subtree are processed. The inOrder traversal of the tree in Fig. 12.21 is:

    6 13 17 27 33 42 48

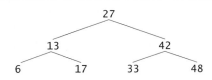

Fig. 12.21 Binary search tree with seven nodes.

Note that the inOrder traversal of a binary search tree prints the node values in ascending order. The process of creating a binary search tree actually sorts the data—and thus this process is called the *binary tree sort*.

The steps for a preOrder traversal are:

1. Process the value in the node.

2. Traverse the left subtree preOrder.

3. Traverse the right subtree preOrder.

The value in each node is processed as the node is visited. After the value in a given node is processed, the values in the left subtree are processed, then the values in the right subtree are processed. The preOrder traversal of the tree in Fig. 12.21 is:

    27 13 6 17 42 33 48

The steps for a postOrder traversal are:

1. Traverse the left subtree postOrder.

2. Traverse the right subtree postOrder.

3. Process the value in the node.

The value in each node is not printed until the values of its children are printed. The post-Order traversal of the tree in Fig. 12.21 is:

```
6  17  13  33  48  42  27
```

The binary search tree facilitates *duplicate elimination*. As the tree is being created, an attempt to insert a duplicate value will be recognized because a duplicate will follow the same "go left" or "go right" decisions on each comparison as the original value did. Thus, the duplicate will eventually be compared with a node in the tree containing the same value. The duplicate value may simply be discarded at this point.

Searching a binary tree for a value that matches a key value is also fast. If the tree is tightly packed, each level contains about twice as many elements as the previous level. So a binary search tree with n elements would have a maximum of $\log_2 n$ levels, and thus a maximum of $\log_2 n$ comparisons would have to be made either to find a match or to determine that no match exists. This means, for example, that when searching a (tightly packed) 1000-element binary search tree, no more than 10 comparisons need to be made because $2^{10} > 1000$. When searching a (tightly packed) 1,000,000 element binary search tree, no more than 20 comparisons need to be made because $2^{20} > 1,000,000$.

In the Exercises, algorithms are presented for several other binary tree operations such as deleting an item from a binary tree, printing a binary tree in a two-dimensional tree format, and performing a level order traversal of a binary tree. The level order traversal of a binary tree visits the nodes of the tree row-by-row starting at the root node level. On each level of the tree, the nodes are visited from left to right. Other binary tree exercises include allowing a binary search tree to contain duplicate values, inserting string values in a binary tree and determining how many levels are contained in a binary tree.

SUMMARY

- Self-referential structures contain members called links that point to structures of the same structure type.

- Self-referential structures enable many structures to be linked together in stacks, queues, lists and trees.

- Dynamic memory allocation reserves a block of bytes in memory to store a data object during program execution.

- Function `malloc` takes the number of bytes to be allocated as an argument and returns a `void` pointer to the allocated memory. Function `malloc` is usually used with the `sizeof` operator. The `sizeof` operator determines the size in bytes of the structure for which memory is being allocated.

- Function `free` deallocates memory.

- A linked list is a collection of data stored in a group of connected self-referential structures.

- A linked list is a dynamic data structure—the length of the list can increase or decrease as necessary.

- Linked lists can continue to grow while memory is available.

- Linked lists provide a mechanism for simple insertion and deletion of data by reassigning pointers.

- Stacks and queues are constrained versions of a linked list.

- New nodes are added to a stack and removed from a stack only at the top. For this reason, a stack is referred to as a last-in, first-out (LIFO) data structure.

- The link member in the last node of the stack is set to NULL to indicate the bottom of the stack.

- The two primary operations used to manipulate a stack are `push` and `pop`. The `push` operation creates a new node and places it on the top of the stack. The `pop` operation removes a node from the top of the stack, frees the memory that was allocated to the popped node and returns the popped value.

- In a queue data structure, nodes are removed from the head and added to the tail. For this reason, a queue is referred to as a first-in, first-out (FIFO) data structure. The add and remove operations are known as enqueue and dequeue.

- Trees are more complex data structures than linked lists, queues and stacks. Trees are two-dimensional data structures requiring two or more links per node.

- Binary trees contain two links per node.

- The root node is the first node in the tree.

- Each of the pointers in the root node refers to a child. The left child is the first node in the left subtree and the right child is the first node in the right subtree. The children of a node are called siblings. If a node does not have any children it is called a leaf node.

- A binary search tree has the characteristic that the value in the left child of a node is less than the parent node value and the value in the right child of a node is greater than or equal to the parent node value. If it can be determined that there are no duplicate data values, the value in the right child is simply greater than the parent node value.

- An inorder traversal of a binary tree traverses the left subtree inorder, processes the value in the node and traverses the right subtree inorder. The value in a node is not processed until the values in its left subtree are processed.

- A preorder traversal processes the value in the node, traverses the left subtree preorder and traverses the right subtree preorder. The value in each node is processed as the node is encountered.

- A postorder traversal traverses the left subtree postorder, traverses the right subtree postorder, and processes the value in the node. The value in each node is not processed until the values in both its subtrees are processed.

TERMINOLOGY

binary search tree
binary tree
binary tree sort
child node
children
deleting a node
dequeue
double indirection
dynamic data structures
dynamic memory allocation
enqueue
FIFO (first-in, first-out)
free
head of a queue
inorder traversal
inserting a node
leaf node
left child
left subtree
LIFO (last-in, first-out)
linear data structure
linked list
malloc (allocate memory)
node

nonlinear data structure
NULL pointer
parent node
pointer to a pointer
pop
postorder traversal
predicate function
preorder traversal
push
queue
right child
right subtree
root node
self-referential structure
siblings
sizeof
stack
subtree
tail of a queue
top
traversal
tree
visit a node

COMMON PROGRAMMING ERRORS

12.1   Not setting the link in the last node of a list to NULL can lead to runtime errors.

12.2   Assuming that the size of a structure is simply the sum of the sizes of its members is a logic error.

12.3   Not returning dynamically allocated memory when it is no longer needed can cause the system to run out of memory prematurely. This is sometimes called a "memory leak."

12.4   Freeing memory not allocated dynamically with malloc.

12.5   Referring to memory that has been freed.

12.6   Not setting the link in the bottom node of a stack to NULL can lead to runtime errors.

12.7   Not setting the link in the last node of a queue to NULL can lead to runtime errors.

12.8   Not setting to NULL the links in leaf nodes of a tree can lead to runtime errors.

ERROR-PREVENTION TIPS

12.1   When using malloc, test for a NULL pointer return value. Print an error message if the requested memory is not allocated.

12.2   Assign NULL to the link member of a new node. Pointers should be initialized before they are used.

GOOD PROGRAMMING PRACTICES

12.1   Use the sizeof operator to determine the size of a structure.

12.2   When memory that was dynamically allocated is no longer needed, use free to return the memory to the system immediately.

PERFORMANCE TIPS

12.1   An array can be declared to contain more elements than the number of data items expected, but this can waste memory. Linked lists can provide better memory utilization in these situations.

12.2   Insertion and deletion in a sorted array can be time consuming—all the elements following the inserted or deleted element must be shifted appropriately.

12.3   The elements of an array are stored contiguously in memory. This allows immediate access to any array element because the address of any element can be calculated directly based on its position relative to the beginning of the array. Linked lists do not afford such immediate access to their elements.

12.4   Using dynamic memory allocation (instead of arrays) for data structures that grow and shrink at execution time can save memory. Keep in mind, however, that the pointers take up space, and that dynamic memory allocation incurs the overhead of function calls.

PORTABILITY TIP

12.1   A structure's size is not necessarily the sum of the sizes of its members. This is so because of various machine-dependent boundary alignment requirements (see Chapter 10).

SELF-REVIEW EXERCISES

12.1   Fill in the blanks in each of the following:
a) A self-_____ structure is used to form dynamic data structures.
b) Function _____ is used to dynamically allocate memory.

c) A(n) _____ is a specialized version of a linked list in which nodes can be inserted and deleted only from the start of the list.

d) Functions that look at a linked list but do not modify it are referred to as _____.

e) A queue is referred to as a(n) _____ data structure.

f) The pointer to the next node in a linked list is referred to as a(n) _____.

g) Function _____ is used to reclaim dynamically allocated memory.

h) A(n) _____ is a specialized version of a linked list in which nodes can be inserted only at the start of the list and deleted only from the end of the list.

i) A(n) _____ is a nonlinear, two-dimensional data structure that contains nodes with two or more links.

j) A stack is referred to as a(n) _____ data structure because the last node inserted is the first node removed.

k) The nodes of a(n) _____ tree contain two link members.

l) The first node of a tree is the _____ node.

m) Each link in a tree node points to a(n) _____ or _____ of that node.

n) A tree node that has no children is called a(n) _____ node.

o) The three traversal algorithms (covered in this chapter) for a binary tree are _____, _____ and _____.

12.2   What are the differences between a linked list and a stack?

12.3   What are the differences between a stack and a queue?

12.4   Write a statement or set of statements to accomplish each of the following. Assume that all the manipulations occur in main (therefore, no addresses of pointer variables are needed), and assume the following definitions:

```
struct gradeNode {
    char lastName[ 20 ];
    double grade;
    struct gradeNode *nextPtr;
};

typedef struct gradeNode GradeNode;
typedef GradeNode *GradeNodePtr;
```

a) Create a pointer to the start of the list called startPtr. The list is empty.

b) Create a new node of type GradeNode that is pointed to by pointer newPtr of type GradeNodePtr. Assign the string "Jones" to member lastName and the value 91.5 to member grade (use strcpy). Provide any necessary declarations and statements.

c) Assume that the list pointed to by startPtr currently consists of 2 nodes—one containing "Jones" and one containing "Smith". The nodes are in alphabetical order. Provide the statements necessary to insert in order nodes containing the following data for lastName and grade:

"Adams"	85.0
"Thompson"	73.5
"Pritchard"	66.5

Use pointers previousPtr, currentPtr and newPtr to perform the insertions. State what previousPtr and currentPtr point to before each insertion. Assume that newPtr always points to the new node, and that the new node has already been assigned the data.

d) Write a while loop that prints the data in each node of the list. Use pointer currentPtr to move along the list.

e) Write a while loop that deletes all the nodes in the list and frees the memory associated with each node. Use pointer currentPtr and pointer tempPtr to walk along the list and free memory, respectively.

12.5 Manually provide the inorder, preorder and postorder traversals of the binary search tree of Fig. 12.22.

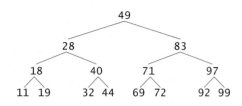

Fig. 12.22 A 15-node binary search tree.

ANSWERS TO SELF-REVIEW EXERCISES

12.1 a) referential. b) `malloc`. c) stack. d) predicates. e) FIFO. f) link. g) `free`. h) queue. i) tree. j) LIFO. k) binary. l) root. m) child, subtree. n) leaf. o) inorder, preorder postorder.

12.2 It is possible to insert a node anywhere in a linked list, and remove a node from anywhere in a linked list. However, nodes in a stack may only be inserted at the top of the stack and removed from the top of a stack.

12.3 A queue has pointers to both its head and its tail so that nodes may be inserted at the tail and deleted from the head. A stack has a single pointer to the top of the stack where both insertion and deletion of nodes is performed.

12.4 a) `GradeNodePtr startPtr = NULL;`
b) `GradeNodePtr newPtr;`
   `newPtr = malloc( sizeof( GradeNode ) );`
   `strcpy( newPtr->lastName, "Jones" );`
   `newPtr->grade = 91.5;`
   `newPtr->nextPtr = NULL;`
c) To insert "Adams":
   `previousPtr` is NULL, `currentPtr` points to the first element in the list.
   `newPtr->nextPtr = currentPtr;`
   `startPtr = newPtr;`

   To insert "Thompson":
   `previousPtr` points to the last element in the list (containing "Smith")
   `currentPtr` is NULL.
   `newPtr->nextPtr = currentPtr;`
   `previousPtr->nextPtr = newPtr;`

   To insert "Pritchard":
   `previousPtr` points to the node containing "Jones"
   `currentPtr` points to the node containing "Smith"
   `newPtr->nextPtr = currentPtr;`
   `previousPtr->nextPtr = newPtr;`
d) `currentPtr = startPtr;`
   `while ( currentPtr != NULL ) {`
   `    printf( "Lastname = %s\nGrade = %6.2f\n",`
   `            currentPtr->lastName, currentPtr->grade );`
   `    currentPtr = currentPtr->nextPtr;`
   `}`

```
e) currentPtr = startPtr;
   while ( currentPtr != NULL ) {
      tempPtr = currentPtr;
      currentPtr = currentPtr->nextPtr;
      free( tempPtr );
   }
   startPtr = NULL;
```

12.5   The inorder traversal is:

   11 18 19 28 32 40 44 49 69 71 72 83 92 97 99

The preorder traversal is:

   49 28 18 11 19 40 32 44 83 71 69 72 97 92 99

The postorder traversal is:

   11 19 18 32 44 40 28 69 72 71 92 99 97 83 49

EXERCISES

12.6   Write a program that concatenates two linked lists of characters. The program should include function `concatenate` that takes pointers to both lists as arguments and concatenates the second list to the first list.

12.7   Write a program that merges two ordered lists of integers into a single ordered list of integers. Function `merge` should receive pointers to the first node of each of the lists to be merged and should return a pointer to the first node of the merged list.

12.8   Write a program that inserts 25 random integers from 0 to 100 in order in a linked list. The program should calculate the sum of the elements and the floating-point average of the elements.

12.9   Write a program that creates a linked list of 10 characters, then creates a copy of the list in reverse order.

12.10   Write a program that inputs a line of text and uses a stack to print the line reversed.

12.11   Write a program that uses a stack to determine if a string is a palindrome (i.e., the string is spelled identically backward and forward). The program should ignore spaces and punctuation.

12.12   Stacks are used by compilers to help in the process of evaluating expressions and generating machine language code. In this and the next exercise, we investigate how compilers evaluate arithmetic expressions consisting only of constants, operators and parentheses.

Humans generally write expressions like 3 + 4 and 7 / 9 in which the operator (+ or / here) is written between its operands—this is called *infix notation*. Computers "prefer" *postfix notation* in which the operator is written to the right of its two operands. The preceding infix expressions would appear in postfix notation as 3 4 + and 7 9 /, respectively.

To evaluate a complex infix expression, a compiler would first convert the expression to postfix notation, and then evaluate the postfix version of the expression. Each of these algorithms requires only a single left-to-right pass of the expression. Each algorithm uses a stack in support of its operation, and in each the stack is used for a different purpose.

In this exercise, you will write a version of the infix-to-postfix conversion algorithm. In the next exercise, you will write a version of the postfix expression evaluation algorithm.

Write a program that converts an ordinary infix arithmetic expression (assume a valid expression is entered) with single digit integers such as

   (6 + 2) * 5 - 8 / 4

to a postfix expression. The postfix version of the preceding infix expression is

```
6  2  +  5  *  8  4  /  -
```

The program should read the expression into character array `infix`, and use modified versions of the stack functions implemented in this chapter to help create the postfix expression in character array `postfix`. The algorithm for creating a postfix expression is as follows:

1) Push a left parenthesis `'('` onto the stack.
2) Append a right parenthesis `')'` to the end of `infix`.
3) While the stack is not empty, read `infix` from left to right and do the following:

   If the current character in `infix` is a digit, copy it to the next element of `postfix`.

   If the current character in `infix` is a left parenthesis, push it onto the stack.

   If the current character in `infix` is an operator,

   Pop operators (if there are any) at the top of the stack while they have equal or higher precedence than the current operator, and insert the popped operators in `postfix`.

   Push the current character in `infix` onto the stack.

   If the current character in `infix` is a right parenthesis

   Pop operators from the top of the stack and insert them in `postfix` until a left parenthesis is at the top of the stack.

   Pop (and discard) the left parenthesis from the stack.

The following arithmetic operations are allowed in an expression:

+   addition
−   subtraction
*   multiplication
/   division
^   exponentiation
%   remainder

The stack should be maintained with the following declarations:

```
struct stackNode {
   char data;
   struct stackNode *nextPtr;
};

typedef struct stackNode StackNode;
typedef StackNode *StackNodePtr;
```

The program should consist of `main` and eight other functions with the following function headers:

`void convertToPostfix( char infix[], char postfix[] )`

Convert the infix expression to postfix notation.

`int isOperator( char c )`

Determine if `c` is an operator.

`int precedence( char operator1, char operator2 )`

Determine if the precedence of `operator1` is less than, equal to, or greater than the precedence of `operator2`. The function returns -1, 0 and 1, respectively.

`void push( StackNodePtr *topPtr, char value )`

Push a value on the stack.

`char pop( StackNodePtr *topPtr )`

Pop a value off the stack.

```
char stackTop( StackNodePtr topPtr )
```

Return the top value of the stack without popping the stack.

```
int isEmpty( StackNodePtr topPtr )
```

Determine if the stack is empty.

```
void printStack( StackNodePtr topPtr )
```

Print the stack.

12.13 Write a program that evaluates a postfix expression (assume it is valid) such as

```
6 2 + 5 * 8 4 / -
```

The program should read a postfix expression consisting of digits and operators into a character array. Using modified versions of the stack functions implemented earlier in this chapter, the program should scan the expression and evaluate it. The algorithm is as follows:

1) Append the null character (`'\0'`) to the end of the postfix expression. When the null character is encountered, no further processing is necessary.
2) While `'\0'` has not been encountered, read the expression from left to right.
   If the current character is a digit,
       Push its integer value onto the stack (the integer value of a digit character is its value in the computer's character set minus the value of `'0'` in the computer's character set).
   Otherwise, if the current character is an *operator*,
       Pop the two top elements of the stack into variables x and y.
       Calculate y *operator* x.
       Push the result of the calculation onto the stack.
3) When the null character is encountered in the expression, pop the top value of the stack. This is the result of the postfix expression.

[*Note:* In 2) above, if the operator is `'/'`, the top of the stack is 2, and the next element in the stack is 8, then pop 2 into x, pop 8 into y, evaluate 8 / 2, and push the result, 4, back on the stack. This note also applies to operator `'-'`.] The arithmetic operations allowed in an expression are:

+	addition
–	subtraction
*	multiplication
/	division
^	exponentiation
%	remainder]

The stack should be maintained with the following declarations:

```
struct stackNode {
   int data;
   struct stackNode *nextPtr;
};

typedef struct stackNode StackNode;
typedef StackNode *StackNodePtr;
```

The program should consist of main and six other functions with the following function headers:

```
int evaluatePostfixExpression( char *expr )
```

Evaluate the postfix expression.

```
int calculate( int op1, int op2, char operator )
```

Evaluate the expression op1 operator op2.

```
void push( StackNodePtr *topPtr, int value )
```

Push a value on the stack.

```
int pop( StackNodePtr *topPtr )
```

Pop a value off the stack.

```
int isEmpty( StackNodePtr topPtr )
```

Determine if the stack is empty.

```
void printStack( StackNodePtr topPtr )
```

Print the stack.

12.14 Modify the postfix evaluator program of Exercise 12.13 so that it can process integer operands larger than 9.

12.15 *(Supermarket Simulation)* Write a program that simulates a check-out line at a supermarket. The line is a queue. Customers arrive in random integer intervals of 1 to 4 minutes. Also, each customer is serviced in random integer intervals of 1 to 4 minutes. Obviously, the rates need to be balanced. If the average arrival rate is larger than the average service rate, the queue will grow infinitely. Even with balanced rates, randomness can still cause long lines. Run the supermarket simulation for a 12-hour day (720 minutes) using the following algorithm:

1) Choose a random integer between 1 and 4 to determine the minute at which the first customer arrives.
2) At the first customer's arrival time:
   Determine customer's service time (random integer from 1 to 4);
   Begin servicing the customer;
   Schedule arrival time of next customer (random integer 1 to 4 added to the current time).
3) For each minute of the day:
   If the next customer arrives,
       Say so;
       Enqueue the customer;
       Schedule the arrival time of the next customer;
   If service was completed for the last customer;
       Say so;
       Dequeue next customer to be serviced;
       Determine customer's service completion time
           (random integer from 1 to 4 added to the current time).

Now run your simulation for 720 minutes and answer each of the following:

a) What is the maximum number of customers in the queue at any time?
b) What is the longest wait any one customer experienced?
c) What happens if the arrival interval is changed from 1 to 4 minutes to 1 to 3 minutes?

12.16 Modify the program of Fig. 12.19 to allow the binary tree to contain duplicate values.

12.17 Write a program based on the program of Fig. 12.19 that inputs a line of text, tokenizes the sentence into separate words, inserts the words in a binary search tree, and prints the inorder, preorder, and postorder traversals of the tree.

[*Hint:* Read the line of text into an array. Use `strtok` to tokenize the text. When a token is found, create a new node for the tree, assign the pointer returned by `strtok` to member `string` of the new node, and insert the node in the tree.]

12.18 In this chapter, we saw that duplicate elimination is straightforward when creating a binary search tree. Describe how you would perform duplicate elimination using only a single subscripted array. Compare the performance of array-based duplicate elimination with the performance of binary-search-tree-based duplicate elimination.

12.19 Write a function `depth` that receives a binary tree and determines how many levels it has.

12.20 (*Recursively Print a List Backwards*) Write a function `printListBackwards` that recursively outputs the items in a list in reverse order. Use your function in a test program that creates a sorted list of integers and prints the list in reverse order.

12.21 (*Recursively Search a List*) Write a function `searchList` that recursively searches a linked list for a specified value. The function should return a pointer to the value if it is found; otherwise, NULL should be returned. Use your function in a test program that creates a list of integers. The program should prompt the user for a value to locate in the list.

12.22 (*Binary Tree Delete*) In this exercise, we discuss deleting items from binary search trees. The deletion algorithm is not as straightforward as the insertion algorithm. There are three cases that are encountered when deleting an item—the item is contained in a leaf node (i.e., it has no children), the item is contained in a node that has one child, or the item is contained in a node that has two children.

If the item to be deleted is contained in a leaf node, the node is deleted and the pointer in the parent node is set to NULL.

If the item to be deleted is contained in a node with one child, the pointer in the parent node is set to point to the child node and the node containing the data item is deleted. This causes the child node to take the place of the deleted node in the tree.

The last case is the most difficult. When a node with two children is deleted, another node must take its place. However, the pointer in the parent node cannot simply be assigned to point to one of the children of the node to be deleted. In most cases, the resulting binary search tree would not adhere to the following characteristic of binary search trees: *The values in any left subtree are less than the value in the parent node, and the values in any right subtree are greater than the value in the parent node.*

Which node is used as a *replacement node* to maintain this characteristic? Either the node containing the largest value in the tree less than the value in the node being deleted, or the node containing the smallest value in the tree greater than the value in the node being deleted. Let us consider the node with the smaller value. In a binary search tree, the largest value less than a parent's value is located in the left subtree of the parent node and is guaranteed to be contained in the rightmost node of the subtree. This node is located by walking down the left subtree to the right until the pointer to the right child of the current node is NULL. We are now pointing to the replacement node which is either a leaf node or a node with one child to its left. If the replacement node is a leaf node, the steps to perform the deletion are as follows:

1) Store the pointer to the node to be deleted in a temporary pointer variable (this pointer is used to delete the dynamically allocated memory).
2) Set the pointer in the parent of the node being deleted to point to the replacement node.
3) Set the pointer in the parent of the replacement node to null.
4) Set the pointer to the right subtree in the replacement node to point to the right subtree of the node to be deleted.
5) Delete the node to which the temporary pointer variable points.

The deletion steps for a replacement node with a left child are similar to those for a replacement node with no children, but the algorithm also must move the child to the replacement node's position. If the replacement node is a node with a left child, the steps to perform the deletion are as follows:

1) Store the pointer to the node to be deleted in a temporary pointer variable.
2) Set the pointer in the parent of the node being deleted to point to the replacement node.
3) Set the pointer in the parent of the replacement node to point to the left child of the replacement node.
4) Set the pointer to the right subtree in the replacement node to point to the right subtree of the node to be deleted.

5) Delete the node to which the temporary pointer variable points.

Write function `deleteNode` which takes as its arguments a pointer to the root node of the tree and the value to be deleted. The function should locate in the tree the node containing the value to be deleted and use the algorithms discussed here to delete the node. If the value is not found in the tree, the function should print a message that indicates whether or not the value is deleted. Modify the program of Fig. 12.19 to use this function. After deleting an item, call the `inOrder`, `preOrder` and `postOrder` traversal functions to confirm that the delete operation was performed correctly.

12.23 (*Binary Tree Search*) Write function `binaryTreeSearch` that attempts to locate a specified value in a binary search tree. The function should take as arguments a pointer to the root node of the binary tree and a search key to be located. If the node containing the search key is found, the function should return a pointer to that node; otherwise, the function should return a `NULL` pointer.

12.24 (*Level Order Binary Tree Traversal*) The program of Fig. 12.19 illustrated three recursive methods of traversing a binary tree—inorder traversal, preorder traversal, and postorder traversal. This exercise presents the *level order traversal* of a binary tree in which the node values are printed level-by-level starting at the root node level. The nodes on each level are printed from left to right. The level order traversal is not a recursive algorithm. It uses the queue data structure to control the output of the nodes. The algorithm is as follows:

1) Insert the root node in the queue
2) While there are nodes left in the queue,
    Get the next node in the queue
    Print the node's value
    If the pointer to the left child of the node is not null
        Insert the left child node in the queue
    If the pointer to the right child of the node is not null
        Insert the right child node in the queue.

Write function `levelOrder` to perform a level order traversal of a binary tree. The function should take as an argument a pointer to the root node of the binary tree. Modify the program of Fig. 12.19 to use this function. Compare the output from this function to the outputs of the other traversal algorithms to see that it worked correctly. [*Note:* You will also need to modify and incorporate the queue processing functions of Fig. 12.13 in this program.]

12.25 (*Printing Trees*) Write a recursive function `outputTree` to display a binary tree on the screen. The function should output the tree row-by-row with the top of the tree at the left of the screen and the bottom of the tree toward the right of the screen. Each row is output vertically. For example, the binary tree illustrated in Fig. 12.22 is output as follows:

Note the rightmost leaf node appears at the top of the output in the rightmost column, and the root node appears at the left of the output. Each column of output starts five spaces to the right of the previous column. Function outputTree should receive as arguments a pointer to the root node of the tree and an integer totalSpaces representing the number of spaces preceding the value to be output (this variable should start at zero so the root node is output at the left of the screen). The function uses a modified inorder traversal to output the tree—it starts at the rightmost node in the tree and works back to the left. The algorithm is as follows:

> While the pointer to the current node is not null
> Recursively call outputTree with the right subtree of the current node and
>   totalSpaces + 5
> Use a for statement to count from 1 to totalSpaces and output spaces
> Output the value in the current node
> Set the pointer to the current node to point to the left subtree of the current node
> Increment totalSpaces by 5.

SPECIAL SECTION: BUILDING YOUR OWN COMPILER

In Exercise 7.18 and Exercise 7.19, we introduced Simpletron Machine Language (SML) and created the Simpletron computer simulator to execute programs written in SML. In this section, we build a compiler that converts programs written in a high-level programming language to SML. This section "ties" together the entire programming process. We will write programs in this new high-level language, compile the programs on the compiler we build, and run the programs on the simulator we built in Exercise 7.19.

12.26 (*The Simple Language*) Before we begin building the compiler, we discuss a simple, yet powerful, high-level language similar to early versions of the popular language BASIC. We call the language *Simple*. Every Simple *statement* consists of a *line number* and a Simple *instruction*. Line numbers must appear in ascending order. Each instruction begins with one of the following Simple *commands*: rem, input, let, print, goto, if...goto or end (see Fig. 12.23). All commands except end can be used repeatedly. Simple evaluates only integer expressions using the +, -, * and / operators. These operators have the same precedence as in C. Parentheses can be used to change the order of evaluation of an expression.

Command	Example statement	Description
rem	50 rem this is a remark	Any text following the command rem is for documentation purposes only and is ignored by the compiler.
input	30 input x	Display a question mark to prompt the user to enter an integer. Read that integer from the keyboard and store the integer in x.
let	80 let u = 4 * (j - 56))	Assign u the value of 4 * (j - 56). Note that an arbitrarily complex expression can appear to the right of the equal sign.
print	10 print w	Display the value of w.
goto	70 goto 45	Transfer program control to line 45.

Fig. 12.23 Simple commands. (Part 1 of 2.)

Command	Example statement	Description
if...goto	35 if i == z goto 80	Compare i and z for equality and transfer program control to line 80 if the condition is true; otherwise, continue execution with the next statement.
end	99 end	Terminate program execution.

Fig. 12.23 Simple commands. (Part 2 of 2.)

Our Simple compiler recognizes only lowercase letters. All characters in a Simple file should be lowercase (uppercase letters result in a syntax error unless they appear in a rem statement in which case they are ignored). A *variable name* is a single letter. Simple does not allow descriptive variable names, so variables should be explained in remarks to indicate their use in the program. Simple uses only integer variables. Simple does not have variable declarations—merely mentioning a variable name in a program causes the variable to be declared and initialized to zero automatically. The syntax of Simple does not allow string manipulation (reading a string, writing a string, comparing strings, etc.). If a string is encountered in a Simple program (after a command other than rem), the compiler generates a syntax error. Our compiler will assume that Simple programs are entered correctly. Exercise 12.29 asks the student to modify the compiler to perform syntax error checking.

Simple uses the conditional if...goto statement and the unconditional goto statement to alter the flow of control during program execution. If the condition in the if...goto statement is true, control is transferred to a specific line of the program. The following relational and equality operators are valid in an if...goto statement: <, >, <=, >=, == or !=. The precedence of these operators is the same as in C.

Let us now consider several Simple programs that demonstrate Simple's features. The first program (Fig. 12.24) reads two integers from the keyboard, stores the values in variables a and b, and computes and prints their sum (stored in variable c).

```
1    10 rem    determine and print the sum of two integers
2    15 rem
3    20 rem    input the two integers
4    30 input a
5    40 input b
6    45 rem
7    50 rem    add integers and store result in c
8    60 let c = a + b
9    65 rem
10   70 rem    print the result
11   80 print c
12   90 rem    terminate program execution
13   99 end
```

Fig. 12.24 Determine the sum of two integers.

Figure 12.25 determines and prints the larger of two integers. The integers are input from the keyboard and stored in s and t. The if...goto statement tests the condition s >= t. If the condition is true, control is transferred to line 90 and s is output; otherwise, t is output and control is transferred to the end statement in line 99 where the program terminates.

```
1    10 rem    determine the larger of two integers
2    20 input s
3    30 input t
4    32 rem
5    35 rem    test if s >= t
6    40 if s >= t goto 90
7    45 rem
8    50 rem    t is greater than s, so print t
9    60 print t
10   70 goto 99
11   75 rem
12   80 rem    s is greater than or equal to t, so print s
13   90 print s
14   99 end
```

Fig. 12.25 Find the larger of two integers .

Simple does not provide a repetition structure (such as C's for, while or do...while). However, Simple can simulate each of C's repetition structures using the if...goto and goto statements. Figure 12.26 uses a sentinel-controlled loop to calculate the squares of several integers. Each integer is input from the keyboard and stored in variable j. If the value entered is the sentinel -9999, control is transferred to line 99 where the program terminates. Otherwise, k is assigned the square of j, k is output to the screen and control is passed to line 20 where the next integer is input.

```
1    10 rem    calculate the squares of several integers
2    20 input j
3    23 rem
4    25 rem    test for sentinel value
5    30 if j == -9999 goto 99
6    33 rem
7    35 rem    calculate square of j and assign result to k
8    40 let k = j * j
9    50 print k
10   53 rem
11   55 rem    loop to get next j
12   60 goto 20
13   99 end
```

Fig. 12.26 Calculate the squares of several integers.

Using the sample programs of Fig. 12.24, Fig. 12.25 and Fig. 12.26 as your guide, write a Simple program to accomplish each of the following:
  a) Input three integers, determine their average and print the result.
  b) Use a sentinel-controlled loop to input 10 integers and compute and print their sum.
  c) Use a counter-controlled loop to input seven integers, some positive and some negative, and compute and print their average.
  d) Input a series of integers and determine and print the largest. The first integer input indicates how many numbers should be processed.
  e) Input 10 integers and print the smallest.
  f) Calculate and print the sum of the even integers from 2 to 30.
  g) Calculate and print the product of the odd integers from 1 to 9.

12.27 (*Building A Compiler; Prerequisite: Complete Exercise 7.18, Exercise 7.19, Exercise 12.12, Exercise 12.13 and Exercise 12.26*) Now that the Simple language has been presented (Exercise 12.26), we discuss how to build our Simple compiler. First, we consider the process by which a Simple program is converted to SML and executed by the Simpletron simulator (see Fig. 12.27). A file containing a Simple program is read by the compiler and converted to SML code. The SML code is output to a file on disk, in which SML instructions appear one per line. The SML file is then loaded into the Simpletron simulator, and the results are sent to a file on disk and to the screen. Note that the Simpletron program developed in Exercise 7.19 took its input from the keyboard. It must be modified to read from a file so it can run the programs produced by our compiler.

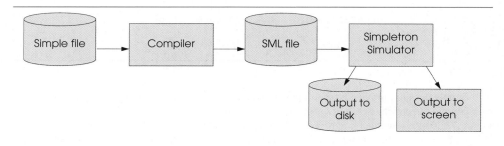

Fig. 12.27 Writing, compiling and executing a Simple language program.

The compiler performs two *passes* of the Simple program to convert it to SML. The first pass constructs a *symbol table* in which every *line number*, *variable name* and *constant* of the Simple program is stored with its type and corresponding location in the final SML code (the symbol table is discussed in detail below). The first pass also produces the corresponding SML instruction(s) for each Simple statement. As we will see, if the Simple program contains statements that transfer control to a line later in the program, the first pass results in an SML program containing some incomplete instructions. The second pass of the compiler locates and completes the unfinished instructions, and outputs the SML program to a file.

First Pass

The compiler begins by reading one statement of the Simple program into memory. The line must be separated into its individual *tokens* (i.e., "pieces" of a statement) for processing and compilation (standard library function `strtok` can be used to facilitate this task). Recall that every statement begins with a line number followed by a command. As the compiler breaks a statement into tokens, if the token is a line number, a variable, or a constant, it is placed in the symbol table. A line number is placed in the symbol table only if it is the first token in a statement. The `symbolTable` is an array of `tableEntry` structures representing each symbol in the program. There is no restriction on the number of symbols that can appear in the program. Therefore, the `symbolTable` for a particular program could be large. Make the `symbolTable` a 100-element array for now. You can increase or decrease its size once the program is working.

The `tableEntry` structure definition is as follows:

```
struct tableEntry {
   int symbol;
   char type;      /* 'C', 'L' or 'V' */
   int location;   /* 00 to 99 */
};
```

Each `tableEntry` structure contains three members. Member `symbol` is an integer containing the ASCII representation of a variable (remember that variable names are single characters), a line number, or a constant. Member `type` is one of the following characters indicating the symbol's type: `'C'` for constant, `'L'` for line number, or `'V'` for variable. Member `location` contains the Simpletron memory location (00 to 99) to which the symbol refers. Simpletron memory is an array of 100 integers in which SML instructions and data are stored. For a line number, the location is the element in the Simpletron memory array at which the SML instructions for the Simple statement begin. For a variable or constant, the location is the element in the Simpletron memory array in which the variable or constant is stored. Variables and constants are allocated from the end of Simpletron's memory backwards. The first variable or constant is stored in location at 99, the next in location at 98, etc.

The symbol table plays an integral part in converting Simple programs to SML. We learned in Chapter 7 that an SML instruction is a four-digit integer that comprises two parts—the *operation code* and the *operand*. The operation code is determined by commands in Simple. For example, the simple command `input` corresponds to SML operation code 10 (read), and the Simple command `print` corresponds to SML operation code 11 (write). The operand is a memory location containing the data on which the operation code performs its task (e.g., operation code 10 reads a value from the keyboard and stores it in the memory location specified by the operand). The compiler searches `symbolTable` to determine the Simpletron memory location for each symbol so the corresponding location can be used to complete the SML instructions.

The compilation of each Simple statement is based on its command. For example, after the line number in a `rem` statement is inserted in the symbol table, the remainder of the statement is ignored by the compiler, because a remark is for documentation purposes only. The `input`, `print`, `goto` and `end` statements correspond to the SML *read*, *write*, *branch* (to a specific location) and *halt* instructions. Statements containing these Simple commands are converted directly to SML [*Note:* That a `goto` statement may contain an unresolved reference if the specified line number refers to a statement further into the Simple program file; this is sometimes called a forward reference.]

When a `goto` statement is compiled with an unresolved reference, the SML instruction must be *flagged* to indicate that the second pass of the compiler must complete the instruction. The flags are stored in 100-element array `flags` of type `int` in which each element is initialized to −1. If the memory location to which a line number in the Simple program refers is not yet known (i.e., it is not in the symbol table), the line number is stored in array `flags` in the element with the same subscript as the incomplete instruction. The operand of the incomplete instruction is set to 00 temporarily. For example, an unconditional branch instruction (making a forward reference) is left as +4000 until the second pass of the compiler. The second pass of the compiler will be described shortly.

Compilation of `if...goto` and `let` statements is more complicated than other statements— they are the only statements that produce more than one SML instruction. For an `if...goto` statement, the compiler produces code to test the condition and to branch to another line if necessary. The result of the branch could be an unresolved reference. Each of the relational and equality operators can be simulated using SML's *branch zero* and *branch negative* instructions (or possibly a combination of both).

For a `let` statement, the compiler produces code to evaluate an arbitrarily complex arithmetic expression consisting of integer variables and/or constants. Expressions should separate each operand and operator with spaces. Exercise 12.12 and Exercise 12.13 presented the infix-to-postfix conversion algorithm and the postfix evaluation algorithm used by compilers to evaluate expressions. Before proceeding with your compiler, you should complete each of these exercises. When a compiler encounters an expression, it converts the expression from infix notation to postfix notation, then evaluates the postfix expression.

How is it that the compiler produces the machine language to evaluate an expression containing variables? The postfix evaluation algorithm contains a "hook" that allows our compiler to generate SML instructions rather than actually evaluating the expression. To enable this "hook" in the compiler, the postfix evaluation algorithm must be modified to search the symbol table for each symbol it encounters (and possibly insert it), determine the symbol's corresponding memory location, and *push the memory location on the stack instead of the symbol.* When an operator is encountered in the postfix expression, the two memory locations at the top of the stack are popped and machine language for effecting the operation is produced using the memory locations as operands. The result of each subexpression is stored in a temporary location in memory and pushed back onto the stack so the evaluation of the postfix expression can continue. When postfix evaluation is complete, the memory location containing the result is the only location left on the stack. This is popped and SML instructions are generated to assign the result to the variable at the left of the `let` statement.

Second Pass

The second pass of the compiler performs two tasks: resolve any unresolved references and output the SML code to a file. Resolution of references occurs as follows:

1) Search the `flags` array for an unresolved reference (i.e., an element with a value other than -1).

2) Locate the structure in array `symbolTable` containing the symbol stored in the `flags` array (be sure that the type of the symbol is `'L'` for line number).

3) Insert the memory location from structure member `location` into the instruction with the unresolved reference (remember that an instruction containing an unresolved reference has operand 00).

4) Repeat steps 1, 2 and 3 until the end of the `flags` array is reached.

After the resolution process is complete, the entire array containing the SML code is output to a disk file with one SML instruction per line. This file can be read by the Simpletron for execution (after the simulator is modified to read its input from a file).

A Complete Example

The following example illustrates a complete conversion of a Simple program to SML as it will be performed by the Simple compiler. Consider a Simple program that inputs an integer and sums the values from 1 to that integer. The program and the SML instructions produced by the first pass are illustrated in Fig. 12.28. The symbol table constructed by the first pass is shown in Fig. 12.29.

Simple program	SML location and instruction		Description
5 rem sum 1 to x		*none*	rem ignored
10 input x	00	+1099	read x into location 99
15 rem check y == x		*none*	rem ignored
20 if y == x goto 60	01	+2098	load y (98) into accumulator
	02	+3199	sub x (99) from accumulator
	03	+4200	*branch zero to unresolved location*
25 rem increment y		*none*	rem ignored
30 let y = y + 1	04	+2098	load y into accumulator
	05	+3097	add 1 (97) to accumulator

Fig. 12.28 SML instructions produced after the compiler's first pass. (Part 1 of 2.)

Simple program	SML location and instruction	Description
	06 +2196	store in temporary location 96
	07 +2096	load from temporary location 96
	08 +2198	store accumulator in y
35 rem add y to total	*none*	rem ignored
40 let t = t + y	09 +2095	load t (95) into accumulator
	10 +3098	add y to accumulator
	11 +2194	store in temporary location 94
	12 +2094	load from temporary location 94
	13 +2195	store accumulator in t
45 rem loop y	*none*	rem ignored
50 goto 20	14 +4001	branch to location 01
55 rem output result	*none*	rem ignored
60 print t	15 +1195	output t to screen
99 end	16 +4300	terminate execution

Fig. 12.28 SML instructions produced after the compiler's first pass. (Part 2 of 2.)

Symbol	Type	Location
5	L	00
10	L	00
'x'	V	99
15	L	01
20	L	01
'y'	V	98
25	L	04
30	L	04
1	C	97
35	L	09
40	L	09
't'	V	95
45	L	14
50	L	14
55	L	15
60	L	15
99	L	16

Fig. 12.29 Symbol table for program of Fig. 12.28.

Most Simple statements convert directly to single SML instructions. The exceptions in this program are remarks, the if...goto statement in line 20, and the let statements. Remarks do not translate into machine language. However, the line number for a remark is placed in the symbol table in case the line number is referenced in a goto statement or an if...goto statement. Line 20 of the program specifies that if the condition y == x is true, program control is transferred to line 60. Because line 60 appears later in the program, the first pass of the compiler has not as yet placed 60 in the symbol table (line numbers are placed in the symbol table only when they appear as the first token in a statement). Therefore, it is not possible at this time to determine the operand of the SML *branch zero* instruction at location 03 in the array of SML instructions. The compiler places 60 in location 03 of the flags array to indicate that the second pass completes this instruction.

We must keep track of the next instruction location in the SML array because there is not a one-to-one correspondence between Simple statements and SML instructions. For example, the if...goto statement of line 20 compiles into three SML instructions. Each time an instruction is produced, we must increment the *instruction counter* to the next location in the SML array. Note that the size of Simpletron's memory could present a problem for Simple programs with many statements, variables and constants. It is conceivable that the compiler will run out of memory. To test for this case, your program should contain a *data counter* to keep track of the location at which the next variable or constant will be stored in the SML array. If the value of the instruction counter is larger than the value of the data counter, the SML array is full. In this case, the compilation process should terminate and the compiler should print an error message indicating that it ran out of memory during compilation.

Step-by-Step View of the Compilation Process

Let us now walk through the compilation process for the Simple program in Fig. 12.28. The compiler reads the first line of the program

```
5 rem sum 1 to x
```

into memory. The first token in the statement (the line number) is determined using strtok (see Chapter 8 for a discussion of C's string manipulation functions). The token returned by strtok is converted to an integer using atoi, so the symbol 5 can be located in the symbol table. If the symbol is not found, it is inserted in the symbol table. Since we are at the beginning of the program and this is the first line, no symbols are in the table yet. So, 5 is inserted into the symbol table as type L (line number) and assigned the first location in SML array (00). Although this line is a remark, a space in the symbol table is allocated for the line number (in case it is referenced by a goto or an if...goto). No SML instruction is generated for a rem statement, so the instruction counter is not incremented.

The statement

```
10 input x
```

is tokenized next. The line number 10 is placed in the symbol table as type L and assigned the first location in the SML array (00 because a remark began the program, so the instruction counter is currently 00). The command input indicates that the next token is a variable (only a variable can appear in an input statement). Because input corresponds directly to an SML operation code, the compiler simply has to determine the location of x in the SML array. Symbol x is not found in the symbol table. So, it is inserted into the symbol table as the ASCII representation of x, given type V, and assigned location 99 in the SML array (data storage begins at 99 and is allocated backwards). SML code can now be generated for this statement. Operation code 10 (the SML read operation code) is multiplied by 100, and the location of x (as determined in the symbol table) is added to complete the instruction. The instruction is then stored in the SML array at location 00. The instruction counter is incremented by 1 because a single SML instruction was produced.

The statement

```
15 rem    check y == x
```

is tokenized next. The symbol table is searched for line number 15 (which is not found). The line number is inserted as type L and assigned the next location in the array, 01 (remember that rem statements do not produce code, so the instruction counter is not incremented).

The statement

```
20 if y == x goto 60
```

is tokenized next. Line number 20 is inserted in the symbol table and given type L with the next location in the SML array 01. The command if indicates that a condition is to be evaluated. The variable y is not found in the symbol table, so it is inserted and given the type V and the SML location 98. Next, SML instructions are generated to evaluate the condition. Since there is no direct equivalent in SML for the if...goto, it must be simulated by performing a calculation using x and y and branching based on the result. If y is equal to x, the result of subtracting x from y is zero, so the *branch zero* instruction can be used with the result of the calculation to simulate the if...goto statement. The first step requires that y be loaded (from SML location 98) into the accumulator. This produces the instruction 01 +2098. Next, x is subtracted from the accumulator. This produces the instruction 02 +3199. The value in the accumulator may be zero, positive or negative. Since the operator is ==, we want to *branch zero*. First, the symbol table is searched for the branch location (60 in this case), which is not found. So, 60 is placed in the flags array at location 03, and the instruction 03 +4200 is generated (we cannot add the branch location because we have not assigned a location to line 60 in the SML array yet). The instruction counter is incremented to 04.

The compiler proceeds to the statement

```
25 rem    increment y
```

The line number 25 is inserted in the symbol table as type L and assigned SML location 04. The instruction counter is not incremented.

When the statement

```
30 let y = y + 1
```

is tokenized, the line number 30 is inserted in the symbol table as type L and assigned SML location 04. Command let indicates that the line is an assignment statement. First, all the symbols on the line are inserted in the symbol table (if they are not already there). The integer 1 is added to the symbol table as type C and assigned SML location 97. Next, the right side of the assignment is converted from infix to postfix notation. Then the postfix expression (y 1 +) is evaluated. Symbol y is located in the symbol table and its corresponding memory location is pushed onto the stack. Symbol 1 is also located in the symbol table, and its corresponding memory location is pushed onto the stack. When the operator + is encountered, the postfix evaluator pops the stack into the right operand of the operator and pops the stack again into the left operand of the operator, then produces the SML instructions

```
04 +2098    (load y)
05 +3097    (add 1)
```

The result of the expression is stored in a temporary location in memory (96) with instruction

```
06 +2196    (store temporary)
```

and the temporary location is pushed on the stack. Now that the expression has been evaluated, the result must be stored in y (i.e., the variable on the left side of =). So, the temporary location is loaded into the accumulator and the accumulator is stored in y with the instructions

```
07  +2096      (load temporary)
08  +2198      (store y)
```

The reader will immediately notice that SML instructions appear to be redundant. We will discuss this issue shortly.

When the statement

```
35 rem    add y to total
```

is tokenized, line number 35 is inserted in the symbol table as type L and assigned location 09.

The statement

```
40 let t = t + y
```

is similar to line 30. The variable t is inserted in the symbol table as type V and assigned SML location 95. The instructions follow the same logic and format as line 30, and the instructions 09 +2095, 10 +3098, 11 +2194, 12 +2094, and 13 +2195 are generated. Note that the result of t + y is assigned to temporary location 94 before being assigned to t (95). Once again, the reader will note that the instructions in memory locations 11 and 12 appear to be redundant. Again, we will discuss this shortly.

The statement

```
45 rem    loop y
```

is a remark, so line 45 is added to the symbol table as type L and assigned SML location 14.

The statement

```
50 goto 20
```

transfers control to line 20. Line number 50 is inserted in the symbol table as type L and assigned SML location 14. The equivalent of goto in SML is the *unconditional branch* (40) instruction that transfers control to a specific SML location. The compiler searches the symbol table for line 20 and finds that it corresponds to SML location 01. The operation code (40) is multiplied by 100 and location 01 is added to it to produce the instruction 14 +4001.

The statement

```
55 rem    output result
```

is a remark, so line 55 is inserted in the symbol table as type L and assigned SML location 15.

The statement

```
60 print t
```

is an output statement. Line number 60 is inserted in the symbol table as type L and assigned SML location 15. The equivalent of print in SML is operation code 11 (*write*). The location of t is determined from the symbol table and added to the result of the operation code multiplied by 100.

The statement

```
99 end
```

is the final line of the program. Line number 99 is stored in the symbol table as type L and assigned SML location 16. The end command produces the SML instruction +4300 (43 is *halt* in SML) which is written as the final instruction in the SML memory array.

This completes the first pass of the compiler. We now consider the second pass. The flags array is searched for values other than -1. Location 03 contains 60, so the compiler knows that instruction 03 is incomplete. The compiler completes the instruction by searching the symbol table for 60, determining its location and adding the location to the incomplete instruction. In this case, the search determines that line 60 corresponds to SML location 15, so the completed instruction 03 +4215 is produced replacing 03 +4200. The Simple program has now been compiled successfully.

To build the compiler, you will have to perform each of the following tasks:

a) Modify the Simpletron simulator program you wrote in Exercise 7.19 to take its input from a file specified by the user (see Chapter 11). Also, the simulator should output its results to a disk file in the same format as the screen output.

b) Modify the infix-to-postfix evaluation algorithm of Exercise 12.12 to process multi-digit integer operands and single-letter variable-name operands. [*Hint:* Standard library function `strtok` can be used to locate each constant and variable in an expression, and constants can be converted from strings to integers using standard library function `atoi`.] [*Note:* The data representation of the postfix expression must be altered to support variable names and integer constants.]

c) Modify the postfix evaluation algorithm to process multi-digit integer operands and variable name operands. Also, the algorithm should now implement the previously discussed "hook" so that SML instructions are produced rather than directly evaluating the expression. [*Hint:* Standard library function `strtok` can be used to locate each constant and variable in an expression, and constants can be converted from strings to integers using standard library function `atoi`.] [*Note:* The data representation of the postfix expression must be altered to support variable names and integer constants.]

d) Build the compiler. Incorporate parts (b) and (c) for evaluating expressions in `let` statements. Your program should contain a function that performs the first pass of the compiler and a function that performs the second pass of the compiler. Both functions can call other functions to accomplish their tasks.

12.28 (*Optimizing the Simple Compiler*) When a program is compiled and converted into SML, a set of instructions is generated. Certain combinations of instructions often repeat themselves, usually in triplets called *productions*. A production normally consists of three instructions such as *load, add* and *store*. For example, Fig. 12.30 illustrates five of the SML instructions that were produced in the compilation of the program in Fig. 12.28. The first three instructions are the production that adds 1 to y. Note that instructions 06 and 07 store the accumulator value in temporary location 96, then load the value back into the accumulator so instruction 08 can store the value in location 98. Often a production is followed by a load instruction for the same location that was just stored. This code can be *optimized* by eliminating the store instruction and the subsequent load instruction that operate on the same memory location. This optimization would enable the Simpletron to execute the program faster because there are fewer instructions in this version. Figure 12.31 illustrates the optimized SML for the program of Fig. 12.28. Note that there are four fewer instructions in the optimized code—a memory-space savings of 25%.

Modify the compiler to provide an option for optimizing the Simpletron Machine Language code it produces. Manually compare the non-optimized code with the optimized code, and calculate the percentage reduction.

```
04  +2098          (load)
05  +3097          (add)
06  +2196          (store)
07  +2096          (load)
08  +2198          (store)
```

Fig. 12.30 Unoptimized code from the program of Fig. 12.28.

Simple program	SML location and instruction	Description
5 rem sum 1 to x	*none*	rem ignored
10 input x	00 +1099	read x into location 99
15 rem check y == x	*none*	rem ignored
20 if y == x goto 60	01 +2098	load y (98) into accumulator
	02 +3199	sub x (99) from accumulator
	03 +4211	branch to location 11 if zero
25 rem increment y	*none*	rem ignored
30 let y = y + 1	04 +2098	load y into accumulator
	05 +3097	add 1 (97) to accumulator
	06 +2198	store accumulator in y (98)
35 rem add y to total	*none*	rem ignored
40 let t = t + y	07 +2096	load t from location (96)
	08 +3098	add y (98) accumulator
	09 +2196	store accumulator in t (96)
45 rem loop y	*none*	rem ignored
50 goto 20	10 +4001	branch to location 01
55 rem output result	*none*	rem ignored
60 print t	11 +1196	output t (96) to screen
99 end	12 +4300	terminate execution

Fig. 12.31 Optimized code for the program of Fig. 12.28.

12.29 (*Modifications to the Simple Compiler*) Perform the following modifications to the Simple compiler. Some of these modifications may also require modifications to the Simpletron Simulator program written in Exercise 7.19.

a) Allow the modulus operator (%) to be used in let statements. Simpletron Machine Language must be modified to include a modulus instruction.

b) Allow exponentiation in a let statement using ∧ as the exponentiation operator. Simpletron Machine Language must be modified to include an exponentiation instruction.

c) Allow the compiler to recognize uppercase and lowercase letters in Simple statements (e.g., 'A' is equivalent to 'a'). No modifications to the Simpletron Simulator are required.

d) Allow input statements to read values for multiple variables such as input x, y. No modifications to the Simpletron Simulator are required.

e) Allow the compiler to output multiple values in a single print statement such as print a, b, c. No modifications to the Simpletron Simulator are required.

f) Add syntax checking capabilities to the compiler so error messages are output when syntax errors are encountered in a Simple program. No modifications to the Simpletron Simulator are required.

g) Allow arrays of integers. No modifications to the Simpletron Simulator are required.

h) Allow subroutines specified by the Simple commands `gosub` and `return`. Command `gosub` passes program control to a subroutine and command `return` passes control back to the statement after the `gosub`. This is similar to a function call in C. The same subroutine can be called from many `gosub`s distributed throughout a program. No modifications to the Simpletron Simulator are required.

i) Allow repetition structures of the form

```
for x = 2 to 10 step 2
    rem Simple statements
next
```

j) This `for` statement loops from 2 to 10 with an increment of 2. The `next` line marks the end of the body of the `for` line. No modifications to the Simpletron Simulator are required.

k) Allow repetition structures of the form

```
for x = 2 to 10
    rem Simple statements
next
```

l) This `for` statement loops from 2 to 10 with a default increment of 1. No modifications to the Simpletron Simulator are required.

m) Allow the compiler to process string input and output. This requires the Simpletron Simulator to be modified to process and store string values. [*Hint*: Each Simpletron word can be divided into two groups, each holding a two-digit integer. Each two-digit integer represents the ASCII decimal equivalent of a character.] Add a machine language instruction that will print a string beginning at a certain Simpletron memory location. The first half of the word at that location is a count of the number of characters in the string (i.e., the length of the string). Each succeeding half word contains one ASCII character expressed as two decimal digits. The machine language instruction checks the length and prints the string by translating each two-digit number into its equivalent character.

n) Allow the compiler to process floating-point values in addition to integers. The Simpletron Simulator must also be modified to process floating-point values.

12.30 (*A Simple Interpreter*) An interpreter is a program that reads a high-level language program statement, determines the operation to be performed by the statement, and executes the operation immediately. The program is not converted into machine language first. Interpreters execute slowly because each statement encountered in the program must first be deciphered. If statements are contained in a loop, the statements are deciphered each time they are encountered in the loop. Early versions of the BASIC programming language were implemented as interpreters.

Write an interpreter for the Simple language discussed in Exercise 12.26. The program should use the infix-to-postfix converter developed in Exercise 12.12 and the postfix evaluator developed in Exercise 12.13 to evaluate expressions in a `let` statement. The same restrictions placed on the Simple language in Exercise 12.26 should be adhered to in this program. Test the interpreter with the Simple programs written in Exercise 12.26. Compare the results of running these programs in the interpreter with the results of compiling the Simple programs and running them in the Simpletron simulator built in Exercise 7.19.

13

C Preprocessor

Objectives

- To be able to use #include for developing large programs.
- To be able to use #define to create macros and macros with arguments.
- To understand conditional compilation.
- To be able to display error messages during conditional compilation.
- To be able to use assertions to test if the values of expressions are correct.

Hold thou the good; define it well.
Alfred, Lord Tennyson

I have found you an argument; but I am not obliged to find you an understanding.
Samuel Johnson

A good symbol is the best argument, and is a missionary to persuade thousands.
Ralph Waldo Emerson

Conditions are fundamentally sound.
Herbert Hoover [December 1929]

The partisan, when he is engaged in a dispute, cares nothing about the rights of the question, but is anxious only to convince his hearers of his own assertions.
Plato

Outline

13.1 Introduction

This chapter describes the *C preprocessor*. Preprocessing occurs before a program is compiled. Some possible actions are the inclusion of other files in the file being compiled, definition of *symbolic constants* and *macros, conditional compilation* of program code and *conditional execution of preprocessor directives*. All preprocessor directives begin with # and only whitespace characters may appear before a preprocessor directive on a line.

13.2 #include Preprocessor Directive

The #include *preprocessor directive* has been used throughout this text. The #include directive causes a copy of a specified file to be included in place of the directive. The two forms of the #include directive are:

```
#include <filename>
#include "filename"
```

The difference between these is the location the preprocessor searches for the file to be included. If the file name is enclosed in quotes, the preprocessor searches in the same directory as the file being compiled for the file to be included. This method is normally used to include programmer-defined headers. If the file name is enclosed in angle brackets (< and >)—used for *standard library headers*—the search is performed in an implementation-dependent manner, normally through predesignated directories.

The #include directive is used to include standard library headers such as stdio.h and stdlib.h (see Fig. 5.6). The #include directive is also used with programs consisting of several source files that are to be compiled together. A header containing declarations common to the separate program files is often created and included in the file. Examples of such declarations are structure and union declarations, enumerations and function prototypes.

13.3 #define Preprocessor Directive: Symbolic Constants

The #define *directive* creates *symbolic constants*—constants represented as symbols—and *macros*—operations defined as symbols. The #define directive format is

>   #define *identifier replacement-text*

When this line appears in a file, all subsequent occurrences of *identifier* will be replaced by *replacement-text* automatically before the program is compiled. For example,

>   #define PI 3.14159

replaces all subsequent occurrences of the symbolic constant PI with the numeric constant 3.14159. Symbolic constants enable the programmer to create a name for a constant and use the name throughout the program. If the constant needs to be modified throughout the program, it can be modified once in the #define directive. When the program is recompiled, all occurrences of the constant in the program will be modified accordingly. [*Note:* Everything to the right of the symbolic constant name replaces the symbolic constant.] For example, #define PI = 3.14159 causes the preprocessor to replace every occurrence of the identifier PI with = 3.14159. This is the cause of many subtle logic and syntax errors. Redefining a symbolic constant with a new value is also an error.

Good Programming Practice 13.1

Using meaningful names for symbolic constants helps make programs more self-documenting.

13.4 #define Preprocessor Directive: Macros

A *macro* is an identifier defined in a #define preprocessor directive. As with symbolic constants, the *macro-identifier* is replaced in the program with the *replacement-text* before the program is compiled. Macros may be defined with or without *arguments*. A macro without arguments is processed like a symbolic constant. In a *macro with arguments*, the arguments are substituted in the replacement text, then the macro is *expanded*—i.e., the replacement-text replaces the identifier and argument list in the program.

Consider the following macro definition with one argument for the area of a circle:

>   #define CIRCLE_AREA(x) ((PI) * (x) * (x))

Wherever CIRCLE_AREA(y) appears in the file, the value of y is substituted for x in the replacement-text, the symbolic constant PI is replaced by its value (defined previously) and the macro is expanded in the program. For example, the statement

>   area = CIRCLE_AREA(4);

is expanded to

>   area = ((3.14159) * (4) * (4));

and the value of the expression is evaluated and assigned to variable area. The parentheses around each x in the replacement text force the proper order of evaluation when the macro argument is an expression. For example, the statement

>   area = CIRCLE_AREA(c + 2);

is expanded to

```
area = ( ( 3.14159 ) * ( c + 2 ) * ( c + 2 ) );
```

which evaluates correctly because the parentheses force the proper order of evaluation. If the parentheses are omitted, the macro expansion is

```
area = 3.14159 * c + 2 * c + 2;
```

which evaluates incorrectly as

```
area = ( 3.14159 * c ) + ( 2 * c ) + 2;
```

because of the rules of operator precedence.

Common Programming Error 13.1

Forgetting to enclose macro arguments in parentheses in the replacement text can lead to logic errors.

Macro CIRCLE_AREA could be defined as a function. Function circleArea

```
double circleArea( double x )
{
    return 3.14159 * x * x;
}
```

performs the same calculation as macro CIRCLE_AREA, but the overhead of a function call is associated with function circleArea. The advantages of macro CIRCLE_AREA are that macros insert code directly in the program—avoiding function call overhead—and the program remains readable because the CIRCLE_AREA calculation is defined separately and named meaningfully. A disadvantage is that its argument is evaluated twice.

Performance Tip 13.1

Macros can sometimes be used to replace a function call with inline code prior to execution time. This eliminates the overhead of a function call.

The following is a macro definition with two arguments for the area of a rectangle:

```
#define RECTANGLE_AREA( x, y )  ( ( x ) * ( y ) )
```

Wherever RECTANGLE_AREA(x, y) appears in the program, the values of x and y are substituted in the macro replacement text and the macro is expanded in place of the macro name. For example, the statement

```
rectArea = RECTANGLE_AREA( a + 4, b + 7 );
```

is expanded to

```
rectArea = ( ( a + 4 ) * ( b + 7 ) );
```

The value of the expression is evaluated and assigned to variable rectArea.

The replacement text for a macro or symbolic constant is normally any text on the line after the identifier in the #define directive. If the replacement text for a macro or symbolic constant is longer than the remainder of the line, a *backslash* (\) must be placed at the end of the line, indicating that the replacement text continues on the next line.

Symbolic constants and macros can be discarded by using the #undef *preprocessor directive*. Directive #undef "undefines" a symbolic constant or macro name. The *scope* of a symbolic constant or macro is from its definition until it is undefined with #undef, or until the end of the file. Once undefined, a name can be redefined with #define.

Functions in the standard library sometimes are defined as macros based on other library functions. A macro commonly defined in the stdio.h header is

```
#define getchar() getc( stdin )
```

The macro definition of getchar uses function getc to get one character from the standard input stream. Function putchar of the stdio.h header and the character handling functions of the ctype.h header often are implemented as macros as well. Note that expressions with side effects (i.e., variable values are modified) should not be passed to a macro because macro arguments may be evaluated more than once.

13.5 Conditional Compilation

Conditional compilation enables the programmer to control the execution of preprocessor directives and the compilation of program code. Each of the conditional preprocessor directives evaluates a constant integer expression. Cast expressions, sizeof expressions and enumeration constants cannot be evaluated in preprocessor directives.

The conditional preprocessor construct is much like the if selection statement. Consider the following preprocessor code:

```
#if !defined(NULL)
    #define NULL 0
#endif
```

These directives determine if NULL is defined. The expression defined(NULL) evaluates to 1 if NULL is defined; 0 otherwise. If the result is 0, !defined(NULL) evaluates to 1 and NULL is defined. Otherwise, the #define directive is skipped. Every #if construct ends with #endif. Directives #ifdef and #ifndef are shorthand for #if defined(*name*) and #if !defined(*name*). A multiple-part conditional preprocessor construct may be tested by using the #elif (the equivalent of else if in an if statement) and the #else (the equivalent of else in an if statement) directives.

During program development, programmers often find it helpful to "comment out" portions of code to prevent it from being compiled. If the code contains comments, /* and */ cannot be used to accomplish this task. Instead, the programmer can use the following preprocessor construct:

```
#if 0
    code prevented from compiling
#endif
```

To enable the code to be compiled, replace the 0 in the preceding construct with 1.

Conditional compilation is commonly used as a debugging aid. Many C implementations provide *debuggers*, which provide much more powerful features than conditional compilation. If a debugger is not available, printf statements are often used to print variable values and to confirm the flow of control. These printf statements can be enclosed in conditional preprocessor directives so the statements are only compiled while the debugging process is not completed. For example,

```
#ifdef DEBUG
    printf( "Variable x = %d\n", x );
#endif
```

causes a `printf` statement to be compiled in the program if the symbolic constant DEBUG has been defined (`#define DEBUG`) before directive `#ifdef DEBUG`. When debugging is completed, the `#define` directive is removed from the source file and the `printf` statements inserted for debugging purposes are ignored during compilation. In larger programs, it may be desirable to define several different symbolic constants that control the conditional compilation in separate sections of the source file.

Common Programming Error 13.2

Inserting conditionally compiled `printf` statements for debugging purposes in locations where C currently expects a single statement. In this case, the conditionally compiled statement should be enclosed in a compound statement. Thus, when the program is compiled with debugging statements, the flow of control of the program is not altered.

13.6 #error and #pragma Preprocessor Directives

The *#error directive*

```
#error tokens
```

prints an implementation-dependent message including the *tokens* specified in the directive. The tokens are sequences of characters separated by spaces. For example,

```
#error 1 - Out of range error
```

contains 6 tokens. When a `#error` directive is processed on some systems, the tokens in the directive are displayed as an error message, preprocessing stops and the program does not compile.

The *#pragma directive*

```
#pragma tokens
```

causes an implementation-defined action. A pragma not recognized by the implementation is ignored. For more information on `#error` and `#pragma`, see the documentation for your C implementation.

13.7 # and ## Operators

The # and ## preprocessor operators are available in standard C. The # operator causes a replacement text token to be converted to a string surrounded by quotes. Consider the following macro definition:

```
#define HELLO(x) printf( "Hello, " #x "\n" );
```

When HELLO(John) appears in a program file, it is expanded to

```
printf( "Hello, " "John" "\n" );
```

The string "John" replaces #x in the replacement text. Strings separated by white space are concatenated during preprocessing, so the preceding statement is equivalent to

```
printf( "Hello, John\n" );
```

Note that the # operator must be used in a macro with arguments because the operand of # refers to an argument of the macro.

The ## operator concatenates two tokens. Consider the following macro definition:

```
#define TOKENCONCAT(x, y)  x ## y
```

When TOKENCONCAT appears in the program, its arguments are concatenated and used to replace the macro. For example, TOKENCONCAT(O, K) is replaced by OK in the program. The ## operator must have two operands.

13.8 Line Numbers

The #line *preprocessor directive* causes the subsequent source code lines to be renumbered starting with the specified constant integer value. The directive

```
#line 100
```

starts line numbering from 100 beginning with the next source code line. A file name can be included in the #line directive. The directive

```
#line 100 "file1.c"
```

indicates that lines are numbered from 100 beginning with the next source code line and that the name of the file for the purpose of any compiler messages is "file1.c". The directive normally is used to help make the messages produced by syntax errors and compiler warnings more meaningful. The line numbers do not appear in the source file.

13.9 Predefined Symbolic Constants

ANSI C provides *predefined symbolic constants* (Fig. 13.1). The identifiers for each of the predefined symbolic constants begin and end with *two* underscores. These identifiers and the defined identifier (used in Section 13.5) cannot be used in #define or #undef directives.

Symbolic constant	Explanation
__LINE__	The line number of the current source code line (an integer constant).
__FILE__	The presumed name of the source file (a string).
__DATE__	The date the source file was compiled (a string of the form "Mmm dd yyyy" such as "Jan 19 2002").
__TIME__	The time the source file was compiled (a string literal of the form "hh:mm:ss").

Fig. 13.1   Some predefined symbolic constants.

13.10 Assertions

The `assert` *macro*—defined in the `assert.h` header—tests the value of an expression. If the value of the expression is 0 (false), `assert` prints an error message and calls function `abort` (of the general utilities library—`stdlib.h`) to terminate program execution. This is a useful debugging tool for testing if a variable has a correct value. For example, suppose variable x should never be larger than 10 in a program. An assertion may be used to test the value of x and print an error message if the value of x is incorrect. The statement would be

```
assert( x <= 10 );
```

If x is greater than 10 when the preceding statement is encountered in a program, an error message containing the line number and file name is printed and the program terminates. The programmer may then concentrate on this area of the code to find the error. If the symbolic constant NDEBUG is defined, subsequent assertions will be ignored. Thus, when assertions are no longer needed, the line

```
#define NDEBUG
```

is inserted in the program file rather than deleting each assertion manually.

SUMMARY

- All preprocessor directives begin with #.
- Only whitespace characters may appear before a preprocessor directive on a line.
- The #include directive includes a copy of the specified file. If the file name is enclosed in quotes, the preprocessor begins searching in the same directory as the file being compiled for the file to be included. If the file name is enclosed in angle brackets (< and >), the search is performed in an implementation-defined manner.
- The #define preprocessor directive is used to create symbolic constants and macros.
- A symbolic constant is a name for a constant.
- A macro is an operation defined in a #define preprocessor directive. Macros may be defined with or without arguments.
- The replacement text for a macro or symbolic constant is any text remaining on the line after the identifier in the #define directive. If the replacement text for a macro or symbolic constant is longer than the remainder of the line, a backslash (\) is placed at the end of the line indicating that the replacement text continues on the next line.
- Symbolic constants and macros can be discarded by using the #undef preprocessor directive. Directive #undef "undefines" the symbolic constant or macro name.
- The scope of a symbolic constant or macro is from its definition until it is undefined with #undef or until the end of the file.
- Conditional compilation enables the programmer to control the execution of preprocessor directives and the compilation of program code.
- The conditional preprocessor directives evaluate constant integer expressions. Cast expressions, `sizeof` expressions and enumeration constants cannot be evaluated in preprocessor directives.
- Every #if construct ends with #endif.
- Directives #ifdef and #ifndef are provided as shorthand for #if defined(*name*) and #if !defined(*name*).

- Multiple-part conditional preprocessor constructs may be tested with directives #elif and #else.
- The #error directive prints an implementation-dependent message that includes the tokens specified in the directive.
- The #pragma directive causes an implementation-defined action. If the pragma is not recognized by the implementation, the pragma is ignored.
- The # operator causes a replacement text token to be converted to a string surrounded by quotes. The # operator must be used in a macro with arguments, because the operand of # must be an argument of the macro.
- The ## operator concatenates two tokens. The ## operator must have two operands.
- The #line preprocessor directive causes the subsequent source code lines to be renumbered starting with the specified constant integer value.
- Constant __LINE__ is the line number of the current source code line (an integer). Constant __FILE__ is the presumed name of the file (a string). Constant __DATE__ is the date the source file is compiled (a string). Constant __TIME__ is the time the source file is compiled (a string). Note that each of the predefined symbolic constants begins and ends with two underbars.
- Macro assert—defined in the assert.h header—tests the value of an expression. If the value of the expression is 0 (false), assert prints an error message and calls function abort to terminate program execution.

TERMINOLOGY

\ (backslash) continuation character
abort
argument
assert
assert.h
C preprocessor
concatenation preprocessor operator ##
conditional compilation
conditional execution of preprocessor directives
convert-to-string preprocessor operator #
__DATE__
debugger
#define
#elif
#else
#endif
#error
expand a macro
__FILE__
#if

#ifdef
#ifndef
#include <filename>
#include "filename"
#line
__LINE__
macro
macro with arguments
#pragma
predefined symbolic constants
preprocessing directive
replacement text
scope of a symbolic constant or macro
standard library headers
stdio.h
stdlib.h
symbolic constant
__TIME__
#undef

COMMON PROGRAMMING ERRORS

13.1 Forgetting to enclose macro arguments in parentheses in the replacement text can lead to logic errors.

13.2 Inserting conditionally compiled printf statements for debugging purposes in locations where C currently expects a single statement. In this case, the conditionally compiled statement should be enclosed in a compound statement. Thus, when the program is compiled with debugging statements, the flow of control of the program is not altered.

GOOD PROGRAMMING PRACTICE

13.1 Using meaningful names for symbolic constants helps make programs more self-documenting.

PERFORMANCE TIP

13.1 Macros can sometimes be used to replace a function call with inline code prior to execution time. This eliminates the overhead of a function call.

SELF-REVIEW EXERCISES

13.1 Fill in the blanks in each of the following:
a) Every preprocessor directive must begin with _____.
b) The conditional compilation construct may be extended to test for multiple cases by using the _____ and the _____ directives.
c) The _____ directive creates macros and symbolic constants.
d) Only _____ characters may appear before a preprocessor directive on a line.
e) The _____ directive discards symbolic constant and macro names.
f) The _____ and _____ directives are provided as shorthand notation for `#if defined(`*name*`)` and `#if !defined(`*name*`)`.
g) _____ enables the programmer to control the execution of preprocessor directives and the compilation of program code.
h) The _____ macro prints a message and terminates program execution if the value of the expression the macro evaluates is 0.
i) The _____ directive inserts a file in another file.
j) The _____ operator concatenates its two arguments.
k) The _____ operator converts its operand to a string.
l) The character _____ indicates that the replacement text for a symbolic constant or macro continues on the next line.
m) The _____ directive causes the source code lines to be numbered from the indicated value beginning with the next source code line.

13.2 Write a program to print the values of the predefined symbolic constants listed in Fig. 13.1.

13.3 Write a preprocessor directive to accomplish each of the following:
a) Define symbolic constant YES to have the value 1.
b) Define symbolic constant NO to have the value 0.
c) Include the header `common.h`. The header is found in the same directory as the file being compiled.
d) Renumber the remaining lines in the file beginning with line number 3000.
e) If symbolic constant TRUE is defined, undefine it and redefine it as 1. Do not use `#ifdef`.
f) If symbolic constant TRUE is defined, undefine it and redefine it as 1. Use the `#ifdef` preprocessor directive.
g) If symbolic constant TRUE is not equal to 0, define symbolic constant FALSE as 0. Otherwise define FALSE as 1.
h) Define macro SQUARE_VOLUME that computes the volume of a square. The macro takes one argument.

ANSWERS TO SELF-REVIEW EXERCISES

13.1 a) `#`. b) `#elif`, `#else`. c) `#define`. d) whitespace. e) `#undef`. f) `#ifdef`, `#ifndef`. g) Conditional compilation. h) `assert`. i) `#include`. j) `##`. k) `#`. l) `\`. m) `#line`.

13.2

```
1    /* Print the values of the predefined macros */
2    #include <stdio.h>
3    int main()
4    {
5       printf( "__LINE__ = %d\n", __LINE__ );
6       printf( "__FILE__ = %s\n", __FILE__ );
7       printf( "__DATE__ = %s\n", __DATE__ );
8       printf( "__TIME__ = %s\n", __TIME__ );
9       return 0;
10   }
```

```
__LINE__ = 5
__FILE__ = macros.c
__DATE__ = Jun  5 2003
__TIME__ = 09:38:58
```

13.3 a) #define YES 1
          b) #define NO 0
          c) #include "common.h"
          d) #line 3000
          e) #if defined(TRUE)
                 #undef TRUE
                 #define TRUE 1
             #endif
          f) #ifdef TRUE
                 #undef TRUE
                 #define TRUE 1
             #endif
          g) #if TRUE
                 #define FALSE 0
             #else
                 #define FALSE 1
             #endif
          h) #define SQUARE_VOLUME(x) (x) * (x) * (x)

EXERCISES

13.4 Write a program that defines a macro with one argument to compute the volume of a sphere. The program should compute the volume for spheres of radius 1 to 10 and print the results in tabular format. The formula for the volume of a sphere is

$$(4.0 / 3) * \pi * r^3$$

where π is 3.14159.

13.5 Write a program that produces the following output:

```
The sum of x and y is 13
```

The program should define macro SUM with two arguments, x and y, and use SUM to produce the output.

13.6 Write a program that defines and uses macro MINIMUM2 to determine the smallest of two numeric values. Input the values from the keyboard.

13.7 Write a program that defines and uses macro MINIMUM3 to determine the smallest of three numeric values. Macro MINIMUM3 should use macro MINIMUM2 defined in Exercise 13.6 to determine the smallest number. Input the values from the keyboard.

13.8 Write a program that defines and uses macro PRINT to print a string value.

13.9 Write a program that defines and uses macro PRINTARRAY to print an array of integers. The macro should receive the array and the number of elements in the array as arguments.

13.10 Write a program that defines and uses macro SUMARRAY to sum the values in a numeric array. The macro should receive the array and the number of elements in the array as arguments.

14

Other C Topics

Objectives

- To be able to redirect keyboard input to come from a file.
- To be able to redirect screen output to be placed in a file.
- To be able to write functions that use variable-length argument lists.
- To be able to process command-line arguments.
- To be able to assign specific types to numeric constants
- To be able to use temporary files.
- To be able to process unexpected events within a program.
- To be able to allocate memory dynamically for arrays.
- To be able to change the size of memory that was dynamically allocated previously.

We'll use a signal I have tried and found

far-reaching and easy to yell. Waa-hoo!
Zane Grey

Use it up, wear it out;
Make it do, or do without.
Anonymous

It is quite a three-pipe problem.
Sir Arthur Conan Doyle

Outline

14.1 Introduction

This chapter presents several additional topics not ordinarily covered in introductory courses. Many of the capabilities discussed here are specific to particular operating systems, especially UNIX and Windows.

14.2 Redirecting Input/Output on UNIX and Windows Systems

Normally the input to a program is from the keyboard (standard input), and the output from a program is displayed on the screen (standard output). On most computer systems—UNIX and Windows systems in particular—it is possible to *redirect* inputs to come from a file rather than the keyboard and redirect outputs to be placed in a file rather than on the screen. Both forms of redirection can be accomplished without using the file processing capabilities of the standard library.

There are several ways to redirect input and output from the UNIX command line. Consider the executable file `sum` that inputs integers one at a time and keeps a running total of the values until the end-of-file indicator is set, then prints the result. Normally the user inputs integers from the keyboard and enters the end-of-file key combination to indicate that no further values will be input. With input redirection, the input can be stored in a file. For example, if the data is stored in file `input`, the command line

```
$ sum < input
```

executes the program `sum`; the *redirect input symbol* (<) indicates that the data in file `input` is to be used as input by the program. Redirecting input on a Windows system is performed identically.

Note that $ is a UNIX command line prompt (some UNIX systems use a % prompt or other symbol). Students often find it difficult to understand that redirection is an operating system function, not another C feature.

The second method of redirecting input is *piping*. A *pipe* (|) causes the output of one program to be redirected as the input to another program. Suppose program `random` outputs a series of random integers; the output of `random` can be "piped" directly to program `sum` using the UNIX command line

```
$ random | sum
```

This causes the sum of the integers produced by `random` to be calculated. Piping is performed identically in UNIX and Windows.

Program output can be redirected to a file by using the *redirect output symbol* (>) (the same symbol is used for UNIX and Windows). For example, to redirect the output of program `random` to file `out`, use

```
$ random > out
```

Finally, program output can be appended to the end of an existing file by using the *append output symbol* (>>) (the same symbol is used for UNIX and Windows). For example, to append the output from program `random` to file `out` created in the preceding command line, use

```
$ random >> out
```

14.3 Variable-Length Argument Lists

It is possible to create functions that receive an unspecified number of arguments. Most programs in the text have used the standard library function `printf` which, as you know, takes a variable number of arguments. As a minimum, `printf` must receive a string as its first argument, but `printf` can receive any number of additional arguments. The function prototype for `printf` is

```
int printf( const char *format, ... );
```

The *ellipsis* (. . .) in the function prototype indicates that the function receives a variable number of arguments of any type. Note that the ellipsis must always be placed at the end of the parameter list.

The macros and definitions of the *variable arguments headers* `stdarg.h` (Fig. 14.1) provide the capabilities necessary to build functions with *variable-length argument lists*. Figure 14.2 demonstrates function `average` (line 28) that receives a variable number of arguments. The first argument of `average` is always the number of values to be averaged.

Identifier	Explanation
va_list	A type suitable for holding information needed by macros `va_start`, `va_arg` and `va_end`. To access the arguments in a variable-length argument list, an object of type `va_list` must be defined.

Fig. 14.1 `stdarg.h` variable-length argument list type and macros. (Part 1 of 2.)

Identifier	Explanation
va_start	A macro that is invoked before the arguments of a variable-length argument list can be accessed. The macro initializes the object declared with va_list for use by the va_arg and va_end macros.
va_arg	A macro that expands to an expression of the value and type of the next argument in the variable-length argument list. Each invocation of va_arg modifies the object declared with va_list so that the object points to the next argument in the list.
va_end	A macro that facilitates a normal return from a function whose variable-length argument list was referred to by the va_start macro.

Fig. 14.1   stdarg.h variable-length argument list type and macros. (Part 2 of 2.)

```
1   /* Fig. 14.2: fig14_02.c
2      Using variable-length argument lists */
3   #include <stdio.h>
4   #include <stdarg.h>
5
6   double average( int i, ... ); /* prototype */
7
8   int main()
9   {
10     double w = 37.5;
11     double x = 22.5;
12     double y = 1.7;
13     double z = 10.2;
14
15     printf( "%s%.1f\n%s%.1f\n%s%.1f\n%s%.1f\n\n",
16        "w = ", w, "x = ", x, "y = ", y, "z = ", z );
17     printf( "%s%.3f\n%s%.3f\n%s%.3f\n",
18        "The average of w and x is ", average( 2, w, x ),
19        "The average of w, x, and y is ", average( 3, w, x, y ),
20        "The average of w, x, y, and z is ",
21        average( 4, w, x, y, z ) );
22
23     return 0; /* indicates successful termination */
24
25   } /* end main */
26
27   /* calculate average */
28   double average( int i, ... )
29   {
30     double total = 0; /* initialize total */
31     int j; /* counter for selecting arguments */
32     va_list ap; /* stores information needed by va_start and va_end */
33
34     va_start( ap, i ); /* initializes the va_list object */
35
```

Fig. 14.2   Using variable-length argument lists. (Part 1 of 2.)

```
36      /* process variable length argument list */
37      for ( j = 1; j <= i; j++ ) {
38         total += va_arg( ap, double );
39      } /* end for */
40
41      va_end( ap ); /* clean up variable-length argument list */
42
43      return total / i; /* calculate average */
44   } /* end function average */
```

```
w = 37.5
x = 22.5
y = 1.7
z = 10.2

The average of w and x is 30.000
The average of w, x, and y is 20.567
The average of w, x, y, and z is 17.975
```

Fig. 14.2   Using variable-length argument lists. (Part 2 of 2.)

Function `average` (lines 20–44) uses all the definitions and macros of header `stdarg.h`. Object `ap`, of type `va_list` (line 32), is used by macros `va_start`, `va_arg` and `va_end` to process the variable-length argument list of function `average`. The function begins by invoking macro `va_start` (line 34) to initialize object `ap` for use in `va_arg` and `va_end`. The macro receives two arguments—object `ap` and the identifier of the rightmost argument in the argument list before the ellipsis—`i` in this case (`va_start` uses `i` here to determine where the variable-length argument list begins). Next function `average` repeatedly adds the arguments in the variable-length argument list to variable `total` (lines 37–39). The value to be added to `total` is retrieved from the argument list by invoking macro `va_arg`. Macro `va_arg` receives two arguments—object `ap` and the type of the value expected in the argument list—`double` in this case. The macro returns the value of the argument. Function `average` invokes macro `va_end` (line 41) with object `ap` as an argument to facilitate a normal return to `main` from `average`. Finally, the average is calculated and returned to `main`.

Common Programming Error 14.1

Placing an ellipsis in the middle of a function parameter list is a syntax error. An ellipsis may only be placed at the end of the parameter list.

The reader may question how function `printf` and function `scanf` know what type to use in each `va_arg` macro. The answer is that `printf` and `scanf` scan the format conversion specifiers in the format control string to determine the type of the next argument to be processed.

14.4 Using Command-Line Arguments

On many systems, it is possible to pass arguments to `main` from a command line by including parameters `int argc` and `char *argv[]` in the parameter list of `main`. Parameter argc receives the number of command-line arguments. Parameter argv is an array of strings in which the actual command-line arguments are stored. Common uses of command-line arguments include printing the arguments, passing options to a program and passing filenames to a program.

Figure 14.3 copies a file into another file one character at a time. We assume that the executable file for the program is called mycopy. A typical command line for the mycopy program on a UNIX system is

```
$ mycopy input output
```

This command line indicates that file input is to be copied to file output. When the program is executed, if argc is not 3 (mycopy counts as one of the arguments), the program prints an error message and terminates. Otherwise, array argv contains the strings "mycopy", "input" and "output". The second and third arguments on the command line are used as file names by the program. The files are opened using function fopen. If both files are opened successfully, characters are read from file input and written to file output until the end-of-file indicator for file input is set. Then the program terminates. The result is an exact copy of file input. See the manuals for your system for more information on command-line arguments.

```
1   /* Fig. 14.3: fig14_03.c
2      Using command-line arguments */
3   #include <stdio.h>
4
5   int main( int argc, char *argv[] )
6   {
7      FILE *inFilePtr;  /* input file pointer */
8      FILE *outFilePtr; /* output file pointer */
9      int c;            /* define c to hold characters input by user */
10
11     /* check number of command-line arguments */
12     if ( argc != 3) {
13        printf( "Usage: copy infile outfile\n" );
14     } /* end if */
15     else {
16
17        /* if input file can be opened */
18        if ( ( inFilePtr = fopen( argv[ 1 ], "r" ) ) != NULL ) {
19
20           /* if output file can be opened */
21           if ( ( outFilePtr = fopen( argv[ 2 ], "w" ) ) != NULL ) {
22
23              /* read and output characters */
24              while ( ( c = fgetc( inFilePtr ) ) != EOF ) {
25                 fputc( c, outFilePtr );
26              } /* end while */
27
28           } /* end if */
```

Fig. 14.3 Using command-line arguments. (Part 1 of 2.)

```
29                else { /* output file could not be opened */
30                    printf( "File \"%s\" could not be opened\n", argv[ 2 ] );
31                } /* end else */
32
33            } /* end if */
34            else { /* input file could not be opened */
35                printf( "File \"%s\" could not be opened\n", argv[ 1 ] );
36            } /* end else */
37
38        } /* end else */
39
40        return 0; /* indicates successful termination */
41
42    } /* end main */
```

Fig. 14.3 Using command-line arguments. (Part 2 of 2.)

14.5 Notes on Compiling Multiple-Source-File Programs

As stated earlier in the text it is possible to build programs that consist of multiple source files (see Chapter 16, C++ Classes and Data Abstraction). There are several considerations when creating programs in multiple files. For example, the definition of a function must be entirely contained in one file—it cannot span two or more files.

In Chapter 5, we introduced the concepts of storage class and scope. We learned that variables declared outside any function definition are of storage class `static` by default and are referred to as global variables. Global variables are accessible to any function defined in the same file after the variable is declared. Global variables also are accessible to functions in other files. However, the global variables must be declared in each file in which they are used. For example, if we define global integer variable `flag` in one file and refer to it in a second file, the second file must contain the declaration

```
extern int flag;
```

prior to the variable's use in that file. This declaration uses the storage class specifier `extern` to indicate that variable `flag` is defined either later in the same file or in a different file. The compiler informs the linker that unresolved references to variable `flag` appear in the file (the compiler does not know where the `flag` is defined, so it lets the linker attempt to find `flag`). If the linker cannot locate a definition of `flag`, the linker issues an error message and does not produce an executable file. If the linker finds a proper global definition, the linker resolves the references by indicating where `flag` is located.

Performance Tip 14.1

Global variables increase performance because they can be accessed directly by any function—the overhead of passing data to functions is eliminated.

Software Engineering Observation 14.1

Global variables should be avoided unless application performance is critical because they violate the principle of least privilege.

Just as `extern` declarations can be used to declare global variables to other program files, function prototypes can extend the scope of a function beyond the file in which it is defined (the `extern` specifier is not required in a function prototype). This is accomplished by including the function prototype in each file in which the function is invoked and compiling the files together (see Section 13.2). Function prototypes indicate to the compiler that the specified function is defined either later in the same file or in a different file. Again, the compiler does not attempt to resolve references to such a function—that task is left to the linker. If the linker cannot locate a proper function definition, the linker issues an error message.

As an example of using function prototypes to extend the scope of a function, consider any program containing the preprocessor directive `#include <stdio.h>`. This directive includes in a file the function prototypes for functions such as `printf` and `scanf`. Other functions in the file can use `printf` and `scanf` to accomplish their tasks. The `printf` and `scanf` functions are defined in other files. We do not need to know where they are defined. We are simply reusing the code in our programs. The linker resolves our references to these functions automatically. This process enables us to use the functions in the standard library.

Software Engineering Observation 14.2

Creating programs in multiple source files facilitates software reusability and good software engineering. Functions may be common to many applications. In such instances, those functions should be stored in their own source files, and each source file should have a corresponding header file containing function prototypes. This enables programmers of different applications to reuse the same code by including the proper header file and compiling their applications with the corresponding source file.

It is possible to restrict the scope of a global variable or function to the file in which it is defined. The storage class specifier `static`, when applied to a global variable or a function, prevents it from being used by any function that is not defined in the same file. This is referred to as *internal linkage*. Global variables and functions that are not preceded by `static` in their definitions have *external linkage*—they can be accessed in other files if those files contain proper declarations and/or function prototypes.

The global variable declaration

```
static double pi = 3.14159;
```

creates variable `pi` of type `double`, initializes it to `3.14159` and indicates that `pi` is known only to functions in the file in which it is defined.

The `static` specifier is commonly used with utility functions that are called only by functions in a particular file. If a function is not required outside a particular file, the principle of least privilege should be enforced by using `static`. If a function is defined before it is used in a file, `static` should be applied to the function definition. Otherwise, `static` should be applied to the function prototype.

When building large programs in multiple source files, compiling the program becomes tedious if small changes are made to one file and the entire program must be recompiled. Many systems provide special utilities that recompile only the modified program file. On UNIX systems the utility is called `make`. Utility `make` reads a file called `makefile` that contains instructions for compiling and linking the program. Products such as Borland C++ Builder and Microsoft Visual C++ provide similar utilities as well. For more information on `make` utilities, see the manual for your development tool.

14.6 Program Termination with `exit` and `atexit`

The general utilities library (`stdlib.h`) provides methods of terminating program execution by means other than a conventional return from function `main`. Function `exit` forces a program to terminate as if it executed normally. The function often is used to terminate a program when an input error is detected, or if a file to be processed by the program cannot be opened. Function `atexit` *registers* a function that should be called upon successful termination of the program—i.e., either when the program terminates by reaching the end of `main`, or when `exit` is invoked.

Function `atexit` takes as an argument a pointer to a function (i.e., the function name). Functions called at program termination cannot have arguments and cannot return a value. Up to 32 functions may be registered for execution at program termination.

Function `exit` takes one argument. The argument is normally the symbolic constant `EXIT_SUCCESS` or the symbolic constant `EXIT_FAILURE`. If `exit` is called with `EXIT_SUCCESS`, the implementation-defined value for successful termination is returned to the calling environment. If `exit` is called with `EXIT_FAILURE`, the implementation-defined value for unsuccessful termination is returned. When function `exit` is invoked, any functions previously registered with `atexit` are invoked in the reverse order of their registration, all streams associated with the program are flushed and closed, and control returns to the host environment. Figure 14.4 tests functions `exit` and `atexit`. The program prompts the user to determine whether the program should be terminated with `exit` or by reaching the end of `main`. Note that function `print` is executed at program termination in each case.

```
1   /* Fig. 14.4: fig14_04.c
2      Using the exit and atexit functions */
3   #include <stdio.h>
4   #include <stdlib.h>
5
6   void print( void ); /* prototype */
7
8   int main()
9   {
10      int answer; /* user's menu choice */
11
12      atexit( print ); /* register function print */
13      printf( "Enter 1 to terminate program with function exit"
14         "\nEnter 2 to terminate program normally\n" );
15      scanf( "%d", &answer );
16
17      /* call exit if answer is 1 */
18      if ( answer == 1 ) {
19         printf( "\nTerminating program with function exit\n" );
20         exit( EXIT_SUCCESS );
21      } /* end if */
22
23      printf( "\nTerminating program by reaching the end of main\n" );
24
25      return 0; /* indicates successful termination */
```

Fig. 14.4   `exit` and `atexit` functions. (Part 1 of 2.)

```
26
27   } /* end main */
28
29   /* display message before termination */
30   void print( void )
31   {
32      printf( "Executing function print at program "
33         "termination\nProgram terminated\n" );
34   } /* end function print */
```

```
Enter 1 to terminate program with function exit
Enter 2 to terminate program normally
1

Terminating program with function exit
Executing function print at program termination
Program terminated
```

```
Enter 1 to terminate program with function exit
Enter 2 to terminate program normally
2

Terminating program by reaching the end of main
Executing function print at program termination
Program terminated
```

Fig. 14.4 exit and atexit functions. (Part 2 of 2.)

14.7 volatile Type Qualifier

In Chapter 6 and Chapter 7, we introduced the const type qualifier. C also provides the volatile type qualifier to suppress various kinds of optimizations. The C standard indicates that when volatile is used to qualify a type, the nature of the access to an object of that type is implementation dependent.

14.8 Suffixes for Integer and Floating-Point Constants

C provides integer and floating-point suffixes for specifying the types of integer and floating-point constants. The integer suffixes are: u or U for an unsigned integer, l or L for a long integer, and ul, lu, UL or LU for an unsigned long integer. The following constants are of type unsigned, long and unsigned long, respectively:

```
174u
8358L
28373ul
```

If an integer constant is not suffixed, its type is determined by the first type capable of storing a value of that size (first int, then long int, then unsigned long int).

The floating-point suffixes are: f or F for a float, and l or L for a long double. The following constants are of type float and long double, respectively:

```
1.28f
3.14159L
```

A floating-point constant that is not suffixed is automatically of type `double`.

14.9 More on Files

Chapter 11 introduced capabilities for processing text files with sequential access and random access. C also provides capabilities for processing binary files, but some computer systems do not support binary files. If binary files are not supported and a file is opened in a binary file mode (Fig. 14.5), the file will be processed as a text file. Binary files should be used instead of text files only in situations where rigid speed, storage and/or compatibility conditions demand binary files. Otherwise, text files are always preferred for their inherent portability and for the ability to use other standard tools to examine and manipulate the file data.

Mode	Description
rb	Open a binary file for reading.
wb	Create a binary file for writing. If the file already exists, discard the current contents.
ab	Append; open or create a binary file for writing at end-of-file.
rb+	Open a binary file for update (reading and writing).
wb+	Create a binary file for update. If the file already exists, discard the current contents.
ab+	Append; open or create a binary file for update; all writing is done at the end of the file.

Fig. 14.5   Binary file open modes.

Performance Tip 14.2

Consider using binary files instead of text files in applications that demand high performance.

Portability Tip 14.1

Use text files when writing portable programs.

In addition to the file processing functions discussed in Chapter 11, the standard library also provides function `tmpfile` that opens a temporary file in mode `"wb+"`. Although this is a binary file mode, some systems process temporary files as text files. A temporary file exists until it is closed with `fclose`, or until the program terminates.

Figure 14.6 changes the tabs in a file to spaces. The program prompts the user to enter the name of a file to be modified. If the file entered by the user and the temporary file are opened successfully, the program reads characters from the file to be modified and writes them to the temporary file. If the character read is a tab (`'\t'`), it is replaced by a space and written to the temporary file. When the end of the file being modified is reached, the file pointers for each file are repositioned to the start of each file with `rewind`. Next, the temporary file is copied into the original file one character at a time. The program prints the original file as it copies characters into the temporary file and prints the new file as it copies characters from the temporary file to the original file to confirm the characters being written.

```
1    /* Fig. 14.6: fig14_06.c
2       Using temporary files */
3    #include <stdio.h>
4
5    int main()
6    {
7       FILE *filePtr;      /* pointer to file being modified */
8       FILE *tempFilePtr; /* temporary file pointer */
9       int c; /* define c to hold characters read from a file */
10      char fileName[ 30 ]; /* create char array */
11
12      printf( "This program changes tabs to spaces.\n"
13         "Enter a file to be modified: " );
14      scanf( "%29s", fileName );
15
16      /* fopen opens the file */
17      if ( ( filePtr = fopen( fileName, "r+" ) ) != NULL ) {
18
19         /* create temporary file */
20         if ( ( tempFilePtr = tmpfile() ) != NULL ) {
21            printf( "\nThe file before modification is:\n" );
22
23            /* read characters from file and place in temporary file */
24            while ( ( c = getc( filePtr ) ) != EOF ) {
25               putchar( c );
26               putc( c == '\t' ? ' ' : c, tempFilePtr );
27            } /* end while */
28
29            rewind( tempFilePtr );
30            rewind( filePtr );
31            printf( "\n\nThe file after modification is:\n" );
32
33            /* read from temporary file and write into original file */
34            while ( ( c = getc( tempFilePtr ) ) != EOF ) {
35               putchar( c );
36               putc( c, filePtr );
37            } /* end while */
38
39         } /* end if */
40         else { /* if temporary file could not be opened */
41            printf( "Unable to open temporary file\n" );
42         } /* end else */
43
44      } /* end if */
45      else { /* if file could not be opened */
46         printf( "Unable to open %s\n", fileName );
47      } /* end else */
48
49      return 0; /* indicates successful termination */
50
51   } /* end main */
```

Fig. 14.6 Temporary files. (Part 1 of 2.)

```
This program changes tabs to spaces.
Enter a file to be modified: data.txt

The file before modification is:
0         1         2         3         4
          5         6         7         8         9


The file after modification is:
0 1 2 3 4
 5 6 7 8 9
```

Fig. 14.6   Temporary files. (Part 2 of 2.)

14.10 Signal Handling

An unexpected *event*, or *signal*, can cause a program to terminate prematurely. Some unexpected events include *interrupts* (typing *<ctrl>-c* on a UNIX or Windows system), *illegal instructions, segmentation violations, termination orders from the operating system* and *floating-point exceptions* (division by zero or multiplying large floating-point values). The *signal handling library* (`signal.h`) provides the capability to *trap* unexpected events with function `signal`. Function `signal` receives two arguments—an integer signal number and a pointer to the signal handling function. Signals can be generated by function `raise` which takes an integer signal number as an argument. Figure 14.7 summarizes the standard signals defined in header file `signal.h`. Figure 14.8 demonstrates functions `signal` and `raise`.

Signal	Explanation
SIGABRT	Abnormal termination of the program (such as a call to function `abort`).
SIGFPE	An erroneous arithmetic operation, such as a divide by zero or an operation resulting in overflow.
SIGILL	Detection of an illegal instruction.
SIGINT	Receipt of an interactive attention signal.
SIGSEGV	An invalid access to storage.
SIGTERM	A termination request set to the program.

Fig. 14.7   `signal.h` standard signals.

```
1   /* Fig. 14.8: fig14_08.c
2      Using signal handling */
3   #include <stdio.h>
4   #include <signal.h>
5   #include <stdlib.h>
6   #include <time.h>
7
8   void signalHandler( int signalValue ); /* prototype */
9
```

Fig. 14.8   Signal handling. (Part 1 of 3.)

```
10   int main()
11   {
12      int i; /* counter used to loop 100 times */
13      int x; /* variable to hold random values between 1-50 */
14
15      signal( SIGINT, signalHandler ); /* register signal handler */
16      srand( clock() );
17
18      /* output numbers 1 to 100 */
19      for ( i = 1; i <= 100; i++ ) {
20         x = 1 + rand() % 50; /* generate random number to raise SIGINT */
21
22         /* raise SIGINT when x is 25 */
23         if ( x == 25 ) {
24            raise( SIGINT );
25         } /* end if */
26
27         printf( "%4d", i );
28
29         /* output \n when i is a multiple of 10 */
30         if ( i % 10 == 0 ) {
31            printf( "\n" );
32         } /* end if */
33
34      } /* end for */
35
36      return 0; /* indicates successful termination */
37
38   } /* end main */
39
40   /* handles signal */
41   void signalHandler( int signalValue )
42   {
43      int response; /* user's response to signal (1 or 2) */
44
45      printf( "%s%d%s\n%s",
46         "\nInterrupt signal ( ", signalValue, " ) received.",
47         "Do you wish to continue ( 1 = yes or 2 = no )? " );
48
49      scanf( "%d", &response );
50
51      /* check for invalid responses */
52      while ( response != 1 && response != 2 ) {
53         printf( "( 1 = yes or 2 = no )? " );
54         scanf( "%d", &response );
55      } /* end while */
56
57      /* determine if it is time to exit */
58      if ( response == 1 ) {
59
60         /* reregister signal handler for next SIGINT */
61         signal( SIGINT, signalHandler );
62      } /* end if */
```

Fig. 14.8 Signal handling. (Part 2 of 3.)

```
63        else {
64            exit( EXIT_SUCCESS );
65        } /* end else */
66
67    } /* end function signalHandler */
```

```
     1   2   3   4   5   6   7   8   9  10
    11  12  13  14  15  16  17  18  19  20
    21  22  23  24  25  26  27  28  29  30
    31  32  33  34  35  36  37  38  39  40
    41  42  43  44  45  46  47  48  49  50
    51  52  53  54  55  56  57  58  59  60
    61  62  63  64  65  66  67  68  69  70
    71  72  73  74  75  76  77  78  79  80
    81  82  83  84  85  86  87  88  89  90
    91  92  93
Interrupt signal ( 2 ) received.
Do you wish to continue ( 1 = yes or 2 = no )? 1
    94  95  96
Interrupt signal ( 2 ) received.
Do you wish to continue ( 1 = yes or 2 = no )? 2
```

Fig. 14.8   Signal handling. (Part 3 of 3.)

Figure 14.8 uses function `signal` to trap an interactive signal (`SIGINT`). Line 15 calls `signal` with `SIGINT` and a pointer to function `signalHandler` (remember that the name of a function is a pointer to the beginning of the function). When a signal of type `SIGINT` occurs, control passes to function `signalHandler`, which prints a message and gives the user the option to continue normal execution of the program. If the user wishes to continue execution, the signal handler is reinitialized by calling `signal` again and control returns to the point in the program at which the signal was detected. In this program, function `raise` (line 24) is used to simulate an interactive signal. A random number between 1 and 50 is chosen. If the number is `25`, `raise` is called to generate the signal. Normally, interactive signals are initiated outside the program. For example, typing *<ctrl>-c* during program execution on a UNIX or Windows system generates an interactive signal that terminates program execution. Signal handling can be used to trap the interactive signal and prevent the program from being terminated.

14.11 Dynamic Memory Allocation: Functions `calloc` and `realloc`

Chapter 12, C Data Structures, introduced the notion of dynamically allocating memory using function `malloc`. As we stated in Chapter 12, arrays are better than linked lists for rapid sorting, searching and data access. However, arrays are normally *static data structures*. The general utilities library (`stdlib.h`) provides two other functions for dynamic memory allocation—`calloc` and `realloc`. These functions can be used to create and modify *dynamic arrays*. As shown in Chapter 7, C Pointers, a pointer to an array can be subscripted like an array. Thus, a pointer to a contiguous portion of memory created by calloc can be manipulated as an array. Function calloc dynamically allocates memory for an array. The prototype for calloc is

```
void *calloc( size_t nmemb, size_t size );
```

Its two arguments represent the number of elements (nmemb) and the size of each element (size). Function calloc also initializes the elements of the array to zero. The function returns a pointer to the allocated memory, or a NULL pointer if the memory is not allocated. The primary difference between malloc and calloc is that calloc clears the memory it allocates and malloc does not.

Function realloc changes the size of an object allocated by a previous call to malloc, calloc or realloc. The original object's contents are not modified provided that the amount of memory allocated is larger than the amount allocated previously. Otherwise, the contents are unchanged up to the size of the new object. The prototype for realloc is

```
void *realloc( void *ptr, size_t size );
```

The two arguments are a pointer to the original object (ptr) and the new size of the object (size). If ptr is NULL, realloc works identically to malloc. If size is 0 and ptr is not NULL, the memory for the object is freed. Otherwise, if ptr is not NULL and size is greater than zero, realloc tries to allocate a new block of memory for the object. If the new space cannot be allocated, the object pointed to by ptr is unchanged. Function realloc returns either a pointer to the reallocated memory, or a NULL pointer to indicate that the memory was not reallocated.

14.12 Unconditional Branching with goto

Throughout the text we have stressed the importance of using structured programming techniques to build reliable software that is easy to debug, maintain and modify. In some cases, performance is more important than strict adherence to structured programming techniques. In these cases, some unstructured programming techniques may be used. For example, we can use break to terminate execution of a repetition structure before the loop continuation condition becomes false. This saves unnecessary repetitions of the loop if the task is completed before loop termination.

Another instance of unstructured programming is the goto *statement*—an unconditional branch. The result of the goto statement is a change in the flow of control of the program to the first statement after the *label* specified in the goto statement. A label is an identifier followed by a colon. A label must appear in the same function as the goto statement that refers to it. Figure 14.9 uses goto statements to loop ten times and print the counter value each time. After initializing count to 1, line 11 tests count to determine whether it is greater than 10 (the label start is skipped because labels do not perform any action). If so, control is transferred from the goto to the first statement after the label end (which appears at line 20). Otherwise, lines 15–16 print and increment count, and control transfers from the goto (line 18) to the first statement after the label start (which appears at line 9).

```
1   /* Fig. 14.9: fig14_09.c
2      Using goto */
3   #include <stdio.h>
4
5   int main()
6   {
7      int count = 1; /* initialize count */
8
9      start: /* label */
10
11         if ( count > 10 ) {
12            goto end;
13         } /* end if */
14
15         printf( "%d   ", count );
16         count++;
17
18         goto start; /* goto start on line 9 */
19
20      end: /* label */
21         putchar( '\n' );
22
23      return 0; /* indicates successful termination */
24
25   } /* end main */
```

1 2 3 4 5 6 7 8 9 10

Fig. 14.9 goto statement.

In Chapter 3, we stated that only three control structures are required to write any program—sequence, selection and repetition. When the rules of structured programming are followed, it is possible to create deeply nested control structures from which it is difficult to efficiently escape. Some programmers use goto statements in such situations as a quick exit from a deeply nested structure. This eliminates the need to test multiple conditions to escape from a control structure.

Performance Tip 14.3

The goto statement can be used to exit deeply nested control structures efficiently.

Software Engineering Observation 14.3

The goto statement should be used only in performance-oriented applications. The goto statement is unstructured and can lead to programs that are more difficult to debug, maintain and modify.

SUMMARY

- On many computer systems it is possible to redirect input to a program and output from a program.
- Input is redirected from the command line using the redirect input symbol (<) or using a pipe (|).

- Output is redirected from the command line using the redirect output symbol (>) or the append output symbol (>>). The redirect output symbol simply stores the program output in a file, and the append output symbol appends the output to the end of a file.

- The macros and definitions of the variable arguments header `stdarg.h` provide the capabilities necessary to build functions with variable-length argument lists.

- An ellipsis (. . .) in a function prototype indicates a variable number of arguments.

- Type `va_list` is suitable for holding information needed by macros `va_start`, `va_arg` and `va_end`. To access the arguments in a variable-length argument list, an object of type `va_list` must be declared.

- Macro `va_start` is invoked before the arguments of a variable-length argument list can be accessed. The macro initializes the object declared with `va_list` for use by the `va_arg` and `va_end` macros.

- Macro `va_arg` expands to an expression of the value and type of the next argument in the variable length argument list. Each invocation of `va_arg` modifies the object declared with `va_list` so that the object points to the next argument in the list.

- Macro `va_end` facilitates a normal return from a function whose variable argument list was referred to by the `va_start` macro.

- On many systems it is possible to pass arguments to `main` from the command line by including the parameters `int argc` and `char *argv[]` in the parameter list of `main`. Parameter `argc` receives the number of command-line arguments. Parameter `argv` is an array of strings in which the actual command-line arguments are stored.

- The definition of a function must be entirely contained in one file—it cannot span two or more files.

- Global variables must be declared in each file in which they are used.

- Function prototypes can extend the scope of a function beyond the file in which it is defined. This is accomplished by including the function prototype in each file in which the function is invoked and compiling the files together.

- The storage class specifier `static`, when applied to a global variable or a function, prevents it from being used by any function that is not defined in the same file. This is referred to as internal linkage. Global variables and functions that are not preceded by `static` in their definitions have external linkage—they can be accessed in other files if those files contain proper declarations or function prototypes.

- The `static` specifier is commonly used with utility functions that are called only by functions in a particular file. If a function is not required outside a particular file, the principle of least privilege should be enforced by using `static`.

- When building large programs in multiple source files, compiling the program becomes tedious if small changes are made to one file and the entire program must be recompiled. Many systems provide special utilities that recompile only the modified program file. On UNIX systems the utility is called `make`. Utility `make` reads a file called `makefile` that contains instructions for compiling and linking the program.

- Function `exit` forces a program to terminate as if it executed normally.

- Function `atexit` registers a function to be called upon normal termination of the program—i.e., either when the program terminates by reaching the end of `main` or when `exit` is invoked.

- Function `atexit` takes a pointer to a function as an argument. Functions called at program termination cannot have arguments and cannot return a value. Up to 32 functions may be registered for execution at program termination.

- Function `exit` takes one argument. The argument is normally the symbolic constant `EXIT_SUCCESS` or the symbolic constant `EXIT_FAILURE`. If `exit` is called with `EXIT_SUCCESS`, the implementation-defined value for successful termination is returned to the calling environment. If exit is called with EXIT_FAILURE, the implementation-defined value for unsuccessful termination is returned.

- When function exit is invoked, any functions registered with atexit are invoked in the reverse order of their registration, all streams associated with the program are flushed and closed, and control returns to the host environment.

- The C standard indicates that when volatile is used to qualify a type, the nature of the access to an object of that type is implementation dependent.

- C provides integer and floating-point suffixes for specifying the types of integer and floating-point constants. The integer suffixes are: u or U for an unsigned integer, l or L for a long integer, and ul or UL for an unsigned long integer. If an integer constant is not suffixed, its type is determined by the first type capable of storing a value of that size (first int, then long int, then unsigned long int). The floating-point suffixes are: f or F for a float, and l or L for a long double. A floating-point constant that is not suffixed is of type double.

- C provides capabilities for processing binary files, but some computer systems do not support binary files. If binary files are not supported and a file is opened in a binary file mode, the file will be processed as a text file.

- Function tmpfile opens a temporary file in mode "wb+". Although this is a binary file mode, some systems process temporary files as text files. A temporary file exists until it is closed with fclose or until the program terminates.

- The signal handling library enables trapping of unexpected events with function signal. Function signal receives two arguments—an integer signal number and a pointer to the signal-handling function.

- Signals can also be generated with function raise and an integer argument.

- The general utilities library (stdlib.h) provides two functions for dynamic memory allocation—calloc and realloc. These functions can be used to create dynamic arrays.

- Function calloc receives two arguments—the number of elements (nmemb) and the size of each element (size)—and initializes the elements of the array to zero. The function returns either a pointer to the allocated memory, or a NULL pointer if the memory is not allocated.

- Function realloc changes the size of an object allocated by a previous call to malloc, calloc or realloc. The original object's contents are not modified provided that the amount of memory allocated is larger than the amount allocated previously.

- Function realloc takes two arguments—a pointer to the original object (ptr) and the new size of the object (size). If ptr is NULL, realloc works identically to malloc. If size is 0 and the pointer received is not NULL, the memory for the object is freed. Otherwise, if ptr is not NULL and size is greater than zero, realloc tries to allocate a new block of memory for the object. If the new space cannot be allocated, the object pointed to by ptr is unchanged. Function realloc returns either a pointer to the reallocated memory, or a NULL pointer.

- The result of the goto statement is a change in the flow of control of the program. Program execution continues at the first statement after the label specified in the goto statement.

- A label is an identifier followed by a colon. A label must appear in the same function as the goto statement that refers to it.

TERMINOLOGY

append output symbol >>	atexit
argc	calloc
argv	command-line arguments

const   `raise`
dynamic arrays   `realloc`
event   redirect input symbol (<)
`exit`   redirect output symbol (>)
`EXIT_FAILURE`   segmentation violation
`EXIT_SUCCESS`   `signal`
external linkage   signal handling library
`extern` storage class specifier   `signal.h`
`float` suffix (f or F)   `static` storage class specifier
floating-point exception   `stdarg.h`
`goto` statement   temporary file
I/O redirection   `tmpfile`
illegal instruction   trap
internal linkage   `unsigned` integer suffix (u or U)
interrupt   `unsigned long` integer suffix (ul or UL)
`long double` suffix (1 or L)   `va_arg`
`long int` suffix (1 or L)   `va_end`
make   `va_list`
`makefile`   variable-length argument list
pipe symbol (|)   `va_start`
piping   `volatile`

COMMON PROGRAMMING ERROR

14.1   Placing an ellipsis in the middle of a function parameter list is a syntax error. An ellipsis may only be placed at the end of the parameter list.

PERFORMANCE TIPS

14.1   Global variables increase performance because they can be accessed directly by any function—the overhead of passing data to functions is eliminated.

14.2   Consider using binary files instead of text files in applications that demand high performance.

14.3   The `goto` statement can be used to exit deeply nested control structures efficiently.

PORTABILITY TIP

14.1   Use text files when writing portable programs.

SOFTWARE ENGINEERING OBSERVATIONS

14.1   Global variables should be avoided unless application performance is critical because they violate the principle of least privilege.

14.2   Creating programs in multiple source files facilitates software reusability and good software engineering. Functions may be common to many applications. In such instances, those functions should be stored in their own source files and each source file should have a corresponding header file containing function prototypes. This enables programmers of different applications to reuse the same code by including the proper header file and compiling their application with the corresponding source file.

14.3   The `goto` statement should be used only in performance-oriented applications. The `goto` statement is unstructured and can lead to programs that are more difficult to debug, maintain and modify.

SELF-REVIEW EXERCISE

14.1   Fill in the blanks in each of the following:

   a) The _____ symbol is used to redirect input data from a file rather than the keyboard.

   b) The _____ symbol is used to redirect the screen output so that it is placed in a file.

   c) The _____ symbol is used to append the output of a program to the end of a file.

   d) A(n) _____ is used to direct the output of one program to be the input of another program.

   e) A(n) _____ in the parameter list of a function indicates that the function can receive a variable number of arguments.

   f) Macro _____ must be invoked before the arguments in a variable-length argument list can be accessed.

   g) Macro _____ is used to access the individual arguments of a variable-length argument list.

   h) Macro _____ facilitates a normal return from a function whose variable argument list was referred to by macro `va_start`.

   i) Argument _____ of `main` receives the number of arguments in a command line.

   j) Argument _____ of `main` stores command-line arguments as character strings.

   k) UNIX utility _____ reads a file called _____ that contains instructions for compiling and linking a program consisting of multiple source files. The utility only recompiles a file if the file has been modified since it was last compiled.

   l) Function _____ forces a program to terminate execution.

   m) Function _____ registers a function to be called upon normal termination of the program.

   n) An integer or floating-point _____ can be appended to an integer or floating-point constant to specify the exact type of the constant.

   o) Function _____ opens a temporary file that exists until it is closed or program execution terminates.

   p) Function _____ can be used to trap unexpected events.

   q) Function _____ generates a signal from within a program.

   r) Function _____ dynamically allocates memory for an array and initializes the elements to zero.

   s) Function _____ changes the size of a block of memory dynamically allocated previously.

ANSWERS TO SELF-REVIEW EXERCISE

14.1   a) redirect input (<). b) redirect output (>). c) append output (>>). d) pipe (|). e) ellipsis (...). f) `va_start`. g) `va_arg`. h) `va_end`. i) `argc`. j) `argv`. k) `make`, `makefile`. l) `exit`. m) `atexit`. n) suffix. o) `tmpfile`. p) `signal`. q) `raise`. r) `calloc`. s) `realloc`.

EXERCISES

14.2   Write a program that calculates the product of a series of integers that are passed to function `product` using a variable-length argument list. Test your function with several calls, each with a different number of arguments.

14.3   Write a program that prints the command-line arguments of the program.

14.4   Write a program that sorts an array of integers into ascending order or descending order. The program should use command-line arguments to pass either argument -a for ascending order or -d for descending order. [*Note:* This is the standard format for passing options to a program in UNIX.]

14.5   Write a program that places a space between each character in a file. The program should first write the contents of the file being modified into a temporary file with spaces between each character, then copy the file back to the original file. This operation should overwrite the original contents of the file.

14.6   Read the manuals for your compiler to determine what signals are supported by the signal handling library (`signal.h`). Write a program that contains signal handlers for the standard signals SIGABRT and SIGINT. The program should test the trapping of these signals by calling function `abort` to generate a signal of type SIGABRT and by typing *<ctrl> c* to generate a signal of type SIGINT.

14.7   Write a program that dynamically allocates an array of integers. The size of the array should be input from the keyboard. The elements of the array should be assigned values input from the keyboard. Print the values of the array. Next, reallocate the memory for the array to 1/2 of the current number of elements. Print the values remaining in the array to confirm that they match the first half of the values in the original array.

14.8   Write a program that takes two command-line arguments that are file names, reads the characters from the first file one at a time and writes the characters in reverse order to the second file.

14.9   Write a program that uses `goto` statements to simulate a nested looping structure that prints a square of asterisks as follows:

```
*****
*   *
*   *
*   *
*****
```

The program should use only the following three `printf` statements:

```
printf( "*" );
printf( " " );
printf( "\n" );
```

15

C++ as a "Better C"

Objectives

- To become familiar with the C++ enhancements to C.
- To become familiar with the C++ standard library.
- To understand the concept of `inline` functions.
- To be able to create and manipulate references.
- To understand the concept of default arguments.
- To understand the role the unary scope resolution operator has in scoping.
- To be able to overload functions.
- To be able to define functions that can perform similar operations on different types of data.

Form ever follows function.
Louis Henri Sullivan

E pluribus unum.
(One composed of many.)
Virgil

O! call back yesterday, bid time return.
William Shakespeare

Call me Ishmael.
Herman Melville

When you call me that, smile.
Owen Wister

Outline

15.1 Introduction

We now begin the second section of this unique text. In the first fourteen chapters, we presented a thorough treatment of procedural programming and top-down program design with C. In the C++ portion of this book (Chapters 15 through 23), we introduce three additional programming paradigms: *object-based programming* (with classes, encapsulation, objects and operator overloading), *object-oriented programming* (with inheritance and polymorphism) and *generic programming* (with function templates and class templates), and we emphasize the creation of reusable software componentry by "crafting valuable classes." After we study C++, we present a thorough introduction to Java programming (Chapters 24 through 30) using class libraries to explore event-driven programming, graphics programming, graphical user interface (GUI) programming and multimedia programming.

15.2 C++

C++ improves on many of C's features and provides *object-oriented-programming (OOP)* capabilities that hold great promise for increasing software productivity, quality and reusability. This chapter discusses many of C++'s enhancements to C.

C's designers and early implementers never anticipated that the language would become such a phenomenon (the same holds true for the UNIX operating system). When a programming language becomes as entrenched as C, new requirements demand that the language evolve rather than simply be displaced by a new language. C++ was developed by Bjarne Stroustrup at Bell Laboratories, and was originally called "C with classes." The name C++ includes C's increment operator (++) to indicate that C++ is an enhanced version of C. C++ is a superset of C, so programmers can use a C++ compiler to compile existing C programs, and then gradually evolve those programs to C++.

Chapters 15 through 23 provide an introduction to the version of C++ standardized in the United States through the *American National Standards Institute (ANSI)* and worldwide through the *International Standards Organization (ISO)*. We have done a careful walk-through of the ANSI/ISO C++ standard document and audited our presentation against it for completeness and accuracy. However, C++ is a rich language, and there are some sub-tleties in the language and advanced subjects we have not covered. If you need additional technical details on C++, we suggest that you read the C++ standard document. You can order the C++ standard document from the ANSI Web site

    http://www.ansi.org/

The title of the document is "Information Technology – Programming Languages – C++" and its document number is ISO/IEC 14882-1998. If you prefer not to purchase the docu-ment, the older draft version of the standard can be viewed at the World Wide Web site

    http://www.cygnus.com/misc/wp/

Many features of the current version of C++ are not compatible with older C++ imple-mentations, so you may find that some of the programs in this text do not work on older C++ compilers.

15.3 A Simple Program: Adding Two Integers

Figure 15.1 revisits the addition program of Fig. 2.5 and illustrates several important fea-tures of the C++ language as well as some differences between C and C++. [Note: C files have the .c (lowercase) extension. C++ files can have a variety of extensions: .cpp, .cxx, .C (uppercase), etc. We use the extension .cpp.]

```
1   // Fig. 15.1: fig15_01.cpp
2   // Addition program
3   #include <iostream>
4
5   int main()
6   {
7      int integer1;
8
9      std::cout << "Enter first integer\n";
10     std::cin >> integer1;
11
12     int integer2, sum;           // declaration
13
14     std::cout << "Enter second integer\n";
15     std::cin >> integer2;
16     sum = integer1 + integer2;
17     std::cout << "Sum is " << sum << std::endl;
18
19     return 0;   // indicate that program ended successfully
20  } // end function main
```

Fig. 15.1   An addition program. (Part 1 of 2.)

```
Enter first integer
45
Enter second integer
72
Sum is 117
```

Fig. 15.1   An addition program. (Part 2 of 2.)

Lines 1 and 2

```
// Fig. 15.1: fig15_01.cpp
// Addition program
```

each begin with //, indicating that the remainder of each line is a comment. C++ allows you to begin a comment with // and use the remainder of the line for comment text. C++ programmers may also use C-style comments.

The C++ preprocessor directive (line 3)

```
#include <iostream>
```

exhibits the ANSI/ISO standard C++ style for including header files from the standard library. This line tells the C++ preprocessor to include the contents of the *input/output stream header file* iostream. This file must be included for any program that outputs data to the screen or inputs data from the keyboard using C++-style stream input/output. We discuss iostream's many features in detail in Chapter 21, C++ Stream Input/Output.

As in C, line 5 is a part of every C++ program. Keyword int to the left of main indicates that main "returns" an integer value. Note that in C, the programmer need not specify a return-value-type for functions. However, C++ does require the programmer to specify the return-value-type for all functions, or else the compiler generates an error.

Common Programming Error 15.1

Omitting the return-value-type in a C++ function definition is a syntax error.

Line 7 is a *familiar variable declaration.* However, unlike in C, where variables must be declared inside a block (i.e., a set of braces, {}) before any executable statements, variable declarations in C++ can be placed almost anywhere inside a block. This is demonstrated in line 12 where variables integer2 and sum are declared.

Good Programming Practice 15.1

If you prefer to place declarations at the beginning of a function, separate those declarations from the executable statements in that function with one blank line to highlight where the declarations end and the executable statements begin.

The statement in line 9 uses the *standard output stream* **cout** and the operator << (the *stream insertion operator*, pronounced *"put to"*) to output a string of text. Output and input in C++ is accomplished with *streams* of characters. Thus, when the preceding statement is executed, it sends the stream of characters Enter first integer to the *standard output stream object—std::cout*—which is normally "connected" to the screen. We like to pronounce the preceding statement as "cout *gets* the character string "Enter first integer\n".

The statement on line 10 uses the *input stream object* **cin** and the *stream extraction operator,* **>>**, to obtain a value from the keyboard. Using the stream extraction operator makes `std::cin` take character input from the standard input stream, which is usually the keyboard. We like to pronounce the preceding statement as, "`std::cin` *gives* a value to `integer1`" or simply "`std::cin` *gives* `integer1`."

When the computer executes the preceding statement, it waits for the user to enter a value for variable `integer1`. The user responds by typing an integer (as characters), then pressing the *Enter* key. The computer then converts the character representation of the number to an integer and assigns this value to the variable `integer1`.

Line 14 prints the words `Enter second integer` on the screen, then positions to the beginning of the next line. This statement prompts the user to take action. Line 15 obtains a value for variable `integer2` from the user.

Line 17 displays the character string `Sum is`, followed by the numerical value of variable `sum`, followed by `std::endl` (endl is an abbreviation for "end line")—a so-called *stream manipulator*. The `std::endl` manipulator outputs a newline, then "flushes the output buffer." This simply means that, on some systems where outputs accumulate in the machine until there are enough to "make it worthwhile to display on the screen," `std::endl` forces any accumulated outputs to be displayed at that moment.

Notice that we placed `std::` before `cout`, `cin` and `endl`. This is required when we use the preprocessor directive `#include <iostream>`. The notation `std::cout` specifies that we are using a name, in this case `cout`, that belongs to "namespace" `std`. Namespaces are an advanced C++ feature that we do not discuss in these introductory C++ chapters. For now, you should simply remember to include `std::` before each mention of `cout`, `cin` and `cerr` in a program. This can be cumbersome—in Fig. 15.3, we introduce the `using` statement, which will enable us to avoid having to place `std::` before each use of a namespace `std` name.

Note that the statement in line 17 outputs multiple values of different types (e.g., strings, `double`s, `int`s, etc.). The stream insertion operator "knows" how to output each piece of data. Using multiple stream insertion operators (`<<`) in a single statement is referred to as *concatenating, chaining* or *cascading stream insertion operations*. Thus, it is unnecessary to have multiple output statements to output multiple pieces of data. For a complete list of C++ operators see Appendix C, Operator Precedence.

Calculations can also be performed in output statements. We could have combined the statements in lines 16 and 17 into the statement

```
std::cout << "Sum is " << integer1 + integer2 << std::endl;
```

thus eliminating the need for the variable `sum`.

A powerful feature of C++ is that users can create their own data types. They can then "teach" C++ how to input and output values of these new data types using the `>>` and `<<` operators (this is called *operator overloading*—a topic we will explore in Chapter 18).

15.4 C++ Standard Library

C++ programs are constructed with two major building blocks, *functions* and user-defined data types called *classes*, which we explore in depth in the next chapter. Most C++ programmers take advantage of the rich collections of existing classes and functions in the C++ standard library. Thus, there are really two parts to learning the C++ "world." The first is learning the C++ language itself and the second is learning how to use the classes and functions in the C++ standard library. Throughout the book, we discuss many of these classes and functions. The standard class libraries are generally provided by compiler vendors. Many special-purpose class libraries are supplied by independent software vendors.

Software Engineering Observation 15.1

Use a "building block approach" to creating programs. Avoid reinventing the wheel. Use existing pieces where possible—this is called "software reuse" and is central to object-oriented programming.

Software Engineering Observation 15.2

When programming in C++, you will typically use the following building blocks: classes and functions from the C++ standard library, classes and functions you create yourself, and classes and functions from various popular libraries provided by third-party vendors.

The advantage of creating your own functions and classes is that you will know exactly how they work. You will be able to examine the C++ code. The disadvantage is the time-consuming and complex effort that goes into designing, developing and maintaining new functions and classes that are correct and that operate efficiently.

Performance Tip 15.1

Using standard library functions and classes instead of writing your own comparable versions can improve program performance because this software is carefully written to perform efficiently and correctly.

Portability Tip 15.1

Using standard library functions and classes instead of writing your own comparable versions can improve program portability because this software is included in virtually all C++ implementations.

15.5 Header Files

Each standard library has a corresponding *header file* containing the function prototypes for all the functions in that library and definitions of various data types and constants needed by those functions.

Software Engineering Observation 15.3

Function prototypes are required in C++. Use the #include preprocessor directives to obtain standard library function prototypes. Also use #include to obtain header files containing function prototypes used by you and/or your group members.

Figure 15.2 lists some common C++ standard library header files that might be included in C++ programs. The header files ending in .h are "old-style" header files that have been superseded by the C++ standard library header files.

The programmer can create custom header files. Programmer-defined header files should end in .h. A programmer-defined header file can be included by using the #include preprocessor directive. For example, the header file square.h can be included in our program by placing the directive

```
#include "square.h"
```

at the beginning of the program.

Standard library header file	Explanation
`<cassert>`	Contains macros and information for adding diagnostics that aid program debugging. The old version of this header file is `<assert.h>`.
`<cctype>`	Contains function prototypes for functions that test characters for certain properties, that can be used to convert lowercase letters to uppercase letters and vice versa. This header file replaces header file `<ctype.h>`.
`<cfloat>`	Contains the floating-point size limits of the system. This header file replaces header file `<float.h>`.
`<climits>`	Contains the integral size limits of the system. This header file replaces header file `<limits.h>`.
`<cmath>`	Contains function prototypes for math library functions. This header file replaces header file `<math.h>`.
`<cstdio>`	Contains function prototypes for the standard input/output library functions and information used by them. This header file replaces header file `<stdio.h>`.
`<cstdlib>`	Contains function prototypes for conversions of numbers to text, text to numbers, memory allocation, random numbers and various other utility functions. This header file replaces header file `<stdlib.h>`.
`<cstring>`	Contains function prototypes for C-style string processing functions. This header file replaces header file `<string.h>`.
`<ctime>`	Contains function prototypes and types for manipulating the time and date. This header file replaces header file `<time.h>`.
`<iostream>`	Contains function prototypes for the standard input and standard output functions. This header file replaces header file `<iostream.h>`.
`<iomanip>`	Contains function prototypes for the stream manipulators that enable formatting of streams of data. This header file replaces `<iomanip.h>`.
`<fstream>`	Contains function prototypes for functions that perform input from files on disk and output to files on disk. This header file replaces header file `<fstream.h>`.
`<utility>`	Contains classes and functions that are used by many standard library header files.
`<vector>`, `<list>`, `<deque>`, `<queue>`, `<stack>`, `<map>`, `<set>`, `<bitset>`	These header files contain classes that implement the standard library containers. Containers are used to store data during a program's execution.
`<functional>`	Contains classes and functions used by standard library algorithms.
`<memory>`	Contains classes and functions used by the standard library to allocate memory to the standard library containers.
`<iterator>`	Contains classes for accessing data in the standard library containers.
`<algorithm>`	Contains functions for manipulating data in standard library containers.

Fig. 15.2   Standard library header files. (Part 1 of 2.)

Standard library header file	Explanation
`<exception>`, `<stdexcept>`	These header files contain classes that are used for exception handling (discussed in Chapter 23).
`<string>`	Contains the definition of class `string` from the standard library.
`<sstream>`	Contains prototypes for functions that perform input from strings in memory and output to strings in memory.
`<locale>`	Contains classes and functions normally used by stream processing to process data in the natural form for different languages (e.g., monetary formats, sorting strings, character presentation, etc.).
`<limits>`	Contains classes for defining the numerical data type limits on each computer platform.
`<typeinfo>`	Contains classes for run-time type identification (determining data types at execution time).

Fig. 15.2   Standard library header files. (Part 2 of 2.)

15.6 Inline Functions

As we saw in Chapter 5, implementing a program in C as a set of functions is good from a software engineering standpoint, but function calls involve execution-time overhead. C++ provides *inline functions* to help reduce function-call overhead—especially for small functions. The qualifier *inline* before a function's return type in the function definition "advises" the compiler to generate a copy of the function's code in place, to avoid a function call. The trade-off is that multiple copies of the function code are inserted in the program (thus making the program larger) rather than a single copy of the function to which control is passed each time the function is called. The compiler can ignore the `inline` qualifier and typically does so for all but the smallest functions.

Software Engineering Observation 15.4

Any change to an `inline` *function could require all clients of the function to be recompiled. This can be significant in some program development and maintenance situations.*

Good Programming Practice 15.2

The `inline` *qualifier should be used only with small, frequently used functions.*

Performance Tip 15.2

Using `inline` *functions can reduce execution time but increase program size.*

Figure 15.3 uses `inline` function `cube` to calculate the volume of a cube. Lines 6–8

```
using std::cout;
using std::cin;
using std::endl;
```

are *using* statements that help us eliminate the need to repeat the std:: prefix. Once we include these using statements, we can write cout instead of std::cout, cin instead of std::cin and endl instead of std::endl, in the remainder of the program. [*Note:* From this point forward, each C++ example contains one or more using statements.]

```cpp
1    // Fig. 15.3: fig15_03.cpp
2    // Using an inline function to calculate
3    // the volume of a cube.
4    #include <iostream>
5
6    using std::cout;
7    using std::cin;
8    using std::endl;
9
10   inline double cube( const double s ) { return s * s * s; }
11
12   int main()
13   {
14      double side;
15
16      for ( int k = 1; k < 4; k++ ) {
17         cout << "Enter the side length of your cube:  ";
18         cin >> side;
19         cout << "Volume of cube with side "
20              << side << " is " << cube( side ) << endl;
21      } // end for
22
23      return 0;
24   } // end function main
```

```
Enter the side length of your cube:  1.0
Volume of cube with side 1 is 1
Enter the side length of your cube:  2.3
Volume of cube with side 2.3 is 12.167
Enter the side length of your cube:  5.4
Volume of cube with side 5.4 is 157.464
```

Fig. 15.3   Using an inline function to calculate the volume of a cube.

Notice the declaration of variable k in the for loop (line 16). C++ gives the programmer the option of declaring a for loop's control variable in the initialization section of the for header. Control variables declared in the for header can be used only in the body of the for structure, as the value of the control variable is unknown outside the for structure's header and body. All other C++ control structures are the same as in C.

Line 16's condition

    k < 4

evaluates to either a 0 value (false) or a nonzero value (true). This is consistent with C. However, C++ does add data type *bool* for representing a boolean value. A bool variable may be assigned an integer value, keyword *true* or keyword *false*. We will begin using keywords `bool`, `true` and `false` in successive C++ chapters. Figure 15.4 lists the keywords common to C and C++ and the keywords unique to C++.

C++ Keywords

Keywords common to the C and C++ programming languages

auto	break	case	char	const
continue	default	do	double	else
enum	extern	float	for	goto
if	int	long	register	return
short	signed	sizeof	static	struct
switch	typedef	union	unsigned	void
volatile	while			

C++ only keywords

asm	bool	catch	class	const_cast
delete	dynamic_cast	explicit	false	friend
inline	mutable	namespace	new	operator
private	protected	public	reinterpret_cast	
static_cast	template	this	throw	true
try	typeid	typename	using	virtual
wchar_t				

Fig. 15.4   C++ keywords.

15.7 References and Reference Parameters

Two ways to invoke functions in many programming languages are *call-by-value* and *call-by-reference*. When an argument is passed call-by-value, a *copy* of the argument's value is made and passed to the called function. Changes to the copy do not affect the original variable's value in the caller. This prevents accidental side effects that so greatly hinder the development of correct and reliable software systems. Each of the arguments that have been passed in the preceding programs in this chapter has been passed call-by-value.

Performance Tip 15.3

One disadvantage of call-by-value is that, if a large data item is being passed, copying that data can take a considerable amount of execution time.

In this section we introduce *reference parameters*—the second technique C++ provides for performing call-by-reference. The first technique, pointers, was introduced in Chapter 7. With call-by-reference, the caller gives the called function the ability to access the caller's data directly, and to modify that data if the called function so chooses.

Performance Tip 15.4

Call-by-reference is good for performance reasons because it eliminates the overhead of copying large amounts of data.

Software Engineering Observation 15.5

Call-by-reference can weaken security because the called function can corrupt the caller's data.

A reference parameter is an alias for its corresponding argument. To indicate that a function parameter is passed by reference, simply follow the parameter's type in the function prototype by an ampersand (&); use the same convention when listing the parameter's type in the function header. For example, the declaration

        int &count

in a function header may be pronounced "count is a reference to an int." In the function call, simply mention the variable by name, and it will be passed by reference. Mentioning the variable by its parameter name in the body of the called function actually refers to the original variable in the calling function, and the original variable can be modified directly by the called function. As always, the function prototype and header must agree.

Figure 15.5 compares call-by-value and call-by-reference with reference parameters. The "styles" of the arguments in the calls to squareByValue and squareByReference are identical, as both variables are simply mentioned by name. Without checking the function prototypes or function definitions, it is not possible to tell from the calls alone whether either function can modify its arguments. Function prototypes are mandatory, however, so the compiler has no trouble resolving the ambiguity.

```
1   // Fig. 15.5: fig15_05.cpp
2   // Comparing call-by-value and call-by-reference
3   // with references.
4   #include <iostream>
5
6   using std::cout;
7   using std::endl;
8
9   int squareByValue( int );
10  void squareByReference( int & );
11
12  int main()
13  {
14     int x = 2, z = 4;
15
16     cout << "x = " << x << " before squareByValue\n"
17          << "Value returned by squareByValue: "
18          << squareByValue( x ) << endl
19          << "x = " << x << " after squareByValue\n" << endl;
20
21     cout << "z = " << z << " before squareByReference" << endl;
22     squareByReference( z );
23     cout << "z = " << z << " after squareByReference" << endl;
24
25     return 0;
26  } // end function main
27
```

Fig. 15.5   An example of call-by-reference. (Part 1 of 2.)

```
28   int squareByValue( int a )
29   {
30      return a *= a;      // caller's argument not modified
31   } // end function squareByValue
32
33   void squareByReference( int &cRef )
34   {
35      cRef *= cRef;      // caller's argument modified
36   } // end function squareByReference
```

```
x = 2 before squareByValue
Value returned by squareByValue: 4
x = 2 after squareByValue

z = 4 before squareByReference
z = 16 after squareByReference
```

Fig. 15.5   An example of call-by-reference. (Part 2 of 2.)

Common Programming Error 15.2

Reference parameters are mentioned only by name in the body of the called function, so the programmer might inadvertently treat reference parameters as call-by-value parameters. This can cause unexpected side effects if the original copies of the variables are changed by the calling function.

Performance Tip 15.5

For passing large objects, use a constant reference parameter to simulate the appearance and security of call-by-value and avoid the overhead of passing a copy of the large object.

Note the placement of & in the parameter list of the squareByReference function. Some C++ programmers prefer to write int& cRef rather than int &cRef.

Software Engineering Observation 15.6

For the combined reasons of clarity and performance, many C++ programmers prefer that modifiable arguments be passed by using pointers, small nonmodifiable arguments be passed call-by-value and large nonmodifiable arguments be passed by using references to constants.

References can also be used as aliases for other variables within a function. For example, the code

```
int count = 1;       // declare integer variable count
int &cRef = count;   // create cRef as an alias for count
++cRef;              // increment count (using its alias)
```

increments variable count by using its alias cRef. Reference variables must be initialized in their declarations (see Fig. 15.6 and Fig. 15.7) and cannot be reassigned as aliases to other variables. Once a reference is declared as an alias for another variable, all operations supposedly performed on the alias (i.e., the reference) are actually performed on the original variable itself. The alias is simply another name for the original variable. Neither taking the address of a reference nor comparing references cause syntax errors; rather, each operation actually occurs on the variable for which the reference is an alias. A reference argument must be an *lvalue*, not a constant or expression that returns an *rvalue*.

```cpp
1   // Fig. 15.6: fig15_06.cpp
2   // References must be initialized
3   #include <iostream>
4
5   using std::cout;
6   using std::endl;
7
8   int main()
9   {
10     int x = 3, &y = x;   // y is now an alias for x
11
12     cout << "x = " << x << endl << "y = " << y << endl;
13     y = 7;
14     cout << "x = " << x << endl << "y = " << y << endl;
15
16     return 0;
17  } // end function main
```

```
x = 3
y = 3
x = 7
y = 7
```

Fig. 15.6 Using an initialized reference.

```cpp
1   // Fig. 15.7: fig15_07.cpp
2   // References must be initialized
3   #include <iostream>
4
5   using std::cout;
6   using std::endl;
7
8   int main()
9   {
10     int x = 3, &y;   // Error: y must be initialized
11
12     cout << "x = " << x << endl << "y = " << y << endl;
13     y = 7;
14     cout << "x = " << x << endl << "y = " << y << endl;
15
16     return 0;
17  } // end function main
```

Borland C++ command-line compiler error message

```
Error E2304 Fig15_07.cpp 10: Reference variable 'y' must be initialized in
function main()
```

Fig. 15.7 Attempting to use an uninitialized reference. (Part 1 of 2.)

Microsoft Visual C++ compiler error message

```
Fig15_07.cpp(10) : error C2530: 'y' : references must be initialized
```

Fig. 15.7   Attempting to use an uninitialized reference. (Part 2 of 2.)

Common Programming Error 15.3

Not initializing a reference variable when it is declared is a syntax error.

Common Programming Error 15.4

Attempting to reassign a previously declared reference to be an alias to another variable is a logic error. The value of the other variable is simply assigned to the location for which the reference is already an alias.

Common Programming Error 15.5

Declaring multiple references in one statement while assuming that the & distributes across a comma-separated list of variable names. To declare variables x, y and z all as references to integers, use the notation int &x = a, &y = b, &z = c; rather than the incorrect notation int& x = a, y = b, z = c; or the other common incorrect notation int &x, y, z;.

Functions can return references, but this can be dangerous. When returning a reference to a variable declared in the called function, the variable should be declared `static` within that function. Otherwise the reference refers to an automatic variable that is discarded when the function terminates; such a variable is said to be "undefined" and the program's behavior would be unpredictable (some compilers issue warnings when this is done). References to undefined variables are called *dangling references*.

Common Programming Error 15.6

Returning a pointer or reference to an automatic variable in a called function is a logic error. Some compilers will issue a warning when this occurs in a program.

15.8 Default Arguments and Empty Parameter Lists

Function calls commonly pass a particular value of an argument. The programmer can specify that such an argument is a *default argument,* and the programmer can provide a default value for that argument. When a default argument is omitted in a function call, the default value of that argument is inserted by the compiler and passed in the call.

Default arguments must be the rightmost (trailing) arguments in a function's parameter list. When one is calling a function with two or more default arguments, if an omitted argument is not the rightmost argument in the argument list, all arguments to the right of that argument also must be omitted. Default arguments should be specified with the first occurrence of the function name—typically, in the prototype. Default values can be constants, global variables or function calls.

Figure 15.8 demonstrates using default arguments in calculating the volume of a box. The function prototype for `boxVolume` in line 8 specifies that all three arguments have been given default values of `1`. Note that the default values should be defined only in the function prototype. Also note that we provided variable names in the function prototype for readability. As always, variable names are not required in function prototypes.

```cpp
1   // Fig. 15.8: fig15_08.cpp
2   // Using default arguments
3   #include <iostream>
4
5   using std::cout;
6   using std::endl;
7
8   int boxVolume( int length = 1, int width = 1, int height = 1 );
9
10  int main()
11  {
12     cout << "The default box volume is: " << boxVolume()
13          << "\n\nThe volume of a box with length 10,\n"
14          << "width 1 and height 1 is: " << boxVolume( 10 )
15          << "\n\nThe volume of a box with length 10,\n"
16          << "width 5 and height 1 is: " << boxVolume( 10, 5 )
17          << "\n\nThe volume of a box with length 10,\n"
18          << "width 5 and height 2 is: " << boxVolume( 10, 5, 2 )
19          << endl;
20
21     return 0;
22  } // end function main
23
24  // Calculate the volume of a box
25  int boxVolume( int length, int width, int height )
26  {
27     return length * width * height;
28  } // end function boxVolume
```

```
The default box volume is: 1

The volume of a box with length 10,
width 1 and height 1 is: 10

The volume of a box with length 10,
width 5 and height 1 is: 50

The volume of a box with length 10,
width 5 and height 2 is: 100
```

Fig. 15.8   Using default arguments.

The first call to boxVolume (line 12) specifies no arguments and thus uses all three default values. The second call (line 14) passes a length argument and thus uses default values for the width and height arguments. The third call (line 16) passes arguments for length and width and thus uses a default value for the height argument. The last call (line 18) passes arguments for length, width and height, thus using no default values.

 Good Programming Practice 15.3

Using default arguments can simplify writing function calls. However, some programmers feel that explicitly specifying all arguments is clearer.

Common Programming Error 15.7

Specifying and attempting to use a default argument that is not a rightmost (trailing) argument (while not simultaneously defaulting all the rightmost arguments) is a syntax error.

C++, like C, allows the programmer to leave the parameter list empty for a function. In C++, an empty parameter list is specified by writing either void or nothing at all in parentheses. The prototypes

```
void print1();
void print2( void );
```

specify that functions print1 and print2 do not take any arguments and do not return values. Other than the function names, these prototypes are equivalent.

Portability Tip 15.2

The meaning of an empty function parameter list in C++ is dramatically different than in C. In C, it means all argument checking is disabled (i.e., the function call can pass any arguments it wants). In C++, it means that the function takes no arguments. Thus, C programs using this feature might report syntax errors when compiled in C++.

15.9 Unary Scope Resolution Operator

Recall from our discussion of scoping rules in Chapter 5 that it is possible to declare local and global variables with the same name. This causes the global variable to be "hidden" by the local variable in the local scope. C++ provides the *unary scope resolution operator (::)* to provide access to a global variable when it has been hidden by a local variable with the same name in a local scope. However, the unary scope resolution operator cannot be used to access a local variable of the same name in an outer block. Just as in C a global variable can be accessed directly without the unary scope resolution operator if the name of the global variable is not the same as the name of a local variable in scope.

Figure 15.9 demonstrates the unary scope resolution operator with local and global variables of the same name. To emphasize that the local and global versions of constant variable PI are distinct, the program declares one of the variables double and one float.

```
1   // Fig. 15.9: fig15_09.cpp
2   // Using the unary scope resolution operator
3   #include <iostream>
4
5   using std::cout;
6   using std::endl;
7   using std::ios;
8
9   #include <iomanip>
10
11  using std::setprecision;
12  using std::setiosflags;
13  using std::setw;
14
15  const double PI = 3.14159265358979;
```

Fig. 15.9   Using the unary scope resolution operator. (Part 1 of 2.)

```
16
17  int main()
18  {
19     const float PI = static_cast< float >( ::PI );
20
21     cout << setprecision( 20 )
22          << "  Local float value of PI = " << PI
23          << "\nGlobal double value of PI = " << ::PI << endl;
24
25     cout << setw( 28 ) << "Local float value of PI = "
26          << setiosflags( ios::fixed | ios::showpoint )
27          << setprecision( 10 ) << PI << endl;
28     return 0;
29  } // end function main
```

Borland C++ command-line compiler output

```
  Local float value of PI = 3.141592741012573242
Global double value of PI = 3.141592653589790007
  Local float value of PI = 3.1415927410
```

Microsoft Visual C++ compiler output

```
  Local float value of PI = 3.1415927410125732
Global double value of PI = 3.14159265358979
  Local float value of PI = 3.1415927410
```

Fig. 15.9   Using the unary scope resolution operator. (Part 2 of 2.)

Common Programming Error 15.8

Attempting to access a nonglobal variable in an outer block by using the unary scope resolution operator is a syntax error if no global variable exists with the same name as the variable in the outer block and a logic error if one does.

Good Programming Practice 15.4

Avoid using variables of the same name for different purposes in a program. Although this is allowed in various circumstances, it can be confusing.

The statement (line 19)

```
const float PI = static_cast< float >( ::PI );
```

includes the cast operator `static_cast< float >( )`, which creates a temporary floating-point copy of its operand in parentheses—`::PI`. In C++, operator `static_cast` replaces the C-style cast discussed in earlier chapters. [*Note*: C++ actually provides four cast operators, including `static_cast`, that collectively replace the C-style cast operator. We do not discuss these other cast operators in this text. Casting operations can become quite complex and are error prone, so the C++ community felt that replacing the C-style cast operator with new cast operators would simplify casting operations and reduce errors.]

The formatting capabilities in Fig. 15.9 are explained in depth in Chapter 21 and discussed here briefly. The call `setprecision( 20 )` in the output statement (lines 21–23)

```
cout << setprecision( 20 )
     << "  Local float value of PI = " << PI
     << "\nGlobal double value of PI = " << ::PI << endl;
```

indicates that `float` constant PI is to be printed with twenty digits of *precision* to the right
of the decimal point (e.g., 3.1415927410125732). This call is referred to as a *parameterized
stream manipulator*. If the precision is not specified, floating-point values are normally
output with six digits of precision (i.e., the *default precision*), although we will see an exception to this in a moment.

Line 25

```
cout << setw( 28 ) << "Local float value of PI = "
```

calls `setw( 28 )` to specify that the next value output (i.e., "Local float value of PI
= ") be printed in a *field width* of 28, i.e., the value is printed with at least 28 character positions. If the value to be output is less than 28 character positions wide, the value is *right
justified* in the field by default. If the value to be output is more than 28 character positions
wide, the field width is extended to accommodate the entire value.

Lines 26 and 27

```
<< setiosflags( ios::fixed | ios::showpoint )
<< setprecision( 10 ) << PI << endl;
```

indicate that constant PI is printed as a *fixed-point* value, with a decimal point (specified
with the stream manipulator `setiosflags( ios::fixed | ios::showpoint )`) and ten
digits of precision to the right of the decimal point (specified with manipulator `setpre-
cision(10)`). When `setprecision` is used in a program, the printed value is *rounded*
to the indicated number of decimal positions, although the value in memory remains unaltered. For example, the values 87.945 and 67.543 are output as 87.95 and 67.54, respectively, when `setprecision` is passed a value of 2.

The stream manipulator `setiosflags( ios::fixed | ios::showpoint )` in the
preceding statement sets two output formatting options, namely *ios::fixed* and
ios::showpoint. The bitwise inclusive OR operator (|)—discussed in Chapter 10—sep-
arates multiple options in a `setiosflags` call. [*Note:* Although commas (,) are often used
to separate a list of items, they cannot be used with the stream manipulator `setiosflags`;
otherwise, only the last option in the list will be set.] The option `ios::fixed` causes a
floating-point value to be output in so-called *fixed-point format* (as opposed to *scientific
notation*, which we will discuss in Chapter 21). The `ios::showpoint` option forces the
decimal point and trailing zeros to print even if the value is a whole number amount such
as 88.00. Without the `ios::showpoint` option, such a value prints in C++ as 88 without
the trailing zeros and without the decimal point.

Programs that use these calls must contain the preprocessor directive (line 9)

```
#include <iomanip>
```

Lines 11 through 13 specify the names from the `<iomanip>` header file that are used in this
program. Note that `endl` is a *nonparameterized stream manipulator* and does not require
the `<iomanip>` header file. We will discuss `iomanip`'s powerful input/output formatting
capabilities in greater detail in Chapter 21.

15.10 Function Overloading

C++ enables several functions of the same name to be defined as long as they have different sets of parameters (at least as far as their types are concerned). This capability is called *function overloading*. When an overloaded function is called, the C++ compiler selects the proper function by examining the number, types and order of the arguments in the call. Function overloading is commonly used to create several functions of the same name that perform similar tasks on different data types.

 Good Programming Practice 15.5

Overloading functions that perform closely related tasks can make programs more readable and understandable.

Figure 15.10 uses overloaded function `square` to calculate the square of an `int` and the square of a `double`. In Chapter 18, we discuss how to overload operators to define how they should operate on objects of user-defined data types. In fact, we have been using many overloaded operators to this point, including the stream insertion operator `<<` and the stream extraction operator `>>`. Section 15.11 introduces function templates for generating overloaded functions that perform identical tasks on different data types.

```cpp
1   // Fig. 15.10: fig15_10.cpp
2   // Using overloaded functions
3   #include <iostream>
4
5   using std::cout;
6   using std::endl;
7
8   int square( int x ) { return x * x; }
9
10  double square( double y ) { return y * y; }
11
12  int main()
13  {
14     cout << "The square of integer 7 is " << square( 7 )
15          << "\nThe square of double 7.5 is " << square( 7.5 )
16          << endl;
17
18     return 0;
19  } // end function main
```

```
The square of integer 7 is 49
The square of double 7.5 is 56.25
```

Fig. 15.10 Using overloaded functions.

Overloaded functions are distinguished by their *signatures*—a signature is a combination of a function's name and its parameter types. The compiler encodes each function identifier with the number and types of its parameters (sometimes referred to as *name mangling* or *name decoration*) to enable *type-safe linkage*. Type-safe linkage ensures that the proper overloaded function is called and that the arguments conform to the parameters. Linkage errors are detected and reported by the compiler.

Common Programming Error 15.9

Creating overloaded functions with identical parameter lists and different return types is a syntax error.

The compiler uses only the parameter lists to distinguish between functions of the same name. Overloaded functions need not have the same number of parameters. Programmers should use caution when overloading functions with default parameters, because this may cause ambiguity.

15.11 Function Templates

Overloaded functions are normally used to perform similar operations that involve different program logic on different data types. If the program logic and operations are identical for each data type, this may be performed more compactly and conveniently by using *function templates*. The programmer writes a single function template definition. Given the argument types provided in calls to this function, C++ generates separate *template functions* to handle each type of call appropriately. Thus, defining a single function template defines a whole family of solutions. In Chapter 22, we will introduce a related C++ feature called class templates.

All function template definitions begin with keyword `template` followed by a list of formal type parameters to the function template enclosed in angle brackets (< and >). Every formal type parameter is preceded by either keyword `typename` or keyword `class`. The *formal type parameters* are built-in types or user-defined types used to specify the types of the arguments to the function, to specify the return type of the function and to declare variables within the body of the function definition.

The following function template definition is also used in Fig. 15.11 (lines 9–21):

```
template < class T >    // or template< typename T >
T maximum( T value1, T value2, T value3 )
{
   T max = value1;

   if ( value2 > max )
      max = value2;

   if ( value3 > max )
      max = value3;

   return max;
} // end function template maximum
```

This function template declares a single formal type parameter T as the type of the data to be tested by function `maximum`. When the compiler detects a `maximum` invocation in the program source code, the type of the data passed to `maximum` is substituted for T throughout the template definition, and C++ creates a complete function for determining the maximum of three values of the specified data type. Then, the newly created function is compiled. Thus, templates really are a means of code generation. In Fig. 15.11, three functions are created—one expects three `int` values, one expects three `double` values and one expects three `char` values. The function template created for type `int` is:

```
int maximum( int value1, int value2, int value3 )
{
   int max = value1;

   if ( value2 > max )
      max = value2;

   if ( value3 > max )
      max = value3;

   return max;
}
```

The name of a type parameter must be unique in the formal parameter list of a particular template definition. Figure 15.11 illustrates the use of the maximum template function to determine the largest of three int values, three double values and three char values.

```
1   // Fig. 15.11: fig15_11.cpp
2   // Using a function template
3   #include <iostream>
4
5   using std::cout;
6   using std::cin;
7   using std::endl;
8
9   template < class T >
10  T maximum( T value1, T value2, T value3 )
11  {
12     T max = value1;
13
14     if ( value2 > max )
15        max = value2;
16
17     if ( value3 > max )
18        max = value3;
19
20     return max;
21  } // end function template maximum
22
23  int main()
24  {
25     int int1, int2, int3;
26
27     cout << "Input three integer values: ";
28     cin >> int1 >> int2 >> int3;
29     cout << "The maximum integer value is: "
30          << maximum( int1, int2, int3 );          // int version
31
32     double double1, double2, double3;
33
34     cout << "\nInput three double values: ";
35     cin >> double1 >> double2 >> double3;
```

Fig. 15.11 Using a function template. (Part 1 of 2.)

```
36      cout << "The maximum double value is: "
37          << maximum( double1, double2, double3 ); // double version
38
39      char char1, char2, char3;
40
41      cout << "\nInput three characters: ";
42      cin >> char1 >> char2 >> char3;
43      cout << "The maximum character value is: "
44          << maximum( char1, char2, char3 )          // char version
45          << endl;
46
47      return 0;
48  } // end function main
```

```
Input three integer values: 1 2 3
The maximum integer value is: 3
Input three double values: 3.3 2.2 1.1
The maximum double value is: 3.3
Input three characters: A C B
The maximum character value is: C
```

Fig. 15.11 Using a function template. (Part 2 of 2.)

Common Programming Error 15.10

Not placing either keyword class or keyword typename before every type parameter of a function template is a syntax error.

SUMMARY

- The C++ standard library contains many functions and classes that programmers can take advantage of in their own programs.

- Single-line C++ comments begin with //.

- The line #include <iostream> tells the C++ preprocessor to include the contents of the input/output stream header file in the program. This file contains information necessary to compile programs that use std::cin, std::cout, std::endl and operators << and >>.

- The output stream object std::cout—normally connected to the screen—is used to output data. Multiple data items can be output by concatenating stream insertion (<<) operators.

- The input stream object std::cin—normally connected to the keyboard—is used to input data. Multiple data items can be input by concatenating stream extraction (>>) operators.

- The statements

```
using std::cout;
using std::cin;
using std::endl;
```

  are using statements that help us eliminate the need to repeat the std:: prefix. Once we include these using statements, we can write cout instead of std::cout, cin instead of std::cin and endl instead of std::endl, in the remainder of a program.

- Inline functions eliminate function-call overhead. The programmer uses the keyword inline to advise the compiler to generate function code in line (when possible) to minimize function calls. The compiler can choose to ignore the inline request.

- C++ provides keyword `bool` for representing boolean values. A `bool` may be assigned 0, a non-zero value, keyword `true` or keyword `false`.

- C++ offers a direct form of call-by-reference using reference parameters. To indicate that a function parameter is passed by reference, follow the parameter's type in the function prototype by an &. In the function call, mention the variable by name and it will be passed call-by-reference. In the called function, mentioning the variable by its local name actually refers to the original variable in the calling function. Thus, the original variable can be modified directly by the called function.

- Reference parameters can also be created for local use as aliases for other variables within a function. Reference variables must be initialized in their declarations, and they cannot be reassigned as aliases to other variables. Once a reference variable is declared as an alias for another variable, all operations supposedly performed on the alias are actually performed on the variable.

- C++ allows the programmer to specify default arguments to functions and their default values. If a default argument is omitted in a call to a function, the default value of that argument is used. Default arguments must be the rightmost (trailing) arguments in a function's parameter list. Default arguments should be specified with the first occurrence of the function name. Default values can be constants, global variables or function calls.

- C++ allows the programmer to specify an empty parameter list by using the `void` keyword or by simply leaving the parameter list empty.

- The unary scope resolution operator (`::`) enables a program to access a global variable when a local variable of the same name is in scope.

- The unary cast operator `static_cast< float >( )` creates a temporary floating-point copy of its operand.

- The stream manipulator `setw` specifies that a value be printed in a field of a specified size—right justified by default. If the value to be output is more than the specified field width, the field width is extended to accommodate the entire value. Programs that use this call must contain the preprocessor directive `#include <iomanip>`.

- The stream manipulator `setiosflags( ios::fixed | ios::showpoint )` sets two output formatting options, namely `ios::fixed` and `ios::showpoint`. The bitwise inclusive OR operator (`|`) separates multiple options in a `setiosflags` call. The option `ios::fixed` causes a floating-point value to be output in *fixed-point format* (as opposed to *scientific notation*). The `ios::showpoint` option forces the decimal point and trailing zeros to print even if the value is a whole number amount. Programs that use these calls must contain the preprocessor directive `#include <iomanip>`.

- It is possible to define several functions with the same name but with different parameter types. This is called function overloading. When an overloaded function is called, the compiler selects the proper function by examining the number and types of arguments in the call.

- Overloaded functions can have different return values and must have different parameter lists. Two functions differing only by return type will produce a compilation error.

- Function templates enable the creation of functions that perform the same operations on different types of data, but the function template is defined only once.

TERMINOLOGY

// for C++ comment
alias
ampersand (&) suffix
argument in a function call
bool

C++
C++ standard library
call a function
call-by-reference
call-by-value

called-function

caller

calling function

`cin`

class

`class`

component

copy of a value

`cout`

dangling reference

default function arguments

`endl`

`false`

field width

fixed-point format

fixed-point value

function call

function overloading

function scope

function signature

global variable

header file

`inline` function

`<iomanip>`

`ios::fixed`

`ios::showpoint`

`<iostream>`

local variable

lvalue

name decoration

name mangling

namespace

nonparameterized stream manipulator

object-oriented programming

overloading

parameter in a function definition

parameterized stream manipulator

reference parameter

reference type

rvalue

scientific notation

scope

`setiosflags`

`setprecision`

`setw`

signature

standard input stream

standard library header files

standard output stream

`static_cast`

`std::` prefix

stream extraction operator (>>)

stream insertion operator (<<)

stream manipulator

streams

`template`

template function

`true`

`typename`

type-safe linkage

unary scope resolution operator (::)

`using`

COMMON PROGRAMMING ERRORS

15.1 Omitting the return-value-type in a C++ function definition is a syntax error.

15.2 Reference parameters are mentioned only by name in the body of the called function, so the programmer might inadvertently treat reference parameters as call-by-value parameters. This can cause unexpected side effects if the original copies of the variables are changed by the calling function.

15.3 Not initializing a reference variable when it is declared is a syntax error.

15.4 Attempting to reassign a previously declared reference to be an alias to another variable is a logic error. The value of the other variable is simply assigned to the location for which the reference is already an alias.

15.5 Declaring multiple references in one statement while assuming that the & distributes across a comma-separated list of variable names. To declare variables x, y and z all as references to integers, use the notation int &x = a, &y = b, &z = c; rather than the incorrect notation int& x = a, y = b, z = c; or the other common incorrect notation int &x, y, z;.

15.6 Returning a pointer or reference to an automatic variable in a called function is a logic error. Some compilers will issue a warning when this occurs in a program.

15.7 Specifying and attempting to use a default argument that is not a rightmost (trailing) argument (while not simultaneously defaulting all the rightmost arguments) is a syntax error.

15.8   Attempting to access a nonglobal variable in an outer block by using the unary scope resolution operator is a syntax error if no global variable exists with the same name as the variable in the outer block and a logic error if one does.

15.9   Creating overloaded functions with identical parameter lists and different return types is a syntax error.

15.10   Not placing either keyword `class` or keyword `typename` before every type parameter of a function template is a syntax error.

GOOD PROGRAMMING PRACTICES

15.1   If you prefer to place declarations at the beginning of a function, separate those declarations from the executable statements in that function with one blank line to highlight where the declarations end and the executable statements begin.

15.2   The `inline` qualifier should be used only with small, frequently used functions.

15.3   Using default arguments can simplify writing function calls. However, some programmers feel that explicitly specifying all arguments is clearer.

15.4   Avoid using variables of the same name for different purposes in a program. Although this is allowed in various circumstances, it can be confusing.

15.5   Overloading functions that perform closely related tasks can make programs more readable and understandable.

PERFORMANCE TIPS

15.1   Using standard library functions and classes instead of writing your own comparable versions can improve program performance because this software is carefully written to perform efficiently and correctly.

15.2   Using `inline` functions can reduce execution time but increase program size.

15.3   One disadvantage of call-by-value is that, if a large data item is being passed, copying that data can take a considerable amount of execution time.

15.4   Call-by-reference is good for performance reasons because it eliminates the overhead of copying large amounts of data.

15.5   For passing large objects, use a constant reference parameter to simulate the appearance and security of call-by-value and avoid the overhead of passing a copy of the large object.

PORTABILITY TIPS

15.1   Using standard library functions and classes instead of writing your own comparable versions can improve program portability because this software is included in virtually all C++ implementations.

15.2   The meaning of an empty function parameter list in C++ is dramatically different than in C. In C, it means all argument checking is disabled (i.e., the function call can pass any arguments it wants). In C++, it means that the function takes no arguments. Thus, C programs using this feature might report syntax errors when compiled in C++.

SOFTWARE ENGINEERING OBSERVATIONS

15.1   Use a "building block approach" to creating programs. Avoid reinventing the wheel. Use existing pieces where possible—this is called "software reuse" and is central to object-oriented programming.

15.2   When programming in C++, you will typically use the following building blocks: classes and functions from the C++ standard library, classes and functions you create yourself, and classes and functions from various popular libraries provided by third-party vendors.

15.3 Function prototypes are required in C++. Use the #include preprocessor directives to obtain standard library function prototypes. Also use #include to obtain header files containing function prototypes used by you and/or your group members.

15.4 Any change to an inline function could require all clients of the function to be recompiled. This can be significant in some program development and maintenance situations.

15.5 Call-by-reference can weaken security because the called function can corrupt the caller's data.

15.6 For the combined reasons of clarity and performance, many C++ programmers prefer that modifiable arguments be passed by using pointers, small nonmodifiable arguments be passed call-by-value and large nonmodifiable arguments be passed by using references to constants.

SELF-REVIEW EXERCISES

15.1 Answer each of the following:
a) In C++, it is possible to have various functions with the same name that operate on different types and/or numbers of arguments. This is called function _____.
b) The _____ enables access to a global variable with the same name as a variable in the current scope.
c) A function _____ enables a single function to be defined to perform a task on many different data types.

15.2 Why would a function prototype contain a parameter type declaration such as double &?

15.3 (True/False) All calls in C++ are performed call-by-value.

15.4 Write a complete program that uses an inline function sphereVolume to prompt the user for the radius of a sphere and to calculate and print the volume of that sphere by using the assignment volume = (4.0 / 3) * 3.14159 * pow(radius, 3).

ANSWERS TO SELF-REVIEW EXERCISES

15.1 a) Overloading. b) Unary scope resolution operator (::). c) template.

15.2 The programmer is declaring a reference parameter of type double to get access through call-by-reference to the original argument variable.

15.3 False. C++ allows direct call-by-reference via the use of reference parameters in addition to the use of pointers.

15.4 See below.

```
1   // ex15_04.cpp
2   // Inline function that calculates the volume of a sphere
3   #include <iostream>
4
5   using std::cout;
6   using std::cin;
7   using std::endl;
8
9   #include <cmath>
10
11  const double PI = 3.14159;
12
13  inline double sphereVolume( const double r )
14     { return 4.0 / 3.0 * PI * pow( r, 3 ); }
```

(Part 1 of 2.)

```
15
16   int main()
17   {
18      double radius;
19
20      cout << "Enter the length of the radius of your sphere: ";
21      cin >> radius;
22      cout << "Volume of sphere with radius " << radius <<
23              " is " << sphereVolume( radius ) << endl;
24      return 0;
25   } // end function main
```

(Part 2 of 2.)

EXERCISES

15.5   Write a C++ program that uses an `inline` function `circleArea` to prompt the user for the radius of a circle and to calculate and print the area of that circle.

15.6   Write a complete C++ program with the two alternate functions specified below, of which each simply triples the variable `count` defined in `main`. Then compare and contrast the two approaches. These two functions are
    a) Function `tripleCallByValue` that passes a copy of `count` call-by-value, triples the copy and returns the new value.
    b) Function `tripleByReference` that passes `count` with true call-by-reference via a reference parameter and triples the original copy of `count` through its alias (i.e., the reference parameter).

15.7   What is the purpose of the unary scope resolution operator?

15.8   Write a program that uses a function template called `min` to determine the smaller of two arguments. Test the program using integer, character and floating-point number pairs.

15.9   Write a program that uses a function template called `max` to determine the largest of three arguments. Test the program using integer, character and floating-point number pairs.

15.10   Determine whether the following program segments contain errors. For each error, explain how it can be corrected. [*Note*: For a particular program segment, it is possible that no errors are present in the segment.]

```
a) template < class A >
   int sum( int num1, int num2, int num3 )
      { return num1 + num2 + num3; }
b) void printResults( int x, int y )
   {
      cout << "The sum is " << x + y << '\n';
      return x + y;
   }
c) template < A >
   A product( A num1, A num2, A num3 )
   {
      return num1 * num2 * num3;
   }
d) double cube( int );
   int cube( int );
```

16

C++ Classes and Data Abstraction

Objectives

- To understand the software engineering concepts of encapsulation and data hiding.
- To understand the notions of data abstraction and abstract data types (ADTs).
- To be able to create C++ ADTs, namely classes.
- To understand how to create, use, and destroy class objects.
- To be able to control access to object data members and member functions.
- To begin to appreciate the value of object orientation.

My object all sublime
I shall achieve in time.
W. S. Gilbert

Is it a world to hide virtues in?
William Shakespeare

Your public servants serve you right.
Adlai Stevenson

Private faces in public places
Are wiser and nicer
Than public faces in private places.
W. H. Auden

16.1 Introduction

Now we begin our introduction to object orientation in C++. In Chapters 1 through 14 we presented structured programming in C. The objects we build in C++ will be composed in part of structured program pieces.

Let us introduce some key concepts and terminology of object orientation. Object-oriented programming (OOP) *encapsulates* data (attributes) and functions (behavior) into packages called *classes;* the data and functions of a class are intimately tied together. A class is like a blueprint. Out of a blueprint, a builder can build a house. Out of a class, a programmer can create an object. One blueprint can be reused many times to make many houses. One class can be reused many times to make many objects of the same class. Classes have the property of *information hiding.* This means that although class objects may know how to communicate with one another across well-defined *interfaces,* classes normally are not allowed to know how other classes are implemented—implementation details are hidden within the classes themselves. Surely it is possible to drive a car effectively without knowing the details of how engines, transmissions and exhaust systems work internally. We will see why information hiding is so crucial to good software engineering.

In C and other *procedural programming languages,* programming tends to be *action-oriented,* whereas ideally in C++ programming is *object-oriented.* In C, the unit of programming is the *function.* In C++, the unit of programming is the *class* from which objects are eventually *instantiated* (i.e., created).

C programmers concentrate on writing functions. Groups of actions that perform some task are formed into functions, and functions are grouped to form programs. Data are certainly important in C, but the view is that data exist primarily in support of the actions that functions perform. The *verbs* in a system specification help the C programmer determine the set of functions that will work together to implement the system.

C++ programmers concentrate on creating their own *user-defined types* called *classes*. Classes are also referred to as *programmer-defined types*. Each class contains data as well as the set of functions that manipulate the data. The data components of a class are called *data members*. The function components of a class are called *member functions* (or *methods* in other object-oriented languages). Just as an instance of a built-in type such as `int` is called a *variable,* an instance of a user-defined type (i.e., a class) is called an *object.* [In the C++ community, the terms variable and object are often used interchangeably.] The focus of attention in C++ is on classes rather than functions. The *nouns* in a system specification help the C++ programmer determine the set of classes that will be used to create the objects that will work together to implement the system.

Classes in C++ are a natural evolution of the C notion of `struct` which we discussed in Chapter 10. Remember that a `struct` is a collection of related variables (data), whereas a class contains both variables (*data members*) and the functions that manipulate those data (*member functions*). In the next section we develop a `Time` abstract data type as a C++ class. We will see that classes provide a robust way to describe new abstract data types.

16.2 Implementing a Time Abstract Data Type with a Class

Classes enable the programmer to model objects that have *attributes* (represented as *data members*) and *behaviors* or *operations* (represented as *member functions*). Types containing data members and member functions are defined in C++ using the keyword `class`.

Member functions are sometimes called *methods* in other object-oriented programming languages, and are invoked in response to *messages* sent to an object. A message corresponds to a member-function call sent from one object to another or sent from a function to an object.

Once a class has been defined, the class name can be used to declare objects of that class. Figure 16.1 contains a simple definition for class `Time`.

```
1   class Time {
2   public:
3       Time();
4       void setTime( int, int, int );
5       void printMilitary();
6       void printStandard();
7   private:
8       int hour;       // 0 - 23
9       int minute;     // 0 - 59
10      int second;     // 0 - 59
11  }; // end class Time
```

Fig. 16.1   Simple definition of `class Time`.

Our `Time` class definition begins with the keyword `class`. The *body* of the class definition is delineated with left and right braces ({ and }). The class definition terminates with a semicolon. Our `Time` class definition contains three integer members `hour`, `minute` and `second`.

Common Programming Error 16.1

Forgetting the semicolon at the end of a class (or structure) definition is a syntax error.

The *public:* and *private:* labels are called *member access specifiers.* Any data member or member function declared after member access specifier public (and before the next member access specifier) is accessible wherever the program has access to an object of class Time. Any data member or member function declared after member access specifier private (and up to the next member access specifier) is accessible only to member functions of the class. Member access specifiers are always followed by a colon (:) and can appear multiple times and in any order in a class definition. For the remainder of the text, we will refer to the member access specifiers as public and private (without the colon). In Chapter 19 we introduce a third member access specifier, called protected, as we study inheritance and the part inheritance plays in object-oriented programming.

Good Programming Practice 16.1

Use each member access specifier only once in a class definition for clarity and readability. Place public members first where they are easy to locate.

The class definition contains prototypes for the following four member functions after the public member access specifier—Time, setTime, printMilitary and print-Standard. These are the *public member functions* or *public services* or *public behaviors* or *interface* of the class. These functions will be used by *clients* (i.e., portions of a program that are users) of the class to manipulate the data of the class. The data members of the class support the delivery of the *services* the class provides to the clients of the class with its member functions. These services allow the client code to interact with an object of the class.

Notice the member function with the same name as the class; it is called a *constructor* function of that class. A constructor is a special member function that initializes the data members of a class object. A class constructor function is called whenever an object of that class is created. We will see that it is common to have several constructors for a class; this is accomplished through function overloading. Note that no return type is specified for the constructor.

Common Programming Error 16.2

Specifying a return type and/or a return value for a constructor is a syntax error.

The three integer members appear after the private member access specifier. This indicates that these data members of the class are only accessible to member functions— and, as we will see in the next chapter, "friends"—of the class. Thus, the data members can only be accessed by the four functions whose prototypes appear in the class definition (or by friends of the class). Data members are normally listed in the private portion of a class and member functions are normally listed in the public portion. It is possible to have private member functions and public data, as we will see later; the latter is uncommon and is considered a poor programming practice.

Once the class has been defined, it can be used as a type in object, array and pointer definitions as follows:

```
Time sunset,                 // object of type Time
    arrayOfTimes[ 5 ],       // array of Time objects
    *pointerToTime,          // pointer to a Time object
    &dinnerTime = sunset;    // reference to a Time object
```

The class name becomes a new type specifier. There may be many objects of a class, just as there may be many variables of a type such as int. The programmer can create new class types as needed. This is one reason why C++ is said to be an *extensible language*.

Figure 16.2 uses the Time class. The program instantiates a single object of class Time called t. When the object is instantiated, the Time constructor is called and initializes each private data member to 0. The time is then printed in military and standard formats to confirm that the members have been initialized properly. The time is then set using the setTime member function and is printed again in both formats. Then setTime attempts to set the data members to invalid values, and the time is again printed in both formats.

```
1    // Fig. 16.2: fig16_02.cpp
2    // Time class.
3    #include <iostream>
4
5    using std::cout;
6    using std::endl;
7
8    // Time abstract data type (ADT) definition
9    class Time {
10   public:
11      Time();                      // constructor
12      void setTime( int, int, int ); // set hour, minute, second
13      void printMilitary();        // print military time format
14      void printStandard();        // print standard time format
15   private:
16      int hour;      // 0 - 23
17      int minute;    // 0 - 59
18      int second;    // 0 - 59
19   }; // end class Time
20
21   // Time constructor initializes each data member to zero.
22   // Ensures all Time objects start in a consistent state.
23   Time::Time() { hour = minute = second = 0; }
24
25   // Set a new Time value using military time. Perform validity
26   // checks on the data values. Set invalid values to zero.
27   void Time::setTime( int h, int m, int s )
28   {
29      hour = ( h >= 0 && h < 24 ) ? h : 0;
30      minute = ( m >= 0 && m < 60 ) ? m : 0;
31      second = ( s >= 0 && s < 60 ) ? s : 0;
32   } // end function setTime
33
34   // Print Time in military format
35   void Time::printMilitary()
36   {
```

Fig. 16.2   Abstract data type Time implementation as a class. (Part 1 of 2.)

```
37        cout << ( hour < 10 ? "0" : "" ) << hour << ":"
38            << ( minute < 10 ? "0" : "" ) << minute;
39   } // end function printMilitary
40
41   // Print Time in standard format
42   void Time::printStandard()
43   {
44        cout << ( ( hour == 0 || hour == 12 ) ? 12 : hour % 12 )
45            << ":" << ( minute < 10 ? "0" : "" ) << minute
46            << ":" << ( second < 10 ? "0" : "" ) << second
47            << ( hour < 12 ? " AM" : " PM" );
48   } // end function printStandard
49
50   // Driver to test simple class Time
51   int main()
52   {
53        Time t;   // instantiate object t of class Time
54
55        cout << "The initial military time is ";
56        t.printMilitary();
57        cout << "\nThe initial standard time is ";
58        t.printStandard();
59
60        t.setTime( 13, 27, 6 );
61        cout << "\n\nMilitary time after setTime is ";
62        t.printMilitary();
63        cout << "\nStandard time after setTime is ";
64        t.printStandard();
65
66        t.setTime( 99, 99, 99 );   // attempt invalid settings
67        cout << "\n\nAfter attempting invalid settings:"
68            << "\nMilitary time: ";
69        t.printMilitary();
70        cout << "\nStandard time: ";
71        t.printStandard();
72        cout << endl;
73        return 0;
74   } // end function main
```

```
The initial military time is 00:00
The initial standard time is 12:00:00 AM

Military time after setTime is 13:27
Standard time after setTime is 1:27:06 PM

After attempting invalid settings:
Military time: 00:00
Standard time: 12:00:00 AM
```

Fig. 16.2   Abstract data type Time implementation as a class. (Part 2 of 2.)

Again, note that the data members hour, minute and second are preceded by the private member access specifier. A class's private data members are normally not accessible outside the class. (Again, we will see in Chapter 17 that friends of a class may access the class's `private` members.) The philosophy here is that the actual data representation used within the class is of no concern to the class's clients. For example, it would be perfectly reasonable for the class to represent the time internally as the number of seconds since midnight. Clients could use the same `public` member functions and get the same results without being aware of this. In this sense, the implementation of a class is said to be *hidden* from its clients. Such *information hiding* promotes program modifiability and simplifies the client's perception of a class.

Software Engineering Observation 16.1

Clients of a class use the class without knowing the internal details of how the class is implemented. If the class implementation is changed (to improve performance, for example), provided the class's interface remains constant, the class's client source code need not change (although the client may need to be recompiled). This makes it much easier to modify systems.

In this program, the `Time` constructor initializes the data members to 0 (i.e., the military time equivalent of 12 AM). This ensures that the object is in a consistent state when it is created. Invalid values cannot be stored in the data members of a `Time` object because the constructor is called whenever the `Time` object is created and all subsequent attempts by a client to modify the data members are scrutinized by function `setTime`.

Software Engineering Observation 16.2

Member functions are usually shorter than functions in non-object-oriented programs because the data stored in data members have ideally been validated by a constructor and/or by member functions that store new data. The data are already in the object, so the member function calls often have no arguments or at least have fewer arguments than typical function calls in non-object-oriented languages. Thus, the calls are shorter, the function definitions are shorter and the function prototypes are shorter.

Note that the data members of a class cannot be initialized where they are declared in the class body. These data members should be initialized by the class's constructor, or they can be assigned values by "set" functions.

Common Programming Error 16.3

Attempting to initialize a data member of a class explicitly in the class definition is a syntax error.

A function with the same name as the class but preceded with a *tilde character (~)* is called the *destructor* of that class (this example does not explicitly include a destructor, so the system "plugs one in" for you). The destructor does "termination housekeeping" on each class object before the memory for the object is reclaimed by the system. Destructors cannot take arguments and hence cannot be overloaded. We will discuss constructors and destructors in more detail later in this chapter and in Chapter 17.

Note that the functions the class provides to the outside world are preceded by the `public` member access specifier. The `public` functions implement the behaviors or services the class provides to its clients—commonly referred to as the class's *interface* or *public interface*.

Software Engineering Observation 16.3

Clients have access to a class's interface but should not have access to a class's implementation.

The class definition contains declarations of the class's data members and the class's member functions. The member function declarations are the function prototypes we discussed in earlier chapters. Member functions can be defined inside a class, but it is a good programming practice to define the functions outside the class definition.

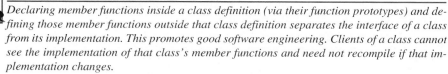

Software Engineering Observation 16.4

Declaring member functions inside a class definition (via their function prototypes) and defining those member functions outside that class definition separates the interface of a class from its implementation. This promotes good software engineering. Clients of a class cannot see the implementation of that class's member functions and need not recompile if that implementation changes.

Note the use of the *binary scope resolution operator (: :)* in each member function definition following the class definition in Fig. 16.2. Once a class is defined and its member functions are declared, the member functions must be defined. Each member function of the class can be defined directly in the class body (rather than including the function prototype of the class), or the member function can be defined after the class body. When a member function is defined after its corresponding class definition, the function name is preceded by the class name and the binary scope resolution operator (: :). Different classes can have the same member names, so the scope resolution operator "ties" the member name to the class name to uniquely identify the member functions of a particular class.

Common Programming Error 16.4

When defining a class's member functions outside that class, omitting the class name and scope resolution operator on the function name is an error.

Even though a member function declared in a class definition may be defined outside that class definition, that member function is still within that *class's scope,* i.e., its name is known only to other members of the class unless referred to via an object of the class, a reference to an object of the class or a pointer to an object of the class. We will say more about class scope shortly.

If a member function is defined in a class definition, the member function is inlined by the compiler. Member functions defined outside a class definition may be made inline by explicitly using the keyword `inline`. Remember that the compiler reserves the right not to inline any function.

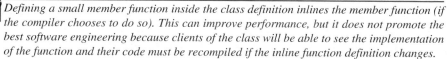

Performance Tip 16.1

Defining a small member function inside the class definition inlines the member function (if the compiler chooses to do so). This can improve performance, but it does not promote the best software engineering because clients of the class will be able to see the implementation of the function and their code must be recompiled if the inline function definition changes.

Software Engineering Observation 16.5

Only the simplest member functions and most stable member functions (i.e., the implementation is unlikely to change) should be defined in the class header.

It is interesting that the `printMilitary` and `printStandard` member functions take no arguments. This is because member functions implicitly know that they are to print the data members of the particular `Time` object for which they are invoked. This makes member function calls more concise than conventional function calls in procedural programming.

Error-Prevention Tip 16.1

The fact that member function calls generally take either no arguments or substantially fewer arguments than conventional function calls in non-object-oriented languages reduces the likelihood of passing the wrong arguments, types of arguments and/or number of arguments.

Software Engineering Observation 16.6

Using an object-oriented programming approach can often simplify function calls by reducing the number of parameters to be passed. This benefit of object-oriented programming derives from the fact that encapsulation of data members and member functions within an object gives the member functions the right to access the data members.

Classes simplify programming because the client (or user of the class object) need only be concerned with the operations encapsulated or embedded in the object. Such operations are usually designed to be client-oriented rather than implementation-oriented. Clients need not be concerned with a class's implementation (although the client, of course, wants a correct and efficient implementation). Interfaces do change, but less frequently than implementations. When an implementation changes, implementation-dependent code must change accordingly. By hiding the implementation we eliminate the possibility of other program parts becoming dependent on the details of the class implementation.

Software Engineering Observation 16.7

A central theme of this book is "reuse, reuse, reuse." We will carefully discuss a number of techniques for "polishing" classes to encourage reuse. We focus on "crafting valuable classes" and creating valuable "software assets."

Often, classes do not have to be created "from scratch." Rather, they may be *derived* from other classes that provide attributes and behaviors the new classes can use. Or classes can include objects of other classes as members. Such *software reuse* can greatly enhance programmer productivity. Deriving new classes from existing classes is called *inheritance* and is discussed in Chapter 19. Including class objects as members of other classes is called *composition* (or *aggregation*) and is discussed in Chapter 17.

People new to object-oriented programming often express concern at the fact that objects must be quite large because they contain data and functions. Logically, this is true—the programmer may think of objects as containing data and functions. Physically, however, this is not true.

Performance Tip 16.2

Actually, objects contain only data, so objects are much smaller than if they also contained functions. Applying operator `sizeof` to a class name or to an object of that class will report only the size of the class's data. The compiler creates one copy (only) of the member functions separate from all objects of the class. All objects of the class share this one copy of the member functions. Each object, of course, needs its own copy of the class's data because these data can vary among the objects. The function code is nonmodifiable (also called reentrant code or pure procedure) and hence can be shared among all objects of one class.

16.3 Class Scope and Accessing Class Members

A class's data members (variables declared in the class definition) and member functions (functions declared in the class definition) belong to that *class's scope*. Nonmember functions are defined as *file scope*.

Within a class's scope, class members are immediately accessible by all that class's member functions and can be referenced by name. Outside a class's scope, class members are referenced through one of the handles on an object—an object name, a reference to an object or a pointer to an object. [We will see in Chapter 17 that an implicit handle is inserted by the compiler on every reference to a data member or member function in an object.]

Member functions of a class can be overloaded, but only by other member functions of the class. To overload a member function, simply provide in the class definition a prototype for each version of the overloaded function, and provide a separate function definition for each version of the function.

Variables defined in a member function have *function scope*—they are known only to that function. If a member function defines a variable with the same name as a variable with class scope, the class-scope variable is hidden by the function-scope variable in the function scope. Such a hidden variable can be accessed by preceding the operator with the class name followed by the scope resolution operator (::). Hidden global variables can be accessed with the unary scope resolution operator (see Chapter 15).

The operators used to access class members are identical to the operators used to access structure members. The *dot member selection operator (.)* is combined with an object's name or with a reference to an object to access the object's members. The *arrow member selection operator (->)* is combined with a pointer to an object to access that object's members.

Figure 16.3 uses a simple class called Count with public data member x of type int, and public member function print to illustrate accessing the members of a class with the member selection operators. The program defines three variables related to type Count—counter, counterRef (a reference to a Count object) and counterPtr (a pointer to a Count object). Variable counterRef is defined to reference counter, and variable counterPtr is defined to point to counter. *It is important to note that data member x has been made public here simply to demonstrate how public members are accessed off handles (i.e., a name, a reference or a pointer). As we have stated, data are typically made private, as we will do in most subsequent examples.* In Chapter 19, C++ Inheritance, we will sometimes make data protected.

```
1    // Fig. 16.3: fig16_03.cpp
2    // Demonstrating the class member access operators . and ->
3    //
4    // CAUTION: IN FUTURE EXAMPLES WE AVOID PUBLIC DATA!
5    #include <iostream>
6
7    using std::cout;
8    using std::endl;
9
10   // Simple class Count
11   class Count {
12   public:
13      int x;
```

Fig. 16.3   Accessing an object's data members and member functions through each type of object handle—through the object's name, through a reference and through a pointer to the object. (Part 1 of 2.)

```
14        void print() { cout << x << endl; }
15    }; // end class Count
16
17    int main()
18    {
19        Count counter,              // create counter object
20              *counterPtr = &counter, // pointer to counter
21              &counterRef = counter;  // reference to counter
22
23        cout << "Assign 7 to x and print using the object's name: ";
24        counter.x = 7;          // assign 7 to data member x
25        counter.print();        // call member function print
26
27        cout << "Assign 8 to x and print using a reference: ";
28        counterRef.x = 8;       // assign 8 to data member x
29        counterRef.print();     // call member function print
30
31        cout << "Assign 10 to x and print using a pointer: ";
32        counterPtr->x = 10;     // assign 10 to data member x
33        counterPtr->print();    // call member function print
34        return 0;
35    } // end function main
```

```
Assign 7 to x and print using the object's name: 7
Assign 8 to x and print using a reference: 8
Assign 10 to x and print using a pointer: 10
```

Fig. 16.3   Accessing an object's data members and member functions through each type of object handle—through the object's name, through a reference and through a pointer to the object. (Part 2 of 2.)

16.4 Separating Interface from Implementation

One of the fundamental principles of good software engineering is to separate interface from implementation. This makes it easier to modify programs. As far as clients of a class are concerned, changes in the class's implementation do not affect the client as long as the class's interface originally provided to the client is unchanged (the class's functionality could be expanded beyond the original interface).

Software Engineering Observation 16.8

Place the class declaration in a header file to be included by any client that wants to use the class. This forms the class's `public` interface (and provides the client with the function prototypes it needs to be able to call the class's member functions). Place the definitions of the class member functions in a source file. This forms the implementation of the class.

Software Engineering Observation 16.9

Clients of a class do not need access to the class's source code to use the class. The clients do, however, need to be able to link to the class's object code. This encourages independent software vendors (ISVs) to provide class libraries for sale or license. The ISVs provide in their products only the header files and the object modules. No proprietary information is revealed—as would be the case if source code were provided. The C++ user community benefits by having more ISV-produced class libraries available.

Actually, the situation is not quite this rosy. Header files do contain some portion of the implementation and hints about other portions of the implementation. Inline member functions, for example, need to be in a header file, so that when the compiler compiles a client, the client can include the `inline` function definition in place. Private members are listed in the class definition in the header file, so these members are visible to clients even though the clients may not access the `private` members.

Software Engineering Observation 16.10

Information important to the interface to a class should be included in the header file. Information that will be used only internally in the class and will not be needed by clients of the class should be included in the unpublished source file. This is yet another example of the principle of least privilege.

Figure 16.4 splits the program of Fig. 16.2 into multiple files. When building a C++ program, each class definition is normally placed in a *header file,* and that class's member function definitions are placed in *source-code files* of the same base name. The header files are included (via #include) in each file in which the class is used, and the source-code file is compiled and linked with the file containing the main program. See your compiler's documentation to determine how to compile and link programs consisting of multiple source files.

Figure 16.4 consists of the header file time1.h in which class Time is declared, the file time1.cpp in which the member functions of class Time are defined and the file fig16_04.cpp in which function main is defined. The output for this program is identical to the output of Fig. 16.2.

```
1   // Fig. 16.4: time1.h
2   // Declaration of the Time class.
3   // Member functions are defined in time1.cpp
4
5   // prevent multiple inclusions of header file
6   #ifndef TIME1_H
7   #define TIME1_H
8
9   // Time abstract data type definition
10  class Time {
11  public:
12     Time();                          // constructor
13     void setTime( int, int, int );   // set hour, minute, second
14     void printMilitary();            // print military time format
15     void printStandard();            // print standard time format
16  private:
17     int hour;      // 0 - 23
18     int minute;    // 0 - 59
19     int second;    // 0 - 59
20  }; // end class Time
21
22  #endif
```

Fig. 16.4   Separating Time class interface and implementation—time1.h.

```
23  // Fig. 16.4: time1.cpp
24  // Member function definitions for Time class.
25  #include <iostream>
26
27  using std::cout;
28
29  #include "time1.h"
30
31  // Time constructor initializes each data member to zero.
32  // Ensures all Time objects start in a consistent state.
33  Time::Time() { hour = minute = second = 0; }
34
35  // Set a new Time value using military time. Perform validity
36  // checks on the data values. Set invalid values to zero.
37  void Time::setTime( int h, int m, int s )
38  {
39     hour   = ( h >= 0 && h < 24 ) ? h : 0;
40     minute = ( m >= 0 && m < 60 ) ? m : 0;
41     second = ( s >= 0 && s < 60 ) ? s : 0;
42  } // end function setTime
43
44  // Print Time in military format
45  void Time::printMilitary()
46  {
47     cout << ( hour < 10 ? "0" : "" ) << hour << ":"
48          << ( minute < 10 ? "0" : "" ) << minute;
49  } // end function printMilitary
50
51  // Print time in standard format
52  void Time::printStandard()
53  {
54     cout << ( ( hour == 0 || hour == 12 ) ? 12 : hour % 12 )
55          << ":" << ( minute < 10 ? "0" : "" ) << minute
56          << ":" << ( second < 10 ? "0" : "" ) << second
57          << ( hour < 12 ? " AM" : " PM" );
58  } // end function printStandard
```

Fig. 16.4 Separating Time class interface and implementation—time1.cpp.

```
59  // Fig. 16.4: fig16_04.cpp
60  // Driver for Time1 class
61  // NOTE: Compile with time1.cpp
62  #include <iostream>
63
64  using std::cout;
65  using std::endl;
66
67  #include "time1.h"
68
```

Fig. 16.4 Separating Time class interface and implementation—fig16_04.cpp.
(Part 1 of 2.)

```
69    // Driver to test simple class Time
70    int main()
71    {
72       Time t;  // instantiate object t of class time
73
74       cout << "The initial military time is ";
75       t.printMilitary();
76       cout << "\nThe initial standard time is ";
77       t.printStandard();
78
79       t.setTime( 13, 27, 6 );
80       cout << "\n\nMilitary time after setTime is ";
81       t.printMilitary();
82       cout << "\nStandard time after setTime is ";
83       t.printStandard();
84
85       t.setTime( 99, 99, 99 );  // attempt invalid settings
86       cout << "\n\nAfter attempting invalid settings:\n"
87            << "Military time: ";
88       t.printMilitary();
89       cout << "\nStandard time: ";
90       t.printStandard();
91       cout << endl;
92       return 0;
93    } // end function main
```

```
The initial military time is 00:00
The initial standard time is 12:00:00 AM

Military time after setTime is 13:27
Standard time after setTime is 1:27:06 PM

After attempting invalid settings:
Military time: 00:00
Standard time: 12:00:00 AM
```

Fig. 16.4   Separating Time class interface and implementation—fig16_04.cpp. (Part 2 of 2.)

Note that the class declaration is enclosed in the following preprocessor code:

```
// prevent multiple inclusions of header file
#ifndef TIME1_H
#define TIME1_H
   ...
#endif
```

When we build larger programs, other definitions and declarations will also be placed in header files. The preceding preprocessor directives prevent the code between #ifndef (if not defined) and #endif from being included if the name TIME1_H has been defined. If the header has not been included previously in a file, the name TIME1_H is defined by the #define directive and the header file statements are included. If the header has been included previously, TIME1_H is defined already and the header file is not included again. Attempts to include a header file multiple times (inadvertently) typically occur in large programs with many header files that may themselves include other header files. [*Note:* The convention we use for the symbolic constant name in the preprocessor directives is simply the header file name with the underscore character replacing the period.]

Error-Prevention Tip 16.2

Use #ifndef, #define and #endif preprocessor directives to prevent header files from being included more than once in a program.

Good Programming Practice 16.2

Use the name of the header file with the period replaced by an underscore in the #ifndef and #define preprocessor directives of a header file.

16.5 Controlling Access to Members

The member access specifiers public and private (and protected, as we will see in Chapter 19, C++ Inheritance) are used to control access to a class's data members and member functions. The default access mode for classes is private so all members after the class header and before the first member access specifier are private. After each member access specifier, the mode that was invoked by that member access specifier applies until the next member access specifier or until the terminating right brace (}) of the class definition. The member access specifiers public, private and protected may be repeated, but such usage is rare and can be confusing.

A class's private members can be accessed only by member functions (and friends, as we will see in Chapter 17) of that class. The public members of a class may be accessed by any function in the program.

The primary purpose of public members is to present to the class's clients a view of the *services* (behaviors) the class provides. This set of services forms the *public interface* of the class. Clients of the class need not be concerned with how the class accomplishes its tasks. The private members of a class as well as the definitions of its public member functions are not accessible to the clients of a class. These components form the *implementation* of the class.

Software Engineering Observation 16.11

C++ encourages programs to be implementation independent. When the implementation of a class used by implementation-independent code changes, that code need not be modified. If any part of the interface of the class changes, the implementation-independent code must be recompiled.

Common Programming Error 16.5

An attempt by a function, which is not a member of a particular class (or a friend of that class), to access a private member of that class is a syntax error.

Figure 16.5 demonstrates that private class members are only accessible through the public class interface using public member functions. When this program is compiled, the compiler generates two errors stating that the private member specified in each statement is not accessible. Figure 16.5 includes time1.h and is compiled with time1.cpp from Fig. 16.4.

```cpp
1   // Fig. 16.5: fig16_05.cpp
2   // Demonstrate errors resulting from attempts
3   // to access private class members.
4   #include <iostream>
5
6   using std::cout;
7
8   #include "time1.h"
9
10  int main()
11  {
12     Time t;
13
14     // Error: 'Time::hour' is not accessible
15     t.hour = 7;
16
17     // Error: 'Time::minute' is not accessible
18     cout << "minute = " << t.minute;
19
20     return 0;
21  } // end function main
```

Borland C++ command-line compiler error messages

```
Time1.cpp:
Fig16_05.cpp:
Error E2247 Fig16_05.cpp 15:
  'Time::hour' is not accessible in function main()
Error E2247 Fig16_05.cpp 18:
  'Time::minute' is not accessible in function main()

*** 2 errors in Compile ***
```

Microsoft Visual C++ compiler error messages

```
Compiling...
Fig16_05.cpp
D:\Fig16_05.cpp(15) : error C2248: 'hour' : cannot access private
member declared in class 'Time'
D:\Fig16_05\time1.h(18) : see declaration of 'hour'
D:\Fig16_05.cpp(18) : error C2248: 'minute' : cannot access private
member declared in class 'Time'
D:\time1.h(19) : see declaration of 'minute'
Error executing cl.exe.

test.exe - 2 error(s), 0 warning(s)
```

Fig. 16.5 Erroneous attempt to access `private` members of a class .

Good Programming Practice 16.3

If you choose to list the `private` members first in a class definition, explicitly use the `private` member access specifier despite the fact that `private` is assumed by default. This improves program clarity. Our preference is to list the `public` members of a class first to emphasize the class's interface.

Good Programming Practice 16.4

Despite the fact that the `public` *and* `private` *member access specifiers may be repeated and intermixed, list all the* `public` *members of a class first in one group; then list all the* `private` *members in another group. This focuses the client's attention on the class's* `public` *interface, rather than on the class's implementation.*

Software Engineering Observation 16.12

Keep all the data members of a class `private`. *Provide* `public` *member functions to* set *the values of* `private` *data members and to* get *the values of* `private` *data members. This architecture helps hide the implementation of a class from its clients, which reduces bugs and improves program modifiability.*

A client of a class may be a member function of another class or it may be a global function (i.e., a C-like "loose" or "free" function in the file that is not a member function of any class).

The default access for members of a class is `private`. Access to members of a class may be explicitly set to `public`, `protected` (as we will see in Chapter 19) or `private`. The default access for `struct` members is `public`. Access to members of a `struct` also may be explicitly set to `public`, `protected` or `private`.

Software Engineering Observation 16.13

Class designers use `private`, `protected` *and* `public` *members to enforce the notion of information hiding and the principle of least privilege.*

Just because class data is `private` does not necessarily mean that clients cannot effect changes to that data. The data can be changed by member functions or `friend`s of that class. As we will see, these functions should be designed to ensure the integrity of the data.

Access to a class's `private` data should be carefully controlled by the use of member functions, called *access functions* (also called *accessor methods*). For example, to allow clients to read the value of `private` data, the class can provide a *get* function. To enable clients to modify `private` data, the class can provide a *set* function. Such modification would seem to violate the notion of `private` data. But a *set* member function can provide data validation capabilities (such as range checking) to ensure that the value is set properly. A *set* function can also translate between the form of the data used in the interface and the form used in the implementation. A *get* function need not expose the data in "raw" format; rather, the *get* function can edit the data and limit the view of the data the client will see.

Software Engineering Observation 16.14

The class designer need not provide set *and/or* get *functions for each* `private` *data item; these capabilities should be provided only when appropriate. If the service is useful to the client code, that service should be provided in the class's* `public` *interface.*

Error-Prevention Tip 16.3

Making the data members of a class `private` *and the member functions of the class* `public` *facilitates debugging because problems with data manipulations are localized to either the class's member functions or the* `friend`s *of the class.*

16.6 Access Functions and Utility Functions

Not all member functions need be made public to serve as part of the interface of a class. Some member functions remain private and serve as *utility functions* to the other functions of the class.

Software Engineering Observation 16.15

Member functions tend to fall into a number of different categories: functions that read and return the value of private data members; functions that set the value of private data members; functions that implement the services of the class; and functions that perform various mechanical chores for the class such as initializing class objects, assigning class objects, converting between classes and built-in types or between classes and other classes and handling memory for class objects.

Access functions can read or display data. Another common use for access functions is to test the truth or falsity of conditions—such functions are often called *predicate functions*. An example of a predicate function would be an isEmpty function for any container class—a class capable of holding many objects—such as a linked list, a stack or a queue. A program would test isEmpty before attempting to read another item from the container object. An isFull predicate function might test a container class object to determine if it has no additional room. A set of useful predicate functions for our Time class might be isAM and isPM.

Figure 16.6 demonstrates the notion of a *utility function* (also called a *helper function*). A utility function is not part of a class's interface; rather, it is a private member function that supports the operation of the class's public member functions. Utility functions are not intended to be used by clients of a class.

```
1   // Fig. 16.6: salesp.h
2   // SalesPerson class definition
3   // Member functions defined in salesp.cpp
4   #ifndef SALESP_H
5   #define SALESP_H
6
7   class SalesPerson {
8   public:
9      SalesPerson();                // constructor
10     void getSalesFromUser();      // get sales figures from keyboard
11     void setSales( int, double ); // User supplies one month's
12                                   // sales figures.
13     void printAnnualSales();
14
15  private:
16     double totalAnnualSales();    // utility function
17     double sales[ 12 ];           // 12 monthly sales figures
18  }; // end class SalesPerson
19
20  #endif
```

Fig. 16.6   Using a utility function—salesp.h.

```
21   // Fig. 16.6: salesp.cpp
22   // Member functions for class SalesPerson
23   #include <iostream>
24
25   using std::cout;
26   using std::cin;
27   using std::endl;
28
29   #include <iomanip>
30
31   using std::setprecision;
32   using std::setiosflags;
33   using std::ios;
34
35   #include "salesp.h"
36
37   // Constructor function initializes array
38   SalesPerson::SalesPerson()
39   {
40      for ( int i = 0; i < 12; i++ )
41         sales[ i ] = 0.0;
42   } // end SalesPerson constructor
43
44   // Function to get 12 sales figures from the user
45   // at the keyboard
46   void SalesPerson::getSalesFromUser()
47   {
48      double salesFigure;
49
50      for ( int i = 1; i <= 12; i++ ) {
51         cout << "Enter sales amount for month " << i << ": ";
52
53         cin >> salesFigure;
54         setSales( i, salesFigure );
55      } // end for
56   } // end function getSalesFromUser
57
58   // Function to set one of the 12 monthly sales figures.
59   // Note that the month value must be from 0 to 11.
60   void SalesPerson::setSales( int month, double amount )
61   {
62      if ( month >= 1 && month <= 12 && amount > 0 )
63         sales[ month - 1 ] = amount; // adjust for subscripts 0-11
64      else
65         cout << "Invalid month or sales figure" << endl;
66   } // end function setSales
67
68   // Print the total annual sales
69   void SalesPerson::printAnnualSales()
70   {
71      cout << setprecision( 2 )
72           << setiosflags( ios::fixed | ios::showpoint )
73           << "\nThe total annual sales are: $"
```

Fig. 16.6 Using a utility function—salesp.cpp. (Part 1 of 2.)

```
74                 << totalAnnualSales() << endl;
75   } // end function printAnnualSales
76
77   // Private utility function to total annual sales
78   double SalesPerson::totalAnnualSales()
79   {
80      double total = 0.0;
81
82      for ( int i = 0; i < 12; i++ )
83         total += sales[ i ];
84
85      return total;
86   } // end function totalAnnualSales
```

Fig. 16.6   Using a utility function—`salesp.cpp`. (Part 2 of 2.)

```
87   // Fig. 16.6: fig16_06.cpp
88   // Demonstrating a utility function
89   // Compile with salesp.cpp
90   #include "salesp.h"
91
92   int main()
93   {
94      SalesPerson s;          // create SalesPerson object s
95
96      s.getSalesFromUser();   // note simple sequential code
97      s.printAnnualSales();   // no control structures in main
98      return 0;
99   } // end function main
```

```
Enter sales amount for month 1: 5314.76
Enter sales amount for month 2: 4292.38
Enter sales amount for month 3: 4589.83
Enter sales amount for month 4: 5534.03
Enter sales amount for month 5: 4376.34
Enter sales amount for month 6: 5698.45
Enter sales amount for month 7: 4439.22
Enter sales amount for month 8: 5893.57
Enter sales amount for month 9: 4909.67
Enter sales amount for month 10: 5123.45
Enter sales amount for month 11: 4024.97
Enter sales amount for month 12: 5923.92

The total annual sales are: $60120.59
```

Fig. 16.6   Using a utility function—`fig16_06.cpp`.

Class `SalesPerson` has an array of 12 monthly sales figures initialized by the constructor to zero and set to user-supplied values by function `setSales`. Member function `printAnnualSales` prints the total sales for the last 12 months. Utility function `totalAnnualSales` totals the 12 monthly sales figures for the benefit of `printAnnualSales`. Member function `printAnnualSales` edits the sales figures into dollar amount format.

Note that `main` includes only a simple sequence of member function calls—there are no control structures.

Software Engineering Observation 16.16

A phenomenon of object-oriented programming is that once a class is defined, creating and manipulating objects of that class usually involves issuing only a simple sequence of member function calls—few, if any, control structures are needed. By contrast, it is common to have control structures in the implementation of a class's member functions.

16.7 Initializing Class Objects: Constructors

When a class object is created, its members can be initialized by that class's *constructor* function. A constructor is a class member function with the same name as the class. The programmer provides the constructor, which is then invoked whenever an object of that class is created (instantiated). Constructors may be overloaded to provide a variety of means for initializing objects of a class. Data members must either be initialized in a constructor of the class or their values may be *set* later after the object is created. However, it is considered a good programming and software engineering practice to ensure that an object is fully initialized before the client code invokes the object's member functions. In general, you should not rely on the client code to ensure that an object gets initialized properly.

Common Programming Error 16.6

Data members of a class cannot be initialized in the class definition.

Common Programming Error 16.7

Attempting to declare a return type for a constructor and/or attempting to return a value from a constructor are syntax errors.

Good Programming Practice 16.5

When appropriate (almost always), provide a constructor to ensure that every object is properly initialized with meaningful values. Pointer data members, in particular, should be initialized to some legitimate pointer value or to 0.

Error-Prevention Tip 16.4

Every member function (and `friend`) that modifies the `private` data members of an object should ensure that the data remains in a consistent state.

When an object of a class is declared, *initializers* can be provided in parentheses to the right of the object name and before the semicolon. These initializers are passed as arguments to the class's constructor. We will soon see several examples of these *constructor calls*. [*Note:* Although programmers do not explicitly call constructors, programmers can still provide data that get passed to constructors as arguments.]

16.8 Using Default Arguments with Constructors

The constructor from `time1.cpp` (Fig. 16.4) initialized `hour`, `minute` and `second` to 0 (i.e., 12 midnight in military time). Constructors can contain default arguments. Figure 16.7 redefines the `Time` constructor function to include default arguments of zero for each variable. By providing default arguments to the constructor, even if no values are provided in a constructor call, the object is still guaranteed to be initialized to a consistent state, due to the default arguments. A programmer-supplied constructor that defaults all its arguments (or explicitly requires no arguments) is also a *default constructor*, i.e., a constructor that can be invoked with no arguments. There can be only one default constructor per class.

```cpp
1   // Fig. 16.7: time2.h
2   // Declaration of the Time class.
3   // Member functions are defined in time2.cpp
4
5   // preprocessor directives that
6   // prevent multiple inclusions of header file
7   #ifndef TIME2_H
8   #define TIME2_H
9
10  // Time abstract data type definition
11  class Time {
12  public:
13     Time( int = 0, int = 0, int = 0 );  // default constructor
14     void setTime( int, int, int );  // set hour, minute, second
15     void printMilitary();           // print military time format
16     void printStandard();           // print standard time format
17  private:
18     int hour;      // 0 - 23
19     int minute;    // 0 - 59
20     int second;    // 0 - 59
21  }; // end class Time
22
23  #endif
```

Fig. 16.7   Using a constructor with default arguments—`time2.h`.

```cpp
24  // Fig. 16.7: time2.cpp
25  // Member function definitions for Time class.
26  #include <iostream>
27
28  using std::cout;
29
30  #include "time2.h"
31
32  // Time constructor initializes each data member to zero.
33  // Ensures all Time objects start in a consistent state.
34  Time::Time( int hr, int min, int sec )
35     { setTime( hr, min, sec ); }
36
37  // Set a new Time value using military time. Perform validity
38  // checks on the data values. Set invalid values to zero.
39  void Time::setTime( int h, int m, int s )
40  {
41     hour   = ( h >= 0 && h < 24 ) ? h : 0;
42     minute = ( m >= 0 && m < 60 ) ? m : 0;
43     second = ( s >= 0 && s < 60 ) ? s : 0;
44  } // end function setTime
```

Fig. 16.7   Using a constructor with default arguments—`time2.cpp`. (Part 1 of 2.)

```
45
46   // Print Time in military format
47   void Time::printMilitary()
48   {
49      cout << ( hour < 10 ? "0" : "" ) << hour << ":"
50           << ( minute < 10 ? "0" : "" ) << minute;
51   } // end function printMilitary
52
53   // Print Time in standard format
54   void Time::printStandard()
55   {
56      cout << ( ( hour == 0 || hour == 12 ) ? 12 : hour % 12 )
57           << ":" << ( minute < 10 ? "0" : "" ) << minute
58           << ":" << ( second < 10 ? "0" : "" ) << second
59           << ( hour < 12 ? " AM" : " PM" );
60   } // end function printStandard
```

Fig. 16.7   Using a constructor with default arguments—`time2.cpp`. (Part 2 of 2.)

```
61   // Fig. 16.7: fig16_07.cpp
62   // Demonstrating a default constructor
63   // function for class Time.
64   #include <iostream>
65
66   using std::cout;
67   using std::endl;
68
69   #include "time2.h"
70
71   int main()
72   {
73      Time t1,                // all arguments defaulted
74           t2( 2 ),           // minute and second defaulted
75           t3( 21, 34 ),      // second defaulted
76           t4( 12, 25, 42 ),  // all values specified
77           t5( 27, 74, 99 );  // all bad values specified
78
79      cout << "Constructed with:\n"
80           << "all arguments defaulted:\n   ";
81      t1.printMilitary();
82      cout << "\n   ";
83      t1.printStandard();
84
85      cout << "\nhour specified; minute and second defaulted:"
86           << "\n   ";
87      t2.printMilitary();
88      cout << "\n   ";
89      t2.printStandard();
90
91      cout << "\nhour and minute specified; second defaulted:"
92           << "\n   ";
93      t3.printMilitary();
```

Fig. 16.7   Using a constructor with default arguments—`fig16_07.cpp`. (Part 1 of 2.)

```
94        cout << "\n    ";
95        t3.printStandard();
96
97        cout << "\nhour, minute, and second specified:"
98             << "\n    ";
99        t4.printMilitary();
100       cout << "\n    ";
101       t4.printStandard();
102
103       cout << "\nall invalid values specified:"
104            << "\n    ";
105       t5.printMilitary();
106       cout << "\n    ";
107       t5.printStandard();
108       cout << endl;
109
110       return 0;
111   } // end function main
```

```
Constructed with:
all arguments defaulted:
    00:00
    12:00:00 AM
hour specified; minute and second defaulted:
    02:00
    2:00:00 AM
hour and minute specified; second defaulted:
    21:34
    9:34:00 PM
hour, minute, and second specified:
    12:25
    12:25:42 PM
all invalid values specified:
    00:00
    12:00:00 AM
```

Fig. 16.7   Using a constructor with default arguments—`fig16_07.cpp`. (Part 2 of 2.)

In this program, the constructor calls member function `setTime` with the values passed to the constructor (or the default values) to ensure that the value supplied for `hour` is in the range 0 to 23, and that the values for `minute` and `second` are each in the range 0 to 59. If a value is out of range, it is set to zero by `setTime` (this is an example of ensuring that a data member remains in a consistent state).

Note that the `Time` constructor could be written to include the same statements as member function `setTime`. This may be slightly more efficient because the extra call to `setTime` is eliminated. However, coding the `Time` constructor and member function `setTime` identically makes maintenance of this program more difficult. If the implementation of member function `setTime` changes, the implementation of the `Time` constructor should change accordingly. Having the `Time` constructor call `setTime` directly requires any changes to the implementation of `setTime` to be made only once. This reduces the likelihood of a programming error when altering the implementation. Also, the performance of the `Time` constructor can be enhanced by explicitly declaring the constructor `inline` or by defining the constructor in the class definition (which implicitly `inlines` the function definition).

Software Engineering Observation 16.17

If a member function of a class already provides all or part of the functionality required by a constructor (or other member function) of the class, call that member function from the constructor (or other member function). This simplifies the maintenance of the code and reduces the likelihood of an error if the implementation of the code is modified. As a general rule: Avoid repeating code.

Good Programming Practice 16.6

Declare default function argument values only in the function prototype within the class definition in the header file.

Common Programming Error 16.8

Specifying default initializers for the same member function in both a header file and in the member function definition.

[*Note:* Any change to the default arguments of a method requires the client code to be recompiled. If it is likely that the default argument values will change, use overloaded functions instead. Thus, if the implementation of a member function changes, the client code need not be recompiled.]

Figure 16.7 initializes five `Time` objects—one with all three arguments defaulted in the constructor call, one with one argument specified, one with two arguments specified, one with three arguments specified and one with three invalid arguments specified. The contents of each object's data members after instantiation and initialization are displayed.

If no constructor is defined for a class, the compiler creates a default constructor. Such a constructor does not perform any initialization, so when the object is created, it is not guaranteed to be in a consistent state.

Software Engineering Observation 16.18

It is possible for a class not to have a default constructor if any constructors are defined and none of them is explicitly a default constructor.

16.9 Using Destructors

A *destructor* is a special member function of a class. The name of the destructor for a class is the *tilde (~)* character followed by the class name. This naming convention has intuitive appeal, because as we will see in a later chapter, the tilde operator is the bitwise complement operator, and, in a sense, the destructor is the complement of the constructor.

A class's destructor is called when an object is destroyed—e.g., for automatic objects when program execution leaves the scope in which an object of that class was instantiated. The destructor does not actually destroy the object—it performs *termination housekeeping* before the system reclaims the memory so that memory may be reused to hold new objects.

A destructor receives no parameters and returns no value. A class may have only one destructor—destructor overloading is not allowed.

Common Programming Error 16.9

It is a syntax error to attempt to pass arguments to a destructor, to specify a return type for a destructor (even `void` cannot be specified), to return values from a destructor or to overload a destructor.

Notice that destructors have not been provided for the classes presented so far. We will soon see several examples of classes with useful destructors. In Chapter 18, we will see that destructors are appropriate for classes whose objects contain dynamically allocated memory (for arrays and strings, for example). In Chapter 17, we discuss how to dynamically allocate and deallocate storage.

Software Engineering Observation 16.19

As we will see (throughout the remainder of the book), constructors and destructors have much greater prominence in C++ and object-oriented programming than is possible to convey after only our brief introduction here.

16.10 When Constructors and Destructors Are Called

Constructors and destructors are called automatically. The order in which these function calls are made depends on the order in which execution enters and leaves the scope in which objects are instantiated. Generally, destructor calls are made in the reverse order of the constructor calls. However, as we will see in Fig. 16.8, the storage class of objects can alter the order in which the destructors are called.

Constructors are called for objects defined in global scope before any other function (including `main`) in that file begins execution (although the order of execution of global object constructors between files is not guaranteed). The corresponding destructors are called when `main` terminates or the `exit` function (see Chapter 14) is called. Destructors are not called for global objects if the program is terminated with a call to function `abort` (see Chapter 14).

Constructors are called for automatic local objects when execution reaches the point where the objects are defined. Corresponding destructors are called when the objects leave scope (i.e., the block in which they are defined exits). Constructors and destructors for automatic objects are called each time the objects enter and leave scope. Destructors are not called for automatic objects if the program is terminated with a call to functions `exit` or `abort`.

Constructors are called for `static` local objects only once when execution first reaches the point where the objects are defined. Corresponding destructors are called when `main` terminates or the `exit` function is called. Destructors are not called for `static` objects if the program is terminated with a call to function `abort`.

The program of Fig. 16.8 demonstrates the order in which constructors and destructors are called for objects of type `CreateAndDestroy` in several scopes. The program defines `first` in global scope. Its constructor is called as the program begins execution and its destructor is called at program termination after all other objects are destroyed.

```
1   // Fig. 16.8: create.h
2   // Definition of class CreateAndDestroy.
3   // Member functions defined in create.cpp.
4   #ifndef CREATE_H
5   #define CREATE_H
6
7   class CreateAndDestroy {
8   public:
```

Fig. 16.8 Demonstrating the order in which constructors and destructors are called—
`create.h`. (Part 1 of 2.)

```
 9        CreateAndDestroy( int );   // constructor
10        ~CreateAndDestroy();       // destructor
11     private:
12        int data;
13     }; // end class CreateAndDestroy
14
15     #endif
```

Fig. 16.8   Demonstrating the order in which constructors and destructors are called—
`create.h`. (Part 2 of 2.)

```
16     // Fig. 16.8: create.cpp
17     // Member function definitions for class CreateAndDestroy
18     #include <iostream>
19
20     using std::cout;
21     using std::endl;
22
23     #include "create.h"
24
25     CreateAndDestroy::CreateAndDestroy( int value )
26     {
27        data = value;
28        cout << "Object " << data << "   constructor";
29     } // end CreateAndDestroy constructor
30
31     CreateAndDestroy::~CreateAndDestroy()
32        { cout << "Object " << data << "   destructor " << endl; }
```

Fig. 16.8   Demonstrating the order in which constructors and destructors are called—
`create.cpp`.

```
33     // Fig. 16.8: fig16_08.cpp
34     // Demonstrating the order in which constructors and
35     // destructors are called.
36     #include <iostream>
37
38     using std::cout;
39     using std::endl;
40
41     #include "create.h"
42
43     void create( void );   // prototype
44
45     CreateAndDestroy first( 1 );   // global object
46
47     int main()
48     {
49        cout << "   (global created before main)" << endl;
50
```

Fig. 16.8   Demonstrating the order in which constructors and destructors are called—
`fig16_08.cpp`. (Part 1 of 2.)

```
51          CreateAndDestroy second( 2 );          // local object
52          cout << "    (local automatic in main)" << endl;
53
54          static CreateAndDestroy third( 3 );   // local object
55          cout << "    (local static in main)" << endl;
56
57          create();   // call function to create objects
58
59          CreateAndDestroy fourth( 4 );          // local object
60          cout << "    (local automatic in main)" << endl;
61          return 0;
62       } // end function main
63
64       // Function to create objects
65       void create( void )
66       {
67          CreateAndDestroy fifth( 5 );
68          cout << "    (local automatic in create)" << endl;
69
70          static CreateAndDestroy sixth( 6 );
71          cout << "    (local static in create)" << endl;
72
73          CreateAndDestroy seventh( 7 );
74          cout << "    (local automatic in create)" << endl;
75       } // end function create
```

```
Object 1    constructor    (global created before main)
Object 2    constructor    (local automatic in main)
Object 3    constructor    (local static in main)
Object 5    constructor    (local automatic in create)
Object 6    constructor    (local static in create)
Object 7    constructor    (local automatic in create)
Object 7    destructor
Object 5    destructor
Object 4    constructor    (local automatic in main)
Object 4    destructor
Object 2    destructor
Object 6    destructor
Object 3    destructor
Object 1    destructor
```

Fig. 16.8   Demonstrating the order in which constructors and destructors are called—
           fig16_08.cpp. (Part 2 of 2.)

Function main declares three objects. Objects second and fourth are local automatic objects, and object third is a static local object. The constructors for each of these objects are called when execution reaches the point where each object is declared. The destructors for objects fourth and second are called in that order when the end of main is reached. Object third is static; therefore, it exists until program termination. The destructor for object third is called before the destructor for first, but after all other objects are destroyed.

Function `create` declares three objects—`fifth` and `seventh` are local automatic objects, and `sixth` is a `static` local object. The destructors for objects `seventh` and `fifth` are called in that order when the end of `create` is reached. Object `sixth` is `static`, so it exists until program termination. The destructor for `sixth` is called before the destructors for `third` and `first`, but after all other objects are destroyed.

16.11 Using Data Members and Member Functions

A class's `private` data members can be accessed only by member functions (and `friend`s) of the class. A typical manipulation might be the adjustment of a customer's bank balance (e.g., a `private` data member of a class `BankAccount`) by a member function `computeInterest`.

Classes often provide `public` member functions to allow clients of the class to *set* (i.e., write) or *get* (i.e., read) the values of `private` data members. These functions need not be called *set* and *get* specifically, but they often are. More specifically, a member function that *set*s data member `interestRate` would typically be named `setInterestRate`, and a member function that *get*s the `interestRate` would typically be called `getInterestRate`. *Get* functions are also commonly called "query" functions.

It may seem that providing both *set* and *get* capabilities is essentially the same as making the data members `public`. This is yet another subtlety of C++ that makes the language so desirable for software engineering. If a data member is `public`, then the data member may be read or written at will by any function in the program. If a data member is `private`, a `public` *get* function would certainly seem to allow other functions to read the data at will, but the *get* function could control the formatting and display of the data. A `public` *set* function could—and most likely would—carefully scrutinize any attempt to modify the value of the data member. This would ensure that the new value is appropriate for that data item. For example, an attempt to *set* the day of the month to 37 could be rejected, an attempt to *set* a person's weight to a negative value could be rejected, an attempt to *set* a numeric quantity to an alphabetic value could be rejected, an attempt to *set* a grade on an exam to 185 (when the proper range is zero to 100) could be rejected, etc.

Software Engineering Observation 16.20

Making data members `private` *and controlling access, especially write access, to those data members through* `public` *member functions helps ensure data integrity.*

Error-Prevention Tip 16.5

The benefits of data integrity are not automatic simply because data members are made `private`*—the programmer must provide the validity checking. C++ does, however, provide a framework in which programmers can design better programs in a convenient manner.*

Good Programming Practice 16.7

Member functions that set *the values of* `private` *data should verify that the intended new values are proper; if they are not, the* set *functions should place the* `private` *data members into an appropriate consistent state.*

The client of a class should be notified when an attempt is made to assign an invalid value to a data member. A class's *set* functions are often written to return values indicating that an attempt was made to assign invalid data to an object of the class. This enables clients of the class to test the return values of *set* functions to determine if the object they are manipulating is a valid object and to take appropriate action if the object is not valid.

Figure 16.9 extends our Time class to include *get* and *set* functions for the hour, minute and second private data members. The *set* functions strictly control the setting of the data members. Attempts to *set* any data member to an incorrect value cause the data member to be set to zero (thus leaving the data member in a consistent state). Each *get* function simply returns the appropriate data member's value. The program first uses the *set* functions to *set* the private data members of Time object t to valid values, then uses the *get* functions to retrieve the values for output. Next, the *set* functions attempt to *set* the hour and second members to invalid values and the minute member to a valid value, then the *get* functions retrieve the values for output. The output confirms that invalid values cause the data members to be *set* to zero. Finally, the program *sets* the time to 11:58:00 and increments the minute value by 3 with a call to function incrementMinutes. Function incrementMinutes is a nonmember function that uses the *get* and *set* member functions to increment the minute member properly. Although this works, it incurs the performance burden of issuing multiple function calls. In the next chapter, we discuss the notion of friend functions as a means of eliminating this performance burden.

```cpp
1   // Fig. 16.9: time3.h
2   // Declaration of the Time class.
3   // Member functions defined in time3.cpp
4
5   // preprocessor directives that
6   // prevent multiple inclusions of header file
7   #ifndef TIME3_H
8   #define TIME3_H
9
10  class Time {
11  public:
12      Time( int = 0, int = 0, int = 0 );   // constructor
13
14      // set functions
15      void setTime( int, int, int );   // set hour, minute, second
16      void setHour( int );    // set hour
17      void setMinute( int );  // set minute
18      void setSecond( int );  // set second
19
20      // get functions
21      int getHour();          // return hour
22      int getMinute();        // return minute
23      int getSecond();        // return second
24
25      void printMilitary();   // output military time
26      void printStandard();   // output standard time
27
28  private:
29      int hour;               // 0 - 23
30      int minute;             // 0 - 59
31      int second;             // 0 - 59
32  }; // end class Time
```

Fig. 16.9 Using *set* and *get* functions—time3.h. (Part 1 of 2.)

```
33
34    #endif
```

Fig. 16.9 Using *set* and *get* functions—`time3.h`. (Part 2 of 2.)

```
35    // Fig. 16.9: time3.cpp
36    // Member function definitions for Time class.
37    #include <iostream>
38
39    using std::cout;
40
41    #include "time3.h"
42
43    // Constructor function to initialize private data.
44    // Calls member function setTime to set variables.
45    // Default values are 0 (see class definition).
46    Time::Time( int hr, int min, int sec )
47       { setTime( hr, min, sec ); }
48
49    // Set the values of hour, minute, and second.
50    void Time::setTime( int h, int m, int s )
51    {
52       setHour( h );
53       setMinute( m );
54       setSecond( s );
55    } // end function setTime
56
57    // Set the hour value
58    void Time::setHour( int h )
59       { hour = ( h >= 0 && h < 24 ) ? h : 0; }
60
61    // Set the minute value
62    void Time::setMinute( int m )
63       { minute = ( m >= 0 && m < 60 ) ? m : 0; }
64
65    // Set the second value
66    void Time::setSecond( int s )
67       { second = ( s >= 0 && s < 60 ) ? s : 0; }
68
69    // Get the hour value
70    int Time::getHour() { return hour; }
71
72    // Get the minute value
73    int Time::getMinute() { return minute; }
74
75    // Get the second value
76    int Time::getSecond() { return second; }
77
78    // Print time is military format
79    void Time::printMilitary()
80    {
81       cout << ( hour < 10 ? "0" : "" ) << hour << ":"
```

Fig. 16.9 Using set and get functions—`time3.cpp`. (Part 1 of 2.)

```
82            << ( minute < 10 ? "0" : "" ) << minute;
83      } // end function printMilitary
84
85      // Print time in standard format
86      void Time::printStandard()
87      {
88         cout << ( ( hour == 0 || hour == 12 ) ? 12 : hour % 12 )
89              << ":" << ( minute < 10 ? "0" : "" ) << minute
90              << ":" << ( second < 10 ? "0" : "" ) << second
91              << ( hour < 12 ? " AM" : " PM" );
92      } // end function printStandard
```

Fig. 16.9   Using set and get functions—`time3.cpp`. (Part 2 of 2.)

```
93      // Fig. 16.9: fig16_09.cpp
94      // Demonstrating the Time class set and get functions
95      #include <iostream>
96
97      using std::cout;
98      using std::endl;
99
100     #include "time3.h"
101
102     void incrementMinutes( Time &, const int );
103
104     int main()
105     {
106        Time t;
107
108        t.setHour( 17 );
109        t.setMinute( 34 );
110        t.setSecond( 25 );
111
112        cout << "Result of setting all valid values:\n"
113             << "  Hour: " << t.getHour()
114             << "  Minute: " << t.getMinute()
115             << "  Second: " << t.getSecond();
116
117        t.setHour( 234 );    // invalid hour set to 0
118        t.setMinute( 43 );
119        t.setSecond( 6373 ); // invalid second set to 0
120
121        cout << "\n\nResult of attempting to set invalid hour and"
122             << " second:\n  Hour: " << t.getHour()
123             << "  Minute: " << t.getMinute()
124             << "  Second: " << t.getSecond() << "\n\n";
125
126        t.setTime( 11, 58, 0 );
127        incrementMinutes( t, 3 );
128
129        return 0;
130     } // end function main
```

Fig. 16.9   Using *set* and *get* functions—`fig16_09.cpp`. (Part 1 of 2.)

```
131
132   void incrementMinutes( Time &tt, const int count )
133   {
134      cout << "Incrementing minute " << count
135           << " times:\nStart time: ";
136      tt.printStandard();
137
138      for ( int i = 0; i < count; i++ ) {
139         tt.setMinute( ( tt.getMinute() + 1 ) % 60 );
140
141         if ( tt.getMinute() == 0 )
142            tt.setHour( ( tt.getHour() + 1 ) % 24 );
143
144         cout << "\nminute + 1: ";
145         tt.printStandard();
146      } // end for
147
148      cout << endl;
149   } // end function incrementMinutes
```

```
Result of setting all valid values:
  Hour: 17  Minute: 34  Second: 25

Result of attempting to set invalid hour and second:
  Hour: 0  Minute: 43  Second: 0
```

```
Incrementing minute 3 times:
Start time: 11:58:00 AM
minute + 1: 11:59:00 AM
minute + 1: 12:00:00 PM
minute + 1: 12:01:00 PM
```

Fig. 16.9   Using *set* and *get* functions—`fig16_09.cpp`. (Part 2 of 2.)

Common Programming Error 16.10

A constructor can call other member functions of the class such as set *or* get *functions, but because the constructor is initializing the object, the data members may not yet be in a consistent state. Using data members before they have been properly initialized can cause logic errors.*

Using *set* functions is certainly important from a software engineering standpoint because they can perform validity checking. Both *set* and *get* functions have another important software engineering advantage.

Software Engineering Observation 16.21

Accessing `private` *data through* set *and* get *member functions not only protects the data members from receiving invalid values, but it also insulates clients of the class from the representation of the data members. Thus, if the representation of the data changes for some reason (typically to reduce the amount of storage required or to improve performance), only the member functions need to change—the clients need not change as long as the interface provided by the member functions remains the same. The clients may, however, need to be recompiled.*

16.12 A Subtle Trap: Returning a Reference to a private Data Member

A reference to an object is an alias for the *name* of the object and hence may be used on the left side of an assignment statement. In this context, the reference makes a perfectly acceptable *lvalue* that can receive a value. One way to use this capability (unfortunately!) is to have a public member function of a class return a non-const reference to a private data member of that class.

Figure 16.10 uses a simplified Time class to demonstrate returning a reference to a private data member. Such a return actually makes a call to function badSetHour an alias for the private data member hour! The function call can be used in any way that the private data member can be used, including as an *lvalue* in an assignment statement!

```
1    // Fig. 16.10: time4.h
2    // Declaration of the Time class.
3    // Member functions defined in time4.cpp
4
5    // preprocessor directives that
6    // prevent multiple inclusions of header file
7    #ifndef TIME4_H
8    #define TIME4_H
9
10   class Time {
11   public:
12      Time( int = 0, int = 0, int = 0 );
13      void setTime( int, int, int );
14      int getHour();
15      int &badSetHour( int );   // DANGEROUS reference return
16   private:
17      int hour;
18      int minute;
19      int second;
20   }; // end class Time
21
22   #endif
```

Fig. 16.10 Returning a reference to a private data member—time4.h.

```
23   // Fig. 16.10: time4.cpp
24   // Member function definitions for Time class.
25   #include "time4.h"
26
27   // Constructor function to initialize private data.
28   // Calls member function setTime to set variables.
29   // Default values are 0 (see class definition).
30   Time::Time( int hr, int min, int sec )
31      { setTime( hr, min, sec ); }
32
33   // Set the values of hour, minute, and second.
34   void Time::setTime( int h, int m, int s )
35   {
```

Fig. 16.10 Returning a reference to a private data member—time4.cpp. (Part 1 of 2.)

```
36      hour   = ( h >= 0 && h < 24 ) ? h : 0;
37      minute = ( m >= 0 && m < 60 ) ? m : 0;
38      second = ( s >= 0 && s < 60 ) ? s : 0;
39   } // end function setTime
40
41   // Get the hour value
42   int Time::getHour() { return hour; }
43
44   // POOR PROGRAMMING PRACTICE:
45   // Returning a reference to a private data member.
46   int &Time::badSetHour( int hh )
47   {
48      hour = ( hh >= 0 && hh < 24 ) ? hh : 0;
49
50      return hour;  // DANGEROUS reference return
51   } // end function badSetHour
```

Fig. 16.10 Returning a reference to a `private` data member—`time4.cpp`. (Part 2 of 2.)

```
52   // Fig. 16.10: fig16_10.cpp
53   // Demonstrating a public member function that
54   // returns a reference to a private data member.
55   // Time class has been trimmed for this example.
56   #include <iostream>
57
58   using std::cout;
59   using std::endl;
60
61   #include "time4.h"
62
63   int main()
64   {
65      Time t;
66      int &hourRef = t.badSetHour( 20 );
67
68      cout << "Hour before modification: " << hourRef;
69      hourRef = 30;  // modification with invalid value
70      cout << "\nHour after modification: " << t.getHour();
71
72      // Dangerous: Function call that returns
73      // a reference can be used as an lvalue!
74      t.badSetHour( 12 ) = 74;
75      cout << "\n\n*********************************\n"
76           << "POOR PROGRAMMING PRACTICE!!!!!!!!\n"
77           << "badSetHour as an lvalue, Hour: "
78           << t.getHour()
79           << "\n*********************************" << endl;
80
81      return 0;
82   }
```

Fig. 16.10 Returning a reference to a `private` data member—`fig16_10.cpp`.
        (Part 1 of 2.)

```
Hour before modification: 20
Hour after modification: 30


**********************************
POOR PROGRAMMING PRACTICE!!!!!!!!
badSetHour as an lvalue, Hour: 74
**********************************
```

Fig. 16.10 Returning a reference to a `private` data member—`fig16_10.cpp`.
(Part 2 of 2.)

 Good Programming Practice 16.8

Never have a `public` member function return a non-`const` reference (or a pointer) to a `private` data member. Returning such a reference violates the encapsulation of the class. In fact, returning any reference or pointer to `private` data still makes the client code dependent on the representation of the class's data. So, returning pointers or references to `private` data should be avoided.

The program begins by declaring `Time` object `t` and reference `hourRef` that is assigned the reference returned by the call `t.badSetHour(20)`. The program displays the value of the alias `hourRef`. Next, the alias is used to set the value of `hour` to 30 (an invalid value) and the value is displayed again. Finally, the function call itself is used as an *lvalue* and assigned the value 74 (another invalid value), and the value is displayed.

16.13 Assignment by Default Memberwise Copy

The assignment operator (=) can be used to assign an object to another object of the same type. Such assignment is by default performed by *memberwise copy*—each member of one object is copied (assigned) individually to the same member in another object (see Fig. 16.11). [*Note:* Memberwise copy can cause serious problems when used with a class whose data members contain dynamically allocated storage; in Chapter 18, C++ Operator Overloading, we will discuss these problems and show how to deal with them.]

```
1   // Fig. 16.11: fig16_11.cpp
2   // Demonstrating that class objects can be assigned
3   // to each other using default memberwise copy
4   #include <iostream>
5
6   using std::cout;
7   using std::endl;
8
9   // Simple Date class
10  class Date {
11  public:
12     Date( int = 1, int = 1, int = 1990 ); // default constructor
13     void print();
14  private:
15     int month;
```

Fig. 16.11 Assigning one object to another with default memberwise copy. (Part 1 of 2.)

```
16       int day;
17       int year;
18    }; // end class Date
19
20    // Simple Date constructor with no range checking
21    Date::Date( int m, int d, int y )
22    {
23       month = m;
24       day = d;
25       year = y;
26    } // end Date constructor
27
28    // Print the Date in the form mm-dd-yyyy
29    void Date::print()
30       { cout << month << '-' << day << '-' << year; }
31
32    int main()
33    {
34       Date date1( 7, 4, 1993 ), date2;  // d2 defaults to 1/1/90
35
36       cout << "date1 = ";
37       date1.print();
38       cout << "\ndate2 = ";
39       date2.print();
40
41       date2 = date1;   // assignment by default memberwise copy
42       cout << "\n\nAfter default memberwise copy, date2 = ";
43       date2.print();
44       cout << endl;
45
46       return 0;
47    } // end function main
```

```
date1 = 7-4-1993
date2 = 1-1-1990

After default memberwise copy, date2 = 7-4-1993
```

Fig. 16.11 Assigning one object to another with default memberwise copy. (Part 2 of 2.)

Objects may be passed as function arguments and may be returned from functions. Such passing and returning is performed call-by-value by default—a copy of the object is passed or returned (we present several examples in Chapter 18).

Performance Tip 16.3

Passing an object call-by-value is good from a security standpoint because the called function has no access to the original object, but call-by-value can degrade performance when making a copy of a large object. An object can be passed call-by-reference by passing either a pointer or a reference to the object. Call-by-reference offers good performance but is weaker from a security standpoint because the called function is given access to the original object. Call-by-const-reference is a safe, good-performing alternative.

16.14 Software Reusability

People who write object-oriented programs concentrate on implementing useful classes. There is a tremendous opportunity to capture and catalog classes so that they can be accessed by large segments of the programming community. Many *class libraries* exist and others are being developed worldwide. There are efforts to make these libraries broadly accessible. Software is increasingly being constructed from existing, well-defined, carefully tested, well-documented, portable, widely available components. This kind of software reusability speeds the development of powerful, high-quality software. *Rapid applications development (RAD)* through the mechanisms of reusable componentry has become an important field.

Significant problems must be solved, however, before the full potential of software reusability can be realized. We need cataloging schemes, licensing schemes, protection mechanisms to ensure that master copies of classes are not corrupted, description schemes so that designers of new systems can determine if existing objects meet their needs, browsing mechanisms to determine what classes are available and how closely they meet software developer requirement and the like. Many interesting research and development problems need to be solved. There is great motivation to solve these problems because the potential value of their solutions is enormous.

SUMMARY

- Structures are aggregate data types built using data of other types.
- The keyword `struct` introduces a structure definition. The body of a structure is delineated by braces (`{` and `}`). Every structure definition must end with a semicolon.
- A structure tag name can be used to declare variables of a structure type.
- Structure definitions do not reserve space in memory; they create new data types that are used to declare variables.
- Members of a structure or a class are accessed using the member access operators—the dot operator (`.`) and the arrow operator (`->`). The dot operator accesses a structure member via the object's variable name or a reference to the object. The arrow operator accesses a structure member via a pointer to the object.
- Drawbacks to creating new data types with `struct`s are the possibility of having uninitialized data; improper initialization; all programs using a `struct` must be changed if the `struct` implementation changes and no protection is provided to ensure that data are kept in a consistent state with proper data values.
- Classes enable the programmer to model objects with attributes and behaviors. Class types can be defined in C++ using the keywords `class` and `struct`, but keyword `class` is normally used for this purpose.
- The class name can be used to declare objects of that class.
- Class definitions begin with the keyword `class`. The body of the class definition is delineated with braces (`{` and `}`). Class definitions terminate with a semicolon.
- Any data member or member function declared after `public:` in a class is visible to any function with access to an object of the class.
- Any data member or member function declared after `private:` is only visible to `friend`s and other members of the class.
- Member access specifiers always end with a colon (`:`) and can appear multiple times and in any order in a class definition.

- Private data are not accessible from outside the class.

- The implementation of a class should be hidden from its clients.

- A constructor is a member function with the same name as the class that is used to initialize the members of a class object. A class's constructor is called when an object of that class is instantiated.

- A destructor has the same name as the class but preceded with a tilde character (~).

- The set of `public` member functions of a class is called the class's interface or `public` interface.

- When a member function is defined outside the class definition, the function name is preceded by the class name and the binary scope resolution operator (`::`).

- Member functions defined using the scope resolution operator outside a class definition are within that class's scope.

- Member functions defined in a class definition are `inlined`. The compiler reserves the right not to `inline` any function.

- Calling member functions is more concise than calling functions in procedural programming because most data used by the member function are directly accessible in the object.

- Within a class's scope, class members may be referenced simply by their names. Outside a class's scope, class members are referenced through either an object name, a reference to an object or a pointer to an object.

- A fundamental principle of good software engineering is to separate interface from implementation.

- Class definitions are normally placed in header files and member function definitions are normally placed in source-code files of the same base name.

- The default access mode for classes is `private` so all members after the class header and before the first member access specifier are considered to be `private`.

- A class's `public` members present a view of the services the class provides to the clients of the class.

- Access to a class's `private` data can be carefully controlled by the use of member functions called access functions. If a class wants to allow clients to read `private` data, the class can provide a *get* function. To enable clients to modify `private` data, the class can provide a *set* function.

- Data members of a class are normally made `private` and member functions of a class are normally made `public`. Some member functions may be `private` and serve as utility functions to the other functions of the class.

- Data members of a class cannot be initialized in a class definition. They must be initialized in a constructor, or their values may be *set* after their object is created.

- Constructors can be overloaded.

- Once a class object is properly initialized, all member functions that manipulate the object should ensure that the object remains in a consistent state.

- When an object of a class is declared, initializers can be provided. These initializers are passed to the class's constructor.

- Constructors can specify default arguments.

- Constructors may not specify return types, nor may they attempt to return values.

- If no constructor is defined for a class, the compiler creates a default constructor. A default constructor supplied by the compiler does not perform any initialization, so when the object is created, it is not guaranteed to be in a consistent state.

- The destructor of an automatic object is called when the object goes out of scope. The destructor itself does not actually destroy the object, but it does perform termination housekeeping before the system reclaims the object's storage.

- Destructors do not receive parameters and do not return values. A class may have only one destructor (destructors cannot be overloaded).

- The assignment operator (=) is used to assign an object to another object of the same type. Such assignment is normally performed by default memberwise copy. Memberwise copy is not ideal for all classes.

TERMINOLOGY

& reference operator
abstract data type (ADT)
access function
arrow member selection operator (->)
attribute
behavior
binary scope resolution operator (::)
class
class definition
class member selector operator (.)
class scope
client of a class
consistent state for a data member
constructor
data member
data type
default constructor
destructor
dot member selection operator (.)
encapsulation
extensibility
file scope
get function
global object
header file
helper function
implementation of a class
information hiding
initialize a class object
inline member function
instance of a class
instantiate an object of a class
interface to a class
member access control

member access specifiers
member function
member initializer
member selection operator (. and ->)
memberwise copy
message
nonmember function
nonstatic local object
object
object-oriented design (OOD)
object-oriented programming (OOP)
predicate function
principle of least privilege
private
procedural programming
programmer-defined type
protected
public
public interface of a class
query function
rapid applications development (RAD)
reusable code
scope resolution operator (::)
self-referential structure
services of a class
set function
software reusability
source-code file
static local object
structure
tilde (~) in destructor name
user-defined type
utility function

COMMON PROGRAMMING ERRORS

16.1   Forgetting the semicolon at the end of a class (or structure) definition is a syntax error.

16.2   Specifying a return type and/or a return value for a constructor is a syntax error.

16.3   Attempting to initialize a data member of a class explicitly in the class definition is a syntax error.

16.4   When defining a class's member functions outside that class, omitting the class name and scope resolution operator on the function name is an error.

16.5 An attempt by a function, which is not a member of a particular class (or a `friend` of that class), to access a `private` member of that class is a syntax error.

16.6 Data members of a class cannot be initialized in the class definition.

16.7 Attempting to declare a return type for a constructor and/or attempting to return a value from a constructor are syntax errors.

16.8 Specifying default initializers for the same member function in both a header file and in the member function definition.

16.9 It is a syntax error to attempt to pass arguments to a destructor, to specify a return type for a destructor (even `void` cannot be specified), to return values from a destructor or to overload a destructor.

16.10 A constructor can call other member functions of the class such as *set* or *get* functions, but because the constructor is initializing the object, the data members may not yet be in a consistent state. Using data members before they have been properly initialized can cause logic errors.

GOOD PROGRAMMING PRACTICES

16.1 Use each member access specifier only once in a class definition for clarity and readability. Place `public` members first where they are easy to locate.

16.2 Use the name of the header file with the period replaced by an underscore in the `#ifndef` and `#define` preprocessor directives of a header file.

16.3 If you choose to list the `private` members first in a class definition, explicitly use the `private` member access specifier despite the fact that `private` is assumed by default. This improves program clarity. Our preference is to list the `public` members of a class first to emphasize the class's interface.

16.4 Despite the fact that the `public` and `private` member access specifiers may be repeated and intermixed, list all the `public` members of a class first in one group, then list all the `private` members in another group. This focuses the client's attention on the class's `public` interface, rather than on the class's implementation.

16.5 When appropriate (almost always), provide a constructor to ensure that every object is properly initialized with meaningful values. Pointer data members, in particular, should be initialized to some legitimate pointer value or to 0.

16.6 Declare default function argument values only in the function prototype within the class definition in the header file.

16.7 Member functions that *set* the values of `private` data should verify that the intended new values are proper; if they are not, the *set* functions should place the `private` data members into an appropriate consistent state.

16.8 Never have a `public` member function return a non-`const` reference (or a pointer) to a `private` data member. Returning such a reference violates the encapsulation of the class. In fact, returning any reference or pointer to `private` data still makes the client code dependent on the representation of the class's data. So, returning pointers or references to `private` data should be avoided.

PERFORMANCE TIPS

16.1 Defining a small member function inside the class definition inlines the member function (if the compiler chooses to do so). This can improve performance, but it does not promote the best software engineering because clients of the class will be able to see the implementation of the function and their code must be recompiled if the inline function definition changes.

16.2   Actually, objects contain only data, so objects are much smaller than if they also contained functions. Applying operator `sizeof` to a class name or to an object of that class will report only the size of the class's data. The compiler creates one copy (only) of the member functions separate from all objects of the class. All objects of the class share this one copy of the member functions. Each object, of course, needs its own copy of the class's data because these data can vary among the objects. The function code is nonmodifiable (also called *reentrant code* or *pure procedure*) and hence can be shared among all objects of one class.

16.3   Passing an object call-by-value is good from a security standpoint because the called function has no access to the original object, but call-by-value can degrade performance when making a copy of a large object. An object can be passed call-by-reference by passing either a pointer or a reference to the object. Call-by-reference offers good performance but is weaker from a security standpoint because the called function is given access to the original object. Call-by-`const`-reference is a safe, good-performing alternative.

SOFTWARE ENGINEERING OBSERVATIONS

16.1   Clients of a class use the class without knowing the internal details of how the class is implemented. If the class implementation is changed (to improve performance, for example), provided the class's interface remains constant, the class's client source code need not change (although the client may need to be recompiled). This makes it much easier to modify systems.

16.2   Member functions are usually shorter than functions in non-object-oriented programs because the data stored in data members have ideally been validated by a constructor and/or by member functions that store new data. The data are already in the object, so the member function calls often have no arguments or at least have fewer arguments than typical function calls in non-object-oriented languages. Thus, the calls are shorter, the function definitions are shorter and the function prototypes are shorter.

16.3   Clients have access to a class's interface but should not have access to a class's implementation.

16.4   Declaring member functions inside a class definition (via their function prototypes) and defining those member functions outside that class definition separates the interface of a class from its implementation. This promotes good software engineering. Clients of a class cannot see the implementation of that class's member functions and need not recompile if that implementation changes.

16.5   Only the simplest member functions and most stable member functions (i.e., the implementation is unlikely to change) should be defined in the class header.

16.6   Using an object-oriented programming approach can often simplify function calls by reducing the number of parameters to be passed. This benefit of object-oriented programming derives from the fact that encapsulation of data members and member functions within an object gives the member functions the right to access the data members.

16.7   A central theme of this book is "reuse, reuse, reuse." We will carefully discuss a number of techniques for "polishing" classes to encourage reuse. We focus on "crafting valuable classes" and creating valuable "software assets."

16.8   Place the class declaration in a header file to be included by any client that wants to use the class. This forms the class's `public` interface (and provides the client with the function prototypes it needs to be able to call the class's member functions). Place the definitions of the class member functions in a source file. This forms the implementation of the class.

16.9   Clients of a class do not need access to the class's source code to use the class. The clients do, however, need to be able to link to the class's object code. This encourages independent software vendors (ISVs) to provide class libraries for sale or license. The ISVs provide in their products only the header files and the object modules. No proprietary information is revealed—as would be the case if source code were provided. The C++ user community benefits by having more ISV-produced class libraries available.

16.10   Information important to the interface to a class should be included in the header file. Information that will be used only internally in the class and will not be needed by clients of the class should be included in the unpublished source file. This is yet another example of the principle of least privilege.

16.11   C++ encourages programs to be implementation independent. When the implementation of a class used by implementation-independent code changes, that code need not be modified. If any part of the interface of the class changes, the implementation-independent code must be recompiled.

16.12   Keep all the data members of a class `private`. Provide `public` member functions to *set* the values of `private` data members and to *get* the values of `private` data members. This architecture helps hide the implementation of a class from its clients, which reduces bugs and improves program modifiability.

16.13   Class designers use `private`, `protected` and `public` members to enforce the notion of information hiding and the principle of least privilege.

16.14   The class designer need not provide *set* and/or *get* functions for each `private` data item; these capabilities should be provided only when appropriate. If the service is useful to the client code, that service should be provided in the class's `public` interface.

16.15   Member functions tend to fall into a number of different categories: functions that read and return the value of `private` data members; functions that set the value of `private` data members; functions that implement the services of the class and functions that perform various mechanical chores for the class such as initializing class objects, assigning class objects, converting between classes and built-in types or between classes and other classes and handling memory for class objects.

16.16   A phenomenon of object-oriented programming is that once a class is defined, creating and manipulating objects of that class usually involves issuing only a simple sequence of member function calls—few, if any, control structures are needed. By contrast, it is common to have control structures in the implementation of a class's member functions.

16.17   If a member function of a class already provides all or part of the functionality required by a constructor (or other member function) of the class, call that member function from the constructor (or other member function). This simplifies the maintenance of the code and reduces the likelihood of an error if the implementation of the code is modified. As a general rule: Avoid repeating code.

16.18   It is possible for a class not to have a default constructor if any constructors are defined and none of them is explicitly a default constructor.

16.19   As we will see (throughout the remainder of the book), constructors and destructors have much greater prominence in C++ and object-oriented programming than is possible to convey after only our brief introduction here.

16.20   Making data members `private` and controlling access, especially write access, to those data members through `public` member functions helps ensure data integrity.

16.21   Accessing `private` data through *set* and *get* member functions not only protects the data members from receiving invalid values, but it also insulates clients of the class from the representation of the data members. Thus, if the representation of the data changes for some reason (typically to reduce the amount of storage required or to improve performance), only the member functions need to change—the clients need not change as long as the interface provided by the member functions remains the same. The clients may, however, need to be recompiled.

ERROR-PREVENTION TIPS

16.1 The fact that member function calls generally take either no arguments or substantially fewer arguments than conventional function calls in non-object-oriented languages reduces the likelihood of passing the wrong arguments, the wrong types of arguments and/or the wrong number of arguments.

16.2 Use `#ifndef`, `#define` and `#endif` preprocessor directives to prevent header files from being included more than once in a program.

16.3 Making the data members of a class `private` and the member functions of the class `public` facilitates debugging because problems with data manipulations are localized to either the class's member functions or the `friend`s of the class.

16.4 Every member function (and `friend`) that modifies the `private` data members of an object should ensure that the data remains in a consistent state.

16.5 The benefits of data integrity are not automatic simply because data members are made `private`—the programmer must provide the validity checking. C++ does, however, provide a framework in which programmers can design better programs in a convenient manner.

SELF-REVIEW EXERCISES

16.1 Fill in the blanks in each of the following:
   a) Class members are accessed via the _____ operator in conjunction with the name of an object of the class or via the _____ operator in conjunction with a pointer to an object of the class.
   b) Members of a class specified as _____ are accessible only to member functions of the class and `friend`s of the class.
   c) A(n) _____ is a special member function used to initialize the data members of a class.
   d) The default access for members of a class is _____.
   e) A(n) _____ function is used to assign values to `private` data members of a class.
   f) _____ can be used to assign an object of a class to another object of the same class.
   g) Member functions of a class are normally made _____ and data members of a class are normally made _____.
   h) A(n) _____ function is used to retrieve values of `private` data of a class.
   i) The set of `public` member functions of a class is referred to as the class's _____.
   j) A class implementation is said to be hidden from its clients or _____.
   k) The keywords _____ and _____ can be used to introduce a class definition.
   l) Members of a class specified as _____ are accessible anywhere an object of the class is in scope.

16.2 Find the error(s) in each of the following and explain how to correct it (them):
   a) Assume the following prototype is declared in class `Time`:

```
void ~Time( int );
```

   b) The following is a partial definition of class `Time`.

```
class Time {
public:
// function prototypes
private:
    int hour = 0;
    int minute = 0;
    int second = 0;
}; // end class Time
```

c) Assume the following prototype is declared in class `Employee`:

```
int Employee( const char *, const char * );
```

ANSWERS TO SELF-REVIEW EXERCISES

16.1 a) dot (.), arrow (->). b) `private`. c) constructor. d) `private`. e) *set*. f) Default memberwise copy (performed by the assignment operator). g) `public`, `private`. h) *get*. i) interface. j) encapsulated. k) `class`, `struct`. l) `public`.

16.2 a) Error: Destructors are not allowed to return values or take arguments.
Correction: Remove the return type `void` and the parameter `int` from the declaration.
b) Error: Members cannot be explicitly initialized in the class definition.
Correction: Remove the explicit initialization from the class definition and initialize the data members in a constructor.
c) Error: Constructors are not allowed to return values.
Correction: Remove the return type `int` from the declaration.

EXERCISES

16.3   What is the purpose of the scope resolution operator?

16.4   Provide a constructor that is capable of using the current time from the `time` function—declared in the C Standard Library header `time.h`—to initialize an object of the `Time` class.

16.5   Create a class called `Complex` for performing arithmetic with complex numbers. Write a driver program to test your class.
Complex numbers have the form

```
realPart + imaginaryPart * i
```

where `i` is

$$\sqrt{-1}$$

Use `double` variables to represent the `private` data of the class. Provide a constructor function that enables an object of this class to be initialized when it is declared. The constructor should contain default values in case no initializers are provided. Provide `public` member functions for each of the following:
a) Addition of two `Complex` numbers: The real parts are added together and the imaginary parts are added together.
b) Subtraction of two `Complex` numbers: The real part of the right operand is subtracted from the real part of the left operand and the imaginary part of the right operand is subtracted from the imaginary part of the left operand.
c) Printing `Complex` numbers in the form (a, b) where a is the real part and b is the imaginary part.

16.6   Create a class called `Rational` for performing arithmetic with fractions. Write a driver program to test your class.
Use integer variables to represent the `private` data of the class—the numerator and the denominator. Provide a constructor function that enables an object of this class to be initialized when it is declared. The constructor should contain default values in case no initializers are provided and should store the fraction in reduced form (i.e., the fraction

$$\frac{2}{4}$$

would be stored in the object as 1 in the numerator and 2 in the denominator). Provide `public` member functions for each of the following:

    a) Addition of two `Rational` numbers. The result should be stored in reduced form.

    b) Subtraction of two `Rational` numbers. The result should be stored in reduced form.

    c) Multiplication of two `Rational` numbers. The result should be stored in reduced form.

    d) Division of two `Rational` numbers. The result should be stored in reduced form.

    e) Printing `Rational` numbers in the form `a/b` where `a` is the numerator and `b` is the denominator.

    f) Printing `Rational` numbers in floating-point format.

16.7   Create a class `Rectangle`. The class has attributes `length` and `width`, each of which defaults to 1. It has member functions that calculate the `perimeter` and the `area` of the rectangle. It has *set* and *get* functions for both `length` and `width`. The *set* functions should verify that `length` and `width` are each floating-point numbers larger than 0.0 and less than 20.0.

16.8   Create a more sophisticated `Rectangle` class than the one you created in Exercise 16.7. This class stores only the Cartesian coordinates of the four corners of the rectangle. The constructor calls a *set* function that accepts four sets of coordinates and verifies that each of these is in the first quadrant with no single *x* or *y* coordinate larger than 20.0. The *set* function also verifies that the supplied coordinates do, in fact, specify a rectangle. Member functions calculate the `length`, `width`, `perimeter` and `area`. The length is the larger of the two dimensions. Include a predicate function `square` that determines if the rectangle is a square.

16.9   Modify the `Rectangle` class of Exercise 16.8 to include a `draw` function that displays the rectangle inside a 25-by-25 box enclosing the portion of the first quadrant in which the rectangle resides. Include a `setFillCharacter` function to specify the character out of which the body of the rectangle will be drawn. Include a `setPerimeterCharacter` function to specify the character that will be used to draw the border of the rectangle. If you feel ambitious, you might include functions to scale the size of the rectangle, rotate it and move it around within the designated portion of the first quadrant.

16.10   Create a class `HugeInteger` that uses a 40-element array of digits to store integers as large as 40-digits each. Provide member functions `inputHugeInteger`, `outputHugeInteger`, `addHugeIntegers` and `substractHugeIntegers`. For comparing `HugeInteger` objects, provide functions `isEqualTo`, `isNotEqualTo`, `isGreaterThan`, `isLessThan`, `IsGreaterThanOrEqualTo` and `isLessThanOrEqualTo`—each of these is a "predicate" function that simply returns `true` if the relationship holds between the two huge integers and returns `false` if the relationship does not hold. Provide a predicate function `isZero`. If you feel ambitious, also provide member functions `multiplyHugeIntegers`, `divideHugeIntegers` and `modulusHugeIntegers`.

16.11   Create a class `TicTacToe` that will enable you to write a complete program to play the game of tic-tac-toe. The class contains as `private` data a 3-by-3 double array of integers. The constructor should initialize the empty board to all zeros. Allow two human players. Wherever the first player moves, place a 1 in the specified square; place a 2 wherever the second player moves. Each move must be to an empty square. After each move, determine if the game has been won or if the game is a draw. If you feel ambitious, modify your program so that the computer makes the moves for one of the players. Also, allow the player to specify whether he or she wants to go first or second. If you feel exceptionally ambitious, develop a program that will play three-dimensional tic-tac-toe on a 4-by-4-by-4 board (Caution: This is an extremely challenging project that could take many weeks of effort!)

17

C++ Classes: Part II

Objectives

- To be able to create and destroy objects dynamically.
- To be able to specify `const` (constant) objects and `const` member functions.
- To understand the purpose of `friend` functions and friend classes.
- To understand how to use `static` data members and member functions.
- To understand the concept of a container class.
- To understand the notion of iterator classes that walk through the elements of container classes.
- To understand the use of the `this` pointer.

But what, to serve our private ends,
Forbids the cheating of our friends?
Charles Churchill

Instead of this absurd division into sexes they ought to class people as static and dynamic.
Evelyn Waugh

This above all: To thine own self be true.
William Shakespeare

Have no friends not equal to yourself.
Confucius

Outline

17.1 Introduction

In this chapter we continue our study of classes and data abstraction. We discuss many more advanced topics and lay the groundwork for the discussion of classes and operator overloading in Chapter 18. The discussion in Chapters 16 through 18 encourages programmers to use objects, what we call *object-based programming (OBP)*. Then, Chapters 19 and 20 introduce inheritance and polymorphism—the techniques of truly *object-oriented programming (OOP)*. In this and several subsequent chapters, we use the C-style strings we introduced in Chapter 8. This will help the reader master the complex topic of C pointers and prepare for the professional world in which the reader will see a great deal of C legacy code that has been put in place over the last two decades.

17.2 `const` (Constant) Objects and `const` Member Functions

We have emphasized the *principle of least privilege* as one of the most fundamental principles of good software engineering. Let us see how this principle applies to objects.

Some objects need to be modifiable and some do not. The programmer may use the keyword `const` to specify that an object is not modifiable, and that any attempt to modify the object is a syntax error. For example,

```
const Time noon( 12, 0, 0 );
```

declares a `const` object `noon` of class `Time` and initializes it to 12 noon.

 Software Engineering Observation 17.1

Declaring an object as `const` helps enforce the principle of least privilege. Attempts to modify the object are caught at compile time rather than causing execution-time errors.

Software Engineering Observation 17.2

Using const *is crucial to proper class design, program design and coding.*

Performance Tip 17.1

Declaring variables and objects const *is not only an effective software engineering practice—it can improve performance as well because today's sophisticated optimizing compilers can perform certain optimizations on constants that cannot be performed on variables.*

C++ compilers disallow any member function calls for const objects unless the member functions themselves are also declared const. This is true even for *get* member functions that do not modify the object. Member functions declared const cannot modify the object—the compiler disallows this.

A function is specified as const *both* in its prototype and in its definition by inserting the keyword const after the function's parameter list, and, in the case of the function definition, before the left brace that begins the function body. For example, the following member function of class A

```
int A::getValue() const { return privateDataMember; }
```

simply returns the value of one of the object's data members, and is appropriately declared const.

Common Programming Error 17.1

Defining as const *a member function that modifies a data member of an object is a syntax error.*

Common Programming Error 17.2

Defining as const *a member function that calls a non-*const *member function of the class on the same instance of the class is a syntax error.*

Common Programming Error 17.3

*Invoking a non-*const *member function on a* const *object is a syntax error.*

Software Engineering Observation 17.3

A const *member function can be overloaded with a non-*const *version. The choice of which overloaded member function to use is made by the compiler based on whether the object is* const *or not.*

An interesting problem arises here for constructors and destructors, each of which often needs to modify objects. The const declaration is not allowed for constructors and destructors of const objects. A constructor must be allowed to modify an object so that the object can be initialized properly. A destructor must be able to perform its termination housekeeping chores before an object is destroyed.

Common Programming Error 17.4

Attempting to declare a constructor or destructor const *is a syntax error.*

Figure 17.1 instantiates two Time objects—one non-const object and one const object. The program attempts to modify the const object noon with non-const member functions setHour (in line 102) and printStandard (in line 108). The program also illustrates the three other combinations of member function calls on objects—a non-const member function on a non-const object (line 100), a const member function on a non-const object (line 104) and a const member function on a const object (line 106 and 107). The messages generated by two popular compilers for non-const member functions called on a const object are shown in the output window.

```
1   // Fig. 17.1: time5.h
2   // Declaration of the class Time.
3   // Member functions defined in time5.cpp
4   #ifndef TIME5_H
5   #define TIME5_H
6
7   class Time {
8   public:
9      Time( int = 0, int = 0, int = 0 );  // default constructor
10
11     // set functions
12     void setTime( int, int, int );  // set time
13     void setHour( int );       // set hour
14     void setMinute( int );     // set minute
15     void setSecond( int );     // set second
16
17     // get functions (normally declared const)
18     int getHour() const;       // return hour
19     int getMinute() const;     // return minute
20     int getSecond() const;     // return second
21
22     // print functions (normally declared const)
23     void printMilitary() const;  // print military time
24     void printStandard();        // print standard time
25   private:
26     int hour;              // 0 - 23
27     int minute;            // 0 - 59
28     int second;            // 0 - 59
29   }; // end class Time
30
31   #endif
```

Fig. 17.1   Using a Time class with const objects and const member functions— time5.h.

```
32   // Fig. 17.1: time5.cpp
33   // Member function definitions for Time class.
34   #include <iostream>
35
36   using std::cout;
37
38   #include "time5.h"
```

Fig. 17.1   Using a Time class with const objects and const member functions— time5.cpp. (Part 1 of 2.)

```
39
40   // Constructor function to initialize private data.
41   // Default values are 0 (see class definition).
42   Time::Time( int hr, int min, int sec )
43      { setTime( hr, min, sec ); }
44
45   // Set the values of hour, minute, and second.
46   void Time::setTime( int h, int m, int s )
47   {
48      setHour( h );
49      setMinute( m );
50      setSecond( s );
51   } // end function setTime
52
53   // Set the hour value
54   void Time::setHour( int h )
55      { hour = ( h >= 0 && h < 24 ) ? h : 0; }
56
57   // Set the minute value
58   void Time::setMinute( int m )
59      { minute = ( m >= 0 && m < 60 ) ? m : 0; }
60
61   // Set the second value
62   void Time::setSecond( int s )
63      { second = ( s >= 0 && s < 60 ) ? s : 0; }
64
65   // Get the hour value
66   int Time::getHour() const { return hour; }
67
68   // Get the minute value
69   int Time::getMinute() const { return minute; }
70
71   // Get the second value
72   int Time::getSecond() const { return second; }
73
74   // Display military format time: HH:MM
75   void Time::printMilitary() const
76   {
77      cout << ( hour < 10 ? "0" : "" ) << hour << ":"
78           << ( minute < 10 ? "0" : "" ) << minute;
79   } // end function printMilitary
80
81   // Display standard format time: HH:MM:SS AM (or PM)
82   void Time::printStandard()   // should be const
83   {
84      cout << ( ( hour == 12 ) ? 12 : hour % 12 ) << ":"
85           << ( minute < 10 ? "0" : "" ) << minute << ":"
86           << ( second < 10 ? "0" : "" ) << second
87           << ( hour < 12 ? " AM" : " PM" );
88   } // end function printStandard
```

Fig. 17.1   Using a Time class with const objects and const member functions—
time5.cpp. (Part 2 of 2.)

```
89   // Fig. 17.1: fig17_01.cpp
90   // Attempting to access a const object with
91   // non-const member functions.
92   #include "time5.h"
93
94   int main()
95   {
96      Time wakeUp( 6, 45, 0 );         // non-constant object
97      const Time noon( 12, 0, 0 );     // constant object
98
99                            // MEMBER FUNCTION   OBJECT
100     wakeUp.setHour( 18 );  // non-const        non-const
101
102     noon.setHour( 12 );    // non-const        const
103
104     wakeUp.getHour();      // const            non-const
105
106     noon.getMinute();      // const            const
107     noon.printMilitary();  // const            const
108     noon.printStandard();  // non-const        const
109     return 0;
110  } // end function main
```

Borland C++ command-line compiler warning messages

```
Fig17_01.cpp:
Warning W8037 Fig17_01.cpp 14: Non-const function Time::setHour(int)
   called for const object in function main()
Warning W8037 Fig17_01.cpp 20: Non-const function Time::printStandard()
   called for const object in function main()
Turbo Incremental Link 5.00 Copyright (c) 1997, 2000 Borland
```

Microsoft Visual C++ compiler error messages

```
Compiling...
Fig17_01.cpp
d:fig17_01.cpp(14) : error C2662: 'setHour' : cannot convert 'this' pointer
from 'const class Time' to 'class Time &'
Conversion loses qualifiers
d:\fig17_01.cpp(20) : error C2662: 'printStandard' : cannot convert 'this'
pointer from 'const class Time' to 'class Time &'
Conversion loses qualifiers
Time5.cpp
Error executing cl.exe.

test.exe - 2 error(s), 0 warning(s)
```

Fig. 17.1   Using a Time class with const objects and const member functions—
fig17_01.cpp.

Good Programming Practice 17.1

Declare as const all member functions that do not need to modify the current object so that you can use them on a const object if you need to.

Notice that even though a constructor must be a non-`const` member function, it can still be called for a `const` object. The definition of the `Time` constructor in lines 42 and 43

```
Time::Time( int hr, int min, int sec )
   { setTime( hr, min, sec ); }
```

shows that the `Time` constructor calls non-`const` member function—`setTime`—to perform the initialization of a `Time` object. Invoking a non-`const` member function from the constructor call for a `const` object is allowed. The `const`ness of an object is enforced from the time the constructor completes initialization of the object until that object's destructor is called.

Software Engineering Observation 17.4

A `const` object cannot be modified by assignment so it must be initialized. When a data member of a class is declared `const`, a member initializer must be used to provide the constructor with the initial value of the data member for an object of the class.

Also notice that line 108 (line 20 in the source file)

```
noon.printStandard();   // non-const          const
```

generates a compiler error even though member function `printStandard` of class `Time` does not modify the object on which it is invoked. Not modifying an object is not sufficient to indicate a `const` method. The method must also explicitly be declared `const`.

Figure 17.2 demonstrates the use of a member initializer to initialize `const` data member `increment` of class `Increment`. The constructor for `Increment` is modified as follows:

```
Increment::Increment( int c, int i )
   : increment( i )
{ count = c; }
```

The notation `: increment( i )` initializes `increment` to the value `i`. If multiple member initializers are needed, simply include them in a comma-separated list after the colon. All data members *can* be initialized using member initializer syntax, but `const`s and references *must* be initialized in this manner. Later in this chapter, we will see that member objects must be initialized this way. In Chapter 19 when we study inheritance, we will see that base class portions of derived classes also must be initialized this way.

```
1   // Fig. 17.2: fig17_02.cpp
2   // Using a member initializer to initialize a
3   // constant of a built-in data type.
4   #include <iostream>
5
6   using std::cout;
7   using std::endl;
8
9   class Increment {
10  public:
```

Fig. 17.2   Using a member initializer to initialize a constant of a built-in data type. (Part 1 of 2.)

```
11        Increment( int c = 0, int i = 1 );
12        void addIncrement() { count += increment; }
13        void print() const;
14
15     private:
16        int count;
17        const int increment;    // const data member
18     }; // end class Increment
19
20     // Constructor for class Increment
21     Increment::Increment( int c, int i )
22        : increment( i )     // initializer for const member
23     { count = c; }
24
25     // Print the data
26     void Increment::print() const
27     {
28        cout << "count = " << count
29             << ", increment = " << increment << endl;
30     } // end function print
31
32     int main()
33     {
34        Increment value( 10, 5 );
35
36        cout << "Before incrementing: ";
37        value.print();
38
39        for ( int j = 0; j < 3; j++ ) {
40           value.addIncrement();
41           cout << "After increment " << j + 1 << ": ";
42           value.print();
43        } // end for
44
45        return 0;
46     } // end function main
```

```
Before incrementing: count = 10, increment = 5
After increment 1: count = 15, increment = 5
After increment 2: count = 20, increment = 5
After increment 3: count = 25, increment = 5
```

Fig. 17.2   Using a member initializer to initialize a constant of a built-in data type. (Part 2 of 2.)

Error-Prevention Tip 17.1

Always declare member functions const *if they do not modify the object. This can help eliminate many bugs.*

Figure 17.3 illustrates the compiler errors issued by two popular C++ compilers for a program that attempts to initialize increment with an assignment statement rather than with a member initializer.

Common Programming Error 17.5

Not providing a member initializer for a const data member is a syntax error.

```cpp
1   // Fig. 17.3: fig17_03.cpp
2   // Attempting to initialize a constant of
3   // a built-in data type with an assignment.
4   #include <iostream>
5
6   using std::cout;
7   using std::endl;
8
9   class Increment {
10  public:
11     Increment( int c = 0, int i = 1 );
12     void addIncrement() { count += increment; }
13     void print() const;
14  private:
15     int count;
16     const int increment;
17  }; // end class Increment
18
19  // Constructor for class Increment
20  Increment::Increment( int c, int i )
21  {              // Constant member 'increment' is not initialized
22     count = c;
23     increment = i;  // ERROR: Cannot modify a const object
24  } // end Increment constructor
25
26  // Print the data
27  void Increment::print() const
28  {
29     cout << "count = " << count
30          << ", increment = " << increment << endl;
31  } // end function print
32
33  int main()
34  {
35     Increment value( 10, 5 );
36
37     cout << "Before incrementing: ";
38     value.print();
39
40     for ( int j = 0; j < 3; j++ ) {
41        value.addIncrement();
42        cout << "After increment " << j << ": ";
43        value.print();
44     } // end for
45
46     return 0;
47  } // end function main
```

Fig. 17.3 Erroneous attempt to initialize a constant of a built-in data type by assignment. (Part 1 of 2.)

Borland C++ command-line compiler warning and error messages

```
Fig17_03.cpp:
Warning W8038 Fig17_03.cpp 21: Constant member 'Increment::increment'
    is not initialized in function Increment::Increment(int,int)
Error E2024 Fig17_03.cpp 23: Cannot modify a const object in function
    Increment::Increment(int,int)
Warning W8057 Fig17_03.cpp 24: Parameter 'i' is never used in function
    Increment::Increment(int,int)
*** 1 errors in Compile ***
```

Microsoft Visual C++ compiler error messages

```
Compiling...
Fig17_03.cpp
D:\Fig17_03.cpp(21) : error C2758: 'increment' : must be initialized in con-
structor base/member initializer list
D:\Fig17_03.cpp(16) : see declaration of 'increment'
D:\Fig17_03.cpp(23) : error C2166: l-value specifies const object
Error executing cl.exe.

test.exe - 2 error(s), 0 warning(s)
```

Fig. 17.3   Erroneous attempt to initialize a constant of a built-in data type by assignment. (Part 2 of 2.)

Software Engineering Observation 17.5

Constant class members (`const` objects and `const` "variables") must be initialized with member initializer syntax; assignments are not allowed.

Note that function `print` (line 27) is declared `const`. It is reasonable, yet strange, to label this function `const` because we will probably never have a `const Increment` object.

Software Engineering Observation 17.6

It is good practice to declare all a class's member functions that do not modify the object in which they operate as `const`. Occasionally, this will be an anomaly because you will have no intention of creating `const` objects of that class. Declaring such member functions `const` does offer a benefit though. If you inadvertently modify the object in that member function, the compiler will issue a syntax error message.

Error-Prevention Tip 17.2

Languages like C++ are "moving targets" as they evolve. More keywords are likely to be added to the language. Avoid using "loaded" words like "object" as identifiers. Even though "object" is not currently a keyword in C++, it could become one, so future compiling with new compilers could "break" existing code.

17.3 Composition: Objects as Members of Classes

An `AlarmClock` class object needs to know when it is supposed to sound its alarm, so why not include a `Time` object as a member of the `AlarmClock` object? Such a capability is called *composition*. A class can have objects of other classes as members.

> ### Software Engineering Observation 17.7
> *The most common form of software reusability is* composition, *in which a class has objects of other classes as members.*

Whenever an object is created, its constructor is called, so we need to specify how arguments are passed to member-object constructors. Member objects are constructed in the order in which they are declared (not in the order they are listed in the constructor's member initializer list) and before their enclosing class objects (sometimes called *host objects*) are constructed.

Figure 17.4 uses class `Employee` and class `Date` to demonstrate objects as members of other objects. Class `Employee` contains `private` data members `firstName`, `last-Name`, `birthDate` and `hireDate`. Members `birthDate` and `hireDate` are `const` objects of class `Date`, which contains `private` data members `month`, `day` and `year`. The program instantiates an `Employee` object, and initializes and displays its data members. Note the syntax of the function header in the `Employee` constructor definition:

```
Employee::Employee( char *fname, char *lname,
                    int bmonth, int bday, int byear,
                    int hmonth, int hday, int hyear )
    : birthDate( bmonth, bday, byear ),
      hireDate( hmonth, hday, hyear )
```

The constructor takes eight arguments (`fname`, `lname`, `bmonth`, `bday`, `byear`, `hmonth`, `hday` and `hyear`). The colon (`:`) in the header separates the member initializers from the parameter list. The member initializers specify the `Employee` arguments being passed to the constructors of the member `Date` objects. Arguments `bmonth`, `bday` and `byear` are passed to object `birthDate`'s constructor, and arguments `hmonth`, `hday` and `hyear` are passed to object `hireDate`'s constructor. Multiple member initializers are separated by commas.

```cpp
1   // Fig. 17.4: date1.h
2   // Declaration of the Date class.
3   // Member functions defined in date1.cpp
4   #ifndef DATE1_H
5   #define DATE1_H
6
7   class Date {
8   public:
9      Date( int = 1, int = 1, int = 1900 ); // default constructor
10     void print() const;   // print date in month/day/year format
11     ~Date();   // provided to confirm destruction order
12  private:
13     int month;   // 1-12
14     int day;    // 1-31 based on month
15     int year;    // any year
16
17     // utility function to test proper day for month and year
18     int checkDay( int );
19  }; // end class Date
```

Fig. 17.4   Using member-object initializers—`date1.h`. (Part 1 of 2.)

```
20
21  #endif
```

Fig. 17.4 Using member-object initializers—`date1.h`. (Part 2 of 2.)

```
22  // Fig. 17.4: date1.cpp
23  // Member function definitions for Date class.
24  #include <iostream>
25
26  using std::cout;
27  using std::endl;
28
29  #include "date1.h"
30
31  // Constructor: Confirm proper value for month;
32  // call utility function checkDay to confirm proper
33  // value for day.
34  Date::Date( int mn, int dy, int yr )
35  {
36     if ( mn > 0 && mn <= 12 )          // validate the month
37        month = mn;
38     else {
39        month = 1;
40        cout << "Month " << mn << " invalid. Set to month 1.\n";
41     } // end else
42
43     year = yr;                          // should validate yr
44     day = checkDay( dy );               // validate the day
45
46     cout << "Date object constructor for date ";
47     print();          // interesting: a print with no arguments
48     cout << endl;
49  } // end Date constructor
50
51  // Print Date object in form  month/day/year
52  void Date::print() const
53     { cout << month << '/' << day << '/' << year; }
54
55  // Destructor: provided to confirm destruction order
56  Date::~Date()
57  {
58     cout << "Date object destructor for date ";
59     print();
60     cout << endl;
61  } // end Date destructor
62
63  // Utility function to confirm proper day value
64  // based on month and year.
65  // Is the year 2000 a leap year?
66  int Date::checkDay( int testDay )
67  {
68     static const int daysPerMonth[ 13 ] =
```

Fig. 17.4 Using member-object initializers—`date1.cpp`. (Part 1 of 2.)

```
69            {0, 31, 28, 31, 30, 31, 30, 31, 31, 30, 31, 30, 31};
70
71      if ( testDay > 0 && testDay <= daysPerMonth[ month ] )
72         return testDay;
73
74      if ( month == 2 &&        // February: Check for leap year
75            testDay == 29 &&
76            ( year % 400 == 0 ||
77              ( year % 4 == 0 && year % 100 != 0 ) ) )
78         return testDay;
79
80      cout << "Day " << testDay << " invalid. Set to day 1.\n";
81
82      return 1;   // leave object in consistent state if bad value
83   } // end function checkDay
```

Fig. 17.4   Using member-object initializers—`date1.cpp`. (Part 2 of 2.)

```
84    // Fig. 17.4: emply1.h
85    // Declaration of the Employee class.
86    // Member functions defined in emply1.cpp
87    #ifndef EMPLY1_H
88    #define EMPLY1_H
89
90    #include "date1.h"
91
92    class Employee {
93    public:
94       Employee( char *, char *, int, int, int, int, int, int );
95       void print() const;
96       ~Employee();   // provided to confirm destruction order
97    private:
98       char firstName[ 25 ];
99       char lastName[ 25 ];
100      const Date birthDate;
101      const Date hireDate;
102   }; // end Employee constructor
103
104   #endif
```

Fig. 17.4   Using member-object initializers—`emply1.h`.

```
105   // Fig. 17.4: emply1.cpp
106   // Member function definitions for Employee class.
107   #include <iostream>
108
109   using std::cout;
110   using std::endl;
111
112   #include <cstring>
113   #include "emply1.h"
```

Fig. 17.4   Using member-object initializers—`emply1.cpp`. (Part 1 of 2.)

```
114  #include "date1.h"
115
116  Employee::Employee( char *fname, char *lname,
117                      int bmonth, int bday, int byear,
118                      int hmonth, int hday, int hyear )
119     : birthDate( bmonth, bday, byear ),
120       hireDate( hmonth, hday, hyear )
121  {
122     // copy fname into firstName and be sure that it fits
123     int length = strlen( fname );
124     length = ( length < 25 ? length : 24 );
125     strncpy( firstName, fname, length );
126     firstName[ length ] = '\0';
127
128     // copy lname into lastName and be sure that it fits
129     length = strlen( lname );
130     length = ( length < 25 ? length : 24 );
131     strncpy( lastName, lname, length );
132     lastName[ length ] = '\0';
133
134     cout << "Employee object constructor: "
135          << firstName << ' ' << lastName << endl;
136  } // end Employee constructor
137
138  void Employee::print() const
139  {
140     cout << lastName << ", " << firstName << "\nHired: ";
141     hireDate.print();
142     cout << "  Birth date: ";
143     birthDate.print();
144     cout << endl;
145  } // end function print
146
147  // Destructor: provided to confirm destruction order
148  Employee::~Employee()
149  {
150     cout << "Employee object destructor: "
151          << lastName << ", " << firstName << endl;
152  } // end Employee destructor
```

Fig. 17.4 Using member-object initializers—`emply1.cpp`. (Part 2 of 2.)

```
153  // Fig. 17.4: fig17_04.cpp
154  // Demonstrating composition: an object with member objects.
155  #include <iostream>
156
157  using std::cout;
158  using std::endl;
159
160  #include "emply1.h"
161
```

Fig. 17.4 Using member-object initializers—`fig17_04.cpp`. (Part 1 of 2.)

```
162  int main()
163  {
164      Employee e( "Bob", "Jones", 7, 24, 1949, 3, 12, 1988 );
165
166      cout << '\n';
167      e.print();
168
169      cout << "\nTest Date constructor with invalid values:\n";
170      Date d( 14, 35, 1994 );   // invalid Date values
171      cout << endl;
172      return 0;
173  } // end function main
```

```
Date object constructor for date 7/24/1949
Date object constructor for date 3/12/1988
Employee object constructor: Bob Jones

Jones, Bob
Hired: 3/12/1988  Birth date: 7/24/1949

Test Date constructor with invalid values:
Month 14 invalid. Set to month 1.
Day 35 invalid. Set to day 1.
Date object constructor for date 1/1/1994

Date object destructor for date 1/1/1994
Employee object destructor: Jones, Bob
Date object destructor for date 3/12/1988
Date object destructor for date 7/24/1949
```

Fig. 17.4 Using member-object initializers—`fig17_04.cpp`. (Part 2 of 2.)

Remember that `const` members and references are also initialized in the member initializer list (in Chapter 19, we will see that base class portions of derived classes are also initialized this way). Class `Date` and class `Employee` each include a destructor function that prints a message when a `Date` object or an `Employee` object is destroyed, respectively. This enables us to confirm in the program output that objects are constructed from the inside out and destructed in the reverse order from the outside in (i.e., the `Date` member objects are destroyed after the `Employee` object that contains them).

A member object does not need to be initialized explicitly through a member initializer. If a member initializer is not provided, the member object's default constructor will be called implicitly. Values, if any, established by the default constructor can be overridden by *set* functions. However, for complex initialization, this approach may require significant additional work and time.

Common Programming Error 17.6

Not providing a default constructor for the class of a member object when no member initializer is provided for that member object is a syntax error.

Performance Tip 17.2

Initialize member objects explicitly through member initializers. This eliminates the overhead of "doubly initializing" member objects—once when the member object's default constructor is called and again when set *functions are used to initialize the member object.*

Software Engineering Observation 17.8

If a class has as a member an object of another class, making that member object `public` does not violate the encapsulation and hiding of that member object's `private` members.

Notice the `Date` member function `print` in line 52. Many member functions of classes in C++ require no arguments. This is because each member function contains an implicit handle (in the form of a pointer) to the object on which it operates. We discuss the implicit pointer—called *this*—in Section 17.5.

In this first version of our `Employee` class (for ease of programming), we use two 25-character arrays to represent the first and last name of the `Employee`. These arrays may be a waste of space for names shorter than 24 characters (remember, one character in each array is for the terminating null character, `'\0'`, of the string). Also, names longer than 24 characters must be truncated to fit into these character arrays. Later in this chapter we will present another version of class `Employee` that dynamically creates the exact amount of space to hold the first and the last name.

17.4 `friend` Functions and `friend` Classes

A *friend function* of a class is defined outside that class's scope, yet has the right to access `private` (and as we will see in Chapter 19, C++ Inheritance, `protected`) members of the class. A function or an entire class may be declared to be a `friend` of another class.

Using `friend` functions can enhance performance. A mechanical example is shown here of how a `friend` function works. Later in the book, `friend` functions are used to overload operators for use with class objects and to create iterator classes. Objects of an iterator class are used to successively select items or perform an operation on items in a container class (see Section 17.9) object. Objects of container classes are capable of storing items. Using `friend`s is often appropriate when a member function cannot be used for certain operations as we will see in Chapter 18, C++ Operator Overloading.

To declare a function as a `friend` of a class, precede the function prototype in the class definition with the keyword `friend`. To declare class `ClassTwo` as a `friend` of class `ClassOne`, place a declaration of the form

```
friend class ClassTwo;
```

in the definition of class `ClassOne`.

Software Engineering Observation 17.9

Even though the prototypes for `friend` functions appear in the class definition, `friend`s are still not member functions.

Software Engineering Observation 17.10

Member access notions of `private`, `protected` and `public` are not relevant to friendship declarations, so friendship declarations can be placed anywhere in the class definition.

Good Programming Practice 17.2

Place all friendship declarations first in the class immediately after the class header and do not precede them with any member-access specifier.

Friendship is granted, not taken, i.e., for class B to be a `friend` of class A, class A must explicitly declare that class B is its `friend`. Also, friendship is neither symmetric nor transitive, i.e., if class A is a `friend` of class B, and class B is a `friend` of class C, you cannot infer that class B is a `friend` of class A (again, friendship is not symmetric), that class C is a `friend` of class B or that class A is a `friend` of class C (again, friendship is not transitive).

Software Engineering Observation 17.11

Some people in the OOP community feel that "friendship" corrupts information hiding and weakens the value of the object-oriented design approach.

Figure 17.5 demonstrates the declaration and use of `friend` function `setX` for setting the `private` data member x of class `count`. Note that the `friend` declaration appears first (by convention) in the class declaration, even before `public` member functions are declared. The program of Fig. 17.6 demonstrates the messages produced by the compiler when non-`friend` function `cannotSetX` is called to modify `private` data member x. Figures 17.5 and 17.6 are intended to introduce the "mechanics" of using `friend` functions—practical examples of using `friend` functions appear in forthcoming chapters.

```cpp
1   // Fig. 17.5: fig17_05.cpp
2   // Friends can access private members of a class.
3   #include <iostream>
4
5   using std::cout;
6   using std::endl;
7
8   // Modified Count class
9   class Count {
10     friend void setX( Count &, int ); // friend declaration
11   public:
12     Count() { x = 0; }                  // constructor
13     void print() const { cout << x << endl; }   // output
14   private:
15     int x;   // data member
16   }; // end class Count
17
18   // Can modify private data of Count because
19   // setX is declared as a friend function of Count
20   void setX( Count &c, int val )
21   {
22     c.x = val;   // legal: setX is a friend of Count
23   } // end function setX
24
25   int main()
26   {
27     Count counter;
28
29     cout << "counter.x after instantiation: ";
30     counter.print();
31     cout << "counter.x after call to setX friend function: ";
32     setX( counter, 8 );   // set x with a friend
33     counter.print();
34     return 0;
35   } // end function main
```

Fig. 17.5 Friends can access `private` members of a class. (Part 1 of 2.)

```
counter.x after instantiation: 0
counter.x after call to setX friend function: 8
```

Fig. 17.5 Friends can access `private` members of a class. (Part 2 of 2.)

```
1   // Fig. 17.6: fig17_06.cpp
2   // Non-friend/non-member functions cannot access
3   // private data of a class.
4   #include <iostream>
5
6   using std::cout;
7   using std::endl;
8
9   // Modified Count class
10  class Count {
11  public:
12     Count() { x = 0; }                      // constructor
13     void print() const { cout << x << endl; }  // output
14  private:
15     int x;  // data member
16  }; // end class Count
17
18  // Function tries to modify private data of Count,
19  // but cannot because it is not a friend of Count.
20  void cannotSetX( Count &c, int val )
21  {
22     c.x = val;  // ERROR: 'Count::x' is not accessible
23  } // end function cannotSetX
24
25  int main()
26  {
27     Count counter;
28
29     cannotSetX( counter, 3 ); // cannotSetX is not a friend
30     return 0;
31  } // end function main
```

Borland C++ command-line compiler error messages

```
Error E2247 Fig17_06.cpp 22: 'Count::x' is not accessible in
   function cannotSetX(Count &,int)
```

Microsoft Visual C++ compiler error messages

```
D:\Fig17_06.cpp(22) :
   error C2248: 'x' : cannot access private member declared in
   class 'Count'
       D:\Fig17_06.cpp(15) : see declaration of 'x'
       Error executing cl.exe.
```

Fig. 17.6 Non-`friend`/non-member functions cannot access `private` members.

Note that function `setX` (line 20) is a C-style, stand-alone function—it is not a member function of class `Count`. For this reason, when `setX` is invoked for object `counter`, we use the statement in line 32

```
setX( counter, 8 );    // set x with a friend
```

that takes `counter` as an argument rather than using a handle (such as the name of the object) to call the function, as in

```
counter.setX( 8 );
```

As we mentioned, Fig. 17.5 is a mechanical example of the `friend` construct. It would normally be appropriate to define function `setX` as a member function of class `Count`.

Software Engineering Observation 17.12

C++ is a hybrid language, so it is common to have a mix of two types of function calls in one program and often back to back—C-like calls that pass primitive data or objects to functions and C++ calls that pass functions (or messages) to objects.

It is possible to specify overloaded functions as `friend`s of a class. Each overloaded function intended to be a `friend` must be explicitly declared in the class definition as a `friend` of the class.

17.5 Using the `this` Pointer

Every object has access to its own address through a pointer called `this`. An object's `this` pointer is not part of the object itself—i.e., the `this` pointer is not reflected in the result of a `sizeof` operation on the object. Rather, the `this` pointer is passed into the object (by the compiler) as an implicit first argument on every non-`static` member function call to the object (`static` members are discussed in Section 17.7).

The `this` pointer is implicitly used to reference both the data members and member functions of an object; it can also be used explicitly. The type of the `this` pointer depends on the type of the object and whether the member function in which `this` is used is declared `const`. In a non-constant member function of class `Employee`, the `this` pointer has type `Employee * const` (a constant pointer to an `Employee` object). In a constant member function of the class `Employee`, the `this` pointer has the data type `const Employee * const` (a constant pointer to an `Employee` object that is constant).

For now, we show a simple example of using the `this` pointer explicitly; later in this chapter and in Chapter 18, we show some substantial and subtle examples of using `this`. Every non-`static` member function has access to the `this` pointer to the object for which the member function is being invoked.

Performance Tip 17.3

For reasons of economy of storage, only one copy of each member function exists per class, and this member function is invoked by every object of that class. Each object, on the other hand, has its own copy of the class's data members.

Figure 17.7 demonstrates the explicit use of the `this` pointer to enable a member function of class `Test` to print the `private` data `x` of a `Test` object.

```cpp
1   // Fig. 17.7: fig17_07.cpp
2   // Using the this pointer to refer to object members.
3   #include <iostream>
4
5   using std::cout;
6   using std::endl;
7
8   class Test {
9   public:
10     Test( int = 0 );              // default constructor
11     void print() const;
12  private:
13     int x;
14  }; // end class Test
15
16  Test::Test( int a ) { x = a; }  // constructor
17
18  void Test::print() const        // ( ) around *this required
19  {
20     cout << "          x = " << x
21        << "\n  this->x = " << this->x
22        << "\n(*this).x = " << ( *this ).x << endl;
23  } // end function print
24
25  int main()
26  {
27     Test testObject( 12 );
28
29     testObject.print();
30
31     return 0;
32  } // end function main
```

```
         x = 12
  this->x = 12
(*this).x = 12
```

Fig. 17.7   Using the this pointer.

For illustration purposes, the print member function in Fig. 17.7 first prints x directly. Then, print uses two different notations for accessing x through the this pointer—the arrow operator (->) off the this pointer and the dot operator (.) off the dereferenced this pointer.

Note the parentheses around *this when used with the dot member selection operator (.). The parentheses are needed because the dot operator has higher precedence than the * operator. Without the parentheses, the expression

    *this.x

would be evaluated as if it were parenthesized as follows:

    *(this.x)

which is a syntax error because the dot operator cannot be used with a pointer.

Common Programming Error 17.7

Attempting to use the member selection operator (.) with a pointer to an object is a syntax error—the dot member selection operator may only be used with an object or with a reference to an object.

One interesting use of the `this` pointer is to prevent an object from being assigned to itself. As we will see in Chapter 18, C++ Operator Overloading, self-assignment can cause serious errors when the objects contain pointers to dynamically allocated storage.

Another use of the `this` pointer is in enabling cascaded member function calls. Figure 17.8 illustrates returning a reference to a `Time` object to enable member function calls of class `Time` to be cascaded. Member functions `setTime`, `setHour`, `setMinute` and `setSecond` each return `*this` with a return type of `Time &`.

```
1   // Fig. 17.8: time6.h
2   // Cascading member function calls.
3
4   // Declaration of class Time.
5   // Member functions defined in time6.cpp
6   #ifndef TIME6_H
7   #define TIME6_H
8
9   class Time {
10  public:
11     Time( int = 0, int = 0, int = 0 );  // default constructor
12
13     // set functions
14     Time &setTime( int, int, int ); // set hour, minute, second
15     Time &setHour( int );     // set hour
16     Time &setMinute( int );   // set minute
17     Time &setSecond( int );   // set second
18
19     // get functions (normally declared const)
20     int getHour() const;      // return hour
21     int getMinute() const;    // return minute
22     int getSecond() const;    // return second
23
24     // print functions (normally declared const)
25     void printMilitary() const;  // print military time
26     void printStandard() const;  // print standard time
27  private:
28     int hour;                 // 0 - 23
29     int minute;               // 0 - 59
30     int second;               // 0 - 59
31  }; // end class Time
32
33  #endif
```

Fig. 17.8 Cascading member function calls—`time6.h`.

```cpp
34   // Fig. 17.8: time6.cpp
35   // Member function definitions for Time class.
36   #include <iostream>
37
38   using std::cout;
39
40   #include "time6.h"
41
42   // Constructor function to initialize private data.
43   // Calls member function setTime to set variables.
44   // Default values are 0 (see class definition).
45   Time::Time( int hr, int min, int sec )
46      { setTime( hr, min, sec ); }
47
48   // Set the values of hour, minute, and second.
49   Time &Time::setTime( int h, int m, int s )
50   {
51      setHour( h );
52      setMinute( m );
53      setSecond( s );
54      return *this;   // enables cascading
55   } // end function setTime
56
57   // Set the hour value
58   Time &Time::setHour( int h )
59   {
60      hour = ( h >= 0 && h < 24 ) ? h : 0;
61
62      return *this;   // enables cascading
63   } // end function setHour
64
65   // Set the minute value
66   Time &Time::setMinute( int m )
67   {
68      minute = ( m >= 0 && m < 60 ) ? m : 0;
69
70      return *this;   // enables cascading
71   } // end function setMinute
72
73   // Set the second value
74   Time &Time::setSecond( int s )
75   {
76      second = ( s >= 0 && s < 60 ) ? s : 0;
77
78      return *this;   // enables cascading
79   } // end function setSecond
80
81   // Get the hour value
82   int Time::getHour() const { return hour; }
83
84   // Get the minute value
85   int Time::getMinute() const { return minute; }
86
```

Fig. 17.8 Cascading member function calls—time6.cpp. (Part 1 of 2.)

```
87   // Get the second value
88   int Time::getSecond() const { return second; }
89
90   // Display military format time: HH:MM
91   void Time::printMilitary() const
92   {
93      cout << ( hour < 10 ? "0" : "" ) << hour << ":"
94           << ( minute < 10 ? "0" : "" ) << minute;
95   } // end function printMilitary
96
97   // Display standard format time: HH:MM:SS AM (or PM)
98   void Time::printStandard() const
99   {
100     cout << ( ( hour == 0 || hour == 12 ) ? 12 : hour % 12 )
101          << ":" << ( minute < 10 ? "0" : "" ) << minute
102          << ":" << ( second < 10 ? "0" : "" ) << second
103          << ( hour < 12 ? " AM" : " PM" );
104  } // end function printStandard
```

Fig. 17.8 Cascading member function calls—`time6.cpp`. (Part 2 of 2.)

```
105  // Fig. 17.8: fig17_08.cpp
106  // Cascading member function calls together
107  // with the this pointer
108  #include <iostream>
109
110  using std::cout;
111  using std::endl;
112
113  #include "time6.h"
114
115  int main()
116  {
117     Time t;
118
119     t.setHour( 18 ).setMinute( 30 ).setSecond( 22 );
120     cout << "Military time: ";
121     t.printMilitary();
122     cout << "\nStandard time: ";
123     t.printStandard();
124
125     cout << "\n\nNew standard time: ";
126     t.setTime( 20, 20, 20 ).printStandard();
127     cout << endl;
128
129     return 0;
130  } // end function main
```

```
Military time: 18:30
Standard time: 6:30:22 PM

New standard time: 8:20:20 PM
```

Fig. 17.8 Cascading member function calls—`fig17_08.cpp`.

Why does the technique of returning *this as a reference work? The dot operator (.) associates from left to right, so the expression

```
t.setHour( 18 ).setMinute( 30 ).setSecond( 22 );
```

first evaluates t.setHour(18) then returns a reference to object t as the value of this function call. The remaining expression is then interpreted as

```
t.setMinute( 30 ).setSecond( 22 );
```

The t.setMinute(30) call executes and returns the equivalent of t. The remaining expression is interpreted as

```
t.setSecond( 22 );
```

Note the calls

```
t.setTime( 20, 20, 20 ).printStandard();
```

also use the cascading feature. These calls must appear in this order in this expression because printStandard as defined in the class does not return a reference to t. Placing the call to printStandard in the preceding statement before the call to setTime results in a syntax error.

17.6 Dynamic Memory Allocation with Operators new and delete

The *new* and *delete* operators provide a nicer means of performing dynamic memory allocation (for any built-in or user-defined type) than do C's malloc and free function calls. Consider the following code

```
TypeName *typeNamePtr;
```

In ANSI C, to dynamically create an object of type TypeName, you would write

```
typeNamePtr = malloc( sizeof( TypeName ) );
```

This requires a function call to malloc and explicit use of the sizeof operator. In versions of C prior to ANSI C, you would also have to cast the pointer returned by malloc with the cast (TypeName *). Function malloc does not provide any method of initializing the allocated block of memory. In C++, you simply write

```
typeNamePtr = new TypeName;
```

The new operator creates an object of the proper size, calls the constructor for the object and returns a pointer of the correct type. If new is unable to find space, it returns a 0 pointer in versions of C++ prior to the ANSI/ISO standard. [*Note:* In Chapter 23, we will show you how to deal with new failures in the context of the ANSI/ISO C++ standard. In particular, we will show how new "throws" an "exception" and we will show how to "catch" that exception and deal with it.] To destroy the object and free the space for this object in C++ you must use the delete operator as follows:

```
delete typeNamePtr;
```

C++ allows you to provide an *initializer* for a newly created object, as in

```
double *thingPtr = new double( 3.14159 );
```

which initializes a newly created `double` object to `3.14159`.

A 10-element integer array can be created and assigned to `arrayPtr` as follows:

```
int *arrayPtr = new int[ 10 ];
```

This array is deleted with the statement

```
delete [] arrayPtr;
```

As we will see, using `new` and `delete` instead of `malloc` and `free` offers other benefits as well. In particular, `new` invokes the constructor and `delete` invokes the class's destructor.

Common Programming Error 17.8

Mixing `new` and `delete` style dynamic memory allocation with `malloc` and `free` style dynamic memory allocation is a logic error: Space created by `malloc` cannot be freed by `delete`; objects created by `new` cannot be deleted by `free`.

Common Programming Error 17.9

Using `delete` instead of `delete []` for arrays can lead to runtime logic errors. To avoid problems, space created as an array should be deleted with the `delete []` operator and space created as an individual element should be deleted with the `delete` operator.

Good Programming Practice 17.3

C++ includes C, so C++ programs can contain storage created by `malloc` and deleted by `free`, and objects created by `new` and deleted by `delete`. It is best to use only `new` and `delete`.

17.7 static Class Members

Each object of a class has its own copy of all the data members of the class. In certain cases only one copy of a variable should be shared by all objects of a class. A `static` class variable is used for these and other reasons. A `static` class variable represents "class-wide" information (i.e., a property of the class, not of a specific object of the class). The declaration of a `static` member begins with the keyword `static`.

Let us motivate the need for `static` class-wide data with a video game example. Suppose we have a video game with `Martian`s and other space creatures. Each `Martian` tends to be brave and willing to attack other space creatures when the `Martian` is aware that there are at least five `Martian`s present. If fewer than five are present, each `Martian` becomes cowardly. So each `Martian` needs to know the `martianCount`. We could endow each instance of class `Martian` with `martianCount` as a data member. If we do this, then every `Martian` will have a separate copy of the data member and every time we create a new `Martian` we will have to update the data member `martianCount` in every `Martian` object. This wastes space with the redundant copies and wastes time in updating the separate copies. Instead, we declare `martianCount` to be `static`. This makes `martianCount` class-wide data. Every `Martian` can see the `martianCount` as if it were a data member of the `Martian`, but only one copy of the static `martianCount` is maintained by C++. This saves space. We save time by having the `Martian` constructor increment the static `martianCount`. There is only one copy, so we do not have to increment separate copies of `martianCount` for each `Martian` object.

Performance Tip 17.4

Use `static` data members to save storage when a single copy of the data will suffice.

Although `static` data members may seem like global variables, `static` data members have class scope. `static` members can be `public`, `private` or `protected`. `static` data members *must* be initialized *once* (and only once) at file scope. A class's `public` `static` class members can be accessed through any object of that class, or they can be accessed through the class name using the binary scope resolution operator. A class's `private` and `protected` `static` members must be accessed through `public` member functions of the class or through `friends` of the class. A class's `static` members exist even when no objects of that class exist. To access a `public` `static` class member when no objects of the class exist, simply prefix the class name and the binary scope resolution operator (`::`) to the name of the data member. To access a `private` or `protected` `static` class member when no objects of the class exist, a `public` `static` member function must be provided and the function must be called by prefixing its name with the class name and binary scope resolution operator.

Figure 17.9 demonstrates a `private` `static` data member and a `public` `static` member function. Data member `count` is initialized to zero at file scope with the statement

```
int Employee::count = 0;
```

Data member `count` maintains a count of the number of objects of class `Employee` that have been instantiated. When objects of class `Employee` exist, member `count` can be referenced through any member function of an `Employee` object—in this example, `count` is referenced by both the constructor and the destructor.

```
1   // Fig. 17.9: employ1.h
2   // An employee class
3   #ifndef EMPLOY1_H
4   #define EMPLOY1_H
5
6   class Employee {
7   public:
8      Employee( const char*, const char* );  // constructor
9      ~Employee();                           // destructor
10     const char *getFirstName() const;      // return first name
11     const char *getLastName() const;       // return last name
12
13     // static member function
14     static int getCount();  // return # objects instantiated
15
16  private:
17     char *firstName;
```

Fig. 17.9 Using a `static` data member to maintain a count of the number of objects of a class—`employ1.h`. (Part 1 of 2.)

```
18        char *lastName;
19
20        // static data member
21        static int count;  // number of objects instantiated
22   }; // end class Employee
23
24   #endif
```

Fig. 17.9   Using a static data member to maintain a count of the number of objects of a class—employ1.h. (Part 2 of 2.)

```
25   // Fig. 17.9: employ1.cpp
26   // Member function definitions for class Employee
27   #include <iostream>
28
29   using std::cout;
30   using std::endl;
31
32   #include <cstring>
33   #include <cassert>
34   #include "employ1.h"
35
36   // Initialize the static data member
37   int Employee::count = 0;
38
39   // Define the static member function that
40   // returns the number of employee objects instantiated.
41   int Employee::getCount() { return count; }
42
43   // Constructor dynamically allocates space for the
44   // first and last name and uses strcpy to copy
45   // the first and last names into the object
46   Employee::Employee( const char *first, const char *last )
47   {
48      firstName = new char[ strlen( first ) + 1 ];
49      assert( firstName != 0 );    // ensure memory allocated
50      strcpy( firstName, first );
51
52      lastName = new char[ strlen( last ) + 1 ];
53      assert( lastName != 0 );     // ensure memory allocated
54      strcpy( lastName, last );
55
56      ++count;   // increment static count of employees
57      cout << "Employee constructor for " << firstName
58           << ' ' << lastName << " called." << endl;
59   } // end Employee constructor
60
61   // Destructor deallocates dynamically allocated memory
62   Employee::~Employee()
63   {
64      cout << "~Employee() called for " << firstName
```

Fig. 17.9   Using a static data member to maintain a count of the number of objects of a class—employ1.cpp. (Part 1 of 2.)

```
65              << ' ' << lastName << endl;
66     delete [] firstName;  // recapture memory
67     delete [] lastName;   // recapture memory
68     --count;  // decrement static count of employees
69  } // end Employee destructor
70
71  // Return first name of employee
72  const char *Employee::getFirstName() const
73  {
74     // Const before return type prevents client from modifying
75     // private data. Client should copy returned string before
76     // destructor deletes storage to prevent undefined pointer.
77     return firstName;
78  } // end function getFirstName
79
80  // Return last name of employee
81  const char *Employee::getLastName() const
82  {
83     // Const before return type prevents client from modifying
84     // private data. Client should copy returned string before
85     // destructor deletes storage to prevent undefined pointer.
86     return lastName;
87  } // end function getLastName
```

Fig. 17.9   Using a `static` data member to maintain a count of the number of objects of a class—`employ1.cpp`. (Part 2 of 2.)

```
88  // Fig. 17.9: fig17_09.cpp
89  // Driver to test the employee class
90  #include <iostream>
91
92  using std::cout;
93  using std::endl;
94
95  #include "employ1.h"
96
97  int main()
98  {
99     cout << "Number of employees before instantiation is "
100         << Employee::getCount() << endl;    // use class name
101
102    Employee *e1Ptr = new Employee( "Susan", "Baker" );
103    Employee *e2Ptr = new Employee( "Robert", "Jones" );
104
105    cout << "Number of employees after instantiation is "
106         << e1Ptr->getCount();
107
108    cout << "\n\nEmployee 1: "
109         << e1Ptr->getFirstName()
110         << " " << e1Ptr->getLastName()
111         << "\nEmployee 2: "
```

Fig. 17.9   Using a `static` data member to maintain a count of the number of objects of a class—`fig17_09.cpp`. (Part 1 of 2.)

```
112                    << e2Ptr->getFirstName()
113                    << " " << e2Ptr->getLastName() << "\n\n";
114
115      delete e1Ptr;    // recapture memory
116      e1Ptr = 0;
117      delete e2Ptr;    // recapture memory
118      e2Ptr = 0;
119
120      cout << "Number of employees after deletion is "
121           << Employee::getCount() << endl;
122
123      return 0;
124  } // end function main
```

```
Number of employees before instantiation is 0
Employee constructor for Susan Baker called.
Employee constructor for Robert Jones called.
Number of employees after instantiation is 2

Employee 1: Susan Baker
Employee 2: Robert Jones

~Employee() called for Susan Baker
~Employee() called for Robert Jones
Number of employees after deletion is 0
```

Fig. 17.9   Using a `static` data member to maintain a count of the number of objects of a class—`fig17_09.cpp`. (Part 2 of 2.)

Common Programming Error 17.10

It is a syntax error to include keyword `static` in the definition of a `static` class variable at file scope.

When no objects of class `Employee` exist, member `count` can still be referenced, but only through a call to `static` member function `getCount` as follows:

        Employee::getCount()

In this example, function `getCount` is used to determine the number of `Employee` objects currently instantiated. Note that when there are no objects instantiated in the program, the `Employee::getCount()` function call is issued. However, when there are objects instantiated, function `getCount` can be called through one of the objects as shown in the statement in lines 105 and 106

        cout << "Number of employees after instantiation is "
             << e1Ptr->getCount();

Note that the calls `e2Ptr->getCount()` and `Employee::getCount()` produce the same result.

Software Engineering Observation 17.13

Some organizations have in their software engineering standards that all calls to `static` member functions be made using the class name and not the object handle.

A member function may be declared `static` if it does not access non-`static` class data members and member functions. Unlike non-`static` member functions, a `static` member function has no `this` pointer because `static` data members and `static` member functions exist independent of any objects of a class.

Common Programming Error 17.11

Referring to the `this` pointer within a `static` member function is a syntax error.

Common Programming Error 17.12

Declaring a `static` member function `const` is a syntax error.

Software Engineering Observation 17.14

A class's `static` data members and `static` member functions exist and can be used even if no objects of that class have been instantiated.

Lines 102 and 103 use operator `new` to dynamically allocate two `Employee` objects. When each `Employee` object is allocated, its constructor is called. When `delete` is used in lines 115 and 117 to deallocate the two `Employee` objects, their destructors are called.

Good Programming Practice 17.4

After deleting dynamically allocated memory, set the pointer that referred to that memory to 0. This disconnects the pointer from the previously allocated space on the free store.

Note the use of *assert* in the `Employee` constructor function. The `assert` "macro"— defined in the `cassert` header file—tests the value of a condition. If the value of the expression is `false`, then `assert` issues an error message and calls function *abort* (of the general utilities header file—`cstdlib`) to terminate program execution. This is a useful debugging tool for testing if a variable has a correct value. [*Note:* Function `abort` immediately terminates program execution without running any destructors.]

In this program, `assert` determines if the `new` operator was able to fulfill the request for memory to be allocated dynamically. For example, in the `Employee` constructor function, the following line (which is also called an *assertion*)

```
assert( firstName != 0 );
```

tests pointer `firstName` to determine if it is not equal to 0. If the condition in the preceding assertion is `true`, the program continues without interruption. If the condition in the preceding assertion is `false`, an error message containing the line number, the condition being tested and the file name in which the assertion appears is printed, and the program terminates. The programmer may then concentrate on this area of the code to find the error. In Chapter 23, C++ Exception Handling, we will provide a better method of dealing with execution time errors.

Assertions do not have to be removed from the program when debugging is completed. When assertions are no longer needed for debugging purposes in a program, the line

```
#define NDEBUG
```

is inserted at the beginning of the program file (typically this can also be specified in the compiler options). This causes the preprocessor to ignore all assertions instead of the programmer having to delete each assertion manually.

Note that the implementations of functions `getFirstName` and `getLastName` return to the client of the class constant character pointers. In this implementation, if the client wishes to retain a copy of the first name or last name, the client is responsible for copying the dynamically allocated memory in the `Employee` object after obtaining the constant character pointer from the object. Note that it is also possible to implement `getFirstName` and `getLastName` so the client is required to pass a character array and the size of the array to each function. Then, the functions could copy the first or last name into the character array provided by the client.

17.8 Data Abstraction and Information Hiding

Classes normally hide their implementation details from the clients of the classes. This is called *information hiding*. As an example of information hiding, let us consider a data structure called a *stack*.

Think of a stack in terms of a pile of dishes. When a dish is placed on the pile, it is always placed at the top (referred to as *pushing onto the stack*), and when a dish is removed from the pile, it is always removed from the top (referred to as *popping off the stack*). Stacks are known as *last-in, first-out (LIFO) data structures*—the last item pushed (inserted) on the stack is the first item popped (removed) from the stack.

The programmer may create a stack class and hide from its clients the implementation of the stack. Stacks can easily be implemented with arrays (or linked lists; see Chapter 12, C Data Structures). A client of a stack class need not know how the stack is implemented. The client simply requires that when data items are placed in the stack, the data items will be recalled in last-in, first-out order. Describing the functionality of a class independent of its implementation is called *data abstraction* and C++ classes define so-called *abstract data types (ADTs)*. Although users may happen to know the details of how a class is implemented, users should not write code that depends on these details. This means that the implementation of a particular class (such as one that implements a stack and its operations of *push* and *pop*) can be altered or replaced without affecting the rest of the system, as long as the `public` interface to that class does not change.

The job of a high-level language is to create a view convenient for programmers to use. There is no single accepted standard view—that is one reason why there are so many programming languages. Object-oriented programming in C++ presents yet another view.

Most programming languages emphasize actions. In these languages, data exist in support of the actions programs need to take. Data are viewed as being "less interesting" than actions, anyway. Data are "crude." There are only a few built-in data types, and it is difficult for programmers to create their own new data types.

This view changes with C++ and the object-oriented style of programming. C++ elevates the importance of data. The primary activity in C++ is creating new types (i.e., classes) and expressing the interactions among objects of those types.

To move in this direction, the programming-languages community needed to formalize some notions about data. The formalization we consider is the notion of abstract data types (ADTs). ADTs receive as much attention today as structured programming did over the last two decades. ADTs do not replace structured programming. Rather, they provide an additional formalization that can further improve the program development process.

What is an abstract data type? Consider the built-in type `int`. What comes to mind is the notion of an integer in mathematics, but `int` on a computer is not precisely what an integer is in mathematics. In particular, computer `int`s are normally quite limited in size. For example, `int` on a 32-bit machine may be limited approximately to the range –2 billion to +2 billion. If the result of a calculation falls outside this range, an "overflow" error occurs and the machine responds in some machine-dependent manner, including the possibility of "quietly" producing an incorrect result. Mathematical integers do not have this problem. So the notion of a computer `int` is really only an approximation to the notion of a real-world integer. The same is true with `double`.

Even `char` is an approximation; `char` values are normally eight-bit patterns of ones and zeros; these patterns look nothing like the characters they represent such as a capital Z, a lowercase z, a dollar sign ($), a digit (5), and so on. Values of type `char` on most computers are quite limited compared with the range of real-world characters. The seven-bit ASCII character set provides for 128 different character values. This is completely inadequate for representing languages such as Japanese and Chinese that require thousands of characters.

The point is that even the built-in data types provided with programming languages like C++ are really only approximations or models of real-world concepts and behaviors. We have taken `int` for granted until this point, but now you have a new perspective to consider. Types like `int`, `double`, `char` and others are all examples of abstract data types. They are essentially ways of representing real-world notions to some satisfactory level of precision within a computer system.

An abstract data type actually captures two notions, namely a *data representation* and the *operations* that are allowed on those data. For example, the notion of `int` defines addition, subtraction, multiplication, division and modulus operations in C++, but division by zero is undefined; and these allowed operations perform in a manner sensitive to machine parameters such as the fixed-word size of the underlying computer system. Another example is the notion of negative integers, whose operations and data representation are clear, but the operation of taking the square root of a negative integer is undefined. In C++, the programmer uses classes to more precisely implement abstract data types and their services.

17.8.1 Example: Array Abstract Data Type

We discussed arrays in Chapter 6. An array is not much more than a pointer and some space. This primitive capability is acceptable for performing array operations if the programmer is cautious and undemanding. There are many operations that would be nice to perform with arrays, but that are not built into C++. With C++ classes, the programmer can develop an array ADT that is preferable to "raw" arrays. The array class can provide many helpful new capabilities such as

- Subscript range checking.
- An arbitrary range of subscripts instead of having to start with 0.
- Array assignment.
- Array comparison.
- Array input/output.
- Arrays that know their sizes.
- Arrays that expand dynamically to accommodate more elements.

We create our own array class in Chapter 18, C++ Operator Overloading. C++ has a small set of built-in types. Classes extend the base programming language.

Software Engineering Observation 17.15

The programmer is able to create new types through the class mechanism. These new types can be designed to be used as conveniently as the built-in types. Thus, C++ is an extensible language. Although the language is easy to extend with these new types, the base language itself is not changeable.

New classes created in C++ environments can be proprietary to an individual, to small groups or to companies. Classes can also be placed in standard class libraries intended for wide distribution. This does not necessarily promote standards although de facto standards are emerging. The full value of C++ can be realized only when substantial and standardized class libraries are used to develop new applications. ANSI (the American National Standards Institute) and ISO (the International Standards Organization) have developed a standard version of C++ that includes a standard class library. The reader who learns C++ and object-oriented programming will be ready to take advantage of the new kinds of rapid, component-oriented software development made possible with increasingly abundant and rich libraries.

17.8.2 Example: String Abstract Data Type

C++ is an intentionally sparse language that provides programmers with only the raw capabilities needed to build a broad range of systems (consider it a tool for making tools). The language is designed to minimize performance burdens. C++ is appropriate for both applications programming and systems programming—the latter places extraordinary performance demands on programs. Certainly, it would have been possible to include a string data type among C++'s built-in data types. Instead, the language was designed to include mechanisms for creating and implementing string abstract data types through classes.

17.8.3 Example: Queue Abstract Data Type

Each of us stands in line from time to time. A waiting line is also called a *queue.* We wait in line at the supermarket checkout counter, we wait in line to get gasoline, we wait in line to board a bus, we wait in line to pay a toll on the highway and students know all too well about waiting in line during registration to get the courses they want. Computer systems use many waiting lines internally, so we need to write programs that simulate what queues are and do.

A queue is a good example of an abstract data type. A queue offers well-understood behavior to its clients. Clients put items in a queue one at a time—using an *enqueue* operation—and the clients get those items back one at a time on demand—using a *dequeue* operation. Conceptually, a queue can become infinitely long. A real queue, of course, is finite. Items are returned from a queue in *first-in, first-out (FIFO)* order—the first item inserted in the queue is the first item removed from the queue.

The queue hides an internal data representation that somehow keeps track of the items currently waiting in line, and it offers a set of operations to its clients, namely *enqueue* and *dequeue.* The clients are not concerned about the implementation of the queue. Clients merely want the queue to operate "as advertised." When a client enqueues a new item, the queue should accept that item and place it internally in some kind of first-in, first-out data structure. When the client wants the next item from the front of the queue, the queue should remove the item from its internal representation and should deliver the item to the outside world (i.e., to the *client* of the queue) in FIFO order, i.e., the item that has been in the queue the longest should be the next one returned by the next *dequeue* operation.

The queue ADT guarantees the integrity of its internal data structure. Clients may not manipulate this data structure directly. Only the queue member functions have access to its internal data. Clients may cause only allowable operations to be performed on the data representation; operations not provided in the ADT's `public` interface are rejected in some appropriate manner. This could mean issuing an error message, terminating execution or simply ignoring the operation request.

17.9 Container Classes and Iterators

Among the most popular types of classes are *container classes* (also called *collection classes*), i.e., classes designed to hold collections of objects. Container classes commonly provide services such as insertion, deletion, searching, sorting, testing an item to determine if it is a member of the collection and the like. Arrays, stacks, queues, trees and linked lists are examples of container classes.

It is common to associate *iterator objects*—or more simply *iterators*—with container classes. An iterator is an object that returns the next item of a collection (or performs some action on the next item of a collection). Once an iterator for a class has been written, obtaining the next element from the class can be expressed simply. Just as a book being shared by several people could have several bookmarks in it at once, a container class can have several iterators operating on it at once. Each iterator maintains its own "position" information.

SUMMARY

- The keyword `const` specifies that an object is not modifiable.
- The C++ compiler disallows non-`const` member function calls on `const` objects.
- An attempt by a `const` member function of a class to modify an object of that class is a syntax error.
- A function is specified as `const` both in its declaration and its definition.
- A `const` member function may be overloaded with a non-`const` version. The choice of which overloaded member function to use is made by the compiler based on whether the object has been declared `const` or not.
- A `const` object must be initialized—member initializers must be provided in the constructor of a class when that class contains `const` data members.
- Classes can be composed of objects of other classes.
- Member objects are constructed in the order in which they are listed in the class definition and before their enclosing class objects are constructed.
- If a member initializer is not provided for a member object, the member object's default constructor is called.
- A `friend` function of a class is a function defined outside that class and that has the right to access all members of the class.
- Friendship declarations can be placed anywhere in the class definition.
- The `this` pointer is implicitly used to reference both the non-`static` member functions and non-`static` data members of the object.
- Each non-`static` member function has access to its object's address by using the `this` keyword.
- The `this` pointer may be used explicitly.

- The new operator allocates space for an object, runs the object's constructor and returns a pointer of the correct type. To free the space for this object, use the delete operator.
- An array of objects can be allocated dynamically with new as in

      int *ptr = new int[100];

  which allocates an array of 100 integers and assigns the starting location of the array to ptr. The preceding array of integers is deleted with the statement

      delete [] ptr;

- A static data member represents "class-wide" information (i.e., a property of the class, not an object). The declaration of a static member begins with the keyword static.
- static data members have class scope.
- static members of a class can be accessed through an object of that class or through the class name using the scope resolution operator (if the member is public).
- A member function may be declared static if it does not access non-static class members. Unlike non-static member functions, a static member function has no this pointer. This is because static data members and static member functions exist independent of any objects of a class.
- Classes normally hide their implementation details from the clients of the classes. This is called information hiding.
- Stacks are known as last-in, first-out (LIFO) data structures—the last item pushed (inserted) on the stack is the first item popped (removed) from the stack.
- Describing the functionality of a class independent of its implementation is called data abstraction and C++ classes define so-called abstract data types (ADTs).
- C++ elevates the importance of data. The primary activity in C++ is creating new data types (i.e., classes) and expressing the interactions among objects of those data types.
- Abstract data types are ways of representing real-world notions to some satisfactory level of precision within a computer system.
- An abstract data type actually captures two notions, namely a data representation and the operations that are allowed on those data.
- C++ is an extensible language. Although the language is easy to extend with these new types, the base language itself is not changeable.
- C++ is an intentionally sparse language that provides programmers with only the raw capabilities needed to build a broad range of systems. The language is designed to minimize performance burdens.
- Items are returned from a queue in first-in, first-out (FIFO) order—the first item inserted in the queue is the first item removed from the queue.
- Container classes (also called collection classes) are designed to hold collections of objects. Container classes commonly provide services such as insertion, deletion, searching, sorting, testing an item for membership in the class and the like.
- It is common to associate iterator objects—or more simply iterators—with container classes. An iterator is an object that returns the next item of a collection (or performs some action on the next item of a collection).
- When a class definition uses only a pointer to another class, the class header file for that other class (which would ordinarily reveal the private data of that class) is not required to be included with

`#include`. You can simply declare that other class as a data type with a forward class declaration before the type is used in the file.

- The implementation file containing the member functions for the proxy class is the only file that includes the header file for the class whose `private` data we would like to hide.
- The implementation file is provided to the client as a precompiled object file along with the header file that includes the function prototypes of the services provided by the proxy class.

TERMINOLOGY

abstract data type (ADT)	`friend` function
binary scope resolution operator (`::`)	host object
cascading member function calls	iterator
class scope	last-in-first-out (LIFO)
composition	member access specifiers
`const` member function	member initializer
`const` object	member object
constructor	member object constructor
container	member selection operator (`.`)
data representations	`new` operator
default constructor	`new []` operator
default destructor	object-based programming
`delete` operator	operations in an ADT
`delete[]` operator	pointer member selection operator (`->`)
dequeue (queue operation)	*pop* (stack operation)
destructor	principle of least privilege
dynamic objects	*push* (stack operation)
enqueue (queue operation)	queue abstract data type
extensible language	stack abstract data type
first-in-first-out (FIFO)	`static` data member
forward class declaration	`static` member function
`friend` class	`this` pointer

COMMON PROGRAMMING ERRORS

17.1 Defining as `const` a member function that modifies a data member of an object is a syntax error.

17.2 Defining as `const` a member function that calls a non-`const` member function of the class on the same instance of the class is a syntax error.

17.3 Invoking a non-`const` member function on a `const` object is a syntax error.

17.4 Attempting to declare a constructor or destructor `const` is a syntax error.

17.5 Not providing a member initializer for a `const` data member is a syntax error.

17.6 Not providing a default constructor for the class of a member object when no member initializer is provided for that member object is a syntax error.

17.7 Attempting to use the member selection operator (`.`) with a pointer to an object is a syntax error—the dot member selection operator may only be used with an object or with a reference to an object.

17.8 Mixing `new` and `delete` style dynamic memory allocation with `malloc` and `free` style dynamic memory allocation is a logic error: Space created by `malloc` cannot be freed by `delete`; objects created by `new` cannot be deleted by `free`.

17.9   Using `delete` instead of `delete []` for arrays can lead to runtime logic errors. To avoid problems, space created as an array should be deleted with the `delete []` operator and space created as an individual element should be deleted with the `delete` operator.

17.10   It is a syntax error to include keyword `static` in the definition of a `static` class variable at file scope.

17.11   Referring to the `this` pointer within a `static` member function is a syntax error.

17.12   Declaring a `static` member function `const` is a syntax error.

GOOD PROGRAMMING PRACTICES

17.1   Declare as `const` all member functions that do not need to modify the current object so that you can use them on a `const` object if you need to.

17.2   Place all friendship declarations first in the class immediately after the class header and do not precede them with any member-access specifier.

17.3   C++ includes C, so C++ programs can contain storage created by `malloc` and deleted by `free`, and objects created by `new` and deleted by `delete`. It is best to use only `new` and `delete`.

17.4   After deleting dynamically allocated memory, set the pointer that referred to that memory to 0. This disconnects the pointer from the previously allocated space on the free store.

PERFORMANCE TIPS

17.1   Declaring variables and objects `const` is not only an effective software engineering practice—it can improve performance as well because today's sophisticated optimizing compilers can perform certain optimizations on constants that cannot be performed on variables.

17.2   Initialize member objects explicitly through member initializers. This eliminates the overhead of "doubly initializing" member objects—once when the member object's default constructor is called and again when *set* functions are used to initialize the member object.

17.3   For reasons of economy of storage, only one copy of each member function exists per class, and this member function is invoked by every object of that class. Each object, on the other hand, has its own copy of the class's data members.

17.4   Use `static` data members to save storage when a single copy of the data will suffice.

SOFTWARE ENGINEERING OBSERVATIONS

17.1   Declaring an object as `const` helps enforce the principle of least privilege. Attempts to modify the object are caught at compile time rather than causing execution-time errors.

17.2   Using `const` is crucial to proper class design, program design and coding.

17.3   A `const` member function can be overloaded with a non-`const` version. The choice of which overloaded member function to use is made by the compiler based on whether the object is `const` or not.

17.4   A `const` object cannot be modified by assignment so it must be initialized. When a data member of a class is declared `const`, a member initializer must be used to provide the constructor with the initial value of the data member for an object of the class.

17.5   Constant class members (`const` objects and `const` "variables") must be initialized with member initializer syntax; assignments are not allowed.

17.6   It is good practice to declare all a class's member functions that do not modify the object in which they operate as `const`. Occasionally, this will be an anomaly because you will have no intention of creating `const` objects of that class. Declaring such member functions `const` does offer a benefit though. If you inadvertently modify the object in that member function, the compiler will issue a syntax error message.

17.7 The most common form of software reusability is *composition,* in which a class has objects of other classes as members.

17.8 If a class has as a member an object of another class, making that member object `public` does not violate the encapsulation and hiding of that member object's `private` members.

17.9 Even though the prototypes for `friend` functions appear in the class definition, `friend`s are still not member functions.

17.10 Member access notions of `private`, `protected` and `public` are not relevant to friendship declarations, so friendship declarations can be placed anywhere in the class definition.

17.11 Some people in the OOP community feel that "friendship" corrupts information hiding and weakens the value of the object-oriented design approach.

17.12 C++ is a hybrid language, so it is common to have a mix of two types of function calls in one program and often back to back—C-like calls that pass primitive data or objects to functions and C++ calls that pass functions (or messages) to objects.

17.13 Some organizations have in their software engineering standards that all calls to `static` member functions be made using the class name and not the object handle.

17.14 A class's `static` data members and `static` member functions exist and can be used even if no objects of that class have been instantiated.

17.15 The programmer is able to create new types through the class mechanism. These new types can be designed to be used as conveniently as the built-in types. Thus, C++ is an extensible language. Although the language is easy to extend with these new types, the base language itself is not changeable.

ERROR-PREVENTION TIPS

17.1 Always declare member functions `const` if they do not modify the object. This can help eliminate many bugs.

17.2 Languages like C++ are "moving targets" as they evolve. More keywords are likely to be added to the language. Avoid using "loaded" words like "object" as identifiers. Even though "object" is not currently a keyword in C++, it could become one, so future compiling with new compilers could "break" existing code.

SELF-REVIEW EXERCISES

17.1 Fill in the blanks in each of the following:

a) _____ syntax is used to initialize constant members of a class.

b) A nonmember function must be declared as a(n) _____ of a class to have access to that class's `private` data members.

c) The _____ operator dynamically allocates memory for an object of a specified type and returns a(n) _____ to that type.

d) A constant object must be _____; it cannot be modified after it is created.

e) A(n) _____ data member represents class-wide information.

f) An object's member functions have access to a "self pointer" to the object called the _____ pointer.

g) The keyword _____ specifies that an object or variable is not modifiable after it is initialized.

h) If a member initializer is not provided for a member object of a class, the object's _____ is called.

i) A member function that is declared `static` cannot access _____ class members.

j) Member objects are constructed _____ their enclosing class object.

k) The _____ operator reclaims memory previously allocated by `new`.

17.2 Find the error(s) in each of the following and explain how to correct it (them):

a)
```cpp
class Example {
public:
    Example( int y = 10 ) { data = y; }
    int getIncrementedData() const { return ++data; }
    static int getCount()
    {
        cout << "Data is " << data << endl;
        return count;
    }
private:
    int data;
    static int count;
};
```

b)
```cpp
char *string;
string = new char[ 20 ];
free( string );
```

ANSWERS TO SELF-REVIEW EXERCISES

17.1 a) Member initializer. b) `friend`. c) `new`, pointer. d) initialized. e) `static`. f) `this`. g) `const`. h) default constructor. i) non-`static`. j) before. k) `delete`.

17.2 a) Error: The class definition for `Example` has two errors. The first occurs in function `getIncrementedData`. The function is declared `const`, but it modifies the object.

Correction: To correct the first error, remove the `const` keyword from the definition of `getIncrementedData`.

Error: The second error occurs in function `getCount`. This function is `static`, so it is not allowed to access any non-`static` member of the class.

Correction: To correct the second error, remove the output line from the definition of `getCount`.

b) Error: Memory dynamically allocated by `new` is deleted by the C Standard Library function `free`.

Correction: Use C++'s `delete` operator to reclaim the memory. C-style dynamic memory allocation should not be mixed with C++'s `new` and `delete` operators.

EXERCISES

17.3 Compare and contrast dynamic memory allocation using the C++'s `new` and `delete` operators, with dynamic memory allocation using the C Standard Library functions `malloc` and `free`.

17.4 Explain the notion of friendship in C++. Explain the negative aspects of friendship as described in the text.

17.5 Can a correct `Time` class definition include both of the following constructors? If not, explain why not.

```cpp
Time( int h = 0, int m = 0, int s = 0 );
Time();
```

17.6 What happens when a return type, even `void`, is specified for a constructor or destructor?

17.7 Create a `Date` class with the following capabilities:

a) Output the date in multiple formats such as

```
DDD  YYYY
MM/DD/YY
June 14, 1992
```

b) Use overloaded constructors to create `Date` objects initialized with dates of the formats in part (a).

c) Create a `Date` constructor that reads the system date using the standard library functions of the `<ctime>` header and sets the `Date` members.

In Chapter 18, we will be able to create operators for testing the equality of two dates and for comparing dates to determine if one date is prior to, or after, another.

17.8   Create a `SavingsAccount` class. Use a `static` data member to contain the `annualInterestRate` for each of the savers. Each member of the class contains a `private` data member `savingsBalance` indicating the amount the saver currently has on deposit. Provide a `calculateMonthlyInterest` member function that calculates the monthly interest by multiplying the `balance` by `annualInterestRate` divided by 12; this interest should be added to `savingsBalance`. Provide a `static` member function `modifyInterestRate` that sets the `static` `annualInterestRate` to a new value. Write a driver program to test class `SavingsAccount`. Instantiate two different `savingsAccount` objects, `saver1` and `saver2`, with balances of $2000.00 and $3000.00, respectively. Set `annualInterestRate` to 3%, then calculate the monthly interest and print the new balances for each of the savers. Then set the `annualInterestRate` to 4% and calculate the next month's interest and print the new balances for each of the savers.

17.9   It would be perfectly reasonable for the `Time` class of Fig. 17.8 to represent the time internally as the number of seconds since midnight rather than the three integer values `hour`, `minute` and `second`. Clients could use the same `public` methods and get the same results. Modify the `Time` class of Fig. 17.8 to implement the `Time` as the number of seconds since midnight and show that there is no visible change in functionality to the clients of the class.

18

C++ Operator Overloading

Objectives

- To understand how to redefine (overload) operators to work with new types.
- To understand how to convert objects from one class to another class.
- To learn when to, and when not to, overload operators.
- To study several interesting classes that use overloaded operators.
- To create an `Array` class.

The whole difference between construction and creation is exactly this: that a thing constructed can only be loved after it is constructed; but a thing created is loved before it exists.
Gilbert Keith Chesterton

The die is cast.
William Shakespeare

Our doctor would never really operate unless it was necessary. He was just that way. If he didn't need the money, he wouldn't lay a hand on you.
Herb Shriner

18.1 Introduction

In Chapters 16 and 17, we introduced the basics of C++ classes and the notion of abstract data types (ADTs). Manipulations on class objects (i.e., instances of ADTs) were accomplished by sending messages (in the form of member function calls) to the objects. This function-call notation is cumbersome for certain kinds of classes, especially mathematical classes. For these kinds of classes it would be nice to use C++'s rich set of built-in operators to specify object manipulations. In this chapter, we show how to enable C++'s operators to work with class objects. This process is called *operator overloading*. It is straightforward and natural to extend C++ with these new capabilities. It also requires great care because when overloading is misused, it can make a program difficult to understand.

Operator << has several purposes in C++—as the stream-insertion operator and as the bitwise left-shift operator. This is an example of operator overloading. Similarly, >> is also overloaded; it is used both as the stream-extraction operator and as the bitwise right-shift operator. Both of these operators are overloaded in the C++ class library. The C++ language itself overloads + and -. These operators perform differently depending on their context in integer arithmetic, floating-point arithmetic and pointer arithmetic.

C++ enables the programmer to overload most operators to be sensitive to the context in which they are used. The compiler generates the appropriate code based on the manner in which the operator is used. Some operators are overloaded frequently, especially the assignment operator and various arithmetic operators such as + and -. The job performed by overloaded operators can also be performed by explicit function calls, but operator notation is often clearer.

We will discuss when to use operator overloading and when not to use operator overloading. We show how to overload operators, and we present many complete programs using overloaded operators.

18.2 Fundamentals of Operator Overloading

C++ programming is a type-sensitive and type-focused process. Programmers can use built-in types and can define new types. The built-in types can be used with C++'s rich collection of operators. Operators provide programmers with a concise notation for expressing manipulations of objects of built-in types.

Programmers can use operators with user-defined types as well. Although C++ does not allow new operators to be created, it does allow most existing operators to be overloaded so that when these operators are used with class objects, the operators have meaning appropriate to the new types. This is one of C++'s most powerful features.

Software Engineering Observation 18.1

Operator overloading contributes to C++'s extensibility, one of the language's most appealing attributes.

Good Programming Practice 18.1

Use operator overloading when it makes a program clearer than accomplishing the same operations with explicit function calls.

Good Programming Practice 18.2

Avoid excessive or inconsistent use of operator overloading as this can make a program cryptic and difficult to read.

Although operator overloading may sound like an exotic capability, most programmers implicitly use overloaded operators regularly. For example, the addition operator (+) operates quite differently on integers, floats and doubles. But addition nevertheless works fine with variables of type `int`, `float`, `double` and a number of other built-in types because the addition operator (+) has been overloaded in the C++ language itself.

Operators are overloaded by writing a function definition (with a header and body) as you normally would, except that the function name now becomes the keyword `operator` followed by the symbol for the operator being overloaded. For example, the function name `operator+` would be used to overload the addition operator (+).

To use an operator on class objects, that operator *must* be overloaded—with two exceptions. The assignment operator (=) may be used with every class without explicit overloading. The default behavior of the assignment operator is a *memberwise assignment* of the data members of the class. We will soon see that such default memberwise assignment is dangerous for classes with pointer members; we will explicitly overload the assignment operator for such classes. The address operator (&) may also be used with objects of any class without overloading; it simply returns the address of the object in memory. The address operator can also be overloaded.

Overloading is most appropriate for mathematical classes. These often require that a substantial set of operators be overloaded to ensure consistency with the way these mathematical classes are handled in the real world. For example, it would be unusual to overload only addition for a complex number class because other arithmetic operators are also commonly used with complex numbers.

C++ is an operator-rich language. C++ programmers who understand the meaning and context of each operator are likely to make reasonable choices when it comes to overloading operators for new classes.

The point of operator overloading is to provide the same concise expressions for user-defined types that C++ provides with its rich collection of operators for built-in types. Operator overloading is not automatic, however; the programmer must write operator overloading functions to perform the desired operations. Sometimes these functions are best made member functions; sometimes they are best as `friend` functions and occasionally they can be made non-member, non-`friend` functions.

Extreme misuses of overloading are possible such as overloading operator + to perform subtraction-like operations or overloading operator / to perform multiplication-like operations. Such uses of overloading make a program extremely difficult to comprehend.

Good Programming Practice 18.3

Overload operators to perform the same function or similar functions on class objects as the operators perform on objects of built-in types. Avoid non-intuitive uses of operators.

Good Programming Practice 18.4

Before writing C++ programs with overloaded operators, consult the manuals for your compiler to become aware of restrictions and requirements unique to particular operators.

18.3 Restrictions on Operator Overloading

Most of C++'s operators can be overloaded. These are shown in Fig. 18.1. Figure 18.2 lists the operators that cannot be overloaded.

Operators that can be overloaded							
+	–	*	/	%	^	&	|
~	!	=	<	>	+=	-=	*=
/=	%=	^=	&=	|=	<<	>>	>>=
<<=	==	!=	<=	>=	&&	||	++
--	->*	,	->	[]	()	new	delete
new[]	delete[]						

Fig. 18.1   Operators that can be overloaded.

Operators that cannot be overloaded				
.	.*	::	?:	sizeof

Fig. 18.2   Operators that cannot be overloaded.

Common Programming Error 18.1

Attempting to overload a non-overloadable operator is a syntax error.

The precedence of an operator cannot be changed by overloading. This can lead to awkward situations in which an operator is overloaded in a manner for which its fixed precedence is inappropriate. However, parentheses can be used to force the order of evaluation of overloaded operators in an expression.

The associativity of an operator cannot be changed by overloading.

It is not possible to change the "arity" of an operator (i.e., the number of operands an operator takes): Overloaded unary operators remain as unary operators; overloaded binary operators remain as binary operators. C++'s only ternary operator (?:) cannot be overloaded (Fig. 18.2). Operators &, *, + and – each have unary and binary versions; these unary and binary versions can be overloaded separately.

It is not possible to create new operators; only existing operators can be overloaded. Unfortunately, this prevents the programmer from using popular notations like the ** operator used in FORTRAN and BASIC for exponentiation.

Common Programming Error 18.2

Attempting to create new operators via operator overloading is a syntax error.

The meaning of how an operator works on objects of built-in types cannot be changed by operator overloading. The programmer cannot, for example, change the meaning of how + adds two integers. Operator overloading works only with objects of user-defined types or with a mixture of an object of a user-defined type and an object of a built-in type.

Common Programming Error 18.3

Attempting to modify how an operator works with objects of built-in types is a syntax error.

Software Engineering Observation 18.2

At least one argument of an operator function must be a class object or a reference to a class object. This prevents programmers from changing how operators work on built-in types.

Overloading an assignment operator and an addition operator to allow statements like

```
object2 = object2 + object1;
```

does not imply that the += operator is also overloaded to allow statements such as

```
object2 += object1;
```

Such behavior can be achieved by explicitly overloading the += operator for that class.

Common Programming Error 18.4

Assuming that overloading an operator such as + overloads related operators such as += or that overloading == overloads a related operator like !=. Operators can be overloaded only explicitly; there is no implicit overloading.

Common Programming Error 18.5

Attempting to change the "arity" of an operator via operator overloading is a syntax error.

Good Programming Practice 18.5

To ensure consistency among related operators, use one to implement the others (i.e., use an overloaded + operator to implement an overloaded += operator).

18.4 Operator Functions as Class Members vs. as `friend` Functions

Operator functions can be member functions or non-member functions; non-member functions are often made `friend`s for performance reasons. Member functions use the `this` pointer implicitly to obtain one of their class object arguments (the left argument for binary operators). Both class arguments must be explicitly listed in a non-member function call.

When overloading (), [], -> or any of the assignment operators, the operator overloading function must be declared as a class member. For the other operators, the operator overloading functions can be non-member functions.

Whether an operator function is implemented as a member function or as a non-member function, the operator is still used the same way in expressions. So which implementation is best?

When an operator function is implemented as a member function, the leftmost (or only) operand must be a class object (or a reference to a class object) of the operator's class. If the left operand must be an object of a different class or a built-in type, this operator function must be implemented as a non-member function (as we will do in Section 18.5 when overloading << and >> as the stream-insertion and stream-extraction operators, respectively). A non-member operator function needs to be a `friend` if that function must access `private` or `protected` members of that class directly.

The overloaded << operator must have a left operand of type `ostream &` (such as `cout` in the expression `cout << classObject`), so it must be a non-member function. Similarly, the overloaded >> operator must have a left operand of type `istream &` (such as `cin` in the expression `cin >> classObject`), so it, too, must be a non-member function. Also, each of these overloaded operator functions may require access to the `private` data members of the class object being output or input, so these overloaded operator functions are sometimes made `friend` functions of the class for performance reasons.

Performance Tip 18.1

It is possible to overload an operator as a non-member, non-`friend` function, but such a function needing access to a class's `private` or `protected` data would need to use set or get functions provided in that class's `public` interface. The overhead of calling these functions could cause poor performance, so these functions can be `inlined` to improve performance.

Operator member functions of a specific class are called only when the left operand of a binary operator is specifically an object of that class, or when the single operand of a unary operator is an object of that class.

Another reason why one might choose a non-member function to overload an operator is to enable the operator to be commutative. For example, suppose we have an object, `number`, of type `long int`, and an object `bigInteger1`, of class `HugeInteger` (a class in which integers may be arbitrarily large rather than being limited by the machine word size of the underlying hardware; class `HugeInteger` is developed in the chapter exercises). The addition operator (+) produces a temporary `HugeInteger` object as the sum of a `HugeInteger` and a `long int` (as in the expression `bigInteger1 + number`), or as the sum of a `long int` and a `HugeInteger` (as in the expression `number + bigInteger1`). Thus, we require the addition operator to be commutative (exactly as it is normally). The problem is that the class object must appear on the left of the addition operator if that operator is to be overloaded as a member function. So, we overload the operator as a non-member `friend` function to allow the `HugeInteger` to appear on the right of the addition. Function `operator+` that deals with the `HugeInteger` on the left can still be a member function. Remember that a non-member function need not necessarily be a `friend` if appropriate *set* and *get* functions exist in the class's `public` interface, and especially if the *set* and *get* functions are `inlined`.

18.5 Overloading Stream-Insertion and Stream-Extraction Operators

C++ is able to input and output the built-in data types using the stream-extraction operator >> and stream-insertion operator <<. These operators are overloaded (in the class libraries provided with C++ compilers) to process each built-in data type including C-like `char *` strings and pointers. The stream-insertion and stream-extraction operators also can be overloaded to perform input and output for user-defined types. Figure 18.3 demonstrates overloading the stream-extraction and stream-insertion operators to handle data of a user-defined telephone number class called `PhoneNumber`. This program assumes telephone numbers are input correctly.

```cpp
1   // Fig. 18.3: fig18_03.cpp
2   // Overloading the stream-insertion and
3   // stream-extraction operators.
4   #include <iostream>
5
6   using std::cout;
7   using std::cin;
8   using std::endl;
9   using std::ostream;
10  using std::istream;
11
12  #include <iomanip>
13
14  using std::setw;
15
16  class PhoneNumber {
17     friend ostream &operator<<( ostream&, const PhoneNumber & );
18     friend istream &operator>>( istream&, PhoneNumber & );
19
20  private:
21     char areaCode[ 4 ];   // 3-digit area code and null
22     char exchange[ 4 ];   // 3-digit exchange and null
23     char line[ 5 ];       // 4-digit line and null
24  }; // end class PhoneNumber
25
26  // Overloaded stream-insertion operator (cannot be
27  // a member function if we would like to invoke it with
28  // cout << somePhoneNumber;).
29  ostream &operator<<( ostream &output, const PhoneNumber &num )
30  {
31     output << "(" << num.areaCode << ") "
32            << num.exchange << "-" << num.line;
```

Fig. 18.3 User-defined stream-insertion and stream-extraction operators. (Part 1 of 2.)

```
33        return output;       // enables cout << a << b << c;
34    } // end operator<< function
35
36    istream &operator>>( istream &input, PhoneNumber &num )
37    {
38        input.ignore();                       // skip (
39        input >> setw( 4 ) >> num.areaCode;   // input area code
40        input.ignore( 2 );                    // skip ) and space
41        input >> setw( 4 ) >> num.exchange;   // input exchange
42        input.ignore();                       // skip dash (-)
43        input >> setw( 5 ) >> num.line;       // input line
44        return input;        // enables cin >> a >> b >> c;
45    } // end operator>> function
46
47    int main()
48    {
49        PhoneNumber phone; // create object phone
50
51        cout << "Enter phone number in the form (123) 456-7890:\n";
52
53        // cin >> phone invokes operator>> function by
54        // issuing the call operator>>( cin, phone ).
55        cin >> phone;
56
57        // cout << phone invokes operator<< function by
58        // issuing the call operator<<( cout, phone ).
59        cout << "The phone number entered was: " << phone << endl;
60        return 0;
61    } // end function main
```

```
Enter phone number in the form (123) 456-7890:
(800) 555-1212
The phone number entered was: (800) 555-1212
```

Fig. 18.3   User-defined stream-insertion and stream-extraction operators. (Part 2 of 2.)

The stream-extraction operator function `operator>>` (line 36) takes an `istream` reference called `input` and a `PhoneNumber` reference called `num` as arguments, and returns an `istream` reference. Operator function `operator>>` is used to input phone numbers of the form

(800) 555-1212

into objects of class `PhoneNumber`. When the compiler sees the expression

cin >> phone

in `main`, the compiler generates the function call

operator>>(cin, phone);

When this call is executed, reference parameter `input` becomes an alias for `cin` and reference parameter `num` becomes an alias for `phone`. The operator function reads as strings the three parts of the telephone number into the `areaCode`, `exchange` and `line` members of the referenced PhoneNumber object (num in the operator function and `phone` in `main`). Stream manipulator `setw` limits the number of characters read into each character array. Remember that, when used with `cin`, `setw` restricts the number of characters read to one less than its argument (i.e., `setw( 4 )` allows three characters to be read and saves one position for a terminating null character). The parentheses, space and dash characters are skipped by calling `istream` member function `ignore`, which discards the specified number of characters in the input stream (one character by default). Function `operator>>` returns `istream` reference `input` (i.e., `cin`). This enables input operations on PhoneNumber objects to be cascaded with input operations on other PhoneNumber objects or on objects of other data types. For example, two PhoneNumber objects could be input as follows:

```
cin >> phone1 >> phone2;
```

First, the expression `cin >> phone1` would execute by making the call

```
operator>>( cin, phone1 );
```

This call would then return a reference to `cin` as the value of `cin >> phone1` so the remaining portion of the expression would be interpreted simply as `cin >> phone2`. This would execute by making the call

```
operator>>( cin, phone2 );
```

The stream-insertion operator takes an `ostream` reference (`output`) and a reference (`num`) to a user-defined type (PhoneNumber) as arguments, and returns an `ostream` reference. Function `operator<<` displays objects of type PhoneNumber. When the compiler sees the expression

```
cout << phone
```

in `main`, the compiler generates the non-member function call

```
operator<<( cout, phone );
```

Function `operator<<` displays the parts of the telephone number as strings because they are stored in string format.

Note that the functions `operator>>` and `operator<<` are declared in `class Pho-neNumber` as non-member, `friend` functions. These operators must be non-members because the object of class PhoneNumber appears in each case as the right operand of the operator; the class operand must appear on the left of the operator to overload that operator as a member function. Overloaded input and output operators are declared as `friends` if they need to access non-`public` class members directly for performance reasons. Also note that the PhoneNumber reference in `operator<<`'s parameter list is `const` (because the PhoneNumber will simply be output) and the PhoneNumber reference in `operator>>`'s parameter list is non-`const` (because the PhoneNumber object must be modified to store the input telephone number in the object).

Software Engineering Observation 18.3

New input/output capabilities for user-defined types can be added to C++ without modifying the declarations or `private` *data members for either the* `ostream` *class or the* `istream` *class. This is another example of the extensibility of the C++ programming language.*

18.6 Overloading Unary Operators

A unary operator for a class can be overloaded as a non-`static` member function with no arguments or as a non-member function with one argument; that argument must be either an object of the class or a reference to an object of the class. Member functions that implement overloaded operators must be non-`static` so they can access the non-`static` data of the class. Remember that `static` member functions can only access `static` data members of the class.

We can overload unary operator `!` to test if an object of the user-defined `String` class is empty and return a `bool` result. When overloading a unary operator such as `!` as a non-`static` member function with no arguments, if `s` is a `String` class object or a reference to a `String` class object, when the compiler sees the expression `!s`, the compiler generates the call `s.operator!()`. The operand `s` is the class object for which the `String` class member function `operator!` is being invoked. The function is declared in the class definition as follows:

```
class String {
public:
    bool operator!() const;
    ...
}; // end class String
```

A unary operator such as `!` may be overloaded as a non-member function with one argument two different ways—either with an argument that is an object (this requires a copy of the object, so the side effects of the function are not applied to the original object), or with an argument that is a reference to an object (no copy of the original object is made, so all side effects of this function are applied to the original object). If `s` is a `String` class object (or a reference to a `String` class object), then `!s` is treated as if the call `operator!(s)` had been written, invoking the non-member `friend` function of class `String` declared below:

```
class String {
    friend bool operator!( const String & );
    ...
}; // end class String
```

Good Programming Practice 18.6

When overloading unary operators, it is preferable to make the operator functions class members instead of non-member `friend` functions. `friend` functions and `friend` classes should be avoided unless they are absolutely necessary. The use of `friend`s violates the encapsulation of a class.

18.7 Overloading Binary Operators

A binary operator can be overloaded as a non-`static` member function with one argument, or as a non-member function with two arguments (one of those arguments must be either a class object or a reference to a class object).

When overloading binary operator `+=` as a non-`static` member function of a user-defined `String` class with one argument, if `y` and `z` are `String` class objects, then `y += z` is treated as if `y.operator+=(z)` had been written, invoking the `operator+=` member function declared below

```
class String {
public:
   const String &operator+=( const String & );
   ...
}; // end class String
```

If binary operator += is to be overloaded as a non-member function, it must take two arguments—one of which must be a class object or a reference to a class object. If y and z are String class objects or references to String class objects, then y += z is treated as if the call operator+=(y, z) had been written in the program, invoking non-member, friend function operator+= declared below

```
class String {
   friend const String &operator+=( String &,
                                     const String & );
   ...
}; // end class String
```

18.8 Case Study: An Array Class

Array notation in C++ is just an alternative to pointers, so arrays have much potential for errors. For example, a program can easily "walk off" either end of an array because C++ does not check whether subscripts fall outside the range of an array. Arrays of size n must number their elements 0, ..., $n - 1$; alternate subscript ranges are not allowed. An entire non-char array cannot be input or output at once; each array element must be read or written individually. Two arrays cannot be meaningfully compared with equality operators or relational operators (because the array names are simply pointers to where the arrays begin in memory). When an array is passed to a general-purpose function designed to handle arrays of any size, the size of the array must be passed as an additional argument. One array cannot be assigned to another with the assignment operator(s) (because array names are const pointers and a constant pointer cannot be used on the left side of an assignment operator). These and other capabilities certainly seem like "naturals" for dealing with arrays, but C++ does not provide such capabilities. However, C++ does provide the means to implement such array capabilities through the mechanisms of operator overloading.

In this example, we develop an array class that performs range checking to ensure that subscripts remain within the bounds of the array. The class allows one array object to be assigned to another with the assignment operator. Objects of this array class know their size, so the size does not need to be passed separately as an argument when passing an array to a function. Entire arrays can be input or output with the stream-extraction and stream-insertion operators, respectively. Array comparisons can be made with the equality operators == and !=. Our array class uses a static member to keep track of the number of array objects that have been instantiated in the program.

This example will sharpen your appreciation of data abstraction. You will probably want to suggest many enhancements to this array class. Class development is an interesting, creative and intellectually challenging activity—always with the goal of "crafting valuable classes."

The program of Fig. 18.4 demonstrates class Array and its overloaded operators. First we walk through the driver program in main. Then we consider the class definition and each of the class's member function and friend function definitions.

```
1    // Fig. 18.4: array1.h
2    // Simple class Array (for integers)
3    #ifndef ARRAY1_H
4    #define ARRAY1_H
5
6    #include <iostream>
7
8    using std::ostream;
9    using std::istream;
10
11   class Array {
12      friend ostream &operator<<( ostream &, const Array & );
13      friend istream &operator>>( istream &, Array & );
14   public:
15      Array( int = 10 );                    // default constructor
16      Array( const Array & );               // copy constructor
17      ~Array();                             // destructor
18      int getSize() const;                  // return size
19      const Array &operator=( const Array & ); // assign arrays
20      bool operator==( const Array & ) const;  // compare equal
21
22      // Determine if two arrays are not equal and
23      // return true, otherwise return false (uses operator==).
24      bool operator!=( const Array &right ) const
25         { return ! ( *this == right ); }
26
27      int &operator[]( int );               // subscript operator
28      const int &operator[]( int ) const;   // subscript operator
29      static int getArrayCount();           // Return count of
30                                            // arrays instantiated.
31   private:
32      int size; // size of the array
33      int *ptr; // pointer to first element of array
34      static int arrayCount;  // # of Arrays instantiated
35   }; // end class Array
36
37   #endif
```

Fig. 18.4 An Array class with operator overloading—array1.h.

```
38   // Fig 18.4: array1.cpp
39   // Member function definitions for class Array
40   #include <iostream>
41
42   using std::cout;
43   using std::cin;
44   using std::endl;
45
46   #include <iomanip>
47
48   using std::setw;
49
```

Fig. 18.4 An Array class with operator overloading—array1.cpp. (Part 1 of 4.)

```
50   #include <cstdlib>
51   #include <cassert>
52   #include "array1.h"
53
54   // Initialize static data member at file scope
55   int Array::arrayCount = 0;    // no objects yet
56
57   // Default constructor for class Array (default size 10)
58   Array::Array( int arraySize )
59   {
60      size = ( arraySize > 0 ? arraySize : 10 );
61      ptr = new int[ size ]; // create space for array
62      assert( ptr != 0 );    // terminate if memory not allocated
63      ++arrayCount;          // count one more object
64
65      for ( int i = 0; i < size; i++ )
66         ptr[ i ] = 0;       // initialize array
67   } // end Array constructor
68
69   // Copy constructor for class Array
70   // must receive a reference to prevent infinite recursion
71   Array::Array( const Array &init ) : size( init.size )
72   {
73      ptr = new int[ size ]; // create space for array
74      assert( ptr != 0 );    // terminate if memory not allocated
75      ++arrayCount;          // count one more object
76
77      for ( int i = 0; i < size; i++ )
78         ptr[ i ] = init.ptr[ i ];  // copy init into object
79   } // end Array constructor
80
81   // Destructor for class Array
82   Array::~Array()
83   {
84      delete [] ptr;         // reclaim space for array
85      --arrayCount;          // one fewer object
86   } // end Array destructor
87
88   // Get the size of the array
89   int Array::getSize() const { return size; }
90
91   // Overloaded assignment operator
92   // const return avoids: ( a1 = a2 ) = a3
93   const Array &Array::operator=( const Array &right )
94   {
95      if ( &right != this ) {  // check for self-assignment
96
97         // for arrays of different sizes, deallocate original
98         // left side array, then allocate new left side array.
99         if ( size != right.size ) {
100           delete [] ptr;         // reclaim space
101           size = right.size;     // resize this object
102           ptr = new int[ size ]; // create space for array copy
```

Fig. 18.4   An Array class with operator overloading—array1.cpp. (Part 2 of 4.)

```
103               assert( ptr != 0 );    // terminate if not allocated
104            } // end if
105
106            for ( int i = 0; i < size; i++ )
107               ptr[ i ] = right.ptr[ i ];  // copy array into object
108         } // end if
109
110         return *this;    // enables x = y = z;
111      } // end operator= function
112
113      // Determine if two arrays are equal and
114      // return true, otherwise return false.
115      bool Array::operator==( const Array &right ) const
116      {
117         if ( size != right.size )
118            return false;    // arrays of different sizes
119
120         for ( int i = 0; i < size; i++ )
121            if ( ptr[ i ] != right.ptr[ i ] )
122               return false; // arrays are not equal
123
124         return true;        // arrays are equal
125      } // end operator== function
126
127      // Overloaded subscript operator for non-const Arrays
128      // reference return creates an lvalue
129      int &Array::operator[]( int subscript )
130      {
131         // check for subscript out of range error
132         assert( 0 <= subscript && subscript < size );
133
134         return ptr[ subscript ]; // reference return
135      } // end operator[] function
136
137      // Overloaded subscript operator for const Arrays
138      // const reference return creates an rvalue
139      const int &Array::operator[]( int subscript ) const
140      {
141         // check for subscript out of range error
142         assert( 0 <= subscript && subscript < size );
143
144         return ptr[ subscript ]; // const reference return
145      } // end operator[] function
146
147      // Return the number of Array objects instantiated
148      // static functions cannot be const
149      int Array::getArrayCount() { return arrayCount; }
150
151      // Overloaded input operator for class Array;
152      // inputs values for entire array.
153      istream &operator>>( istream &input, Array &a )
154      {
```

Fig. 18.4 An Array class with operator overloading—array1.cpp. (Part 3 of 4.)

```
155     for ( int i = 0; i < a.size; i++ )
156         input >> a.ptr[ i ];
157
158     return input;    // enables cin >> x >> y;
159  } // end operator>> function
160
161  // Overloaded output operator for class Array
162  ostream &operator<<( ostream &output, const Array &a )
163  {
164     int i;
165
166     for ( i = 0; i < a.size; i++ ) {
167         output << setw( 12 ) << a.ptr[ i ];
168
169         if ( ( i + 1 ) % 4 == 0 ) // 4 numbers per row of output
170             output << endl;
171     } // end for
172
173     if ( i % 4 != 0 )
174         output << endl;
175
176     return output;    // enables cout << x << y;
177  } // end operator<< function
```

Fig. 18.4 An Array class with operator overloading—`array1.cpp`. (Part 4 of 4.)

```
178  // Fig. 18.4: fig18_04.cpp
179  // Driver for simple class Array
180  #include <iostream>
181
182  using std::cout;
183  using std::cin;
184  using std::endl;
185
186  #include "array1.h"
187
188  int main()
189  {
190     // no objects yet
191     cout << "# of arrays instantiated = "
192         << Array::getArrayCount() << '\n';
193
194     // create two arrays and print Array count
195     Array integers1( 7 ), integers2;
196     cout << "# of arrays instantiated = "
197         << Array::getArrayCount() << "\n\n";
198
199     // print integers1 size and contents
200     cout << "Size of array integers1 is "
201         << integers1.getSize()
202         << "\nArray after initialization:\n"
203         << integers1 << '\n';
```

Fig. 18.4 An Array class with operator overloading—`fig18_04.cpp`. (Part 1 of 3.)

```
204
205     // print integers2 size and contents
206     cout << "Size of array integers2 is "
207         << integers2.getSize()
208         << "\nArray after initialization:\n"
209         << integers2 << '\n';
210
211     // input and print integers1 and integers2
212     cout << "Input 17 integers:\n";
213     cin >> integers1 >> integers2;
214     cout << "After input, the arrays contain:\n"
215         << "integers1:\n" << integers1
216         << "integers2:\n" << integers2 << '\n';
217
218     // use overloaded inequality (!=) operator
219     cout << "Evaluating: integers1 != integers2\n";
220     if ( integers1 != integers2 )
221         cout << "They are not equal\n";
222
223     // create array integers3 using integers1 as an
224     // initializer; print size and contents
225     Array integers3( integers1 );
226
227     cout << "\nSize of array integers3 is "
228         << integers3.getSize()
229         << "\nArray after initialization:\n"
230         << integers3 << '\n';
231
232     // use overloaded assignment (=) operator
233     cout << "Assigning integers2 to integers1:\n";
234     integers1 = integers2;
235     cout << "integers1:\n" << integers1
236         << "integers2:\n" << integers2 << '\n';
237
238     // use overloaded equality (==) operator
239     cout << "Evaluating: integers1 == integers2\n";
240     if ( integers1 == integers2 )
241         cout << "They are equal\n\n";
242
243     // use overloaded subscript operator to create rvalue
244     cout << "integers1[5] is " << integers1[ 5 ] << '\n';
245
246     // use overloaded subscript operator to create lvalue
247     cout << "Assigning 1000 to integers1[5]\n";
248     integers1[ 5 ] = 1000;
249     cout << "integers1:\n" << integers1 << '\n';
250
251     // attempt to use out of range subscript
252     cout << "Attempt to assign 1000 to integers1[15]" << endl;
253     integers1[ 15 ] = 1000;  // ERROR: out of range
254
255     return 0;
256  } // end function main
```

Fig. 18.4 An Array class with operator overloading—`fig18_04.cpp`. (Part 2 of 3.)

```
# of arrays instantiated = 0
# of arrays instantiated = 2

Size of array integers1 is 7
Array after initialization:
            0            0            0            0
            0            0            0

Size of array integers2 is 10
Array after initialization:
            0            0            0            0
            0            0            0            0
            0            0

Input 17 integers:
1 2 3 4 5 6 7 8 9 10 11 12 13 14 15 16 17
After input, the arrays contain:
integers1:
            1            2            3            4
            5            6            7
integers2:
            8            9           10           11
           12           13           14           15
           16           17

Evaluating: integers1 != integers2
They are not equal

Size of array integers3 is 7
Array after initialization:
            1            2            3            4
            5            6            7

Assigning integers2 to integers1:
integers1:
            8            9           10           11
           12           13           14           15
           16           17
integers2:
            8            9           10           11
           12           13           14           15
           16           17

Evaluating: integers1 == integers2
They are equal

integers1[5] is 13
Assigning 1000 to integers1[5]
integers1:
            8            9           10           11
           12         1000           14           15
           16           17

Attempt to assign 1000 to integers1[15]
Assertion failed: 0 <= subscript && subscript < size, file Array1.cpp, line 95
abnormal program termination
```

Fig. 18.4   An Array class with operator overloading—fig18_04.cpp. (Part 3 of 3.)

The `static` class variable `arrayCount` of class `Array` contains the number of `Array` objects instantiated during program execution. The program begins by using `static` member function `getArrayCount` (line 192) to retrieve the number of arrays instantiated so far. Next, the program instantiates two objects of class `Array` (line 195)— `integers1` with seven elements and `integers2` with default size 10 elements (the default value specified by the `Array` default constructor). Line 197 calls function `getArrayCount` again to retrieve the value of class variable `arrayCount`. Lines 200 through 203 use member function `getSize` to determine the size of `Array` `integers1` and output `integers1` using the `Array` overloaded stream-insertion operator to confirm that the array elements were initialized correctly by the constructor. Next, lines 206 through 209 output the size of array `integers2` and output `integers2` using the `Array` over-loaded stream-insertion operator.

The user is then prompted to input 17 integers. The `Array` overloaded stream-extraction operator is used to read these values into both arrays with line 213

```
cin >> integers1 >> integers2;
```

The first seven values are stored in `integers1` and the remaining 10 values are stored in `integers2`. In lines 214 through 216, the two arrays are output with the `Array` stream-insertion operator to confirm that the input was performed correctly.

Line 220 tests the overloaded inequality operator by evaluating the condition

```
integers1 != integers2
```

and the program reports that the arrays are indeed not equal.

Line 225 instantiates a third `Array` called `integers3` and initializes it with `Array` `integers1`. This invokes the `Array` copy constructor to copy the elements of `integers1` into `integers3`. We discuss the details of the copy constructor shortly.

Lines 227 through 230 output the size of `integers3` and output `integers3` using the `Array` overloaded stream-insertion operator to confirm that the array elements were initialized correctly by the constructor.

Next, line 234 tests the overloaded assignment operator (=) with the statement

```
integers1 = integers2;
```

Both `Array`s are printed in lines 235 and 236 to confirm that the assignment was successful. Note that `integers1` originally held 7 integers and needed to be resized to hold a copy of the 10 elements in `integers2`. As we will see, the overloaded assignment operator performs this resizing in a manner transparent to the invoker of the operator.

Next, line 240 uses the overloaded equality operator (==) to confirm that objects `integers1` and `integers2` are indeed identical after the assignment.

Line 244 uses the overloaded subscript operator to refer to `integers1[ 5 ]`—an in-range element of `integers1`. This subscripted name is used as an *rvalue* to print the value in `integers1[ 5 ]`. Line 248, uses `integers1[ 5 ]` as an *lvalue* on the left side of an assignment statement to assign a new value, `1000`, to element 5 of `integers1`. Note that `operator[]` returns the reference to use as the *lvalue* after it determines that 5 is in range for `integers1`.

Line 253 attempts to assign the value `1000` to `integers1[ 15 ]`—an out-of-range element. The `Array` overloaded `[]` operator catches this error and program execution terminates abnormally.

Interestingly, the array subscript operator [] is not restricted for use only with arrays; it can be used to select elements from other kinds of ordered container classes such as linked lists, strings, dictionaries, and so on. Also, subscripts no longer have to be integers; characters, strings, floats or even objects of user-defined classes also could be used.

Now that we have seen how this program operates, let us walk through the class header and the member function definitions. Lines 32 through 34

```
int size; // size of the array
int *ptr; // pointer to first element of array
static int arrayCount;  // # of Arrays instantiated
```

represent the private data members of the class. The array consists of a size member indicating the number of elements in the array, an int pointer—ptr—that will point to the dynamically allocated array of integers stored in an Array object, and static member arrayCount indicating the number of array objects that have been instantiated.

Lines 12 and 13

```
friend ostream &operator<<( ostream &, const Array & );
friend istream &operator>>( istream &, Array & );
```

declare the overloaded stream-insertion operator and the overloaded stream-extraction operator to be friends of class Array. When the compiler sees an expression like

```
cout << arrayObject
```

it invokes the operator<<(ostream &, const Array &) function by generating the call

```
operator<<( cout, arrayObject )
```

When the compiler sees an expression like

```
cin >> arrayObject
```

it invokes the operator>>(istream &, Array &) function by generating the call

```
operator>>( cin, arrayObject )
```

We note again that these stream-insertion and stream-extraction operator functions cannot be members of class Array because the Array object is always mentioned on the right side of a stream-insertion operator and a stream-extraction operator. If these operator functions were to be members of class Array, the following awkward statements would have to be used to output and input an Array:

```
arrayObject << cout;
arrayObject >> cin;
```

Function operator<< (defined in line 162) prints the number of elements indicated by the size from the array stored at ptr. Function operator>> (defined in line 153) inputs directly into the array pointed to by ptr. Each of these operator functions returns an appropriate reference to enable cascaded output or input statements, respectively.

Line 15

```
Array( int = 10 );                      // default constructor
```

declares the default constructor for the class and specifies that the array size defaults to 10 elements. When the compiler sees a declaration like

```
Array integers1( 7 );
```

or the equivalent form

```
Array integers1 = 7;
```

it invokes the default constructor (remember that the default constructor in this example actually receives a single `int` argument that has a default value of 10). The default constructor (defined in line 58) validates and assigns the argument to the `size` data member, uses `new` to obtain the space to hold the internal representation of this array and assigns the pointer returned by `new` to data member `ptr`, uses `assert` to test that `new` was successful, increments `arrayCount`, then uses a `for` loop to initialize all the elements of the array to zero. It is possible to have an `Array` class that does not initialize its members if, for example, these members are to be read at some later time. But this is considered to be a poor programming practice. `Array`s, and objects in general, should be maintained at all times in a properly initialized and consistent state.

Line 16

```
Array( const Array & );            // copy constructor
```

declares a *copy constructor* (defined in line 71) that initializes an `Array` by making a copy of an existing `Array` object. Such copying must be done carefully to avoid the pitfall of leaving both `Array` objects pointing to the same dynamically allocated storage, exactly the problem that would occur with default memberwise copy. Copy constructors are invoked whenever a copy of an object is needed, such as in call-by-value, when returning an object by value from a called function or when initializing an object to be a copy of another object of the same class. The copy constructor is called in a definition when an object of class `Array` is instantiated and initialized with another `Array` object as in the following declaration:

```
Array integers3( integers1 );
```

or the equivalent declaration

```
Array integers3 = integers1;
```

Common Programming Error 18.6

Note that the copy constructor must use call-by-reference, not call-by-value. Otherwise, the copy constructor call results in infinite recursion (a fatal logic error) because, for call-by-value, a copy of the object passed to the copy constructor must be made, which results in the copy constructor being called recursively!

The copy constructor for `Array` uses a member initializer to copy the `size` of the array used for initialization into the `size` data member, uses `new` to obtain the space to hold the internal representation of this array and assigns the pointer returned by `new` to data member `ptr`, uses `assert` to test that `new` was successful, increments `arrayCount`, then uses a `for` loop to copy all the elements of the initializer array into this array.

Common Programming Error 18.7

If the copy constructor simply copied the pointer in the source object to the target object's pointer, then both objects would point to the same dynamically allocated storage. The first destructor to execute would then delete the dynamically allocated storage, and the other object's `ptr` would then be undefined, a situation called a "dangling pointer" and likely to result in a serious run-time error.

Software Engineering Observation 18.4

A constructor, a destructor, an overloaded assignment operator and a copy constructor are usually provided as a group for any class that uses dynamically allocated memory.

Line 17

```
~Array();                                // destructor
```

declares the destructor (defined in line 82) for the class. The destructor is invoked when the life of an object of class `Array` is terminated. The destructor uses `delete []` to reclaim the dynamic storage allocated by `new` in the constructor, then decrements `arrayCount`.

Line 18

```
int getSize() const;                     // return size
```

declares a function that reads the size of the array.

Line 19

```
const Array &operator=( const Array & ); // assign arrays
```

declares the overloaded assignment operator function for the class. When the compiler sees an expression like

```
integers1 = integers2;
```

it invokes the `operator=` function by generating the call

```
integers1.operator=( integers2 )
```

The `operator=` member function (defined in line 93) tests for *self assignment*. If a self assignment is being attempted, the assignment is skipped (i.e., the object already is itself; in a moment we will see why self assignment is dangerous). If it is not a self assignment, then the member function determines if the sizes of the two arrays are identical—in which case the original array of integers in the left-side `Array` object is not reallocated. Otherwise, `operator=` uses `delete` to reclaim the space originally allocated in the target array, copies the `size` of the source array to the `size` of the target array, uses `new` to allocate that amount of space for the target array and places the pointer returned by `new` into the array's `ptr` member and uses `assert` to verify that `new` succeeded. Then, `operator=` uses a `for` loop to copy the array elements from the source array to the target array. Regardless of whether this is a self assignment or not, the member function then returns the current object (i.e., `*this`) as a constant reference; this enables cascaded `Array` assignments such as `x = y = z`.

Common Programming Error 18.8

Not providing an overloaded assignment operator and a copy constructor for a class when objects of that class contain pointers to dynamically allocated storage is a logic error.

Software Engineering Observation 18.5

It is possible to prevent one class object from being assigned to another. This is done by declaring the assignment operator as a private member of the class.

Software Engineering Observation 18.6

It is possible to prevent class objects from being copied; to do this, simply make both the overloaded assignment operator and the copy constructor `private`*.*

Line 20

```
bool operator==( const Array & ) const;   // compare equal
```

declares the overloaded equality operator (==) for the class. When the compiler sees the expression

```
integers1 == integers2
```

in `main`, the compiler invokes the `operator==` member function by generating the call

```
integers1.operator==( integers2 )
```

The `operator==` member function (defined in line 115) immediately returns `false` if the `size` members of the arrays are different. Otherwise, the member function compares each pair of elements. If they are all the same, `true` is returned. The first pair of elements to differ causes `false` to be returned immediately.

Lines 24 and 25

```
bool operator!=( const Array &right ) const
   { return ! ( *this == right ); }
```

define the overloaded inequality operator (`!=`) for the class. The `operator!=` member function is defined in terms of the overloaded equality operator. The function definition uses the overloaded `operator==` function to determine if one `Array` is equal to another, then returns the opposite of that result. Writing the `operator!=` function in this manner enables the programmer to reuse the `operator==` function and reduces the amount of code that must be written in the class. Also, note that the full function definition for `operator!=` is in the `Array` header file. This allows the compiler to `inline` the definition of `operator!=` to eliminate the overhead of the extra function call.

Lines 27 and 28

```
int &operator[]( int );                 // subscript operator
const int &operator[]( int ) const;     // subscript operator
```

declare two overloaded subscript operators (defined in lines 129 and 139, respectively) for the class. When the compiler sees the expression

```
integers1[ 5 ]
```

in `main`, the compiler invokes the appropriate overloaded `operator[]` member function by generating the call

```
integers1.operator[]( 5 )
```

The compiler creates a call to the `const` version of `operator[]` when the subscript operator is used on a `const Array` object. For example, if `const` object `z` is instantiated with the statement

```
const Array z( 5 );
```

then a `const` version of `operator[]` is required when a statement such as

```
cout << z[ 3 ] << endl;
```

is executed. A `const` object can have only its `const` member functions called.

Each definition of `operator[]` tests if the subscript is in range, and, if it is not, the program terminates abnormally. If the subscript is in range, the appropriate element of the array is returned as a reference so that it may be used as an *lvalue* (for example, on the left side of an assignment statement) in the case of the non-`const` version of `operator[]`, or an *rvalue* in the case of the `const` version of `operator[]`.

Line 29

```
static int getArrayCount();        // return count of Arrays
```

declares `static` function `getArrayCount` that returns the value of `static` data member `arrayCount`, even if no objects of class `Array` exist.

18.9 Converting between Types

Most programs process information of a variety of types. Sometimes all the operations "stay within a type." For example, adding an integer to an integer produces an integer (as long as the result is not too large to be represented as an integer). But, it is often necessary to convert data of one type to data of another type. This can happen in assignments, in calculations, in passing values to functions and in returning values from functions. The compiler knows how to perform certain conversions among built-in types. Programmers can force conversions among built-in types by casting.

But what about user-defined types? The compiler cannot know how to convert among user-defined types and built-in types. The programmer must specify how such conversions are to occur. Such conversions can be performed with *conversion constructors*—single-argument constructors that turn objects of other types (including built-in types) into objects of a particular class.

A *conversion operator* (also called a *cast operator*) can be used to convert an object of one class into an object of another class or into an object of a built-in type. Such a conversion operator must be a non-`static` member function; this kind of conversion operator cannot be a `friend` function.

The function prototype

```
A::operator char *() const;
```

declares an overloaded cast operator function for creating a temporary `char *` object out of an object of user-defined type A. An overloaded *cast operator function* does not specify a return type—the return type is the type to which the object is being converted. If `s` is a class object, when the compiler sees the expression `(char *) s` the compiler generates the call `s.operator char *()`. The operand `s` is the class object `s` for which the member function `operator char *` is being invoked.

Overloaded cast operator functions can be defined for converting objects of user-defined types into built-in types or into objects of other user-defined types. The prototypes

```
A::operator int() const;
A::operator otherClass() const;
```

declare overloaded cast operator functions for converting an object of user-defined type A into an integer and for converting an object of user-defined type A into an object of user-defined type `otherClass`.

One of the nice features of cast operators and conversion constructors is that, when necessary, the compiler can call these functions to create temporary objects. For example, if an object s of a user-defined `String` class appears in a program at a location where an ordinary `char` * is expected, such as

```
cout << s;
```

the compiler calls the overloaded cast operator function `operator char *` to convert the object into a `char` * and uses the resulting `char` * in the expression. With this cast operator provided for our `String` class, the stream-insertion operator does not have to be overloaded to output a `String` using `cout`.

18.10 Overloading ++ and --

The increment and decrement operators—preincrement, postincrement, predecrement and postdecrement—can all be overloaded. We will see how the compiler distinguishes between the prefix version and the postfix version of an increment or decrement operator.

To overload the increment operator to allow both preincrement and postincrement usage, each overloaded operator function must have a distinct signature so the compiler will be able to determine which version of ++ is intended. The prefix versions are overloaded exactly as any other prefix unary operator would be.

Suppose, for example, that we want to add 1 to the day in the user-defined `Date` object d1. When the compiler sees the preincrementing expression

```
++d1
```

the compiler generates the member function call

```
d1.operator++()
```

whose prototype would be

```
Date &operator++();
```

If the preincrementing is implemented as a non-member function, when the compiler sees the expression

```
++d1
```

the compiler generates the function call

```
operator++( d1 )
```

whose prototype would be declared in the `Date` class as

```
friend Date &operator++( Date & );
```

Overloading the postincrementing operator presents a bit of a challenge because the compiler must be able to distinguish between the signatures of the overloaded preincrement and postincrement operator functions. The convention that has been adopted in C++ is that when the compiler sees the postincrementing expression

    d1++

it will generate the member-function call

    d1.operator++(0)

whose prototype is

    Date operator++(int)

The 0 is strictly a "dummy value" to make the argument list of operator++, used for postincrementing, distinguishable from the argument list of operator++, used for preincrementing.

If the postincrementing is implemented as a non-member function, when the compiler sees the expression

    d1++

the compiler generates the function call

    operator++(d1, 0)

whose prototype would be

    friend Date operator++(Date &, int);

Once again, the 0 argument is used by the compiler so the argument list of operator++, used for postincrementing, is distinguishable from the argument list for preincrementing.

Everything stated in this section for overloading preincrement and postincrement operators applies to overloading predecrement and postdecrement operators.

SUMMARY

- Operator << is used for multiple purposes in C++—as the stream-insertion operator and as the left-shift operator. This is an example of operator overloading. Similarly, >> is also overloaded; it is used both as the stream-extraction operator and as the right-shift operator.

- C++ enables the programmer to overload most operators to be sensitive to the context in which they are used. The compiler generates the appropriate code based on the operator's use.

- Operator overloading contributes to C++'s extensibility.

- To overload an operator, write a function definition; the function name must be the keyword operator followed by the symbol for the operator being overloaded.

- To use an operator on class objects, that operator *must* be overloaded—with two exceptions. The assignment operator (=) may be used with two objects of the same class to perform a default memberwise copy without overloading. The address operator (&) may also be used with objects of any class without overloading; it returns the address of the object in memory.

- Operator overloading provides the same concise expressions for user-defined types that C++ provides with its rich collection of operators that work on built-in types.

- The precedence and associativity of an operator cannot be changed by overloading.

- It is not possible to change the number of operands an operator takes: Overloaded unary operators remain as unary operators; overloaded binary operators remain as binary operators. C++'s only ternary operator, ?:, cannot be overloaded.

- It is not possible to create symbols for new operators; only existing operators may be overloaded.

- The meaning of how an operator works on built-in types cannot be changed by overloading.

- When overloading (), [], -> or any assignment operator, the operator overloading function must be declared as a class member.

- Operator functions can be member functions or non-member functions.

- When an operator function is implemented as a member function, the leftmost operand must be a class object (or a reference to a class object) of the operator's class.

- If the left operand must be an object of a different class, this operator function must be implemented as a non-member function.

- Operator member functions are called only when the left operand of a binary operator is an object of that class, or when the single operand of a unary operator is an object of that class.

- One might choose a non-member function to overload an operator to enable the operator to be commutative (i.e., given the proper overloaded operator definitions, the left argument of an operator can be an object of another data type).

- A unary operator can be overloaded as a non-static member function with no arguments or as a non-member function with one argument; that argument must be either an object of a user-defined type or a reference to an object of a user-defined type.

- A binary operator can be overloaded as a non-static member function with one argument, or as a non-member function with two arguments (one of those arguments must be either a class object or a reference to a class object).

- Array subscript operator [] is not restricted for use only with arrays; it can be used to select elements from other kinds of ordered container classes such as linked lists, strings, dictionaries etc. Also, subscripts no longer have to be integers; characters or strings could be used, for example.

- A copy constructor is used to initialize an object with another object of the same class. Copy constructors are also invoked whenever a copy of an object is needed, such as in call-by-value, and when returning a value from a called function. In a copy constructor, the object being copied must be passed in by reference.

- The compiler does not know how to convert between user-defined types and built-in types—the programmer must explicitly specify how such conversions are to occur. Such conversions can be performed with conversion constructors (i.e., single-argument constructors) that simply turn objects of other types into objects of a particular class.

- A conversion operator (or cast operator) can be used to convert an object of one class into an object of another class or into an object of a built-in type. Such a conversion operator must be a non-static member function; this kind of conversion operator cannot be a friend function.

- A conversion constructor is a single-argument constructor used to convert the argument into an object of the constructor's class. The compiler can call such a constructor implicitly.

- The assignment operator is the most frequently overloaded operator. It is normally used to assign an object to another object of the same class, but through the use of conversion constructors, it can also be used to assign between different classes.

- If an overloaded assignment operator is not defined, assignment is still allowed, but it defaults to a memberwise copy of each data member. In some cases this is acceptable. For objects that contain pointers to dynamically allocated storage, memberwise copy results in two different objects pointing to the same dynamically allocated storage. When the destructor for either of these objects is called, the dynamically allocated storage is released. If the other object then refers to that storage, the result is undefined.

- To overload the increment operator to allow both preincrement and postincrement usage, each overloaded operator function must have a distinct signature so the compiler will be able to determine which version of ++ is intended. The prefix versions are overloaded exactly as any other prefix unary operator. Providing a unique signature to the postincrement operator function is achieved by providing a second argument—which must be of type `int`. Actually, the user does not supply a value for this special integer argument. It is there simply to help the compiler distinguish between prefix and postfix versions of increment and decrement operators.

TERMINOLOGY

cascaded overloaded operators
cast operator function
class `Array`
class `Date`
class `HugeInteger`
class `PhoneNumber`
class `String`
conversion constructor
conversion function
conversion operator
conversions between built-in types and classes
conversions between class types
copy constructor
dangling pointer
default memberwise copy
explicit type conversions (with casts)
`friend` overloaded operator function
function call operator
implicit type conversions
member function overloaded operator
memory leak
non-overloadable operators
`operator!`
`operator!=`
`operator()`
`operator+`
`operator++`
`operator++( int )`
`operator+=`
`operator--`
`operator<`
`operator<<`
`operator<=`
`operator=`
`operator==`
`operator>`

`operator>=`
`operator>>`
`operator[]`
`operator char *`
operators implemented as functions
`operator int`
operator keyword
operator overloading
overloaded <= operator
overloaded = operator
overloaded == operator
overloaded > operator
overloaded >= operator
overloaded >> operator
overloaded assignment (=) operator
overloaded [] operator
overloading
overloading a binary operator
overloadable operators
overloaded != operator
overloaded + operator
overloaded ++ operator
overloaded += operator
overloaded -- operator
overloaded < operator
overloaded << operator
overloading a unary operator
postfix unary operator overloading
prefix unary operator overloading
self assignment
single-argument constructor
string concatenation
substring
user-defined conversion
user-defined type

COMMON PROGRAMMING ERRORS

18.1   Attempting to overload a non-overloadable operator is a syntax error.

18.2   Attempting to create new operators via operator overloading is a syntax error.

18.3   Attempting to modify how an operator works with objects of built-in types is a syntax error.

18.4   Assuming that overloading an operator such as + overloads related operators such as += or that overloading == overloads a related operator like !=. Operators can be overloaded only explicitly; there is no implicit overloading.

18.5   Attempting to change the "arity" of an operator via operator overloading is a syntax error.

18.6   Note that the copy constructor *must* use call-by-reference, not call-by-value. Otherwise, the copy constructor call results in infinite recursion (a fatal logic error) because, for call-by-value, a copy of the object passed to the copy constructor must be made, which results in the copy constructor being called recursively!

18.7   If the copy constructor simply copied the pointer in the source object to the target object's pointer, then both objects would point to the same dynamically allocated storage. The first destructor to execute would then delete the dynamically allocated storage, and the other object's `ptr` would then be undefined, a situation called a "dangling pointer" and likely to result in a serious run-time error.

18.8   Not providing an overloaded assignment operator and a copy constructor for a class when objects of that class contain pointers to dynamically allocated storage is a logic error.

GOOD PROGRAMMING PRACTICES

18.1   Use operator overloading when it makes a program clearer than accomplishing the same operations with explicit function calls.

18.2   Avoid excessive or inconsistent use of operator overloading as this can make a program cryptic and difficult to read.

18.3   Overload operators to perform the same function or similar functions on class objects as the operators perform on objects of built-in types. Avoid non-intuitive uses of operators.

18.4   Before writing C++ programs with overloaded operators, consult the manuals for your compiler to become aware of restrictions and requirements unique to particular operators.

18.5   To ensure consistency among related operators, use one to implement the others (i.e., use an overloaded + operator to implement an overloaded += operator).

18.6   When overloading unary operators, it is preferable to make the operator functions class members instead of non-member `friend` functions. `friend` functions and `friend` classes should be avoided unless they are absolutely necessary. The use of `friend`s violates the encapsulation of a class.

PERFORMANCE TIP

18.1   It is possible to overload an operator as a non-member, non-`friend` function, but such a function needing access to a class's `private` or `protected` data would need to use *set* or *get* functions provided in that class's `public` interface. The overhead of calling these functions could cause poor performance, so these functions can be `inline`d to improve performance.

SOFTWARE ENGINEERING OBSERVATIONS

18.1   Operator overloading contributes to C++'s extensibility, one of the language's most appealing attributes.

18.2   At least one argument of an operator function must be a class object or a reference to a class object. This prevents programmers from changing how operators work on built-in types.

18.3 New input/output capabilities for user-defined types can be added to C++ without modifying the declarations or `private` data members for either the `ostream` class or the `istream` class. This is another example of the extensibility of the C++ programming language.

18.4 A constructor, a destructor, an overloaded assignment operator and a copy constructor are usually provided as a group for any class that uses dynamically allocated memory.

18.5 It is possible to prevent one class object from being assigned to another. This is done by declaring the assignment operator as a `private` member of the class.

18.6 It is possible to prevent class objects from being copied; to do this, simply make both the overloaded assignment operator and the copy constructor `private`.

SELF-REVIEW EXERCISES

18.1 Fill in the blanks in each of the following:
  a) Suppose a and b are integer variables and we form the sum a + b. Now suppose c and d are floating-point variables and we form the sum c + d. The two + operators here are clearly being used for different purposes. This is an example of _____.
  b) Keyword _____ introduces an overloaded operator function definition.
  c) To use operators on class objects, they must be overloaded, with the exception of the operators _____ and _____.
  d) The _____, _____ and _____ of an operator cannot be changed by overloading the operator.

18.2 Explain the multiple meanings of the operators << and >> in C++.

18.3 In what context might the name `operator/` be used in C++?

18.4 (True/False) In C++, only existing operators can be overloaded.

18.5 How does the precedence of an overloaded operator in C++ compare with the precedence of the original operator?

ANSWERS TO SELF-REVIEW EXERCISES

18.1 a) operator overloading. b) `operator`. c) assignment (=), address(&). d) precedence, associativity, "arity."

18.2 Operator >> is both the right-shift operator and the stream-extraction operator depending, on its context. Operator << is both the left-shift operator and the stream-insertion operator depending, on its context.

18.3 For operator overloading: It would be the name of a function that would provide an overloaded version of the / operator.

18.4 True.

18.5 Identical.

EXERCISES

18.6 Give as many examples as you can of operator overloading implicit in C++. Give a reasonable example of a situation in which you might want to overload an operator explicitly in C++.

18.7 The C++ operators that cannot be overloaded are _____, _____, _____, _____ and _____.

18.8 *(Project)* C++ is an evolving language, and new languages are always being developed. What additional operators would you recommend adding to C++ or to a future language like C++ that would support both procedural programming and object-oriented programming? Write a careful justification. You might consider sending your suggestions to the ANSI C++ Committee or the newsgroup `comp.std.c++`.

18.9 Overload the subscript operator to return the largest element of a collection, the second largest, the third largest, etc.

18.10 Consider class `Complex` shown in Fig. 18.5. The class enables operations on so-called *complex numbers*. These are numbers of the form `realPart + imaginaryPart * i` where *i* has the value:

$$\sqrt{-1}$$

a) Modify the class to enable input and output of complex numbers through the overloaded `>>` and `<<` operators, respectively (you should remove the `print` function from the class).

b) Overload the multiplication operator to enable multiplication of two complex numbers as in algebra.

c) Overload the `==` and `!=` operators to allow comparisons of complex numbers.

```
1   // Fig. 18.5: complex1.h
2   // Definition of class Complex
3   #ifndef COMPLEX1_H
4   #define COMPLEX1_H
5
6   class Complex {
7   public:
8      Complex( double = 0.0, double = 0.0 );      // constructor
9      Complex operator+( const Complex & ) const;  // addition
10     Complex operator-( const Complex & ) const;  // subtraction
11     const Complex &operator=( const Complex & ); // assignment
12     void print() const;                          // output
13  private:
14     double real;        // real part
15     double imaginary;   // imaginary part
16  }; // end class Complex
17
18  #endif
```

Fig. 18.5 A complex number class—`complex1.h`.

```
19  // Fig. 18.5: complex1.cpp
20  // Member function definitions for class Complex
21  #include <iostream>
22
23  using std::cout;
24
25  #include "complex1.h"
26
27  // Constructor
28  Complex::Complex( double r, double i )
29     : real( r ), imaginary( i ) { }
```

Fig. 18.5 A complex number class—`complex1.cpp`. (Part 1 of 2.)

```
30
31    // Overloaded addition operator
32    Complex Complex::operator+( const Complex &operand2 ) const
33    {
34       return Complex( real + operand2.real,
35                       imaginary + operand2.imaginary );
36    } // end operator+ function
37
38    // Overloaded subtraction operator
39    Complex Complex::operator-( const Complex &operand2 ) const
40    {
41       return Complex( real - operand2.real,
42                       imaginary - operand2.imaginary );
43    } // end operator- function
44
45    // Overloaded = operator
46    const Complex& Complex::operator=( const Complex &right )
47    {
48       real = right.real;
49       imaginary = right.imaginary;
50       return *this;    // enables cascading
51    } // end operator= function
52
53    // Display a Complex object in the form: (a, b)
54    void Complex::print() const
55       { cout << '(' << real << ", " << imaginary << ')'; }
```

Fig. 18.5   A complex number class—`complex1.cpp`. (Part 2 of 2.)

```
56    // Fig. 18.5: fig18_05.cpp
57    // Driver for class Complex
58    #include <iostream>
59
60    using std::cout;
61    using std::endl;
62
63    #include "complex1.h"
64
65    int main()
66    {
67       Complex x, y( 4.3, 8.2 ), z( 3.3, 1.1 );
68
69       cout << "x: ";
70       x.print();
71       cout << "\ny: ";
72       y.print();
73       cout << "\nz: ";
74       z.print();
75
76       x = y + z;
77       cout << "\n\nx = y + z:\n";
78       x.print();
```

Fig. 18.5   A complex number class—`fig18_05.cpp`. (Part 1 of 2.)

```
79        cout << " = ";
80        y.print();
81        cout << " + ";
82        z.print();
83
84        x = y - z;
85        cout << "\n\nx = y - z:\n";
86        x.print();
87        cout << " = ";
88        y.print();
89        cout << " - ";
90        z.print();
91        cout << endl;
92
93        return 0;
94    } // end function main
```

```
x: (0, 0)
y: (4.3, 8.2)
z: (3.3, 1.1)

x = y + z:
(7.6, 9.3) = (4.3, 8.2) + (3.3, 1.1)

x = y - z:
(1, 7.1) = (4.3, 8.2) - (3.3, 1.1)
```

Fig. 18.5 A complex number class—`fig18_05.cpp`. (Part 2 of 2.)

18.11   The program of Fig. 18.3 contains the comment

```
// Overloaded stream-insertion operator (cannot be
// a member function if we would like to invoke it with
// cout << somePhoneNumber;)
```

Actually, it cannot be a member function of class `ostream`, but it can be a member function of class `PhoneNumber` if we were willing to invoke it in either of the following ways:

```
somePhoneNumber.operator<<( cout );
```

or

```
somePhoneNumber << cout;
```

Rewrite the program of Fig. 18.3 with the overloaded stream-insertion `operator<<` as a member function and try the two preceding statements in the program to prove that they work.

19

C++ Inheritance

Objectives

- To be able to create new classes by inheriting from existing classes.
- To understand how inheritance promotes software reusability.
- To understand the notions of base classes and derived classes.

Say not you know another entirely, till you have divided an inheritance with him.
Johann Kasper Lavater

This method is to define as the number of a class the class of all classes similar to the given class.
Bertrand Russell

A deck of cards was built like the purest of hierarchies, with every card a master to those below it, a lackey to those above it.
Ely Culbertson

Good as it is to inherit a library, it is better to collect one.
Augustine Birrell

Save base authority from others' books.
William Shakespeare

Outline

19.1 Introduction

In this and the next chapter we discuss two of the most important capabilities of object-oriented programming—*inheritance* and *polymorphism.* Inheritance is a form of software reusability in which new classes are created from existing classes by absorbing their attributes and behaviors and overriding or embellishing these with capabilities the new classes require. Software reusability saves time in program development. It encourages the reuse of proven and debugged high-quality software, thus reducing problems after a system becomes functional. These are exciting possibilities. Polymorphism enables us to write programs in a general fashion to handle a wide variety of existing and yet-to-be-specified related classes. Inheritance and polymorphism are effective techniques for managing software complexity.

When creating a new class, instead of writing completely new data members and member functions, the programmer can designate that the new class is to *inherit* the data members and member functions of a previously defined *base class.* The new class is referred to as a *derived class.* Each derived class itself becomes a candidate to be a base class for some future derived class. With *single inheritance,* a class is derived from one base class. With *multiple inheritance,* a derived class inherits from multiple (possibly unrelated) base classes. Single inheritance is straightforward—we show several examples that should enable the reader to become proficient quickly. Multiple inheritance is complex and error prone—we briefly discuss this advanced topic here and issue a strong caution urging the reader to pursue further study before using this powerful capability.

A derived class can add data members and member functions of its own, so a derived class can be larger than its base class. A derived class is more specific than its base class and represents a smaller group of objects. With single inheritance, the derived class starts out essentially the same as the base class. The real strength of inheritance comes from the ability to define in the derived class additions, replacements or refinements to the features inherited from the base class.

C++ offers three kinds of inheritance—`public`, `protected` and `private`. In this chapter we concentrate on `public` inheritance and briefly explain the other two kinds. The second form, `private` inheritance, can be used as an alternative form of composition. The third form, `protected` inheritance, is a relatively recent addition to C++ and is rarely used. With `public` inheritance, every object of a derived class may also be treated as an object of that derived class's base class. However, the converse is not true—base-class objects are not objects of that base class's derived classes. We will take advantage of this "derived-class-object-is-a-base-class-object" relationship to perform some interesting manipulations. For example, we can thread a wide variety of different objects related through inheritance into a linked list of base-class objects. This allows a variety of objects to be processed in a general way. As we will see in the next chapter, this capability—called polymorphism—is a key thrust of object-oriented programming.

We add a new form of member access control in this chapter, namely, `protected` access. Derived classes and their `friend`s can access `protected` base-class members, whereas non-`friend`, non-derived-class-member functions cannot.

Experience in building software systems indicates that significant portions of the code deal with closely related special cases. It becomes difficult in such systems to see the "big picture," because the designer and the programmer become preoccupied with the special cases. Object-oriented programming provides several ways of "seeing the forest through the trees"—a process called *abstraction.*

If a program is loaded with closely related special cases, then it is common to see `switch` statements that distinguish among the special cases and provide the processing logic to deal with each case individually. In Chapter 20, we will show how to use inheritance and polymorphism to replace such `switch` logic with simpler logic.

We distinguish between *is a relationships* and *has a relationships. Is a* is inheritance. In an *is a* relationship, an object of a derived-class type may also be treated as an object of the base-class type. *Has a* is composition (see Fig. 17.4). In a *has a* relationship, a class object *has* one or more objects of other classes as members.

A derived class cannot access the `private` members of its base class; allowing this would violate the encapsulation of the base class. A derived class can, however, access the `public` and `protected` members of its base class. Base-class members that should not be accessible to a derived class via inheritance are declared `private` in the base class. A derived class can access `private` members of the base class only through access functions provided in the base class's `public` and `protected` interfaces.

One problem with inheritance is that a derived class can inherit `public` member function implementations that it does not need to have or should expressly not have. When a base-class member implementation is inappropriate for a derived class, that member can be overridden in the derived class with an appropriate implementation. In some cases, `public` inheritance is simply inappropriate.

Perhaps most exciting is the notion that new classes can inherit from existing *class libraries.* Organizations develop their own class libraries and can take advantage of other libraries available worldwide. Eventually, software will be constructed predominantly from *standardized reusable components* just as hardware is often constructed today. This will help to meet the challenges of developing the ever more powerful software we will need in the future.

19.2 Inheritance: Base Classes and Derived Classes

Often an object of one class really "is an" object of another class as well. A rectangle certainly *is a* quadrilateral (as is a square, a parallelogram and a trapezoid). Thus, the class Rectangle can be said to *inherit* from class Quadrilateral. In this context, class Quadrilateral is called a *base class* and class Rectangle is called a *derived class*. A rectangle *is a* specific type of quadrilateral, but it is incorrect to claim that a quadrilateral *is a* rectangle (the quadrilateral could, for example, be a parallelogram). Figure 19.1 shows several simple inheritance examples.

Base class	Derived classes
Student	GraduateStudent
	UndergraduateStudent
Shape	Circle
	Triangle
	Rectangle
Loan	CarLoan
	HomeImprovementLoan
	MortgageLoan
Employee	FacultyMember
	StaffMember
Account	CheckingAccount
	SavingsAccount

Fig. 19.1 Some simple inheritance examples.

Other object-oriented programming languages such as Smalltalk and Java use different terminology: In inheritance, the base class is called the *superclass* (represents a superset of objects) and the derived class is called the *subclass* (represents a subset of objects).

Inheritance normally produces derived classes with *more* features than their base classes, so the terms superclass and subclass can be confusing; we will avoid these terms. Derived class objects may be thought of as objects of their base classes; this implies that more objects are associated with base classes and fewer objects are associated with derived classes, so it is reasonable to call base classes "superclasses" and derived classes "subclasses."

Inheritance forms tree-like hierarchical structures. A base class exists in a hierarchical relationship with its derived classes. A class can certainly exist by itself, but it is when a class is used with the mechanism of inheritance that the class becomes either a base class that supplies attributes and behaviors to other classes, or the class becomes a derived class that inherits attributes and behaviors.

Let us develop a simple inheritance hierarchy. A typical university community has thousands of people who are community members. These people consist of employees, students and alumni. Employees are either faculty members or staff members. Faculty members are either administrators (such as deans and department chairpersons) or teaching faculty. This yields the inheritance hierarchy shown in Fig. 19.2. Note that some administrators also teach classes, so we have used multiple inheritance to create a class called `AdministratorTeacher`. Students often work for their universities, and employees often take courses, so it would also be reasonable to use multiple inheritance to create a class called `EmployeeStudent`.

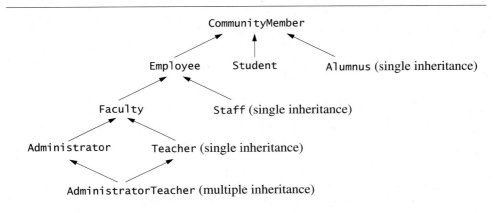

Fig. 19.2   An inheritance hierarchy for university community members.

Another substantial inheritance hierarchy is the `Shape` hierarchy of Fig. 19.3. A common observation among students learning object-oriented programming is that there are abundant examples of hierarchies in the real world. It is just that these students are not accustomed to categorizing the real world in this manner, so it takes some adjustment in their thinking.

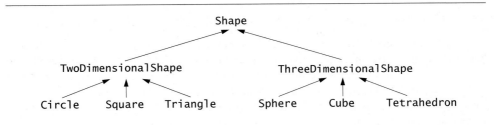

Fig. 19.3   A portion of a `Shape` class hierarchy.

Let us consider the syntax for indicating inheritance in a class. To specify that class `CommissionWorker` is derived from class `Employee`, class `CommissionWorker` would typically be defined as follows:

```
class CommissionWorker : public Employee {
   ...
}; // end class CommissionWorker
```

This is called *public inheritance* and is the most commonly used type of inheritance. We will also discuss *private inheritance* and *protected inheritance*. With `public` inheritance, the `public` and `protected` base class members are inherited as `public` and `protected` members of the derived class, respectively. Remember that `private` members of a base class are not accessible from that class's derived classes. Note that `friend` functions are not inherited.

It is possible to treat base-class objects and derived-class objects similarly; that commonality is expressed in the attributes and behaviors of the base class. Objects of any class derived with `public` inheritance from a common base class can all be treated as objects of that base class. We will consider many examples in which we can take advantage of this relationship with an ease of programming not available in non-object-oriented languages, such as C.

19.3 Protected Members

A base class's `public` members are accessible by all functions in the program. A base class's `private` members are accessible only by member functions and `friend`s of the base class.

We introduced `protected` access as an intermediate level of protection between `public` access and `private` access. A base class's `protected` members may be accessed only by members and `friend`s of the base class and by members and `friend`s of derived classes. Derived-class members can refer to `public` and `protected` members of the base class simply by using the member names. Note that `protected` data "breaks" encapsulation—a change to `protected` members of a base class may require modification of all derived classes.

Software Engineering Observation 19.1

In general, declare data members of a class `private` *and use* `protected` *only as a "last resort" when systems need to be tuned to meet unique performance requirements.*

19.4 Casting Base-Class Pointers to Derived-Class Pointers

An object of a publicly derived class can also be treated as an object of its corresponding base class. This makes possible some interesting manipulations. For example, despite the fact that objects of a variety of classes derived from a particular base class may be quite different from one another, we can still create a linked list of them—again, as long as we treat them as base-class objects. But the reverse is not true: A base-class object is not always a derived-class object.

Common Programming Error 19.1

Treating a base-class object as a derived-class object can cause errors.

The programmer may, however, use an explicit cast to convert a base-class pointer to a derived-class pointer. This process is often called *downcasting a pointer*. But be careful—if such a pointer is to be dereferenced, then the programmer should be sure that the type of the pointer matches the type of the object to which it points. Our treatment in this section uses techniques widely available in most compilers.

Common Programming Error 19.2

Explicitly casting a base-class pointer that points to a base-class object into a derived-class pointer, then referring to derived-class members that do not exist in that object, can lead to run-time logic errors.

Our first example is shown in Fig. 19.4. Lines 1–43 show the `Point` class definition and `Point` member function definitions. Lines 44–106 show the `Circle` class definition and `Circle` member function definitions. Lines 107–147 show a driver program in which we demonstrate assigning derived-class pointers to base-class pointers (often called *upcasting a pointer*) and casting base-class pointers to derived-class pointers.

```cpp
1   // Fig. 19.4: point.h
2   // Definition of class Point
3   #ifndef POINT_H
4   #define POINT_H
5
6   #include <iostream>
7
8   using std::ostream;
9
10  class Point {
11      friend ostream &operator<<( ostream &, const Point & );
12  public:
13      Point( int = 0, int = 0 );        // default constructor
14      void setPoint( int, int );        // set coordinates
15      int getX() const { return x; }    // get x coordinate
16      int getY() const { return y; }    // get y coordinate
17  protected:          // accessible by derived classes
18      int x, y;       // x and y coordinates of the Point
19  }; // end class Point
20
21  #endif
```

Fig. 19.4   Casting base-class pointers to derived-class pointers—`point.h`.

```cpp
22  // Fig. 19.4: point.cpp
23  // Member functions for class Point
24  #include <iostream>
25  #include "point.h"
26
27  // Constructor for class Point
28  Point::Point( int a, int b ) { setPoint( a, b ); }
29
30  // Set x and y coordinates of Point
31  void Point::setPoint( int a, int b )
32  {
33      x = a;
34      y = b;
35  } // end function setPoint
```

Fig. 19.4   Casting base-class pointers to derived-class pointers—`point.cpp`. (Part 1 of 2.)

```
36
37   // Output Point (with overloaded stream insertion operator)
38   ostream &operator<<( ostream &output, const Point &p )
39   {
40      output << '[' << p.x << ", " << p.y << ']';
41
42      return output;    // enables cascaded calls
43   } // end operator<< function
```

Fig. 19.4 Casting base-class pointers to derived-class pointers—point.cpp. (Part 2 of 2.)

```
44   // Fig. 19.4: circle.h
45   // Definition of class Circle
46   #ifndef CIRCLE_H
47   #define CIRCLE_H
48
49   #include <iostream>
50
51   using std::ostream;
52
53   #include <iomanip>
54
55   using std::ios;
56   using std::setiosflags;
57   using std::setprecision;
58
59   #include "point.h"
60
61   class Circle : public Point {  // Circle inherits from Point
62      friend ostream &operator<<( ostream &, const Circle & );
63   public:
64      // default constructor
65      Circle( double r = 0.0, int x = 0, int y = 0 );
66
67      void setRadius( double );    // set radius
68      double getRadius() const;    // return radius
69      double area() const;         // calculate area
70   protected:
71      double radius;
72   }; // end class Circle
73
74   #endif
```

Fig. 19.4 Casting base-class pointers to derived-class pointers—circle.h.

```
75   // Fig. 19.4: circle.cpp
76   // Member function definitions for class Circle
77   #include "circle.h"
78
```

Fig. 19.4 Casting base-class pointers to derived-class pointers—circle.cpp. (Part 1 of 2.)

```
79   // Constructor for Circle calls constructor for Point
80   // with a member initializer then initializes radius.
81   Circle::Circle( double r, int a, int b )
82      : Point( a, b )          // call base-class constructor
83   { setRadius( r ); }
84
85   // Set radius of Circle
86   void Circle::setRadius( double r )
87      { radius = ( r >= 0 ? r : 0 ); }
88
89   // Get radius of Circle
90   double Circle::getRadius() const { return radius; }
91
92   // Calculate area of Circle
93   double Circle::area() const
94      { return 3.14159 * radius * radius; }
95
96   // Output a Circle in the form:
97   // Center = [x, y]; Radius = #.##
98   ostream &operator<<( ostream &output, const Circle &c )
99   {
100     output << "Center = " << static_cast< Point >( c )
101            << "; Radius = "
102            << setiosflags( ios::fixed | ios::showpoint )
103            << setprecision( 2 ) << c.radius;
104
105     return output;     // enables cascaded calls
106  } // end operator<< function
```

Fig. 19.4 Casting base-class pointers to derived-class pointers—`circle.cpp`. (Part 2 of 2.)

```
107  // Fig. 19.4: fig19_04.cpp
108  // Casting base-class pointers to derived-class pointers
109  #include <iostream>
110
111  using std::cout;
112  using std::endl;
113
114  #include <iomanip>
115
116  #include "point.h"
117  #include "circle.h"
118
119  int main()
120  {
121     Point *pointPtr = 0, p( 30, 50 );
122     Circle *circlePtr = 0, c( 2.7, 120, 89 );
123
124     cout << "Point p: " << p << "\nCircle c: " << c << '\n';
125
```

Fig. 19.4 Casting base-class pointers to derived-class pointers—`fig19_04.cpp`. (Part 1 of 2.)

```
126     // Treat a Circle as a Point (see only the base class part)
127     pointPtr = &c;    // assign address of Circle to pointPtr
128     cout << "\nCircle c (via *pointPtr): "
129          << *pointPtr << '\n';
130
131     // Treat a Circle as a Circle (with some casting)
132     // cast base-class pointer to derived-class pointer
133     circlePtr = static_cast< Circle * >( pointPtr );
134     cout << "\nCircle c (via *circlePtr):\n" << *circlePtr
135          << "\nArea of c (via circlePtr): "
136          << circlePtr->area() << '\n';
137
138     // DANGEROUS: Treat a Point as a Circle
139     pointPtr = &p;    // assign address of Point to pointPtr
140
141     // cast base-class pointer to derived-class pointer
142     circlePtr = static_cast< Circle * >( pointPtr );
143     cout << "\nPoint p (via *circlePtr):\n" << *circlePtr
144          << "\nArea of object circlePtr points to: "
145          << circlePtr->area() << endl;
146     return 0;
147  } // end function main
```

```
Point p: [30, 50]
Circle c: Center = [120, 89]; Radius = 2.70

Circle c (via *pointPtr): [120, 89]

Circle c (via *circlePtr):
Center = [120, 89]; Radius = 2.70
Area of c (via circlePtr): 22.90

Point p (via *circlePtr):
Center = [30, 50]; Radius = 0.00
Area of object circlePtr points to: 0.00
```

Fig. 19.4   Casting base-class pointers to derived-class pointers—`fig19_04.cpp`. (Part 2 of 2.)

Let us examine the `Point` class definition. The `public` interface to `Point` includes member functions `setPoint`, `getX` and `getY`. The data members `x` and `y` of `Point` are specified as `protected`. This prevents clients of `Point` objects from directly accessing the data, but enables classes derived from `Point` to access the inherited data members directly. If the data were `private`, the `public` member functions of `Point` would be used to access the data, even by derived classes. Note that the `Point` overloaded stream-insertion operator function is able to reference variables `x` and `y` directly because the stream-insertion operator function is a `friend` of class `Point`. Note also that it is necessary to reference `x` and `y` through objects as in `p.x` and `p.y`. This is because the stream-insertion operator function is not a member function of the class `Point`, so we must use an explicit handle so the compiler knows what object we are referencing. Note that this class offers `inlined` `public` member functions `getX` and `getY`, so `operator<<` does not need to be a friend to achieve good performance. However, needed public member functions may not be provided in the public interface of every class, so friendship is often appropriate.

Class Circle inherits from class Point with public inheritance. This is specified in the first line of the class definition:

```
class Circle : public Point {   // Circle inherits from Point
```

The colon (:) in the header of the class definition indicates inheritance. The keyword public indicates the type of inheritance. (In Section 19.7 we will discuss protected and private inheritance.) All the public and protected members of class Point are inherited as public and protected members, respectively, into class Circle. This means that the public interface to Circle includes the Point public members as well as the Circle public members area, setRadius and getRadius.

The Circle constructor must invoke the Point constructor to initialize the Point base-class portion of a Circle object. This is accomplished with a member initializer (introduced in Chapter 17) as follows:

```
Circle::Circle( double r, int a, int b )
   : Point( a, b )       // call base-class constructor
```

The second line of the constructor header invokes the Point constructor by name. Values a and b are passed from the Circle constructor to the Point constructor to initialize the base-class members x and y. If the Circle constructor did not invoke the Point constructor explicitly, the default Point constructor would be invoked implicitly with the default values for x and y (i.e., 0 and 0). If in this case the Point class did not provide a default constructor, the compiler would issue a syntax error. Note that the Circle overloaded operator<< function is able to output the Point part of the Circle by casting the Circle reference c to a Point. This results in a call to operator<< for Point and outputs the x and y coordinates using the proper Point formatting.

The driver program creates pointPtr as a pointer to a Point object and instantiates Point object p, then creates circlePtr as a pointer to a Circle object and instantiates Circle object c. The objects p and c are output using their overloaded stream-insertion operators to show that they were initialized correctly. Next, the driver assigns a derived-class pointer (the address of object c) to base-class pointer pointPtr and outputs the Circle object c using operator<< for Point and the dereferenced pointer *pointPtr. Note that only the Point portion of the Circle object c is displayed. With public inheritance, it is always valid to assign a derived-class pointer to a base-class pointer because a derived-class object *is a* base-class object. The base-class pointer "sees" only the base-class part of the derived-class object. The compiler performs an implicit conversion of the derived-class pointer to a base-class pointer.

Then, the driver program demonstrates casting pointPtr back to a Circle *. The result of the cast operation is assigned to circlePtr. The Circle object c is output using the overloaded stream-insertion operator for Circle and the dereferenced pointer *circlePtr. The area of Circle object c is output via circlePtr. This results in a valid area value because the pointers are always pointing to a Circle object.

A base-class pointer cannot be assigned directly to a derived-class pointer, because this is an inherently dangerous assignment—derived-class pointers expect to be pointing to derived-class objects. The compiler does not perform an implicit conversion in this case. Using an explicit cast informs the compiler that the programmer knows this type of pointer conversion is dangerous—the programmer assumes responsibility for using the pointer appropriately, so the compiler is willing to allow the dangerous conversion.

Next, the driver assigns a base-class pointer (the address of object p) to base-class pointer pointPtr and casts pointPtr back to a Circle *. The result of the cast operation is assigned to circlePtr. Point object p is output using operator<< for Circle and the dereferenced pointer *circlePtr. Note the zero value output for the radius member (which actually does not exist, because circlePtr is really aimed at a Point object). Outputting a Point as a Circle results in an undefined value (in this case it happens to be zero) for the radius, because the pointers are always pointing to a Point object. A Point object does not have a radius member. Therefore, the program outputs whatever value happens to be in memory at the location that circlePtr expects the radius data member to be. The area of the object pointed to by circlePtr (Point object p) is also output via circlePtr. Note that the value for the area is 0.00 because this calculation is based on the "undefined" value of the radius. Obviously, accessing data members that are not there is dangerous. Calling member functions that do not exist can crash a program.

In this section we have shown the mechanics of pointer conversions. This material establishes the foundation we will need for our deeper treatment of object-oriented programming with polymorphism in the next chapter.

19.5 Using Member Functions

A derived class's member functions may need to access certain base class data members and member functions.

Software Engineering Observation 19.2

A derived class cannot directly access private members of its base class.

This is a crucial aspect of software engineering in C++. If a derived class could access the base class's private members, this would violate the encapsulation of the base class. Hiding private members is a huge help in testing, debugging and correctly modifying systems. If a derived class could access its base class's private members, it would then be possible for classes derived from that derived class to access those data as well, and so on. This would propagate access to what is supposed to be private data, and the benefits of encapsulation would be lost throughout the class hierarchy.

19.6 Overriding Base-Class Members in a Derived Class

A derived class can override a base-class member function by supplying a new version of that function with the same signature (if the signature were different, this would be function overloading rather than function overriding). When that function is mentioned by name in the derived class, the derived-class version is selected. The scope-resolution operator may be used to access the base-class version from the derived class.

Common Programming Error 19.3

When a base-class member function is overridden in a derived class, it is common to have the derived-class version call the base-class version and do some additional work. Not using the scope-resolution operator to reference the base class's member function causes infinite recursion because the derived-class member function actually calls itself. This will eventually cause the system to exhaust memory, a fatal execution-time error.

Consider a simplified class `Employee`. It stores the employee's `firstName` and `lastName`. This information is common to all employees including classes derived from class `Employee`. From class `Employee` now derive `HourlyWorker`, `PieceWorker`, `Boss` and `CommissionWorker`. The `HourlyWorker` gets paid by the hour with "time-and-a-half" for overtime hours in excess of 40 hours per week. The `PieceWorker` gets paid a fixed rate per item produced—for simplicity, assume this person makes only one type of item, so the `private` data members are number of items produced and rate per item. The `Boss` gets a fixed wage per week. The `CommissionWorker` gets a small fixed weekly base salary plus a fixed percentage of that person's gross sales for the week. For simplicity, we study only class `Employee` and derived class `HourlyWorker`.

Our next example is shown in Fig. 19.5. Lines 1 through 50 show the `Employee` class definition and `Employee` member function definitions. Lines 51 through 106 show the `HourlyWorker` class definition and `HourlyWorker` member function definition. Lines 107 through 117 show a driver program for the `Employee/HourlyWorker` inheritance hierarchy that simply instantiates an `HourlyWorker` object, initializes it and calls `HourlyWorker` member function `print` to output the object's data.

```
1    // Fig. 19.5: employ.h
2    // Definition of class Employee
3    #ifndef EMPLOY_H
4    #define EMPLOY_H
5
6    class Employee {
7    public:
8       Employee( const char *, const char * );   // constructor
9       void print() const;   // output first and last name
10      ~Employee();          // destructor
11   private:
12      char *firstName;      // dynamically allocated string
13      char *lastName;       // dynamically allocated string
14   }; // end class Employee
15
16   #endif
```

Fig. 19.5 Overriding base-class members in a derived class—`employ.h`.

```
17   // Fig. 19.5: employ.cpp
18   // Member function definitions for class Employee
19   #include <iostream>
20
21   using std::cout;
22
23   #include <cstring>
24   #include <cassert>
25   #include "employ.h"
26
27   // Constructor dynamically allocates space for the
28   // first and last name and uses strcpy to copy
29   // the first and last names into the object.
```

Fig. 19.5 Overriding base-class members in a derived class—`employ.cpp`. (Part 1 of 2.)

```
30   Employee::Employee( const char *first, const char *last )
31   {
32      firstName = new char[ strlen( first ) + 1 ];
33      assert( firstName != 0 ); // terminate if not allocated
34      strcpy( firstName, first );
35
36      lastName = new char[ strlen( last ) + 1 ];
37      assert( lastName != 0 );   // terminate if not allocated
38      strcpy( lastName, last );
39   } // end Employee constructor
40
41   // Output employee name
42   void Employee::print() const
43      { cout << firstName << ' ' << lastName; }
44
45   // Destructor deallocates dynamically allocated memory
46   Employee::~Employee()
47   {
48      delete [] firstName;    // reclaim dynamic memory
49      delete [] lastName;     // reclaim dynamic memory
50   } // end Employee destructor
```

Fig. 19.5   Overriding base-class members in a derived class—`employ.cpp`. (Part 2 of 2.)

```
51   // Fig. 19.5: hourly.h
52   // Definition of class HourlyWorker
53   #ifndef HOURLY_H
54   #define HOURLY_H
55
56   #include "employ.h"
57
58   class HourlyWorker : public Employee {
59   public:
60      HourlyWorker( const char*, const char*, double, double );
61      double getPay() const;   // calculate and return salary
62      void print() const;      // overridden base-class print
63   private:
64      double wage;             // wage per hour
65      double hours;            // hours worked for week
66   }; // end class HourlyWorker
67
68   #endif
```

Fig. 19.5   Overriding base-class members in a derived class—`hourly.h`.

```
69   // Fig. 19.5: hourly.cpp
70   // Member function definitions for class HourlyWorker
71   #include <iostream>
72
73   using std::cout;
74   using std::endl;
```

Fig. 19.5   Overriding base-class members in a derived class—`hourly.cpp`. (Part 1 of 2.)

```
75
76   #include <iomanip>
77
78   using std::ios;
79   using std::setiosflags;
80   using std::setprecision;
81
82   #include "hourly.h"
83
84   // Constructor for class HourlyWorker
85   HourlyWorker::HourlyWorker( const char *first,
86                               const char *last,
87                               double initHours, double initWage )
88      : Employee( first, last )   // call base-class constructor
89   {
90      hours = initHours;   // should validate
91      wage = initWage;     // should validate
92   } // end HourlyWorker constructor
93
94   // Get the HourlyWorker's pay
95   double HourlyWorker::getPay() const { return wage * hours; }
96
97   // Print the HourlyWorker's name and pay
98   void HourlyWorker::print() const
99   {
100     cout << "HourlyWorker::print() is executing\n\n";
101     Employee::print();   // call base-class print function
102
103     cout << " is an hourly worker with pay of $"
104          << setiosflags( ios::fixed | ios::showpoint )
105          << setprecision( 2 ) << getPay() << endl;
106  } // end function print
```

Fig. 19.5   Overriding base-class members in a derived class—`hourly.cpp`. (Part 2 of 2.)

```
107  // Fig. 19.5: fig19_05.cpp
108  // Overriding a base-class member function in a
109  // derived class.
110  #include "hourly.h"
111
112  int main()
113  {
114     HourlyWorker h( "Bob", "Smith", 40.0, 10.00 );
115     h.print();
116     return 0;
117  } // end function main
```

```
HourlyWorker::print() is executing

Bob Smith is an hourly worker with pay of $400.00
```

Fig. 19.5   Overriding base-class members in a derived class—`fig19_05.cpp`.

The `Employee` class definition consists of two `private char *` data members—`firstName` and `lastName`—and three member functions—a constructor, a destructor and `print`. The constructor function receives two strings and dynamically allocates character arrays to store the strings. Note that the `assert` macro is used to determine if memory was allocated to `firstName` and `lastName`. If not, the program terminates with an error message indicating the condition tested, the line number on which the condition appears and the file in which the condition is located. [*Note:* Once again, in the C++ standard, `new` "throws" an exception if insufficient memory is available; we discuss this in Chapter 23.] The data of `Employee` are `private`, so the only access to the data is through member function `print`, which simply outputs the first name and last name of the employee. The destructor function returns the dynamically allocated memory to the system (to avoid a "memory leak").

Class `HourlyWorker` inherits from class `Employee` with `public` inheritance. Again, this is specified in the first line of the class definition using the colon (`:`) notation as follows:

```
class HourlyWorker : public Employee
```

The `public` interface to `HourlyWorker` includes the `Employee print` function and `HourlyWorker` member functions `getPay` and `print`. Note that `HourlyWorker` defines its own `print` function with the same prototype as `Employee::print()`—this is an example of function overriding. Therefore, class `HourlyWorker` has access to two `print` functions. Class `HourlyWorker` also contains `private` data members `wage` and `hours` for calculating the employee's weekly salary.

The `HourlyWorker` constructor uses member initializer syntax to pass the strings `first` and `last` to the `Employee` constructor so the base-class members can be initialized, then initializes members `hours` and `wage`. Member function `getPay` calculates the salary of the `HourlyWorker`.

`HourlyWorker` member function `print` overrides the `Employee print` member function. Often, base-class member functions are overridden in a derived class to provide more functionality. The overridden functions sometimes call the base-class version of the function to perform part of the new task. In this example, the derived-class `print` function calls the base-class `print` function to output the employee's name (the base-class `print` is the only function with access to the `private` data of the base class). The derived-class `print` function also outputs the employee's pay. Note how the base-class version of `print` is called

```
Employee::print();
```

The base-class function and the derived-class function have the same name and signature, so the base-class function must be preceded by its class name and the scope resolution operator. Otherwise, the derived-class version of the function would be called causing infinite recursion (i.e., the `HourlyWorker print` function would call itself).

19.7 Public, Protected and Private Inheritance

When deriving a class from a base class, the base class may be inherited as `public`, `protected` or `private`. Use of `protected` and `private` inheritance is rare, and each should be used only with great care; we normally use `public` inheritance in this book. Figure 19.6 summarizes for each type of inheritance the accessibility of base-class members in a derived class. The first column contains the base-class member-access specifiers.

When deriving a class from a `public` base class, `public` members of the base class become `public` members of the derived class and `protected` members of the base class become `protected` members of the derived class. A base class's `private` members are never directly accessible from a derived class, but can be accessed through calls to the `public` and `protected` members of the base class.

Base class member access specifier	Type of inheritance		
	public inheritance	protected inheritance	private inheritance
public	public in derived class. Can be accessed directly by any non-`static` member functions, `friend` functions and non-member functions.	protected in derived class. Can be accessed directly by all non-`static` member functions and `friend` functions.	private in derived class. Can be accessed directly by all non-`static` member functions and `friend` functions.
protected	protected in derived class. Can be accessed directly by all non-`static` member functions and `friend` functions.	protected in derived class. Can be accessed directly by all non-`static` member functions and `friend` functions.	private in derived class. Can be accessed directly by all non-`static` member functions and `friend` functions.
private	Hidden in derived class. Can be accessed by non-`static` member functions and `friend` functions through `public` or `protected` member functions of the base class.	Hidden in derived class. Can be accessed by non-`static` member functions and `friend` functions through `public` or `protected` member functions of the base class.	Hidden in derived class. Can be accessed by non-`static` member functions and `friend` functions through `public` or `protected` member functions of the base class.

Fig. 19.6   Summary of base-class member accessibility in a derived class.

When deriving from a `protected` base class, `public` and `protected` members of the base class become `protected` members of the derived class. When deriving from a `private` base class, `public` and `protected` members of the base class become `private` members (e.g., the functions become utility functions) of the derived class. `Private` and `protected` inheritance are not *is a* relationships.

19.8 Direct Base Classes and Indirect Base Classes

A base class may be a *direct base class* of a derived class, or a base class may be an *indirect base class* of a derived class. A direct base class of a derived class is explicitly listed in that derived class's header with the colon (`:`) notation when that derived class is declared. An indirect base class is not explicitly listed in the derived class's header; rather, the indirect base class is inherited from two or more levels up the class hierarchy.

19.9 Using Constructors and Destructors in Derived Classes

A derived class inherits its base class's members, so when an object of a derived class is instantiated, each base class's constructor must be called to initialize the base-class members of the derived-class object. A *base-class initializer* (which uses the member-initializer syntax we have seen) can be provided in the derived-class constructor to call the base-class constructor explicitly; otherwise, the derived class's constructor will call the base class's default constructor implicitly.

Base-class constructors and base-class assignment operators are not inherited by derived classes. Derived-class constructors and assignment operators, however, can call base-class constructors and assignment operators.

A derived-class constructor always calls the constructor for its base class first to initialize the derived class's base-class members. If the derived-class constructor is omitted, the derived class's default constructor calls the base class's default constructor. Destructors are called in the reverse order of constructor calls, so a derived-class destructor is called before its base-class destructor.

Software Engineering Observation 19.3

Suppose we create an object of a derived class where both the base class and the derived class contain objects of other classes. When an object of that derived class is created, first the constructors for the base class's member objects execute, then the base-class constructor executes, then the constructors for the derived class's member objects execute, then the derived class's constructor executes. Destructors are called in the reverse of the order in which their corresponding constructors are called.

Software Engineering Observation 19.4

The order in which member objects are constructed is the order in which those objects are declared within the class definition. The order in which the member initializers are listed does not affect the order of construction.

Software Engineering Observation 19.5

In inheritance, base-class constructors are called in the order in which inheritance is specified in the derived-class definition. The order in which the base-class constructors are specified in the derived-class member initializer list does not affect the order of construction.

Figure 19.7 demonstrates the order in which base-class and derived-class constructors and destructors are called. Lines 1 through 39 show a simple `Point` class containing a constructor, a destructor and `protected` data members `x` and `y`. The constructor and destructor both print the `Point` object for which they are invoked.

```
1   // Fig. 19.7: point2.h
2   // Definition of class Point
3   #ifndef POINT2_H
4   #define POINT2_H
5
6   class Point {
7   public:
```

Fig. 19.7   Order in which base-class and derived-class constructors and destructors are called—`point2.h`. (Part 1 of 2.)

```
 8       Point( int = 0, int = 0 );   // default constructor
 9       ~Point();      // destructor
10    protected:        // accessible by derived classes
11       int x, y;      // x and y coordinates of Point
12    }; // end class Point
13
14    #endif
```

Fig. 19.7   Order in which base-class and derived-class constructors and destructors are called—point2.h. (Part 2 of 2.)

```
15    // Fig. 19.7: point2.cpp
16    // Member function definitions for class Point
17    #include <iostream>
18
19    using std::cout;
20    using std::endl;
21
22    #include "point2.h"
23
24    // Constructor for class Point
25    Point::Point( int a, int b )
26    {
27       x = a;
28       y = b;
29
30       cout << "Point  constructor: "
31            << '[' << x << ", " << y << ']' << endl;
32    } // end Point constructor
33
34    // Destructor for class Point
35    Point::~Point()
36    {
37       cout << "Point  destructor:  "
38            << '[' << x << ", " << y << ']' << endl;
39    } // end Point destructor
```

Fig. 19.7   Order in which base-class and derived-class constructors and destructors are called—point2.cpp.

```
40    // Fig. 19.7: circle2.h
41    // Definition of class Circle
42    #ifndef CIRCLE2_H
43    #define CIRCLE2_H
44
45    #include "point2.h"
46
47    class Circle : public Point {
48    public:
```

Fig. 19.7   Order in which base-class and derived-class constructors and destructors are called—circle2.h. (Part 1 of 2.)

```
49        // default constructor
50        Circle( double r = 0.0, int x = 0, int y = 0 );
51
52        ~Circle();
53     private:
54        double radius;
55     }; // end class Circle
56
57     #endif
```

Fig. 19.7   Order in which base-class and derived-class constructors and destructors are called—`circle2.h`. (Part 2 of 2.)

```
58     // Fig. 19.7: circle2.cpp
59     // Member function definitions for class Circle
60     #include <iostream>
61
62     using std::cout;
63     using std::endl;
64
65     #include "circle2.h"
66
67     // Constructor for Circle calls constructor for Point
68     Circle::Circle( double r, int a, int b )
69        : Point( a, b )    // call base-class constructor
70     {
71        radius = r;   // should validate
72        cout << "Circle constructor: radius is "
73             << radius << " [" << x << ", " << y << ']' << endl;
74     } // end Circle constructor
75
76     // Destructor for class Circle
77     Circle::~Circle()
78     {
79        cout << "Circle destructor:  radius is "
80             << radius << " [" << x << ", " << y << ']' << endl;
81     } // end Circle destructor
```

Fig. 19.7   Order in which base-class and derived-class constructors and destructors are called—`circle2.cpp`.

```
82     // Fig. 19.7: fig19_07.cpp
83     // Demonstrate when base-class and derived-class
84     // constructors and destructors are called.
85     #include <iostream>
86
87     using std::cout;
88     using std::endl;
89
90     #include "point2.h"
```

Fig. 19.7   Order in which base-class and derived-class constructors and destructors are called—`fig19_07.cpp`. (Part 1 of 2.)

```
91   #include "circle2.h"
92
93   int main()
94   {
95       // Show constructor and destructor calls for Point
96       {
97           Point p( 11, 22 );
98       } // end block
99
100      cout << endl;
101      Circle circle1( 4.5, 72, 29 );
102      cout << endl;
103      Circle circle2( 10, 5, 5 );
104      cout << endl;
105      return 0;
106  } // end function main
```

```
Point  constructor:  [11, 22]
Point  destructor:   [11, 22]

Point  constructor:  [72, 29]
Circle constructor:  radius is 4.5 [72, 29]

Point  constructor:  [5, 5]
Circle constructor:  radius is 10 [5, 5]

Circle destructor:   radius is 10 [5, 5]
Point  destructor:   [5, 5]
Circle destructor:   radius is 4.5 [72, 29]
Point  destructor:   [72, 29]
```

Fig. 19.7   Order in which base-class and derived-class constructors and destructors are called—fig19_07.cpp. (Part 2 of 2.)

Lines 40 through 81 show a simple Circle class derived from Point with public inheritance. Class Circle provides a constructor, a destructor and a private data member radius. The constructor and destructor both print the Circle object for which they are invoked. The Circle constructor also invokes the Point constructor using member initializer syntax and passes the values a and b so the base-class data members x and y can be initialized.

Lines 82 through 106 are the driver program for this Point/Circle hierarchy. The program begins by instantiating a Point object in a scope inside main. The object goes in and out of scope immediately, so the Point constructor and destructor are both called. Next, the program instantiates Circle object circle1. This invokes the Point constructor to perform output with values passed from the Circle constructor, then performs the output specified in the Circle constructor. Circle object circle2 is instantiated next. Again, the Point and Circle constructors are both called. Note that the body of the Point constructor is performed before the body of the Circle constructor. The end of main is reached, so the destructors are called for objects circle1 and circle2. Destructors are called in the reverse order of their corresponding constructors. Therefore, the Circle destructor and Point destructor are called in that order for object circle2, then the Circle and Point destructors are called in that order for object circle1.

19.10 Implicit Derived-Class Object to Base-Class Object Conversion

Despite the fact that a derived-class object also *is a* base-class object, the derived-class type and the base-class type are different. Under `public` inheritance, derived-class objects can be treated as base-class objects. This makes sense because the derived class has members corresponding to each of the base-class members—remember that the derived class can have more members than the base class. Assignment in the other direction is not allowed because assigning a base-class object to a derived-class object would leave the additional derived-class members undefined. Although such assignment is not "naturally" allowed, it could be made legitimate by providing a properly overloaded assignment operator and/or conversion constructor (see Chapter 18). Note that what we say about pointers in the remainder of this section also applies to references.

Common Programming Error 19.4

Assigning a derived-class object to an object of a corresponding base class, then attempting to reference derived-class-only members in the new base-class object is a syntax error.

With `public` inheritance, a pointer to a derived-class object may be implicitly converted into a pointer to a base-class object, because a derived-class object is a base-class object.

There are four possible ways to mix and match base-class pointers and derived-class pointers with base-class objects and derived-class objects:

1. Referring to a base-class object with a base-class pointer is straightforward.

2. Referring to a derived-class object with a derived-class pointer is straightforward.

3. Referring to a derived-class object with a base-class pointer is safe because the derived-class object is an object of its base class as well. Such code can only refer to base-class members. If this code refers to derived-class-only members through the base-class pointer, the compiler will report a syntax error.

4. Referring to a base-class object with a derived-class pointer is a syntax error. The derived-class pointer must first be cast to a base-class pointer.

Common Programming Error 19.5

Casting a base-class pointer to a derived-class pointer can cause errors if that pointer is then used to reference a base-class object that does not have the desired derived-class members.

As convenient as it may be to treat derived-class objects as base-class objects, and to do this by manipulating all these objects with base-class pointers, there is a problem. In a payroll system, for example, we would like to be able to walk through a linked list of employees and calculate the weekly pay for each person. But using base-class pointers enables the program to call only the base-class payroll calculation routine (if indeed there were such a routine in the base class). We need a way to invoke the proper payroll calculation routine for each object, whether it is a base-class object or a derived-class object, and to do this simply by using the base-class pointer. The solution is to use `virtual` functions and polymorphism, as will be discussed in Chapter 20.

19.11 Software Engineering with Inheritance

We can use inheritance to customize existing software. We inherit the attributes and behaviors of an existing class, then add attributes and behaviors (or override base-class behaviors) to customize the class to meet our needs. This is done in C++ without the derived class having access to the base class's source code, but the derived class does need to be able to link to the base class's object code. This powerful capability is attractive to independent software vendors (ISVs). The ISVs can develop proprietary classes for sale or license and make these classes available to users in object-code format. Users can then derive new classes from these library classes rapidly and without accessing the ISVs' proprietary source code. All the ISVs need to supply with the object code are the header files.

Software Engineering Observation 19.6

In theory, users do not need to see the source code of classes from which they inherit. In practice, people who license classes tell us that the customers often demand the source code. Programmers still seem reluctant to incorporate code into their programs when this code has been written by other people.

Performance Tip 19.1

When performance is a major concern, programmers may want to see source code of classes they are inheriting from so they can tune the code to meet their performance requirements.

It can be difficult for students to appreciate the problems faced by designers and implementors on large-scale software projects. People experienced on such projects will invariably state that a key to improving the software development process is software reuse. Object-oriented programming, in general, and C++, in particular, certainly do this.

The availability of substantial and useful class libraries delivers the maximum benefits of software reuse through inheritance. As interest in C++ grows, interest in class libraries is growing exponentially. Just as shrink-wrapped software produced by independent software vendors became an explosive growth industry with the arrival of the personal computer, so, too, is the creation and sale of class libraries. Application designers build their applications with these libraries, and library designers are being rewarded by having their libraries wrapped with the applications. Libraries currently being shipped with C++ compilers tend to be rather general-purpose and limited in scope. A massive worldwide commitment to the development of class libraries is coming, for a huge variety of applications arenas.

Software Engineering Observation 19.7

Creating a derived class does not affect its base class's source code or object code; the integrity of a base class is preserved by inheritance.

A base class specifies commonality—all classes derived from a base class inherit the capabilities of that base class. In the object-oriented design process, the designer looks for commonality and "factors it out" to form desirable base classes. Derived classes are then customized beyond the capabilities inherited from the base class.

Software Engineering Observation 19.8

In an object-oriented system, classes are often closely related. "Factor out" common attributes and behaviors and place these in a base class. Then use inheritance to form derived classes.

Just as the designer of non-object-oriented systems seeks to avoid unnecessary proliferation of functions, the designer of object-oriented systems should avoid unnecessary proliferation of classes. Such a proliferation of classes creates management problems and can hinder software reusability simply because it is more difficult for a potential reuser of a class to locate that class in a huge collection. The trade-off is to create fewer classes, each providing substantial additional functionality. Such classes might be too rich for certain reusers; they can mask the excessive functionality, thus "toning down" the classes to meet their needs.

Performance Tip 19.2

If classes produced through inheritance are larger than they need to be, memory and processing resources may be wasted. Inherit from the class "closest" to what you need.

Note that reading a set of derived-class declarations can be confusing because inherited members are not shown, but they are nevertheless present in the derived classes. A similar problem can exist in the documentation of derived classes.

Software Engineering Observation 19.9

A derived class contains the attributes and behaviors of its base class. A derived class can also contain additional attributes and behaviors. With inheritance, the base class can be compiled independently of the derived class. Only the derived class's incremental attributes and behaviors need to be compiled to be able to combine these with the base class to form the derived class.

Software Engineering Observation 19.10

Modifications to a base class do not require derived classes to change as long as the `public` and `protected` interfaces to the base class remain unchanged. Derived classes may, however, need to be recompiled.

19.12 Composition vs. Inheritance

We have discussed *is a* relationships, which are supported by `public` inheritance. We have also discussed *has a* relationships (and seen examples in preceding chapters) in which a class may have other classes as members—such relationships create new classes by *composition* of existing classes. For example, given the classes `Employee`, `BirthDate` and `TelephoneNumber`, it is improper to say that an `Employee` *is a* `BirthDate` or that an Employee *is a* `TelephoneNumber`. But it is certainly appropriate to say that each `Employee` *has a* `BirthDate` and that each `Employee` *has a* `TelephoneNumber`.

Software Engineering Observation 19.11

Program modifications to a class that is a member of another class do not require the enclosing class to change as long as the `public` interface to the member class remains unchanged. Note that the composite class may, however, need to be recompiled.

19.13 *Uses A* and *Knows A* Relationships

Inheritance and composition each encourage software reuse by creating new classes that have much in common with existing classes. There are other ways to use the services of classes. Although a person object is not a car and a person object does not contain a car, a person object certainly *uses a* car. A function uses an object by calling a non-`private` member function of that object using a pointer, reference or the object name itself.

An object can be *aware of* another object. Knowledge networks frequently have such relationships. One object can contain a pointer handle or a reference handle to another object to be aware of that object. In this case, one object is said to have a *knows a* relationship with the other object; this is sometimes called an *association*.

19.14 Case Study: Point, Circle, Cylinder

Now let us consider the capstone exercise for this chapter. We consider a point, circle, cylinder hierarchy. First we develop and use class Point (Fig. 19.8). Then we present an example in which we derive class Circle from class Point (Fig. 19.9). Finally, we present an example in which we derive class Cylinder from class Circle (Fig. 19.10).

Figure 19.8 shows class Point. Lines 1 through 42 are the class Point header file and implementation file. Note that Point's data members are protected. Thus, when class Circle is derived from class Point, the member functions of class Circle will be able to directly reference coordinates x and y rather than using access functions. This may result in better performance.

```
1   // Fig. 19.8: point2.h
2   // Definition of class Point
3   #ifndef POINT2_H
4   #define POINT2_H
5
6   #include <iostream>
7
8   using std::ostream;
9
10  class Point {
11     friend ostream &operator<<( ostream &, const Point & );
12  public:
13     Point( int = 0, int = 0 );      // default constructor
14     void setPoint( int, int );      // set coordinates
15     int getX() const { return x; }  // get x coordinate
16     int getY() const { return y; }  // get y coordinate
17  protected:         // accessible to derived classes
18     int x, y;           // coordinates of the point
19  }; // end class Point
20
21  #endif
```

Fig. 19.8 Demonstrating class Point—point2.h.

```
22  // Fig. 19.8: point2.cpp
23  // Member functions for class Point
24  #include "point2.h"
25
26  // Constructor for class Point
27  Point::Point( int a, int b ) { setPoint( a, b ); }
28
```

Fig. 19.8 Demonstrating class Point—point2.cpp. (Part 1 of 2.)

```
29   // Set the x and y coordinates
30   void Point::setPoint( int a, int b )
31   {
32      x = a;
33      y = b;
34   } // end function setPoint
35
36   // Output the Point
37   ostream &operator<<( ostream &output, const Point &p )
38   {
39      output << '[' << p.x << ", " << p.y << ']';
40
41      return output;              // enables cascading
42   } // end operator<< function
```

Fig. 19.8   Demonstrating class `Point`—`point2.cpp`. (Part 2 of 2.)

```
43   // Fig. 19.8: fig19_08.cpp
44   // Driver for class Point
45   #include <iostream>
46
47   using std::cout;
48   using std::endl;
49
50   #include "point2.h"
51
52   int main()
53   {
54      Point p( 72, 115 );   // instantiate Point object p
55
56      // protected data of Point inaccessible to main
57      cout << "X coordinate is " << p.getX()
58           << "\nY coordinate is " << p.getY();
59
60      p.setPoint( 10, 10 );
61      cout << "\n\nThe new location of p is " << p << endl;
62
63      return 0;
64   } // end function main
```

```
X coordinate is 72
Y coordinate is 115

The new location of p is [10, 10]
```

Fig. 19.8   Demonstrating class `Point`—`fig19_08.cpp`.

Lines 43 through 64 comprise the driver program for class `Point`. Note that `main` must use the access functions `getX` and `getY` to read the values of `protected` data members `x` and `y`; remember that `protected` data members are accessible only to members and `friends` of their class and members and `friends` of their derived classes.

Our next example is shown in Fig. 19.9. The Point class definition and the member function definitions from Fig. 19.8 are reused here. Lines 1 through 62 show the Circle class definition and Circle member function definitions. Lines 63 through 90 are the driver program for class Circle. Note that class Circle inherits from class Point with public inheritance. This means that the public interface to Circle includes the Point member functions as well as the Circle member functions setRadius, getRadius and area.

```cpp
1   // Fig. 19.9: circle2.h
2   // Definition of class Circle
3   #ifndef CIRCLE2_H
4   #define CIRCLE2_H
5
6   #include <iostream>
7
8   using std::ostream;
9
10  #include "point2.h"
11
12  class Circle : public Point {
13     friend ostream &operator<<( ostream &, const Circle & );
14  public:
15     // default constructor
16     Circle( double r = 0.0, int x = 0, int y = 0 );
17     void setRadius( double );      // set radius
18     double getRadius() const;      // return radius
19     double area() const;           // calculate area
20  protected:         // accessible to derived classes
21     double radius;   // radius of the Circle
22  }; // end class Circle
23
24  #endif
```

Fig. 19.9 Demonstrating class Circle—circle2.h.

```cpp
25  // Fig. 19.9: circle2.cpp
26  // Member function definitions for class Circle
27  #include <iomanip>
28
29  using std::ios;
30  using std::setiosflags;
31  using std::setprecision;
32
33  #include "circle2.h"
34
35  // Constructor for Circle calls constructor for Point
36  // with a member initializer and initializes radius
37  Circle::Circle( double r, int a, int b )
38     : Point( a, b )         // call base-class constructor
39  { setRadius( r ); }
```

Fig. 19.9 Demonstrating class Circle—circle2.cpp. (Part 1 of 2.)

```
40
41   // Set radius
42   void Circle::setRadius( double r )
43      { radius = ( r >= 0 ? r : 0 ); }
44
45   // Get radius
46   double Circle::getRadius() const { return radius; }
47
48   // Calculate area of Circle
49   double Circle::area() const
50      { return 3.14159 * radius * radius; }
51
52   // Output a circle in the form:
53   // Center = [x, y]; Radius = #.##
54   ostream &operator<<( ostream &output, const Circle &c )
55   {
56      output << "Center = " << static_cast< Point > ( c )
57             << "; Radius = "
58             << setiosflags( ios::fixed | ios::showpoint )
59             << setprecision( 2 ) << c.radius;
60
61      return output;    // enables cascaded calls
62   } // end operator<< function
```

Fig. 19.9 Demonstrating class `Circle`—`circle2.cpp`. (Part 2 of 2.)

```
63   // Fig. 19.9: fig19_09.cpp
64   // Driver for class Circle
65   #include <iostream>
66
67   using std::cout;
68   using std::endl;
69
70   #include "point2.h"
71   #include "circle2.h"
72
73   int main()
74   {
75      Circle c( 2.5, 37, 43 );
76
77      cout << "X coordinate is " << c.getX()
78           << "\nY coordinate is " << c.getY()
79           << "\nRadius is " << c.getRadius();
80
81      c.setRadius( 4.25 );
82      c.setPoint( 2, 2 );
83      cout << "\n\nThe new location and radius of c are\n"
84           << c << "\nArea " << c.area() << '\n';
85
86      Point &pRef = c;
87      cout << "\nCircle printed as a Point is: " << pRef << endl;
88
```

Fig. 19.9 Demonstrating class `Circle`—`fig19_09.cpp`. (Part 1 of 2.)

```
89      return 0;
90  } // end function main
```

```
X coordinate is 37
Y coordinate is 43
Radius is 2.5

The new location and radius of c are
Center = [2, 2]; Radius = 4.25
Area 56.74

Circle printed as a Point is: [2, 2]
```

Fig. 19.9   Demonstrating class `Circle`—`fig19_09.cpp`. (Part 2 of 2.)

Note that the `Circle` overloaded `operator<<` function which, as a `friend` of class `Circle`, is able to output the `Point` part of the `Circle` by casting the `Circle` reference c to a `Point`. This results in a call to `operator<<` for `Point` and outputs the x and y coordinates using the proper `Point` formatting.

The driver program instantiates an object of class `Circle` then uses *get* functions to obtain the information about the `Circle` object. Again, `main` is neither a member function nor a `friend` of class `Circle`, so it cannot directly reference the `protected` data of class `Circle`. The program then uses *set* functions `setRadius` and `setPoint` to reset the radius and coordinates of the center of the circle. Finally, the driver initializes reference variable pRef of type "reference to `Point` object" (`Point &`) to `Circle` object c. The driver then prints pRef, which, despite the fact that it is initialized with a `Circle` object, "thinks" it is a `Point` object, so the `Circle` object actually prints as a `Point` object.

Our last example is shown in Fig. 19.10. The `Point` class and `Circle` class definitions and their member function definitions from Fig. 19.8 and Fig. 19.9 are reused here. Lines 1 through 65 show the `Cylinder` class definition and `Cylinder` member function definitions. Lines 66 through 109 are the driver program for class `Cylinder`. Note that class `Cylinder` inherits from class `Circle` with `public` inheritance. This means that the `public` interface to `Cylinder` includes the `Circle` member functions and `Point` member functions as well as the `Cylinder` member functions `setHeight`, `getHeight`, `area` (overridden from `Circle`) and `volume`. Note that the `Cylinder` constructor is required to invoke the constructor for its direct base class `Circle`, but not for its indirect base class `Point`. Each derived class constructor is only responsible for calling the constructors of that class's immediate base class (or classes, in the case of multiple inheritance). Also, note that the `Cylinder` overloaded `operator<<` function, which is a `friend` of class `Cylinder`, is able to output the `Circle` part of the `Cylinder` by casting the `Cylinder` reference c to a `Circle`. This results in a call to `operator<<` for `Circle` and outputs the x and y coordinates and the `radius` using the proper `Circle` formatting.

```
1    // Fig. 19.10: cylindr2.h
2    // Definition of class Cylinder
3    #ifndef CYLINDR2_H
4    #define CYLINDR2_H
5
6    #include <iostream>
7
8    using std::ostream;
9
10   #include "circle2.h"
11
12   class Cylinder : public Circle {
13      friend ostream &operator<<( ostream &, const Cylinder & );
14
15   public:
16      // default constructor
17      Cylinder( double h = 0.0, double r = 0.0,
18               int x = 0, int y = 0 );
19
20      void setHeight( double );    // set height
21      double getHeight() const;    // return height
22      double area() const;         // calculate and return area
23      double volume() const;       // calculate and return volume
24
25   protected:
26      double height;               // height of the Cylinder
27   }; // end class Cylinder
28
29   #endif
```

Fig. 19.10 Demonstrating class `Cylinder`—`cylindr2.h`.

```
30   // Fig. 19.10: cylindr2.cpp
31   // Member and friend function definitions
32   // for class Cylinder.
33   #include "cylindr2.h"
34
35   // Cylinder constructor calls Circle constructor
36   Cylinder::Cylinder( double h, double r, int x, int y )
37      : Circle( r, x, y )    // call base-class constructor
38   { setHeight( h ); }
39
40   // Set height of Cylinder
41   void Cylinder::setHeight( double h )
42      { height = ( h >= 0 ? h : 0 ); }
43
44   // Get height of Cylinder
45   double Cylinder::getHeight() const { return height; }
46
47   // Calculate area of Cylinder (i.e., surface area)
48   double Cylinder::area() const
49   {
```

Fig. 19.10 Demonstrating class `Cylinder`—`cylindr2.cpp`. (Part 1 of 2.)

```
50      return 2 * Circle::area() +
51             2 * 3.14159 * radius * height;
52   } // end function area
53
54   // Calculate volume of Cylinder
55   double Cylinder::volume() const
56      { return Circle::area() * height; }
57
58   // Output Cylinder dimensions
59   ostream &operator<<( ostream &output, const Cylinder &c )
60   {
61      output << static_cast< Circle >( c )
62             << "; Height = " << c.height;
63
64      return output;     // enables cascaded calls
65   } // end operator<< function
```

Fig. 19.10 Demonstrating class Cylinder—cylindr2.cpp. (Part 2 of 2.)

```
66   // Fig. 19.10: fig19_10.cpp
67   // Driver for class Cylinder
68   #include <iostream>
69
70   using std::cout;
71   using std::endl;
72
73   #include "point2.h"
74   #include "circle2.h"
75   #include "cylindr2.h"
76
77   int main()
78   {
79      // create Cylinder object
80      Cylinder cyl( 5.7, 2.5, 12, 23 );
81
82      // use get functions to display the Cylinder
83      cout << "X coordinate is " << cyl.getX()
84           << "\nY coordinate is " << cyl.getY()
85           << "\nRadius is " << cyl.getRadius()
86           << "\nHeight is " << cyl.getHeight() << "\n\n";
87
88      // use set functions to change the Cylinder's attributes
89      cyl.setHeight( 10 );
90      cyl.setRadius( 4.25 );
91      cyl.setPoint( 2, 2 );
92      cout << "The new location, radius, and height of cyl are:\n"
93           << cyl << '\n';
94
95      cout << "The area of cyl is:\n"
96           << cyl.area() << '\n';
97
```

Fig. 19.10 Demonstrating class Cylinder—fig19_10.cpp. (Part 1 of 2.)

```
98      // display the Cylinder as a Point
99      Point &pRef = cyl;     // pRef "thinks" it is a Point
100     cout << "\nCylinder printed as a Point is: "
101          << pRef << "\n\n";
102
103     // display the Cylinder as a Circle
104     Circle &circleRef = cyl;   // circleRef thinks it is a Circle
105     cout << "Cylinder printed as a Circle is:\n" << circleRef
106          << "\nArea: " << circleRef.area() << endl;
107
108     return 0;
109 } // end function main
```

```
X coordinate is 12
Y coordinate is 23
Radius is 2.5
Height is 5.7

The new location, radius, and height of cyl are:
Center = [2, 2]; Radius = 4.25; Height = 10.00
The area of cyl is:
380.53

Cylinder printed as a Point is: [2, 2]

Cylinder printed as a Circle is:
Center = [2, 2]; Radius = 4.25
Area: 56.74
```

Fig. 19.10 Demonstrating class `Cylinder`—`fig19_10.cpp`. (Part 2 of 2.)

The driver program instantiates an object of class `Cylinder` then uses *get* functions to obtain the information about the `Cylinder` object. Again, `main` is neither a member function nor a `friend` of class `Cylinder`, so it cannot directly reference the `protected` data of class `Cylinder`. The driver program then uses *set* functions `setHeight`, `setRadius` and `setPoint` to reset the height, radius and coordinates of the cylinder. Finally, the driver initializes reference variable `pRef` of type "reference to `Point` object" (`Point &`) to `Cylinder` object `cyl`. It then prints `pRef`, which, despite the fact that it is initialized with a `Cylinder` object, "thinks" it is a `Point` object, so the `Cylinder` object actually prints as a `Point` object. The driver then initializes reference variable `circleRef` of type "reference to `Circle` object" (`Circle &`) to `Cylinder` object `cyl`. The driver program then prints `circleRef`, which, despite the fact that it is initialized with a `Cylinder` object, "thinks" it is a `Circle` object, so the `Cylinder` object actually prints as a `Circle` object. The area of the `Circle` is also output.

This example nicely demonstrates `public` inheritance and defining and referencing `protected` data members. The reader should now be confident with the basics of inheritance. In the next chapter, we show how to program with inheritance hierarchies in a general manner using polymorphism. Data abstraction, inheritance and polymorphism are the crux of object-oriented programming.

SUMMARY

- One of the keys to the power of object-oriented programming is achieving software reusability through inheritance.

- The programmer can designate that the new class is to inherit the data members and member functions of a previously defined base class. In this case, the new class is referred to as a derived class.

- With single inheritance, a class is derived from only one base class. With multiple inheritance, a derived class inherits from multiple (possibly unrelated) base classes.

- A derived class normally adds data members and member functions of its own, so a derived class generally has a larger definition than its base class. A derived class is more specific than its base class and normally represents fewer objects.

- A derived class cannot access the `private` members of its base class; allowing this would violate the encapsulation of the base class. A derived class can, however, access the `public` and `protected` members of its base class.

- A derived-class constructor always calls the constructor for its base class first to create and initialize the derived class's base-class members.

- Destructors are called in the reverse order of constructor calls, so a derived-class destructor is called before its base-class destructor.

- Inheritance enables software reusability, which saves time in development and encourages the use of previously proven and debugged high-quality software.

- Inheritance can be accomplished from existing class libraries.

- Someday most software will be constructed from standardized reusable components, as most hardware is constructed today.

- The implementor of a derived class does not need access to the source code of a base class, but it does need the interface to the base class and the base class's object code.

- An object of a derived class can be treated as an object of its corresponding public base class. However, the reverse is not true.

- A base class exists in a hierarchical relationship with its singly derived classes.

- A class can exist by itself. When that class is used with the mechanism of inheritance, it becomes either a base class that supplies attributes and behaviors to other classes, or the class becomes a derived class that inherits those attributes and behaviors.

- An inheritance hierarchy can be arbitrarily deep within the physical limitations of a particular system.

- Hierarchies are useful tools for understanding and managing complexity. With software becoming increasingly complex, C++ provides mechanisms for supporting hierarchical structures through inheritance and polymorphism.

- An explicit cast can be used to convert a base-class pointer to a derived-class pointer. Such a pointer should not be dereferenced unless it actually points to an object of the derived class type.

- `Protected` access serves as an intermediate level of protection between `public` access and `private` access. `Protected` members of a base class may be accessed by members and `friends` of the base class and by members and `friends` of derived classes; no other functions can access the `protected` members of a base class.

- `Protected` members are used to extend privileges to derived classes while denying those privileges to nonclass, non-`friend` functions.

- When deriving a class from a base class, the base class may be declared as either `public`, `protected` or `private`.

- When deriving a class from a `public` base class, `public` members of the base class become `public` members of the derived class, and `protected` members of the base class become `protected` members of the derived class.

- When deriving a class from a `protected` base class, `public` and `protected` members of the base class become `protected` members of the derived class.

- When deriving a class from a `private` base class, `public` and `protected` members of the base class become `private` members of the derived class.

- A base class may be either a direct base class of a derived class or an indirect base class of a derived class. A direct base class is explicitly listed where the derived class is declared. An indirect base class is not explicitly listed; rather it is inherited from several levels up the class hierarchy tree.

- When a base-class member is inappropriate for a derived class, we may simply redefine that member in the derived class.

- It is important to distinguish between *is a* relationships and *has a* relationships. In a *has a* relationship, a class object has an object of another class as a member. In an *is a* relationship, an object of a derived-class type may also be treated as an object of the base-class type. *Is a* is inheritance. *Has a* is composition.

- A derived-class object can be assigned to a base-class object. This kind of assignment makes sense because the derived class has members corresponding to each of the base-class members.

- A pointer to a derived-class object can be implicitly converted into a pointer for a base-class object.

- It is possible to convert a base-class pointer to a derived-class pointer by using an explicit cast. The target should be a derived-class object.

- A base class specifies commonality. All classes derived from a base class inherit the capabilities of that base class. In the object-oriented design process, the designer looks for commonality and factors it out to form desirable base classes. Derived classes are then customized beyond the capabilities inherited from the base class.

- Reading a set of derived-class declarations can be confusing because not all the members of the derived class are present in these declarations. In particular, inherited members are not listed in the derived-class declarations, but these members are indeed present in the derived classes.

- *Has a* relationships are examples of creating new classes by composition of existing classes.

- *Knows a* relationships are examples of objects containing pointers or references to other objects so they can be aware of those objects.

- Member object constructors are called in the order in which the objects are declared. In inheritance, base-class constructors are called in the order in which inheritance is specified and before the derived-class constructor.

- For a derived-class object, first the base-class constructor is called, then the derived-class constructor is called (which may call member object constructors).

- When the derived-class object is destroyed, the destructors are called in the reverse order of the constructors—first the derived-class destructor is called, then the base-class destructor is called.

- A class may be derived from more than one base class; such derivation is called multiple inheritance.

- Indicate multiple inheritance by following the colon (`:`) inheritance indicator with a comma-separated list of base classes.

- The derived-class constructor calls base-class constructors for each of its base classes through the member-initializer syntax. Base-class constructors are called in the order in which the base classes are declared during inheritance.

TERMINOLOGY

abstraction	inheritance
ambiguity in multiple inheritance	*is a* relationship
association	*knows a* relationship
base class	member access control
base-class constructor	member class
base class default constructor	member object
base-class destructor	multiple inheritance
base-class initializer	object-oriented programming (OOP)
base-class pointer	override a base-class member function
class hierarchy	pointer to a base-class object
class libraries	pointer to a derived-class object
client of a class	`private` base class
composition	`private` inheritance
customize software	`protected` base class
derived class	`protected` inheritance
derived-class constructor	`protected` keyword
derived-class destructor	`protected` member of a class
derived-class pointer	`public` base class
direct-base class	`public` inheritance
downcasting a pointer	single inheritance
`friend` of a base class	software reusability
`friend` of a derived class	standardized software components
function overriding	subclass
has a relationship	superclass
hierarchical relationship	upcasting a pointer
indirect base class	*uses* a relationship

COMMON PROGRAMMING ERRORS

19.1 Treating a base-class object as a derived-class object can cause errors.

19.2 Explicitly casting a base-class pointer that points to a base-class object into a derived-class pointer, then referring to derived-class members that do not exist in that object, can lead to run-time logic errors.

19.3 When a base-class member function is overridden in a derived class, it is common to have the derived-class version call the base-class version and do some additional work. Not using the scope-resolution operator to reference the base class's member function causes infinite recursion because the derived-class member function actually calls itself. This will eventually cause the system to exhaust memory, a fatal execution-time error.

19.4 Assigning a derived-class object to an object of a corresponding base class, then attempting to reference derived-class-only members in the new base-class object is a syntax error.

19.5 Casting a base-class pointer to a derived-class pointer can cause errors if that pointer is then used to reference a base-class object that does not have the desired derived-class members.

PERFORMANCE TIPS

19.1 When performance is a major concern, programmers may want to see source code of classes they are inheriting from so they can tune the code to meet their performance requirements.

19.2 If classes produced through inheritance are larger than they need to be, memory and processing resources may be wasted. Inherit from the class "closest" to what you need.

SOFTWARE ENGINEERING OBSERVATIONS

19.1   In general, declare data members of a class `private` and use `protected` only as a "last resort" when systems need to be tuned to meet unique performance requirements.

19.2   A derived class cannot directly access `private` members of its base class.

19.3   Suppose we create an object of a derived class where both the base class and the derived class contain objects of other classes. When an object of that derived class is created, first the constructors for the base class's member objects execute, then the base-class constructor executes, then the constructors for the derived class's member objects execute, then the derived class's constructor executes. Destructors are called in the reverse of the order in which their corresponding constructors are called.

19.4   The order in which member objects are constructed is the order in which those objects are declared within the class definition. The order in which the member initializers are listed does not affect the order of construction.

19.5   In inheritance, base-class constructors are called in the order in which inheritance is specified in the derived-class definition. The order in which the base-class constructors are specified in the derived-class member initializer list does not affect the order of construction.

19.6   In theory, users do not need to see the source code of classes from which they inherit. In practice, people who license classes tell us that the customers often demand the source code. Programmers still seem reluctant to incorporate code into their programs when this code has been written by other people.

19.7   Creating a derived class does not affect its base class's source code or object code; the integrity of a base class is preserved by inheritance.

19.8   In an object-oriented system, classes are often closely related. "Factor out" common attributes and behaviors and place these in a base class. Then use inheritance to form derived classes.

19.9   A derived class contains the attributes and behaviors of its base class. A derived class can also contain additional attributes and behaviors. With inheritance, the base class can be compiled independently of the derived class. Only the derived class's incremental attributes and behaviors need to be compiled to be able to combine these with the base class to form the derived class.

19.10   Modifications to a base class do not require derived classes to change as long as the `public` and `protected` interfaces to the base class remain unchanged. Derived classes may, however, need to be recompiled.

19.11   Program modifications to a class that is a member of another class do not require the enclosing class to change as long as the `public` interface to the member class remains unchanged. Note that the composite class may, however, need to be recompiled.

SELF-REVIEW EXERCISES

19.1   Fill in the blanks in each of the following:

    a) If the class `Alpha` inherits from the class `Beta`, class `Alpha` is called the _____ class and class `Beta` is called the _____ class.

    b) C++ provides for _____, which allows a derived class to inherit from many base classes, even if these base classes are unrelated.

    c) Inheritance enables _____, which saves time in development and encourages using previously proven and high-quality software.

    d) An object of a(n) _____ class can be treated as an object of its corresponding _____ class.

    e) To convert a base-class pointer to a derived-class pointer, a(n) _____ must be used because the compiler considers this a dangerous operation.

    f) The three member access specifiers are _____, _____ and _____.

g) When deriving a class from a base class with public inheritance, public members of the base class become _____ members of the derived class, and protected members of the base class become _____ members of the derived class.

h) When deriving a class from a base class with protected inheritance, public base class members become _____ members of the derived class and protected base class members become _____ members of the derived class.

i) A *has a* relationship between classes represents _____ and an *is a* relationship between classes represents _____.

ANSWERS TO SELF-REVIEW EXERCISES

19.1 a) derived, base. b) multiple inheritance. c) software reusability. d) derived, base. e) cast. f) public, protected, private.   g) public, protected.   h) protected, protected. i) composition, inheritance.

EXERCISES

19.2 Consider the class Bicycle. Given your knowledge of some common components of bicycles, show a class hierarchy in which the class Bicycle inherits from other classes, which, in turn, inherit from yet other classes. Discuss the instantiation of various objects of class Bicycle. Discuss inheritance from class Bicycle for other closely related derived classes.

19.3 Briefly define each of the following terms: inheritance, multiple inheritance, base class and derived class.

19.4 Discuss why converting a base-class pointer to a derived-class pointer is considered dangerous by the compiler.

19.5 (True/False) A derived class is often called a subclass because it represents a subset of its base class (i.e., a derived class is generally smaller than its base class).

19.6 (True/False) A derived-class object is also an object of that derived class's base class.

19.7 Some programmers prefer not to use protected access because it breaks the encapsulation of the base class. Discuss the relative merits of using protected access vs. insisting on using private access in base classes.

19.8 Many programs written with inheritance could be solved with composition instead, and vice versa. Discuss the relative merits of these approaches in the context of the Point, Circle, Cylinder class hierarchy in this chapter. Rewrite the program of Fig. 19.10 (and the supporting classes) to use composition rather than inheritance. After you do this, reassess the relative merits of the two approaches both for the Point, Circle, Cylinder problem and for object-oriented programs in general.

19.9 In the chapter, we stated, "When a base-class member is inappropriate for a derived class, that member can be overridden in the derived class with an appropriate implementation." If this is done, does the derived-class-is-a-base-class-object relationship still hold? Explain your answer.

19.10 Study the inheritance hierarchy of Fig. 19.2. For each class, indicate some common attributes and behaviors consistent with the hierarchy. Add some other classes (UndergraduateStudent, GraduateStudent, Freshman, Sophomore, Junior, Senior, etc.) to enrich the hierarchy.

19.11 Write an inheritance hierarchy for class Quadrilateral, Trapezoid, Parallelogram, Rectangle and Square. Use Quadrilateral as the base class of the hierarchy. Make the hierarchy as deep (i.e., as many levels) as possible. The private data of Quadrilateral should be the (*x, y*) coordinate pairs for the four endpoints of the Quadrilateral. Write a driver program that instantiates and displays objects of each of these classes.

19.12 Write down all the shapes you can think of—both two-dimensional and three-dimensional—and form those shapes into a shape hierarchy. Your hierarchy should have base class Shape from which class TwoDimensionalShape and class ThreeDimensionalShape are derived. Once you have developed the hierarchy, define each of the classes in the hierarchy. We will use this hierarchy in the exercises of Chapter 20 to process all shapes as objects of base-class Shape. This is a technique called polymorphism.

20

C++ Virtual Functions and Polymorphism

Objectives

- To understand the notion of polymorphism.
- To understand how to declare and use `virtual` functions to effect polymorphism.
- To understand the distinction between abstract classes and concrete classes.
- To learn how to declare pure `virtual` functions to create abstract classes.
- To appreciate how polymorphism makes systems extensible and maintainable.
- To understand how C++ implements `virtual` functions and dynamic binding "under the hood."

One Ring to rule them all, One Ring to find them,
One Ring to bring them all and in the darkness bind them.
John Ronald Reuel Tolkien

The silence often of pure innocence
Persuades when speaking fails.
William Shakespeare

General propositions do not decide concrete cases.
Oliver Wendell Holmes

A philosopher of imposing stature doesn't think in a vacuum.
Even his most abstract ideas are, to some extent, conditioned
by what is or is not known in the time when he lives.
Alfred North Whitehead

Outline

20.1 Introduction

With *virtual functions* and *polymorphism,* it is possible to design and implement systems that are more easily *extensible.* Programs can be written to generically process—as base-class objects—objects of all existing classes in a hierarchy. Classes that do not exist during program development can be added with little or no modifications to the generic part of the program—as long as those classes are part of the hierarchy that is being processed generically. The only parts of a program that will need modification are those parts that require direct knowledge of the particular class that is added to the hierarchy.

20.2 Type Fields and `switch` Statements

One means of dealing with objects of different types is to use a `switch` statement to take an appropriate action on each object based on that object's type. For example, in a hierarchy of shapes in which each shape specifies its type as a data member, a `switch` structure could determine which `print` function to call based on the type of the particular object.

There are many problems with using `switch` logic. The programmer might forget to make such a type test when one is warranted. The programmer may forget to test all possible cases in a `switch`. If a `switch`-based system is modified by adding new types, the programmer might forget to insert the new cases in all existing `switch` statements. Every addition or deletion of a class to handle new types demands that every `switch` statement in the system be modified; tracking these down can be time consuming and prone to error.

As we will see, `virtual` functions and polymorphic programming can eliminate the need for `switch` logic. The programmer can use the `virtual` function mechanism to perform the equivalent logic, thus avoiding the kinds of errors typically associated with `switch` logic.

Software Engineering Observation 20.1

An interesting consequence of using virtual functions and polymorphism is that programs take on a simplified appearance. They contain less branching logic in favor of simpler sequential code. This facilitates testing, debugging, program maintenance and bug avoidance.

20.3 virtual Functions

Suppose a set of shape classes such as Circle, Triangle, Rectangle, Square, etc. are all derived from base class Shape. In object-oriented programming, each of these classes might be endowed with the ability to draw itself. Although each class has its own draw function, the draw function for each shape is quite different. When drawing a shape, whatever that shape may be, it would be nice to be able to treat all these shapes generically as objects of the base class Shape. Then to draw any shape, we could simply call function draw of base class Shape and let the program determine *dynamically* (i.e., at run time) which derived class draw function to use.

To enable this kind of behavior, we declare draw in the base class as a *virtual function* and we *override* draw in each of the derived classes to draw the appropriate shape. A virtual function is declared by preceding the function's prototype with the keyword virtual in the base class. For example,

```
virtual void draw() const;
```

may appear in base class Shape. The preceding prototype declares that function draw is a constant function that takes no arguments, returns nothing and is a virtual function.

Software Engineering Observation 20.2

Once a function is declared virtual, it remains virtual all the way down the inheritance hierarchy from that point even if it is not declared virtual when a class overrides it.

Good Programming Practice 20.1

Even though certain functions are implicitly virtual because of a declaration made higher in the class hierarchy, explicitly declare these functions virtual at every level of the hierarchy to promote program clarity.

Software Engineering Observation 20.3

When a derived class chooses not to define a virtual function, the derived class simply inherits its immediate base class's virtual function definition.

If function draw in the base class has been declared virtual, and if we then use a base-class pointer or reference to point to the derived-class object and invoke the draw function using this pointer (e.g., shapePtr->draw()) or reference, the program will choose the correct derived class's draw function dynamically (i.e., at run time) based on the object type—not the pointer or reference type. Such *dynamic binding* will be illustrated in the case study in Section 20.8.

When a virtual function is called by referencing a specific object by name and using the dot member selection operator (e.g., squareObject.draw()), the reference is resolved at compile time (this is called *static binding*) and the virtual function that is called is the one defined for (or inherited by) the class of that particular object.

20.4 Abstract Base Classes and Concrete Classes

When we think of a class as a type, we assume that objects of that type will be instantiated. However, there are cases in which it is useful to define classes for which the programmer never intends to instantiate any objects. Such classes are called *abstract classes*. These are used as base classes in inheritance situations, so we normally will refer to them as *abstract base classes*. No objects of an abstract base class can be instantiated.

The sole purpose of an abstract class is to provide an appropriate base class from which classes may inherit interface and/or implementation. Classes from which objects can be instantiated are called *concrete classes*.

We could have an abstract base class TwoDimensionalShape and derive concrete classes such as Square, Circle, Triangle, etc. We could also have an abstract base class ThreeDimensionalShape and derive concrete classes such as Cube, Sphere, Cylinder, etc. Abstract base classes are too generic to define real objects; we need to be more specific before we can think of instantiating objects. That is what concrete classes do; they provide the specifics that make it reasonable to instantiate objects.

A class is made abstract by declaring one or more of its virtual functions to be "pure." A *pure virtual function* is one with an *initializer of* = 0 in its declaration as in

```
virtual double earnings() const = 0;   // pure virtual
```

Software Engineering Observation 20.4

If a class is derived from a class with a pure virtual function, and if no definition is supplied for that pure virtual function in the derived class, then that virtual function remains pure in the derived class. Consequently, the derived class is also an abstract class.

Common Programming Error 20.1

Attempting to instantiate an object of an abstract class (i.e., a class that contains one or more pure virtual functions) is a syntax error.

A hierarchy does not need to contain any abstract classes, but as we will see, many good object-oriented systems have class hierarchies headed by an abstract base class. In some cases, abstract classes constitute the top few levels of the hierarchy. A good example of this is a shape hierarchy. The hierarchy could be headed by abstract base class Shape. On the next level, we can have two more abstract base classes—namely TwoDimensionalShape and ThreeDimensionalShape. The next level down would start defining concrete classes for two-dimensional shapes such as circles and squares, and concrete classes for three-dimensional shapes such as spheres and cubes.

20.5 Polymorphism

C++ enables *polymorphism*—the ability for objects of different classes related by inheritance to respond differently to the same message (i.e., member function call). The same message sent to many different types of objects takes on "many forms"—hence the term polymorphism. If, for example, class Rectangle is derived from Quadrilateral, then a Rectangle object *is a* more specific version of a Quadrilateral object. An operation (e.g., calculating the perimeter) that can be performed on a Quadrilateral object also can be performed on a Rectangle object.

Polymorphism is implemented via `virtual` functions. When a request is made through a base-class pointer (or reference) to use a `virtual` function, C++ chooses the correct overridden function in the appropriate derived class associated with the object.

Sometimes a non-`virtual` member function is defined in a base class and overridden in a derived class. If such a member function is called through a base-class pointer to the derived-class object, the base-class version is used. If the member function is called through a derived-class pointer, the derived-class version is used. This is non-polymorphic behavior.

Consider the following example using base class `Employee` and derived class `HourlyWorker` of Fig. 19.5:

```
Employee e, *ePtr = &e;
HourlyWorker h, *hPtr = &h;
ePtr->print();    // call base-class print function
hPtr->print();    // call derived-class print function
ePtr = &h;        // allowable implicit conversion
ePtr->print();    // still calls base-class print
```

Our `Employee` base class and `HourlyWorker` derived class both have their own `print` functions defined. The functions were not declared `virtual` and they have the same signature, so calling the `print` function through an `Employee` pointer results in `Employee::print()` being called (regardless of whether the `Employee` pointer is pointing to a base-class `Employee` object or a derived-class `HourlyWorker` object) and calling the `print` function through an `HourlyWorker` pointer results in function `HourlyWorker::print()` being called. The base-class `print` function is also available to the derived class, but to call the base-class `print` for a derived-class object through a pointer to a derived-class object, for example, the function must be called explicitly as follows:

```
hPtr->Employee::print();  // call base-class print function
```

This specifies that the base-class `print` should be called explicitly.

Through the use of `virtual` functions and polymorphism, one member function call can cause different actions to occur depending on the type of the object receiving the call (we will see that a small amount of execution-time overhead is required). This gives the programmer tremendous expressive capability. We will see examples of the power of polymorphism and `virtual` functions in the next several sections.

Software Engineering Observation 20.5

With `virtual` functions and polymorphism, the programmer can deal in generalities and let the execution-time environment concern itself with the specifics. The programmer can command a wide variety of objects to behave in manners appropriate to those objects without even knowing the types of those objects.

Software Engineering Observation 20.6

Polymorphism promotes extensibility: Software written to invoke polymorphic behavior is written independently of the types of the objects to which messages are sent. Thus, new types of objects that can respond to existing messages can be added into such a system without modifying the base system. Except for client code that instantiates new objects, programs need not be recompiled.

Software Engineering Observation 20.7

An abstract class defines an interface for the various members of a class hierarchy. The abstract class contains pure virtual *functions that will be defined in the derived classes. All functions in the hierarchy can use this same interface through polymorphism.*

Although we cannot instantiate objects of abstract base classes, we *can* declare pointers and references to abstract base classes. Such pointers and references can then be used to enable polymorphic manipulations of derived-class objects when such objects are instantiated from concrete classes.

Let us consider applications of polymorphism and virtual functions. A screen manager needs to display many objects of different classes, including new object types that will be added to the system even after the screen manager is written. The system may need to display various shapes (i.e., base class is Shape) such as squares, circles, triangles, rectangles, points, lines and the like (each shape class is derived from the base class Shape). The screen manager uses base-class pointers or references (to Shape) to manage all the objects to be displayed. To draw any object (regardless of the level at which that object appears in the inheritance hierarchy), the screen manager uses a base-class pointer (or reference) to the object and simply sends a draw message to the object. Function draw has been declared pure virtual in base class Shape and has been overridden in each of the derived classes. Each Shape object knows how to draw itself. The screen manager does not have to worry about what type each object is or whether the object is of a type the screen manager has seen before—the screen manager simply tells each object to draw itself.

Polymorphism is particularly effective for implementing layered software systems. In operating systems, for example, each type of physical device may operate differently from the others. Regardless of this, commands to *read* or *write* data from and to devices can have a certain uniformity. The *write* message sent to a device-driver object needs to be interpreted specifically in the context of that device driver and how that device driver manipulates devices of a specific type. However, the *write* call itself is really no different from the *write* to any other device in the system—it simply places some number of bytes from memory onto that device. An object-oriented operating system might use an abstract base class to provide an interface appropriate for all device drivers. Then, through inheritance from that abstract base class, derived classes are formed that all operate similarly. The capabilities (i.e., the public interface) offered by the device drivers are provided as pure virtual functions in the abstract base class. Implementations of these virtual functions are provided in the derived classes that correspond to the specific types of device drivers.

With polymorphic programming, a program might walk through a container, such as an array of pointers to objects from various levels of a class hierarchy. The pointers in such an array would all be base-class pointers to derived-class objects. For example, an array of objects of class TwoDimensionalShape could contain TwoDimensionalShape * pointers to objects from the derived classes Square, Circle, Triangle, Rectangle, Line, etc. Sending a message to draw each object in the array would, using polymorphism, draw the correct picture on the screen.

20.6 New Classes and Dynamic Binding

Polymorphism and virtual functions work nicely when all possible classes are not known in advance. But they also work when new kinds of classes are added to systems.

New classes are accommodated by dynamic binding (also called *late binding*). An object's type need not be known at compile time for a `virtual` function call to be compiled. At run time, the `virtual` function call is matched with the appropriate member function of the called object.

A screen manager program can now display new kinds of objects as they are added to the system without the screen manager needing to be recompiled. The `draw` function call remains the same. The new objects themselves contain the actual drawing capabilities. This makes it easy to add new capabilities to systems with minimal impact. It also promotes software reuse.

Dynamic binding enables independent software vendors (ISVs) to distribute software without revealing proprietary secrets. Software distributions can consist of only header files and object files. No source code needs to be revealed. Software developers can then use inheritance to derive new classes from those provided by the ISVs. Software that works with the classes the ISVs provide will continue to work with the derived classes and will use (via dynamic binding) the overridden `virtual` functions provided in these classes.

In Section 20.8, we present a comprehensive polymorphism case study. In Section 20.9, we describe in depth precisely how polymorphism, virtual functions and dynamic binding are implemented in C++.

20.7 Virtual Destructors

A problem can occur when using polymorphism to process dynamically allocated objects of a class hierarchy. If an object (with a non-`virtual` destructor) is destroyed explicitly by applying the `delete` operator to a base-class pointer to the object, the base-class destructor function (matching the pointer type) is called on the object. This occurs regardless of the type of the object to which the base-class pointer is pointing and regardless of the fact that each class's destructor has a different name.

There is a simple solution to this problem—declare a `virtual` base-class destructor. This makes all derived-class destructors `virtual` even though they do not have the same name as the base-class destructor. Now, if an object in the hierarchy is destroyed explicitly by applying the `delete` operator to a base-class pointer to a derived-class object, the destructor for the appropriate class is called. Remember, when a derived-class object is destroyed, the base-class part of the derived-class object is also destroyed—the base-class destructor always executes after the derived-class destructor.

Good Programming Practice 20.2

If a class has `virtual` functions, provide a `virtual` destructor, even if one is not required for the class. Classes derived from this class may contain destructors that must be called properly.

Common Programming Error 20.2

Constructors cannot be `virtual`. Declaring a constructor as a `virtual` function is a syntax error.

20.8 Case Study: Inheriting Interface and Implementation

Our next example (Fig. 20.1) re-examines the `Point`, `Circle`, `Cylinder` hierarchy from the previous chapter except that we now head the hierarchy with abstract base class `Shape`. `Shape` has two pure `virtual` functions—`printShapeName` and `print`—so `Shape` is an abstract base class. `Shape` contains two other `virtual` functions, `area` and `volume`, each of which has a default implementation that returns a value of zero. Point inherits these implementations from Shape. This makes sense because both the area and volume of a point are zero. Circle inherits the volume function from Point, but Circle provides its own implementation for the area function. Cylinder provides its own implementations for both the area function and the volume function.

```
1   // Fig. 20.1: shape.h
2   // Definition of abstract base class Shape
3   #ifndef SHAPE_H
4   #define SHAPE_H
5
6   class Shape {
7   public:
8      virtual double area() const { return 0.0; }
9      virtual double volume() const { return 0.0; }
10
11     // pure virtual functions overridden in derived classes
12     virtual void printShapeName() const = 0;
13     virtual void print() const = 0;
14  }; // end class Shape
15
16  #endif
```

Fig. 20.1   Demonstrating interface inheritance with the Shape class hierarchy—
shape.h.

```
17  // Fig. 20.1: point1.h
18  // Definition of class Point
19  #ifndef POINT1_H
20  #define POINT1_H
21
22  #include <iostream>
23
24  using std::cout;
25
26  #include "shape.h"
27
28  class Point : public Shape {
29  public:
30     Point( int = 0, int = 0 );  // default constructor
31     void setPoint( int, int );
32     int getX() const { return x; }
33     int getY() const { return y; }
34     virtual void printShapeName() const { cout << "Point: "; }
35     virtual void print() const;
36  private:
37     int x, y;   // x and y coordinates of Point
38  }; // end class Point
39
40  #endif
```

Fig. 20.1   Demonstrating interface inheritance with the Shape class hierarchy—
point1.h.

```
41    // Fig. 20.1: point1.cpp
42    // Member function definitions for class Point
43    #include "point1.h"
44
45    Point::Point( int a, int b ) { setPoint( a, b ); }
46
47    void Point::setPoint( int a, int b )
48    {
49       x = a;
50       y = b;
51    } // end function setPoint
52
53    void Point::print() const
54       { cout << '[' << x << ", " << y << ']'; }
```

Fig. 20.1   Demonstrating interface inheritance with the **Shape** class hierarchy—
           point1.cpp.

```
55    // Fig. 20.1: circle1.h
56    // Definition of class Circle
57    #ifndef CIRCLE1_H
58    #define CIRCLE1_H
59    #include "point1.h"
60
61    class Circle : public Point {
62    public:
63       // default constructor
64       Circle( double r = 0.0, int x = 0, int y = 0 );
65
66       void setRadius( double );
67       double getRadius() const;
68       virtual double area() const;
69       virtual void printShapeName() const { cout << "Circle: "; }
70       virtual void print() const;
71    private:
72       double radius;   // radius of Circle
73    }; // end class Circle
74
75    #endif
```

Fig. 20.1   Demonstrating interface inheritance with the **Shape** class hierarchy—
           circle1.h.

```
76    // Fig. 20.1: circle1.cpp
77    // Member function definitions for class Circle
78    #include <iostream>
79
80    using std::cout;
81
82    #include "circle1.h"
```

Fig. 20.1   Demonstrating interface inheritance with the **Shape** class hierarchy—
           circle1.cpp. (Part 1 of 2.)

```
83
84    Circle::Circle( double r, int a, int b )
85       : Point( a, b )  // call base-class constructor
86    { setRadius( r ); }
87
88    void Circle::setRadius( double r ) { radius = r > 0 ? r : 0; }
89
90    double Circle::getRadius() const { return radius; }
91
92    double Circle::area() const
93       { return 3.14159 * radius * radius; }
94
95    void Circle::print() const
96    {
97       Point::print();
98       cout << "; Radius = " << radius;
99    } // end function print
```

Fig. 20.1   Demonstrating interface inheritance with the Shape class hierarchy—
circle1.cpp. (Part 2 of 2.)

```
100   // Fig. 20.1: cylindr1.h
101   // Definition of class Cylinder
102   #ifndef CYLINDR1_H
103   #define CYLINDR1_H
104   #include "circle1.h"
105
106   class Cylinder : public Circle {
107   public:
108      // default constructor
109      Cylinder( double h = 0.0, double r = 0.0,
110               int x = 0, int y = 0 );
111
112      void setHeight( double );
113      double getHeight();
114      virtual double area() const;
115      virtual double volume() const;
116      virtual void printShapeName() const { cout << "Cylinder: "; }
117      virtual void print() const;
118   private:
119      double height;   // height of Cylinder
120   }; // end class Cylinder
121
122   #endif
```

Fig. 20.1   Demonstrating interface inheritance with the Shape class hierarchy—
cylindr1.h.

```
123   // Fig. 20.1: cylindr1.cpp
124   // Member and friend function definitions for class Cylinder
```

Fig. 20.1   Demonstrating interface inheritance with the Shape class hierarchy—
cylindr1.cpp. (Part 1 of 2.)

```
125  #include <iostream>
126
127  using std::cout;
128
129  #include "cylindr1.h"
130
131  Cylinder::Cylinder( double h, double r, int x, int y )
132     : Circle( r, x, y )   // call base-class constructor
133  { setHeight( h ); }
134
135  void Cylinder::setHeight( double h )
136     { height = h > 0 ? h : 0; }
137
138  double Cylinder::getHeight() { return height; }
139
140  double Cylinder::area() const
141  {
142     // surface area of Cylinder
143     return 2 * Circle::area() +
144            2 * 3.14159 * getRadius() * height;
145  } // end function area
146
147  double Cylinder::volume() const
148     { return Circle::area() * height; }
149
150  void Cylinder::print() const
151  {
152     Circle::print();
153     cout << "; Height = " << height;
154  } // end function print
```

Fig. 20.1   Demonstrating interface inheritance with the **Shape** class hierarchy—
           `cylindr1.cpp`. (Part 2 of 2.)

```
155  // Fig. 20.1: fig20_01.cpp
156  // Driver for shape, point, circle, cylinder hierarchy
157  #include <iostream>
158
159  using std::cout;
160  using std::endl;
161
162  #include <iomanip>
163
164  using std::ios;
165  using std::setiosflags;
166  using std::setprecision;
167
168  #include "shape.h"
169  #include "point1.h"
170  #include "circle1.h"
171  #include "cylindr1.h"
```

Fig. 20.1   Demonstrating interface inheritance with the **Shape** class hierarchy—
           `fig20_01.cpp`. (Part 1 of 4.)

```
172
173  void virtualViaPointer( const Shape * );
174  void virtualViaReference( const Shape & );
175
176  int main()
177  {
178     cout << setiosflags( ios::fixed | ios::showpoint )
179          << setprecision( 2 );
180
181     Point point( 7, 11 );                    // create a Point
182     Circle circle( 3.5, 22, 8 );             // create a Circle
183     Cylinder cylinder( 10, 3.3, 10, 10 );    // create a Cylinder
184
185     point.printShapeName();    // static binding
186     point.print();             // static binding
187     cout << '\n';
188
189     circle.printShapeName();   // static binding
190     circle.print();            // static binding
191     cout << '\n';
192
193     cylinder.printShapeName(); // static binding
194     cylinder.print();          // static binding
195     cout << "\n\n";
196
197     Shape *arrayOfShapes[ 3 ];   // array of base-class pointers
198
199     // aim arrayOfShapes[0] at derived-class Point object
200     arrayOfShapes[ 0 ] = &point;
201
202     // aim arrayOfShapes[1] at derived-class Circle object
203     arrayOfShapes[ 1 ] = &circle;
204
205     // aim arrayOfShapes[2] at derived-class Cylinder object
206     arrayOfShapes[ 2 ] = &cylinder;
207
208     // Loop through arrayOfShapes and call virtualViaPointer
209     // to print the shape name, attributes, area, and volume
210     // of each object using dynamic binding.
211     cout << "Virtual function calls made off "
212          << "base-class pointers\n";
213
214     for ( int i = 0; i < 3; i++ )
215        virtualViaPointer( arrayOfShapes[ i ] );
216
217     // Loop through arrayOfShapes and call virtualViaReference
218     // to print the shape name, attributes, area, and volume
219     // of each object using dynamic binding.
220     cout << "Virtual function calls made off "
221          << "base-class references\n";
222
```

Fig. 20.1   Demonstrating interface inheritance with the **Shape** class hierarchy—
`fig20_01.cpp`. (Part 2 of 4.)

```
223        for ( int j = 0; j < 3; j++ )
224            virtualViaReference( *arrayOfShapes[ j ] );
225
226        return 0;
227    } // end function main
228
229    // Make virtual function calls off a base-class pointer
230    // using dynamic binding.
231    void virtualViaPointer( const Shape *baseClassPtr )
232    {
233        baseClassPtr->printShapeName();
234        baseClassPtr->print();
235        cout << "\nArea = " << baseClassPtr->area()
236            << "\nVolume = " << baseClassPtr->volume() << "\n\n";
237    } // end function virtualViaPointer
238
239    // Make virtual function calls off a base-class reference
240    // using dynamic binding.
241    void virtualViaReference( const Shape &baseClassRef )
242    {
243        baseClassRef.printShapeName();
244        baseClassRef.print();
245        cout << "\nArea = " << baseClassRef.area()
246            << "\nVolume = " << baseClassRef.volume() << "\n\n";
247    } // end function virtualViaReference
```

```
Point: [7, 11]
Circle: [22, 8]; Radius = 3.50
Cylinder: [10, 10]; Radius = 3.30; Height = 10.00

Virtual function calls made off base-class pointers
Point: [7, 11]
Area = 0.00
Volume = 0.00

Circle: [22, 8]; Radius = 3.50
Area = 38.48
Volume = 0.00

Cylinder: [10, 10]; Radius = 3.30; Height = 10.00
Area = 275.77
Volume = 342.12

Virtual function calls made off base-class references
Point: [7, 11]
Area = 0.00
Volume = 0.00

Circle: [22, 8]; Radius = 3.50
Area = 38.48
Volume = 0.00
```

Fig. 20.1   Demonstrating interface inheritance with the **Shape** class hierarchy—
`fig20_01.cpp`. (Part 3 of 4.)

```
Cylinder: [10, 10]; Radius = 3.30; Height = 10.00
Area = 275.77
Volume = 342.12
```

Fig. 20.1   Demonstrating interface inheritance with the Shape class hierarchy—
fig20_01.cpp. (Part 4 of 4.)

Note that although Shape is an abstract base class, it still contains implementations of certain member functions, and these implementations are inheritable. The Shape class provides an inheritable interface in the form of four virtual functions that all members of the hierarchy will contain. Class Shape also provides some implementations that derived classes in the first few levels of the hierarchy will use.

Software Engineering Observation 20.8

A class can inherit interface and/or implementation from a base class. Hierarchies designed for implementation inheritance *tend to have their functionality high in the hierarchy—each new derived class inherits one or more member functions that were defined in a base class, and the new derived class uses the base-class definitions. Hierarchies designed for* interface inheritance *tend to have their functionality lower in the hierarchy—a base class specifies one or more functions that should be defined for each class in the hierarchy (i.e., they have the same signature), but the individual derived classes provide their own implementations of the function(s).*

Base class Shape (lines 1–16) consists of four public virtual functions and does not contain any data. Functions printShapeName and print are pure virtual, so they are overridden in each of the derived classes. Functions area and volume are defined to return 0.0. These functions are overridden in derived classes when it is appropriate for those classes to have a different area calculation and/or a different volume calculation. Note that Shape is an abstract class and it contains some "impure" virtual functions (area and volume). Abstract classes can also include non-virtual functions and data, which will be inherited by derived classes.

Class Point (lines 17–54) is derived from Shape with public inheritance. A Point has an area of 0.0 and a volume of 0.0, so the base-class member functions area and volume are not overridden here—they are simply inherited as defined in Shape. Functions printShapeName and print are implementations of virtual functions that were defined as pure virtual in the base class—if we did not override these functions in class Point, then Point would also be an abstract class and we would not be able to instantiate Point objects. Other member functions include a *set* function to assign new x and y coordinates to a Point and *get* functions to return the x and y coordinates of a Point.

Class Circle (lines 55–99) is derived from Point with public inheritance. A Circle has a volume of 0.0, so base-class member function volume is not overridden here—it is inherited from Point, which previously inherited volume from Shape. A Circle has nonzero area, so the area function is overridden in this class. Functions printShapeName and print are implementations of virtual functions that were defined as pure virtual in the Shape class. If these functions are not overridden here, the Point versions of these functions would be inherited. Other member functions include a *set* function to assign a new radius to a Circle and a *get* function to return the radius of a Circle.

Class Cylinder (lines 100–154) is derived from Circle with public inheritance. A Cylinder has area and volume different from those of Circle, so the area and volume functions are both overridden in this class. Functions printShapeName and print are implementations of virtual functions that were defined as pure virtual in the Shape class. If these functions are not overridden here, the Circle versions of these functions would be inherited. Other member functions include *set* and *get* functions to assign a new height and return the height of a Cylinder, respectively.

The driver program (lines 155–247) begins by instantiating Point object point, Circle object circle and Cylinder object cylinder. Functions printShapeName and print are invoked for each object to print the name of the object and to illustrate that the objects are initialized correctly. Each call to printShapeName and print in lines 185 through 194 uses static binding—at compile time the compiler knows the type of each object for which printShapeName and print are called.

Next, array arrayOfShapes, each element of which is of type Shape *, is declared. This array of base-class pointers is used to point to each of the derived-class objects. The address of object point is assigned to arrayOfShapes[0] (line 200), the address of object circle is assigned to arrayOfShapes[1] (line 203) and the address of object cylinder is assigned to arrayOfShapes[2] (line 206).

Next, a for structure (line 214) walks through the array arrayOfShapes and invokes function virtualViaPointer (line 215)

```
virtualViaPointer( arrayOfShapes[ i ] );
```

for each element of the array. Function virtualViaPointer receives in parameter baseClassPtr (of type const Shape *) the address stored in an element of arrayOf-Shapes. Each time virtualViaPointer executes, the following four virtual function calls are made

```
baseClassPtr->printShapeName()
baseClassPtr->print()
baseClassPtr->area()
baseClassPtr->volume()
```

Each of these calls invokes a virtual function on the object to which baseClassPtr points at run time—an object whose type cannot be determined here at compile time. The output illustrates that the appropriate functions for each class are invoked. First, the string "Point: " and the coordinates of the object point are output; the area and volume are both 0.00. Next, the string "Circle: ", the coordinates of the center of object circle and the radius of object circle are output; the area of circle is calculated and the volume is returned as 0.00. Finally, the string "Cylinder: ", the coordinates of the center of the base of object cylinder, the radius of object cylinder and the height of object cylinder are output; the area of cylinder is calculated and the volume of cylinder is calculated. All the virtual function calls to printShapeName, print, area and volume are resolved at run-time with dynamic binding.

Finally, a for structure (line 223) walks through arrayOfShapes and invokes function virtualViaReference (line 224)

```
virtualViaReference( *arrayOfShapes[ j ] );
```

for each element of the array. Function virtualViaReference receives in its parameter baseClassRef (of type const Shape &), a reference formed by dereferencing the address stored in an element of the array. During each call to `virtualViaReference`, the following `virtual` function calls are made

```
baseClassRef.printShapeName()
baseClassRef.print()
baseClassRef.area()
baseClassRef.volume()
```

Each of the preceding calls invokes these functions on the object to which `baseClassRef` refers. The output produced using base-class references is identical to the output produced using base-class pointers.

20.9 Polymorphism, `virtual` Functions and Dynamic Binding "Under the Hood"

C++ makes polymorphism easy to program. It is certainly possible to program for polymorphism in non-object-oriented languages such as C, but doing so requires complex and potentially dangerous pointer manipulations. In this section we discuss how C++ implements polymorphism, `virtual` functions and dynamic binding internally. This will give you a solid understanding of how these capabilities really work. More importantly, it will help you appreciate the overhead of polymorphism—in additional memory consumption and processor time. This will help you determine when to use polymorphism and when to avoid it.

First, we will explain the data structures the C++ compiler builds at compile time to support polymorphism at run time. Then, we will show how an executing program uses these data structures to execute `virtual` functions and achieve the dynamic binding associated with polymorphism.

When C++ compiles a class that has one or more `virtual` functions, it builds a *virtual function table (vtable)* for that class. The *vtable* is used by the executing program to select the proper function implementations each time a `virtual` function of that class is to be executed. Figure 20.2 illustrates the `virtual` function tables for classes `Shape`, `Point`, `Circle` and `Cylinder`.

In the *vtable* for class `Shape`, the first function pointer points to the implementation of the `area` function for that class, namely a function that returns an area of `0.0`. The second function pointer points to the `volume`, function which also returns `0.0`. The `printShapeName` and `print` functions are each pure `virtual`—they lack implementations so their function pointers are each set to 0. Any class that has one or more 0 pointers in its *vtable* is an abstract class. Classes without any 0 *vtable* pointers (as `Point`, `Circle` and `Cylinder`) are concrete classes.

Class `Point` inherits the `area` and `volume` functions of class `Shape`, so the compiler simply sets these two pointers in the *vtable* for class `Point` to be copies of the `area` and `volume` pointers in class `Shape`. Class `Point` overrides function `printShapeName` to print `"Point: "` so the function pointer points to the `printShapeName` function of class `Point`. `Point` also overrides `print` so the corresponding function pointer points to the `Point` class function that prints `[ x, y ]`.

The `Circle` `area` function pointer in the *vtable* for class `Circle` points to the `Circle` `area` function that returns πr^2. The `volume` function pointer is simply copied from the `Point` class—that pointer was previously copied into `Point` from `Shape`. The `printShapeeName` function pointer points to the `Circle` version of the function that prints `"Circle: "`. The `print` function pointer points to `Circle`'s `print` function that prints `[ x, y ] r`.

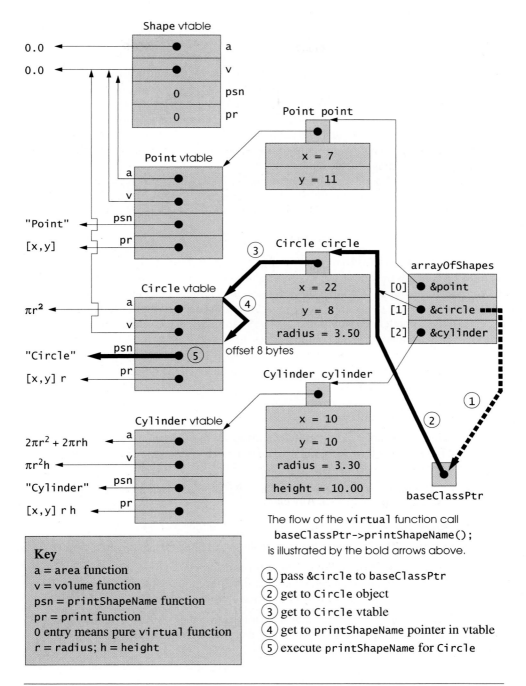

Fig. 20.2 Flow of control of a virtual function call.

The $\texttt{area}$ function pointer in the *vtable* for class $\texttt{Cylinder}$ points to the $\texttt{Cylinder}$ $\texttt{area}$ function that calculates the surface area of the $\texttt{Cylinder}$, namely $2\pi r^2 + 2\pi rh$. The $\texttt{Cylinder}$ $\texttt{volume}$ function pointer points to a $\texttt{volume}$ function that returns $\pi r^2 h$. The $\texttt{Cylinder}$ $\texttt{printShapeName}$ function pointer points to a function that prints "$\texttt{Cylinder:}$ ". The $\texttt{Cylinder}$ $\texttt{print}$ function pointer points to its function that prints [$\texttt{x, y}$] $\texttt{r}$ $\texttt{h}$.

Polymorphism is accomplished through a complex data structure involving three levels of pointers. We have discussed one level—the function pointers in the *vtable*. These pointers point to the actual functions to be executed when a $\texttt{virtual}$ function is invoked.

Now we consider the second level of pointers. Whenever an object of a class with $\texttt{virtual}$ functions is instantiated, the compiler attaches to the front of the object a pointer to the *vtable* for that class. [*Note:* This pointer is normally at the front of the object, but it is not required to be implemented that way.]

The third level of pointer is simply the handle on the object that is receiving the $\texttt{virtual}$ function call (this handle may also be a reference).

Now let us see how a typical $\texttt{virtual}$ function call is executed. Consider the call

```
baseClassPtr->printShapeName()
```

in function $\texttt{virtualViaPointer}$. Assume for the following discussion that $\texttt{baseClassPtr}$ contains the address in $\texttt{arrayOfShapes[1]}$ (i.e., the address of object $\texttt{circle}$). When the compiler compiles this statement, it determines that the call is indeed being made off a base-class pointer and that $\texttt{printShapeName}$ is a $\texttt{virtual}$ function.

Next, the compiler determines that $\texttt{printShapeName}$ is the third entry in each of the *vtables*. To locate this entry, the compiler notes that it will need to skip the first two entries. Thus, the compiler compiles an *offset* or *displacement* of 8 bytes (4 bytes for each pointer on today's popular 32-bit machines) into the machine language object code that will execute the $\texttt{virtual}$ function call.

Then, the compiler generates code that will [*Note:* The numbers in the list below correspond to the circled numbers in Fig. 20.2]:

1. Select the *ith* entry from $\texttt{arrayOfShapes}$ (in this case the address of object $\texttt{circle}$) and pass it to $\texttt{virtualViaPointer}$. This sets $\texttt{baseClassPtr}$ to point to $\texttt{circle}$.

2. Dereference that pointer to get to the $\texttt{circle}$ object—which as you recall, begins with a pointer to the $\texttt{Circle}$ *vtable*.

3. Dereference $\texttt{circle}$'s *vtable* pointer to get to the $\texttt{Circle}$ *vtable*.

4. Skip the offset of 8 bytes to pick up the $\texttt{printShapeName}$ function pointer.

5. Dereference the $\texttt{printShapeName}$ function pointer to form the name of the actual function to be executed and use the function call operator () to execute the appropriate $\texttt{printShapeName}$ function and print the character string "$\texttt{Circle:}$ ".

The data structures of Fig. 20.2 may appear to be complex, but most of this complexity is managed by the compiler and hidden from the programmer, making polymorphic programming straightforward in C++.

The pointer dereferencing operations and memory accesses that occur on every $\texttt{virtual}$ function call do require some additional run time. The *vtables* and the *vtable* pointers added to the objects require some additional memory.

Hopefully, you now have enough information about how virtual functions operate to determine if using them is appropriate for each application you are considering.

Performance Tip 20.1

Polymorphism as implemented with virtual functions and dynamic binding is efficient. Programmers may use these capabilities with nominal impact on system performance.

Performance Tip 20.2

Virtual functions and dynamic binding enable polymorphic programming as opposed to switch logic programming. C++ optimizing compilers normally generate code that runs at least as efficiently as hand-coded switch-based logic. One way or the other, the overhead of polymorphism is acceptable for most applications. But in some situations—real-time applications with stringent performance requirements, for example—the overhead of polymorphism may be too high.

SUMMARY

- With virtual functions and polymorphism, it becomes possible to design and implement systems that are more easily extensible. Programs can be written to process objects of types that may not exist when the program is under development.

- Polymorphic programming with virtual functions can eliminate the need for switch logic. The programmer can use the virtual function mechanism to perform the equivalent logic, thus avoiding the kinds of errors typically associated with switch logic. Client code making decisions about object types and representations indicates poor class design.

- Derived classes can provide their own implementations of a base class virtual function if necessary, but if they do not, the base class's implementation is used.

- If a virtual function is called by referencing a specific object by name and using the dot member selection operator, the reference is resolved at compile time (this is called *static binding*) and the virtual function that is called is the one defined for (or inherited by) the class of that particular object.

- There are many situations in which it is useful to define classes for which the programmer never intends to instantiate any objects. Such classes are called abstract classes. These are used only as base classes, so we will normally refer to them as abstract base classes. No objects of an abstract class may be instantiated in a program.

- Classes from which objects can be instantiated are called concrete classes.

- A class is made abstract by declaring one or more of its virtual functions to be pure. A pure virtual function is one with an initializer of = 0 in its declaration.

- If a class is derived from a class with a pure virtual function without supplying a definition for that pure virtual function in the derived class, then that virtual function remains pure in the derived class. Consequently, the derived class is also an abstract class.

- C++ enables polymorphism—the ability for objects of different classes related by inheritance to respond differently to the same member function call.

- Polymorphism is implemented via virtual functions.

- When a request is made through a base-class pointer or reference to use a virtual function, C++ chooses the correct overridden function in the appropriate derived class associated with the object.

- Through the use of virtual functions and polymorphism, one member function call can cause different actions depending on the type of the object receiving the call.

- Although we cannot instantiate objects of abstract base classes, we can declare pointers to abstract base classes. Such pointers can be used to enable polymorphic manipulations of derived-class objects when such objects are instantiated from concrete classes.

- New kinds of classes are regularly added to systems. New classes are accommodated by dynamic binding (also called late binding). The type of an object need not be known at compile time for a virtual function call to be compiled. At run time, the virtual function call is matched with the member function of the receiving object.

- Dynamic binding enables independent software vendors (ISVs) to distribute software without revealing proprietary secrets. Software distributions can consist of only header files and object files. No source code needs to be revealed. Software developers can then use inheritance to derive new classes from those provided by the ISVs. The software that works with the classes the ISVs provide will continue to work with the derived classes and will use (via dynamic binding) the overridden virtual functions provided in these classes.

- Dynamic binding requires that at run time, the call to a virtual member function be routed to the virtual function version appropriate for the class. A virtual function table called the *vtable* is implemented as an array containing function pointers. Each class with virtual functions has a *vtable*. For each virtual function in the class, the *vtable* has an entry containing a function pointer to the version of the virtual function to use for an object of that class. The virtual function to use for a particular class could be the function defined in that class, or it could be a function inherited either directly or indirectly from a base class higher in the hierarchy.

- When a base class provides a virtual member function, derived classes can override the virtual function, but they do not have to override it. Thus, a derived class can use a base class's version of a virtual member function, and this would be indicated in the *vtable*.

- Each object of a class with virtual functions contains a pointer to the *vtable* for that class. The appropriate function pointer in the *vtable* is obtained and dereferenced to complete the call at run time. This *vtable* lookup and pointer dereferencing require nominal run time overhead, usually less than the best possible client code.

- Declare the base-class destructor virtual if the class contains virtual functions. This makes all derived-class destructors virtual even though they do not have the same name as the base-class destructor. If an object in the hierarchy is destroyed explicitly by applying the delete operator to a base-class pointer to a derived-class object, the destructor for the appropriate class is called.

- Any class that has one or more 0 pointers in its *vtable* is an abstract class. Classes without any 0 *vtable* pointers (like Point, Circle and Cylinder) are concrete classes.

TERMINOLOGY

abstract base class	eliminating switch statements
abstract class	explicit pointer conversion
base-class virtual function	extensibility
class hierarchy	implementation inheritance
concrete class	independent software vendor (ISV)
convert derived-class pointer to base-class pointer	indirect base class
derived class	inheritance
derived-class constructor	interface inheritance
direct base class	late binding
displacement into *vtable*	offset into *vtable*
dynamic binding	override a pure virtual function
early binding	override a virtual function

20.9 (True/False) All virtual functions in an abstract base class must be declared as pure virtual functions.

20.10 Suggest one or more levels of abstract base classes for the Shape hierarchy discussed in this chapter (the first level is Shape and the second level consists of the classes TwoDimensionalShape and ThreeDimensionalShape).

20.11 How does polymorphism promote extensibility?

20.12 You have been asked to develop a flight simulator that will have elaborate graphical outputs. Explain why polymorphic programming would be especially effective for a problem of this nature.

20.13 Develop a basic graphics package. Use the Shape class inheritance hierarchy from Chapter 19. Limit yourself to two-dimensional shapes such as squares, rectangles, triangles and circles. Interact with the user. Let the user specify the position, size, shape and fill characters to be used in drawing each shape. The user can specify many items of the same shape. As you create each shape, place a Shape * pointer to each new Shape object into an array. Each class has its own draw member function. Write a polymorphic screen manager that walks through the array (preferably using an iterator) sending draw messages to each object in the array to form a screen image. Redraw the screen image each time the user specifies an additional shape.

20.14 In Exercise 19.12, you developed a Shape class hierarchy and defined the classes in the hierarchy. Modify the hierarchy so that class Shape is an abstract base class containing the interface to the hierarchy. Derive TwoDimensionalShape and ThreeDimensionalShape from class Shape— these classes should also be abstract. Use a virtual print function to output the type and dimensions of each class. Also include virtual area and volume functions so these calculations can be performed for objects of each concrete class in the hierarchy. Write a driver program that tests the Shape class hierarchy.

21

C++ Stream Input/Output

Objectives

- To understand how to use C++ object-oriented stream input/output.
- To be able to format inputs and outputs.
- To understand the stream I/O class hierarchy.
- To understand how to input/output objects of user-defined types.
- To be able to create user-defined stream manipulators.
- To be able to determine the success or failure of input/output operations.
- To be able to tie output streams to input streams.

Consciousness ... does not appear to itself chopped up in bits ... A "river" or a "stream" are the metaphors by which it is most naturally described.
William James

All the news that's fit to print.
Adolph S. Ochs

Outline

Summary • Terminology • Common Programming Errors • Good Programming Practices • Performance Tip • Portability Tip • Software Engineering Observations • Self-Review Exercises • Answers to Self-Review Exercises • Exercises

21.1 Introduction

The C++ standard libraries provide an extensive set of input/output capabilities. This chapter discusses a range of capabilities sufficient for performing most common I/O operations and overviews the remaining capabilities. Some of the features presented here were discussed earlier in the text, but this chapter provides a more complete discussion of the input/output capabilities of C++.

Many of the I/O features described here are object oriented. The reader should find it interesting to see how such capabilities are implemented. This style of I/O makes use of other C++ features, such as references, function overloading and operator overloading.

As we will see, C++ uses *type-safe I/O*. Each I/O operation is automatically performed in a manner sensitive to the data type. If an I/O function has been properly defined to handle a particular data type, then that function is called to handle that data type. If there is no match between the type of the actual data and a function for handling that data type, a compiler error indication is set. Thus, improper data cannot sneak through the system (as can occur in C—a hole in C that allows for some rather subtle and often bizarre errors).

Users may specify I/O of user-defined types, as well as standard types. This *extensibility* is one of the most valuable features of C++.

Good Programming Practice 21.1

Use the C++ form of I/O exclusively in C++ programs, despite the fact that C-style I/O is available to C++ programmers.

Software Engineering Observation 21.1

C++ style I/O is type safe.

Software Engineering Observation 21.2

C++ enables a common treatment of I/O of predefined types and user-defined types. This kind of commonality facilitates software development in general and software reuse in particular.

21.2 Streams

C++ I/O occurs in *streams* of bytes. A stream is simply a sequence of bytes. In input operations, the bytes flow from a device (e.g., a keyboard, a disk drive, or a network connection) to main memory. In output operations, bytes flow from main memory to a device (e.g., a display screen, a printer, a disk drive, a network connection).

The application associates meaning with bytes. The bytes may represent ASCII characters, internal format raw data, graphics images, digital speech, digital video or any other kind of information an application may require.

The job of the system I/O mechanisms is to move bytes from devices to memory and vice versa in a consistent and reliable manner. Such transfers often involve mechanical motion such as the rotation of a disk or a tape, or typing keystrokes at a keyboard. The time these transfers take is normally huge compared to the time the processor takes to manipulate data internally. Thus, I/O operations require careful planning and tuning to ensure maximum performance.

C++ provides both "low-level" and "high-level" I/O capabilities. Low-level I/O capabilities (i.e., unformatted I/O) typically specify that some number of bytes should simply be transferred device-to-memory or memory-to-device. In such transfers, the individual byte is the item of interest. Such low-level capabilities do provide high-speed, high-volume transfers, but these capabilities are not particularly convenient for people.

People prefer a higher-level view of I/O (i.e., *formatted I/O*), in which bytes are grouped into meaningful units such as integers, floating-point numbers, characters, strings and user-defined types. These type-oriented capabilities are satisfactory for most I/O other than high-volume file processing.

Performance Tip 21.1

Use unformatted I/O for the best performance in high-volume file processing.

21.2.1 Iostream Library Header Files

The C++ `iostream` library provides hundreds of I/O capabilities. Several header files contain portions of the library interface.

Most C++ programs include the `<iostream>` header file, which declares basic services required for all stream-I/O operations. The `<iostream>` header file defines the `cin`, `cout`, `cerr` and `clog` objects which correspond to the standard input stream, the standard output stream, the unbuffered standard error stream and the buffered standard error stream, respectively. Both unformatted- and formatted-I/O services are provided.

The `<iomanip>` header declares services useful for performing formatted I/O with so-called *parameterized stream manipulators*.

C++ implementations generally contain other I/O-related libraries that provide system-specific capabilities such as controlling special-purpose devices for audio and video I/O.

21.2.2 Stream Input/Output Classes and Objects

The `iostream` library contains many classes for handling a wide variety of I/O operations. The `istream` class supports stream-input operations. The `ostream` class supports stream-output operations. The `iostream` class supports both stream-input and stream-output operations.

The `istream` class and the `ostream` class are each derived through single inheritance from the `ios` base class. The `iostream` class is derived through multiple inheritance from both the `istream` class and the `ostream` class. These inheritance relationships are summarized in Fig. 21.1.

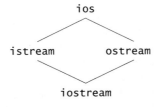

Fig. 21.1   Portion of the stream I/O class hierarchy.

Operator overloading provides a convenient notation for performing input/output. The left shift operator (<<) is overloaded to designate stream output and is referred to as the *stream-insertion operator.* The right shift operator (>>) is overloaded to designate stream input and is referred to as the *stream-extraction operator.* These operators are used with the standard stream objects cin, cout, cerr and clog, and commonly with user-defined stream objects.

The predefined object cin is an instance of the istream class and is said to be "tied to" (or connected to) the standard input device, normally the keyboard. The stream-extraction operator (>>) as used in the following statement causes a value for the integer variable grade (assuming that grade has been declared as an int variable) to be input from cin to memory:

```
cin >> grade;  // data "flows" in the direction of the arrows
               // to the right
```

Note that the stream-extraction operation is "smart enough" to "know" what the type of the data is. Assuming that grade has been properly declared, no additional type information needs to be specified for use with the stream-extraction operator (as is the case, incidentally, in C-style I/O).

The predefined object cout is an instance of the ostream class and is said to be "tied to" the standard output device, normally the display screen. The stream-insertion operator (<<), as used in the following statement, causes the value of the integer variable grade (assuming that grade has been declared as an int variable) to be output from memory to the standard output device:

```
cout << grade; // data "flows" in the direction of the arrows
               // to the left
```

Note that the stream-insertion operator is "smart enough" to "know" the type of grade (assuming it has been properly declared), so no additional type information needs to be specified for use with the stream-insertion operator.

The predefined object cerr is an instance of the ostream class and is said to be "tied to" the standard error device. Outputs to object cerr are unbuffered. This means that each stream insertion to cerr causes its output to appear immediately; this is appropriate for promptly notifying a user about errors.

The predefined object clog is an instance of the ostream class and is also said to be "tied to" the standard error device. Outputs to clog are buffered. This means that each insertion to clog could cause its output to be held in a buffer until the buffer is filled or until the buffer is flushed.

C++ file processing uses the classes ifstream to perform file input operations, ofstream for file output operations and fstream for file input/output operations. The ifstream class inherits from class istream, the ofstream class inherits from class ostream and the fstream class inherits from class iostream. The various inheritance relationships of the input/output-related classes are summarized in Fig. 21.2. There are many more classes in the full stream-I/O class hierarchy supported at most installations, but the classes shown here provide the vast majority of the capabilities most programmers will need. See the class library reference for your C++ system for more information about file processing.

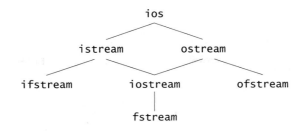

Fig. 21.2   Portion of stream-I/O class hierarchy with key file-processing classes.

21.3 Stream Output

The C++ `ostream` class provides the ability to perform formatted and unformatted output. Capabilities for output include output of standard data types with the stream-insertion operator; output of characters with the `put` member function; unformatted output with the `write` member function (Section 21.5); output of integers in decimal, octal and hexadecimal formats (Section 21.6.1); output of floating-point values with various precisions (Section 21.6.2), with forced decimal points (Section 21.7.2), in scientific notation and in fixed notation (Section 21.7.6); output of data justified in fields of designated field widths (Section 21.7.3); output of data in fields padded with specified characters (Section 21.7.4); and output of uppercase letters in scientific notation and hexadecimal notation (Section 21.7.7).

21.3.1 Stream-Insertion Operator

Stream output may be performed with the stream-insertion operator (i.e., the overloaded `<<` operator). The `<<` operator is overloaded to output data items of built-in types, to output strings and to output pointer values. Section 21.9 shows how to overload `<<` to output data items of user-defined types. Figure 21.3 demonstrates output of a string using a single stream-insertion statement. Multiple insertion statements may be used, as in Fig. 21.4. When this program is run, it produces the same output as the previous program.

```
1   // Fig. 21.3: fig21_03.cpp
2   // Outputting a string using stream insertion.
3   #include <iostream>
4
5   using std::cout;
6
7   int main()
8   {
9      cout << "Welcome to C++!\n";
10
11     return 0;
12  } // end function main
```

```
Welcome to C++!
```

Fig. 21.3   Outputting a string using stream insertion.

```
1    // Fig. 21.4: fig21_04.cpp
2    // Outputting a string using two stream insertions.
3    #include <iostream>
4
5    using std::cout;
6
7    int main()
8    {
9       cout << "Welcome to ";
10      cout << "C++!\n";
11
12      return 0;
13   } // end function main
```

```
Welcome to C++!
```

Fig. 21.4   Outputting a string using two stream insertions.

The effect of the \n (newline) escape sequence is also achieved by the **endl** (end line) *stream manipulator*, as in Fig. 21.5. The **endl** stream manipulator issues a newline character and, in addition, flushes the output buffer (i.e., causes the output buffer to be output immediately even if it is not full). The output buffer may also be flushed simply by

        cout << flush;

Stream manipulators are discussed in detail in Section 21.6.

```
1    // Fig. 21.5: fig21_05.cpp
2    // Using the endl stream manipulator.
3    #include <iostream>
4
5    using std::cout;
6    using std::endl;
7
8    int main()
9    {
10      cout << "Welcome to ";
11      cout << "C++!";
12      cout << endl;    // end line stream manipulator
13
14      return 0;
15   } // end function main
```

```
Welcome to C++!
```

Fig. 21.5   Using the endl stream manipulator.

Expressions can be output as shown in Fig. 21.6.

Good Programming Practice 21.2

When outputting expressions, place them in parentheses to prevent operator precedence problems between the operators in the expression and the << operator.

```
1    // Fig. 21.6: fig21_06.cpp
2    // Outputting expression values.
3    #include <iostream>
4
5    using std::cout;
6    using std::endl;
7
8    int main()
9    {
10       cout << "47 plus 53 is ";
11
12       // parentheses not needed; used for clarity
13       cout << ( 47 + 53 );          // expression
14       cout << endl;
15
16       return 0;
17   } // end function main
```

```
47 plus 53 is 100
```

Fig. 21.6 Outputting expression values.

21.3.2 Cascading Stream-Insertion/Extraction Operators

The overloaded << and >> operators may each be used in a *cascaded form,* as shown in Fig. 21.7.

```
1    // Fig. 21.7: fig21_07.cpp
2    // Cascading the overloaded << operator.
3    #include <iostream>
4
5    using std::cout;
6    using std::endl;
7
8    int main()
9    {
10       cout << "47 plus 53 is " << ( 47 + 53 ) << endl;
11
12       return 0;
13   } // end function main
```

```
47 plus 53 is 100
```

Fig. 21.7 Cascading the overloaded << operator.

The multiple stream insertions in Fig. 21.7 are executed as if they had been written

$$(((\text{cout} << \text{"47 plus 53 is "}) << (47 + 53)) << \text{endl});$$

(i.e., << associates from left to right). This kind of cascading of stream-insertion operators is allowed because the overloaded << operator returns a reference to its left-operand object, (i.e., cout). Thus the leftmost parenthesized expression

```
( cout << "47 plus 53 is " )
```

outputs the specified character string and returns a reference to `cout`. This allows the middle parenthesized expression to be evaluated as

```
( cout << ( 47 + 53 ) )
```

which outputs the integer value 100 and returns a reference to `cout`. The rightmost parenthesized expression is then evaluated as

```
cout << endl
```

which outputs a newline, flushes `cout` and returns a reference to `cout`. This last return is not used.

21.3.3 Output of char * Variables

In C-style I/O, it is necessary for the programmer to supply type information. C++ determines data types automatically—a nice improvement over C. But sometimes this "gets in the way." For example, we know that a character string is of type `char *`. Suppose we want to print the value of that pointer, i.e., the memory address of the first character of that string. But the `<<` operator has been overloaded to print data of type `char *` as a null-terminated string. The solution is to cast the pointer to `void *` (this should be done to any pointer variable the programmer wishes to output as an address). Figure 21.8 demonstrates printing a `char *` variable in both string and address formats. Note that the address prints as a hexadecimal (base-16) number. We say more about controlling the bases of numbers in Sections 21.6.1, 21.7.4, 21.7.5 and 21.7.7. [*Note:* The output of the program in Fig. 21.8 may differ from compiler to compiler.]

```
1   // Fig. 21.8: fig21_08.cpp
2   // Printing the address stored in a char* variable
3   #include <iostream>
4
5   using std::cout;
6   using std::endl;
7
8   int main()
9   {
10      const char *string = "test";
11
12      cout << "Value of string is: " << string
13          << "\nValue of static_cast< void * >( string ) is: "
14          << static_cast< void * >( string ) << endl;
15      return 0;
16   } // end function main
```

```
Value of string is: test
Value of static_cast< void *>( string ) is: 0046C070
```

Fig. 21.8 Printing the address stored in a `char *` variable.

21.3.4 Character Output with Member Function put; Cascading puts

The put member function outputs one character as in

```
cout.put( 'A' );
```

which displays A on the screen. Calls to put may be cascaded as in

```
cout.put( 'A' ).put( '\n' );
```

which outputs the letter A followed by a newline character. As with <<, the preceding statement executes in this manner because the dot operator (.) associates from left to right, and the put member function returns a reference to the ostream object that received the put message (function call). The put function may also be called with an ASCII-valued expression, as in cout.put(65), which also outputs A.

21.4 Stream Input

Now let us consider stream input. This may be performed with the stream-extraction operator (i.e., the overloaded >> operator). This operator normally skips *whitespace characters* (such as blanks, tabs and newlines) in the input stream. Later we will see how to change this behavior. The stream-extraction operator returns zero (false) when end-of-file is encountered on a stream; otherwise, the stream-extraction operator returns a reference to the object that received the extraction message (e.g., cin in the expression cin >> grade). Each stream contains a set of *state bits* used to control the state of the stream (i.e., formatting, setting error states, etc.). Stream extraction causes the stream's failbit to be set if data of the wrong type are input and causes the stream's badbit to be set if the operation fails. We will soon see how to test these bits after an I/O operation. Sections 21.7 and 21.8 discuss the stream state bits in detail.

21.4.1 Stream-Extraction Operator

To read two integers, use the cin object and the overloaded >> stream-extraction operator as in Fig. 21.9. Note that stream-extraction operations can also be cascaded.

```
1   // Fig. 21.9: fig21_09.cpp
2   // Calculating the sum of two integers input from the keyboard
3   // with cin and the stream-extraction operator.
4   #include <iostream>
5
6   using std::cout;
7   using std::cin;
8   using std::endl;
9
10  int main()
11  {
12     int x, y;
13
```

Fig. 21.9   Calculating the sum of two integers input from the keyboard with cin and the stream-extraction operator. (Part 1 of 2.)

```
14        cout << "Enter two integers: ";
15        cin >> x >> y;
16        cout << "Sum of " << x << " and " << y << " is: "
17             << ( x + y ) << endl;
18
19        return 0;
20   } // end function main
```

```
Enter two integers: 30 92
Sum of 30 and 92 is: 122
```

Fig. 21.9 Calculating the sum of two integers input from the keyboard with `cin` and the stream-extraction operator. (Part 2 of 2.)

The relatively high precedence of the >> and << operators can cause problems. For example, the program of Fig. 21.10 will not compile properly without the parentheses around the conditional expression. The reader should verify this.

```
1    // Fig. 21.10: fig21_10.cpp
2    // Avoiding a precedence problem between the stream-insertion
3    // operator and the conditional operator.
4    // Need parentheses around the conditional expression.
5    #include <iostream>
6
7    using std::cout;
8    using std::cin;
9    using std::endl;
10
11   int main()
12   {
13      int x, y;
14
15      cout << "Enter two integers: ";
16      cin >> x >> y;
17      cout << x << ( x == y ? " is" : " is not" )
18           << " equal to " << y << endl;
19
20      return 0;
21   } // end function main
```

```
Enter two integers: 7 5
7 is not equal to 5
```

```
Enter two integers: 8 8
8 is equal to 8
```

Fig. 21.10 Avoiding a precedence problem between the stream-insertion operator and the conditional operator.

Common Programming Error 21.1

Attempting to read from an ostream *(or from any other output-only stream).*

Common Programming Error 21.2

Attempting to write to an istream *(or to any other input-only stream).*

Common Programming Error 21.3

Not providing parentheses to force proper precedence when using the relatively high precedence stream-insertion operator << *or stream-extraction operator* >>.

A popular way to input a series of values is to use the stream-extraction operation in the loop-continuation condition of a while loop. The extraction returns false (0) when end-of-file is encountered. Consider the program of Fig. 21.11, which finds the highest grade on an exam. Assume that the number of grades is not known in advance and that the user will type end-of-file to indicate that all the grades have been entered. The while condition, (cin >> grade), becomes 0 (interpreted as false) when the user enters end-of-file.

```cpp
1    // Fig. 21.11: fig21_11.cpp
2    // Stream-extraction operator returning false on end-of-file.
3    #include <iostream>
4
5    using std::cout;
6    using std::cin;
7    using std::endl;
8
9    int main()
10   {
11       int grade, highestGrade = -1;
12
13       cout << "Enter grade (enter end-of-file to end): ";
14       while ( cin >> grade ) {
15           if ( grade > highestGrade )
16               highestGrade = grade;
17
18           cout << "Enter grade (enter end-of-file to end): ";
19       } // end while
20
21       cout << "\n\nHighest grade is: " << highestGrade << endl;
22       return 0;
23   } // end function main
```

```
Enter grade (enter end-of-file to end): 67
Enter grade (enter end-of-file to end): 87
Enter grade (enter end-of-file to end): 73
Enter grade (enter end-of-file to end): 95
Enter grade (enter end-of-file to end): 34
Enter grade (enter end-of-file to end): 99
Enter grade (enter end-of-file to end): ^Z
Highest grade is: 99
```

Fig. 21.11 Stream-extraction operator returning false on end-of-file.

Portability Tip 21.1

When prompting the user on how to end input from the keyboard, ask the user to "enter end-of-file to end input" rather than prompting for <ctrl>-d (UNIX and Macintosh) or <ctrl>-z (PC and VAX).

In Fig. 21.11, `cin >> grade` can be used as a condition, because the base class `ios` (from which `istream` is inherited) provides an overloaded cast operator that converts a stream into a pointer of type `void *`. The value of the returned pointer is 0 (`false`) if an error occurred while attempting to read a value or the end-of-file indicator was encountered. The compiler is able to use the `void *` cast operator implicitly.

21.4.2 get and getline Member Functions

The `get` member function with no arguments inputs one character from the designated stream (even if this is whitespace) and returns this character as the value of the function call. This version of `get` returns EOF when end-of-file on the stream is encountered.

Figure 21.12 demonstrates the use of member functions `eof` and `get` on input stream `cin` and member function `put` on output stream `cout`. The program first prints the value of `cin.eof()` [i.e., `false` (0 on the output)] to show that end-of-file has not occurred on `cin`. The user enters a line of text and presses *Enter* followed by end-of-file (*<ctrl>-z* on IBM PC-compatible systems, *<ctrl>-d* on UNIX and Macintosh systems). The program reads each character and outputs it to `cout` using member function `put`. When the end-of-file is encountered, the `while` ends, and `cin.eof()`—now `true`—is printed again (1 on the output) to show that end-of-file has been set on `cin`. Note that this program uses the version of `istream` member function `get` that takes no arguments and returns the character being input.

```cpp
1   // Fig. 21.12: fig21_12.cpp
2   // Using member functions get, put and eof.
3   #include <iostream>
4
5   using std::cout;
6   using std::cin;
7   using std::endl;
8
9   int main()
10  {
11     char c;
12
13     cout << "Before input, cin.eof() is " << cin.eof()
14          << "\nEnter a sentence followed by end-of-file:\n";
15
16     while ( ( c = cin.get() ) != EOF )
17        cout.put( c );
18
19     cout << "\nEOF in this system is: " << c;
20     cout << "\nAfter input, cin.eof() is " << cin.eof() << endl;
21     return 0;
22  } // end function main
```

Fig. 21.12 Using member functions get, put and eof. (Part 1 of 2.)

```
Before input, cin.eof() is 0
Enter a sentence followed by end-of-file:
Testing the get and put member functions
Testing the get and put member functions
^Z

EOF in this system is: -1
After input cin.eof() is 1
```

Fig. 21.12 Using member functions get, put and eof. (Part 2 of 2.)

The get member function with a character reference argument inputs the next character from the input stream (even if this is a whitespace character) and stores it in the character argument. This version of get returns 0 when end-of-file is encountered; otherwise this version of get returns a reference to the istream object for which the get member function is being invoked.

A third version of the get member function takes three arguments—a character array, a size limit and a delimiter (with default value '\n'). This version reads characters from the input stream. It reads up to one less than the specified maximum number of characters and terminates, or terminates as soon as the delimiter is read. A null character is inserted to terminate the input string in the character array used as a buffer by the program. The delimiter is not placed in the character array, but does remain in the input stream (the delimiter will be the next character read). Thus, the result of a second consecutive get is an empty line unless the delimiter character is flushed from the input stream. Figure 21.13 compares input using cin with stream extraction (which reads characters until a whitespace character is encountered) and input with cin.get. Note that the call to cin.get does not specify a delimiter character, so the default '\n' is used.

```
1   // Fig. 21.13: fig21_13.cpp
2   // Contrasting input of a string with cin and cin.get.
3   #include <iostream>
4
5   using std::cout;
6   using std::cin;
7   using std::endl;
8
9   int main()
10  {
11     const int SIZE = 80;
12     char buffer1[ SIZE ], buffer2[ SIZE ];
13
14     cout << "Enter a sentence:\n";
15     cin >> buffer1;
16     cout << "\nThe string read with cin was:\n"
17          << buffer1 << "\n\n";
18
19     cin.get( buffer2, SIZE );
```

Fig. 21.13 Contrasting input of a string using cin with stream extraction and input with cin.get. (Part 1 of 2.)

```
20      cout << "The string read with cin.get was:\n"
21          << buffer2 << endl;
22
23      return 0;
24   } // end function main
```

```
Enter a sentence:
Contrasting string input with cin and cin.get

The string read with cin was:
Contrasting

The string read with cin.get was:
 string input with cin and cin.get
```

Fig. 21.13 Contrasting input of a string using `cin` with stream extraction and input with `cin.get`. (Part 2 of 2.)

The `getline` member function operates like the third version of the `get` member function and inserts a null character after the line in the character array. The `getline` function removes the delimiter from the stream (i.e., reads the character and discards it), but does not store it in the character array. The program of Fig. 21.14 demonstrates the use of the `getline` member function to input a line of text.

```
1    // Fig. 21.14: fig21_14.cpp
2    // Character input with member function getline.
3    #include <iostream>
4
5    using std::cout;
6    using std::cin;
7    using std::endl;
8
9    int main()
10   {
11      const SIZE = 80;
12      char buffer[ SIZE ];
13
14      cout << "Enter a sentence:\n";
15      cin.getline( buffer, SIZE );
16
17      cout << "\nThe sentence entered is:\n" << buffer << endl;
18      return 0;
19   } // end function main
```

```
Enter a sentence:
Using the getline member function

The sentence entered is:
Using the getline member function
```

Fig. 21.14 Character input with member function `getline`.

21.4.3 `istream` Member Functions `peek`, `putback` and `ignore`

The `ignore` member function skips over a designated number of characters (the default is one character) or terminates upon encountering a designated delimiter (the default delimiter is `EOF`, which causes `ignore` to skip to the end of the file when reading from a file).

The `putback` member function places the previous character obtained by a `get` from an input stream back onto that stream. This function is useful for applications that scan an input stream looking for a field beginning with a specific character. When that character is input, the application puts the character back on the stream so that the character can be included in the data about to be input.

The `peek` member function returns the next character from an input stream, but does not remove the character from the stream.

21.4.4 Type-Safe I/O

C++ offers *type-safe I/O*. The << and >> operators are overloaded to accept data items of specific types. If unexpected data are processed, various error flags are set that the user may test to determine if an I/O operation succeeded or failed. In this manner, the program "stays in control." We discuss these error flags in Section 21.8.

21.5 Unformatted I/O with `read`, `gcount` and `write`

Unformatted input/output is performed with the `read` and `write` member functions. Each of these inputs or outputs some number of bytes to or from a character array in memory. These bytes are not formatted in any way. They are simply input or output as raw bytes. For example, the call

```
char buffer[] = "HAPPY BIRTHDAY";
cout.write( buffer, 10 );
```

outputs the first 10 bytes of `buffer` (including null characters that would cause output with `cout` and << to terminate). Since a character string evaluates to the address of its first character, the call

```
cout.write( "ABCDEFGHIJKLMNOPQRSTUVWXYZ", 10 );
```

displays the first 10 characters of the alphabet.

The `read` member function inputs a designated number of characters into a character array. If fewer than the designated number of characters are read, `failbit` is set. We will soon see how to determine if `failbit` has been set (see Section 21.8). Member function `gcount` reports the number of characters read by the last input operation.

Figure 21.15 demonstrates `istream` member functions `read` and `gcount` and `ostream` member function `write`. The program inputs 20 characters (from a longer input sequence) into character array `buffer` with `read`, determines the number of characters input with `gcount` and outputs the characters in `buffer` with `write`.

```
1   // Fig. 21.15: fig21_15.cpp
2   // Unformatted I/O with read, gcount and write.
```

Fig. 21.15 Unformatted I/O with `read`, `gcount` and `write`. (Part 1 of 2.)

```
3    #include <iostream>
4
5    using std::cout;
6    using std::cin;
7    using std::endl;
8
9    int main()
10   {
11       const int SIZE = 80;
12       char buffer[ SIZE ];
13
14       cout << "Enter a sentence:\n";
15       cin.read( buffer, 20 );
16       cout << "\nThe sentence entered was:\n";
17       cout.write( buffer, cin.gcount() );
18       cout << endl;
19       return 0;
20   } // end function main
```

```
Enter a sentence:
Using the read, write and gcount member functions
The sentence entered was:
Using the read, writ
```

Fig. 21.15 Unformatted I/O with read, gcount and write. (Part 2 of 2.)

21.6 Stream Manipulators

C++ provides various *stream manipulators* that perform formatting tasks. The stream manipulators provide capabilities such as setting field widths, setting precisions, setting and unsetting format flags, setting the fill character in fields, flushing streams, inserting a newline in the output stream and flushing the stream, inserting a null character in the output stream and skipping whitespace in the input stream. These features are described in the following sections.

21.6.1 Integral Stream Base: dec, oct, hex and setbase

Integers are normally interpreted as decimal (base-10) values. To change the base in which integers are interpreted on a stream, insert the manipulator hex to set the base to hexadecimal (base 16) or insert the manipulator oct to set the base to octal (base 8). Insert the dec stream manipulator to reset the stream base to decimal.

The base of a stream may also be changed by the stream manipulator setbase, which takes one integer argument of 10, 8 or 16 to set the base. Stream manipulator setbase takes an argument, so it is called a *parameterized stream manipulator*. Using setbase or any other parameterized manipulator requires the inclusion of the <iomanip> header file. The stream base remains the same until it is explicitly changed. Figure 21.16 shows the use of the hex, oct, dec and setbase stream manipulators.

```
1    // Fig. 21.16: fig21_16.cpp
2    // Using hex, oct, dec and setbase stream manipulators.
3    #include <iostream>
4
5    using std::cout;
6    using std::cin;
7    using std::endl;
8
9    #include <iomanip>
10
11   using std::hex;
12   using std::dec;
13   using std::oct;
14   using std::setbase;
15
16   int main()
17   {
18      int n;
19
20      cout << "Enter a decimal number: ";
21      cin >> n;
22
23      cout << n << " in hexadecimal is: "
24           << hex << n << '\n'
25           << dec << n << " in octal is: "
26           << oct << n << '\n'
27           << setbase( 10 ) << n << " in decimal is: "
28           << n << endl;
29
30      return 0;
31   } // end function main
```

```
Enter a decimal number: 20
20 in hexadecimal is: 14
20 in octal is: 24
20 in decimal is: 20
```

Fig. 21.16 Using the hex, oct, dec and setbase stream manipulators .

21.6.2 Floating-Point Precision (precision, setprecision)

We can control the *precision* of floating-point numbers (i.e., the number of digits to the right of the decimal point) by using either the setprecision stream manipulator or the precision member function. A call to either of these sets the precision for all subsequent output operations until the next precision-setting call. The precision member function with no argument returns the current precision setting. The program of Fig. 21.17 uses both the precision member function and the setprecision manipulator to print a table showing the square root of 2 with precisions varying from 0 through 9.

```cpp
1    // Fig. 21.17: fig21_17.cpp
2    // Controlling precision of floating-point values
3    #include <iostream>
4
5    using std::cout;
6    using std::cin;
7    using std::endl;
8
9    #include <iomanip>
10
11   using std::ios;
12   using std::setiosflags;
13   using std::setprecision;
14
15   #include <cmath>
16
17   int main()
18   {
19       double root2 = sqrt( 2.0 );
20       int places;
21
22       cout << setiosflags( ios::fixed )
23            << "Square root of 2 with precisions 0-9.\n"
24            << "Precision set by the "
25            << "precision member function:" << endl;
26
27       for ( places = 0; places <= 9; places++ ) {
28          cout.precision( places );
29          cout << root2 << '\n';
30       } // end for
31
32       cout << "\nPrecision set by the "
33            << "setprecision manipulator:\n";
34
35       for ( places = 0; places <= 9; places++ )
36          cout << setprecision( places ) << root2 << '\n';
37
38       return 0;
39   } // end function main
```

```
Square root of 2 with precisions 0-9.
Precision set by the precision member function:
1
1.4
1.41
1.414
1.4142
1.41421
1.414214
1.4142136
1.41421356
1.414213562
```

Fig. 21.17 Controlling precision of floating-point values. (Part 1 of 2.)

```
Precision set by the setprecision manipulator:
1
1.4
1.41
1.414
1.4142
1.41421
1.414214
1.4142136
1.41421356
1.414213562
```

Fig. 21.17 Controlling precision of floating-point values. (Part 2 of 2.)

21.6.3 Field Width (`setw`, `width`)

The `ios width` member function sets the field width (i.e., the number of character positions in which a value should be output or the number of characters that should be input) and returns the previous width. If values processed are smaller than the field width, *fill characters* are inserted as *padding*. A value wider than the designated width will not be truncated—the full number will be printed.

Common Programming Error 21.4

The width setting applies only for the next insertion or extraction; afterward, the width is implicitly set to 0 (i.e., output values will simply be as wide as they need to be). The width function with no argument returns the current setting. It is a logic error to assume that the width setting applies to all subsequent outputs.

Common Programming Error 21.5

When not providing a sufficiently wide field to handle outputs, the outputs print as wide as they need to be, possibly causing difficult-to-read outputs.

Figure 21.18 demonstrates the use of the `width` member function on both input and output. Note that on input into a `char` array, a maximum of one fewer characters than the width will be read, because provision is made for the null character to be placed in the input string. Remember that stream extraction terminates when nonleading whitespace is encountered. The `setw` stream manipulator also may be used to set the field width. [*Note:* When the user is prompted for input, the user should enter a line of text and press *Enter* followed by end-of-file (*<ctrl>-z* on IBM PC-compatible systems, *<ctrl>-d* on UNIX and Macintosh systems).] Note that when inputting anything other than a `char` array, `width` and `setw` are ignored.

```
1   // fig21_18.cpp
2   // Demonstrating the width member function
3   #include <iostream>
4
5   using std::cout;
6   using std::cin;
```

Fig. 21.18 Demonstrating the `width` member function. (Part 1 of 2.)

```
 7    using std::endl;
 8
 9    int main()
10    {
11       int w = 4;
12       char string[ 10 ];
13
14       cout << "Enter a sentence:\n";
15       cin.width( 5 );
16
17       while ( cin >> string ) {
18          cout.width( w++ );
19          cout << string << endl;
20          cin.width( 5 );
21       } // end while
22
23       return 0;
24    } // end function main
```

```
Enter a sentence:
This is a test of the width member function
This
   is
      a
   test
      of
      the
      widt
          h
        memb
           er
         func
          tion
```

Fig. 21.18 Demonstrating the `width` member function. (Part 2 of 2.)

21.6.4 User-Defined Manipulators

Users may create their own stream manipulators. Figure 21.19 shows the creation and use of new stream manipulators `bell`, `ret` (carriage return), `tab` and `endLine`. Users may also create their own parameterized stream manipulators—consult your installation's manuals for instructions on how to do this.

```
1    // Fig. 21.19: fig21_19.cpp
2    // Creating and testing user-defined, nonparameterized
3    // stream manipulators.
4    #include <iostream>
5
6    using std::ostream;
```

Fig. 21.19 Creating and testing user-defined, nonparameterized stream manipulators. (Part 1 of 2.)

```
 7    using std::cout;
 8    using std::flush;
 9
10    // bell manipulator (using escape sequence \a)
11    ostream& bell( ostream& output ) { return output << '\a'; }
12
13    // ret manipulator (using escape sequence \r)
14    ostream& ret( ostream& output ) { return output << '\r'; }
15
16    // tab manipulator (using escape sequence \t)
17    ostream& tab( ostream& output ) { return output << '\t'; }
18
19    // endLine manipulator (using escape sequence \n
20    // and the flush member function)
21    ostream& endLine( ostream& output )
22    {
23       return output << '\n' << flush;
24    } // end function endLine
25
26    int main()
27    {
28       cout << "Testing the tab manipulator:" << endLine
29            << 'a' << tab << 'b' << tab << 'c' << endLine
30            << "Testing the ret and bell manipulators:"
31            << endLine << "..........";
32       cout << bell;
33       cout << ret << "-----" << endLine;
34       return 0;
35    } // end function main
```

```
Testing the tab manipulator:
a       b       c
Testing the ret and bell manipulators:
-----.....
```

Fig. 21.19 Creating and testing user-defined, nonparameterized stream manipulators. (Part 2 of 2.)

21.7 Stream Format States

Various *format flags* specify the kinds of formatting to be performed during stream I/O operations. The setf, unsetf and flags member functions control the flag settings.

21.7.1 Format State Flags

Each of the format state flags shown in Fig. 21.20 (and some that are not shown) is defined as an enumeration in class ios and is explained in the next several sections.

  These flags can be controlled by the flags, setf and unsetf member functions, but many C++ programmers prefer to use stream manipulators (see Section 21.7.8). The programmer may use the bitwise-or operation, |, to combine various options into a single long value (see Fig. 21.23). Calling the flags member function for a stream and specifying these "or-ed" options sets the options on that stream and returns a long value containing the prior options. This value is often saved so that `flags` may be called with this saved value to restore the previous stream options.

Format state flag	Description
ios::skipws	Skip whitespace characters on an input stream.
ios::left	Left-justify output in a field. Padding characters appear to the right if necessary.
ios::right	Right-justify output in a field. Padding characters appear to the left if necessary.
ios::internal	Indicate that a number's sign should be left-justified in a field and a number's magnitude should be right-justified in that same field (i.e., padding characters appear between the sign and the number).
ios::dec	Specify that integers should be treated as decimal (base 10) values.
ios::oct	Specify that integers should be treated as octal (base 8) values.
ios::hex	Specify that integers should be treated as hexadecimal (base 16) values.
ios::showbase	Specify that the base of a number is to be output ahead of the number (a leading 0 for octals; a leading 0x or 0X for hexadecimals).
ios::showpoint	Specify that floating-point numbers should be output with a decimal point. This is normally used with `ios::fixed` to guarantee a certain number of digits to the right of the decimal point.
ios::uppercase	Specify that uppercase letters (i.e., X and A through F) should be used in the hexadecimal integer and that uppercase E should be used when representing a floating-point value in scientific notation.
ios::showpos	Specify that positive and negative numbers should be preceded by a + or – sign, respectively.
ios::scientific	Specify output of a floating-point value in scientific notation.
ios::fixed	Specify output of a floating-point value in fixed-point notation with a specific number of digits to the right of the decimal point.

Fig. 21.20 Format state flags.

The `flags` function must specify a value representing the settings of all the flags. The one-argument `setf` function, on the other hand, specifies one or more "or-ed" flags and "ors" them with the existing flag settings to form a new format state.

The `setiosflags` parameterized stream manipulator performs the same functions as the `setf` member function. The `resetiosflags` stream manipulator performs the same functions as the `unsetf` member function. To use either of these stream manipulators, be sure to `#include <iomanip>`.

The `skipws` flag indicates that `>>` should skip whitespace on an input stream. The default behavior of `>>` is to skip whitespace. To change this, use the call `unsetf(ios::skipws)`. The `ws` stream manipulator also may be used to specify that whitespace should be skipped.

21.7.2 Trailing Zeros and Decimal Points (`ios::showpoint`)

The `showpoint` flag is set to force a floating-point number to be output with its decimal point and trailing zeros. A floating-point value of 79.0 will print as 79 without the flag `showpoint` set and as 79.000000 (or as many trailing zeros as are specified by the current precision) with `showpoint` set. The program in Fig. 21.21 shows the use of the `setf` member function to set the `showpoint` flag to control trailing zeros and the printing of the decimal point for floating-point values.

```
1    // Fig. 21.21: fig21_21.cpp
2    // Controlling the printing of trailing zeros and decimal
3    // points for floating-point values.
4    #include <iostream>
5
6    using std::cout;
7    using std::endl;
8
9    #include <iomanip>
10
11   using std::ios;
12
13   #include <cmath>
14
15   int main()
16   {
17      cout << "Before setting the ios::showpoint flag\n"
18           << "9.9900 prints as: " << 9.9900
19           << "\n9.9000 prints as: " << 9.9000
20           << "\n9.0000 prints as: " << 9.0000
21           << "\n\nAfter setting the ios::showpoint flag\n";
22      cout.setf( ios::showpoint );
23      cout << "9.9900 prints as: " << 9.9900
24           << "\n9.9000 prints as: " << 9.9000
25           << "\n9.0000 prints as: " << 9.0000 << endl;
26      return 0;
27   } // end function main
```

```
Before setting the ios::showpoint flag
9.9900 prints as: 9.99
9.9000 prints as: 9.9
9.0000 prints as: 9

After setting the ios::showpoint flag
9.9900 prints as: 9.99000
9.9000 prints as: 9.90000
9.0000 prints as: 9.00000
```

Fig. 21.21 Controlling the printing of trailing zeros and decimal points with float values.

21.7.3 Justification (`ios::left`, `ios::right`, `ios::internal`)

The `left` and `right` flags enable fields to be left-justified with padding characters to the right, or right-justified with padding characters to the left, respectively. The character to be used for padding is specified by the `fill` member function or the `setfill` parameterized stream manipulator (see Section 21.7.4). Figure 21.22 shows the use of the manipulators `setw`, `setiosflags` and `resetiosflags` and the `setf` and `unsetf` member functions to control the left- and right-justification of integer data in a field.

```cpp
1    // Fig. 21.22: fig21_22.cpp
2    // Left-justification and right-justification.
3    #include <iostream>
4
5    using std::cout;
6    using std::endl;
7
8    #include <iomanip>
9
10   using std::ios;
11   using std::setw;
12   using std::setiosflags;
13   using std::resetiosflags;
14
15   int main()
16   {
17      int x = 12345;
18
19      cout << "Default is right justified:\n"
20           << setw(10) << x << "\n\nUSING MEMBER FUNCTIONS"
21           << "\nUse setf to set ios::left:\n" << setw(10);
22
23      cout.setf( ios::left, ios::adjustfield );
24      cout << x << "\nUse unsetf to restore default:\n";
25      cout.unsetf( ios::left );
26      cout << setw( 10 ) << x
27           << "\n\nUSING PARAMETERIZED STREAM MANIPULATORS"
28           << "\nUse setiosflags to set ios::left:\n"
29           << setw( 10 ) << setiosflags( ios::left ) << x
30           << "\nUse resetiosflags to restore default:\n"
31           << setw( 10 ) << resetiosflags( ios::left )
32           << x << endl;
33      return 0;
34   } // end function main
```

```
Default is right justified:
     12345

USING MEMBER FUNCTIONS
Use setf to set ios::left:
12345
Use unsetf to restore default:
     12345
```

Fig. 21.22 Left-justification and right-justification. (Part 1 of 2.)

```
USING PARAMETERIZED STREAM MANIPULATORS
Use setiosflags to set ios::left:
12345
Use resetiosflags to restore default:
    12345
```

Fig. 21.22 Left-justification and right-justification. (Part 2 of 2.)

The `internal` flag indicates that a number's sign (or base when the `ios::showbase` flag is set; see Section 21.7.5) should be left-justified within a field, the number's magnitude should be right-justified and intervening spaces should be padded with the fill character. The `left`, `right` and `internal` flags are contained in static data member `ios::adjustfield`. The `ios::adjustfield` argument must be provided as the second argument to `setf` when setting the `left`, `right` or `internal` justification flags. This enables `setf` to ensure that only one of the three justification flags is set (they are mutually exclusive). Figure 21.23 shows the use of the `setiosflags` and `setw` stream manipulators to specify internal spacing. Note the use of the `ios::showpos` flag to force the printing of the plus sign.

```
1   // Fig. 21.23: fig21_23.cpp
2   // Printing an integer with internal spacing and
3   // forcing the plus sign.
4   #include <iostream>
5
6   using std::cout;
7   using std::endl;
8
9   #include <iomanip>
10
11  using std::ios;
12  using std::setiosflags;
13  using std::setw;
14
15  int main()
16  {
17     cout << setiosflags( ios::internal | ios::showpos )
18          << setw( 10 ) << 123 << endl;
19     return 0;
20  } // end function main
```

```
+       123
```

Fig. 21.23 Printing an integer with internal spacing and forcing the plus sign.

21.7.4 Padding (`fill`, `setfill`)

The *fill member function* specifies the fill character to be used with adjusted fields; if no value is specified, spaces are used for padding. The `fill` function returns the prior padding character. The *setfill manipulator* also sets the padding character. Figure 21.24 demonstrates the use of the `fill` member function and the `setfill` manipulator to control the setting and resetting of the fill character.

```cpp
1   // Fig. 21.24: fig21_24.cpp
2   // Using the fill member function and the setfill
3   // manipulator to change the padding character for
4   // fields larger than the values being printed.
5   #include <iostream>
6
7   using std::cout;
8   using std::endl;
9
10  #include <iomanip>
11
12  using std::ios;
13  using std::setw;
14  using std::hex;
15  using std::dec;
16  using std::setfill;
17
18  int main()
19  {
20     int x = 10000;
21
22     cout << x << " printed as int right and left justified\n"
23          << "and as hex with internal justification.\n"
24          << "Using the default pad character (space):\n";
25     cout.setf( ios::showbase );
26     cout << setw( 10 ) << x << '\n';
27     cout.setf( ios::left, ios::adjustfield );
28     cout << setw( 10 ) << x << '\n';
29     cout.setf( ios::internal, ios::adjustfield );
30     cout << setw( 10 ) << hex << x;
31
32     cout << "\n\nUsing various padding characters:\n";
33     cout.setf( ios::right, ios::adjustfield );
34     cout.fill( '*' );
35     cout << setw( 10 ) << dec << x << '\n';
36     cout.setf( ios::left, ios::adjustfield );
37     cout << setw( 10 ) << setfill( '%' ) << x << '\n';
38     cout.setf( ios::internal, ios::adjustfield );
39     cout << setw( 10 ) << setfill( '^' ) << hex << x << endl;
40     return 0;
41  } // end function main
```

Fig. 21.24 Using the `fill` member function and the `setfill` manipulator to change the padding character for fields larger than the values being printed. (Part 1 of 2.)

```
10000 printed as int right and left justified
and as hex with internal justification.
Using the default pad character (space):
     10000
10000
0x    2710

Using various padding characters:
*****10000
10000%%%%%
0x^^^^2710
```

Fig. 21.24 Using the `fill` member function and the `setfill` manipulator to change the padding character for fields larger than the values being printed. (Part 2 of 2.)

21.7.5 Integral Stream Base (`ios::dec`, `ios::oct`, `ios::hex`, `ios::showbase`)

The *ios::basefield static member* (used similarly to `ios::adjustfield` with `setf`) includes the `ios::oct`, `ios::hex` and `ios::dec` flag bits to specify that integers are to be treated as octal, hexadecimal and decimal values, respectively. Stream insertions default to decimal if none of these bits is set. The default for stream extractions is to process the data in the form in which they are supplied—integers starting with 0 are treated as octal values, integers starting with 0x or 0X are treated as hexadecimal values and all other integers are treated as decimal values. Once a particular base is specified for a stream, all integers on that stream are processed with that base until a new base is specified or until the end of the program.

Set the `showbase` flag to force the base of an integral value to be output. Decimal numbers are output normally, octal numbers are output with a leading 0 and hexadecimal numbers are output with either a leading 0x or a leading 0X (the `uppercase` flag determines which option is chosen; see Section 21.7.7). Figure 21.25 demonstrates the use of the `showbase` flag to force an integer to print in decimal, octal and hexadecimal formats.

```
1   // Fig. 21.25: fig21_25.cpp
2   // Using the ios::showbase flag
3   #include <iostream>
4
5   using std::cout;
6   using std::endl;
7
8   #include <iomanip>
9
10  using std::ios;
11  using std::setiosflags;
12  using std::oct;
13  using std::hex;
14
```

Fig. 21.25 Using the `ios::showbase` flag. (Part 1 of 2.)

```
15   int main()
16   {
17      int x = 100;
18
19      cout << setiosflags( ios::showbase )
20          << "Printing integers preceded by their base:\n"
21          << x << '\n'
22          << oct << x << '\n'
23          << hex << x << endl;
24      return 0;
25   } // end function main
```

```
Printing integers preceded by their base:
100
0144
0x64
```

Fig. 21.25 Using the `ios::showbase` flag. (Part 2 of 2.)

21.7.6 Floating-Point Numbers; Scientific Notation (`ios::scientific`, `ios::fixed`)

The *ios::scientific flag* and the *ios::fixed flag* are contained in the *static data member ios::floatfield* (these flags are used similarly to `ios::adjustfield` and `ios::basefield` in `setf`). These flags control the output format of floating-point numbers. The `scientific` flag forces the output of a floating-point number in scientific format. The `fixed` flag forces a floating-point number to display a specific number of digits (as specified by the `precision` member function) to the right of the decimal point. Without these flags set, the value of the floating-point number determines the output format.

The call `cout.setf(0, ios::floatfield)` restores the default format for outputting floating-point numbers. Figure 21.26 demonstrates displaying floating-point numbers in fixed and scientific formats using the two-argument `setf` with `ios::floatfield`. The exponent format in scientific notation may differ between compilers.

```
1    // Fig. 21.26: fig21_26.cpp
2    // Displaying floating-point values in system default,
3    // scientific, and fixed formats.
4    #include <iostream>
5
6    using std::cout;
7    using std::endl;
8    using std::ios;
9
10   int main()
11   {
12      double x = .001234567, y = 1.946e9;
13
```

Fig. 21.26 Displaying floating-point values in system default, scientific and fixed format. (Part 1 of 2.)

```
14      cout << "Displayed in default format:\n"
15          << x << '\t' << y << '\n';
16      cout.setf( ios::scientific, ios::floatfield );
17      cout << "Displayed in scientific format:\n"
18          << x << '\t' << y << '\n';
19      cout.unsetf( ios::scientific );
20      cout << "Displayed in default format after unsetf:\n"
21          << x << '\t' << y << '\n';
22      cout.setf( ios::fixed, ios::floatfield );
23      cout << "Displayed in fixed format:\n"
24          << x << '\t' << y << endl;
25      return 0;
26  } // end function main
```

```
Displayed in default format:
0.00123457      1.946e+009
Displayed in scientific format:
1.234567e-003    1.946000e+009
Displayed in default format after unsetf:
0.00123457      1.946e+009
Displayed in fixed format:
0.001235        1946000000.000000
```

Fig. 21.26 Displaying floating-point values in system default, scientific and fixed format. (Part 2 of 2.)

21.7.7 Uppercase/Lowercase Control (`ios::uppercase`)

The `ios::uppercase` flag forces an uppercase X or E to be output with hexadecimal integers or with scientific notation floating-point values, respectively (Fig. 21.27). When set, the `ios::uppercase` flag causes all letters in a hexadecimal value to be uppercase.

```
1   // Fig. 21.27: fig21_27.cpp
2   // Using the ios::uppercase flag
3   #include <iostream>
4
5   using std::cout;
6   using std::endl;
7
8   #include <iomanip>
9
10  using std::setiosflags;
11  using std::ios;
12  using std::hex;
13
14  int main()
15  {
16      cout << setiosflags( ios::uppercase )
17          << "Printing uppercase letters in scientific\n"
18          << "notation exponents and hexadecimal values:\n"
19          << 4.345e10 << '\n' << hex << 123456789 << endl;
```

Fig. 21.27 Using the `ios::uppercase` flag. (Part 1 of 2.)

```
20        return 0;
21    } // end function main
```

```
Printing uppercase letters in scientific
notation exponents and hexadecimal values:
4.345E+010
75BCD15
```

Fig. 21.27 Using the `ios::uppercase` flag. (Part 2 of 2.)

21.7.8 Setting and Resetting the Format Flags (`flags`, `setiosflags`, `resetiosflags`)

The `flags` member function without an argument simply returns (as a `long` value) the current settings of the format flags. The `flags` member function with a `long` argument sets the format flags as specified by the argument and returns the prior flag settings. Any format flags not specified in the argument to `flags` are reset. Note that the initial settings of the flags on each system may differ. The program of Fig. 21.28 demonstrates the use of the `flags` member function to set a new format state and save the previous format state, then restore the original format settings.

```
1    // Fig. 21.28: fig21_28.cpp
2    // Demonstrating the flags member function.
3    #include <iostream>
4
5    using std::cout;
6    using std::endl;
7    using std::ios;
8
9
10   int main()
11   {
12       int i = 1000;
13       double d = 0.0947628;
14
15       cout << "The value of the flags variable is: "
16            << cout.flags()
17            << "\nPrint int and double in original format:\n"
18            << i << '\t' << d << "\n\n";
19       long originalFormat =
20            cout.flags( ios::oct | ios::scientific );
21       cout << "The value of the flags variable is: "
22            << cout.flags()
23            << "\nPrint int and double in a new format\n"
24            << "specified using the flags member function:\n"
25            << i << '\t' << d << "\n\n";
26       cout.flags( originalFormat );
27       cout << "The value of the flags variable is: "
28            << cout.flags()
```

Fig. 21.28 Demonstrating the `flags` member function. (Part 1 of 2.)

```
29                 << "\nPrint values in original format again:\n"
30                 << i << '\t' << d << endl;
31        return 0;
32  } // end function main
```

```
The value of the flags variable is: 513
Print int and double in original format:
1000      0.0947628

The value of the flags variable is: 12000
Print int and double in a new format
specified using the flags member function:
1750      9.476280e-002

The value of the flags variable is: 513
Print values in original format again:
1000      0.0947628
```

Fig. 21.28 Demonstrating the flags member function. (Part 2 of 2.)

The setf member function sets the format flags provided in its argument and returns the previous flag settings as a long value, as in

```
long previousFlagSettings =
        cout.setf( ios::showpoint | ios::showpos );
```

The setf member function with two long arguments, as in

```
cout.setf( ios::left, ios::adjustfield );
```

first clears the bits of ios::adjustfield, then sets the ios::left flag. This version of setf is used with the bit fields associated with ios::basefield (represented by ios::dec, ios::oct and ios::hex), ios::floatfield (represented by ios::scientific and ios::fixed) and ios::adjustfield (represented by ios::left, ios::right and ios::internal).

The unsetf member function resets the designated flags and returns the value of the flags prior to being reset.

21.8 Stream Error States

The state of a stream may be tested through bits in class ios—the base class for the classes istream, ostream and iostream we are using for I/O.

The eofbit is set for an input stream after end-of-file is encountered. A program can use the eof member function to determine if end-of-file has been encountered on a stream after an attempt to extract data beyond the end of the stream. The call

```
cin.eof()
```

returns true if end-of-file has been encountered on cin and false otherwise.

The failbit is set for a stream when a format error occurs on the stream. For example, a format error occurs when the program is inputting integers and a nondigit character is encountered in the input stream. When such an error occurs, the characters are not lost. The `fail` member function reports if a stream operation has failed; it is normally possible to recover from such errors.

The `badbit` is set for a stream when an error occurs that results in the loss of data. The `bad` member function reports if a stream operation has failed. Such serious failures are normally nonrecoverable.

The `goodbit` is set for a stream if none of the bits `eofbit`, `failbit` or `badbit` are set for the stream.

The `good` member function returns `true` if the `bad`, `fail` and `eof` functions would all return false. I/O operations should only be performed on "good" streams.

The `rdstate` member function returns the error state of the stream. A call to `cout.rdstate`, for example, would return the state of the stream, which could then be tested by a `switch` statement that examines `ios::eofbit`, `ios::badbit`, `ios::failbit` and `ios::goodbit`. The preferred means of testing the state of a stream is to use the member functions `eof`, `bad`, `fail` and `good`—using these functions does not require the programmer to be familiar with particular status bits.

The `clear` member function is normally used to restore a stream's state to "good" so that I/O may proceed on that stream. The default argument for `clear` is `ios::goodbit`, so the statement

```
cin.clear();
```

clears `cin` and sets `goodbit` for the stream. The statement

```
cin.clear( ios::failbit )
```

sets the `failbit`. The user might want to do this when performing input on `cin` with a user-defined type and encountering a problem. The name `clear` seems inappropriate in this context, but it is correct.

The program of Fig. 21.29 illustrates the use of the `rdstate`, `eof`, `fail`, `bad`, `good` and `clear` member functions. [*Note:* The actual values output may differ from compiler to compiler.]

```
1    // Fig. 21.29: fig21_29.cpp
2    // Testing error states.
3    #include <iostream>
4
5    using std::cout;
6    using std::endl;
7    using std::cin;
8
9    int main()
10   {
11      int x;
12      cout << "Before a bad input operation:"
13           << "\ncin.rdstate(): " << cin.rdstate()
14           << "\n    cin.eof(): " << cin.eof()
15           << "\n   cin.fail(): " << cin.fail()
```

Fig. 21.29 Testing error states. (Part 1 of 2.)

```
16              << "\n    cin.bad(): " << cin.bad()
17              << "\n    cin.good(): " << cin.good()
18              << "\n\nExpects an integer, but enter a character: ";
19      cin >> x;
20
21      cout << "\nAfter a bad input operation:"
22              << "\ncin.rdstate(): " << cin.rdstate()
23              << "\n    cin.eof(): " << cin.eof()
24              << "\n    cin.fail(): " << cin.fail()
25              << "\n    cin.bad(): " << cin.bad()
26              << "\n    cin.good(): " << cin.good() << "\n\n";
27
28      cin.clear();
29
30      cout << "After cin.clear()"
31              << "\ncin.fail(): " << cin.fail()
32              << "\ncin.good(): " << cin.good() << endl;
33      return 0;
34   } // end function main
```

```
Before a bad input operation:
cin.rdstate(): 0
    cin.eof(): 0
   cin.fail(): 0
    cin.bad(): 0
   cin.good(): 1

Expects an integer, but enter a character: A

After a bad input operation:
cin.rdstate(): 2
    cin.eof(): 0
   cin.fail(): 1
    cin.bad(): 0
   cin.good(): 0

After cin.clear()
cin.fail(): 0
cin.good(): 1
```

Fig. 21.29 Testing error states. (Part 2 of 2.)

The `operator!` member function returns `true` if either the `badbit` is set, the `failbit` is set or both are set. The `operator void*` member function returns `false` (0) if either the `badbit` is set, the `failbit` is set or both are set. These functions are useful in file processing when a true/false condition is being tested under the control of a selection structure or repetition structure.

21.9 Tying an Output Stream to an Input Stream

Interactive applications generally involve an `istream` for input and an `ostream` for output. When a prompting message appears on the screen, the user responds by entering the appropriate data. Obviously, the prompt needs to appear before the input operation proceeds. With output buffering, outputs appear only when the buffer fills, when outputs are flushed explicitly by the program or automatically at the end of the program. C++ provides member function `tie` to synchronize (i.e., "tie together") the operation of an `istream` and an `ostream` to ensure that outputs appear before their subsequent inputs. The call

```
cin.tie( &cout );
```

ties `cout` (an `ostream`) to `cin` (an `istream`). Actually, this particular call is redundant because C++ performs this operation automatically to create a user's standard input/output environment. The user would, however, explicitly tie together other `istream`/`ostream` pairs. To untie an input stream, `inputStream`, from an output stream, use the call

```
inputStream.tie( 0 );
```

SUMMARY

- I/O operations are performed in a manner sensitive to the type of the data.
- C++ I/O occurs in streams of bytes. A stream is simply a sequence of bytes.
- I/O mechanisms of the system move bytes from devices to memory and vice versa in an efficient and reliable manner.
- C++ provides "low-level" and "high-level" I/O capabilities. Low-level I/O-capabilities specify that some number of bytes should be transferred device-to-memory or memory-to-device. High-level I/O is performed with bytes grouped into meaningful units such as integers, floats, characters, strings and user-defined types.
- C++ provides both unformatted I/O and formatted I/O operations. Unformatted I/O transfers are fast, but process raw data that are difficult for people to use. Formatted I/O processes data in meaningful units, but requires extra processing time that can negatively impact high-volume data transfers.
- Most C++ programs include the `<iostream>` header file that declares all stream I/O operations.
- Header `<iomanip>` declares the formatted input/output with parameterized stream manipulators.
- The `<fstream>` header declares file processing operations.
- The `istream` class supports stream input operations.
- The `ostream` class supports stream output operations.
- The `iostream` class supports both stream input and stream output operations.
- The `istream` class and the `ostream` class are each derived through single inheritance from the `ios` base class.
- The `iostream` class is derived through multiple inheritance from both the `istream` class and the `ostream` class.
- The left shift operator (`<<`) is overloaded to designate stream output and is referred to as the stream-insertion operator.
- The right shift operator (`>>`) is overloaded to designate stream input and is referred to as the stream-extraction operator.
- The `istream` object `cin` is tied to the standard input device, normally the keyboard.
- The `ostream` class object `cout` is tied to the standard output device, normally the screen.
- The `ostream` class object `cerr` is tied to the standard error device. Outputs to `cerr` are unbuffered; each insertion to `cerr` appears immediately.

- Stream manipulator `endl` issues a newline character and flushes the output buffer.
- The C++ compiler determines data types automatically for input and output.
- Addresses are displayed in hexadecimal format by default.
- To print the address in a pointer variable, cast the pointer to `void*`.
- Member function `put` outputs one character. Calls to `put` may be cascaded.
- Stream input is performed with the stream-extraction operator `>>`. This operator automatically skips whitespace characters in the input stream.
- The `>>` operator returns `false` after end-of-file is encountered on a stream.
- Stream extraction causes `failbit` to be set for improper input and `badbit` to be set if the operation fails.
- A series of values can be input using the stream-extraction operation in a `while` loop header. The extraction returns 0 when end-of-file is encountered.
- The `get` member function with no arguments inputs one character and returns the character; EOF is returned if end-of-file is encountered on the stream.
- Member function `get` with an argument of type `char` reference inputs one character. EOF is returned when end-of-file is encountered; otherwise, the `istream` object for which the `get` member function is being invoked is returned.
- Member function `get` with three arguments—a character array, a size limit and a delimiter (with default value newline)—reads characters from the input stream up to a maximum of limit - 1 characters and terminates, or terminates when the delimiter is read. The input string is terminated with a null character. The delimiter is not placed in the character array, but remains in the input stream.
- The `getline` member function operates like the three-argument `get` member function. The `getline` function removes the delimiter from the input stream, but does not store it in the string.
- Member function `ignore` skips the specified number of characters (the default is 1) in the input stream; it terminates if the specified delimiter is encountered (the default delimiter is EOF).
- The `putback` member function places the previous character obtained by a `get` on a stream back onto that stream.
- The `peek` member function returns the next character from an input stream, but does not extract (remove) the character from the stream.
- C++ offers type-safe I/O. If unexpected data are processed by the `<<` and `>>` operators, various error flags are set which the user may test to determine if an I/O operation succeeded or failed.
- Unformatted I/O is performed with member functions `read` and `write`. These input or output some number of bytes to or from memory beginning at a designated memory address. They are input or output as raw bytes with no formatting.
- The `gcount` member function returns the number of characters input by the previous `read` operation on that stream.
- Member function `read` inputs a specified number of characters into a character array. `failbit` is set if fewer than the specified number of characters are read.
- To change the base in which integers output, use the manipulator `hex` to set the base to hexadecimal (base 16) or `oct` to set the base to octal (base 8). Use manipulator `dec` to reset the base to decimal. The base remains the same until explicitly changed.
- The parameterized stream manipulator `setbase` also sets the base for integer output. `setbase` takes one integer argument of 10, 8 or 16 to set the base.
- Floating-point precision can be controlled using either the `setprecision` stream manipulator or the `precision` member function. Both set the precision for all subsequent output operations until

the next precision-setting call. The `precision` member function with no argument returns the current precision value.

• Parameterized manipulators require the inclusion of the `<iomanip>` header file.

• Member function `width` sets the field width and returns the previous width. Values smaller than the field are padded with fill characters. The field width setting applies only for the next insertion or extraction; the field width is implicitly set to 0 afterward (subsequent values will be output as large as they need to be). Values larger than a field are printed in their entirety. Function `width` with no argument returns the current width setting. Manipulator `setw` also sets the width.

• For input, the `setw` stream manipulator establishes a maximum string size; if a larger string is entered, the larger line is broken into pieces no larger than the designated size.

• Users may create their own stream manipulators.

• Member functions `setf`, `unsetf` and `flags` control the flag settings.

• The `skipws` flag indicates that `>>` should skip whitespace on an input stream. The `ws` stream manipulator also skips over leading whitespace in an input stream.

• Format flags are defined as an enumeration in class `ios`.

• Format flags are controlled by the `flags` and `setf` member functions, but many C++ programmers prefer to use stream manipulators. The bitwise-or operation, `|`, can be used to combine various options into a single `long` value. Calling the `flags` member function for a stream and specifying these "or-ed" options sets the options on that stream and returns a `long` value containing the prior options. This value is often saved so `flags` may be called with this saved value to restore the previous stream options.

• The `flags` function must specify a value representing the total settings of all the flags. The `setf` function with one argument, on the other hand, automatically "ors" the specified flags with the existing flag settings to form a new format state.

• The `showpoint` flag is set to force a floating-point number to be output with a decimal point and number of significant digits specified by the precision.

• The `left` and `right` flags cause fields to be left-justified with padding characters to the right or right-justified with padding characters to the left.

• The `internal` flag indicates that a number's sign (or base when the flag `ios::showbase` is set) should be left-justified within a field, magnitude should be right-justified and intervening spaces should be padded with the fill character.

• `ios::adjustfield` contains the flags `left`, `right` and `internal`.

• Member function `fill` specifies the fill character to be used with `left`, `right` and `internal` adjusted fields (space is the default); the prior padding character is returned. Stream manipulator `setfill` also sets the fill character.

• Static member `ios::basefield` has `oct`, `hex` and `dec` bits to specify that integers are to be treated as octal, hexadecimal and decimal values, respectively. Integer output defaults to decimal if none of these bits is set; stream extractions process the data in the form the data is supplied.

• Set the `showbase` flag to force the base of an integral value to be output.

• Static data member `ios::floatfield` contains the flags `scientific` and `fixed`. Set the `scientific` flag to output a floating-point number in scientific format. Set the `fixed` flag to output a floating-point number with the precision specified by the `precision` member function.

• The call `cout.setf(0, ios::floatfield)` restores the default format for displaying floating-point numbers.

- Set the `uppercase` flag to force an uppercase X or E to be output with hexadecimal integers or with scientific notation floating-point values, respectively. When set, the `ios::uppercase` flag causes all letters in a hexadecimal value to be uppercase.

- Member function `flags` with no argument returns the `long` value of the current settings of the format flags. Member function `flags` with a `long` argument sets the format flags specified by the argument and returns the prior flag settings.

- Member function `setf` sets the format flags in its argument and returns the previous flag settings as a `long` value.

- Member function `setf(long setBits, long resetBits)` clears the bits of `resetBits`, then sets the bit in `setBits`.

- Member function `unsetf` resets the designated flags and returns prior value of the flags.

- Parameterized stream manipulator `setiosflags` performs the same functions as member function `flags`.

- Parameterized stream manipulator `resetiosflags` performs the same functions as member function `unsetf`.

- The state of a stream may be tested through bits in class `ios`.

- The `eofbit` is set for an input stream after end-of-file is encountered during an input operation. The `eof` member function reports if the `eofbit` has been set.

- The `failbit` is set for a stream when a format error occurs on the stream. No characters are lost. The `fail` member function reports if a stream operation has failed; it is normally possible to recover from such errors.

- The `badbit` is set for a stream when an error occurs that results in data loss. The `bad` member function reports if a stream operation failed. Such serious failures are normally nonrecoverable.

- The `good` member function returns true if the `bad`, `fail` and `eof` functions would all return false. I/O operations should only be performed on "good" streams.

- The `rdstate` member function returns the error state of the stream.

- Member function `clear` is normally used to restore a stream's state to "good" so that I/O may proceed on that stream.

- C++ provides the `tie` member function to synchronize `istream` and `ostream` operations to ensure that outputs appear before subsequent inputs.

TERMINOLOGY

bad member function
badbit
cerr
cin
clear member function
clog
cout
dec stream manipulator
default fill character (space)
default precision
end-of-file
endl
eof member function
eofbit

fail member function
failbit
field width
fill character
fill member function
flags member function
flush member function
flush stream manipulator
format flags
format states
formatted I/O
fstream class
gcount member function
get member function

COMMON PROGRAMMING ERRORS

21.1 Attempting to read from an ostream (or from any other output-only stream).

21.2 Attempting to write to an istream (or to any other input-only stream).

21.3 Not providing parentheses to force proper precedence when using the relatively high precedence stream-insertion operator << or stream-extraction operator >>.

21.4 The width setting applies only for the next insertion or extraction; afterward, the width is implicitly set to 0 (i.e., output values will simply be as wide as they need to be). The width function with no argument returns the current setting. It is a logic error to assume that the width setting applies to all subsequent outputs.

21.5 When not providing a sufficiently wide field to handle outputs, the outputs print as wide as they need to be, possibly causing difficult-to-read outputs.

GOOD PROGRAMMING PRACTICES

21.1 Use the C++ form of I/O exclusively in C++ programs, despite the fact that C-style I/O is available to C++ programmers.

21.2 When outputting expressions, place them in parentheses to prevent operator precedence problems between the operators in the expression and the << operator.

PERFORMANCE TIP

21.1 Use unformatted I/O for the best performance in high-volume file processing.

PORTABILITY TIP

21.1 When prompting the user on how to end input from the keyboard, ask the user to "enter end-of-file to end input" rather than prompting for *<ctrl>-d* (UNIX and Macintosh) or *<ctrl>-z* (PC and VAX).

SOFTWARE ENGINEERING OBSERVATIONS

21.1 C++ style I/O is type safe.

21.2 C++ enables a common treatment of I/O of predefined types and user-defined types. This kind of commonality facilitates software development in general and software reuse in particular.

SELF-REVIEW EXERCISES

21.1 Answer each of the following:

a) Overloaded stream operators are often defined as _____ functions of a class.

b) The format justification bits that can be set include _____, _____ and _____.

c) Input/output in C++ occurs as _____ of bytes.

d) Parameterized stream manipulators _____ and _____ can be used to set and re-set format state flags.

e) Most C++ programs should include the _____ header file that contains the declarations required for all stream I/O operations.

f) Member functions _____ and _____ set and reset format state flags.

g) Header file _____ contains the declarations required for performing "in-memory" formatting.

h) When using parameterized manipulators, the header file _____ must be included.

i) Header _____ contains the declarations required for user-controlled file processing.

j) The _____ stream manipulator inserts a newline character in the output stream and flushes the output stream.

k) Header file _____ is used in programs that mix C-style and C++-style I/O.

l) The `ostream` member function _____ is used to perform unformatted output.

m) Input operations are supported by the _____ class.

n) Outputs to the standard error stream are directed to either the _____ or the _____ stream object.

o) Output operations are supported by the _____ class.

p) The symbol for the stream-insertion operator is _____.

q) The four objects that correspond to the standard devices on the system include _____, _____, _____ and _____.

r) The symbol for the stream-extraction operator is _____.

s) The stream manipulators _____, _____ and _____ specify that integers should be displayed in octal, hexadecimal and decimal formats, respectively.

t) The default precision for displaying floating-point values is _____.

u) When set, the _____ flag causes positive numbers to display with a plus sign.

21.2 State whether the following are *true* or *false*. If the answer is *false*, explain why.

a) The stream member function `flags()` with a long argument sets the `flags` state variable to its argument and returns its previous value.

b) The stream-insertion operator << and the stream-extraction operator >> are overloaded to handle all standard data types—including strings and memory addresses (stream-insertion only)—and all user-defined data types.

c) The stream member function flags() with no arguments resets all the flag bits in the flags state variable.

d) The stream-extraction operator >> can be overloaded with an operator function that takes an istream reference and a reference to a user-defined type as arguments and returns an istream reference.

e) The ws stream manipulator skips leading whitespace in an input stream.

f) The stream-insertion operator << can be overloaded with an operator function that takes an istream reference and a reference to a user-defined type as arguments and returns an istream reference.

g) Input with the stream-extraction operator >> always skips leading whitespace characters in the input stream.

h) The input and output features are provided as part of C++.

i) The stream member function rdstate() returns the current state of the stream.

j) The cout stream is normally connected to the display screen.

k) The stream member function good() returns true if the bad(), fail() and eof() member functions all return false.

l) The cin stream is normally connected to the display screen.

m) If a nonrecoverable error occurs during a stream operation, the bad member function will return true.

n) Output to cerr is unbuffered and output to clog is buffered.

o) When the ios::showpoint flag is set, floating-point values are forced to print with the default six digits of precision—provided that the precision value has not been changed, in which case floating-point values print with the specified precision.

p) The ostream member function put outputs the specified number of characters.

q) The stream manipulators dec, oct and hex only affect the next integer output operation.

r) When output, memory addresses are displayed as long integers by default.

21.3   For each of the following, write a single statement that performs the indicated task.

a) Output the string "Enter your name: ".

b) Set a flag to cause the exponent in scientific notation and the letters in hexadecimal values to print in capital letters.

c) Output the address of the variable string of type char *.

d) Set a flag so that floating-point values print in scientific notation.

e) Output the address of the variable integerPtr of type int *.

f) Set a flag so that when integer values are output, the integer base for octal and hexadecimal values is displayed.

g) Output the value pointed to by floatPtr of type float *.

h) Use a stream member function to set the fill character to '*' for printing in field widths larger than the values being output. Write a separate statement to do this with a stream manipulator.

i) Output the characters 'O' and 'K' in one statement with ostream function put.

j) Get the value of the next character in the input stream without extracting it from the stream.

k) Input a single character into variable c of type char using the istream member function get in two different ways.

l) Input and discard the next six characters in the input stream.

m) Use the istream member function read to input 50 characters into array line of type char.

n) Read 10 characters into character array name. Stop reading characters if the '.' delimiter is encountered. Do not remove the delimiter from the input stream. Write another statement that performs this task and removes the delimiter from the input.

o) Use the istream member function gcount to determine the number of characters input into character array line by the last call to istream member function read and output that number of characters using ostream member function write.

p) Write separate statements to flush the output stream using a member function and a stream manipulator.

q) Output the following values: 124, 18.376, 'Z', 1000000 and "String".

r) Print the current precision setting using a member function.

s) Input an integer value into int variable months and a floating-point value into float variable percentageRate.

t) Print 1.92, 1.925 and 1.9258 with 3 digits of precision using a manipulator.

u) Print integer 100 in octal, hexadecimal and decimal using stream manipulators.

v) Print integer 100 in decimal, octal and hexadecimal using a single stream manipulator to change the base.

w) Print 1234 right-justified in a 10-digit field.

x) Read characters into character array line until the character 'z' is encountered up to a limit of 20 characters (including a terminating null character). Do not extract the delimiter character from the stream.

y) Use integer variables x and y to specify the field width and precision used to display the double value 87.4573 and display the value.

21.4 Identify the error in each of the following statements and explain how to correct it.

a) cout << "Value of x <= y is: " << x <= y;

b) The following statement should print the integer value of 'c'.
   cout << 'c';

c) cout << ""A string in quotes"";

21.5 For each of the following, show the output.

a) cout << "12345" << endl;
   cout.width(5);
   cout.fill('*');
   cout << 123 << endl << 123;

b) cout << setw(10) << setfill('$') << 10000;

c) cout << setw(8) << setprecision(3) << 1024.987654;

d) cout << setiosflags(ios::showbase) << oct << 99
        << endl << hex << 99;

e) cout << 100000 << endl
        << setiosflags(ios::showpos) << 100000;

f) cout << setw(10) << setprecision(2) <<
        << setiosflags(ios::scientific) << 444.93738;

ANSWERS TO SELF-REVIEW EXERCISES

21.1 a) friend b) ios::left, ios::right and ios::internal. c) streams.
d) setiosflags, resetiosflags. e) iostream. f) setf, unsetf. g) strstream. h) iomanip.
i) fstream. j) endl. k) stdiostream. l) write. m) istream. n) cerr or clog. o) ostream.
p) <<. q) cin, cout, cerr and clog. r) >>. s) oct, hex and dec. t) six digits of precision.
u) ios::showpos.

21.2 a) True.

    b) False. The stream-insertion and stream-extraction operators are not overloaded for all user-defined types. The programmer of a class must specifically provide the overloaded operator functions to overload the stream operators for use with each user-defined type.

    c) False. The stream member function `flags()` with no arguments simply returns the current value of the `flags` state variable.

    d) True.

    e) True.

    f) False. To overload the stream-insertion operator `<<`, the overloaded operator function must take an `ostream` reference and a reference to a user-defined type as arguments and return an `ostream` reference.

    g) True. Unless `ios::skipws` is off.

    h) False. The I/O features of C++ are provided as part of the C++ Standard Library. The C++ language does not contain capabilities for input, output or file processing.

    i) True.

    j) True.

    k) True.

    l) False. The `cin` stream is connected to the standard input of the computer, which is normally the keyboard.

    m) True.

    n) True.

    o) True.

    p) False. The `ostream` member function `put` outputs its single-character argument.

    q) False. The stream manipulators `dec`, `oct` and `hex` set the output format state for integers to the specified base until the base is changed again or the program terminates.

    r) False. Memory addresses are displayed in hexadecimal format by default. To display addresses as `long` integers, the address must be cast to a `long` value.

21.3   a) `cout << "Enter your name: ";`

    b) `cout.setf(ios::uppercase);`

    c) `cout << (void *) string;`

    d) `cout.setf(ios::scientific, ios::floatfield);`

    e) `cout << integerPtr;`

    f) `cout << setiosflags(ios::showbase);`

    g) `cout << *floatPtr;`

    h) `cout.fill( '*' );`
       `cout << setfill( '*' );`

    i) `cout.put( 'O' ).put( 'K' );`

    j) `cin.peek();`

    k) `c = cin.get();`
       `cin.get( c );`

    l) `cin.ignore( 6 );`

    m) `cin.read( line, 50 );`

    n) `cin.get( name, 10, '.' );`
       `cin.getline( name, 10, '.' );`

    o) `cout.write( line, cin.gcount() );`

    p) `cout.flush();`
       `cout << flush;`

    q) `cout << 124 << 18.376 << 'Z' << 1000000 << "String";`

    r) `cout << cout.precision();`

    s) `cin >> months >> percentageRate;`

```
t) cout << setprecision( 3 ) << 1.92 << '\t'
        << 1.925 << '\t' << 1.9258;
u) cout << oct << 100 << hex << 100 << dec << 100;
v) cout << 100 << setbase( 8 ) << 100 << setbase( 16 ) << 100;
w) cout << setw( 10 ) << 1234;
x) cin.get( line, 20, 'z' );
y) cout << setw( x ) << setprecision( y ) << 87.4573;
```

21.4 a) Error: The precedence of the << operator is higher than the precedence of <=, which
          causes the statement to be evaluated improperly and also causes a compiler error.
          Correction: To correct the statement, add parentheses around the expression x <= y.
          This problem will occur with any expression that uses operators of lower precedence than
          the << operator if the expression is not placed in parentheses.
      b) Error: In C++, characters are not treated as small integers, as they are in C.
          Correction: To print the numerical value for a character in the computer's character set,
          the character must be cast to an integer value as in the following:
            cout << int('c');
      c) Error: Quote characters cannot be printed in a string unless an escape sequence is used.
          Correction: Print the string in one of the following ways:
            cout << '"' << "A string in quotes" << '"';
            cout << "\"A string in quotes\"";

21.5 a) 12345
         **123
         123
      b) $$$$$10000
      c) 1024.988
      d) 0143
         0x63
      e) 100000
         +100000
      f)   4.45e+02

EXERCISES

21.6   Write a statement for each of the following:
      a) Print integer 40000 left-justified in a 15-digit field.
      b) Read a string into character array variable state.
      c) Print 200 with and without a sign.
      d) Print the decimal value 100 in hexadecimal form preceded by 0x.
      e) Read characters into array s until the character 'p' is encountered up to a limit of 10
         characters (including the terminating null character). Extract the delimiter from the input
         stream and discard it.
      f) Print 1.234 in a 9-digit field with preceding zeros.
      g) Read a string of the form "characters" from the standard input. Store the string in
         character array s. Eliminate the quotation marks from the input stream. Read a maximum
         of 50 characters (including the terminating null character).

21.7   Write a program to test inputting integer values in decimal, octal and hexadecimal format.
Output each integer read by the program in all three formats. Test the program with the following
input data: 10, 010, 0x10.

21.8   Write a program that prints pointer values using casts to all the integer data types. Which
ones print strange values? Which ones cause errors?

21.9   Write a program to test the results of printing the integer value 12345 and the floating-point value 1.2345 in various-size fields. What happens when the values are printed in fields containing fewer digits than the values?

21.10   Write a program that prints the value 100.453627 rounded to the nearest digit, tenth, hundredth, thousandth and ten thousandth.

21.11   Write a program that inputs a string from the keyboard and determines the length of the string. Print the string using twice the length as the field width.

21.12   Write a program that converts integer Fahrenheit temperatures from 0 to 212 degrees to floating-point Celsius temperatures with 3 digits of precision. Use the formula

```
celsius = 5.0 / 9.0 * ( fahrenheit - 32 );
```

to perform the calculation. The output should be printed in two right-justified columns and the Celsius temperatures should be preceded by a sign for both positive and negative values.

21.13   In some programming languages, strings are entered surrounded by either single or double quotation marks. Write a program that reads the three strings suzy, "suzy" and 'suzy'. Are the single and double quotes ignored or read as part of the string?

21.14   In Fig. 18.3, the stream-extraction and -insertion operators were overloaded for input and output of objects of the PhoneNumber class. Rewrite the stream-extraction operator to perform the following error checking on input. The operator>> function will need to be entirely recoded.

   a) Input the entire phone number into an array. Test that the proper number of characters has been entered. There should be a total of 14 characters read for a phone number of the form (800) 555-1212. Use the stream member function clear to set ios::failbit for improper input.

   g) The area code and exchange do not begin with 0 or 1. Test the first digit of the area code and exchange portions of the phone number to be sure that neither begins with 0 or 1. Use stream member function clear to set ios::failbit for improper input.

   h) The middle digit of an area code used to always be 0 or 1 (although this has changed recently). Test the middle digit for a value of 0 or 1. Use the stream member function clear to set ios::failbit for improper input. If none of the above operations results in ios::failbit being set for improper input, copy the three parts of the telephone number into the areaCode, exchange and line members of the PhoneNumber object. In the main program, if ios::failbit has been set on the input, have the program print an error message and end rather than print the phone number.

21.15   Write a program that accomplishes each of the following:

   a) Create the user-defined class Point that contains the private integer data members xCoordinate and yCoordinate and declares stream-insertion and stream-extraction overloaded operator functions as friends of the class.

   i) Define the stream-insertion and stream-extraction operator functions. The stream-extraction operator function should determine if the data entered are valid data, and if not, it should set the ios::failbit to indicate improper input. The stream-insertion operator should not be able to display the point after an input error occurred.

   j) Write a main function that tests input and output of user-defined class Point using the overloaded stream-extraction and stream-insertion operators.

21.16   Write a program that accomplishes each of the following:

   a) Create the user-defined class Complex that contains the private integer data members real and imaginary and declares stream-insertion and stream-extraction overloaded operator functions as friends of the class.

    k) Define the stream-insertion and -extraction operator functions. The stream-extraction operator function should determine if the data entered are valid, and if not, it should set `ios::failbit` to indicate improper input. The input should be of the form

        3 + 8i

    l) The values can be negative or positive, and it is possible that one of the two values is not provided. If a value is not provided, the appropriate data member should be set to 0. The stream-insertion operator should not be able to display the point if an input error occurred. The output format should be identical to the input format shown above. For negative imaginary values, a minus sign should be printed rather than a plus sign.

    m) Write a `main` function that tests input and output of user-defined class `Complex` using the overloaded stream-extraction and stream-insertion operators.

21.17 Write a program that uses a `for` structure to print a table of ASCII values for the characters in the ASCII character set from 33 to 126. The program should print the decimal value, octal value, hexadecimal value and character value for each character. Use the stream manipulators `dec`, `oct` and `hex` to print the integer values.

21.18 Write a program to show that the `getline` and three-argument `get` `istream` member functions each end the input string with a string-terminating null character. Also, show that `get` leaves the delimiter character on the input stream while `getline` extracts the delimiter character and discards it. What happens to the unread characters in the stream?

21.19 Write a program that creates the user-defined manipulator `skipwhite` to skip leading whitespace characters in the input stream. The manipulator should use the `isspace` function from the `<cctype>` library to test if the character is a whitespace character. Each character should be input using the `istream` member function `get`. When a nonwhitespace character is encountered, the `skipwhite` manipulator finishes its job by placing the character back on the input stream and returning an `istream` reference.

    Test the manipulator by creating a `main` function in which the `ios::skipws` flag is unset so that the stream-extraction operator does not automatically skip whitespace. Then test the manipulator on the input stream by entering a character preceded by whitespace as input. Print the character that was input to confirm that a whitespace character was not input.

22

C++ Templates

Objectives

- To be able to use class templates to create a group of related types.
- To be able to distinguish between class templates and template classes.
- To understand how to overload template functions.
- To understand the relationships among templates, `friend`s, inheritance and `static` members.

Behind that outside pattern
the dim shapes get clearer every day.
It is always the same shape, only very numerous.
Charlotte Perkins Gilman

If you are able to slip through the parameters
of the skies and the earth, then do so.
The *Koran*

A Mighty Maze! but not without a plan.
Alexander Pope

22.1 Introduction

In this chapter we discuss one of C++'s more powerful features, namely templates. Templates enable us to specify, with a single code segment, an entire range of related (overloaded) functions—called template functions—or an entire range of related classes—called *template classes.*

As we discussed in Chapter 15, we might write a single *function template* for an array sort function, then have C++ generate separate template functions that will sort an int array, sort a float array, sort an array of strings and so on.

We might write a single *class template* for a stack class, then have C++ generate separate template classes such as a stack-of-int class, a stack-of-float class, a stack-of-string class and so on.

Note the distinction between class templates and template classes: Class templates are like stencils out of which we trace shapes; template classes are like the separate tracings that all have the same shape but could be drawn in different colors, for example.

Software Engineering Observation 22.1

Templates are one of C++'s most powerful capabilities for software reuse.

In this chapter, we will present examples of class templates. We will also consider the relationships between templates and other C++ features such as inheritance, friends and static members.

The design and details of the template mechanisms discussed here are based on the work of Bjarne Stroustrup as presented in his paper, *Parameterized Types for C++*, and published in the *Proceedings of the USENIX C++ Conference* held in Denver, Colorado, in October 1988.

22.2 Class Templates

It is possible to understand what a stack is (a data structure into which we insert items in one order and retrieve them in last-in-first-out order) independent of the type of the items being placed in the stack. But when it comes to actually instantiating a stack, a data type must be specified. This creates a wonderful opportunity for software reusability. We need the means for describing the notion of a stack generically and instantiating classes that are type-specific versions of this generic class. This capability is provided by *class templates* in C++.

Software Engineering Observation 22.2

Class templates encourage software reusability by enabling type-specific versions of generic classes to be instantiated.

Class templates are called *parameterized types* because they require one or more type parameters to specify how to customize a "generic class" template to form a specific template class.

The programmer who wishes to produce a variety of template classes simply writes one class template definition. Each time the programmer needs a new type-specific instantiation, the programmer uses a concise, simple notation and the compiler writes the source code for the template class the programmer requires. One Stack class template, for example, could thus become the basis for creating many Stack classes (such as "Stack of double," "Stack of int," "Stack of char," "Stack of Employee" etc.) used in a program.

Note the definition of the Stack class template in Fig. 22.1. It looks like a conventional class definition except that it is preceded by the header (line 6)

```
template< class T >
```

to specify that this is a class template definition with type parameter T indicating the type of the Stack class to be created. The programmer need not specifically use identifier T—any identifier can be used. The type of element to be stored on this Stack is mentioned only generically as T throughout the Stack class header and member function definitions. We will show momentarily how T becomes associated with a specific type, such as double or int. There are two constraints for nonprimitive data types used with this Stack: They must have a default constructor and they must support the assignment operator. If an object of the class used with this Stack contains dynamically allocated memory, the assignment operator should be overloaded for that type as shown in Chapter 18.

```
1   // Fig. 22.1: tstack1.h
2   // Class template Stack
3   #ifndef TSTACK1_H
4   #define TSTACK1_H
5
6   template< class T >
7   class Stack {
8   public:
9      Stack( int = 10 );     // default constructor (stack size 10)
10     ~Stack() { delete [] stackPtr; } // destructor
11     bool push( const T& ); // push an element onto the stack
12     bool pop( T& );        // pop an element off the stack
13  private:
14     int size;              // # of elements in the stack
15     int top;               // location of the top element
16     T *stackPtr;           // pointer to the stack
17
```

Fig. 22.1   Demonstrating class template Stack—tstack1.h. (Part 1 of 2.)

```
18      bool isEmpty() const { return top == -1; }        // utility
19      bool isFull() const { return top == size - 1; } // functions
20   }; // end class template Stack
21
22   // Constructor with default size 10
23   template< class T >
24   Stack< T >::Stack( int s )
25   {
26      size = s > 0 ? s : 10;
27      top = -1;                  // Stack is initially empty
28      stackPtr = new T[ size ]; // allocate space for elements
29   } // end Stack constructor
30
31   // Push an element onto the stack
32   // return 1 if successful, 0 otherwise
33   template< class T >
34   bool Stack< T >::push( const T &pushValue )
35   {
36      if ( !isFull() ) {
37         stackPtr[ ++top ] = pushValue; // place item in Stack
38         return true;   // push successful
39      } // end if
40      return false;        // push unsuccessful
41   } // end function template push
42
43   // Pop an element off the stack
44   template< class T >
45   bool Stack< T >::pop( T &popValue )
46   {
47      if ( !isEmpty() ) {
48         popValue = stackPtr[ top-- ];  // remove item from Stack
49         return true;   // pop successful
50      } // end if
51      return false;        // pop unsuccessful
52   } // end function template pop
53
54   #endif
```

Fig. 22.1   Demonstrating class template Stack—tstack1.h. (Part 2 of 2.)

```
55   // Fig. 22.1: fig22_01.cpp
56   // Test driver for Stack template
57   #include <iostream>
58
59   using std::cout;
60   using std::cin;
61   using std::endl;
62
63   #include "tstack1.h"
64
65   int main()
66   {
```

Fig. 22.1   Demonstrating class template Stack—fig22_01.cpp. (Part 1 of 2.)

```
67       Stack< double > doubleStack( 5 );
68       double f = 1.1;
69       cout << "Pushing elements onto doubleStack\n";
70
71       while ( doubleStack.push( f ) ) { // success true returned
72          cout << f << ' ';
73          f += 1.1;
74       } // end while
75
76       cout << "\nStack is full. Cannot push " << f
77           << "\n\nPopping elements from doubleStack\n";
78
79       while ( doubleStack.pop( f ) )   // success true returned
80          cout << f << ' ';
81
82       cout << "\nStack is empty. Cannot pop\n";
83
84       Stack< int > intStack;
85       int i = 1;
86       cout << "\nPushing elements onto intStack\n";
87
88       while ( intStack.push( i ) ) { // success true returned
89          cout << i << ' ';
90          ++i;
91       } // end while
92
93       cout << "\nStack is full. Cannot push " << i
94           << "\n\nPopping elements from intStack\n";
95
96       while ( intStack.pop( i ) )   // success true returned
97          cout << i << ' ';
98
99       cout << "\nStack is empty. Cannot pop\n";
100      return 0;
101   } // end function main
```

```
Pushing elements onto doubleStack
1.1 2.2 3.3 4.4 5.5
Stack is full. Cannot push 6.6

Popping elements from doubleStack
5.5 4.4 3.3 2.2 1.1
Stack is empty. Cannot pop

Pushing elements onto intStack
1 2 3 4 5 6 7 8 9 10
Stack is full. Cannot push 11

Popping elements from intStack
10 9 8 7 6 5 4 3 2 1
Stack is empty. Cannot pop
```

Fig. 22.1 Demonstrating class template Stack—fig22_01.cpp. (Part 2 of 2.)

Now let us consider the driver (function main) that exercises the Stack class template (see the output in Fig. 22.1). The driver begins by instantiating object doubleStack of size 5. This object is declared to be of class Stack< double > (pronounced "Stack of double"). The compiler associates type double with type parameter T in the template to produce the source code for a Stack class of type double. Although the programmer does not see this source code, it is included in the source code and compiled.

The driver then successively pushes the double values 1.1, 2.2, 3.3, 4.4 and 5.5 onto doubleStack. The push loop terminates when the driver attempts to push a sixth value onto doubleStack (which is already full because it was created to hold a maximum of five elements).

The driver now pops the five values off the stack (note in Fig. 22.1, that the values do pop off in last-in-first-out order). The driver attempts to pop a sixth value, but doubleStack is now empty, so the pop loop terminates.

Next, the driver instantiates integer stack intStack with the declaration

```
Stack< int > intStack;
```

(pronounced "intStack is a Stack of int"). No size is specified, so the size defaults to 10 as specified in the default constructor (line 24). Once again, the driver loops pushing values onto intStack until it is full, then loops popping values off intStack until it is empty. Once again, the values pop off in last-in-first-out order.

The member function definitions outside the class each begin with the header (line 23)

```
template< class T >
```

Then each definition resembles a conventional function definition except that the Stack element type is always listed generically as type parameter T. The binary scope resolution operator is used with the class template name Stack<T> to tie each member function definition to the class template's scope. In this case, the class name is Stack< T >. When doubleStack is instantiated to be of type Stack< double >, the Stack constructor uses new to create an array of elements of type double to represent the stack (line 28). The statement

```
stackPtr = new T[ size ];
```

in the Stack class template definition is generated by the compiler in the Stack< double > template class as

```
stackPtr = new double[ size ];
```

Notice that the code in function main of Fig. 22.1 is almost identical for both the doubleStack manipulations in the top half of main and the intStack manipulations in the bottom half of main. This presents us with another opportunity to use a function template. Figure 22.2 uses function template testStack to perform the same tasks as main in Fig. 22.1—push a series of values onto a Stack< T > and pop the values off a Stack< T >. Function template testStack uses formal type parameter T to represent the data type stored in the Stack< T >. The function template takes four arguments—a reference to an object of type Stack< T >, a value of type T that will be the first value pushed onto the Stack< T >, a value of type T used to increment the values pushed onto the Stack< T > and a character string of type const char * that represents the name of the

Stack< T > object for output purposes. Function `main` now simply instantiates an object of type Stack< double > called `doubleStack` and an object of type Stack< int > called `intStack` and uses these objects in lines 42 and 43

```
testStack( doubleStack, 1.1, 1.1, "doubleStack" );
testStack( intStack, 1, 1, "intStack" );
```

Note that the output of Fig. 22.2 precisely matches the output of Fig. 22.1.

```
1   // Fig. 22.2: fig22_02.cpp
2   // Test driver for Stack template.
3   // Function main uses a function template to manipulate
4   // objects of type Stack< T >.
5   #include <iostream>
6
7   using std::cout;
8   using std::cin;
9   using std::endl;
10
11  #include "tstack1.h"
12
13  // Function template to manipulate Stack< T >
14  template< class T >
15  void testStack(
16     Stack< T > &theStack,    // reference to the Stack< T >
17     T value,                 // initial value to be pushed
18     T increment,             // increment for subsequent values
19     const char *stackName ) // name of the Stack < T > object
20  {
21     cout << "\nPushing elements onto " << stackName << '\n';
22
23     while ( theStack.push( value ) ) { // success true returned
24        cout << value << ' ';
25        value += increment;
26     } // end while
27
28     cout << "\nStack is full. Cannot push " << value
29          << "\n\nPopping elements from " << stackName << '\n';
30
31     while ( theStack.pop( value ) )   // success true returned
32        cout << value << ' ';
33
34     cout << "\nStack is empty. Cannot pop\n";
35  } // end function template testStack
36
37  int main()
38  {
39     Stack< double > doubleStack( 5 );
40     Stack< int > intStack;
41
42     testStack( doubleStack, 1.1, 1.1, "doubleStack" );
43     testStack( intStack, 1, 1, "intStack" );
```

Fig. 22.2   Passing a Stack template object to a function template. (Part 1 of 2.)

```
44
45     return 0;
46  } // end function main
```

```
Pushing elements onto doubleStack
1.1 2.2 3.3 4.4 5.5
Stack is full. Cannot push 6.6

Popping elements from doubleStack
5.5 4.4 3.3 2.2 1.1
Stack is empty. Cannot pop

Pushing elements onto intStack
1 2 3 4 5 6 7 8 9 10
Stack is full. Cannot push 11

Popping elements from intStack
10 9 8 7 6 5 4 3 2 1
Stack is empty. Cannot pop
```

Fig. 22.2   Passing a `Stack` template object to a function template. (Part 2 of 2.)

22.3 Class Templates and Nontype Parameters

The `Stack` class template of the previous section used only type parameters in the template header. It is also possible to use *nontype parameters*; a nontype parameter can have a default argument and the nontype parameter is treated as `const`. For example, the template header could be modified to take an `int elements` parameter as follows:

```
template< class T, int elements >  // note non-type parameter
```

Then, a declaration such as

```
Stack< double, 100 > mostRecentSalesFigures;
```

would instantiate (at compile time) a 100-element `Stack` template class named `mostRecentSalesFigures` of `double` values; this template class would be of type `Stack< double, 100 >`. The class header might then contain a `private` data member with an array declaration such as

```
T stackHolder[ elements ];   // array to hold stack contents
```

Performance Tip 22.1

When it is possible to do so, specifying the size of a container class (such as an array class or a stack class) at compile time (possibly through a nontype template size parameter) eliminates the execution time overhead of creating the space dynamically with **new.**

Software Engineering Observation 22.3

When it is possible to do so, specifying the size of a container at compile time (possibly through a nontype template size parameter) avoids the possibility of a potentially fatal execution-time error if **new** *is unable to obtain the needed memory.*

In the Exercises, you will use a nontype parameter to create a template for the `Array` class developed in Chapter 18, C++ Operator Overloading. This template will enable `Array` objects to be instantiated with a specified number of elements of a specified type at compile time, rather than dynamically creating space for the `Array` objects at execution time.

A class for a specific type that does not match a common class template can be provided to override the class template for that type. For example, an `Array` class template can be used to instantiate an array of any type. The programmer may choose to take control of instantiating the `Array` class of a specific type, such as `Martian`. This is done simply by forming the new class with a class name of `Array<Martian>`.

22.4 Templates and Inheritance

Templates and inheritance relate in several ways:

- A class template can be derived from a template class.

- A class template can be derived from a non-template class.

- A template class can be derived from a class template.

- A non-template class can be derived from a class template.

22.5 Templates and `friends`

We have seen that functions and entire classes can be declared as `friend`s of non-template classes. With class templates, the obvious kinds of friendship arrangements can be declared. Friendship can be established between a class template and a global function, a member function of another class (possibly a template class), or even an entire class (possibly a template class). The notations required to establish these friendship relationships can be cumbersome.

Inside a class template for class X that has been declared with

```
template< class T > class X
```

a friendship declaration of the form

```
friend void f1();
```

makes function `f1` a `friend` of every template class instantiated from the preceding class template.

Inside a class template for class X that has been declared with

```
template< class T > class X
```

a friendship declaration of the form

```
friend void f2( X< T > & );
```

for a particular type T such as `float` makes function `f2( X< float > & )` a `friend` of `X< float >` only.

Inside a class template, you can declare that a member function of another class is a `friend` of any template class generated from the class template. Simply name the member function of the other class using the class name and the binary scope-resolution operator. For example, inside a class template for class X that has been declared with

```
template< class T > class X
```

a friendship declaration of the form

```
friend void A::f4();
```

makes member function `f4` of class A a `friend` of every template class instantiated from the preceding class template.

Inside a class template for class X that has been declared with

```
template< class T > class X
```

a friendship declaration of the form

```
friend void C< T >::f5( X< T > & );
```

for a particular type T such as `float` makes member function

```
C< float >::f5( X< float > & )
```

a `friend` function of *only* template class X< `float` >.

Inside a class template for class X that has been declared with

```
template< class T > class X
```

a second class Y can be declared with

```
friend class Y;
```

making every member function of class Y a `friend` of every template class produced from the class template for X.

Inside a class template for class X that has been declared with

```
template< class T > class X
```

a second class Z can be declared with

```
friend class Z< T >;
```

then when a template class is instantiated with a particular type for T such as `float`, all members of `class Z< float >` become `friend`s of template class X< `float` >.

22.6 Templates and `static` Members

What about `static` data members? Remember that with a non-template class, one copy of a `static` data member is shared among all objects of the class and the `static` data member must be initialized at file scope.

Each template class instantiated from a class template has its own copy of each `static` data member of the class template; all objects of that template class share that one `static` data member. And as with `static` data members of non-template classes, `static` data members of template classes must be initialized at file scope. Each template class gets its own copy of the class template's `static` member functions.

SUMMARY

- Templates enable us to specify a range of related (overloaded) functions—called template functions—or a range of related classes—called template classes.

- Class templates provide the means for describing a class generically and instantiating classes that are type-specific versions of this generic class.

- Class templates are called parameterized types; they require type parameters to specify how to customize a generic class template to form a specific template class.

- The programmer who wishes to use template classes writes one class template. When the programmer needs a new type-specific class, the programmer uses a concise notation and the compiler writes the source code for the template class.

- A class template definition looks like a conventional class definition except that it is preceded by `template< class T >` (or `template< typename T >`) to indicate this is a class template definition with type parameter `T` indicating the type of the class to be created. The type `T` is mentioned throughout the class header and member function definitions as a generic type name.

- The member function definitions outside the class each begin with the header `template< class T >` (or `template< typename T >`). Then each function definition resembles a conventional function definition except that the generic data in the class are always listed generically as type parameter `T`. The binary scope resolution operator is used with the class template name to tie each member function definition to the class template's scope as in `ClassName< T >`.

- It is possible to use nontype parameters in the header of a class template.

- A class for a specific type can be provided to override the class template for that type.

- A class template can be derived from a template class. A class template can be derived from a non-template class. A template class can be derived from a class template. A non-template class can be derived from a class template.

- Functions and entire classes can be declared as `friend`s of non-template classes. With class templates, the obvious kinds of friendship arrangements can be declared. Friendship can be established between a class template and a global function, a member function of another class (possibly a template class) or even an entire class (possibly a template class).

- Each template class instantiated from a class template has its own copy of each `static` data member of the class template; all objects of that template class share that one `static` data member. And as with `static` data members of non-template classes, `static` data members of template classes must be initialized at file scope.

- Each template class gets a copy of the class template's `static` member functions.

TERMINOLOGY

angle brackets (< and >)	nontype parameter in a template header
class template	overloading a template function
class template name	parameterized type
formal type parameter in a template header	`static` data member of a class template
`friend` of a template	`static` data member of a template class
keyword `class` in a template type parameter	`static` member function of a class template
keyword `template`	`static` member function of a template class

template argument   template parameter
template class   `template< class T >`
template class member function   type parameter in a template header
template function   `typename`
template name

PERFORMANCE TIP

22.1   When it is possible to do so, specifying the size of a container class (such as an array class or a stack class) at compile time (possibly through a nontype template size parameter) eliminates the execution time overhead of creating the space dynamically with `new`.

SOFTWARE ENGINEERING OBSERVATIONS

22.1   Templates are one of C++'s most powerful capabilities for software reuse.

22.2   Class templates encourage software reusability by enabling type-specific versions of generic classes to be instantiated.

22.3   When it is possible to do so, specifying the size of a container at compile time (possibly through a nontype template size parameter) avoids the possibility of a potentially fatal execution-time error if `new` is unable to obtain the needed memory.

SELF-REVIEW EXERCISES

22.1   Answer each of the following *true* or *false*. If *false*, explain why.
   a) If several template classes are generated from a single class template with a single `static` data member, each of the template classes shares a single copy of the class template's `static` data member.
   b) The name of a formal type parameter can be used only once in the formal type parameter list of the template definition. Formal type parameter names among template definitions must be unique.
   c) Keywords `class` and `typename` as used with a template type parameter specifically mean "any user-defined class type."

22.2   Fill in the blanks in each of the following:
   a) Templates enable us to specify, with a single code segment, an entire range of related classes called _____.
   b) Class templates are also called _____ types.
   c) The _____ operator is used with a template class name to tie each member function definition to the class template's scope.
   d) As with `static` data members of non-template classes, `static` data members of template classes must also be initialized at _____ scope.

ANSWERS TO SELF-REVIEW EXERCISES

22.1   a) False. Each template class will have a copy of the `static` data member. b) False. Formal type parameter names among template functions need not be unique. c) False. Keywords `class` and `typename` in this context also allow for a type parameter of a built-in type.

22.2   a) template classes. b) parameterized. c) binary scope resolution. d) file.

EXERCISES

22.3   Use a nontype parameter `numberOfElements` and a type parameter `elementType` to help create a template for the `Array` class we developed in Chapter 18, C++ Operator Overloading. This template will enable `Array` objects to be instantiated with a specified number of elements of a specified element type at compile time.

22.4   Write a program with class template `Array`. The template can instantiate an `Array` of any element type. Override the template with a specific definition for an `Array` of `float` elements (`class Array< float >`). The driver should demonstrate the instantiation of an `Array` of `int` through the template and should show that an attempt to instantiate an `Array` of `float` uses the definition provided in `class Array< float >`.

22.5   Which is more like a stencil—a class template or a template class? Explain your answer.

22.6   What performance problem can result from using class templates?

22.7   Why is it appropriate to call a class template a parameterized type?

22.8   Explain why you might use the statement

```
Array< Employee > workerList( 100 );
```

in a C++ program.

22.9   Review your answer to Exercise 22.8. Now, why might you use the statement

```
Array< Employee > workerList;
```

in a C++ program?

22.10 Explain the use of the following notation in a C++ program:

```
template< class T > Array< T >::Array( int s )
```

22.11 Why might you typically use a nontype parameter with a class template for a container such as an array or stack?

22.12 Describe how to provide a class for a specific type to override the class template for that type.

22.13 Describe the relationship between class templates and inheritance.

22.14 Suppose a class template has the header

```
template< class T1 > class C1
```

Describe the friendship relationships established by placing each of the following friendship declarations inside this class template header. Identifiers beginning with "f" are functions, identifiers beginning with "C" are classes and identifiers beginning with "T" can represent any type (i.e., built-in types or class types).

    a) `friend void f1();`
    b) `friend void f2( C1< T1 > &);`
    c) `friend void C2::f4();`
    d) `friend void C3< T1 >::f5( C1< T1 > & );`
    e) `friend class C5;`
    f) `friend class C6< T1 >;`

22.15 Suppose class template `Employee` has a `static` data member `count`. Suppose three template classes are instantiated from the class template. How many copies of the `static` data member will exist? How will the use of each be constrained (if at all)?

23

C++ Exception Handling

Objectives

- To use `try`, `throw` and `catch` to watch for, indicate and handle exceptions, respectively.
- To process uncaught and unexpected exceptions.
- To be able to process `new` failures.
- To use `auto_ptr` to prevent memory leaks.
- To understand the standard exception hierarchy.

I never forget a face, but in your case I'll make an exception.
Groucho (Julius Henry) Marx

No rule is so general, which admits not some exception.
Robert Burton

It is common sense to take a method and try it. If it fails, admit it frankly and try another. But above all, try something.
Franklin Delano Roosevelt

O! throw away the worser part of it,
And live the purer with the other half.
William Shakespeare

If they're running and they don't look where they're going
I have to come out from somewhere and catch them.
Jerome David Salinger

And oftentimes excusing of a fault
Doth make the fault the worse by the excuse.
William Shakespeare

To err is human, to forgive divine.
Alexander Pope

Outline

23.1 Introduction

In this chapter, we introduce *exception handling*. The extensibility of C++ can increase substantially the number and kinds of errors that can occur. The features presented here enable programmers to write clearer, more robust, more fault-tolerant programs. Recent systems developed with these and/or similar techniques have reported positive results. We also mention when exception handling should not be used.

The style and details of exception handling presented in this chapter are based on the work of Andrew Koenig and Bjarne Stroustrup as presented in their paper, "Exception Handling for C++ (revised)," published in the *Proceedings of the USENIX C++ Conference* held in San Francisco in April, 1990.

Error-handling code varies in nature and amount among software systems depending on the application and whether or not the software is a product for release. Commercial products tend to contain far more error-handling code than "casual" software.

There are many popular means of dealing with errors. Most commonly, error-handling code is interspersed throughout a system's code. Errors are dealt with at the places in the code where the errors can occur. The advantage to this approach is that a programmer reading code can see the error processing in the immediate vicinity of the code and determine if the proper error checking has been implemented.

The problem with this scheme is that the code in a sense becomes "polluted" with the error processing. It becomes more difficult for a programmer concerned with the application itself to read the code and determine if the code is functioning correctly. This makes it more difficult to understand and to maintain the code.

Some common examples of exceptions are failure of new to obtain a requested amount of memory, an out-of-bounds array subscript, arithmetic overflow, division by zero and invalid function parameters.

C++'s exception-handling features enable the programmer to remove the error-handling code from the "main line" of a program's execution. This improves program readability and modifiability. With the C++ style of exception handling, it is possible to catch all kinds of exceptions, to catch all exceptions of a certain type or to catch all exceptions of related types. This makes programs more robust by reducing the likelihood that errors will not be caught by a program. Exception handling is provided to enable programs to catch and handle errors rather than letting them occur and suffering the consequences. If the programmer does not provide a means of handling a fatal error, the program terminates.

Exception handling is designed for dealing with *synchronous errors* such as an attempt to divide by zero (that occurs as the program executes the divide instruction). With exception handling, before the program executes the division, it checks the denominator and "throws" (issues) an exception if the denominator is zero.

Exception handling is not designed to deal with asynchronous situations such as disk I/O completions, network message arrivals, mouse clicks and the like; these are best handled through other means, such as interrupt processing.

Exception handling is used in situations in which the system can recover from the error causing the exception. The recovery procedure is called an *exception handler*. Exception handling is typically used when the error will be dealt with by a different part of the program (i.e., a different scope) from that which detected the error. A program that carries on an interactive dialog with a user should not use exceptions to process input errors.

Exception handling is especially appropriate for situations in which the program will not be able to recover, but needs to provide orderly cleanup, then shut down "gracefully."

Good Programming Practice 23.1

Use exceptions for errors that must be processed in a different scope from that in which they occur. Use other means of error handling for errors that will be processed in the scope in which they occur.

Good Programming Practice 23.2

Avoid using exception handling for purposes other than error handling, because this can reduce program clarity.

There is another reason to avoid using exception-handling techniques for conventional program control. Exception handling is designed for error processing, which is an infrequent activity that is often used because a program is about to terminate. Given this, it is not required that C++ compiler writers implement exception handling for the kind of optimal performance that might be expected of regular application code.

Performance Tip 23.1

Although it is possible to use exception handling for purposes other than error handling, this can reduce program performance.

Performance Tip 23.2

Exception handling is generally implemented in compilers in such a manner that when an exception does not occur, little or no overhead is imposed by the presence of exception-handling code. When exceptions happen, they do incur execution-time overhead. Certainly the presence of exception-handling code makes the program consume more memory.

Software Engineering Observation 23.1

Flow of control with conventional control structures is generally clearer and more efficient than with exceptions.

Common Programming Error 23.1

Another reason exceptions can be dangerous as an alternative to normal flow of control is that the stack is unwound and resources allocated prior to the occurrence of the exception may not be freed. This problem can be avoided by careful programming.

Exception handling helps improve a program's fault tolerance. It becomes "more pleasant" to write error-processing code, so programmers are more likely to provide it. It also becomes possible to catch exceptions in a variety of ways, such as by type, or even to specify that exceptions of any type are to be caught.

The majority of programs written today support only a single thread of execution. Multithreading is receiving great attention in recent operating systems like Windows NT, OS/2 and various versions of UNIX. The techniques discussed in this chapter apply even for multithreaded programs, although we do not discuss multithreaded programs specifically.

We will show how to deal with "uncaught" exceptions. We will consider how unexpected exceptions are handled. We will show how related exceptions can be represented by exception classes derived from a common base exception class.

The exception-handling features of C++ are becoming widely used as a result of the C++ standard. Standardization is especially important on large software projects where dozens or even hundreds of people work on separate components of a system and these components need to interact for the overall system to function properly.

Software Engineering Observation 23.2

Exception handling is well suited to systems of separately developed components. Exception handling makes it easier to combine the components. Each component can perform its own exception detection separate from the handling of the exceptions in another scope.

Exception handling can be viewed as another means of returning control from a function or exiting a block of code. Normally, when an exception occurs, it will be handled by a caller of the function generating the exception, by a caller of that caller or however far back in the call chain it becomes necessary to go to find a handler for that exception.

23.2 When Exception Handling Should Be Used

Exception handling should be used to process only exceptional situations, despite the fact that there is nothing to prevent the programmer from using exceptions as an alternative to program control; to process exceptions for program components that are not geared to handling those exceptions directly; to process exceptions from software components, such as functions, libraries and classes that are likely to be widely used, and where it does not make sense for those components to handle their own exceptions; and on large projects to handle error processing in a uniform manner project wide.

Good Programming Practice 23.3

Use conventional error-handling techniques rather than exception handling for straightfor-ward, local error processing in which a program is easily able to deal with its own errors.

Software Engineering Observation 23.3

When dealing with libraries, the caller of the library function will likely have unique error pro-cessing in mind for an exception generated in the library function. It is unlikely that a library function will perform error processing that would meet the unique needs of all users. Therefore, exceptions are an appropriate means for dealing with errors produced by library functions.

23.3 Other Error-Handling Techniques

We have presented a variety of ways of dealing with exceptional situations prior to this chapter. The following summarizes these and other useful techniques:

- Use `assert` to test for coding and design errors. If an assertion is `false`, the pro-gram terminates and the code must be corrected. This is useful at debugging time.

- Simply ignore the exceptions. This would be devastating for software products re-leased to the general public or for special-purpose software needed for mission-critical situations. But for your own software developed for your own purposes, it is quite common to ignore many kinds of errors.

- Abort the program. This, of course, prevents a program from running to completion and producing incorrect results. Actually, for many types of errors this is appropri-ate, especially for nonfatal errors that enable a program to run to completion, per-haps misleading the programmer to think that the program functioned correctly. Here, too, such a strategy is inappropriate for mission-critical applications. Resource issues are also important here. If a program obtains a resource, the program should normally return that resource before program termination.

Common Programming Error 23.2

Aborting a program could leave a resource in a state in which other programs would not be able to acquire the resource; hence the program would have a so-called "resource leak."

- Set some error indicator. The problem with this is that programs may not check these error indicators at all points at which the errors could be troublesome.

- Test for the error condition, issue an error message and call `exit` to pass an ap-propriate error code to the program's environment.

- `setjump` and `longjump`. These `<csetjmp>` `library functions` enable the programmer to specify an immediate jump out of deeply nested function calls back to an error handler. Without `setjump`/`longjump`, a program must execute several returns to get out of the deeply nested function calls. These could be used to jump to some error handler. But they are dangerous in because they unwind the stack without calling destructors for automatic objects. This can lead to serious problems.

- Certain specific kinds of errors have dedicated capabilities for handling them. For example, when `new` fails to allocate memory, it can cause a `new_handler` function to execute to deal with the error. This function can be varied by supplying a function name as the argument to `set_new_handler`. We discuss function `set_new_handler` in detail in Section 23.14.

23.4 Basics of C++ Exception Handling: `try`, `throw`, `catch`

C++ exception handling is geared to situations in which the function that detects an error is unable to deal with it. Such a function will *throw an exception*. There is no guarantee that there will be "anything out there"—i.e., an *exception handler* specifically geared to processing that kind of exception. If there is, the exception will be *caught* and *handled*. If there is no exception handler for that particular kind of exception, the program terminates.

The programmer encloses in a *try block* the code that may generate an error that will produce an exception. The `try` block is followed by one or more *catch blocks*. Each `catch` block specifies the type of exception it can catch and handle. Each `catch` block contains an exception handler. If the exception matches the type of the parameter in one of the `catch` blocks, the code for that `catch` block is executed. If no handler is found, function `terminate` is called, which by default calls function `abort`.

Program control on a thrown exception leaves the `try` block and searches the `catch` blocks in order for an appropriate handler. (We will soon discuss what makes a handler "appropriate.") If no exceptions are thrown in the `try` block, the exception handlers for that block are skipped and the program resumes execution after the last `catch` block.

We can specify the exceptions a function `throw`s. As an option, we can specify that a function shall not `throw` any exceptions at all.

The exception is thrown in a `try` block in the function, or the exception is thrown from a function called directly or indirectly from the `try` block. The point at which the `throw` is executed is called the *throw point*. This term is also used to describe the `throw` expression itself. Once an exception is thrown, control cannot return to the `throw` point.

When an exception occurs, it is possible to communicate information to the exception handler from the point of the exception. That information is the type of the thrown object itself or information placed in the thrown object.

The thrown object is typically a character string (for an error message) or a class object. The thrown object conveys information to the exception handler that will process that exception.

Software Engineering Observation 23.4

A key to exception handling is that the portion of a program or system that will handle the exception can be quite different or distant from the portion of the program that detected and generated the exceptional situation.

23.5 A Simple Exception-Handling Example: Divide by Zero

Now let us consider a simple example of exception handling. Figure 23.1 uses `try`, `throw` and `catch` to detect a division by zero, indicate a divide-by-zero exception and handle a divide-by-zero exception.

```cpp
1   // Fig. 23.1: fig23_01.cpp
2   // A simple exception handling example.
3   // Checking for a divide-by-zero exception.
4   #include <iostream>
5
6   using std::cout;
7   using std::cin;
8   using std::endl;
9
10  // Class DivideByZeroException to be used in exception
11  // handling for throwing an exception on a division by zero.
12  class DivideByZeroException {
13  public:
14     DivideByZeroException()
15        : message( "attempted to divide by zero" ) { }
16     const char *what() const { return message; }
17  private:
18     const char *message;
19  }; // end class DivideByZeroException
20
21  // Definition of function quotient. Demonstrates throwing
22  // an exception when a divide-by-zero exception is encountered.
23  double quotient( int numerator, int denominator )
24  {
25     if ( denominator == 0 )
26        throw DivideByZeroException();
27
28     return static_cast< double > ( numerator ) / denominator;
29  } // end function quotient
30
31  // Driver program
32  int main()
33  {
34     int number1, number2;
35     double result;
36
37     cout << "Enter two integers (end-of-file to end): ";
38
39     while ( cin >> number1 >> number2 ) {
40
41        // the try block wraps the code that may throw an
42        // exception and the code that should not execute
43        // if an exception occurs
44        try {
45           result = quotient( number1, number2 );
46           cout << "The quotient is: " << result << endl;
47        } // end try
48        catch ( DivideByZeroException ex ) { // exception handler
49           cout << "Exception occurred: " << ex.what() << '\n';
50        } // end catch
51
52        cout << "\nEnter two integers (end-of-file to end): ";
53     } // end while
```

Fig. 23.1 A simple exception-handling example with divide by zero. (Part 1 of 2.)

```
54
55      cout << endl;
56      return 0;        // terminate normally
57   } // end function main
```

```
Enter two integers (end-of-file to end): 100 7
The quotient is: 14.2857

Enter two integers (end-of-file to end): 100 0
Exception occurred: attempted to divide by zero

Enter two integers (end-of-file to end): 33 9
The quotient is: 3.66667

Enter two integers (end-of-file to end):^Z
```

Fig. 23.1 A simple exception-handling example with divide by zero. (Part 2 of 2.)

Now consider the driver program in main. Note the "localized" declaration of number1 and number2.

The program contains a try block (line 44) which wraps the code that may throw an exception. Note that the actual division that may cause the error is not explicitly listed inside the try block. Rather, the call to function quotient contains the code that attempts the actual division. Function quotient (defined in line 23) actually throws the divide-by-zero exception object, as we will see momentarily. In general, errors may surface through explicitly mentioned code in the try block, through calls to a function or even through deeply nested function calls initiated by code in the try block.

The try block is immediately followed by a catch block containing the exception handler for the divide-by-zero error. In general, when an exception is thrown within a try block, the exception is caught by a catch block which specifies the appropriate type that matches the thrown exception. In Fig. 23.1, the catch block specifies that it will catch exception objects of type DivideByZeroException; this type matches the type of the object thrown in function quotient. The body of this exception handler prints the error message returned by calling function what. Exception handlers can be much more elaborate than this.

If, when executed, the code in a try block does not throw an exception, then all the catch handlers immediately following the try block are skipped and execution resumes with the first line of code after the catch handlers; in Fig. 23.1 a return statement is executed that returns 0, indicating normal termination.

Now let us examine the definitions of class DivideByZeroException and function quotient. In function quotient, when the if statement determines that the denominator is zero, the body of the if statement issues a throw statement that specifies the name of the constructor for the exception object. This causes an object of class DivideByZeroException to be created. This object will be caught by the catch statement (specifying type DivideByZeroException) after the try block. The constructor for class DivideByZeroException simply points data member message at the string "attempted to divide by zero". The thrown object is received in the parameter specified in the catch handler (in this case, parameter ex), and the message is printed there through a call to function what.

Good Programming Practice 23.4

Associating each type of execution-time error with an appropriately named exception object improves program clarity.

23.6 Throwing an Exception

Keyword `throw` is used to indicate that an exception has occurred. This is called *throwing an exception*. A `throw` normally specifies one operand. (A special case we will discuss specifies no operands.) The operand of a `throw` can be of any type. If the operand is an object, we call it an *exception object*. The value of any expression can be `throw`n instead of an object. It is possible to `throw` objects not intended for error handling.

Where is an exception caught? Upon being thrown, the exception will be caught by the closest exception handler (for the `try` block from which the exception was thrown) specifying an appropriate type. The exception handlers for a `try` block are listed immediately following the `try` block.

As part of throwing an exception, a temporary copy of the `throw` operand is created and initialized. This object then initializes the parameter in the exception handler. The temporary object is destroyed when the exception handler completes execution and exits.

Software Engineering Observation 23.5

If it is necessary to pass information about the error that caused an exception, such information can be placed in the thrown object. The `catch` handler will then contain a parameter name through which that information could be referenced.

Software Engineering Observation 23.6

An object can be thrown without containing information to be passed; in this case, mere knowledge that an exception of this type has been thrown may provide sufficient information for the handler to do its job correctly.

When an exception is thrown, control exits the current `try` block and proceeds to an appropriate `catch` handler (if one exists) after that `try` block. It is possible that the `throw` point could be in a deeply nested scope within a `try` block; control will still proceed to the `catch` handler. It is also possible that the `throw` point could be in a deeply nested function call; still, control will proceed to the `catch` handler.

A `try` block may appear to contain no error checking and include no `throw` statements, but code referenced in the `try` block could certainly cause error-checking code in constructors to execute. Code in a `try` block could perform array subscripting on an array class object whose `operator[]` member function is overloaded to `throw` an exception on a subscript-out-of-range error. Any function call can invoke code that might `throw` an exception or call another function that `throw`s an exception.

Although an exception can terminate program execution, it is not required to do so. However, an exception does terminate the block in which the exception occurred.

Common Programming Error 23.3

Exceptions should be thrown only within a `try` block. An exception thrown outside a `try` block causes a call to `terminate`.

Common Programming Error 23.4

It is possible to throw *a conditional expression. But be careful because promotion rules may cause the value returned by the conditional expression to be of a different type than you may expect. For example, when throwing an* int *or a* double *from the same conditional expression, the conditional expression will convert the* int *to a* double. *Therefore the result will always be caught by a* catch *with a* double *argument rather than sometimes catching* double *(for the actual* double*) and sometimes catching* int.

23.7 Catching an Exception

Exception handlers are contained in catch blocks. Each catch block starts with the keyword catch followed by parentheses containing a type (indicating the type of exception this catch block handles) and an optional parameter name. This is followed by braces delineating the exception-handling code. When an exception is caught, the code in the catch block is executed.

The catch handler defines its own scope. A catch specifies in parentheses the type of the object to be caught. The parameter in a catch handler can be named or unnamed. If the parameter is named, the parameter can be referenced in the handler. If the parameter is unnamed (i.e., only a type is listed for purposes of matching with the thrown object type), then information is not conveyed from the throw point to the handler; only control passes from the throw point to the handler. For many exceptions, this is acceptable.

Common Programming Error 23.5

Specifying a comma-separated list of catch *arguments is a syntax error.*

An exception whose thrown object's type matches the type of the argument in the catch header causes the catch block, i.e., the exception handler for exceptions of that type, to execute.

The catch handler that catches an exception is the first one listed after the currently active try block that matches the type of the thrown object. The matching rules are discussed shortly.

An exception that is not caught causes a call to terminate, which by default terminates a program by calling abort. It is possible to specify customized behavior by designating another function to be executed by providing that function's name as the argument in a set_terminate function call.

A catch followed by parentheses enclosing an ellipsis

```
catch( ... )
```

means to catch all exceptions.

Common Programming Error 23.6

Placing catch(...) *before other* catch *blocks would prevent those blocks from ever being executed;* catch(...) *must be placed last in the list of handlers following a* try *block.*

Software Engineering Observation 23.7

A weakness with catching exceptions with catch(...) *is that you normally cannot be sure what the exception type is. Another weakness is that without a named parameter, there is no way to refer to the exception object inside the exception handler.*

It is possible that no handler will match a particular thrown object. This causes the search for a match to continue in the next enclosing try block. As this process continues, it may eventually be determined that there is no handler in the program that matches the type of the thrown object; in this case function `terminate` is called, which by default calls function `abort`.

The exception handlers are searched in order for an appropriate match. The first handler that yields a match is executed. When that handler finishes executing, control resumes with the first statement after the last `catch` block (i.e., the first statement after the last exception handler for that `try` block).

It is possible that several exception handlers will provide an acceptable match to the type of the exception that was thrown. In this case, the first exception handler that matches the exception type is executed. If several handlers match, and if each of these handles the exception differently, then the order of the handlers will affect the manner in which the exception is handled.

It is possible that several `catch` handlers could contain a class type that would match the type of a particular thrown object. This can happen for several reasons. First, there can be a "catch-all" handler `catch(...)` that will catch any exception. Second, because of inheritance hierarchies, it is possible that a derived-class object can be caught either by a handler specifying the derived-class type, or by handlers specifying the types of any base classes of that derived class.

Common Programming Error 23.7

Placing a `catch` that catches a base-class object before a `catch` that catches an object of a class derived from that base class is a logic error. The base-class `catch` will catch all objects of classes derived from that base class, so the derived-class `catch` will never be executed.

Error-Prevention Tip 23.1

The programmer determines the order in which the exception handlers are listed. This order can affect how exceptions originating in that `try` block are handled. If you are getting unexpected behavior in your program's handling of exceptions, it may be because an early `catch` block is intercepting and handling the exceptions before they reach your intended `catch` handler.

Sometimes a program may process many closely related types of exceptions. Instead of providing separate exception classes and `catch` handlers for each, a programmer can provide a single exception class and `catch` handler for a group of exceptions. As each exception occurs, the exception object can be created with different `private` data. The `catch` handler can examine this `private` data to distinguish the type of the exception.

When does a match occur? The type of the `catch` handler parameter matches the type of the thrown object if

*   They are indeed of the same type.

*   The `catch` handler parameter type is a `public` base class of the class of the thrown object.

*   The handler parameter is of a base-class pointer or reference type and the thrown object is of a derived-class pointer or reference type.

*   The `catch` handler is of the form `catch( ... )`.

Common Programming Error 23.8

Placing an exception handler with a **void** * *argument type before exception handlers with other pointer types causes a logic error. The* **void** * *handler would catch all exceptions of pointer types, so the other handlers would never execute. Only* **catch (...)** *should follow* **catch (void *)**.

An exact type match is required. No promotions or conversions are performed when looking for a handler except for derived-class-to-base-class conversions.

It is possible to **throw const** objects. In this case, the **catch** handler argument type must also be declared **const**.

If no handler is found for an exception, the program terminates. Although this may seem acceptable, it is not what programmers are used to doing. Rather, errors often simply happen then program execution continues, possibly only "hobbling" along.

A **try** block followed by several **catch**es resembles a **switch** statement. It is not necessary to use **break** to exit an exception handler in a manner that skips over the remaining exception handlers. Each **catch** block defines a distinct scope, whereas all the cases in a **switch** statement are contained within the scope of the **switch**.

Common Programming Error 23.9

Placing a semicolon after a **try** *block or after any* **catch** *handler (other than the last* **catch**) *following a* **try** *block is a syntax error.*

An exception handler cannot access automatic objects defined within its **try** block, because, when an exception occurs, the **try** block terminates and all the automatic objects inside the **try** block are destroyed before the handler begins executing.

What happens when an exception occurs in an exception handler? The original exception that was caught is officially handled when the exception handler begins executing. So exceptions occurring in an exception handler need to be processed outside the **try** block in which the original exception was thrown.

Exception handlers can be written in a variety of ways. They could take a closer look at an error and decide to call **terminate**. They could *rethrow* an exception (Section 23.8). They could convert one type of exception into another by throwing a different exception. They could perform any necessary recovery and resume execution after the last exception handler. They could look at the situation causing the error, remove the cause of the error and retry by calling the original function that caused an exception. (This would not create infinite recursion.) They could return some status value to their environment, etc.

Software Engineering Observation 23.8

It is best to incorporate your exception-handling strategy into a system from the inception of the design process. It is difficult to add effective exception handling after a system has been implemented.

When a **try** block does not **throw** exceptions and the **try** block completes normal execution, control passes to the first statement after the last **catch** following the **try**.

It is not possible to return to the **throw** point by issuing a **return** statement in a **catch** handler. Such a **return** simply returns to the function that called the function containing the **catch** block.

Common Programming Error 23.10

Assuming that after an exception is processed, control will return to the first statement after the throw *is a logic error.*

Software Engineering Observation 23.9

Another reason not to use exceptions for conventional flow of control is that these "additional" exceptions can get in the way of genuine error-type exceptions. It becomes more difficult for the programmer to keep track of the number of exception cases. For example, when a program processes an excessive variety of exceptions, can we really be sure of just what is being caught by a catch(...)? *Exceptional situations should be rare, not commonplace.*

When an exception is caught, it is possible that resources may have been allocated, but not yet released in the try block. The catch handler, if possible, should release these resources. For example, the catch handler should delete space allocated by new and should close any files opened in the try block that threw the exception.

A catch block can process the error in a manner that enables the program to continue executing correctly. Or the catch block can terminate the program.

A catch handler itself can discover an error and throw an exception. Such an exception will not be processed by catch handlers associated with the same try block as the catch handler throwing the exception. Rather, the thrown exception will be caught, if possible, by a catch handler associated with the next outer try block.

Common Programming Error 23.11

Assuming that an exception thrown from a catch *handler will be processed by that handler or any other handler associated with the* try *block that threw the exception which caused the original* catch *handler to execute is a logic error.*

23.8 Rethrowing an Exception

It is possible that the handler that catches an exception may decide that it cannot process the exception, or it may simply want to release resources before letting someone else handle it. In this case, the handler can simply rethrow the exception with the statement

        throw;

Such a throw with no arguments rethrows the exception. If no exception was thrown to begin with, then the rethrow causes a call to terminate.

Common Programming Error 23.12

Placing an empty throw *statement outside a* catch *handler; executing such a* throw *causes a call to* terminate.

Even if a handler can process an exception, regardless of whether it does any processing on that exception, the handler can still rethrow the exception for further processing outside the handler.

A rethrown exception is detected by the next enclosing try block and is handled by an exception handler listed after that enclosing try block.

Software Engineering Observation 23.10

Use catch(...) *to perform recovery that does not depend on the type of the exception, such as releasing common resources. The exception can be rethrown to alert more specific enclosing* catch *blocks.*

The program of Fig. 23.2 demonstrates rethrowing an exception. In the `try` block of main, function `throwException` is called in line 31. In the `try` block of function `throwException`, the `throw` statement in line 17 `throws` an instance of standard library class `exception` (defined in header file `<exception>`). This exception is caught immediately in the `catch` handler in line 19, which prints an error message, then rethrows the exception. This terminates function `throwException` and returns control to the `try`/`catch` block in main. The exception is caught again in line 34, and an error message is printed.

```cpp
1   // Fig. 23.2: fig23_02.cpp
2   // Demonstration of rethrowing an exception.
3   #include <iostream>
4
5   using std::cout;
6   using std::endl;
7
8   #include <exception>
9
10  using std::exception;
11
12  void throwException()
13  {
14     // Throw an exception and immediately catch it.
15     try {
16        cout << "Function throwException\n";
17        throw exception();   // generate exception
18     } // end try
19     catch( exception e )
20     {
21        cout << "Exception handled in function throwException\n";
22        throw;  // rethrow exception for further processing
23     } // end catch
24
25     cout << "This also should not print\n";
26  } // end function throwException
27
28  int main()
29  {
30     try {
31        throwException();
32        cout << "This should not print\n";
33     } // end try
34     catch ( exception e )
35     {
36        cout << "Exception handled in main\n";
37     } // end catch
38
39     cout << "Program control continues after catch in main"
40          << endl;
41     return 0;
42  } // end function main
```

Fig. 23.2   Rethrowing an exception. (Part 1 of 2.)

```
Function throwException
Exception handled in function throwException
Exception handled in main
Program control continues after catch in main
```

Fig. 23.2   Rethrowing an exception. (Part 2 of 2.)

23.9 Exception Specifications

An *exception specification* enumerates a list of exceptions that can be thrown by a function to be specified:

```
int g( double h ) throw ( a, b, c )
{
    // function body
}
```

It is possible to restrict the exception types thrown from a function. The exception types are specified in the function declaration as an *exception specification* (also called a *throwlist*). The exception specification lists the exceptions that may be thrown. A function may throw the indicated exceptions or derived types. Despite this supposed guarantee that other exception types will not be thrown, it is possible to do so. If an exception not listed in the exception specification is thrown, function unexpected is called.

Placing throw() (i.e., an *empty exception specification*) after a function's parameter list states that the function will not throw any exceptions. Such a function could, in fact, throw an exception; this, too, would generate a call to unexpected.

Common Programming Error 23.13

Throwing an exception not in a function's exception specification causes a call to unexpected.

A function with no exception specification can throw any exception:

```
void g();       // this function can throw any exception
```

The meaning of the unexpected function can be redefined by calling function set_unexpected.

One interesting aspect of exception handling is that the compiler will not consider it a syntax error if a function contains a throw expression for an exception not listed in the function's exception specification. The function must attempt to throw that exception at execution time before the error will be caught.

If a function throws an exception of a particular class type, that function can also throw exceptions of all classes derived from that class with public inheritance.

23.10 Processing Unexpected Exceptions

Function unexpected calls the function specified with the set_unexpected function. If no function has been specified in this manner, terminate is called by default.

Function terminate can be called explicitly if a thrown exception cannot be caught, if the stack is corrupted during exception handling, as the default action on a call to unexpected, and if during stack unwinding initiated by an exception, an attempt by a destructor to throw an exception causes terminate to be called.

Function set_terminate can specify the function that will be called when function terminate is called. Otherwise, terminate calls abort.

Prototypes for functions set_terminate and set_unexpected are located in header file <exception>.

Function set_terminate and function set_unexpected each return a pointer to the last function called by terminate and unexpected. This enables the programmer to save the function pointer so it can be restored later.

Functions set_terminate and set_unexpected take pointers to functions as arguments. Each argument must point to a function with void return type and no arguments.

If the last action of a user-defined termination function is not to exit a program, function abort will automatically be called to end program execution after the other statements of the user-defined termination function are executed.

23.11 Stack Unwinding

When an exception is thrown but not caught in a particular scope, the function-call stack is unwound and an attempt is made to catch the exception in the next outer try/catch block. Unwinding the function-call stack means that the function in which the exception was not caught terminates, all local variables in that function are destroyed and control returns to the point at which that function was called. If that point in the program is in a try block, an attempt is made to catch the exception. If that point in the program is not in a try block or the exception is not caught, stack unwinding occurs again. As mentioned in the previous section, if the exception is not caught in the program, function terminate is called to terminate the program. The program of Fig. 23.3 demonstrates stack unwinding.

```
1   // Fig. 23.3: fig23_03.cpp
2   // Demonstrating stack unwinding.
3   #include <iostream>
4
5   using std::cout;
6   using std::endl;
7
8   #include <stdexcept>
9
10  using std::runtime_error;
11
12  void function3() throw ( runtime_error )
13  {
14     throw runtime_error( "runtime_error in function3" );
15  } // end function function3
16
17  void function2() throw ( runtime_error )
18  {
19     function3();
20  } // end function function2
21
```

Fig. 23.3   Demonstration of stack unwinding. (Part 1 of 2.)

```
22   void function1() throw ( runtime_error )
23   {
24      function2();
25   } // end function function1
26
27   int main()
28   {
29      try {
30         function1();
31      } // end try
32      catch ( runtime_error e )
33      {
34         cout << "Exception occurred: " << e.what() << endl;
35      } // end catch
36
37      return 0;
38   } // end function main
```

```
Exception occurred: runtime_error in function3
```

Fig. 23.3 Demonstration of stack unwinding. (Part 2 of 2.)

In main, the try block calls function1 (line 30). Next, function1 (defined in line 22) calls function2. Then, function2 (defined in line 17) calls function3. Line 14 of function3 throws an exception object. Line 14 is not in a try block, so stack unwinding occurs—function3 terminates in line 19 and control returns to function2. Line 19 is not in a try block, so stack unwinding occurs again—function2 terminates in line 24 and control returns to function1. Line 24 is not in a try block, so stack unwinding occurs one more time—function1 terminates in line 30 and control returns to main. Line 30 is in a try block, so the exception can be caught and processed in the first matching catch handler after the try block (in line 32).

23.12 Constructors, Destructors and Exception Handling

First, let us deal with an issue we have mentioned, but that has yet to be satisfactorily resolved: What happens when an error is detected in a constructor? For example, how should a String constructor respond when new fails and indicates that it was unable to obtain the space needed to hold the String's internal representation? The problem is that a constructor cannot return a value, so how do we let the outside world know that the object has not been properly constructed? One scheme is simply to return the improperly constructed object and hope that anyone using the object would make appropriate tests to determine that the object was in fact bad. Another scheme is to set some variable outside the constructor. A thrown exception passes to the outside world the information about the failed constructor and the responsibility to deal with the failure.

To catch an exception, the exception handler must have access to a copy constructor for the thrown object. (Default memberwise copy is also valid.)

Exceptions thrown in constructors cause destructors to be called for any objects built as part of the object being constructed before the exception is thrown.

Destructors are called for every automatic object constructed in a `try` block before an exception is thrown. An exception is handled at the moment the handler begins executing; stack unwinding is guaranteed to have been completed at that point. If a destructor invoked as a result of stack unwinding `throws` an exception, `terminate` is called.

If an object has member objects and if an exception is thrown before the outer object is fully constructed, then destructors will be executed for the member objects that have been fully constructed prior to the occurrence of the exception.

If an array of objects has been partially constructed when an exception occurs, only the destructors for the constructed array elements will be called.

An exception could preclude the operation of code that would normally release a resource, thus causing a *resource leak*. One technique to resolve this problem is to initialize a local object when the resource is acquired. When an exception occurs, the destructor will be invoked and can free the resource.

It is possible to `catch` exceptions thrown from destructors by enclosing the function that calls the destructor in a `try` block and providing a `catch` handler with the proper type. The thrown object's destructor executes after an exception handler completes execution.

23.13 Exceptions and Inheritance

Various exception classes can be derived from a common base class. If a `catch` catches a pointer or reference to an exception object of a base-class type, it can also `catch` a pointer or reference to all objects of classes derived from that base class. This can allow for polymorphic processing of related errors.

Error-Prevention Tip 23.2

Using inheritance with exceptions enables an exception handler to `catch` related errors with a rather concise notation. One could certainly `catch` each type of pointer or reference to a derived-class exception object individually, but it is more concise to `catch` pointers or references to base-class exception objects instead. Also, catching pointers or references to derived-class exception objects individually is subject to error if the programmer forgets to explicitly test for one or more of the derived-class pointer or reference types.

23.14 Processing new Failures

There are several methods of dealing with `new` failures. To this point, we have used macro `assert` to test the value returned from `new`. If that value is 0, the `assert` macro terminates the program. This is not a robust mechanism for dealing with `new` failures—it does not allow us to recover from the failure in any way. The C++ standard specifies that when `new` fails, it `throws` a `bad_alloc` exception (defined in header file `<new>`). However, some compilers may not be compliant with the C++ standard and therefore use the version of `new` that returns 0 on failure. In this section we present three examples of `new` failing. The first example returns 0 when `new` fails. The second and third examples use the version of `new` that `throws` a `bad_alloc` exception when `new` fails.

Figure 23.4 demonstrates `new` returning 0 on failure to allocate the requested amount of memory. The `for` structure in line 12 is supposed to loop 50 times and allocate an array of 5,000,000 `double` values (i.e., 40,000,000 bytes, because a `double` is normally 8 bytes) each time through the loop. The `if` structure in line 15 tests the result of each `new` operation to determine if the memory was allocated. If new fails and returns 0, the message "Memory allocation failed" is printed and the loop terminates.

```
1   // Fig. 23.4: fig23_04.cpp
2   // Demonstrating new returning 0
3   // when memory is not allocated
4   #include <iostream>
5
6   using std::cout;
7
8   int main()
9   {
10      double *ptr[ 50 ];
11
12      for ( int i = 0; i < 50; i++ ) {
13         ptr[ i ] = new double[ 5000000 ];
14
15         if ( ptr[ i ] == 0 ) { // new failed to allocate memory
16            cout << "Memory allocation failed for ptr[ "
17                 << i << " ]\n";
18            break;
19         } // end if
20         else
21            cout << "Allocated 5000000 doubles in ptr[ "
22                 << i << " ]\n";
23      } // end for
24
25      return 0;
26   } // end function main
```

```
Allocated 5000000 doubles in ptr[ 0 ]
Allocated 5000000 doubles in ptr[ 1 ]
Allocated 5000000 doubles in ptr[ 2 ]
Allocated 5000000 doubles in ptr[ 3 ]
Memory allocation failed for ptr[ 4 ]
```

Fig. 23.4 Demonstrating new returning 0 on failure.

The output shows that only four iterations of the loop were performed before new failed and the loop terminated. Your output may differ based on the physical memory, disk space available for virtual memory on your system and the compiler used to compile the program.

Figure 23.5 demonstrates new throwing bad_alloc when it fails to allocate the requested memory. The for structure in line 18 inside the try block is supposed to loop 50 times and on each pass allocate an array of 5,000,000 double values (i.e., 40,000,000 bytes, because a double is normally 8 bytes). If new fails and throws a bad_alloc exception, the loop terminates and the program continues in the exception-handling flow of control in line 24, where the exception is caught and processed. The message "Exception occurred: " is printed, followed by the string (containing the exception-specific message "Allocation Failure") returned from exception.what(). The output shows that only four iterations of the loop were performed before new failed and threw the bad_alloc exception. Your output may differ based on the physical memory, disk space available for virtual memory on your system and the compiler you use to compile the program.

```cpp
1   // Fig. 23.5: fig23_05.cpp
2   // Demonstrating new throwing bad_alloc
3   // when memory is not allocated
4   #include <iostream>
5
6   using std::cout;
7   using std::endl;
8
9   #include <new>
10
11  using std::bad_alloc;
12
13  int main()
14  {
15     double *ptr[ 50 ];
16
17     try {
18        for ( int i = 0; i < 50; i++ ) {
19           ptr[ i ] = new double[ 5000000 ];
20           cout << "Allocated 5000000 doubles in ptr[ "
21                << i << " ]\n";
22        } // end for
23     } // end try
24     catch ( bad_alloc exception ) {
25        cout << "Exception occurred: "
26             << exception.what() << endl;
27     } // end catch
28
29     return 0;
30  } // end function main
```

```
Allocated 5000000 doubles in ptr[ 0 ]
Allocated 5000000 doubles in ptr[ 1 ]
Allocated 5000000 doubles in ptr[ 2 ]
Allocated 5000000 doubles in ptr[ 3 ]
Exception occurred: Allocation Failure
```

Fig. 23.5   Demonstrating new throwing bad_alloc on failure.

Compilers vary in their support for new failure handling. Many C++ compilers return 0 by default when new fails. Some of these compilers support new throwing an exception if the header file <new> (or <new.h>) is included. Other compilers throw bad_alloc by default whether or not you include header file <new>. Read the documentation for your compiler to determine your compiler's support for new failure handling.

The C++ standard specifies that standard-compliant compilers can still use a version of new that returns 0 when it fails. For this purpose, the header file <new> defines nothrow (of type nothrow_t), which is used as follows:

```cpp
double *ptr = new( nothrow ) double[ 5000000 ];
```

The preceding statement indicates that the version of new that does not throw bad_alloc exceptions (i.e., nothrow) should be used to allocate an array of 5,000,000 doubles.

Software Engineering Observation 23.11

The C++ standard recommends that to make programs more robust, programmers should use the version of new that throws bad_alloc exceptions on failure.

There is an additional feature that can be used to perform handling of new failures. Function set_new_handler (prototyped in header file <new>) takes as its argument a function pointer for a function that takes no arguments and returns void. The function pointer is registered as the function to call when new fails. This provides the programmer with a uniform method of processing every new failure regardless of where the failure occurs in the program. Once a *new handler* is registered in the program with set_new_handler, new will not throw bad_alloc on failure.

Operator new is actually a loop that attempts to acquire memory. If the memory is allocated, new returns a pointer to that memory. If new fails to allocate memory and no new handler function has been registered with set_new_handler, new throws a bad_alloc exception. If new fails to allocate memory and a new handler function has been registered, the new handler function is called. The C++ standard specifies that the new handler function should perform one of the following tasks:

1. Make more memory available by deleting other dynamically allocated memory and return to the loop in operator new to attempt to allocate the memory again.

2. Throw an exception of type bad_alloc.

3. Call function abort or exit (both from header file <cstdlib>) to terminate the program.

Figure 23.6 demonstrates set_new_handler. Function customNewHandler simply prints an error message and terminates the program with a call to abort. The output shows that only four iterations of the loop were performed before new failed and threw the bad_alloc exception. Your output may differ, based on the physical memory, disk space available for virtual memory on your system and the compiler you use to compile the program.

```
1   // Fig. 23.6: fig23_06.cpp
2   // Demonstrating set_new_handler
3   #include <iostream>
4
5   using std::cout;
6   using std::cerr;
7
8   #include <new>
9   #include <cstdlib>
10
11  using std::set_new_handler;
12
13  void customNewHandler()
14  {
```

Fig. 23.6 Demonstrating set_new_handler. (Part 1 of 2.)

```
15          cerr << "customNewHandler was called";
16          abort();
17      } // end function customNewHandler
18
19      int main()
20      {
21          double *ptr[ 50 ];
22          set_new_handler( customNewHandler );
23
24          for ( int i = 0; i < 50; i++ ) {
25              ptr[ i ] = new double[ 5000000 ];
26
27              cout << "Allocated 5000000 doubles in ptr[ "
28                  << i << " ]\n";
29          } // end for
30
31          return 0;
32      } // end function main
```

```
Allocated 5000000 doubles in ptr[ 0 ]
Allocated 5000000 doubles in ptr[ 1 ]
Allocated 5000000 doubles in ptr[ 2 ]
Allocated 5000000 doubles in ptr[ 3 ]
customNewHandler was called
```

Fig. 23.6   Demonstrating `set_new_handler`. (Part 2 of 2.)

23.15 Class `auto_ptr` and Dynamic Memory Allocation

A common programming practice is to allocate dynamic memory (possibly an object) on the free store, assign the address of that memory to a pointer, use the pointer to manipulate the memory and deallocate the memory with `delete` when the memory is no longer needed. If an exception occurs after the memory has been allocated and before the `delete` statement is executed, a memory leak could occur. The C++ standard provides class template `auto_ptr` in header file <memory> to deal with this situation.

An object of class `auto_ptr` maintains a pointer to dynamically allocated memory. When an `auto_ptr` object goes out of scope, it performs a `delete` operation on its pointer data member. Class template `auto_ptr` provides operators * and -> so an `auto_ptr` object can be used like a regular pointer variable. Figure 23.7 demonstrates an `auto_ptr` object that points to an object of class `Integer` (defined in lines 12–22).

```
1   // Fig. 23.7: fig23_07.cpp
2   // Demonstrating auto_ptr
3   #include <iostream>
4
5   using std::cout;
6   using std::endl;
7
8   #include <memory>
```

Fig. 23.7   Demonstrating `auto_ptr`. (Part 1 of 2.)

```
 9
10   using std::auto_ptr;
11
12   class Integer {
13   public:
14      Integer( int i = 0 ) : value( i )
15         { cout << "Constructor for Integer " << value << endl; }
16      ~Integer()
17         { cout << "Destructor for Integer " << value << endl; }
18      void setInteger( int i ) { value = i; }
19      int getInteger() const { return value; }
20   private:
21      int value;
22   }; // end class Integer
23
24   int main()
25   {
26      cout << "Creating an auto_ptr object that points "
27           << "to an Integer\n";
28
29      auto_ptr< Integer > ptrToInteger( new Integer( 7 ) );
30
31      cout << "Using the auto_ptr to manipulate the Integer\n";
32      ptrToInteger->setInteger( 99 );
33      cout << "Integer after setInteger: "
34           << ( *ptrToInteger ).getInteger()
35           << "\nTerminating program" << endl;
36
37      return 0;
38   } // end function main
```

```
Creating an auto_ptr object that points to an Integer
Constructor for Integer 7
Using the auto_ptr to manipulate the Integer
Integer after setInteger: 99
Terminating program
Destructor for Integer 99
```

Fig. 23.7 Demonstrating auto_ptr. (Part 2 of 2.)

Line 29

```
auto_ptr< Integer > ptrToInteger( new Integer( 7 ) );
```

creates auto_ptr object ptrToInteger and initializes it with a pointer to a dynamically allocated Integer object containing the value 7.

Line 32

```
ptrToInteger->setInteger( 99 );
```

uses the auto_ptr overloaded -> operator and the function call operator () to call function setInteger on the Integer object pointed to by ptrToInteger. The call

```
( *ptrToInteger ).getInteger()
```

in line 34 uses the `auto_ptr` overloaded * operator to dereference `ptrToInteger`, then uses the dot (.) operator and the function call operator () to call function `getInteger` on the `Integer` object pointed to by `ptrToInteger`.

Variable `ptrToInteger` is a local automatic variable in `main`, so `ptrToInteger` is destroyed when `main` terminates. This forces a `delete` of the `Integer` object pointed to by `ptrToInteger`, which, of course, forces a call to the `Integer` class destructor. Most importantly, this technique can prevent memory leaks.

23.16 Standard Library Exception Hierarchy

Experience has shown that exceptions fall nicely into a number of categories. The C++ standard includes a hierarchy of exception classes. This hierarchy is headed by base class `exception` (defined in header file `<exception>`), which contains function `what()` that is overridden in each derived class to issue an appropriate error message.

From base class `exception`, some of the immediate derived classes are `runtime_error` and `logic_error` (both defined in header `<stdexcept>`), each of which has several derived classes.

Also derived from `exception` are the exceptions thrown by C++ language features—for example, `bad_alloc` is thrown by `new` (Section 23.14), `bad_cast` is thrown by `dynamic_cast` and `bad_typeid` is thrown by `typeid`. By including `std::bad_exception` in the `throw` list of a function, if an unexpected exception occurs, `unexpected()` can throw `bad_exception` instead of terminating (by default) or instead of calling another function specified with `set_unexpected`.

Class `logic_error` is the base class of several standard exception classes that indicate errors in program logic that can often be prevented by writing proper code. Descriptions of some of these classes follow. Class `invalid_argument` indicates that an invalid argument was passed to a function. (Proper coding can, of course, prevent invalid arguments from reaching a function.) Class `length_error` indicates that a length larger than the maximum size allowed for the object being manipulated was used for that object. Class `out_of_range` indicates that a value such as a subscript into an array or `string` was out of range.

Class `runtime_error` is the base class of several other standard exception classes that indicate errors in a program and that can only be detected at execution time. Class `overflow_error` indicates that an arithmetic overflow error occurred. Class `underflow_error` indicates that an arithmetic underflow error occurred.

Software Engineering Observation 23.12

The standard `exception` *hierarchy is meant to serve as a starting point. Users can* `throw` *standard exceptions,* `throw` *exceptions derived from the standard exceptions or* `throw` *their own exceptions not derived from the standard exceptions.*

Common Programming Error 23.14

User-defined exception classes need not be derived from class `exception`. *Thus, writing* `catch( exception e )` *is not guaranteed to* `catch` *all exceptions a program may encounter.*

Error-Prevention Tip 23.3

To `catch` *all exceptions that might be thrown in a* `try` *block, use* `catch( ... )`.

SUMMARY

- Some common examples of exceptions are an out-of-bounds array subscript, arithmetic overflow, division by zero, invalid function parameters and determining that there is insufficient memory to satisfy an allocation request by new.

- The spirit behind exception handling is to enable programs to catch and handle errors rather than letting them occur and simply suffering the consequences. With exception handling, if the programmer does not provide a means of handling a fatal error, the program will terminate; nonfatal errors normally allow a program to continue executing, but produce incorrect results.

- Exception handling is designed for dealing with synchronous errors (i.e., errors that occur as the result of a program's execution).

- Exception handling is not designed to deal with asynchronous situations such as network message arrivals, disk I/O completions, and mouse clicks; these are best handled through other means, such as interrupt processing.

- Exception handling is typically used in situations in which the error will be dealt with by a different part of the program (i.e., a different scope) from that which detected the error.

- Exceptions should not be used as a mechanism for specifying flow of control. Flow of control with conventional control structures is generally clearer and more efficient than with exceptions.

- Exception handling should be used to process exceptions for program components that are not geared to handling those exceptions directly.

- Exception handling should be used to process exceptions from software components such as functions, libraries, and classes that are likely to be widely used and where it does not make sense for those components to handle their own exceptions.

- Exception handling should be used on large projects to handle error processing in a uniform manner for the entire project.

- C++ exception handling is geared to situations in which the function that detects an error is unable to deal with it. Such a function will throw an exception. If the exception matches the type of the parameter in one of the catch blocks, the code for that catch block is executed. Otherwise, function terminate is called, which by default calls function abort.

- The programmer encloses in a try block the code that may generate an error that will produce an exception. The try block is immediately followed by one or more catch blocks. Each catch block specifies the type of exception it can catch and handle. Each catch block contains an exception handler.

- Program control on a thrown exception leaves the try block and searches the catch blocks in order for an appropriate handler. If no exceptions are thrown in the try block, the exception handlers for that block are skipped and the program resumes execution after the last catch block.

- Exceptions are thrown in a try block in a function or from a function called directly or indirectly from the try block.

- Once an exception is thrown, control cannot return directly to the throw point.

- It is possible to communicate information to the exception handler from the point of the exception. That information is the type of thrown object or information placed in the thrown object.

- A popular exception type thrown is char *. It is common to simply include an error message as the operand of the throw.

- The exceptions thrown by a particular function can be specified with an exception specification. An empty exception specification states that the function will not throw any exceptions.

- Exceptions are caught by the closest exception handler (for the try block from which the exception was thrown) specifying an appropriate type.

- As part of throwing an exception, a temporary copy of the `throw` operand is created and initialized. This temporary object then initializes the proper variable in the exception handler. The temporary object is destroyed when the exception handler is exited.

- Errors are not always checked explicitly. A `try` block, for example, may appear to contain no error checking and include no `throw` statements. But code referenced in the `try` block could certainly cause error-checking code to execute.

- An exception terminates the block in which the exception occurred.

- Exception handlers are contained in `catch` blocks. Each `catch` block starts with the keyword `catch`, followed by parentheses containing a type and an optional parameter name. This is followed by braces delineating the exception-handling code. When an exception is caught, the code in the `catch` block is executed. The `catch` handler defines its own scope.

- The parameter in a `catch` handler can be named or unnamed. If the parameter is named, the parameter can be referenced in the handler. If the parameter is unnamed (i.e., only a type is listed for the purpose of matching with the thrown object type or an ellipsis for all types), then the handler will ignore the thrown object. The handler may rethrow the object to an outer `try` block.

- It is possible to specify customized behavior to replace function `terminate` by designating another function to be executed and providing that function's name as the argument in a `set_terminate` function call.

- `catch(...)` means to `catch` all exceptions.

- It is possible that no handler will match a particular thrown object. This causes the search for a match to continue in an enclosing `try` block.

- The exception handlers are searched in order for an appropriate match. The first handler that yields a match is executed. When that handler finishes executing, control resumes with the first statement after the last `catch` block.

- The order of the exception handlers affects how an exception is handled.

- A derived-class object can be caught either by a handler specifying the derived-class type or by handlers specifying the types of any base classes of that derived class.

- Sometimes a program may process many closely related types of exceptions. Instead of providing separate exception classes and `catch` handlers for each, a programmer can provide a single exception class and `catch` handler for a group of exceptions. As each exception occurs, the exception object can be created with different `private` data. The `catch` handler can examine these `private` data to distinguish the type of the exception.

- It is possible that even though a precise match is available, a match requiring standard conversions will be made because that handler appears before the one that would result in a precise match.

- By default, if no handler is found for an exception, the program terminates.

- An exception handler cannot directly access variables in the scope of its `try` block. Information the handler needs is normally passed in the thrown object.

- Exception handlers can take a closer look at an error and decide to call `terminate`. They can rethrow an exception. They can convert one type of exception into another by throwing a different exception. They can perform any necessary recovery and resume execution after the last exception handler. They can look at the situation causing the error, remove the cause of the error and retry by calling the original function that caused an exception. (This would not create infinite recursion.) They can simply return some status value to their environment, etc.

- A handler that catches a derived-class object should be placed before a handler that catches a base-class object. If the base-class handler were first, it would catch both the base-class objects and the object of classes derived from that base class.

- When an exception is caught, it is possible that resources may have been allocated, but not yet released in the `try` block. The `catch` handler should release these resources.

- It is possible that a `catch` handler may decide that it cannot process the exception. In this case, the handler can simply rethrow the exception. A `throw` with no arguments rethrows the exception. If no exception was thrown to begin with, then the rethrow causes a call to `terminate`.

- Even if a handler can process an exception, and regardless of whether it does any processing on that exception, the handler can rethrow the exception for further processing outside the handler. A rethrown exception is detected by the next enclosing `try` block and is handled by an exception handler listed after that enclosing `try` block.

- A function with no exception specification can `throw` any exception.

- Function `unexpected` calls a function specified with function `set_unexpected`. If no function has been specified in this manner, `terminate` is called by default.

- Function `terminate` can be called in various ways: explicitly; if a thrown exception cannot be caught; if the stack is corrupted during exception handling; as the default action on a call to function `unexpected`; or if, during stack unwinding initiated by an exception, an attempt by a destructor to `throw` an exception causes `terminate` to be called.

- Prototypes for functions `set_terminate` and `set_unexpected` are found in header file `<exception>`.

- Functions `set_terminate` and `set_unexpected` return pointers to the last function called by `terminate` and `unexpected`. This enables the programmer to save the function pointer so it can be restored later.

- Functions `set_terminate` and `set_unexpected` take pointers to functions as arguments. Each argument must point to a function with `void` return type and no arguments.

- If the last action of a user-defined termination function is not to exit a program, function `abort` will be called to end program execution after the other statements of the user-defined termination function are executed.

- An exception thrown outside a `try` block will cause the program to terminate.

- If a handler cannot be found after a `try` block, stack unwinding continues until an appropriate handler is found. If a handler is ultimately not found, then `terminate` is called, which by default aborts the program with `abort`.

- Exception specifications list the exceptions that may be thrown from a function. A function may `throw` the indicated exceptions, or it may `throw` derived types. If an exception not listed in the exception specification is thrown, `unexpected` is called.

- If a function `throws` an exception of a particular class type, that function can also `throw` exceptions of all classes derived from that class with `public` inheritance.

- To `catch` an exception, the handler must have access to a copy constructor for the thrown object.

- Exceptions thrown from constructors cause destructors to be called for all completed base-class objects and member objects of the object being constructed before the exception is thrown.

- If an array of objects has been partially constructed when an exception occurs, only the destructors for the fully constructed array elements will be called.

- Exceptions thrown from destructors can be caught by enclosing the function that calls the destructor in a `try` block and provide a `catch` handler with the proper type.

- A powerful reason for using inheritance with exceptions is to create the ability to `catch` a variety of related errors easily with concise notation. One could certainly `catch` each type of derived-class exception object individually, but if all derived exceptions are handled the same, it is much more concise to simply catch the base-class exception object.

- The C++ standard specifies that when new fails, it throws a bad_alloc exception (bad_alloc is defined in header file <new>).

- Some compilers are not compliant with the C++ standard and still use the version of new that returns 0 on failure.

- Function set_new_handler (prototyped in header file <new>) takes as its argument a function pointer to a function that takes no arguments and returns void. The function pointer is registered as the function to call when new fails. Once a new *handler* is registered with set_new_handler, new will not throw bad_alloc on failure.

- An object of class auto_ptr maintains a pointer to dynamically allocated memory. Whenever an auto_ptr object goes out of scope, it performs a delete operation on its pointer data member. Class template auto_ptr provides operators * and -> so an auto_ptr object can be used like a regular pointer variable.

- The C++ standard includes a hierarchy of exception classes headed by base class exception (defined in header file <exception>), which offers the service what() that is overridden in each derived class to issue an appropriate error message.

- By including std::bad_exception in the throw list of a function definition, if an unexpected exception occurs, unexpected() will throw bad_exception instead of terminating (by default) or instead of calling another function specified with set_unexpected.

TERMINOLOGY

abort()
assert macro
auto_ptr
bad_alloc
bad_cast
bad_typeid
catch(...)
catch a group of exceptions
catch an exception
catch argument
catch block
catch(void *)
dynamic_cast
empty exception specification
empty throw specification
enclosing try block
exception
exception declaration
exception handler
<exception> header file
exception list
exception object
exception specification
exceptional condition
exit
fault tolerance
function with no exception specification
handle an exception
handler for a base class

handler for a derived class
invalid_argument
length_error
logic_error
<memory> header file
mission-critical application
nested exception handlers
new_handler
<new> header file
nothrow
out_of_range
overflow_error
rethrow an exception
robustness
runtime_error
set_new_handler
set_terminate
set_unexpected
stack unwinding
std::bad_exception
<stdexcept> header file
terminate
throw an exception
throw an unexpected exception
throw expression
throw list
throw point
throw without arguments
throw

try block   underflow_error
uncaught exception   unexpected

COMMON PROGRAMMING ERRORS

23.1 Another reason exceptions can be dangerous as an alternative to normal flow of control is that the stack is unwound and resources allocated prior to the occurrence of the exception may not be freed. This problem can be avoided by careful programming.

23.2 Aborting a program could leave a resource in a state in which other programs would not be able to acquire the resource; hence the program would have a so-called "resource leak."

23.3 Exceptions should be thrown only within a try block. An exception thrown outside a try block causes a call to terminate.

23.4 It is possible to throw a conditional expression. But be careful because promotion rules may cause the value returned by the conditional expression to be of a different type than you may expect. For example, when throwing an int or a double from the same conditional expression, the conditional expression will convert the int to a double. Therefore the result will always be caught by a catch with a double argument rather than sometimes catching double (for the actual double) and sometimes catching int.

23.5 Specifying a comma-separated list of catch arguments is a syntax error.

23.6 Placing catch(...) before other catch blocks would prevent those blocks from ever being executed; catch(...) must be placed last in the list of handlers following a try block.

23.7 Placing a catch that catches a base-class object before a catch that catches an object of a class derived from that base class is a logic error. The base-class catch will catch all objects of classes derived from that base class, so the derived-class catch will never be executed.

23.8 Placing an exception handler with a void * argument type before exception handlers with other pointer types causes a logic error. The void * handler would catch all exceptions of pointer types, so the other handlers would never execute. Only catch (...) should follow catch (void *).

23.9 Placing a semicolon after a try block or after any catch handler (other than the last catch) following a try block is a syntax error.

23.10 Assuming that after an exception is processed, control will return to the first statement after the throw is a logic error.

23.11 Assuming that an exception thrown from a catch handler will be processed by that handler or any other handler associated with the try block that threw the exception which caused the original catch handler to execute is a logic error.

23.12 Placing an empty throw statement outside a catch handler; executing such a throw causes a call to terminate.

23.13 Throwing an exception not in a function's exception specification causes a call to unexpected.

23.14 User-defined exception classes need not be derived from class exception. Thus, writing catch(exception e) is not guaranteed to catch all exceptions a program may encounter.

GOOD PROGRAMMING PRACTICES

23.1 Use exceptions for errors that must be processed in a different scope from where they occur. Use other means of error handling for errors that will be processed in the scope in which they occur.

23.2 Avoid using exception handling for purposes other than error handling, because this can reduce program clarity.

23.3 Use conventional error-handling techniques rather than exception handling for straightforward, local error processing in which a program is easily able to deal with its own errors.

23.4 Associating each type of execution-time error with an appropriately named exception object improves program clarity.

PERFORMANCE TIPS

23.1 Although it is possible to use exception handling for purposes other than error handling, this can reduce program performance.

23.2 Exception handling is generally implemented in compilers in such a manner that when an exception does not occur, little or no overhead is imposed by the presence of exception-handling code. When exceptions happen, they do incur execution-time overhead. Certainly the presence of exception-handling code makes the program consume more memory.

SOFTWARE ENGINEERING OBSERVATIONS

23.1 Flow of control with conventional control structures is generally clearer and more efficient than with exceptions.

23.2 Exception handling is well suited to systems of separately developed components. Exception handling makes it easier to combine the components. Each component can perform its own exception detection separate from the handling of the exceptions in another scope.

23.3 When dealing with libraries, the caller of the library function will likely have unique error processing in mind for an exception generated in the library function. It is unlikely that a library function will perform error processing that would meet the unique needs of all users. Therefore, exceptions are an appropriate means for dealing with errors produced by library functions.

23.4 A key to exception handling is that the portion of a program or system that will handle the exception can be quite different or distant from the portion of the program that detected and generated the exceptional situation.

23.5 If it is necessary to pass information about the error that caused an exception, such information can be placed in the thrown object. The `catch` handler will then contain a parameter name through which that information could be referenced.

23.6 An object can be thrown without containing information to be passed; in this case, mere knowledge that an exception of this type has been thrown may provide sufficient information for the handler to do its job correctly.

23.7 A weakness with catching exceptions with `catch( ... )` is that you normally cannot be sure what the exception type is. Another weakness is that without a named parameter, there is no way to refer to the exception object inside the exception handler.

23.8 It is best to incorporate your exception-handling strategy into a system from the inception of the design process. It is difficult to add effective exception handling after a system has been implemented.

23.9 Another reason not to use exceptions for conventional flow of control is that these "additional" exceptions can get in the way of genuine error-type exceptions. It becomes more difficult for the programmer to keep track of the number of exception cases. For example, when a program processes an excessive variety of exceptions, can we really be sure of just what is being caught by a `catch( ... )`? Exceptional situations should be rare, not commonplace.

23.10 Use `catch( ... )` to perform recovery that does not depend on the type of the exception, such as releasing common resources. The exception can be rethrown to alert more specific enclosing `catch` blocks.

23.11   The C++ standard recommends that to make programs more robust, programmers should use the version of new that throws bad_alloc exceptions on failure.

23.12   The standard exception hierarchy is meant to serve as a starting point. Users can throw standard exceptions, throw exceptions derived from the standard exceptions or throw their own exceptions not derived from the standard exceptions.

ERROR-PREVENTION TIPS

23.1   The programmer determines the order in which the exception handlers are listed. This order can affect how exceptions originating in that try block are handled. If you are getting unexpected behavior in your program's handling of exceptions, it may be because an early catch block is intercepting and handling the exceptions before they reach your intended catch handler.

23.2   Using inheritance with exceptions enables an exception handler to catch related errors with a rather concise notation. One could certainly catch each type of pointer or reference to a derived-class exception object individually, but it is more concise to catch pointers or references to base-class exception objects instead. Also, catching pointers or references to derived-class exception objects individually is subject to error if the programmer forgets to explicitly test for one or more of the derived-class pointer or reference types.

23.3   To catch all exceptions that might be thrown in a try block, use catch(...).

SELF-REVIEW EXERCISES

23.1   List five common examples of exceptions.

23.2   Give several reasons why exception-handling techniques should not be used for conventional program control.

23.3   Why are exceptions appropriate for dealing with errors produced by library functions?

23.4   What is a "resource leak?"

23.5   If no exceptions are thrown in a try block, where does control proceed to after the try block completes execution?

23.6   What happens if an exception is thrown outside a try block?

23.7   Give a key advantage and a key disadvantage of using catch(...).

23.8   What happens if no catch handler matches the type of a thrown object?

23.9   What happens if several handlers match the type of the thrown object?

23.10   Why would a programmer specify a base-class type as the type of a catch handler, then throw objects of derived-class types?

23.11   How might a catch handler be written to process related types of errors without using inheritance among exception classes?

23.12   What pointer type is used in a catch handler to catch any exception of any pointer type?

23.13   Suppose a catch handler with a precise match to an exception object type is available. Under what circumstances might a different handler be executed for exception objects of that type?

23.14   Must throwing an exception cause program termination?

23.15   What happens when a catch handler throws an exception?

23.16   What does the statement throw; do?

23.17   How does the programmer restrict the exception types that can be thrown from a function?

23.18   What happens if a function does `throw` an exception of a type not allowed by the exception specification for the function?

23.19   What happens to the automatic objects that have been constructed in a `try` block when that block `throws` an exception?

ANSWERS TO SELF-REVIEW EXERCISES

23.1   Insufficient memory to satisfy a `new` request, array subscript out of bounds, arithmetic overflow, division by zero, invalid function parameters.

23.2   (a) Exception handling is designed to handle infrequently occurring situations that often result in program termination, so compiler writers are not required to implement exception handling to perform optimally.   (b) Flow of control with conventional control structures is generally clearer and more efficient than with exceptions.   (c) Problems can occur because the stack is unwound when an exception occurs and resources allocated prior to the exception may not be freed.   (d) The "additional" exceptions can get in the way of genuine error-type exceptions. It becomes more difficult for the programmer to keep track of the larger number of exception cases. What does a `catch(...)` really catch?

23.3   It is unlikely that a library function will perform error processing that will meet the unique needs of all users.

23.4   An aborting program could leave a resource in a state in which other programs would not be able to acquire the resource.

23.5   The exception handlers (in the `catch` blocks) for that `try` block are skipped and the program resumes execution after the last `catch` block.

23.6   An exception thrown outside a `try` block causes a call to `terminate`.

23.7   The form `catch(...)` catches any type of error thrown in a `try` block. An advantage is that no thrown error can slip by. A disadvantage is that the `catch` has no parameter, so it cannot reference information in the thrown object and cannot know the cause of the error.

23.8   This causes the search for a match to continue in the next enclosing `try` block. As this process continues, it may eventually be determined that there is no handler in the program that matches the type of the thrown object; in this case `terminate` is called, which by default calls `abort`. An alternative `terminate` function can be provided as an argument to `set_terminate`.

23.9   The first matching exception handler after the `try` block is executed.

23.10   This is a nice way to `catch` related types of exceptions.

23.11   Provide a single exception class and `catch` handler for a group of exceptions. As each exception occurs, the exception object can be created with different `private` data. The `catch` handler can examine these `private` data to distinguish the type of the exception.

23.12   `void *`.

23.13   A handler requiring standard conversions may appear before one with a precise match.

23.14   No, but it does terminate the block in which the exception is thrown.

23.15   The exception will be processed by a `catch` handler (if one exists) associated with the `try` block (if one exists) enclosing the `catch` handler that caused the exception.

23.16   It rethrows the exception.

23.17   Provide an exception specification listing the exception types that can be thrown from the function.

23.18   Function `unexpected` is called.

23.19   Through the process of stack unwinding, destructors are called for each of these objects.

EXERCISES

23.20   Under what circumstances would the programmer not provide a parameter name when defining the type of the object that will be caught by a handler?

23.21   A program contains the statement

```
throw;
```

Where would you normally expect to find such a statement? What if that statement appeared in a different part of the program?

23.22   Under what circumstances would you use the following statement?

```
catch(...) { throw; }
```

23.23   Compare and contrast exception handling with the various other error-processing schemes discussed in the text.

23.24   List the advantages of exception handling over conventional means of error processing.

23.25   Use inheritance to create a base exception class and various derived exception classes. Then show that a `catch` handler specifying the base class can `catch` derived-class exceptions.

23.26   Write a program designed to generate and handle a memory exhaustion error. Your program should loop on a request to create dynamic storage through operator `new`.

Introduction to Java Applications and Applets

Objectives

- To be able to write simple Java applications.
- To be able to use input and output statements.
- To observe some of Java's exciting capabilities through several demonstration applets provided with the Java 2 Software Development Kit.
- To understand the difference between an applet and an application.
- To be able to write simple Java applets.
- To be able to write simple Hypertext Markup Language (HTML) files to load an applet into the `appletviewer` or a World Wide Web browser.

Comment is free, but facts are sacred.
C. P. Scott

The creditor hath a better memory than the debtor.
James Howell

When faced with a decision, I always ask, "What would be the most fun?"
Peggy Walker

Classes struggle, some classes triumph, others are eliminated.
Mao Zedong

Outline

24.1 Introduction

We now proceed to study Java—a powerful object-oriented language that is fun to use for
novices but also appropriate for experienced programmers building substantial information
systems. Java is certain to become the language of choice in the new millennium for implementing Internet-based and Intranet-based applications as well as software for devices that
communicate over networks (such as cellular phones, pagers and personal digital assistants). Do not be surprised when your new stereo and other devices in your home will be
networked together using Java technology!

In the C chapters of this text we presented a thorough treatment of procedural programming and top-down program design. In the C++ chapters, we presented additional programming paradigms—object-based programming (with classes, encapsulation, objects, and
operator overloading), object-oriented programming (with inheritance and polymorphism),
and generic programming (with function templates and class templates). These programming paradigms are crucial for developing elegant, robust, and maintainable software systems. In the Java chapters we discuss graphics, graphical user interfaces, multimedia and
event-driven programming; Sun Microsystems developed Java with these popular technologies in mind.

Mastering these varied development paradigms and the technologies discussed in *C
How to Program: Fourth Edition* will help you build a solid foundation in programming.
We have worked hard to create what we hope will be an informative, entertaining and chal-
lenging learning experience for you.

An implementation of Java is available free at the Sun Web site

```
java.sun.com
```

These chapters are based on Sun's most recent Java release—the *Java 2 Platform*. Sun provides an implementation of the *Java 2 Platform* called the *Java 2 Software Development Kit (J2SDK), version 1.4* that includes the tools you need to write software in Java. Java's extraordinary portability means the programs in this book should work correctly with any version of J2SDK 1.4

In Chapters 24 through 30, we present Java programming in reasonably substantial depth for an introductory book like this. You will learn how to create Java programs called applications and applets; key differences between Java, C and C++; object-based and object-oriented programming in Java; graphics programming with a variety of colors, fonts, outline shapes, and filled shapes; graphical user interface (GUI) programming with Java's so-called Swing components; and multimedia programming with effects such as audio clips, image processing, image maps and animation.

24.2 Basics of a Typical Java Environment

Java systems generally consist of several parts: an environment, the language, the Java Applications Programming Interface (API), and various class libraries. The following discussion explains a typical Java program development environment as shown in Fig. 24.1.

Java programs normally go through five phases to be executed (Fig. 24.1). These are: *edit, compile, load, verify* and *execute*. If you are not using UNIX, Windows 95/98 or Windows NT, refer to the manuals for your system's Java environment, or ask your instructor how to accomplish these tasks in your environment (that will probably be similar to the environment in Fig. 24.1).

Phase 1 consists of editing a file. This is accomplished with an *editor program*. The programmer types a Java program using the editor and makes corrections if necessary. When the programmer specifies that the file in the editor should be saved, the program is stored on a secondary storage device such as a disk. Java program file names end with the `.java` *extension*. Two editors widely used on UNIX systems are `vi` and emacs. On Windows 95/98 and Windows NT simple edit programs like the DOS Edit command and the Windows Notepad will suffice. Java integrated development environments (IDEs) such as Sun's Forte for Java, Borland's JBuilder, Symantec's Visual Cafe and Microsoft's Visual J++ have built-in editors that are smoothly integrated into the programming environment. We assume the reader knows how to edit a file.

In Phase 2, the programmer gives the command `javac` to *compile* the program. The Java compiler translates the Java program into *bytecodes*—the language understood by the Java interpreter. To compile a program called `Welcome.java`, type

```
javac Welcome.java
```

at the command window of your system (i.e., the MS-DOS prompt in Windows 95/98 and Windows NT or the shell prompt in UNIX). If the program compiles correctly, a file called `Welcome.class` is produced. This is the file containing the bytecodes that will be interpreted during the execution phase.

Phase 3 is called *loading*. The program must first be placed in memory before it can be executed. This is done by the *class loader*, which takes the `.class` file (or files) containing the bytecodes and transfers it to memory. The `.class` file can be loaded from a disk on your system or over a network (such as your local university or company network or even the Internet). There are two types of programs for which the class loader loads `.class`

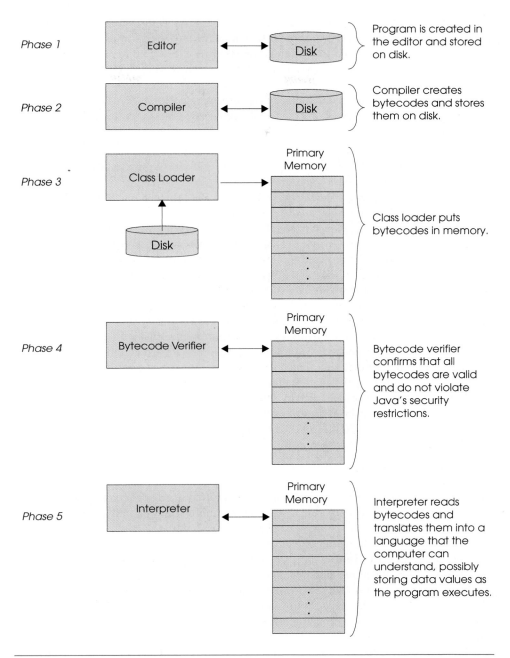

Phase 1   Editor ◄──► Disk   } Program is created in the editor and stored on disk.

Phase 2   Compiler ◄──► Disk   } Compiler creates bytecodes and stores them on disk.

Phase 3   Class Loader ──► Primary Memory

Disk ──► Class Loader

} Class loader puts bytecodes in memory.

Phase 4   Bytecode Verifier ◄──► Primary Memory   } Bytecode verifier confirms that all bytecodes are valid and do not violate Java's security restrictions.

Phase 5   Interpreter ◄──► Primary Memory   } Interpreter reads bytecodes and translates them into a language that the computer can understand, possibly storing data values as the program executes.

Fig. 24.1   A typical Java environment.

files—*applications* and *applets*. A Java application is a program such as a word processor program, a spreadsheet program, a drawing program, an email program, etc. that is normally stored and executed from the user's local computer. A Java applet is a small program that is normally stored on a remote computer that users connect to via a World Wide Web browser. Applets are loaded from a remote computer into the browser, executed in the browser and discarded when execution completes. To execute an applet again, the user must point their browser at the appropriate location on the World Wide Web and reload the program into the browser.

Applications are loaded into memory and executed using the *Java interpreter* via the command *java*. When executing a Java application called `Welcome`, the command

    java Welcome

invokes the interpreter for the `Welcome` application and causes the class loader to load information used in the `Welcome` program.

The class loader also is executed when a Java applet is loaded into a World Wide Web browser such as *Netscape's Communicator, Microsoft's Internet Explorer* or *Sun's Hot-Java*. Browsers are used to view documents on the World Wide Web called *HTML (Hypertext Markup Language)* documents. HTML is used to format a document in a manner that is easily understood by the browser application (we will introduce HTML in Section 24.7; for a detailed treatment of HTML and other Internet programming technologies, please see our text *Internet and World Wide Web How to Program*). An HTML document may refer to a Java applet. When the browser sees an applet referenced in an HTML document, the browser launches the Java class loader to load the applet (normally from the location where the HTML document is stored). Browsers that support Java each have a built-in Java interpreter. Once the applet is loaded, the browser's Java interpreter executes the applet. Applets can also be executed from the command line using the *appletviewer command* provided with the J2SDK—the set of tools including the compiler (`javac`), interpreter (`java`), `appletviewer` and other tools used by Java programmers. Like Netscape Communicator, Internet Explorer and HotJava, the `appletviewer` requires an HTML document to invoke an applet. For example, if the `Welcome.html` file refers to the `Welcome` applet, the `appletviewer` command is used as follows:

    appletviewer Welcome.html

This causes the class loader to load the information used in the `Welcome` applet. The `appletviewer` is commonly referred to as a "minimal browser"—it only knows how to interpret applets.

Before the bytecodes in an applet are executed by the Java interpreter built into a browser or the `appletviewer`, they are verified by the *bytecode verifier* in Phase 4 (this also happens in applications that download bytecodes from a network). This ensures that the bytecodes for classes that are loaded from the Internet (referred to as *downloaded classes*) are valid and that they do not violate Java's security restrictions. Java enforces strong security because Java programs arriving over the network should not be able to cause damage to your files and your system (as computer viruses might).

Finally, in Phase 5, the computer, under the control of its CPU, interprets the program one bytecode at a time, thus performing the actions specified by the program.

Programs may not work on the first try. Each of the preceding phases can fail because of various errors that we will discuss in this text. For example, an executing program might attempt to divide by zero (an illegal operation in Java just as it is in arithmetic). This would cause the Java program to print an error message. The programmer would return to the edit phase, make the necessary corrections and proceed through the remaining phases again to determine if the corrections work properly.

Common Programming Error 24.1

Errors like division-by-zero occur as a program runs, so these errors are called run-time er-rors *or* execution-time errors. *Fatal run-time errors cause programs to terminate immediately without having successfully performed their jobs.* Nonfatal run-time errors *allow programs to run to completion, often producing incorrect results.*

Most programs in Java input and/or output data. When we say that a program prints a result, we normally mean that the result is displayed on a screen. Data may be output to other devices such as disks and hardcopy printers.

24.3 General Notes about Java and This Book

Java is a powerful language. Experienced programmers sometimes take pride in being able to create some weird, contorted, convoluted usage of a language. This is a poor program-ming practice. It makes programs more difficult to read, more likely to behave strangely, more difficult to test and debug, and more difficult to adapt to changing requirements. These chapters are also geared for novice programmers, so we stress *clarity*. The following is our first Java "good programming practice."

Good Programming Practice 24.1

Write your Java programs in a simple and straightforward manner. This is sometimes re-ferred to as KIS *("keep it simple").* Do not "stretch" the language by trying bizarre usages.

You have heard that Java is a portable language, and that programs written in Java can run on many different computers. *Portability is an elusive goal.* The ANSI C standard doc-ument contains a lengthy list of portability issues, and complete books have been written that discuss portability.

Portability Tip 24.1

Although it is easier to write portable programs in Java than in most other programming lan-guages, there are differences among compilers, interpreters and computers that can make portability difficult to achieve. Simply writing programs in Java does not guarantee porta-bility. The programmer will occasionally need to deal directly with compiler and computer variations.

Error-Prevention Tip 24.1

Always test your Java programs on all systems on which you intend to run those programs.

We have done a careful walkthrough of Sun's Java documentation and audited our pre-sentation against it for completeness and accuracy. However, Java is a rich language, and there are some subtleties in the language and some topics we have not covered. If you need additional technical details on Java, we suggest that you read the most current Java docu-mentation available over the Internet at `java.sun.com`.

Good Programming Practice 24.2

Read the documentation for the version of Java you are using. Refer to this documentation frequently to be sure you are aware of the rich collection of Java features and that you are using these features correctly.

Good Programming Practice 24.3

Your computer and compiler are good teachers. If after carefully reading your Java documentation manual you are not sure how a feature of Java works, experiment and see what happens. Study each error or warning message you get when you compile your programs and correct the programs to eliminate these messages.

We explain how Java works in its current implementation. Perhaps the most striking problem with the early versions of Java is that Java programs execute interpretively on the client's machine. Interpreters execute slowly compared to fully compiled machine code.

Performance Tip 24.1

Interpreters have an advantage over compilers for the Java world, namely that an interpreted program can begin execution immediately as soon as it is downloaded to the client's machine, whereas a source program to be compiled must first suffer a potentially long delay as the program is compiled before it can be executed.

Although only Java interpreters were available to execute bytecodes at the client's site on early Java systems, Java compilers have been written for most popular platforms. These compilers take the Java bytecodes (or in some cases the Java source code) and compile them into the native machine code of the client's machine. These compiled programs perform comparably to compiled C or C++ code. There are not compilers for every Java platform, so Java programs will not perform at the same level on all platforms.

Applets present some more interesting issues. Remember, an applet could be coming from virtually any *Web server* in the world. So the applet will have to be able to run on any possible Java platform. Short, fast-executing Java applets can certainly still be interpreted. But what about more substantial, compute-intensive applets. Here the user may be willing to suffer the compilation delay to get better execution performance. For some especially performance-intensive applets the user may have no choice; interpreted code would run too slowly for the applet to perform properly, so the applet would have to be compiled.

An intermediate step between interpreters and compilers is a *just-in-time (JIT) compiler* that, as the interpreter runs, produces compiled code for the programs and executes the programs in machine language rather than reinterpreting them. JIT compilers do not produce machine language that is as efficient as a full compiler. Full compilers for Java are under development now. For the latest information on high-speed Java program translation you may want to read about Sun's *HotSpot* compiler, visit

```
java.sun.com/products/hotspot/
```

For organizations wanting to do heavy-duty information systems development, Integrated Development Environments (IDEs) are available from the major software suppliers. The IDEs provide many tools for supporting the software development process. Several Java IDEs on the market today are just as powerful as those available for C and C++ systems development. This is a strong signal that Java has been accepted as a viable language for developing substantial software systems.

24.4 A Simple Program: Printing a Line of Text

We begin by considering a simple Java *application* that displays a line of text. An application is a program that executes using the `java` interpreter (discussed later in this section). The program and its output are shown in Fig. 24.2.

```
1   // Fig. 24.2: Welcome1.java
2   // A first program in Java
3
4   public class Welcome1 {
5      public static void main( String args[] )
6      {
7         System.out.println( "Welcome to Java Programming!" );
8      } // end main
9   } // end class Welcome1
```

```
Welcome to Java Programming!
```

Fig. 24.2   A first program in Java.

This program illustrates several important features of the Java language. We consider each line of the program in detail. Each program has line numbers for the reader's convenience; those line numbers are not part of Java programs. Line 7 does the "real work" of the program, namely displaying the phrase `Welcome to Java Programming!` on the screen. But let us consider each line in order. Line 1

```
// Fig. 24.2: Welcome1.java
```

begins with //, indicating that the remainder of the line is a *comment*. We begin every program with a comment indicating figure number and file name. As in C++, a comment that begins with // is called a *single-line comment* because the comment terminates at the end of the current line.

Java also supports C-style multiple-line comment (delimited with /* and */), which we introduced in Chapter 2. A similar form of comment called a *documentation comment* is delimited with /** and */.

Common Programming Error 24.2

Forgetting one of the delimiters of a multiple-line comment is a syntax error.

Java programmers generally use C++-style single-line comments in preference to C-style comments. Throughout this book, we use C++-style single-line comments. Java introduced the documentation comment syntax to enable programmers to highlight portions of programs that the *javadoc* utility program (provided by Sun Microsystems with the Java 2 Software Development Kit) can read and use to prepare documentation for your program automatically. There are subtle issues to using `javadoc`-style comments properly in a program. We do not use `javadoc`-style comments in-line in the book.

Line 4

```
public class Welcome1 {
```

begins a *class definition* for class `Welcome1`. Every program in Java consists of at least one class definition that is defined by you—the programmer. These classes are known as *programmer-defined classes* or *user-defined classes*. In Chapter 26, Java Object-Based Programming, we discuss programs that contain several programmer-defined classes. The *class keyword* introduces a class definition in Java and is immediately followed by the *class name* (Welcome1 in this program). Keywords (or *reserved words*) are reserved for use by Java (we discuss the keywords throughout the text) and are always spelled with all lowercase letters. By convention, all class names in Java begin with a capital first letter and have a capital first letter for every word in the class name (e.g., SampleClassName). The name of the class is called an *identifier*. An identifier is a series of characters consisting of letters, digits, underscores (_) and dollar signs ($) that does not begin with a digit and does not contain any spaces. Some valid identifiers are Welcome1, $value, _value, m_inputField1 and button7. The name 7button is not a valid identifier because it begins with a digit, and the name input field is not a valid identifier because it contains a space. Java is *case sensitive*—uppercase and lowercase letters are different, so a1 and A1 are different identifiers.

Common Programming Error 24.3

Java is case sensitive. Not using the proper uppercase and lowercase letters for an identifier is normally a syntax error.

Good Programming Practice 24.4

By convention, you should always begin a class name with a capital first letter.

Good Programming Practice 24.5

When reading a Java program, look for identifiers that start with capital first letters. These normally represent Java classes.

Software Engineering Observation 24.1

Avoid using identifiers containing dollar signs ($) as these are often used by the compiler to create identifier names.

In Chapters 24 and 25, every class we define begins with the *public keyword*. For now, we will simply require this keyword. The public keyword is discussed in detail in Chapter 26, where we also discuss classes that do not begin with keyword public. [*Note:* Several times early in this text, we ask you to simply mimic certain Java features we introduce as you write your own Java programs. We specifically do this when it is not yet important to know all the details of a feature to use that feature in Java. All programmers initially learn how to program by mimicking what other programmers have done before them. For each detail we ask you to mimic, we indicate where the full discussion will be presented later in the text.]

When you save your class definition in a file, the class name must be used as part of the file name. For our application, the file name is Welcome1.java. All Java class definitions are stored in files ending with the .java file name extension.

Common Programming Error 24.4

For a public class, it is an error if the file name is not identical to the class name in both spelling and capitalization. Therefore, it is also an error for a file to contain two or more public classes.

Common Programming Error 24.5

It is an error not to end a file name with the .java extension for a file containing an application's class definition. The Java compiler will not be able to compile the class definition.

A *left brace* (at the end of line 4 in this program), {, begins the *body* of every class definition. A corresponding *right brace* (at line 9 in this program), }, must end each class definition. Notice that lines 5 through 8 are indented. This is a spacing convention used to make programs more readable. We define each spacing convention as a *Good Programming Practice*.

Common Programming Error 24.6

If braces do not occur in matching pairs, the compiler indicates an error.

Good Programming Practice 24.6

Whenever you type an opening left brace, {, in your program, immediately type the closing right brace, }, then reposition the cursor between the braces to begin typing the body. This helps prevent missing braces.

Good Programming Practice 24.7

Indent the entire body of each class definition one "level" of indentation between the left brace, {, and the right brace, }, that define the body of the class. This emphasizes the structure of the class definition and helps make the class definition easier to read.

Good Programming Practice 24.8

Set a convention for the indent size you prefer, then uniformly apply that convention. The Tab key may be used to create indents, but tab stops may vary between editors. We recommend using either 1/4-inch tab stops or (preferably) three spaces to form a level of indent.

Line 5

```
public static void main( String args[] )
```

is a part of every Java application. Java applications automatically begin executing at `main`. The parentheses after `main` indicate that `main` is a program *method*, or what a C or C++ programmer would call a function. Java class definitions normally contain one or more methods. For a Java application class, exactly one of those methods must be called `main` and must be defined as shown in line 5; otherwise, the `java` interpreter will not execute the application. Methods are able to perform tasks and return information when they complete their tasks. The *void* keyword indicates that this method will perform a task (displaying a line of text in this program), but will not return any information when it completes its task. We will see that many methods return information when they complete their task. Methods are explained in detail in Chapter 25. For now, simply mimic `main`'s first line in each of your Java applications.

The left brace, {, in line 6 begins the *body of the method definition*. A corresponding right brace, }, must end the method definition's body (line 8 of the program). Notice that the line in the body of the method is indented between these braces.

Good Programming Practice 24.9

Indent the entire body of each method definition one "level" of indentation between the left brace, {, and the right brace, }, that define the body of the method. This makes the structure of the method stand out and helps make the method definition easier to read.

Line 7

```
System.out.println( "Welcome to Java Programming!" );
```

instructs the computer to print the *string* of characters contained between the double quotation marks. A string is sometimes called a *character string*, a *message* or a *string literal*. We refer to characters between double quotation marks generically as strings. Whitespace characters in strings are not ignored by the compiler.

System.out is known as the *standard output object*. System.out allows Java applications to display strings and other types of information in the *command window* from which the Java application is executed. On Microsoft Windows 95/98, the command window is the *MS-DOS prompt*. On Microsoft Windows NT, the command window is the *Command Prompt*. On UNIX, the command window is normally called a *command window*, a *command tool*, a *shell tool* or a *shell*. On computers running an operating system that does not have a command window (such as a Macintosh), the java interpreter normally displays a window containing the information displayed by the program.

Method *System.out.println displays (or prints) a line* of text in the command window. When System.out.println completes its task, it positions the *output cursor* (the location where the next character will be displayed) to the beginning of the next line in the command window (this is similar to your pressing the *Enter* key when typing in a text editor—the cursor is repositioned at the beginning of the next line in your file).

The entire line, including System.out.println, its *argument* in the parentheses (the string) and the *semicolon* (;), is called a *statement*. Every statement must end with a semicolon (also known as the *statement terminator*). When this statement executes, it displays the message Welcome to Java Programming! in the command window.

Common Programming Error 24.7

Omitting the semicolon at the end of a statement is a syntax error.

Error-Prevention Tip 24.2

When the compiler reports a syntax error, the error may not be on the line indicated by the error messages. First, check the line where the error was reported. If that line does not contain syntax errors, check the preceding several lines in the program.

We are now ready to compile and execute our program. To compile the program, we open a command window, change to the directory where the program is stored and type

```
javac Welcome1.java
```

If the program contains no syntax errors, the preceding command creates a new file called Welcome1.class containing the Java bytecodes that represent our application. These bytecodes will be interpreted by the java interpreter when we tell it to execute the program by typing the command

```
java Welcome1
```

which launches the java interpreter and indicates that it should load the .class file for class Welcome1. Note that the .class file name extension is omitted from the preceding command; otherwise the interpreter will not execute the program. The interpreter automatically calls method main. Next, the statement at line 7 of main displays "Welcome to Java Programming!" Figure 24.3 shows the execution of the application in a Microsoft Windows **Command Prompt** window.

Fig. 24.3   Executing the `Welcome1` application in a Microsoft Windows **Command Prompt**.

Although this first program displays output in the command window, most Java applications that display output use windows or *dialog boxes* to display output. For example, World Wide Web browsers such as Netscape Communicator or Microsoft Internet Explorer display Web pages in their own windows. Email programs typically allow you to type messages in a window provided by the email program or read messages you receive in a window provided by the email program. Dialog boxes are windows that typically are used to display important messages to the user of an application. Java 2 already includes class *JOptionPane* that allows you to easily display a dialog box containing information. The program of Fig. 24.4 displays a similar string to the one shown in Fig. 24.2 in a predefined dialog box called a *message dialog*. Notice that this new version of the program also makes use of the C-style \n *escape sequence* to insert newline characters into the string.

```java
1  // Fig. 24.4: Welcome2.java
2  // Printing multiple lines in a dialog box
3  import javax.swing.JOptionPane;  // import class JOptionPane
4
5  public class Welcome2 {
6     public static void main( String args[] )
7     {
8        JOptionPane.showMessageDialog(
9           null, "Welcome\nto\nJava\nProgramming!" );
10
11       System.exit( 0 );  // terminate the program
12    } // end main
13 } // end class Welcome2
```

```
Message                         ×
 i    Welcome
      to
      Java
      Programming!
          OK
```

Fig. 24.4   Displaying multiple lines in a dialog box.

One of the great strengths of Java is its rich set of predefined classes that programmers can reuse rather than "reinventing the wheel." We use a large number of these classes in this book. Java's many predefined classes are grouped into categories of related classes called *packages*. The packages are referred to collectively as the *Java class library* or the *Java applications programming interface (Java API)*. Class JOptionPane is defined for us in a package called *javax.swing*.

Line 3

```
import javax.swing.JOptionPane;
```

is an *import* statement. The compiler uses import statements to identify and load classes required to compile a Java program. When you use classes from the Java API, the compiler attempts to ensure that you use them correctly. The import statements help the compiler locate the classes you intend to use. Each piece of the package name is a directory (or folder) on disk. All the packages in the Java API are stored in the directory java or javax that contain many subdirectories including swing (a subdirectory of javax). Packages are discussed in detail in Chapter 26, Java Object-Based Programming.

The preceding line tells the compiler to load the *JOptionPane* class from the *javax.swing* package. This package contains many classes that help Java programmers define *graphical user interfaces (GUIs)* for their application. *GUI components* facilitate data entry by the user of your program and formatting or presenting data outputs to the user of your program. For example, Fig. 24.5 contains a Netscape Communicator window. In the window, there is a bar containing *menus* (**File**, **Edit**, **View**, etc.). Below the menu bar there is a set of *buttons* that each have a defined task in Netscape Communicator. Below the buttons there is a *text field* in which the user can type the name of the World Wide Web site to visit. To the left of the text field is a *label* that indicates the purpose of the text field. The menus, buttons, text fields and labels are part of Netscape Communicator's GUI. They enable you to interact with the Communicator program. Java contains classes that implement the GUI components described here and others that will be described in Chapter 29, Java Graphical User Interface Components. In main, lines 8 and 9

```
JOptionPane.showMessageDialog(
    null, "Welcome\nto\nJava\nProgramming!" );
```

indicate a call to method *showMessageDialog* of class JOptionPane. The method requires two arguments. When a method requires multiple arguments, the arguments are separated with *commas* (,). Until we discuss JOptionPane in detail in Chapter 29, the first argument will always be the keyword *null*. The second argument is the string to display.

Good Programming Practice 24.10

Place a space after each comma in an argument list (,) to make programs more readable.

Method JOptionPane.showMessageDialog is a special method of the class JOptionPane called a *static method*. Such methods are always called using their class name followed by a dot operator (.) and the method name. We discuss static methods in Chapter 26, Java Object-Based Programming.

Executing the preceding statement displays the dialog box shown in Fig. 24.6. The *title bar* of the dialog contains the string **Message** to indicate that the dialog is presenting a message to the user. The dialog box automatically includes an **OK** button that allows the user to *dismiss (hide) the dialog* by pressing the button. This is accomplished by positioning the *mouse cursor* (also called the *mouse pointer*) over the **OK** button and clicking the mouse.

button   label   menu   menu bar   text field

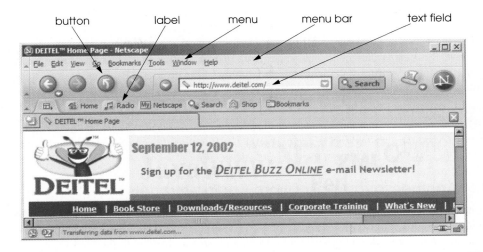

Fig. 24.5   Netscape Navigator window with GUI components.

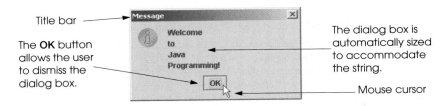

Title bar

The **OK** button
allows the user
to dismiss the
dialog box.

The dialog box is
automatically sized
to accommodate
the string.

Mouse cursor

Fig. 24.6   Message dialog.

Remember that all statements in Java end with a semicolon (;). Therefore, lines 8 and
9 represent one statement. Java allows large statements to be split over many lines. However, you cannot split a statement in the middle of an identifier or in the middle of a string.

Common Programming Error 24.8

Splitting a statement in the middle of an identifier or a string is a syntax error.

Line 11

```
System.exit( 0 );  // terminate the program
```

uses `static` method *exit* of class `System` to terminate the application. This line is required in any application that displays a graphical user interface to terminate the application. Notice once again the syntax used to call the method—the class name (`System`), a dot
(`.`) and the method name (`exit`). Remember that identifiers starting with capital first letters
normally represent class names. So, you can assume that `System` is a class. The argument
0 to method `exit` indicates that the application terminated successfully (a non-zero value
normally indicates that an error occurred). This value is passed to the command window
that executed the program. This is useful if the program is executed from a batch file (on
Windows 95/98/NT systems) or a shell script (on UNIX systems). Batch files and shell

scripts are typically used to execute several programs in sequence such that when the first program ends, the next program begins execution automatically. For more information on batch files or shell scripts, see your operating system's documentation.

Class `System` is part of the package *java.lang*. Notice that class `System` is not imported with an `import` statement at the beginning of the program. Package `java.lang` is automatically imported in every Java program.

Common Programming Error 24.9

Forgetting to call `System.exit` in an application that displays a graphical user interface prevents the program from terminating properly. This normally results in the command window preventing you from typing any other commands.

24.5 Another Java Application: Adding Integers

Our next application inputs two integers (whole numbers) typed by a user at the keyboard, computes the sum of these values and displays the result. As the user types each integer and presses the *Enter* key, the integer is read into the program and added to the total.

This program uses another predefined dialog box from class `JOptionPane` called an *input dialog* that allows the user to input a value for use in the program. The program also uses a message dialog to display the results of the addition. Figure 24.7 shows the application and sample screen captures.

```
1  // Fig. 24.7: Addition.java
2  // An addition program
3
4  import javax.swing.JOptionPane;  // import class JOptionPane
5
6  public class Addition {
7     public static void main( String args[] )
8     {
9        String firstNumber,     // first string entered by user
10              secondNumber;    // second string entered by user
11       int number1,            // first number to add
12           number2,            // second number to add
13           sum;                // sum of number1 and number2
14
15       // read in first number from user as a string
16       firstNumber =
17          JOptionPane.showInputDialog( "Enter first integer" );
18
19       // read in second number from user as a string
20       secondNumber =
21          JOptionPane.showInputDialog( "Enter second integer" );
22
23       // convert numbers from type String to type int
24       number1 = Integer.parseInt( firstNumber );
25       number2 = Integer.parseInt( secondNumber );
26
27       // add the numbers
28       sum = number1 + number2;
```

Fig. 24.7   An addition program "in action." (Part 1 of 2.)

```
29
30        // display the results
31        JOptionPane.showMessageDialog(
32          null, "The sum is " + sum, "Results",
33          JOptionPane.PLAIN_MESSAGE );
34
35        System.exit( 0 );    // terminate the program
36      } // end main
37    } // end class Addition
```

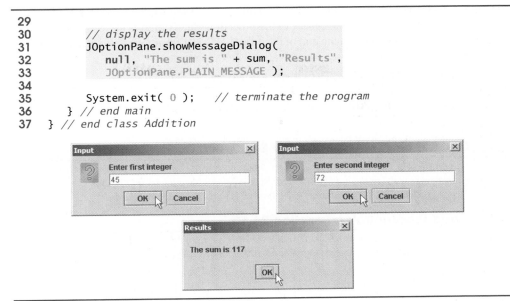

Fig. 24.7   An addition program "in action." (Part 2 of 2.)

Line 4

```
import javax.swing.JOptionPane;   // import class JOptionPane
```

specifies to the compiler where to locate class `JOptionPane` for use in this application.
As stated earlier, every Java program consists of at least one class definition. Line 6

```
public class Addition {
```

begins the definitions of class `Addition`. The file name for this `public` class must be Ad-
dition.java.

Remember that all class definitions start with an opening left brace (end of line 6), {,
and end with a closing right brace, } (line 37).

As stated earlier, every application begins execution with method `main` (line 7). The
left brace (line 8) marks the beginning of `main`'s body and the corresponding right brace
(line 36) marks the end of `main`.

Lines 9 and 10

```
String firstNumber,     // first string entered by user
       secondNumber;    // second string entered by user
```

are a *declaration*. The words `firstNumber` and `secondNumber` are the names of *variables*. All variables must be declared with a name and a data type before they can be used
in a program. This declaration specifies that the variables `firstNumber` and `secondNum-
ber` are data of type *String* (from package java.lang), which means that these variables
will hold strings. A variable name can be any valid identifier. Declarations end with a semicolon (;) and can be split over several lines with each variable in the declaration separated
by a comma (i.e., a *comma-separated list* of variable names). Several variables of the same

type may be declared in one declaration or in multiple declarations. We could have written two declarations, one for each variable, but the preceding declaration is more concise. Notice the single-line comments at the end of each line. This is a common syntax used by programmers to indicate the purpose of each variable in the program.

Good Programming Practice 24.11

Choosing meaningful variable names helps a program to be "self-documenting" (i.e., it becomes easier to understand a program simply by reading it rather than having to read manuals or use excessive comments).

Good Programming Practice 24.12

By convention, variable name identifiers begin with a lowercase first letter. As with class names every word in the name after the first word should begin with a capital first letter. For example, identifier firstNumber *has a capital N in its second word* Number.

Good Programming Practice 24.13

Some programmers prefer to declare each variable on a separate line. This format allows for easy insertion of a descriptive comment next to each declaration.

Lines 11 through 13

```
int number1,    // first number to add
    number2,    // second number to add
    sum;        // sum of number1 and number2
```

declare that variables number1, number2 and sum are data of type *int*.

We will soon discuss the data types float and double for specifying real numbers and variables of type char for specifying character data. A char variable may hold only a single lowercase letter, a single uppercase letter, a single digit, or a single special character such as x, $, 7, * and escape sequences (such as the newline character \n). Java is also capable of representing characters from many other languages.

Types such as int, double and char are often called *primitive data types* or *built-in data types*. Primitive type names are keywords. The eight primitive types (boolean, char, byte, short, int, long, float and double) are summarized in Chapter 25.

Lines 15 through 17

```
// read in first number from user as a string
firstNumber =
    JOptionPane.showInputDialog( "Enter first integer" );
```

read from the user a String representing the first of the two integers that will be added. Method JOptionPane.showInputDialog displays the following input dialog:

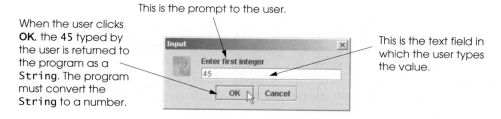

The argument to `showInputDialog` indicates to the user what to do in the text field. This message is called a *prompt* because it directs the user to take a specific action. The user types characters in the text field, then clicks the **OK** button to return the string to the program. [If you type and nothing appears in the text field, position the mouse pointer in the text field and click the mouse to activate the text field.] Unfortunately, Java does not provide a simple form of input that is analogous to displaying output in the command window with `System.out.print` and `System.out.println`. For this reason, we normally receive input from a user through a GUI component (an input dialog in this program).

Technically, the user can type anything in the text field of the input. For this program, if the user either types a noninteger value or clicks the **Cancel** button, a run-time logic error will occur.

The result of the call to `JOptionPane.showInputDialog` (a `String` containing the characters typed by the user) is given to variable `firstNumber` with the *assignment operator* `=`. The statement is read as, "`firstNumber` *gets* the value of `JOptionPane.showInputDialog( "Enter first integer" )`." The = operator is a *binary operator* because it has two *operands*—`firstNumber` and the result of the expression `JOptionPane.showInputDialog( "Enter first integer" )`. This whole statement is called an *assignment statement* because it assigns a value to a variable. The expression to the right side of the assignment operator = is always evaluated first.

Lines 19 through 21

```
// read in second number from user as a string
secondNumber =
    JOptionPane.showInputDialog( "Enter second integer" );
```

displays an input dialog in which the user types a `String` representing the second of the two integers that will be added.

Lines 23 through 25

```
// convert numbers from type String to type int
number1 = Integer.parseInt( firstNumber );
number2 = Integer.parseInt( secondNumber );
```

convert the two strings input by the user to `int` values that can be used in a calculation. Method *Integer.parseInt* (a `static` method of class `Integer`) converts its `String` argument to an integer. Class `Integer` is part of the package `java.lang`. The integer returned by `Integer.parseInt` in line 24 is assigned to variable `number1`. Any subsequent references to `number1` in the program use this same integer value. The integer returned by `Integer.parseInt` in line 25 is assigned to variable `number2`. Any subsequent references to `number2` in the program use this same integer value.

The assignment statement at line 28

```
sum = number1 + number2;
```

calculates the sum of the variables `number1` and `number2`, and assigns the result to variable `sum` using the assignment operator `=`. The statement is read as, "`sum` *gets* the value of `number1 + number2`." Most calculations are performed in assignment statements.

 Good Programming Practice 24.14

Place spaces on either side of a binary operator. This makes the operator stand out and makes the program more readable.

After performing the calculation, lines 31 through 33

```
JOptionPane.showMessageDialog(
    null, "The sum is " + sum, "Results",
    JOptionPane.PLAIN_MESSAGE );
```

use method `JOptionPane.showMessageDialog` to display the result of the addition. The expression

```
"The sum is " + sum
```

from the preceding statement uses the operator + to "add" a string (the literal `"The sum is "`) and `sum` (the `int` variable containing the result of the addition in line 28). Java has a version of the + operator for *string concatenation* that enables a string and a value of another data type (including another string) to be concatenated—the result of this operation is a new (and normally longer) string. If we assume `sum` contains the value 117, the expression evaluates as follows: Java determines that the two operands of the + operator (the string `"The sum is "` and the integer `sum`) are different types and one of them is a string. Next, `sum` is automatically converted to a string and concatenated with `"The sum is "`, which results in the string `"The sum is 117"`. This string is displayed in the dialog box. Note that the automatic conversion of integer `sum` only occurs because it is concatenated with the string literal `"The sum is "`. Also note that the space between `is` and `117` is part of the string `"The sum is "`.

Common Programming Error 24.10

Confusing the + operator used for string concatenation with the + operator used for addition can lead to strange results. For example, assuming integer variable y has the value 5, the expression "y + 2 = " + y + 2 results in the string "y + 2 = 52", not "y + 2 = 7", because first the value of y is concatenated with the string "y + 2 = ", then the value 2 is concatenated with the new larger string "y + 2 = 5". The expression "y + 2 = " + (y + 2) produces the desired result.

The version of method `showMessageDialog` used in Fig. 24.7 is different from the one discussed in Fig. 24.4 in that it requires four arguments. The following dialog box illustrates two of the four arguments. As with the first version, the first argument will always be `null` until we discuss class `JOptionPane` in detail in Chapter 29. The second argument is the message to display. The third argument is the string to display in the title bar of the dialog. The fourth argument (`JOptionPane.PLAIN_MESSAGE`) is a value indicating the type of message dialog to display—this 'type of message dialog does not display an icon to the left of the message.

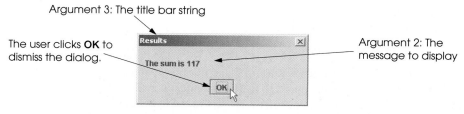

The message dialog types are shown in Fig. 24.8. All message dialog types except `PLAIN_MESSAGE` dialogs display an icon to the user indicating the type of message.

Message dialog type	Icon	Description
`JOptionPane.ERROR_MESSAGE`		Displays a dialog that indicates an error to the application user.
`JOptionPane.INFORMATION_MESSAGE`		Displays a dialog with an informational message to the application user—the user can simply dismiss the dialog.
`JOptionPane.WARNING_MESSAGE`		Displays a dialog that warns the application user of a potential problem.
`JOptionPane.QUESTION_MESSAGE`		Displays a dialog that poses a question to the application user. This normally requires a response such as clicking a **Yes** or **No** button.
`JOptionPane.PLAIN_MESSAGE`	no icon	Displays a dialog that simply contains a message with no icon.

Fig. 24.8   `JOptionPane` constants for message dialogs.

24.6 Sample Applets from the Java 2 Software Development Kit

Let us now take a look at another type of Java program: the Java applet. We begin our introduction to Java applets by considering several samples provided with the Java 2 Software Development Kit (J2SDK) version 1.4. The applets demonstrate a small portion of Java's powerful capabilities. Each J2SDK sample program also comes with its Java *source code*—the .java files containing the Java applet programs. This source code will be helpful as you enhance your Java knowledge—you can read the source code provided to learn new and exciting features of Java. Remember, all programmers initially learn new programming concepts by mimicking the use of those concepts in existing programs. The J2SDK comes with many such programs and there are a tremendous number of Java resources on the Internet and World Wide Web that include Java source code.

The demonstration programs provided with the J2SDK are located in your J2SDK install directory in a subdirectory called **demo**. For the Java 2 Software Development Kit version 1.4, the default location of the **demo** directory on Windows is

       `c:\j2sdk1.4.1\demo`

On UNIX/Linux/Mac OS X, it is the directory in which you install the J2SDK followed by `j2sdk1.4.1/demo`—for example,

       `/usr/local/j2sdk1.4.1/demo`

For other platforms, there will be a similar directory (or folder) structure. This chapter assumes that the J2SDK is installed in `c:\j2sdk1.4.1` on Windows and in your home directory in ~/j2sdk1.4.1 on UNIX/Linux/Max OS X.[1]

---

1. You may need to update these locations to reflect your chosen installation directory and disk drive, or a different version of the J2SDK.

If you are using a Java development tool that does not come with the Sun Java demos, you can download the J2SDK (with the demos) from the Sun Microsystems Java Web site

```
java.sun.com/j2se/1.4.1/
```

24.6.1 The TicTacToe Applet

The first applet we demonstrate from the J2SDK demos is the TicTacToe applet, which allows you to play Tic-Tac-Toe against the computer. To execute this applet, open a command window (MS-DOS Prompt on Windows 95/98/ME, Command Prompt on Windows NT/2000/XP or a terminal window/shell on UNIX/Linux/Max OS X) and change directories to the J2SDK's demo directory. Each operating system mentioned here uses the command *cd* to *change directories*. For example,

```
cd c:\j2sdk1.4.1\demo
```

changes to the demo directory on Windows and

```
cd ~/j2sdk1.4.1/demo
```

changes to the demo directory on UNIX/Linux/Max OS X.

The demo directory contains several subdirectories. You can list these directories by issuing in the command window the dir command on Windows or the ls command on UNIX/Linux/Max OS X. We discuss the directories *applets* and *jfc*. The applets directory contains many demonstration applets. The jfc (Java Foundation Classes) directory contains many examples of Java's graphics and GUI features (some of these examples are also applets). Change directories to the applets directory by issuing the command

```
cd applets
```

on either Windows or UNIX/Linux/Max OS X.

List the contents of the applets directory to see the directory names for the demonstration applets. Figure 24.9 provides a brief description of each example.

Example	Description
Animator	Performs one of four separate animations.
ArcTest	Demonstrates drawing arcs. You can interact with the applet to change attributes of the arc that is displayed.
BarChart	Draws a simple bar chart.
Blink	Displays blinking text in different colors.
CardTest	Demonstrates several GUI components and a variety of ways in which GUI components can be arranged on the screen. (The arrangement of GUI components is also known as the *layout* of the GUI components.)
Clock	Draws a clock with rotating "hands," the current date and the current time. The clock is updated once per second.

Fig. 24.9   The examples from the applets directory. (Part 1 of 2.)

Example	Description
DitherTest	Demonstrates drawing with a graphics technique known as dithering that allows gradual transformation from one color to another.
DrawTest	Allows the user to drag the mouse to draw lines and points on the applet in different colors.
Fractal	Draws a fractal. Fractals typically require complex calculations to determine how they are displayed.
GraphicsTest	Draws a variety of shapes to illustrate graphics capabilities.
GraphLayout	Draws a graph consisting of many nodes (represented as rectangles) connected by lines. Drag a node to see the other nodes in the graph adjust on the screen and demonstrate complex graphical interactions.
ImageMap	Demonstrates an image with *hot spots*. Positioning the mouse pointer over certain areas of the image highlights the area and a message is displayed in the lower-left corner of the appletviewer window. Position over the mouth in the image to hear the applet say "hi."
JumpingBox	Moves a rectangle randomly around the screen. Try to catch it by clicking it with the mouse!
MoleculeViewer	Presents a three-dimensional view of several different chemical molecules. Drag the mouse to view the molecule from different angles.
NervousText	Draws text that jumps around the screen.
SimpleGraph	Draws a complex curve.
SortDemo	Compares three sorting techniques. Sorting arranges information in order—like alphabetizing words. When you execute the applet, three appletviewer windows appear. Click in each one to start the sort. Notice that the sorts all operate at different speeds.
SpreadSheet	Demonstrates a simple spreadsheet of rows and columns.
SymbolTest	Draws characters from the Java character set.
TicTacToe	Allows the user to play Tic-Tac-Toe against the computer.
WireFrame	Draws a three-dimensional shape as a wire frame. Drag the mouse to view the shape from different angles.

Fig. 24.9   The examples from the applets directory. (Part 2 of 2.)

Change directories to subdirectory TicTacToe. In that directory is an HTML file (example1.html) that is used to execute the applet. In the command window, type

```
appletviewer example1.html
```

and press the *Enter* key. This executes the appletviewer. The appletviewer loads the HTML file specified as its *command-line argument* (example1.html), determines from the file which applet to load (we discuss the details of HTML files in section 24.7 on page 877) and begins execution of the applet. Figure 24.9 shows several screen captures of playing Tic-Tac-Toe with this applet.

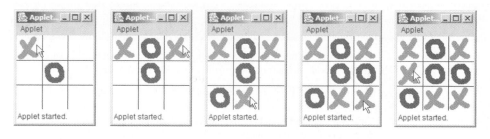

Fig. 24.10 Sample execution of the TicTacToe applet.

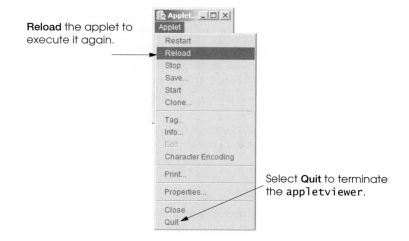

Reload the applet to
execute it again.

Select **Quit** to terminate
the appletviewer.

Fig. 24.11 Selecting Reload from the appletviewer's Applet menu.

Error-Prevention Tip 24.3

If the appletviewer command does not work and/or the system indicates that the applet-viewer command cannot be found, the PATH environment variable may not be defined properly on your computer. Review the installation directions for the Java 2 Software Development Kit to ensure that the PATH environment variable is correctly defined for your system (on some computers, you may need to restart your computer after defining the PATH environment variable).

You are player **X**. To interact with the applet, point the mouse at the square where you want to place an **X** and click the mouse button (normally, the left mouse button). The applet plays a sound (assuming your computer supports audio playback) and places an **X** in the square if the square is open. If the square is occupied, this is an invalid move and the applet plays a different sound indicating that you cannot make the specified move. After you make a valid move, the applet responds by making its own move (this happens immediately).

To play again, re-execute the applet by clicking the appletviewer's **Applet** *menu* and selecting the **Reload** *menu item* from the menu. To terminate the appletviewer, click the appletviewer's **Applet** menu and select the **Quit** *menu item*.

24.6.2 The DrawTest Applet

The next applet we demonstrate from the demos allows you to draw lines and points in different colors. To draw, you simply drag the mouse on the applet by pressing a mouse button and holding it while you drag the mouse. For this example, change directories to directory **applets**, then to subdirectory **DrawTest**. In that directory is the **example1.html** file that is used to execute the applet. In the command window, type the command

```
appletviewer example1.html
```

and press the *Enter* key. This executes the **appletviewer**. The **appletviewer** loads the HTML file specified as its command-line argument (**example1.html** again), determines from the file which applet to load and begins execution of the applet. Fig. 24.12 shows a screen capture of this applet after drawing some lines and points.

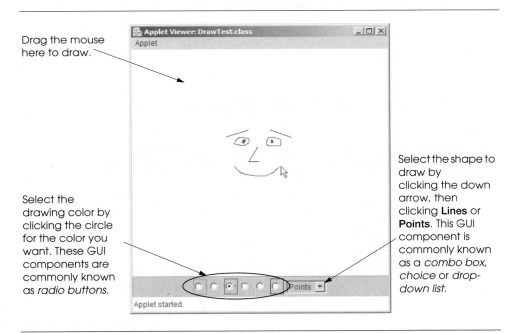

Drag the mouse here to draw.

Select the drawing color by clicking the circle for the color you want. These GUI components are commonly known as *radio buttons*.

Select the shape to draw by clicking the down arrow, then clicking **Lines** or **Points**. This GUI component is commonly known as a *combo box*, *choice* or *drop-down list*.

Fig. 24.12 Sample execution of the **DrawTest** applet.

The default shape to draw is a line and the default color is black, so you can immediately draw black lines by dragging the mouse across the applet. To drag the mouse, press and hold the mouse button and move the mouse. Notice that the line follows the mouse pointer around the applet. The line is not permanent until you let go of the mouse button. You can then start a new line by repeating the process.

Select a color by clicking the circle inside one of the colored rectangles at the bottom of the applet. You can select from red, green, blue, pink, orange and black. The GUI components used to present these options are commonly known as *radio buttons*. If you think of a car radio, only one radio station can be selected at a time. Similarly, only one drawing color can be selected at a time.

Try changing the shape from **Lines** to **Points** by clicking the down arrow to the right of the word **Lines** at the bottom of the applet. A list drops down from the GUI component containing the two choices—**Lines** and **Points**. To select **Points**, click the word **Points** in the list. The GUI component closes the list and **Points** are now the current shape. This GUI component is commonly known as a *choice*, *combo box* or *drop-down list*.

To start a new drawing, select **Reload** from the `appletviewer`'s **Applet** menu. To terminate the applet, select **Quit** from the `appletviewer`'s **Applet** menu.

24.6.3 The Java2D Applet

The last applet we demonstrate (Fig. 24.13) before defining applets of our own shows many of the complex new two-dimensional drawing capabilities built into Java 2—known as the *Java2D API*. For this example, change directories to the `jfc` directory in the J2SDK's

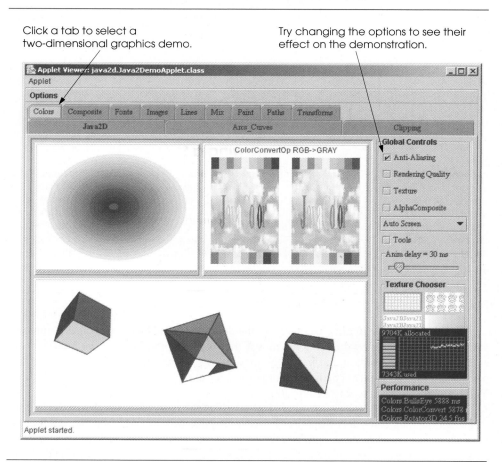

Fig. 24.13 Sample execution of the `Java2D` applet.

demo directory, then change to the Java2D directory (you can move up the directory tree toward demo using the command "cd .." in both Windows and UNIX). In that directory is an HTML file (Java2DemoApplet.html) that is used to execute the applet. In the command window, type the command

```
appletviewer Java2DemoApplet.html
```

and press the *Enter* key. This executes the appletviewer. The appletviewer loads the HTML file specified as its command-line argument (Java2DemoApplet.html), determines from the file which applet to load and begins execution of the applet. This particular demo takes some time to load as it is quite large. Fig. 24.12 shows a screen capture of one of this applet's many demonstrations of Java's new two-dimensional graphics capabilities.

At the top of this demo you see tabs that look like file folders in a filing cabinet. This demo provides 11 different tabs with several different features on each tab. To change to a different part of the demo, simply click one of the tabs. Also, try changing the options in the upper-right corner of the applet. Some of these affect the speed with which the applet draws the graphics. For example, click the small box with a check in it (a GUI component known as a *checkbox*) to the left of the word **Anti-Aliasing** to turn off anti-aliasing (a graphics technique for producing smoother on-screen graphics in which the edges of the graphic are blurred). When this feature is turned off (i.e., its *checkbox* is unchecked), the animation speed increases for the animated shapes at the bottom of the demo shown in Fig. 24.13. This is because an animated shape displayed with anti-aliasing takes longer to draw than an animated shape without anti-aliasing.

24.7 A Simple Java Applet: Drawing a String

Now, we begin with some applets of our own. Remember, we are just getting started—we have many more topics to learn before we can write applets similar to those demonstrated in Section 24.6. However, we will cover many of the same techniques in upcoming chapters.

We begin by considering a simple applet that mimics the program of Fig. 24.2 by displaying the string "Welcome to Java Programming!". The applet and its screen output are shown in Fig. 24.14. The HTML document to load the applet into the appletviewer is shown and discussed in Fig. 24.15.

```
1   // Fig. 24.14: WelcomeApplet.java
2   // A first applet in Java
3   import javax.swing.JApplet;   // import class JApplet
4   import java.awt.Graphics;     // import class Graphics
5
6   public class WelcomeApplet extends JApplet {
7      public void paint( Graphics g )
8      {
9         g.drawString( "Welcome to Java Programming!", 25, 25 );
10     } // end method paint
11  } // end class WelcomeApplet
```

Fig. 24.14 A first applet in Java and the applet screen output. (Part 1 of 2.)

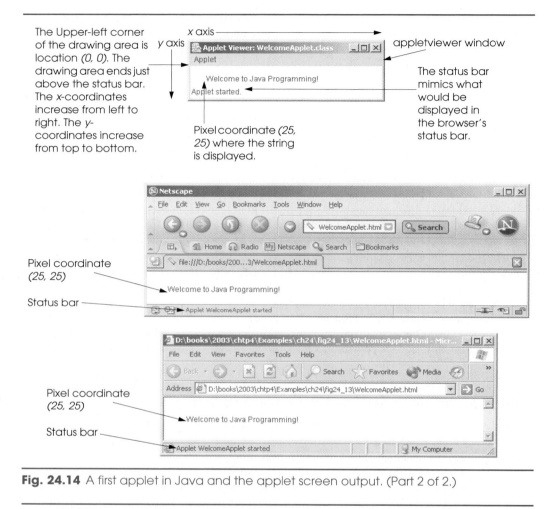

The Upper-left corner of the drawing area is location (0, 0). The drawing area ends just above the status bar. The x-coordinates increase from left to right. The y-coordinates increase from top to bottom.

x axis

y axis

appletviewer window

The status bar mimics what would be displayed in the browser's status bar.

Pixel coordinate (25, 25) where the string is displayed.

Pixel coordinate (25, 25)

Status bar

Pixel coordinate (25, 25)

Status bar

Fig. 24.14 A first applet in Java and the applet screen output. (Part 2 of 2.)

```
1   <html>
2   <applet code="WelcomeApplet.class" width=300 height=30>
3   </applet>
4   </html>
```

Fig. 24.15 The WelcomeApplet.html file, which loads the WelcomeApplet class of Fig. 24.14 into the appletviewer.

This program illustrates several important Java features. We consider each line of the program in detail. Line 9 does the "real work" of the program, namely drawing the string Welcome to Java Programming! on the screen. But let us consider each line of the program in order. Lines 1 and 2

```
// Fig. 24.14: WelcomeApplet.java
// A first applet in Java
```

begin with //, indicating that the remainder of each line is a comment. The comment in line 1 indicates the figure number and file name for the applet source code. The comment `A first applet in Java` in line 2 simply describes the purpose of the program.

As stated in earlier, Java contains many predefined pieces called classes (or data types) that are grouped into packages in the Java API. Lines 3 and 4

```
import javax.swing.JApplet;  // import class JApplet
import java.awt.Graphics;   // import class Graphics
```

are `import` statements that tell the compiler where to locate the classes required to compile this Java applet. These specific lines tell the compiler that class *JApplet* is located in package `javax.swing` and class *Graphics* is located in package *java.awt*. When you create an applet in Java, you normally import the `JApplet` class. You import the `Graphics` class so the program can draw graphics (such as lines, rectangles, ovals and strings of characters) on a Java applet (or application later in the book). [*Note:* There is an older class called *Applet* from package *java.applet* that is not used with Java's newest GUI components from the `javax.swing` package. In this book, we use only class `JApplet` with applets.]

Each piece of the package name is a directory (or folder) on disk. All the packages in the Java API are stored in the directory `java` or `javax` that contain many subdirectories, including `awt` and `swing`. [*Note:* If you look for these directories on disk, you will not find them because they are stored in a special compressed file called a *Java archive file (JAR file)*. In the J2SDK installation directory structure is a file called *rt.jar* that contains the `.class` files for the entire Java API.]

As with applications, every Java applet is composed of at least one class definition. One key feature of class definitions that was not mentioned earlier is that you rarely create a class definition "from scratch." In fact, when you create a class definition, you normally use pieces of an existing class definition. Java uses *inheritance* (discussed further in Chapter 27) to create new classes from existing class definitions. Line 6

```
public class WelcomeApplet extends JApplet {
```

begins a `class` definition for class `WelcomeApplet`. Once again, keyword `class` introduces a class definition and is immediately followed by the class name (`WelcomeApplet` in this class). The *extends keyword* followed by a class name indicates the class (in this case `JApplet`) from which our new class inherits existing pieces. In this inheritance relationship, `JApplet` is called the *superclass* or *base class* and `WelcomeApplet` is called the *subclass* or *derived class*. We discuss inheritance in detail in Chapter 27, Java Object-Oriented Programming. Using inheritance here results in a new class definition that has the *attributes* (data) and *behaviors* (methods) of the `JApplet` class as well as the new features we are adding in our `WelcomeApplet` class definition (specifically, the ability to display `Welcome to Java Programming!` on the screen).

A key benefit of extending class `JApplet` is that someone else has already defined "what it means to be an applet." The `appletviewer` and World Wide Web browsers that support applets expect every Java applet to have certain capabilities (attributes and behaviors) and class `JApplet` already provides all those capabilities—programmers do not need to define all these capabilities on their own (again, programmers do not need to "reinvent the wheel"). In fact, an applet requires well over 200 different methods to be defined. In our programs to this point, we have defined one method in every program. If we had to define over 200 methods just to display Welcome to Java Programming!, we would probably never create an applet! By simply using extends to inherit from class JApplet, all the methods of JApplet are now part of our WelcomeApplet.

The inheritance mechanism is easy to use; the programmer does not need to know every detail of class JApplet or any other class from which new classes are inherited. The programmer needs to know only that class JApplet has already defined the capabilities required to create the minimum applet. To make the best use of any class, however, the programmer should study all the capabilities of the class that is extended.

Good Programming Practice 24.15

Investigate the capabilities of any class in the Java API documentation carefully before inheriting a subclass from it. This helps ensure that the programmer does not unintentionally redefine a capability that is already provided.

Classes are used as "templates" or "blueprints" to *instantiate* (or *create*) *objects* for use in a program. An object (or *instance*) resides in the computer's memory and contains information used by the program. The term object normally implies that attributes (data) and behaviors (methods) are associated with the object. The object's methods use the attributes to provide useful services to the *client of the object* (i.e., the code that calls the methods).

Our WelcomeApplet class is used to create an object that implements the applet's attributes and behaviors. The default behavior of method paint in class JApplet is to do nothing. Class WelcomeApplet *overrides* (*replaces* or *redefines*) that behavior such that paint draws a message on the screen. When the appletviewer or browser tells the applet to "draw itself" on the screen by calling method paint, our message Welcome to Java Programming! appears rather than a blank screen.

The appletviewer or browser in which the applet executes is responsible for creating an object (instance) of class WelcomeApplet. [*Note:* The terms instance and object are often used interchangeably.] The keyword *public* in line 6 is required to enable the browser to create an object of class WelcomeApplet and execute the applet. The class that inherits from JApplet to create an applet must be a public class. The public keyword and related keywords (such as private and protected) are discussed in detail in Chapter 26, Java Object-Based Programming. For now, we ask you simply to start all class definitions with the public keyword until the discussion of public in Chapter 26.

When you save a public class in a file, the class's name is used as part of the file name. For our applet, the file name must be WelcomeApplet.java. Please note that the file name must be spelled exactly the same as the class name and have the .java file name extension.

Error-Prevention Tip 24.4

The compiler error message "Public class ClassName must be defined in a file called Class-Name.java" indicates either 1) that the file name does not exactly match the name of the public class in the file (including all uppercase and lowercase letters), or 2) that you typed the class name incorrectly when compiling the class (the name must be spelled with the proper uppercase and lowercase letters).

At the end of line 6, the left brace, {, begins the body of the class definition. The corresponding right brace, }, on line 11 ends the class definition. Line 7

```
public void paint( Graphics g )
```

begins the definition of the applet's *paint method*. Method `paint` is one of three methods (behaviors) that are guaranteed to be called automatically for you when any applet begins execution. These three methods are `init` (discussed later in this chapter), `start` (discussed later in the book) and `paint`, and they are guaranteed to be called in that order. These methods are called from the `appletviewer` or browser in which the applet is executing. Your applet class gets a "free" version of each of these methods from class `JApplet` when you specify `extends JApplet` in the first line of your applet's class definition. There are several other methods that are also guaranteed to be called during an applet's execution—these methods are discussed in Chapter 25.

The free version of each of these methods is defined with an empty body (i.e., by default each of these methods does not perform a task). One of the reasons we inherit all applets from class `JApplet` is to get our free copies of the methods that get called automatically during execution of an applet (and many other methods too).

Why would you want a free copy of a method that does nothing? The predefined start-up sequence of method calls made by the `appletviewer` or browser for every applet is always `init`, `start` and `paint`—this provides an applet programmer a guaranteed start-up sequence of method calls as every applet begins execution. Every applet does not need all three of these methods. However, the `appletviewer` or browser expects each of these methods to be defined so it can provide a consistent start-up sequence for an applet. [*Note:* This is similar to applications always starting execution with `main`.] Inheriting the default versions of these methods guarantees the browser that it can treat each applet uniformly by calling `init`, `start` and `paint` as applet execution begins. Also, the programmer can concentrate on defining only the methods required for a particular applet.

Lines 7 through 10 are the definition of `paint`. The task of method `paint` is to draw graphics (such as lines, ovals and strings of characters) on the screen. Keyword `void` indicates that this method does not return any results when it completes its task. The set of parentheses after `paint` defines the method's *parameter list*. Recall that the parameter list is where methods receive data required to perform their tasks. Normally, this data is passed by the programmer to the method through a *method call* (also known as *invoking a method* or *sending a message*). For example, in Fig. 24.4 we passed data to `JOptionPane.show-MessageDialog` including the message to display and the type of message dialog. However, method `paint`—which is called for us to draw in the applet's viewable area on the screen—receives the information it needs automatically when the method is called. Method `paint`'s parameter list indicates that it requires a `Graphics` object (named `g`) to perform its task. The `Graphics` object is used by `paint` to draw graphics on the applet. The `public` keyword at the beginning of line 7 is required so the `appletviewer` or browser can call your `paint` method. For now, all method definitions should begin with the `public` keyword. Other alternatives are introduced in Chapter 26.

The left brace, {, in line 8 begins the method definition's body. The corresponding right brace, }, in line 10 ends the method definition's body. Line 9

```
g.drawString( "Welcome to Java Programming!", 25, 25 );
```

is a statement that instructs the computer to perform an action (or task), namely to display the characters of the character string `Welcome to Java Programming!` on the applet. This statement uses method `drawString` defined by class `Graphics` (this class defines all the graphical drawing capabilities of a Java program, such as drawing strings of characters and drawing shapes such as rectangles, ovals and lines). Method `drawString` is called using the `Graphics` object g (in `paint`'s parameter list) followed by a dot operator (`.`) followed by the method name `drawString`. The method name is followed by a set of parentheses containing the argument list `drawString` needs to perform its task.

The first argument to `drawString` is the `String` to draw. The last two arguments in the list—25 and 25—are the *coordinates* (or *position*) at which the bottom-left corner of the string should be drawn in the applet's on-screen area. Coordinates are measured from the upper-left corner of the applet in *pixels* (the upper-left corner of the white area in the screen capture of Fig. 24.14). A pixel ("picture element") is the unit of display for your computer's screen. On a color screen, a pixel appears as one colored dot on the screen. Many personal computers have 640 pixels for the width of the screen and 480 pixels for the height of the screen, for a total of 640 times 480 or 307,200 displayable pixels. Many computer screens have higher screen resolutions, i.e., they have more pixels for the width and height of the screen. The higher the screen resolution, the smaller the applet appears on the screen. Drawing methods from class `Graphics` require coordinates to specify where to draw on the applet (later in the text we demonstrate drawing in applications). The first coordinate is the *x-coordinate* (the number of pixels from the left side of the applet), and the second coordinate is the *y-coordinate* (representing the number of pixels from the top of the applet).

When the preceding statement is executed, it draws the message `Welcome to Java Programming!` on the applet at the coordinates 25 and 25. Note that the quotation marks enclosing the character string are *not* displayed on the screen.

After class `WelcomeApplet` is defined and saved in file `WelcomeApplet.java`, the class must be compiled using the Java compiler `javac`. In the command window, type the command

```
javac WelcomeApplet.java
```

to compile class `WelcomeApplet`. If there are no syntax errors, the resulting bytecodes are stored in the file `WelcomeApplet.class`.

After compiling the program of Fig. 24.14, we must create an *HTML (Hypertext Markup Language)* file to load the applet into the `appletviewer` (or a browser) to execute. Typically, an HTML file ends with the `.html` or `.htm` file name extension. Browsers display the contents of documents that contain text (also known as *text files*). To execute a Java applet, you must provide an HTML text file that indicates which applet the `appletviewer` (or browser) should load and execute. Figure 24.15 contains a simple HTML file—`WelcomeApplet.html`—that is used to load into the `appletviewer` (or a browser) the applet defined in Fig. 24.14. [*Note*: For this book, we always demonstrate applets with the `appletviewer`.]

Good Programming Practice 24.16

Always test a Java applet in the `appletviewer` and ensure that it is executing correctly before loading the applet into a World Wide Web browser. Browsers often save a copy of an applet in memory until the current browsing session terminates (i.e., all browser windows are closed). Thus, if you change an applet, recompile the applet, then reload the applet in the browser, you may not see the changes because the browser may still be executing the original version of the applet. Close all your browser windows to remove the old version of the applet from memory. Open a new browser window and load the applet to see your changes.

Software Engineering Observation 24.2

If your World Wide Web browser does not support Java 2, most of the applets in this book will not execute in your browser. This is because most of the applets in this book use features that are new to Java 2 or are not provided by browsers that support Java 1.1

Many HTML codes (or *tags*) come in pairs. For example, lines 1 and 4 of Fig. 24.15 indicate the beginning and the end, respectively, of the HTML tags in the file. All HTML tags begin with a *left angle bracket, <,* and end with a *right angle bracket, >.* Lines 2 and 3 are special HTML tags for Java applets. They tell the appletviewer (or browser) to load a specific applet and define the size of the applet's display area (its *width* and *height* in pixels) in the appletviewer (or browser). Normally, the applet and its corresponding HTML file are stored in the same directory on disk.

Typically, an HTML file is loaded into your browser from a computer other than your own that is connected to the Internet. However, HTML files also can reside on your computer (as we demonstrated in section 24.6 on page 871). Whenever an HTML file that specifies an applet to execute is loaded into the appletviewer (or a browser), the appletviewer (or browser) loads the applet's .class file (or files) from the same directory on the computer from which the HTML file was loaded.

The *<applet>* tag has several components. The first component of the <applet> tag in line 2 (code="WelcomeApplet.class") indicates that the file WelcomeApplet.class contains the compiled applet class. Remember, when you compile your Java programs, every class is compiled into a separate file that has the same name as the class and ends with the .class extension. The second and third components of the <applet> tag indicate the *width* and the *height* of the applet in pixels. The upper-left corner of the applet's display area is always at *x*-coordinate 0 and *y*-coordinate 0. The width of this applet is 300 pixels and its height is 30 pixels. You may want (or need) to use larger width and height values to define a larger drawing area for your applets. In line 3, the </applet> tag terminates the <applet> tag that began in line 2. In line 4, the </html> tag specifies the end of the HTML tags that began in line 1 with <html>.

Software Engineering Observation 24.3

Generally, each applet should be less than 640 pixels wide and 480 pixels tall (most computer screens support these dimensions as the minimum width and height).

Common Programming Error 24.11

Placing additional characters such as commas (,) between the components in the <applet> tag may cause the appletviewer or browser to produce an error message indicating a MissingResourceException when loading the applet.

Common Programming Error 24.12

Forgetting the ending </applet> tag prevents the applet from loading into the appletviewer or browser properly.

Error-Prevention Tip 24.5

If you receive a MissingResourceException error message when loading an applet into the appletviewer or a browser, check the <applet> tag in the HTML file carefully for syntax errors. Compare your HTML file to the file in Fig. 24.15 to confirm proper syntax.

The appletviewer only understands the <applet> and </applet> HTML tags, so it is sometimes referred to as the "minimal browser" (it ignores all other HTML tags). The `appletviewer` is an ideal place to test an applet's execution and ensure that the applet executes properly. Once the applet's execution is verified, you can add `<applet>` and `</applet>` tags to an HTML file that will be viewed by people browsing the Internet. The `appletviewer` is invoked for the `WelcomeApplet` from your computer's command window as follows:

```
appletviewer WelcomeApplet.html
```

Note that the `appletviewer` *requires* an HTML file to load an applet. This is different from the `java` interpreter for applications which required the class name of the application class. Also, the preceding command must be issued from the directory in which the HTML file and the applet's `.class` file are located.

Common Programming Error 24.13

Running the `appletviewer` with a file name that does not end with `.html` or `.htm` is an error that prevents the `appletviewer` from loading your applet for execution.

Portability Tip 24.2

Test your applets in every browser used by people who view your applet. This will help ensure that people who view your applet experience the functionality you expect. [Note: A goal of the Java Plug-In (discussed later in the book) is to provide consistent applet execution across many different browsers.]

24.8 Two More Simple Applets: Drawing Strings and Lines

Let us consider another applet. `Welcome to Java Programming!` can be displayed several ways. Two `drawString` statements in the `paint` method can print multiple lines as in Fig. 24.16 (the corresponding HTML file is in Fig. 24.17).

```java
1   // Fig. 24.16: WelcomeApplet2.java
2   // Displaying multiple strings
3   import javax.swing.JApplet;   // import class JApplet
4   import java.awt.Graphics;     // import class Graphics
5
6   public class WelcomeApplet2 extends JApplet {
7      public void paint( Graphics g )
8      {
9         g.drawString( "Welcome to", 25, 25 );
10        g.drawString( "Java Programming!", 25, 40 );
11     } // end method paint
12  } // end class WelcomeApplet2
```

Pixel coordinate *(25, 25)*, where
Welcome to is displayed

Pixel coordinate *(25, 40)*, where
Java Programming! is displayed

Applet Viewer: WelcomeApplet2.class
Applet
Welcome to
Java Programming!
Applet started.

Fig. 24.16 Displaying multiple strings.

```
1   <html>
2   <applet code="WelcomeApplet2.class" width=300 height=45>
3   </applet>
4   </html>
```

Fig. 24.17 The `WelcomeApplet2.html` file, which loads the `WelcomeApplet2` class of Fig. 24.16 into the `appletviewer`.

Note that each `drawString` can draw at any pixel location on the applet. The reason the two output lines appear as shown in the output window is that we specified the same *x*- coordinate (`25`) for each `drawString` so the strings appear aligned at their left sides, and we specified different *y*- coordinates (`25` in line 9 and `40` in line 10) so the strings appear at different vertical locations on the applet. If we reverse lines 9 and 10 in the program, the output window will still appear as shown because the pixel coordinates specified in each `drawString` statement are completely independent of the coordinates specified in all other `drawString` statements (and all other drawing operations). The concept of lines of text as previously shown with methods `System.out.println` and `JOptionPane.showMessageDialog` does not exist when drawing graphics. In fact, if you try to output a string containing a newline character (`\n`), you will simply see a small black box at that position in the string.

To make drawing more interesting, the applet of Fig. 24.18 draws two lines and a string. The HTML file to load the applet into the `appletviewer` is shown in Fig. 24.19.

```
1   // Fig. 24.18: WelcomeLines.java
2   // Displaying text and lines
3   import javax.swing.JApplet;  // import class JApplet
4   import java.awt.Graphics;    // import class Graphics
5
6   public class WelcomeLines extends JApplet {
7      public void paint( Graphics g )
8      {
9         g.drawLine( 15, 10, 210, 10 );
10        g.drawLine( 15, 30, 210, 30 );
11        g.drawString( "Welcome to Java Programming!", 25, 25 );
12     } // end method paint
13  } // end class WelcomeLines
```

Coordinate *(15, 10)* — Coordinate *(210, 10)*
Coordinate *(15, 30)* — Coordinate *(210, 30)*

Fig. 24.18 Drawing strings and lines.

```
1   <html>
2   <applet code="WelcomeLines.class" width=300 height=40>
3   </applet>
4   </html>
```

Fig. 24.19 The `WelcomeLines.html` file, which loads the `WelcomeLines` class of Fig. 24.19 into the `appletviewer`.

Lines 9 and 10 of method `paint`

```
g.drawLine( 15, 10, 210, 10 );
g.drawLine( 15, 30, 210, 30 );
```

use *method drawLine* of class `Graphics` to indicate that the `Graphics` object that g refers to should draw lines. Method `drawLine` requires four arguments that represent the two end points of the line on the applet—the *x*-coordinate and *y*-coordinate of the first end point in the line and the *x*-coordinate and *y*-coordinate of the second end point in the line. All coordinate values are specified with respect to the upper-left corner *(0, 0)* coordinate of the applet. When method `drawLine` is called, it simply draws a line between the two specified end points.

24.9 Another Java Applet: Adding Integers

Our next applet (Fig. 24.20) mimics the application of Fig. 24.7 for adding two integers. However, this applet requests that the user enter two *floating-point numbers* (i.e., numbers with a decimal point such as 7.33, 0.0975 and 1000.12345). To store floating-point numbers in memory we introduce primitive data type *double*, which is used to represent *double-precision floating-point* numbers. There is also primitive data type *float* for *storing single-precision floating-point* numbers. A `double` requires more memory to store a floating-point value, but stores it with approximately twice the precision of a `float` (15 significant digits for `double` vs. seven significant digits for `float`).

Once again, we use `JOptionPane.showInputDialog` to request input from the user. The applet then computes the sum of the input values and displays the result by drawing a string inside a rectangle on the applet. The HTML file to load this applet into the `appletviewer` is shown in Fig. 24.21.

```
1   // Fig. 24.20: AdditionApplet.java
2   // Adding two floating-point numbers
3   import java.awt.Graphics;    // import class Graphics
4   import javax.swing.*;        // import package javax.swing
5
6   public class AdditionApplet extends JApplet {
7      double sum;   // sum of the values entered by the user
8
9      public void init()
10     {
11        String firstNumber,     // first string entered by user
12               secondNumber;    // second string entered by user
13        double number1,         // first number to add
14               number2;         // second number to add
15
16        // read in first number from user
17        firstNumber =
18           JOptionPane.showInputDialog(
19              "Enter first floating-point value" );
20
```

Fig. 24.20 An addition program "in action." (Part 1 of 2.)

```
21          // read in second number from user
22          secondNumber =
23             JOptionPane.showInputDialog(
24                "Enter second floating-point value" );
25
26          // convert numbers from type String to type double
27          number1 = Double.parseDouble( firstNumber );
28          number2 = Double.parseDouble( secondNumber );
29
30          // add the numbers
31          sum = number1 + number2;
32       } // end method init
33
34       public void paint( Graphics g )
35       {
36          // draw the results with g.drawString
37          g.drawRect( 15, 10, 270, 20 );
38          g.drawString( "The sum is " + sum, 25, 25 );
39       } // end method paint
40    } // end class AdditionApplet
```

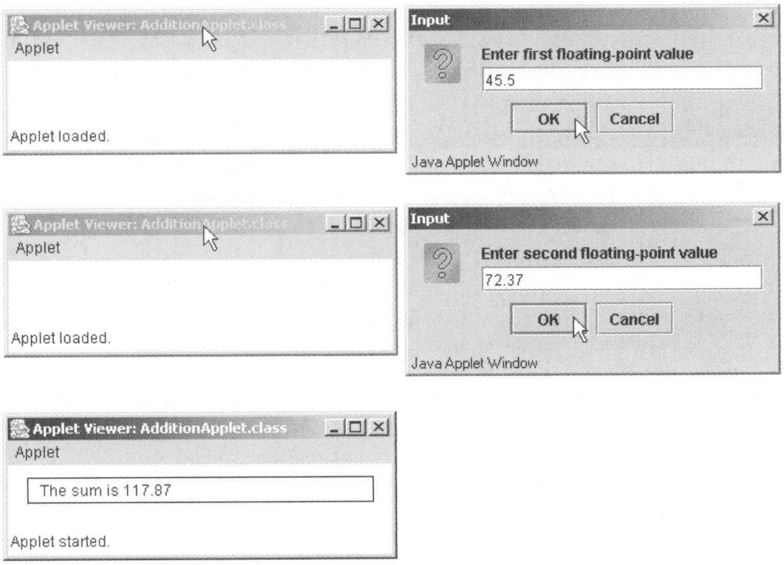

Fig. 24.20 An addition program "in action." (Part 2 of 2.)

```
1    <html>
2    <applet code="AdditionApplet.class" width=300 height=50>
3    </applet>
4    </html>
```

Fig. 24.21 The AdditionApplet.html file, which loads the AdditionApplet class of Fig. 24.20 into the appletviewer.

Line 3

```
import java.awt.Graphics;    // import class Graphics
```

specifies to the compiler where to locate class `Graphics` (package `java.awt`) for use in this application. Actually, the `import` statement at line 3 is not required if we always use the complete name of class `Graphics`—*java.awt.Graphics*—which includes the full package name and class name. For example, the first line of method `paint` can be defined as

```
public void paint( java.awt.Graphics g )
```

Software Engineering Observation 24.4

The Java compiler does not need `import` *statements in a Java source code file if the complete class name—the full package name and class name (e.g.,* java.awt.Graphics*)—is specified every time a class name is used in the source code.*

Line 4

```
import javax.swing.*;        // import package javax.swing
```

specifies to the compiler where to locate the entire `javax.swing` package. The asterisk (*****) indicates that all classes in the `javax.swing` package (such as `JApplet` and `JOption-Pane`) should be available to the compiler so the compiler can ensure that we use the classes correctly. This allows programmers to use the *shorthand name* (the class name by itself) of any class from the `javax.swing` package in the program. Remember that our last two programs only imported class `JApplet` from the `javax.swing` package. In this program, we use classes `JApplet` and `JOptionPane` from the `javax.swing` package. Importing an entire package into a program is also a shorthand notation so the programmer does not have to provide a separate `import` statement for every class used from that package. Remember that you can always use the complete name of every class, i.e., `javax.swing.JApplet` and `javax.swing.JOptionPane` rather than `import` statements.

Software Engineering Observation 24.5

The compiler does not load every class in a package when it encounters an `import` *statement that uses the* * *(e.g.,* javax.swing.**) notation to indicate that multiple classes from the package are used in the program. The compiler searches the package only for those classes used in the program.*

Software Engineering Observation 24.6

Many package directories have subdirectories. For example, the java.awt *package directory contains subdirectory* event *for the package* java.awt.event*. When the compiler encounters an* `import` *statement that uses the* * *(e.g.,* java.awt.**) notation to indicate that multiple classes from the package are used in the program, the compiler does not search the subdirectory* event*. This means that you cannot define an* `import` *of* java.* *to search for classes from all packages.*

Software Engineering Observation 24.7

When using `import` *statements, separate* `import` *statements must be specified for each package used in a program.*

Common Programming Error 24.14

Assuming that an `import` statement for an entire package (e.g., `java.awt.*`) also imports classes from subdirectories in that package (e.g., `java.awt.event.*`) results in syntax errors for the classes from the subdirectories. There must be separate `import` statements for every package from which classes are used.

Remember that applets inherit from the `JApplet` class, so they have all the methods required by the `appletviewer` or a browser to execute the applet. Line 6

```
public class AdditionApplet extends JApplet {
```

begins class `AdditionApplet`'s definition and indicates that it inherits from `JApplet`.

All class definitions start with an opening left brace (end of line 6), {, and end with a closing right brace, } (line 40).

Common Programming Error 24.15

If braces do not occur in matching pairs, the compiler indicates a syntax error.

Line 7

```
double sum;   // sum of the values entered by the user
```

is an *instance variable declaration*—every instance (object) of the class contains one copy of each instance variable. For example, if there are 10 instances of this applet executing, each instance has its own copy of `sum`. Thus, there would be 10 separate copies of `sum` (one for each applet). Instance variables are declared in the body of the class definition, but not in the body of any method of the class definition. The preceding declaration states that `sum` is a variable of primitive type `double`.

An important benefit of instance variables is that their identifiers can be used throughout the class definition (i.e., in all methods of the class). Until now, we declared all variables in an application's `main` method. Variables defined in the body of a method are known as *local variables* and can only be used in the body of the method in which they are defined. Another distinction between instance variables and local variables is that instance variables are always assigned a default value and local variables are not. The variable `sum` is initialized to 0.0 automatically because it is an instance variable.

Common Programming Error 24.16

Using a local variable that is not initialized before it is used is a syntax error. Each local variable must be assigned a value before an attempt is made to use that variable's value.

Good Programming Practice 24.17

Initializing instance variables rather than relying on automatic initialization improves program readability.

This applet contains two methods—`init` (definition in lines 9 through 32) and `paint` (definition in lines 34 through 39). Method `init` is a special applet method that is normally the first method defined by the programmer in an applet and is guaranteed to be the first method called in every applet. Method `init` is called once during an applet's execution. The method normally *initializes* the applet's instance variables (if they need to be initialized to a value other than their default value) and performs any tasks that need to be performed once at the beginning of an applet's execution.

Software Engineering Observation 24.8

The order in which methods are defined in a class definition has no effect on when those methods are called at execution time.

The first line of the `init` method always appears as

```
public void init()
```

indicating that `init` is a `public` method that returns no information (`void`) when it completes and receives no arguments (empty parentheses after `init`) to perform its task.

The left brace (line 10) marks the beginning of `init`'s body, and the corresponding right brace (line 32) marks the end of `init`. Lines 11 and 12

```
String firstNumber,     // first string entered by user
       secondNumber;    // second string entered by user
```

are a declaration for the local `String` variables `firstNumber` and `secondNumber`.

Lines 13 and 14

```
double number1,     // first number to add
       number2;     // second number to add
```

declare that variables `number1` and `number2` are of primitive data type `double`, which means that these variables hold floating-point values. These are instance variables, so they are automatically initialized to 0.0 (the default for `double` instance variables).

Note that there are actually two types of variables in Java—*primitive data type variables* (normally called *variables*) and *reference variables* (normally called *references*). The identifiers `firstNumber` and `secondNumber` are actually references—names that are used to *refer to objects* in the program. Such references actually contain the location in the computer's memory of an object. In our preceding applets, method `paint` actually receives a reference called g that refers to a `Graphics` object. That reference is used to send messages to (i.e., call methods on) the `Graphics` object in memory that allows us to draw on the applet. For example, the statement

```
g.drawString( "Welcome to Java Programming!", 25, 25 );
```

sends the `drawString` message to (calls the `drawString` method on) the `Graphics` object to which g refers. As part of the message (method call), we provide the data that `drawString` requires to do its task. The `Graphics` object then draws the `String` at the specified location.

The identifiers `number1`, `number2` and `sum` are the names of *variables*. A variable is similar to an object. The main difference between a variable and an object is that an object is defined by a class definition that can contain both data (instance variables) and methods, whereas a variable is defined by a *primitive (or built-in) data type* (one of `char`, `byte`, `short`, `int`, `long`, `float`, `double` or `boolean`) that can contain only data. A variable can store exactly one value at a time, whereas one object can contain many individual pieces of data. The distinction between a variable and a reference is based on the data type of the identifier (as stated in a declaration). If the data type is a class name, the identifier is a reference to an object and that reference can be used to send messages to (call methods on) that object. If the data type is one of the primitive data types, the identifier is a variable that can be used to store in memory or retrieve from memory a single value of the declared primitive type.

Software Engineering Observation 24.9

A hint to help you determine if an identifier is a variable or a reference is the variable's data type. By convention all class names in Java start with a capitalized first letter. Therefore, if the data type starts with a capitalized first letter, you can normally assume that the identifier is a reference to an object of the declared type (e.g., Graphics g indicates that g is a reference to a Graphics object).

Lines 16 through 19

```
// read in first number from user
firstNumber =
    JOptionPane.showInputDialog(
        "Enter first floating-point value" );
```

read the first floating-point number from the user. Method JOptionPane.showInputDialog displays an input dialog that prompts the user to enter a value. The user types a value in the input dialog's text field, then clicks the **OK** button to return the string the user typed to the program. [If you type and nothing appears in the text field, position the mouse pointer in the text field and click the mouse to make the text field active.]

Technically, the user can type anything he or she wants here. For this program if the user either types a non-numeric value or clicks the **Cancel** button, a run-time error will occur and a message will be displayed in the command window from which the appletviewer was executed.

Variable firstNumber is given the result of the call to JOptionPane.showInputDialog operation with an assignment statement. The statement is read as "firstNumber *gets* the value of JOptionPane.showInputDialog("Enter first floating-point value")."

Lines 21 through 24

```
// read in second number from user
secondNumber =
    JOptionPane.showInputDialog(
        "Enter second floating-point value" );
```

read the second floating-point value from the user by displaying an input dialog.

Lines 26 through 28

```
// convert numbers from type String to type int
number1 = Double.parseDouble( firstNumber );
number2 = Double.parseDouble( secondNumber );
```

convert the two strings input by the user to double values that can be used in a calculation. Method *Double.parseDouble* (a static method of class Double) converts its String argument to a double floating-point value Double is part of the package java.lang. The floating-point value returned by Double.parseDouble in line 27 is assigned to variable number1. Any subsequent references to number1 in the method use this same floating-point value. The floating-point value returned by Double.parseDouble in line 28 is assigned to variable number2. Any subsequent references to number2 in the method use this same floating-point value.

Software Engineering Observation 24.10

For each primitive data type (such as `int` *or* `double`*) there is a corresponding class (such as* `Integer` *or* `Double`*) in package* `java.lang`*. These classes (commonly known as type-wrappers) provide methods for processing primitive data type values (such as converting a* `String` *to a primitive data type value or converting a primitive data type value to a* `String`*). Primitive data types do not have methods. Therefore, methods related to a primitive data type are located in the corresponding type-wrapper class (i.e., method* `parseDouble` *that converts a* `String` *to a* `double` *value is located in class* `Double`*).*

The assignment statement in line 31

```
sum = number1 + number2;
```

calculates the sum of the variables `number1` and `number2` and assigns the result to variable `sum` using the assignment operator `=`. The statement is read as "`sum` *gets* the value of `number1 + number2`." Most calculations are performed in assignment statements. Notice that instance variable `sum` is used in the preceding statement in method `init` even though `sum` was not defined in method `init`. We defined `sum` as an instance variable, so we can use it in `init` and all other methods of the class.

The applet's `init` method returns and the `appletviewer` or browser calls the applet's `start` method. We did not define method `start` in this applet so the one provided by class `JApplet` is used here. The `start` method is primarily used with an advanced concept called multithreading, which we do not discuss in these introductory chapters.

Next, the browser calls the applet's `paint` method. In this example, method `paint` draws a rectangle containing the string with the result of the addition. Line 37

```
g.drawRect( 15, 10, 270, 20 );
```

sends the `drawRect` message to the `Graphics` object to which g refers (calls the `Graphics` object's `drawRect` method). Method `drawRect` draws a rectangle based on its four arguments. The first two integer values represent the *upper-left x-coordinate* and *upper-left y-coordinate* where the `Graphics` object begins drawing the rectangle. The third and fourth arguments are non-negative integers that represent the *width* of the rectangle in pixels and the *height* of the rectangle in pixels, respectively. This particular statement draws a rectangle starting at coordinate *(15, 10)* that is 270 pixels wide and 20 pixels high.

Common Programming Error 24.17

It is a logic error to supply a negative width or negative height as an argument to `Graphics` *method* `drawRect`*. The rectangle will not be displayed and no error will be indicated.*

Common Programming Error 24.18

It is a logic error to supply two points (i.e., pairs of x- and y-coordinates) as the arguments to `Graphics` *method* `drawRect`*. The third argument must be the width in pixels and the fourth argument must be the height in pixels of the rectangle to draw.*

Common Programming Error 24.19

It is normally a logic error to supply arguments to `Graphics` *method* `drawRect` *that cause the rectangle to draw outside the applet's viewable area (i.e., the width and height of the applet as specified in the HTML document that references the applet). Either increase the applet's width and height in the HTML document or pass arguments to method* `drawRect` *that cause the rectangle to draw inside the applet's viewable area.*

Line 38

```
g.drawString( "The sum is " + sum, 25, 25 );
```

sends the **drawString** message to the **Graphics** object to which **g** refers (calls the **Graphics** object's **drawString** method). The expression

```
"The sum is " + sum
```

from the preceding statement uses the string concatenation operator + to concatenate the string **"The sum is "** and **sum** (converted to a string) to create the string displayed by **drawString**. Notice again that instance variable **sum** is used in the preceding statement even though it was not defined in method **paint**.

The benefit of defining **sum** as an instance variable is that we were able to assign **sum** a value in **init** and use **sum**'s value in the **paint** method later in the program. All methods of a class are capable of using the instance variables in the class definition.

Software Engineering Observation 24.11

*The only statements that should be placed in an applet's **init** method are those that are directly related to the one-time initialization of an applet's instance variables. The applet's results should be displayed from other methods of the applet class. Results that involve drawing should be displayed from the applet's **paint** method.*

Software Engineering Observation 24.12

*The only statements that should be placed in an applet's **paint** method are those that are directly related to drawing (i.e., calls to methods of class **Graphics**) and the logic of drawing. Generally, dialog boxes should not be displayed from an applet's **paint** method.*

In this chapter we have introduced many important features of Java, including applications, applets, displaying data on the screen, inputting data from the keyboard, performing calculations and making decisions. In the next chapter we introduce some of the differences between Java and C/C++, such as arrays, operators and method definitions. In later chapters we introduce object-based and object-oriented programming as well as Java's graphics, graphical user interface (GUI) and multimedia features.

SUMMARY

- Java is one of today's most popular software development languages.
- Java was developed by Sun Microsystems. Sun provides an implementation of the Java 2 Platform called the Java 2 Software Development Kit (J2SDK) that includes the minimum set of tools you need to write software in Java.
- Java is a fully object-oriented language with strong support for proper software engineering techniques.
- Java systems generally consist of several parts: an environment, the language, the Java Applications Programming Interface (API), and various class libraries.
- Java programs normally go through five phases to be executed—edit, compile, load, verify and execute.
- Java program file names end with the **.java** extension.
- The Java compiler (**javac**) translates a Java program into bytecodes—the language understood by the Java interpreter. If a program compiles correctly, a file with the **.class** extension is produced. This is the file containing the bytecodes that are interpreted during the execution phase.

- A Java program must first be placed in memory before it can be executed. This is done by the class loader, which takes the .class file (or files) containing the bytecodes and transfers it to memory. The .class file can be loaded from a disk on your system or over a network.

- An application is a program that executes using the java interpreter.

- A comment that begins with // is called a single-line comment. Programmers insert comments to document programs and improve program readability.

- A string of characters contained between double quotation marks is called a string, a character string, a message or a string literal.

- Keyword class introduces a class definition and is immediately followed by the class name.

- Keywords (or reserved words) are reserved for use by Java.

- By convention, all class names in Java begin with a capital first letter. If a class name has more than one word, each word should be capitalized.

- An identifier is a series of characters consisting of letters, digits, underscores (_) and dollar signs ($) that does not begin with a digit, does not contain any spaces and is not a keyword.

- Java is case sensitive—uppercase and lowercase letters are different.

- A left brace, {, begins the body of every class definition. A corresponding right brace, }, ends each class definition.

- Java applications begin executing at method main.

- The first line of method main must be defined as

      public static void main(String args[])

- A left brace, {, begins the body of a method definition. A corresponding right brace, }, ends the method definition's body.

- System.out is known as the standard output object. System.out allows Java applications to display strings and other types of information in the command window from which the Java application is executed.

- The escape sequence \n means newline. Other escape sequences include \t (tab), \r (carriage return), \\ (backslash) and \" (double quote).

- Method println of the System.out object displays (or prints) a line of information in the command window. When println completes its task, it automatically positions to the beginning of the next line in the command window.

- Every statement must end with a semicolon (also known as the statement terminator).

- The difference between System.out.print and System.out.println is that System.out.print does not position to the beginning of the next line in the command window when it finishes displaying its argument. The next character that is displayed in the command window will appear immediately after the last character displayed with System.out.print.

- Java contains many predefined classes that are grouped by directories on disk into categories of related classes called packages. The packages are referred to collectively as the Java class library or the Java applications programming interface (Java API).

- Class JOptionPane is defined for us in a package called javax.swing. Class JOptionPane contains methods that display a dialog box containing information.

- The compiler uses import statements to locate classes required to compile a Java program.

- The javax.swing package contains many classes that help define a graphical user interface (GUI) for an application. GUI components facilitate data entry by the user of a program and data outputs by a program.

- Method showMessageDialog of class JOptionPane requires two arguments. Until we discuss JOptionPane in detail in Chapter 29, the first argument will always be the keyword null. The second argument is the string to display.

- A static method is called by following its class name by a dot (.) and the method name.

- Method exit of class System terminates an application. Class System is part of the package java.lang. Package java.lang is automatically imported in every Java program.

- Variables of type int hold integer values (i.e., whole numbers such as 7, –11, 0, 31914).

- Types such as int, float, double and char are often called primitive data types. Primitive type names are keywords of the Java programming language.

- Method Integer.parseInt (a static method of class Integer) converts its String argument to an integer.

- Java has a version of the + operator for string concatenation that enables a string and a value of another data type (including another string) to be concatenated.

- Variable names correspond to locations in the computer's memory. Every variable has a name, a type, a size and a value.

- Every variable declared in a method must be initialized before it can be used in an expression.

- An applet is a Java program that runs in the appletviewer (a test utility for applets that is included with the J2SDK) or a World Wide Web browser such as Netscape Communicator or Microsoft Internet Explorer. The appletviewer (or browser) executes an applet when a Hypertext Markup Language (HTML) document containing the applet is opened in the appletviewer (or browser).

- In the appletviewer, you can execute an applet again by clicking the appletviewer's **Applet** menu and selecting the Reload option from the menu. To terminate an applet, click the appletviewer's **Applet** menu and select the Quit option.

- Class Graphics is located in package java.awt. Import the Graphics class so the program can draw graphics.

- Class JApplet is located in package javax.swing. When you create an applet in Java, you normally import the JApplet class.

- Each piece of the package name is a directory (or folder) on disk. All the packages in the Java API are stored in the directory java or javax, which contain many subdirectories.

- Java uses inheritance to create new classes from existing class definitions. Keyword extends followed by a class name indicates the class from which a new class inherits.

- In the inheritance relationship, the class following extends is called the superclass or base class and the new class is called the subclass or derived class. Using inheritance results in a new class definition that has the attributes (data) and behaviors (methods) of the superclass as well as the new features added in the subclass definition.

- A benefit of extending class JApplet is that someone else has already defined "what it means to be an applet." The appletviewer and World Wide Web browsers that support applets expect every Java applet to have certain capabilities (attributes and behaviors), and class JApplet already provides all those capabilities.

- Classes are used as "templates" or "blueprints" to instantiate (or create) objects in memory for use in a program. An object (or instance) is a region in the computer's memory in which information is stored for use by the program. The term object normally implies that attributes (data) and behaviors (methods) are associated with the object and that those behaviors perform operations on the attributes of the object.

- Method paint is one of three methods (behaviors) that are guaranteed to be called automatically for you when any applet begins execution. These three methods are init, start and paint, and they are guaranteed to be called in that order. These methods are called from the `appletviewer` or browser in which the applet is executing.

- Method `drawString` of class `Graphics` draws a string at the specified location on the applet. The first argument to `drawString` is the `String` to draw. The last two arguments in the list are the coordinates (or position) at which the string should be drawn. Coordinates are measured from the upper-left corner of the applet in pixels.

- You must create an HTML (Hypertext Markup Language) file to load an applet into the `appletviewer` (or a browser) to execute.

- Many HTML codes (referred to as tags) come in pairs. HTML tags begin with a left angle bracket < and end with a right angle bracket >.

- Normally, the applet and its corresponding HTML file are stored in the same directory on disk.

- The first component of the `<applet>` tag indicates the file containing the compiled applet class. The second and third components of the `<applet>` tag indicate the `width` and the `height` of the applet in pixels. Generally, each applet should be less than 640 pixels wide and 480 pixels high (most computer screens support these dimensions as the minimum width and height).

- The `appletviewer` only understands the `<applet>` and `</applet>` HTML tags, so it is sometimes referred to as the "minimal browser" (it ignores all other HTML tags).

- Method `drawLine` of class `Graphics` draws lines. The method requires four arguments representing the two end points of the line on the applet—the x-coordinate and y-coordinate of the first end point in the line and the x-coordinate and y-coordinate of the second end point in the line. All coordinate values are specified with respect to the upper-left corner (0, 0) coordinate of the applet.

- Primitive data type `double` stores double-precision floating-point numbers. Primitive data type `float` stores single-precision floating-point numbers. A `double` requires more memory to store a floating-point value, but stores it with approximately twice the precision of a `float` (15 significant digits for `double` vs. seven significant digits for `float`).

- The `import` statements are not required if you always use the complete name of a class, including the full package name and class name.

- The asterisk (`*`) notation after a package name in an `import` indicates that all classes in the package should be available to the compiler so the compiler can ensure that the classes are used correctly. This allows programmers to use the shorthand name (the class name by itself) of any class from the package in the program.

- Every instance (object) of the class contains one copy of each instance variable. Instance variables are declared in the body of the class definition, but not in the body of any method of the class definition. An important benefit of instance variables is that their identifiers can be used throughout the class definition (i.e., in all methods of the class).

- Method `init` is called once during an applet's execution. The method normally initializes the applet's instance variables and performs any tasks that need to be performed once at the beginning of an applet's execution.

- Method `Double.parseDouble` (a `static` method of class `Double`) converts its `String` argument to a `double` floating-point value. Class `Double` is part of the package `java.lang`.

TERMINOLOGY

!= "is not equal to"
< "is less than"
<= "is less than or equal to"
== "is equal to"

> "is greater than"
>= "is greater than or equal to"
addition operator (+)
applet

application
argument to a method
assignment operator (=)
assignment statement
associativity of operators
backslash (\) escape character
binary operator
body of a class definition
body of a method definition
braces ({ and })
case sensitive
character string
class
class definition
.class file extension
class keyword
class name
command tool
command window
comma-separated list
comment (//)
compilation error
compile error
compiler
compile-time error
declaration
dialog box
division operator (/)
document a program
empty string ("")
equality operators
escape sequence
false
graphical user interface (GUI)
identifier
import statement
input dialog
int primitive type
integer (int)
Integer class
integer division
interpreter
Java
Java 2 Software Development Kit (J2SDK)
Java applications programming interface (API)
Java class library
Java documentation comment
.java file extension
java interpreter
java.lang package

javax.swing package
JOptionPane class
JOptionPane.ERROR_MESSAGE
JOptionPane.INFORMATION_MESSAGE
JOptionPane.PLAIN_MESSAGE
JOptionPane.QUESTION_MESSAGE
JOptionPane.showInputDialog
JOptionPane.showMessageDialog
JOptionPane.WARNING_MESSAGE
left brace { begins the body of a class
left brace { begins the body of a method
literal
main method
memory
memory location
message
message dialog
method
Microsoft Internet Explorer browser
modulus operator (%)
mouse cursor
mouse pointer
MS-DOS Prompt
multiple-line comment
multiplication operator (*)
nested parentheses
Netscape Communicator browser
newline character (\n)
object
operand
operator
package
parentheses ()
parseInt method of class Integer
precedence
primitive data type
programmer-defined class
prompt
public keyword
relational operators
reserved words
right brace } ends the body of a class
right brace } ends the body of a method
right-to-left associativity
rules of operator precedence
semicolon (;) statement terminator
shell tool
single-line comment
standard output object
statement

statement terminator (;)	`System.out`
`static` method	`System.out.print` method
straight-line form	`System.out.println` method
string	title bar of a dialog
`String` class	`true`
string concatenation	user-defined class
string concatenation operator (+)	variable
subtraction operator (-)	variable name
syntax error	variable value
`System` class	`void` keyword
`System.exit` method	white-space characters

COMMON PROGRAMMING ERRORS

24.1 Errors like division-by-zero errors occur as a program runs, so these errors are called *run-time errors* or *execution-time errors*. *Fatal run-time errors* cause programs to terminate immediately without having successfully performed their jobs. *Nonfatal run-time errors* allow programs to run to completion, often producing incorrect results.

24.2 Forgetting one of the delimiters of a multiple-line comment is a syntax error.

24.3 Java is case sensitive. Not using the proper uppercase and lowercase letters for an identifier is normally a syntax error.

24.4 For a `public` class, it is an error if the file name is not identical to the class name in both spelling and capitalization. Therefore, it is also an error for a file to contain two or more `public` classes.

24.5 It is an error not to end a file name with the `.java` extension for a file containing an application's class definition. The Java compiler will not be able to compile the class definition.

24.6 If braces do not occur in matching pairs, the compiler indicates an error.

24.7 Omitting the semicolon at the end of a statement is a syntax error.

24.8 Splitting a statement in the middle of an identifier or a string is a syntax error.

24.9 Forgetting to call `System.exit` in an application that displays a graphical user interface prevents the program from terminating properly. This normally results in the command window preventing you from typing any other commands.

24.10 Confusing the + operator used for string concatenation with the + operator used for addition can lead to strange results. For example, assuming integer variable y has the value 5, the expression `"y + 2 = " + y + 2` results in the string `"y + 2 = 52"`, not `"y + 2 = 7"`, because first the value of y is concatenated with the string `"y + 2 = "`, then the value 2 is concatenated with the new larger string `"y + 2 = 5"`. The expression `"y + 2 = " + (y + 2)` produces the desired result.

24.11 Placing additional characters such as commas (,) between the components in the `<applet>` tag may cause the `appletviewer` or browser to produce an error message indicating a `MissingResourceException` when loading the applet.

24.12 Forgetting the ending `</applet>` tag prevents the applet from loading into the `appletviewer` or browser properly.

24.13 Running the `appletviewer` with a file name that does not end with `.html` or `.htm` is an error that prevents the `appletviewer` from loading your applet for execution.

24.14 Assuming that an `import` statement for an entire package (e.g., `java.awt.*`) also `imports` classes from subdirectories in that package (e.g., `java.awt.event.*`) results in syntax errors for the classes from the subdirectories. There must be separate import statements for every package from which classes are used.

24.15 If braces do not occur in matching pairs, the compiler indicates a syntax error.

24.16 Using a local variable that is not initialized before it is used is a syntax error. Each local variable must be assigned a value before an attempt is made to use that variable's value.

24.17 It is a logic error to supply a negative width or negative height as an argument to Graphics method drawRect. The rectangle will not be displayed and no error will be indicated.

24.18 It is a logic error to supply two points (i.e., pairs of *x*- and *y*-coordinates) as the arguments to Graphics method drawRect. The third argument must be the width in pixels and the fourth argument must be the height in pixels of the rectangle to draw.

24.19 It is normally a logic error to supply arguments to Graphics method drawRect that cause the rectangle to draw outside the applet's viewable area (i.e., the width and height of the applet as specified in the HTML document that references the applet). Either increase the applet's width and height in the HTML document or pass arguments to method drawRect that cause the rectangle to draw inside the applet's viewable area.

ERROR-PREVENTION TIPS

24.1 Always test your Java programs on all systems on which you intend to run those programs.

24.2 When the compiler reports a syntax error, the error may not be on the line indicated by the error messages. First, check the line where the error was reported. If that line does not contain syntax errors, check the preceding several lines in the program.

24.3 If the appletviewer command does not work and/or the system indicates that the appletviewer command cannot be found, the PATH environment variable may not be defined properly on your computer. Review the installation directions for the Java 2 Software Development Kit to ensure that the PATH environment variable is correctly defined for your system (on some computers, you may need to restart your computer after defining the PATH environment variable).

24.4 The compiler error message "Public class ClassName must be defined in a file called *ClassName*.java" indicates either 1) that the file name does not exactly match the name of the public class in the file (including all uppercase and lowercase letters), or 2) that you typed the class name incorrectly when compiling the class (the name must be spelled with the proper uppercase and lowercase letters).

24.5 If you receive a MissingResourceException error message when loading an applet into the appletviewer or a browser, check the <applet> tag in the HTML file carefully for syntax errors. Compare your HTML file to the file in Fig. 24.15 to confirm proper syntax.

GOOD PROGRAMMING PRACTICES

24.1 Write your Java programs in a simple and straightforward manner. This is sometimes referred to as *KIS ("keep it simple")*. Do not "stretch" the language by trying bizarre usages.

24.2 Read the documentation for the version of Java you are using. Refer to this documentation frequently to be sure you are aware of the rich collection of Java features and that you are using these features correctly.

24.3 Your computer and compiler are good teachers. If after carefully reading your Java documentation manual you are not sure how a feature of Java works, experiment and see what happens. Study each error or warning message you get when you compile your programs and correct these programs to eliminate the messages.

24.4 By convention, you should always begin a class name with a capital first letter.

24.5 When reading a Java program, look for identifiers that start with capital first letters. These normally represent Java classes.

24.6 Whenever you type an opening left brace, {, in your program, immediately type the closing right brace, }, then reposition the cursor between the braces to begin typing the body. This helps prevent missing braces.

24.7   Indent the entire body of each class definition one "level" of indentation between the left brace, {, and the right brace, }, that define the body of the class. This emphasizes the structure of the class definition and helps make the class definition easier to read.

24.8   Set a convention for the indent size you prefer, then uniformly apply that convention. The *Tab* key may be used to create indents, but tab stops may vary between editors. We recommend using either 1/4-inch tab stops or (preferably) three spaces to form a level of indent.

24.9   Indent the entire body of each method definition one "level" of indentation between the left brace, {, and the right brace, }, that define the body of the method. This makes the structure of the method stand out and helps make the method definition easier to read.

24.10   Place a space after each comma in an argument list (,) to make programs more readable.

24.11   Choosing meaningful variable names helps a program to be "self-documenting" (i.e., it becomes easier to understand a program simply by reading it rather than having to read manuals or use excessive comments).

24.12   By convention, variable name identifiers begin with a lowercase first letter. As with class names every word in the name after the first word should begin with a capital first letter. For example, identifier `firstNumber` has a capital N in its second word `Number`.

24.13   Some programmers prefer to declare each variable on a separate line. This format allows for easy insertion of a descriptive comment next to each declaration.

24.14   Place spaces on either side of a binary operator. This makes the operator stand out and makes the program more readable.

24.15   Investigate the capabilities of any class in the Java API documentation carefully before inheriting a subclass from it. This helps ensure that the programmer does not unintentionally redefine a capability that is already provided.

24.16   Always test a Java applet in the `appletviewer` and ensure that it is executing correctly before loading the applet into a World Wide Web browser. Browsers often save a copy of an applet in memory until the current browsing session terminates (i.e., all browser windows are closed). Thus, if you change an applet, recompile the applet, then reload the applet in the browser, you may not see the changes because the browser may still be executing the original version of the applet. Close all your browser windows to remove the old version of the applet from memory. Open a new browser window and load the applet to see your changes.

24.17   Initializing instance variables rather than relying on automatic initialization improves program readability.

PORTABILITY TIPS

24.3   Although it is easier to write portable programs in Java than in most other programming languages, there are differences among compilers, interpreters and computers that can make portability difficult to achieve. Simply writing programs in Java does not guarantee portability. The programmer will occasionally need to deal directly with compiler and computer variations.

24.4   Test your applets in every browser used by people who view your applet. This will help ensure that people who view your applet experience the functionality you expect. [*Note:* A goal of the Java Plug-In (discussed later in the book) is to provide consistent applet execution across many different browsers.]

SOFTWARE ENGINEERING OBSERVATIONS

24.1   Avoid using identifiers containing dollar signs ($) as these are often used by the compiler to create identifier names.

24.2 If your World Wide Web browser does not support Java 2, most of the applets in this book will not execute in your browser. This is because most of the applets in this book use features that are new to Java 2 or are not provided by browsers that support Java 1.1.

24.3 Generally, each applet should be less than 640 pixels wide and 480 pixels tall (most computer screens support these dimensions as the minimum width and height).

24.4 The Java compiler does not need `import` statements in a Java source code file if the complete class name—the full package name and class name (e.g., `java.awt.Graphics`)—is specified every time a class name is used in the source code.

24.5 The compiler does not load every class in a package when it encounters an `import` statement that uses the * (e.g., `javax.swing.*`) notation to indicate that multiple classes from the package are used in the program. The compiler searches the package only for those classes used in the program.

24.6 Many package directories have subdirectories. For example, the `java.awt` package directory contains subdirectory `event` for the package `java.awt.event`. When the compiler encounters an `import` statement that uses the * (e.g., `java.awt.*`) notation to indicate that multiple classes from the package are used in the program, the compiler does not search the subdirectory `event`. This means that you cannot define an `import` of `java.*` to search for classes from all packages.

24.7 When using `import` statements, separate `import` statements must be specified for each package used in a program.

24.8 The order in which methods are defined in a class definition has no effect on when those methods are called at execution time.

24.9 A hint to help you determine if an identifier is a variable or a reference is the variable's data type. By convention all class names in Java start with a capitalized first letter. Therefore, if the data type starts with a capitalized first letter, you can normally assume that the identifier is a reference to an object of the declared type (e.g., `Graphics g` indicates that `g` is a reference to a `Graphics` object).

24.10 For each primitive data type (such as `int` or `double`) there is a corresponding class (such as `Integer` or `Double`) in package `java.lang`. These classes (commonly known as typewrappers) provide methods for processing primitive data type values (such as converting a `String` to a primitive data type value or converting a primitive data type value to a `String`). Primitive data types do not have methods. Therefore, methods related to a primitive data type are located in the corresponding type-wrapper class (i.e., method `parseDouble` that converts a `String` to a `double` value is located in class `Double`).

24.11 The only statements that should be placed in an applet's `init` method are those that are directly related to the one-time initialization of an applet's instance variables. The applet's results should be displayed from other methods of the applet class. Results that involve drawing should be displayed from the applet's `paint` method.

24.12 The only statements that should be placed in an applet's `paint` method are those that are directly related to drawing (i.e., calls to methods of class `Graphics`) and the logic of drawing. Generally, dialog boxes should not be displayed from an applet's `paint` method.

SELF-REVIEW EXERCISES

24.1 Fill in the blanks in each of the following.

a) _____ begins a single-line comment.

b) Class _____ displays message dialogs and input dialogs.

c) _____ are reserved for use by Java.

d) Java applications begin execution at method _____.

e) Methods _____ and _____ display information in the command window.

f) A(n) _____ method is always called using its class name followed by a dot (.) and its method name.

24.2   State whether each of the following is *true* or *false*. If *false*, explain why.

a) Comments cause the computer to print the text after the // on the screen when the program is executed.

b) All variables must be given a type when they are declared.

c) Java considers the variables number and NuMbEr to be identical.

d) Method Integer.parseInt converts an integer to a String.

24.3   Write Java statements to accomplish each of the following:

a) Declare variables c, thisIsAVariable, q76354 and number to be of type int.

b) Display a dialog asking the user to enter an integer.

c) Convert a String to an integer and store the converted value in integer variable age. Assume that the String is stored in stringValue.

d) If the variable number is not equal to 7, display "The variable number is not equal to 7" in a message dialog. [*Hint:* Use the version of the message dialog that requires two arguments.]

e) Print the message "This is a Java program" on one line in the command window.

f) Print the message "This is a Java program" on two lines in the command window where the first line ends with Java. Use only one statement.

24.4   Identify and correct the errors in the following statement:

```
if ( c => 7 )
    JOptionPane.showMessageDialog( null,
    "c is equal to or greater than 7" );
```

24.5   Fill in the blanks in each of the following.

a) Class _____ provides methods for drawing.

b) Java applets begin execution with a series of three method calls: _____, _____ and _____.

c) Methods _____ and _____ display lines and rectangles.

d) Keyword _____ is used to indicate that a new class is a subclass of an existing class.

e) Every Java applet should extend either class _____ or class _____.

f) A class definition describes the _____ and _____ of an object.

g) Java's eight primitive data types are _____, _____, _____, _____, _____, _____, _____ and _____.

24.6   State whether each of the following is *true* or *false*. If *false*, explain why.

a) Method drawRect requires four arguments that specify two points on the applet to draw a rectangle.

b) Method drawLine requires four arguments that specify two points on the applet to draw a line.

c) Type Double is a primitive data type.

d) Data type int is used to declare a floating-point number.

e) Method Double.parseDouble converts a String to a primitive double value.

24.7   Write Java statements to accomplish each of the following:

a) Display a dialog asking the user to enter a floating-point number.

b) Convert a String to a floating-point number and store the converted value in double variable age. Assume that the String is stored in stringValue.

c) Draw the message "This is a Java program" on one line on an applet (assume you are defining this statement in the applet's paint method) at position *(10, 10)*.

d) Draw the message "This is a Java program" on two lines on an applet (assume these statements are defined in applet method paint) starting at position *(10, 10)* and where the first line ends with Java. Make the two lines start at the same *x* coordinate.

ANSWERS TO SELF-REVIEW EXERCISES

24.1 a) //. b) JOptionPane. c) Keywords. d) main. e) System.out.print and System.out.println. f) static.

24.2 a) False. Comments do not cause any action to be performed when the program is executed. They are used to document programs and improve their readability.
  b) True.
  c) False. Java is case sensitive, so these variables are distinct.
  d) False. Integer.parseInt method converts a String to an integer (int) value.

24.3 a) int c, thisIsAVariable, q76354, number;
  b) value = JOptionPane.showInputDialog("Enter an integer");
  c) age = Integer.parseInt(stringValue);
  d) if (number != 7)
          JOptionPane.showMessageDialog(null,
              "The variable number is not equal to 7");
  e) System.out.println("This is a Java program");
  f) System.out.println("This is a Java\nprogram");

24.4 Error: The relational operator => is incorrect.
  Correction: Change => to >=.

24.5 a) Graphics. b) init, start and paint. c) drawLine and drawRect. d) extends.
e) JApplet, Applet. f) attributes and behaviors. g) byte, short, int, long, float, double, char and boolean.

24.6 a) False. Method drawRect requires four arguments—two that specify the upper-left corner of the rectangle and two that specify the width and height of the rectangle.
  b) True.
  c) False. Type Double is a class in the java.lang package. Remember that names that start with a capital first letter are normally class names.
  d) False. Data type double or data type float can be used to declare a floating-point number. Data type int is used to declare integers.
  e) True.

24.7 a) value = JOptionPane.showInputDialog(
              "Enter a floating-point number");
  b) age = Double.parseDouble(stringValue);
  c) g.drawString("This is a Java program", 10, 10);
  d) g.drawString("This is a Java", 10, 10);
      g.drawString("program", 10, 25);

EXERCISES

24.8 Fill in the blanks in each of the following:
  a) _____ are used to document a program and improve its readability.
  b) An input dialog capable of receiving input from the user is displayed with method _____ of class _____.

24.9 Write Java statements that accomplish each of the following:
  a) Display the message "Enter two numbers" using class JOptionPane.

    b) Assign the product of variables b and c to variable a.

    c) State that a program performs a sample payroll calculation (i.e., use text that helps to document a program).

24.10 What displays in the message dialog when each of the following Java statements is performed? Assume x = 2 and y = 3.

    a) `JOptionPane.showMessageDialog( null, "x = " + x );`

    b) `JOptionPane.showMessageDialog( null,`
           `"The value of x + x is " + ( x + x ) );`

    c) `JOptionPane.showMessageDialog( null, "x =" );`

    d) `JOptionPane.showMessageDialog(null,`
           `( x + y ) + " = " + ( y + x ) );`

24.11 Write an application that asks the user to enter two numbers, obtains the two numbers from the user and prints the sum, product, difference and quotient of the two numbers. Use the techniques shown in Fig. 24.7.

24.12 Write an application that asks the user to enter two integers, obtains the numbers from the user and displays the larger number followed by the words "is larger" in an information message dialog. If the numbers are equal, print the message "These numbers are equal." Use the techniques shown in Fig. 24.7.

24.13 Write an application that inputs three integers from the user and displays the sum, average, product, smallest and largest of these numbers in an information message dialog. Use the GUI techniques shown in Fig. 24.7. [*Note:* The average calculation in this exercise should result in an integer representation of the average. So, if the sum of the values is 7, the average will be 2 not 2.3333...]

24.14 Write an application that inputs from the user the radius of a circle and prints the circle's diameter, circumference and area. Use the constant value 3.14159 for π. Use the GUI techniques shown in Fig. 24.7. [*Note:* You may also use the predefined constant Math.PI for the value of π. This constant is more precise than the value 3.14159. Class Math is defined in the java.lang package, so you do not need to import it.] Use the following formulas (*r* is the radius): *diameter = 2r, circumference = 2πr, area = πr²*.

24.15 Write an application that displays in the command window a box, an oval, an arrow and a diamond using asterisks (*) as follows:

```
*********        ***           *              *
*       *       *   *         ***            *  *
*       *      *     *       *****          *    *
*       *      *     *         *           *      *
*       *      *     *         *          *        *
*       *      *     *         *          *        *
*       *      *     *         *           *      *
*       *      *     *         *            *    *
*       *       *   *          *             *  *
*********        ***           *              *
```

24.16 Modify the program you created in Exercise 24.15 to display the shapes in a JOptionPane.PLAIN_MESSAGE dialog.

24.17 Write a program that reads a first name and a last name from the user as two separate inputs and concatenates the first name and last name separated by a space. Display in a message dialog the concatenated name.

25

Beyond C and C++: Operators, Methods and Arrays in Java

Objectives

- To understand primitive types and logical operators as they are used in Java.
- To introduce the common math methods available in the Java API.
- To be able to create new methods.
- To understand the mechanisms used to pass information between methods.
- To introduce simulation techniques using random number generation.
- To understand array objects in Java.
- To understand how to write and use methods that call themselves.

Form ever follows function.
Louis Henri Sullivan

E pluribus unum.
(One composed of many.)
Virgil

O! call back yesterday, bid time return.
William Shakespeare, *Richard II*

Call me Ishmael.
Herman Melville, *Moby Dick*

When you call me that, smile.
Owen Wister

25.1 Introduction

In this chapter we introduce some of the key differences between Java, C and C++. We begin by introducing primitive data types and keywords in Java. We then discuss Java's logical operators and methods as well as the packages that comprise the Java *Application Programming Interface (API)*.

In Chapter 5 we wrote a simulator for playing the game of craps. We revisit this example in Section 25.7 on page 926, where we add a *graphical user interface (GUI) and discuss how to generate random numbers in Java. We end the chapter with a discussion of Java arrays and how they improve upon arrays in C and C++.*

25.2 Primitive Data Types and Keywords

The table in Fig. 25.1 lists the primitive data types in Java. The primitive types are the building blocks for more complicated types. Like its predecessor languages C and C++, Java requires all variables to have a type before they can be used in a program. For this reason, Java is referred to as a *strongly typed language.*

Type	Size in bits	Values	Standard
boolean		true or false	
char	16	'\u0000' to '\uFFFF'	(ISO Unicode character set)

Fig. 25.1   The Java primitive data types. (Part 1 of 2.)

Type	Size in bits	Values	Standard
byte	8	−128 to +127	
short	16	−32,768 to +32,767	
int	32	−2,147,483,648 to +2,147,483,647	
long	64	−9,223,372,036,854,775,808 to +9,223,372,036,854,775,807	
float	32	−3.40292347E+38 to +3.40292347E+38	(IEEE 754 floating point)
double	64	−1.79769313486231570E+308 to +1.79769313486231570E+308	(IEEE 754 floating point)

Fig. 25.1   The Java primitive data types. (Part 2 of 2.)

Unlike C and C++, the primitive types in Java are portable across all computer platforms that support Java. This and many other portability features of Java enable programmers to write programs once without knowing which computer platform will execute the program. This is sometimes referred to as "WORA" (Write Once Run Anywhere).

In C and C++ programs, programmers frequently had to write separate versions of programs to support different computer platforms because the primitive data types were not guaranteed to be identical from computer to computer. For example, an int value on one machine might be represented by 16 bits (2 bytes) of memory and an int value on another machine might be represented by 32 bits (4 bytes) of memory. In Java, int values are always 32 bits (4 bytes).

Portability Tip 25.1

All primitive data types in Java are portable across all platforms that support Java.

Each data type in the table is listed with its size in bits (there are 8 bits to a byte) and its range of values. The designers of Java want maximum portability, so they chose to use internationally recognized standards for both character formats (Unicode) and for floating-point numbers (IEEE 754).

Whenever instance variables of the primitive data types are declared in a class, they are assigned default values unless specified otherwise by the programmer. Variables of types char, byte, short, int, long, float and double are all given the value 0 by default. Variables of type boolean are given false by default.

Each of the words boolean, char, byte, short, int, long, float and double are Java keywords. These words are reserved by the language to implement various features, such as Java's primitive data types. Keywords cannot be used as identifiers such as for variable names. A complete list of Java keywords is shown in Fig. 25.2.

Common Programming Error 25.1

Using a keyword as an identifier is a syntax error.

Java Keywords				
abstract	boolean	break	byte	case
catch	char	class	continue	default
do	double	else	extends	false
final	finally	float	for	if
implements	import	instanceof	int	interface
long	native	new	null	package
private	protected	public	return	short
static	super	switch	synchronized	this
throw	throws	transient	true	try
void	volatile	while		
Keywords that are reserved but not used by Java				
const	goto			

Fig. 25.2   Java keywords.

25.3 Logical Operators

Java provides *logical operators* that may be used to form complex conditions for control structures by combining simple conditions. The logical operators are **&&** *(logical AND),* **&** *(boolean logical AND),* **| |** *(logical OR),* **|** *(boolean logical inclusive OR),* **^** *(boolean logical exclusive OR)* and **!** *(logical NOT,* also called *logical negation).* We will consider examples of each of these.

Suppose we wish to ensure at some point in a program that two conditions are *both* true before we choose a certain path of execution. In this case we can use the logical **&&** operator as follows:

```
if ( gender == 1 && age >= 65 )
    ++seniorFemales;
```

This `if` statement contains two simple conditions. The condition `gender == 1` might be evaluated, for example, to determine if a person is a female. The condition `age >= 65` is evaluated to determine if a person is a senior citizen. The two simple conditions are evaluated first because the precedences of `==` and `>=` are both higher than the precedence of `&&`. The `if` statement then considers the combined condition

```
gender == 1 && age >= 65
```

This condition is `true` *if and only if* both of the simple conditions are `true`. Finally, if this combined condition is indeed `true`, the count of `seniorFemales` is incremented by `1`. If either or both of the simple conditions are `false`, the program skips the incrementing and proceeds to the statement following the `if` structure. The preceding combined condition can be made more readable by adding redundant parentheses:

```
( gender == 1 ) && ( age >= 65 )
```

The table of Fig. 25.3 summarizes the **&&** operator. The table shows all four possible combinations of `false` and `true` values for *expression1* and *expression2*. Such tables are often called *truth tables*. Java evaluates to `false` or `true` all expressions that include relational operators, equality operators and/or logical operators.

expression1	expression2	expression1 && expression2
false	false	false
false	true	false
true	false	false
true	true	true

Fig. 25.3   Truth table for the && (logical AND) operator.

Now let us consider the || (logical OR) operator. Suppose we wish to ensure that either *or* both of two conditions are `true` before we choose a certain path of execution. In this case we use the || operator as in the following program segment:

```
if ( semesterAverage >= 90 || finalExam >= 90 )
    System.out.println( "Student grade is A" );
```

This statement also contains two simple conditions. The condition `semesterAverage >= 90` is evaluated to determine if the student deserves an "A" in the course because of a solid performance throughout the semester. The condition `finalExam >= 90` is evaluated to determine if the student deserves an "A" in the course because of an outstanding performance on the final exam. The `if` statement then considers the combined condition

```
semesterAverage >= 90 || finalExam >= 90
```

and awards the student an "A" if either or both of the simple conditions are `true`. Note that the message "`Student grade is A`" is *not* printed only when both of the simple conditions are `false`. Figure 25.4 is a truth table for the logical OR operator (||).

expression1	expression2	expression1 || expression2
false	false	false
false	true	true
true	false	true
true	true	true

Fig. 25.4   Truth table for the || (logical OR) operator.

The && operator has a higher precedence than the || operator. Both operators associate from left to right. An expression containing && or || operators is evaluated only until truth or falsity is known. Thus, evaluation of the expression gender == 1 && age >= 65 will stop immediately if `gender` is not equal to 1 (i.e., the entire expression is `false`), and continue if `gender` is equal to 1 (i.e., the entire expression could still be `true` if the condition `age >= 65` is `true`). This performance feature for evaluation of logical AND and logical OR expressions is called *short-circuit evaluation.*

Common Programming Error 25.2

*In expressions using operator **&&**, it is possible that a condition—we will call this the dependent condition—may require another condition to be **true** for it to be meaningful to evaluate the dependent condition. In this case, the dependent condition should be placed after the other condition or an error might occur.*

Performance Tip 25.1

*In expressions using operator **&&**, if the separate conditions are independent of one another, make the condition that is most likely to be **false** the leftmost condition. In expressions using operator **||**, make the condition that is most likely to be **true** the leftmost condition. This can reduce a program's execution time.*

The *boolean logical AND (**&**)* and *boolean logical inclusive OR (**|**)* operators work identically to the regular logical AND and logical OR operators with one exception—the boolean logical operators always evaluate both of their operands (i.e., there is no short-circuit evaluation). Therefore, the expression

```
gender == 1 & age >= 65
```

evaluates `age >= 65` regardless of whether `gender` is equal to 1. This is useful if the right operand of the boolean logical AND or boolean logical inclusive OR operator has a needed *side effect*—a modification of a variable's value. For example, the expression

```
birthday == true | ++age >= 65
```

guarantees that the condition `++age >= 65` will be evaluated. Thus, the variable `age` will be incremented in the preceding expression regardless of whether the overall expression is `true` or `false`.

Good Programming Practice 25.1

For clarity, avoid expressions with side effects in conditions. The side effects may look clever, but they are often more trouble than they are worth.

A condition containing the *boolean logical exclusive OR (^)* operator is `true` *if and only if one of its operands results in a **true** value and one results in a **false** value.* If both operands are `true` or both are `false`, the result of the entire condition is `false`. Figure 25.5 is a truth table for the boolean logical exclusive OR operator (^). This operator is also guaranteed to evaluate both of its operands (i.e., there is no short-circuit evaluation).

expression1	expression2	expression1 ^ expression2
false	false	false
false	true	true
true	false	true
true	true	false

Fig. 25.5   Truth table for the boolean logical exclusive OR (^) operator.

Java provides the ! (logical negation) operator to enable a programmer to "reverse" the meaning of a condition. Unlike the logical operators &&, &, ||, | and ^ which combine two conditions (binary operators), the logical negation operator has only a single condition as an operand (unary operator). The logical negation operator is placed before a condition to choose a path of execution if the original condition (without the logical negation operator) is `false`, such as in the following program segment:

```
if ( ! ( grade == sentinelValue ) )
    System.out.println( "The next grade is " + grade );
```

The parentheses around the condition `grade == sentinelValue` are needed because the logical negation operator has a higher precedence than the equality operator. Figure 25.6 is a truth table for the logical negation operator.

expression	! expression
false	true
true	false

Fig. 25.6   Truth table for operator ! (logical NOT).

In most cases, the programmer can avoid using logical negation by expressing the condition differently with an appropriate relational or equality operator. For example, the preceding statement may also be written as follows:

```
if ( grade != sentinelValue )
    System.out.println( "The next grade is " + grade );
```

This flexibility can help a programmer express a condition in a more convenient manner. The application of Fig. 25.7 demonstrates all the logical operators and boolean logical operators by producing their truth tables. The program uses string concatenation to create the string that is displayed in a `JTextArea`.

```
1   // Fig. 25.7: LogicalOperators.java
2   // Demonstrating the logical operators
3   import javax.swing.*;
4
5   public class LogicalOperators {
6      public static void main( String args[] )
7      {
8         JTextArea outputArea = new JTextArea( 17, 20 );
9         JScrollPane scroller = new JScrollPane( outputArea );
10        String output = "";
11
12        output += "Logical AND (&&)" +
13                    "\nfalse && false: " + ( false && false ) +
14                    "\nfalse && true: " + ( false && true ) +
15                    "\ntrue && false: " + ( true && false ) +
16                    "\ntrue && true: " + ( true && true );
```

Fig. 25.7   Demonstrating the logical operators. (Part 1 of 2.)

```
17
18          output += "\n\nLogical OR (||)" +
19                    "\nfalse || false: " + ( false || false ) +
20                    "\nfalse || true: " + ( false || true ) +
21                    "\ntrue || false: " + ( true || false ) +
22                    "\ntrue || true: " + ( true || true );
23
24          output += "\n\nBoolean logical AND (&)" +
25                    "\nfalse & false: " + ( false & false ) +
26                    "\nfalse & true: " + ( false & true ) +
27                    "\ntrue & false: " + ( true & false ) +
28                    "\ntrue & true: " + ( true & true );
29
30          output += "\n\nBoolean logical inclusive OR (|)" +
31                    "\nfalse | false: " + ( false | false ) +
32                    "\nfalse | true: " + ( false | true ) +
33                    "\ntrue | false: " + ( true | false ) +
34                    "\ntrue | true: " + ( true | true );
35
36          output += "\n\nBoolean logical exclusive OR (^)" +
37                    "\nfalse ^ false: " + ( false ^ false ) +
38                    "\nfalse ^ true: " + ( false ^ true ) +
39                    "\ntrue ^ false: " + ( true ^ false ) +
40                    "\ntrue ^ true: " + ( true ^ true );
41
42          output += "\n\nLogical NOT (!)" +
43                    "\n!false: " + ( !false ) +
44                    "\n!true: " + ( !true );
45
46          outputArea.setText( output );
47          JOptionPane.showMessageDialog( null, scroller,
48             "Truth Tables", JOptionPane.INFORMATION_MESSAGE );
49          System.exit( 0 );
50       } // end main
51    } // end class LogicalOperators
```

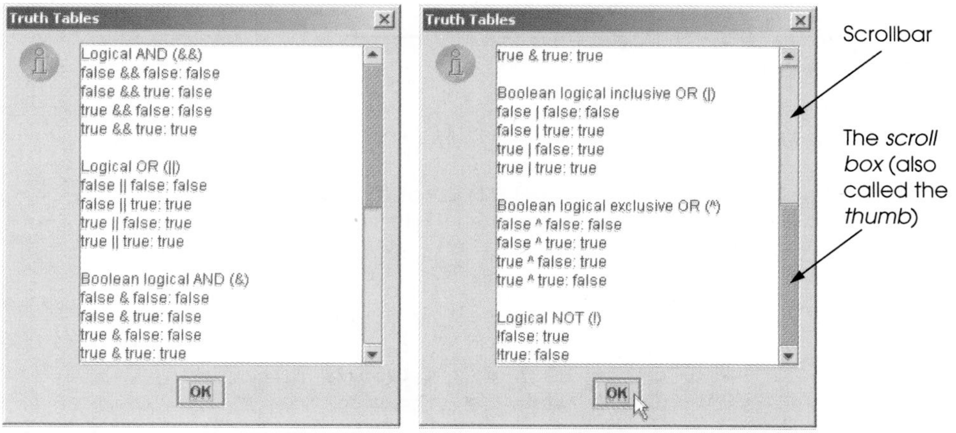

Fig. 25.7   Demonstrating the logical operators. (Part 2 of 2.)

In the output of Fig. 25.7, the strings "false" and "true" indicate `false` and `true` for the operands in each condition. The result of the condition is shown as `true` or `false`. Note that whenever you add a `boolean` value to a `String`, Java adds the string "false" or "true" based on the `boolean` value.

Line 8 in method `main`

```
JTextArea outputArea = new JTextArea( 17, 20 );
```

creates a `JTextArea` with 17 rows and 20 columns. Line 9

```
JScrollPane scroller = new JScrollPane( outputArea );
```

declares `JScrollPane` reference `scroller` and initializes it with a new `JScrollPane` object. Class `JScrollPane` (from package `javax.swing`) provides a GUI component with scrolling functionality.

When you execute this application, notice the *scrollbar* on the right side of the `JText-Area`. You can click the *arrows* at the top or bottom of the scrollbar to scroll up or down through the text in the `JTextArea` one line at a time. You can also drag the *scroll box* (also called the *thumb*) up or down to rapidly scroll through the text. A `JScrollPane` object is initialized with the GUI component for which it will provide scrolling functionality (`out-putArea` here). This attaches the GUI component to the `JScrollPane`.

Lines 12 through 44 build the `output` string that is to be displayed in the `output-Area`. Line 46 uses method `setText` to replace the text in `outputArea` with the `output` string. Lines 47 and 48 display a message dialog. The second argument, `scroller`, indicates that the `scroller` and the `outputArea` attached to it should be displayed as the message in the message dialog.

25.4 Method Definitions

Each program we have presented has consisted of a class definition that contained at least one method definition that called Java API methods to accomplish its tasks. We now consider how programmers write their own customized methods.

Consider an applet (Fig. 25.8) that uses a method `square` (invoked from the applet's `init` method) to calculate the squares of the integers from 1 to 10.

```
1   // Fig. 25.8: SquareInt.java
2   // A programmer-defined square method
3   import java.awt.Container;
4   import javax.swing.*;
5
6   public class SquareInt extends JApplet {
7      public void init()
8      {
9         String output = "";
10
11        JTextArea outputArea = new JTextArea( 10, 20 );
12
13        // get the applet's GUI component display area
14        Container c = getContentPane();
15
```

Fig. 25.8   Using programmer-defined method `square` . (Part 1 of 2.)

```
16          // attach outputArea to Container c
17          c.add( outputArea );
18
19          int result;
20
21          for ( int x = 1; x <= 10; x++ ) {
22              result = square( x );
23              output += "The square of " + x +
24                        " is " + result + "\n";
25          } // end for
26
27          outputArea.setText( output );
28      } // end method init
29
30      // square method definition
31      public int square( int y )
32      {
33          return y * y;
34      } // end method square
35  } // end class SquareInt
```

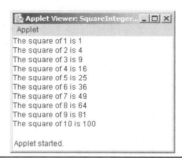

Fig. 25.8   Using programmer-defined method `square`. (Part 2 of 2.)

When the applet begins execution, its `init` method is called first. Line 9 declares `String` reference `output` and initializes it with the empty string. This `String` will contain the results of squaring the values from 1 to 10. Line 11 declares `JTextArea` reference `outputArea` and initializes it with a new `JTextArea` object of 10 rows and 20 columns. The `output` string will be displayed in `outputArea`.

This program is the first in which we display a GUI component on an applet. The on-screen display area for a `JApplet` has a *content pane* to which the GUI components must be attached so they can be displayed at execution time. The content pane is an object of class *Container* from the *java.awt package*. This class was `imported` on line 3 for use in the applet. Line 14

```
Container c = getContentPane();
```

declares `Container` reference `c` and assigns it the result of a call to method *getContentPane*—one of the many methods that our class `SquareInt` inherits from class `JApplet`. Method `getContentPane` returns a reference to the applet's content pane that can be used to attach GUI components like a `JTextArea` to the user interface of the applet.

Line 17

```
c.add( outputArea );
```

places the `JTextArea` GUI component object to which `outputArea` refers on the applet so it can be displayed when the applet is executed. `Container` method `add` attaches a GUI component to a container. For the moment, we can attach only one GUI component to the applet's content pane and that GUI component will automatically occupy the applet's entire drawing area on the screen (as defined by the `width` and `height` of the applet in pixels in the applet's HTML document). Later, we will discuss how to lay out many GUI components on an applet.

Line 19 declares `int` variable `result`, in which the result of each square calculation is stored. Lines 21 through 25 are a `for` repetition structure in which each iteration of the loop calculates the `square` of the current value of control variable x, stores the value in `result` and concatenates the `result` to the end of `output`.

Method `square` is *invoked* or *called* in line 22 with the statement

```
result = square( x );
```

When program control reaches this statement, method `square` (defined in line 31) is called. In fact, the () represent the *method call operator* which has high precedence. At this point, a copy of the value of x (the *argument* to the method call) is made automatically by the program and program control transfers to the first line of method `square`. Method `square` receives the copy of the value of x in the *parameter* y. Then `square` calculates y * y. The result is passed back to the point in `init` where `square` was invoked. The value returned is then assigned to variable `result`. Lines 23 and 24

```
output += "The square of " + x +
          " is " + result + "\n";
```

concatenate "The `square of` ", the value of x, " `is` ", the value of `result` and a newline character to the end of `output`. This process is repeated ten times using the `for` repetition structure. Line 27

```
outputArea.setText( output );
```

uses method `setText` to set `outputArea`'s text to the `String output`. Note that references `output`, `outputArea` and c, and variable `result` are declared as local variables in `init` because they are used only in `init`. Variables should be declared as instance variables only if they are required for use in more than one method of the class or if their values must be saved between calls to the methods of the class.

The definition of method `square` (line 31) shows that `square` expects an integer parameter y—this will be the name used to manipulate the value passed to `square` in the body of method `square`. Keyword `int` preceding the method name indicates that `square` returns an integer result. The *return statement* in `square` passes the result of the calculation y * y back to the calling method. Note that the entire method definition is contained between the braces of the class `SquareInt`. All methods must be defined inside a class definition.

Good Programming Practice 25.2

Place a blank line between method definitions to separate the methods and enhance program readability.

Common Programming Error 25.3

Defining a method outside the braces of a class definition is a syntax error.

The format of a method definition is

return-value-type method-name(parameter-list)
{
    declarations and statements
}

The *method-name* is any valid identifier. The *return-value-type* is the data type of the result returned from the method to the caller. The return-value-type `void` indicates that a method does not return a value. Methods can return at most one value.

Common Programming Error 25.4

Omitting the return-value-type in a method definition is a syntax error.

Common Programming Error 25.5

Forgetting to return a value from a method that is supposed to return a value is a syntax error. If a return-value-type other than `void` is specified, the method must contain a `return` statement.

Common Programming Error 25.6

Returning a value from a method whose return type has been declared `void` is a syntax error.

The *parameter-list* is a comma-separated list containing the declarations of the parameters received by the method when it is called. There must be one argument in the method call for each parameter in the method definition. The arguments must also be compatible with the type of the parameter. For example, a parameter of type `double` could receive values of 7.35, 22 or –.03546, but not `"hello"` (because a `double` variable cannot contain a `String`). If a method does not receive any values, the *parameter-list* is empty (i.e., the method name is followed by an empty set of parentheses). A type must be listed explicitly for each parameter in the parameter list of a method or a syntax error occurs.

Common Programming Error 25.7

Declaring method parameters of the same type as `float x, y` instead of `float x, float y` is a syntax error because types are required for each parameter in the parameter list.

Common Programming Error 25.8

Placing a semicolon after the right parenthesis enclosing the parameter list of a method definition is a syntax error.

Common Programming Error 25.9

Redefining a method parameter as a local variable in the method is a syntax error.

Common Programming Error 25.10

Passing to a method an argument that is not compatible with the corresponding parameter's type is a syntax error.

Good Programming Practice 25.3

Although it is not incorrect to do so, do not use the same names for the arguments passed to a method and the corresponding parameters in the method definition. This helps avoid ambiguity.

The *declarations* and *statements* within braces form the *method body*. The method body is also referred to as a *block*. A block is a compound statement that includes declarations. Variables can be declared in any block and blocks can be nested. A method cannot be defined inside another method.

Common Programming Error 25.11

Defining a method inside another method is a syntax error.

Good Programming Practice 25.4

Choosing meaningful method names and meaningful parameter names makes programs more readable and helps avoid excessive use of comments.

Software Engineering Observation 25.1

A method should usually be no longer than one page. Better yet, a method should usually be no longer than half a page. Regardless of how long a method is, it should perform one task well. Small methods promote software reusability.

Error-Prevention Tip 25.1

Small methods are easier to test, debug and understand than large ones.

Software Engineering Observation 25.2

Programs should be written as collections of small methods. This makes programs easier to write, debug, maintain and modify.

Software Engineering Observation 25.3

A method requiring a large number of parameters may be performing too many tasks. Consider dividing the method into smaller methods that perform the separate tasks. The method header should fit on one line if possible.

Software Engineering Observation 25.4

The method header and method calls must all agree in the number, type and order of parameters and arguments.

There are three ways to return control to the point at which a method was invoked. If the method does not return a result, control is returned when the method-ending right brace is reached or by executing the statement

```
return;
```

If the method does return a result, the statement

```
return expression;
```

returns the value of *expression* to the caller. When a `return` statement is executed, control returns immediately to the point at which a method was invoked.

Note that the example of Fig. 25.8 actually contains two method definitions—`init` (line 7) and `square` (line 31). Remember that the `init` method is automatically called to initialize the applet. In this example, method `init` repeatedly invokes the `square` method to perform a calculation, then displays the results in the `JTextArea` that is attached to the applet's content pane.

Notice the syntax used to invoke method `square`—we use just the method name followed by the arguments to the method in parentheses. Methods in a class definition are allowed to invoke all other methods in the same class definition using this syntax (there is an exception to this discussed in Chapter 26). Methods in the same class definition are both the methods defined in that class and the inherited methods (the methods from the class that the current class `extends`—`JApplet` in the last example). We have now seen three ways to call a method—a method name by itself (as shown with `square( x )` in this example), a reference to an object followed by the dot (`.`) operator and the method name (such as `g.drawLine( x1, y1, x2, y2 )`) and a class name followed by a method name (such as `Integer.parseInt( stringToConvert )`). The last syntax is only for `static` methods of a class (discussed in detail in Chapter 26).

25.5 Java API Packages

As we have seen, Java contains many predefined classes that are grouped by directories on disk into categories of related classes called packages. Together, these packages are referred to as the Java applications programming interface (Java API).

Type	Allowed promotions
double	None
float	double
long	float or double
int	long, float or double
char	int, long, float or double
short	int, long, float or double
byte	short, int, long, float or double
boolean	None (boolean values are not considered to be numbers in Java)

Fig. 25.9 Allowed promotions for primitive data types.

Throughout the text, `import` statements are used to specify the location of classes required to compile a Java program. For example, to tell the compiler to load the `JApplet` class from the `javax.swing` package, the statement

```
import javax.swing.JApplet;
```

is used. One of the great strengths of Java is the large number of classes in the packages of the Java API that programmers can reuse rather than "reinventing the wheel." We exercise a large number of these classes in this book. Figure 25.10 lists alphabetically the packages of the Java API and provides a brief description of each package. Other packages are available for download from `http://java.sun.com`. Note that most of these packages have not yet been discussed. This table is provided to give you a sense of the variety of reusable components available in the Java API. When learning Java, you should spend time reading the descriptions of the packages and classes in the Java API documentation.

Package	Description
`java.applet`	*The Java Applet Package.* This package contains the `Applet` class and several interfaces that enable the creation of applets, interaction of applets with the browser and playing audio clips. In Java 2, class `javax.swing.JApplet` is used to define an applet that uses the *Swing GUI components.*
`java.awt`	*The Java Abstract Windowing Toolkit Package.* This package contains the classes and interfaces required to create and manipulate graphical user interfaces in Java 1.0 and 1.1. In Java 2, these classes can still be used, but the *Swing GUI components* of the `javax.swing` packages are often used instead.
`java.awt.color`	*The Java Color Space Package.* This package contains classes that support color spaces.
`java.awt.datatransfer`	*The Java Data Transfer Package.* This package contains classes and interfaces that enable transfer of data between a Java program and the computer's clipboard (a temporary storage area for data).
`java.awt.dnd`	*The Java Drag-and-Drop Package.* This package contains classes and interfaces that provide drag-and-drop support between programs.
`java.awt.event`	*The Java Abstract Windowing Toolkit Event Package.* This package contains classes and interfaces that enable event handling for GUI components in both the `java.awt` and `javax.swing` packages.
`java.awt.font`	*The Java Font Manipulation Package.* This package contains classes and interfaces for manipulating many different fonts.
`java.awt.geom`	*The Java Two-Dimensional Objects Package.* This package contains classes for manipulating objects that represent two-dimensional graphics.
`java.awt.im`	*The Java Input Method Framework Package.* This package contains classes and an interface that support Japanese, Chinese and Korean language input into a Java program.

`java.awt.image`
`java.awt.image.`
  `renderable`
	The Java Image Packages. These packages contain classes and interfaces that enable storing and manipulation of images in a program.

Fig. 25.10 Packages of the Java API. (Part 1 of 4.)

Package	Description
`java.awt.print`	*The Java Printing Package.* This package contains classes and interfaces that support printing from Java programs.
`java.beans` `java.beans.beancontext`	*The Java Beans Packages.* These packages contain classes and interfaces that enable the programmer to create reusable software components.
`java.io`	*The Java Input/Output Package.* This package contains classes that enable programs to input and output data.
`java.lang`	*The Java Language Package.* This package contains classes and interfaces required by many Java programs (many are discussed throughout the text) and is automatically imported by the compiler into all programs.
`java.lang.ref`	*The Reference Objects Package.* This package contains classes that enable interaction between a Java program and the garbage collector.
`java.lang.reflect`	*The Java Core Reflection Package.* This package contains classes and interfaces that enable a program to discover the accessible variables and methods of a class dynamically during the execution of a program.
`java.math`	*The Java Arbitrary Precision Math Package.* This package contains classes for performing arbitrary-precision arithmetic.
`java.net`	*The Java Networking Package.* This package contains classes that enable programs to communicate via networks.

`java.rmi`
`java.rmi.activation`
`java.rmi.dgc`
`java.rmi.registry`
`java.rmi.server`
	The Java Remote Method Invocation Packages.
	These packages contain classes and interfaces that enable the programmer to create distributed Java programs. Using remote method invocation, a program can call a method of a separate program on the same computer or on a computer anywhere on the Internet.

`java.security`
`java.security.acl`
`java.security.cert`
`java.security.`
`  interfaces`
`java.security.spec`
	The Java Security Packages.
	These packages contains classes and interfaces that enable a Java program to encrypt data and control the access privileges provided to a Java program for security purposes.

`java.sql`	*The Java Database Connectivity Package.* This package contain classes and interfaces that enable a Java program to interact with a database.

Fig. 25.10 Packages of the Java API. (Part 2 of 4.)

Package	Description
`java.text`	*The Java Text Package.* This package contains classes and interfaces that enable a Java program to manipulate numbers, dates, characters and strings. This package provides many of Java's internationalization capabilities for customizing applications to a specific locale (or geographical region).
`java.util`	*The Java Utilities Package.* This package contains utility classes and interfaces such as: date and time manipulations, random number processing capabilities (`Random`), storing and processing large amounts of data, breaking strings into smaller pieces called tokens (`StringTokenizer`) and other capabilities.
`java.util.jar` `java.util.zip`	*The Java Utilities JAR and ZIP Packages.* These packages contain utility classes and interfaces that enable a Java program to combine Java `.class` files and other resource files (such as images and audio) into compressed file called *Java archive (JAR) files* or *ZIP files.*
`javax.accessibility`	*The Java Accessibility Package.* This package contains classes and interfaces that allow a Java program to support technologies for people with disabilities; examples are screen readers and screen magnifiers.
`javax.swing`	*The Java Swing GUI Components Package.* This package contains classes and interfaces for Java's Swing GUI components that provide support for portable GUIs.
`javax.swing.border`	*The Java Swing Borders Package.* This package contains classes and an interface for drawing borders around areas in a GUI.
`javax.swing.` `  colorchooser`	*The Java Swing Color Chooser Package.* This package contains classes and interfaces for the `JColorChooser` predefined dialog for choosing colors.
`javax.swing.event`	*The Java Swing Event Package.* This package contains classes and interfaces that enable event handling for GUI components in the `javax.swing` package.
`javax.swing.` `  filechooser`	*The Java Swing File Chooser Package.* This package contains classes and interfaces for the `JFileChooser` predefined dialog for locating files on disk.

`javax.swing.plaf`
`javax.swing.plaf.basic`
`javax.swing.plaf.metal`
`javax.swing.plaf.multi`
	The Java Swing Pluggable-Look-and-Feel Packages.
	These packages contain classes and an interface used to change the look-and-feel of a Swing-based GUI between the Java look-and-feel, Microsoft Windows look-and-feel and the UNIX Motif look-and-feel. The package also supports development of a customized look-and-feel for a Java program.

Fig. 25.10 Packages of the Java API. (Part 3 of 4.)

Package	Description
`javax.swing.table`	*The Java Swing Table Package.* This package contains classes and interfaces for creating and manipulating spreadsheet-like tables.
`javax.swing.text`	*The Java Swing Text Package.* This package contains classes and interfaces to manipulate text-based GUI components in Swing.

`javax.swing.text.html`
`javax.swing.text.html.`
  `parser`
	The Java Swing HTML Text Packages.
	These packages contain classes that provide support for building HTML text editors.

`javax.swing.text.rtf`	*The Java Swing RTF Text Package.* This package contains a class that provides support for building editors that support rich-text formatting.
`javax.swing.tree`	*The Java Swing Tree Package.* This package contains classes and interfaces for creating and manipulating expanding tree GUI components.
`javax.swing.undo`	*The Java Swing Undo Package.* This package contains classes and interfaces that support providing undo and redo capabilities in a Java program.

`org.omg.CORBA`
`org.omg.CORBA.`
  `DynAnyPackage`
`org.omg.CORBA.`
  `ORBPackage`
`org.omg.CORBA.portable`
`org.omg.CORBA.`
  `TypeCodePackage`
`org.omg.CosNaming`
`org.omg.CosNaming.`
  `NamingContextPackage`
	The Object Management Group (OMG) CORBA Packages.
	These packages contain classes and interfaces that implement OMG's CORBA APIs that allow a Java program to communicate with programs written in other programming languages in a similar fashion to using Java's RMI packages to communicate between Java programs.

Fig. 25.10 Packages of the Java API. (Part 4 of 4.)

25.6 Random Number Generation

We now take another look at simulation and game playing (see Chapter 5). Like C, Java provides the programmer with methods for generating random numbers. In this section and the next section, we will develop Java versions of some of the game-playing programs that we previously wrote in C.

You will remember that in C we used the function `rand` to generate random numbers. The `rand` function returned an integer value between 0 and the symbolic constant RAND_MAX. Random numbers are generated differently in Java. The `Math` class provides the *random* method. Consider the following statement:

```
double randomValue = Math.random();
```

The `random` method generates a `double` value greater than or equal to 0.0 but less than 1.0. If `random` truly produces values at random, every value greater than or equal to 0.0 but less than 1.0 has an equal *chance* (or *probability*) of being chosen each time `random` is called.

The range of values produced directly by `random` is often different than what is needed in a specific application. For example, a program that simulates coin tossing might require only 0 for "heads" and 1 for "tails." A program that simulates rolling a six-sided die would require random integers in the range 1 to 6. A program that randomly predicts the next type of spaceship (out of four possibilities) that will fly across the horizon in a video game would require random integers in the range 1 through 4.

To demonstrate `random`, let us develop a Java version of the program from Chapter 5 that simulates 20 rolls of a six-sided die and prints the value of each roll. We use the multiplication operator (*) in conjunction with `random` as follows:

```
(int) ( Math.random() * 6 )
```

to produce integers in the range 0 to 5. You will recall that in C we used the modulus operator (%) to *scale* the return value of `rand`. Since the `random` method in Java returns a `double` value greater than or equal to 0.0 but less than 1.0 we must multiply the random number by a *scaling factor* (in this case, 6) to scale correctly. The integer cast operator is used to truncate the floating-point part (the part after the decimal point) of each value produced by the preceding expression. We then *shift* the range of numbers produced by adding 1 to our previous result, as in

```
1 + (int) ( Math.random() * 6 )
```

Figure 25.11 confirms that the results are in the range 1 to 6.

```java
1   // Fig. 25.11: RandomInt.java
2   // Shifted, scaled random integers
3   import javax.swing.JOptionPane;
4
5   public class RandomInt {
6      public static void main( String args[] )
7      {
8         int value;
9         String output = "";
10
11        for ( int i = 1; i <= 20; i++ ) {
12           value = 1 + (int) ( Math.random() * 6 );
13           output += value + "   ";
14
15           if ( i % 5 == 0 )
16              output += "\n";
17        }
18
19        JOptionPane.showMessageDialog( null, output,
20           "20 Random Numbers from 1 to 6",
21           JOptionPane.INFORMATION_MESSAGE );
22
23        System.exit( 0 );
24     } // end main
25  } // end class RandomInt
```

Fig. 25.11 Shifted and scaled random integers. (Part 1 of 2.)

Fig. 25.11 Shifted and scaled random integers. (Part 2 of 2.)

To show that these numbers occur approximately with equal likelihood, let us simulate 6000 rolls of a die with the program of Fig. 25.12. Each integer from 1 to 6 should appear approximately 1000 times.

```java
1    // Fig. 25.12: RollDie.java
2    // Roll a six-sided die 6000 times
3    import javax.swing.*;
4
5    public class RollDie {
6       public static void main( String args[] )
7       {
8          int frequency1 = 0, frequency2 = 0,
9                frequency3 = 0, frequency4 = 0,
10               frequency5 = 0, frequency6 = 0, face;
11
12         // summarize results
13         for ( int roll = 1; roll <= 6000; roll++ ) {
14            face = 1 + (int) ( Math.random() * 6 );
15
16            switch ( face ) {
17               case 1:
18                  ++frequency1;
19                  break;
20               case 2:
21                  ++frequency2;
22                  break;
23               case 3:
24                  ++frequency3;
25                  break;
26               case 4:
27                  ++frequency4;
28                  break;
29               case 5:
30                  ++frequency5;
31                  break;
32               case 6:
33                  ++frequency6;
34                  break;
35            } // end switch
36         } // end for
37
```

Fig. 25.12 Rolling a six-sided die 6000 times. (Part 1 of 2.)

```
38              JTextArea outputArea = new JTextArea( 7, 10 );
39
40              outputArea.setText(
41                 "Face\tFrequency" +
42                 "\n1\t" + frequency1 +
43                 "\n2\t" + frequency2 +
44                 "\n3\t" + frequency3 +
45                 "\n4\t" + frequency4 +
46                 "\n5\t" + frequency5 +
47                 "\n6\t" + frequency6 );
48
49              JOptionPane.showMessageDialog( null, outputArea,
50                 "Rolling a Die 6000 Times",
51                 JOptionPane.INFORMATION_MESSAGE );
52              System.exit( 0 );
53           } // end main
54        } // end class RollDie
```

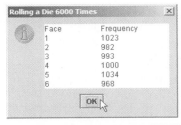

Fig. 25.12 Rolling a six-sided die 6000 times. (Part 2 of 2.)

As the program output shows, by scaling and shifting we have utilized the `random` method to realistically simulate the rolling of a six-sided die. The `for` loop in line 13 iterates 6000 times. During each iteration of the loop, line 14 produces a value from 1 to 6. The nested `switch` structure in line 16 uses the `face` value that was randomly chosen as its controlling expression. Based on the value of `face`, one of the six counter variables is incremented during each iteration of the loop. Note that *no* `default` case is provided in the `switch` structure. After we study arrays in Section 25.9 on page 935 and Section 25.10 on page 936 we will show how to replace the entire `switch` sturcture in this program with a single-line statement. Run the program several times and observe the results. Notice that a *different* sequence of random numbers is obtained each time the program is executed, so the program results should vary.

Previously we demonstrated how to write a single statement to simulate the rolling of a six-sided die with the statement

```
face = 1 + (int) ( Math.random() * 6 );
```

which always assigns an integer (at random) to variable `face` in the range $1 \le face \le 6$. Note that the width of this range (i.e., the number of consecutive integers in the range) is 6 and the starting number in the range is 1. Referring to the preceding statement, we see that the width of the range is determined by the number used to scale `random` with the multiplication operator (i.e., 6) and the starting number of the range is equal to the number (i.e., 1) added to `(int) ( Math.random() * 6 )`. We can generalize this result as follows:

```
n = a + (int) ( Math.random() * b );
```

where a is the *shifting value* (which is equal to the first number in the desired range of consecutive integers) and b is the *scaling factor* (which is equal to the width of the desired range of consecutive integers).

25.7 Example: A Game of Chance

Recall our example "craps" game from Chapter 5. We now present a new version of the craps simulator as a Java applet in Fig. 25.13.

```java
1   // Fig. 25.13: Craps.java
2   // Craps
3   import java.awt.*;
4   import java.awt.event.*;
5   import javax.swing.*;
6
7   public class Craps extends JApplet implements ActionListener {
8       // constant variables for status of game
9       final int WON = 0, LOST = 1, CONTINUE = 2;
10
11      // other variables used in program
12      boolean firstRoll = true;    // true if first roll
13      int sumOfDice = 0;           // sum of the dice
14      int myPoint = 0;    // point if no win/loss on first roll
15      int gameStatus = CONTINUE;   // game not over yet
16
17      // graphical user interface components
18      JLabel die1Label, die2Label, sumLabel, pointLabel;
19      JTextField firstDie, secondDie, sum, point;
20      JButton roll;
21
22      // setup graphical user interface components
23      public void init()
24      {
25          Container c = getContentPane();
26          c.setLayout( new FlowLayout() );
27
28          die1Label = new JLabel( "Die 1" );
29          c.add( die1Label );
30          firstDie = new JTextField( 10 );
31          firstDie.setEditable( false );
32          c.add( firstDie );
33
34          die2Label = new JLabel( "Die 2" );
35          c.add( die2Label );
36          secondDie = new JTextField( 10 );
37          secondDie.setEditable( false );
38          c.add( secondDie );
39
40          sumLabel = new JLabel( "Sum is" );
41          c.add( sumLabel );
```

Fig. 25.13 Program to simulate the game of craps. (Part 1 of 4.)

```java
42          sum = new JTextField( 10 );
43          sum.setEditable( false );
44          c.add( sum );
45
46          pointLabel = new JLabel( "Point is" );
47          c.add( pointLabel );
48          point = new JTextField( 10 );
49          point.setEditable( false );
50          c.add( point );
51
52          roll = new JButton( "Roll Dice" );
53          roll.addActionListener( this );
54          c.add( roll );
55      } // end method init
56
57      // call method play when button is pressed
58      public void actionPerformed( ActionEvent e )
59      {
60          play();
61      } // end method actionPerformed
62
63      // process one roll of the dice
64      public void play()
65      {
66          if ( firstRoll ) {              // first roll of the dice
67              sumOfDice = rollDice();
68
69              switch ( sumOfDice ) {
70                  case 7: case 11:        // win on first roll
71                      gameStatus = WON;
72                      point.setText( "" );  // clear point text field
73                      break;
74                  case 2: case 3: case 12: // lose on first roll
75                      gameStatus = LOST;
76                      point.setText( "" );  // clear point text field
77                      break;
78                  default:                // remember point
79                      gameStatus = CONTINUE;
80                      myPoint = sumOfDice;
81                      point.setText( Integer.toString( myPoint ) );
82                      firstRoll = false;
83                      break;
84              } // end switch
85          } // end if
86          else {
87              sumOfDice = rollDice();
88
89              if ( sumOfDice == myPoint )    // win by making point
90                  gameStatus = WON;
91              else
92                  if ( sumOfDice == 7 )      // lose by rolling 7
93                      gameStatus = LOST;
94          } // end else
```

Fig. 25.13 Program to simulate the game of craps. (Part 2 of 4.)

```
95
96            if ( gameStatus == CONTINUE )
97               showStatus( "Roll again." );
98            else {
99               if ( gameStatus == WON )
100                  showStatus( "Player wins. " +
101                     "Click Roll Dice to play again." );
102               else
103                  showStatus( "Player loses. " +
104                     "Click Roll Dice to play again." );
105
106               firstRoll = true;
107            } // end else
108      } // end method play
109
110      // roll the dice
111      public int rollDice()
112      {
113         int die1, die2, workSum;
114
115         die1 = 1 + ( int ) ( Math.random() * 6 );
116         die2 = 1 + ( int ) ( Math.random() * 6 );
117         workSum = die1 + die2;
118
119         firstDie.setText( Integer.toString( die1 ) );
120         secondDie.setText( Integer.toString( die2 ) );
121         sum.setText( Integer.toString( workSum ) );
122
123         return workSum;
124      } // end method rollDice
125 } // end class Craps
```

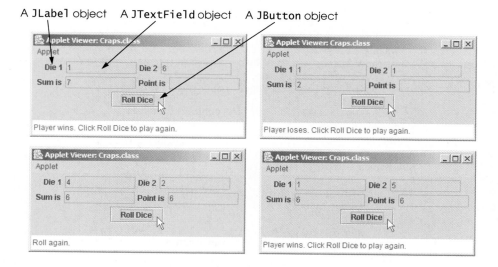

Fig. 25.13 Program to simulate the game of craps. (Part 3 of 4.)

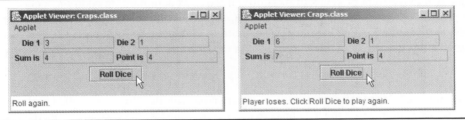

Fig. 25.13 Program to simulate the game of craps. (Part 4 of 4.)

Notice that just as in the C version of the simulator the player must roll two dice on the first and all subsequent rolls. When you execute the applet, click the **Roll Dice** button to play the game. The lower-left corner of the `appletviewer` window displays the results of each roll. The screen captures show four separate executions of the applet (a win and a loss on the first roll, and a win and a loss after the first roll).

Until now, all user interactions with applications and applets have been through either an input dialog (in which the user could type an input value for the program) or a message dialog (in which a message was displayed to the user and the user could click **OK** to dismiss the dialog). Although these are valid ways to receive input from a user and display output in a Java program, they are fairly limited in their capabilities—an input dialog can obtain only one value at a time from the user and a message dialog can display only one message. It is much more common to receive multiple inputs from the user at once (such as the user entering name and address information) or display many pieces of data at once (such as the values of the dice, the sum of the dice and the point in this example). To begin our introduction to more elaborate user interfaces, this program illustrates two new graphical user interface concepts—attaching several GUI components to an applet and graphical user interface *event handling*.

Lines 3 through 5

```
import java.awt.*;
import java.awt.event.*;
import javax.swing.*;
```

specify to the compiler where to locate the classes used in this applet. The first `import` specifies that the program uses classes from package `java.awt` (specifically, classes `Container` and `FlowLayout`). The second `import` specifies that the program uses classes from package `java.awt.event`. This package contains many data types that enable a program to process a user's interactions with a program's GUI. In this program, we use the `ActionListener` and `ActionEvent` data types from package `java.awt.event`. The last `import` statement specifies that the program uses classes from package `javax.swing` (specifically, classes `JApplet`, `JLabel`, `JTextField` and `JButton`).

As stated earlier, every Java program is based on at least one class definition that extends and enhances an existing class definition via inheritance. Remember that applets inherit from class `JApplet`. Line 7

```
public class Craps extends JApplet implements ActionListener
```

indicates that class `Craps` inherits from `JApplet` and *implements ActionListener*. A class can inherit existing attributes and behaviors (data and methods) from another class specified to the right of keyword `extends` in the class definition. In addition, a class can implement one or more *interfaces*. An interface specifies one or more behaviors (i.e., methods) *that you must define* in your class definition. The interface `ActionListener` specifies that this class *must define a method* with the first line

```
public void actionPerformed( ActionEvent e )
```

This method's task is to process a user's interaction with the `JButton` (called **Roll Dice** on the user interface) in this example. When the user presses the button, this method will be called automatically in response to the user interaction. This process is called *event handling*. The *event* is the user interaction (pressing the button). The *event handler* is the `actionPerformed` method, which is called automatically in response to the event. We discuss the details of this interaction and method `actionPerformed` shortly. Chapter 27, Java Object-Oriented Programming, discusses interfaces in detail. For now, mimic the features we illustrate that support event handling of the GUI components we present.

The game is reasonably involved. The player may win or lose on the first roll, or may win or lose on any roll. Line 9 of the program

```
final int WON = 0, LOST = 1, CONTINUE = 2;
```

creates variables that define the three states of a game of craps—game won, game lost or continue rolling the dice. Keyword *final* at the beginning of the declaration indicates that these are *constant variables*. Constant variables must be initialized once only before they are used and cannot be modified thereafter. Constant variables are often called *named constants* or *read-only variables*.

Common Programming Error 25.12

After a `final` variable has been initialized, attempting to assign another value to that variable is a syntax error.

Good Programming Practice 25.5

Use only uppercase letters (with underscores between words) in the names of `final` variables. This makes these constants stand out in a program.

Good Programming Practice 25.6

Using meaningfully named `final` variables rather than integer constants (such as 2) makes programs more readable.

Lines 12 through 15

```
boolean firstRoll = true;    // true if first roll
int sumOfDice = 0;           // sum of the dice
int myPoint = 0;    // point if no win/loss on first roll
int gameStatus = CONTINUE;   // game not over yet
```

declare several instance variables that are used throughout the `Craps` applet. Variable `firstRoll` indicates if the next roll of the dice is the first roll in the current game. Variable `sumOfDice` maintains the sum of the dice for the last roll. Variable `myPoint` stores the "point" if the player does not win or lose on the first roll. Variable `gameStatus` keeps track of the current state of the game (WON, LOST or CONTINUE).

Lines 18 through 20

```
JLabel die1Label, die2Label, sumLabel, pointLabel;
JTextField firstDie, secondDie, sum, point;
JButton roll;
```

declare references to the GUI components used in this applet's graphical user interface. References die1Label, die2Label, sumLabel and pointLabel all refer to *JLabel* objects. A JLabel contains a string of characters to display on the screen. Normally, a JLabel indicates the purpose of another graphical user interface element on the screen. In the screen captures of Fig. 25.13, the JLabel objects are the text to the left of each rectangle in the first two rows of the user interface. References firstDie, secondDie, sum and point all refer to *JTextField* objects. JTextFields are used to get a single line of information from the user at the keyboard or to display information on the screen. In the screen captures of Fig. 25.13, the JTextField objects are the rectangles to the right of each JLabel in the first two rows of the user interface. Reference roll refers to a *JButton* object. When the user presses a JButton, normally the program responds by performing a task (rolling the dice in this example). The JButton object is the rectangle containing the words **Roll Dice** at the bottom of the user interface in Fig. 25.13. We have already used JTextFields and JButtons in prior examples. Every message dialog and every input dialog contained an **OK** button to dismiss the message dialog or send the user's input to the program. Every input dialog also contained a JTextField in which the user typed an input value.

Method init (line 23) creates the GUI component objects and attaches them to the user interface. Line 25

```
Container c = getContentPane();
```

declares Container reference c and assigns it the result of a call to method getContentPane. Remember, method getContentPane returns a reference to the applet's content pane that can be used to attach GUI components to the user interface of the applet.

Line 26

```
c.setLayout( new FlowLayout() );
```

uses Container method *setLayout* to define the *layout manager* for the applet's user interface. Layout managers are provided to arrange GUI components on a Container for presentation purposes. The layout managers determine the position and size of every GUI component attached to the container. This enables the programmer to concentrate on the basic "look and feel" and lets the layout managers process most of the layout details.

FlowLayout is the most basic layout manager. GUI components are placed on a Container from left to right in the order in which they are attached to the Container with method add. When the edge of the container is reached, components are continued on the next line. The preceding statement creates a new object of class FlowLayout and passes it to method setLayout. Normally, the layout is set before any GUI components are added to a Container.

[*Note:* Each Container can have only one layout manager at a time (separate Containers in the same program can have different layout managers). Most Java programming environments provide GUI design tools that help a programmer graphically design a GUI, then automatically write Java code to create the GUI. Some of these GUI designers also allow the programmer to use the layout managers. Chapter 29 discusses several layout managers that allow more precise control over the layout of the GUI components.]

Lines 28 through 32, 34 through 38, 40 through 44 and 46 through 50 each create a JLabel and JTextField pair and attach them to the user interface. These lines are all quite similar, so we concentrate on lines 28 through 32.

```
die1Label = new JLabel( "Die 1" );
c.add( die1Label );
firstDie = new JTextField( 10 );
firstDie.setEditable( false );
c.add( firstDie );
```

Line 28 creates a new JLabel object, initializes it with the string "Die 1" and assigns the object to reference die1Label. This labels the corresponding JTextField firstDie in the user interface so the user can determine the purpose of the value displayed in first-Die. Line 29 attaches the JLabel to which die1Label refers to the applet's content pane. Line 30 creates a new JTextField object, initializes it to be 10 characters wide and assigns the object to reference firstDie. This JTextField will display the value of the first die after each roll of the dice. Line 31 uses JTextField method setEditable with the argument false to indicate that the user should not be able to type in the JTextField (i.e., make the JTextField *uneditable*). An uneditable JTextField has a gray background by default. An editable JTextField has a white background by default (as seen in input dialogs). Line 32 attaches the JTextField to which firstDie refers to the applet's content pane.

Line 52

```
roll = new JButton( "Roll Dice" );
```

creates a new JButton object, initializes it with the string "Roll Dice" (this string will appear on the button) and assigns the object to reference roll.

Line 53

```
roll.addActionListener( this );
```

specifies that *this* applet should *listen* for events from the JButton roll. The this keyword enables the applet to refer to itself (we discuss this in detail in Chapter 26). When the user interacts with a GUI component an *event* is sent to the applet. GUI events are messages indicating that the user of the program interacted with one of the program's GUI components. For example, when you press JButton roll in this program, an event is sent to the applet indicating that the user pressed the button. This indicates to the applet that *an action was performed* by the user on the JButton and automatically calls method actionPerformed to process the user's interaction.

This style of programming is known as *event-driven programming*—the user interacts with a GUI component, the program is notified of the event and the program processes the event. The user's interaction with the GUI "drives" the program. The methods that are called when an event occurs are also known as *event-handling methods*. When a GUI event occurs in a program, Java creates an object containing information about the event that occurred and *automatically calls* an appropriate event handling method. Before any event can be processed, each GUI component must know which object in the program defines the event handling method that will be called when an event occurs. In line 53, JButton method *addActionListener* is used to tell `roll` that the applet (`this`) can *listen* for *action events* and defines method `actionPerformed`. This is called *registering the event handler* with the GUI component (we also like to call it the *start listening* line because the applet is now listening for events from the button). To respond to an action event, we must define a class that `implements` `ActionListener` (this requires that the class also define method `actionPerformed`) and we must register the event handler with the GUI component. Finally, the last line in `init` attaches the `JButton` to which `roll` refers to the applet's content pane, thus completing the user interface.

Method `actionPerformed` (line 58) is one of several methods that process interactions between the user and GUI components. The first line of the method

```
public void actionPerformed( ActionEvent e )
```

indicates that `actionPerformed` is a `public` method that returns nothing (`void`) when it completes its task. Method `actionPerformed` receives one argument—an `Action-Event`—when it is called automatically in response to an action performed on a GUI component by the user (in this case pressing the `JButton`). The `ActionEvent` argument contains information about the action that occurred.

We define a method `rollDice` (line 111) to roll the dice and compute and display their sum. Method `rollDice` is defined once, but it is called from two places in the program (lines 67 and 87). Method `rollDice` takes no arguments, so it has an empty parameter list. Method `rollDice` returns the sum of the two dice, so a return type of `int` is indicated in the method header.

The user clicks the "Roll Dice" button to roll the dice. This invokes method `action-Performed` (line 58) of the applet, which then invokes method `play` (defined in line 64). Method `play` checks the `boolean` variable `firstRoll` (line 66) to determine if it is `true` or `false`. If it is `true`, this is the first roll of the game. Line 67 calls `rollDice` (defined in line 111), which picks two random values from 1 to 6, displays the value of the first die, second die and the sum of the dice in the first three `JTextFields`, and returns the sum of the dice. Note that the integer values are converted to `Strings` with `static` method `Integer.toString` because `JTextFields` can only display `Strings`. After the first roll, the nested `switch` structure in line 69 determines if the game is won or lost, or if the game should continue with another roll. After the first roll, if the game is not over, `sum` is saved in `myPoint` and displayed in `JTextField point`.

The program proceeds to the nested `if/else` structure in line 96, which uses applet method *showStatus* to display in the `appletviewer` status bar

```
    Roll again.
```

if `gameStatus` is equal to `CONTINUE` and

```
    Player wins. Click Roll Dice to play again.
```

if `gameStatus` is equal to `WON` and

```
    Player loses. Click Roll Dice to play again.
```

if `gameStatus` is equal to `LOST`. Method `showStatus` receives a `String` argument and displays it in the status bar of the `appletviewer` or browser. If the game was won or lost, line 106 sets `firstRoll` to `true` to indicate that the next roll of the dice is the first roll of the next game.

The program then waits for the user to click button "Roll Dice" again. Each time the user presses "Roll Dice", method `actionPerformed` invokes method `play` and method `rollDice` is called to produce a new `sum`. If `sum` matches `myPoint`, `gameStatus` is set to WON, the `if/else` structure in line 96 executes and the game is complete. If `sum` is equal to 7, `gameStatus` is set to LOST, `if/else` structure in line 96 executes and the game is complete. Clicking the "Roll Dice" button starts a new game. Throughout the program, the four `JTextFields` are updated with the new values of the dice and the sum on each roll, and the `JTextField` `point` is updated each time a new game is started.

25.8 Methods of Class `JApplet`

We have written many applets to this point in the text, but we have not yet discussed the key methods of class `JApplet` class that are called automatically during the execution of an applet. Figure 25.14 lists the key methods of class `JApplet`, when they get called and the purpose of each method.

These `JApplet` methods are defined by the Java API to do nothing unless you provide a definition in your applet's class definition. If you would like to use one of these methods in an applet you are defining, you *must* define the first line of the method as shown in Fig. 25.14. Otherwise, the method will not get called automatically during the applet's execution.

Method	When the method is called and its purpose
`public void init()`	This method is called once by the `appletviewer` or browser when an applet is loaded for execution. It performs initialization of an applet. Typical actions performed here are initialization of instance variables and GUI components of the applet, loading of sounds to play or images to display (Chapter 30, Java Multimedia) and creation of threads.
`public void start()`	This method is called after the `init` method completes execution and every time the user of the browser returns to the HTML page on which the applet resides (after browsing another HTML page). This method performs any tasks that must be completed when the applet is loaded for the first time into the browser and that must be performed every time the HTML page on which the applet resides is revisited. Typical actions performed here include starting an animation (Chapter 30, Java Multimedia) and starting other threads of execution.
`public void paint( Graphics g )`	This method is called to draw on the applet after the `init` method completes execution and the `start` method has started executing. It is also called automatically every time the applet needs to be repainted. For example, if the user of the browser covers the applet with another open window on the screen, then uncovers the applet, the `paint` method is called. Typical actions performed here involve drawing with the `Graphics` object g that is passed to the `paint` method for you.

Fig. 25.14 `JApplet` methods called automatically during an applet's execution. (Part 1 of 2.)

Method	When the method is called and its purpose

`public void stop()`

    This method is called when the applet should stop executing—normally when the user of the browser leaves the HTML page on which the applet resides. This method performs any tasks that are required to suspend the applet's execution. Typical actions performed here are to stop execution of animations and threads.

`public void destroy()`

    This method is called when the applet is being removed from memory—normally when the user of the browser exits the browsing session. This method performs any tasks that are required to destroy resources allocated to the applet.

Fig. 25.14 JApplet methods called automatically during an applet's execution. (Part 2 of 2.)

 Common Programming Error 25.13

Providing a definition for one of the JApplet methods init, start, paint, stop or de-stroy that does not match the method headers shown in Fig. 25.14 results in a method that will not be called automatically during execution of the applet.

    Method *repaint* is also of interest to many applet programmers. The applet's `paint` method is normally called automatically. What if you would like to change the appearance of the applet in response to the user's interactions with the applet? In such situations, you may want to call `paint` directly. However, to call `paint`, we must pass it the `Graphics` parameter it expects. This poses a problem for us. We do not have a `Graphics` object at our disposal to pass to `paint` (we discuss this issue in Chapter 30, Java Multimedia). For this reason, the `repaint` method is provided for you. The statement

    `repaint();`

invokes another method called *update* and passes it the `Graphics` object for you. The update method erases any drawing that was previously done on the applet, then invokes the `paint` method and passes it the `Graphics` object for you. The `repaint` and `update` methods are discussed in detail in Chapter 30, Java Multimedia.

25.9 Declaring and Allocating Arrays

Arrays occupy space in memory. The programmer specifies the type of the elements and uses operator `new` to dynamically allocate the number of elements required by each array. Arrays are allocated with `new` because arrays are considered to be objects and all objects must be created with `new`. To allocate 12 elements for integer array c, the declaration

    `int c[] = new int[ 12 ];`

is used. The preceding statement can also be performed in two steps as follows:

```
int c[];              // declares the array
c = new int[ 12 ];   // allocates the array
```

When arrays are allocated, the elements are initialized to zero for the numeric primitive-data-type variables, to `false` for `boolean` variables or to `null` for references (any non-primitive type).

Common Programming Error 25.14

Unlike C or C++ the number of elements in the array is never specified in the square brackets after the array name in a declaration. The declaration `int c[ 12 ]`; causes a syntax error.

Memory may be reserved for several arrays with a single declaration. The following declaration reserves 100 elements for `String` array b and 27 elements for `String` array x:

```
String b[] = new String[ 100 ], x[] = new String[ 27 ];
```

When declaring an array, the type of the array and the square brackets can be combined at the beginning of the declaration to indicate that all identifiers in the declaration represent arrays, as in

```
double[] array1, array2;
```

which declares both `array1` and `array2` as arrays of `double` values. As shown previously, the declaration and initialization of the array can be combined in the declaration. The following declaration reserves 10 elements for `array1` and 20 elements for `array2`:

```
double[] array1 = new double[ 10 ], array2 = new double[ 20 ];
```

Arrays may be declared to contain any data type. It is important to remember that in an array of primitive data type, every element of the array contains one value of the declared data type of the array. For example, every element of an `int` array is an `int` value. However, in an array of a nonprimitive type, every element of the array is a reference to an object of the data type of the array. For example, every element of a `String` array is a reference to a `String` that has the value `null` by default.

25.10 Examples Using Arrays

The application of Fig. 25.15 uses the new operator to dynamically allocate an array of 10 elements which are initially zero, then it prints the array in tabular format.

```
1   // Fig. 25.15: InitArray.java
2   // initializing an array
3   import javax.swing.*;
4
5   public class InitArray {
6      public static void main( String args[] )
7      {
8         String output = "";
9         int n[];                // declare reference to an array
10
11        n = new int[ 10 ];  // dynamically allocate array
12
13        output += "Subscript\tValue\n";
```

Fig. 25.15 Initializing the elements of an array to zeros. (Part 1 of 2.)

```
14
15            for ( int i = 0; i < n.length; i++ )
16               output += i + "\t" + n[ i ] + "\n";
17
18            JTextArea outputArea = new JTextArea( 11, 10 );
19            outputArea.setText( output );
20
21            JOptionPane.showMessageDialog( null, outputArea,
22               "Initializing an Array of int Values",
23               JOptionPane.INFORMATION_MESSAGE );
24
25            System.exit( 0 );
26         } // end main
27      } // end class InitArray
```

Fig. 25.15 Initializing the elements of an array to zeros. (Part 2 of 2.)

Line 9 declares n as a reference capable of referring to array of integers. Line 11 allocates the 10 elements of the array with new an initializes the reference. Line 13 appends to String output the headings for the columns of output displayed by the program.

Lines 15 and 16

```
for ( int i = 0; i < n.length; i++ )
   output += i + "\t" + n[ i ] + "\n";
```

use a for structure to build the output String that will be displayed in a JTextArea on a message dialog. Note the use of zero-based counting (remember, subscripts start at 0) so the loop can access every element of the array. Also, note the expression n.length in the for structure condition to determine the length of the array. In this example, the length of the array is 10, so the loop continues executing as long as the value of control variable i is less than 10. For a 10-element array, the subscript values are 0 through 9, so using the less than operator < guarantees that the loop does not attempt to access an element beyond the end of the array. The elements of an array can be allocated and initialized in the array declaration by following the declaration with an equal sign and a comma-separated *initializer list enclosed* in braces ({ and }). In this case, the array size is determined by the number of elements in the initializer list. For example, the statement

```
int n[] = { 10, 20, 30, 40, 50 };
```

creates a five-element array with subscripts of 0, 1, 2, 3 and 4. Note that the preceding declaration does not require the new operator to create the array object—this is provided by the compiler whenever it encounters an array declaration that includes an initializer list.

The application of Fig. 25.16 initializes an integer array with 10 values (line 12) and displays the array in tabular format in a `JTextArea` on a message dialog.

```java
1   // Fig. 25.16: InitArray.java
2   // initializing an array with a declaration
3   import javax.swing.*;
4
5   public class InitArray {
6      public static void main( String args[] )
7      {
8         String output = "";
9
10        // Initializer list specifies number of elements and
11        // value for each element.
12        int n[] = { 32, 27, 64, 18, 95, 14, 90, 70, 60, 37 };
13
14        output += "Subscript\tValue\n";
15
16        for ( int i = 0; i < n.length; i++ )
17           output += i + "\t" + n[ i ] + "\n";
18
19        JTextArea outputArea = new JTextArea( 11, 10 );
20        outputArea.setText( output );
21
22        JOptionPane.showMessageDialog( null, outputArea,
23           "Initializing an Array with a Declaration",
24           JOptionPane.INFORMATION_MESSAGE );
25
26        System.exit( 0 );
27     } // end main
28  } // end class InitArray
```

Fig. 25.16 Initializing the elements of an array with a declaration.

The application of Fig. 25.17 initializes the elements of a 10-element array s to the even integers 2, 4, 6, …, 20 and prints the array in tabular format. These numbers are generated by multiplying each successive value of the loop counter by 2 and adding 2.

```
1   // Fig. 25.17: InitArray.java
2   // initialize array n to the even integers from 2 to 20
3   import javax.swing.*;
4
5   public class InitArray {
6      public static void main( String args[] )
7      {
8         final int ARRAY_SIZE = 10;
9         int n[];                         // reference to int array
10        String output = "";
11
12        n = new int[ ARRAY_SIZE ];   // allocate array
13
14        // Set the values in the array
15        for ( int i = 0; i < n.length; i++ )
16           n[ i ] = 2 + 2 * i;
17
18        output += "Subscript\tValue\n";
19
20        for ( int i = 0; i < n.length; i++ )
21           output += i + "\t" + n[ i ] + "\n";
22
23        JTextArea outputArea = new JTextArea( 11, 10 );
24        outputArea.setText( output );
25
26        JOptionPane.showMessageDialog( null, outputArea,
27           "Initializing to Even Numbers from 2 to 20",
28           JOptionPane.INFORMATION_MESSAGE );
29
30        System.exit( 0 );
31     } // end main
32  } // end class InitArray
```

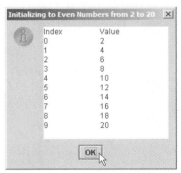

Fig. 25.17 Generating values to be placed into elements of an array.

Line 8

```
final int ARRAY_SIZE = 10;
```

uses the `final` qualifier to declare a so-called constant variable ARRAY_SIZE whose value is 10. Constant variables must be initialized before they are used and cannot be modified thereafter. If an attempt is made to modify a `final` variable after it is declared as shown in the preceding statement, the compiler issues a message like

```
Can't assign a value to a final variable
```

If an attempt is made to modify a `final` variable after it is declared, then initialized in a separate statement, the compiler issues the error message

```
Can't assign a second value to a blank final variable
```

If an attempt is made to use a `final` local variable before it is initialized, the compiler issues the error message

```
Variable variableName may not have been initialized
```

If an attempt is made to use a `final` instance variable before it is initialized, the compiler issues the error message

```
Blank final variable 'variableName' may not have been initialized. It
must be assigned a value in an initializer, or in every constructor.
```

Constant variables are also called *named constants* or *read-only variables*. They are often used to make a program more readable. Note that the term "constant variable" is an oxymoron—a contradiction in terms—like "jumbo shrimp" or "freezer burn."

Common Programming Error 25.15

Assigning a value to a constant variable after the variable has been initialized is a syntax error.

The application of Fig. 25.18 sums the values contained in the 10-element integer array a (declared, allocated and initialized in line 8). The statement (line 12) in the body of the for loop does the totaling. It is important to remember that the values being supplied as initializers for array a normally would be read into the program. For example, in an applet the user could enter the values through a JTextField, or in an application the values could be read from a file on disk.

```
1   // Fig. 25.18: SumArray.java
2   // Compute the sum of the elements of the array
3   import javax.swing.*;
4
5   public class SumArray {
6      public static void main( String args[] )
7      {
8         int a[] = { 1, 2, 3, 4, 5, 6, 7, 8, 9, 10 };
9         int total = 0;
10
11        for ( int i = 0; i < a.length; i++ )
12           total += a[ i ];
13
14        JOptionPane.showMessageDialog( null,
15           "Total of array elements: " + total,
16           "Sum the Elements of an Array",
17           JOptionPane.INFORMATION_MESSAGE );
```

Fig. 25.18 Computing the sum of the elements of an array. (Part 1 of 2.)

```
18
19              System.exit( 0 );
20      } // end main
21  } // end class SumArray
```

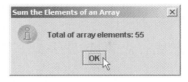

Fig. 25.18 Computing the sum of the elements of an array. (Part 2 of 2.)

Our next example uses arrays to summarize the results of data collected in a survey. Consider the problem statement:

> *Forty students were asked to rate the quality of the food in the student cafeteria on a scale of 1 to 10 (1 means awful and 10 means excellent). Place the 40 responses in an integer array and summarize the results of the poll.*

This is a typical array processing application (see Fig. 25.19). We wish to summarize the number of responses of each type (i.e., 1 through 10). The array `responses` is a 40-element integer array of the students' responses to the survey. We use an 11-element array `frequency` to count the number of occurrences of each response. We ignore the first element, `frequency[ 0 ]`, because it is more logical to have the response 1 increment `frequency[ 1 ]` than `frequency[ 0 ]`. This allows us to use each response directly as a subscript on the `frequency` array. Each element of the array is used as a counter for one of the survey responses.

```
1   // Fig. 25.19: StudentPoll.java
2   // Student poll program
3   import javax.swing.*;
4
5   public class StudentPoll {
6      public static void main( String args[] )
7      {
8         int responses[] = { 1, 2, 6, 4, 8, 5, 9, 7, 8, 10,
9                             1, 6, 3, 8, 6, 10, 3, 8, 2, 7,
10                            6, 5, 7, 6, 8, 6, 7, 5, 6, 6,
11                            5, 6, 7, 5, 6, 4, 8, 6, 8, 10 };
12        int frequency[] = new int[ 11 ];
13        String output = "";
14
15        for ( int answer = 0;                    // initialize
16              answer < responses.length;         // condition
17              answer++ )                         // increment
18           ++frequency[ responses[ answer ] ];
19
20        output += "Rating\tFrequency\n";
21
```

Fig. 25.19 A simple student-poll analysis program. (Part 1 of 2.)

```
22          for ( int rating = 1;
23               rating < frequency.length;
24               rating++ )
25            output += rating + "\t" + frequency[ rating ] + "\n";
26
27          JTextArea outputArea = new JTextArea( 11, 10 );
28          outputArea.setText( output );
29
30          JOptionPane.showMessageDialog( null, outputArea,
31             "Student Poll Program",
32             JOptionPane.INFORMATION_MESSAGE );
33
34          System.exit( 0 );
35       } // end main
36    } // end class StudentPoll
```

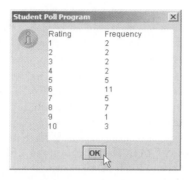

Fig. 25.19 A simple student-poll analysis program. (Part 2 of 2.)

 Good Programming Practice 25.7

Strive for program clarity. It is sometimes worthwhile to trade off the most efficient use of memory or processor time in favor of writing clearer programs.

 Performance Tip 25.2

Sometimes performance considerations far outweigh clarity considerations.

The for loop (lines 15 through 18) takes the responses one at a time from the array response and increments one of the 10 counters in the frequency array (frequency[1] to frequency[10]). The key statement in the loop is

```
++frequency[ responses[ answer ] ];
```

This statement increments the appropriate frequency counter depending on the value of responses[answer].

Let's consider several iterations of the for loop. When counter answer is 0, responses[answer] is the value of the first element of array responses (i.e., 1), so ++frequency[responses[answer]]; is actually interpreted as

```
++frequency[ 1 ];
```

which increments array element one. In evaluating the expression, start with the value in the innermost set of square brackets (`answer`). Once you know the value of `answer`, plug that value into the expression and evaluate the next outer set of square brackets (`responses[ answer ]`). Then, use that value as the subscript for the `frequency` array to determine which counter to increment.

When `answer` is 1, `responses[ answer ]` is the value of the second element of array `responses` (i.e., 2), so `++frequency[ responses[ answer ] ];` is actually interpreted as

```
++frequency[ 2 ];
```

which increments array element two (the third element of the array).

When `answer` is 2, `responses[ answer ]` is the value of the third element of array `responses` (i.e., 6), so `++frequency[ responses[ answer ] ];` is actually interpreted as

```
++frequency[ 6 ];
```

which increments array element six (the seventh element of the array) and so on. Note that regardless of the number of responses processed in the survey, only an 11-element array is required (ignoring element zero) to summarize the results because all the response values are between 1 and 10 and the subscript values for an 11-element array are 0 through 10. Also note that the results are correct because the elements of the `frequency` array were automatically initialized to zero when the array was allocated with `new`.

If the data contained invalid values, such as 13, the program would attempt to add 1 to `frequency[ 13 ]`, which is outside the array bounds. In C and C++, such a reference would be allowed by the compiler and at execution time. The program would "walk" past the end of the array to where it thought element number 13 was located and add 1 to whatever happened to be at that location in memory. This could potentially modify another variable in the program or even result in premature program termination. Java provides mechanisms to prevent accessing elements outside the bounds of the array.

Error-Prevention Tip 25.2

When a Java program is executed, the Java interpreter checks array element subscripts to be sure they are valid (i.e., all subscripts must be greater than or equal to 0 and less than the length of the array). If there is an invalid subscript, Java generates an exception.

Error-Prevention Tip 25.3

Exceptions are used to indicate that an error occurred in a program. They enable the programmer to recover from an error and continue execution of the program instead of abnormally terminating the program. When an invalid array reference is made, an ArrayIndexOutOfBoundsException *is generated.*

Common Programming Error 25.16

Referring to an element outside the array bounds is a logic error.

Error-Prevention Tip 25.4

When looping through an array, the array subscript should never go below 0 and should always be less than the total number of elements in the array (one less than the size of the array). Make sure the loop terminating condition prevents accessing elements outside this range.

Error-Prevention Tip 25.5

Programs should validate the correctness of all input values to prevent erroneous information from affecting a program's calculations.

Our next application (Fig. 25.20) reads numbers from an array and graphs the information in the form of a bar chart (or histogram)—each number is printed, then a bar consisting of that many asterisks is displayed beside the number. The nested `for` loop (lines 13 through 18) actually appends the bars to the `String` that will be displayed in `JTextArea` `outputArea` on a message dialog. Note the loop continuation condition of the inner `for` structure in line 16 (j <= n[i]). Each time the inner `for` structure is reached, it counts from 1 to n[i], thus using a value in array n to determine the final value of the control variable j and the number of asterisks to display.

```java
1   // Fig. 25.20: Histogram.java
2   // Histogram printing program
3   import javax.swing.*;
4
5   public class Histogram {
6      public static void main( String args[] )
7      {
8         int n[] = { 19, 3, 15, 7, 11, 9, 13, 5, 17, 1 };
9         String output = "";
10
11        output += "Element\tValue\tHistogram";
12
13        for ( int i = 0; i < n.length; i++ ) {
14           output += "\n" + i + "\t" + n[ i ] + "\t";
15
16           for ( int j = 1; j <= n[ i ]; j++ ) // print a bar
17              output += "*";
18        } // end for
19
20        JTextArea outputArea = new JTextArea( 11, 30 );
21        outputArea.setText( output );
22
23        JOptionPane.showMessageDialog( null, outputArea,
24           "Histogram Printing Program",
25           JOptionPane.INFORMATION_MESSAGE );
26
27        System.exit( 0 );
28     } // end main
29  } // end class Histogram
```

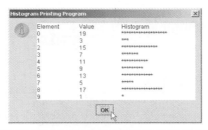

Fig. 25.20 A program that prints histograms.

Section 25.6 on page 922 indicated that there is a more elegant method of writing the dice-rolling program of Fig. 25.12. The program rolled a single six-sided die 6000 times. An array version of this application is shown in Fig. 25.21. Lines 16 through 35 of Fig. 25.12 are replaced by line 13 of this program, which uses the random `face` value as the subscript for array `frequency` to determine which element should be incremented during each iteration of the loop. The random number calculation in line 12 produces numbers from 1 to 6 (the values for a six-sided die), so the `frequency` array must be large enough to allow subscript values of 1 to 6. The smallest number of elements required for an array to have these subscript values is seven elements (subscript values from 0 to 6). In this program, we ignore element 0 of array `frequency`. Also, lines 18 and 19 of this program replace lines 40 through 47 from Fig. 25.12. We can loop through array `frequency`, so we do not have to enumerate each line of text to display in the `JTextArea` as we did in Fig. 25.12.

```java
1   // Fig. 25.21: RollDie.java
2   // Roll a six-sided die 6000 times
3   import javax.swing.*;
4
5   public class RollDie {
6      public static void main( String args[] )
7      {
8         int face, frequency[] = new int[ 7 ];
9         String output = "";
10
11        for ( int roll = 1; roll <= 6000; roll++ ) {
12           face = 1 + ( int ) ( Math.random() * 6 );
13           ++frequency[ face ];
14        }
15
16        output += "Face\tFrequency";
17
18        for ( face = 1; face < frequency.length; face++ )
19           output += "\n" + face + "\t" + frequency[ face ];
20
21        JTextArea outputArea = new JTextArea( 7, 10 );
22        outputArea.setText( output );
23
24        JOptionPane.showMessageDialog( null, outputArea,
25           "Rolling a Die 6000 Times",
26           JOptionPane.INFORMATION_MESSAGE );
27
28        System.exit( 0 );
29     } // end main
30  } // end class RollDie
```

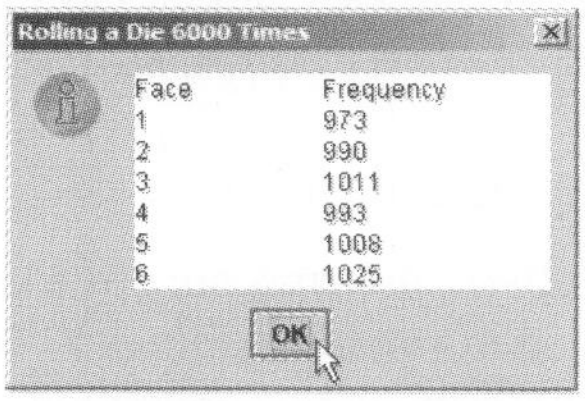

Fig. 25.21 Dice-rolling program using arrays instead of `switch`.

25.11 References and Reference Parameters

Two ways to pass arguments to methods (or functions) in many programming languages (like C and C++) are *call-by-value* and *call-by-reference* (also called *pass-by-value* and *pass-by-reference*). When an argument is passed call-by-value, a *copy* of the argument's value is made and passed to the called method.

Error-Prevention Tip 25.6

With call-by-value, changes to the called method's copy do not affect the original variable's value in the calling method. This prevents the accidental side effects that so greatly hinder the development of correct and reliable software systems.

With call-by-reference, the caller gives the called method the ability to directly access the caller's data and to modify that data if the called method so chooses. Call-by-reference can improve performance because it can eliminate the overhead of copying large amounts of data, but call-by-reference can weaken security because the called method can access the caller's data.

Software Engineering Observation 25.5

Unlike other languages, Java does not allow the programmer to choose whether to pass each argument call-by-value or call-by-reference. Primitive data type variables are always passed call-by-value. Objects are not passed to methods; rather, references to objects are passed to methods. The references themselves are also passed call-by-value. When a method receives a reference to an object, the method can manipulate the object directly.

Software Engineering Observation 25.6

When returning information from a method via a return *statement, primitive-data-type variables are always returned by value (i.e., a copy is returned) and objects are always returned by reference (i.e., a reference to the object is returned).*

To pass a reference to an object into a method, simply specify in the method call the reference name. Mentioning the reference by its parameter name in the body of the called method actually refers to the original object in memory, and the original object can be accessed directly by the called method.

Arrays are treated as objects by Java, so arrays are passed to methods call-by-reference—a called method can access the elements of the caller's original arrays. The name of an array is actually a reference to an object that contains the array elements and the `length` instance variable, which indicates the number of elements in the array. In the next section, we demonstrate call-by-value and call-by-reference using arrays.

Performance Tip 25.3

Passing arrays by reference makes sense for performance reasons. If arrays were passed by value, a copy of each element would be passed. For large, frequently passed arrays, this would waste time and would consume considerable storage for the copies of the arrays.

25.12 Multiple-Subscripted Arrays

Multiple-subscripted arrays with two subscripts are often used to represent *tables* of values consisting of information arranged in *rows* and *columns*. To identify a particular table element, we must specify the two subscripts—by convention, the first identifies the element's row and the second identifies the element's column. Arrays that require two subscripts to identify a particular element are called *double-subscripted arrays.* Note that multiple-subscripted arrays can have more than two subscripts. Java does not support multiple-subscripted arrays directly, but does allow the programmer to specify single-subscripted arrays whose elements are also single-subscripted arrays, thus achieving the same effect. Figure 25.22 illustrates a double-subscripted array, a, containing three rows and four columns (i.e., a 3-by-4 array). In general, an array with *m* rows and *n* columns is called an *m-by-n array*

Every element in array a is identified in Fig. 25.22 by an element name of the form a[i][j]; a is the name of the array and i and j are the subscripts that uniquely identify the row and column of each element in a. Notice that the names of the elements in the first row all have a first subscript of 0; the names of the elements in the fourth column all have a second subscript of 3.

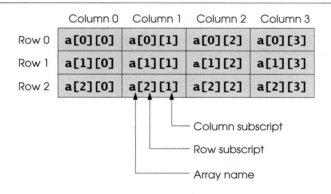

Fig. 25.22 A double-subscripted array with three rows and four columns.

Multiple-subscripted arrays can be initialized in declarations like a single-subscripted array. A double-subscripted array b[2][2] could be declared and initialized with

```
int b[][] = { { 1, 2 }, { 3, 4 } };
```

The values are grouped by row in braces. So, 1 and 2 initialize b[0][0] and b[0][1], and 3 and 4 initialize b[1][0] and b[1][1]. The compiler determines the number of rows by counting the number of sub-initializer lists (represented by sets of braces) in the main initializer list. The compiler determines the number of columns in each row by counting the number of initializer values in the sub-initializer list for that row.

Multiple-subscripted arrays are maintained as arrays of arrays. The declaration

```
int b[][] = { { 1, 2 }, { 3, 4, 5 } };
```

creates integer array b with row 0 containing two elements (1 and 2) and row 1 containing three elements (3, 4 and 5).

A multiple-subscripted array with the same number of columns in every row can be allocated dynamically. For example, a 3-by-3 array is allocated as follows:

```
int b[][];
b = new int[ 3 ][ 3 ];
```

As with single-subscripted arrays, the elements of a double-subscripted array are initialized when new creates the array object.

A multiple-subscripted array in which each row has a different number of columns can be allocated dynamically as follows:

```
int b[][];
b = new int[ 2 ][ ];    // allocate rows
b[ 0 ] = new int[ 5 ];  // allocate columns for row 0
b[ 1 ] = new int[ 3 ];  // allocate columns for row 1
```

The preceding code creates a two-dimensional array with two rows. Row 0 has five columns and row 1 has three columns.

The applet of Fig. 25.23 demonstrates initializing double-subscripted arrays in declarations and using nested for loops to traverse the arrays (i.e., manipulate every element of the array).

```
1   // Fig. 25.23: InitArray.java
2   // Initializing multidimensional arrays
3   import java.awt.Container;
4   import javax.swing.*;
5
6   public class InitArray extends JApplet {
7      JTextArea outputArea;
8
9      // initialize the applet
10     public void init()
11     {
12        outputArea = new JTextArea();
13        Container c = getContentPane();
14        c.add( outputArea );
15
16        int array1[][] = { { 1, 2, 3 }, { 4, 5, 6 } };
17        int array2[][] = { { 1, 2 }, { 3 }, { 4, 5, 6 } };
18
19        outputArea.setText( "Values in array1 by row are\n" );
20        buildOutput( array1 );
21
22        outputArea.append( "\nValues in array2 by row are\n" );
23        buildOutput( array2 );
24     } // end method init
25
26     public void buildOutput( int a[][] )
27     {
28        for ( int i = 0; i < a.length; i++ ) {
29
30           for ( int j = 0; j < a[ i ].length; j++ )
31              outputArea.append( a[ i ][ j ] + "  " );
32
33           outputArea.append( "\n" );
34        } // end for
35     } // end method buildOutput
36  } // end class InitArray
```

Fig. 25.23 Initializing multidimensional arrays. (Part 1 of 2.)

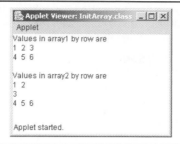

Fig. 25.23 Initializing multidimensional arrays. (Part 2 of 2.)

The program declares two arrays in method `init`. The declaration of `array1` (line 16) provides six initializers in two sublists. The first sublist initializes the first row of the array to the values 1, 2 and 3; and the second sublist initializes the second row of the array to the values 4, 5 and 6. The declaration of `array2` (line 17) provides six initializers in three sublists. The sublist for the first row explicitly initializes the first row to have two elements with values 1 and 2, respectively. The sublist for the second row initializes the second row to have one element with value 3. The sublist for the third row initializes the third row to the values 4, 5 and 6.

Method `init` calls method `buildOutput` from lines 20 and 23 to append each array's elements to `JTextArea outputArea`. The `buildOutput` method definition specifies the array parameter as `int a[][]` to indicate that a double-subscripted array will be received as an argument. Note the use of a nested `for` structure to output the rows of each double-subscripted array. In the outer `for` structure, the expression `a.length` determines the number of rows in the array. In the inner `for` structure, the expression `a[i].length` determines the number of columns in each row of the array. This condition enables the loop to determine for each row the exact number of columns.

Many common array manipulations use `for` repetition structures. For example, the following `for` structure sets all the elements in the third row of array a in Fig. 25.22 to zero:

```
for ( int col = 0; col < a[ 2 ].length; col++)
    a[ 2 ][ col ] = 0;
```

We specified the *third* row, therefore we know that the first subscript is always 2 (0 is the first row and 1 is the second row). The `for` loop varies only the second subscript (i.e., the column subscript). The preceding `for` structure is equivalent to the assignment statements

```
a[ 2 ][ 0 ] = 0;
a[ 2 ][ 1 ] = 0;
a[ 2 ][ 2 ] = 0;
a[ 2 ][ 3 ] = 0;
```

The following nested `for` structure determines the total of all the elements in array a:

```
int total = 0;

for ( int row = 0; row < a.length; row++ )
    for ( int col = 0; col < a[ row ].length; col++ )
        total += a[ row ][ col ];
```

The `for` structure totals the elements of the array one row at a time. The outer `for` structure begins by setting the `row` subscript to 0 so the elements of the first row may be totaled by the inner `for` structure. The outer `for` structure then increments `row` to 1, so the second row can be totaled. Then, the outer `for` structure increments `row` to 2, so the third row can be totaled. The result can be displayed when the nested `for` structure terminates.

SUMMARY

- The primitive types (`boolean`, `char`, `byte`, `short`, `int`, `long`, `float` and `double`) are the building blocks for more complicated types in Java.

- Java requires all variables to have a type before they can be used in a program. For this reason, Java is referred to as a strongly typed language.

- Primitive types in Java are portable across all computer platforms that support Java.

- Java uses internationally recognized standards for both character formats (Unicode) and for floating-point numbers (IEEE 754).

- Variables of types `char`, `byte`, `short`, `int`, `long`, `float` and `double` are all given the value 0 by default. Variables of type `boolean` are given `false` by default.

- Logical operators may be used to form complex conditions by combining conditions. The logical operators are `&&`, `&`, `||`, `|`, `∧` and `!`, meaning logical AND, boolean logical AND, logical OR, boolean logical inclusive OR, boolean logical exclusive OR and logical NOT (negation), respectively.

- The best way to develop and maintain a large program is to divide it into several smaller program modules each of which is more manageable than the original program. Modules are written in Java as classes and methods.

- The on-screen display area for a `JApplet` has a content pane to which the GUI components must be attached so they can be displayed at execution time. The content pane is an object of class `Container` from the `java.awt` package.

- Method `getContentPane` returns a reference to the applet's content pane.

- The general format for a method definition is

    return-value-type method-name (*parameter-list*)
    {
        declarations and statements
    }

The *return-value-type* states the type of the value returned to the calling method. If a method does not return a value, the *return-value-type* is `void`. The *method-name* is any valid identifier. The *parameter-list* is a comma-separated list containing the declarations of the variables that will be passed to the method. If a method does not receive any values, *parameter-list* is empty. The method body is the set of *declarations and statements* that constitute the method.

- An empty parameter list is specified with empty parentheses.

- The arguments passed to a method should match in number, type and order with the parameters in the method definition.

- When a program encounters a method, control is transferred from the point of invocation to the called method, the method is executed and control returns to the caller.

- A called method can return control to the caller in one of three ways. If the method does not return a value, control is returned when the method-ending right brace is reached or by executing the statement

```
return;
```

- If the method does return a value, the statement

```
return expression;
```

returns the value of *expression*.

- Method `Math.random` generates a `double` value greater than or equal to 0.0 but less than 1.0.
- Values produced by `Math.random` can be scaled and shifted to produce values in a particular range.
- The general equation for scaling and shifting a random number is

```
n = a + (int) ( Math.random() * b );
```

- where `a` is the shifting value (the first number in the desired range of consecutive integers) and `b` is the scaling factor (the width of the desired range of consecutive integers).
- A class can inherit existing attributes and behaviors (data and methods) from another class specified to the right of keyword `extends` in the class definition. In addition, a class can implement one or more interfaces. An interface specifies one or more behaviors (i.e., methods) that you must define in your class definition.
- The interface `ActionListener` specifies that this class must define a method with the first line

```
public void actionPerformed( ActionEvent e )
```

- The task of method `actionPerformed` is to process a user's interaction with a GUI component that generates an action event. This method is called automatically in response to the user interaction. This process is called event handling. The event is the user interaction (pressing the button). The event handler is the `actionPerformed` method, which is called automatically in response to the event. This style of programming is known as event-driven programming.
- Keyword `final` is used to declare constant variables. Constant variables must be initialized once before they are used and cannot be modified thereafter. Constant variables are often called named constants or read-only variables.
- A `JLabel` contains a string of characters to display on the screen. Normally, a `JLabel` indicates the purpose of another graphical user interface element on the screen.
- `JTextField`s are used to get information from the user at the keyboard or to display information on the screen.
- When the user presses a `JButton`, normally the program responds by performing a task (rolling the dice in this example).
- `Container` method `setLayout` defines the layout manager for the applet's user interface. Layout managers are provided to arrange GUI components on a `Container` for presentation purposes. The layout managers provide basic layout capabilities that determine the position and size of every GUI component attached to the container. This enables the programmer to concentrate on the basic "look and feel" and lets the layout managers process most of the layout details.
- `FlowLayout` is the most basic layout manager. GUI components are placed on a `Container` from left to right in the order in which they are attached to the `Container` with method `add`. When the edge of the container is reached, components are continued on the next line.
- Before any event can be processed, each GUI component must know which object in the program defines the event handling method that will be called when an event occurs. Method `addAction-Listener` is used to tell a `JButton` that another object is listening for action events and defines

method `actionPerformed`. This is called registering the event handler with the GUI component (we also like to call it the start listening line because the applet is now listening for events from the button). To respond to an action event, we must define a class that `implements ActionListener` (this requires that the class also define method `actionPerformed`) and we must register the event handler with the GUI component.

- Method `showStatus` receives a `String` argument and displays it in the status bar of the `appletviewer` or browser.

- The applet's `init` method is called once by the `appletviewer` or browser when an applet is loaded for execution. It performs initialization of an applet. The applet's `start` method is called after the `init` method completes execution and every time the user of the browser returns to the HTML page on which the applet resides (after browsing another HTML page).

- The applet's `paint` method is called after the `init` method completes execution and the `start` method has started executing to draw on the applet. It is also called automatically every time the applet needs to be repainted.

- The applet's `stop` method is called when the applet should suspend execution—normally when the user of the browser leaves the HTML page on which the applet resides.

- The applet's `destroy` method is called when the applet is being removed from memory—normally when the user of the browser exits the browsing session.

- Method `repaint` can be called in an applet to cause a fresh call to `paint`. Method `repaint` invokes another method called `update` and passes it the `Graphics` object. The `update` method erases any drawing that was previously done on the applet, then invokes the `paint` method and passes it the `Graphics` object.

- When declaring an array, the type of the array and the square brackets can be combined at the beginning of the declaration to indicate that all identifiers in the declaration represent arrays, as in

    ```
    double[] array1, array2;
    ```

- The elements of an array can be initialized by declaration (using initializer lists), by assignment and by input.

- Java prevents referencing elements beyond the bounds of an array.

- To pass an array to a method, the name of the array is passed. To pass a single element of an array to a method, simply pass the name of the array followed by the subscript (contained in square brackets) of the particular element.

- Arrays are passed to methods call-by-reference—therefore, the called methods can modify the element values in the caller's original arrays. Single elements of primitive-data-type arrays are passed to methods call-by-value.

- Arrays may be used to represent tables of values consisting of information arranged in rows and columns. To identify a particular element of a table, two subscripts are specified: The first identifies the row in which the element is contained and the second identifies the column in which the element is contained. Tables or arrays that require two subscripts to identify a particular element are called double-subscripted arrays.

- A double-subscripted array can be initialized with a initializer list of the form

    arrayType arrayName`[][]` = { { *row1 sub-list* }, { *row2 sub-list* }, ... };

- To dynamically create an array with a fixed number of rows and columns, use

    arrayType arrayName`[][]` = **new** *arrayType*`[` *numRows* `][` *numColumns* `]`;

- To pass one row of a double-subscripted array to a method that receives a single-subscripted array, simply pass the name of the array followed by the row subscript.

TERMINOLOGY

! operator
&& operator
| | operator
a[i]
a[i][j]
ActionEvent class
ActionListener interface
actionPerformed method
append method of class JTextArea
argument in a method call
array
array initializer list
boolean logical AND (&)
boolean logical exclusive OR (^)
boolean logical inclusive OR (|)
bounds checking
break
call a method
called method
caller
calling method
class
column subscript
declare an array
destroy method of JApplet
divide and conquer
double
double-subscripted array
duration
element of an array
element of chance
final
FlowLayout class
Font class from java.awt
Font.BOLD
Font.ITALIC
Font.PLAIN
init method of JApplet
initialize an array
initializer
invoke a method
ISO Unicode character set
Java API (Java class library)
JButton class of package javax.swing
JLabel class of package javax.swing
JScrollPane class

JTextArea class
JTextField class of package javax.swing
logical AND (&&)
logical negation (!)
logical operators
logical OR (||)
long
Math class methods
Math.E
Math.PI
Math.random method
m-by-n array
method
method call
method call operator, ()
method declaration
method definition
method overloading
mixed-type expression
modular program
multiple-subscripted array
name of an array
named constant
off-by-one error
paint method of JApplet
pass-by-reference
pass-by-value
passing arrays to methods
programmer-defined method
random number generation
reference parameter
reference types
repaint method of JApplet
return
return value type
row subscript
scaling
scroll box
scrollbar
setFont method
setLayout method of JApplet
shifting
short-circuit evaluation
showStatus method of JApplet
side effects
simulation

single-subscripted array
software engineering
software reusability
square brackets []
start method of JApplet
stop method of JApplet
subscript
table of values

tabular format
thumb of a scrollbar
unary operator
update method of JApplet
value of an element
void
zeroth element

COMMON PROGRAMMING ERRORS

25.1 Using a keyword as an identifier is a syntax error.

25.2 In expressions using operator &&, it is possible that a condition—we will call this the dependent condition—may require another condition to be true for it to be meaningful to evaluate the dependent condition. In this case, the dependent condition should be placed after the other condition or an error might occur.

25.3 Defining a method outside the braces of a class definition is a syntax error.

25.4 Omitting the return-value-type in a method definition is a syntax error.

25.5 Forgetting to return a value from a method that is supposed to return a value is a syntax error. If a return-value-type other than void is specified, the method must contain a return statement.

25.6 Returning a value from a method whose return type has been declared void is a syntax error.

25.7 Declaring method parameters of the same type as float x, y instead of float x, float y is a syntax error because types are required for each parameter in the parameter list.

25.8 Placing a semicolon after the right parenthesis enclosing the parameter list of a method definition is a syntax error.

25.9 Redefining a method parameter as a local variable in the method is a syntax error.

25.10 Passing to a method an argument that is not compatible with the corresponding parameter's type is a syntax error.

25.11 Defining a method inside another method is a syntax error.

25.12 After a final variable has been initialized, attempting to assign another value to that variable is a syntax error.

25.13 Providing a definition for one of the JApplet methods init, start, paint, stop or destroy that does not match the method headers shown in Fig. 25.14 results in a method that will not be called automatically during execution of the applet.

25.14 Unlike C or C++ the number of elements in the array is never specified in the square brackets after the array name in a declaration. The declaration int c[12]; causes a syntax error.

25.15 Assigning a value to a constant variable after the variable has been initialized is a syntax error.

25.16 Referring to an element outside the array bounds is a logic error.

ERROR-PREVENTION TIPS

25.1 Small methods are easier to test, debug and understand than large ones.

25.2 When a Java program is executed, the Java interpreter checks array element subscripts to be sure they are valid (i.e., all subscripts must be greater than or equal to 0 and less than the length of the array). If there is an invalid subscript, Java generates an exception.

25.3 Exceptions are used to indicate that an error occurred in a program. They enable the programmer to recover from an error and continue the execution of the program instead of abnormally terminating the program. When an invalid array reference is made, an `ArrayIndexOutOf-BoundsException` is generated.

25.4   When looping through an array, the array subscript should never go below 0 and should always be less than the total number of elements in the array (one less than the size of the array). Make sure the loop terminating condition prevents accessing elements outside this range.

25.5   Programs should validate the correctness of all input values to prevent erroneous information from affecting a program's calculations.

25.6   With call-by-value, changes to the called method's copy do not affect the original variable's value in the calling method. This prevents the accidental side effects that so greatly hinder the development of correct and reliable software systems.

GOOD PROGRAMMING PRACTICES

25.1   For clarity, avoid expressions with side effects in conditions. The side effects may look clever, but they are often more trouble than they are worth.

25.2   Place a blank line between method definitions to separate the methods and enhance program readability.

25.3   Although it is not incorrect to do so, do not use the same names for the arguments passed to a method and the corresponding parameters in the method definition. This helps avoid ambiguity.

25.4   Choosing meaningful method names and meaningful parameter names makes programs more readable and helps avoid excessive use of comments.

25.5   Use only uppercase letters (with underscores between words) in the names of `final` variables. This makes these constants stand out in a program.

25.6   Using meaningfully named `final` variables rather than integer constants (such as 2) makes programs more readable.

25.7   Strive for program clarity. It is sometimes worthwhile to trade off the most efficient use of memory or processor time in favor of writing clearer programs.

PERFORMANCE TIPS

25.1   In expressions using operator `&&`, if the separate conditions are independent of one another, make the condition that is most likely to be false the leftmost condition. In expressions using operator `||`, make the condition that is most likely to be true the leftmost condition. This can reduce a program's execution time.

25.2   Sometimes performance considerations far outweigh clarity considerations.

25.3   Passing arrays by reference makes sense for performance reasons. If arrays were passed by value, a copy of each element would be passed. For large, frequently passed arrays, this would waste time and would consume considerable storage for the copies of the arrays.

PORTABILITY TIP

25.1   All primitive data types in Java are portable across all platforms that support Java.

SOFTWARE ENGINEERING OBSERVATIONS

25.1   A method should usually be no longer than one page. Better yet, a method should usually be no longer than half a page. Regardless of how long a method is, it should perform one task well. Small methods promote software reusability.

25.2   Programs should be written as collections of small methods. This makes programs easier to write, debug, maintain and modify.

25.3   A method requiring a large number of parameters may be performing too many tasks. Consider dividing the method into smaller methods that perform the separate tasks. The method header should fit on one line if possible.

25.4   The method header and method calls must all agree in the number, type and order of parameters and arguments.

25.5   Unlike other languages, Java does not allow the programmer to choose whether to pass each argument call-by-value or call-by-reference. Primitive data type variables are always passed call-by-value. Objects are not passed to methods; rather, references to objects are passed to methods. The references themselves are also passed call-by-value. When a method receives a reference to an object, the method can manipulate the object directly.

25.6   When returning information from a method via a `return` statement, primitive-data-type variables are always returned by value (i.e., a copy is returned) and objects are always returned by reference (i.e., a reference to the object is returned).

SELF-REVIEW EXERCISES

25.1   Answer each of the following:
   a) Program modules in Java are called _____ and _____.
   b) A method is invoked with a(n) _____.
   c) A variable known only within the method in which it is defined is called a(n) _____.
   d) The _____ statement in a called method can be used to pass the value of an expression back to the calling method.
   e) The keyword _____ is used in a method header to indicate that a method does not return a value.
   f) The three ways to return control from a called method to a caller are _____, _____ and _____.
   g) The _____ method is invoked once when an applet begins execution.
   h) The _____ method is used to produce random numbers.
   i) The _____ method is invoked each time the user of a browser revisits the HTML page on which an applet resides.
   j) The _____ method is invoked to draw on an applet.
   k) The _____ method invokes the applet's `update` method, which in turn invokes the applet's `paint` method.
   l) The _____ method is invoked for an applet each time the user of a browser leaves an HTML page on which the applet resides.
   m) The _____ qualifier is used to declare read-only variables.

25.2   Give the method header for each of the following methods.
   a) Method `hypotenuse`, which takes two double-precision, floating-point arguments `side1` and `side2` and returns a double-precision, floating-point result.
   b) Method `smallest`, which takes three integers, `x`, `y`, `z` and returns an integer.
   c) Method `instructions`, which does not take any arguments and does not return a value. [*Note*: Such methods are commonly used to display instructions to a user.]
   d) Method `intToFloat`, which takes an integer argument, `number` and returns a floating-point result.

25.3   Find the error in each of the following program segments and explain how the error can be corrected:

```
a) int g() {
       System.out.println( "Inside method g" );
       int h() {
           System.out.println( "Inside method h" );
       }
   }
b) int sum( int x, int y ) {
       int result;
       result = x + y;
   }
c) int sum( int n ) {
       if ( n == 0 )
           return 0;
       else
           n + sum( n - 1 );
   }
d) void f( float a ); {
       float a;
       System.out.println( a );
   }
e) void product() {
       int a = 6, b = 5, c = 4, result;
       result = a * b * c;
       System.out.println( "Result is " + result );
       return result;
   }
```

25.4   State whether each of the following is *true* or *false*. If *false*, explain why.
   a) An array can store many different types of values.
   b) An array subscript should normally be of data type `float`.
   c) An individual array element that is passed to a method and modified in that method will
      contain the modified value when the called method completes execution.

ANSWERS TO SELF-REVIEW EXERCISES

25.1   a) Methods and classes. b) Method call. c) Local variable. d) `return`. e) `void`. f) `return`;
or `return` *expression*; or encountering the closing right brace of a method. g) `init`. h) `Math.ran-`
`dom`. i) `start`. j) `paint`. k) `repaint`. l) `stop`. m) `final`.

25.2   a) `double hypotenuse( double side1, double side2 )`
   b) `int smallest( int x, int y, int z )`
   c) `void instructions()`
   d) `float intToFloat( int number )`

25.3   a) Error: Method `h` is defined in method `g`.
      Correction: Move the definition of `h` out of the definition of `g`.
   b) Error: The method is supposed to return an integer, but does not.
      Correction: Delete variable `result` and place the following statement in the method:
         `return x + y;`
      or add the following statement at the end of the method body:
         `return result;`

c) Error: The result of n + sum(n - 1) is not returned by this recursive method, resulting in a syntax error.
Correction: Rewrite the statement in the else clause as **return** n + sum(n - 1);

d) Error: The semicolon after the right parenthesis that encloses the parameter list and re-defining the parameter a in the method definition are each incorrect.
Correction: Delete the semicolon after the right parenthesis of the parameter list and delete the declaration float a;.

e) Error: The method returns a value when it is not supposed to.
Correction: Change the return type to int.

25.4 a) False. An array can store only values of the same type.

b) False. An array subscript must be an integer or an integer expression.

c) False for individual primitive-type array elements because they are passed call-by-value. If a reference to an array is passed, then modifications to the array elements are reflected in the original. Also, an individual element of a class type passed to a method is passed call-by-reference and changes to the object will be reflected in the original array element.

EXERCISES

25.5 Answer each of the following questions:
a) What does it mean to choose numbers "at random?"
b) Why is the Math.random method useful for simulating games of chance?
c) Why is it often necessary to scale and/or shift the values produced by Math.random?
d) Why is computerized simulation of real-world situations a useful technique?

25.6 Write statements that assign random integers to the variable n in the following ranges:
a) $1 \leq n \leq 2$
b) $1 \leq n \leq 100$
c) $0 \leq n \leq 9$
d) $1000 \leq n \leq 1112$
e) $-1 \leq n \leq 1$
f) $-3 \leq n \leq 11$

25.7 For each of the following sets of integers, write a single statement that will print a number at random from the set.
a) 2, 4, 6, 8, 10.
b) 3, 5, 7, 9, 11.
c) 6, 10, 14, 18, 22.

25.8 Define a method hypotenuse that calculates the length of the hypotenuse of a right triangle when the other two sides are given. The method should take two arguments of type double and return the hypotenuse as a double. Incorporate this method into an applet that reads integer values for side1 and side2 from JTextFields and performs the calculation with the hypotenuse method. Determine the length of the hypotenuse for each of the following triangles. [*Note*: Register for event handling on only the second JTextField. The user should interact with the program by typing numbers in both JTextFields and pressing *Enter* in the second JTextField.]

Triangle	Side 1	Side 2
1	3.0	4.0
2	5.0	12.0
3	8.0	15.0

25.9   Write a method `multiple` that determines for a pair of integers whether the second integer is a multiple of the first. The method should take two integer arguments and return `true` if the second is a multiple of the first and `false` otherwise. Incorporate this method into an applet that inputs a series of pairs of integers (one pair at a time using `JTextFields`). [*Note:* Register for event handling on only the second `JTextField`. The user should interact with the program by typing numbers in both `JTextFields` and pressing *Enter* in the second `JTextField`.]

25.10   Write an applet that inputs integers (one at a time) and passes them one at a time to method `isEven`, which uses the modulus operator to determine if an integer is even. The method should take an integer argument and return `true` if the integer is even and `false` otherwise. Use an input dialog to obtain the data from the user.

25.11   Write a method `squareOfAsterisks` that displays a solid square of asterisks whose side is specified in integer parameter `side`. For example, if `side` is 4, the method displays

```
****
****
****
****
```

Incorporate this method into an applet that reads an integer value for `side` from the user at the keyboard and performs the drawing with the `squareOfAsterisks` method. Note that this method should be called from the applet's `paint` method and should be passed the `Graphics` object from `paint`.

25.12   Implement the following integer methods:

    a) Method `celsius` returns the Celsius equivalent of a Fahrenheit temperature using the calculation

```
C = 5.0 / 9.0 * ( F - 32 );
```

    b) Method `fahrenheit` returns the Fahrenheit equivalent of a Celsius temperature.

```
F = 9.0 / 5.0 * C + 32;
```

    c) Use these methods to write an applet that enables the user to enter either a Fahrenheit temperature and display the Celsius equivalent or enter a Celsius temperature and display the Fahrenheit equivalent.

[*Note:* This applet will require that two `JTextField` objects that have registered action events. When `actionPerformed` is invoked, the `ActionEvent` parameter has method `getSource()` to determine the GUI component with which the user interacted. Your `actionPerformed` method should contain an `if/else` structure of the following form:

```
if ( e.getSource() == input1 ) {
    // process input1 interaction here
}
else {  // e.getSource() == input2
    // process input2 interaction here
}
```

where `input1` and `input2` are `JTextField` references.]

25.13   An integer is said to be *prime* if it is divisible only by 1 and itself. For example, 2, 3, 5 and 7 are prime, but 4, 6, 8 and 9 are not.

    a) Write a method that determines if a number is prime.

b) Use this method in an applet that determines and prints all the prime numbers between 1 and 10,000. How many of these 10,000 numbers do you really have to test before being sure that you have found all the primes? Display the results in a **JTextArea** that has scrolling functionality.

c) Initially you might think that *n*/2 is the upper limit for which you must test to see if a number is prime, but you need only go as high as the square root of *n*. Why? Rewrite the program and run it both ways. Estimate the performance improvement.

25.14 Write a method that takes an integer value and returns the number with its digits reversed. For example, given the number 7631, the method should return 1367. Incorporate the method into an applet that reads a value from the user. Display the result of the method in the status bar.

25.15 The *greatest common divisor (GCD)* of two integers is the largest integer that evenly divides each of the two numbers. Write a method **gcd** that returns the greatest common divisor of two integers. Incorporate the method into an applet that reads two values from the user. Display the result of the method in the status bar.

25.16 Write a method **qualityPoints** that inputs a student's average and returns 4 if a student's average is 90–100, 3 if the average is 80–89, 2 if the average is 70–79, 1 if the average is 60–69 and 0 if the average is lower than 60. Incorporate the method into an applet that reads a value from the user. Display the result of the method in the status bar.

25.17 Write an applet that simulates coin tossing. Let the program toss the coin each time the user presses the "**Toss**" button. Count the number of times each side of the coin appears. Display the results. The program should call a separate method **flip** that takes no arguments and returns **false** for tails and **true** for heads. [*Note:* If the program realistically simulates the coin tossing, each side of the coin should appear approximately half the time.]

25.18 Computers are playing an increasing role in education. Write a program that will help an elementary school student learn multiplication. Use **Math.random** to produce two positive one-digit integers. It should then display a question in the status bar such as

```
How much is 6 times 7?
```

The student then types the answer into a **JTextField**. Your program checks the student's answer. If it is correct, draw the string "**Very good!**" on the applet, then ask another multiplication question. If the answer is wrong, draw the string "**No. Please try again.**" on the applet, then let the student try the same question again repeatedly until the student finally gets it right. A separate method should be used to generate each new question. This method should be called once when the applet begins execution and each time the user answers the question correctly. All drawing on the applet should be performed by the **paint** method.

25.19 Write an applet that plays the "guess the number" game as follows: Your program chooses the number to be guessed by selecting a random integer in the range 1 to 1000. The applet displays the prompt **Guess a number between 1 and 1000** next to a **JTextField**. The player types a first guess into the **JTextField** and presses the *Enter* key. If the player's guess is incorrect, your program should display **Too high. Try again.** or **Too low. Try again.** in the status bar to help the player "zero in" on the correct answer and should clear the **JTextField** so the user can enter the next guess. When the user enters the correct answer, display **Congratulations. You guessed the number!** in the status bar and clear the **JTextField** so the user can play again. [*Note:* The guessing technique employed in this problem is similar to a *binary search*.]

25.20 The greatest common divisor of integers x and y is the largest integer that evenly divides both x and y. Write a recursive method **gcd** that returns the greatest common divisor of x and y. The **gcd** of x and y is defined recursively as follows: If y is equal to 0, then **gcd(x, y)** is x; otherwise, **gcd(**

x, y) is gcd(y, x % y), where % is the modulus operator. Use this method to replace the one you wrote in the applet of Exercise 25.15.

25.21 Modify the craps program of Fig. 25.13 to allow wagering. Initialize variable bankBalance to 1000 dollars. Prompt the player to enter a wager. Check that wager is less than or equal to bank-Balance, and if not, have the user reenter wager until a valid wager is entered. After a correct wager is entered, run one game of craps. If the player wins, increase bankBalance by wager and print the new bankBalance. If the player loses, decrease bankBalance by wager, print the new bank-Balance, check if bankBalance has become zero, and if so, print the message "Sorry. You busted!" As the game progresses, print various messages to create some "chatter," such as "Oh, you're going for broke, huh?" or "Aw c'mon, take a chance!" or "You're up big. Now's the time to cash in your chips!". Implement the "chatter" as a separate method that randomly chooses the string to display.

25.22 Write a program to simulate the rolling of two dice. The program should use Math.random to roll the first die and should use Math.random again to roll the second die. The sum of the two values should then be calculated. [*Note:* Since each die can show an integer value from 1 to 6, the sum of the values will vary from 2 to 12, with 7 being the most frequent sum and 2 and 12 being the least frequent sums. Figure 25.24 shows the 36 possible combinations of the two dice. Your program should roll the dice 36,000 times. Use a single-subscripted array to tally the numbers of times each possible sum appears. Print the results in a tabular format. Also, determine if the totals are reasonable (i.e., there are six ways to roll a 7, so approximately one sixth of all the rolls should be 7).

	1	2	3	4	5	6
1	2	3	4	5	6	7
2	3	4	5	6	7	8
3	4	5	6	7	8	9
4	5	6	7	8	9	10
5	6	7	8	9	10	11
6	7	8	9	10	11	12

Fig. 25.24 The 36 possible outcomes of rolling two dice.

26

Java Object-Based Programming

Objectives

- To understand encapsulation and data hiding.
- To understand the notions of data abstraction and abstract data types (ADTs).
- To create Java ADTs, namely classes.
- To be able to create, use and destroy objects.
- To be able to control access to object instance variables and methods.
- To appreciate the value of object orientation.
- To understand the use of the `this` reference.
- To understand class variables and class methods.

My object all sublime
I shall achieve in time.
W. S. Gilbert

Is it a world to hide virtues in?
William Shakespeare

Your public servants serve you right.
Adlai Stevenson

But what, to serve our private ends,
Forbids the cheating of our friends?
Charles Churchill

This above all: to thine own self be true.
William Shakespeare

Have no friends not equal to yourself.
Confucius

Outline

26.1 Introduction

Now we investigate object orientation in Java. If you have already read the introduction to object orientation in C++ (Chapter 16) you may want to jump right into Section 26.2, Implementing a Time Abstract Data Type with a Class, where we take our first look at an object-oriented implementation in Java

Let us introduce some key concepts and terminology of object orientation. OOP *encapsulates* data (*attributes*) and methods (*behaviors*) into *objects;* the data and methods of an object are intimately tied together. Objects have the property of *information hiding.* This means that although objects may know how to communicate with one another across well-defined *interfaces,* objects normally are not allowed to know how other objects are implemented—implementation details are hidden within the objects themselves. Surely it is possible to drive a car effectively without knowing the details of how engines, transmissions and exhaust systems work internally. We will see why information hiding is so crucial to good software engineering.

In C and other *procedural programming languages,* programming tends to be *action-oriented.* In Java, programming is *object-oriented.* In C, the unit of programming is the *function* (called *methods* in Java). In Java, the unit of programming is the *class* from which objects are eventually *instantiated* (i.e., created). Functions do not disappear in Java; rather they are encapsulated as methods with the data they process within the "walls" of classes.

C programmers concentrate on writing functions. Groups of actions that perform some task are formed into functions and functions are grouped to form programs. Data is certainly important in C, but the view is that data exists primarily in support of the actions that functions perform. The *verbs* in a system-requirements document help the C programmer determine the set of functions that will work together to implement the system.

Java programmers concentrate on creating their own *user-defined types* called *classes.* Classes are also referred to as *programmer-defined types.* Each class contains data as well as the set of methods that manipulate the data. The data components of a class are called *instance variables* (or *data members* in C++). Just as an instance of a built-in type such as `int` is called a *variable,* an instance of a user-defined type (i.e., a class) is called an *object.* The focus of attention in Java is on objects rather than methods. The *nouns* in a system-requirements document help the Java programmer determine an initial set of classes with which to begin the design process. These classes are then used to instantiate objects that will work together to implement the system.

This chapter explains how to create and use objects, a subject we like to call *object-based programming (OBP).* Chapter 27 introduces *inheritance* and *polymorphism*—two key technologies that enable true *object-oriented programming (OOP).* Although inheritance is not discussed in detail until Chapter 27, inheritance is part of every Java class definition.

Performance Tip 26.1

All Java objects are passed by reference. Only a memory address is passed, not a copy of a possibly large object (as would be the case in a pass-by-value).

Software Engineering Observation 26.1

It is important to write programs that are understandable and easy to maintain. Change is the rule rather than the exception. Programmers should anticipate that their code will be modified. As we will see, classes facilitate program modifiability.

26.2 Implementing a Time Abstract Data Type with a Class

The application of Fig. 26.1 consists of two classes—`Time1` and `TimeTest`. Class `Time1` is defined in file `Time1.java` (specified in the comment in line 1) and the class `TimeTest` is defined in file `TimeTest.java` (specified in the comment in line 49). [*Note:* Every program in this book that contains more than one file begins the file with a comment indicating the figure number and file name.] Although these two classes are defined in separate files, we number the lines in the program consecutively across both files for discussion purposes in the text. It is important to note that these classes *must* be defined in separate files.

Software Engineering Observation 26.2

Class definitions that begin with keyword `public` must be stored in a file that has exactly the same name as the class and ends with the `.java` file name extension.

Common Programming Error 26.1

Defining more than one `public` class in the same file is a syntax error.

```
1   // Fig. 26.1: Time1.java
2   // Time1 class definition
3   import java.text.DecimalFormat;  // used for number formatting
4
5   // This class maintains the time in 24-hour format
6   public class Time1 extends Object {
7       private int hour;    // 0 - 23
8       private int minute;  // 0 - 59
9       private int second;  // 0 - 59
10
```

Fig. 26.1   Abstract data type `Time1` implementation as a class—`Time1.java`. (Part 1 of 2.)

```
11        // Time1 constructor initializes each instance variable
12        // to zero. Ensures that each Time1 object starts in a
13        // consistent state.
14        public Time1()
15        {
16           setTime( 0, 0, 0 );
17        } // end Time1 constructor
18
19        // Set a new time value using universal time. Perform
20        // validity checks on the data. Set invalid values to zero.
21        public void setTime( int h, int m, int s )
22        {
23           hour   = ( ( h >= 0 && h < 24 ) ? h : 0 );
24           minute = ( ( m >= 0 && m < 60 ) ? m : 0 );
25           second = ( ( s >= 0 && s < 60 ) ? s : 0 );
26        } // end method setTime
27
28        // Convert to String in universal-time format
29        public String toUniversalString()
30        {
31           DecimalFormat twoDigits = new DecimalFormat( "00" );
32
33           return twoDigits.format( hour ) + ":" +
34                  twoDigits.format( minute ) + ":" +
35                  twoDigits.format( second );
36        } // end method toUniversalString
37
38        // Convert to String in standard-time format
39        public String toString()
40        {
41           DecimalFormat twoDigits = new DecimalFormat( "00" );
42
43           return ( ( hour == 12 || hour == 0 ) ? 12 : hour % 12 ) +
44                  ":" + twoDigits.format( minute ) +
45                  ":" + twoDigits.format( second ) +
46                  ( hour < 12 ? " AM" : " PM" );
47        } // end method toString
48     } // end class Time1
```

Fig. 26.1   Abstract data type Time1 implementation as a class—Time1.java. (Part 2 of 2.)

```
49     // Fig. 26.1: TimeTest.java
50     // Class TimeTest to exercise class Time1
51     import javax.swing.JOptionPane;
52
53     public class TimeTest {
54        public static void main( String args[] )
55        {
56           Time1 t = new Time1();   // calls Time1 constructor
57           String output;
```

Fig. 26.1   Abstract data type Time1 implementation as a class—TimeTest.java. (Part 1 of 2.)

```
58
59        output = "The initial universal time is: " +
60                t.toUniversalString() +
61                "\nThe initial standard time is: " +
62                t.toString() +
63                "\nImplicit toString() call: " + t;
64
65        t.setTime( 13, 27, 6 );
66        output += "\n\nUniversal time after setTime is: " +
67                t.toUniversalString() +
68                "\nStandard time after setTime is: " +
69                t.toString();
70
71        t.setTime( 99, 99, 99 );  // all invalid values
72        output += "\n\nAfter attempting invalid settings: " +
73                "\nUniversal time: " + t.toUniversalString() +
74                "\nStandard time: " + t.toString();
75
76        JOptionPane.showMessageDialog( null, output,
77            "Testing Class Time1",
78            JOptionPane.INFORMATION_MESSAGE );
79
80        System.exit( 0 );
81    } // end main
82 } // end class TimeTest
```

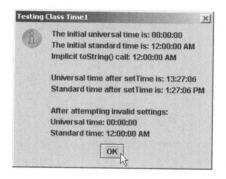

Fig. 26.1   Abstract data type `Time1` implementation as a class—`TimeTest.java`. (Part 2 of 2.)

Figure 26.1 (lines 1 through 48) contains a simple definition for class `Time1`. Our `Time1` class definition begins with line 6

```
public class Time1 extends Object {
```

indicating that class `Time1` `extends` class *Object* (from package `java.lang`). Remember that you never really create a class definition "from scratch." In fact, when you create a class definition, you always use pieces of an existing class definition. Java uses *inheritance* to create new classes from existing class definitions. Keyword `extends` followed by class name `Object` indicates the class (in this case `Time1`) from which our new class inherits existing pieces. In this inheritance relationship, `Object` is called the *superclass* or *base class* and `Time1` is called the *subclass* or *derived class*. Using inheritance results in a new class definition that has the *attributes* (data) and *behaviors* (methods) of class `Object` as well as new features we add in our `Time1` class definition. Every class in Java is a subclass of `Object`. Therefore, every class inherits the eleven methods defined by class `Object`. One key `Object` method is *toString*, discussed later in this section. Other methods of class `Object` are discussed as they are needed throughout the text.

Software Engineering Observation 26.3

Every class defined in Java must extend another class. If a class does not explicitly use keyword `extends` *in its definition, the class implicitly* `extends Object`.

The *body* of the class definition is delineated with left and right braces ({ and }) in lines 6 and 48. Class `Time1` contains three integer instance variables—hour, `minute` and second—that represent the time in *universal-time* format (*24-hour clock* format).

Keywords *public* and *private* are *member access modifiers*. Instance variables or methods declared with member access modifier `public` are accessible wherever the program has a reference to a `Time1` object. Instance variables or methods declared with member access modifier `private` are accessible *only* to methods of the class. Every instance variable or method definition should be preceded by a member access modifier. Member access modifiers can appear multiple times and in any order in a class definition.

Good Programming Practice 26.1

Group members by member access modifier in a class definition for clarity and readability.

Common Programming Error 26.2

An attempt by a method which is not a member of a particular class to access a `private` *member of that class is a syntax error.*

The three integer instance variables hour, `minute` and second are each declared (lines 7 through 9) with member access modifier `private`. This indicates that these instance variables of the class are only accessible to methods of the class. When an object of the class is instantiated (created), such instance variables are encapsulated in the object and can be accessed only through methods of that object's class (normally through the class's `public` methods). Instance variables are normally declared `private` and methods are normally declared `public`. It is possible to have `private` methods and `public` data, as we will see later. The `private` methods are often called *utility methods* or *helper methods* because they can only be called by other methods of that class and are used to support the operation of those methods. Using `public` data is uncommon and is a dangerous programming practice.

Good Programming Practice 26.2

Our preference is to list the `private` *instance variables of a class first so as you read the code, you see the names and types of the instance variables before they are used in the methods of the class.*

Good Programming Practice 26.3

Despite the fact that `private` *and* `public` *members may be repeated and intermixed, list all the* `private` *members of a class first in one group, then list all the* `public` *members in another group.*

Software Engineering Observation 26.4

Keep all the instance variables of a class `private`. When necessary provide `public` methods to set the values of `private` instance variables and to get the values of `private` instance variables. This architecture helps hide the implementation of a class from its clients, which reduces bugs and improves program modifiability.

Software Engineering Observation 26.5

Methods tend to fall into a number of different categories: methods that get the values of `private` instance variables; methods that set the values of `private` instance variables; methods that implement the services of the class; and methods that perform various mechanical chores for the class, such as initializing class objects, assigning class objects, and converting between classes and built-in types or between classes and other classes.

Access methods can read or display data. Another common use for access methods is to test the truth or falsity of conditions—such methods are often called *predicate methods*. An example of a predicate method would be an `isEmpty` method for any container class—a class capable of holding many objects—such as a linked list, a stack or a queue. A program might test `isEmpty` before attempting to read another item from the container object. A program might test `isFull` before attempting to insert another item into a container object.

Class `Time1` contains the following `public` methods—`Time1` (line 14), `setTime` (line 21), `toUniversalString` (line 29) and `toString` (line 39). These are the *public methods*, *public services* or *public interface* of the class. These methods are used by *clients* (i.e., portions of a program that are users of a class) of the class to manipulate the data stored in objects of the class.

The clients of a class use references to interact with an object of the class. For example, method `paint` in an applet is a client of class `Graphics`—`paint` uses a reference to a `Graphics` object (such as g) that it receives as an argument to draw on the applet by calling methods that are `public` services of class `Graphics` (such as `drawString`, `drawLine`, `drawOval` and `drawRect`).

Notice the method with the same name as the class (line 14); it is the *constructor* method of that class. A constructor is a special method that initializes the instance variables of a class object. A class's constructor method is called whenever an object of that class is instantiated. This constructor simply calls the class's `setTime` method (discussed shortly) with hour, minute and second values specified as 0.

Constructors can take arguments but cannot return a value. An important difference between constructors and other methods is that constructors *are not allowed to specify a return data type* (not even `void`). Normally, constructors are `public` methods of a class. Non-`public` methods are discussed later.

Common Programming Error 26.3

Attempting to declare a return type for a constructor and/or attempting to `return` a value from a constructor is a logic error. Java allows other methods of the class to have the same name as the class and to specify return types. Such methods are not constructors and will not be called when an object of the class is instantiated.

Method `setTime` (line 21) is a `public` method that receives three integer arguments and uses them to set the time. Each argument is tested in a conditional expression that determines if the value is in range. For example, the hour value must be greater than or equal to 0 and less than 24 because we represent the time in universal time format (0–23 for the hour, 0–59 for the minute and 0–59 for the second). Any value outside this range is an invalid value and is set to zero—ensuring that a `Time1` object always contains valid data. This is also known as *keeping the object in a consistent state*. In cases where invalid data is supplied to `setTime`, the program may want to indicate that an invalid time setting was attempted. We explore this possibility in the exercises.

Good Programming Practice 26.4

Always define a class so its instance variables are maintained in a consistent state.

The `toUniversalString` method (line 29) takes no arguments and returns a `String`. This method produces a universal-time-format string consisting of six digits—two for the hour, two for the minute and two for the second. For example, 13:30:07 represents 1:30:07 PM. Line 31 creates an instance of class `DecimalFormat` (from package `java.text` imported in line 3) to help format the universal time. The object `twoDigits` is initialized with the *format control string* `"00"`, which indicates that the number format should consist of two digits—each 0 is a placeholder for a digit. If the number being formatted is a single digit, it is preceded by a leading 0 (i.e., 8 is formatted as 08). The `return` statement in lines 33 through 35 uses the `format` method (that returns a formatted `String` containing the number) from object `twoDigits` to format the `hour`, `minute` and `second` values into two-digit strings. Those strings are concatenated with the + operator (separated by colons) and returned from the `toUniversalString` method.

Method `toString` (line 39) takes no arguments and returns a `String`. This method produces a standard-time-format string consisting of the `hour`, `minute` and `second` values separated by colons and an AM or PM indicator as in `1:27:06 PM`. This method uses the same `DecimalFormat` techniques as method `toUniversalString` to guarantee that the `minute` and `second` values each appear with two digits. Method `toString` is special in that we inherited from class `Object` a `toString` method with exactly the same first line as our `toString` in line 39. The original `toString` method of class `Object` is a generic version that is used mainly as a placeholder that can be redefined by a subclass (similar to methods `init`, `start` and `paint` from class `JApplet`). Our version replaces the version we inherited to provide a `toString` method that is more appropriate for our class. This is known as *overriding* the original method definition (discussed in detail in Chapter 27).

Once the class has been defined, it can be used as a type in declarations such as

```
Time1 sunset,        // reference to object of type Time1
      timeArray[];   // reference to array of Time1 objects
```

The class name is a new type specifier. There may be many objects of a class, just as there may be many variables of a primitive data type such as `int`. The programmer can create new class types as needed; this is one of the reasons why Java is known as an *extensible language*.

The application of Fig. 26.1 (lines 48 through 82) uses class `Time1`. Method `main` of class `TimeTest` declares and initializes an instance of class `Time1` called `t` with line 56

```
Time1 t = new Time1();  // calls Time1 constructor
```

When the object is instantiated, operator `new` allocates the memory in which the `Time1` object will be stored, then `new` calls the `Time1` constructor to initialize the instance variables of the new Time1 object. The constructor invokes method setTime to explicitly initialize each private instance variable to 0. Operator new then returns a reference to the new object, and that reference is assigned to t. Similarly, line 31 in class Time1 uses new to allocate the memory for a DecimalFormat object, then calls the DecimalFormat constructor with the argument "00" to indicate the number format control string.

Software Engineering Observation 26.6

Every time new creates an object of a class, that class's constructor is called to initialize the instance variables of the new object.

Note that class Time1 was not imported into the TimeTest.java file. Actually, every class in Java is part of a *package* (like the classes from the Java API). If the programmer does not specify the package for a class, the class is automatically placed in the *default package* which includes the compiled classes in the current directory. If a class is in the same package as the class that uses it, an import statement is not required. We import classes from the Java API because their .class files are not in the same package with each program we write. Section 26.4 illustrates how to define your own packages of classes.

Line 57 declares a String reference output that will store the string containing the results to be displayed in a message dialog. Lines 59 through 63 append to output the time in universal-time format (by sending message toUniversalString to the object to which t refers) and standard-time format (by sending message toString to the object to which t refers) to confirm that the data were initialized properly. Notice line 63

```
"\nImplicit toString() call: " + t;
```

In Java, the + operator can be used to concatenate Strings. Applying the + operator to a String and an object results in an implicit call to the object's toString method, which converts the object into a String. The + operator then concatenates the two Strings to produce a single String. Lines 62 and 63 illustrate that you can call toString both explicitly and implicitly in a String concatenation operation.

Line 65

```
t.setTime( 13, 27, 6 );
```

sends the setTime message to the object to which t refers to change the time. Then lines 66 through 69 append the time to output again in both formats to confirm that the time was set correctly.

To illustrate that method setTime validates the values passed to it, line 71

```
t.setTime( 99, 99, 99 );  // all invalid values
```

calls method setTime and attempts to set the instance variables to invalid values. Then lines 72 through 74 append the time to output again in both formats to confirm that setTime validated the data. Lines 76 through 78 display a message box with the results of our program. Notice in the last two lines of the output window that the time is set to midnight—the default value of a Time1 object.

Now that we have seen our first nonapplet nonapplication class, let us consider several issues of class design.

Again, note that the instance variables hour, minute and second are each declared private. Instance variables declared private are not accessible outside the class in which they are defined. The philosophy here is that the actual data representation used within the class is of no concern to the class's clients. For example, it would be perfectly reasonable for the class to represent the time internally as the number of seconds since midnight. Clients could use the same `public` methods and get the same results without being aware of this. In this sense, implementation of a class is said to be *hidden* from its clients. Exercise 26.10 asks you to make precisely this modification to the `Time1` class of Fig. 26.1 and show that there is no visible change to the clients of the class.

Software Engineering Observation 26.7

Information hiding promotes program modifiability and simplifies the client's perception of a class.

Software Engineering Observation 26.8

Clients of a class can (and should) use the class without knowing the internal details of how the class is implemented. If the class implementation is changed (to improve performance, for example), provided the class's interface remains constant, the class clients' source code need not change. This makes it much easier to modify systems.

In this program, the `Time1` constructor simply initializes the instance variables to 0 (i.e., the military time equivalent of 12 AM). This ensures that the object is created in a *consistent state* (i.e., all instance variable values are valid). Invalid values cannot be stored in the instance variables of a `Time1` object because the constructor is called when the `Time1` object is created, and subsequent attempts by a client to modify the instance variables are scrutinized by the method `setTime`.

Instance variables can be initialized where they are declared in the class body, by the class's constructor, or they can be assigned values by *set* methods. Instance variables that are not explicitly initialized by the programmer are initialized by the compiler (primitive numeric variables are set to 0, `boolean`s are set to `false` and references are set to `null`).

Good Programming Practice 26.5

Initialize instance variables of a class in that class's constructor.

It is interesting that the `toUniversalString` and `toString` methods take no arguments. This is because these methods implicitly know that they are to manipulate the instance variables of the particular `Time1` object for which they are invoked. This makes method calls more concise than conventional function calls in procedural programming. It also reduces the likelihood of passing the wrong arguments, the wrong types of arguments and/or the wrong number of arguments as often happens in C function calls.

Software Engineering Observation 26.9

Using an object-oriented programming approach can often simplify method calls by reducing the number of parameters to be passed. This benefit of object-oriented programming derives from the fact that encapsulation of instance variables and methods within an object gives the methods the right to access the instance variables.

Classes simplify programming because the client (or user of the class object) need only be concerned with the `public` operations encapsulated in the object. Such operations are usually designed to be client oriented rather than implementation oriented. Clients need not be concerned with a class's implementation. Interfaces do change, but less frequently than implementations. When an implementation changes, implementation-dependent code must change accordingly. By hiding the implementation we eliminate the possibility of other program parts becoming dependent on the details of the class implementation.

Often, classes do not have to be created "from scratch." Rather, they may be *derived* from other classes that provide operations the new classes can use, or classes can include objects of other classes as members. Such *software reuse* can greatly enhance programmer productivity. Deriving new classes from existing classes is called *inheritance* and is discussed in detail in Chapter 27. Including class objects as members of other classes is called *composition* or *aggregation* and is discussed later in this chapter.

26.3 Class Scope

A class's instance variables and methods belong to that *class's scope*. Within a class's scope, class members are immediately accessible to all that class's methods and can be referenced simply by name. Outside a class's scope, class members cannot be referenced directly by name. Those class members (such as `public` members) that are visible can only be accessed off a "handle" (i.e., primitive data type members can be referred to by `objectReferenceName.primitiveVariableName` and object members can be referenced by `objectReferenceName.objectMemberName`).

Variables defined in a method are known only to that method (i.e., they are local variables to that method). Such variables are said to have block scope. If a method defines a variable with the same name as a variable with class scope (i.e., an instance variable), the class-scope variable is hidden by the local variable in the method scope. A hidden instance variable can be accessed in the method by preceding its name with the keyword `this` and the dot operator, as in `this.x`. Keyword `this` is discussed later in THIS chapter.

26.4 Creating Packages

As we have seen in almost every example in the text, classes and *interfaces* (discussed in Chapter 27) from preexisting libraries such as the Java API can be imported into a Java program. Each class and interface in the Java API belongs to a specific package that contains a group of related classes and interfaces. Packages are actually directory structures used to organize classes and interfaces. Packages provide a mechanism for *software reuse*. One of our goals as programmers is to create reusable software components so we are not required to repeatedly redefine code in separate programs. Another benefit of packages is that they provide a convention for *unique class names*. With hundreds of thousands of Java programmers around the world, there is a good chance that the names you choose for classes will conflict with the names that other programmers choose for their classes.

The application of Fig. 26.2 illustrates how to create your own package and use a class from that package in a program.

```
1   // Fig. 26.2: Time1.java
2   // Time1 class definition
3   package com.deitel.chtp4.ch26;
4   import java.text.DecimalFormat;   // used for number formatting
```

Fig. 26.2   Creating a package for software reuse—`Time1.java`. (Part 1 of 2.)

```
 5
 6    // This class maintains the time in 24-hour format
 7    public class Time1 extends Object {
 8       private int hour;      // 0 - 23
 9       private int minute;    // 0 - 59
10       private int second;    // 0 - 59
11
12       // Time1 constructor initializes each instance variable
13       // to zero. Ensures that each Time1 object starts in a
14       // consistent state.
15       public Time1()
16       {
17          setTime( 0, 0, 0 );
18       } // end Time1 constructor
19
20       // Set a new time value using military time. Perform
21       // validity checks on the data. Set invalid values
22       // to zero.
23       public void setTime( int h, int m, int s )
24       {
25          hour = ( ( h >= 0 && h < 24 ) ? h : 0 );
26          minute = ( ( m >= 0 && m < 60 ) ? m : 0 );
27          second = ( ( s >= 0 && s < 60 ) ? s : 0 );
28       } // end method setTime
29
30       // Convert to String in universal-time format
31       public String toUniversalString()
32       {
33          DecimalFormat twoDigits = new DecimalFormat( "00" );
34
35          return twoDigits.format( hour ) + ":" +
36                 twoDigits.format( minute ) + ":" +
37                 twoDigits.format( second );
38       } // end method toUniversalString
39
40       // Convert to String in standard-time format
41       public String toString()
42       {
43          DecimalFormat twoDigits = new DecimalFormat( "00" );
44
45          return ( (hour == 12 || hour == 0) ? 12 : hour % 12 ) +
46                 ":" + twoDigits.format( minute ) +
47                 ":" + twoDigits.format( second ) +
48                 ( hour < 12 ? " AM" : " PM" );
49       } // end method toString
50    } // end class Time1
```

Fig. 26.2 Creating a package for software reuse—`Time1.java`. (Part 2 of 2.)

```
51   // Fig. 26.2: TimeTest.java
52   // Class TimeTest to use imported class Time1
53   import javax.swing.JOptionPane;
```

Fig. 26.2 Creating a package for software reuse—`TimeTest.java`. (Part 1 of 2.)

```
54    import com.deitel.chtp4.ch26.Time1;   // import Time1 class
55
56    public class TimeTest {
57       public static void main( String args[] )
58       {
59          Time1 t = new Time1();
60
61          t.setTime( 13, 27, 06 );
62          String output =
63             "Universal time is: " + t.toUniversalString() +
64             "\nStandard time is: " + t.toString();
65
66          JOptionPane.showMessageDialog( null, output,
67             "Packaging Class Time1 for Reuse",
68             JOptionPane.INFORMATION_MESSAGE );
69
70          System.exit( 0 );
71       } // end main
72    } // end class TimeTest
```

Fig. 26.2   Creating a package for software reuse—TimeTest.java. (Part 2 of 2.)

The steps for creating a reusable class are:

1. Declare a public class. If the class is not public, it can be used only by other classes in the same package.

2. Choose a package name, and add a *package statement* to the source code file for the reusable class declaration. There can be only one package statement in a Java source code file and it must precede all other declarations and statements in the file.

3. Compile the class so it is placed in the appropriate package directory structure.

4. Import the reusable class into a program, and use the class.

For *Step 1*, we chose to use the public class Time1 defined in Fig. 26.1. No modifications have been made to the implementation of the class, so we will not discuss the implementation details of the class again here.

To satisfy *Step 2*, we added a package statement at the beginning of the file. Line 3

```
package com.deitel.chtp4.ch26;   // place Time1 in a package
```

uses a package *statement* to define a package named com.deitel.chtp4.ch26. Placing a package statement at the beginning of a Java source file indicates that the class defined in the file is part of the specified package. The only statements in Java that can appear outside the braces of a class definition are package and import statements.

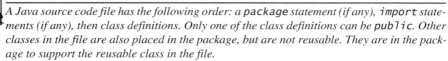

Software Engineering Observation 26.10

A Java source code file has the following order: a package *statement (if any),* import *statements (if any), then class definitions. Only one of the class definitions can be* public. *Other classes in the file are also placed in the package, but are not reusable. They are in the package to support the reusable class in the file.*

In an effort to provide a unique name for each package, Sun Microsystems specifies a convention for package naming. Every package name should start with your Internet domain name in reverse order. For example, our Internet domain name is `deitel.com` so we began our package name with `com.deitel`. If your domain name is *yourcollege*`.edu`, the package name you would use is `edu.`*yourcollege*. After the domain name is reversed, you can choose any other names you want for your package. If you are part of a company with many divisions or a university with many schools, you may want to use the name of your division or school as the next name in the package. We chose to use `chtp4` as the next name in our package name to indicate that this class is from *C How to Program: Fourth Edition*. The last name in our package name specifies that this package is for Chapter 26 (`ch26`). [*Note*: We use our own packages several times throughout the book. You can determine the chapter in which one of our reusable classes is defined by looking at the last name in the `import` statement.]

Step 3 is to compile the class so it is stored in the appropriate package. When a Java file containing a `package` statement is compiled, the resulting class file is placed in the directory structure specified by the `package` statement. The `package` statement of Fig. 26.2 indicates that class `Time1` should be placed in the directory `ch26`. The other names—`com`, `deitel` and `chtp4`—are also directories. The directory names in the `package` statement specify the exact location of the classes in the package. If these directories do not exist before the class is compiled, the compiler can create them.

When a Java file containing a `package` statement is compiled, the resulting `.class` file is placed in the directory specified by the `package` statement. The preceding `package` statement indicates that class `Time1` should be placed in the directory `ch26`. The other names—`com`, `deitel` and `chtp4`—are also directories. The directory names in the `package` statement specify the exact location of the classes in the package. If these directories do not exist before the class is compiled, the compiler creates them.

When compiling a class in a package, the (*-d*) command-line option causes the `javac` compiler to create appropriate directories based on the class's `package` statement. The option also specifies where to create (or locate) the directories. For example, in a command window, we used the compilation command

```
javac -d . Time1.java
```

to specify that the first directory in our package name should be placed in the current directory. The `.` after `-d` in the preceding command represents the current directory on the Windows, UNIX and Linux operating systems (and several others as well). After executing the compilation command, the current directory contains a directory called `com`, `com` contains a directory called `deitel`, `deitel` contains a directory called `chtp4` and `chtp4` contains a directory called `ch26`. In the `ch26` directory, you can find the file `Time1.class`. [*Note:* If you do not use the `-d` option, then you must copy or move the class file to the appropriate package directory after compiling it.]

The `package` name is part of the class name. The class name in this example is actually `com.deitel.chtp4.ch26.Time1`. You can use this *fully qualified* name in your programs, or you can `import` the class and use its simple name (`Time1`) in the program. If another package also contains a `Time1` class, the fully qualified class names can be used to distinguish between the classes in the program and prevent a *name conflict* (also called a *name collision*).

Once the class is compiled and stored in its package, the class can be imported into programs (*Step 4*). Line 54

```
import com.deitel.chtp4.ch26.Time1;  // import Time1 class
```

specifies that class `Time1` should be imported for use in class `TimeTest`. [*Note:* Classes in a package never need to import other classes from the same package.]

26.5 Initializing Class Objects: Constructors

When an object is created, its members can be initialized by a *constructor* method. A constructor is a method with the same name as the class (including case sensitivity). The programmer provides the constructor which is invoked automatically each time an object of that class is instantiated. Instance variables can be initialized implicitly to their default values (0 for primitive numeric types, `false` for `boolean`s and `null` for references), can be initialized in a constructor of the class, or their values may be set later after the object is created. Constructors cannot specify return types or return values. A class may contain overloaded constructors to provide a variety of means for initializing objects of that class.

Good Programming Practice 26.6

When appropriate (almost always), provide a constructor to ensure that every object is properly initialized with meaningful values.

When an object of a class is created, *initializers* can be provided in parentheses to the right of the class name. These initializers are passed as arguments to the class's constructor. This technique is demonstrated in the next example. We have also seen this technique several times previously as we created new objects of classes like `DecimalFormat`, `JLabel`, `JTextField`, `JTextArea` and `JButton`. For each of these classes we have seen statements of the form

```
ref = new ClassName( arguments );
```

where `ref` is a reference of the appropriate data type, `new` indicates that a new object is being created, *ClassName* indicates the type of the new object and *arguments* specifies the values used by the class's constructor to initialize the object.

If no constructors are defined for a class, the compiler creates a *default constructor* that takes no arguments (also called a *no-argument constructor*). The default constructor for a class calls the default constructor for the class that this class `extends`, then proceeds to initialize the instance variables in the manner we discussed previously (i.e., primitive numeric data type variables to 0, `boolean`s to `false` and references to `null`). If the class that this class extends does not have a default constructor, the compiler issues an error message. It is also possible for the programmer to provide a no-argument constructor as we showed in class `Time1` and will see in the next example. If any constructors are defined for a class by the programmer, Java will not create a default constructor for the class.

Common Programming Error 26.4

If constructors are provided for a class, but none of the public constructors are no-argument constructors, and an attempt is made to call a no-argument constructor to initialize an object of the class, a syntax error occurs. A constructor may be called with no arguments only if there are no constructors for the class (the default constructor is called) or if there is a no-argument constructor.

26.6 Using *Set* and *Get* Methods

Private instance variables can be manipulated only by methods of the class. A typical manipulation might be the adjustment of a customer's bank balance (e.g., a private instance variable of a class BankAccount) by a method computeInterest.

Classes often provide public methods to allow clients of the class to *set* (i.e., assign values to) or *get* (i.e., obtain the values of) private instance variables. These methods need not be called *set* and *get*, but they often are. If you pursue further study of Java you will see that this naming convention is important for creating reusable Java software components called *JavaBeans*.

As a naming example, a method that sets instance variable interestRate would typically be named setInterestRate and a method that gets the interestRate would typically be called getInterestRate. *Get* methods are also commonly called *accessor methods* or *query methods*. *Set* methods are also commonly called *mutator methods* (because they typically change a value).

It would seem that providing *set* and *get* capabilities is essentially the same as making the instance variables public. This is another subtlety of Java that makes the language so desirable for software engineering. If an instance variable is public, the instance variable may be read or written at will by any method in the program. If an instance variable is private, a public *get* method certainly seems to allow other methods to read the data at will, but the *get* method controls the formatting and display of the data. A public *set* method can—and most likely will—carefully scrutinize attempts to modify the instance variable's value. This ensures that the new value is appropriate for that data item. For example, an attempt to *set* the day of the month for a date to 37 would be rejected, an attempt to *set* a person's weight to a negative value would be rejected, and so on. So, although *set* and *get* methods may provide access to private data, the access is restricted by the programmer's implementation of the methods.

The benefits of data integrity are not automatic simply because instance variables are made private—the programmer must provide validity checking. Java provides the framework in which programmers can design better programs in a convenient manner.

Software Engineering Observation 26.11

Methods that set the values of private data should verify that the intended new values are proper; if they are not, the set *methods should place the private instance variables into an appropriate consistent state.*

A class's *set* methods can return values indicating that attempts were made to assign invalid data to objects of the class. This enables clients of the class to test the return values of *set* methods to determine if the objects they are manipulating are valid and to take appropriate action if the objects are not valid.

Good Programming Practice 26.7

Every method that modifies the `private` *instance variables of an object should ensure that the data remains in a consistent state.*

The applet of Fig. 26.3 enhances our `Time` class (now called `Time2`) to include *get* and *set* methods for the `hour`, `minute` and `second` `private` instance variables. The *set* methods strictly control the setting of the instance variables to valid values. Attempts to set any instance variable to an incorrect value cause the instance variable to be set to zero (thus leaving the instance variable in a consistent state). Each *get* method simply returns the appropriate instance variable's value. This applet also introduces enhanced GUI event handling techniques as we move toward defining our first full-fledged windowed application.

```java
1   // Fig. 26.3: Time2.java
2   // Time2 class definition
3   package com.deitel.chtp4.ch26;    // place Time2 in a package
4   import java.text.DecimalFormat;   // used for number formatting
5
6   // This class maintains the time in 24-hour format
7   public class Time2 extends Object {
8       private int hour;      // 0 - 23
9       private int minute;    // 0 - 59
10      private int second;    // 0 - 59
11
12      // Time2 constructor initializes each instance variable
13      // to zero. Ensures that Time object starts in a
14      // consistent state.
15      public Time2() { setTime( 0, 0, 0 ); }
16
17      // Set Methods
18      // Set a new time value using universal time. Perform
19      // validity checks on the data. Set invalid values to zero.
20      public void setTime( int h, int m, int s )
21      {
22          setHour( h );     // set the hour
23          setMinute( m );   // set the minute
24          setSecond( s );   // set the second
25      } // end method setTime
26
27      // set the hour
28      public void setHour( int h )
29          { hour = ( ( h >= 0 && h < 24 ) ? h : 0 ); }
30
31      // set the minute
32      public void setMinute( int m )
33          { minute = ( ( m >= 0 && m < 60 ) ? m : 0 ); }
34
35      // set the second
36      public void setSecond( int s )
37          { second = ( ( s >= 0 && s < 60 ) ? s : 0 ); }
38
```

Fig. 26.3 Using *set* and *get* methods—`Time2.java`. (Part 1 of 2.)

```
39        // Get Methods
40        // get the hour
41        public int getHour() { return hour; }
42
43        // get the minute
44        public int getMinute() { return minute; }
45
46        // get the second
47        public int getSecond() { return second; }
48
49        // Convert to String in universal-time format
50        public String toUniversalString()
51        {
52           DecimalFormat twoDigits = new DecimalFormat( "00" );
53
54           return twoDigits.format( getHour() ) + ":" +
55                  twoDigits.format( getMinute() ) + ":" +
56                  twoDigits.format( getSecond() );
57        } // end method toUniversalString
58
59        // Convert to String in standard-time format
60        public String toString()
61        {
62           DecimalFormat twoDigits = new DecimalFormat( "00" );
63
64           return ( ( getHour() == 12 || getHour() == 0 ) ?
65                    12 : getHour() % 12 ) + ":" +
66                  twoDigits.format( getMinute() ) + ":" +
67                  twoDigits.format( getSecond() ) +
68                  ( getHour() < 12 ? " AM" : " PM" );
69        } // end method toString
70     } // end class Time2
```

Fig. 26.3   Using *set* and *get* methods—Time2.java. (Part 2 of 2.)

```
71     // Fig. 26.3: TimeTest.java
72     // Demonstrating the Time2 class set and get methods
73     import java.awt.*;
74     import java.awt.event.*;
75     import javax.swing.*;
76     import com.deitel.chtp4.ch26.Time2;
77
78     public class TimeTest extends JApplet
79                           implements ActionListener {
80        private Time2 t;
81        private JLabel hourLabel, minuteLabel, secondLabel;
82        private JTextField hourField, minuteField,
83                           secondField, display;
84        private JButton tickButton;
85
86        public void init()
87        {
```

Fig. 26.3   Using *set* and *get* methods—TimeTest.java. (Part 1 of 4.)

```
 88            t = new Time2();
 89
 90            Container c = getContentPane();
 91
 92            c.setLayout( new FlowLayout() );
 93            hourLabel = new JLabel( "Set Hour" );
 94            hourField = new JTextField( 10 );
 95            hourField.addActionListener( this );
 96            c.add( hourLabel );
 97            c.add( hourField );
 98
 99            minuteLabel = new JLabel( "Set minute" );
100            minuteField = new JTextField( 10 );
101            minuteField.addActionListener( this );
102            c.add( minuteLabel );
103            c.add( minuteField );
104
105            secondLabel = new JLabel( "Set Second" );
106            secondField = new JTextField( 10 );
107            secondField.addActionListener( this );
108            c.add( secondLabel );
109            c.add( secondField );
110
111            display = new JTextField( 30 );
112            display.setEditable( false );
113            c.add( display );
114
115            tickButton = new JButton( "Add 1 to Second" );
116            tickButton.addActionListener( this );
117            c.add( tickButton );
118
119            updateDisplay();
120       } // end method init
121
122       public void actionPerformed( ActionEvent e )
123       {
124            if ( e.getSource() == tickButton )
125               tick();
126            else if ( e.getSource() == hourField ) {
127               t.setHour(
128                  Integer.parseInt( e.getActionCommand() ) );
129               hourField.setText( "" );
130            }
131            else if ( e.getSource() == minuteField ) {
132               t.setMinute(
133                  Integer.parseInt( e.getActionCommand() ) );
134               minuteField.setText( "" );
135            }
136            else if ( e.getSource() == secondField ) {
137               t.setSecond(
138                  Integer.parseInt( e.getActionCommand() ) );
139               secondField.setText( "" );
140            }
```

Fig. 26.3 Using *set* and *get* methods—TimeTest.java. (Part 2 of 4.)

```
141
142        updateDisplay();
143     } // end method actionPerformed
144
145     public void updateDisplay()
146     {
147        display.setText( "Hour: " + t.getHour() +
148           "; Minute: " + t.getMinute() +
149           "; Second: " + t.getSecond() );
150        showStatus( "Standard time is: " + t.toString() +
151           "; Universal time is: " + t.toUniversalString() );
152     } // end method updateDisplay
153
154     public void tick()
155     {
156        t.setSecond( ( t.getSecond() + 1 ) % 60 );
157
158        if ( t.getSecond() == 0 ) {
159           t.setMinute( ( t.getMinute() + 1 ) % 60 );
160
161           if ( t.getMinute() == 0 )
162              t.setHour( ( t.getHour() + 1 ) % 24 );
163        } // end if
164     } // end method tick
165  } // end class TimeTest
```

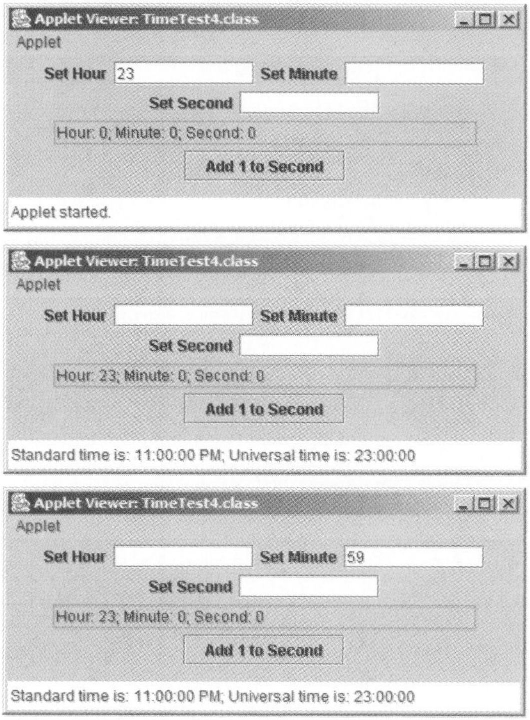

Fig. 26.3   Using *set* and *get* methods—`TimeTest.java`. (Part 3 of 4.)

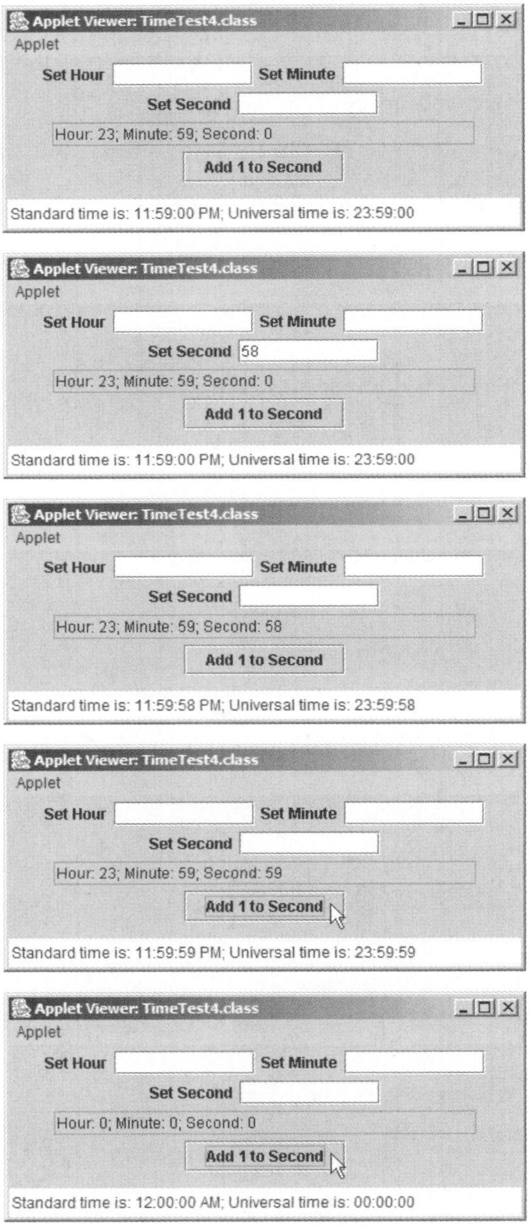

Fig. 26.3 Using *set* and *get* methods—`TimeTest.java`. (Part 4 of 4.)

The new *set* methods of the class are defined in lines 28, 32 and 36 respectively. Notice that each method performs the same conditional statement that was previously in method setTime for setting the hour, minute or second. With the addition of these methods we were able to redefine the body of method setTime (line 20) to use these three methods to set the time.

Software Engineering Observation 26.12

If a method of a class already provides all or part of the functionality required by another method of the class, call that method from the other method. This simplifies the maintenance of the code and reduces the likelihood of an error if the implementation of the code is modified. It is also an effective example of reuse.

Due to the changes in class Time2 just described, we have minimized the changes that will have to occur in the class definition if the data representation is changed from hour, minute and second to another representation (such as total elapsed seconds in the day). Only the new *set* and *get* method bodies will have to change. This allows the programmer to change the implementation of the class without affecting the clients of the class (as long as all the public methods of the class are still called the same way).

The TimeTest applet provides a graphical user interface that enables the user to exercise the methods of class Time2. The user can set the hour, minute or second value by typing a value in the appropriate JTextField and pressing the *Enter* key. The user can also click the **Add 1 to second** button to increment the time by one second. The JText-Field and JButton events in this applet are all processed in method actionPerformed (line 122). Notice that lines 95, 101, 107 and 116 all call addActionListener to indicate that the applet should start listening to JTextFields hourField, minuteField, secondField and JButton tickButton, respectively. Also, notice that all four calls use this as the argument, indicating that the object of our applet class TimeTest has its actionPerformed method invoked for each user interaction with these four GUI components. This poses an interesting question—how do we determine the GUI component with which the user interacted?

In actionPerformed, notice the use of e.getSource() to determine which GUI component generated the event. For example, line 124

```
if ( e.getSource() == tickButton )
```

determines if tickButton was clicked by the user. If so, the body of the if structure is executed. Otherwise, the condition in the if structure in line 126 is tested, etc. Every event has a *source*—the GUI component with which the user interacted to signal the program to do a task. The ActionEvent parameter that is supplied to actionPerformed whenever the event occurs contains a reference to the source. The preceding condition simply asks, "Is the *source* of the event the tickButton?"

After each operation, the resulting time is displayed as a string in the status bar of the applet. The output windows illustrate the applet before and after the following operations: setting the hour to 23, setting the minute to 59, setting the second to 58 and incrementing the second twice with the **Add 1 to second** button.

Note that when the **Add 1 to second** button is clicked, the applet's tick method (line 154) is called by method actionPerformed. Method tick uses all the new *set* and *get* methods to increment the second properly. Although this works, it incurs the performance burden of issuing multiple method calls.

Common Programming Error 26.5

A constructor can call other methods of the class, such as set or get methods, but because the constructor is initializing the object, the instance variables may not yet be in a consistent state. Using instance variables before they have been properly initialized is an error.

Set methods are certainly important from a software engineering standpoint because they can perform validity checking. *Set* and *get* methods have another important software engineering advantage as discussed in *Software Engineering Observation* 26.13.

Software Engineering Observation 26.13

Accessing `private` data through set and get methods not only protects the instance variables from receiving invalid values, but also insulates clients of the class from representation of the instance variables. Thus, if representation of the data changes (typically, to reduce the amount of storage required or to improve performance), only the method implementations need to change—the clients need not change as long as the interface provided by the methods remains the same.

26.7 Using the `this` Reference

When a method of a class references another member of that class for a specific object of that class, how does Java ensure that the proper object is referenced? The answer is that each object has access to a reference to itself—called the *`this` reference*.

The `this` reference is implicitly used to refer to both the instance variables and methods of an object. For now, we show a simple example of using the `this` reference explicitly; later, we show some substantial and subtle examples of using `this`.

Performance Tip 26.2

Java conserves storage by maintaining only one copy of each method per class; this method is invoked by every object of that class. Each object, on the other hand, has its own copy of the class's instance variables.

The application of Fig. 26.4 demonstrates implicit and explicit use of the `this` reference to enable the `main` method of class `ThisTest` to display the `private` data of a `SimpleTime` object.

```
1   // Fig. 26.4: ThisTest.java
2   // Using the this reference to refer to
3   // instance variables and methods.
4   import javax.swing.*;
5   import java.text.DecimalFormat;
6
7   public class ThisTest {
8      public static void main( String args[] )
9      {
10        SimpleTime t = new SimpleTime( 12, 30, 19 );
11
12        JOptionPane.showMessageDialog( null, t.buildString(),
13           "Demonstrating the \"this\" Reference",
14           JOptionPane.INFORMATION_MESSAGE );
```

Fig. 26.4   Using the `this` reference. (Part 1 of 2.)

```
15
16              System.exit( 0 );
17         } // end method main
18    } // end class ThisTest
19
20    class SimpleTime {
21       private int hour, minute, second;
22
23       public SimpleTime( int hour, int minute, int second )
24       {
25          this.hour = hour;
26          this.minute = minute;
27          this.second = second;
28       } // end SimpleTime constructor
29
30       public String buildString()
31       {
32          return "this.toString(): " + this.toString() +
33                 "\ntoString(): " + toString() +
34                 "\nthis (with implicit toString() call): " +
35                 this;
36       } // end method buildString
37
38       public String toString()
39       {
40          DecimalFormat twoDigits = new DecimalFormat( "00" );
41
42          return twoDigits.format( this.hour ) + ":" +
43                 twoDigits.format( this.minute ) + ":" +
44                 twoDigits.format( this.second );
45       } // end method toString
46    } // end class SimpleTime
```

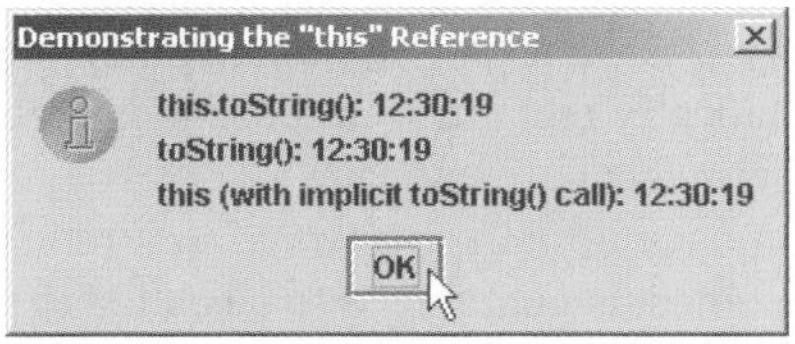

Demonstrating the "this" Reference

　　this.toString(): 12:30:19
　　toString(): 12:30:19
　　this (with implicit toString() call): 12:30:19

OK

Fig. 26.4 Using the this reference. (Part 2 of 2.)

Class SimpleTime (lines 20 through 46) defines three private instance variables—
hour, minute and second. The constructor (line 23) receives three int arguments to initialize a SimpleTime object. Notice that the parameter names for the constructor are the
same as the instance variable names. Remember that a local variable of a method with the
same name as an instance variable of a class hides the instance variable in the scope of the
method. For this reason, we use the this reference to explicitly refer to the instance variables on lines 25 through 27.

Common Programming Error 26.6

*In a method in which a method parameter has the same name as one of the class members,
use this explicitly if you want to access the class member; otherwise, you will incorrectly
reference the method parameter.*

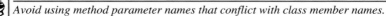

Good Programming Practice 26.8

Avoid using method parameter names that conflict with class member names.

Method `buildString` (lines 30–36) returns a `String` created with the statement

```
return "this.toString(): " + this.toString() +
       "\ntoString(): " + toString() +
       "\nthis (with implicit toString() call): " +
       this;
```

that uses the `this` reference three ways. The first line explicitly invokes the class's `toString` method via `this.toString()`. The second line implicitly uses the `this` reference to perform the same task. The third line appends `this` to the string that will be returned. Remember that the `this` reference is a reference to an object—the current `SimpleTime` object being manipulated. As before, any reference added to a `String` results in a call to the `toString` method for the referenced object. Method `buildString` is invoked in line 12 to display the results of the three calls to `toString`. Note that the same time is displayed on all three lines of the output because all three calls to `toString` are for the same object.

26.8 Finalizers

We have seen that constructor methods are capable of initializing data in an object of a class when the class is created. Often, constructors acquire various system resources such as memory (when the `new` operator is used). We need a disciplined way to give resources back to the system when they are no longer needed to avoid resource leaks. The most common resource acquired by constructors is memory. Java performs automatic *garbage collection* of memory to help return memory back to the system. When an object is no longer used in the program (i.e., there are no references to the object), the object is *marked for garbage collection*. The memory for such an object can be reclaimed when the *garbage collector* executes. Therefore, memory leaks that are common in other languages like C and C++ (because memory is not automatically reclaimed in those languages) are less likely to happen in Java. However, other resource leaks can occur.

Every class in Java can have a *finalizer method* that returns resources to the system. The finalizer method for an object is guaranteed to be called to perform *termination housekeeping* on the object just before the garbage collector reclaims the memory for the object. A class's finalizer method always has the name `finalize`, receives no parameters and returns no value (i.e., its return type is `void`). A class should have only one `finalize` method that takes no arguments. Method `finalize` is originally defined in class `Object` as a placeholder that does nothing. This guarantees that every class has a `finalize` method for the garbage collector to call.

Finalizers have not been provided for the classes presented so far. Actually, finalizers are rarely used with simple classes. We will see a sample `finalize` method and discuss the garbage collector further in Fig. 26.5.

26.9 Static Class Members

Each object of a class has its own copy of all the instance variables of the class. In certain cases only one copy of a particular variable should be shared by all objects of a class. A *static class variable* is used for these and other reasons. A static class variable represents *class-wide information*—all objects of the class share the same piece of data. The declaration of a static member begins with the keyword static.

Let us motivate the need for static class-wide data with a video game example. Suppose we have a video game with Martians and other space creatures. Each Martian tends to be brave and willing to attack other space creatures when the Martian is aware that there are at least five Martians present. If there are fewer than five Martians present, each Martian becomes cowardly. So each Martian needs to know the martianCount. We could endow class Martian with martianCount as instance data. If we do this, then every Martian will have a separate copy of the instance data and every time we create a new Martian we will have to update the instance variable martianCount in every Martian. This wastes space with the redundant copies and wastes time in updating the separate copies. Instead, we declare martianCount to be static. This makes martianCount class-wide data. Every Martian can see the martianCount as if it were instance data of the Martian, but only one copy of the static martianCount is maintained by Java. This saves space. We save time by having the Martian constructor increment the static martianCount. There is only one copy, so we do not have to increment separate copies of martianCount for each Martian object.

Performance Tip 26.3

Use static class variables to save storage when a single copy of the data will suffice.

Although static class variables may seem like global variables, static class variables have class scope. A class's public static class members can be accessed through a reference to any object of that class, or they can be accessed through the class name using the dot operator (e.g., Math.random()). A class's private static class members can be accessed only through methods of the class. Actually, static class members exist even when no objects of that class exist—they are available as soon as the class is loaded into memory at execution time. To access a private static class member when no objects of the class exist, a public static method must be provided and the method must be called by prefixing its name with the class name and dot operator.

The program of Fig. 26.5 demonstrates the use of a private static class variable and a public static method. The class variable count is initialized to zero by default. Class variable count maintains a count of the number of objects of class Employee that have been instantiated and currently reside in memory. This includes objects that have already been marked for garbage collection but have not yet been reclaimed.

```
1   // Fig. 26.5: Employee.java
2   // Declaration of the Employee class.
3   public class Employee extends Object {
4       private String firstName;
5       private String lastName;
6       private static int count;  // # of objects in memory
7
```

Fig. 26.5   Using a static class variable to maintain a count of the number of objects of a class—Employee.java. (Part 1 of 2.)

```
 8      public Employee( String fName, String lName )
 9      {
10         firstName = fName;
11         lastName = lName;
12
13         ++count;   // increment static count of employees
14         System.out.println( "Employee object constructor: " +
15                              firstName + " " + lastName );
16      } // end Employee constructor
17
18      protected void finalize()
19      {
20         --count;   // decrement static count of employees
21         System.out.println( "Employee object finalizer: " +
22                              firstName + " " + lastName +
23                              "; count = " + count );
24      } // end method finalize
25
26      public String getFirstName() { return firstName; }
27
28      public String getLastName() { return lastName; }
29
30      public static int getCount() { return count; }
31   } // end class Employee
```

Fig. 26.5   Using a `static` class variable to maintain a count of the number of objects of a class—`Employee.java`. (Part 2 of 2.)

```
32   // Fig. 8.12: EmployeeTest.java
33   // Test Employee class with static class variable,
34   // static class method, and dynamic memory.
35   import javax.swing.*;
36
37   public class EmployeeTest {
38      public static void main( String args[] )
39      {
40         String output;
41
42         output = "Employees before instantiation: " +
43                  Employee.getCount();
44
45         Employee e1 = new Employee( "Susan", "Baker" );
46         Employee e2 = new Employee( "Bob", "Jones" );
47
48         output += "\n\nEmployees after instantiation: " +
49                   "\nvia e1.getCount(): " + e1.getCount() +
50                   "\nvia e2.getCount(): " + e2.getCount() +
51                   "\nvia Employee.getCount(): " +
52                   Employee.getCount();
53
```

Fig. 26.5   Using a `static` class variable to maintain a count of the number of objects of a class—`EmployeeTest.java`. (Part 1 of 2.)

```
54          output += "\n\nEmployee 1: " + e1.getFirstName() +
55                     " " + e1.getLastName() +
56                     "\nEmployee 2: " + e2.getFirstName() +
57                     " " + e2.getLastName();
58
59          // mark objects referred to by e1 and e2
60          // for garbage collection
61          e1 = null;
62          e2 = null;
63
64          System.gc(); // suggest that garbage collector be called
65
66          output += "\n\nEmployees after System.gc(): " +
67                     Employee.getCount();
68
69          JOptionPane.showMessageDialog( null, output,
70             "Static Members and Garbage Collection",
71             JOptionPane.INFORMATION_MESSAGE );
72          System.exit( 0 );
73       } // end main
74    } // end class EmployeeTest
```

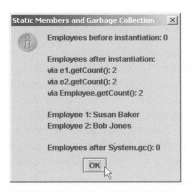

```
Employee object constructor: Susan Baker
Employee object constructor: Bob Jones
Employee object finalizer: Susan Baker; count = 1
Employee object finalizer: Bob Jones; count = 0
```

Fig. 26.5 Using a `static` class variable to maintain a count of the number of objects of a class—`EmployeeTest.java`. (Part 2 of 2.)

When objects of class `Employee` exist, member `count` can be used in any method of an `Employee` object—in this example, `count` is incremented (line 13) by the constructor and decremented (line 20) by the finalizer. When no objects of class `Employee` exist, member `count` can still be referenced, but only through a call to `public static` method `getCount` as follows:

```
Employee.getCount()
```

In this example, method `getCount` determines the number of `Employee` objects currently in memory. Note that when there are no objects instantiated in the program, the `Employee.getCount()` method call is issued. However, when there are objects instantiated, method `getCount` can also be called through a reference to one of the objects, as in

```
e1.getCount()
```

Good Programming Practice 26.9

Always invoke `static` *methods using the class name and the dot operator (.). This emphasizes to other programmers reading your code that the method being called is a* `static` *method.*

Notice that the `Employee` class has a `finalize` method (line 18). This method is included to show when it is called by the garbage collector in a program. Method `finalize` is normally declared *protected* so it is not part of the `public` services of a class. We will discuss the `protected` access modifier in detail in Chapter 27.

Method `main` of the `EmployeeTest` application instantiates two `Employee` objects (lines 45 and 46). When each `Employee` object's constructor is invoked, lines 10 and 11 store references to that `Employee`'s first name and last name `String` objects. Note that these two statements *do not* make copies of the original `String`s arguments. Actually, `String` objects in Java are *immutable*—they cannot be modified after they are created (class `String` does not provide any *set* methods). A reference cannot be used to modify a `String`, so it is safe to have many references to one `String` object in a Java program. This is not normally the case for most other classes in Java.

When `main` is done with the two `Employee` objects, the references `e1` and `e2` are set to `null` in lines 61 and 62. At this point references `e1` and `e2` no longer refer to the objects that were instantiated in lines 45 and 46. This *marks the objects for garbage collection* because there are no more references to the objects in the program.

Eventually, the garbage collector reclaims the memory for these objects (or the memory is reclaimed by the operating system when the program terminates). It is not guaranteed when the garbage collector will execute, so we make an explicit call to the garbage collector with the line 64

```
System.gc();  // explicit call to garbage collector
```

that uses `public static` method gc from class `System` (`java.lang` package) to suggest that the garbage collector execute immediately. However, this is just a suggestion to the Java Virtual Machine (the interpreter)—the suggestion can be ignored. In our example, the garbage collector did execute before lines 69 through 71 displayed the results of the program. The last line of the output indicates that the number of `Employee` objects in memory is 0 after the call to `System.gc()`. Also, the last two lines of the command window output show that the `Employee` object for `Susan Baker` was finalized before the `Employee` object for `Bob Jones`. The garbage collector is not guaranteed to execute when `System.gc()` is invoked and the garbage collector is not guaranteed to collect objects in a specific order, so it is possible that the output of this program on your system may differ.

[*Note*: A method declared `static` cannot access non-`static` class members. Unlike non-`static` methods, a `static` method has no `this` reference because `static` class variables and `static` class methods exist independent of any objects of a class and before any objects of the class have been instantiated.]

Common Programming Error 26.7

Referring to the this *reference in a* static *method is a syntax error.*

Common Programming Error 26.8

It is a syntax error for a static *method to call an instance method or to access an instance variable.*

Software Engineering Observation 26.14

Any static *class variables and* static *class methods exist and can be used even if no objects of that class have been instantiated.*

SUMMARY

- OOP encapsulates data (attributes) and methods (behaviors) into objects; the data and methods of an object are intimately tied together.

- Objects have the property of information hiding. Objects may know how to communicate with one another across well-defined interfaces, but they normally are not allowed to know how other objects are implemented.

- Java programmers concentrate on creating their own user-defined types called classes. The data components of a class are called instance variables.

- Java uses inheritance to create new classes from existing class definitions.

- Every class in Java is a subclass of Object. Thus, every new class definition has the attributes (data) and behaviors (methods) of class Object.

- Keywords public and private are member access modifiers.

- Instance variables and methods declared with member access modifier public are accessible wherever the program has a reference to an object of the class in which the they are defined.

- Instance variables and methods declared with member access modifier private are accessible only to methods of the class in which they are defined.

- Instance variables are normally declared private and methods are normally declared public.

- The public methods (or public services) of a class are used by clients of the class to manipulate the data stored in objects of the class.

- A constructor is a method with the exact same name as the class that initializes the instance variables of an object of the class when the object is instantiated. Constructor methods can be overloaded for a class. Constructors can take arguments but cannot return a value.

- Constructors and other methods that change instance variable values should always maintain objects in a consistent state.

- Method toString takes no arguments and returns a String. The original toString method of class Object is a placeholder that is normally redefined by a subclass.

- When an object is instantiated, operator new allocates the memory for the object, then new calls the constructor for the class to initialize the instance variables of the object.

- If the .class files for the classes used in a program are in the same directory as the class that uses them, import statements are not required.

- Concatenating a String and any object results in an implicit call to the object's toString method to convert the object to a String, then the Strings are concatenated.

- Within a class's scope, class members are immediately accessible to all that class's methods and can be referenced simply by name. Outside a class's scope, class members can only be accessed off a "handle" (i.e., a reference to an object of the class).

- If a method defines a variable with the same name as a variable with class scope, the class-scope variable is hidden by the method-scope variable in the method. A hidden instance variable can be accessed in the method by preceding its name with the keyword `this` and the dot operator.

- Each class and interface in the Java API belongs to a specific package that contains a group of related classes and interfaces.

- Packages are actually directory structures used to organize classes and interfaces. Packages provide a mechanism for software reuse and a convention for unique class names.

- Creating a reusable class requires: defining a `public` class, adding a `package` statement to the class definition file, compiling the class into the appropriate package directory structure to make the new class available to the compiler and the interpreter, and importing the class into a program.

- Java 2 has a directory called `classes` where the compiled version of new reusable classes are placed that is well known to both the compiler and the interpreter.

- When compiling a class in a package, the option `-d` must be passed to the compiler to specify where to create (or locate) all the directories in the `package` statement.

- The `package` directory names become part of the class name when the class is compiled. Use this fully qualified name in programs or `import` the class and use its short name (the name of the class by itself) in the program.

- If no constructors are defined for a class, the compiler creates a default constructor that takes no arguments.

- When one object of a class has a reference to another object of the same class, the first object can access all the second object's data and methods.

- Classes often provide `public` methods to allow clients of the class to *set* (i.e., assign values to) or *get* (i.e., obtain the values of) `private` instance variables. *Get* methods are also commonly called accessor methods or query methods. *Set* methods are also commonly called mutator methods (because they typically change a value).

- Every event has a source—the GUI component with which the user interacted to signal the program to do a task.

- When no member access modifier is provided for a method or variable when it is defined in a class, the method or variable is considered to have package access.

- If a program uses multiple classes from the same package, these classes can access each other's package-access methods and data directly through a reference to an object.

- Each object has access to a reference to itself called the `this` reference that can be used inside the methods of the class to refer to the object's data and other methods explicitly.

- Any time you have a reference in a program (even as the result of a method call), the reference can be followed by a dot operator and a call to one of the methods for the reference type.

- Every class in Java can have a finalizer method that returns resources to the system. A class's finalizer method always has the name `finalize`, receives no parameters and returns no value. Method `finalize` is originally defined in class `Object` as a placeholder that does nothing. This guarantees that every class has a `finalize` method for the garbage collector to call.

- A `static` class variable represents class-wide information—all objects of the class share the same piece of data. A class's `public static` members can be accessed through a reference to any object of that class, or they can be accessed through the class name using the dot operator.

- `public static` method `gc` from class `System` suggests that the garbage collector execute immediately. This suggestion can be ignored. The garbage collector is not guaranteed to collect objects in a specific order.

- A method declared `static` cannot access non-`static` class members. Unlike non-`static` methods, a `static` method has no `this` reference because `static` class variables and `static` class methods exist independent of any objects of a class.

- `static` class members exist even when no objects of that class exist—they are available as soon as the class is loaded into memory at execution time.

TERMINOLOGY

abstract data type (ADT)
access method
attribute
behavior
class
class definition
class library
class method (`static`)
class scope
class variable
client of a class
consistent state for an instance variable
constructor
container class
`-d` compiler option
data type
default constructor
dot operator (`.`)
encapsulation
extends
extensibility
finalizer
get method
helper method
implementation of a class
information hiding
initialize a class object
instance method
instance of a class
instance variable

instantiate an object of a class
interface to a class
member access control
member access modifiers
method
method calls
mutator method
`new` operator
no-argument constructor
object
object-based programming (OBP)
object-oriented programming (OOP)
package access
`package` statement
predicate method
principle of least privilege
`private`
programmer-defined type
`public`
public interface of a class
query method
reusable code
services of a class
set method
software reusability
`static` class variable
`static` method
`this` reference
user-defined type
utility method

COMMON PROGRAMMING ERRORS

26.1   Defining more than one `public` class in the same file is a syntax error.

26.2   An attempt by a method which is not a member of a particular class to access a `private` member of that class is a syntax error.

26.3   Attempting to declare a return type for a constructor and/or attempting to `return` a value from a constructor is a logic error. Java allows other methods of the class to have the same name as the class and to specify return types. Such methods are not constructors and will not be called when an object of the class is instantiated.

26.4   If constructors are provided for a class, but none of the public constructors are no-argument constructors, and an attempt is made to call a no-argument constructor to initialize an object of the class, a syntax error occurs. A constructor may be called with no arguments only if there are no constructors for the class (the default constructor is called) or if there is a no-argument constructor.

26.5   A constructor can call other methods of the class, such as *set* or *get* methods, but because the constructor is initializing the object, the instance variables may not yet be in a consistent state. Using instance variables before they have been properly initialized is an error.

26.6   In a method in which a method parameter has the same name as one of the class members, use this explicitly if you want to access the class member; otherwise, you will incorrectly reference the method parameter.

26.7   Referring to the this reference in a static method is a syntax error.

26.8   It is a syntax error for a static method to call an instance method or to access an instance variable.

GOOD PROGRAMMING PRACTICES

26.1   Group members by member access modifier in a class definition for clarity and readability.

26.2   Our preference is to list the private instance variables of a class first so as you read the code, you see the names and types of the instance variables before they are used in the methods of the class.

26.3   Despite the fact that private and public members may be repeated and intermixed, list all the private members of a class first in one group, then list all the public members in another group.

26.4   Always define a class so its instance variables are maintained in a consistent state.

26.5   Initialize instance variables of a class in that class's constructor.

26.6   When appropriate (almost always), provide a constructor to ensure that every object is properly initialized with meaningful values.

26.7   Every method that modifies the private instance variables of an object should ensure that the data remains in a consistent state.

26.8   Avoid using method parameter names that conflict with class member names.

26.9   Always invoke static methods using the class name and the dot operator (.). This emphasizes to other programmers reading your code that the method being called is a static method.

PERFORMANCE TIPS

26.1   All Java objects are passed by reference. Only a memory address is passed, not a copy of a possibly large object (as would be the case in a pass-by-value).

26.2   Java conserves storage by maintaining only one copy of each method per class; this method is invoked by every object of that class. Each object, on the other hand, has its own copy of the class's instance variables.

26.3   Use static class variables to save storage when a single copy of the data will suffice.

SOFTWARE ENGINEERING OBSERVATIONS

26.1   It is important to write programs that are understandable and easy to maintain. Change is the rule rather than the exception. Programmers should anticipate that their code will be modified. As we will see, classes facilitate program modifiability.

26.2   Class definitions that begin with keyword public must be stored in a file that has exactly the same name as the class and ends with the .java file name extension.

26.3   Every class defined in Java must extend another class. If a class does not explicitly use key-word `extends` in its definition, the class implicitly `extends Object`.

26.4   Keep all the instance variables of a class `private`. When necessary provide `public` meth-ods to set the values of `private` instance variables and to get the values of `private` in-stance variables. This architecture helps hide the implementation of a class from its clients, which reduces bugs and improves program modifiability.

26.5   Methods tend to fall into a number of different categories: methods that get the values of `private` instance variables; methods that set the values of `private` instance variables; methods that implement the services of the class; and methods that perform various mechan-ical chores for the class, such as initializing class objects, assigning class objects, and con-verting between classes and built-in types or between classes and other classes.

26.6   Every time `new` creates an object of a class, that class's constructor is called to initialize the instance variables of the new object.

26.7   Information hiding promotes program modifiability and simplifies the client's perception of a class.

26.8   Clients of a class can (and should) use the class without knowing the internal details of how the class is implemented. If the class implementation is changed (to improve performance, for example), provided the class's interface remains constant, the class clients' source code need not change. This makes it much easier to modify systems.

26.9   Using an object-oriented programming approach can often simplify method calls by reducing the number of parameters to be passed. This benefit of object-oriented programming derives from the fact that encapsulation of instance variables and methods within an object gives the methods the right to access the instance variables.

26.10 A Java source code file has the following order: a `package` statement (if any), `import` state-ments (if any), then class definitions. Only one of the class definitions can be `public`. Other classes in the file are also placed in the package, but are not reusable. They are in the package to support the reusable class in the file.

26.11 Methods that set the values of `private` data should verify that the intended new values are proper; if they are not, the *set* methods should place the `private` instance variables into an appropriate consistent state.

26.12 If a method of a class already provides all or part of the functionality required by another method of the class, call that method from the other method. This simplifies the maintenance of the code and reduces the likelihood of an error if the implementation of the code is modi-fied. It is also an effective example of reuse.

26.13 Accessing `private` data through *set* and *get* methods not only protects the instance variables from receiving invalid values, but also insulates clients of the class from representation of the instance variables. Thus, if representation of the data changes (typically, to reduce the amount of storage required or to improve performance), only the method implementations need to change—the clients need not change as long as the interface provided by the methods remains the same.

26.14 Any `static` class variables and `static` class methods exist and can be used even if no ob-jects of that class have been instantiated.

SELF-REVIEW EXERCISE

26.1   Fill in the blanks in each of the following:
   a) Class members are accessed via the _____ operator in conjunction with a reference to an object of the class.
   b) Members of a class specified as _____ are accessible only to methods of the class.

c) A(n) _____ is a special method used to initialize the instance variables of a class.
d) A(n) _____ method is used to assign values to `private` instance variables of a class.
e) Methods of a class are normally made _____ and instance variables of a class are normally made _____.
f) A(n) _____ method is used to retrieve values of `private` data of a class.
g) The keyword _____ introduces a class definition.
h) Members of a class specified as _____ are accessible anywhere an object of the class is in scope.
i) The _____ operator dynamically allocates memory for an object of a specified type and returns a(n) _____ to that type.
j) A(n) _____ instance variable represents class-wide information.
k) A method declared `static` cannot access _____ class members.

ANSWERS TO SELF-REVIEW EXERCISE

26.1   a) dot (`.`). b) `private`. c) constructor. d) set. e) `public`, `private`. f) get. g) `class`. h) `public`. i) new, reference. j) `static`. k) non-`static`.

EXERCISES

26.2   Create a class called `Rational` for performing arithmetic with fractions. Write a driver program to test your class.

Use integer variables to represent the `private` instance variables of the class—the `numerator` and the `denominator`. Provide a constructor method that enables an object of this class to be initialized when it is declared. The constructor should store the fraction in reduced form (i.e., the fraction

2/4

would be stored in the object as 1 in the `numerator` and 2 in the `denominator`). Provide a no-argument constructor that sets default values in case no initializers are provided. Provide `public` methods for each of the following:

a) Addition of two `Rational` numbers. The result of the addition should be stored in reduced form.
b) Subtraction of two `Rational` numbers. The result of the subtraction should be stored in reduced form.
c) Multiplication of two `Rational` numbers. The result of the multiplication should be stored in reduced form.
d) Division of two `Rational` numbers. The result of the division should be stored in reduced form.
e) Printing `Rational` numbers in the form a/b, where a is the `numerator` and b is the `denominator`.
f) Printing `Rational` numbers in floating-point format. (Consider providing formatting capabilities that enable the user of the class to specify the number of digits of precision to the right of the decimal point.)

26.3   Modify the `Time2` class of Fig. 26.3 to include the `tick` method that increments the time stored in a `Time2` object by one second. Also provide method `incrementMinute` to increment the minute and method `incrementHour` to increment the hour. The `Time2` object should always remain in a consistent state. Write a driver program that tests the `tick` method, the `incrementMinute` method and the `incrementHour` method to ensure that they work correctly. Be sure to test the following cases:

a) Incrementing into the next minute.
b) Incrementing into the next hour.
c) Incrementing into the next day (i.e., 11:59:59 PM to 12:00:00 AM).

26.4   Create a class `Rectangle`. The class has attributes `length` and `width`, each of which defaults to 1. It has methods that calculate the `perimeter` and the `area` of the rectangle. It has *set* and *get* methods for both `length` and `width`. The *set* methods should verify that `length` and `width` are each floating-point numbers larger than 0.0 and less than 20.0.

26.5   Create a more sophisticated `Rectangle` class than the one you created in Exercise 26.4. This class stores only the Cartesian coordinates of the four corners of the rectangle. The constructor calls a *set* method that accepts four sets of coordinates and verifies that each of these is in the first quadrant with no single *x*- or *y*-coordinate larger than 20.0. The *set* method also verifies that the supplied coordinates do, in fact, specify a rectangle. Provide methods to calculate the `length`, `width`, `perimeter` and `area`. The length is the larger of the two dimensions. Include a predicate method `isSquare` which determines if the rectangle is a square.

26.6   Modify the `Rectangle` class of Exercise 26.5 to include a `draw` method that displays the rectangle inside a 25-by-25 box enclosing the portion of the first quadrant in which the rectangle resides. Use the methods of the `Graphics` class to help output the `Rectangle`. If you feel ambitious, you might include methods to scale the size of the rectangle, rotate it and move it around within the designated portion of the first quadrant.

26.7   Create a class `HugeInteger` which uses a 40-element array of digits to store integers as large as 40 digits each. Provide methods `inputHugeInteger`, `outputHugeInteger`, `add-HugeIntegers` and `subtractHugeIntegers`. For comparing `HugeInteger` objects, provide methods `isEqualTo`, `isNotEqualTo`, `isGreaterThan`, `isLessThan`, `IsGreaterThanOrEqualTo` and `isLessThanOrEqualTo`—each of these is a "predicate" method that simply returns `true` if the relationship holds between the two `HugeInteger`s and returns `false` if the relationship does not hold. Provide a predicate method `isZero`. If you feel ambitious, also provide the method `multiply-HugeIntegers`, the method `divideHugeIntegers` and the method `modulusHugeIntegers`.

26.8   Create class `SavingsAccount`. Use a `static` variable to store the `annualInterestRate` for all account holders. Each object of the class contains a `private` instance variable `savingsBalance` indicating the amount the saver currently has on deposit. Provide method `calculateMonthly-Interest`, which multiplies the `savingsBalance` by `annualInterestRate` divided by 12; this interest should be added to `savingsBalance`. Provide a `static` method `modifyInterestRate` that sets the `annualInterestRate` to a new value. Write a program to test class `SavingsAccount`. Instantiate two `savingsAccount` objects, `saver1` and `saver2`, with balances of $2000.00 and $3000.00, respectively. Set `annualInterestRate` to 4%, then calculate the monthly interest and print the new balances for each account. Then set the `annualInterestRate` to 5% and calculate the next month's interest and print the new balances for each account.

26.9   Create class `IntegerSet`. Each object of the class can hold integers in the range 0 through 100. A set is represented internally as an array of `boolean`s. Array element `a[i]` is `true` if integer *i* is in the set. Array element `a[j]` is `false` if integer *j* is not in the set. The no-argument constructor initializes a set to the so-called "empty set" (i.e., a set whose array representation contains all `false` values).

Provide the following methods: Method `unionOfIntegerSets` creates a third set which is the set-theoretic union of two existing sets (i.e., an element of the third set's array is set to `true` if that element is `true` in either or both of the existing sets; otherwise, the element of the third set is set to `false`). Method `intersectionOfIntegerSets` creates a third set which is the set-theoretic intersection of two existing sets i.e., an element of the third set's array is set to `false` if that element is `false` in either or both of the existing sets; otherwise, the element of the third set is set to `true`). Method `insertElement` inserts a new integer *k* into a set (by setting `a[k]` to `true`). Method `deleteElement` deletes integer *m* (by setting `a[m]` to `false`). Method `setPrint` prints a set as a list of numbers separated by spaces. Print only those elements that are present in the set. Print `---` for an empty set. Method `isEqualTo` determines if two sets are equal. Write a program to test your `IntegerSet` class. Instantiate several `IntegerSet` objects. Test that all your methods work properly.

26.10 It would be perfectly reasonable for the Time1 class of Fig. 26.1 to represent the time internally as the number of seconds since midnight rather than the three integer values hour, minute and second. Clients could use the same public methods and get the same results. Modify the Time1 class of Fig. 26.1 to implement the Time1 as the number of seconds since midnight and show that there is no visible change to the clients of the class.

26.11 *(Drawing Program)* Create a drawing applet that randomly draws lines, rectangles and ovals. For this purpose, create a set of "smart" shape classes where objects of these classes know how to draw themselves if provided with a Graphics object that tells them where to draw (i.e., the applet's Graphics object allows a shape to draw on the applet's background). The class names should be MyLine, MyRect and MyOval.

The data for class MyLine should include *x1*, *y1*, *x2* and *y2* coordinates. Method drawLine method of class Graphics will connect the two points supplied with a line. The data for classes MyRect and MyOval should include an upper-left *x*-coordinate value, an upper-left *y*-coordinate value, a *width* (must be nonnegative) and a *height* (must be nonnegative). All data in each class must be private.

In addition to the data, each class should define at least the following public methods:

   a) A constructor with no arguments that sets the coordinates to 0.

   b) A constructor with arguments that sets the coordinates to the supplied values.

   c) *Set* methods for each individual piece of data that allow the programmer to independently set any piece of data in a shape (e.g., if you have an instance variable x1, you should have a method setX1).

   d) *Get* methods for each individual piece of data that allow the programmer to independently retrieve any piece of data in a shape (e.g., if you have an instance variable x1, you should have a method getX1).

   e) A draw method with the first line

```
public void draw( Graphics g )
```

   f) will be called from the applet's paint method to draw a shape onto the screen.

The preceding methods are required. If you would like to provide more methods for flexibility, please do so.

Begin by defining class MyLine and an applet to test your classes. The applet should have a MyLine instance variable line that can refer to one MyLine object (created in the applet's init method with random coordinates). The applet's paint method should draw the shape with a statement like

```
line.draw( g );
```

where line is the MyLine reference and g is the Graphics object that the shape will use to draw itself on the applet.

Next, change the single MyLine reference into an array of MyLine references and hard code several MyLine objects into the program for drawing. The applet's paint method should walk through the array of MyLine objects and draw every one.

After the preceding part is working, you should define the MyOval and MyRect classes and add objects of these classes into the MyRect and MyOval arrays. The applet's paint method should walk through each array and draw every shape. Create five shapes of each type.

Once the applet is running, select Reload from the appletviewer's **Applet** menu to reload the applet. This will cause the applet to choose new random numbers for the shapes and draw the shapes again.

In Chapter 27, we will modify this exercise to take advantage of the similarities between the classes and to avoid reinventing the wheel.

27

Java Object-Oriented Programming

Objectives

- To understand inheritance and software reusability.
- To understand superclasses and subclasses.
- To appreciate how polymorphism makes systems extensible and maintainable.
- To understand the distinction between abstract classes and concrete classes.
- To learn how to create abstract classes and interfaces.

Say not you know another entirely, till you have divided an inheritance with him.
Johann Kasper Lavater

This method is to define as the number of a class the class of all classes similar to the given class.
Bertrand Russell

Good as it is to inherit a library, it is better to collect one.
Augustine Birrell

General propositions do not decide concrete cases.
Oliver Wendell Holmes

A philosopher of imposing stature doesn't think in a vacuum. Even his most abstract ideas are, to some extent, conditioned by what is or is not known in the time when he lives.
Alfred North Whitehead

27.1 Introduction

In this chapter we discuss object-oriented programming (OOP) and its key component technologies—*inheritance* and *polymorphism.* Inheritance is a form of software reusability in which new classes are created from existing classes by absorbing their attributes and behaviors and embellishing these with capabilities the new classes require. Software reusability saves time in program development. It encourages reuse of proven and debugged high-quality software, thus reducing problems after a system becomes operational. These are exciting possibilities. Polymorphism enables us to write programs in a general fashion to handle a wide variety of existing and yet-to-be-specified related classes. Polymorphism makes it easy to add new capabilities to a system. Inheritance and polymorphism are effective techniques for dealing with software complexity.

When creating a new class, instead of writing completely new instance variables and instance methods, the programmer can designate that the new class is to *inherit* the instance variables and instance methods of a previously defined *superclass.* The new class is referred to as a *subclass.* Each subclass itself becomes a candidate to be a superclass for some future subclass.

The *direct superclass* of a subclass is the superclass from which the subclass explicitly inherits (via the keyword `extends`). An indirect superclass is inherited from two or more levels up the class hierarchy.

With *single inheritance,* a class is derived from one superclass. Java does not support *multiple inheritance* (as C++ does) but it does support the notion of *interfaces.* Interfaces help Java achieve many of the advantages of multiple inheritance without the associated problems. We will discuss the details of interfaces in this chapter where we consider both general principles as well as a detailed specific example of creating and using interfaces.

A subclass normally adds instance variables and instance methods of its own, so a subclass is generally larger than its superclass. A subclass is more specific than its superclass and represents a smaller group of objects. With single inheritance, the subclass starts out essentially the same as the superclass. The real strength of inheritance comes from the ability to define in the subclass additions to, or replacements for, the features inherited from the superclass.

Every object of a subclass is also an object of that subclass's superclass. However, the converse is not true—superclass objects are not objects of that superclass's subclasses. We will take advantage of this "subclass-object-is-a-superclass-object" relationship to perform some powerful manipulations. For example, we can link a wide variety of different objects related to a common superclass through inheritance into a linked list of superclass objects. This allows a variety of objects to be processed in a general way. As we will see in this chapter, this is a key thrust of object-oriented programming.

We add a new form of member access control in this chapter, namely `protected` access. Subclass methods and methods of other classes in the same package as the superclass can access `protected` superclass members.

Experience in building software systems indicates that significant portions of the code deal with closely related special cases. It becomes difficult in such systems to see the "big picture" because the designer and the programmer become preoccupied with the special cases. Object-oriented programming provides several ways of "seeing the forest through the trees"—a process called *abstraction.*

If a procedural program has many closely related special cases, then it is common to see `switch` structures or nested `if/else` structures that distinguish among the special cases and provide the processing logic to deal with each case individually. We will show how to use inheritance and polymorphism to replace such `switch` logic with much simpler logic.

We distinguish between the *is a relationship* and the *has a relationship. Is a* is inheritance. In an *is a* relationship, an object of a subclass type may also be treated as an object of its superclass type. *Has a* is composition (as we discussed in Chapter 26). In a *has a* relationship, a class object has one or more objects of other classes as members. For example, a car *has a* steering wheel.

A subclass's methods may need to access certain of its superclass's instance variables and methods.

Software Engineering Observation 27.1

 A subclass cannot directly access `private` members of its superclass.

This is a crucial aspect of software engineering in Java. If a subclass could access the superclass's `private` members, this would violate information hiding in the superclass.

Error-Prevention Tip 27.1

Hiding private *members is a huge help in testing, debugging and correctly modifying systems. If a subclass could access its superclass's* private *members, it would then be possible for classes derived from that subclass to access that data as well, and so on. This would propagate access to what is supposed to be* private *data, and the benefits of information hiding would be lost throughout the class hierarchy.*

A subclass in the same package as its superclass can access the *public, protected* and package access members of its superclass. Superclass members that should not be accessible to a subclass via inheritance are declared *private* in the superclass. A subclass can effect state changes in superclass *private* members only through *public, protected* and package access methods provided in the superclass and inherited into the subclass.

A problem with inheritance is that a subclass can inherit methods that it does not need or should not have. When a superclass member is inappropriate for a subclass, that member can be *overridden* (redefined) in the subclass with an appropriate implementation.

Perhaps most exciting is the notion that new classes can inherit from abundant *class libraries*. Organizations develop their own class libraries and can take advantage of other libraries available worldwide. Someday, most software may be constructed from *standardized reusable components* just as hardware is often constructed today. This will help meet the challenges of developing the ever more powerful software we will need in the future.

27.2 Superclasses and Subclasses

Often an object of one class *is an* object of another class as well. A rectangle certainly *is a* quadrilateral (as are squares, parallelograms and trapezoids). Thus, class Rectangle can be said to *inherit* from class Quadrilateral. In this context, class Quadrilateral is a superclass and class Rectangle is a subclass. A rectangle *is a* specific type of quadrilateral, but it is incorrect to claim that a quadrilateral *is a* rectangle (the quadrilateral could be a parallelogram). Figure 27.1 shows several simple inheritance examples of superclasses and potential subclasses.

Superclass	Subclasses
Student	GraduateStudent UndergraduateStudent
Shape	Circle Triangle Rectangle
Loan	CarLoan HomeImprovementLoan MortgageLoan
Employee	FacultyMember StaffMember
Account	CheckingAccount SavingsAccount

Fig. 27.1   Some simple inheritance examples .

Inheritance normally produces subclasses with *more* features than their superclasses, so the terms superclass and subclass can be confusing. There is another way, however, to view these terms that clarifies the relationship. Every subclass object *is an* object of its superclass, and one superclass can have many subclasses, so the set of objects represented by a superclass is normally larger than the set of objects represented by any of that superclass's subclasses. For example, the superclass Vehicle represents in a generic manner all vehicles, such as cars, trucks, boats, bicycles, etc. However, subclass Car represents only a small subset of all the Vehicles in the world.

Inheritance relationships form tree-like hierarchical structures. A superclass exists in a hierarchical relationship with its subclasses. A class can certainly exist by itself, but it is when a class is used with the mechanism of inheritance that the class becomes either a superclass that supplies attributes and behaviors to other classes, or the class becomes a subclass that inherits those attributes and behaviors.

Let us develop a simple inheritance hierarchy for shapes. Circles, squares, cubes and tetrahedrons are all different kinds of shapes. Some of these shapes can be drawn in two dimensions and some must be modeled in three dimensions. This yields the inheritance hierarchy shown in Fig. 27.2. Note that the inheritance hierarchy could contain many other classes. For example, squares and rectangles are both kinds of quadrilaterals. The arrows in the hierarchy represent the *is a* relationship. For example, based on this class hierarchy that we can state, "a Square *is a* TwoDimensionalShape," or "a Cube *is a* ThreeDimensionalShape." Shape is the *direct superclass* of both TwoDimensionalShape and ThreeDimensionalShape. Shape is an *indirect superclass* of all the other classes in the hierarchy diagram.

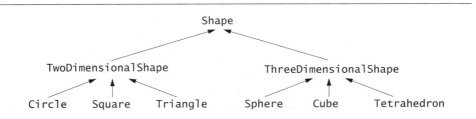

Fig. 27.2 A portion of a Shape class hierarchy.

Also, starting from the bottom of the diagram you can follow the arrows and apply the *is a* relationship all the way up to the topmost superclass in the hierarchy. For example, a Tetrahedron *is a* ThreeDimensionalShape and also *is a* Shape. In Java, a Tetrahedron also *is an* Object because all classes in Java have Object as one of their direct or indirect superclasses. Thus, all classes in Java are related in a hierarchical relationship in which they share the 11 methods defined by class Object that include the toString and finalize methods discussed previously. Other methods of class Object are discussed as they are needed in the text.

There are abundant examples of hierarchies in the real world but students are not accustomed to categorizing the real world in this manner, so it takes some adjustment in their thinking. Actually, biology students have had some practice with hierarchies. Everything we study in biology is grouped into a hierarchy headed by living things and these can be plants or animals and so on.

To specify that class `TwoDimensionalShape` is derived from (or inherits from) class `Shape`, class `TwoDimensionalShape` could be defined in Java as follows:

```
class TwoDimensionalShape extends Shape { ... }
```

With inheritance, `private` members of a superclass are not directly accessible from that class's subclasses. Package access members of the superclass are only accessible in a subclass if both the superclass and its subclass are in the same package. All other superclass members become members of the subclass using their original member access (i.e., `public` members of the superclass become `public` members of the subclass and `protected` members of the superclass become `protected` members of the subclass).

Software Engineering Observation 27.2

Constructors are never inherited—they are specific to the class in which they are defined.

It is possible to treat superclass objects and subclass objects similarly; that commonality is expressed in the attributes and behaviors of the superclass. Objects of all classes derived from a common superclass can all be treated as objects of that superclass.

We will consider many examples in which we can take advantage of this relationship with an ease of programming not available in non-object-oriented languages such as C.

27.3 protected Members

A superclass's `public` members are accessible anywhere the program has a reference to that superclass type or one of its subclass types. A superclass's `private` members are accessible only in methods of that superclass.

A superclass's `protected` access members serve as an intermediate level of protection between `public` and `private` access. A superclass's `protected` members may be accessed only by methods of the superclass, by methods of subclasses and by methods of other classes in the same package (`protected` members have package access).

Subclass methods can normally refer to `public` and `protected` members of the superclass simply by using the member names. When a subclass method *overrides* a superclass method (discussed in Sec. 27.4), the superclass method may be accessed from the subclass by preceding the superclass method name with keyword `super` followed by the dot operator (`.`). This technique is illustrated several times throughout the chapter.

27.4 Relationship between Superclass Objects and Subclass Objects

An object of a subclass can be treated as an object of its superclass. This makes possible some interesting manipulations. For example, despite the fact that objects of a variety of classes derived from a particular superclass may be quite different from one another, we can create an array of references to them—as long as we treat them as superclass objects. But the reverse is not true: A superclass object is not also automatically a subclass object.

Common Programming Error 27.1

Treating a superclass object as a subclass object can cause errors.

However, an explicit cast can be used to convert a superclass reference to a subclass reference. This can only be done when the superclass reference is actually referencing a subclass object; otherwise, Java will indicate a *ClassCastException*—an indication that the cast operation is not allowed.

Common Programming Error 27.2

Assigning an object of a superclass to a subclass reference (without a cast) is a syntax error.

Software Engineering Observation 27.3

If an object has been assigned to a reference of one of its superclasses, it is acceptable to cast that object back to its own type. In fact, this must be done to send that object any of its messages that do not appear in that superclass.

Our first example of inheritance is shown in Fig. 27.3. Every applet we defined has used some of the techniques presented here. We now formalize the inheritance concept.

```
1   // Fig. 27.3: Point.java
2   // Definition of class Point
3
4   public class Point {
5      protected int x, y; // coordinates of the Point
6
7      // No-argument constructor
8      public Point()
9      {
10        // implicit call to superclass constructor occurs here
11        setPoint( 0, 0 );
12     } // end Point constructor
13
14     // Constructor
15     public Point( int a, int b )
16     {
17        // implicit call to superclass constructor occurs here
18        setPoint( a, b );
19     } // end Point constructor
20
21     // Set x and y coordinates of Point
22     public void setPoint( int a, int b )
23     {
24        x = a;
25        y = b;
26     } // end method setPoint
27
28     // get x coordinate
29     public int getX() { return x; }
30
31     // get y coordinate
32     public int getY() { return y; }
33
```

Fig. 27.3   Assigning subclass references to superclass references—Point.java. (Part 1 of 2.)

```
34        // convert the point into a String representation
35        public String toString()
36           { return "[" + x + ", " + y + "]"; }
37     } // end class Point
```

Fig. 27.3   Assigning subclass references to superclass references—`Point.java`. (Part 2 of 2.)

```
38     // Fig. 27.3: Circle.java
39     // Definition of class Circle
40
41     public class Circle extends Point {  // inherits from Point
42        protected double radius;
43
44        // No-argument constructor
45        public Circle()
46        {
47           // implicit call to superclass constructor occurs here
48           setRadius( 0 );
49        } // end Circle constructor
50
51        // Constructor
52        public Circle( double r, int a, int b )
53        {
54           super( a, b );  // call to superclass constructor
55           setRadius( r );
56        } // end Circle constructor
57
58        // Set radius of Circle
59        public void setRadius( double r )
60           { radius = ( r >= 0.0 ? r : 0.0 ); }
61
62        // Get radius of Circle
63        public double getRadius() { return radius; }
64
65        // Calculate area of Circle
66        public double area() { return Math.PI * radius * radius; }
67
68        // convert the Circle to a String
69        public String toString()
70        {
71           return "Center = " + "[" + x + ", " + y + "]" +
72                  "; Radius = " + radius;
73        } // end method toString
74     } // end class Circle
```

Fig. 27.3   Assigning subclass references to superclass references—`Circle.java`.

```
75     // Fig. 27.3: InheritanceTest.java
76     // Demonstrating the "is a" relationship
77     import java.text.DecimalFormat;
```

Fig. 27.3   Assigning subclass references to superclass references—`InheritanceTest.java` (Part 1 of 3.).

```
78    import javax.swing.JOptionPane;
79
80    public class InheritanceTest {
81       public static void main( String args[] )
82       {
83          Point pointRef, p;
84          Circle circleRef, c;
85          String output;
86
87          p = new Point( 30, 50 );
88          c = new Circle( 2.7, 120, 89 );
89
90          output = "Point p: " + p.toString() +
91                   "\nCircle c: " + c.toString();
92
93          // use the "is a" relationship to refer to a Circle
94          // with a Point reference
95          pointRef = c;    // assign Circle to pointRef
96
97          output += "\n\nCircle c (via pointRef): " +
98                    pointRef.toString();
99
100         // Use downcasting (casting a superclass reference to a
101         // subclass data type) to assign pointRef to circleRef
102         circleRef = (Circle) pointRef;
103
104         output += "\n\nCircle c (via circleRef): " +
105                   circleRef.toString();
106
107         DecimalFormat precision2 = new DecimalFormat( "0.00" );
108         output += "\nArea of c (via circleRef): " +
109                   precision2.format( circleRef.area() );
110
111         // Attempt to refer to Point object
112         // with Circle reference
113         if ( p instanceof Circle ) {
114            circleRef = (Circle) p;  // line 40 in Test.java
115            output += "\n\ncast successful";
116         }
117         else
118            output += "\n\np does not refer to a Circle";
119
120         JOptionPane.showMessageDialog( null, output,
121            "Demonstrating the \"is a\" relationship",
122            JOptionPane.INFORMATION_MESSAGE );
123
124         System.exit( 0 );
125      } // end main
126   } // end class InheritanceTest
```

Fig. 27.3 Assigning subclass references to superclass references—
InheritanceTest.java (Part 2 of 3.).

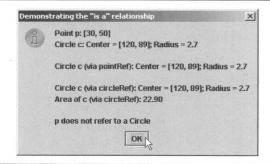

Fig. 27.3   Assigning subclass references to superclass references—
          `InheritanceTest.java` (Part 3 of 3.).

Every class definition in Java must extend another class. However, notice that class `Point` (line 4) does not explicitly use the **extends** keyword. If a new class definition does not explicitly extend an existing class definition, Java implicitly uses class `Object` (package `java.lang`) as the superclass for the new class definition. Class `Object` provides a set of methods that can be used with any object of any class.

Software Engineering Observation 27.4

Every class in Java extends `Object` unless specified otherwise in the first line of the class definition. Thus, class `Object` is the superclass of the entire Java class hierarchy.

Lines 1 through 37 show a `Point` class definition. Lines 38 through 74 show a `Circle` class definition; we will see that class `Circle` inherits from class `Point`. Lines 75–126 show an application that demonstrates assigning subclass references to superclass references and casting superclass references to subclass references.

Let us first examine the `Point` class definition in lines 1 through 37. The **public** services of class `Point` include methods `setPoint`, `getX`, `getY`, `toString` and two `Point` constructors. The instance variables x and y of `Point` are specified as **protected**. This prevents clients of `Point` objects from directly accessing the data (unless they are classes in the same package), but enables classes derived from `Point` to access the inherited instance variables directly. If the data were specified as **private**, the non-**private** methods of `Point` would have to be used to access the data, even by subclasses. Note that class `Point`'s `toString` method overrides the original `toString` from class `Object`.

Class `Point`'s constructors (lines 8 and 15) must call class `Object`'s constructor. In fact, every subclass constructor is required to call its direct superclass's constructor as its first task either implicitly or explicitly (the syntax for this call is discussed with class `Circle` momentarily). If there is no explicit call to the superclass constructor, Java attempts to call the superclass's default constructor. Note that lines 10 and 17 are comments indicating where the call to the superclass `Object`'s default constructor occurs.

Class `Circle` (lines 38 through 74) inherits from class `Point`. This is specified in the first line of the class definition

```
public class Circle extends Point {  // inherits from Point
```

Keyword **extends** in the class definition indicates inheritance. All the (non–**private**) members of class `Point` (except the constructors) are inherited into class `Circle`. Thus, the `public` interface to `Circle` includes the `Point public` methods as well as the two overloaded `Circle` constructors and `Circle` methods `setRadius, getRadius, area` and `toString`. Notice that method `area` (line 66) uses predefined constant `Math.PI` from class `Math` (package `java.lang`) to calculate the area of a circle.

The `Circle` constructors (lines 45 and 52) must invoke a `Point` constructor to initialize the superclass portion (variables x and y inherited from `Point`) of a `Circle` object. The default constructor in line 45 does not explicitly call a `Point` constructor, so Java calls class `Point`'s default constructor (defined in line 8) that initializes superclass members x and y to zeros. If the `Point` class contained only the constructor of line 15 (i.e., did not provide a default constructor), a compiler error would occur.

Line 54 in the body of the second `Circle` constructor

```
super( a, b );  // explicit call to superclass constructor
```

explicitly invokes the `Point` constructor (defined in line 11) using the *superclass constructor call syntax* [i.e., keyword *super* followed by a set of parentheses containing the arguments to the superclass constructor (in this case the values a and b are passed to initialize the superclass members x and y)]. The call to the superclass constructor must be the first line in the body of the subclass constructor. To explicitly call the superclass default constructor use the statement

```
super();  // explicit call to superclass default constructor
```

Common Programming Error 27.3

It is a syntax error if a **super** *call by a subclass to its superclass constructor is not the first statement in the subclass constructor.*

Common Programming Error 27.4

It is a syntax error if the arguments to a **super** *call by a subclass to its superclass constructor do not match the parameters specified in one of the superclass constructor definitions.*

A subclass can redefine a superclass method using the same signature; this is called *overriding* a superclass method. Whenever that method is mentioned by name in the subclass, the subclass version is called. We have actually been overriding methods in every applet in the book. When we extend `JApplet` to create a new applet class, the new class inherits versions of `init` and `paint` (and many other methods). Each time we defined `init` or `paint`, we were overriding the original version that was inherited. Also, when we provided method `toString` for the classes in Chapter 26, we were overriding the original version of `toString` provided by class `Object`. As we will soon see, the `super` reference followed by the dot operator may be used to access the original superclass version of that method from the subclass.

Note that class `Circle`'s `toString` method (line 69) overrides the `Point` class `toString` method (line 35). Class `Point`'s `toString` method overrides the original `toString` method provided by class `Object`. Class `Object` provides the original `toString` method, so every class inherits a `toString` method. This method is used to convert any object of any class into a `String` representation and is sometimes called implicitly by the program (e.g., when an object is added to a `String`). `Circle` method `toString` directly accesses the `protected` instance variables x and y that were inherited from class `Point`. The values of x and y are used as part of the `Circle`'s `String` representation. Actually, if you study class `Point`'s `toString` method and class `Circle`'s `toString` method, you will notice that `Circle`'s `toString` uses exactly the same formatting as `Point`'s `toString` for the `Point` parts of the `Circle`. To call `Point`'s `toString` from class `Circle` use the expression

```
super.toString()
```

Software Engineering Observation 27.5

A redefinition of a superclass method in a subclass need not have the same signature as the superclass method. Such a redefinition is not method overriding but is simply an example of method overloading.

Software Engineering Observation 27.6

Any object can be converted to a `String` *with an explicit or implicit call to the object's* `toString` *method.*

Software Engineering Observation 27.7

Each class should override method `toString` *to return useful information about objects of that class.*

Common Programming Error 27.5

It is a syntax error if a method in a superclass and a method in its subclass have the same signature but a different return type.

The application (lines 75 through 126) instantiates `Point` object p and `Circle` object c in lines 87 and 88 in `main`. The `String` representations of each object are appended to `String output` to show that they were initialized correctly (lines 90 and 91). See the first two lines in the output screen capture to confirm this.

Line 95

```
pointRef = c;   // assign Circle to pointRef
```

assigns `Circle` c (a reference to a subclass object) to `pointRef` (a superclass reference). It is always acceptable in Java to assign a subclass reference to a superclass reference (because of the *is a* relationship of inheritance). A `Circle` *is a* `Point` because class `Circle` extends class `Point`. Assigning a superclass reference to a subclass reference is dangerous, as we will see.

Lines 97 and 98 append the result of `pointRef.toString()` to the `String output`. Interestingly, when this `pointRef` is sent the `toString` message, Java knows that the object really is a `Circle`, so it chooses the `Circle` `toString` method instead of using the `Point` `toString` method as you might have expected. This is an example of *polymorphism* and *dynamic binding*, concepts we treat in depth later in this chapter. The compiler looks at the preceding expression and asks the question, "Does the data type of the reference `pointRef` (i.e., `Point`) have a `toString` method with no arguments?" The answer to this question is yes (see `Point`'s `toString` definition in line 35). The compiler is simply checking the syntax of the expression and ensuring that the method exists. At execution time, the interpreter asks the question, "What type is the object to which `pointRef` refers?" Every object in Java knows its own data type, so the answer to the question is `pointRef` refers to a `Circle` object. Based on this answer, the interpreter calls the `toString` method of the actual object's data type (i.e., class `Circle`'s `toString` method). See the third line of the output to confirm this. The two key programming techniques we used to achieve this effect are 1) extending class `Point` to create class `Circle` and 2) overriding method `toString` with the exact same signature in class `Point` and class `Circle`.

Line 102

```
circleRef = (Circle) pointRef;
```

casts `pointRef` (which admittedly is referencing a `Circle` at this time in the program's execution) to a `Circle` and assigns the result to `circleRef` (this cast would be dangerous if `pointRef` were really referencing a `Point`, as we will soon discuss). Then we use `circleRef` to append to `String output` the various facts about `Circle circleRef`. Lines 104 and 105 invoke method `toString` to append the `String` representation of the `Circle`. Lines 107 through 109 append the `area` of the `Circle` formatted with an instance of class `DecimalFormat` (package `java.text`) called `precision2` that formats a number with two digits to the right of the decimal point. The format `"0.00"` (specified in line 107) uses 0 twice to indicate the proper number of digits after the decimal point. Each 0 is a required decimal place. The 0 to the left of the decimal point indicates a minimum of one digit to the left of the decimal point.

Next, the `if/else` structure in lines 113 through 118 attempts a dangerous cast in line 114. We cast `Point p` to a `Circle`. At execution time if this is attempted, Java would determine that p really references a `Point`, recognize the cast to `Circle` as being dangerous and indicate an improper cast with `ClassCastException` message. However, we prevent this statement from executing with the `if` condition

```
if ( p instanceof Circle ) {
```

that uses operator *instanceof* to determine if the object to which p refers *is a* `Circle`. This condition evaluates to `true` only if the object to which p refers *is a* `Circle`; otherwise, the condition evaluates to `false`. Reference p does not refer to a `Circle`, so the condition fails and a `String` indicating that p does not refer to a `Circle` is appended to `output`.

If we remove the `if` test from the program and execute the program, the following message is generated at execution time:

```
Exception in thread "main"
java.lang.ClassCastException: Point
    at InheritanceTest.main(InheritanceTest.java:40)
```

Such error messages normally include the file name (`InheritanceTest.java`) and line number at which the error occurred (40) so you can go to that specific line in the program for debugging. Note that the line number specified—`InheritanceTest.java:40`—is different from the line numbers for file `InheritanceTest.java` shown in the text. This is because the examples in the text are numbered with consecutive line numbers for all files in the same program for discussion purposes. If you open the file `InheritanceTest.java` in an editor, you will find that the error did indeed occur in line 40 (which is line 114 in the whole program).

27.5 Implicit Subclass-Object-to-Superclass-Object Conversion

Despite the fact that a subclass object also *is a* superclass object, the subclass type and the superclass type are different. Subclass objects can be treated as superclass objects. This makes sense because the subclass has members corresponding to each of the superclass members—remember that the subclass normally has more members than the superclass has. Assignment in the other direction is not allowed because assigning a superclass object to a subclass reference would leave the additional subclass members undefined.

A reference to a subclass object may be implicitly converted into a reference to a superclass object because a subclass object *is a* superclass object through inheritance.

There are four possible ways to mix and match superclass references and subclass references with superclass objects and subclass objects:

1. Referring to a superclass object with a superclass reference is straightforward.

2. Referring to a subclass object with a subclass reference is straightforward.

3. Referring to a subclass object with a superclass reference is safe because the subclass object *is an* object of its superclass as well. Such code can only refer to superclass members. If this code refers to subclass-only members through the superclass reference, the compiler will report a syntax error.

4. Referring to a superclass object with a subclass reference is a syntax error. The subclass reference must first be cast to a superclass reference.

Common Programming Error 27.6

Assigning a subclass object to a superclass reference, then attempting to reference subclass-only members with the superclass reference, is a syntax error.

As convenient as it may be to treat subclass objects as superclass objects, and to do this by manipulating all these objects with superclass references, there appears to be a problem. In a payroll system, for example, we would like to be able to walk through an array of employees and calculate the weekly pay for each person. But intuition suggests that using superclass references would enable the program to call only the superclass payroll calculation routine (if indeed there is such a routine in the superclass). We need a way to invoke the proper payroll calculation routine for each object, whether it is a superclass object or a subclass object, and to do this simply by using the superclass reference. Actually, this is precisely how Java behaves and is discussed in this chapter when we consider polymorphism and dynamic binding.

27.6 Software Engineering with Inheritance

We can use inheritance to customize existing software. When we use inheritance to create a new class from an existing class, the new class inherits the attributes and behaviors of an existing class, then we can add attributes and behaviors or override superclass behaviors to customize the class to meet our needs.

It can be difficult for students to appreciate the problems faced by designers and implementers on large-scale software projects in industry. People experienced on such projects will invariably state that a key to improving the software development process is encouraging software reuse. Object-oriented programming in general, and Java in particular, certainly does this.

It is the availability of substantial and useful class libraries that delivers the maximum benefits of software reuse through inheritance. As interest in Java grows, interest in Java class libraries will increase. Just as shrink-wrapped software produced by independent software vendors became an explosive growth industry with the arrival of the personal computer, so, too, will the creation and sale of Java class libraries. Application designers will build their applications with these libraries, and library designers will be rewarded by having their libraries wrapped with the applications. What we see coming is a massive worldwide commitment to the development of Java class libraries for a huge variety of applications arenas.

Software Engineering Observation 27.8

Creating a subclass does not affect its superclass's source code or the superclass's Java bytecodes; the integrity of a superclass is preserved by inheritance.

A superclass specifies commonality. All classes derived from a superclass inherit the capabilities of that superclass. In the object-oriented design process, the designer looks for commonality among a set of classes and factors it out to form desirable superclasses. Subclasses are then customized beyond the capabilities inherited from the superclass.

Software Engineering Observation 27.9

Just as the designer of non-object-oriented systems should avoid unnecessary proliferation of functions, the designer of object-oriented systems should avoid unnecessary proliferation of classes. Proliferating classes creates management problems and can hinder software reusability simply because it is more difficult for a potential user of a class to locate that class in a huge collection. The trade-off is to create fewer classes, each providing substantial additional functionality, but such classes might be too rich for certain users.

Performance Tip 27.1

If classes produced through inheritance are larger than they need to be, memory and processing resources may be wasted. Inherit from the class "closest" to what you need.

Note that reading a set of subclass declarations can be confusing because inherited members are not shown, but inherited members are nevertheless present in the subclasses. A similar problem can exist in the documentation of subclasses.

Software Engineering Observation 27.10

In an object-oriented system, classes are often closely related. "Factor out" common attributes and behaviors and place these in a superclass. Then use inheritance to form subclasses without having to repeat common attributes and behaviors.

Software Engineering Observation 27.11

Modifications to a superclass do not require subclasses to change as long as the public interface to the superclass remains unchanged.

27.7 Composition vs. Inheritance

We have discussed *is a* relationships that are implemented by inheritance. We have also discussed *has a* relationships (and seen examples in preceding chapters) in which a class may have objects of other classes as members—such relationships create new classes by *composition* of existing classes. For example, given the classes `Employee`, `BirthDate` and `TelephoneNumber`, it is improper to say that an `Employee` *is a* `BirthDate` or that an `Employee` *is a* `TelephoneNumber`. But it is certainly appropriate to say that an `Employee` *has a* `BirthDate` and that an `Employee` *has a* `TelephoneNumber`.

27.8 Introduction to Polymorphism

With *polymorphism,* it is possible to design and implement systems that are more easily *extensible.* Programs can be written to process generically—as superclass objects—objects of all existing classes in a hierarchy. Classes that do not exist during program development can be added with little or no modifications to the generic part of the program—as long as those classes are part of the hierarchy that is being processed generically. The only parts of a program that need modification are those parts that require direct knowledge of the particular class that is added to the hierarchy. We will study two substantial class hierarchies and will show how objects throughout those hierarchies are manipulated polymorphically.

27.9 Type Fields and switch Statements

One means of dealing with objects of many different types is to use a `switch` statement to take an appropriate action on each object based on that object's type. For example, in a hierarchy of shapes in which each shape has a `shapeType` instance variable, a `switch` structure could determine which `print` method to call based on the object's `shapeType`.

There are many problems with using `switch` logic. The programmer might forget to make such a type test when one is warranted. The programmer may forget to test all possible cases in a `switch`. If a `switch`-based system is modified by adding new types, the programmer might forget to insert the new cases in existing `switch` statements. Every addition or deletion of a class demands that every `switch` statement in the system be modified; tracking these down can be time consuming and error-prone.

As we will see, polymorphic programming can eliminate the need for `switch` logic. The programmer can use Java's polymorphism mechanism to perform the equivalent logic, thus avoiding the kinds of errors typically associated with `switch` logic.

Error-Prevention Tip 27.2

An interesting consequence of using polymorphism is that programs take on a simplified appearance. They contain less branching logic in favor of simpler sequential code. This simplification facilitates testing, debugging and program maintenance.

27.10 Dynamic Method Binding

Suppose a set of shape classes such as `Circle`, `Triangle`, `Rectangle`, `Square`, etc. are all derived from superclass `Shape`. In object-oriented programming, each of these classes might be endowed with the ability to draw itself. Each class has its own `draw` method, and the `draw` method implementation for each shape is quite different. When drawing a shape, whatever that shape may be, it would be nice to be able to treat all these shapes generically as objects of the superclass `Shape`. Then to draw any shape, we could simply call method `draw` of superclass `Shape` and let the program determine dynamically (i.e., at execution time) which subclass `draw` method to use based on the actual object's type.

To enable this kind of behavior, we declare `draw` in the superclass, then we override `draw` in each of the subclasses to draw the appropriate shape.

Software Engineering Observation 27.12

When a subclass chooses not to redefine a method, the subclass simply inherits its immediate superclass's method definition.

If we use a superclass reference to refer to a subclass object and invoke the `draw` method, the program will choose the correct subclass's `draw` method dynamically (i.e., at execution time). This is called *dynamic method binding* and will be illustrated in the case studies later in this chapter.

27.11 `final` Methods and Classes

Variables can be declared `final` to indicate that they cannot be modified after they are declared and that they must be initialized when they are declared. It is also possible to define methods and classes with the `final` modifier.

A method that is declared `final` cannot be overridden in a subclass. Methods that are declared `static` and methods that are declared `private` are implicitly `final`. A `final` method's definition can never change, so the compiler can optimize the program by removing calls to `final` methods and replacing them with the expanded code of their definitions at each method call location—a technique known as *inlining the code*.

A class that is declared `final` cannot be a superclass (i.e., a class cannot inherit from a `final` class). All methods in a `final` class are implicitly `final`.

Performance Tip 27.2

The compiler can decide to inline a `final` method call and will do so for small, simple `final` methods. Inlining does not violate encapsulation or information hiding (but does improve performance because it eliminates the overhead of making a method call).

Performance Tip 27.3

Pipelined processors can improve performance by executing portions of the next several instructions simultaneously, but not if those instructions follow a method call. Inlining (which the compiler can perform on a `final` method) can improve performance in these processors because it eliminates the out-of-line transfer of control associated with a method call.

Software Engineering Observation 27.13

A class declared `final` cannot be extended and every method is implicitly `final`.

27.12 Abstract Superclasses and Concrete Classes

When we think of a class as a type, we assume that objects of that type will be instantiated. However, there are cases in which it is useful to define classes for which the programmer never intends to instantiate any objects. Such classes are called *abstract classes and contain one or more abstract methods.* These are used as superclasses in inheritance situations, so we will normally refer to them as *abstract superclasses.* No objects of abstract superclasses can be instantiated.

Common Programming Error 27.7

Attempting to instantiate an object of an abstract *class (i.e., a class that contains one or more* abstract *methods) is a syntax error.*

Software Engineering Observation 27.14

An abstract *class can still have instance data and non-*abstract *methods subject to the normal rules of inheritance by subclasses. An* abstract *class can also have constructors.*

The sole purpose of an abstract class is to provide an appropriate superclass from which other classes may inherit interface and/or implementation (we will see examples of each shortly). Classes from which objects can be instantiated are called *concrete classes*.

Software Engineering Observation 27.15

If a subclass is derived from a superclass with an abstract *method, and if no definition is supplied in the subclass for that* abstract *method (i.e., if that method is not overridden in the subclass), that method remains* abstract *in the subclass. Consequently, the subclass is also an* abstract *class and must be explicitly declared as an* abstract *class.*

Software Engineering Observation 27.16

The ability to declare an abstract *method gives the class designer considerable power over how subclasses will be implemented in a class hierarchy. Any new class that wants to inherit from this class is forced to override the* abstract *method (either directly or by inheriting from a class that has overridden the method). Otherwise, that new class will contain an* abstract *method and thus be an* abstract *class unable to instantiate objects.*

We could have an abstract superclass TwoDimensionalObject and derive concrete classes such as Square, Circle, Triangle, etc. We could also have an abstract superclass ThreeDimensionalObject and derive concrete classes such as Cube, Sphere, Cylinder, etc. Abstract superclasses are too generic to define real objects; we need to be more specific before we can think of instantiating objects. For example, if someone tells you to "draw the shape," what shape would you draw? Concrete classes provide the specifics that make it reasonable to instantiate objects.

A class is made abstract by declaring it with keyword *abstract*. A hierarchy does not need to contain any abstract classes, but as we will see, many good object-oriented systems have class hierarchies headed by abstract superclasses. In some cases, abstract classes constitute the top few levels of the hierarchy. A good example of this is the shape hierarchy in Fig. 27.2. The hierarchy begins with abstract superclass Shape. On the next level down we have two more abstract superclasses, namely TwoDimensionalShape and ThreeDimensionalShape. The next level down would start defining concrete classes for two-dimensional shapes such as Circle and Square, and concrete classes for three-dimensional shapes such as Sphere and Cube.

Common Programming Error 27.8

It is a syntax error if a class with one or more abstract *methods is not explicitly declared* abstract.

27.13 Polymorphism Example

Here we present an example of polymorphism. If class Rectangle is derived from class Quadrilateral, then a Rectangle object *is a* more specific version of a Quadrilateral object. An operation (such as calculating the perimeter or the area) that can be performed on an object of class `Quadrilateral` can also be performed on an object of class `Rectangle`. Such operations can also be performed on other "kinds of" `Quadrilaterals`, such as `Squares`, `Parallelograms` and `Trapezoids`. When a request is made through a superclass reference to use a method, Java chooses the correct overridden method polymorphically in the appropriate subclass associated with the object.

Through the use of polymorphism, one method call can cause different actions to occur depending on the type of the object receiving the call. This gives the programmer tremendous expressive capability. We will see examples of the power of polymorphism in the next several sections.

Software Engineering Observation 27.17

With polymorphism, the programmer can deal in generalities and let the execution-time environment concern itself with the specifics. The programmer can command a wide variety of objects to behave in manners appropriate to those objects without even knowing the types of those objects.

Software Engineering Observation 27.18

Polymorphism promotes extensibility: Software written to invoke polymorphic behavior is written independent of the types of the objects to which messages (i.e., method calls) are sent. Thus, new types of objects that can respond to existing messages can be added into such a system without modifying the base system.

Software Engineering Observation 27.19

If a method is declared `final` it cannot be overridden in subclasses, so that method calls may not be sent polymorphically to objects of those subclasses. The method call may still be sent to subclasses but they will all respond identically rather than polymorphically.

Software Engineering Observation 27.20

An `abstract` class defines a common interface for the various members of a class hierarchy. The `abstract` class contains methods that will be defined in the subclasses. All classes in the hierarchy can use this same interface through polymorphism.

Although we cannot instantiate objects of `abstract` superclasses, we *can* declare references to `abstract` superclasses. Such references can be used to enable polymorphic manipulations of subclass objects when such objects are instantiated from concrete classes.

Let us consider more applications of polymorphism. A screen manager needs to display a variety of objects, including new types of objects that will be added to the system even after the screen manager is written. The system may need to display various shapes (i.e., the superclass is `Shape`) such as `Circle`, `Triangle`, `Rectangle`, etc. (each shape class is derived from superclass `Shape`). The screen manager uses superclass references (to `Shape`) to manage the objects to be displayed. To draw any object (regardless of the level at which that object appears in the inheritance hierarchy), the screen manager uses a superclass reference to the object and simply sends a `draw` message to the object. Method `draw` has been declared `abstract` in superclass `Shape` and has been overridden in each of the subclasses. Each `Shape` object knows how to draw itself. The screen manager does not have to worry about what type each object is or whether the screen manager has seen objects of that type before—the screen manager simply tells each object to `draw` itself.

Polymorphism is particularly effective for implementing layered software systems. In operating systems, for example, each type of physical device may operate quite differently from the others. Even so, commands to *read* or *write* data from and to devices can have a certain uniformity. The *write* message sent to a device-driver object needs to be interpreted specifically in the context of that device driver and how that device driver manipulates devices of a specific type. However, the *write* call itself is really no different from the *write* to any other device in the system—simply place some number of bytes from memory onto that device. An object-oriented operating system might use an `abstract` superclass to provide an interface appropriate for all device drivers. Then, through inheritance from that `abstract` superclass, subclasses are formed that all operate similarly. The capabilities (i.e., the `public` interface) offered by the device drivers are provided as `abstract` methods in the `abstract` superclass. The implementations of these `abstract` methods are provided in the subclasses that correspond to the specific types of device drivers.

It is common in object-oriented programming to define an *iterator class* that can walk through all the objects in a container (such as an array). If you want to print a list of objects in a linked list, for example, an iterator object can be instantiated that will return the next element of the linked list each time the iterator is called. Iterators are commonly used in polymorphic programming to walk through an array or a linked list of objects from various levels of a hierarchy. The references in such a list would all be superclass references. A list of objects of superclass class `TwoDimensionalShape` could contain objects from the classes `Square`, `Circle`, `Triangle`, etc. Sending a `draw` message to each object in the list would, using polymorphism, draw the correct picture on the screen.

27.14 New Classes and Dynamic Binding

Polymorphism certainly works nicely when all possible classes are known in advance. But it also works when new kinds of classes are added to systems.

New classes are accommodated by dynamic method binding (also called *late binding*). An object's type need not be known at compile time for a polymorphic call to be compiled. At execution time, the call is matched with the method of the called object.

A screen manager program can now handle (without recompilation) new types of display objects as they are added to the system. The `draw` method call remains the same. The new objects themselves each contain a `draw` method implementing the actual drawing capabilities. This makes it easy to add new capabilities to systems with minimal impact. It also promotes software reuse.

Performance Tip 27.4

Polymorphism as implemented with dynamic method binding is efficient.

Performance Tip 27.5

The kinds of polymorphic manipulations made possible with dynamic binding can also be accomplished by using hand-coded `switch` logic based on type fields in objects. The polymorphic code generated by the Java compiler runs with comparable performance to efficiently coded `switch` logic.

27.15 Case Study: Inheriting Interface and Implementation

Now let us consider a substantial inheritance example. We consider a `Point`, `Circle`, `Cylinder` hierarchy in Fig. 27.4. We have as the head of the hierarchy `abstract` superclass `Shape`. This hierarchy mechanically demonstrates the power of polymorphism. In the exercises, we explore a more realistic hierarchy of shapes.

```java
1  // Fig. 27.4: Shape.java
2  // Definition of abstract base class Shape
3
4  public abstract class Shape extends Object {
5     public double area() { return 0.0; }
6     public double volume() { return 0.0; }
7     public abstract String getName();
8  } // end class Shape
```

Fig. 27.4   Shape, point, circle, cylinder hierarchy—`Shape.java`.

```java
9   // Fig. 27.4: Point.java
10  // Definition of class Point
11
12  public class Point extends Shape {
13     protected int x, y; // coordinates of the Point
14
15     // no-argument constructor
16     public Point() { setPoint( 0, 0 ); }
17
18     // constructor
19     public Point( int a, int b ) { setPoint( a, b ); }
20
21     // Set x and y coordinates of Point
22     public void setPoint( int a, int b )
23     {
24        x = a;
25        y = b;
26     } // end method setPoint
27
28     // get x coordinate
29     public int getX() { return x; }
30
31     // get y coordinate
32     public int getY() { return y; }
33
34     // convert the point into a String representation
35     public String toString()
36        { return "[" + x + ", " + y + "]"; }
37
38     // return the class name
39     public String getName() { return "Point"; }
40  } // end class Point
```

Fig. 27.4   Shape, point, circle, cylinder hierarchy—`Point.java`.

```
41    // Fig. 27.4: Circle.java
42    // Definition of class Circle
43
44    public class Circle extends Point {  // inherits from Point
45       protected double radius;
46
47       // no-argument constructor
48       public Circle()
49       {
50          // implicit call to superclass constructor here
51          setRadius( 0 );
52       } // end Circle constructor
53
54       // Constructor
55       public Circle( double r, int a, int b )
56       {
57          super( a, b );   // call the superclass constructor
58          setRadius( r );
59       } // end Circle constructor
60
61       // Set radius of Circle
62       public void setRadius( double r )
63          { radius = ( r >= 0 ? r : 0 ); }
64
65       // Get radius of Circle
66       public double getRadius() { return radius; }
67
68       // Calculate area of Circle
69       public double area() { return Math.PI * radius * radius; }
70
71       // convert the Circle to a String
72       public String toString()
73          { return "Center = " + super.toString() +
74                   "; Radius = " + radius; }
75
76       // return the class name
77       public String getName() { return "Circle"; }
78    } // end class Circle
```

Fig. 27.4 Shape, point, circle, cylinder hierarchy—`Circle.java`.

```
79    // Fig. 27.4: Cylinder.java
80    // Definition of class Cylinder
81
82    public class Cylinder extends Circle {
83       protected double height;   // height of Cylinder
84
85       // no-argument constructor
86       public Cylinder()
87       {
88          // implicit call to superclass constructor here
89          setHeight( 0 );
```

Fig. 27.4 Shape, point, circle, cylinder hierarchy—`Cylinder.java`. (Part 1 of 2.)

```
90      } // end Cylinder constructor
91
92      // constructor
93      public Cylinder( double h, double r, int a, int b )
94      {
95         super( r, a, b );    // call superclass constructor
96         setHeight( h );
97      } // end Cylinder constructor
98
99      // Set height of Cylinder
100     public void setHeight( double h )
101        { height = ( h >= 0 ? h : 0 ); }
102
103     // Get height of Cylinder
104     public double getHeight() { return height; }
105
106     // Calculate area of Cylinder (i.e., surface area)
107     public double area()
108     {
109        return 2 * super.area() +
110               2 * Math.PI * radius * height;
111     } // end method area
112
113     // Calculate volume of Cylinder
114     public double volume() { return super.area() * height; }
115
116     // Convert a Cylinder to a String
117     public String toString()
118        { return super.toString() + "; Height = " + height; }
119
120     // Return the class name
121     public String getName() { return "Cylinder"; }
122  } // end class Cylinder
```

Fig. 27.4   Shape, point, circle, cylinder hierarchy—Cylinder.java. (Part 2 of 2.)

```
123  // Fig. 27.4: Test.java
124  // Driver for point, circle, cylinder hierarchy
125  import javax.swing.JOptionPane;
126  import java.text.DecimalFormat;
127
128  public class Test {
129     public static void main( String args[] )
130     {
131        Point point = new Point( 7, 11 );
132        Circle circle = new Circle( 3.5, 22, 8 );
133        Cylinder cylinder = new Cylinder( 10, 3.3, 10, 10 );
134
135        Shape arrayOfShapes[];
136
137        arrayOfShapes = new Shape[ 3 ];
138
```

Fig. 27.4   Shape, point, circle, cylinder hierarchy—Test.java. (Part 1 of 2.)

```
139          // aim arrayOfShapes[0] at subclass Point object
140          arrayOfShapes[ 0 ] = point;
141
142          // aim arrayOfShapes[1] at subclass Circle object
143          arrayOfShapes[ 1 ] = circle;
144
145          // aim arrayOfShapes[2] at subclass Cylinder object
146          arrayOfShapes[ 2 ] = cylinder;
147
148          String output =
149             point.getName() + ": " + point.toString() + "\n" +
150             circle.getName() + ": " + circle.toString() + "\n" +
151             cylinder.getName() + ": " + cylinder.toString();
152
153          DecimalFormat precision2 = new DecimalFormat( "0.00" );
154
155          // Loop through arrayOfShapes and print the name,
156          // area, and volume of each object.
157          for ( int i = 0; i < arrayOfShapes.length; i++ ) {
158             output += "\n\n" +
159                arrayOfShapes[ i ].getName() + ": " +
160                arrayOfShapes[ i ].toString() +
161                "\nArea = " +
162                precision2.format( arrayOfShapes[ i ].area() ) +
163                "\nVolume = " +
164                precision2.format( arrayOfShapes[ i ].volume() );
165          } // end for
166
167          JOptionPane.showMessageDialog( null, output,
168             "Demonstrating Polymorphism",
169             JOptionPane.INFORMATION_MESSAGE );
170
171          System.exit( 0 );
172       } // end main
173    } // end class Test
```

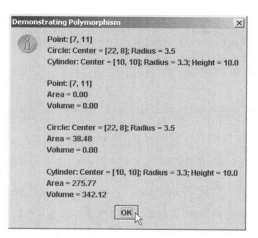

Fig. 27.4   Shape, point, circle, cylinder hierarchy—Test.java. (Part 2 of 2.)

Shape contains `abstract` method `getName` so Shape must be declared an abstract superclass. Shape contains two other methods, `area` and `volume`, each of which has an implementation that returns zero by default. Point inherits these implementations from Shape. This makes sense because both the area and volume of a point are zero. Circle inherits the `volume` method from Point, but Circle provides its own implementation for the area method. Cylinder provides its own implementations for both the `area` (interpreted as the surface area of the cylinder) and `volume` methods.

In this example, class Shape is used to define a set of methods that all Shapes in our hierarchy have in common. Defining these methods in class Shape enables us to generically call these methods through a Shape reference. Remember, the only methods that can be called through any reference are those `public` methods defined in the reference's declared class type and any `public` methods inherited into that class. Thus, we can call Object and Shape methods through a Shape reference.

Note that although Shape is an `abstract` superclass, it still contains implementations of methods `area` and `volume`, and these implementations are inheritable. The Shape class provides an inheritable interface (set of services) in the form of three methods that all classes of the hierarchy will contain. The Shape class also provides some implementations that subclasses in the first few levels of the hierarchy will use.

This case study emphasizes that a subclass can inherit interface and/or implementation from a superclass.

Software Engineering Observation 27.21

Hierarchies designed for implementation inheritance tend to have their functionality high in the hierarchy—each new subclass inherits one or more methods that were defined in a superclass and uses the superclass definitions.

Software Engineering Observation 27.22

Hierarchies designed for interface inheritance tend to have their functionality lower in the hierarchy—a superclass specifies one or more methods that should be called identically for each object in the hierarchy (i.e., they have the same signature), but the individual subclasses provide their own implementations of the method(s).

Superclass Shape (Fig. 27.4, lines 1 through 8) extends Object, consists of three `public` methods and does not contain any data (although it could). Method `getName` is `abstract`, so it is overridden in each of the subclasses. Methods `area` and `volume` are defined to return 0.0. These methods are overridden in subclasses when it is appropriate for those classes to have a different `area` calculation (classes Circle and Cylinder) and/or a different `volume` calculation (class Cylinder).

Class Point (Fig. 27.4, lines 9 through 40) is derived from Shape. A Point has an area of 0.0 and a volume of 0.0, so the superclass methods `area` and `volume` are not overridden here—they are inherited as defined in Shape. Other methods include `setPoint` to assign new x and y coordinates to a Point and `getX` and `getY` to return the x and y coordinates of a Point. Method `getName` is an implementation of the `abstract` method in the superclass. If this method were not defined, class Point would be an `abstract` class.

Class Circle (Fig. 27.4, lines 41 through 78) is derived from Point. A Circle has a volume of 0.0, so superclass method `volume` is not overridden—it is inherited from class Point, which inherited it from Shape. A Circle has an area different from that of a Point, so the `area` method is overridden. Method `getName` is an implementation of the abstract method in the superclass. If this method is not overridden here, the `Point` version of `getName` would be inherited. Other methods include `setRadius` to assign a new radius to a `Circle` and `getRadius` to return the `radius` of a `Circle`.

 Software Engineering Observation 27.23

A subclass always inherits the most recently defined version of each `public` *and* `protected` *method from its direct and indirect superclasses.*

Class `Cylinder` (Fig. 27.4, lines 79 through 122) is derived from `Circle`. A `Cylinder` has area and volume different from those of class `Circle`, so the `area` and `volume` methods are both overridden. Method `getName` is an implementation of the abstract method in the superclass. If this method had not been overridden here, the `Circle` version of `getName` would be inherited. Other methods include `setHeight` to assign a new height to a `Cylinder` and `getHeight` to return the `height` of a `Cylinder`.

Method `main` of class `Test` (Fig. 27.4, lines 123 through 173) instantiates `Point` object `point`, `Circle` object `circle` and `Cylinder` object `cylinder` (lines 131 through 133). Next, array `arrayOfShapes` is instantiated (line 137). This array of superclass `Shape` references will refer to each subclass object instantiated. In line 140, the reference `point` is assigned to array element `arrayOfShapes[0]`. In line 143, the reference `circle` is assigned to array element `arrayOfShapes[1]`. In line 146, the reference `cylinder` is assigned to array element `arrayOfShapes[2]`. Now, each superclass `Shape` reference in the array refers to a subclass object of type `Point`, `Circle` or `Cylinder`.

Lines 148 through 151 invoke methods `getName` and `toString` to illustrate that the objects are initialized correctly (see the first three lines of the output).

Next, the `for` structure in lines 157 through 165 walks through `arrayOfShapes` and the following calls are made during each iteration of the loop:

```
arrayOfShapes[ i ].getName()
arrayOfShapes[ i ].toString()
arrayOfShapes[ i ].area()
arrayOfShapes[ i ].volume()
```

Each of these method calls is invoked on the object to which `arrayOfShapes[i]` currently refers. When the compiler looks at each of these calls, it is simply trying to determine if a `Shape` reference (`arrayOfShapes[i]`) can be used to call these methods. For methods `getName`, `area` and `volume` the answer is yes, because each of these methods is defined in class `Shape`. For method `toString`, the compiler first looks at class `Shape` to determine that `toString` is not defined there, then the compiler proceeds to `Shape`'s superclass (`Object`) to determine if `Shape` inherited a `toString` method that takes no arguments (which it did, because all `Object`s have a `toString` method).

The output illustrates that all four methods are invoked properly based on the type of the referenced object. First, the string `"Point: "` and the coordinates of the object `point` (`arrayOfShapes[0]`) are output; the area and volume are both 0. Next, the string `"Circle: "`, the coordinates of object `circle`, and the radius of object `circle` (`arrayOfShapes[1]`) are output; the area of `circle` is calculated and the volume is 0. Finally, the string `"Cylinder: "`, the coordinates of object `cylinder`, the radius of object `cylinder` and the height of object `cylinder` (`arrayOfShapes[2]`) are output; the area of `cylinder` is calculated and the volume of `cylinder` is calculated. All the method calls to `getName`, `toString`, `area` and `volume` are resolved at run-time with dynamic binding.

27.16 Case Study: Creating and Using Interfaces

Our next example (Fig. 27.5) reexamines the Point, Circle, Cylinder hierarchy, replacing abstract superclass Shape with the interface Shape. An interface definition begins with the keyword *interface* and contains a set of public abstract methods. Interfaces may also contain public final static data. To use an interface, a class must specify that it implements the interface and the class must define every method in the interface with the number of arguments and the return type specified in the interface definition. If the class leaves one method in the interface undefined, the class becomes an abstract class and must be declared abstract in the first line of its class definition. Implementing an interface is like signing a contract with the compiler that states, "I will define all the methods specified by the interface."

Common Programming Error 27.9

Leaving a method of an interface undefined in a class that implements the interface results in a compile error indicating that the class must be declared abstract.

An interface is typically used in place of an abstract class when there is no default implementation to inherit—i.e., no instance variables and no default method implementations. Like public abstract classes, interfaces are typically public data types, so they are normally defined in files by themselves with the same name as the interface and the .java extension.

The definition of interface Shape begins in line 4. Interface Shape has abstract methods area, volume and getName. By coincidence, all three methods take no arguments. However, this is not a requirement of methods in an interface.

```
1   // Fig. 27.5: Shape.java
2   // Definition of interface Shape
3
4   public interface Shape {
5       public abstract double area();
6       public abstract double volume();
7       public abstract String getName();
8   } // end interface Shape
```

Fig. 27.5 Point, circle, cylinder hierarchy with a Shape interface—Shape.java.

```
9    // Fig. 27.5: Point.java
10   // Definition of class Point
11
12   public class Point extends Object implements Shape {
13       protected int x, y; // coordinates of the Point
14
15       // no-argument constructor
16       public Point() { setPoint( 0, 0 ); }
17
18       // constructor
19       public Point( int a, int b ) { setPoint( a, b ); }
```

Fig. 27.5 Point, circle, cylinder hierarchy with a Shape interface—Point.java. (Part 1 of 2.)

```
20
21      // Set x and y coordinates of Point
22      public void setPoint( int a, int b )
23      {
24         x = a;
25         y = b;
26      } // end method setPoint
27
28      // get x coordinate
29      public int getX() { return x; }
30
31      // get y coordinate
32      public int getY() { return y; }
33
34      // convert the point into a String representation
35      public String toString()
36         { return "[" + x + ", " + y + "]"; }
37
38      // return the area
39      public double area() { return 0.0; }
40
41      // return the volume
42      public double volume() { return 0.0; }
43
44      // return the class name
45      public String getName() { return "Point"; }
46   } // end class Point
```

Fig. 27.5   Point, circle, cylinder hierarchy with a Shape interface—`Point.java`. (Part 2 of 2.)

Line 12

```
public class Point extends Object implements Shape {
```

indicates that class `Point` extends class `Object` and implements interface `Shape`. Class `Point` provides definitions of all three methods in the interface. Method `area` is defined in line 39. Method `volume` is defined in line 42. Method `getName` is defined in line 45. These three methods satisfy the implementation requirement for the three methods defined in the interface. We have fulfilled our contract with the compiler.

When a class `implements` an interface, the same *is a* relationship provided by inheritance applies. In our example, class `Point` implements `Shape`. Therefore, a `Point` object *is a* `Shape`. In fact, objects of any class that extends `Point` are also `Shape` objects. Using this relationship, we have maintained the original definitions of class `Circle`, class `Cylinder` and application class `Test` from Fig. 27.4 to illustrate that an interface can be used instead of an `abstract` class to polymorphically process `Shape`s. Notice that the output for the program is identical to Fig. 27.4. Also, notice that `Object` method `toString` is called through a `Shape` interface reference (line 166).

Software Engineering Observation 27.24

All methods of class `Object` can be called using a reference of an interface data type—a reference refers to an object and all objects have the methods defined by class `Object`

```
1    // Fig. 27.5: Circle.java
2    // Definition of class Circle
3
4    public class Circle extends Point {  // inherits from Point
5       protected double radius;
6
7       // no-argument constructor
8       public Circle()
9       {
10          // implicit call to superclass constructor here
11          setRadius( 0 );
12       } // end Circle constructor
13
14       // Constructor
15       public Circle( double r, int a, int b )
16       {
17          super( a, b );  // call the superclass constructor
18          setRadius( r );
19       } // end Circle constructor
20
21       // Set radius of Circle
22       public void setRadius( double r )
23          { radius = ( r >= 0 ? r : 0 ); }
24
25       // Get radius of Circle
26       public double getRadius() { return radius; }
27
28       // Calculate area of Circle
29       public double area() { return Math.PI * radius * radius; }
30
31       // convert the Circle to a String
32       public String toString()
33          { return "Center = " + super.toString() +
34                   "; Radius = " + radius; }
35
36       // return the class name
37       public String getName() { return "Circle"; }
38    } // end class Circle
```

Fig. 27.5　Point, circle, cylinder hierarchy with a Shape interface—Circle.java.

```
39    // Fig. 27.5: Cylinder.java
40    // Definition of class Cylinder
41
42    public class Cylinder extends Circle {
43       protected double height;  // height of Cylinder
44
```

Fig. 27.5　Point, circle, cylinder hierarchy with a Shape interface—Cylinder.java.
(Part 1 of 2.)

```
45          // no-argument constructor
46          public Cylinder()
47          {
48             // implicit call to superclass constructor here
49             setHeight( 0 );
50          } // end Cylinder constructor
51
52          // constructor
53          public Cylinder( double h, double r, int a, int b )
54          {
55             super( r, a, b );    // call superclass constructor
56             setHeight( h );
57          } // end Cylinder constructor
58
59          // Set height of Cylinder
60          public void setHeight( double h )
61             { height = ( h >= 0 ? h : 0 ); }
62
63          // Get height of Cylinder
64          public double getHeight() { return height; }
65
66          // Calculate area of Cylinder (i.e., surface area)
67          public double area()
68          {
69             return 2 * super.area() +
70                    2 * Math.PI * radius * height;
71          } // end method area
72
73          // Calculate volume of Cylinder
74          public double volume() { return super.area() * height; }
75
76          // Convert a Cylinder to a String
77          public String toString()
78             { return super.toString() + "; Height = " + height; }
79
80          // Return the class name
81          public String getName() { return "Cylinder"; }
82       } // end class Cylinder
```

Fig. 27.5   Point, circle, cylinder hierarchy with a Shape interface—Cylinder.java.
(Part 2 of 2.)

One benefit of using interfaces is that a class can implement as many interfaces as it needs in addition to extending a class. To implement more than one interface, simply provide a comma-separated list of interface names after keyword implements in the class definition. This is particularly useful in the GUI event handling mechanism. A class that implements more than one event-listener interface (such as ActionListener in earlier examples) can process different types of GUI events, as we will see in Chapter 29.

```
83    // Fig. 27.5: Test.java
84    // Driver for point, circle, cylinder hierarchy
85    import javax.swing.JOptionPane;
86    import java.text.DecimalFormat;
87
88    public class Test {
89       public static void main( String args[] )
90       {
91          Point point = new Point( 7, 11 );
92          Circle circle = new Circle( 3.5, 22, 8 );
93          Cylinder cylinder = new Cylinder( 10, 3.3, 10, 10 );
94
95          Shape arrayOfShapes[];
96
97          arrayOfShapes = new Shape[ 3 ];
98
99          // aim arrayOfShapes[0] at subclass Point object
100         arrayOfShapes[ 0 ] = point;
101
102         // aim arrayOfShapes[1] at subclass Circle object
103         arrayOfShapes[ 1 ] = circle;
104
105         // aim arrayOfShapes[2] at subclass Cylinder object
106         arrayOfShapes[ 2 ] = cylinder;
107
108         String output =
109            point.getName() + ": " + point.toString() + "\n" +
110            circle.getName() + ": " + circle.toString() + "\n" +
111            cylinder.getName() + ": " + cylinder.toString();
112
113         DecimalFormat precision2 = new DecimalFormat( "#0.00" );
114
115         // Loop through arrayOfShapes and print the name,
116         // area, and volume of each object.
117         for ( int i = 0; i < arrayOfShapes.length; i++ ) {
118            output += "\n\n" +
119               arrayOfShapes[ i ].getName() + ": " +
120               arrayOfShapes[ i ].toString() +
121               "\nArea = " +
122               precision2.format( arrayOfShapes[ i ].area() ) +
123               "\nVolume = " +
124               precision2.format( arrayOfShapes[ i ].volume() );
125         }
126
127         JOptionPane.showMessageDialog( null, output,
128            "Demonstrating Polymorphism",
129            JOptionPane.INFORMATION_MESSAGE );
130
131         System.exit( 0 );
132      } // end main
133   } // end class Test
```

Fig. 27.5 Point, circle, cylinder hierarchy with a **Shape** interface. (Part 1 of 2.)

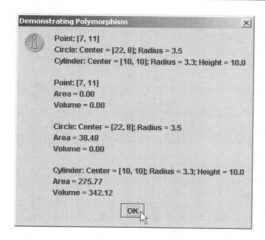

Fig. 27.5   Point, circle, cylinder hierarchy with a Shape interface. (Part 2 of 2.)

Another use of interfaces is to define a set of constants that can be used in many class definitions. Consider interface `Constants`

```
public interface Constants {
    public static final int ONE = 1;
    public static final int TWO = 2;
    public static final int THREE = 3;
}
```

Classes that implement interface `Constants` can use constants ONE, TWO and THREE anywhere in the class definition. A class can even use these constants by simply importing the interface, then referring to each constant as `Constants.ONE`, `Constants.TWO` and `Constants.THREE`. No methods are declared in this interface, so a class that implements the interface is not required to provide any implementation.

27.17 Inner Class Definitions

All the class definitions discussed to this point were defined at file scope—the classes have been defined in files, but not inside other classes in those files. Java provides a facility called *inner classes* in which classes can be defined inside other classes. Such classes can be complete class definitions or *anonymous inner class* definitions (classes without a name). Inner classes are used mainly in event handling. However, they have other benefits. For example, when defining a queue abstract data type one might use an inner class to represent the objects that store each item currently in the queue. Only the queue data structure requires knowledge of how the objects are stored internally, so the implementation can be hidden by defining an inner class as part of class `Queue`.

Inner classes are frequently used with GUI event handling, so we take this opportunity not only to show you inner class definitions, but also to demonstrate an application that executes in its own window. After you complete this example, you will be able to use in your applications the GUI techniques shown only in applets so far.

To demonstrate an inner class definition, Fig. 27.6 uses a simplified version of the Time2 class (renamed Time here) from Fig. 26.3. Class Time provides a default constructor, the same *set/get* methods as Fig. 26.3 and a toString method. Also, this program defines class TimeTestWindow as an application. The application executes in its own window.

```
1   // Fig. 27.6: Time.java
2   // Time class definition
3   import java.text.DecimalFormat;   // used for number formatting
4
5   // This class maintains the time in 24-hour format
6   public class Time extends Object {
7      private int hour;      // 0 - 23
8      private int minute;    // 0 - 59
9      private int second;    // 0 - 59
10
11     // Time constructor initializes each instance variable
12     // to zero. Ensures that Time object starts in a
13     // consistent state.
14     public Time() { setTime( 0, 0, 0 ); }
15
16     // Set a new time value using universal time. Perform
17     // validity checks on the data. Set invalid values to zero.
18     public void setTime( int h, int m, int s )
19     {
20        setHour( h );      // set the hour
21        setMinute( m );    // set the minute
22        setSecond( s );    // set the second
23     } // end method setTime
24
25     // set the hour
26     public void setHour( int h )
27        { hour = ( ( h >= 0 && h < 24 ) ? h : 0 ); }
28
29     // set the minute
30     public void setMinute( int m )
31        { minute = ( ( m >= 0 && m < 60 ) ? m : 0 ); }
32
33     // set the second
34     public void setSecond( int s )
35        { second = ( ( s >= 0 && s < 60 ) ? s : 0 ); }
36
37     // get the hour
38     public int getHour() { return hour; }
39
40     // get the minute
41     public int getMinute() { return minute; }
42
43     // get the second
44     public int getSecond() { return second; }
45
```

Fig. 27.6 Demonstrating an inner class in a windowed application—Time.java. (Part 1 of 2.)

```
46        // Convert to String in standard-time format
47        public String toString()
48        {
49            DecimalFormat twoDigits = new DecimalFormat( "00" );
50
51            return ( ( getHour() == 12 || getHour() == 0 ) ?
52                    12 : getHour() % 12 ) + ":" +
53                twoDigits.format( getMinute() ) + ":" +
54                twoDigits.format( getSecond() ) +
55                ( getHour() < 12 ? " AM" : " PM" );
56        } // end method toString
57    } // end class Time
```

Fig. 27.6   Demonstrating an inner class in a windowed application—Time.java. (Part 2 of 2.)

```
58    // Fig. 27.6: TimeTestWindow.java
59    // Demonstrating the Time class set and get methods
60    import java.awt.*;
61    import java.awt.event.*;
62    import javax.swing.*;
63
64    public class TimeTestWindow extends JFrame {
65        private Time t;
66        private JLabel hourLabel, minuteLabel, secondLabel;
67        private JTextField hourField, minuteField,
68                            secondField, display;
69        private JButton exitButton;
70
71        public TimeTestWindow()
72        {
73            super( "Inner Class Demonstration" );
74
75            t = new Time();
76
77            Container c = getContentPane();
78
79            // create an instance of the inner class
80            ActionEventHandler handler = new ActionEventHandler();
81
82            c.setLayout( new FlowLayout() );
83            hourLabel = new JLabel( "Set Hour" );
84            hourField = new JTextField( 10 );
85            hourField.addActionListener( handler );
86            c.add( hourLabel );
87            c.add( hourField );
88
89            minuteLabel = new JLabel( "Set minute" );
90            minuteField = new JTextField( 10 );
91            minuteField.addActionListener( handler );
92            c.add( minuteLabel );
```

Fig. 27.6   Demonstrating an inner class in a windowed application—TimeTestWindow.java. (Part 1 of 3.)

```
93          c.add( minuteField );
94
95          secondLabel = new JLabel( "Set Second" );
96          secondField = new JTextField( 10 );
97          secondField.addActionListener( handler );
98          c.add( secondLabel );
99          c.add( secondField );
100
101         display = new JTextField( 30 );
102         display.setEditable( false );
103         c.add( display );
104
105         exitButton = new JButton( "Exit" );
106         exitButton.addActionListener( handler );
107         c.add( exitButton );
108      } // end TimeTestWindow constructor
109
110      public void displayTime()
111      {
112         display.setText( "The time is: " + t );
113      } // end method displayTime
114
115      public static void main( String args[] )
116      {
117         TimeTestWindow window = new TimeTestWindow();
118
119         window.setSize( 400, 140 );
120         window.show();
121      } // end main
122
123      // Inner class definition for event handling
124      private class ActionEventHandler implements ActionListener {
125         public void actionPerformed( ActionEvent e )
126         {
127            if ( e.getSource() == exitButton )
128               System.exit( 0 );   // terminate the application
129            else if ( e.getSource() == hourField ) {
130               t.setHour(
131                  Integer.parseInt( e.getActionCommand() ) );
132               hourField.setText( "" );
133            }
134            else if ( e.getSource() == minuteField ) {
135               t.setMinute(
136                  Integer.parseInt( e.getActionCommand() ) );
137               minuteField.setText( "" );
138            }
139            else if ( e.getSource() == secondField ) {
140               t.setSecond(
141                  Integer.parseInt( e.getActionCommand() ) );
142               secondField.setText( "" );
143            }
144
```

Fig. 27.6 Demonstrating an inner class in a windowed application—
TimeTestWindow.java. (Part 2 of 3.)

```
145              displayTime();
146          } // end method actionPerformed
147      } // end class ActionEventHandler
148  } // end class TimeTestWindow
```

Line 64

```
public class TimeTestWindow extends JFrame {
```

indicates that class `TimeTestWindow` extends class *JFrame* (from package `jav-ax.swing`) rather than class `JApplet` (as shown in Fig. 26.3). Superclass `JFrame` provides the basic attributes and behaviors of a window—a *title bar* and buttons to *minimize*, *maximize* and *close* the window (all labeled in the first screen capture). Class `Time-TestWindow` uses the same GUI components as the applet of Fig. 26.3 except that the button (line 69) is now called `exitButton` and is used to terminate the application.

The `init` method of the applet has been replaced by a constructor (line 71) to guarantee that the window's GUI components are created as the application begins executing. Method `main` (line 115) defines a `new` object of class `TimeTestWindow` that results in a call to the constructor. Remember, `init` is a special method that is guaranteed to be called when an applet begins execution. However, this program is not an applet, so the `init` method is not guaranteed to be called.

Several new features appear in the constructor. Line 73 calls the superclass `JFrame` constructor with the string `"Inner Class Demonstration"`. This string is displayed in the title bar of the window by class `JFrame`'s constructor. Line 80

```
ActionEventHandler handler = new ActionEventHandler();
```

defines one instance of our inner class `ActionEventHandler` and assigns it to `handler`. This reference is passed to each of the four calls to `addActionListener` (lines 85, 91, 97 and 106) that register the event handlers for each GUI component that generates events in this example (`hourField`, `minuteField`, `secondField` and `exitButton`). Each call to `addActionListener` requires an object of type `ActionListener` to be passed as an argument. Actually, `handler` *is an* `ActionListener`. Line 124 (the first line of the inner class definition)

```
private class ActionEventHandler implements ActionListener {
```

indicates that inner class `ActionEventHandler` implements `ActionListener`. Thus, every object of type `ActionEventHandler` *is an* `ActionListener`. The requirement that `addActionListener` be passed an object of type `ActionListener` is satisfied! The *is a* relationship is used extensively in the GUI event handling mechanism, as you will see over the next several chapters. The inner class is defined as `private` because it will be used only in this class definition. Inner classes can be `private`, `protected` or `public`.

An inner class object has a special relationship with the outer class object that creates it. The inner class object is allowed to access directly all the instance variables and methods of the outer class object. The `actionPerformed` method (line 125) of class `Action-EventHandler` does just that. Throughout the method, the instance variables `t`, `exit-Button`, `hourField`, `minuteField` and `secondField` are used, as is method `displayTime`. Notice that none of these needs a "handle" to the outer class object. This is a free relationship created by the compiler between the outer class and its inner classes.

Software Engineering Observation 27.25

An inner class object is allowed to access directly all the instance variables and methods of the outer class object that defined it.

[*Note*: This application must be terminated by pressing the **Exit** button. Remember, an application that displays a window must be terminated with a call to System.exit(0). Also note that a window in Java is 0 pixels wide, 0 pixels high and not displayed by default. Lines 119 and 120 resize the window and show it on the screen.]

An inner class can also be defined inside a method of a class. Such an inner class has access to its outer class's members. However, it has limited access to the local variables for the method in which it is defined.

Software Engineering Observation 27.26

An inner class defined in a method is allowed to access directly all the instance variables and methods of the outer class object that defined it and any final local variables in the method.

The application of Fig. 27.7 modifies class TimeTestWindow to use *anonymous inner classes* defined in methods. An anonymous inner class has no name, so one object of the anonymous inner class must be created at the point where the class is defined in the program. We demonstrate anonymous inner classes two ways in this example. First, we use separate anonymous inner classes that implement an interface (ActionListener) to create event handlers for each of the three JTextFields hourField, minuteField and secondField. We also demonstrate how to terminate an application when the user clicks the Close box on the window. The event handler is defined as an anonymous inner class that extends a class (WindowAdapter). The Time class used is identical to Fig. 27.6, so it is not included here. Also, the **Exit** button has been removed from this example.

```java
1   // Fig. 27.7: TimeTestWindow.java
2   // Demonstrating the Time class set and get methods
3   import java.awt.*;
4   import java.awt.event.*;
5   import javax.swing.*;
6
7   public class TimeTestWindow extends JFrame {
8      private Time t;
9      private JLabel hourLabel, minuteLabel, secondLabel;
10     private JTextField hourField, minuteField,
11                        secondField, display;
12
13     public TimeTestWindow()
14     {
15        super( "Inner Class Demonstration" );
16
17        t = new Time();
18
19        Container c = getContentPane();
20
21        c.setLayout( new FlowLayout() );
22        hourLabel = new JLabel( "Set Hour" );
23        hourField = new JTextField( 10 );
24        hourField.addActionListener(
25           new ActionListener() {  // anonymous inner class
26              public void actionPerformed( ActionEvent e )
```

Fig. 27.7 Demonstrating anonymous inner classes—TimeTestWindow.java. (Part 1 of 4.)

```
27                   {
28                      t.setHour(
29                         Integer.parseInt( e.getActionCommand() ) );
30                      hourField.setText( "" );
31                      displayTime();
32                   } // end method actionPerformed
33                } // end anonymous inner class
34             ); // end addActionListener
35             c.add( hourLabel );
36             c.add( hourField );
37
38             minuteLabel = new JLabel( "Set minute" );
39             minuteField = new JTextField( 10 );
40             minuteField.addActionListener(
41                new ActionListener() {  // anonymous inner class
42                   public void actionPerformed( ActionEvent e )
43                   {
44                      t.setMinute(
45                         Integer.parseInt( e.getActionCommand() ) );
46                      minuteField.setText( "" );
47                      displayTime();
48                   }
49                }
50             );
51             c.add( minuteLabel );
52             c.add( minuteField );
53
54             secondLabel = new JLabel( "Set Second" );
55             secondField = new JTextField( 10 );
56             secondField.addActionListener(
57                new ActionListener() {  // anonymous inner class
58                   public void actionPerformed( ActionEvent e )
59                   {
60                      t.setSecond(
61                         Integer.parseInt( e.getActionCommand() ) );
62                      secondField.setText( "" );
63                      displayTime();
64                   } // end method actionPerformed
65                } // end anonymous inner class
66             ); // end addActionListener
67             c.add( secondLabel );
68             c.add( secondField );
69
70             display = new JTextField( 30 );
71             display.setEditable( false );
72             c.add( display );
73          } // end TimeTestWindow constructor
74
75          public void displayTime()
76          {
77             display.setText( "The time is: " + t );
78          } // end method displayTime
```

Fig. 27.7   Demonstrating anonymous inner classes—TimeTestWindow.java. (Part 2 of 4.)

```
79
80     public static void main( String args[] )
81     {
82        TimeTestWindow window = new TimeTestWindow();
83
84        window.addWindowListener(
85           new WindowAdapter() {
86              public void windowClosing( WindowEvent e )
87              {
88                 System.exit( 0 );
89              } // end method windowClosing
90           } // end anonymous inner class
91        ); // end addWindowListener
92
93        window.setSize( 400, 120 );
94        window.show();
95     } // end main
96  } // end class TimeTestWindow
```

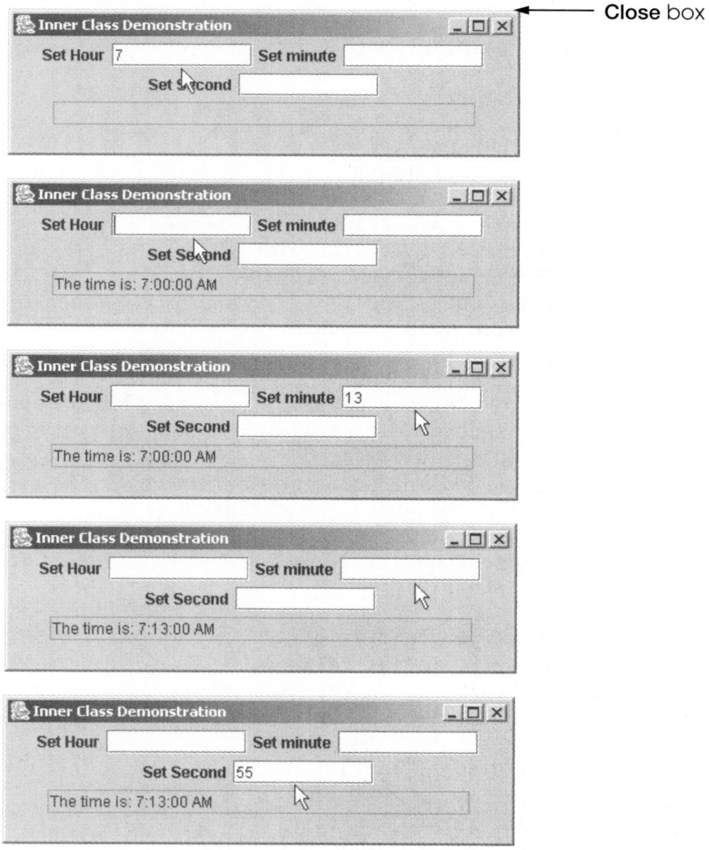

Fig. 27.7 Demonstrating anonymous inner classes—`TimeTestWindow.java`. (Part 3 of 4.)

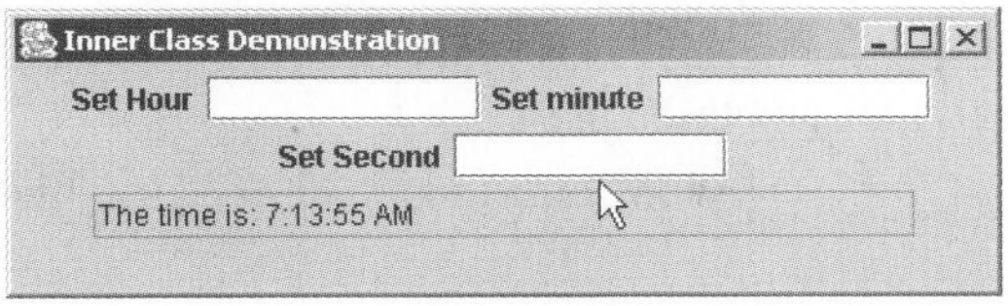

Fig. 27.7   Demonstrating anonymous inner classes—`TimeTestWindow.java`. (Part 4 of 4.)

Each of the three `JTextFields` that generate events in this program has a similar anonymous inner class to handle its events, so we discuss only the anonymous inner class for `hourField` here. Lines 24 through 34

```
hourField.addActionListener(
   new ActionListener() {  // anonymous inner class
      public void actionPerformed( ActionEvent e )
      {
         t.setHour(
            Integer.parseInt( e.getActionCommand() ) );
         hourField.setText( "" );
         displayTime();
      } // end method actionPerformed
   } // end anonymous inner class
); // end addActionListener
```

call `hourField`'s `addActionListener` method. The argument to this method must be an object that *is an* `ActionListener` (i.e., any object of a class that implements `Action-Listener`). Lines 25 through 33 use special Java syntax to define an anonymous inner class and create one object of that class that is passed as the argument to `addActionListener`. Line 25

```
new ActionListener() {  // anonymous inner class
```

uses operator `new` to create an object. The syntax `ActionListener()` begins the definition of an anonymous inner class that implements interface `ActionListener`. This is similar to beginning a class definition with

```
public class MyHandler implements ActionListener {
```

The parentheses after `ActionListener` indicate a call to the default constructor of the anonymous inner class.

The opening left brace ({) at the end of line 25 and the closing right brace (}) in line 33 define the body of the class. Lines 26 through 32 define the one method—`actionPer-formed`—that is required in any class that implements `ActionListener`. Method `actionPerformed` is called when the user presses *Enter* while typing in `hourField`.

Software Engineering Observation 27.27

When an anonymous inner class implements an interface, the class must define every method in the interface.

Method `main` creates one instance of class `TimeTestWindow` (line 82), sizes the window (line 93) and displays the window (line 94).

Windows generate a variety of events that are discussed in Chapter 29. For this example we discuss the one event generated when the user clicks the window's close box—a *window closing event*. Lines 84 through 91

```
window.addWindowListener(
    new WindowAdapter() {
        public void windowClosing( WindowEvent e )
        {
            System.exit( 0 );
        } // end method windowClosing
    } // end anonymous inner class
); // end addWindowListener
```

enable the user to terminate the application by clicking the window's **Close** box (labeled in the first screen capture. Method *addWindowListener* registers a window event listener. The argument to addWindowListener must be a reference to an object that *is a WindowListener* (package java.awt.event) (i.e., any object of a class that implements WindowListener). However, there are seven different methods that must be defined in every class that implements WindowListener and we only need one in this example—*windowClosing*. For event handling interfaces with more than one method, Java provides a corresponding class (called an *adapter class*) that already implements all the methods in the interface for you. All you need to do is extend the adapter class and override the methods you require in your program.

Common Programming Error 27.10

Extending an adapter class and misspelling the name of the method you are overriding is a logic error.

Lines 85 through 90 use special Java syntax to define an anonymous inner class and create one object of that class that is passed as the argument to addWindowListener. Line 85

```
new WindowAdapter() {
```

uses operator new to create an object. The syntax WindowAdapter() begins the definition of an anonymous inner class that extends class WindowAdapter. This is similar to beginning a class definition with

```
public class MyHandler extends WindowAdapter {
```

The parentheses after WindowAdapter indicate a call to the default constructor of the anonymous inner class. Class WindowAdapter implements interface WindowListener, so every WindowAdapter object *is a* WindowListener—the exact type required for the argument to addWindowListener.

The opening left brace ({) at the end of line 85 and the closing right brace (}) in line 90 define the body of the class. Lines 86 through 89 override the one method of WindowAdapter—windowClosing—that is called when the user clicks the window's **Close** box. In this example, windowClosing terminates the application with a call to System.exit(0).

In the last two examples, we have seen that inner classes can be used to create event handlers and that separate anonymous inner classes can be defined to handle events individually for each GUI component. In Chapter 29, we will revisit this concept as we discuss the event handling mechanism in detail.

27.18 Notes on Inner Class Definitions

This section presents several notes of interest to programmers regarding the definition and use of inner classes.

1. Compiling a class that contains inner classes results in a separate .class file for every class. Inner classes with names have the file name *OuterClassName$Inner-ClassName*.class. Anonymous inner classes have the file name *OuterClass-Name$#*.class, where # starts at 1 and is incremented for each anonymous inner class encountered during compilation.

2. Inner classes with class names can be defined as public, protected, package access or private and are subject to the same usage restrictions as other members of a class.

3. To access the outer class's this reference, use *OuterClassName*.this.

4. The outer class is responsible for creating objects of its inner classes. To create an object of another class's inner class, first create an object of the outer class and assign it to a reference (we will call it ref). Then use a statement of the following form to create an inner class object:

    OuterClassName.InnerClassName innerRef = ref.new *InnerClassName*();

5. An inner class can be declared static. A static inner class does not require an object of its outer class to be defined (whereas a non-static inner class does). A static inner class does not have access to the outer class's non-static members.

27.19 Type-Wrapper Classes for Primitive Types

Each of the primitive types has a *type-wrapper class*. These classes are called Character, Byte, Short, Integer, Long, Float, Double and Boolean. Each type-wrapper class enables you to manipulate primitive types as objects of class Object. Therefore, values of the primitive data types can be processed polymorphically if they are maintained as objects of the type-wrapper classes. Many of the classes we will develop or reuse manipulate and share Objects. These classes cannot polymorphically manipulate variables of primitive types, but they can polymorphically manipulate objects of the type-wrapper classes, because every class ultimately is derived from class Object.

Each of the numeric classes—Byte, Short, Integer, Long, Float and Double— inherits from class Number. Each of the type wrappers is declared final, so their methods are implicitly final and may not be overridden. Note that many of the methods that process the primitive data types are defined as static methods of the type-wrapper classes. If you need to manipulate a primitive value in your program, first refer to the documentation for the type-wrapper classes—the method you need may already be defined.

SUMMARY

- One of the keys to the power of object-oriented programming is achieving software reusability through inheritance.
- Through inheritance, a new class inherits the instance variables and methods of a previously defined superclass. In this case, the new class is referred to as a subclass.
- With single inheritance, a class is derived from one superclass. With multiple inheritance, a subclass inherits from multiple superclasses. Java does not support multiple inheritance, but Java does provide the notion of interfaces, which offer many of the benefits of multiple inheritance without the associated problems.
- A subclass normally adds instance variables and methods of its own, so a subclass generally is larger than its superclass. A subclass is more specific than its superclass and normally represents fewer objects.
- A subclass cannot access the `private` members of its superclass. A subclass can, however, access the `public`, `protected` and package access members of its superclass; the subclass must be in the superclass's package to use superclass members with package access.
- Inheritance enables software reusability, which saves time in development and encourages the use of previously proven and debugged high-quality software.
- Someday most software will be constructed from standardized reusable components exactly as hardware often is today.
- An object of a subclass can be treated as an object of its corresponding superclass, but the reverse is not true.
- A superclass exists in a hierarchical relationship with its subclasses.
- When a class is used with the mechanism of inheritance, it becomes either a superclass that supplies attributes and behaviors to other classes, or the class becomes a subclass that inherits those attributes and behaviors.
- An inheritance hierarchy can be arbitrarily deep within the physical limitations of a particular system, but most inheritance hierarchies have only a few levels.
- Hierarchies are useful for understanding and managing complexity. With software becoming increasingly complex, Java provides mechanisms for supporting hierarchical structures through inheritance and polymorphism.
- `protected` access serves as an intermediate level of protection between `public` access and `private` access. `protected` members of a superclass may be accessed by methods of the superclass, by methods of subclasses and by methods of classes in the same package; no other methods can access the `protected` members of a superclass.
- A superclass may be either a direct superclass of a subclass or an indirect superclass of a subclass. A direct superclass is the class that a subclass explicitly `extends`. An indirect superclass is inherited from several levels up the class hierarchy tree.
- When a superclass member is inappropriate for a subclass, the programmer may override that member in the subclass.
- It is important to distinguish between *is a* relationships and *has a* relationships. In a *has a* relationship, a class object has a reference to an object of another class as a member. In an *is a* relationship, an object of a subclass type may also be treated as an object of the superclass type. *Is a* is inheritance. *Has a* is composition.
- A subclass object can be assigned to a superclass reference. This kind of assignment makes sense because the subclass has members corresponding to each of the superclass members.

- A reference to a subclass object may be implicitly converted to a reference for a superclass object.

- It is possible to convert a superclass reference to a subclass reference by using an explicit cast. If the target is not a subclass object, a `ClassCastException` is thrown.

- A superclass specifies commonality. All classes derived from a superclass inherit the capabilities of that superclass. In the object-oriented design process, the designer looks for commonality among classes and factors it out to form superclasses. Subclasses are then customized beyond the capabilities inherited from the superclass.

- Reading a set of subclass declarations can be confusing because inherited superclass members are not listed in the subclass declarations, but these members are indeed present in the subclasses.

- With polymorphism, it becomes possible to design and implement systems that are more easily extensible. Programs can be written to process objects of types that may not exist when the program is under development.

- Polymorphic programming can eliminate the need for `switch` logic, thus avoiding the kinds of errors associated with `switch` logic.

- An abstract method is declared by preceding the method's definition with the keyword `abstract` in the superclass.

- There are many situations in which it is useful to define classes for which the programmer never intends to instantiate any objects. Such classes are called `abstract` classes. These are used only as superclasses, so we will normally refer to them as `abstract` superclasses. No objects of an `abstract` class may be instantiated.

- Classes from which objects can be instantiated are called concrete classes.

- A class is made abstract by declaring it with the keyword `abstract`.

- If a subclass is derived from a superclass with an `abstract` method without supplying a definition for that `abstract` method in the subclass, that method remains `abstract` in the subclass. Consequently, the subclass is also an `abstract` class (and cannot instantiate any objects).

- When a request is made through a superclass reference to use a method, Java chooses the correct overridden method in the subclass associated with the object.

- Through the use of polymorphism, one method call can cause different actions to occur, depending on the type of the object receiving the call.

- Although we cannot instantiate objects of `abstract` superclasses, we can declare references to `abstract` superclasses. Such references can then be used to enable polymorphic manipulations of subclass objects when such objects are instantiated from concrete classes.

- New classes are regularly added to systems. New classes are accommodated by dynamic method binding (also called late binding). The type of an object need not be known at compile time for a method call to be compiled. At execution time, the appropriate method of the receiving object is selected.

- With dynamic method binding, at execution time the call to a method is routed to the method version appropriate for the class of the object receiving the call.

- When a superclass provides a method, subclasses can override the method, but they do not have to override it. Thus a subclass can use a superclass's version of a method.

- An interface definition begins with the keyword `interface` and contains a set of `public abstract` methods. Interfaces may also contain `public final static` data.

- To use an interface, a class must specify that it `implements` the interface and that class must define every method in the interface with the number of arguments and the return type specified in the interface definition.

- An interface is typically used in place of an `abstract` class when there is no default implementation to inherit.
- When a class implements an interface, the same *is a* relationship provided by inheritance applies.
- To implement more than one interface, simply provide a comma-separated list of interface names after keyword `implements` in the class definition.
- Inner classes are defined inside the scope of other classes.
- An inner class can also be defined inside a method of a class. Such an inner class has access to its outer class's members and to the `final` local variables for the method in which it is defined.
- Inner class definitions are used mainly in event handling.
- Class `JFrame` provides the basic attributes and behaviors of a window—a title bar and buttons to minimize, maximize and close the window.
- An inner class object has a special relationship with the outer class object that creates it. The inner class object is allowed to access directly all the instance variables and methods of the outer class object.
- An anonymous inner class has no name, so one object of the anonymous inner class must be created at the point where the class is defined in the program.
- An anonymous inner class can implement an interface or extend a class.
- The event generated when the user clicks the window's **Close** box is a window closing event.
- Method `addWindowListener` registers a window event listener. Its argument must be a reference to an object that is a `WindowListener` (package `java.awt.event`).
- For event handling interfaces with more than one method, Java provides a corresponding class (called an adapter class) that already implements all the methods in the interface for you. Class `WindowAdapter` implements interface `WindowListener`, so every `WindowAdapter` object *is a* `WindowListener`.
- Compiling a class that contains inner classes results in a separate `.class` file for every class.
- Inner classes with class names can be defined as `public`, `protected`, package access or `private` and are subject to the same usage restrictions as other members of a class.
- To access the outer class's `this` reference, use *OuterClassName*.`this`.
- The outer class is responsible for creating objects of its non-`static` inner classes.
- An inner class can be declared `static`.

TERMINOLOGY

`abstract` class	dynamic method binding
`abstract` method	`extends`
`abstract` superclass	extensibility
abstraction	`final` class
anonymous inner class	`final` instance variable
base class	`final` method
`Boolean` class	garbage collection
`Character` class	*has a* relationship
class hierarchy	hierarchical relationship
client of a class	implementation inheritance
composition	implicit reference conversion
direct superclass	indirect superclass
`Double` class	inheritance

inheritance hierarchy
inner class
`Integer` class
interface
interface inheritance
is a relationship
`JFrame` class
late binding
`Long` class
member access control
member object
method overriding
multiple inheritance
`Number` class
`Object` class
object-oriented programming (OOP)
override a method
override an `abstract` method
overriding vs. overloading
polymorphism

`protected` member of a class
reference to an `abstract` class
`show` method
single inheritance
software reusability
standardized software components
subclass
subclass constructor
subclass reference
`super`
superclass
superclass constructor
superclass reference
`switch` logic
`this`
type-wrapper class
`WindowAdapter` class
`windowClosing` method
`WindowEvent` class
`WindowListener` interface

COMMON PROGRAMMING ERRORS

27.1   Treating a superclass object as a subclass object can cause errors.

27.2   Assigning an object of a superclass to a subclass reference (without a cast) is a syntax error.

27.3   It is a syntax error if a `super` call by a subclass to its superclass constructor is not the first statement in the subclass constructor.

27.4   It is a syntax error if the arguments to a `super` call by a subclass to its superclass constructor do not match the parameters specified in one of the superclass constructor definitions.

27.5   It is a syntax error if a method in a superclass and a method in its subclass have the same signature but a different return type.

27.6   Assigning a subclass object to a superclass reference, then attempting to reference subclass-only members with the superclass reference, is a syntax error.

27.7   Attempting to instantiate an object of an `abstract` class (i.e., a class that contains one or more `abstract` methods) is a syntax error.

27.8   It is a syntax error if a class with one or more `abstract` methods is not explicitly declared `abstract`.

27.9   Leaving a method of an `interface` undefined in a class that `implements` the interface results in a compile error indicating that the class must be declared `abstract`.

27.10 Extending an adapter class and misspelling the name of the method you are overriding is a logic error.

ERROR-PREVENTION TIPS

27.1   Hiding `private` members is a huge help in testing, debugging and correctly modifying systems. If a subclass could access its superclass's `private` members, it would then be possible for classes derived from that subclass to access that data as well, and so on. This would propagate access to what is supposed to be `private` data, and the benefits of information hiding would be lost throughout the class hierarchy.

27.2   An interesting consequence of using polymorphism is that programs take on a simplified appearance. They contain less branching logic in favor of simpler sequential code. This simplification facilitates testing, debugging and program maintenance.

PERFORMANCE TIPS

27.1   If classes produced through inheritance are larger than they need to be, memory and processing resources may be wasted. Inherit from the class "closest" to what you need.

27.2   The compiler can decide to inline a `final` method call and will do so for small, simple `final` methods. Inlining does not violate encapsulation or information hiding (but does improve performance because it eliminates the overhead of making a method call).

27.3   Pipelined processors can improve performance by executing portions of the next several instructions simultaneously, but not if those instructions follow a method call. Inlining (which the compiler can perform on a `final` method) can improve performance in these processors because it eliminates the out-of-line transfer of control associated with a method call.

27.4   Polymorphism as implemented with dynamic method binding is efficient.

27.5   The kinds of polymorphic manipulations made possible with dynamic binding can also be accomplished by using hand-coded `switch` logic based on type fields in objects. The polymorphic code generated by the Java compiler runs with comparable performance to efficiently coded `switch` logic.

SOFTWARE ENGINEERING OBSERVATIONS

27.1   A subclass cannot directly access `private` members of its superclass.

27.2   Constructors are never inherited—they are specific to the class in which they are defined.

27.3   If an object has been assigned to a reference of one of its superclasses, it is acceptable to cast that object back to its own type. In fact, this must be done to send that object any of its messages that do not appear in that superclass.

27.4   Every class in Java extends `Object` unless specified otherwise in the first line of the class definition. Thus, class `Object` is the superclass of the entire Java class hierarchy.

27.5   A redefinition of a superclass method in a subclass need not have the same signature as the superclass method. Such a redefinition is not method overriding but is simply an example of method overloading.

27.6   Any object can be converted to a `String` with an explicit or implicit call to the object's `toString` method.

27.7   Each class should override method `toString` to return useful information about objects of that class.

27.8   Creating a subclass does not affect its superclass's source code or the superclass's Java bytecodes; the integrity of a superclass is preserved by inheritance.

27.9   Just as the designer of non-object-oriented systems should avoid unnecessary proliferation of functions, the designer of object-oriented systems should avoid unnecessary proliferation of classes. Proliferating classes creates management problems and can hinder software reusability simply because it is more difficult for a potential user of a class to locate that class in a huge collection. The trade-off is to create fewer classes, each providing substantial additional functionality, but such classes might be too rich for certain users.

27.10   In an object-oriented system, classes are often closely related. "Factor out" common attributes and behaviors and place these in a superclass. Then use inheritance to form subclasses without having to repeat common attributes and behaviors.

27.11 Modifications to a superclass do not require subclasses to change as long as the public interface to the superclass remains unchanged.

27.12 When a subclass chooses not to redefine a method, the subclass simply inherits its immediate superclass's method definition.

27.13 A class declared `final` cannot be extended and every method is implicitly `final`.

27.14 An `abstract` can still have instance data and non-`abstract` methods subject to the normal rules of inheritance by subclasses. An `abstract` class can also have constructors.

27.15 If a subclass is derived from a superclass with an `abstract` method, and if no definition is supplied in the subclass for that `abstract` method (i.e., if that method is not overridden in the subclass), that method remains `abstract` in the subclass. Consequently, the subclass is also an `abstract` class and must be explicitly declared as an `abstract` class.

27.16 The ability to declare an `abstract` method gives the class designer considerable power over how subclasses will be implemented in a class hierarchy. Any new class that wants to inherit from this class is forced to override the `abstract` method (either directly or by inheriting from a class that has overridden the method). Otherwise, that new class will contain an `abstract` method and thus be an `abstract` class unable to instantiate objects.

27.17 With polymorphism, the programmer can deal in generalities and let the execution-time environment concern itself with the specifics. The programmer can command a wide variety of objects to behave in manners appropriate to those objects without even knowing the types of those objects.

27.18 Polymorphism promotes extensibility: Software written to invoke polymorphic behavior is written independent of the types of the objects to which messages (i.e., method calls) are sent. Thus, new types of objects that can respond to existing messages can be added into such a system without modifying the base system.

27.19 If a method is declared `final` it cannot be overridden in subclasses, so that method calls may not be sent polymorphically to objects of those subclasses. The method call may still be sent to subclasses but they will all respond identically rather than polymorphically.

27.20 An `abstract` class defines a common interface for the various members of a class hierarchy. The `abstract` class contains methods that will be defined in the subclasses. All classes in the hierarchy can use this same interface through polymorphism.

27.21 Hierarchies designed for implementation inheritance tend to have their functionality high in the hierarchy—each new subclass inherits one or more methods that were defined in a superclass and uses the superclass definitions.

27.22 Hierarchies designed for interface inheritance tend to have their functionality lower in the hierarchy—a superclass specifies one or more methods that should be called identically for each object in the hierarchy (i.e., they have the same signature), but the individual subclasses provide their own implementations of the method(s).

27.23 A subclass always inherits the most recently defined version of each `public` and `protected` method from its direct and indirect superclasses.

27.24 All methods of class `Object` can be called using a reference of an interface data type—a reference refers to an object and all objects have the methods defined by class `Object`.

27.25 An inner class object is allowed to access directly all the instance variables and methods of the outer class object that defined it.

27.26 An inner class defined in a method is allowed to access directly all the instance variables and methods of the outer class object that defined it and any `final` local variables in the method.

27.27 When an anonymous inner class implements an interface, the class must define every method in the interface.

SELF-REVIEW EXERCISES

27.1   Fill in the blanks in each of the following:

    a) If the class `Alpha` inherits from the class `Beta`, class `Alpha` is called the _____ class and class `Beta` is called the class.

    b) Inheritance enables _____, which saves time in development and encourages using previously proven and high-quality software components.

    c) An object of a class can be treated as an object of its corresponding _____ class.

    d) The four member access specifiers are _____, _____, and _____.

    e) A *has a* relationship between classes represents _____ and an *is a* relationship between classes represents _____.

    f) Using polymorphism helps eliminate _____ logic.

    g) If a class contains one or more `abstract` methods, it is a(n) _____ class.

    h) A method call resolved at run-time is referred to as _____ binding.

27.2   a) A subclass may call any non-`private` superclass method by prepending _____ to the method call.

    b) A superclass typically represents a larger number of objects than its subclass represents. (*true/false*).

    c) A subclass typically encapsulates less functionality than does its superclass. (*true/false*).

ANSWERS TO SELF-REVIEW EXERCISES

27.1   a) sub, super. b) software reusability. c) sub, super. d) `public`, `protected`, `private` and package access. e) composition, inheritance. f) `switch`. g) `abstract`. h) dynamic.

27.2   a) `super`
    b) true
    c) false

EXERCISES

27.3   Consider the class `Bicycle`. Given your knowledge of some common components of bicycles, show a class hierarchy in which the class `Bicycle` inherits from other classes, which, in turn, inherit from yet other classes. Discuss the instantiation of various objects of class `Bicycle`. Discuss inheritance from class `Bicycle` for other closely related subclasses.

27.4   Define each of the following terms: single inheritance, multiple inheritance, interface, superclass and subclass.

27.5   Discuss why casting a superclass reference to a subclass reference is potentially dangerous.

27.6   Distinguish between single inheritance and multiple inheritance. Why does Java not support multiple inheritance? What feature of Java helps realize the benefits of multiple inheritance?

27.7   (*True/False*) A subclass is generally smaller than its superclass.

27.8   (*True/False*) A subclass object is also an object of that subclass's superclass.

27.9   Rewrite the `Point`, `Circle`, `Cylinder` program of Fig. 27.4 as a `Point`, `Square`, `Cube` program. Do this two ways—once with inheritance and once with composition.

27.10   In the chapter, we stated, "When a superclass method is inappropriate for a subclass, that method can be overridden in the subclass with an appropriate implementation." If this is done, does the subclass-is-a-superclass-object relationship still hold? Explain your answer.

27.11   How is it that polymorphism enables you to program "in the general" rather than "in the specific"? Discuss the key advantages of programming "in the general."

27.12 Discuss the problems of programming with switch logic. Explain why polymorphism is an effective alternative to using switch logic.

27.13 Distinguish between inheriting interface and inheriting implementation. How do inheritance hierarchies designed for inheriting interface differ from those designed for inheriting implementation?

27.14 Distinguish between non-abstract methods and abstract methods.

27.15 (*True/False*) All methods in an abstract superclass must be declared abstract.

27.16 Suggest one or more levels of abstract superclasses for the Shape hierarchy discussed in the beginning of this chapter (the first level is Shape and the second level consists of the classes TwoDimensionalShape and ThreeDimensionalShape).

27.17 How does polymorphism promote extensibility?

27.18 You have been asked to develop a flight simulator that will have elaborate graphical outputs. Explain why polymorphic programming would be especially effective for a problem of this nature.

27.19 (*Drawing Application*) Modify the drawing program of Exercise 26.11 to create a drawing application that draws random lines, rectangles and ovals. [*Note:* Like an applet, a JFrame has a paint method that you can override to draw on the background of the JFrame.]

For this exercise, modify the MyLine, MyOval and MyRect classes of Exercise 26.11 to create the class hierarchy in Figure 27.8. The classes of the MyShape hierarchy should be "smart" shape classes where objects of these classes know how to draw themselves (if provided with a Graphics object that tells them where to draw). The only switch or if/else logic in this program should be to determine the type of shape object to create (use random numbers to pick the shape type and the coordinates of each shape). Once an object from this hierarchy is created, it will be manipulated for the rest of its lifetime as a superclass MyShape reference.

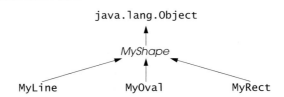

Fig. 27.8 The MyShape hierarchy.

Class MyShape in Figure 27.8 *must* be abstract. The only data representing the coordinates of the shapes in the hierarchy should be defined in class MyShape. Lines, rectangles and ovals can all be drawn if you know two points in space. Lines require *x1*, *y1*, *x2* and *y2* coordinates. The drawLine method of the Graphics class will connect the two points supplied with a line. If you have the same four coordinate values (*x1*, *y1*, *x2* and *y2*) for ovals and rectangles, you can calculate the four arguments needed to draw them. Each requires an upper-left *x*-coordinate value (minimum of the two *x*-coordinate values), an upper-left *y*-coordinate value (minimum of the two *y*-coordinate values), a *width* (difference between the two *x*-coordinate values; must be nonnegative) and a *height* (difference between the two *y*-coordinate values; must be nonnegative). [*Note:* In Chapter 29, each *x,y* pair will be captured using mouse events from mouse interactions between the user and the program's background. These coordinates will be stored in an appropriate shape object as selected by the user. As you begin the exercise, you will use random coordinate values as arguments to the constructor.]

In addition to the data for the hierarchy, class MyShape should define at least the following methods:

a) A constructor with no arguments that sets the coordinates to 0.
b) A constructor with arguments that sets the coordinates to the supplied values.
c) *Set* methods for each individual piece of data that allow the programmer to independently set any piece of data for a shape in the hierarchy (e.g., if you have an instance variable x1, you should have a method setX1).
d) *Get* methods for each individual piece of data that allow the programmer to independently retrieve any piece of data for a shape in the hierarchy (e.g., if you have an instance variable x1, you should have a method getX1).
e) The abstract method
```
public abstract void draw( Graphics g );
```
This method will be called from the program's paint method to draw a shape onto the screen.

The preceding methods are required. If you would like to provide more methods for flexibility, please do so. However, be sure that any method you define in this class is a method that would be used by *all* shapes in the hierarchy.

All data *must* be private to class MyShape in this exercise (this forces you to use proper encapsulation of the data and provide proper *set/get* methods to manipulate the data). You are not allowed to define new data that can be derived from existing information. As explained previously, the upper-left *x*, upper-left *y*, *width* and *height* needed to draw an oval or rectangle can be calculated if you already know two points in space. All subclasses of MyShape should provide two constructors that mimic those provided by class MyShape.

Objects of the MyOval and MyRect classes should not calculate their upper-left *x*-coordinate, upper-left *y*-coordinate, *width* and *height* until they are about to draw. Never modify the *x1*, *y1*, *x2* and *y2* coordinates of a MyOval or MyRect object to prepare to draw them. Instead, use the temporary results of the calculations described above. This will help us enhance the program in Chapter 29 by allowing the user to select each shape's coordinates with the mouse.

There should be no MyLine, MyOval or MyRect references in the program—only MyShape references that refer to MyLine, MyOval and MyRect objects are allowed. The program should keep an array of MyShape references containing all shapes. The program's paint method should walk through the array of MyShape references and draw every shape (i.e., call every shape's draw method).

Begin by defining class MyShape, class MyLine and an application to test your classes. The application should have a MyShape instance variable that can refer to one MyLine object (created in the application's constructor). The paint method (for your subclass of JFrame) should draw the shape with a statement like

```
currentShape.draw( g );
```

where currentShape is the MyShape reference and g is the Graphics object that the shape will use to draw itself on the background of the window.

Next, change the single MyShape reference into an array of MyShape references and hard code several MyLine objects into the program for drawing. The application's paint method should walk through the array of shapes and draw every shape.

After the preceding part is working, you should define the MyOval and MyRect classes and add objects of these classes into the existing array. For now, all the shape objects should be created in the constructor for your subclass of JFrame. In Chapter 29, we will create the objects when the user chooses a shape and begins drawing it with the mouse.

28

Java Graphics and Java2D

Objectives

- To understand graphics contexts and graphics objects.
- To understand and be able to manipulate colors.
- To understand and be able to manipulate fonts.
- To understand and be able to use Graphics methods for drawing lines, rectangles, rectangles with rounded corners, three-dimensional rectangles, ovals, arcs and polygons.
- To use methods of class Graphics2D from the Java2D API to draw lines, rectangles, rectangles with rounded corners, ellipses, arcs and general paths.
- To be able to specify Paint and Stroke characteristics of shapes displayed with Graphics2D.

One picture is worth ten thousand words.
Chinese proverb

Treat nature in terms of the cylinder, the sphere, the cone, all in perspective.
Paul Cézanne

Nothing ever becomes real till it is experienced—even a proverb is no proverb to you till your life has illustrated it.
John Keats

A picture shows me at a glance what it takes dozens of pages of a book to expound.
Ivan Sergeyevich

Outline

28.1 Introduction

In this chapter, we overview several of Java's capabilities for drawing two-dimensional
shapes, controlling colors and controlling fonts. One of Java's initial appeals was its support for graphics that enabled Java programmers to visually enhance their applets and applications. Java now contains many more sophisticated drawing capabilities as part of the
Java2D API. The chapter begins with an introduction to many of the original drawing capabilities of Java. Next, we present several of the new and more powerful Java2D capabilities, such as controlling the style of lines used to draw shapes and controlling how shapes
are filled with color and patterns.

Figure 28.1 shows a portion of the Java class hierarchy that includes several of the
basic graphics classes and Java2D API classes and interfaces covered in this chapter. Class
`Color` contains methods and constants for manipulating colors. Class `Font` contains
methods and constants for manipulating fonts. Class `FontMetrics` contains methods for
obtaining font information. Class `Polygon` contains methods for creating polygons. Class
`Graphics` contains methods for drawing strings, lines, rectangles and other shapes. The
bottom half of the figure lists several classes and interfaces from the Java2D API. Class
`BasicStroke` helps specify the drawing characteristics of lines. Classes `GradientPaint`
and `TexturePaint` help specify the characteristics for filling shapes with colors or patterns. Classes `GeneralPath`, `Arc2D`, `Ellipse2D`, `Line2D`, `Rectangle2D` and
`RoundRectangle2D` define a variety of Java2D shapes.

To begin drawing in Java, we must first understand Java's *coordinate system*
(Fig. 28.2), which is a scheme for identifying every possible point on the screen. By
default, the upper-left corner of a GUI component (such as an applet or a window) has the
coordinates (0, 0). A coordinate pair is composed of an *x-coordinate* (the *horizontal coor-
dinate*) and a *y-coordinate* (the *vertical coordinate*). The *x*-coordinate is the horizontal distance moving right from the upper-left corner. The *y*-coordinate is the vertical distance
moving down from the upper-left corner. The *x-axis* describes every horizontal coordinate,
and the *y-axis* describes every vertical coordinate.

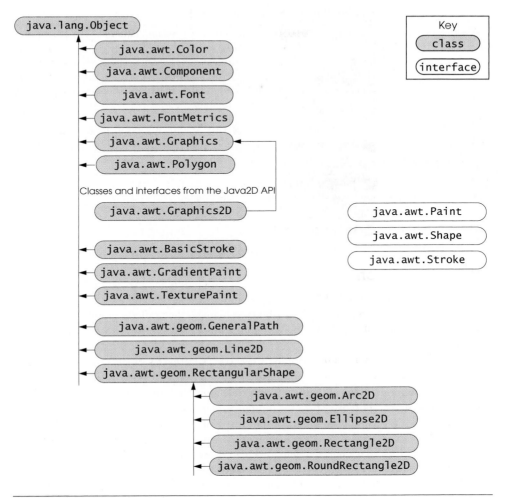

Fig. 28.1 Some classes and interfaces used in this chapter from Java's original graphics capabilities and from the Java2D API.

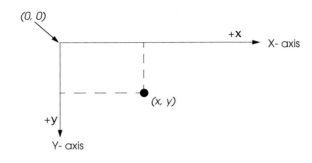

Fig. 28.2 Java coordinate system. Units are measured in pixels.

Software Engineering Observation 28.1

The upper-left coordinate (0, 0) of a window is actually behind the title bar of the window. For this reason, drawing coordinates should be adjusted to draw inside the borders of the window. Class Container *(a superclass of all windows in Java) has method* getInsets *that returns an* Insets *object (package* java.awt*) for this purpose. An* Insets *object has four* public *members—*top, bottom, left *and* right*—that represent the number of pixels from each edge of the window to the drawing area for the window.*

Text and shapes are displayed on the screen by specifying coordinates. Coordinate units are measured in *pixels*. A pixel is a display monitor's smallest unit of resolution.

Portability Tip 28.1

Different display monitors have different resolutions (i.e., the density of pixels varies). This may cause graphics to appear to be different sizes on different monitors.

28.2 Graphics Contexts and Graphics Objects

A Java *graphics context* enables drawing on the screen. A Graphics object manages a graphics context by controlling how information is drawn. Graphics objects contain methods for drawing, font manipulation, color manipulation and the like. Every applet we have seen in the text that performs drawing on the screen has used the Graphics object g (the argument to the applet's paint method) to manage the applet's graphics context. In this chapter, we demonstrate drawing in applications. However, every technique shown here can be used in applets.

The Graphics class is an abstract class (i.e., Graphics objects cannot be instantiated). This contributes to Java's portability. Drawing is performed differently on each platform that supports Java, so there cannot be one class that implements drawing capabilities on all systems. For example, the graphics capabilities that enable a PC running Microsoft Windows to draw a rectangle are different from the graphics capabilities that enable a UNIX workstation to draw a rectangle—and those are both different from the graphics capabilities that enable a Macintosh to draw a rectangle. When Java is implemented on each platform, a derived class of Graphics is created that actually implements all the drawing capabilities. This implementation is hidden from us by the Graphics class, which supplies the interface that enables us to write programs that use graphics in a platform-independent manner.

Class Component is the superclass for many of the classes in the java.awt package (we discuss class Component in Chapter 29). Component method paint takes a Graphics object as an argument. This object is passed to the paint method by the system when a paint operation is required for a Component. The header for the paint method is

```
public void paint( Graphics g )
```

The paint object paint receives a reference to an object of the system's derived Graphics class. The preceding method header should look familiar to you—it is the same one we have been using in our applet classes. Actually, the Component class is an indirect base class of class JApplet—the superclass of every applet in this book. Many capabilities of class JApplet are inherited from class Component. The paint method defined in class Component does nothing by default—it must be overridden by the programmer.

The `paint` method is seldom called directly by the programmer because drawing graphics is an *event-driven process*. When an applet executes, the `paint` method is automatically called (after calls to the `JApplet`'s `init` and `start` methods). For `paint` to be called again, an *event* must occur (such as covering and uncovering the applet). Similarly, when any `Component` is displayed, that `Component`'s `paint` method is called.

If the programmer needs to call `paint`, a call is made to the `paint` class `repaint` method. Method `repaint` requests a call to the `Component` class `update` method as soon as possible to clear the `Component`'s background of any previous drawing, then `update` calls `paint` directly. The `repaint` method is frequently called by the programmer to force a `paint` operation. Method `repaint` should not be overridden because it performs some system-dependent tasks. The `update` method is seldom called directly and sometimes overridden. Overriding the `update` method is useful for "smoothing" animations (i.e., reducing "flicker") as we will discuss in Chapter 30, Java Multimedia: Images, Animation and Audio. The headers for `repaint` and `update` are

```
public void repaint()
public void update( Graphics g )
```

Method `update` takes a `Graphics` object as an argument, which is supplied automatically by the system when `update` is called.

In this chapter we focus on the `paint` method. In the next chapter we concentrate more on the event-driven nature of graphics and discuss the `repaint` and `update` methods in more detail. We also discuss class `JComponent`—a superclass of many GUI components in package `javax.swing`. Subclasses of `JComponent` typically paint from their `paint-Component` methods.

28.3 Color Control

Colors enhance the appearance of a program and help convey meaning. For example, a traffic light has three different color lights—red indicates stop, yellow indicates caution and green indicates go.

Class *Color* defines methods and constants for manipulating colors in a Java program. The predefined color constants are summarized in Fig. 28.3, and several color methods and constructors are summarized in Fig. 28.4. Note that two of the methods in Fig. 28.4 are `Graphics` methods that are specific to colors.

Color Constant	Color	RGB value
`public final static Color orange`	orange	255, 200, 0
`public final static Color pink`	pink	255, 175, 175
`public final static Color cyan`	cyan	0, 255, 255
`public final static Color magenta`	magenta	255, 0, 255
`public final static Color yellow`	yellow	255, 255, 0
`public final static Color black`	black	0, 0, 0

Fig. 28.3 *Color* class `static` constants and RGB values. (Part 1 of 2.)

Color Constant	Color	RGB value
public final static Color white	white	255, 255, 255
public final static Color gray	gray	128, 128, 128
public final static Color lightGray	light gray	192, 192, 192
public final static Color darkGray	dark gray	64, 64, 64
public final static Color red	red	255, 0, 0
public final static Color green	green	0, 255, 0
public final static Color blue	blue	0, 0, 255

Fig. 28.3 Color class static constants and RGB values. (Part 2 of 2.)

Method	Description

public Color(int r, int g, int b)

Creates a color based on red, green and blue contents expressed as integers from 0 to 255.

public Color(float r, float g, float b)

Creates a color based on red, green and blue contents expressed as floating-point values from 0.0 to 1.0.

public int getRed()   // Color class

Returns a value between 0 and 255 representing the red content.

public int getGreen()   // Color class

Returns a value between 0 and 255 representing the green content.

public int getBlue()   // Color class

Returns a value between 0 and 255 representing the blue content.

public Color getColor()   // Graphics class

Returns a Color object representing the current color for the graphics context.

public void setColor(Color c) // Graphics class

Sets the current color for drawing with the graphics context.

Fig. 28.4 Color methods and color-related Graphics methods.

Every color is created from a red, a green and a blue component. Together these components are called *RGB values*. All three RGB components can be integers in the range 0 to 255, or all three RGB parts can be floating-point values in the range 0.0 to 1.0. The first RGB part defines the amount of red, the second defines the amount of green and the third defines the amount of blue. The larger the RGB value, the greater the amount of that particular color. Java enables the programmer to choose from $256 \times 256 \times 256$ (or approximately 16.7 million) colors. However, not all computers are capable of displaying all these colors. If this is the case, the computer will display the closest color it can.

Common Programming Error 28.1

Spelling any static Color class constant with an initial capital letter is a syntax error.

Two Color constructors are shown in Fig. 28.4—one that takes three int arguments and one that takes three float arguments, with each argument specifying the amount of red, green and blue, respectively. The int values must be between 0 and 255 and the float values must be between 0.0 and 1.0. The new Color object will have the specified amounts of red, green and blue. Color methods getRed, getGreen and getBlue return integer values from 0 to 255 representing the amount of red, green and blue, respectively. Graphics method getColor returns a Color object representing the current drawing color. Graphics method setColor sets the current drawing color.

The application of Fig. 28.5 demonstrates several methods from Fig. 28.4 by drawing filled rectangles and strings in several different colors.

```java
1   // Fig. 28.5: ShowColors.java
2   // Demonstrating Colors
3   import java.awt.*;
4   import javax.swing.*;
5   import java.awt.event.*;
6
7   public class ShowColors extends JFrame {
8      public ShowColors()
9      {
10         super( "Using colors" );
11
12         setSize( 400, 130 );
13         show();
14      } // end ShowColors constructor
15
16      public void paint( Graphics g )
17      {
18         // set new drawing color using integers
19         g.setColor( new Color( 255, 0, 0 ) );
20         g.fillRect( 25, 25, 100, 20 );
21         g.drawString( "Current RGB: " + g.getColor(), 130, 40 );
22
23         // set new drawing color using floats
24         g.setColor( new Color( 0.0f, 1.0f, 0.0f ) );
25         g.fillRect( 25, 50, 100, 20 );
26         g.drawString( "Current RGB: " + g.getColor(), 130, 65 );
27
28         // set new drawing color using static Color objects
29         g.setColor( Color.blue );
30         g.fillRect( 25, 75, 100, 20 );
31         g.drawString( "Current RGB: " + g.getColor(), 130, 90 );
32
33         // display individual RGB values
34         Color c = Color.magenta;
35         g.setColor( c );
```

Fig. 28.5 Demonstrating setting and getting a Color. (Part 1 of 2.)

```
36            g.fillRect( 25, 100, 100, 20 );
37            g.drawString( "RGB values: " + c.getRed() + ", " +
38               c.getGreen() + ", " + c.getBlue(), 130, 115 );
39       } // end method paint
40
41       public static void main( String args[] )
42       {
43          ShowColors app = new ShowColors();
44
45          app.addWindowListener(
46             new WindowAdapter() {
47                public void windowClosing( WindowEvent e )
48                {
49                   System.exit( 0 );
50                } // end method windowClosing
51             } // end anonymous inner class
52          ); // end addWindowListener
53       } // end method main
54    } // end class ShowColors
```

Fig. 28.5   Demonstrating setting and getting a Color. (Part 2 of 2.)

When the application begins execution, class ShowColors's paint method is called to paint the window. Line 19

```
g.setColor( new Color( 255, 0, 0 ) );
```

uses Graphics method setColor to set the current drawing color. Method setColor receives a Color object. The expression new Color(255, 0, 0) creates a new Color object that represents red (red value 255 and 0 for the green and blue values). Line 20

```
g.fillRect( 25, 25, 100, 20 );
```

uses Graphics method fillRect to draw a filled rectangle in the current color. The first two parameters to method fillRect are the *x* and *y* coordinates of the upper-left-hand corner of the rectangle. The third and fourth parameters are the width and height of the rectangle, respectively. Line 21

```
g.drawString( "Current RGB: " + g.getColor(), 130, 40 );
```

uses Graphics method drawString to draw a String in the current color. The expression g.getColor() retrieves the current color from the Graphics object. The returned Color is concatenated with string "Current RGB: " resulting in an implicit call to class Color's toString method. Notice that the String representation of the Color object contains the class name and package (java.awt.Color), and the red, green and blue values.

Lines 24 through 26 and lines 29 through 31 perform the same tasks again. Line 24

    g.setColor(new Color(0.0f, 1.0f, 0.0f));

uses the Color constructor with three float arguments to create the color green (0.0f for red, 1.0f for green and 0.0f for blue). Note the syntax of the constants. The letter f appended to a floating-point constant indicates that the constant should be treated as type float. Normally, floating-point constants are treated as type double.

Line 29 sets the current drawing color to one of the predefined Color constants (Color.blue). Note that the new operator is not needed to create the constant. The Color constants are static, so they are defined when class Color is loaded into memory at execution time.

The statement in lines 37 and 38 demonstrates Color methods getRed, getGreen and getBlue on the predefined Color.magenta object.

Software Engineering Observation 28.2

To change the color, you must create a new Color object (or use one of the predefined Color constants); there are no set *methods in class Color to change the characteristics of the current color.*

One of the newer features of Java is the predefined GUI component *JColorChooser* (package javax.swing) for selecting colors. The application of Fig. 28.6 enables you to press a button to display a JColorChooser dialog. When you select a color and press the dialog's **OK** button, the background color of the application window changes colors.

```
1   // Fig. 28.6: ShowColors2.java
2   // Demonstrating JColorChooser
3   import java.awt.*;
4   import javax.swing.*;
5   import java.awt.event.*;
6
7   public class ShowColors2 extends JFrame {
8       private JButton changeColor;
9       private Color color = Color.lightGray;
10      private Container c;
11
12      public ShowColors2()
13      {
14          super( "Using JColorChooser" );
15
16          c = getContentPane();
17          c.setLayout( new FlowLayout() );
18
19          changeColor = new JButton( "Change Color" );
20          changeColor.addActionListener(
21             new ActionListener() {
22                public void actionPerformed( ActionEvent e )
23                {
24                   color =
25                      JColorChooser.showDialog( ShowColors2.this,
26                         "Choose a color", color );
```

Fig. 28.6   Demonstrating the JColorChooser dialog. (Part 1 of 3.)

```
27
28                    if ( color == null )
29                        color = Color.lightGray;
30
31                    c.setBackground( color );
32                    c.repaint();
33                } // end method actionPerformed
34             } // end anonymous inner class
35          ); // end addActionListener
36          c.add( changeColor );
37
38          setSize( 400, 130 );
39          show();
40       } // end ShowColors2 constructor
41
42       public static void main( String args[] )
43       {
44          ShowColors2 app = new ShowColors2();
45
46          app.addWindowListener(
47             new WindowAdapter() {
48                public void windowClosing( WindowEvent e )
49                {
50                   System.exit( 0 );
51                } // end method windowClosing
52             } // end anonymous inner class
53          ); // end addWindowListener
54       } // end main
55    } // end class ShowColors2
```

Select a color
from one of
the color
swatches.

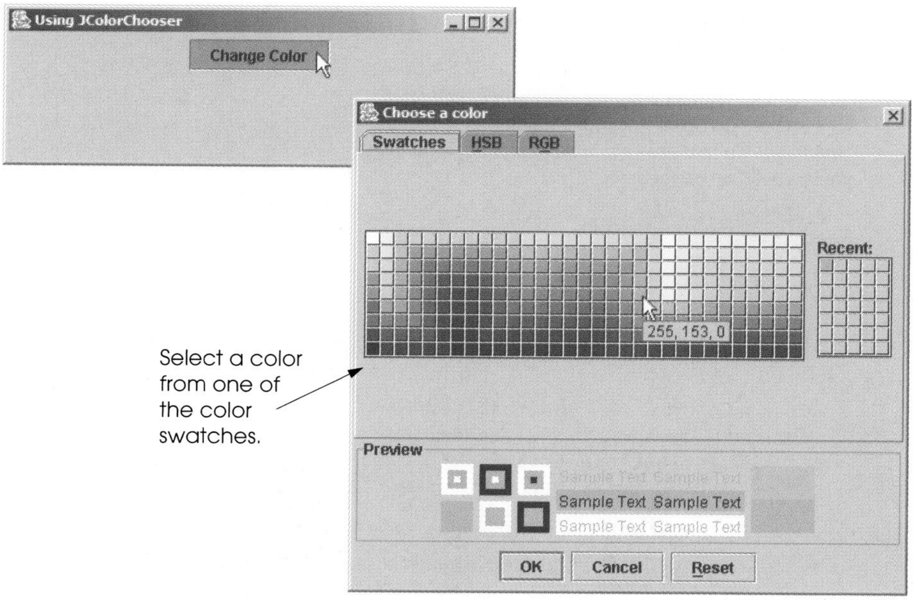

Fig. 28.6 Demonstrating the JColorChooser dialog. (Part 2 of 3.)

Fig. 28.6   Demonstrating the `JColorChooser` dialog. (Part 3 of 3.)

Lines 24 through 26 (from method `actionPerformed` for `changeColor`)

```
color =
    JColorChooser.showDialog( ShowColors2.this,
        "Choose a color", color );
```

use `static` method *showDialog* of class `JColorChooser` to display the color chooser dialog. This method returns the selected `Color` object (or `null` if the user presses **Cancel** or closes the dialog without pressing **OK**).

Method `showDialog` takes three arguments—a reference to its parent `Component`, a `String` to display in the title bar of the dialog and the initial selected `Color` for the dialog. The parent component is the window from which the dialog is displayed. While the color chooser dialog is on the screen, the user cannot interact with the parent component. This type of dialog is called a *modal dialog* and is discussed in Chapter 29. Notice the special syntax `ShowColors2.this` used in the preceding statement. When using an inner class, you can access the outer class object's `this` reference by qualifying `this` with the name of the outer class and the dot (`.`) operator.

After the user selects a color, lines 28 and 29 determine if `color` is `null`, and if so, set `color` to the default `Color.lightGray`. Line 31

```
c.setBackground( color );
```

uses method `setBackground` to change the background color of the content pane (represented by `Container c` in this program). Method `setBackground` is one of the many `Component` methods that can be used on most GUI components. Line 32

```
c.repaint();
```

ensures that the background is repainted by calling `repaint` for the content pane. This schedules a call to the content pane's `update` method, which repaints the background of the content pane in the current background color.

The second screen capture of Fig. 28.6 demonstrates the default `JColorChooser` dialog that allows the user to select a color from a variety of *color swatches*. Notice that there are actually three tabs across the top of the dialog—**Swatches**, **HSB** and **RGB**. These represent three different ways to select a color. The **HSB** tab allows you to select a color based on *hue, saturation* and *brightness*. The **RGB** tab allows you to select a color using sliders to select the red, green and blue components of the color. The **HSB** and **RGB** tabs are shown in Fig. 28.7.

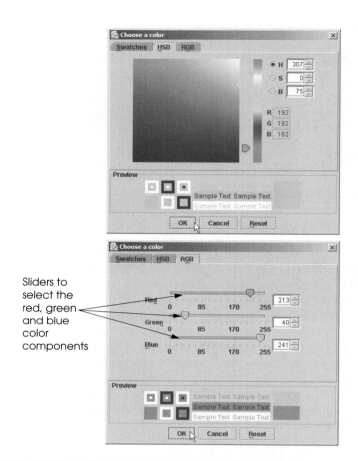

Sliders to
select the
red, green
and blue
color
components

Fig. 28.7   The HSB and RGB tabs of the `JColorChooser` dialog.

28.4 Font Control

This section introduces methods and constants for font control. Most font methods and font constants are part of class `Font`. Some methods of class `Font` and class `Graphics` are summarized in Fig. 28.8.

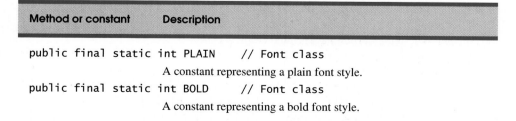

Method or constant	Description
`public final static int PLAIN    // Font class`	
	A constant representing a plain font style.
`public final static int BOLD     // Font class`	
	A constant representing a bold font style.

Fig. 28.8   `Font` methods, constants and font-related `Graphics` methods. (Part 1 of 2.)

Method or constant	Description

`public final static int ITALIC   // Font class`
> A constant representing an italic font style.

`public Font( String name, int style, int size )`
> Creates a Font object with the specified font, style and size.

`public int getStyle()           // Font class`
> Returns an integer value indicating the current font style.

`public int getSize()            // Font class`
> Returns an integer value indicating the current font size.

`public String getName()         // Font class`
> Returns the current font name as a string.

`public String getFamily()       // Font class`
> Returns the font's family name as a string.

`public boolean isPlain()        // Font class`
> Tests a font for a plain font style. Returns true if the font is plain.

`public boolean isBold()         // Font class`
> Tests a font for a bold font style. Returns true if the font is bold.

`public boolean isItalic()       // Font class`
> Tests a font for an italic font style. Returns true if the font is italic.

`public Font getFont()           // Graphics class`
> Returns a Font object reference representing the current font.

`public void setFont(Font f)     // Graphics class`
> Sets the current font to the font, style and size specified by the Font object reference f.

Fig. 28.8   Font methods, constants and font-related Graphics methods. (Part 2 of 2.)

Class Font's constructor takes three arguments—the *font name, font style* and *font size*. The font name is any font currently supported by the system where the program is running, such as standard Java fonts Monospaced, SansSerif and Serif. The font style is Font.PLAIN, Font.ITALIC or Font.BOLD (static constants of class Font). Font styles can be used in combination (e.g., Font.ITALIC + Font.BOLD). The font size is measured in points. A *point* is 1/72 of an inch. Graphics method setFont sets the current drawing font—the font in which text will be displayed—to its Font argument.

Portability Tip 28.2

The number of fonts varies greatly across systems. The JDK guarantees that the fonts Serif, Monospaced, SansSerif, Dialog and DialogInput will be available.

Common Programming Error 28.2

Specifying a font that is not available on a system is a logic error. Java will substitute that system's default font.

The program of Fig. 28.9 displays text in four different fonts with each font in a different size. The program uses the Font constructor to initialize Font objects in lines 20, 25, 30 and 37 (each in a call to Graphics method setFont to change the drawing font). Each call to the Font constructor passes a font name (Serif, Monospaced or SansSerif) as a String, a font style (Font.PLAIN, Font.ITALIC or Font.BOLD) and a font size. Once Graphics method setFont is invoked, all text displayed following the call will appear in the new font until the font is changed. Note that line 35 changes the drawing color to red, so the next string displayed appears in red.

Software Engineering Observation 28.3

To change the font, you must create a new Font object; there are no set methods in class Font to change the characteristics of the current font.

```java
1   // Fig. 28.9: Fonts.java
2   // Using fonts
3   import java.awt.*;
4   import javax.swing.*;
5   import java.awt.event.*;
6
7   public class Fonts extends JFrame {
8      public Fonts()
9      {
10         super( "Using fonts" );
11
12         setSize( 420, 125 );
13         show();
14      } // end Fonts constructor
15
16      public void paint( Graphics g )
17      {
18         // set current font to Serif (Times), bold, 12pt
19         // and draw a string
20         g.setFont( new Font( "Serif", Font.BOLD, 12 ) );
21         g.drawString( "Serif 12 point bold.", 20, 50 );
22
23         // set current font to Monospaced (Courier),
24         // italic, 24pt and draw a string
25         g.setFont( new Font( "Monospaced", Font.ITALIC, 24 ) );
26         g.drawString( "Monospaced 24 point italic.", 20, 70 );
27
28         // set current font to SansSerif (Helvetica),
29         // plain, 14pt and draw a string
30         g.setFont( new Font( "SansSerif", Font.PLAIN, 14 ) );
31         g.drawString( "SansSerif 14 point plain.", 20, 90 );
32
33         // set current font to Serif (times), bold/italic,
34         // 18pt and draw a string
35         g.setColor( Color.red );
36         g.setFont(
37            new Font( "Serif", Font.BOLD + Font.ITALIC, 18 ) );
38         g.drawString( g.getFont().getName() + " " +
```

Fig. 28.9   Using Graphics method setFont to change Fonts . (Part 1 of 2.)

```
39                              g.getFont().getSize() +
40                              " point bold italic.", 20, 110 );
41       } // end method paint
42
43       public static void main( String args[] )
44       {
45          Fonts app = new Fonts();
46
47          app.addWindowListener(
48             new WindowAdapter() {
49                public void windowClosing( WindowEvent e )
50                {
51                   System.exit( 0 );
52                } // end method windowClosing
53             } // end anonymous inner class
54          ); // end addWindowListener
55       } // end main
56    } // end class Fonts
```

Using fonts

Serif 12 point bold.

Monospaced 24 point italic.

SansSerif 14 point plain.

Serif 18 point bold italic.

Fig. 28.9   Using `Graphics` method `setFont` to change `Fonts`. (Part 2 of 2.)

Often it is necessary to get information about the current font such as the font name, the font style and the font size. Several `Font` methods used to get font information are summarized in Fig. 28.8. Method `getStyle` returns an integer value representing the current style. The integer value returned is either `Font.PLAIN`, `Font.ITALIC`, `Font.BOLD` or any combination of `Font.PLAIN`, `Font.ITALIC` and `Font.BOLD`.

Method `getSize` returns the font size in points. Method `getName` returns the current font name as a `String`. Method `getFamily` returns the name of the font family to which the current font belongs. The name of the font family is platform-specific.

Portability Tip 28.3

Java uses standardized font names and maps these into system-specific font names for portability. This is transparent to the programmer.

`Font` methods are also available to test the style of the current font and are summarized in Fig. 28.8. The `isPlain` method returns `true` if the current font style is plain. The `isBold` method returns `true` if the current font style is bold. The `isItalic` method returns `true` if the current font style is italic.

Sometimes precise information about a font's metrics must be known—such as *height*, *descent* (the amount a character dips below the baseline), *ascent* (the amount a character rises above the baseline) and *leading* (the difference between the height and the ascent). Figure 28.10 illustrates some of the common *font metrics*. Note that the coordinate passed to `drawString` corresponds to the lower-left corner of the baseline of the font.

Class *FontMetrics* defines several methods for obtaining font metrics. These methods and `Graphics` method *getFontMetrics* are summarized in Fig. 28.11.

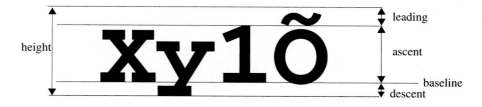

Fig. 28.10 Font metrics.

The program of Fig. 28.12 uses the methods of Fig. 28.11 to obtain font metric information for two fonts.

Method	Description

```
public int getAscent()                          // FontMetrics class
```
Returns a value representing the ascent of a font in points.
```
public int getDescent()                         // FontMetrics class
```
Returns a value representing the descent of a font in points.
```
public int getLeading()                         // FontMetrics class
```
Returns a value representing the leading of a font in points.
```
public int getHeight()                          // FontMetrics class
```
Returns a value representing the height of a font in points.
```
public FontMetrics getFontMetrics()             // Graphics class
```
Returns the FontMetrics object for the current drawing Font.
```
public FontMetrics getFontMetrics( Font f ) // Graphics class
```
Returns the FontMetrics object for the specified Font argument.

Fig. 28.11 FontMetrics and Graphics methods for obtaining font metrics.

```java
1   // Fig. 28.12: Metrics.java
2   // Demonstrating methods of class FontMetrics and
3   // class Graphics useful for obtaining font metrics
4   import java.awt.*;
5   import java.awt.event.*;
6   import javax.swing.*;
7
8   public class Metrics extends JFrame {
9      public Metrics()
10     {
11        super( "Demonstrating FontMetrics" );
12
13        setSize( 510, 210 );
14        show();
15     } // end Metrics constructor
```

Fig. 28.12 Obtaining font metric information. (Part 1 of 2.)

```
16
17      public void paint( Graphics g )
18      {
19         g.setFont( new Font( "SansSerif", Font.BOLD, 12 ) );
20         FontMetrics fm = g.getFontMetrics();
21         g.drawString( "Current font: " + g.getFont(), 10, 40 );
22         g.drawString( "Ascent: " + fm.getAscent(), 10, 55 );
23         g.drawString( "Descent: " + fm.getDescent(), 10, 70 );
24         g.drawString( "Height: " + fm.getHeight(), 10, 85 );
25         g.drawString( "Leading: " + fm.getLeading(), 10, 100 );
26
27         Font font = new Font( "Serif", Font.ITALIC, 14 );
28         fm = g.getFontMetrics( font );
29         g.setFont( font );
30         g.drawString( "Current font: " + font, 10, 130 );
31         g.drawString( "Ascent: " + fm.getAscent(), 10, 145 );
32         g.drawString( "Descent: " + fm.getDescent(), 10, 160 );
33         g.drawString( "Height: " + fm.getHeight(), 10, 175 );
34         g.drawString( "Leading: " + fm.getLeading(), 10, 190 );
35      } // end method paint
36
37      public static void main( String args[] )
38      {
39         Metrics app = new Metrics();
40
41         app.addWindowListener(
42            new WindowAdapter() {
43               public void windowClosing( WindowEvent e )
44               {
45                  System.exit( 0 );
46               } // end method windowClosing
47            } // end anonymous inner class
48         ); // end addWindowListener
49      } // end main
50   } // end class Metrics
```

Fig. 28.12 Obtaining font metric information. (Part 2 of 2.)

Line 19 creates and sets the current drawing font to a SansSerif, bold, 12-point font. Line 20 uses Graphics method getFontMetrics to obtain the FontMetrics object for the current font. Line 21 uses an implicit call to class Font's toString method to output the string representation of the font. Lines 22 through 25 use FontMetric methods to obtain the ascent, descent, height and leading for the font.

Line 27 creates a new `Serif`, italic, 14-point font. Line 28 uses a second version of `Graphics` method `getFontMetrics`, which receives a `Font` argument and returns a corresponding `FontMetrics` object. Lines 31 to 34 obtain the ascent, descent, height and leading for the font. Notice that the font metrics are slightly different for the two fonts.

28.5 Drawing Lines, Rectangles and Ovals

This section presents a variety of `Graphics` methods for drawing lines, rectangles and ovals. The methods and their parameters are summarized in Fig. 28.13. For each drawing method that requires a `width` and `height` parameter, the `width` and `height` must each be a nonnegative value. Otherwise, the shape will not display.

Method	Description
`public void drawLine( int x1, int y1, int x2, int y2 )`	
	Draws a line between the point (x1, y1) and the point (x2, y2).
`public void drawRect( int x, int y, int width, int height )`	
	Draws a rectangle of the specified `width` and `height`. The top-left corner of the rectangle has the coordinates (x, y).
`public void fillRect( int x, int y, int width, int height )`	
	Draws a solid rectangle with the specified `width` and `height`. The top-left corner of the rectangle has the coordinate (x, y).
`public void clearRect( int x, int y, int width, int height )`	
	Draws a solid rectangle with the specified `width` and `height` in the current background color. The top-left corner of the rectangle has the coordinate (x, y).
`public void drawRoundRect( int x, int y, int width, int height,` `int arcWidth, int arcHeight )`	
	Draws a rectangle with rounded corners in the current color with the specified `width` and `height`. The `arcWidth` and `arcHeight` determine the rounding of the corners (see Fig. 28.15).
`public void fillRoundRect( int x, int y, int width, int height,` `int arcWidth, int arcHeight )`	
	Draws a solid rectangle with rounded corners in the current color with the specified `width` and `height`. The `arcWidth` and `arcHeight` determine the rounding of the corners (see Fig. 28.15).
`public void draw3DRect( int x, int y, int width, int height, boolean b )`	
	Draws a three-dimensional rectangle in the current color with the specified `width` and `height`. The top-left corner of the rectangle has the coordinates (x, y). The rectangle appears raised when b is `true` and is lowered when b is `false`.
`public void fill3DRect( int x, int y, int width, int height, boolean b )`	
	Draws a filled three-dimensional rectangle in the current color with the specified `width` and `height`. The top-left corner of the rectangle has the coordinates (x, y). The rectangle appears raised when b is `true` and is lowered when b is `false`.

Fig. 28.13 `Graphics` methods that draw lines, rectangles and ovals. (Part 1 of 2.)

Method	Description

public void drawOval(int x, int y, int width, int height)

> Draws an oval in the current color with the specified width and height. The
> bounding rectangle's top-left corner is at the coordinates *(x, y)*. The oval
> touches all four sides of the bounding rectangle at the center of each side (see
> Fig. 28.16).

public void fillOval(int x, int y, int width, int height)

> Draws a filled oval in the current color with the specified width and height.
> The bounding rectangle's top-left corner is at the coordinates *(x, y)*. The oval
> touches all four sides of the bounding rectangle at the center of each side (see
> Fig. 28.16).

Fig. 28.13 Graphics methods that draw lines, rectangles and ovals. (Part 2 of 2.)

The application of Fig. 28.14 demonstrates drawing a variety of lines, rectangles, 3D
rectangles, rounded rectangles and ovals.

```
1   // Fig. 28.14: LinesRectsOvals.java
2   // Drawing lines, rectangles and ovals
3   import java.awt.*;
4   import java.awt.event.*;
5   import javax.swing.*;
6
7   public class LinesRectsOvals extends JFrame {
8      private String s = "Using drawString!";
9
10     public LinesRectsOvals()
11     {
12        super( "Drawing lines, rectangles and ovals" );
13
14        setSize( 400, 165 );
15        show();
16     } // end LinesRectsOvals constructor
17
18     public void paint( Graphics g )
19     {
20        g.setColor( Color.red );
21        g.drawLine( 5, 30, 350, 30 );
22
23        g.setColor( Color.blue );
24        g.drawRect( 5, 40, 90, 55 );
25        g.fillRect( 100, 40, 90, 55 );
26
27        g.setColor( Color.cyan );
28        g.fillRoundRect( 195, 40, 90, 55, 50, 50 );
29        g.drawRoundRect( 290, 40, 90, 55, 20, 20 );
30
```

Fig. 28.14 Demonstrating Graphics method drawLine. (Part 1 of 2.)

```
31              g.setColor( Color.yellow );
32              g.draw3DRect( 5, 100, 90, 55, true );
33              g.fill3DRect( 100, 100, 90, 55, false );
34
35              g.setColor( Color.magenta );
36              g.drawOval( 195, 100, 90, 55 );
37              g.fillOval( 290, 100, 90, 55 );
38        } // end method paint
39
40        public static void main( String args[] )
41        {
42              LinesRectsOvals app = new LinesRectsOvals();
43
44              app.addWindowListener(
45                 new WindowAdapter() {
46                    public void windowClosing( WindowEvent e )
47                    {
48                       System.exit( 0 );
49                    } // end method windowClosing
50                 } // end anonymous inner class
51              ); // end addWindowListener
52        } // end main
53  } // end class LinesRectsOvals
```

Fig. 28.14 Demonstrating Graphics method drawLine. (Part 2 of 2.)

Methods fillRoundRect (line 28) and drawRoundRect (line 29) draw rectangles
with rounded corners. Their first two arguments specify the coordinates of the upper-left
corner of the *bounding rectangle*—the area in which the rounded rectangle will be drawn.
Note that the upper-left corner coordinates are not the edge of the rounded rectangle but the
coordinates where the edge would be if the rectangle had square corners. The third and
fourth arguments specify the width and height of the rectangle. Their last two arguments—arcWidth and arcHeight—determine the horizontal and vertical diameters of
the arcs used to represent the corners.

Methods draw3DRect (line 32) and fill3DRect (line 33) take the same arguments.
The first two arguments specify the top-left corner of the rectangle. The next two arguments
specify the width and height of the rectangle, respectively. The last argument determines
if the rectangle is *raised* (true) or *lowered* (false). The three-dimensional effect of
draw3DRect appears as two edges of the rectangle in the original color and two edges in
a slightly darker color. The three-dimensional effect of fill3DRect appears as two edges
of the rectangle in the original drawing color and the fill and other two edges in a slightly
darker color. Raised rectangles have the original drawing color edges at the top and left of

the rectangle. Lowered rectangles have the original drawing color edges at the bottom and right of the rectangle. The three-dimensional effect is difficult to see in some colors.

Figure 28.15 labels the arc width, arc height, width and height of a rounded rectangle. Using the same value for `arcWidth` and `arcHeight` produces a quarter circle at each corner. When `width`, `height`, `arcWidth` and `arcHeight` have the same values, the result is a circle. If the values for `width` and `height` are the same and the values of `arcWidth` and `arcHeight` are 0, the result is a square.

Both the `drawOval` and `fillOval` methods take the same four arguments. The first two arguments specify the top-left coordinate of the bounding rectangle that contains the oval. The last two arguments specify the `width` and `height` of the bounding rectangle, respectively. Figure 28.16 shows an oval bounded by a rectangle. Note that the oval touches the center of all four sides of the bounding rectangle (the bounding rectangle is not displayed on the screen).

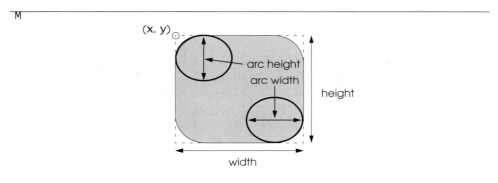

Fig. 28.15 The arc width and arc height for rounded rectangles.

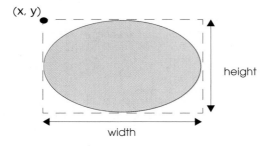

Fig. 28.16 An oval bounded by a rectangle.

28.6 Drawing Arcs

An *arc* is a portion of a oval. Arc angles are measured in degrees. Arcs *sweep* from a *starting angle* the number of degrees specified by their *arc angle*. The starting angle indicates in degrees where the arc begins. The arc angle specifies the total number of degrees through which the arc sweeps. Figure 28.17 illustrates two arcs. The left set of axes shows an arc sweeping from zero degrees to approximately 110 degrees. Arcs that sweep in a counter-clockwise direction are measured in *positive degrees*. The right set of axes shows an arc sweeping from zero degrees to approximately –110 degrees. Arcs that sweep in a clockwise direction are measured in *negative degrees*. Notice the dashed boxes around the arcs in Fig. 28.17. When drawing an arc, we specify a bounding rectangle for an oval. The arc will sweep along part of the oval. The `Graphics` methods—*drawArc* and *fillArc*—for drawing arcs are summarized in Fig. 28.18.

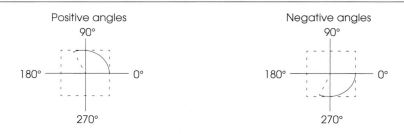

Fig. 28.17 Positive and negative arc angles.

Method	Description
`public void drawArc( int x, int y, int width, int height,` `                int startAngle, int arcAngle )`	
	Draws an arc relative to the bounding rectangle's top-left coordinates *(x, y)* with the specified `width` and `height`. The arc segment is drawn starting at `startAngle` and sweeps `arcAngle` degrees.
`public void fillArc( int x, int y, int width, int height,` `                int startAngle, int arcAngle )`	
	Draws a solid arc (i.e., a sector) relative to the bounding rectangle's top-left coordinates *(x, y)* with the specified `width` and `height`. The arc segment is drawn starting at `startAngle` and sweeps `arcAngle` degrees.

Fig. 28.18 `Graphics` methods for drawing arcs.

The program of Fig. 28.19 demonstrates the arc methods of Fig. 28.18. The program draws six arcs (three unfilled and three filled). To illustrate the bounding rectangle that helps determine where the arc appears, the first three arcs are displayed inside a yellow rectangle that has the same `x`, `y`, `width` and `height` arguments as the arcs.

```
1   // Fig. 28.19: DrawArcs.java
2   // Drawing arcs
3   import java.awt.*;
4   import javax.swing.*;
5   import java.awt.event.*;
6
7   public class DrawArcs extends JFrame {
```

Fig. 28.19 Demonstrating `drawArc` and `fillArc`. (Part 1 of 3.)

```
 8        public DrawArcs()
 9        {
10           super( "Drawing Arcs" );
11
12           setSize( 300, 170 );
13           show();
14        } // end DrawArcs constructor
15
16        public void paint( Graphics g )
17        {
18           // start at 0 and sweep 360 degrees
19           g.setColor( Color.yellow );
20           g.drawRect( 15, 35, 80, 80 );
21           g.setColor( Color.black );
22           g.drawArc( 15, 35, 80, 80, 0, 360 );
23
24           // start at 0 and sweep 110 degrees
25           g.setColor( Color.yellow );
26           g.drawRect( 100, 35, 80, 80 );
27           g.setColor( Color.black );
28           g.drawArc( 100, 35, 80, 80, 0, 110 );
29
30           // start at 0 and sweep -270 degrees
31           g.setColor( Color.yellow );
32           g.drawRect( 185, 35, 80, 80 );
33           g.setColor( Color.black );
34           g.drawArc( 185, 35, 80, 80, 0, -270 );
35
36           // start at 0 and sweep 360 degrees
37           g.fillArc( 15, 120, 80, 40, 0, 360 );
38
39           // start at 270 and sweep -90 degrees
40           g.fillArc( 100, 120, 80, 40, 270, -90 );
41
42           // start at 0 and sweep -270 degrees
43           g.fillArc( 185, 120, 80, 40, 0, -270 );
44        } // end method paint
45
46        public static void main( String args[] )
47        {
48           DrawArcs app = new DrawArcs();
49
50           app.addWindowListener(
51              new WindowAdapter() {
52                 public void windowClosing( WindowEvent e )
53                 {
54                    System.exit( 0 );
55                 } // end method windowClosing
56              } // end anonymous inner class
57           ); // end addWindowListener
58        } // end main
59     } // end class DrawArcs
```

Fig. 28.19 Demonstrating drawArc and fillArc. (Part 2 of 3.)

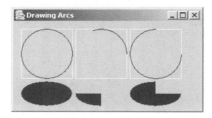

Fig. 28.19 Demonstrating drawArc and fillArc. (Part 3 of 3.)

28.7 Drawing Polygons and Polylines

Polygons are multi-sided shapes. *Polylines* are a series of connected points. Graphics methods for drawing polygons and polylines are discussed in Fig. 28.19. Note that some methods require a *Polygon* object (package java.awt). Class Polygon's constructors are also described in Fig. 28.20.

Method	Description
public void drawPolygon(int xPoints[], int yPoints[], int points)	
	Draws a polygon. The *x*-coordinate of each point is specified in the xPoints array and the *y*-coordinate of each point is specified in the yPoints array. The last argument specifies the number of points. This method draws a closed polygon—even if the last point is different from the first point.
public void drawPolyline(int xPoints[], int yPoints[], int points)	
	Draws a series of connected lines. The *x*-coordinate of each point is specified in the xPoints array and the *y*-coordinate of each point is specified in the yPoints array. The last argument specifies the number of points. If the last point is different from the first point, the polyline is not closed.
public void drawPolygon(Polygon p)	
	Draws the specified closed polygon.
public void fillPolygon(int xPoints[], int yPoints[], int points)	
	Draws a solid polygon. The *x*-coordinate of each point is specified in the xPoints array and the *y*-coordinate of each point is specified in the yPoints array. The last argument specifies the number of points. This method draws a closed polygon—even if the last point is different from the first point.
public void fillPolygon(Polygon p)	
	Draws the specified solid polygon. The polygon is closed.
public Polygon() // Polygon class	
	Constructs a new polygon object. The polygon does not contain any points.

Fig. 28.20 Graphics methods for drawing polygons and class Polygon constructors. (Part 1 of 2.)

Method	Description

```
public Polygon( int xValues[], int yValues[],      // Polygon class
                int numberOfPoints )
```
Constructs a new polygon object. The polygon has `numberOfPoints` sides, with each point consisting of an *x*-coordinate from `xValues` and a *y*-coordinate from `yValues`.

Fig. 28.20 `Graphics` methods for drawing polygons and class `Polygon` constructors. (Part 2 of 2.)

The program of Fig. 28.21 draws polygons and polylines using the methods and constructors in Fig. 28.20.

```
1   // Fig. 28.21: DrawPolygons.java
2   // Drawing polygons
3   import java.awt.*;
4   import java.awt.event.*;
5   import javax.swing.*;
6
7   public class DrawPolygons extends JFrame {
8      public DrawPolygons()
9      {
10        super( "Drawing Polygons" );
11
12        setSize( 275, 230 );
13        show();
14     } // end DrawPolygons constructor
15
16     public void paint( Graphics g )
17     {
18        int xValues[] = { 20, 40, 50, 30, 20, 15 };
19        int yValues[] = { 50, 50, 60, 80, 80, 60 };
20        Polygon poly1 = new Polygon( xValues, yValues, 6 );
21
22        g.drawPolygon( poly1 );
23
24        int xValues2[] = { 70, 90, 100, 80, 70, 65, 60 };
25        int yValues2[] = { 100, 100, 110, 110, 130, 110, 90 };
26
27        g.drawPolyline( xValues2, yValues2, 7 );
28
29        int xValues3[] = { 120, 140, 150, 190 };
30        int yValues3[] = { 40, 70, 80, 60 };
31
32        g.fillPolygon( xValues3, yValues3, 4 );
33
34        Polygon poly2 = new Polygon();
35        poly2.addPoint( 165, 135 );
```

Fig. 28.21 Demonstrating `drawPolygon` and `fillPolygon`. (Part 1 of 2.)

```
36          poly2.addPoint( 175, 150 );
37          poly2.addPoint( 270, 200 );
38          poly2.addPoint( 200, 220 );
39          poly2.addPoint( 130, 180 );
40
41          g.fillPolygon( poly2 );
42       } // end method paint
43
44       public static void main( String args[] )
45       {
46          DrawPolygons app = new DrawPolygons();
47
48          app.addWindowListener(
49             new WindowAdapter() {
50                public void windowClosing( WindowEvent e )
51                {
52                   System.exit( 0 );
53                } // end method windowClosing
54             } // end anonymous inner class
55          ); // end addWindowListener
56       } // end main
57    } // end class DrawPolygons
```

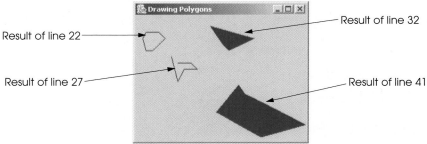

Fig. 28.21 Demonstrating `drawPolygon` and `fillPolygon`. (Part 2 of 2.)

Lines 18 through 20 create two `int` arrays and use them to specify the points for Polygon `poly1`. The `Polygon` constructor call at line 20 receives array `xValues`, which contains the *x*-coordinate of each point, array `yValues`, which contains the *y*-coordinate of each point, and 6 (the number of points in the polygon). Line 22 displays `poly1` by passing it as an argument to `Graphics` method `drawPolygon`.

Lines 24 and 25 create two `int` arrays and use them to specify the points for a series of connected lines. Array `xValues2` contains the *x*-coordinate of each point and array `yValues2` contains the *y*-coordinate of each point. Line 27 uses `Graphics` method `drawPolyline` to display the series of connected lines specified with the arguments `xValues2`, `yValues2` and 7 (the number of points).

Lines 29 through 30 create two `int` arrays and use them to specify the points of a polygon. Array `xValues3` contains the *x*-coordinate of each point and array `yValues3` contains the *y*-coordinate of each point. Line 32 displays a polygon by passing to `Graphics` method `fillPolygon` the two arrays (`xValues3` and `yValues3`) and the number of points to draw (4).

Common Programming Error 28.3

An ArrayIndexOutOfBoundsException is thrown if the number of points specified in the third argument to method drawPolygon or method fillPolygon is greater than the number of elements in the arrays of coordinates that define the polygon to display.

Line 34 creates Polygon poly2 with no points. Lines 35 through 39 use Polygon method *addPoint* to add pairs of *x*- and *y*-coordinates to the Polygon. Line 41 displays Polygon poly2 by passing it to Graphics method fillPolygon.

28.8 The Java2D API

The *Java2D API* provides advanced two-dimensional graphics capabilities for programmers who require detailed and complex graphical manipulations. The API includes features for processing line art, text and images in packages java.awt, java.awt.image, java.awt.color, java.awt.font, java.awt.geom, java.awt.print and java.awt.image.renderable. The capabilities of the API are far too broad to cover in this textbook. In this section, we present an overview of several Java2D capabilities.

Drawing with the Java2D API is accomplished with an instance of class *Graphics2D* (package java.awt). Class Graphics2D is a subclass of class Graphics, so it has all the graphics capabilities demonstrated earlier in this chapter. In fact, the actual object we have used to draw in every paint method is a Graphics2D object that is passed to method paint and accessed via the superclass Graphics reference g. To access the Graphics2D capabilities, we must downcast the Graphics reference passed to paint to a Graphics2D reference with a statement such as

```
Graphics2D g2d = ( Graphics2D ) g;
```

The programs of the next several sections use this technique.

28.9 Java2D Shapes

Next, we present several Java2D shapes from package java.awt.geom, including *Ellipse2D.Double*, *Rectangle2D.Double*, *Arc2D.Double*, *Line2D.Double* and *RoundRectangle2D.Double*. Note the syntax of each class name. Each of these classes represents a shape with dimensions specified as double-precision floating-point values. There is a separate version of each represented with single-precision floating-point values (such as *Ellipse2D.Float*). In each case, Double is a static inner class of the class to the left of the dot operator (e.g., Ellipse2D). To use the static inner class, we simply qualify its name with the outer class name.

The program of Fig. 28.22 demonstrates several Java2D shapes and drawing characteristics, such as thick lines, filling shapes with patterns and drawing dashed lines. These are just a few of the many capabilities provided by Java2D..

```
1   // Fig. 28.22: Shapes.java
2   // Demonstrating some Java2D shapes
3   import javax.swing.*;
4   import java.awt.event.*;
```

Fig. 28.22 Demonstrating some Java2D shapes. (Part 1 of 3.)

```java
5    import java.awt.*;
6    import java.awt.geom.*;
7    import java.awt.image.*;
8
9    public class Shapes extends JFrame {
10      public Shapes()
11      {
12         super( "Drawing 2D shapes" );
13
14         setSize( 425, 160 );
15         show();
16      } // end Shapes constructor
17
18      public void paint( Graphics g )
19      {
20         // create 2D by casting g to Graphics2D
21         Graphics2D g2d = ( Graphics2D ) g;
22
23         // draw 2D ellipse filled with a blue-yellow gradient
24         g2d.setPaint(
25            new GradientPaint( 5, 30,          // x1, y1
26                               Color.blue,     // initial Color
27                               35, 100,        // x2, y2
28                               Color.yellow,   // end Color
29                               true ) );       // cyclic
30         g2d.fill( new Ellipse2D.Double( 5, 30, 65, 100 ) );
31
32         // draw 2D rectangle in red
33         g2d.setPaint( Color.red );
34         g2d.setStroke( new BasicStroke( 10.0f ) );
35         g2d.draw(
36            new Rectangle2D.Double( 80, 30, 65, 100 ) );
37
38         // draw 2D rounded rectangle with a buffered background
39         BufferedImage buffImage =
40            new BufferedImage(
41               10, 10, BufferedImage.TYPE_INT_RGB );
42
43         Graphics2D gg = buffImage.createGraphics();
44         gg.setColor( Color.yellow ); // draw in yellow
45         gg.fillRect( 0, 0, 10, 10 ); // draw a filled rectangle
46         gg.setColor( Color.black );  // draw in black
47         gg.drawRect( 1, 1, 6, 6 );   // draw a rectangle
48         gg.setColor( Color.blue );   // draw in blue
49         gg.fillRect( 1, 1, 3, 3 );   // draw a filled rectangle
50         gg.setColor( Color.red );    // draw in red
51         gg.fillRect( 4, 4, 3, 3 );   // draw a filled rectangle
52
53         // paint buffImage onto the JFrame
54         g2d.setPaint(
55            new TexturePaint(
56               buffImage, new Rectangle( 10, 10 ) ) );
57         g2d.fill(
```

Fig. 28.22 Demonstrating some Java2D shapes. (Part 2 of 3.)

```
58              new RoundRectangle2D.Double(
59                  155, 30, 75, 100, 50, 50 ) );
60
61          // draw 2D pie-shaped arc in white
62          g2d.setPaint( Color.white );
63          g2d.setStroke( new BasicStroke( 6.0f ) );
64          g2d.draw(
65              new Arc2D.Double(
66                  240, 30, 75, 100, 0, 270, Arc2D.PIE ) );
67
68          // draw 2D lines in green and yellow
69          g2d.setPaint( Color.green );
70          g2d.draw( new Line2D.Double( 395, 30, 320, 150 ) );
71
72          float dashes[] = { 10 };
73
74          g2d.setPaint( Color.yellow );
75          g2d.setStroke(
76              new BasicStroke( 4,
77                               BasicStroke.CAP_ROUND,
78                               BasicStroke.JOIN_ROUND,
79                               10, dashes, 0 ) );
80          g2d.draw( new Line2D.Double( 320, 30, 395, 150 ) );
81      } // end method paint
82
83      public static void main( String args[] )
84      {
85          Shapes app = new Shapes();
86
87          app.addWindowListener(
88              new WindowAdapter() {
89                  public void windowClosing( WindowEvent e )
90                  {
91                      System.exit( 0 );
92                  } // end method windowClosing
93              } // end anonymous inner class
94          ); // end addWindowListener
95      } // end main
96 } // end class Shapes
```

Fig. 28.22 Demonstrating some Java2D shapes. (Part 3 of 3.)

Line 21 casts the Graphics reference received by paint to a Graphics2D reference and assigns it to g2d to allow access to the Java2D features.

The first shape we draw is an oval filled with gradually changing colors. Lines 24 through 29

```
g2d.setPaint(
    new GradientPaint( 5, 30,            // x1, y1
                       Color.blue,       // initial Color
                       35, 100,          // x2, y2
                       Color.yellow,     // end Color
                       true ) );         // cyclic
```

invoke `Graphics2D` method *setPaint* to set the *Paint* object that determines the color for the shape to display. A `Paint` object is an object of any class that implements interface `java.awt.Paint`. The `Paint` object can be something as simple as one of the predefined `Color` objects introduced in Section 28.3 (class `Color` implements `Paint`) or the `Paint` object can be an instance of the Java2D API's *GradientPaint, SystemColor* or *TexturePaint* classes. In this case, we use a `GradientPaint` object.

Class `GradientPaint` helps draw a shape in a gradually changing colors—called a *gradient*. The `GradientPaint` constructor used here requires seven arguments. The first two arguments specify the starting coordinate for the gradient. The third argument specifies the starting `Color` for the gradient. The fourth and fifth arguments specify the ending coordinate for the gradient. The sixth argument specifies the ending `Color` for the gradient. The last argument specifies if the gradient is cyclic (`true`) or acyclic (`false`). The two coordinates determine the direction of the gradient. The second coordinate *(35, 100)* is down and to the right of the first coordinate *(5, 30)*, so the gradient goes down and to the right at an angle. This gradient is cyclic (`true`), so the color starts with blue, gradually becomes yellow, then gradually returns to blue. If the gradient is acyclic, the color transitions from the first color specified (e.g., blue) to the second color (e.g., yellow).

Line 30

```
g2d.fill( new Ellipse2D.Double( 5, 30, 65, 100 ) );
```

uses `Graphics2D` method *fill* to draw a filled *Shape* object. The `Shape` object is an instance of any class that implements interface `Shape` (package `java.awt`)—in this case, an instance of class `Ellipse2D.Double`. The `Ellipse2D.Double` constructor receives four arguments specifying the bounding rectangle for the ellipse to display.

Next we draw a red rectangle with a thick border. Line 33 uses `setPaint` to set the `Paint` object to `Color.red`. Line 34

```
g2d.setStroke( new BasicStroke( 10.0f ) );
```

uses `Graphics2D` method *setStroke* to set the characteristics of the rectangle's border (or the lines for any other shape). Method `setStroke` requires a *Stroke* object as its argument. The `Stroke` object is an instance of any class that implements interface `Stroke` (package `java.awt`)—in this case, an instance of class *BasicStroke*. Class `BasicStroke` provides a variety of constructors to specify the width of the line, how the line ends (called the *end caps*), how lines join together (called *line joins*) and the dash attributes of the line (if it is a dashed line). The constructor here specifies that the line should be 10 pixels wide.

Lines 35 and 36

```
g2d.draw(
    new Rectangle2D.Double( 80, 30, 65, 100 ) );
```

use `Graphics2D` method *draw* to draw a *Shape* object—in this case, an instance of class `Rectangle2D.Double`. The `Rectangle2D.Double` constructor receives four arguments specifying the upper-left *x*-coordinate, upper-left *y*-coordinate, width and height of the rectangle.

Next we draw a rounded rectangle filled with a pattern created in a *BufferedImage* (package `java.awt.image`) object. Lines 39 through 41

```
BufferedImage buffImage =
    new BufferedImage(
        10, 10, BufferedImage.TYPE_INT_RGB );
```

create the `BufferedImage` object. Class `BufferedImage` can be used to produce images in color and gray scale. This particular `BufferedImage` is 10 pixels wide and 10 pixels high. The third constructor argument `BufferedImage.TYPE_INT_RGB` indicates that the image is stored in color using the RGB color scheme.

To create the fill pattern for the rounded rectangle, we must first draw into the `BufferedImage`. Line 43

```
Graphics2D gg = buffImage.createGraphics();
```

creates a `Graphics2D` object that can be used to draw into the `BufferedImage`. Lines 44 through 51 use methods `setColor`, `fillRect` and `drawRect` (discussed earlier in this chapter) to create the pattern.

Lines 54 through 56

```
g2d.setPaint(
    new TexturePaint(
        buffImage, new Rectangle( 10, 10 ) ) );
```

set the `Paint` object to a new `TexturePaint` (package `java.awt`) object. A `Texture-Paint` object uses the image stored in its associated `BufferedImage` as the fill texture for a filled-in shape. The second argument specifies the `Rectangle` area from the `BufferedImage` that will be replicated through the texture. In this case, the `Rectangle` is the same size as the `BufferedImage`. However, a smaller portion of the `BufferedImage` can be used.

Lines 57 through 59

```
g2d.fill(
    new RoundRectangle2D.Double(
        155, 30, 75, 100, 50, 50 ) );
```

use `Graphics2D` method `fill` to draw a filled `Shape` object—in this case, an instance of class *RoundRectangle2D.Double*. The RoundRectangle2D.Double constructor receives six arguments specifying the rectangle dimensions and the arc width and arc height used to determine the rounding of the corners.

Next we draw a pie-shaped arc with a thick white line. Line 62 sets the `Paint` object to `Color.white`. Line 63 sets the `Stroke` object to a new `BasicStroke` for a line 6 pixels wide. Lines 64 through 66

```
g2d.draw(
    new Arc2D.Double(
        240, 30, 75, 100, 0, 270, Arc2D.PIE ) );
```

use `Graphics2D` method `draw` to draw a `Shape` object—in this case, an `Arc2D.Double`. The `Arc2D.Double` constructor's first four arguments specifying the upper-left *x*-coordinate, upper-left *y*-coordinate, width and height of the bounding rectangle for the arc. The fifth argument specifies the start angle. The sixth argument specifies the arc angle. The last argument specifies how the arc is closed. Constant *Arc2D.PIE* indicates that the arc is closed by drawing two lines—one from the arc's starting point to the center of the bounding rectangle, and one from the center of the bounding rectangle to the ending point. Class Arc2D provides two other `static` constants for specifying how the arc is closed. Constant *Arc2D.CHORD* draws a line from the starting point to the ending point. Constant *Arc2D.OPEN* specifies that the arc is not closed.

Finally, we draw two lines using *Line2D* objects—one solid and one dashed. Line 69 sets the `Paint` object to `Color.green`. Line 70

```
g2d.draw( new Line2D.Double( 395, 30, 320, 150 ) );
```

uses `Graphics2D` method `draw` to draw a `Shape` object—in this case, an instance of class `Line2D.Double`. The `Line2D.Double` constructor's arguments specify starting coordinates and ending coordinates of the line.

Line 72 defines a one-element `float` array containing the value 10. This array will be used to describe the dashes in the dashed line. In this case, each dash will be 10 pixels long. To create dashes of different lengths in a pattern, simply provide the lengths of each dash as an element in the array. Line 74 sets the `Paint` object to `Color.yellow`. Lines 75 through 79

```
g2d.setStroke(
    new BasicStroke( 4,
                     BasicStroke.CAP_ROUND,
                     BasicStroke.JOIN_ROUND,
                 10, dashes, 0 ) );
```

set the `Stroke` object to a new `BasicStroke`. The line will be 4 pixels wide and will have rounded ends (`BasicStroke.CAP_ROUND`). If lines join together (as in a rectangle at the corners), the joining of the lines will be rounded (`BasicStroke.JOIN_ROUND`). The `dashes` argument specifies the dash lengths for the line. The last argument indicates the starting subscript in the `dashes` array for the first dash in the pattern. Line 80 then draws a line with the current `Stroke`.

A general path is a shape constructed from straight lines and complex curves. A general path is represented with an object of class *GeneralPath* (package `java.awt.geom`). The program of Fig. 28.23 demonstrates drawing a general path in the shape of a five-pointed star.

```
1    // Fig. 28.23: Shapes2.java
2    // Demonstrating a general path
3    import javax.swing.*;
4    import java.awt.event.*;
5    import java.awt.*;
6    import java.awt.geom.*;
7
8    public class Shapes2 extends JFrame {
9       public Shapes2()
10      {
```

Fig. 28.23 Demonstrating Java2D `GeneralPaths`. (Part 1 of 3.)

```
11          super( "Drawing 2D Shapes" );
12
13          setBackground( Color.yellow );
14          setSize( 400, 400 );
15          show();
16       } // end Shapes2 constructor
17
18       public void paint( Graphics g )
19       {
20          int xPoints[] =
21             { 55, 67, 109, 73, 83, 55, 27, 37, 1, 43 };
22          int yPoints[] =
23             { 0, 36, 36, 54, 96, 72, 96, 54, 36, 36 };
24
25          Graphics2D g2d = ( Graphics2D ) g;
26
27          // create a star from a series of points
28          GeneralPath star = new GeneralPath();
29
30          // set the initial coordinate of the General Path
31          star.moveTo( xPoints[ 0 ], yPoints[ 0 ] );
32
33          // create the star--this does not draw the star
34          for ( int k = 1; k < xPoints.length; k++ )
35             star.lineTo( xPoints[ k ], yPoints[ k ] );
36
37          // close the shape
38          star.closePath();
39
40          // translate the origin to (200, 200)
41          g2d.translate( 200, 200 );
42
43          // rotate around origin and draw stars in random colors
44          for ( int j = 1; j <= 20; j++ ) {
45             g2d.rotate( Math.PI / 10.0 );
46             g2d.setColor(
47                new Color( ( int ) ( Math.random() * 256 ),
48                           ( int ) ( Math.random() * 256 ),
49                           ( int ) ( Math.random() * 256 ) ) );
50             g2d.fill( star );    // draw a filled star
51          } // end for
52       } // end method paint
53
54       public static void main( String args[] )
55       {
56          Shapes2 app = new Shapes2();
57
58          app.addWindowListener(
59             new WindowAdapter() {
60                public void windowClosing( WindowEvent e )
61                {
62                   System.exit( 0 );
63                } // end method windowClosing
```

Fig. 28.23 Demonstrating Java2D GeneralPaths. (Part 2 of 3.)

```
64                 } // end anonymous inner class
65            ); // end addWindowListener
66         } // end main
67    } // end class Shapes2
```

Fig. 28.23 Demonstrating Java2D `GeneralPaths`. (Part 3 of 3.)

Lines 20 through 23 define two `int` arrays representing the *x*- and *y*-coordinates of the points in the star. Line 28

```
GeneralPath star = new GeneralPath();
```

defines `GeneralPath` object `star`.
Line 31

```
star.moveTo( xPoints[ 0 ], yPoints[ 0 ] );
```

uses `GeneralPath` method *moveTo* to specify the first point in the `star`. The `for` structure in lines 34 and 35

```
for ( int k = 1; k < xPoints.length; k++ )
    star.lineTo( xPoints[ k ], yPoints[ k ] );
```

use `GeneralPath` method *lineTo* to draw a line to the next point in the `star`. Each new call to `lineTo` draws a line from the previous point to the current point. Line 38

```
star.closePath();
```

uses `GeneralPath` method *closePath* to draw a line from the last point to the point specified in the last call to `moveTo`. This completes the general path.
Line 41

```
g2d.translate( 200, 200 );
```

uses Graphics2D method *translate* to move the drawing origin to location *(200, 200)*. All drawing operations now use location *(200, 200)* as *(0, 0)*.

The for structure in line 44 draws the star 20 times by rotating it around the new origin point. Line 45

```
g2d.rotate( Math.PI / 10.0 );
```

uses Graphics2D method *rotate* to rotate the next displayed shape. The argument specifies the rotation angle in radians (with $360° = 2\pi$ radians). Line 50 uses Graphics2D method fill to draw a filled version of the star.

SUMMARY

- A coordinate system is a scheme for identifying every possible point on the screen.
- The upper-left corner of a GUI component has the coordinates *(0, 0)*. A coordinate pair is composed of an *x*-coordinate (the horizontal coordinate) and a *y*-coordinate (the vertical coordinate).
- Coordinate units are measured in pixels. A pixel is a display monitor's smallest unit of resolution.
- A graphics context enables drawing on the screen in Java. A Graphics object manages a graphics context by controlling how information is drawn.
- Graphics objects contain methods for drawing, font manipulation, color manipulation, etc.
- Method paint is normally called in response to an *event* such as uncovering a window.
- Method repaint requests a call to Component method update as soon as possible to clear the Component's background of any previous drawing, then update calls paint directly.
- Class Color defines methods and constants for manipulating colors in a Java program.
- Java uses RGB colors in which the red, green and blue color components are integers in the range 0 to 255 or floating-point values in the range 0.0 to 1.0. The larger the RGB value, the greater the amount of that particular color.
- Color methods getRed, getGreen and getBlue return integer values from 0 to 255 representing the amount of red, green and blue in a Color.
- Class Color provides 13 predefined Color objects.
- Graphics method getColor returns a Color object representing the current drawing color. Graphics method setColor sets the current drawing color.
- Java provides class JColorChooser to display a dialog for selecting colors.
- static method showDialog of class JColorChooser displays a color chooser dialog. This method returns the selected Color object (or null if none is selected).
- The default JColorChooser dialog allows you to select a color from a variety of *color swatches*. The **HSB** tab allows you to select a color based on *hue*, *saturation* and *brightness*. The **RGB** tab allows you to select a color using sliders for the red, green and blue components of the color.
- Component method setBackground (one of the many Component methods that can be used on most GUI components) changes the background color of a component.
- Class Font's constructor takes three arguments—the font name, the *font style* and the *font size*. The font name is any font currently supported by the system. The font style is Font.PLAIN, Font.ITALIC or Font.BOLD. The font size is measured in points.
- Graphics method setFont sets the drawing font.

- Class `FontMetrics` defines several methods for obtaining font metrics.
- `Graphics` method `getFontMetrics` with no arguments obtains the `FontMetrics` object for the current font. A `Graphics` method `getFontMetrics` object that receives a `Font` argument returns a corresponding `FontMetrics` object.
- Methods `draw3DRect` and `fill3DRect` take five arguments specifying the top-left corner of the rectangle, the `width` and `height` of the rectangle, and whether the rectangle is *raised* (`true`) or lowered (`false`).
- Methods `drawRoundRect` and `fillRoundRect` draw rectangles with rounded corners. Their first two arguments specify the upper-left corner, the third and fourth arguments specify the `width` and `height`, and the last two arguments—`arcWidth` and `arcHeight`—determine the horizontal and vertical diameters of the arcs used to represent the corners.
- Methods `drawOval` and `fillOval` take the same arguments—the top-left coordinate and the `width` and the `height` of the bounding rectangle that contains the oval.
- An arc is a portion of an oval. Arcs sweep from a starting angle the number of degrees specified by their arc angle. The starting angle specifies where the arc begins and the arc angle specifies the total number of degrees through which the arc sweeps. Arcs that sweep counterclockwise are measured in positive degrees and arcs that sweep clockwise are measured in negative degrees.
- Methods `drawArc` and `fillArc` take the same arguments—the top-left coordinate, the `width` and the `height` of the bounding rectangle that contains the arc, and the `startAngle` and `arcAngle` that define the sweep of the arc.
- Polygons are multi-sided shapes. `Polylines` are a series of connected points.
- One `Polygon` constructor receives an array containing the *x*-coordinate of each point, an array containing the *y*-coordinate of each point and the number of points in the polygon.
- One version of `Graphics` method `drawPolygon` displays a `Polygon` object. Another version receives an array containing the *x*-coordinate of each point, an array containing the *y*-coordinate of each point and the number of points in the polygon and displays the corresponding polygon.
- `Graphics` method `drawPolyline` displays a series of connected lines specified by its arguments (an array containing the *x*-coordinate of each point, an array containing the *y*-coordinate of each point and the number of points).
- `Polygon` method `addPoint` adds pairs of *x*- and *y*-coordinates to a `Polygon`.
- The Java2D API provides advanced two-dimensional graphics capabilities for processing line art, text and images.
- To access the `Graphics2D` capabilities, downcast the `Graphics` reference passed to `paint` to a `Graphics2d` reference as in (`Graphics2D`) g.
- `Graphics2D` method `setPaint` sets the `Paint` object that determines the color and texture for the shape to display. A `Paint` object is an object of any class that implements interface `java.awt.Paint`. The `Paint` object can be a `Color` or an instance of the Java2D API's `GradientPaint`, `SystemColor` or `TexturePaint` classes.
- Class `GradientPaint` draws a shape in a gradually changing color—called a *gradient*.
- `Graphics2D` method `fill` draws a filled `Shape` object. The `Shape` object is an instance of any class that implements interface `Shape`.
- The `Ellipse2D.Double` constructor receives four arguments specifying the bounding rectangle for the ellipse to display.
- `Graphics2D` method `setStroke` sets the characteristics of the lines used to draw a shape. Method `setStroke` requires a `Stroke` object as its argument. The `Stroke` object is an instance of any class that implements interface `Stroke`, such as a `BasicStroke`.

- Graphics2D method draw draws a Shape object. The Shape object is an instance of any class that implements interface Shape.
- The Rectangle2D.Double constructor receives four arguments specifying the upper-left *x*-coordinate, upper-left *y*-coordinate, width and height of the rectangle.
- Class BufferedImage can be used to produce images in color and gray scale.
- A TexturePaint object uses the image stored in its associated BufferedImage as the fill texture for a filled-in shape.
- The RoundRectangle2D.Double constructor receives six arguments specifying the rectangle dimensions and the arc width and arc height used to determine the rounding of the corners.
- The Arc2D.Double constructor's first four arguments specify the upper-left *x*-coordinate, upper-left *y*-coordinate, width and height of the bounding rectangle for the arc. The fifth argument specifies the start angle. The sixth argument specifies the end angle. The last argument specifies the type of arc (Arc2D.PIE, Arc2D.CHORD or Arc2D.OPEN).
- The Line2D.Double constructor's arguments specify starting and ending line coordinates.
- A general path is a shape constructed from straight lines and complex curves represented with an object of class GeneralPath (package java.awt.geom).
- GeneralPath method moveTo specifies the first point in a general path. GeneralPath method lineTo draws a line to the next point in the general path. Each new call to lineTo draws a line from the previous point to the current point. GeneralPath method closePath draws a line from the last point to the point specified in the last call to moveTo.
- Graphics2D method translate moves the drawing origin to a new location. All drawing operations now use that location as *(0, 0)*.

TERMINOLOGY

addPoint method
angle
arc bounded by a rectangle
arc height
arc sweeping through an angle
arc width
Arc2D.Double class
ascent
background color
baseline
bounding rectangle
BufferedImage class
closed polygon
closePath method
Color class
Component class
coordinate
coordinate system
degree
descent
draw an arc
draw method
draw3DRect method

drawArc method
drawLine method
drawOval method
drawPolygon method
drawPolyline method
drawRect method
drawRoundRect method
Ellipse2D.Double class
event
event-driven process
fill method
fill3DRect method
fillArc method
filled polygon
fillOval method
fillPolygon method
fillRect method
fillRoundRect method
font
Font class
font metrics
font name
font style

COMMON PROGRAMMING ERRORS

28.1 Spelling any `static Color` class constant with an initial capital letter is a syntax error.

28.2 Specifying a font that is not available on a system is a logic error. Java will substitute that system's default font.

28.3 An `ArrayIndexOutOfBoundsException` is thrown if the number of points specified in the third argument to method `drawPolygon` or method `fillPolygon` is greater than the number of elements in the arrays of coordinates that define the polygon to display.

PORTABILITY TIPS

28.1 Different display monitors have different resolutions (i.e., the density of pixels varies). This may cause graphics to appear to be different sizes on different monitors.

28.2 The number of fonts varies greatly across systems. The JDK guarantees that the fonts `Serif`, `Monospaced`, `SansSerif`, `Dialog` and `DialogInput` will be available.

28.3 Java uses standardized font names and maps these into system-specific font names for portability. This is transparent to the programmer.

SOFTWARE ENGINEERING OBSERVATIONS

28.1   The upper-left coordinate *(0, 0)* of a window is actually *behind* the title bar of the window. For this reason, drawing coordinates should be adjusted to draw inside the borders of the window. Class `Container` (a superclass of all windows in Java) has method `getInsets` that returns an `Insets` object (package `java.awt`) for this purpose. An `Insets` object has four `public` members—`top`, `bottom`, `left` and `right`—that represent the number of pixels from each edge of the window to the drawing area for the window.

28.2   To change the color, you must create a new `Color` object (or use one of the predefined `Color` constants); there are no *set* methods in class `Color` to change the characteristics of the current color.

28.3   To change the font, you must create a new `Font` object; there are no *set* methods in class `Font` to change the characteristics of the current font.

SELF-REVIEW EXERCISES

28.1   Fill in the blanks in each of the following:
   a) In Java2D, method _____ of class _____ sets the characteristics of a line used to draw a shape.
   b) Class _____ helps define the fill for a shape such that the fill gradually changes from one color to another.
   c) The _____ method of class `Graphics` draws a line between two points.
   d) RGB is short for _____, _____ and _____.
   e) Font sizes are measured in units called _____.
   f) Class _____ helps define the fill for a shape using a pattern drawn in an object of class `BufferedImage`.

28.2   State whether each of the following is *true* or *false*. If *false*, explain why.
   a) The first two arguments of `Graphics` method `drawOval` specify the center coordinate of the oval.
   b) In the Java coordinate system, *x* values increase from left to right.
   c) Method `fillPolygon` draws a solid polygon in the current color.
   d) Method `drawArc` allows negative angles.
   e) Method `getSize` returns the size of the current font in centimeters.
   f) Pixel coordinate *(0, 0)* is located at the exact center of the monitor.

28.3   Find the error(s) in each of the following and explain how to correct the error(s). Assume that g is a `Graphics` object.
```
a) g.setFont( "SansSerif" );
b) g.erase( x, y, w, h );    // clear rectangle at (x, y)
c) Font f = new Font( "Serif", Font.BOLDITALIC, 12 );
d) g.setColor( Color.Yellow );  // change color to yellow
```

ANSWERS TO SELF-REVIEW EXERCISES

28.1   a) `setStroke`, `Graphics2D`. b) `GradientPaint`. c) `drawLine`. d) red, green, blue. e) points. f) `TexturePaint`.

28.2   a) False. The first two arguments specify the upper-left corner of the bounding rectangle.
   b) True.
   c) True.
   d) True.
   e) False. Font sizes are measured in points.

f) False. The coordinate *(0,0)* corresponds to the upper-left corner of a GUI component on which drawing occurs.

28.3   a) The `setFont` method takes a `Font` object as an argument—not a `String`.

b) The `Graphics` class does not have an `erase` method. The `clearRect` method should be used.

c) `Font.BOLDITALIC` is not a valid font style. To get a bold italic font, use `Font.BOLD` + `Font.ITALIC`.

d) `Yellow` should begin with a lowercase letter: `g.setColor( Color.yellow );`.

EXERCISES

28.4   Fill in the blanks in each of the following:

a) Class _____ of the Java2D API is used to define ovals.

b) Methods `draw` and `fill` of class `Graphics2D` require an object of type _____ as their argument.

c) The three constants that specify font style are _____, _____ and _____.

d) `Graphics2D` method _____ sets the painting color for Java2D shapes.

28.5   State whether each of the following is *true* or *false*. If *false*, explain why.

a) The `drawPolygon` method automatically connects the endpoints of the polygon.

b) The `drawLine` method draws a line between two points.

c) The `fillArc` method uses degrees to specify the angle.

d) In the Java coordinate system, *y* values increase from top to bottom.

e) The `Graphics` class inherits directly from class `Object`.

f) The `Graphics` class is an `abstract` class.

g) The `Font` class inherits directly from class `Graphics`.

28.6   Write a program that draws a series of eight concentric circles. The circles should be separated by 10 pixels. Use the `drawOval` method of class `Graphics`.

28.7   Write a program that draws a series of eight concentric circles. The circles should be separated by 10 pixels. Use the `drawArc` method.

28.8   Modify your solution to Exercise 28.6 to draw the ovals using instances of class `Ellipse2D.Double` and method `draw` of class `Graphics2D`.

28.9   Write a program that draws lines of random lengths in random colors.

28.10   Modify your solution to Exercise 28.9 to draw random lines, in random colors and random line thicknesses. Use class `Line2D.Double` and method `draw` of class `Graphics2D` to draw the lines.

28.11   Write a program that displays randomly generated triangles in different colors. Each triangle should be filled with a different color. Use class `GeneralPath` and method `fill` of class `Graphics2D` to draw the triangles.

28.12   Write a program that randomly draws characters in different font sizes and colors.

28.13   Write a program that draws an 8-by-8 grid. Use the `drawLine` method.

28.14   Modify your solution to Exercise 28.13 to draw the grid using instances of class `Line2D.Double` and method `draw` of class `Graphics2D`.

28.15   Write a program that draws a 10-by-10 grid. Use the `drawRect` method.

28.16   Modify your solution to Exercise 28.15 to draw the grid using instances of class `Rectangle2D.Double` and method `draw` of class `Graphics2D`.

28.17   Write a program that draws a tetrahedron (a pyramid). Use class `GeneralPath` and method draw of class `Graphics2D`.

28.18   Write a program that draws a cube. Use class `GeneralPath` and method `draw` of class `Graphics2D`.

28.19   Write an application that simulates a screen saver. The application should randomly draw lines using method `drawLine` of class `Graphics`. After drawing 100 lines, the application should clear itself and start drawing lines again. To allow the program to draw continuously, place a call to `repaint` as the last line in method `paint`. Do you notice any problems with this on your system?

28.20   Here is a peek ahead. Package `javax.swing` contains a class called `Timer` that is capable of calling method `actionPerformed` of interface `ActionListener` at a fixed time interval (specified in milliseconds). Modify your solution to Exercise 28.19 to remove the call to `repaint` from method `paint`. Define your class so it implements `ActionListener` (the `actionPerformed` method should simply call `repaint`). Define an instance variable of type `Timer` called `timer` in your class. In the constructor for your class, write the following statements:

```
timer = new Timer( 1000, this );
timer.start();
```

This creates an instance of class `Timer` that will call `this` object's `actionPerformed` method every 1000 milliseconds (i.e., every second).

28.21   Modify your solution to Exercise 28.20 to enable the user to enter the number of random lines that should be drawn before the application clears itself and starts drawing lines again. Use a `JText-Field` to obtain the value. The user should be able to type a new number into the `JTextField` at any time during the program's execution. [*Note*: Combining Swing GUI components and drawing leads to interesting problems for which we present solutions in Chapter 29.] For now, the first line of your `paint` method should be

```
super.paint( g );
```

to ensure that the GUI components are displayed properly. You will notice that some of the randomly drawn lines will obscure the `JTextField`. Use an inner class definition to perform event handling for the `JTextField`.

28.22   Modify your solution to Exercise 28.20 to randomly choose different shapes to display (use methods of class `Graphics`).]

28.23   Modify your solution to Exercise 28.22 to use classes and drawing capabilities of the Java2D API. For shapes such as rectangles and ellipses, draw them with randomly generated gradients (use class `GradientPaint` to generate the gradient).

28.24   Write a program that uses method `drawPolyline` to draw a spiral.

28.25   Write a program that inputs four numbers and graphs the numbers as a pie chart. Use class `Arc2D.Double` and method `fill` of class `Graphics2D` to perform the drawing. Draw each piece of the pie in a separate color.

28.26   Write an applet that inputs four numbers and graphs the numbers as a bar graph. Use class `Rectangle2D.Double` and method `fill` of class `Graphics2D` to perform the drawing. Draw each bar in a different color.

29

Java Graphical User Interface Components

Objectives

- To understand the design principles of graphical user interfaces.
- To be able to build graphical user interfaces.
- To understand the packages containing graphical user interface components and event handling classes and interfaces.
- To be able to create and manipulate buttons, labels, lists, text fields and panels.
- To understand mouse events and keyboard events.
- To understand and be able to use layout managers.

… the wisest prophets make sure of the event first.
Horace Walpole

Do you think I can listen all day to such stuff?
Lewis Carroll

Speak the affirmative; emphasize your choice by utter ignoring of all that you reject.
Ralph Waldo Emerson

You pays your money and you takes your choice.
Punch

Guess if you can, choose if you dare.
Pierre Corneille

All hope abandon, ye who enter here!
Dante Alighieri

Outline

29.1 Introduction

A *graphical user interface (GUI)* presents a pictorial interface to a program. A GUI (pronounced "GOO-EE") gives a program a distinctive "look" and "feel." By providing different applications with a consistent set of intuitive user interface components, GUIs allow the user to spend less time trying to remember which keystroke sequences do what and spend more time using the program in a productive manner.

Look-and-Feel Observation 29.1

Consistent user interfaces enable a user to learn new applications faster.

As an example of a GUI, Figure 29.1 contains a Netscape Communicator window with some of its GUI components labeled. In the window, there is a *menu bar* containing *menus* (**File**, **Edit**, **View**, etc.). Below the menu bar there is a set of *buttons* that each have a defined task in Netscape Communicator. Below the buttons there is a *text field* in which the user can type the name of a World Wide Web site to visit. To the left of the text field is a *label* that indicates the purpose of the text field. The menus, buttons, text fields and labels are part of Netscape Communicator's GUI. They enable you to interact with the Communicator program. In this chapter and the next, we will demonstrate these GUI components.

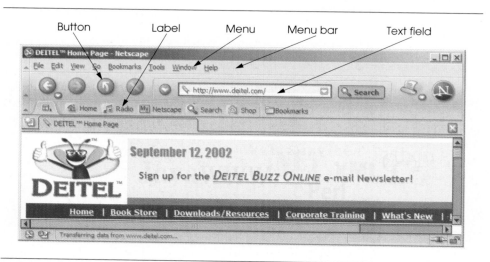

Fig. 29.1   A sample Netscape Communicator window with GUI components.

GUIs are built from *GUI components* (sometimes called *controls* or *widgets*—shorthand notation for *window gadgets*). A GUI component is an object with which the user interacts via the mouse or the keyboard. Several common GUI components are listed in Figure 29.2. In the sections that follow, we discuss each of these GUI components in detail. In the next chapter, we discuss more advanced GUI components.

Component	Description
JLabel	An area where uneditable text or icons can be displayed.
JTextField	An area in which the user inputs data from the keyboard. The area can also display information.
JButton	An area that triggers an event when clicked.
JCheckBox	A GUI component that is either selected or not selected.
JComboBox	A drop-down list of items from which the user can make a selection by clicking an item in the list or by typing into the box, if permitted.
JList	An area where a list of items is displayed from which the user can make a selection by clicking once on any element in the list. Double-clicking an element in the list generates an action event. Multiple elements can be selected.
JPanel	A container in which components can be placed.

Fig. 29.2   Some basic GUI components.

29.2 Swing Overview

The classes that are used to create the GUI components of Figure 29.2 are part of the *Swing GUI components* from package `javax.swing`. These are the newest GUI components of the Java 2 platform. *Swing components* (as they are commonly called) are written, manipulated and displayed completely in Java (so-called *pure Java* components).

The original GUI components from the *Abstract Windowing Toolkit* package `java.awt` (also called the *AWT*) are tied directly to the local platform's graphical user interface capabilities. So, a Java program executing on different Java platforms has a different appearance and sometimes even different user interactions on each platform. Together, the appearance and how the user interacts with the program are known as that program's *look and feel*. The Swing components allow the programmer to specify a different look and feel for each platform, or a uniform look and feel across all platforms, or even to change the look-and-feel while the program is running.

Look-and-Feel Observation 29.2

Swing components are written in Java, so they provide a greater level of portability and flexibility than the original Java GUI components from package `java.awt`.

Swing components are often referred to as *lightweight components*—they are written completely in Java so they are not "weighed down" by the complex GUI capabilities of the platform on which they are used. AWT components (many of which parallel the Swing components) that are tied to the local platform are correspondingly called *heavyweight components*—they rely on the local platform's *windowing system* to determine their functionality and their look and feel. Each heavyweight component has a *peer* (from package `java.awt.peer`) that is responsible for the interactions between the component and the local platform to display and manipulate the component. Several Swing components are still heavyweight components. In particular, subclasses of `java.awt.Window` (such as `JFrame` used in previous chapters) that display windows on the screen still require direct interaction with the local windowing system. As such, heavyweight Swing GUI components are less flexible than many of the lightweight components we will demonstrate.

Portability Tip 29.1

The look of a GUI defined with heavyweight GUI components from package `java.awt` may vary across platforms. Heavyweight components "tie" into the "local" platform GUI, which varies from platform to platform.

Figure 29.3 shows an inheritance hierarchy of the classes that define attributes and behaviors that are common to most Swing components. Each class is displayed with its fully qualified package name and class name. Much of each GUI component's functionality is derived from these classes. A class that inherits from the `Component` class *is a component*. For example, class *`Container`* inherits from class `Component`, and class `Component` inherits from `Object`. Thus, a `Container` *is a* `Component` and *is an* `Object`, and a `Component` *is an* `Object`. A class that inherits from class `Container` *is a* `Container`. Thus, a `JComponent` *is a* `Container`.

Software Engineering Observation 29.1

To effectively use GUI components, the `javax.swing` and `java.awt` inheritance hierarchies must be understood—especially class `Component`, class `Container` and class `JComponent`, which define features common to most Swing components.

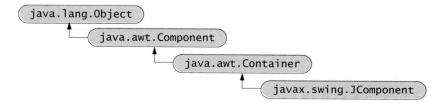

Fig. 29.3   Common superclasses of many of the Swing components.

Class `Component` defines the methods that can be applied to an object of any subclass of `Component`. Two of the methods that originate in class `Component` have been used frequently to this point in the text—`paint` and `repaint`. It is important to understand the methods of class `Component` because much of the functionality inherited by every subclass of `Component` is defined by the `Component` class originally. Operations common to most GUI components (both Swing and AWT) are found in class `Component`.

Good Programming Practice 29.1

Study the methods of class `Component` *in the Java 2 SDK on-line documentation to learn the capabilities common to most GUI components.*

A `Container` is a collection of related components. In applications with `JFrame`s and in applets, we attach components to the content pane—a `Container`. Class `Container` defines the set of methods that can be applied to an object of any subclass of `Container`. One method that originates in class `Container` that has been used frequently to this point in the text is `add` for adding components to a content pane. Another method that originates in class `Container` is `setLayout`, which has been used to specify the layout manager that helps a `Container` position and size its components.

Good Programming Practice 29.2

Study the methods of class `Container` *in the Java 2 SDK on-line documentation to learn the capabilities common to every container for GUI components.*

Class `JComponent` is the superclass to most Swing components. This class defines the set of methods that can be applied to an object of any subclass of `JComponent`.

Good Programming Practice 29.3

Study the methods of class `JComponent` *in the Java 2 SDK on-line documentation to learn the capabilities common to every container for GUI components.*

Swing components that subclass `JComponent` have many features, including:

1. A *pluggable look and feel* that can be used to customize the look and feel when the program executes on different platforms.

2. Shortcut keys (called *mnemonics*) for direct access to GUI components through the keyboard.

3. Common event handling capabilities for cases where several GUI components initiate the same actions in a program.

4. Brief descriptions of a GUI component's purpose (called *tool tips*) that are displayed when the mouse cursor is positioned over the component for a short time.

5. Support for assistive technologies such as braille screen readers for blind people.

6. Support for user interface *localization*—customizing the user interface for display in different languages and cultural conventions.

These are just some of the many features of the Swing components. We discuss several of these features in the remainder of this chapter.

29.3 JLabel

Labels provide text instructions or information on a GUI. Labels are defined with class *JLabel*—a subclass of JComponent. A label displays a single line of *read-only text*. Once labels are created, programs rarely change a label's contents. The application of Figure 29.4 demonstrates JLabels.

Good Programming Practice 29.4

Study the methods of class javax.swing.JLabel in the Java 2 SDK on-line documentation to learn the complete capabilities of the class before using it.

```
1   // Fig. 29.4: LabelTest.java
2   // Demonstrating the JLabel class.
3   import javax.swing.*;
4   import java.awt.*;
5   import java.awt.event.*;
6
7   public class LabelTest extends JFrame {
8      private JLabel label1, label2, label3;
9
10     public LabelTest()
11     {
12        super( "Testing JLabel" );
13
14        Container c = getContentPane();
15        c.setLayout( new FlowLayout() );
16
17        // JLabel constructor with a string argument
18        label1 = new JLabel( "Label with text" );
19        label1.setToolTipText( "This is label1" );
20        c.add( label1 );
21
22        // JLabel constructor with string, Icon and
23        // alignment arguments
24        Icon bug = new ImageIcon( "bug1.gif" );
25        label2 = new JLabel( "Label with text and icon",
26                             bug, SwingConstants.LEFT );
27        label2.setToolTipText( "This is label2" );
28        c.add( label2 );
29
30        // JLabel constructor no arguments
31        label3 = new JLabel();
32        label3.setText( "Label with icon and text at bottom" );
33        label3.setIcon( bug );
```

Fig. 29.4 Demonstrating class JLabel. (Part 1 of 2.)

```
34            label3.setHorizontalTextPosition(
35                SwingConstants.CENTER );
36            label3.setVerticalTextPosition(
37                SwingConstants.BOTTOM );
38            label3.setToolTipText( "This is label3" );
39            c.add( label3 );
40
41            setSize( 275, 170 );
42            show();
43        } // end LabelTest constructor
44
45        public static void main( String args[] )
46        {
47            LabelTest app = new LabelTest();
48
49            app.addWindowListener(
50                new WindowAdapter() {
51                    public void windowClosing( WindowEvent e )
52                    {
53                        System.exit( 0 );
54                    } // end method windowClosing
55                } // end anonymous inner class
56            ); // end addWindowListener
57        } // end main
58    } // end class LabelTest
```

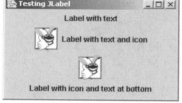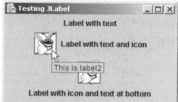

Fig. 29.4   Demonstrating class JLabel. (Part 2 of 2.)

The program declares three JLabel references with line 8

```
private JLabel label1, label2, label3;
```

The JLabel objects are instantiated in the constructor (line 10). The statement

```
label1 = new JLabel( "Label with text" );
```

in line 18 creates a JLabel object with the text **"Label with text"**. The text is displayed on the label. Line 19

```
label1.setToolTipText( "This is label1" );
```

uses method *setToolTipText* (inherited into class JLabel from class JComponent) to specify the tool tip (see the right screen capture in Figure 29.4) that is displayed whenever the user positions the mouse cursor over the label in the GUI. When you execute this program, try positioning the mouse over each label to see its tool tip. Line 20 adds label1 to the content pane.

Look-and-Feel Observation 29.3

Use tool tips (set with JComponent method setToolTipText) to add descriptive text to your GUI components. This text helps the user determine the GUI component's purpose in the user interface.

Many Swing components can display images by specifying an *Icon* as an argument to their constructor or by using a method that is normally called *setIcon*. An Icon is an object of any class that implements interface *Icon* (package javax.swing). One such class is *ImageIcon* (package javax.swing), which supports two image formats— *Graphics Interchange Format (GIF)* and *Joint Photographic Experts Group (JPEG)*. File names for each of these types typically end with .gif or .jpg (or .jpeg), respectively. We discuss images in more detail in Chapter 30, Java Multimedia. Line 24

```
Icon bug = new ImageIcon( "bug1.gif" );
```

defines an ImageIcon object. The file bug1.gif contains the image to load and store in the ImageIcon object. This file is assumed to be in the same directory as the program (we will discuss locating the file elsewhere in Chapter 30). The ImageIcon object is assigned to Icon reference bug. Remember, class ImageIcon implements interface Icon, therefore an ImageIcon *is an* Icon.

Class JLabel supports the display of Icons. Lines 25 and 26

```
label2 = new JLabel( "Label with text and icon",
                bug, SwingConstants.LEFT );
```

use another JLabel constructor to create a label that displays the text "Label with text and icon" and the Icon to which bug refers, and is *left-justified* or *left-aligned* (i.e., the icon and text are at the left side of the label's area on the screen). Interface *SwingConstants* (package javax.swing) defines a set of common integer constants (such as SwingConstants.LEFT) that are used with many Swing components. By default, the text appears to the right of the image when a label contains both text and an image. Both the horizontal and vertical alignments of a label can be set with methods *setHorizontalAlignment* and *setVerticalAlignment*, respectively. Line 27 specifies the tool tip text for label2. Line 28 adds label2 to the content pane.

Common Programming Error 29.1

Forgetting to add a component to a container so it can be displayed is a run-time logic error.

Common Programming Error 29.2

Adding to a container a component that has not been instantiated throws a NullPointerException.

Class JLabel provides many methods to configure a label after it has been instantiated. Line 31 creates a JLabel and invokes the no-argument (default constructor). Such a label has no text or Icon. Line 32

```
label3.setText( "Label with icon and text at bottom" );
```

uses JLabel method *setText* to set the text displayed on the label. A corresponding method *getText* retrieves the current text displayed on a label. Line 33

```
label3.setIcon( bug );
```

uses JLabel method *setIcon* to set the Icon displayed on the label. A corresponding method *getIcon* retrieves the current Icon displayed on a label. Lines 34 through 37

```
label3.setHorizontalTextPosition(
    SwingConstants.CENTER );
label3.setVerticalTextPosition(
    SwingConstants.BOTTOM );
```

use JLabel methods *setHorizontalTextPosition* and *setVerticalTextPosition* to specify the text position in the label. The preceding statements indicate that the text will be centered horizontally and will appear at the bottom of the label. Thus, the Icon will appear above the text. Line 38 sets the tool tip text for the label3. Line 39 adds label3 to the content pane.

29.4 Event Handling Model

In the preceding section, we did not discuss event handling because there are no specific events for JLabel objects. GUIs are *event driven* (i.e., they generate *events* when the user of the program interacts with the GUI). Some common interactions are moving the mouse, clicking the mouse, clicking a button, typing in a text field, selecting an item from a menu, closing a window, etc. Whenever a user interaction occurs, an event is sent to the program. GUI event information is stored in an object of a class that extends AWTEvent. Figure 29.5 illustrates a hierarchy containing many of the event classes we use from package *java.awt.event*. Many of these event classes are discussed throughout this chapter. The event types from package java.awt.event are still used with the Swing components. Additional event types have also been added that are specific to several types of Swing components. New Swing component event types are defined in package *javax.swing.event*.

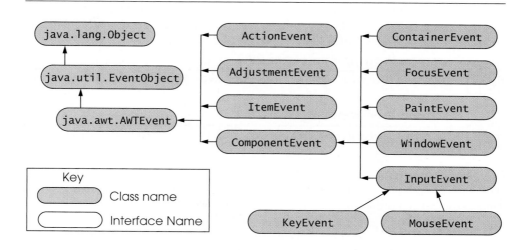

Fig. 29.5 Some event classes of package java.awt.event.

To process a graphical user interface event, the programmer must perform two key tasks—register an *event listener* and implement an *event handler*. An event listener for a GUI event is an object of a class that implements one or more of the event-listener interfaces from package `java.awt.event` and package `javax.swing.event`. Many of the event listener types are common to both Swing and AWT components. Such types are defined in package `java.awt.event` and many of these are shown in Figure 29.6 [*Note*: A shaded background indicates an interface in the diagram.] Additional event listener types that are specific to Swing components are defined in package `javax.swing.event`.

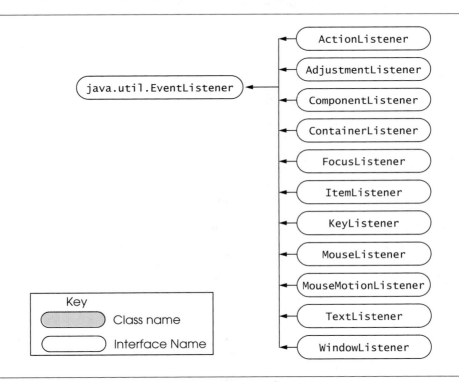

Fig. 29.6 Event-listener interfaces of package `java.awt.event`.

An event listener object "listens" for specific types of events generated in the same object or by other objects (normally GUI components) in a program. An event handler is a method that is automatically called in response to a particular type of event. Each event-listener interface specifies one or more event handling methods that *must* be defined in the class that implements the event-listener interface. Remember that interfaces define `abstract` methods. Any class that implements an interface must define all the methods of that interface; otherwise, the class is an `abstract` class and cannot be used to create objects. The use of event listeners in event handling is known as the *delegation event model*—the processing of an event is delegated to a particular object in the program.

When an event occurs, the GUI component with which the user interacted notifies its registered listeners by calling each listener's appropriate event handling method. For example, when the user presses the *Enter* key in a `JTextField`, the registered listener's actionPerformed method is called. How did the event handler get registered? How does the GUI component know to call actionPerformed as opposed to some other event handling method? We answer these questions and diagram the interaction as part of the next example.

29.5 JTextField and JPasswordField

JTextFields and *JPasswordFields* (package javax.swing) are single-line areas in which text can be entered by the user from the keyboard or text can simply be displayed. A JPasswordField shows that a character was typed as the user enters characters, but hides the characters assuming that they represent a password that should remain known only to the user. When the user types data into a JTextField or JPasswordField and presses the *Enter* key, an action event occurs. If an event listener is registered, the event is processed and the data in the JTextField or JPasswordField can be used in the program. Class JTextField extends class *JTextComponent* (package javax.swing.text), which provides many features common to Swing's text-based components. Class JPasswordField extends JTextField and adds several methods that are specific to processing passwords.

Common Programming Error 29.3

Using a lowercase f in the class names JTextFieldor JPasswordFieldis a syntax error.

The application of Figure 29.7 uses classes JTextField and JPasswordField to create and manipulate four fields. When the user presses *Enter* in the current-active field (the current-active component "has the *focus*"), a message dialog box containing the text in the field is displayed. When an event occurs in the JPasswordField, the password is revealed.

```
1   // Fig. 29.7: TextFieldTest.java
2   // Demonstrating the JTextField class.
3   import java.awt.*;
4   import java.awt.event.*;
5   import javax.swing.*;
6
7   public class TextFieldTest extends JFrame {
8      private JTextField text1, text2, text3;
9      private JPasswordField password;
10
11     public TextFieldTest()
12     {
13        super( "Testing JTextField and JPasswordField" );
14
15        Container c = getContentPane();
16        c.setLayout( new FlowLayout() );
17
18        // construct textfield with default sizing
19        text1 = new JTextField( 10 );
20        c.add( text1 );
```

Fig. 29.7   Demonstrating JTextFields and JPasswordFields. (Part 1 of 3.)

```
21
22          // construct textfield with default text
23          text2 = new JTextField( "Enter text here" );
24          c.add( text2 );
25
26          // construct textfield with default text and
27          // 20 visible elements and no event handler
28          text3 = new JTextField( "Uneditable text field", 20 );
29          text3.setEditable( false );
30          c.add( text3 );
31
32          // construct textfield with default text
33          password = new JPasswordField( "Hidden text" );
34          c.add( password );
35
36          TextFieldHandler handler = new TextFieldHandler();
37          text1.addActionListener( handler );
38          text2.addActionListener( handler );
39          text3.addActionListener( handler );
40          password.addActionListener( handler );
41
42          setSize( 325, 100 );
43          show();
44      } // end TextFieldTest constructor
45
46      public static void main( String args[] )
47      {
48          TextFieldTest app = new TextFieldTest();
49
50          app.addWindowListener(
51              new WindowAdapter() {
52                  public void windowClosing( WindowEvent e )
53                  {
54                      System.exit( 0 );
55                  } // end method windowClosing
56              } // end anonymous inner class
57          ); // end addWindowListener
58      } // end main
59
60      // inner class for event handling
61      private class TextFieldHandler implements ActionListener {
62          public void actionPerformed( ActionEvent e )
63          {
64              String s = "";
65
66              if ( e.getSource() == text1 )
67                  s = "text1: " + e.getActionCommand();
68              else if ( e.getSource() == text2 )
69                  s = "text2: " + e.getActionCommand();
70              else if ( e.getSource() == text3 )
71                  s = "text3: " + e.getActionCommand();
72              else if ( e.getSource() == password ) {
```

Fig. 29.7   Demonstrating JTextFields and JPasswordFields. (Part 2 of 3.)

```
73                    JPasswordField pwd =
74                        (JPasswordField) e.getSource();
75                s = "password: " +
76                        new String( pwd.getPassword() );
77                } // end else if
78
79                JOptionPane.showMessageDialog( null, s );
80            } // end method actionPerformed
81        } // end class TextFieldHandler
82    } // end class TextFieldText
```

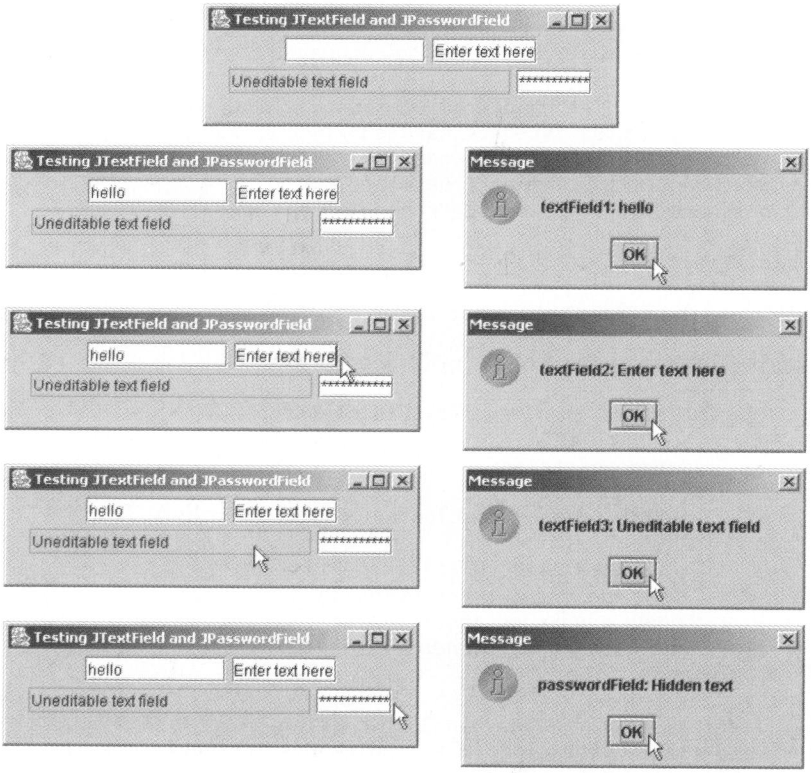

Fig. 29.7 Demonstrating `JTextField`s and `JPasswordField`s. (Part 3 of 3.)

Lines 8 and 9 declare three references for `JTextField`s (`text1`, `text2` and `text3`) and a `JPasswordField` (`password`). Each of these is instantiated in the constructor (line 11). Line 19

```
text1 = new JTextField( 10 );
```

defines `JTextField text1` with 10 columns of text. The width of the text field will be the width in pixels of the average character in the text field's current font multiplied by 10. Line 20 adds `text1` to the content pane.

Line 23

```
text2 = new JTextField( "Enter text here" );
```

defines JTextField text2 with the initial text "Enter text here" to display in the text field. The width of the text field is determined by the text. Line 24 adds text2 to the content pane.

Line 28

```
text3 = new JTextField( "Uneditable text field", 20 );
```

defines JTextField text3 and call the JTextField constructor with two arguments—the default text "Uneditable text field" to display in the text field and the number of columns (20). The width of the text field is determined by the number of columns specified.

Line 29

```
text3.setEditable( false );
```

uses method *setEditable* (inherited into JTextField from class JTextComponent) to indicate that the user cannot modify the text in the text field. Line 30 adds text3 to the content pane.

Line 33

```
password = new JPasswordField( "Hidden text" );
```

defines JPasswordField password with the text "Hidden text" to display in the text field. The width of the text field is determined by the text. Notice that the text is displayed as a string of asterisks when the program executes. Line 34 adds password to the content pane.

For the event handling in this example, we defined inner class TextFieldHandler (lines 61 to 81). Class JTextField handler (discussed in detail shortly) implements interface ActionListener. Thus, every instance of class TextFieldHandler *is an* ActionListener. Line 36

```
TextFieldHandler handler = new TextFieldHandler();
```

defines an instance of class TextFieldHandler and assigns it to reference handler. This one instance will be used as the event-listener object for the JTextFields and the JPasswordField in this example.

Lines 37 through 40

```
text1.addActionListener( handler );
text2.addActionListener( handler );
text3.addActionListener( handler );
password.addActionListener( handler );
```

are the event registration statements that specify the event listener object for each of the three JTextFields and for the JPasswordField. After these statements execute, the object to which handler refers is *listening for events* (i.e., it will be notified when an event occurs) on these four objects. In each case, method addActionListener of class JTextField is called to register the event. Method addActionListener receives as its argument an ActionListener object. Thus, any object of a class that implements interface

ActionListener (i.e., any object that *is an* ActionListener) can be supplied as an argument to this method. The object to which handler refers *is an* ActionListener because its class implements interface ActionListener. Now, when the user presses *Enter* in any of these four fields, method actionPerformed (line 62) in class TextFieldHandler is called to handle the event.

Software Engineering Observation 29.2

The event listener for an event must implement the appropriate event-listener interface.

Method actionPerformed uses its ActionEvent argument's method getSource to determine the GUI component with which the user interacted and creates a String to display in a message dialog box. ActionEvent method getActionCommand returns the text in the JTextField that generated the event. If the user interacted with the JPasswordField, lines 73 and 74

```
JPasswordField pwd =
    (JPasswordField) e.getSource();
```

cast the Component reference returned by e.getSource() to a JPasswordField reference so that lines 75 and 76

```
s = "password: " +
    new String( pwd.getPassword() );
```

can use JPasswordField method *getPassword* to obtain the password and create the String to be displayed. Method getPassword returns the password as an array of type char that is used as an argument to a String constructor to create a String. Line 79 displays a message box indicating the GUI component reference name and the text the user typed in the field.

Note that even an uneditable JTextField can generate an event. Also note that the actual text of the password is displayed when you press *Enter* in the JPasswordField (of course, you would normally not do this!).

Common Programming Error 29.4

Forgetting to register an event handler object for a particular GUI component's event type results in no events being handled for that component for that event type.

Using a separate class to define an event listener is a common programming practice for separating the GUI interface from the implementation of its event handler. For the remainder of this chapter many programs use separate event-listener classes to process GUI events in an attempt to make the code more reusable. Any class that has potential for reuse beyond the example in which the class is introduced has been placed in a package so it can be imported into other programs for reuse.

Good Programming Practice 29.5

Use separate classes to process GUI events.

Software Engineering Observation 29.3

Using separate classes to handle GUI events leads to more reusable, reliable and readable software components that can be placed in packages and used in many programs.

29.5.1 How Event Handling Works

Let us illustrate how the event handling mechanism works using `JTextField text1` from the preceding example. We have two remaining open questions from Section 29.4:

1. How did the event handler get registered?

2. How does the GUI component know to call `actionPerformed` as opposed to some other event handling method?

The first question is answered by the event-registration performed in lines 37 through 40 of the program. Figure 29.8 diagrams `JTextField text1` and its registered event handler.

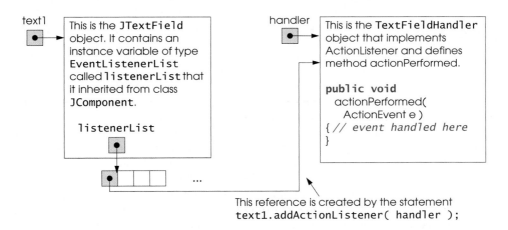

Fig. 29.8   Event registration for `JTextField text1`.

Every `JComponent` has an object of class *`EventListenerList`* (package `javax.swing.event`) called *`listenerList`* as an instance variable. All registered listeners are stored in the `listenerList` (diagramed as an array in Figure 29.8). When the statement

```
text1.addActionListener( handler );
```

executes in Figure 29.7, a new entry is placed in the `listenerList` for `JTextField text1` indicating both the reference to the listener object and the type of listener (in this case `ActionListener`).

The type is important in answering the second question—how does the GUI component know to call `actionPerformed` rather than another event handling method? Every `JComponent` actually supports several different event types, including *mouse events*, *key events* and others. When an event occurs, the event is *dispatched* only to the event listeners of the appropriate type. The dispatching of an event is simply calling the event handling method for each registered listener for that event type.

Each event type has a corresponding event-listener interface. For example, `Action-Events` are handled by `ActionListeners`, *MouseEvents* are handled by *MouseLis-*

teners (and *MouseMotionListeners* as we will see) and *KeyEvents* are handled by *KeyListeners*. When an event is generated by a user interaction with a component, the component is handed a unique *event ID* specifying the event type that occurred. The GUI component uses the event ID to decide the type of listener to which the event should be dispatched and the method to call. In the case of an `ActionEvent`, the event is dispatched to every registered `ActionListener`'s `actionPerformed` method (the only method in interface `ActionListener`). In the case of a `MouseEvent`, the event is dispatched to every registered `MouseListener` (or `MouseMotionListener`). The event ID of the `Mouse-Event` determines which of the seven different mouse event handling methods are called. All this decision logic is handled for you by the GUI components. We discuss other event types and event-listener interfaces as they are needed with each new component we cover.

29.6 JTextArea

JTextAreas provide an area for manipulating multiple lines of text. Like class `JText-Field`, class `JTextArea` inherits from `JTextComponent`, which defines common methods for `JTextFields`, `JTextAreas` and several other text-based GUI components.

The application of Figure 29.9 demonstrates `JTextAreas`. One `JTextArea` displays text that the user can select. The second `JTextArea` is uneditable, and its purpose is to display the text the user selected in the first `JTextArea`. `JTextAreas` do not have action events like `JTextFields`. Often, an *external event*, (i.e., an event generated by a different GUI component) indicates when the text in a `JTextArea` should be processed. For example, to send an email message, a user often clicks a **Send** button to take the text of the message and send it to the recipient. Similarly, when editing a document in a word processor, you normally save the file by selecting a menu item called **Save** or **Save As….** In this program, the button **Copy >>>** generates the external event that causes the selected text in the left `JTextArea` to be copied and displayed in the right `JTextArea`.

Look-and-Feel Observation 29.4

Often an external event determines when the text in a JTextArea should be processed.

```
1   // Fig. 29.9: TextAreaDemo.java
2   // Copying selected text from one text area to another.
3   import java.awt.*;
4   import java.awt.event.*;
5   import javax.swing.*;
6
7   public class TextAreaDemo extends JFrame {
8      private JTextArea t1, t2;
9      private JButton copy;
10
11     public TextAreaDemo()
12     {
13        super( "TextArea Demo" );
14
15        Box b = Box.createHorizontalBox();
16
```

Fig. 29.9   Copying selected text from one text area to another. (Part 1 of 3.)

```
17            String s = "This is a demo string to\n" +
18                       "illustrate copying text\n" +
19                       "from one TextArea to \n" +
20                       "another TextArea using an\n"+
21                       "external event\n";
22
23            t1 = new JTextArea( s, 10, 15 );
24            b.add( new JScrollPane( t1 ) );
25
26            copy = new JButton( "Copy >>>" );
27            copy.addActionListener(
28               new ActionListener() {
29                  public void actionPerformed( ActionEvent e )
30                  {
31                     t2.setText( t1.getSelectedText() );
32                  } // end method actionPerformed
33               } // end anonymous inner class
34            ); // end addActionListener
35            b.add( copy );
36
37            t2 = new JTextArea( 10, 15 );
38            t2.setEditable( false );
39            b.add( new JScrollPane( t2 ) );
40
41            Container c = getContentPane();
42            c.add( b );
43            setSize( 425, 200 );
44            show();
45         } // end TextAreaDemo constructor
46
47         public static void main( String args[] )
48         {
49            TextAreaDemo app = new TextAreaDemo();
50
51            app.addWindowListener(
52               new WindowAdapter() {
53                  public void windowClosing( WindowEvent e )
54                  {
55                     System.exit( 0 );
56                  } // end method windowClosing
57               } // end anonymous inner class
58            ); // end addWindowListener
59         } // end main
60      } // end class TextAreaDemo
```

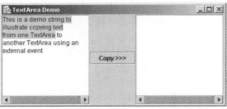

Fig. 29.9 Copying selected text from one text area to another. (Part 2 of 3.)

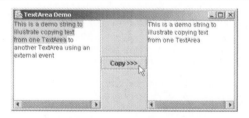

Fig. 29.9   Copying selected text from one text area to another. (Part 3 of 3.)

In the constructor method, line 15

```
Box b = Box.createHorizontalBox();
```

creates a *Box container* (package `javax.swing`) to which the GUI components will be attached. Class `Box` is a subclass of `java.awt.Container` that uses a *BoxLayout* layout manager to arrange the GUI components either horizontally or vertically. We will discuss layout managers further in section 29.11 on page 1124. Class `Box` provides `static` method *createHorizontalBox* to create a `Box` that automatically arranges the components attached to it from left to right in the order that the components are attached.

The application instantiates `JTextArea` objects and assigns them to references `t1` (line 23) and `t2` (line 37). Each `JTextArea` has 10 visible rows and 15 visible columns. Line 23

```
t1 = new JTextArea( s, 10, 15 );
```

specifies that the default string `s` should be displayed in the `JTextArea`. A `JTextArea` does not provide scrollbars in the event that there is more text than can be displayed in the `JTextArea`. For this reason, line 24

```
b.add( new JScrollPane( t1 ) );
```

creates a `JScrollPane` object that is initialized with `JTextArea t1` and both horizontal and vertical scrolling as necessary. The `JScrollPane` object is then added directly to the `Box` container `b`.

Lines 26 through 35 instantiate a `JButton` object and assign it to reference `copy` with the label `"Copy >>>"`, create an anonymous inner class to handle `copy`'s `ActionEvent` and add `copy` to the `Box` container object referenced by `b`. This button provides the external event that determines when the selected text in `t1` should be copied to `t2`. When the user clicks **Copy >>>**, line 31

```
t2.setText( t1.getSelectedText() );
```

in `actionPerformed` indicates that method *getSelectedText* (inherited into `JText-Area` from `JTextComponent`) should return the *selected text* from `t1`. Text is selected by dragging the mouse over the desired text to highlight it. Method `setText` then changes the text in `t2` to the returned `String`.

Lines 37 through 39 create `JTextArea t2` and add it to the `Box` container `b`. Lines 41 and 42 obtain the content pane for the window and add the `Box` to the content pane. The layout of the content pane is managed by a BorderLayout, which we will discuss in section 29.11.2 on page 1128.

[*Note:* It is sometimes desirable when text reaches the right side of a JTextArea to have the text wrap to the next line. This is referred to as *automatic word wrap.*]

Look-and-Feel Observation 29.5

To provide automatic word wrap functionality for a JTextArea, invoke JTextArea method setLineWrap with a true argument.

[*Note:* You can set the horizontal and vertical *scrollbar policies* for the JScrollPane when a JScrollPane is constructed or with methods *setHorizontalScrollBarPolicy* and *setVerticalScrollBarPolicy* of class JScrollPane at any time.] Class JScrollPane provides the constants

```
JScrollPane.VERTICAL_SCROLLBAR_ALWAYS
JScrollPane.HORIZONTAL_SCROLLBAR_ALWAYS
```

to indicate that a scrollbar should always appear, constants

```
JScrollPane.VERTICAL_SCROLLBAR_AS_NEEDED
JScrollPane.HORIZONTAL_SCROLLBAR_AS_NEEDED
```

to indicate that a scrollbar should appear only if necessary, and constants

```
JScrollPane.VERTICAL_SCROLLBAR_NEVER
JScrollPane.HORIZONTAL_SCROLLBAR_NEVER
```

to indicate that a scrollbar should never appear. If the horizontal scrollbar policy is set to JScrollPane.HORIZONTAL_SCROLLBAR_NEVER, a JTextArea attached to the JScrollPane will exhibit automatic word wrap behavior.

29.7 JButton

A *button* is a component the user clicks to trigger a specific action. A Java program can use several types of buttons, including *command buttons*, *check boxes*, *toggle buttons* and *radio buttons*. Figure 29.10 shows the inheritance hierarchy of the Swing buttons we cover in this chapter. As you can see in the diagram, all the button types are subclasses of *AbstractButton* (package javax.swing), which defines many of the features that are common to Swing buttons. In this section, we concentrate on buttons that are typically used to initiate a command. Other button types are covered in the next several sections.

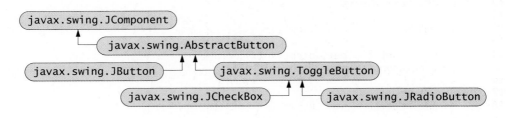

Fig. 29.10 The button hierarchy.

A command button generates an `ActionEvent` when the user clicks the button with the mouse. Command buttons are created with class *JButton*, which inherits from class `AbstractButton`. The text on the face of a `JButton` is called a *button label*. A GUI can have many `JButtons`, but each button label should typically be unique.

Look-and-Feel Observation 29.6

Having more than one JButton with the same label makes the JButtons ambiguous to the user. Be sure to provide a unique label for each button.

The application of Figure 29.11 creates two `JButtons` and demonstrates that `JBut-tons` (like `JLabels`) support the display of `Icons`. Event handling for the buttons is performed by a single instance of inner class `ButtonHandler` (line 52).

Line 8 declares two references to instances of class `JButton`—`plainButton` and `fancyButton`—that are instantiated in the constructor (line 10).

Line 18

```
plainButton = new JButton( "Plain Button" );
```

creates `plainButton` with the button label `"Plain Button"`. Line 19 adds the button to the content pane.

A `JButton` can display `Icons`. To provide the user with an extra level of visual interactivity with the GUI, a `JButton` can also have a *rollover* `Icon`—an `Icon` that is displayed when the mouse is positioned over the button. The icon on the button changes as the mouse moves in and out of the button's area on the screen. Lines 21 and 22

```
Icon bug1 = new ImageIcon( "bug1.gif" );
Icon bug2 = new ImageIcon( "bug2.gif" );
```

create two `ImageIcon` objects that represent the default `Icon` and rollover `Icon` for the `JButton` created in line 23. Both statements assume the image files are stored in the same directory as the program (this is commonly the case for applications that use images).

```
1   // Fig. 29.11: ButtonTest.java
2   // Creating JButtons.
3   import java.awt.*;
4   import java.awt.event.*;
5   import javax.swing.*;
6
7   public class ButtonTest extends JFrame {
8      private JButton plainButton, fancyButton;
9
10     public ButtonTest()
11     {
12        super( "Testing Buttons" );
13
14        Container c = getContentPane();
15        c.setLayout( new FlowLayout() );
16
17        // create buttons
18        plainButton = new JButton( "Plain Button" );
```

Fig. 29.11 Demonstrating command buttons and action events. (Part 1 of 3.)

```
19          c.add( plainButton );
20
21          Icon bug1 = new ImageIcon( "bug1.gif" );
22          Icon bug2 = new ImageIcon( "bug2.gif" );
23          fancyButton = new JButton( "Fancy Button", bug1 );
24          fancyButton.setRolloverIcon( bug2 );
25          c.add( fancyButton );
26
27          // create an instance of inner class ButtonHandler
28          // to use for button event handling
29          ButtonHandler handler = new ButtonHandler();
30          fancyButton.addActionListener( handler );
31          plainButton.addActionListener( handler );
32
33          setSize( 275, 100 );
34          show();
35       } // end ButtonTest constructor
36
37       public static void main( String args[] )
38       {
39          ButtonTest app = new ButtonTest();
40
41          app.addWindowListener(
42             new WindowAdapter() {
43                public void windowClosing( WindowEvent e )
44                {
45                   System.exit( 0 );
46                } // end method windowClosing
47             } // end anonymous inner class
48          ); // end addWindowListener
49       } // end main
50
51       // inner class for button event handling
52       private class ButtonHandler implements ActionListener {
53          public void actionPerformed( ActionEvent e )
54          {
55             JOptionPane.showMessageDialog( null,
56                "You pressed: " + e.getActionCommand() );
57          } // end method actionPerformed
58       } // end class ButtonHandler
59    } // end class ButtonTest
```

Fig. 29.11 Demonstrating command buttons and action events. (Part 2 of 3.)

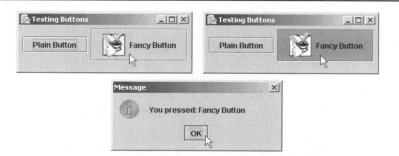

Fig. 29.11 Demonstrating command buttons and action events. (Part 3 of 3.)

Line 23

```
fancyButton = new JButton( "Fancy Button", bug1 );
```

creates fancyButton with default text "Fancy Button" and the Icon bug1. By default, the text is displayed to the right of the icon. Line 24

```
fancyButton.setRolloverIcon( bug2 );
```

uses method *setRolloverIcon* (inherited from class AbstractButton into class JButton) to specify the image displayed on the button when the user positions the mouse over the button. Line 25 adds the button to the content pane.

Look-and-Feel Observation 29.7

Using rollover icons for JButtons provides the user with visual feedback indicating that if they click the mouse, the button's action will occur.

JButtons (like JTextFields) generate ActionEvents. As mentioned previously, an ActionEvent can be processed by any ActionListener object. Lines 29 through 31

```
ButtonHandler handler = new ButtonHandler();
fancyButton.addActionListener( handler );
plainButton.addActionListener( handler );
```

register an ActionListener object for each JButton. Inner class ButtonHandler (lines 52 through 58) defines actionPerformed to display a message dialog box containing the label for the button that was pressed by the user. ActionEvent method getActionCommand returns the label on the button that generated the event.

29.8 JCheckBox

The Swing GUI components contain three types of *state buttons*—*JToggleButton*, *JCheckBox* and *JRadioButton*—that have on/off or true/false values. JToggleButtons are frequently used with *toolbars* (sets of small buttons typically located on a bar across the top of a window). Classes JCheckBox and JRadioButton are subclasses of JToggle-Button. A JRadioButton is different from a JCheckBox in that there are normally several JRadioButtons that are grouped together and only one of the JRadioButtons in the group can be selected (true) at any time. We discuss class JCheckBox in this section.

Look-and-Feel Observation 29.8

Class `AbstractButton` *supports displaying text and images on a button, so all subclasses of* `AbstractButton` *also support displaying text and images.*

The application of Figure 29.12 uses two `JCheckBox` objects to change the font style of the text displayed in a `JTextField`. One `JCheckBox` applies a bold style when selected and the other applies an italic style when selected. If both are selected, the style of the font is bold and italic. When the program is initially executed, neither `JCheckBox` is checked (`true`).

```java
1   // Fig. 29.12: CheckBoxTest.java
2   // Creating Checkbox buttons.
3   import java.awt.*;
4   import java.awt.event.*;
5   import javax.swing.*;
6
7   public class CheckBoxTest extends JFrame {
8      private JTextField t;
9      private JCheckBox bold, italic;
10
11     public CheckBoxTest()
12     {
13        super( "JCheckBox Test" );
14
15        Container c = getContentPane();
16        c.setLayout(new FlowLayout());
17
18        t = new JTextField( "Watch the font style change", 20 );
19        t.setFont( new Font( "TimesRoman", Font.PLAIN, 14 ) );
20        c.add( t );
21
22        // create checkbox objects
23        bold = new JCheckBox( "Bold" );
24        c.add( bold );
25
26        italic = new JCheckBox( "Italic" );
27        c.add( italic );
28
29        CheckBoxHandler handler = new CheckBoxHandler();
30        bold.addItemListener( handler );
31        italic.addItemListener( handler );
32
33        addWindowListener(
34           new WindowAdapter() {
35              public void windowClosing( WindowEvent e )
36              {
37                 System.exit( 0 );
38              } // end method windowClosing
39           } // end anonymous inner class
40        ); // end addWindowListener
41
```

Fig. 29.12 Program that creates two `JCheckBox` buttons. (Part 1 of 2.)

```
42              setSize( 275, 100 );
43              show();
44           } // end CheckBoxTest constructor
45
46           public static void main( String args[] )
47           {
48              new CheckBoxTest();
49           }
50
51           private class CheckBoxHandler implements ItemListener {
52              private int valBold = Font.PLAIN;
53              private int valItalic = Font.PLAIN;
54
55              public void itemStateChanged( ItemEvent e )
56              {
57                 if ( e.getSource() == bold )
58                    if ( e.getStateChange() == ItemEvent.SELECTED )
59                       valBold = Font.BOLD;
60                    else
61                       valBold = Font.PLAIN;
62
63                 if ( e.getSource() == italic )
64                    if ( e.getStateChange() == ItemEvent.SELECTED )
65                       valItalic = Font.ITALIC;
66                    else
67                       valItalic = Font.PLAIN;
68
69                 t.setFont(
70                    new Font( "TimesRoman", valBold + valItalic, 14 ) );
71                 t.repaint();
72              } // end method itemStateChanged
73           } // end inner class CheckBoxHandler
74        } // end class CheckBoxTest
```

Fig. 29.12 Program that creates two JCheckBox buttons. (Part 2 of 2.)

After the JTextField is created and initialized, line 19

```
t.setFont( new Font( "TimesRoman", Font.PLAIN, 14 ) );
```

sets the font of the JTextField to TimesRoman, PLAIN style and 14-point size. Next, the constructor creates two JCheckBox objects with lines 23 and 26

```
bold = new JCheckBox( "Bold" );
italic = new JCheckBox( "Italic" );
```

The `String` passed to the constructor is the *check box label* that appears to the right of the `JCheckBox` by default.

When the user clicks a `JCheckBox`, an `ItemEvent` is generated that can be handled by an `ItemListener` (any object of a class that implements interface `ItemListener`). An `ItemListener` must define method *itemStateChanged*. In this example, the event handling is performed by an instance of inner class `CheckBoxHandler` (lines 51 through 73). Lines 29 through 31

```
CheckBoxHandler handler = new CheckBoxHandler();
bold.addItemListener( handler );
italic.addItemListener( handler );
```

create an instance of class `CheckBoxHandler` and register it with method *addItemListener* as the `ItemListener` for both the `bold` and `italic` `JCheckBox`es.

Method `itemStateChanged` (line 55) is called when the uses clicks either the `bold` or `italic` `JCheckBox`. The method uses `e.getSource()` to determine which `JCheckBox` was clicked. If it was `JCheckBox bold`, the `if/else` structure in lines 58 through 61

```
if ( e.getStateChange() == ItemEvent.SELECTED )
    valBold = Font.BOLD;
else
    valBold = Font.PLAIN;
```

uses `ItemEvent` method *getStateChange* to determine the state of the button (`ItemEvent.SELECTED` or `ItemEvent.DESELECTED`). If the state is selected, integer `valBold` is assigned `Font.BOLD`; otherwise, `valBold` is assigned `Font.PLAIN`. A similar `if/else` structure is executed if `JCheckBox italic` is clicked. If the `italic` state is selected, integer `valItalic` is assigned `Font.ITALIC`; otherwise, `valItalic` is assigned `Font.PLAIN`. The sum of `valBold` and `valItalic` is used in lines 69 and 70 as the style of the new font for the `JTextField`.

29.9   JComboBox

A *combo box* (sometimes called a *drop-down list*) provides a list of items from which the user can make a selection. Combo boxes are implemented with class *JComboBox*, which inherits from class `JComponent`. `JComboBox`es generate `ItemEvents` like `JCheckBox`es and `JRadioButtons`.

The application of Figure 29.13 uses a `JComboBox` to provide a list of four image file names. When an image file name is selected, the corresponding image is displayed as an `Icon` on a `JLabel`. The screen captures for this program show the `JComboBox` list after the selection was made to illustrate which image file name was selected.

```
1   // Fig. 29.13: ComboBoxTest.java
2   // Using a JComboBox to select an image to display.
3   import java.awt.*;
```

Fig. 29.13 Program that uses a `JComboBox` to select an icon. (Part 1 of 3.)

```
4    import java.awt.event.*;
5    import javax.swing.*;
6
7    public class ComboBoxTest extends JFrame {
8       private JComboBox images;
9       private JLabel label;
10      private String names[] =
11         { "bug1.gif", "bug2.gif",
12           "travelbug.gif", "buganim.gif" };
13      private Icon icons[] =
14         { new ImageIcon( names[ 0 ] ),
15           new ImageIcon( names[ 1 ] ),
16           new ImageIcon( names[ 2 ] ),
17           new ImageIcon( names[ 3 ] ) };
18
19      public ComboBoxTest()
20      {
21         super( "Testing JComboBox" );
22
23         Container c = getContentPane();
24         c.setLayout( new FlowLayout() );
25
26         images = new JComboBox( names );
27         images.setMaximumRowCount( 3 );
28
29         images.addItemListener(
30            new ItemListener() {
31               public void itemStateChanged( ItemEvent e )
32               {
33                  label.setIcon(
34                     icons[ images.getSelectedIndex() ] );
35               } // end method itemStateChanged
36            } // end anonymous inner class
37         ); // end addItemListener
38
39         c.add( images );
40
41         label = new JLabel( icons[ 0 ] );
42         c.add( label );
43
44         setSize( 350, 100 );
45         show();
46      } // end ComboBoxText constructor
47
48      public static void main( String args[] )
49      {
50         ComboBoxTest app = new ComboBoxTest();
51
52         app.addWindowListener(
53            new WindowAdapter() {
54               public void windowClosing( WindowEvent e )
55               {
```

Fig. 29.13 Program that uses a JComboBox to select an icon. (Part 2 of 3.)

```
56                    System.exit( 0 );
57                } // end method windowClosing
58             } // end anonymous inner class
59          ); // end addWindowListener
60       } // end main
61    } // end class ComboBoxTest
```

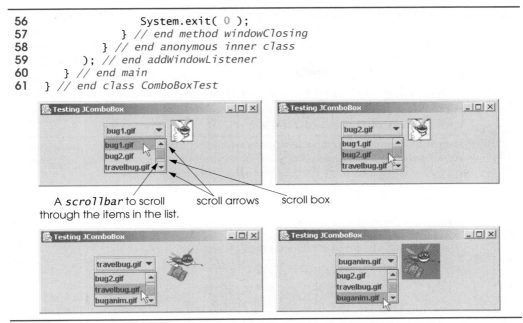

A *scrollbar* to scroll   scroll arrows   scroll box
through the items in the list.

Fig. 29.13 Program that uses a JComboBox to select an icon. (Part 3 of 3.)

Lines 13 through 17

```
private Icon icons[] =
   { new ImageIcon( names[ 0 ] ),
     new ImageIcon( names[ 1 ] ),
     new ImageIcon( names[ 2 ] ),
     new ImageIcon( names[ 3 ] ) };
```

declare and initialize array icons with four new ImageIcon objects. String array names (defined in lines 10 through 12) contains the names of the four image files that are stored in the same directory as the application.

Line 26

```
images = new JComboBox( names );
```

creates a JComboBox object using the Strings in array names as the elements in the list. A numeric *index* keeps track of the ordering of items in the JComboBox. The first item is added at index 0; the next item is added at index 1, and so forth. The first item added to a JComboBox appears as the currently selected item when the JComboBox is displayed. Other items are selected by clicking the JComboBox. When clicked, the JComboBox expands into a list from which the user can make a selection.

Line 27

```
images.setMaximumRowCount( 3 );
```

uses JComboBox method *setMaximumRowCount* to set the maximum number of elements that are displayed when the user clicks the JComboBox. If there are more items in the

JComboBox than the maximum number of elements that are displayed, the JComboBox automatically provides a *scrollbar* (see the first screen capture) that allows the user to view all the elements in the list. The user can click the *scroll arrows* at the top and bottom of the scrollbar to move up and down through the list one element at a time, or the user can drag the *scroll box* in the middle of the scrollbar up and down to move through the list. To drag the scroll box, hold the mouse button down with the mouse cursor on the scroll box and move the mouse.

Look-and-Feel Observation 29.9

Set the maximum row count for a JComboBox to a number of rows that prevents the list from expanding outside the bounds of the window or applet in which it is used. This will ensure that the list displays correctly when it is expanded by the user.

Lines 29 through 37

```
images.addItemListener(
    new ItemListener() {
        public void itemStateChanged( ItemEvent e )
        {
            label.setIcon(
                icons[ images.getSelectedIndex() ] );
        } // end method itemStateChanged
    } // end anonymous inner class
); // end addItemListener
```

register an instance of an anonymous inner class that implements ItemListener as the listener for JComboBox images. When the user makes a selection from images, method itemStateChanged (line 31) sets the Icon for label. The Icon is selected from array icons by determining the index number of the selected item in the JComboBox with method *getSelectedIndex* in line 34.

29.10 Mouse Event Handling

This section presents the *MouseListener* and *MouseMotionListener* event-listener interfaces for handling *mouse events*. Mouse events can be trapped for any GUI component that derives from java.awt.Component. The methods of interfaces MouseListener and MouseMotionListener are summarized in Figure 29.14.

MouseListener and MouseMotionListener interface methods

```
public void mousePressed( MouseEvent e )   // MouseListener
```
   Called when a mouse button is pressed with the mouse cursor on a component.
```
public void mouseClicked( MouseEvent e )   // MouseListener
```
   Called when a mouse button is pressed and released on a component without moving the mouse cursor.

Fig. 29.14 MouseListener and MouseMotionListener interface methods. (Part 1 of 2.)

MouseListener and MouseMotionListener interface methods

```
public void mouseReleased( MouseEvent e )   // MouseListener
```
Called when a mouse button is released after being pressed. This event is always preceded by a mousePressed event.

```
public void mouseEntered( MouseEvent e )    // MouseListener
```
Called when the mouse cursor enters the bounds of a component.

```
public void mouseExited( MouseEvent e )     // MouseListener
```
Called when the mouse cursor leaves the bounds of a component.

```
public void mouseDragged( MouseEvent e )    // MouseMotionListener
```
Called when the mouse button is pressed and the mouse is moved. This event is always preceded by a call to mousePressed.

```
public void mouseMoved( MouseEvent e )      // MouseMotionListener
```
Called when the mouse is moved with the mouse cursor on a component.

Fig. 29.14 MouseListener and MouseMotionListener interface methods. (Part 2 of 2.)

Each of the mouse event handling methods takes a *MouseEvent* object as its argument. A MouseEvent object contains information about the mouse event that occurred, including the *x*- and *y*-coordinates of the location where the event occurred. Methods of MouseListener and MouseMotionListener are called whenever the mouse interacts with a Component if listener objects are registered for a particular Component. Method *mousePressed* is called when a mouse button is pressed with the mouse cursor over a component. Using methods and constants of class *InputEvent* (the superclass of MouseEvent), a program can determine which mouse button the user clicked. Method *mouseClicked* is called whenever a mouse button is released without moving the mouse after a mousePressed operation. Method *mouseReleased* is called whenever a mouse button is released. Method *mouseEntered* is called when the mouse cursor enters the physical boundaries of a Component. Method *mouseExited* is called when the mouse cursor leaves the physical boundaries of a Component. Method *mouseDragged* is called when the mouse button is pressed and held, and the mouse is moved (a process known as *dragging*). The mouseDragged event is preceded by a *mousePressed* event and followed by a *mouseReleased* event. Method *mouseMoved* is called when the mouse is moved with the mouse cursor over a component (and no mouse buttons pressed).

Look-and-Feel Observation 29.10

Method calls to mouseDragged are sent to the MouseMotionListener for the Component on which the drag operation started. Similarly, the mouseReleased method call is sent to the MouseListener for the Component on which the drag operation started.

The MouseTracker application (Figure 29.15) demonstrates the MouseListener and MouseMotionListener methods. The application class implements both interfaces so it can listen for its own mouse events. Note that all seven methods from these two interfaces must be defined by the programmer when a class implements both interfaces.

```java
1   // Fig. 29.15: MouseTracker.java
2   // Demonstrating mouse events.
3
4   import java.awt.*;
5   import java.awt.event.*;
6   import javax.swing.*;
7
8   public class MouseTracker extends JFrame
9                 implements MouseListener, MouseMotionListener {
10     private JLabel statusBar;
11
12     public MouseTracker()
13     {
14        super( "Demonstrating Mouse Events" );
15
16        statusBar = new JLabel();
17        getContentPane().add( statusBar, BorderLayout.SOUTH );
18
19        // application listens to its own mouse events
20        addMouseListener( this );
21        addMouseMotionListener( this );
22
23        setSize( 275, 100 );
24        show();
25     } // end MouseTracker constructor
26
27     // MouseListener event handlers
28     public void mouseClicked( MouseEvent e )
29     {
30        statusBar.setText( "Clicked at [" + e.getX() +
31                           ", " + e.getY() + "]" );
32     } // end method mouseClicked
33
34     public void mousePressed( MouseEvent e )
35     {
36        statusBar.setText( "Pressed at [" + e.getX() +
37                           ", " + e.getY() + "]" );
38     } // end method mousePressed
39
40     public void mouseReleased( MouseEvent e )
41     {
42        statusBar.setText( "Released at [" + e.getX() +
43                           ", " + e.getY() + "]" );
44     } // end method mouseReleased
45
46     public void mouseEntered( MouseEvent e )
47     {
48        statusBar.setText( "Mouse in window" );
49     } // end method mouseEntered
50
51     public void mouseExited( MouseEvent e )
52     {
53        statusBar.setText( "Mouse outside window" );
```

Fig. 29.15 Demonstrating mouse event handling. (Part 1 of 2.)

```
54        } // end method mouseExited
55
56        // MouseMotionListener event handlers
57        public void mouseDragged( MouseEvent e )
58        {
59            statusBar.setText( "Dragged at [" + e.getX() +
60                                ", " + e.getY() + "]" );
61        } // end method mouseDragged
62
63        public void mouseMoved( MouseEvent e )
64        {
65            statusBar.setText( "Moved at [" + e.getX() +
66                                ", " + e.getY() + "]" );
67        } // end method mouseMoved
68
69        public static void main( String args[] )
70        {
71            MouseTracker app = new MouseTracker();
72
73            app.addWindowListener(
74                new WindowAdapter() {
75                    public void windowClosing( WindowEvent e )
76                    {
77                        System.exit( 0 );
78                    } // end method windowClosing
79                } // end anonymous inner class
80            ); // end addWindowListener
81        } // end main
82    } // end class MouseTracker
```

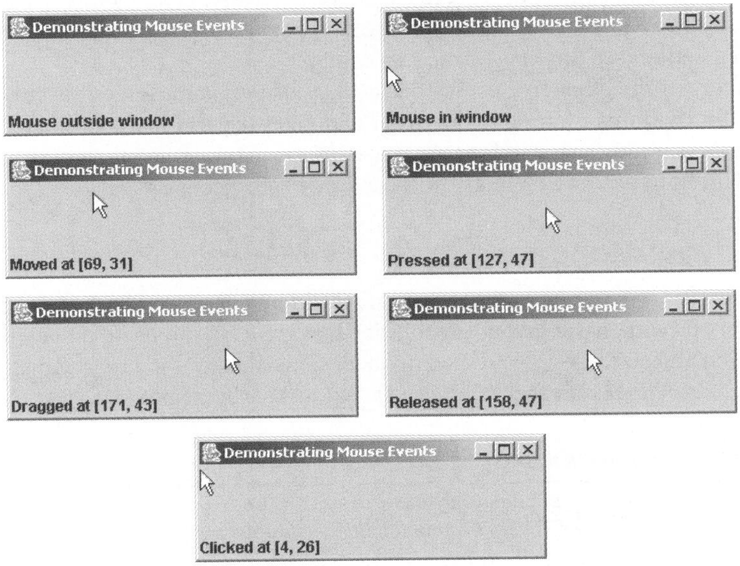

Fig. 29.15 Demonstrating mouse event handling. (Part 2 of 2.)

Each mouse event results in a `String` displayed in `JLabel` `statusBar` at the bottom of the window.

Lines 16 and 17 in the constructor

```
statusBar = new JLabel();
getContentPane().add( statusBar, BorderLayout.SOUTH );
```

define `JLabel` `statusBar` and attach it to the content pane. Until now, each time we used the content pane, method `setLayout` was called to set the content pane's layout manager to a `FlowLayout`. This allowed the content pane to display the GUI components we attached to it from left to right. If the GUI components do not fit on one line, the `FlowLayout` creates additional lines to continue displaying the GUI components. Actually, the default layout manager is a *BorderLayout* that divides the content pane's area into five regions—north, south, east, west and center. Line 17 uses a new version of `Container` method `add` to attach `statusBar` to the region *BorderLayout.SOUTH*, which extends across the entire bottom of the content pane. We discuss `BorderLayout` and several other layout managers in detail later in this chapter.

Lines 20 and 21 in the constructor

```
addMouseListener( this )
addMouseMotionListener( this );
```

register the `MouseTracker` window object as the listener for its own mouse events. Methods *addMouseListener* and *addMouseMotionListener* are `Component` methods that can be used to register mouse event listeners for an object of any class that extends `Component`.

When the mouse enters or exits the application area, method `mouseEntered` (line 46) and method `mouseExited` (line 51) are called, respectively. Both methods display a message in `statusBar` indicating that the mouse is inside the application or the mouse is outside the application (see the first two screen captures).

When any of the other five events occur, they display a message in `statusBar` that includes a `String` that represents the event that occurred and the coordinates where the mouse event occurred. The *x* and *y* coordinates of the mouse when the event occurred are obtained with `MouseEvent` methods *getX* and *getY*, respectively.

29.11 Layout Managers

Layout managers arrange GUI components on a container for presentation purposes. Layout managers provide basic layout capabilities that are easier to use than determining the exact position and size of every GUI component. This enables the programmer to concentrate on the basic "look and feel" and lets the layout managers process most of the layout details.

Look-and-Feel Observation 29.11

Most Java programming environments provide GUI design tools that help a programmer graphically design a GUI, then automatically write Java code to create the GUI.

Some GUI designers also allow the programmer to use the layout managers described here. Figure 29.16 summarizes the layout managers presented in this chapter.

Layout manager	Description
FlowLayout	Default for java.awt.Applet, java.awt.Panel and javax.swing.JPanel. Places components sequentially (left to right) in the order they were added. It is also possible to specify the order of the components using the Container method add that takes a Component and an integer index position as arguments.
BorderLayout	Default for the content panes of JFrames (and other windows) and JApplets. Arranges the components into five areas: North, South, East, West and Center.
GridLayout	Arranges the components into rows and columns.

Fig. 29.16 Layout managers.

Most previous applet and application examples in which we created our own GUI used layout manager *FlowLayout*. Class *FlowLayout* inherits from class Object and implements interface *LayoutManager*, which defines the methods a layout manager uses to arrange and size GUI components on a container.

29.11.1 FlowLayout

FlowLayout is the most basic layout manager. GUI components are placed on a container from left to right in the order in which they are added to the container. When the edge of the container is reached, components are continued on the next line. Class FlowLayout allows GUI components to be *left-aligned*, *centered* (the default) and *right-aligned*.

The application of Figure 29.17 creates three JButton objects and adds them to the application using a FlowLayout layout manager. The components are automatically center-aligned. When the user clicks **Left**, the alignment for the layout manager is changed to a left-aligned FlowLayout. When the user clicks **Right**, the alignment for the layout manager is changed to a right-aligned FlowLayout. When the user clicks **Center**, the alignment for the layout manager is changed to a center-aligned FlowLayout. Each button has its own event handler that is defined with an inner class that implements ActionListener.

```
1   // Fig. 29.17: FlowLayoutDemo.java
2   // Demonstrating FlowLayout alignments.
3   import java.awt.*;
4   import java.awt.event.*;
5   import javax.swing.*;
6
7   public class FlowLayoutDemo extends JFrame {
8       private JButton left, center, right;
9       private Container c;
10      private FlowLayout layout;
11
12      public FlowLayoutDemo()
13      {
```

Fig. 29.17 Program that demonstrates components in FlowLayout. (Part 1 of 3.)

```java
14          super( "FlowLayout Demo" );
15
16          layout = new FlowLayout();
17
18          c = getContentPane();
19          c.setLayout( layout );
20
21          left = new JButton( "Left" );
22          left.addActionListener(
23             new ActionListener() {
24                public void actionPerformed( ActionEvent e )
25                {
26                   layout.setAlignment( FlowLayout.LEFT );
27
28                   // re-align attached components
29                   layout.layoutContainer( c );
30                } // end method actionPerformed
31             } // end anonymous inner class
32          ); // end addActionListener
33          c.add( left );
34
35          center = new JButton( "Center" );
36          center.addActionListener(
37             new ActionListener() {
38                public void actionPerformed( ActionEvent e )
39                {
40                   layout.setAlignment( FlowLayout.CENTER );
41
42                   // re-align attached components
43                   layout.layoutContainer( c );
44                } // end method actionPerformed
45             } // end anonymous inner class
46          ); // end addActionListener
47          c.add( center );
48
49          right = new JButton( "Right" );
50          right.addActionListener(
51             new ActionListener() {
52                public void actionPerformed( ActionEvent e )
53                {
54                   layout.setAlignment( FlowLayout.RIGHT );
55
56                   // re-align attached components
57                   layout.layoutContainer( c );
58                } // end method actionPerformed
59             } // end anonymous inner class
60          ); // end addActionListener
61          c.add( right );
62
63          setSize( 300, 75 );
64          show();
65       } // end FlowLayoutDemo constructor
66
```

Fig. 29.17 Program that demonstrates components in FlowLayout. (Part 2 of 3.)

```
67      public static void main( String args[] )
68      {
69          FlowLayoutDemo app = new FlowLayoutDemo();
70
71          app.addWindowListener(
72              new WindowAdapter() {
73                  public void windowClosing( WindowEvent e )
74                  {
75                      System.exit( 0 );
76                  } // end method windowClosing
77              } // end anonymous inner class
78          ); // end addWindowListener
79      } // end main
80  } // end class FlowLayoutDemo
```

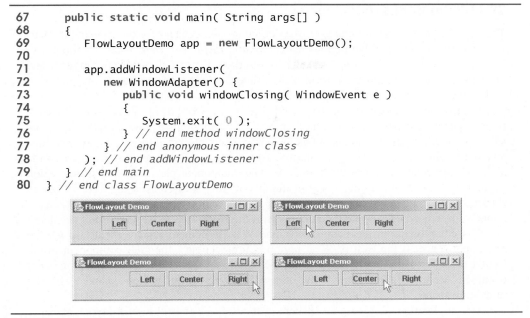

Fig. 29.17 Program that demonstrates components in FlowLayout. (Part 3 of 3.)

As seen previously, a container's layout is set with method *setLayout* of class Container. Line 19

```
c.setLayout( layout );
```

sets the content pane's layout manager to the FlowLayout defined in line 16. Normally, the layout is set before any GUI components are added to a container.

Look-and-Feel Observation 29.12

Each container can have only one layout manager at a time (separate containers in the same program can have different layout managers).

Each button's `actionPerformed` event handler executes two statements. For example, line 26 in method `actionPerformed` for button left

```
layout.setAlignment( FlowLayout.LEFT );
```

uses FlowLayout method *setAlignment* to change the alignment for the FlowLayout to a left-aligned (*FlowLayout.LEFT*) FlowLayout. Line 29

```
layout.layoutContainer( c );
```

uses LayoutManager interface method *layoutContainer* to specify that the content pane should be rearranged based on the adjusted layout.

According to which button was clicked, the `actionPerformed` method for each button sets the FlowLayout's alignment to FlowLayout.LEFT, *FlowLayout.CENTER* or *FlowLayout.RIGHT*.

29.11.2 BorderLayout

The *BorderLayout* layout manager (the default layout manager for the content pane) arranges components into five regions: *North, South, East, West and Center* (North corresponds to the top of the container). Class BorderLayout inherits from Object and implements interface *LayoutManager2* (a subinterface of LayoutManager that adds several methods for enhanced layout processing).

Up to five components can be added directly to a BorderLayout—one for each region. The components placed in the North and South regions extend horizontally to the sides of the container and are as tall as the components placed in those regions. The East and West regions expand vertically between the North and South regions and are as wide as the components placed in those regions. The component placed in the Center region expands to take all remaining space in the layout (this is the reason the JTextArea in Figure 29.18 occupies the entire window). If all five regions are occupied, the entire container's space is covered by GUI components. If the North or South region is not occupied, the GUI components in the East, Center and West regions expand vertically to fill the remaining space. If the East or West region is not occupied, the GUI component in the Center region expands horizontally to fill the remaining space. If the Center region is not occupied, the area is left empty—the other GUI components do not expand to fill the remaining space.

The application of Figure 29.18 demonstrates the BorderLayout layout manager using five JButtons.

```
1   // Fig. 29.18: BorderLayoutDemo.java
2   // Demonstrating BorderLayout.
3   import java.awt.*;
4   import java.awt.event.*;
5   import javax.swing.*;
6
7   public class BorderLayoutDemo extends JFrame
8                                 implements ActionListener {
9      private JButton b[];
10     private String names[] =
11        { "Hide North", "Hide South", "Hide East",
12          "Hide West", "Hide Center" };
13     private BorderLayout layout;
14
15     public BorderLayoutDemo()
16     {
17        super( "BorderLayout Demo" );
18
19        layout = new BorderLayout( 5, 5 );
20
21        Container c = getContentPane();
22        c.setLayout( layout );
23
24        // instantiate button objects
25        b = new JButton[ names.length ];
26
```

Fig. 29.18 Demonstrating components in BorderLayout. (Part 1 of 3.)

```
27              for ( int i = 0; i < names.length; i++ ) {
28                  b[ i ] = new JButton( names[ i ] );
29                  b[ i ].addActionListener( this );
30              } // end for
31
32              // order not important
33              c.add( b[ 0 ], BorderLayout.NORTH );   // North position
34              c.add( b[ 1 ], BorderLayout.SOUTH );   // South position
35              c.add( b[ 2 ], BorderLayout.EAST );    // East position
36              c.add( b[ 3 ], BorderLayout.WEST );    // West position
37              c.add( b[ 4 ], BorderLayout.CENTER ); // Center position
38
39              setSize( 300, 200 );
40              show();
41          } // end BorderLayoutDemo constructor
42
43          public void actionPerformed( ActionEvent e )
44          {
45              for ( int i = 0; i < b.length; i++ )
46                  if ( e.getSource() == b[ i ] )
47                      b[ i ].setVisible( false );
48                  else
49                      b[ i ].setVisible( true );
50
51              // re-layout the content pane
52              layout.layoutContainer( getContentPane() );
53          } // end method actionPerformed
54
55          public static void main( String args[] )
56          {
57              BorderLayoutDemo app = new BorderLayoutDemo();
58
59              app.addWindowListener(
60                  new WindowAdapter() {
61                      public void windowClosing( WindowEvent e )
62                      {
63                          System.exit( 0 );
64                      } // end method windowClosing
65                  } // end anonymous inner class
66              ); // end addWindowListener
67          } // end main
68      } // end class BorderLayoutDemo
```

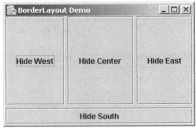

Fig. 29.18 Demonstrating components in `BorderLayout`. (Part 2 of 3.)

Fig. 29.18 Demonstrating components in `BorderLayout`. (Part 3 of 3.)

Line 19 in the constructor

```
layout = new BorderLayout( 5, 5 );
```

defines a `BorderLayout`. The arguments specify the number of pixels between components that are arranged horizontally (*horizontal gap space*) and the number of pixels between components that are arranged vertically (*vertical gap space*), respectively. The default `BorderLayout` constructor supplies 0 pixels of gap space horizontally and vertically. Line 22 uses method `setLayout` to set the content pane's layout to `layout`.

Adding `Components` to a `BorderLayout` requires a different add method from class `Container`, which takes two arguments—the `Component` to add and the region in which the `Component` will be placed. For example, line 33

```
add( b[ 0 ], BorderLayout.NORTH );  // North position
```

specifies that the `b[0]` is to be placed in the NORTH position. The components can be added in any order, but only one component can be added to each region.

Look-and-Feel Observation 29.13

If no region is specified when adding a Component *to a* BorderLayout, *it is assumed that the* Component *should be added to region* BorderLayout.CENTER.

Common Programming Error 29.5

Adding more than one component to a particular region in a BorderLayout *results in only the last component added being displayed. There is no error message to indicate this problem.*

When the user clicks a particular `JButton` in the layout, method `actionPerformed` (line 43) is called. The `for` loop in line 46 uses the following `if/else` structure:

```
if ( e.getSource() == b[ i ] )
   b[ i ].setVisible( false );
else
   b[ i ].setVisible( true );
```

to hide the particular JButton that generated the event. Method *setVisible* (inherited into JButton from class Component) is called with a false argument to hide the JButton. If the current JButton in the array is not the one that generated the event, method setVisible is called with a true argument to ensure that the JButton is displayed on the screen. Line 52

```
layout.layoutContainer( getContentPane() );
```

uses LayoutManager method layoutContainer to recalculate the layout of the content pane. Notice in the screen captures of Figure 29.18 that certain regions in the BorderLayout change shape as JButtons are hidden and displayed in other regions. Try resizing the application window to see how the various regions resize based on the width and height of the window.

29.11.3 GridLayout

The *GridLayout* layout manager divides the container into a grid so that components can be placed in rows and columns. Class GridLayout inherits directly from class Object and implements interface LayoutManager. Every Component in a GridLayout has the same width and height. Components are added to a GridLayout starting at the top-left cell of the grid and proceeding left-to-right until the row is full. Then the process continues left-to-right on the next row of the grid, etc. Figure 29.19 demonstrates the GridLayout layout manager using six JButtons.

```
1   // Fig. 29.19: GridLayoutDemo.java
2   // Demonstrating GridLayout.
3   import java.awt.*;
4   import java.awt.event.*;
5   import javax.swing.*;
6
7   public class GridLayoutDemo extends JFrame
8                               implements ActionListener {
9      private JButton b[];
10     private String names[] =
11        { "one", "two", "three", "four", "five", "six" };
12     private boolean toggle = true;
13     private Container c;
14     private GridLayout grid1, grid2;
15
16     public GridLayoutDemo()
17     {
18        super( "GridLayout Demo" );
19
20        grid1 = new GridLayout( 2, 3, 5, 5 );
21        grid2 = new GridLayout( 3, 2 );
```

Fig. 29.19 Program that demonstrates components in GridLayout. (Part 1 of 2.)

```
22
23          c = getContentPane();
24          c.setLayout( grid1 );
25
26          // create and add buttons
27          b = new JButton[ names.length ];
28
29          for (int i = 0; i < names.length; i++ ) {
30             b[ i ] = new JButton( names[ i ] );
31             b[ i ].addActionListener( this );
32             c.add( b[ i ] );
33          }
34
35          setSize( 300, 150 );
36          show();
37       } // end GridLayoutDemo constructor
38
39       public void actionPerformed( ActionEvent e )
40       {
41          if ( toggle )
42             c.setLayout( grid2 );
43          else
44             c.setLayout( grid1 );
45
46          toggle = !toggle;
47          c.validate();
48       } // end method actionPerformed
49
50       public static void main( String args[] )
51       {
52          GridLayoutDemo app = new GridLayoutDemo();
53
54          app.addWindowListener(
55             new WindowAdapter() {
56                public void windowClosing( WindowEvent e )
57                {
58                   System.exit( 0 );
59                } // end method windowClosing
60             } // end anonymous inner class
61          ); // end addWindowListener
62       } // end main
63    } // end class GridLayoutDemo
```

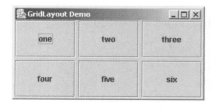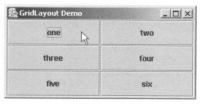

Fig. 29.19 Program that demonstrates components in GridLayout. (Part 2 of 2.)

Lines 20 and 21 in the constructor

```
grid1 = new GridLayout( 2, 3, 5, 5 );
grid2 = new GridLayout( 3, 2 );
```

define two `GridLayout` objects. The `GridLayout` constructor used in line 20 specifies a `GridLayout` with 2 rows, 3 columns, 5 pixels of horizontal-gap space between `Components` in the grid and 5 pixels of vertical-gap space between `Components` in the grid. The `GridLayout` constructor used in line 21 specifies a `GridLayout` with 3 rows, 2 columns and no gap space.

The `JButton` objects in this example initially are arranged using `grid1` (set for the content pane in line 24 with method `setLayout`). The first component is added to the first column of the first row. The next component is added to the second column of the first row, etc. When a `JButton` is pressed, method `actionPerformed` (line 39) is called. Every call to `actionPerformed` toggles the layout between `grid2` and `grid1`.

Line 47

```
c.validate();
```

illustrates a way to re-layout a container for which the layout has changed. `Container` method *validate* recomputes the container's layout based on the current layout manager for the `Container` and the current set of displayed GUI components.

29.12 Panels

Complex GUIs (like Figure 29.1) require that each component be placed in an exact location. They often consist of multiple *panels* with each panel's components arranged in a specific layout. Panels are created with class *JPanel*—a subclass of `JComponent`. The class `JComponent` inherits from `java.awt.Container`, so every `JPanel` is a `Container`. Thus `JPanel`s may have components, including other panels, added to them.

The program of Figure 29.20 demonstrates how a `JPanel` can be used to create a more complex layout for `Components`.

```
1   // Fig. 29.20: PanelDemo.java
2   // Using a JPanel to help lay out components.
3   import java.awt.*;
4   import java.awt.event.*;
5   import javax.swing.*;
6
7   public class PanelDemo extends JFrame {
8      private JPanel buttonPanel;
9      private JButton buttons[];
10
11     public PanelDemo()
12     {
13        super( "Panel Demo" );
14
15        Container c = getContentPane();
```

Fig. 29.20 A `JPanel` with five `JButtons` in a `GridLayout` attached to the SOUTH region of a `BorderLayout`. (Part 1 of 2.)

```
16              buttonPanel = new JPanel();
17              buttons = new JButton[ 5 ];
18
19              buttonPanel.setLayout(
20                  new GridLayout( 1, buttons.length ) );
21
22              for ( int i = 0; i < buttons.length; i++ ) {
23                  buttons[ i ] = new JButton( "Button " + (i + 1) );
24                  buttonPanel.add( buttons[ i ] );
25              }
26
27              c.add( buttonPanel, BorderLayout.SOUTH );
28
29              setSize( 425, 150 );
30              show();
31          } // end PanelDemo constructor
32
33          public static void main( String args[] )
34          {
35              PanelDemo app = new PanelDemo();
36
37              app.addWindowListener(
38                  new WindowAdapter() {
39                      public void windowClosing( WindowEvent e )
40                      {
41                          System.exit( 0 );
42                      } // end method windowClosing
43                  } // end anonymous inner class
44              ); // end addWindowListener
45          } // end main
46      } // end class PanelDemo
```

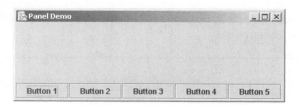

Fig. 29.20 A JPanel with five JButtons in a GridLayout attached to the SOUTH region of a BorderLayout. (Part 2 of 2.)

After JPanel buttonPanel is created in line 16, lines 19 and 20

```
buttonPanel.setLayout(
    new GridLayout( 1, buttons.length ) );
```

set buttonPanel's layout to a GridLayout of one row and five columns (there are five JButtons in array buttons). The five JButtons in array buttons are added to the JPanel in the loop in line 24 with the statement

```
buttonPanel.add( buttons[ i ] );
```

Notice that the buttons are added directly to the `JPanel`—class `JPanel` does not have a content pane like an applet or a `JFrame`. Line 27

```
c.add( buttonPanel, BorderLayout.SOUTH );
```

uses the content pane's default `BorderLayout` to add `buttonPanel` to the SOUTH region. Note that the SOUTH region is as tall as the buttons on `buttonPanel`. A `JPanel` is sized to the components it contains. As more components are added, the `JPanel` grows (according to the restrictions of its layout manager) to accommodate the components. Resize the window to see how the layout manager affects the size of the `JButton`s.

29.13 Creating a Self-Contained Subclass of `JPanel`

A `JPanel` can be used as a *dedicated drawing area* that can receive mouse events and is often extended to create new components. In earlier exercises you may have noticed that combining Swing GUI components and drawing in one window or applet often leads to improper display of the GUI components or the graphics. This is because Swing GUI components are displayed using the same graphics techniques as the drawings and are displayed in the same area as the drawings. The order in which the GUI components are displayed and the drawing is performed may result in drawing over the GUI components or GUI components obscuring the graphics. To fix this problem, we can separate the GUI and the graphics by creating dedicated drawing areas as subclasses of `JPanel`.

Look-and-Feel Observation 29.14

Combining graphics and Swing GUI components may lead to incorrect display of the graphics, the GUI components or both. Using `JPanel`*s for drawing can eliminate this problem by providing a dedicated area for graphics.*

Swing components that inherit from class `JComponent` contain method *paintComponent* that helps them draw properly in the context of a Swing GUI. When customizing a `JPanel` for use as a dedicated drawing area, method `paintComponent` should be overridden as follows:

```
public void paintComponent( Graphics g )
{
    super.paintComponent( g );

    // your additional drawing code
}
```

Notice the call to the superclass version of `paintComponent` appears as the first statement in the body of the overridden method. This ensures that painting occurs in the proper order and that Swing's painting mechanism remains intact. If the superclass version of `paintComponent` is not called, typically the customized GUI component (the subclass of `JPanel` in this case) will not be displayed properly on the user interface. Also, if the superclass version is called after performing the customized drawing statements, the results will typically be erased.

Look-and-Feel Observation 29.15

When a `JComponent`*'s* `paintComponent` *method is overridden, the first statement in the body should always be a call to the superclass's original version of the method.*

Common Programming Error 29.6

When a JComponent's paintComponent method is overridden, not calling the superclass's original version of paintComponent prevents the GUI component from displaying properly on the GUI.

Common Programming Error 29.7

When a JComponent's paintComponent method is overridden, calling the superclass's original version of paintComponent after other drawing is performed erases the other drawings.

Classes JFrame and JApplet are not subclasses of JComponent; therefore, they do not contain method paintComponent. To draw directly on subclasses of JFrame and JApplet, override method paint.

Look-and-Feel Observation 29.16

Calling repaint for a Swing GUI component indicates that the component should be painted as soon as possible. The background of the GUI component is cleared only if the component is opaque. Most Swing components are transparent by default. JComponent method setOpaque can be passed a boolean argument indicating if the component is opaque (true) or transparent (false). The GUI components of package java.awt are different from Swing components in that repaint results in a call to Component method update (which clears the component's background) and update calls method paint (rather than paintComponent).

JPanels do not generate conventional events like buttons, text fields and windows, but are capable of recognizing lower-level events such as mouse events and key events. Figure 29.21 allows the user to draw an oval on a subclass of JPanel with the mouse. Class SelfContainedPanel listens for its own mouse events and draws an oval on itself. The location and size of the oval are determined by the user pressing and holding the mouse button, dragging the mouse and releasing the mouse button. Class SelfContainedPanel is placed in package com.deitel.chtp3.ch29 for future reuse. For this reason, it is imported (line 7) into the SelfContainedPanelTest application class.

```
1    // Fig. 29.21: SelfContainedPanelTest.java
2    // Creating a self-contained subclass of JPanel
3    // that processes its own mouse events.
4    import java.awt.*;
5    import java.awt.event.*;
6    import javax.swing.*;
7    import com.deitel.chtp4.ch29.SelfContainedPanel;
8
9    public class SelfContainedPanelTest extends JFrame {
10       private SelfContainedPanel myPanel;
11
12       public SelfContainedPanelTest()
13       {
14          myPanel = new SelfContainedPanel();
15          myPanel.setBackground( Color.yellow );
```

Fig. 29.21 Capturing mouse events with a JPanel—
SelfContainedPanelTest.java. (Part 1 of 2.)

```
16
17          Container c = getContentPane();
18          c.setLayout( new FlowLayout() );
19          c.add( myPanel );
20
21          addMouseMotionListener(
22             new MouseMotionListener() {
23                public void mouseDragged( MouseEvent e )
24                {
25                   setTitle( "Dragging: x=" + e.getX() +
26                             "; y=" + e.getY() );
27                } // end method mouseDragged
28
29                public void mouseMoved( MouseEvent e )
30                {
31                   setTitle( "Moving: x=" + e.getX() +
32                             "; y=" + e.getY() );
33                } // end method mouseMoved
34             } // end anonymous inner class
35          ); // end addMouseMotionListener
36
37          setSize( 300, 200 );
38          show();
39       } // end SelfContainedPanelTest constructor
40
41       public static void main( String args[] )
42       {
43          SelfContainedPanelTest app =
44             new SelfContainedPanelTest();
45
46          app.addWindowListener(
47             new WindowAdapter() {
48                public void windowClosing( WindowEvent e )
49                {
50                   System.exit( 0 );
51                } // end method windowClosing
52             } // end anonymous inner class
53          ); // end addWindowListener
54       } // end main
55    } // end class SelfContainedPanelTest
```

Fig. 29.21 Capturing mouse events with a JPanel—
        SelfContainedPanelTest.java. (Part 2 of 2.)

```
56    // Fig. 29.21: SelfContainedPanel.java
57    // A self-contained JPanel class that
58    // handles its own mouse events.
59    package com.deitel.chtp4.ch29;
60
```

Fig. 29.21 Capturing mouse events with a JPanel—SelfContainedPanel.java.
        (Part 1 of 3.)

```java
61   import java.awt.*;
62   import java.awt.event.*;
63   import javax.swing.*;
64
65   public class SelfContainedPanel extends JPanel {
66      private int x1, y1, x2, y2;
67
68      public SelfContainedPanel()
69      {
70         addMouseListener(
71            new MouseAdapter() {
72               public void mousePressed( MouseEvent e )
73               {
74                  x1 = e.getX();
75                  y1 = e.getY();
76               } // end method mousePressed
77
78               public void mouseReleased( MouseEvent e )
79               {
80                  x2 = e.getX();
81                  y2 = e.getY();
82                  repaint();
83               } // end method mouseReleased
84            } // end anonymous inner class
85         ); // end addMouseListener
86
87         addMouseMotionListener(
88            new MouseMotionAdapter() {
89               public void mouseDragged( MouseEvent e )
90               {
91                  x2 = e.getX();
92                  y2 = e.getY();
93                  repaint();
94               } // end method mouseDragged
95            } // end anonymous inner class
96         ); // end addMouseMotionListener
97      } // end SelfContainedPanel constructor
98
99      public Dimension getPreferredSize()
100     {
101        return new Dimension( 150, 100 );
102     } // end method getPreferredSize
103
104     public void paintComponent( Graphics g )
105     {
106        super.paintComponent( g );
107
108        g.drawOval( Math.min( x1, x2 ), Math.min( y1, y2 ),
109                    Math.abs( x1 - x2 ), Math.abs( y1 - y2 ) );
110     } // end method paintComponent
111  } // end class SelfContainedPanel
```

Fig. 29.21 Capturing mouse events with a JPanel—SelfContainedPanel.java. (Part 2 of 3.)

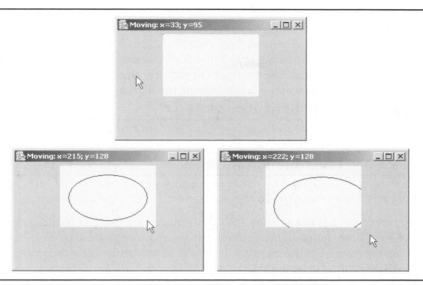

Fig. 29.21 Capturing mouse events with a `JPanel`—`SelfContainedPanel.java`. (Part 3 of 3.)

The constructor method (line 12) of application class `SelfContainedPanelTest` creates an instance of class `SelfContainedPanel` and sets the background color of the `SelfContainedPanel` to yellow so that its area is visible against the background of the application window.

So we can demonstrate the difference between mouse motion events on the `SelfContainedPanel` and mouse motion events on the application window, lines 21 through 35 create an anonymous inner class to handle the application's mouse motion events. Event handlers `mouseDragged` and `mouseMoved` use method `setTitle` (inherited from class `java.awt.Frame`) to display a `String` in the window's title bar indicating the *x* and *y* coordinates where the mouse motion event occurred.

Class `SelfContainedPanel` (lines 65 through 111) extends class `JPanel`. Instance variables `x1` and `y1` store the initial coordinates where the `mousePressed` event occurs on the `SelfContainedPanel`. Instance variables `x2` and `y2` store the coordinates where the user drags the mouse or releases the mouse button. All the coordinates are with respect to the upper-left corner of the `SelfContainedPanel`.

Look-and-Feel Observation 29.17

Drawing on any GUI component is performed with coordinates that are measured from the upper-left corner (0, 0) of that GUI component.

The `SelfContainedPanel` constructor (line 68) uses methods `addMouseListener` and `addMouseMotionListener` to register anonymous inner class objects to handle both the mouse events and the mouse motion events for the `SelfContainedPanel`. Only `mousePressed` (line 72), `mouseReleased` (line 78) and `mouseDragged` (line 89) are actually overridden to perform tasks. The other mouse event handling methods are inherited from class `MouseAdapter` and class `MouseMotionAdapter` when the anonymous inner classes are defined.

By extending class JPanel, we are actually creating a new GUI component. Layout managers often use a GUI component's *getPreferredSize* method (inherited from class java.awt.Component) to determine the preferred width and height of a component when laying out that component as part of a GUI. If a new component has a preferred width and height, it should override method getPreferredSize (lines 99 through 102) to return that width and height as an object of class *Dimension* (package java.awt).

Look-and-Feel Observation 29.18

The default size of a JPanel object is 0 pixels wide and 0 pixels high.

Look-and-Feel Observation 29.19

When subclassing JPanel (or any other JComponent), override method getPreferredSize if the new component should have a specific preferred width and height.

Method paintComponent (line 104) is overridden in class SelfContainedPanel to draw an oval. The width, height and upper-left corner are determined by the user pressing and holding the mouse button, dragging the mouse and releasing the mouse button on the SelfContainedPanel drawing area.

The initial coordinates x1 and y1 on the SelfContainedPanel drawing area are captured in method mousePressed (line 72). As the user drags the mouse after the initial mousePressed operation, the program generates a series of calls to mouseDragged (line 89) while the user continues to hold the mouse button and move the mouse. Each call captures in variables x2 and y2 the current location of the mouse with respect to the upper-left corner of the SelfContainedPanel and calls repaint to draw the current version of the oval. Drawing is strictly confined to the SelfContainedPanel even if the user drags outside the SelfContainedPanel drawing area. Anything drawn off the SelfContainedPanel is *clipped*—pixels are not displayed outside the bounds of the SelfContainedPanel.

The calculations provided in method paintComponent determine the proper upper-left corner using method Math.min twice to find the smaller *x*-coordinate and *y*-coordinate. The oval's width and height must be positive values or the oval is not displayed. Method Math.abs gets the absolute value of the subtractions x1 - x2 and y1 - y2 that determine the width and height of the oval's bounding rectangle, respectively. When the calculations are complete, paintComponent draws the oval. The call to the superclass version of paintComponent at the beginning of the method guarantees that the previous oval displayed on the SelfContainedPanel is erased before the new one is displayed.

Look-and-Feel Observation 29.20

Most Swing GUI components can be transparent or opaque. If a Swing GUI component is opaque, when its paintComponent method is called, its background will be cleared. Otherwise, its background will not be cleared.

Look-and-Feel Observation 29.21

Class JComponent provides method setOpaque that takes a boolean argument to determine if a JComponent is opaque (true) or transparent (false).

Look-and-Feel Observation 29.22

JPanel objects are opaque by default.

When the user releases the mouse button, method `mouseReleased` (line 78) captures in variables `x2` and `y2` the final location of the mouse and invokes `repaint` to draw the final version of the oval.

When executing this program try dragging from the background of the application window into the `SelfContainedPanel` area to see that the drag events are sent to the application window rather than the `SelfContainedPanel`. Then, start a new drag operation in the `SelfContainedPanel` area and drag out to the background of the application window to see that the drag events are sent to the `SelfContainedPanel` rather than to the application window.

Look-and-Feel Observation 29.23

A mouse drag operation begins with a mouse pressed event. All subsequent mouse drag events (for which `mouseDragged` will be called) are sent to the GUI component that received the original mouse pressed event.

29.14 Windows

To this point, we have seen many applications that have used a subclass of `JFrame` as the application's GUI. In this section, we discuss several important issues regarding `JFrame`s.

A `JFrame` is a *window* with a *title bar* and a *border*. Class `JFrame` is a subclass of `java.awt.Frame` (which is a subclass of `java.awt.Window`). As such, `JFrame` is one of the few Swing GUI components that is not considered to be a lightweight GUI component. Unlike most Swing components, `JFrame` is not written completely in Java. In fact, when you display a window from a Java program, the window is part of the local platform's set of GUI components—the window will look like all other windows displayed on that platform. When a Java program executes on a Macintosh and displays a window, the window's title bar and borders will look like other Macintosh applications. When a Java program executes on Microsoft Windows and displays a window, the window's title bar and borders will look like other Microsoft Windows applications. And when a Java program executes on a Unix platform and displays a window, the window's title bar and borders will look like other Unix applications on that platform.

Class `JFrame` supports three operations when the user closes the window. By default, a window is hidden (i.e., removed from the screen) when the user closes a window. This can be controlled with `JFrame` method *setDefaultCloseOperation*. Interface *WindowConstants* (package `javax.swing`) defines three constants for use with this method—DISPOSE_ON_CLOSE, DO_NOTHING_ON_CLOSE and HIDE_ON_CLOSE (the default). Most platforms allow a limited number of total windows to be displayed on the screen. As such, a window is a valuable resource that should be given back to the system when it is no longer needed. Class `Window` (an indirect superclass of `JFrame`) defines method *dispose* for this purpose. When a `Window` is no longer needed in an application, you should explicitly `dispose` of the `Window`. This can be done by explicitly calling the `Window`'s `dispose` method or by calling method `setDefaultCloseOperation` with the argument `WindowConstants.DISPOSE_ON_CLOSE`. Also, terminating an application will return window resources to the system. Setting the default close operation to DO_NOTHING_ON_CLOSE indicates that you will determine what to do when the user indicates that the window should be closed.

Software Engineering Observation 29.4

Windows are a valuable system resource that should be returned to the system when they are no longer needed.

By default, a window is not displayed on the screen until its *show* method is called. A window can also be displayed by calling its `setVisible` method (inherited from class `java.awt.Component`) with `true` as an argument. Also, a window's size should be set with a call to method `setSize` (inherited from class `java.awt.Component`). The position of a window when it appears on the screen is specified with the `setLocation` method (inherited from class `java.awt.Component`).

Common Programming Error 29.8

Forgetting to call method `show` or method `setVisible` on a window is a run-time logic error; the window is not displayed.

Common Programming Error 29.9

Forgetting to call the `setSize` method on a window is a run-time logic error—only the title bar appears.

All windows generate *window events* when the user manipulates the window. Event listeners are registered for window events with `Window` method *addWindowListener*. Interface *WindowListener* (implemented by window event listeners) provides seven methods for handling window events—*windowActivated* (called when the window is made active by clicking the window), *windowClosed* (called after the window is closed), *windowClosing* (called when the user initiates closing of the window), *windowDeactivated* (called when another window is made active), *windowIconified* (called when the user minimizes a window), *windowDeiconified* (called when a window is restored from being minimized) and *windowOpened* (called when a window is first displayed on the screen).

Most windows have an icon at the top-left or right corner that enables a user to close the window and terminate a program. Most windows also have an icon in the upper-left corner of the window that displays a menu when the user clicks the icon. This menu normally contains a **Close** option to close the window and other options for manipulating the window.

29.15 Using Menus with Frames

Menus are an integral part of GUIs. Menus allow the user to perform actions without unnecessarily "cluttering" a graphical user interface with extra GUI components. In Swing GUIs, menus can only be attached to objects of the classes that provide method `setJMenuBar`. Two such classes are `JFrame` and `JApplet`. The classes used to define menus are *JMenuBar*, *JMenuItem*, *JMenu*, *JCheckBoxMenuItem* and class *JRadioButtonMenuItem*.

Look-and-Feel Observation 29.24

Menus simplify GUIs by reducing the number of components the user views.

Class `JMenuBar` (a subclass of `JComponent`) contains the methods necessary to manage a *menu bar*. A menu bar, which is a container for menus.

Class `JMenuItem` (a subclass of `javax.swing.AbstractButton`) contains the methods necessary to manage *menu items*. A menu item is a GUI component inside a menu that when selected causes an action to be performed. A menu item can be used to initiate an action or it can be a *submenu* that provides more menu items from which the user can select. Submenus are useful for grouping related menu items in a menu.

Class JMenu (a subclass of javax.swing.JMenuItem) contains the methods necessary for managing *menus*. Menus contain menu items and are added to menu bars or to other menus as submenus. When a menu is clicked, the menu expands to show its list of menu items. Clicking a menu item generates an action event.

Class JCheckBoxMenuItem (a subclass of javax.swing.JMenuItem) contains the methods necessary to manage menu items that can be toggled on or off. When a JCheckBoxMenuItem is selected, a check appears to the left of the menu item. When the JCheckBoxMenuItem is selected again, the check to the left of the menu item is removed.

Class JRadioButtonMenuItem (a subclass of javax.swing.JMenuItem) contains the methods necessary to manage menu items that can be toggled on or off like JCheckBoxMenuItems. When multiple JRadioButtonMenuItems are maintained as part of a ButtonGroup, only one item in the group can be selected at a given time. When a JRadioButtonMenuItem is selected, a filled circle appears to the left of the menu item. When another JRadioButtonMenuItem is selected, the filled circle to the left of the previously selected menu item is removed.

The application of Figure 29.22 demonstrates various types of menu items. The program also demonstrates how to specify special characters called mnemonics that can provide quick access to a menu or menu item from the keyboard. Mnemonics can be used with objects of all classes that are subclasses of javax.swing.AbstractButton.

```java
1   // Fig. 29.22: MenuTest.java
2   // Demonstrating menus
3   import javax.swing.*;
4   import java.awt.event.*;
5   import java.awt.*;
6
7   public class MenuTest extends JFrame {
8      private Color colorValues[] =
9         { Color.black, Color.blue, Color.red, Color.green };
10     private JRadioButtonMenuItem colorItems[], fonts[];
11     private JCheckBoxMenuItem styleItems[];
12     private JLabel display;
13     private ButtonGroup fontGroup, colorGroup;
14     private int style;
15
16     public MenuTest()
17     {
18        super( "Using JMenus" );
19
20        JMenuBar bar = new JMenuBar();  // create menubar
21        setJMenuBar( bar );  // set the menubar for the JFrame
22
23        // create File menu and Exit menu item
24        JMenu fileMenu = new JMenu( "File" );
25        fileMenu.setMnemonic( 'F' );
26        JMenuItem aboutItem = new JMenuItem( "About..." );
27        aboutItem.setMnemonic( 'A' );
```

Fig. 29.22 Using JMenus and mnemonics. (Part 1 of 5.)

```
28          aboutItem.addActionListener(
29             new ActionListener() {
30                public void actionPerformed( ActionEvent e )
31                {
32                   JOptionPane.showMessageDialog( MenuTest.this,
33                      "This is an example\nof using menus",
34                      "About", JOptionPane.PLAIN_MESSAGE );
35                } // end method actionPerformed
36             } // end anonymous inner class
37          ); // end addActionListener
38          fileMenu.add( aboutItem );
39
40          JMenuItem exitItem = new JMenuItem( "Exit" );
41          exitItem.setMnemonic( 'x' );
42          exitItem.addActionListener(
43             new ActionListener() {
44                public void actionPerformed( ActionEvent e )
45                {
46                   System.exit( 0 );
47                } // end method actionPerformed
48             } // end anonymous inner class
49          ); // end addActionListener
50          fileMenu.add( exitItem );
51          bar.add( fileMenu );      // add File menu
52
53          // create the Format menu, its submenus and menu items
54          JMenu formatMenu = new JMenu( "Format" );
55          formatMenu.setMnemonic( 'r' );
56
57          // create Color submenu
58          String colors[] =
59             { "Black", "Blue", "Red", "Green" };
60          JMenu colorMenu = new JMenu( "Color" );
61          colorMenu.setMnemonic( 'C' );
62          colorItems = new JRadioButtonMenuItem[ colors.length ];
63          colorGroup = new ButtonGroup();
64          ItemHandler itemHandler = new ItemHandler();
65
66          for ( int i = 0; i < colors.length; i++ ) {
67             colorItems[ i ] =
68                new JRadioButtonMenuItem( colors[ i ] );
69             colorMenu.add( colorItems[ i ] );
70             colorGroup.add( colorItems[ i ] );
71             colorItems[ i ].addActionListener( itemHandler );
72          } // end for
73
74          colorItems[ 0 ].setSelected( true );
75          formatMenu.add( colorMenu );
76          formatMenu.addSeparator();
77
78          // create Font submenu
79          String fontNames[] =
80             { "TimesRoman", "Courier", "Helvetica" };
```

Fig. 29.22 Using JMenus and mnemonics. (Part 2 of 5.)

```
81         JMenu fontMenu = new JMenu( "Font" );
82         fontMenu.setMnemonic( 'n' );
83         fonts = new JRadioButtonMenuItem[ fontNames.length ];
84         fontGroup = new ButtonGroup();
85
86         for ( int i = 0; i < fonts.length; i++ ) {
87            fonts[ i ] =
88               new JRadioButtonMenuItem( fontNames[ i ] );
89            fontMenu.add( fonts[ i ] );
90            fontGroup.add( fonts[ i ] );
91            fonts[ i ].addActionListener( itemHandler );
92         } // end for
93
94         fonts[ 0 ].setSelected( true );
95         fontMenu.addSeparator();
96
97         String styleNames[] = { "Bold", "Italic" };
98         styleItems = new JCheckBoxMenuItem[ styleNames.length ];
99         StyleHandler styleHandler = new StyleHandler();
100
101        for ( int i = 0; i < styleNames.length; i++ ) {
102           styleItems[ i ] =
103              new JCheckBoxMenuItem( styleNames[ i ] );
104           fontMenu.add( styleItems[ i ] );
105           styleItems[ i ].addItemListener( styleHandler );
106        } // end for
107
108        formatMenu.add( fontMenu );
109        bar.add( formatMenu );   // add Format menu
110
111        display = new JLabel(
112           "Sample Text", SwingConstants.CENTER );
113        display.setForeground( colorValues[ 0 ] );
114        display.setFont(
115           new Font( "TimesRoman", Font.PLAIN, 72 ) );
116
117        getContentPane().setBackground( Color.cyan );
118        getContentPane().add( display, BorderLayout.CENTER );
119
120        setSize( 500, 200 );
121        show();
122     } // end MenuTest constructor
123
124     public static void main( String args[] )
125     {
126        MenuTest app = new MenuTest();
127
128        app.addWindowListener(
129           new WindowAdapter() {
130              public void windowClosing( WindowEvent e )
131              {
132                 System.exit( 0 );
133              } // end method windowClosing
```

Fig. 29.22 Using JMenus and mnemonics. (Part 3 of 5.)

```
134              } // end anonymous inner class
135          ); // end addWindowListener
136      } // end main
137
138      class ItemHandler implements ActionListener {
139          public void actionPerformed( ActionEvent e )
140          {
141              for ( int i = 0; i < colorItems.length; i++ )
142                  if ( colorItems[ i ].isSelected() ) {
143                      display.setForeground( colorValues[ i ] );
144                      break;
145                  }
146
147              for ( int i = 0; i < fonts.length; i++ )
148                  if ( e.getSource() == fonts[ i ] ) {
149                      display.setFont( new Font(
150                          fonts[ i ].getText(), style, 72 ) );
151                      break;
152                  }
153
154              repaint();
155          } // end method actionPerformed
156      } // end inner class ItemHandler
157
158      class StyleHandler implements ItemListener {
159          public void itemStateChanged( ItemEvent e )
160          {
161              style = 0;
162
163              if ( styleItems[ 0 ].isSelected() )
164                  style += Font.BOLD;
165
166              if ( styleItems[ 1 ].isSelected() )
167                  style += Font.ITALIC;
168
169              display.setFont( new Font(
170                  display.getFont().getName(), style, 72 ) );
171
172              repaint();
173          } // end method itemStateChanged
174      } // end inner class StyleHandler
175  } // end class MenuTest
```

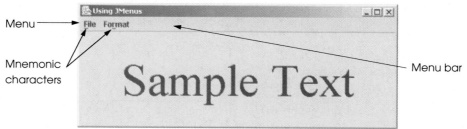

Fig. 29.22 Using `JMenus` and mnemonics. (Part 4 of 5.)

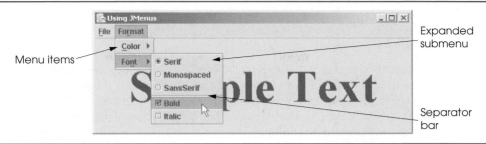

Menu items

Expanded submenu

Separator bar

Fig. 29.22 Using `JMenus` and mnemonics. (Part 5 of 5.)

Class `MenuTest` (line 7) is a completely self-contained class—it defines all the GUI components and event handling for the menu items. Most of the code for this application appears in the class's constructor (line 16).

Lines 20 and 21

```
JMenuBar bar = new JMenuBar();  // create menubar
setJMenuBar( bar );  // set the menubar for the JFrame
```

create the `JMenuBar` and attach it to the application window with `JFrame` method *setJ-MenuBar*.

Common Programming Error 29.10

Forgetting to set the menu bar with `JFrame` *method* `setJMenuBar` *results in the menu bar not being displayed on the* `JFrame`.

Lines 24 through 51 set up the **File** menu and attach it to the menu bar. The **File** menu contains an **About...** menu item that displays a message dialog when the menu item is selected and an **Exit** menu item that can be selected to terminate the application.

Line 24

```
JMenu fileMenu = new JMenu( "File" );
```

creates a `JMenu` object and assigns it to reference `fileMenu` and passes to the constructor the string `"File"` as the name of the menu. Line 25

```
fileMenu.setMnemonic( 'F' );
```

uses `AbstractButton` method *setMnemonic* (inherited into class `JMenu`) to indicate that F is the *mnemonic* for this menu. Pressing the *Alt* key and the letter *F* opens the menu just as clicking the menu name with the mouse would. In the GUI, the mnemonic character in the menu's name is displayed with an underline (see the screen captures).

Look-and-Feel Observation 29.25

Mnemonics provide quick keyboard access to menu commands and button commands.

Look-and-Feel Observation 29.26

*Different mnemonics should be used for each button or menu item. Normally, the first letter in the label on the menu item or button is used as the mnemonic. If multiple buttons or menu items start with the same letter, choose the next most prominent letter in the name (e.g., **x** is commonly chosen for a button or menu item called **Exit**).*

Lines 26 and 27

```
JMenuItem aboutItem = new JMenuItem( "About..." );
aboutItem.setMnemonic( 'A' );
```

define `JMenuItem aboutItem` with the name `"About..."` and set its mnemonic to the letter A. This menu item is added to `fileMenu` in line 38. To access the **About...** item through the keyboard, press the *Alt* key and letter *F* to open the **File** menu, then press *A* to select the **About...** menu item. Lines 28 through 37 create an `ActionListener` to listen for selection of `aboutItem`. Lines 32 through 34

```
JOptionPane.showMessageDialog( MenuTest.this,
    "This is an example\nof using menus",
    "About", JOptionPane.PLAIN_MESSAGE );
```

display a message dialog box. In most prior uses of `showMessageDialog`, the first argument has been `null`. The purpose of the first argument is to specify the *parent window* for the dialog box. The parent window helps determine where the dialog box will be displayed. If the parent window is specified as `null`, the dialog box is normally displayed in the center of the screen. If the parent window is not `null`, the dialog box is normally displayed centered horizontally over the parent window and just below the top of the window.

Dialog boxes can be either *modal* or *modeless*. A *modal dialog box* does not allow any other window in the application to be accessed until the dialog box is dismissed. A *modeless dialog box* allows other windows to be accessed while the dialog is displayed. By default, the dialogs displayed with class `JOptionPane` are modal dialogs. Class *JDialog* can be used to create your own modeless or modal dialogs.

Line 38

```
fileMenu.add( aboutItem );
```

adds `aboutItem` to `fileMenu` with `JMenu` method *add*.

Lines 40 through 50 define menu item `exitItem`, set its mnemonic to x and register an `ActionListener` that terminates the application when `exitItem` is selected.

Line 51

```
bar.add( fileMenu );    // add File menu
```

uses `JMenuBar` method *add* to attach the `fileMenu` to `bar`.

 Look-and-Feel Observation 29.27

Menus normally appear left to right in the order that they are added.

Lines 54 and 55 create menu `formatMenu` and set its mnemonic to r (F is not used because that is the **File** menu's mnemonic).

Lines 60 and 61 create menu `colorMenu` (this will be a submenu in the **Format** menu) and set its mnemonic to C. Line 62 creates `JRadioButtonMenuItem` array `colorItems` that will refer to the menu items in `colorMenu`. Line 63 creates the `ButtonGroup` `colorGroup` that will ensure that only one of the menu items in the **Color** submenu is selected at a time. Line 64 defines an instance of inner class `ItemHandler` (defined in lines 138 to 156) that will be used to respond to selections from the **Color** submenu and the **Font** submenu (discussed shortly). The `for` structure in lines 66 through 72 creates each `JRa-dioButtonMenuItem` in array `colorItems`, adds each menu item to `colorMenu`, adds each menu item to `colorGroup` and registers the `ActionListener` for each menu item.

Line 74

```
colorItems[ 0 ].setSelected( true );
```

uses `AbstractButton` method `setSelected` to indicate that the first element in the `colorItems` array should be selected. Line 75 adds the `colorMenu` as a submenu of the `formatMenu`.

Look-and-Feel Observation 29.28

Adding a menu as a menu item in another menu automatically makes the added menu a submenu. When the mouse is positioned over a submenu (or the submenu's mnemonic is pressed), the submenu expands to show its menu items.

Line 76

```
formatMenu.addSeparator();
```

adds a *separator* line to the menu. The separator appears as a horizontal line in the menu.

Look-and-Feel Observation 29.29

Separators can be added to a menu to logically group menu items.

Lines 79 through 94 create the **Font** submenu and several `JRadioButtonMenuItems` and indicate that the first element of `JRadioButtonMenuItem` array `fonts` should be selected. Line 98 creates a `JCheckBoxMenuItem` array to represent the menu items for specifying bold and italic styles for the fonts. Line 99 defines an instance of inner class `StyleHandler` (defined in lines 158 through 174) to respond to the `JCheckBoxMenuItem` events. The `for` structure in lines 101 through 106 creates each `JCheckBoxMenuItem`, adds each menu item to `fontMenu` and registers the `ItemListener` for each menu item. Line 108 adds `fontMenu` as a submenu of `formatMenu`. Line 109 adds the `formatMenu` to `bar`.

Lines 111 through 115 create a `JLabel` for which the font, font color and font style are controlled through the **Format** menu. The initial foreground color is set to the first element of array `colorValues` (`Color.black`) and the initial font is set to `TimesRoman` with PLAIN style and 72-point size. Line 117 sets the background color of the window's content pane to `Color.cyan`, and line 118 attaches the `JLabel` to the CENTER of the content pane's `BorderLayout`.

Method `actionPerformed` of class `ItemHandler` (line 138) uses two `for` structures to determine which font or color menu item generated the event and sets the font or color of the `JLabel` `display`, respectively. The `if` condition in line 142 uses `AbstractButton` method *isSelected* to determine which `JRadioButtonMenuItem` for selecting colors is selected. The `if` condition in line 148 uses `EventSource` method *getSource* to get a reference to the `JRadioButtonMenuItem` that generated the event. Line 150 uses `AbstractButton` method *getText* to obtain the name of the font from the menu item.

Method `itemStateChanged` of class `StyleHandler` (line 158) is called if the user selects a `JCheckBoxMenuItem` in the `fontMenu`. Lines 163 and 166 determine if either or both of the `JCheckBoxMenuItems` are selected and use their combined state to determine the new style of the font.

Look-and-Feel Observation 29.30

Any lightweight GUI component (i.e., a component that subclasses JComponent) can be added to a JMenu or to a JMenuBar.

SUMMARY

- A graphical user interface (GUI) presents a pictorial interface to a program. A GUI (pronounced "GOO-EE") gives a program a distinctive "look" and "feel."

- By providing different applications with a consistent set of intuitive user interface components, GUIs allow the user to spend more time using the program in a productive manner.

- GUIs are built from GUI components (sometimes called controls or widgets). A GUI component is a visual object with which the user interacts via the mouse or the keyboard.

- Swing GUI components are defined in package javax.swing. Swing components are written, manipulated and displayed completely in Java.

- The original GUI components from the Abstract Windowing Toolkit package java.awt are tied directly to the local platform's graphical user interface capabilities.

- Swing components are lightweight components. AWT components are tied to the local platform and are called heavyweight components—they must rely on the local platform's windowing system to determine their functionality and their look and feel.

- Several Swing GUI components are heavyweight GUI components: in particular, subclasses of java.awt.Window (such as JFrame) that display windows on the screen. Heavyweight Swing GUI components are less flexible than lightweight components.

- Much of each Swing GUI component's functionality is inherited from classes Component, Container and JComponent (the superclass to most Swing components).

- A Container is an area where components can be placed.

- JLabels provide text instructions or information on a GUI.

- JComponent method setToolTipText specifies the tool tip that is displayed whenever the user positions the mouse cursor over a JComponent in the GUI.

- Many Swing components can display images by specifying an Icon as an argument to their constructor or by using a method setIcon.

- Class ImageIcon (package javax.swing) supports two image formats—Graphics Interchange Format (GIF) and Joint Photographic Experts Group (JPEG).

- Interface SwingConstants (package javax.swing) defines a set of common integer constants (such as SwingConstants.LEFT) that are used with many Swing components.

- By default, the text of a JComponent appears to the right of the image when the JComponent contains both text and an image.

- The horizontal and vertical alignments of a JLabel can be set with methods setHorizontalAlignment and setVerticalAlignment. Method setText sets the text displayed on the label. Method getText retrieves the current text displayed on a label. Methods setHorizontalTextPosition and setVerticalTextPosition specify the text position in a label.

- JComponent method setIcon sets the Icon displayed on a JComponent. Method getIcon retrieves the current Icon displayed on a JComponent.

- GUIs generate events when the user interacts with the GUI. Information about a GUI event is stored in an object of a class that extends AWTEvent.

- To process an event, the programmer must register an event listener and implement one or more event handlers.

- The use of event listeners in event handling is known as the delegation event model—the processing of an event is delegated to a particular object in the program.

- When an event occurs, the GUI component with which the user interacted notifies its registered listeners by calling each listener's appropriate event handling method.

- JTextFields and JPasswordFields are single-line areas in which text can be entered by the user from the keyboard or text can simply be displayed. A JPasswordField shows that a character was typed as the user enters characters, but automatically hides the characters.

- When the user types data into a JTextField or JPasswordField and presses the *Enter* key, an ActionEvent occurs.

- JTextComponent method setEditable determines whether the user can modify the text in a JTextComponent.

- JPasswordField method getPassword returns the password as an array of type char.

- Every JComponent contains an object of class EventListenerList (package javax.swing.event) called listenerList in which all registered listeners are stored.

- Every JComponent supports several different event types, including mouse events, key events and others. When an event occurs, the event is dispatched only to the event listeners of the appropriate type. Each event type has a corresponding event-listener interface.

- When an event is generated by a user interaction with a component, the component is handed a unique event ID specifying the event type. The GUI component uses the event ID to decide the type of listener to which the event should be dispatched and the event handler method to call.

- A JButton generates an ActionEvent when the user clicks the button with the mouse.

- An AbstractButton can have a rollover Icon that is displayed when the mouse is positioned over the button. The icon changes as the mouse moves in and out of the button's area on the screen. AbstractButton method setRolloverIcon specifies the image displayed on a button when the user positions the mouse over the button.

- The Swing GUI components contain three state button types—JToggleButton, JCheckBox and JRadioButton—that have on/off or true/false values. Classes JCheckBox and JRadioButton are subclasses of JToggleButton.

- When the user clicks a JCheckBox, an ItemEvent is generated that can be handled by an ItemListener. ItemListeners must define method itemStateChanged. ItemEvent method getStateChange determines the state of a JToggleButton.

- JRadioButtons are similar to JCheckBoxes in that they have two states—selected and not selected (also called deselected). JRadioButtons normally appear as a group in which only one radio button can be selected at a time.

- A JComboBox (sometimes called a drop-down list) provides a list of items from which the user can make a selection. JComboBoxes generate ItemEvents. A numeric index keeps track of the ordering of items in a JComboBox. The first item is added at index 0; the next item is added at index 1, and so forth. The first item added to a JComboBox appears as the currently selected item when the JComboBox is displayed. JComboBox method getSelectedIndex returns the index number of the selected item.

- Mouse events can be trapped for any GUI component that derives from java.awt.Component using MouseListeners and MouseMotionListeners.

- Each mouse event handling method takes as its argument a MouseEvent object containing information about the mouse event and the location where the event occurred.

- Methods addMouseListener and addMouseMotionListener are Component methods used to register mouse event listeners for an object of any class that extends Component.

- Many of the event-listener interfaces provide multiple methods. For each there is a corresponding event listener adapter class that provides a default implementation of every method in the interface. The programmer can extend the adapter class to inherit the default implementation of every method and simply override the method or methods needed for event handling in the program.
- `MouseEvent` method `getClickCount` returns the number of mouse clicks.
- `InputEvent` methods `isMetaDown` and `isAltDown` are used to determine which mouse button the user clicked.
- Layout managers arrange GUI components on a container for presentation purposes.
- `FlowLayout` lays out components from left to right in the order in which they are added to the container. When the edge of the container is reached, components are continued on the next line.
- `FlowLayout` method `setAlignment` changes the alignment for the `FlowLayout` to `FlowLayout.LEFT`, `FlowLayout.CENTER` or `FlowLayout.RIGHT`.
- The `BorderLayout` layout manager arranges components into five regions: North, South, East, West and Center. One component can be added to each region.
- `LayoutManager` method `layoutContainer` recalculates the layout of its `Container` argument.
- The `GridLayout` layout manager divides the container into a grid of rows and columns. Components are added to a `GridLayout` starting at the top-left cell and proceeding left-to-right until the row is full. Then the process continues left-to-right on the next row of the grid, etc.
- `Container` method `validate` recomputes the container's layout based on the current layout manager for the `Container` and the current set of displayed GUI components.
- Panels are created with class `JPanel`, which inherits from class `JComponent`. `JPanel`s may have components, including other panels, added to them.
- `JTextArea`s provide an area for manipulating multiple lines of text. Like class `JTextField`, class `JTextArea` inherits from `JTextComponent`.
- An external event (i.e., an event generated by a different GUI component) normally indicates when the text in a `JTextArea` should be processed.
- Scrollbars are provided for a `JTextArea` by attaching it to a `JScrollPane` object.
- Method `getSelectedText` returns the selected text from a `JTextArea`. Text is selected by dragging the mouse over the desired text to highlight it.
- Method `setText` sets the text in a `JTextArea`.
- To provide automatic word wrap in a `JTextArea`, attach it to a `JScrollPane` with horizontal scrollbar policy `JScrollPane.HORIZONTAL_SCROLLBAR_NEVER`.
- The horizontal and vertical scrollbar policies for a `JScrollPane` are set when a `JScrollPane` is constructed or with methods `setHorizontalScrollBarPolicy` and `setVerticalScrollBarPolicy` of class `JScrollPane`.
- A `JPanel` can be used as a dedicated drawing area that can receive mouse events and is often extended to create new GUI components.
- Swing components that inherit from class `JComponent` contain method `paintComponent`, which helps them draw properly in the context of a Swing GUI. `JComponent` method `paintComponent` should be overridden as follows:

```java
public void paintComponent( Graphics g )
{
   super.paintComponent( g );

   // your additional drawing code
}
```

- The call to the superclass version of paintComponent ensures that painting occurs in the proper order and that Swing's painting mechanism remains intact. If the superclass version of paint-Component is not called, typically the customized GUI component will not be displayed properly on the user interface. Also, if the superclass version is called after performing the customized drawing statements, the results will typically be erased.

- Classes JFrame and JApplet are not subclasses of JComponent; therefore, they do not contain method paintComponent (they have method paint).

- Calling repaint for a Swing GUI component indicates that the component should be painted as soon as possible. The background of the GUI component is cleared only if the component is opaque. Most Swing components are transparent by default. JComponent method setOpaque can be passed a boolean argument indicating if the component is opaque (true) or transparent (false). The GUI components of package java.awt are different from Swing components in that repaint results in a call to Component method update (which clears the component's background) and update calls method paint (rather than paintComponent).

- Method setTitle displays a String in a window's title bar.

- Drawing on any GUI component is performed with coordinates that are measured from the upper-left corner (0, 0) of that GUI component.

- Layout managers often use a GUI component's getPreferredSize method to determine the preferred width and height of a component when laying out that component as part of a GUI. If a new component has a preferred width and height, it should override method getPreferredSize to return that width and height as an object of class Dimension (package java.awt).

- The default size of a JPanel object is 0 pixels wide and 0 pixels high.

- A mouse drag operation begins with a mouse pressed event. All subsequent mouse drag events (for which mouseDragged will be called) are sent to the GUI component that received the original mouse pressed event.

- A JFrame is a window with a title bar and a border. Class JFrame is a subclass of java.awt.Frame (which is a subclass of java.awt.Window).

- Class JFrame supports three operations when the user closes the window. By default, a JFrame is hidden when the user closes a window. This can be controlled with JFrame method setDefaultCloseOperation. Interface WindowConstants (package javax.swing) defines three constants for use with this method—DISPOSE_ON_CLOSE, DO_NOTHING_ON_CLOSE and HIDE_ON_CLOSE (the default).

- By default, a window is not displayed on the screen until its show method is called. A window can also be displayed by calling its setVisible method with true as an argument.

- A window's size should be set with a call to method setSize. The position of a window when it appears on the screen is specified with method setLocation.

- All windows generate window events when the user manipulates the window. Event listeners are registered for window events with method addWindowListener of class Window. The WindowListener interface provides seven methods for handling window events—windowActivated (called when the window is made active by clicking the window), windowClosed (called after the window is closed), windowClosing (called when the user initiates closing of the window), windowDeactivated (called when another window is made active), windowIconified (called when the user minimizes a window), windowDeiconified (called when a window is restored from being minimized) and windowOpened (called when a window is first displayed on the screen).

- The command-line arguments are automatically passed to main as the array of Strings called args. The first argument after the application class name is the first String in the array args, and the length of the array is the total number of command-line arguments.

- Menus are an integral part of GUIs. Menus allow the user to perform actions without unnecessarily "cluttering" a graphical user interface with extra GUI components.

- In Swing GUIs, menus can only be attached to objects of the classes that provide method `set-JMenuBar`. Two such classes are `JFrame` and `JApplet`.

- The classes used to define menus are `JMenuBar`, `JMenuItem`, `JMenu`, `JCheckBoxMenuItem` and class `JRadioButtonMenuItem`.

- A `JMenuBar` is a container for menus.

- A `JMenuItem` is a GUI component inside a menu that, when selected, causes an action to be performed. A `JMenuItem` can be used to initiate an action or it can be a submenu that provides more menu items from which the user can select.

- A `JMenu` contains menu items and can be added to a `JMenuBar` or to other `JMenus` as submenus. When a menu is clicked, the menu expands to show its list of menu items.

- When a `JCheckBoxMenuItem` is selected, a check appears to the left of the menu item. When the `JCheckBoxMenuItem` is selected again, the check to the left of the menu item is removed.

- When multiple `JRadioButtonMenuItems` are maintained as part of a `ButtonGroup`, only one item in the group can be selected at a given time. When a `JRadioButtonMenuItem` is selected, a filled circle appears to the left of the menu item. When another `JRadioButtonMenuItem` is selected, the filled circle to the left of the previously selected menu item is removed.

- `JFrame` method `setJMenuBar` attaches a menu bar to a `JFrame`.

- `AbstractButton` method `setMnemonic` (inherited into class `JMenu`) specifies the mnemonic for an `AbstractButton` object. Pressing the *Alt* key and the mnemonic performs the `AbstractButton`'s action (in the case of a menu, it opens the menu).

- Mnemonic characters are normally displayed with an underline.

- Dialog boxes can be either modal or modeless. A modal dialog box does not allow any other window in the application to be accessed until the dialog box is dismissed. A modeless dialog box allows other windows to be accessed while the dialog is displayed. By default, the dialogs displayed with class `JOptionPane` are modal dialogs. Class `JDialog` can be used to create your own modeless or modal dialogs.

- `JMenu` method `addSeparator` adds a separator line to a menu.

TERMINOLOGY

Abstract Windowing Toolkit	`BorderLayout.NORTH`
`AbstractButton` class	`BorderLayout.SOUTH`
`ActionEvent` class	`BorderLayout.WEST`
`ActionListener` interface	Box class
`actionPerformed` method	`BoxLayout` layout manager
adapter class	button
add method of class `Container`	button label
`addItemListener` method	check box
`addMouseListener` method	check box label
`addMouseMotionListener` method	command button
`addSeparator` method of class `JMenu`	`Component` class
`addWindowListener` method of `Window`	`ComponentAdapter` class
automatic word wrap	`ComponentListener` interface
`BorderLayout` class	`Container` class
`BorderLayout.CENTER`	`ContainerAdapter` class
`BorderLayout.EAST`	`ContainerListener` interface

mouseMoved method
mousePressed method
mouseReleased method
multiple-selection list
paintComponent method of JComponent
radio button
read-only text
register an event listener
right-aligned
rollover icon
scroll arrow
scroll box
scrollbar
scrollbar policies for a JScrollPane
selection mode
setAlignment method
setBackground method
setDefaultCloseOperation method
setEditable method
setHorizontalScrollBarPolicy method
setIcon method
setJMenuBar method
setLayout method of class Container
setListData method of JList
setMaximumRowCount method
setMnemonic method of AbstractButton
setOpaque method of class JComponent
setRolloverIcon method
setSelected method of AbstractButton
setSelectionMode method
setText method
setTitle method of class Frame

setToolTipText method
setVerticalAlignment method
setVerticalScrollBarPolicy method
setVerticalTextPosition method
setVisible method
setVisibleRowCount method
shortcut key (mnemonics)
single-selection list
submenu
SwingConstants.HORIZONTAL
SwingConstants.VERTICAL
SwingConstants interface
Swing GUI component
tool tips
toolbar
user interface localization
validate method
valueChanged method
vertical gap space
widget (window gadget)
window
windowActivated method
WindowAdapter class
windowClosed method
windowClosing method
WindowConstants.DISPOSE_ON_CLOSE
windowDeactivated method
windowDeiconified method
windowIconified method
windowing system
WindowListener interface
windowOpened method

COMMON PROGRAMMING ERRORS

29.1   Forgetting to add a component to a container so it can be displayed is a run-time logic error.

29.2   Adding to a container a component that has not been instantiated throws a NullPointer-Exception.

29.3   Using a lowercase f in the class names JTextField or JPasswordField is a syntax error.

29.4   Forgetting to register an event handler object for a particular GUI component's event type results in no events being handled for that component for that event type.

29.5   Adding more than one component to a particular region in a BorderLayout results in only the last component added being displayed. There is no error message to indicate this problem.

29.6   When a JComponent's paintComponent method is overridden, not calling the superclass's original version of paintComponent prevents the GUI component from displaying properly on the GUI.

29.7   When a JComponent's paintComponent method is overridden, calling the superclass's original version of paintComponent after other drawing is performed erases the other drawings.

29.8   Forgetting to call method show or method setVisible on a window is a run-time logic error; the window is not displayed.

29.9 Forgetting to call the setSize method on a window is a run-time logic error—only the title bar appears.

29.10 Forgetting to set the menu bar with JFrame method setJMenuBar results in the menu bar not being displayed on the JFrame.

GOOD PROGRAMMING PRACTICES

29.1 Study the methods of class Component in the Java 2 SDK on-line documentation to learn the capabilities common to most GUI components.

29.2 Study the methods of class Container in the Java 2 SDK on-line documentation to learn the capabilities common to every container for GUI components.

29.3 Study the methods of class JComponent in the Java 2 SDK on-line documentation to learn the capabilities common to every container for GUI components.

29.4 Study the methods of class javax.swing.JLabel in the Java 2 SDK on-line documentation to learn the complete capabilities of the class before using it.

29.5 Use separate classes to process GUI events.

LOOK-AND-FEEL OBSERVATIONS

29.1 Consistent user interfaces enable a user to learn new applications faster.

29.2 Swing components are written in Java, so they provide a greater level of portability and flexibility than the original Java GUI components from package java.awt.

29.3 Use tool tips (set with JComponent method setToolTipText) to add descriptive text to your GUI components. This text helps the user determine the GUI component's purpose in the user interface.

29.4 Often an external event determines when the text in a JTextArea should be processed.

29.5 To provide automatic word wrap functionality for a JTextArea, invoke JTextArea method setLineWrap with a true argument.

29.6 Having more than one JButton with the same label makes the JButtons ambiguous to the user. Be sure to provide a unique label for each button.

29.7 Using rollover icons for JButtons provides the user with visual feedback indicating that if they click the mouse the button's action will occur.

29.8 Class AbstractButton supports displaying text and images on a button, so all subclasses of AbstractButton also support displaying text and images.

29.9 Set the maximum row count for a JComboBox to a number of rows that prevents the list from expanding outside the bounds of the window or applet in which it is used. This will ensure that the list displays correctly when it is expanded by the user.

29.10 Method calls to mouseDragged are sent to the MouseMotionListener for the Component on which the drag operation started. Similarly, the mouseReleased method call is sent to the MouseListener for the Component on which the drag operation started.

29.11 Most Java programming environments provide GUI design tools that help a programmer graphically design a GUI, then automatically write Java code to create the GUI.

29.12 Each container can have only one layout manager at a time (separate containers in the same program can have different layout managers).

29.13 If no region is specified when adding a Component to a BorderLayout, it is assumed that the Component should be added to region BorderLayout.CENTER.

29.14 Combining graphics and Swing GUI components may lead to incorrect display of the graphics, the GUI components or both. Using JPanels for drawing can eliminate this problem by providing a dedicated area for graphics.

29.15 When a `JComponent`'s `paintComponent` method is overridden, the first statement in the body should always be a call to the superclass's original version of the method.

29.16 Calling `repaint` for a Swing GUI component indicates that the component should be painted as soon as possible. The background of the GUI component is cleared only if the component is opaque. Most Swing components are transparent by default. `JComponent` method `setOpaque` can be passed a `boolean` argument indicating if the component is opaque (`true`) or transparent (`false`). The GUI components of package `java.awt` are different from Swing components in that `repaint` results in a call to `Component` method `update` (which clears the component's background) and `update` calls method `paint` (rather than `paintComponent`).

29.17 Drawing on any GUI component is performed with coordinates that are measured from the upper-left corner *(0, 0)* of that GUI component.

29.18 The default size of a `JPanel` object is 0 pixels wide and 0 pixels tall.

29.19 When subclassing `JPanel` (or any other `JComponent`), override method `getPreferredSize` if the new component should have a specific preferred width and height.

29.20 Most Swing GUI components can be transparent or opaque. If a Swing GUI component is opaque, when its `paintComponent` method is called, its background will be cleared. Otherwise, its background will not be cleared.

29.21 Class `JComponent` provides method `setOpaque` that takes a `boolean` argument to determine if a `JComponent` is opaque (`true`) or transparent (`false`).

29.22 `JPanel` objects are opaque by default.

29.23 A mouse drag operation begins with a mouse pressed event. All subsequent mouse drag events (for which `mouseDragged` will be called) are sent to the GUI component that received the original mouse pressed event.

29.24 Menus simplify GUIs by reducing the number of components the user views.

29.25 Mnemonics provide quick keyboard access to menu commands and button commands.

29.26 Different mnemonics should be used for each button or menu item. Normally, the first letter in the label on the menu item or button is used as the mnemonic. If multiple buttons or menu items start with the same letter, choose the next most prominent letter in the name (e.g., `x` is commonly chosen for a button or menu item called `Exit`).

29.27 Menus normally appear left to right in the order that they are added.

29.28 Adding a menu as a menu item in another menu automatically makes the added menu a submenu. When the mouse is positioned over a submenu (or the submenu's mnemonic is pressed), the submenu expands to show its menu items.

29.29 Separators can be added to a menu to logically group menu items.

29.30 Any lightweight GUI component (i.e., a component that subclasses `JComponent`) can be added to a `JMenu` or to a `JMenuBar`.

PORTABILITY TIP

29.1 The look of a GUI defined with heavyweight GUI components from package `java.awt` may vary across platforms. Heavyweight components "tie" into the "local" platform GUI, which varies from platform to platform.

SOFTWARE ENGINEERING OBSERVATIONS

29.1 To effectively use GUI components, the `javax.swing` and `java.awt` inheritance hierarchies must be understood—especially class `Component`, class `Container` and class `JComponent`, which define features common to most Swing components.

29.2   The event listener for an event must implement the appropriate event-listener interface.

29.3   Using separate classes to handle GUI events leads to more reusable, reliable and readable software components that can be placed in packages and used in many programs.

29.4   Windows are a valuable system resource that should be returned to the system when they are no longer needed.

SELF-REVIEW EXERCISES

29.1   Fill in the blanks in each of the following:
   a)   Method _____ is called when the mouse is moved and an event listener is registered to handle the event.
   b)   Text that cannot be modified by the user is called _____ text.
   c)   A(n) _____ arranges GUI components on a Container.
   d)   The add method for attaching GUI components is a(n) _____ class method.
   e)   GUI is an acronym for _____.
   f)   Method _____ is used to set the layout manager for a container.
   g)   A mouseDragged method call is preceded by a(n) _____ method call and followed by a(n) _____ method call.

29.2   State whether each of the following is *true* or *false*. If *false*, explain why.
   a)   BorderLayout is the default layout manager for a content pane.
   b)   When the mouse cursor is moved into the bounds of a GUI component, method mouse-Over is called.
   c)   A JPanel cannot be added to another JPanel.
   d)   In a BorderLayout, two buttons added to the NORTH region will be placed side-by-side.
   e)   When using BorderLayout, a maximum of five components may be used.

29.3   Find the error(s) in each of the following and explain how to correct it (them).
   a)   `buttonName = JButton( "Caption" );`
   b)   `JLabel aLabel, JLabel;      // create references`
   c)   `txtField = new JTextField( 50, "Default Text" );`
   d)   ```
Container c = getContentPane();
setLayout(new BorderLayout());
button1 = new JButton("North Star");
button2 = new JButton("South Pole");
c.add(button1);
c.add(button2);
```

## ANSWERS TO SELF-REVIEW EXERCISES

**29.1**   a) mouseMoved. b) uneditable (read-only). c) layout manager. d) Container. e) graphical user interface. f) setLayout. g) mousePressed, mouseReleased.

**29.2**   a)   True.
   b)   False. Method mouseEntered is called.
   c)   False. A JPanel can be added to another JPanel because JPanel derives indirectly from Component. Therefore, a JPanel is a Component. Any Component can be added to a Container.
   d)   False. Only the last button added will be displayed. Remember that only one component can be added to each region in a BorderLayout.
   e)   True.

**29.3**   a)   new is needed to instantiate the object.
   b)   JLabel is a class name and cannot be used as a variable name.
```

c) The arguments passed to the constructor are reversed. The `String` must be passed first.
d) `BorderLayout` has been set and components are being added without specifying the region. Proper `add` statements might be
```
c.add( button1, BorderLayout.NORTH );
c.add( button2, BorderLayout.SOUTH );
```

EXERCISES

29.4 Fill in the blanks in each of the following:
a) The `JTextField` class inherits directly from _____.
b) The layout managers discussed in this chapter are _____, _____ and _____.
c) `Container` method _____ attaches a GUI component to a container.
d) Method _____ is called when a mouse button is released (without moving the mouse).

29.5 State whether each of the following is *true* or *false*. If *false*, explain why.
a) Only one layout manager can be used per `Container`.
b) GUI components can be added to a `Container` in any order in a `BorderLayout`.
c) `Graphics` method `setFont` is used to set the font for text fields.
d) A `Mouse` object contains a method called `mouseDragged`.

29.6 State whether each of the following is *true* or *false*. If *false*, explain why.
a) A `JApplet` does not have a content pane.
b) A `JPanel` is a `JComponent`.
c) A `JPanel` is a `Component`.
d) A `JLabel` is a `Container`.
e) An `AbstractButton` is a `JButton`.
f) A `JTextField` is an `Object`.

29.7 Find any error(s) in each of the following and explain how to correct it (them).
a) `import javax.swing.*;`   `// include swing package`
b) `panelObject.GridLayout( 8, 8 ); // set GridLayout`
c) `c.setLayout( new FlowLayout( FlowLayout.DEFAULT ) );`
d) `c.add( eastButton, EAST );  // BorderLayout`

29.8 Create the following GUI. You do not have to provide any functionality.

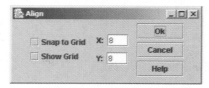

29.9 Create the following GUI. You do not have to provide any functionality.

29.10   Create the following GUI. You do not have to provide any functionality.

29.11   Write a temperature conversion program that converts from Fahrenheit to Celsius. The Fahrenheit temperature should be entered from the keyboard (via a JTextField). A JLabel should be used to display the converted temperature. Use the following formula for the conversion:

```
Celsius = 5 /9 ∞ (Fahrenheit - 32)
```

29.12   Write an application that allows the user to draw a rectangle by dragging the mouse on the application window. The upper-left coordinate should be the location where the user presses the mouse button, and the lower-right coordinate should be the location where the user releases the mouse button. Also display the area of the rectangle in a JLabel in the SOUTH region of a BorderLayout. All drawing should be done on a subclass of JPanel. Use the following formula for the area:

```
area = width ∞ height
```

29.13   Write a program that displays a circle of random size and calculates and displays the area, radius, diameter and circumference. Use the following equations: *diameter = 2 ∞ radius, area = π ∞ radius^2, circumference = 2 ∞ π ∞ radius*. Use the constant Math.PI for pi (π). All drawing should be done on a subclass of JPanel and the results of the calculations should be displayed in a read-only JTextArea.

29.14   Write a program that uses System.out.println statements to print out events as they occur. Provide a JComboBox with a minimum of four items. The user should be able to choose an event to "monitor" from the JComboBox. When that particular event occurs, display information about the event in a message dialog box. Use method toString on the event object to convert it to a string representation.

29.15   Write a program using methods from interface MouseListener that allows the user to press the mouse button, drag the mouse and release the mouse button. When the mouse is released, draw a rectangle with the appropriate upper-left corner, width and height. [*Hint*: The mousePressed method should capture the set of coordinates at which the user presses and holds the mouse button initially, and the mouseReleased method should capture the set of coordinates at which the user releases the mouse button. Both methods should store the appropriate coordinate values. All drawing should be done on a subclass of JPanel and all calculations of the width, height and upper-left corner should be performed by the paintComponent method before the shape is drawn.]

29.16   Modify Exercise 29.15 to provided a "rubber-banding" effect. As the user drags the mouse, the user should be able to see the current size of the rectangle to know exactly what the rectangle will look like when the mouse button is released. [*Hint*: Method mouseDragged should perform the same tasks as mouseReleased.]

29.17   Modify Exercise 29.16 to allow the user to select which shape to draw. A JComboBox should provide options including at least rectangle, oval, line and rounded rectangle.

29.18   Modify Exercise 29.17 to allow the user to select the drawing color from a JColorChooser dialog box.

29.19   Modify Exercise 29.18 to allow the user to specify if a shape should be filled or empty when it is drawn. The user should click a JCheckBox to indicate filled or empty.

29.20   *(Complete Drawing Application)* Using the techniques developed in Exercises 29.12 through 29.19, create a complete drawing program. The program should use the GUI components of this chapter to enable the user to select the shape, color and fill characteristics. For this program, create your own classes (like those in the class hierarchy described in Exercise 27.19) from which objects will be created to store each shape the user draws. The classes should store the location, dimensions and color of each shape and should indicate if the shape is filled or unfilled. Your classes should all derive from a class called MyShape that has all the common features of every shape type. Every subclass of My-Shape should have its own method draw, which returns void and receives a Graphics object as its argument. Create a subclass of JPanel called DrawPanel for drawing the shapes. When the Draw-Panel's paintComponent method is called, it should walk through the array of shapes and display each shape by polymorphically calling the shape's draw method (passing the Graphics object as an argument). Each shape's draw method should know how to draw the shape. As a minimum, your program should provide the following classes: MyLine, MyOval, MyRect, MyRoundRect. Design the class hierarchy for maximum software reuse and place all your classes in the package shapes. Import this package into your program. Each shape should be stored in an array of MyShape objects, where MyShape is the superclass in your hierarchy of shape classes (see Exercise 27.19).

29.21   Modify Exercise 29.20 to provide an **Undo** button that can be used repeatedly to undo the last painting operation. If there are no shapes in the array of shapes, the **Undo** button should be disabled.

30

Java Multimedia: Images, Animation and Audio

Objectives

- To understand how to get and display images.
- To be able to create animations from sequences of images; to control animation speed and flicker.
- To be able to get, play, loop and stop sounds.
- To be able to monitor the loading of images with class `MediaTracker`; to create image maps.
- To customize applets with the `param` tag.

The wheel that squeaks the loudest … gets the grease.
John Billings (Henry Wheeler Shaw)

Noise proves nothing. Often a hen who has merely laid an egg cackles as if she had laid an asteroid.
Mark Twain

We'll use a signal I have tried and found far-reaching and easy to yell. Waa-hoo!
Zane Grey

A wide screen just makes a bad film twice as bad.
Samuel Goldwyn

There is a natural hootchy-kootchy motion to a goldfish.
Walt Disney

Between the motion and the act falls the shadow.
Thomas Stearns Eliot

What we experience of nature is in models, and all of nature's models are so beautiful.
Richard Buckminster Fuller

Outline

30.1 Introduction

Welcome to what may be the largest revolution in the history of the computer industry. Those of us who entered the field decades ago were primarily interested in using computers to do arithmetic calculations at high speed. But as the computer field evolves, we are beginning to realize that the data manipulation capabilities of computers are now equally important. The "sizzle" of Java is *multimedia*, the use of *sound*, *images*, *graphics* and *video* to make applications "come alive." Today many people consider two-dimensional color video to be the "ultimate" in multimedia. But within the decade, we expect all kinds of exciting new three-dimensional applications. Multimedia programming offers many new challenges. The field is already enormous and will grow rapidly.

People are rushing to equip their computers for multimedia. Most new computers are sold "multimedia ready" with CD or DVD drives, audio boards and sometimes special video capabilities.

Among users who want graphics, two-dimensional graphics no longer suffice. Now many people want three-dimensional, high-resolution, color graphics. True three-dimensional imaging may become available within the next decade. Imagine having ultra-high-resolution, "theater-in-the-round," three-dimensional television. Sporting and entertainment events will take place on your living room floor! Medical students worldwide will see operations being performed thousands of miles away as if they were occurring in the same room. People will be able to learn how to drive with extremely realistic driving simulators in their homes before they get behind the wheel. The possibilities are exciting and endless.

Multimedia demands extraordinary computing power. Until recently, affordable computers with this kind of power were not available. But today's ultra-fast processors like the SPARC Ultra from Sun Microsystems, the Pentium from Intel, the Alpha from Compaq Computer Corporation and the R8000 from MIPS/Silicon Graphics (among others) are making effective multimedia possible. The computer and communications industries will be primary beneficiaries of the multimedia revolution. Users will be willing to pay for the faster processors, larger memories and wider communications bandwidths that will be needed to support multimedia applications. Ironically, users may not have to pay more as fierce competition in these industries forces prices down.

We need programming languages that make creating multimedia applications easy. Most programming languages do not have built-in multimedia capabilities. But Java, through the packages of classes that are an integral part of the Java programming world, provides extensive multimedia facilities that will enable you to start developing powerful multimedia applications immediately.

In this chapter we present a series of "live-code" examples that cover many of the interesting multimedia features you will need to build useful applications. We will cover the basics of manipulating images, creating smooth animations, playing sounds, playing videos, creating image maps that can sense when the cursor is over them even without a mouse click and customizing applets via parameters supplied from the HTML file that invokes an applet. The chapter exercises suggest challenging and interesting projects and even mention some "million-dollar" ideas that may help you make your fortune! When we were creating these exercises, the ideas just kept flowing. Multimedia will surely leverage creativity in ways that we have not experienced with "conventional" computer capabilities.

30.2 Loading, Displaying and Scaling Images

Java's multimedia capabilities include graphics, images, animations, sounds and video. We begin our multimedia discussion with images.

The applet of Fig. 30.1 demonstrates loading an *Image* (package java.awt) and loading an *ImageIcon* (package javax.swing). The applet displays the Image in its original size and scaled to twice its original width and twice its original height using two versions of Graphics method *drawImage*. The applet also draws the ImageIcon using its method *paintIcon*. Class ImageIcon is particularly useful because it can be used to easily load an image into any applet or application.

```
1   // Fig. 30.1: LoadImageAndScale.java
2   // Load an image and display it in its original size
3   // and scale it to twice its original width and height.
4   // Load and display the same image as an ImageIcon.
5   import java.applet.Applet;
6   import java.awt.*;
7   import javax.swing.*;
8
9   public class LoadImageAndScale extends JApplet {
10      private Image logo1;
11      private ImageIcon logo2;
12
13      // load the image when the applet is loaded
14      public void init()
15      {
16          logo1 = getImage( getDocumentBase(), "logo.gif" );
17          logo2 = new ImageIcon( "logo.gif" );
18      } // end method init
19
20      // display the image
21      public void paint( Graphics g )
22      {
```

Fig. 30.1   Loading and displaying an image in an applet. (Part 1 of 2.)

```
23          // draw the original image
24          g.drawImage( logo1, 0, 0, this );
25
26          // draw the image scaled to fit the width of the applet
27          // and the height of the applet minus 120 pixels
28          g.drawImage( logo1, 0, 120,
29                      getWidth(), getHeight() - 120, this );
30
31          // draw the icon using its paintIcon method
32          logo2.paintIcon( this, g, 180, 0 );
33       } // end method pain
34    } // end class LoadImageAndSacle
```

Fig. 30.1   Loading and displaying an image in an applet. (Part 2 of 2.)

Lines 10 and 11 declare an `Image` reference and an `ImageIcon` reference, respectively. Class `Image` is an `abstract` class; therefore, you cannot create an object of class `Image` directly. Rather, you must request that an `Image` be loaded and returned to you. Class `Applet` (the superclass of `JApplet`) provides a method that does just that. Line 16 in the applet's `init` method,

```
logo1 = getImage( getDocumentBase(), "logo.gif" );
```

uses `Applet` method *getImage* to load an `Image` into the applet. This version of `getImage` takes two arguments—a location where the image is stored and the file name of the image. In the first argument, `Applet` method `getDocumentBase` is used to determine the location of the image on the Internet (or on your computer if that is where the applet came from). We assume that the image to be loaded is stored in the same directory as the HTML file that invoked the applet. Method `getDocumentBase` returns the location of the HTML file on the Internet as an object of class *URL* (package `java.net`). A URL stores a *Uniform (or Universal) Resource Locator*—a standard format for an address of a piece of information on the Internet. The second argument specifies an image file name. Java currently supports two image formats—*Graphics Interchange Format (GIF)* and *Joint Photographic Experts Group (JPEG)*. File names for each of these types end with `.gif` or `.jpg` (or `.jpeg`) respectively.

Portability Tip 30.1

Class Image *is an* abstract *class, so* Image *objects cannot be created directly. To achieve platform independence, the Java implementation on each platform provides its own subclass of* Image *to store image information.*

When method `getImage` is invoked, it launches a separate thread of execution in which the image is loaded (or downloaded from the Internet). This enables the program to continue execution while the image is being loaded. [*Note:* If the requested file is not available, method `getImage` does not indicate an error.]

Class `ImageIcon` is not an `abstract` class; therefore, you can create an `ImageIcon` object. Line 17 in the applet's `init` method,

```
logo2 = new ImageIcon( "logo.gif" );
```

creates an `ImageIcon` object that loads the same `logo.gif` image. Class `ImageIcon` provides several constructors that allow an `ImageIcon` object to be initialized with an image from the local computer or with an image stored on a Web server on the Internet.

The applet's `paint` method displays the images. Line 24

```
g.drawImage( logo1, 0, 0, this );
```

uses `Graphics` method `drawImage` which receives four arguments (there are actually six overloaded versions of this method). The first argument is a reference to the `Image` object in which the image is stored (`logo1`). The second and third arguments are the *x*- and *y*-coordinates where the image should be displayed on the applet (the coordinates indicate the upper-left corner of the image). The last argument is a reference to an *ImageObserver* object. Normally, the `ImageObserver` is the object on which the image is displayed—we used `this` to indicate the applet. An `ImageObserver` can be any object that implements the `ImageObserver` interface. Interface `ImageObserver` is implemented by class `Component` (one of class `Applet`'s indirect superclasses). Therefore, all `Component`s can be `ImageObserver`s. This argument is important when displaying large images that require a long time to download from the Internet. It is possible that a program will display the image before it is completely downloaded. The `ImageObserver` is automatically notified to update the image that was displayed as the remainder of the image is loaded. When you run this applet, watch carefully as pieces of the image are displayed while the image loads. [*Note:* On faster computers, you may not notice this effect.]

Lines 28 and 29

```
g.drawImage( logo1, 0, 120,
             getWidth(), getHeight() - 120, this );
```

use another version of `Graphics` method `drawImage` to output a *scaled* version of the image. The fourth and fifth arguments specify the *width* and *height* of the image for display purposes. The image is automatically scaled to fit the specified width and height. The fourth argument indicates that the width of the scaled image should be the width of the applet and the fifth argument indicates that the height should be 120 pixels less than the height of the applet. The width and height of the applet are determined with methods `getWidth` and `getHeight` (inherited from class `Component`).

Line 33

```
logo2.paintIcon( this, g, 180, 0 );
```

uses `ImageIcon` method *paintIcon* to display the image. The method requires four arguments—a reference to the `Component` on which the image will be displayed, a reference to the `Graphics` object that will be used to render the image, the *x*-coordinate of the upper-left corner of the image and the *y*-coordinate of the upper-left corner of the image.

If you compare the two ways in which we loaded and displayed images in this example, you can see that using `ImageIcon` is simpler. You can create objects of class `ImageIcon` directly and there is no need to use an `ImageObserver` reference when displaying the image. For this reason, we use class `ImageIcon` for the remainder of the chapter. [*Note:* Class `ImageIcon`'s `paintIcon` method does not allow scaling of an image. However, the class provides method `getImage`, which returns an `Image` reference that can be used with `Graphics` method `drawImage` to display a scaled image.]

30.3 Loading and Playing Audio Clips

Java programs can manipulate and play *audio clips*. It is easy for users to capture their own audio clips and there are a variety of clips available in software products and over the Internet. Your system needs to be equipped with audio hardware (speakers and a sound board) to be able to play the audio clips.

Java provides two mechanisms for playing sounds in an applet—the `Applet`'s *play* method and the *play* method from the *AudioClip interface*. If you would like to play a sound once in a program, the `Applet` method `play` will load the sound and play it for you once; the sound is marked for garbage collection when it is done playing. The `Applet` method `play` method has two forms:

```
public void play( URL location, String soundFileName );
public void play( URL soundURL );
```

The first version loads the audio clip stored in file `soundFileName` from `location` and plays the sound. The first argument is normally a call to the applet's `getDocumentBase` or *getCodeBase method*. Method `getDocumentBase` indicates the location of the HTML file that loaded the applet. Method `getCodeBase` indicates where the `.class` file for the applet is located. The second version of method `play` takes a URL that contains the location and the file name of the audio clip. The statement

```
play( getDocumentBase(), "hi.au" );
```

loads the audio clip in file `hi.au` and plays it once.

The *sound engine* that plays the audio clips supports several audio file formats including *Sun Audio file format (.au extension), Windows Wave file format (.wav extension), Macintosh AIFF file format (.aif or .aiff extension)* and *Musical Instrument Digital Interface (MIDI) file format (.mid or .rmi extensions)*.

Figure 30.2 shows loading and playing an *AudioClip* (package `java.applet`). This technique is more flexible than `Applet` method `play`. It allows the audio to be stored in the program so the audio can be reused throughout the program's execution. `Applet` method *getAudioClip* has two forms that take the same arguments as the `play` method described above. Method `getAudioClip` returns a reference to an `AudioClip`. Once an `AudioClip` is loaded, three methods can be invoked for the object—*play*, *loop* and *stop*. Method `play` plays the audio once. Method `loop` continuously loops the audio clip in the background. Method `stop` terminates an audio clip that is currently playing. In the program, each of these methods is associated with a button on the applet.

```java
1   // Fig. 30.2: LoadAudioAndPlay.java
2   // Load an audio clip and play it.
3   import java.applet.*;
4   import java.awt.*;
5   import java.awt.event.*;
6   import javax.swing.*;
7
8   public class LoadAudioAndPlay extends JApplet {
9      private AudioClip sound1, sound2, currentSound;
10     private JButton playSound, loopSound, stopSound;
11     private JComboBox chooseSound;
12
13     // load the image when the applet begins executing
14     public void init()
15     {
16        Container c = getContentPane();
17        c.setLayout( new FlowLayout() );
18
19        String choices[] = { "Welcome", "Hi" };
20        chooseSound = new JComboBox( choices );
21        chooseSound.addItemListener(
22           new ItemListener() {
23              public void itemStateChanged( ItemEvent e )
24              {
25                 currentSound.stop();
26
27                 currentSound =
28                    chooseSound.getSelectedIndex() == 0 ?
29                       sound1 : sound2;
30              } // end method itemStateChanged
31           } // end anonymous inner class
32        ); // end addItemListener
33        c.add( chooseSound );
34
35        ButtonHandler handler = new ButtonHandler();
36        playSound = new JButton( "Play" );
37        playSound.addActionListener( handler );
38        c.add( playSound );
39        loopSound = new JButton( "Loop" );
40        loopSound.addActionListener( handler );
41        c.add( loopSound );
42        stopSound = new JButton( "Stop" );
43        stopSound.addActionListener( handler );
```

Fig. 30.2 Loading and playing an `AudioClip`. (Part 1 of 2.)

```
44          c.add( stopSound );
45
46          sound1 = getAudioClip(
47                  getDocumentBase(), "welcome.wav" );
48          sound2 = getAudioClip(
49                  getDocumentBase(), "hi.au" );
50          currentSound = sound1;
51      } // end method init
52
53      // stop the sound when the user switches Web pages
54      // (i.e., be polite to the user)
55      public void stop()
56      {
57          currentSound.stop();
58      } // end method stop
59
60      private class ButtonHandler implements ActionListener {
61          public void actionPerformed( ActionEvent e )
62          {
63              if ( e.getSource() == playSound )
64                  currentSound.play();
65              else if ( e.getSource() == loopSound )
66                  currentSound.loop();
67              else if ( e.getSource() == stopSound )
68                  currentSound.stop();
69          } // end method actionPerformed
70      } // end inner class ButtonHandler
71  } // end class LoadAudioAndPlay
```

Fig. 30.2   Loading and playing an AudioClip. (Part 2 of 2.)

Lines 46 through 49 in the applet's init method

```
sound1 = getAudioClip(
        getDocumentBase(), "welcome.wav" );
sound2 = getAudioClip(
        getDocumentBase(), "hi.au" );
```

use getAudioClip to load two audio files—a Windows Wave file (welcome.wav) and a Sun Audio file (hi.au). The user can select which audio clip to play from JComboBox chooseSound. Notice that the applet's stop method is overridden in line 55. When the user switches Web pages, the applet's stop method is called. This version of stop ensures that a playing audio clip is stopped. Otherwise the audio clip will continue to play in the background. This is not really a problem, but can be annoying to the user if the audio clip is looping. The stop method is provided here to be polite to the user.

Good Programming Practice 30.1

When playing audio clips in an applet or application, provide a mechanism for the user to disable the audio.

30.4 Animating a Series of Images

The next example demonstrates animating a series of images that are stored in an array. The application uses the same techniques to load and display `ImageIcon`s as shown in Fig. 30.1. In previous editions of this text, we used a series of animation examples to demonstrate various techniques for smoothing an animation. One of the key techniques involved a concept called *graphics double buffering*. However, because of new features of Swing GUI components that already implement the smoothing techniques, we can simply concentrate on the animation concept.

The animation presented in Fig. 30.3 is designed as a subclass of `JPanel` (called `LogoAnimator`) so it can be attached to an application window or possibly to a `JApplet`. Class `LogoAnimator` also defines a `main` method (defined in line 71 to execute the animation as an application. Method `main` defines an instance of class `JFrame` and attaches a `LogoAnimator` object to the `JFrame` to display the animation.

```
1    // Fig. 30.3: LogoAnimator.java
2    // Animation a series of images
3    import java.awt.*;
4    import java.awt.event.*;
5    import javax.swing.*;
6
7    public class LogoAnimator extends JPanel
8                            implements ActionListener {
9       protected ImageIcon images[];
10      protected int totalImages = 30,
11                    currentImage = 0,
12                    animationDelay = 50; // 50 millisecond delay
13      protected Timer animationTimer;
14
15      public LogoAnimator()
16      {
17         setSize( getPreferredSize() );
18
19         images = new ImageIcon[ totalImages ];
20
21         for ( int i = 0; i < images.length; ++i )
22            images[ i ] =
23               new ImageIcon( "images/deitel" + i + ".gif" );
24
25         startAnimation();
26      } // end LogoAnimator constructor
27
28      public void paintComponent( Graphics g )
29      {
30         super.paintComponent( g );
31
```

Fig. 30.3 Animating a series of images. (Part 1 of 3.)

```
32            if ( images[ currentImage ].getImageLoadStatus() ==
33                 MediaTracker.COMPLETE ) {
34               images[ currentImage ].paintIcon( this, g, 0, 0 );
35               currentImage = ( currentImage + 1 ) % totalImages;
36            }
37         } // end method paintComponent
38
39         public void actionPerformed( ActionEvent e )
40         {
41            repaint();
42         } // end method actionPerformed
43
44         public void startAnimation()
45         {
46            if ( animationTimer == null ) {
47               currentImage = 0;
48               animationTimer = new Timer( animationDelay, this );
49               animationTimer.start();
50            }
51            else  // continue from last image displayed
52               if ( ! animationTimer.isRunning() )
53                  animationTimer.restart();
54         } // end method startAnimation
55
56         public void stopAnimation()
57         {
58            animationTimer.stop();
59         } // end method stopAnimation
60
61         public Dimension getMinimumSize()
62         {
63            return getPreferredSize();
64         } // end method getMinimumSize
65
66         public Dimension getPreferredSize()
67         {
68            return new Dimension( 160, 80 );
69         } // end method getPreferredSize
70
71         public static void main( String args[] )
72         {
73            LogoAnimator anim = new LogoAnimator();
74
75            JFrame app = new JFrame( "Animator test" );
76            app.getContentPane().add( anim, BorderLayout.CENTER );
77
78            app.addWindowListener(
79               new WindowAdapter() {
80                  public void windowClosing( WindowEvent e )
81                  {
82                     System.exit( 0 );
83                  } // end method windowClosing
84               } // end anonymous inner class
```

Fig. 30.3   Animating a series of images. (Part 2 of 3.)

```
85              ); // end addWindowListener
86
87              // The constants 10 and 30 are used below to size the
88              // window 10 pixels wider than the animation and
89              // 30 pixels taller than the animation.
90              app.setSize( anim.getPreferredSize().width + 10,
91                           anim.getPreferredSize().height + 30 );
92              app.show();
93          } // end main
94      } // end class LogoAnimator
```

Fig. 30.3   Animating a series of images. (Part 3 of 3.)

Class `LogoAnimator` loads an array of `ImageIcons` in its constructor. As each `ImageIcon` object is instantiated in the `for` structure in line 21, the `ImageIcon` constructor loads one image for the animation (there are 30 total images) with the statement

```
images[ i ] =
    new ImageIcon( "images/deitel" + i + ".gif" );
```

The argument uses string concatenation to assemble the file name from the pieces `"images/deitel"`, `i` and `".gif"`. Each of the images in the animation is in one of the files "deitel0.gif" through "deitel29.gif." The value of the control variable in the `for` structure is used to select one of the 30 images.

Performance Tip 30.1

It is more efficient to load the frames of the animation as one image than to load each image separately (a painting program can be used to combine the frames of the animation into one image). If the images are being loaded from the World Wide Web, every image loaded requires a separate connection to the site where the images are stored.

Performance Tip 30.2

Loading all the frames of an animation as one large image may force your program to wait to begin displaying the animation.

After loading the images, the constructor calls `startAnimation` (defined in line 44) to begin the animation. The animation is driven by an instance of class *Timer* (package `javax.swing`). An object of class `Timer` generates `ActionEvents` at a fixed interval in milliseconds (normally specified as an argument to the `Timer`'s constructor) and notifies all its registered `ActionListeners` that the event occurred. Lines 46 through 50

```
if ( animationTimer == null ) {
    currentImage = 0;
    animationTimer = new Timer( animationDelay, this );
    animationTimer.start();
}
```

determine if the `Timer` reference `animationTimer` is `null`. If so, `currentImage` is set to 0 to indicate that the animation should begin with the image in the first element of array `images`. Line 48 assigns a new `Timer` object to `animationTimer`. The `Timer` constructor receives two arguments—the delay in milliseconds (`animationDelay` is 50 in this example) and the `ActionListener` that will respond to the `Timer`'s `ActionEvents` (`this` `LogoAnimator` implements `ActionListener` in line 8). Line 49 starts the `Timer` object. Once started, `animationTimer` will generate an `ActionEvent` every 50 milliseconds in this example. Lines 51 through 53

```
else  // continue from last image displayed
    if ( ! animationTimer.isRunning() )
        animationTimer.restart();
```

are for programs that may stop the animation and restart it. For example, to make an animation "browser friendly" in an applet, the animation should be stopped when the user switches Web pages. If the user returns to the Web page with the animation, method `startAnimation` can be called to restart the animation. The `if` condition in line 52 uses `Timer` method `isRunning` to determine if the `Timer` is currently running (i.e., generating events). If it is not running, line 53 calls `Timer` method `restart` to indicate that the `Timer` should start generating events again.

In response to every `Timer` event in this example, method `actionPerformed` (line 39) calls method `repaint`. This schedules a call to the `LogoAnimator`'s `update` method (inherited from class `JPanel`), which, in turn, results in a call to the `LogoAnimator`'s `paintComponent` method (line 28). Remember that any subclass of `JComponent` that performs drawing should do so in its `paintComponent` method. As mentioned in Chapter 29, the first statement in any `paintComponent` method should be a call to the superclass's `paintComponent` method to ensure that Swing components are displayed correctly. The `if` condition in lines 32 and 33

```
if ( images[ currentImage ].getImageLoadStatus() ==
    MediaTracker.COMPLETE ) {
```

uses `ImageIcon` method *getImageLoadStatus* to determine if the image to display is completely loaded into memory. Only complete images should be displayed to make the animation as smooth as possible. When the image is fully loaded, the method returns *MediaTracker.COMPLETE*. An object of class *MediaTracker* (package `java.awt`) is used by class `ImageIcon` to track the loading of an image.

When loading images into a program, the images can be registered with an object of class `MediaTracker` to enable the program to determine when an image is loaded completely. Class `MediaTracker` also provides the ability to wait for an image or several images to load before allowing a program to continue and to determine if an error occurred while loading an image. We do not need to create a `MediaTracker` directly in this example, because class `ImageIcon` does this for us. However, when using class `Image` (as shown in Fig. 30.1), you may want to create your own `MediaTracker`.

Performance Tip 30.3

Some people who are experienced with MediaTracker objects have reported that they can have a detrimental effect on performance. Keep this in mind as an area to scrutinize if you need to tune your multimedia applications.

Performance Tip 30.4

Using MediaTracker method waitForAll to wait for all registered images to completely load may result in a long delay after the program begins execution until the images are actually displayed. The more images and the larger the images, the more time the user will have to wait. Use MediaTracker method waitForAll only to wait for small numbers of images to load completely.

If the image is fully loaded, lines 34 and 35,

```
images[ currentImage ].paintIcon( this, g, 0, 0 );
currentImage = ( currentImage + 1 ) % totalImages;
```

paint the `ImageIcon` at element `currentImage` in the array and prepare for the next image to be displayed by incrementing `currentImage` by 1. Notice the modulus calculation to ensure that the value of `currentImage` is set to 0 when it is incremented past 29 (the last element subscript in the array).

Method `stopAnimation` (line 56), stops the animation with line 58,

```
animationTimer.stop();
```

which uses `Timer` method *stop* to indicate that the `Timer` should stop generating events. This, in turn, prevents `actionPerformed` from calling `repaint` to initiate the painting of the next image in the array.

Software Engineering Observation 30.1

When creating an animation for use in an applet, provide a mechanism for disabling the animation when the user browses a new Web page separate from the page on which the animation applet resides.

Methods `getMinimumSize` (line 61) and `getPreferredSize` (line 66) are overridden to help a layout manager determine the appropriate size of a `LogoAnimator` in a layout. In this example, the images are 160 pixels wide and 80 pixels high, so method `getPreferredSize` returns a `Dimension` object containing 160 and 80. Method `getMinimumSize` simply calls `getPreferredSize` (a common programming practice). Notice in `main` (line 71) that the size of the application window is set (lines 90 and 91) to the preferred width of the animation plus 10 pixels and the preferred height of the animation plus 30 pixels. This is because a window's width and height specify the outer bounds of the window, not the window's *client area* (the area in which GUI components can be attached).

In this example, we were able to take advantage of several features that help produce a smooth animation and controllable animation—`ImageIcon` objects loaded the images, an object of a subclass of `JPanel` displayed the images and a `Timer` object controlled the animation.

30.5 Animation Issues

When you execute the application in Fig. 30.3, you may notice that the images take time to load. If an animation is not designed correctly, this often results in partial images being displayed. You may be able to see that each image displays in pieces. This is often the result of the image format that is used. For example, GIF images can be stored in *interlaced* and *non-interlaced* formats. The format indicates the order in which the pixels of the image are stored. The pixels of a non-interlaced image are stored in the same order that the pixels appear on the screen. As a non-interlaced image is displayed, it appears in chunks from top to bottom as the pixel information is read. The pixels of an interlaced image are stored in rows of pixels, but the rows are out of order. For example, the rows of pixels in the image may be stored in the order 1, 5, 9, 13, ..., followed by 2, 6, 10, 14, ..., and so on. When the image is displayed, it appears to fade in as the first batch of rows presents a rough outline of the picture and the subsequent batches of rows refine the displayed image until the entire image is complete. To help prevent partial images from appearing in previous versions of Java, we tracked the loading of images using a `MediaTracker` object. Only fully loaded images are displayed to produce the smoothest animation. Every image to track must be registered with the `MediaTracker`. This is now performed by class `ImageIcon`'s constructor.

Software Engineering Observation 30.2

Class `ImageIcon` *uses a* `MediaTracker` *object to determine the status of the image it is loading.*

Good Programming Practice 30.2

In an applet, always display something while images load. The longer users must wait to see information appear on the screen, the more likely they will leave the Web page before the information appears.

Another common problem with animations is that the animation *flickers* as each image is displayed. This is due to the `update` method being called in response to each `repaint`. In AWT GUI components, when `update` clears the background of the GUI component, it does so by drawing a filled rectangle the size of the component in the current background color. This would cover the image that was just displayed. Thus, the animation would draw an image, sleep for a fraction of a second, clear the background (causing a flicker) and draw the next image. In subclasses of Swing's `JPanel` (or any other Swing component), method `update` is overridden to prevent clearing of the background if the component is transparent (the background will be cleared if the component is opaque). This helps eliminate flicker.

Look-and-Feel Observation 30.1

Swing components override method `update` *to prevent clearing of the background (for transparent components) in response to* `repaint` *messages.*

If you want to develop multimedia-based applications, your users will want smooth sound and animations. Choppy presentations are unacceptable. This often happens when you write applications that draw directly to the screen. One other technique used to produce smooth animation (and other graphics) is *graphics double buffering.* While the program renders one image on the screen, it can build the next image in an *off-screen buffer.* Then, when it is time for that next image to be displayed, it can be placed on the screen smoothly. Of course, there is a *space/time trade-off.* The extra memory required can be substantial, but the improved display performance may be well worth it.

Graphics double buffering is also useful in programs that need to use drawing capabilities in methods other than `paint` or `paintComponent` (where we have done all our drawing to this point). The off-screen buffer can be passed between methods or even between objects of different classes to allow other methods or objects to draw on the off-screen buffer. The results of the drawing can then be displayed at a later time.

Performance Tip 30.5

Double buffering can reduce or eliminate flicker in an animation, but it can visibly slow the speed at which the animation runs.

When all the pixels of an image do not display at once, an animation has more flicker. When an image is drawn using graphics double buffering, by the time the image is displayed, it will have already been drawn off the screen and the partial images that the user normally would see are hidden from the user. All the pixels will be displayed for the user in one "blast" so the flicker is substantially reduced or eliminated.

The basic concept of a graphics double buffer is as follows: create a blank `Image`, draw on the blank `Image` (using methods of the `Graphics` class) and display the image. The `Image` stores the pixels that will be copied to the screen. The `Graphics` reference is used to draw the pixels. Every image has an associated graphics context—i.e., an object of class `Graphics` that enables drawing to be performed. The `Image` and `Graphics` references used for graphics double buffering are often referred to as the *off-screen image* and the *off-screen graphics context* because they are not actually manipulating screen pixels.

Swing GUI components are displayed using Java's drawing capabilities. Therefore, Swing GUI components are subject to many of the same drawing problems encountered with a typical animation. By default, Swing uses graphics double buffering to render all Swing GUI components. By designing our `LogoAnimator` as a subclass of `JPanel`, we are able to take advantage of Swing's built-in graphics double-buffering to produce the smoothest possible animation.

Look-and-Feel Observation 30.2

Swing GUI components are rendered using graphics double buffering by default.

30.6 Customizing Applets via the HTML param Tag

When browsing the World Wide Web you will often come across applets that are in the public domain—you can use them free of charge on your own Web pages (normally in exchange for crediting the applet's creator). One common feature of such applets is the ability to customize the applet via parameters that are supplied from the HTML file that invokes the applet. For example, the following HTML from file `LogoApplet.html`

```html
<html>
<applet code="LogoApplet.class" width=400 height=400>
<param name="totalimages" value="30">
<param name="imagename" value="deitel">
<param name="animationdelay" value="200">
</applet>
</html>
```

invokes the applet `LogoApplet` (Fig. 30.4) and specifies three parameters. The *param tag* lines must appear between the starting and ending `applet` tags. These values can then be used to customize the applet. Any number of `param` tags can appear between the starting and ending `applet` tags. Each parameter has a *name* and a *value*. `Applet` method *getParameter* is used to get the `value` associated with a specific parameter and return the `value` as a `String`. The argument passed to `getParameter` is a `String` containing the name of the parameter in the `param` tag. For example, the statement

```
                 parameter = getParameter( "animationdelay" );
```

gets the value associated with the `animationdelay` parameter and assigns it to `String`
reference `parameter`. If there is no `param` tag containing the specified parameter, `get-`
`Parameter` returns `null`.

```
1    // Fig. 30.4: LogoAnimator.java
2    // Animating a series of images
3    import java.awt.*;
4    import java.awt.event.*;
5    import javax.swing.*;
6
7    public class LogoAnimator extends JPanel
8                             implements ActionListener {
9       protected ImageIcon images[];
10      protected int totalImages = 30,
11                    currentImage = 0,
12                    animationDelay = 50; // 50 millisecond delay
13      protected String imageName = "deitel";
14      protected Timer animationTimer;
15
16      public LogoAnimator()
17      {
18         initializeAnim();
19      } // end LogoAnimator constructor
20
21      // new constructor to support customization
22      public LogoAnimator( int num, int delay, String name )
23      {
24         totalImages = num;
25         animationDelay = delay;
26         imageName = name;
27
28         initializeAnim();
29      } // end LogoAnimator constructor
30
31      private void initializeAnim()
32      {
33         images = new ImageIcon[ totalImages ];
34
35         for ( int i = 0; i < images.length; ++i )
36            images[ i ] = new ImageIcon( "images/" +
37                              imageName + i + ".gif" );
38
39         // moved here so getPreferredSize can check the size of
40         // the first loaded image.
41         setSize( getPreferredSize() );
42
43         startAnimation();
44      } // end method initializeAnim
45
46      public void paintComponent( Graphics g )
47      {
```

Fig. 30.4   Customizing an applet via the `param` HTML tag. (Part 1 of 3.)

```
48          super.paintComponent( g );
49
50          if ( images[ currentImage ].getImageLoadStatus() ==
51             MediaTracker.COMPLETE ) {
52            images[ currentImage ].paintIcon( this, g, 0, 0 );
53            currentImage = ( currentImage + 1 ) % totalImages;
54          } // end if
55       } // end method paintComponent
56
57       public void actionPerformed( ActionEvent e )
58       {
59          repaint();
60       } // end method actionPerformed
61
62       public void startAnimation()
63       {
64          if ( animationTimer == null ) {
65             currentImage = 0;
66             animationTimer = new Timer( animationDelay, this );
67             animationTimer.start();
68          }
69          else  // continue from last image displayed
70             if ( ! animationTimer.isRunning() )
71                animationTimer.restart();
72       } // end method startAnimation
73
74       public void stopAnimation()
75       {
76          animationTimer.stop();
77       } // end method stopAnimation
78
79       public Dimension getMinimumSize()
80       {
81          return getPreferredSize();
82       } // end method getMinimumSize
83
84       public Dimension getPreferredSize()
85       {
86          return new Dimension( images[ 0 ].getIconWidth(),
87                                images[ 0 ].getIconHeight() );
88       } // end method getPreferredSize
89
90       public static void main( String args[] )
91       {
92          LogoAnimator anim = new LogoAnimator();
93
94          JFrame app = new JFrame( "Animator test" );
95          app.getContentPane().add( anim, BorderLayout.CENTER );
96
97          app.addWindowListener(
98             new WindowAdapter() {
99                public void windowClosing( WindowEvent e )
100               {
```

Fig. 30.4   Customizing an applet via the param HTML tag. (Part 2 of 3.)

```
101                    System.exit( 0 );
102                 } // end method windowClosing
103              } // end anonymous inner class
104           ); // end addWindowListener
105
106           app.setSize( anim.getPreferredSize().width + 10,
107                        anim.getPreferredSize().height + 30 );
108           app.show();
109        } // end main
110     } // end class LogoAnimator
```

Fig. 30.4   Customizing an applet via the `param` HTML tag. (Part 3 of 3.)

```
111    // Fig. 30.4: LogoApplet.java
112    // Customizing an applet via HTML parameters
113    //
114    // HTML parameter "animationdelay" is an int indicating
115    // milliseconds to sleep between images (default 50).
116    //
117    // HTML parameter "imagename" is the base name of the images
118    // that will be displayed (i.e., "deitel" is the base name
119    // for images "deitel0.gif," "deitel1.gif," etc.). The applet
120    // assumes that images are in an "images" subdirectory of
121    // the directory in which the applet resides.
122    //
123    // HTML parameter "totalimages" is an integer representing the
124    // total number of images in the animation. The applet assumes
125    // images are numbered from 0 to totalimages - 1 (default 30).
126
127    import java.awt.*;
128    import javax.swing.*;
129
130    public class LogoApplet extends JApplet{
131       public void init()
132       {
133          String parameter;
134
135          parameter = getParameter( "animationdelay" );
136          int animationDelay = ( parameter == null ? 50 :
137                            Integer.parseInt( parameter ) );
138
139          String imageName = getParameter( "imagename" );
140
141          parameter = getParameter( "totalimages" );
142          int totalImages = ( parameter == null ? 0 :
143                            Integer.parseInt( parameter ) );
144
145          // Create an instance of LogoAnimator
146          LogoAnimator animator;
147
```

Fig. 30.4   Customizing an applet via the `param` HTML tag—`LogoApplet.java`. (Part 1 of 2.)

```
148          if ( imageName == null || totalImages == 0 )
149             animator = new LogoAnimator();
150          else
151             animator = new LogoAnimator( totalImages,
152                               animationDelay, imageName );
153
154          setSize( animator.getPreferredSize().width,
155                   animator.getPreferredSize().height );
156          getContentPane().add( animator, BorderLayout.CENTER );
157
158          animator.startAnimation();
159       } // end method init
160    } // end class LogoApplet
```

Fig. 30.4 Customizing an applet via the `param` HTML tag—`LogoApplet.java`. (Part 2 of 2.)

In Fig. 30.4 we modified class `LogoAnimator` so it can be used from an applet and customized via parameters in the applet's HTML file. Class `LogoApplet` allows Web page designers to customize the animation to use their own images. Three parameters are provided. Parameter `animationdelay` is the number of milliseconds to sleep between images being displayed. This value will be converted to an integer and used as the value for instance variable `sleepTime`. Parameter `imagename` is the base name of the images to be loaded. This `String` will be assigned to instance variable `imageName`. The applet assumes that the images are in a subdirectory named `images` that can be found in the same directory as the applet. The applet also assumes that the image file names are numbered from 0. Parameter `totalimages` represents the total number of images in the animation. Its value will be converted to an integer and assigned to instance variable `totalImages`.

Class `LogoAnimator` has several new features to enable it to be used in and customized by the `LogoApplet`. In line 13, instance variable `imageName` is defined. This will store either the default base name `"deitel"` that is part of every file name, or it will store the customized name passed to the applet from the HTML document.

There are now two constructors—a default constructor (line 16) and a constructor that takes arguments to customize the animation (line 22). Both constructors call our new utility method `initializeAnim` (line 31) to load the images and start the animation. The statements in `initializeAnim` were originally in the default constructor. The `setSize` method call in line 41 (which used to precede the loading of the images) was moved to line 41 so the `LogoAnimator` can be resized based on the width and height of the first image in the animation. To accommodate resizing based on the first image, method `getPreferredSize` (line 84) now returns a `Dimension` object containing the width and height of the first image in the animation.

Class `LogoApplet` (line 130) defines an `init` method in which the three HTML parameters are read with `Applet` method `getParameter` (lines 135, 139 and 141). After the parameters are read and the two integer parameters are converted to `int` values, the `if`/`else` structure in lines 148 through 152 creates a `LogoAnimator`. If the `imageName` is `null` or `totalImages` is 0, the default `LogoAnimator` constructor is called and the default animation will be used. Otherwise, the `totalImages`, `animationDelay` and `imageName` are passed to the three-argument `LogoAnimator` constructor, and the constructor uses those arguments to customize the animation.

30.7 Image Maps

A common technique for creating interesting Web pages is the use of *image maps*. An image map is an image that has *hot areas* that the user can click to accomplish a task such as loading a different Web page into a browser. When the user positions the mouse pointer over a hot area, normally a descriptive message is displayed in the status area of the browser. This technique can be used to implement a *bubble help* system. When the user positions the mouse pointer over a particular element on the screen, a system with bubble help usually displays a message in a small window that appears over the screen element. In Java, the message can be displayed in the status bar.

Figure 30.5 loads an image containing several icons from the *Java Multimedia Cyber Classroom*—the interactive-CD, multimedia version of this text. These icons may look familiar; they are designed to mimic the icons used in this book. The program allows the user to position the mouse pointer over an icon and display a descriptive message for the icon. Event handler `mouseMoved` (line 24) takes the *x*-coordinate of the mouse and passes it to method `translateLocation` (line 42). The *x*-coordinate is tested to determine the icon over which the mouse was positioned when the `mouseMoved` method was called. Method `translateLocation` then returns a message indicating what the icon represents. This message is displayed in the `appletviewer`'s (or browser's) status bar.

```
1   // Fig. 30.5: ImageMap.java
2   // Demonstrating an image map.
3   import java.awt.*;
4   import java.awt.event.*;
5   import javax.swing.*;
6
7   public class ImageMap extends JApplet {
8      private ImageIcon mapImage;
9      private int width, height;
10
11     public void init()
12     {
13        addMouseListener(
14           new MouseAdapter() {
15              public void mouseExited( MouseEvent e )
16              {
17                 showStatus( "Pointer outside applet" );
18              } // end method mouseExited
19           } // end anonymous inner class
```

Fig. 30.5   Demonstrating an image map. (Part 1 of 3.)

```
20          ); // end addMouseListener
21
22          addMouseMotionListener(
23             new MouseMotionAdapter() {
24                public void mouseMoved( MouseEvent e )
25                {
26                   showStatus( translateLocation( e.getX() ) );
27                } // end method mouseMoved
28             } // end anonymous inner class
29          ); // end addMouseMotionListener
30
31          mapImage = new ImageIcon( "icons2.gif" );
32          width = mapImage.getIconWidth();
33          height = mapImage.getIconHeight();
34          setSize( width, height );
35       } // end method init
36
37       public void paint( Graphics g )
38       {
39          mapImage.paintIcon( this, g, 0, 0 );
40       } // end method paint
41
42       public String translateLocation( int x )
43       {
44          // determine width of each icon (there are 6)
45          int iconWidth = width / 6;
46
47          if ( x >= 0 && x <= iconWidth )
48             return "Common Programming Error";
49          else if ( x > iconWidth && x <= iconWidth * 2 )
50             return "Good Programming Practice";
51          else if ( x > iconWidth * 2 && x <= iconWidth * 3 )
52             return "Performance Tip";
53          else if ( x > iconWidth * 3 && x <= iconWidth * 4 )
54             return "Portability Tip";
55          else if ( x > iconWidth * 4 && x <= iconWidth * 5 )
56             return "Software Engineering Observation";
57          else if ( x > iconWidth * 5 && x <= iconWidth * 6 )
58             return "Testing and Debugging Tip";
59
60          return "";
61       } // end method translateLocation
62    } // end class ImageMap
```

Fig. 30.5   Demonstrating an image map. (Part 2 of 3.)

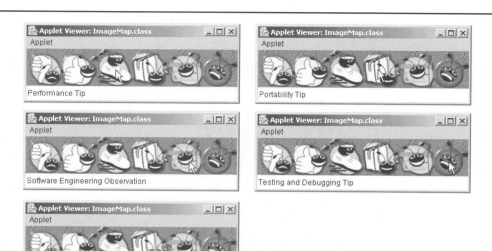

Fig. 30.5 Demonstrating an image map. (Part 3 of 3.)

Clicking in this applet will not cause any action. If we were to add networking capabilities, we could modify this applet to enable each icon to be associated with a different URL.

30.8 Internet and World Wide Web Resources

This section presents several Internet and Web resources for multimedia related sites.

`http://www.nasa.gov/gallery/index.html`
The *NASA multimedia gallery* contains a wide variety of images, audio clips and video clips that you can download and use to test your Java multimedia programs.

`http://sunsite.sut.ac.jp/multimed/`
The *Sunsite Japan Multimedia Collection* also provides a wide variety of images, audio clips and video clips that you can download for educational purposes.

`http://www.anbg.gov.au/anbg/index.html`
The *Australian National Botanic Gardens* Web site provides links to sounds of many animals. Try the *Common Birds* link.

SUMMARY

- `Applet` method `getImage` loads an `Image`. One version of `getImage` takes two arguments—a location where the image is stored and the file name of the image.

- `Applet` method `getDocumentBase` returns the location of the applet's HTML file on the Internet as an object of class `URL` (package `java.net`).

- A URL stores a Uniform (or Universal) Resource Locator—a standard format for an address of a piece of information on the Internet.

- Java supports two image formats—Graphics Interchange Format (GIF) and Joint Photographic Experts Group (JPEG). File names for these types end with `.gif` or `.jpg` (or `.jpeg`), respectively.

- Class `ImageIcon` provides constructors that allow an `ImageIcon` object to be initialized with an image from the local computer or with an image stored on a Web server on the Internet.

- `Graphics` method `drawImage` receives four arguments—a reference to the `Image` object in which the image is stored, the *x*- and *y*-coordinates where the image should be displayed and a reference to an `ImageObserver` object.

- Another version of `Graphics` method `drawImage` outputs a *scaled* image. The fourth and fifth arguments specify the width and height of the image for display purposes.

- Interface `ImageObserver` is implemented by class `Component` (an indirect superclass of `Applet`). `ImageObserver`s are notified to update an image that was displayed as the remainder of the image is loaded.

- `ImageIcon` method `paintIcon` displays the `ImageIcon`'s image. The method requires four arguments—a reference to the `Component` on which the image will be displayed, a reference to the `Graphics` object used to render the image, the *x*-coordinate of the upper-left corner of the image and the *y*-coordinate of the upper-left corner of the image.

- Class `ImageIcon`'s `paintIcon` method does not allow scaling of an image. The class provides method `getImage` which returns an `Image` reference that can be used with `Graphics` method `drawImage` to display a scaled version of an image.

- `Applet` method `play` has two forms:

```
public void play( URL location, String soundFileName );
public void play( URL soundURL );
```

One version loads the audio clip stored in file `soundFileName` from `location` and plays the sound. The other takes a URL that contains the location and the file name of the audio clip.

- `Applet` method `getDocumentBase` indicates the location of the HTML file that loaded the applet. Method `getCodeBase` indicates where the `.class` file for an applet is located.

- The sound engine that plays audio clips supports several audio file formats including Sun Audio file format (`.au` extension), Windows Wave file format (`.wav` extension), Macintosh AIFF file format (`.aif` or `.aiff` extension) and Musical Instrument Digital Interface (MIDI) file format (`.mid` or `.rmi` extensions).

- `Applet` method `getAudioClip` has two forms that take the same arguments as the `play` method. Method `getAudioClip` returns a reference to an `AudioClip`. `AudioClip`s have three methods—`play`, `loop` and `stop`. Method `play` plays the audio once. Method `loop` continuously loops the audio clip. Method `stop` terminates an audio clip that is currently playing.

- `Timer` objects generate `ActionEvents` at fixed intervals in milliseconds and notify their registered `ActionListener`s that the events occurred. The `Timer` constructor receives two arguments—the delay in milliseconds and the `ActionListener`. `Timer` method `start` indicates that the `Timer` should start generating events. `Timer` method `stop` indicates that the `Timer` should stop generating events. `Timer` method `restart` indicates that the `Timer` should start generating events again.

- `ImageIcon` method `getImageLoadStatus` determines if an image is completely loaded into memory. The method returns `MediaTracker.COMPLETE` if the image is fully loaded.

- Images can be registered with an object of class `MediaTracker` to enable the program to determine when an image is loaded completely.

- GIF images can be stored in interlaced and non-interlaced formats. The format indicates the order in which the pixels of the image are stored. The pixels of a non-interlaced image are stored in the same order that the pixels appear on the screen. As a non-interlaced image is displayed, it appears in chunks from top to bottom as the pixel information is read. The pixels of an interlaced image are stored in rows of pixels, but the rows are out of order. When the image is displayed, it appears to fade in as the first batch of rows presents a rough outline of the picture and the subsequent batches of rows refine the displayed image until the entire image is complete.

- A common problem with animations is that the animation flickers as each image is displayed. This is normally due to the `update` method being called in response to each `repaint`. In subclasses of Swing's `JPanel` (or any other Swing component), method `update` is overridden to prevent clearing of the background.

- A technique used to produce smooth animation is graphics double buffering. While the program renders one image on the screen, it can build the next image in an off-screen buffer. Then, when it is time for that next image to be displayed, it can be placed on the screen smoothly.

- Swing GUI components are displayed using Java's drawing capabilities. Therefore, Swing GUI components are subject to many of the same drawing problems encountered with a typical animation. By default, Swing uses graphics double buffering to render all Swing GUI components.

- Applets can be customized via parameters (the `<param>` tag) that are supplied from the HTML file that invokes the applet. The `<param>` tag lines must appear between the starting `applet` tag and the ending `applet` tag. Each parameter has a `name` and a `value`.

- `Applet` method `getParameter` gets the `value` associated with a specific parameter and returns the `value` as a `String`. The argument passed to `getParameter` is a `String` containing the name of the parameter in the `param` tag. If there is no `param` tag containing the specified parameter, `getParameter` returns `null`.

- An image map is an image that has hot areas that the user can click to accomplish a task such as loading a different Web page into a browser.

TERMINOLOGY

`.aif` file name extension
`.aiff` file name extension
animating a series of images
animation
`.au` file name extension
audio clip
bubble help system
customize an applet
`drawImage` method of class `Graphics`
`getAudioClip` method of class `Applet`
`getCodeBase` method of class `Applet`
`getDocumentBase` method of class `Applet`
`getHeight` method of class `Component`
`getIconHeight` method of class `ImageIcon`
`getIconWidth` method of class `ImageIcon`
`getImage` method of class `Applet`
`getImage` method of class `ImageIcon`
`getImageLoadStatus` method
`getParameter` method of class `Applet`
`getWidth` method of class `Component`
`.gif` file name extension
graphics
graphics double buffering
Graphics Interchange Format (GIF)

height of an image
hot area of an image map
HTML file
`Image` class
image map
`ImageIcon` class
`ImageObserver` interface
images
interlaced GIF image
Java Runtime Environment (JRE)
Joint Photographic Experts Group (JPEG)
`.jpeg` file name extension
`.jpg` file name extension
`loop` method of interface `AudioClip`
Macintosh AIFF file (`.aif` or `.aiff`)
`MediaTracker` class
`MediaTracker.COMPLETE`
`.mid` file name extension
multimedia
name attribute of `param` tag
non-interlaced GIF image
off-screen buffer
off-screen graphics context
off-screen image

GOOD PROGRAMMING PRACTICES

30.1   When playing audio clips in an applet or application, provide a mechanism for the user to disable the audio.

30.2   In an applet, always display something while images load. The longer users must wait to see information appear on the screen, the more likely they will leave the Web page before the information appears.

LOOK-AND-FEEL OBSERVATIONS

30.1   Swing components override method update to prevent clearing of the background (for transparent components) in response to repaint messages.

30.2   Swing GUI components are rendered using graphics double buffering by default.

PERFORMANCE TIPS

30.1   It is more efficient to load the frames of the animation as one image than to load each image separately (a painting program can be used to combine the frames of the animation into one image). If the images are being loaded from the World Wide Web, every image loaded requires a separate connection to the site where the images are stored.

30.2   Loading all the frames of an animation as one large image may force your program to wait to begin displaying the animation.

30.3   Some people who are experienced with MediaTracker objects have reported that they can have a detrimental effect on performance. Keep this in mind as an area to scrutinize if you need to tune your multimedia applications.

30.4   Using MediaTracker method waitForAll to wait for all registered images to completely load may result in a long delay after the program begins execution until the images are actually displayed. The more images and the larger the images, the more time the user will have to wait. Use MediaTracker method waitForAll only to wait for small numbers of images to load completely.

30.5   Double buffering can reduce or eliminate flicker in an animation, but it can visibly slow the speed at which the animation runs.

PORTABILITY TIP

30.1   Class Image is an abstract class, so Image objects cannot be created directly. To achieve platform independence, the Java implementation on each platform provides its own subclass of Image to store image information.

SOFTWARE ENGINEERING OBSERVATIONS

30.1   When creating an animation for use in an applet, provide a mechanism for disabling the animation when the user browses a new Web page separate from the page on which the animation applet resides.

30.2   Class `ImageIcon` uses a `MediaTracker` object to determine the status of the image it is loading.

SELF-REVIEW EXERCISES

30.1   Fill in the blanks in each of the following:
a) `Applet` method _____ loads an image into an applet.
b) `Applet` method _____ returns as an object of class URL the location on the Internet of the HTML file that invoked the applet.
c) A(n) _____ is a standard format for an address of a piece of information on the Internet.
d) `Graphics` method _____ displays an image on an applet.
e) With the technique of _____, while the program renders one image on the screen, it can be building the next image in an off-screen buffer. Then, when it is time for that next image to be displayed, it can be placed on the screen smoothly.
f) As a(n) _____ image is displayed, it appears to fade in as the first batch of rows presents a rough outline of the picture and the subsequent batches of rows refine the displayed image until the entire image is complete.
g) There are two key pieces to implementing a graphics double buffer—a(n) _____ reference and a(n) _____ reference. The first is where the actual pixels to be displayed are stored; the second is used to draw the pixels.
h) Images can be registered with a(n) _____ object to enable the program to determine when an image is loaded completely.
i) Java provides two mechanisms for playing sounds in an applet—the `Applet`'s `play` method and the `play` method from the _____ *interface*.
j) A(n) _____ is an image that has *hot areas* that the user can click to accomplish a task such as loading a different Web page.
k) Method _____ of class `ImageIcon` displays the `ImageIcon`'s image.

30.2   State whether each of the following is *true* or *false*. If *false*, explain why.
a) Java currently supports two image formats. File names for each of these types end with `.jif` or `.gpg`, respectively.
b) Overriding the applet's `update` method to call `paint` without clearing the applet will significantly reduce animation flicker.
c) A sound will be garbage-collected as soon as it is done playing.
d) Swing GUI components have built-in graphics double buffering.

ANSWERS TO SELF-REVIEW EXERCISES

30.1   a) `getImage`. b) `getDocumentBase`. c) URL. d) `drawImage`. e) graphics double buffering. f) interlaced. g) `Image`, `Graphics`. h) `MediaTracker`. i) `AudioClip`. j) image map. k) `paintIcon`.

30.2   a) False; should be `.gif` or `.jpg` b) True. c) False, the sound will be marked for garbage collection (if it is not referenced by an `AudioClip`) and will be garbage collected when the garbage collector is able to run. d) True.

EXERCISES

30.3   Describe how to make an animation "browser friendly."

30.4   Discuss the various aspects of flicker elimination in Java.

30.5   Explain the technique of graphics double buffering.

30.6   Describe the Java methods for playing and manipulating audio clips.

30.7   *(Animation)* Create a a general-purpose Java animation program. Your program should allow the user to specify the sequence of frames to be displayed, the speed at which the images are displayed, audios that should be played while the animation is running and so on.

30.8   *(Screensaver)* Use animation of a series of your favorite images to create a screensaver program. Create various special effects that explode the images, spin the images, fade them in and out, move them off the edge of the screen and the like.

30.9   *(Randomly Erasing an Image)* Suppose an image is displayed in a rectangular screen area. One way to erase the image is simply to set every pixel to the same color immediately, but this is a dull visual effect. Write a Java program that displays an image then erases it by using random-number generation to select individual pixels to erase. After most of the image is erased, erase all the remaining pixels at once. You can refer to individual pixels by having a line that starts and ends at the same point. You might try several variants of this problem. For example, you might display lines randomly or you might display shapes randomly to erase regions of the screen.

30.10   *(Text Flasher)* Create a Java program that repeatedly flashes text on the screen. Do this by interspersing the text with a plain background color image. Allow the user to control the "blink speed" and the background color or pattern.

30.11   *(Image Flasher)* Create a Java program that repeatedly flashes an image on the screen. Do this by interspersing the image with a plain background color image.

30.12   *(Digital Clock)* Implement a program that displays a digital clock on the screen. You might add options to scale the clock; display day, month and year; issue an alarm; play certain audios at designated times and the like.

30.13   *(Calling Attention to an Image)* If you want to emphasize an image, you might place a row of simulated light bulbs around your image. You can let the light bulbs flash in unison or you can let them fire on and off in sequence one after the other.

30.14   *(Image Zooming)* Create a program that enables you to zoom in on, or away from, an image.

Internet and Web Resources

This appendix contains a list of valuable C/C++ and Java™ resources on the Internet and the World Wide Web. These resources include FAQs (Frequently Asked Questions), tutorials, how to obtain the ANSI/ISO C++ standard, information about popular compilers and how to obtain free compilers, demos, books, tutorials, software tools, articles, interviews, conferences, journals and magazines, on-line courses, newsgroups and career resources.

For more information about the American National Standards Institute (ANSI) or to purchase standards documents, visit ANSI at **www.ansi.org**.

A.1 C/C++ Resources

sunir.org/booklist/
The Programmer's Book List has a section for C++ books with 30+ titles.

www.possibility.com/Cpp/CppCodingStandard.html
The C++ Coding Standard site has an extensive amount of information about the C++ programming language as well as a great list of C++ resources on the Web.

help-site.com/cpp.html
Help-site.com provides links to C++ resources on the Web.

www.glenmccl.com/tutor.htm
This site is a good reference for users with C/C++ knowledge. Topics are accompanied by detailed explanations and example code.

www.programmersheaven.com/zone3/cat353/index.htm
This site offers an extensive collection of C++ libraries. These libraries are available for free download.

www.programmersheaven.com/zone3/cat155/index.htm
This site is a great resource for programmers. The site offers many utilities for C/C++.

www.programmersheaven.com/c/MsgBoard/wwwboard.asp?Board=3
This message board allows users to post C/C++ programming questions and comments for other members to answer.

www.hal9k.com/cug/
This site provides C++ resources, journals, shareware, freeware and more.

www.codeguru.com/cpp_mfc/index.shtml
A popular Web site for programmers, CodeGuru.com provides an extensive list of resources for programmers using C and C++.

www.dinkumware.com/refxc.html
The Dinkum C Library Reference Manual is written by P.J. Plauger, and is completely available on the Web. It provides a full reference to all functions and macros in the C Standard Library.

www.thinkage.ca/english/products/index.shtml
This Web site is full of shareware goodies, including a source code viewer and an input parser.

www.devx.com/cplus/
DevX is a comprehensive resource for programmers. Each section provides the latest news, tools and techniques for various programming languages. The C++ zone section of the site is dedicated to C++.

A.2 C++ Tutorials

www.icce.rug.nl/documents/cplusplus/
This tutorial, written by a university professor, is designed for C programmers who want to learn C++ programming.

cc.southeasttech.mnscu.edu/msc/index.shtml
Minnesota State College Southeast Technical offers online C++ courses for credit.

www.cplusplus.com/doc/tutorial/
This tutorial covers C++ basics up through advanced object-oriented programming with C++.

www.cprogramming.com/tutorial.html
This site includes a step-by-step tutorial that includes sample code.

www.programmersheaven.com/zone3/cat34/index.htm
This site contains a list of tutorial topics. Tutorial levels range from beginner to expert.

A.3 C/C++ FAQs

www.cs.ruu.nl/wais/html/na-dir/C-faq/diff.html
This Web site contains updates and changes to the comp.lang.c FAQ (www.eskimo.com/~scs/C-faq/top.html).

www.faqs.org/faqs/by-newsgroup/comp/comp.lang.c++.html
This site consists of a series of links to FAQs and tutorials gathered from the comp.lang.c++ newsgroup.

A.4 comp.lang.c++

kom.net/~dbrick/newspage/comp.lang.c++.html
Visit this site to connect to newsgroups related to the comp.lang.c++ hierarchy.

www.csci.csusb.edu/dick/c++std/
This site has links to the ANSI/ISO C++ Draft Standard and the Usenet group comp.std.c++, which provides new information about the standard.

www.research.att.com/~bs/homepage.html
This is the home page for Bjarne Stroustrup, designer of the C++ programming language. He provides a list of C++ resources, FAQs and other useful C++ information.

www.austinlinks.com/CPlusPlus/
This site has a list of C++ resources, including suggested books, career resources, information about the C++ programming language and links to sites with lists of C++ resources.

www.cyberdiem.com/vin/learn.html
Learn C/C++ Today is the title of this site, which provides a number of in depth tutorials on C/C++.

www.trumphurst.com/cpplibs1.html
The C++ Libraries FAQ is compiled by programming professionals for the use and benefit of other C++ programmers. The Library is updated regularly and is a good source for current information.

www.experts-exchange.com/Programming/Programming_Languages/Cplusplus/
The Experts Exchange is a free resource for high-tech professionals who wish to share information with their colleagues. Members can post questions and answers.

cplus.about.com/compute/cplus/
This is the About.com site for C/C++ programming languages. You will find tutorials, freeware/shareware, dictionaries, jobs, magazines and many other related items.

pent21.infosys.tuwien.ac.at/cetus/
oo_c_plus_plus.html#oo_c_plus_plus_general_newsgroups
This site contains links to many different types of C++ resources, such as newsgroups, tutorials, FAQs, articles, utilities and libraries.

news:comp.lang.c++
This is a newsgroup dedicated to object-oriented C++ language issues.

news:comp.lang.c++.moderated
This is a more technically oriented newsgroup dedicated to the C++ language.

A.5 C/C++ Compilers

ftp://gcc.gnu.org/pub/gcc/releases/index.html
A complete index of the latest GCC releases (in C++ and Java, too), free of charge.

www.comeaucomputing.com/features.html
Comeau Computing offers their free compiler, which supports some C99 features.

www.compilers.net/
Compilers.net is a site designed to help you find compilers.

msdn.microsoft.com/visualc/
The Microsoft Visual C++ home page provides product information, overviews, supplemental materials and ordering information for the Visual C++ compiler.

www.borland.com/cbuilder/tsuite/index.html
The Borland Turbo C++ Suite for Windows compiler Web site.

www.metrowerks.com/MW/Develop/Desktop/Windows/default.htm
Metrowerks CodeWarrior is a development environment for coding in C/C++ or Java.

www.faqs.org/faqs/by-newsgroup/comp/comp.compilers.html
This is a site containing a list of FAQs generated within the comp.compilers newsgroup.

www.borland.com/cbuilder/
This is a link to the Borland C++ Builder 6. A free command-line version is available for download.

sunset.backbone.olemiss.edu/%7Ebobcook/eC/
This C++ compiler is designed for beginning C++ users who wish to transition from Pascal to C++.

www.intel.com/software/products/compilers/cwin/
The Intel C++ compiler. Platforms supported include Windows 98, NT, 2000 and XP.

A.6 Java Resources

`java.sun.com`
The Sun Microsystems, Inc. Java Web site is an essential stop when searching the web for Java information. Go to this site to download the Java 2 Software Development Kit (J2SDK). This site is also a complete resource with news, information, online support, code samples and more.

`www.gamelan.com`
Gamelan, which is now part of `developer.com`, has been a wonderful Java resource since the early days of Java. The Gamelan site calls itself the "Official Directory for Java." This site was originally a large Java repository where individuals traded ideas on Java and examples of Java programming. One of its early benefits was the volume of Java source code that was available to the many people learning Java. It is now an all-around Java resource with Java references, free Java downloads, areas where you can ask questions to Java experts, discussion groups on Java, a glossary of Java-related terminology, upcoming Java-related events, directories for specialized industry topics and hundreds of other Java resources.

`www.jars.com`
Another `developer.com` Web site is JARS—originally called the Java Applet Rating Service. The JARS site calls itself the "#1 Java Review Service." This site originally was a large Java repository for applets. Its benefit was that it rated every applet registered at the site as top 1%, top 5% and top 25%, so you could immediately view the best applets on the Web. Early in the development of the Java language, having your applet rated here was a great way to demonstrate your Java programming abilities. JARS is now another all-around resource for Java programmers. Many of the resources for this site, Gamelan and `developer.com`, are now shared as these sites are both owned by EarthWeb.

`developer.java.sun.com`
On the Sun Microsystems Java Web site, visit Java Developer Services. This free site has close to one million members. The site includes technical support, discussion forums, on-line training courses, technical articles, resources, announcements of new Java features, early access to new Java technologies, and links to other important Java Web sites. Even though the site is free, you must register to use it.

`javawoman.com/index.html`
The Java Woman Web site has one of the most extensive list of Java related links we have found on the web. You will find lists of links for Java books, Integrated Development Environments, FAQs, examples, documentation, tutorials, tools and advanced topics.

`www.nikos.com/javatoys/`
The Java Toys Web site includes links to the latest Java news, Java User Groups (JUGs), FAQs, tools, Java-related mailing lists, books and white papers.

`www.devx.com/java`
The Development Exchange Java Zone site includes Java discussion groups, recent Java news and many other Java resources as well.

`www.acme.com/java/`
This page has an animated Java applet with the source code provided. This site is an excellent resource for information on Java. The page provides software, notes and a list of hyperlinks to other resources. Under "software," you will find some animated applets, utility classes and applications.

`www.ibiblio.org/javafaq/`
This site provides the latest Java news. It also has helpful Java resources, including the Java FAQ List, a tutorial called Brewing Java, Java User Groups, Java Links, the Java Book List, Java Trade Shows, Java Training and Exercises.

`www.teamjava.com`
Team Java assists Java consultants in search of contracts and helps to promote Java. They have also listed some useful sites. A few of the sites are included in this list of resources.

`dir.yahoo.com/Computers_and_Internet/Programming_and_Development/`
`Languages/Java/`
Yahoo, a popular World Wide Web search engine, provides links to many Java resources. You can initiate a search using keywords or explore the categories listed at the site, including games, contests, events, tutorials and documentation, mailing lists, security and more.

`www-106.ibm.com/developerworks/java/`
The IBM Developers Java Technology Zone site lists the latest news, tools, code, case studies and events related to IBM and Java.

A.7 Java Products

`java.sun.com/products/`
Download the Java 2 SDK and other Java products from the *Sun Microsystems Java Products page.*

`wwws.sun.com/software/sundev/jde/index.html`
The Sun One Studio IDE is a customizable, platform independent, visual programming development environment.

`www.borland.com/jbuilder/`
The Borland JBuilder IDE home page has news, product information and customer support.

`www-3.ibm.com/software/awdtools/studiositedev/`
Download or read more about the IBM WebSphere Studio for Java development environment.

`www.metrowerks.com/MW/Develop/Desktop/Windows/default.htm`
The Metrowerks CodeWarrior IDE supports a few programming languages, including Java.

A.8 Java FAQs

`javawoman.com/index.html`
The Java Woman Web site has one of the most extensive list of Java related links we have found on the Web. You will find lists of links for Java books, Integrated Development Environments, FAQs, examples, documentation, tutorials, tools and advanced topics.

`www.nikos.com/javatoys/`
The Java Toys Web site includes links to the latest Java news, Java User Groups (JUGs), FAQs, tools, Java-related mailing lists, books and white papers.

`www.devx.com/java`
The Development Exchange Java Zone site includes Java discussion groups, recent Java news and many other Java resources as well.

`www.ibiblio.org/javafaq/`
This site provides the latest Java news. It also has helpful Java resources, including the Java FAQ List, a tutorial called Brewing Java, Java User Groups, Java Links, the Java Book List, Java Trade Shows, Java Training and Exercises.

A.9 Java Tutorials

`java.sun.com/docs/books/tutorial/`
The Java Tutorial Site has a number of tutorials, including sections on JavaBeans, JDBC, RMI, Servlets, Collections and Java Native Interface.

`javawoman.com/index.html`
The Java Woman Web site has one of the most extensive list of Java related links we have found on the web. You will find lists of links for Java books, Integrated Development Environments, FAQs, examples, documentation, tutorials, tools and advanced topics.

`www.ibiblio.org/javafaq/`
This site provides the latest Java news. It also has helpful Java resources, including the Java FAQ List, a tutorial called Brewing Java, Java User Groups, Java Links, the Java Book List, Java Trade Shows, Java Training and Exercises.

A.10 Java Magazines

`www.javaworld.com`
JavaWorld, an online magazine, is an excellent resource for current Java information. You will find news clips, conference information and links to Java-related Web sites.

`www.sys-con.com/java/`
Catch up with the latest Java news at the *Java Developer's Journal* site. This magazine is one of the premier resources for Java news.

`www.javareport.com/`
The *Java Report* is a great resource for Java Developers. You will find the latest industry news, sample code, event listings, products and jobs.

A.11 Java Applets

`java.sun.com`
There are a large number of Java applet resources available on the Web. The best place to start is at the source—the Sun Microsystems, Inc. Java Web site. In the upper-left corner of the Web page is an Applets hyperlink to the Sun Applets Web page.

`java.sun.com/applets/index.html`
This page contains a variety of Java applet resources, including free applets you can use on your own Web site, the demonstration applets from the J2SDK and a variety of other applets (many of which can be downloaded and used on your own computer). There is also a section entitled "Applets at Work" where you can read about uses of applets in industry.

`developer.java.sun.com`
On the Sun Microsystems Java Web site, visit the Java Developer Services. This free site has close to one million members. The site includes technical support, discussion forums, on-line training courses, technical articles, resources, announcements of new Java features, early access to new Java technologies, and links to other important Java Web sites. Even though the site is free, you must register to use it.

`www.gamelan.com`
Gamelan, which is now part of `developer.com`, has been a wonderful Java resource since the early days of Java. The Gamelan site calls itself the "Official Directory for Java." This site originally was a large Java repository where individuals traded ideas on Java and examples of Java programming. One of its early benefits was the volume of Java source code that was available to the many people learning Java. It is now an all-around Java resource with Java references, free Java downloads, areas where you can ask questions to Java experts, discussion groups on Java, a glossary of Java-related terminology, upcoming Java-related events, directories for specialized industry topics and hundreds of other Java resources.

`www.jars.com`
Another `developer.com` Web site is JARS—originally called the Java Applet Rating Service. The JARS site calls itself the "#1 Java Review Service." This site originally was a large Java repository for applets. Its benefit was that it rated every applet registered at the site as top 1%, top 5% and top 25%, so you could immediately view the best applets on the Web. Early in the development of the Java language, having your applet rated here was a great way to demonstrate your Java programming abilities. JARS is now another all-around resource for Java programmers. Many of the resources for this site, `Gamelan` and `developer.com`, are now shared as these sites are both owned by EarthWeb.

A.12 Multimedia

java.sun.com/products/java-media/jmf/
The Java Media Framework home page on the Java Web site. Here you can download the latest Sun implementation of the JMF. The site also contains the documentation for the JMF.

www.nasa.gov/multimedia/highlights/index.html
The NASA multimedia gallery contains a wide variety of images, audio clips and video clips that you can download and use to test your Java multimedia programs.

sunsite.sut.ac.jp/multimed/
The Sunsite Japan Multimedia Collection also provides a wide variety of images, audio clips and video clips that you can download for educational purposes.

A.13 Java Newsgroups

news:comp.lamg.java
news:comp.lang.java.advocacy
news:comp.lang.java.announce
news:comp.lang.java.beans
news:comp.lang.java.corba
news:comp.lang.java.databases
news:comp.lang.java.gui
news:comp.lang.java.help
news:comp.lang.java.machine
news:comp.lang.java.programmer
news:comp.lang.java.softwaretools
news:cz.comp.lang.java
news:fj.comp.lang.java

C99 Internet and Web Resources

This appendix contains C99 Internet and Web resources, including FAQs (Frequently Asked Questions), tutorials, how to obtain the ANSI/ISO C99 standard, demos, books, tutorials, software tools, articles, interviews, conferences, journals, magazines, on-line courses, newsgroups and career resources.

C99 is the latest ANSI standard for the C programming language. It was developed to evolve the C language to keep pace with today's powerful hardware and with increasingly demanding user requirements. The C99 Standard is more capable (than earlier C Standards) of competing with languages like FORTRAN for mathematical applications. C99 capabilities include the `long long` type for 64-bit machines, complex numbers for engineering applications and greater support of floating-point arithmetic. C99 also makes C more consistent with C++ by enabling polymorphism through type-generic mathematical functions and through the creation of a defined boolean type.

The C99 standard contains many changes from earlier versions of the language. These include enhanced floating point functionality, boolean and `long long` variable types, removal of the implicit `int` and allowing variables to be defined in the header of a `for` loop. Detailed explanations of all the changes in C99 can be found in the ANSI/ISO standard document and in many of the links below.

C99 compliant compilers are not yet widely available. Some C libraries and compilers that support the new standard include Dinkumware's C99 library (`www.dinkumware.com`) and Comeau Computing's C99 compiler (`www.comeaucomputing.com`).

The international standard document for C99 can be purchased from the American National Standards Institute (`www.ansi.org`). A technical corrigendum listing errors in the Standard can be downloaded for free. The InterNational Committee for Information Technology Standards (INCITS) serves as ANSI's Technical Advisory Group for ISO/IEC Joint Technical Committee 1. The C99 documentation can be purchased from their Web site, `www.incits.org`.

B.1 C99 Resources

`www.ansi.org`
All ANSI documents including the C99 standard can be found and purchased here.

`www.incits.org/tc_home/j11.htm`
This Web site documents INCITS's (InterNational Committee of Information Technology Support) progress in the development of the C standard.

anubis.dkuug.dk/JTC1/SC22/WG14/
ISO/IEC JTC1/SC22/WG14 is the international standardization working group for the C programming language. The latest revisions and updates to C99 can be found here.

wwwold.dkuug.dk/JTC1/SC22/WG14/www/newinc9x.htm
Contains a list of the features of C99.

www.comeaucomputing.com/features.html
Comeau Computing offers their free compiler, which supports many C99 features.

www.dinkumware.com/libraries_ref.html
Dinkumware licenses C and C++ libraries that conform to ANSI standards and provides on-line documentation.

www.thefreecountry.com/compilers/cpp.shtml
This Web site lists many free C and C++ compilers including some that are moving toward C99 compliance.

david.tribble.com/text/cdiffs.htm
David R. Tribble discusses the compatibility between C99 and ANSI/ISO C++.

gcc.gnu.org/c9xstatus.html
This Web site lists the latest C99 features that are supported by the GNU Compiler Collection (GCC).

www.cs.ruu.nl/wais/html/na-dir/C-faq/diff.html
This Web site contains updates and changes to the comp.lang.c FAQ site, which can be found at www.eskimo.com/~scs/C-faq/top.html.

www-ccs.ucsd.edu/c/
This Web site is a comprehensive reference for programming in Standard C. It contains and documents all of the standard libraries.

www.lysator.liu.se/c/q8/index.html
Doug Gwyn provides a sample of C99 libraries all under public domain.

www.ramtex.dk/standard/iostand.htm
A proposal for C99 revisions addressing I/O-hardware issues.

home.att.net/~jackklein/c/standards.html
Answers to FAQ about ANSI and ISO and why C and C++ Standards are important.

www.cl.cam.ac.uk/~mgk25/c-time/
Proposed new time library for the latest draft of C.

www.devworld.apple.com/tools/mpw-tools/c9x.html
This Web site posts the official Committee Document for the C99 document.

www.eskimo.com/~scs/C-faq/top.html
This FAQ list contains topics such as pointers, memory allocation and strings.

comp.lang.c
Come to this newsgroup for the latest buzz on C99.

comp.std.c
This newsgroup offers a discussion on the C99 standard.

gcc.gnu.org/ml/gcc/
A GNU newsgroup covering many issues such as the C99 standard.

Operator Precedence Charts

Operators are shown in decreasing order of precedence from top to bottom.

C Operator	Type	Associativity
()	parentheses (function call operator)	left to right
[]	array subscript	
.	member selection via object	
->	member selection via pointer	
++	unary preincrement	right to left
--	unary predecrement	
+	unary plus	
-	unary minus	
!	unary logical negation	
~	unary bitwise complement	
(*type*)	C-style unary cast	
*	dereference	
&	address	
sizeof	determine size in bytes	
*	multiplication	left to right
/	division	
%	modulus	
+	addition	left to right
-	subtraction	
<<	bitwise left shift	left to right
>>	bitwise right shift	

Fig. C.1   C operator precedence chart. (Part 1 of 2.)

C Operator	Type	Associativity
< <= > >=	relational less than relational less than or equal to relational greater than relational greater than or equal to	left to right
== !=	relational is equal to relational is not equal to	left to right
&	bitwise AND	left to right
^	bitwise exclusive OR	left to right
|	bitwise inclusive OR	left to right
&&	logical AND	left to right
||	logical OR	left to right
?:	ternary conditional	right to left
= += -= *= /= %= &= ^= |= <<= >>=	assignment addition assignment subtraction assignment multiplication assignment division assignment modulus assignment bitwise AND assignment bitwise exclusive OR assignment bitwise inclusive OR assignment bitwise left shift assignment bitwise right shift with sign	right to left
,	comma	left to right

Fig. C.1   C operator precedence chart. (Part 2 of 2.)

C++ Operator	Type	Associativity
`::`	binary scope resolution	left to right
`::`	unary scope resolution	
`()`	parentheses (function call operator)	left to right
`[]`	array subscript	
`.`	member selection via object	
`->`	member selection via pointer	
`++`	unary postincrement	
`--`	unary postdecrement	
`typeid`	runtime type information	
`dynamic_cast< type >`	runtime type-checked cast	
`static_cast< type >`	compile-time type-checked cast	
`reinterpret_cast< type >`	cast for nonstandard conversions	
`const_cast< type >`	cast away `const`-ness	
`++`	unary preincrement	right to left
`--`	unary predecrement	
`+`	unary plus	
`-`	unary minus	
`!`	unary logical negation	
`~`	unary bitwise complement	
`( type )`	C-style unary cast	
`sizeof`	determine size in bytes	
`&`	address	
`*`	dereference	
`new`	dynamic memory allocation	
`new[]`	dynamic array allocation	
`delete`	dynamic memory deallocation	
`delete[]`	dynamic array deallocation	
`.*`	pointer to member via object	left to right
`->*`	pointer to member via pointer	
`*`	multiplication	left to right
`/`	division	
`%`	modulus	
`+`	addition	left to right
`-`	subtraction	
`<<`	bitwise left shift	left to right
`>>`	bitwise right shift	
`<`	relational less than	left to right
`<=`	relational less than or equal to	
`>`	relational greater than	
`>=`	relational greater than or equal to	
`==`	relational is equal to	left to right
`!=`	relational is not equal to	

Fig. C.2   C++ operator precedence chart (Part 1 of 2.).

C++ Operator	Type	Associativity
&	bitwise AND	left to right
^	bitwise exclusive OR	left to right
|	bitwise inclusive OR	left to right
&&	logical AND	left to right
||	logical OR	left to right
? :	ternary conditional	right to left
=	assignment	right to left
+=	addition assignment	
-=	subtraction assignment	
*=	multiplication assignment	
/=	division assignment	
%=	modulus assignment	
&=	bitwise AND assignment	
^=	bitwise exclusive OR assignment	
|=	bitwise inclusive OR assignment	
<<=	bitwise left shift assignment	
>>=	bitwise right shift with sign	
,	comma	left to right

Fig. C.2   C++ operator precedence chart (Part 2 of 2.).

Java Operator	Type	Associativity
++ --	unary postincrement unary postdecrement	right to left
++ -- + - ! ~ (*type*)	unary preincrement unary predecrement unary plus unary minus unary logical negation unary bitwise complement unary cast	right to left
* / %	multiplication division modulus	left to right
+ -	addition subtraction	left to right
<< >> >>>	bitwise left shift bitwise right shift with sign extension bitwise right shift with zero extension	left to right

Fig. C.3   Java operator precedence chart (Part 1 of 2.).

Java Operator	Type	Associativity
 <= > >= instanceof	relational less than relational less than or equal to relational greater than relational greater than or equal to type comparison	left to right
== !=	relational is equal to relational is not equal to	left to right
&	bitwise AND	left to right
^	bitwise exclusive OR boolean logical exclusive OR	left to right
|	bitwise inclusive OR boolean logical inclusive OR	left to right
&&	logical AND	left to right
||	logical OR	left to right
?:	ternary conditional	right to left
= += -= *= /= %= &= ^= |= <<= >>= >>>=	assignment addition assignment subtraction assignment multiplication assignment division assignment modulus assignment bitwise AND assignment bitwise exclusive OR assignment bitwise inclusive OR assignment bitwise left shift assignment bitwise right shift with sign extension assignment bitwise right shift with zero extension assignment	right to left

Fig. C.3   Java operator precedence chart (Part 2 of 2.).

ASCII Character Set

	0	1	2	3	4	5	6	7	8	9
0	nul	soh	stx	etx	eot	enq	ack	bel	bs	ht
1	lf	vt	ff	cr	so	si	dle	dc1	dc2	dc3
2	dc4	nak	syn	etb	can	em	sub	esc	fs	gs
3	rs	us	sp	!	"	#	$	%	&	'
4	(	)	*	+	,	-	.	/	0	1
5	2	3	4	5	6	7	8	9	:	;
6	<	=	>	?	@	A	B	C	D	E
7	F	G	H	I	J	K	L	M	N	O
8	P	Q	R	S	T	U	V	W	X	Y
9	Z	[	\	]	^	_	'	a	b	c
10	d	e	f	g	h	i	j	k	l	m
11	n	o	p	q	r	s	t	u	v	w
12	x	y	z	{			}	~	del		

Fig. D.1 ASCII Character Set.

The digits at the left of the table are the left digits of the decimal equivalent (0-127) of the character code, and the digits at the top of the table are the right digits of the character code. For example, the character code for "F" is 70, and the character code for "&" is 38.

Number Systems

Objectives

- To understand basic number systems concepts such as base, positional value and symbol value.
- To understand how to work with numbers represented in the binary, octal and hexadecimal number systems
- To be able to abbreviate binary numbers as octal numbers or hexadecimal numbers.
- To be able to convert octal numbers and hexadecimal numbers to binary numbers.
- To be able to convert back and forth between decimal numbers and their binary, octal and hexadecimal equivalents.
- To understand binary arithmetic and how negative binary numbers are represented using two's complement notation.

Here are only numbers ratified.
William Shakespeare

Nature has some sort of arithmetic-geometrical coordinate system, because nature has all kinds of models. What we experience of nature is in models, and all of nature's models are so beautiful.
It struck me that nature's system must be a real beauty, because in chemistry we find that the associations are always in beautiful whole numbers—there are no fractions.
Richard Buckminster Fuller

Outline

E.1 Introduction

In this appendix, we introduce the key number systems that C programmers use, especially when they are working on software projects that require close interaction with "machine-level" hardware. Projects like this include operating systems, computer networking software, compilers, database systems and applications requiring high performance.

When we write an integer, such as 227 or –63, in a C program, the number is assumed to be in the *decimal (base 10) number system*. The *digits* in the decimal number system are 0, 1, 2, 3, 4, 5, 6, 7, 8 and 9. The lowest digit is 0, and the highest digit is 9—one less than the base of 10. Internally, computers use the *binary (base 2) number system*. The binary number system has only two digits, namely 0 and 1. Its lowest digit is 0, and its highest digit is 1—one less than the base of 2.

As we will see, binary numbers tend to be much longer than their decimal equivalents. Programmers who work in assembly languages and in high-level languages like C that enable programmers to reach down to the "machine level" find it cumbersome to work with binary numbers. So two other number systems—the *octal number system (base 8)* and the *hexadecimal number system (base 16)*—are popular, primarily because they make it convenient to abbreviate binary numbers.

In the octal number system, the digits range from 0 to 7. Because both the binary number system and the octal number system have fewer digits than the decimal number system, their digits are the same as the corresponding digits in decimal.

The hexadecimal number system poses a problem because it requires sixteen digits—a lowest digit of 0 and a highest digit with a value equivalent to decimal 15 (one less than the base of 16). By convention, we use the letters A through F to represent the hexadecimal digits corresponding to decimal values 10 through 15. Thus in hexadecimal we can have numbers like 876 consisting solely of decimal-like digits, numbers like 8A55F consisting of digits and letters and numbers like FFE consisting solely of letters. Occasionally, a hexadecimal number spells a common word such as FACE or FEED—this can appear strange to programmers accustomed to working with numbers. The digits of the binary, octal, decimal and hexadecimal number systems are summarized in Fig. E.1–Fig. E.2.

Each of these number systems uses *positional notation*—each position in which a digit is written has a different *positional value*. For example, in the decimal number 937 (the 9, the 3 and the 7 are referred to as *symbol values*), we say that the 7 is written in the ones position, the 3 is written in the tens position and the 9 is written in the hundreds position. Notice that each of these positions is a power of the base (base 10) and that these powers begin at 0 and increase by 1 as we move left in the number (Fig. E.3).

Binary digit	Octal digit	Decimal digit	Hexadecimal digit
0	0	0	0
1	1	1	1
	2	2	2
	3	3	3
	4	4	4
	5	5	5
	6	6	6
	7	7	7
		8	8
		9	9
			A (decimal value of 10)
			B (decimal value of 11)
			C (decimal value of 12)
			D (decimal value of 13)
			E (decimal value of 14)
			F (decimal value of 15)

Fig. E.1   Digits of the binary, octal, decimal and hexadecimal number systems.

Attribute	Binary	Octal	Decimal	Hexadecimal
Base	2	8	10	16
Lowest digit	0	0	0	0
Highest digit	1	7	9	F

Fig. E.2   Comparing the binary, octal, decimal and hexadecimal number systems.

Positional values in the decimal number system			
Decimal digit	9	3	7
Position name	Hundreds	Tens	Ones
Positional value	100	10	1
Positional value as a power of the base (10)	10^2	10^1	10^0

Fig. E.3   Positional values in the decimal number system.

For longer decimal numbers, the next positions to the left would be the thousands position (10 to the 3rd power), the ten-thousands position (10 to the 4th power), the hundred-thousands position (10 to the 5th power), the millions position (10 to the 6th power), the ten-millions position (10 to the 7th power) and so on.

In the binary number 101, we say that the rightmost 1 is written in the ones position, the 0 is written in the twos position and the leftmost 1 is written in the fours position. Notice that each of these positions is a power of the base (base 2) and that these powers begin at 0 and increase by 1 as we move left in the number (Fig. E.4).

For longer binary numbers, the next positions to the left would be the eights position (2 to the 3rd power), the sixteens position (2 to the 4th power), the thirty-twos position (2 to the 5th power), the sixty-fours position (2 to the 6th power) and so on.

In the octal number 425, we say that the 5 is written in the ones position, the 2 is written in the eights position and the 4 is written in the sixty-fours position. Notice that each of these positions is a power of the base (base 8) and that these powers begin at 0 and increase by 1 as we move left in the number (Fig. E.5).

For longer octal numbers, the next positions to the left would be the five-hundred-and-twelves position (8 to the 3rd power), the four-thousand-and-ninety-sixes position (8 to the 4th power), the thirty-two-thousand-seven-hundred-and-sixty eights position (8 to the 5th power) and so on.

In the hexadecimal number 3DA, we say that the A is written in the ones position, the D is written in the sixteens position and the 3 is written in the two-hundred-and-fifty-sixes position. Notice that each of these positions is a power of the base (base 16) and that these powers begin at 0 and increase by 1 as we move left in the number (Fig. E.6).

Positional values in the binary number system			
Binary digit	1	0	1
Position name	Fours	Twos	Ones
Positional value	4	2	1
Positional value as a power of the base (2)	2^2	2^1	2^0

Fig. E.4   Positional values in the binary number system.

Positional values in the octal number system			
Decimal digit	4	2	5
Position name	Sixty-fours	Eights	Ones
Positional value	64	8	1
Positional value as a power of the base (8)	8^2	8^1	8^0

Fig. E.5   Positional values in the octal number system.

Positional values in the hexadecimal number system			
Decimal digit	3	D	A
Position name	Two-hundred-and-fifty-sixes	Sixteens	Ones
Positional value	256	16	1
Positional value as a power of the base (16)	16^2	16^1	16^0

Fig. E.6   Positional values in the hexadecimal number system.

For longer hexadecimal numbers, the next positions to the left would be the four-thousand-and-ninety-sixes position (16 to the 3rd power), the sixty-five-thousand-five-hundred-and-thirty-sixes position (16 to the 4th power) and so on.

E.2 Abbreviating Binary Numbers as Octal Numbers and Hexadecimal Numbers

The main use for octal and hexadecimal numbers in computing is for abbreviating lengthy binary representations. Figure E.7 highlights the fact that lengthy binary numbers can be expressed concisely in number systems with higher bases than the binary number system.

Decimal number	Binary representation	Octal representation	Hexadecimal representation
0	0	0	0
1	1	1	1
2	10	2	2
3	11	3	3
4	100	4	4
5	101	5	5
6	110	6	6
7	111	7	7
8	1000	10	8
9	1001	11	9
10	1010	12	A
11	1011	13	B
12	1100	14	C
13	1101	15	D
14	1110	16	E
15	1111	17	F
16	10000	20	10

Fig. E.7   Decimal, binary, octal and hexadecimal equivalents.

A particularly important relationship that both the octal number system and the hexadecimal number system have to the binary system is that the bases of octal and hexadecimal (8 and 16 respectively) are powers of the base of the binary number system (base 2). Consider the following 12-digit binary number and its octal and hexadecimal equivalents. See if you can determine how this relationship makes it convenient to abbreviate binary numbers in octal or hexadecimal. The answer follows the numbers.

```
Binary NumberOctal equivalentHexadecimal equivalent
10001101000143218D1
```

To see how the binary number converts easily to octal, simply break the 12-digit binary number into groups of three consecutive bits each and write those groups over the corresponding digits of the octal number as follows

```
100 011 010 001
 4   3   2   1
```

Notice that the octal digit you have written under each group of three bits corresponds precisely to the octal equivalent of that three-digit binary number as shown in Fig. E.7.

The same kind of relationship can be observed in converting from binary to hexadecimal. Break the 12-digit binary number into groups of four consecutive bits each and write those groups over the corresponding digits of the hexadecimal number as follows

```
100011010001
 8   D   1
```

Notice that the hexadecimal digit you wrote under each group of four bits corresponds precisely to the hexadecimal equivalent of that four-digit binary number as shown in Fig. E.7.

E.3 Converting Octal Numbers and Hexadecimal Numbers to Binary Numbers

In the previous section, we saw how to convert binary numbers to their octal and hexadecimal equivalents by forming groups of binary digits and simply rewriting these groups as their equivalent octal digit values or hexadecimal digit values. This process may be used in reverse to produce the binary equivalent of a given octal or hexadecimal number.

For example, the octal number 653 is converted to binary simply by writing the 6 as its three-digit binary equivalent 110, the 5 as its three-digit binary equivalent 101 and the 3 as its three-digit binary equivalent 011 to form the nine-digit binary number 110101011.

The hexadecimal number FAD5 is converted to binary simply by writing the F as its four-digit binary equivalent 1111, the A as its four-digit binary equivalent 1010, the D as its four-digit binary equivalent 1101 and the 5 as its four-digit binary equivalent 0101 to form the 16-digit 1111101011010101.

E.4 Converting from Binary, Octal or Hexadecimal to Decimal

Because we are accustomed to working in decimal, it is often convenient to convert a binary, octal or hexadecimal number to decimal to get a sense of what the number is "really" worth. Our diagrams in Section E.1 express the positional values in decimal. To convert a number to decimal from another base, multiply the decimal equivalent of each digit by its positional value and sum these products. For example, the binary number 110101 is converted to decimal 53 as shown in Fig. E.8.

Converting a binary number to decimal

Positional values:	32	16	8	4	2	1
Symbol values:	1	1	0	1	0	1
Products:	1*32=32	1*16=16	0*8=0	1*4=4	0*2=0	1*1=1
Sum:	= 32 + 16 + 0 + 4 + 0s + 1 = 53					

Fig. E.8   Converting a binary number to decimal.

To convert octal 7614 to decimal 3980, we use the same technique, this time using appropriate octal positional values as shown in Fig. E.9.

To convert hexadecimal AD3B to decimal 44347, we use the same technique, this time using appropriate hexadecimal positional values as shown in Fig. E.10.

E.5 Converting from Decimal to Binary, Octal or Hexadecimal

The conversions in Section E.4 follow naturally from the positional notation conventions. Converting from decimal to binary, octal, or hexadecimal also follows these conventions.

Suppose we wish to convert decimal 57 to binary. We begin by writing the positional values of the columns right to left until we reach a column whose positional value is greater than the decimal number. We do not need that column, so we discard it. Thus, we first write:

Positional values:6432168421

Then we discard the column with positional value 64 leaving:

Positional values:3216842 1

Converting an octal number to decimal

Positional values:	512	64	8	1
Symbol values:	7	6	1	4
Products	7*512=3584	6*64=384	1*8=8	4*1=4
Sum:	= 3584 + 384 + 8 + 4 = 3980			

Fig. E.9   Converting an octal number to decimal.

Converting a hexadecimal number to decimal

Positional values:	4096	256	16	1
Symbol values:	A	D	3	B
Products	A*4096=40960	D*256=3328	3*16=48	B*1=11
Sum:	= 40960 + 3328 + 48 + 11 = 44347			

Fig. E.10   Converting a hexadecimal number to decimal.

Next, we work from the leftmost column to the right. We divide 32 into 57 and observe that there is one 32 in 57 with a remainder of 25, so we write 1 in the 32 column. We divide 16 into 25 and observe that there is one 16 in 25 with a remainder of 9 and write 1 in the 16 column. We divide 8 into 9 and observe that there is one 8 in 9 with a remainder of 1. The next two columns each produce quotients of zero when their positional values are divided into 1, so we write 0s in the 4 and 2 columns. Finally, 1 into 1 is 1, so we write 1 in the 1 column. This yields:

```
Positional values:3216842  1
Symbol values:11  10  0   1
```

and thus decimal 57 is equivalent to binary 111001.

To convert decimal 103 to octal, we begin by writing the positional values of the columns until we reach a column whose positional value is greater than the decimal number. We do not need that column, so we discard it. Thus, we first write:

```
Positional values:5126481
```

Then we discard the column with positional value 512, yielding:

```
Positional values:6481
```

Next, we work from the leftmost column to the right. We divide 64 into 103 and observe that there is one 64 in 103 with a remainder of 39, so we write 1 in the 64 column. We divide 8 into 39 and observe that there are four 8s in 39 with a remainder of 7 and write 4 in the 8 column. Finally, we divide 1 into 7 and observe that there are seven 1s in 7 with no remainder, so we write 7 in the 1 column. This yields:

```
Positional values:6481
Symbol values:14  7
```

and thus decimal 103 is equivalent to octal 147.

To convert decimal 375 to hexadecimal, we begin by writing the positional values of the columns until we reach a column whose positional value is greater than the decimal number. We do not need that column, so we discard it. Thus, we first write

```
Positional values:4096256161
```

Then we discard the column with positional value 4096, yielding:

```
Positional values:256161
```

Next, we work from the leftmost column to the right. We divide 256 into 375 and observe that there is one 256 in 375 with a remainder of 119, so we write 1 in the 256 column. We divide 16 into 119 and observe that there are seven 16s in 119 with a remainder of 7 and write 7 in the 16 column. Finally, we divide 1 into 7 and observe that there are seven 1s in 7 with no remainder, so we write 7 in the 1 column. This yields:

```
Positional values:256161
Symbol values:17  7
```

and thus decimal 375 is equivalent to hexadecimal 177.

E.6 Negative Binary Numbers: Two's Complement Notation

The discussion in this appendix has been focussed on positive numbers. In this section, we explain how computers represent negative numbers using *two's complement notation*. First, we explain how the two's complement of a binary number is formed and then we show why it represents the *negative value* of the given binary number.

Consider a machine with 32-bit integers. Suppose

```
int value = 13;
```

The 32-bit representation of `value` is

```
00000000 00000000 00000000 00001101
```

To form the negative of `value` we first form its *one's complement* by applying C's *bitwise complement operator (~)*:

```
onesComplementOfValue = ~value;
```

Internally, `~value` is now `value` with each of its bits reversed—ones become zeros and zeros become ones as follows:

```
value:
00000000 00000000 00000000 00001101
```

```
~value  (i.e., value's ones complement):
11111111 11111111 11111111 11110010
```

To form the two's complement of `value` we simply add one to `value`'s one's complement. Thus

```
Two's complement of value:
11111111 11111111 11111111 11110011
```

Now if this is in fact equal to −13, we should be able to add it to binary 13 and obtain a result of 0. Let us try this:

```
 00000000 00000000 00000000 00001101
+11111111 11111111 11111111 11110011
------------------------------------
 00000000 00000000 00000000 00000000
```

The carry bit coming out of the leftmost column is discarded, and we indeed get zero as a result. If we add the one's complement of a number to the number, the result would be all 1s. The key to getting a result of all zeros is that the two's complement is 1 more than the one's complement. The addition of 1 causes each column to add to 0 with a carry of 1. The carry keeps moving leftward until it is discarded from the leftmost bit and hence the resulting number is all zeros.

Computers actually perform a subtraction such as

```
x = a - value;
```

by adding the two's complement of `value` to a as follows:

```
x = a + (~value + 1);
```

Suppose a is 27 and `value` is 13 as before. If the two's complement of `value` is actually the negative of `value`, then adding the two's complement of value to a should produce the result 14. Let us try this:

```
a (i.e., 27)  00000000 00000000 00000000 00011011
+(~value + 1)+11111111 11111111 11111111 11110011
              -----------------------------------
              00000000 00000000 00000000 00001110
```

which is indeed equal to 14.

SUMMARY

- An integer, such as 19, 227 or –63, in a C program is assumed to be in the decimal (base 10) number system. The digits in the decimal number system are 0, 1, 2, 3, 4, 5, 6, 7, 8 and 9. The lowest digit is 0 and the highest digit is 9—one less than the base of 10.

- Internally, computers use the binary (base 2) number system. The binary number system has only two digits, namely 0 and 1. Its lowest digit is 0 and its highest digit is 1—one less than the base of 2.

- The octal number system (base 8) and the hexadecimal number system (base 16) are popular primarily because they make it convenient to abbreviate binary numbers.

- The digits of the octal number system range from 0 to 7.

- The hexadecimal number system poses a problem because it requires sixteen digits—a lowest digit of 0 and a highest digit with a value equivalent to decimal 15 (one less than the base of 16). By convention, we use the letters A through F to represent the hexadecimal digits corresponding to decimal values 10 through 15.

- Each number system uses positional notation—each position in which a digit is written has a different positional value.

- A particularly important relationship that both the octal number system and the hexadecimal number system have to the binary system is that the bases of octal and hexadecimal (8 and 16 respectively) are powers of the base of the binary number system (base 2).

- To convert an octal to a binary number, replace each octal digit with its three-digit binary equivalent.

- To convert a hexadecimal number to a binary number, simply replace each hexadecimal digit with its four-digit binary equivalent.

- Because we are accustomed to working in decimal, it is convenient to convert a binary, octal or hexadecimal number to decimal to get a sense of the number's "real" worth.

- To convert a number to decimal from another base, multiply the decimal equivalent of each digit by its positional value and sum these products.

- Computers represent negative numbers using two's complement notation.

- To form the negative of a value in binary, first form its one's complement by applying C's bitwise complement operator (~). This reverses the bits of the value. To form the two's complement of a value, simply add one to the value's one's complement.

TERMINOLOGY

base	digit
base 2 number system	hexadecimal number system
base 8 number system	negative value
base 10 number system	octal number system
base 16 number system	one's complement notation
binary number system	positional notation
bitwise complement operator (~)	positional value
conversions	symbol value
decimal number system	two's complement notation

SELF-REVIEW EXERCISES

E.1   The bases of the decimal, binary, octal and hexadecimal number systems are _____,
_____, _____ and _____ respectively.

E.2   In general, the decimal, octal and hexadecimal representations of a given binary number contain (more/fewer) digits than the binary number contains.

E.3   (*True/False*) A popular reason for using the decimal number system is that it forms a convenient notation for abbreviating binary numbers simply by substituting one decimal digit per group of four binary bits.

E.4   The (octal / hexadecimal / decimal) representation of a large binary value is the most concise (of the given alternatives).

E.5   (*True/False*) The highest digit in any base is one more than the base.

E.6   (*True/False*) The lowest digit in any base is one less than the base.

E.7   The positional value of the rightmost digit of any number in either binary, octal, decimal or hexadecimal is always _____.

E.8   The positional value of the digit to the left of the rightmost digit of any number in binary, octal, decimal or hexadecimal is always equal to _____.

E.9   Fill in the missing values in this chart of positional values for the rightmost four positions in each of the indicated number systems:

decimal	1000	100	10	1
hexadecimal	...	256	...	...
binary	...	...	...	...
octal	512	...	8	...

E.10   Convert binary 110101011000 to octal and to hexadecimal.

E.11   Convert hexadecimal FACE to binary.

E.12   Convert octal 7316 to binary.

E.13   Convert hexadecimal 4FEC to octal. [*Hint*: First convert 4FEC to binary then convert that binary number to octal.]

E.14   Convert binary 1101110 to decimal.

E.15   Convert octal 317 to decimal.

E.16   Convert hexadecimal EFD4 to decimal.

E.17   Convert decimal 177 to binary, to octal and to hexadecimal.

E.18   Show the binary representation of decimal 417. Then show the one's complement of 417 and the two's complement of 417.

E.19   What is the result when the two's complement of a number is added to itself?

ANSWERS TO SELF-REVIEW EXERCISES

E.1   10, 2, 8, 16.

E.2   Fewer.

E.3   False.

E.4   Hexadecimal.

E.5   False. The highest digit in any base is one less than the base.

E.6   False. The lowest digit in any base is zero.

E.7   1 (the base raised to the zero power).

E.8   The base of the number system.

E.9   Fill in the missing values in this chart of positional values for the rightmost four positions in each of the indicated number systems:

decimal	1000	100	10	1
hexadecimal	4096	256	16	1
binary	8	4	2	1
octal	512	64	8	1

E.10   Octal 6530; Hexadecimal D58.

E.11   Binary 1111 1010 1100 1110.

E.12   Binary 111 011 001 110.

E.13   Binary 0 100 111 111 101 100; Octal 47754.

E.14   Decimal 2+4+8+32+64=110.

E.15   Decimal 7+1*8+3*64=7+8+192=207.

E.16   Decimal 4+13*16+15*256+14*4096=61396.

E.17   Decimal 177
to binary:

```
256 128 64 32 16 8 4 2 1
128 64 32 16 8 4 2 1
(1*128)+(0*64)+(1*32)+(1*16)+(0*8)+(0*4)+(0*2)+(1*1)
10110001
```

to octal:

```
512 64 8 1
64 8 1
(2*64)+(6*8)+(1*1)
261
```

to hexadecimal:

```
256 16 1
16 1
(11*16)+(1*1)
(B*16)+(1*1)
B1
```

E.18   Binary:

```
512 256 128 64 32 16 8 4 2 1
256 128 64 32 16 8 4 2 1
(1*256)+(1*128)+(0*64)+(1*32)+(0*16)+(0*8)+(0*4)+(0*2)+
(1*1)
110100001
```

```
One's complement: 001011110
Two's complement: 001011111
Check: Original binary number + its two's complement

110100001
001011111
---------
000000000
```

E.19   Zero.

EXERCISES

E.20   Some people argue that many of our calculations would be easier in the base 12 number system because 12 is divisible by so many more numbers than 10 (for base 10). What is the lowest digit in base 12? What might the highest symbol for the digit in base 12 be? What are the positional values of the rightmost four positions of any number in the base 12 number system?

E.21   How is the highest symbol value in the number systems we discussed related to the positional value of the first digit to the left of the rightmost digit of any number in these number systems?

E.22   Complete the following chart of positional values for the rightmost four positions in each of the indicated number systems:

	1000	100	10	1
decimal	1000	100	10	1
base 6	...	...	6	...
base 13	...	169	...	...
base 3	27	...	...	...

E.23   Convert binary 100101111010 to octal and to hexadecimal.

E.24   Convert hexadecimal 3A7D to binary.

E.25   Convert hexadecimal 765F to octal. [Hint: First convert 765F to binary, then convert that binary number to octal.)

E.26   Convert binary 1011110 to decimal.

E.27   Convert octal 426 to decimal.

E.28   Convert hexadecimal FFFF to decimal.

E.29   Convert decimal 299 to binary, to octal and to hexadecimal.

E.30   Show the binary representation of decimal 779. Then show the one's complement of 779 and the two's complement of 779.

E.31   What is the result when the two's complement of a number is added to itself?

E.32   Show the two's complement of integer value −1 on a machine with 32-bit integers.

C Standard Library Resources

This appendix contains a list of valuable C standard libarary resources on the Internet and the World Wide Web. These functions, types and macros are defined by the American National Standards Institute and designed to ensure portability among operating systems and increase efficiency. Though they are not part of the C language, any compiler that supports ANSI C will normally provide definitions of these libraries.

In 1999, the International Standards Organization approved a new version of C, known as C99. This version supports many new features as described in Appendix B. Many of the resources listed below provide information on the C99 additions to the C standard library.

For more information about ANSI or to purchase standards documents, visit ANSI at www.ansi.org.

F.1 C Standard Library Resources

www.ansi.org
All ANSI documents including the C99 standard can be found and purchased here.

www.incits.org
The InterNational Committee of Information Technology Support is ANSI's Technical Advisory Group for ISO/IEC Joint Technical Committee 1. The C99 standard can be found and purchased here.

msdn.microsoft.com/visualc/
The Visual C++ home page contains links to many newsgroups, discussions and related sites, as well as information about this product's C/C++ language support and enhancements.

www.dinkumware.com/libraries_ref.html
Dinkumware licenses C and C++ libraries that conform to ANSI standards and provides on-line documentation.

www.cplusplus.com/ref/
This Web site for the C++ Resources Network contains references for C++ and C Standard libraries.

ccs.ucsd.edu/c/
A comprehensive site for Standard C provided by the University of California, San Diego.

`www.infosys.utas.edu.au/info/documentation/C/CStdLib.html`
Standard C reference materials provided by the University of Tasmania's School of Information Systems.

`www.acm.uiuc.edu/webmonkeys/book/c_guide/`
A C library reference posted by the University of Illinois' chapter of the Association of Computing Machinery.

`www.thefreecountry.com/compilers/cpp.shtml`
This Web site offers free C/C++ libraries, editors, IDEs, compilers and books.

`www.freeprogrammingresources.com/cpplib.html`
This Web site offers many free programming resources including free C and C++ libraries.

`www.programmersheaven.com/`
A complete resource for programmers in any language and environment. This site also offers tools and libraries for C and C++.

`www.gnu.org/manual/glibc-2.0.6/html_mono/libc.html`
A Web site that describes the ISO C standard and all extensions related to the GNU system.

`www.lysator.liu.se/c/rat/title.html`
This Web site presents the complete rationale for the creation of ANSI C.

`www.lysator.liu.se/c/`
A collection of articles and books relating to the history of C and the ANSI standard.

P.J. Plauger, former Convener for the committee responsible for developing the ISO C Standard, has written several books on the Standard C libraries as well as other programming topics. P.J. Plauger was also involved in the development of the C++ Standard and has written books on that library as well. Some of his works include:

- *The Standard C Library*, P.J. Plauger, Prentice Hall, 1993-1994.
- *Standard C: A Reference*, P.J. Plauger and Jim Brodie, Prentice Hall, 1996.
- *The Draft Standard C++ Library*, P.J Plauger, Prentice Hall, 1995.

Index

The DEITEL® Suite of Products...

Getting Started with Microsoft® Visual C++™ 6 with an Introduction to MFC

BOOK / CD-ROM

©2000, 163 pp., paper
(0-13-016147-0)

Visual C++ .NET How To Program

BOOK / CD-ROM

©2004, 1400 pp., paper
(0-13-437377-4)

Written by the authors of the world's best-selling introductory/intermediate C and C++ textbooks, this comprehensive book thoroughly examines Visual C++® .NET. *Visual C++® .NET How to Program* begins with a strong foundation in the introductory and intermediate programming principles students will need in industry, including fundamental topics such as arrays, functions and control structures. Readers learn the concepts of object-oriented programming, including how to create reusable software components with classes and assemblies. The text then explores such essential topics as networking, databases, XML and multimedia. Graphical user interfaces are also extensively covered, giving students the tools to build compelling and fully interactive programs using the "drag-and-drop" techniques provided by the latest version of Visual Studio .NET, Visual Studio .NET 2003.

Advanced Java™ 2 Platform How to Program

BOOK / CD-ROM

©2002, 1811 pp., paper
(0-13-089560-1)

Expanding on the world's best-selling Java textbook—*Java™ How to Program*—*Advanced Java™ 2 Platform How To Program* presents advanced Java topics for developing sophisticated, user-friendly GUIs; significant, scalable enterprise applications; wireless applications and distributed systems. Primarily based on Java 2 Enterprise Edition (J2EE), this textbook integrates technologies such as XML, JavaBeans, security, JDBC™, JavaServer Pages (JSP™), servlets, Remote Method Invocation (RMI), Enterprise JavaBeans™ (EJB) and design patterns into a production-quality system that allows developers to benefit from the leverage and platform independence Java 2 Enterprise Edition provides. The book also features the development of a complete, end-to-end e-business solution using advanced Java technologies. Additional topics include Swing, Java 2D and 3D,

XML, design patterns, CORBA, Jini™, JavaSpaces™, Jiro™, Java Management Extensions (JMX) and Peer-to-Peer networking with an introduction to JXTA. This textbook also introduces the Java 2 Micro Edition (J2ME™) for building applications for handheld and wireless devices using MIDP and MIDlets. Wireless technologies covered include WAP, WML and i-mode.

C# How to Program

BOOK / CD-ROM

©2002, 1568 pp., paper
(0-13-062221-4)

An exciting addition to the *How to Program Series*, *C# How to Program* provides a comprehensive introduction to Microsoft's new object-oriented language. C# builds on the skills already mastered by countless C++ and Java programmers, enabling them to create powerful Web applications and components—ranging from XML-based Web services on Microsoft's .NET platform to middle-tier business objects and system-level applications. *C# How to Program* begins with a strong foundation in the introductory- and intermediate-programming principles students will need in industry. It then explores such essential topics as object-oriented programming and exception handling. Graphical user interfaces are extensively covered, giving readers the tools to build compelling and fully interactive programs. Internet technologies such as XML, ADO .NET and Web services are covered as well as topics including regular expressions, multithreading, networking, databases, files and data structures.

Visual Basic® .NET How to Program Second Edition

BOOK / CD-ROM

©2002, 1400 pp., paper
(0-13-029363-6)

Learn Visual Basic .NET programming from the ground up! The introduction of Microsoft's .NET Framework marks the beginning of major revisions to all of Microsoft's programming languages. This book provides a comprehensive introduction to the next version of Visual Basic— Visual Basic .NET—featuring extensive updates and increased functionality. *Visual Basic .NET How to Program, Second Edition* covers introductory programming techniques as well as more advanced topics, featuring enhanced treatment of developing Web-based applications. Other topics discussed include an extensive treatment of XML and wireless applications, databases, SQL and ADO .NET, Web forms, Web services and ASP .NET.

Internet & World Wide Web How to Program
Second Edition

BOOK / CD-ROM

©2002, 1428 pp., paper
(0-13-030897-8)

The revision of this groundbreaking book offers a thorough treatment of programming concepts that yield visible or audible results in Web pages and Web-based applications. This book discusses effective Web-based design, server- and client-side scripting, multitier Web-based applications development, ActiveX® controls and electronic commerce essentials. This book offers an alternative to traditional programming courses using markup languages (such as XHTML, Dynamic HTML and XML) and scripting languages (such as JavaScript, VBScript, Perl/CGI, Python and PHP) to teach the fundamentals of programming "wrapped in the metaphor of the Web." Updated material on www.deitel.com and www.prenhall.com/deitel provides additional resources for instructors who want to cover Microsoft® or non-Microsoft technologies. The Web site includes an extensive treatment of Netscape® 6 and alternate versions of the code from the Dynamic HTML chapters that will work with non-Microsoft environments as well.

Python
How to Program

BOOK / CD-ROM

©2002, 1376 pp., paper
(0-13-092361-3)

This exciting new textbook provides a comprehensive introduction to Python—a powerful object-oriented programming language with clear syntax and the ability to bring together various technologies quickly and easily. This book covers introductory-programming techniques and more advanced topics such as graphical user interfaces, databases, wireless Internet programming, networking, security, process management, multithreading, XHTML, CSS, PSP and multimedia. Readers will learn principles that are applicable to both systems development and Web programming. The book features the consistent and applied pedagogy that the *How to Program Series* is known for, including the Deitels' signature *LIVE-CODE Approach*, with thousands of lines of code in hundreds of working programs; hundreds of valuable programming tips identified with icons throughout the text; an extensive set of exercises, projects and case studies; two-color four-way syntax coloring and much more.

Wireless Internet & Mobile Business
How to Program

© 2002, 1292 pp., paper
(0-13-062226-5)

While the rapid expansion of wireless technologies, such as cell phones, pagers and personal digital assistants (PDAs), offers many new opportunities for businesses and programmers, it also presents numerous challenges related to issues such as security and standardization. This book offers a thorough treatment of both the management and technical aspects of this growing area, including coverage of current practices and future trends. The first half explores the business issues surrounding wireless technology and mobile business, including an overview of existing and developing communication technologies and the application of business principles to wireless devices. It also discusses location-based services and location-identifying technologies, a topic that is revisited throughout the book. Wireless payment, security, legal and social issues, international communications and more are also discussed. The book then turns to programming for the wireless Internet, exploring topics such as WAP (including 2.0), WML, WMLScript, XML, XHTML™, wireless Java programming (J2ME™), Web Clipping and more. Other topics covered include career resources, wireless marketing, accessibility, Palm™, PocketPC, Windows CE, i-mode, Bluetooth, MIDP, MIDlets, ASP, Microsoft .NET Mobile Framework, BREW™, multimedia, Flash™ and VBScript.

e-Business & e-Commerce for Managers

©2001, 794 pp., cloth
(0-13-032364-0)

This comprehensive overview of building and managing e-businesses explores topics such as the decision to bring a business online, choosing a business model, accepting payments, marketing strategies and security, as well as many other important issues (such as career resources). The book features Web resources and online demonstrations that supplement the text and direct readers to additional materials. The book also includes an appendix that develops a complete Web-based shopping-cart application using HTML, JavaScript, VBScript, Active Server Pages, ADO, SQL, HTTP, XML and XSL. Plus, company-specific sections provide "real-world" examples of the concepts presented in the book.

XML How to Program

BOOK / CD-ROM

©2001, 934 pp., paper
(0-13-028417-3)

This book is a comprehensive guide to programming in XML. It teaches how to use XML to create customized tags and includes chapters that address markup languages for science and technology, multimedia, commerce and many other fields. Concise introductions to Java,

JavaServer Pages, VBScript, Active Server Pages and Perl/CGI provide readers with the essentials of these programming languages and server-side development technologies to enable them to work effectively with XML. The book also covers cutting-edge topics such as XSL, DOM™ and SAX, plus a real-world e-commerce case study and a complete chapter on Web accessibility that addresses Voice XML. It includes tips such as Common Programming Errors, Software Engineering Observations, Portability Tips and Debugging Hints. Other topics covered include XHTML, CSS, DTD, schema, parsers, XPath, XLink, namespaces, XBase, XInclude, XPointer, XSLT, XSL Formatting Objects, JavaServer Pages, XForms, topic maps, X3D, MathML, OpenMath, CML, BML, CDF, RDF, SVG, Cocoon, WML, XBRL and BizTalk™ and SOAP™ Web resources.

Perl How to Program

BOOK / CD-ROM

©2001, 1057 pp., paper (0-13-028418-1)

This comprehensive guide to Perl programming emphasizes the use of the Common Gateway Interface (CGI) with Perl to create powerful, dynamic multi-tier Web-based client/server applications. The book begins with a clear and careful introduction to programming concepts at a level suitable for beginners, and proceeds through advanced topics such as references and complex data structures. Key Perl topics such as regular expressions and string manipulation are covered in detail. The authors address important and topical issues such as object-oriented programming, the Perl database interface (DBI), graphics and security. Also included is a treatment of XML, a bonus chapter introducing the Python programming language, supplemental material on career resources and a complete chapter on Web accessibility. The text includes tips such as Common Programming Errors, Software Engineering Observations, Portability Tips and Debugging Hints.

e-Business & e-Commerce How to Program

BOOK / CD-ROM

©2001, 1254 pp., paper (0-13-028419-X)

This innovative book explores programming technologies for developing Web-based e-business and e-commerce solutions, and covers e-business and e-commerce models and business issues. Readers learn a full range of options, from "build-your-own" to turnkey solutions. The book examines scores of the top e-businesses (examples include Amazon, eBay, Priceline, Travelocity, etc.), explaining the technical details of building successful e-business and e-commerce sites and their underlying business premises. Learn how to implement the dominant e-commerce models—shopping carts, auctions, name-your-own-price, comparison shopping and bots/intelligent agents—by using markup languages (HTML, Dynamic HTML and XML), scripting languages (JavaScript, VBScript and Perl), server-side technologies (Active Server Pages and Perl/CGI) and database (SQL and ADO), security and online payment technologies. Updates are regularly posted to www.deitel.com and the book includes a CD-ROM with software tools, source code and live links.

Visual Basic® 6 How to Program

BOOK / CD-ROM

©1999, 1015 pp., paper (0-13-456955-5)

Visual Basic® 6 How to Program was developed in cooperation with Microsoft to cover important topics such as graphical user interfaces (GUIs), multimedia, object-oriented programming, networking, database programming, VBScript®, COM/DCOM and ActiveX®.

Presenting the DEITEL® DEVELOPER SERIES!

Deitel & Associates is recognized worldwide for its best-selling *How to Program Series* of books for college and university students and its signature *LIVE-CODE Approach* to teaching programming languages. Now, for the first time, Deitel & Associates brings its proven teaching methods to a new series of books specifically designed for professionals.

THREE TYPES OF BOOKS FOR THREE DISTINCT AUDIENCES:

| *A Technical Introduction* | **A Technical Introduction** books provide programmers, technical managers, project managers and other technical professionals with introductions to broad new technology areas. |

| *A Programmer's Introduction* | **A Programmer's Introduction** books offer focused treatments of programming fundamentals for practicing programmers. These books are also appropriate for novices. |

| *For Experienced Programmers* | **For Experienced Programmers** books are for experienced programmers who want a detailed treatment of a programming language or technology. These books contain condensed introductions to programming language fundamentals and provide extensive intermediate level coverage of high-end topics. |

Java™ Web Services for Experienced Programmers

©2003, 700 pp., paper (0-13-046134-2)

Java™ Web Services for Experienced Programmers from the *DEITEL® Developer Series* provides the experienced Java programmer with 103 *LIVE-CODE* examples and covers industry standards including XML, SOAP, WSDL and UDDI. Learn how to build and integrate Web services using the Java API for XML RPC, the Java API for XML Messaging, Apache Axis and the Java Web services Developer Pack. Develop and deploy Web services on several major Web services platforms. Register and discover Web services through public registries and the Java API for XML Registries. Build Web services clients for several platforms, including J2ME. Significant Web services case studies also are included.

Web Services: A Technical Introduction

©2003, 400 pp., paper (0-13-046135-0)

Web Services: A Technical Introduction from the *DEITEL® Developer Series* familiarizes programmers, technical managers and project managers with key Web services concepts, including what Web services are and why they are revolutionary. The book covers the business case for Web services—the underlying technologies, ways in which Web services can provide competitive advantages and opportunities for Web services-related lines of business. Readers learn the latest Web-services standards, including XML, SOAP, WSDL and UDDI; learn about Web services implementations in .NET and Java; benefit from an extensive comparison of Web services products and vendors; and read about Web services security options. Although this is not a programming book, the appendices show .NET and Java code examples to demonstrate the structure of Web services applications and documents. In addition, the book includes numerous case studies describing ways in which organizations are implementing Web services to increase efficiency, simplify business processes, create new revenue streams and interact better with partners and customers.

Complete Training Courses

Each complete package includes the corresponding *How to Program Series* textbook and interactive multimedia Windows-based CD-ROM Cyber Classroom. *Complete Training Courses* are perfect for anyone interested in Web and e-commerce programming. They are affordable resources for college students and professionals learning programming for the first time or reinforcing their knowledge.

Intuitive Browser-Based Interface

You'll love the *Complete Training Courses'* new browser-based interface, designed to be easy and accessible to anyone who's ever used a Web browser. Every *Complete Training Course* features the full text, illustrations and program listings of its corresponding *How to Program* book—all in full color—with full-text searching and hyperlinking.

Further Enhancements to the Deitels' Signature *Live-Code Approach*

Every code sample from the main text can be found in the interactive, multimedia, CD-ROM-based *Cyber Classrooms* included in the *Complete Training Courses*. Syntax coloring of code is included for the *How to Program* books that are published in full color. Even the recent two-color and one-color books use effective syntax shading. The *Cyber Classroom* products are always in full color.

Audio Annotations

Hours of detailed, expert audio descriptions of thousands of lines of code help reinforce concepts.

Easily Executable Code

With one click of the mouse, you can execute the code or save it to your hard drive to manipulate using the programming environment of your choice. With selected *Complete Training Courses*, you can also load all of the code into a development environment such as Microsoft® Visual C++™, enabling you to modify and execute the programs with ease.

Abundant Self-Assessment Material

Practice exams test your understanding of key concepts with hundreds of test questions and answers in addition to those found in the main text. The textbook includes hundreds of programming exercises, while the *Cyber Classrooms* include answers to about half the exercises.

www.phptr.com/phptrinteractive

e-LEARNING • from Deitel & Associates, Inc.

Cyber Classrooms, Web-Based Training and Course Management Systems

DEITEL is committed to continuous research and development in e-Learning.

We are pleased to announce that we have incorporated examples of Web-based training, including a five-way Macromedia® Flash™ animation of a for loop in Java™, into the *Java 2 Multimedia Cyber Classroom, 5/e* (which is included in *The Complete Java 2 Training Course, 5/e*). Our instructional designers and Flash animation team are developing additional simulations that demonstrate key programming concepts.

We are enhancing the *Multimedia Cyber Classroom* products to include more audio, pre- and post-assessment questions and Web-based labs with solutions for the benefit of professors and students alike. In addition, our *Multimedia Cyber Classroom* products, currently available in CD-ROM format, are being ported to Pearson's CourseCompass course-management system—*a powerful e-platform for teaching and learning*. Many DEITEL® materials are available in WebCT, Blackboard and CourseCompass formats for colleges, and will soon be available for various corporate learning management systems. For more information on course management systems, please visit us on the Web at www.prenhall.com/cms.

WHAT'S COMING FROM THE DEITELS

Future Publications

Here are some new books we are considering for 2003/2004 release:

Simply Series: *Simply C++, Simply C#.*

Computer Science Series: *Java Software Design, C++ Software Design.*

Internet and Web Programming Series: *Internet and World Wide Web How to Program 3/e; Open Source Software Development: Linux, Apache, MySQL, Perl and PHP.*

DEITEL® Developer Series: *ASP .NET with Visual Basic .NET, ASP .NET with C#.*

Object Technology Series: *OOAD with the UML, Design Patterns, Java and XML.*

Java Series: *Advanced Java™ 2 Platform How to Program 2/e.*

Operating Systems, Third Edition

This fall we will wrap up the first book in our new *Computer Science Series, Operating Systems, Third Edition.* This book will be entirely updated to reflect current core operating system concepts and design considerations. Using Java™ code to illustrate key points, *Operating Systems* will introduce processes, concurrent programming, deadlock and indefinite postponement, mutual exclusion, physical and virtual memory, file systems, disk performance, distributed systems, security and more. To complement the discussion of operating system concepts, the book will feature extensive case studies on the latest operating systems, including the soon-to-be-released Linux kernel version 2.4 and the Windows XP operating system. This book covers all of the core topics and many elective topics recommended by the Joint Task Force on Computing Curricula 2001 developed by the IEEE Computer Society and ACM, making it an ideal textbook for undergraduate operating systems courses.

Our official e-mail newsletter, the *DEITEL® BUZZ ONLINE*, is a free publication designed to keep you updated on our publishing program, instructor-led corporate training courses, hottest industry trends and topics and more.

Issues of our newsletter include:

- **Technology Spotlights** that feature articles and information on the hottest industry topics drawn directly from our publications or written during the research and development process.

- **Anecdotes** and/or **challenges** that allow our readers to interact with our newsletter and with us. We always welcome and appreciate your comments, answers and feedback. We will summarize all responses we receive in future issues.

- **Announcements** on what's happening at Deitel as well as updated information on our publishing plans.

- **Highlights** and **Announcements** on current and upcoming products that are of interest to professionals, students and instructors.

- Information on our **instructor-led corporate training courses delivered at organizations worldwide**. Complete course listings and special course highlights provide readers with additional details on DEITEL® training offerings.

- Our newsletter is available in both **full-color HTML** or **plain-text** formats depending on your viewing preferences and e-mail client capabilities.

- Learn about the history of Deitel & Associates, our brands, the bugs and more in the **Lore and Legends** section of the newsletter.

- **Hyperlinked Table of Contents** allows readers to navigate quickly through the newsletter by jumping directly to specific topics of interest.

To sign up for the *DEITEL® BUZZ ONLINE* newsletter, visit `www.deitel.com/newsletter/subscribe.html`.

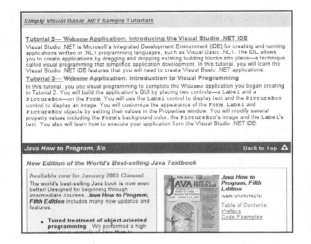

Turn the page to find out more about Deitel & Associates!

The Deitels are the authors of best-selling Java™, C++, C#, C, Visual Basic® and Internet and World Wide Web books and multimedia packages.

Corporate Training Delivered Worldwide

Deitel & Associates, Inc. provides intensive, lecture-and-laboratory courses to organizations worldwide. The programming courses use our signature *LIVE-CODE Approach*, presenting complete working programs.

Deitel & Associates, Inc. has trained over one million students and professionals worldwide through corporate training courses, public seminars, university teaching, *How to Program Series* textbooks, *DEITEL® Developer Series* textbooks, *Simply Series* textbooks, *Cyber Classroom Series* multimedia packages, *Complete Training Course Series* textbook and multimedia packages, broadcast-satellite courses and Web-based training.

Educational Consulting

Deitel & Associates, Inc. offers complete educational consulting services for corporate training programs and professional schools including:

- Curriculum design and development
- Preparation of Instructor Guides
- Customized courses and course materials
- Design and implementation of professional training certificate programs
- Instructor certification
- Train-the-trainers programs
- Delivery of software-related corporate training programs

Visit our Web site for more information on our corporate training curriculum and to purchase our training products.

www.deitel.com/training

Would you like to review upcoming publications?

If you are a professor or senior industry professional interested in being a reviewer of our forthcoming publications, please contact us by email at **deitel@deitel.com**. Insert "Content Reviewer" in the subject heading.

Are you interested in a career in computer education, publishing and training?

We offer a limited number of full-time positions available for college graduates in computer science, information systems, information technology, management information systems, English and communications, marketing, multimedia technology and other areas. Please check our Web site for the latest job postings or contact us by email at **deitel@deitel.com**. Insert "Full-time Job" in the subject heading.

Are you a Boston-area college student looking for an internship?

We have a limited number of competitive summer positions and 20-hr./week school-year opportunities for computer science, English and business majors. Students work at our worldwide headquarters west of Boston. We also offer full-time internships for students taking a semester off from school. This is an excellent opportunity for students looking to gain industry experience and earn money to pay for school. Please contact us by email at **deitel@deitel.com**. Insert "Internship" in the subject heading.

Would you like to explore contract training opportunities with us?

Deitel & Associates, Inc. is looking for contract instructors to teach software-related topics at our clients' sites in the United States and worldwide. Applicants should be experienced professional trainers or college professors. For more information, please visit **www.deitel.com** and send your resume to Abbey Deitel at **abbey.deitel@deitel.com**.

Are you a training company in need of quality course materials?

Corporate training companies worldwide use our *Complete Training Course Series* book and multimedia packages, our *Web-Based Training Series* courses and our *DEITEL® Developer Series* books in their classes. We have extensive ancillary instructor materials for each of our products. For more details, please visit **www.deitel.com** or contact us by email at **deitel@deitel.com**.

License Agreement and Limited Warranty

The software is distributed on an "AS IS" basis, without warranty. Neither the authors, the software developers, nor Prentice Hall make any representation, or warranty, either express or implied, with respect to the software programs, their quality, accuracy, or fitness for a specific purpose. Therefore, neither the authors, the software developers, nor Prentice Hall shall have any liability to you or any other person or entity with respect to any liability, loss, or damage caused or alleged to have been caused directly or indirectly by the programs contained on the media. This includes, but is not limited to, interruption of service, loss of data, loss of classroom time, loss of consulting or anticipatory profits, or consequential damages from the use of these programs. If the media itself is defective, you may return it for a replacement. Use of this software is subject to the Binary Code License terms and conditions at the back of this book. Read the licenses carefully. By opening this package, you are agreeing to be bound by the terms and conditions of these licenses. If you do not agree, do not open the package.

Please refer to end-user license agreements on the CD-ROM for further details.

Using the CD-ROM

The contents of this CD are designed to be accessed through the interface provided in the file **AUTORUN.EXE**. If a startup screen does not pop up automatically when you insert the CD into your computer, double click on the icon for **AUTORUN.EXE** to launch the program or refer to the file **README.TXT** on the CD.

Contents of the CD-ROM

- Microsoft® Visual C++® 6.0 Introductory Edition
- Live links to websites mentioned in this book
- Live code examples from this book

Microsoft® Visual C++® 6.0 Introductory Edition - System Requirements

- PC with a Pentium-class processor, 90 MHz or higher
- Microsoft Windows 95 or later or Microsoft Windows NT 4.0 with service pack 3 or later (service pack 3 included)
- Microsoft Internet Explorer 4.01 Service Pack 1 (included) or later
- CD-ROM drive
- VGA or higher-resolution monitor; Super VGA recommended
- Microsoft Mouse or compatible pointing device
- 24 MB RAM for Windows 95 or later (48 MB recommended)
- 32 MB for Windows NT 4.0 or later (48 MB recommended)
- Disk space required for basic install of VC++ only:
  266 MB typical, 370 MB maximum
- Disk Space required for VC++ and Service Pack install: 345 MB
  (NOTE: Because the Service Pack mostly replaces files, it only adds about 30 MB typically)
- Internet connection

Windows 2000 and XP Users

Microsoft Visual C++ 6.0 Introductory Edition can be installed on either version of Windows. To successfully install the program you will need to be logged in as 'administrator'. The 'MS-DOS Prompt' has been replaced by the 'Command Prompt' on both Windows 2000 and XP.

Note: Pearson Education Product Support and Microsoft no longer offer support for Windows 95.

pointer to a base class
pointer to a derived class
pointer to an abstract class
polymorphism
programming "in the general"
programming "in the specific"
pure `virtual` function (= 0)
reference to a base class
reference to a derived class

reference to an abstract class
software reusability
static binding
`switch` logic
`virtual` destructor
`virtual` function
`virtual` function table
vtable
vtable pointer

COMMON PROGRAMMING ERRORS

20.1 Attempting to instantiate an object of an abstract class (i.e., a class that contains one or more pure `virtual` functions) is a syntax error.

20.2 Constructors cannot be `virtual`. Declaring a constructor as a `virtual` function is a syntax error.

GOOD PROGRAMMING PRACTICES

20.1 Even though certain functions are implicitly `virtual` because of a declaration made higher in the class hierarchy, explicitly declare these functions `virtual` at every level of the hierarchy to promote program clarity.

20.2 If a class has `virtual` functions, provide a `virtual` destructor, even if one is not required for the class. Classes derived from this class may contain destructors that must be called properly.

PERFORMANCE TIPS

20.1 Polymorphism as implemented with `virtual` functions and dynamic binding is efficient. Programmers may use these capabilities with nominal impact on system performance.

20.2 Virtual functions and dynamic binding enable polymorphic programming as opposed to `switch` logic programming. C++ optimizing compilers normally generate code that runs at least as efficiently as hand-coded `switch`-based logic. One way or the other, the overhead of polymorphism is acceptable for most applications. But in some situations—real-time applications with stringent performance requirements, for example—the overhead of polymorphism may be too high.

SOFTWARE ENGINEERING OBSERVATIONS

20.1 An interesting consequence of using `virtual` functions and polymorphism is that programs take on a simplified appearance. They contain less branching logic in favor of simpler sequential code. This facilitates testing, debugging, program maintenance and bug avoidance.

20.2 Once a function is declared `virtual`, it remains `virtual` all the way down the inheritance hierarchy from that point even if it is not declared `virtual` when a class overrides it.

20.3 When a derived class chooses not to define a `virtual` function, the derived class simply inherits its immediate base class's `virtual` function definition.

20.4 If a class is derived from a class with a pure `virtual` function, and if no definition is supplied for that pure `virtual` function in the derived class, then that `virtual` function remains pure in the derived class. Consequently, the derived class is also an abstract class.

20.5 With `virtual` functions and polymorphism, the programmer can deal in generalities and let the execution-time environment concern itself with the specifics. The programmer can command a wide variety of objects to behave in manners appropriate to those objects without even knowing the types of those objects.

20.6   Polymorphism promotes extensibility: Software written to invoke polymorphic behavior is written independently of the types of the objects to which messages are sent. Thus, new types of objects that can respond to existing messages can be added into such a system without modifying the base system. Except for client code that instantiates new objects, programs need not be recompiled.

20.7   An abstract class defines an interface for the various members of a class hierarchy. The abstract class contains pure `virtual` functions that will be defined in the derived classes. All functions in the hierarchy can use this same interface through polymorphism.

20.8   A class can inherit interface and/or implementation from a base class. Hierarchies designed for *implementation inheritance* tend to have their functionality high in the hierarchy—each new derived class inherits one or more member functions that were defined in a base class, and the new derived class uses the base-class definitions. Hierarchies designed for *interface inheritance* tend to have their functionality lower in the hierarchy—a base class specifies one or more functions that should be defined for each class in the hierarchy (i.e., they have the same signature), but the individual derived classes provide their own implementations of the function(s).

SELF-REVIEW EXERCISE

20.1   Fill in the blanks in each of the following:
a)   Using inheritance and polymorphism helps eliminate _____ logic.
b)   A pure `virtual` function is specified by placing _____ at the end of its prototype in the class definition.
c)   If a class contains one or more pure `virtual` functions, it is a(n) _____.
d)   A function call resolved at compile time is referred to as _____ binding.
e)   A function call resolved at run time is referred to as _____ binding.

ANSWERS TO SELF-REVIEW EXERCISE

20.1   a)   `switch`. b) = 0. c) abstract base class. d) static or early. e) dynamic or late.

EXERCISES

20.2   What are `virtual` functions? Describe a circumstance in which `virtual` functions would be appropriate.

20.3   Given that constructors cannot be `virtual`, describe a scheme for how you might achieve a similar effect.

20.4   How is it that polymorphism enables you to program "in the general" rather than "in the specific." Discuss the key advantages of programming "in the general."

20.5   Discuss the problems of programming with `switch` logic. Explain why polymorphism is an effective alternative to using `switch` logic.

20.6   Distinguish between static binding and dynamic binding. Explain the use of `virtual` functions and the vtable in dynamic binding.

20.7   Distinguish between inheriting interface and inheriting implementation. How do inheritance hierarchies designed for inheriting interface differ from those designed for inheriting implementation?

20.8   Distinguish between `virtual` functions and pure `virtual` functions.